PEARSON

COMMON CORE

Literature

THE BRITISH TRADITION

PEARSON

HOBOKEN, NEW JERSEY • BOSTON, MASSACHUSETTS
CHANDLER, ARIZONA • GLENVIEW, ILLINOIS

PEARSON

COMMON CORE

Literature

THE BRITISH TRADITION

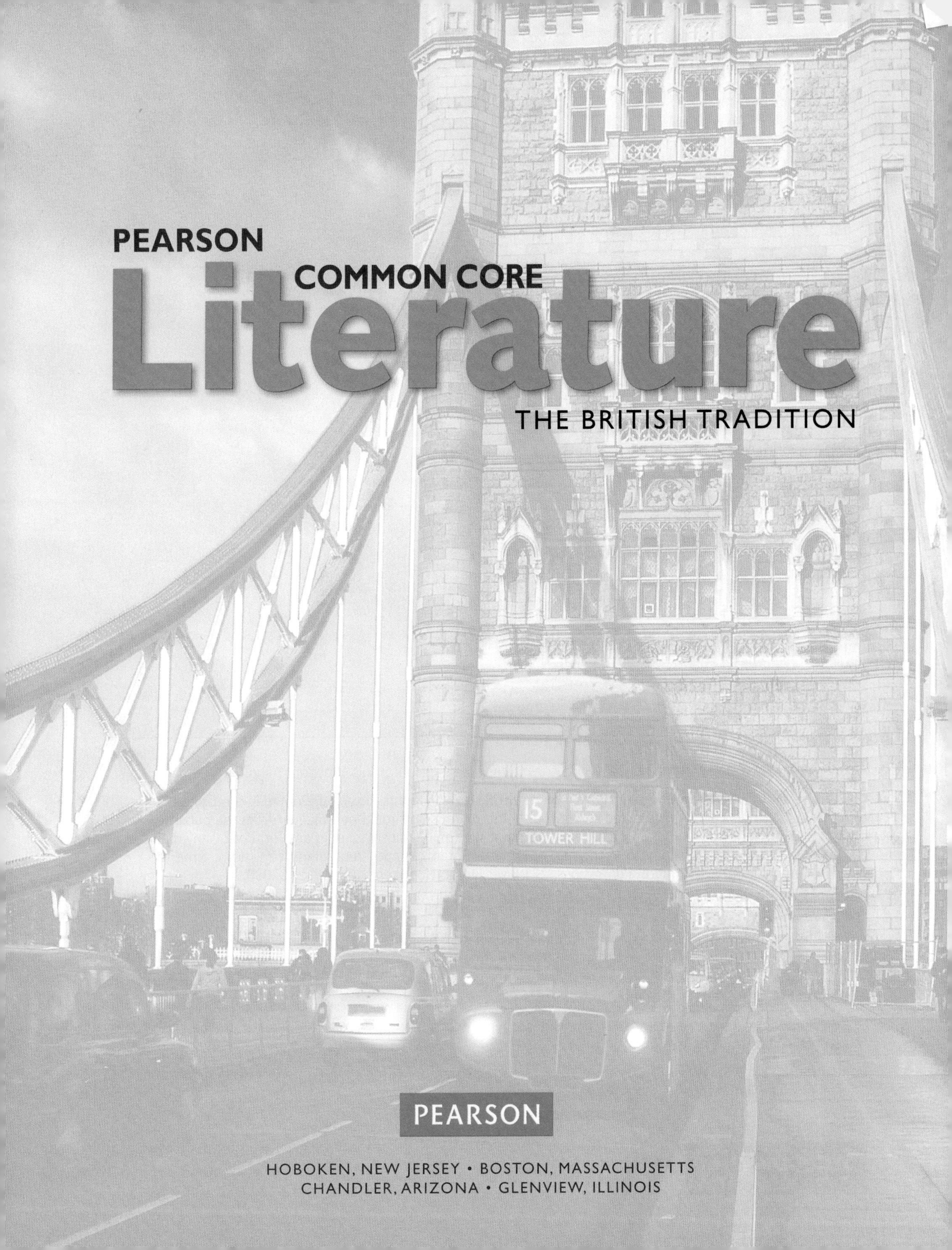

PEARSON

HOBOKEN, NEW JERSEY • BOSTON, MASSACHUSETTS
CHANDLER, ARIZONA • GLENVIEW, ILLINOIS

ISBN-13:   978-0-13-326856-0
ISBN-10:   0-13-326856-X
7 8 9 10 11 12 13 V057 18 17 16 15 14

PEARSON

COMMON CORE

Literature

THE BRITISH TRADITION

PEARSON

HOBOKEN, NEW JERSEY • BOSTON, MASSACHUSETTS
CHANDLER, ARIZONA • GLENVIEW, ILLINOIS

The contributing authors guided the direction and philosophy of Pearson Common Core Literature. They helped to build the pedagogical integrity of the program by contributing content expertise, knowledge of the Common Core State Standards, and support for the shifts in instruction the Common Core will bring. Their knowledge, combined with classroom and professional experience, ensures Pearson Common Core Literature is relevant for both teachers and students.

William G. Brozo, Ph.D., is a Professor of Literacy in the Graduate School of Education at George Mason University in Fairfax, Virginia. He earned his bachelor's degree from the University of North Carolina and his master's and doctorate from the University of South Carolina. He has taught reading and language arts in the Carolinas and is the author of numerous articles on literacy development for children and young adults. His books include *To Be a Boy, To Be a Reader: Engaging Teen and Preteen Boys in Active Literacy; Readers, Teachers, Learners: Expanding Literacy Across the Content Areas; Content Literacy for Today's Adolescents: Honoring Diversity and Building Competence; Supporting Content Area Literacy with Technology* (Pearson); and *Setting the Pace: A Speed, Comprehension, and Study Skills Program.* His newest book is *RTI and the Adolescent Reader: Responsive Literacy Instruction in Secondary Schools.* As an international consultant, Dr. Brozo has provided technical support to teachers from the Balkans to the Middle East, and he is currently a member of a European Union research grant team developing curriculum and providing adolescent literacy professional development for teachers across Europe.

Diane Fettrow spent the majority of her teaching career in Broward County, Florida, teaching high school English courses and serving as department chair. She also worked as an adjunct instructor at Broward College, Nova Southeastern University, and Florida Atlantic University. After she left the classroom, she served as Secondary Language Arts Curriculum Supervisor for several years, working with more than 50 of the district's high schools, centers, and charter schools. During her time as curriculum supervisor, she served on numerous local and state committees; she also served as Florida's K–12 ELA content representative to the PARCC Model Content Frameworks Rapid Response Feedback Group and the PARCC K–12 and Upper Education Engagement Group. Currently she presents workshops on the Common Core State Standards and is working with Pearson on aligning materials to the CCSS.

Kelly Gallagher is a full-time English teacher at Magnolia High School in Anaheim, California, where he has taught for twenty-seven years. He is the former co-director of the South Basin Writing Project at California State University, Long Beach, and the author of *Reading Reasons: Motivational Mini-Lessons for Middle and High School; Deeper Reading: Comprehending Challenging Texts, 4–12; Teaching Adolescent Writers;* and *Readicide: How Schools Are Killing Reading and What You Can Do About It.* He is also a principal author of *Prentice Hall Writing Coach* (Pearson, 2012). Kelly's latest book is *Write Like This* (Stenhouse). Follow Kelly on Twitter @KellyGToGo, and visit him at www.kellygallagher.org.

Elfrieda "Freddy' Hiebert, Ph.D., is President and CEO of TextProject, a nonprofit that provides resources to support higher reading levels. She is also a research associate at the University of California, Santa Cruz. Dr. Hiebert received her Ph.D. in Educational Psychology from the University of Wisconsin-Madison. She has worked in the field of early reading acquisition for 45 years, first as a teacher's aide and teacher of primary-level students in California and, subsequently, as a teacher educator and researcher at the universities of Kentucky, Colorado-Boulder, Michigan, and California-Berkeley. Her research addresses how fluency, vocabulary, and knowledge can be fostered through appropriate texts. Professor Hiebert's research has been published in numerous scholarly journals, and she has authored or edited nine books. Professor Hiebert's model of accessible texts for beginning and struggling readers—TExT—has been used to develop numerous reading programs that are widely used in schools. Dr. Hiebert is the 2008 recipient of the William S. Gray Citation of Merit, awarded by the International Reading Association; is a member of the Reading Hall of Fame; and has chaired a group of experts on early childhood literacy who served in an advisory capacity to the CCSS writers.

Donald J. Leu, Ph.D., is the John and Maria Neag Endowed Chair in Literacy and Technology and holds a joint appointment in Curriculum and Instruction and Educational Psychology in the Neag School of Education at the University of Connecticut. Don is an international authority on literacy education, especially the new skills and strategies required to read, write, and learn with Internet technologies and the best instructional practices that prepare students for these new literacies. He is a member of the Reading Hall of Fame, a Past President of the National Reading Conference, and a former member of the Board of Directors of the International Reading Association. Don is a Principal Investigator on a number of federal research grants, and his work has been funded by the U.S. Department of Education, the National Science Foundation, and the Bill and Melinda Gates Foundation, among others. He recently edited the *Handbook of Research on New Literacies* (Erlbaum, 2008).

Ernest Morrell, Ph.D., is a professor of English Education at Teachers College, Columbia University, and the president-elect of the National Council of Teachers of English (NCTE). He is also the Director of Teachers College's Harlem-based Institute for Urban and Minority Education (IUME). Dr. Morrell was an award-winning high school English teacher in California, and he now works with teachers and schools across the country to infuse multicultural literature, youth popular culture, and media production into standards-based literacy curricula and after-school programs. He is the author of nearly 100 articles and book chapters and five books, including *Critical Media Pedagogy: Achievement, Production, and Justice in City Schools* and *Linking Literacy and Popular Culture*. In his spare time he coaches youth sports and writes poems and plays.

Karen Wixson, Ph.D., is Dean of the School of Education at the University of North Carolina, Greensboro. She has published widely in the areas of literacy curriculum, instruction, and assessment. Dr. Wixson has been an advisor to the National Research Council and helped develop the National Assessment of Educational Progress (NAEP) reading tests. She is a former member of the IRA Board of Directors and co-chair of the IRA Commission on RTI. Recently, Dr. Wixson served on the English Language Arts Work Team that was part of the Common Core State Standards Initiative.

Grant Wiggins, Ed.D., is the President of Authentic Education in Hopewell, New Jersey. He earned his Ed.D. from Harvard University and his B.A. from St. John's College in Annapolis. Grant consults with schools, districts, and state education departments on a variety of reform matters; organizes conferences and workshops; and develops print materials and Web resources on curricular change. He is perhaps best known for being the co-author, with Jay McTighe, of *Understanding by Design* and *The Understanding by Design Handbook*, the award-winning and highly successful materials on curriculum published by ASCD.

The selections in this book are presented through the lens of three Essential Questions:

What is the relationship between literature and place?

How does literature shape or reflect society?

What is the relationship of the writer to tradition?

From Legend to History

The Old English and Medieval Periods (A.D. 449 to 1485)

PART ONE TEXT SET: **EARTHLY EXILE, HEAVENLY HOME**

PART TWO TEXT SET: **THE EPIC**

★ INFORMATIONAL TEXT HIGHLIGHTED

PART THREE TEXT SET: **A NATIONAL SPIRIT**

PART FOUR TEXT SET: **PERILS AND ADVENTURES**

DIGITAL ASSETS KEY

These digital resources, as well as audio and the Online Writer's Notebook, can be found at **pearsonrealize.com**.

- Interactive Whiteboard Activities
- Virtual Tour
- Close Reading Notebook
- Video
- Close Reading Tool for Annotating Texts
- Grammar Tutorials

Contents **xi**

Celebrating Humanity

The English Renaissance Period (1485 to 1625)

DIGITAL ASSETS KEY

These digital resources, as well as audio and the Online Writer's Notebook, can be found at **pearsonrealize.com**.

- Interactive Whiteboard Activities
- Virtual Tour
- Close Reading Notebook
- Video
- Close Reading Tool for Annotating Texts
- Grammar Tutorials

A Turbulent Time

The Seventeenth and Eighteenth Centuries (1625 to 1798)

PART FOUR TEXT SET: **THE ESSAY**

DIGITAL ASSETS KEY

These digital resources, as well as audio and the Online Writer's Notebook, can be found at **pearsonrealize.com**.

- Interactive Whiteboard Activities
- Virtual Tour
- Close Reading Notebook
- Video
- Close Reading Tool for Annotating Texts
- Grammar Tutorials

Rebels and Dreamers

The Romantic Period (1798 to 1832)

PART TWO TEXT SET: **LYRIC POETRY**

PART THREE TEXT SET: **THE REACTION TO SOCIETY'S ILLS**

DIGITAL ASSETS KEY

These digital resources, as well as audio and the Online Writer's Notebook, can be found at **pearsonrealize.com**.

- Interactive Whiteboard Activities
- Virtual Tour
- Close Reading Notebook
- Video
- Close Reading Tool for Annotating Texts
- Grammar Tutorials

Progress and Decline

The Victorian Period (1833 to 1901)

DIGITAL ASSETS KEY

These digital resources, as well as audio and the Online Writer's Notebook, can be found at **pearsonrealize.com**.

▢ **Interactive Whiteboard Activities**

🌐 **Virtual Tour**

▤ **Close Reading Notebook**

▶ **Video**

◎ **Close Reading Tool for Annotating Texts**

G **Grammar Tutorials**

A Time of Rapid Change

The Modern and Postmodern Periods (1901 to Present)

Multiple Perspectives on the Era

PART ONE TEXT SET: FORGING MODERNISM

Extended Study: T. S. Eliot

Comparing Literary Works: Allegory and Pastoral

PART TWO TEXT SET: MODERNISM IN FICTION

Extended Study: Virginia Woolf

DIGITAL ASSETS KEY

These digital resources, as well as audio and the Online Writer's Notebook, can be found at **pearsonrealize.com**.

- Interactive Whiteboard Activities
- Video
- Virtual Tour
- Close Reading Tool for Annotating Texts
- Close Reading Notebook
- G Grammar Tutorials

Literature

▶ Stories

▶ Drama

▶ Poetry

COMMON CORE
Skills Workshops

▶ Writing Workshops

▶ Speaking and Listening

▶ Language Study

▶ Text Set Workshops

SAT PREP ACT Test-Taking Practice

The Common Core State Standards will prepare you to succeed in college and your future career. They are separated into four sections—Reading (Literature and Informational Text), Writing, Speaking and Listening, and Language. Beginning each section, the College and Career Readiness Anchor Standards define what you need to achieve by the end of high school. The grade-specific standards that follow define what you need to know by the end of your current grade level.

ⓒ Common Core Reading Standards

College and Career Readiness Anchor Standards

Key Ideas and Details

1. Read closely to determine what the text says explicitly and to make logical inferences from it; cite specific textual evidence when writing or speaking to support conclusions drawn from the text.

2. Determine central ideas or themes of a text and analyze their development; summarize the key supporting details and ideas.

3. Analyze how and why individuals, events, and ideas develop and interact over the course of a text.

Craft and Structure

4. Interpret words and phrases as they are used in a text, including determining technical, connotative, and figurative meanings, and analyze how specific word choices shape meaning or tone.

5. Analyze the structure of texts, including how specific sentences, paragraphs, and larger portions of the text (e.g., a section, chapter, scene, or stanza) relate to each other and the whole.

6. Assess how point of view or purpose shapes the content and style of a text.

Integration of Knowledge and Ideas

7. Integrate and evaluate content presented in diverse formats and media, including visually and quantitatively, as well as in words.

8. Delineate and evaluate the argument and specific claims in a text, including the validity of the reasoning as well as the relevance and sufficiency of the evidence.

9. Analyze how two or more texts address similar themes or topics in order to build knowledge or to compare the approaches the authors take.

Range of Reading and Level of Text Complexity

10. Read and comprehend complex literary and informational texts independently and proficiently.

Grade 12 Reading Standards for Literature

Key Ideas and Details

1. Cite strong and thorough textual evidence to support analysis of what the text says explicitly as well as inferences drawn from the text, including determining where the text leaves matters uncertain.

2. Determine two or more themes or central ideas of a text and analyze their development over the course of the text, including how they interact and build on one another to produce a complex account; provide an objective summary of the text.

3. Analyze the impact of the author's choices regarding how to develop and relate elements of a story or drama (e.g., where a story is set, how the action is ordered, how the characters are introduced and developed).

Craft and Structure

4. Determine the meaning of words and phrases as they are used in the text, including figurative and connotative meanings; analyze the impact of specific word choices on meaning and tone, including words with multiple meanings or language that is particularly fresh, engaging, or beautiful. (Include Shakespeare as well as other authors.)

5. Analyze how an author's choices concerning how to structure specific parts of a text (e.g., the choice of where to begin or end a story, the choice to provide a comedic or tragic resolution) contribute to its overall structure and meaning as well as its aesthetic impact.

6. Analyze a case in which grasping point of view requires distinguishing what is directly stated in a text from what is really meant (e.g., satire, sarcasm, irony, or understatement).

Integration of Knowledge and Ideas

7. Analyze multiple interpretations of a story, drama, or poem (e.g., recorded or live production of a play or recorded novel or poetry), evaluating how each version interprets the source text. (Include at least one play by Shakespeare and one play by an American dramatist.)

8. (Not applicable to literature)

9. Demonstrate knowledge of eighteenth-, nineteenth-, and early-twentieth-century foundational works of American literature, including how two or more texts from the same period treat similar themes or topics.

Range of Reading and Level of Text Complexity

10. By the end of grade 12, read and comprehend literature, including stories, dramas, and poems, at the high end of the grades 11–CCR text complexity band independently and proficiently.

Grade 12 Reading Standards for Informational Text

Key Ideas and Details

1. Cite strong and thorough textual evidence to support analysis of what the text says explicitly as well as inferences drawn from the text, including determining where the text leaves matters uncertain.

2. Determine two or more central ideas of a text and analyze their development over the course of the text, including how they interact and build on one another to provide a complex analysis; provide an objective summary of the text.

3. Analyze a complex set of ideas or sequence of events and explain how specific individuals, ideas, or events interact and develop over the course of the text.

Craft and Structure

4. Determine the meaning of words and phrases as they are used in a text, including figurative, connotative, and technical meanings; analyze how an author uses and refines the meaning of a key term or terms over the course of a text (e.g., how Madison defines *faction* in *Federalist* No. 10).

5. Analyze and evaluate the effectiveness of the structure an author uses in his or her exposition or argument, including whether the structure makes points clear, convincing, and engaging.

6. Determine an author's point of view or purpose in a text in which the rhetoric is particularly effective, analyzing how style and content contribute to the power, persuasiveness, or beauty of the text.

Integration of Knowledge and Ideas

7. Integrate and evaluate multiple sources of information presented in different media or formats (e.g., visually, quantitatively) as well as in words in order to address a question or solve a problem.

8. Delineate and evaluate the reasoning in seminal U.S. texts, including the application of constitutional principles and use of legal reasoning (e.g., in U.S. Supreme Court majority opinions and dissents) and the premises, purposes, and arguments in works of public advocacy (e.g., *The Federalist,* presidential addresses).

9. Analyze seventeenth-, eighteenth-, and nineteenth-century foundational U.S. documents of historical and literary significance (including The Declaration of Independence, the Preamble to the Constitution, the Bill of Rights, and Lincoln's Second Inaugural Address) for their themes, purposes, and rhetorical features.

Range of Reading and Level of Text Complexity

10. By the end of grade 12, read and comprehend literary nonfiction at the high end of the grades 11–CCR text complexity band independently and proficiently.

ⓒ Common Core Writing Standards

College and Career Readiness Anchor Standards

Text Types and Purposes

1. Write arguments to support claims in an analysis of substantive topics or texts, using valid reasoning and relevant and sufficient evidence.

2. Write informative/explanatory texts to examine and convey complex ideas and information clearly and accurately through the effective selection, organization, and analysis of content.

3. Write narratives to develop real or imagined experiences or events using effective technique, well-chosen details, and well-structured event sequences.

Production and Distribution of Writing

4. Produce clear and coherent writing in which the development, organization, and style are appropriate to task, purpose, and audience.

5. Develop and strengthen writing as needed by planning, revising, editing, rewriting, or trying a new approach.

6. Use technology, including the Internet, to produce and publish writing and to interact and collaborate with others.

Research to Build and Present Knowledge

7. Conduct short as well as more sustained research projects based on focused questions, demonstrating understanding of the subject under investigation.

8. Gather relevant information from multiple print and digital sources, assess the credibility and accuracy of each source, and integrate the information while avoiding plagiarism.

9. Draw evidence from literary or informational texts to support analysis, reflection, and research.

Range of Writing

10. Write routinely over extended time frames (time for research, reflection, and revision) and shorter time frames (a single sitting or a day or two) for a range of tasks, purposes, and audiences.

Grade 12 Writing Standards

Text Types and Purposes

1. Write arguments to support claims in an analysis of substantive topics or texts, using valid reasoning and relevant and sufficient evidence.

   a. Introduce precise, knowledgeable claim(s), establish the significance of the claim(s), distinguish the claim(s) from alternate or opposing claims, and create an organization that logically sequences claim(s), counterclaims, reasons, and evidence.

   b. Develop claim(s) and counterclaims fairly and thoroughly, supplying the most relevant evidence for each while pointing out the strengths and limitations of both in a manner that anticipates the audience's knowledge level, concerns, values, and possible biases.

   c. Use words, phrases, and clauses as well as varied syntax to link the major sections of the text, create cohesion, and clarify the relationships between claim(s) and reasons, between reasons and evidence, and between claim(s) and counterclaims.

   d. Establish and maintain a formal style and objective tone while attending to the norms and conventions of the discipline in which they are writing.

   e. Provide a concluding statement or section that follows from and supports the argument presented.

2. Write informative/explanatory texts to examine and convey complex ideas, concepts, and information clearly and accurately through the effective selection, organization, and analysis of content.

   a. Introduce a topic; organize complex ideas, concepts, and information so that each new element builds on that which precedes it to create a unified whole; include formatting (e.g., headings), graphics (e.g., figures, tables), and multimedia when useful to aiding comprehension.

   b. Develop the topic thoroughly by selecting the most significant and relevant facts, extended definitions, concrete details, quotations, or other information and examples appropriate to the audience's knowledge of the topic.

   c. Use appropriate and varied transitions and syntax to link the major sections of the text, create cohesion, and clarify the relationships among complex ideas and concepts.

   d. Use precise language, domain-specific vocabulary, and techniques such as metaphor, simile, and analogy to manage the complexity of the topic.

   e. Establish and maintain a formal style and objective tone while attending to the norms and conventions of the discipline in which they are writing.

   f. Provide a concluding statement or section that follows from and supports the information or explanation presented (e.g., articulating implications or the significance of the topic).

3. Write narratives to develop real or imagined experiences or events using effective technique, well-chosen details, and well-structured event sequences.

   a. Engage and orient the reader by setting out a problem, situation, or observation and its significance, establishing one or multiple point(s) of view, and introducing a narrator and/or characters; create a smooth progression of experiences or events.

b. Use narrative techniques, such as dialogue, pacing, description, reflection, and multiple plot lines, to develop experiences, events, and/or characters.

c. Use a variety of techniques to sequence events so that they build on one another to create a coherent whole and build toward a particular tone and outcome (e.g., a sense of mystery, suspense, growth, or resolution).

d. Use precise words and phrases, telling details, and sensory language to convey a vivid picture of the experiences, events, setting, and/or characters.

e. Provide a conclusion that follows from and reflects on what is experienced, observed, or resolved over the course of the narrative.

Production and Distribution of Writing

4. Produce clear and coherent writing in which the development, organization, and style are appropriate to task, purpose, and audience.

5. Develop and strengthen writing as needed by planning, revising, editing, rewriting, or trying a new approach, focusing on addressing what is most significant for a specific purpose and audience.

6. Use technology, including the Internet, to produce, publish, and update individual or shared writing products in response to ongoing feedback, including new arguments or information.

Research to Build and Present Knowledge

7. Conduct short as well as more sustained research projects to answer a question (including a self-generated question) or solve a problem; narrow or broaden the inquiry when appropriate; synthesize multiple sources on the subject, demonstrating understanding of the subject under investigation.

8. Gather relevant information from multiple authoritative print and digital sources, using advanced searches effectively; assess the strengths and limitations of each source in terms of the task, purpose, and audience; integrate information into the text selectively to maintain the flow of ideas, avoiding plagiarism and overreliance on any one source and following a standard format for citation.

9. Draw evidence from literary or informational texts to support analysis, reflection, and research.

a. Apply *grades 11–12 Reading standards* to literature (e.g., "Demonstrate knowledge of eighteenth-, nineteenth-, and early-twentieth-century foundational works of American literature, including how two or more texts from the same period treat similar themes or topics").

b. Apply *grades 11–12 Reading standards* to literary nonfiction (e.g., "Delineate and evaluate the reasoning in seminal U.S. texts, including the application of constitutional principles and use of legal reasoning [e.g., in U.S. Supreme Court Case majority opinions and dissents] and the premises, purposes, and arguments in works of public advocacy [e.g., *The Federalist,* presidential addresses]").

Range of Writing

10. Write routinely over extended time frames (time for research, reflection, and revision) and shorter time frames (a single sitting or a day or two) for a range of tasks, purposes, and audiences.

© Common Core Speaking and Listening Standards

College and Career Readiness Anchor Standards

Comprehension and Collaboration

1. Prepare for and participate effectively in a range of conversations and collaborations with diverse partners, building on others' ideas and expressing their own clearly and persuasively.

2. Integrate and evaluate information presented in diverse media and formats, including visually, quantitatively, and orally.

3. Evaluate a speaker's point of view, reasoning, and use of evidence and rhetoric.

Presentation of Knowledge and Ideas

4. Present information, findings, and supporting evidence such that listeners can follow the line of reasoning and the organization, development, and style are appropriate to task, purpose, and audience.

5. Make strategic use of digital media and visual displays of data to express information and enhance understanding of presentations.

6. Adapt speech to a variety of contexts and communicative tasks, demonstrating command of formal English when indicated or appropriate.

Grade 12 Speaking and Listening Standards

Comprehension and Collaboration

1. Initiate and participate effectively in a range of collaborative discussions (one-on-one, in groups, and teacher-led) with diverse partners on *grades 11–12 topics, texts, and issues,* building on others' ideas and expressing their own clearly and persuasively.

    a. Come to discussions prepared, having read and researched material under study; explicitly draw on that preparation by referring to evidence from texts and other research on the topic or issue to stimulate a thoughtful, wellreasoned exchange of ideas.

    b. Work with peers to promote civil, democratic discussions and decision-making, set clear goals and deadlines, and establish individual roles as needed.

    c. Propel conversations by posing and responding to questions that probe reasoning and evidence; ensure a hearing for a full range of positions on a topic or issue; clarify, verify, or challenge ideas and conclusions; and promote divergent and creative perspectives.

    d. Respond thoughtfully to diverse perspectives; synthesize comments, claims, and evidence made on all sides of an issue; resolve contradictions when possible; and determine what additional information or research is required to deepen the investigation or complete the task.

2. Integrate multiple sources of information presented in diverse formats and media (e.g., visually, quantitatively, orally) in order to make informed decisions and solve problems, evaluating the credibility and accuracy of each source and noting any discrepancies among the data.

3. Evaluate a speaker's point of view, reasoning, and use of evidence and rhetoric, assessing the stance, premises, links among ideas, word choice, points of emphasis, and tone used.

Presentation of Knowledge and Ideas

4. Present information, findings, and supporting evidence, conveying a clear and distinct perspective, such that listeners can follow the line of reasoning, alternative or opposing perspectives are addressed, and the organization, development, substance, and style are appropriate to purpose, audience, and a range of formal and informal tasks.

5. Make strategic use of digital media (e.g., textual, graphical, audio, visual, and interactive elements) in presentations to enhance understanding of findings, reasoning, and evidence and to add interest.

6. Adapt speech to a variety of contexts and tasks, demonstrating a command of formal English when indicated or appropriate. (See grades 11–12 Language standards 1 and 3 for specific expectations.)

© Common Core Language Standards

College and Career Readiness Anchor Standards

Conventions of Standard English

1. Demonstrate command of the conventions of standard English grammar and usage when writing or speaking.

2. Demonstrate command of the conventions of standard English capitalization, punctuation, and spelling when writing.

Knowledge of Language

3. Apply knowledge of language to understand how language functions in different contexts, to make effective choices for meaning or style, and to comprehend more fully when reading or listening.

Vocabulary Acquisition and Use

4. Determine or clarify the meaning of unknown and multiple-meaning words and phrases by using context clues, analyzing meaningful word parts, and consulting general and specialized reference materials, as appropriate.

5. Demonstrate understanding of figurative language, word relationships, and nuances in word meanings.

6. Acquire and use accurately a range of general academic and domain-specific words and phrases sufficient for reading, writing, speaking, and listening at the college and career readiness level; demonstrate independence in gathering vocabulary knowledge when considering a word or phrase important to comprehension or expression.

Grade 12 Language Standards

Conventions of Standard English

1. Demonstrate command of the conventions of standard English grammar and usage when writing or speaking.
   a. Apply the understanding that usage is a matter of convention, can change over time, and is sometimes contested.
   b. Resolve issues of complex or contested usage, consulting references (e.g., *Merriam-Webster's Dictionary of English Usage, Garner's Modern American Usage*) as needed.

2. Demonstrate command of the conventions of standard English capitalization, punctuation, and spelling when writing.
   a. Observe hyphenation conventions.
   b. Spell correctly.

Knowledge of Language

3. Apply knowledge of language to understand how language functions in different contexts, to make effective choices for meaning or style, and to comprehend more fully when reading or listening.

   a. Vary syntax for effect, consulting references (e.g., Tufte's *Artful Sentences*) for guidance as needed; apply an understanding of syntax to the study of complex texts when reading.

Vocabulary Acquisition and Use

4. Determine or clarify the meaning of unknown and multiple-meaning words and phrases based on *grades 11–12 reading and content,* choosing flexibly from a range of strategies.

   a. Use context (e.g., the overall meaning of a sentence, paragraph, or text; a word's position or function in a sentence) as a clue to the meaning of a word or phrase.

   b. Identify and correctly use patterns of word changes that indicate different meanings or parts of speech (e.g., *conceive, conception, conceivable*).

   c. Consult general and specialized reference materials (e.g., dictionaries, glossaries, thesauruses), both print and digital, to find the pronunciation of a word or determine or clarify its precise meaning, its part of speech, its etymology, or its standard usage.

   d. Verify the preliminary determination of the meaning of a word or phrase (e.g., by checking the inferred meaning in context or in a dictionary).

5. Demonstrate understanding of figurative language, word relationships, and nuances in word meanings.

   a. Interpret figures of speech (e.g., hyperbole, paradox) in context and analyze their role in the text.

   b. Analyze nuances in the meaning of words with similar denotations.

6. Acquire and use accurately general academic and domain-specific words and phrases, sufficient for reading, writing, speaking, and listening at the college and career readiness level; demonstrate independence in gathering vocabulary knowledge when considering a word or phrase important to comprehension or expression.

COMMON CORE WORKSHOPS

- BUILDING ACADEMIC VOCABULARY

- WRITING AN OBJECTIVE SUMMARY

- COMPREHENDING COMPLEX TEXTS

- ANALYZING ARGUMENTS

- CONDUCTING RESEARCH

 **Common Core
State Standards**

Reading Literature 2, 4
**Reading Informational Text 2, 4,
6, 8, 9**
Writing 1.a, 1.b, 1.e, 7, 8, 9, 9.b
Language 6

Building Academic Vocabulary

Academic vocabulary is the language used in school, on standardized tests, and—often—in the business world. Academic terms are more formal and specific than the informal vocabulary most people use among friends and family members. Success in school and later in work requires a clear understanding of different types of academic language. The Common Core State Standards require that you acquire and use grade-appropriate academic words and phrases.

Technical Domain-Specific Academic Vocabulary The literary concepts you will learn throughout this book are one type of academic language. These words are specific to the content area—the subject or discipline—of literature. Other disciplines, such as social studies, the sciences, mathematics, and the arts, have their own academic vocabularies. Some content-area words cross disciplines, or have different meanings when applied to different areas of study.

Technical words are an even more specialized type of domain-specific academic vocabulary. These are words and phrases, such as the following, that identify a precise element in the content area and usually do not appear in other disciplines:

> *Science:* pipette; genome
> *Music:* clef; libretto

Critical Reading and Thinking Terms Many academic terms define modes of thinking, discussing, or writing about ideas. In this book, these words appear in the Critical Reading questions at the ends of the selections. Such academic terms also appear in instructions and writing prompts.

A Note on Etymology

Etymology is the branch of linguistics that deals with word origins and the development of languages. Etymologists trace the history of a word in its own language, and then to even earlier sources in other, more ancient languages. Knowledge of a word's etymology will contribute to your understanding of its meaning and help you determine the meaning of other words that share its history. Etymological information for content-area words appears in the charts on the following pages.

Common Core State Standards

Language

6. Acquire and use accurately general academic and domain-specific words and phrases, sufficient for reading, writing, speaking, and listening at the college and career readiness level; demonstrate independence in gathering vocabulary knowledge when considering a word or phrase important to comprehension or expression.

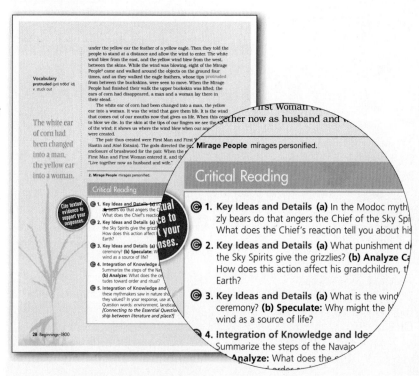

Technical Domain-Specific Academic Vocabulary

Knowledge of technical content-area academic words, and the roots and affixes that compose them, will help you in all your school courses. As you review the charts below, recognize words that apply to content areas other than those specified here.

Technical Domain-Specific Academic Vocabulary: Science

Term	Meaning	Root/Affix
Accelerate	*v.* increase speed	Latin root -*celer*- = swift Words with the same root: accelerator *n.*; celerity *n.*
Catalyst	*n.* something that acts to bring about a result	Latin root -*cata*- = down; away Words with the same root: cataclysm *n.*; catapult *n.*
Chlorophyll	*n.* green pigment found in plant cells	Greek root -*chloro*- = green Words with the same root: chlorine *n.*; chlorosis *n.*
Chromosome	*n.* strand of proteins that carries the genes of a living creature	Greek prefix *chromo*- = color; pigment Words with the same prefix: chromatic *adj.*; chromate *n.*
Cytoplasm	*n.* colorless substance of a cell; outside the nucleus	Greek suffix -*plasm* = molded; formed Words with the same suffix: bioplasm *n.*; protoplasm *n.*
Entropy	*n.* lack of order which increases over time in a system	Greek root -*tropos*- = turning; deviation Words with the same root: tropical *adj.*; trophy *n.*; heliotrope *n.*
Enzyme	*n.* chemical substance produced by living cells that causes changes in other chemicals	Greek suffix -*zyme* = leavening (an agent that causes fermentation) Words with the same suffix: vitazyme *n.*; microzyme *n.*
Mitosis	*n.* method of cell division	Greek suffix -*osis* = action; process Words with the same suffix: prognosis *n.*; psychosis *n.*
Thermometer	*n.* instrument for measuring temperature	Greek root -*therme*- = hot Words with the same root: thermonuclear *adj.*; thermostat *n.*
Viscous	*adj.* having a thick and sticky fluid consistency	Latin prefix *visco*- = sticky Words with the same prefix: viscometer *n.*; viscosity *n.*

Ordinary Language: Ice cubes placed in water will begin to **break down.**

Academic Language: Ice cubes placed in water will begin the process of **entropy.**

Exploring Academic Vocabulary: Science

The word *thermometer* combines the Greek roots -*therme*-, which means "heat," and -*metr*-, which means "measure." Using this knowledge, determine the meaning of the following words derived from the same roots:

dynameter　　**odometer**　　**hypothermia**　　**thermography**

Then, use a dictionary to confirm the definitions you proposed. If a general dictionary is not sufficient, consult a specialized science dictionary to find the information you need. Explain how the meaning of each word relates to those of its Greek origins.

Technical Domain-Specific Academic Vocabulary: Mathematics

Term	Meaning	Root/Affix
Correlate	*v.* show mutual relationship between items	Latin prefix *cor-* = together; with Words with the same prefix: correspond *v.*; corrosion *n.*
Exponent	*n.* symbol placed above and to the right of a number or letter to show how many times that quantity is to be multiplied by itself	Latin suffix *-ponent* = to put; place; set Words with the same suffix: component *n.*; proponent *n.*
Inflection	*n.* change of a curve or arc from convex to concave or the reverse	Latin root *-flectere-* = to bend Words with the same root: reflection *n.*; deflect *v.*
Logarithm	*n.* power to which a base must be raised to produce a given number	Greek prefix *logos-* = word; speech; reason Words with the same prefix: logic *n.*; logotype *n.*
Statistics	*n.* numerical facts or data	Latin root *-stat-* = condition; position; state Words with the same root: statistical *adj.*; static *adj.*
Permutation	*n.* one of the ways in which a set of things can be arranged or ordered	Latin root *-mutare-* = change Words with the same root: mutable *adj.*; mutation *n.*
Estimate	*v.* calculate approximately	Middle French root *-estimer-* = value; appraise Words with the same root: estimation *n.*; esteem *v.*
Graphic	*adj.* relating to the use of diagrams, graphs, curves	Greek root *-graph-* = writing; drawing Words with the same root: telegraph *n.*; biography *n.*; autograph *n.*
Configure	*v.* construct; arrange	Latin root *-figura-* = shape; form; figure Words with the same root: disfigure *v.*; effigy *n.*

> **Ordinary Language:**
> We arranged the **numerical information** in different charts.
>
> **Academic Language:**
> We incorporated **statistical data** into charts.

Exploring Academic Vocabulary: Mathematics

The word *correlate* is built on the Latin prefix *cor-* (also *com-* or *con-*), which means "with" or "together." Using this knowledge, determine the meaning of the following words derived from the same prefix:

correspond   **concert**   **compress**   **congruent**

Then, use an online or print dictionary to confirm the definitions you proposed. Explain how the meaning of each word relates to that of its Latin ancestor.

Technical Domain-Specific Academic Vocabulary: Social Studies

Term	Meaning	Root/Affix
Corporation	*n.* organization of many people authorized to act as a single person	Latin root *-corpus-* = body Words with the same root: corporeal *adj.*; incorporate *v.*
Demography	*n.* study of human populations	Greek prefix *demos-* = people Words with the same prefix: demographic *n.*; democracy *n.*
Economy	*n.* system by which a country's money and goods are used and produced	Greek suffix *-nomy* = law; received knowledge Words with the same suffix: agronomy *n.*; taxonomy *n.*
Invest	*v.* give money to a company in order to receive a profit	Latin root *-vestire-* = dress; clothe Words with the same root: vestment *n.*; investigation *n.*
Admiral	*n.* high-ranking naval officer	Arabic root *-amir-* = leader Words with the same root: emirate *n.;* admiralship *n.*
Curfew	*n.* law requiring a population to stay indoors at a stated hour	Old French root *-covrir-* = to cover Words with the same root: covert *adj.*; coverlet *n.*
Lieutenant	*n.* someone who substitutes for another person of greater authority	Old French root *-lieu-* = place Word with the same root: milieu *n.*
Absolutism	*n.* system of government in which a ruler has unlimited power	Latin prefix *ab-* = away; from Word with the same prefix: absolve *v.*
Civic	*adj.* of a city, citizens, or citizenship	Latin root *-civ-* = citizen Words with the same root: civilian *n.*; civilization *n.*

> **Ordinary Language:**
> The government urges citizens to **put money into** local businesses.
>
> **Academic Language:**
> The government urges citizens to **invest in** local businesses.

Exploring Academic Vocabulary: Social Studies

The word *economy* is built on the Greek suffix *-nomy*, which means "law; body of received knowledge." Using this knowledge, determine the meaning of the following words derived from the same suffix:

taxonomy   **autonomy**   **astronomy**   **gastronomy**

Then, use an online or print dictionary to confirm the definitions you proposed. Explain how the meaning of each word relates to that of its Greek ancestor.

Technical Domain-Specific Academic Vocabulary: Technology

Term	Meaning	Root/Affix
Gigabyte	*n.* unit of storage capacity in a computer system equal to 1,073,741,824 bytes	Greek prefix *giga-* = giant Words with the same prefix: gigahertz *n.*; gigantic *adj.*
Macro	*n.* single computer instruction that represents a sequence of operations	Greek prefix *macro-* = long, tall, deep, large Words with the same prefix: macrobiotic *adj.*; macrocosm *n.*
Pixel	*n.* smallest unit of an image on a television or computer screen	Old French suffix *–el* = small one Words with the same suffix: satchel *n.*; model *n.*
Processor	*n.* central part of a computer that does the calculations needed to deal with the information it is given	from Latin root *-cedere-* = to go Words with the same root: proceed *v.*; recede *v.*
Simulation	*n.* situation that produces conditions that are not real but appear real	Latin root *-sim-* = like derived through Indo-European base *sem-/som-* = same; as one Words with the same root: ensemble *v.*; simultaneous *adj.*
Streaming	*n.* method of transmitting data so that it can be delivered and received in a steady stream	German root *-strom-* = current; river Words with the same root: mainstream *n.*; streamline *v.*
Transmitter	*n.* equipment that sends out radio or television signals	Latin prefix *trans-* = across Words with the same prefix: transportation *n.*; transcontinental *adj.*
Debug	*v.* find and correct defects	Latin prefix *de-* = down; from Words with the same prefix: defuse *v.*; defrost *v.*
Export	*v.* in computers, to save data in a format usable by another program	Latin root *-portare-* = to carry Words with the same root: import *v.*; airport *n.*
Binary	*adj.* made up of two parts or things; twofold	Latin root *-bin-* = together; double Words with the same root: binocular *n.*; binomial *n.*

Ordinary Language:
I asked the technician to **clean up** my computer.

Academic Language:
I asked the technician to **debug** my operating system.

Exploring Academic Vocabulary: Technology

The word *simulation* comes from the Latin root *-sim-*, which means "like." This Latin root derives from the Indo-European base *sem-/som-*, which means "same; as one." Using your knowledge of these origins, determine the meaning of the following words derived from the same roots:

resemble **facsimile** **verisimilitude** **semblance**

Then, use a dictionary to confirm the definitions you proposed. Explain how the meaning of each word relates to that of its Indo-European base.

Technical Domain-Specific Academic Vocabulary: The Arts

Term	Meaning	Root/Affix
Allegro	*adv.* faster than allegretto but not so fast as presto	Latin root *-alacer-/-alacris-* = lively; brisk Words with the same root: allegretto *adj.*; *adv.*; alacrity *n.*
Alignment	*n.* arrangement in a straight line	Old French root *-lignier-* = to line Words with the same root: align *v.*; realign *v.*
Craftmanship	*n.* skill used in making handmade objects	Middle English suffix *-schipe*; derived through Anglian suffix *-scip* = state; condition; quality Words with the same suffix: friendship *n.*; dictatorship *n.*
Decrescendo	*n.* gradual decrease in volume	Old French *creissant*; derived through Latin root *-crescere-* = come forth; spring up; grow; thrive Words with the same root: crescent *n.*; increase *v.*
Baritone	*n.* male singing voice lower than a tenor and higher than a bass	Latin root *-tonus-* = sound; tone Words with the same root: monotone *n.*; intonation *n.*
Medium	*n.* material or technique used in art	Latin root *-medius-* = middle Words with the same root: media *n.*; mediate *v.*; median *adj.*
Musicality	*n.* sensitivity to, knowledge of, or talent for music	Latin suffix *-ity* = quality; state; or degree Words with the same suffix: normality *n.*; publicity *n.*
Technique	*n.* method or procedure in rendering an artistic work	Indo-European prefix *tek-* = shape; make Words with the same prefix: technical *adj.*; technician *n.*
Tempo	*n.* speed at which a composition is performed	Latin root *-tempus-* = time Words with the same root: temporal *adj.*; temporary *adj.*

> **Ordinary Language:** The dancers moved in a perfectly **straight line.**
>
> **Academic Language:** The dancers moved in perfect **alignment** on stage.

Exploring Academic Vocabulary: The Arts

The word *craftsmanship* is built on the Anglian suffix *–scip*, which means "state, condition, quality." Using this knowledge, determine the meaning of the following words derived from the same suffix:

musicianship   **readership**   **friendship**   **partnership**

Then, use an online or print dictionary to confirm the definitions you proposed. Explain how the meaning of each word relates to that of its Anglian ancestor.

Vocabulary Across Content Areas

You might recognize words that apply to content areas other than those specified in the charts on the previous pages. For example, notice how the word *accelerator* relates to two different content areas:

Science: accelerator *n.* nerve or muscle that speeds up a body function

Automotive Technology: accelerator *n.* device, such as the foot throttle of an automobile, for increasing the speed of a machine

While the objects referred to in each definition are different, both of their functions relate to the Latin root *–celer–,* meaning "swift." As you read texts for school, recognize similarities in roots or affixes among words in different content areas. This will help you better understand specific terms and make meaningful connections among topics.

Academic Vocabulary: Critical Thinking Terms

Throughout this book, you will encounter academic vocabulary related to the process of critical thinking. Unlike content-area vocabulary, these words apply equally in all school studies. Being familiar with these academic vocabulary words will be useful as you approach high-stakes standardized tests such as the SAT and ACT. Academic vocabulary will also aid you as you encounter business materials in the workplace.

Term (verb form)	Meaning	Root/Affix
Advocate	Speak or write in support of	Latin root *-voc-* = speak; call Related words: advocate *n.*; advocacy *n.*
Anticipate	Prepare for or signal something	Latin prefix *ante-* = before Related words: anticipatory *adj.*; anticipation *n.*
Arrange	Put into order or sequence	Old French root *-rang-* = rank Related words: arrangement *n.*
Assess	Determine importance; size; or value	Latin root *-sed-/-sess-* = sit Related words: assessment *n.*
Categorize	Place in related groups	Greek prefix *kata-/cata-* = down; against Related words: category *n.*; categorical *adj.*
Compare	Examine in order to discover similarities	Latin root *-par-* = equal Related words: comparison *n.*; comparable *adj.*
Conclude	Determination reached through logical reasoning	Latin root *-clud-* = shut Related words: conclusion *n.*; conclusive *adj.*
Contrast	Examine in order to discover differences	Latin prefix *con-/com-* = with; together Related words: contrastable *adj.*
Debate	Discuss opposing reasons; argue	French root *-batre-* = to beat Related words: debatable *adj.*

Term (verb form)	Meaning	Root/Affix
Deduce	Infer from a general principle	Latin root -duc- = to lead Related words: deduction n.; deductive adj.
Defend	Maintain or support in the face of argument	Latin root -fend- = to strike; push Related words: defense n.; defendant n.
Describe	Represent in words	Latin root -scrib- = to write Related words: description n.; descriptive adj.
Design	Create; fashion or construct according to plan	Latin root -sign- = to mark Related words: design n.; designer n.
Devise	Form in the mind by new combinations of ideas; invent	Latin root -vid- = to separate Related words: devisable adj.
Differentiate	Recognize a difference	Latin suffix -ate = act Related words: different adj.; differentiation n.
Evaluate	Determine significance, worth, or condition through careful study	Old French root -val- = worth; value Related words: evaluation n.; evaluative adj.
Format	Arrange according to a design or plan	Latin root -form- = form, shape Related words: format n.; formation n.
Generalize	Draw a larger principle from details	Latin root -genus- = stock; kind Related words: generalization n.
Hypothesize	Develop a theory about	Greek prefix hypo- = under, beneath Related words: hypothesis n.; hypothetically adv.
Illustrate	Give examples that support an idea	Latin root -lus- = brighten; illuminate Related words: illustration n.; illustrative adj.
Interpret	Explain the meaning of	Latin root -inter- = between Related words: interpretation n.; interpreter n.
Investigate	Make a systematic examination	French root -vestige- = mark; trace; sign Related words: investigation n.; investigative adj.
Paraphrase	Express in one's own words what another person has said or written	Greek prefix para- = beside Related words: paraphraser n.
Predict	Foretell on the basis of observation, experience, or reason	Latin root -dic- = speak, tell, say Related words: prediction n.; predictable adj.
Refute	Prove an argument or statement false or wrong	Latin root -fut- = beat Related words: refutable adj.; refutably adv.
Sort	Put in place according to kind, class, or nature	Old French root -sortir- = allot; assort Related words: sorter n.
Speculate	Use evidence to guess what might happen	Latin root -spec- = look at; view Related words: speculation n.; speculative adj.
Structure	Create a general plot or outline	Latin root -struct- = to build; assemble Related words: structure n.; structural adj.
Validate	Prove to be factual or effective	Latin root -val- = be strong Related words: valid adj.; validity n.

Ordinary Language:
She **explained the meaning of** the story's symbols.

Academic Language:
She **interpreted** the meaning of the story's symbols.

Writing an Objective Summary

The ability to write objective summaries is important in college course work and in many careers, such as journalism, business, law, various medical fields, social work, and research. Writing an effective objective summary involves recording the key ideas of a text as well as demonstrating your understanding of the text.

Characteristics of an Objective Summary

An effective objective summary is a concise, overview of a text. Following are important elements of an objective summary:

- It is **focused,** relaying the main theme or central idea of a text. It includes specific, relevant details that support that theme or central idea and leaves out unnecessary supporting details.
- It is **brief,** although the writer must be careful to balance brevity and thoroughness and not misrepresent the text by eliminating important parts.
- It is **accurate.** It captures the essence of the longer text it is describing.
- It is **objective.** The writer should refrain from inserting his or her own opinions, judgments, reactions, or personal reflections into the summary.

Remember that an objective summary is *not* a collection of sentences or paragraphs copied from the original source. It is *not* a long retelling of every event, detail, or point in the original text. Finally, a good summary does *not* include evaluative comments, such as the reader's overall opinion of or reaction to the text.

Checklist for Writing an Objective Summary

Before writing an objective summary, be sure you are well acquainted with the text.

- **Understand the entire passage.** You must clearly understand the text's meaning, including any advanced or technical terminology. In your summary, refer to details from the beginning, middle, and end of the text.
- **Prioritize ideas and details.** Determine the main or central ideas of a text and identify the key supporting details. Make sure you recognize which details are less important so that you do not include them in your objective summary.
- **Identify the author's audience and purpose.** Knowing what the author intended to accomplish in the text as well as what audience it was designed to reach will help you summarize accurately.

**Common Core
State Standards**

Reading Informational Text
2. Determine two or more central ideas of a text and analyze their development over the course of the text, including how they interact and build on one another to provide a complex analysis; provide an objective summary of the text.

Reading Literature
2. Determine two or more themes or central ideas of a text and analyze their development over the course of the text, including how they interact and build on one another to produce a complex account; provide an objective summary of the text.

INFORMATIONAL TEXT

Model Objective Summary

Note the key elements of an effective objective summary, called out in the sidenotes. Then, write an objective summary of a text you have recently read. Review your summary, and delete any unnecessary details, opinions, or evaluations.

Summary of "The Story of an Hour"

"The Story of an Hour" by the under-appreciated Kate Chopin is a short story about a woman who is told her husband is dead. Set in the late nineteenth century, the story takes place in the home of Mrs. Louise Mallard.

Because of Mrs. Mallard's heart condition, her sister Josephine tells her the news gently. Richards, a family friend, had been in the newspaper office when a telegram was received that told of a railroad disaster, and Brently Mallard was listed as dead. Mrs. Mallard immediately takes in the news and begins to weep, heading to her room alone.

She sits in an armchair and looks out the window. She notices signs of life everywhere, which contrast with her loss. It is so very sad.

Then a thought begins to come to her as she looks at the blue patches in the sky. She breathes heavily as she struggles with the full comprehension of the thought that is trying to possess her, but she gives in. She whispers the word: "Free." She repeats the word over and over. Her eyes brighten, her heart beats quickly, and her body relaxes.

She decides that she will cry at the dead body of the man who loved her, but she welcomes the years beyond that. She looks forward to living independently. The thought of freedom is exhilarating.

Josephine begs her to open the door, but Louise refuses.

She imagines the days ahead and prays that her life will be long, remembering that the day before she had dreaded the thought of a long life. She finally lets her sister in and holds her tight around her waist. Together they go downstairs to meet Richards.

Brently Mallard, alive and unharmed, then walks through the front door. He was unaware of the accident at the railroad and surprised at the cry of his wife.

The doctors said her weak heart could not stand such joy; they called it the "joy that kills."

A one-sentence synopsis highlighting the theme or central idea of the story can be an effective start to a summary. Relating the setting of the text gives the summary context.

Opinions should not be included in an objective summary.

These sentences are too detailed and too interpretative to be included in an objective summary. More appropriate would be a simpler statement, such as, "Suddenly a thought came to her."

Eliminate unnecessary details.

The writer includes the last phrase in the story because the irony is a key element of the story.

Comprehending Complex Texts

As you prepare for higher education and the workplace, you will be required to read increasingly complex texts. A complex text features one or more of the following qualities:

- challenging vocabulary
- long, complex sentences
- figurative language
- multiple levels of meaning
- unfamiliar settings and situations

The selections in this textbook provide you with a range of readings in many genres. Some of these texts will be quite accessible, while others will be, and should be, more challenging. In order to comprehend and interpret complex texts, practice the reading strategies described here.

Strategy 1: Multidraft Reading

Good readers develop the habit of rereading texts in order to comprehend them completely. Similar to listening to a song over and over in order to better understand the lyrics and relive the emotional experience, returning to a text enables readers to more fully enjoy and comprehend it. To fully understand a text, try this multidraft reading strategy:

1st Reading

The first time you read a text, read to gain its basic meaning. If you are reading a narrative text, look for the basics of the plot, character, and setting. If the text is nonfiction, look for central ideas. If you are reading poetry, read first to get a sense of speaker, topic, and mood.

2nd Reading

During your second reading of a text, look for deeper meaning by applying your literary analysis skills. Focus on the artistry or effectiveness of the writing. Look for text structures. Think about why the author chose those organizational patterns. Examine the author's use of language and its effect. For example, consider the effect of rhyme, figurative language, or words with distinct connotations.

3rd Reading

In this reading, search for multiple levels of meaning, considering historical and cultural context. Now is the time to compare and contrast the text with others of its kind you have read. Consider it in the context of its genre, and make connections between texts. You may also make connections between the text and your own experiences. After your third reading, you should be able to evaluate the text's overall effectiveness and its central idea or theme.

Common Core State Standards

Reading Literature

4. Determine the meaning of words and phrases as they are used in the text, including figurative and connotative meanings; analyze the impact of specific word choices on meaning and tone, including words with multiple meanings or language that is particularly fresh, engaging, or beautiful.

Reading Informational Text

4. Determine the meaning of words and phrases as they are used in a text, including figurative, connotative, and technical meanings; analyze how an author uses and refines the meaning of a key term or terms over the course of a text (e.g., how Madison defines *faction* in *Federalist* No. 10).

9. Analyze seventeenth-, eighteenth- and nineteenth-century foundational U.S. documents of historical and literary significance (including the Declaration of Independence, the Preamble to the Constitution, the Bill of Rights, and Lincoln's Second Inaugural Address) for their themes, purposes, and rhetorical features.

Independent Practice

As you read this poem by John Keats, practice the multidraft reading strategy by completing a chart like the one below.

On the Grasshopper and Cricket
by John Keats

The poetry of earth is never dead:

When all the birds are faint with the hot sun,

And hide in cooling trees, a voice will run

From hedge to hedge about the new-mown mead;

That is the Grasshopper's—he takes the lead

In summer luxury—he has never done

With his delights; for when tired out with fun

He rests at ease beneath some pleasant weed.

The poetry of earth is ceasing never:

On a lone winter evening, when the frost

Has wrought a silence, from the stove there shrills

The Cricket's song, in warmth increasing ever,

And seems to one in drowsiness half lost,

The Grasshopper's among some grassy hills.

Multidraft Reading Chart

	My Understanding
1st Reading Look for key ideas and details that reveal basic meaning.	
2nd Reading Read for deeper meanings. Look for ways in which the author used text structures and language to create effects.	
3rd Reading Integrate knowledge and ideas. Consider cultural and historical context and genre. Connect the text to your own experience.	

Strategy 2: Close Read the Text

Complex texts require close reading and a careful analysis of the writer's choice of words, phrases, and sentences. An awareness of literary and rhetorical techniques and elements, such as parallelism, symbolism, analogy, and text structure, contributes to a deep understanding of a complex text. However, a starting point for close reading is comprehension, which is the foundation for interpretation and analysis. Use the following tips to comprehend the text:

Tips for Close Reading
1. Break down long sentences into parts. Look for the subject of the sentence and its verb. Then identify which parts of the sentence modify, or give more information about, its subject.
2. Reread passages. When reading complex texts, be sure to reread passages to confirm that you understand their meaning. Look for rhetorical devices and persuasive techniques.

3. Look for context clues, such as
 	
   a. Restatement of an idea. For example, in this sentence, *small* restates the adjective *diminutive.*
 	
     She received only a **diminutive** sum, but she was able to make the <u>small</u> amount last the rest of the month.
 	
   b. Definition of sophisticated words. In this sentence, the word *depravity* defines the verb *turpitude.*
 	
     The **turpitude**, or <u>depravity</u>, of the young character in the film stunned the audience to silence.
 	
   c. Examples of concepts and topics. In the following sentence, the underlined text provides examples of words that suggest the meaning of the adjective *melancholy.*
 	
     The **melancholy** territory of gothic literature includes <u>gloomy</u> settings, <u>eerie</u> occurrences, and <u>emotionally troubled</u> characters.
 	
   d. Contrasts of ideas and topics.
 	
     Their **banter** evolved into a <u>serious conversation.</u>

4. Identify pronoun antecedents. If long sentences contain pronouns, reread the text to make sure you know to what the pronouns refer. The pronoun *it* in the following sentence refers to the infinitive phrase *to protest injustices,* not to the government. The government should assume that **it** is not harmful <u>to protest injustices.</u> (The government should assume that to protest injustices is not harmful.)
5. Look for conjunctions, such as *and, or, however, accordingly,* and *yet,* to help you understand relationships between ideas.
6. Paraphrase, or restate in your own words, passages of difficult text in order to check your understanding. Remember that a paraphrase is essentially a word-for-word restatement of an original text; it is not a summary.

INFORMATIONAL TEXT

Close-Read Model

As you read this document, take note of the sidenotes that model ways to unlock meaning in the text.

from "Defending Nonviolent Resistance"
by Mohandas K. Gandhi

Affection cannot be manufactured or regulated by law. If one has an affection for a person or system, one should be free to give the fullest expression to his disaffection, so long as he does not contemplate, promote, or incite to violence. But the section under which Mr. Banker [a colleague in nonviolence] and I are charged is one under which mere promotion of disaffection is a crime. I have studied some of the cases tried under it, and I know that some of the most loved of India's patriots have been convicted under it. I consider it a privilege, therefore, to be charged under that section. I have endeavored to give in their briefest outline the reasons for my disaffection. I have no personal ill will against any single administrator, much less can I have any disaffection toward the king's person. But I hold it to be a virtue to be disaffected toward a government which in its totality has done more harm to India than any previous system. India is less manly under the British rule than she ever was before. Holding such a belief, I consider it to be a sin to have affection for the system. And it has been a precious privilege for me to be able to write what I have in the various articles, tendered in evidence against me.

In fact, I believe that I have rendered a service to India and England by showing in non-cooperation the way out of the unnatural state in which both are living. In my humble opinion, non-cooperation with evil is as much a duty as is cooperation with good. But in the past, non-cooperation has been deliberately expressed in violence to the evildoer. I am endeavoring to show to my countrymen that violent non-cooperation only multiplies evil and that as evil can only be sustained by violence, withdrawal of support of evil requires complete abstention from violence. Nonviolence implies voluntary submission to the penalty for non-cooperation with evil. I am here, therefore, to invite and submit cheerfully to the highest penalty that be inflicted upon me for what in law is a deliberate crime and what appears to me to be the highest duty of a citizen. The only course open to you, the judge, is either to resign your post, and thus dissociate yourself from evil if you feel that the law you are called upon to administer is an evil and that in reality I am innocent, or to inflict on me the severest penalty if you believe that the system and the law you are assisting to administer are good for the people of this country and that my activity is therefore injurious to the public weal.

Note rhetorical devices, such as Gandhi's use of antithesis—connecting contrasting ideas—here.

The conjunction *But* indicates a contrasting idea: Gandhi has no ill will toward a single person, but he does have disaffection toward the totality of the government.

Look for antecedents. The antecedent of the word *it* comes after the pronoun: *to be disaffected toward a government...*

Search for context clues. The words in blue are context clues that help you figure out the meaning of the word that appears in yellow.

Break down this long sentence into parts. The text highlighted in yellow conveys the basic meaning of the sentence. The text highlighted in blue provides additional information.

Strategy 3: Ask Questions

Be an attentive reader by asking questions as you read. Throughout this program, we have provided questions for you following each selection. Those questions are sorted into three basic categories that build in sophistication and lead you to a deeper understanding of the texts. Here is an example from this textbook:

Some questions are about **Key Ideas and Details** in the text. You will need to locate and cite explicit information in the text or draw inferences from what you have read.

Some questions are about **Craft and Structure** in the text. To answer these questions, you will need to analyze how the author developed and structured the text. You will also look for ways in which the author artfully used language and how those word choices impacted the meaning and tone of the work.

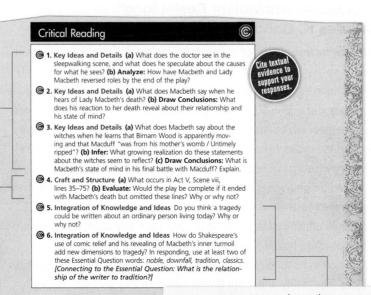

Critical Reading

1. **Key Ideas and Details (a)** What does the doctor see in the sleepwalking scene, and what does he speculate about the causes for what he sees? **(b) Analyze:** How have Macbeth and Lady Macbeth reversed roles by the end of the play?

2. **Key Ideas and Details (a)** What does Macbeth say when he hears of Lady Macbeth's death? **(b) Draw Conclusions:** What does his reaction to her death reveal about their relationship and his state of mind?

3. **Key Ideas and Details (a)** What does Macbeth say about the witches when he learns that Birnam Wood is apparently moving and that Macduff "was from his mother's womb / Untimely ripped"? **(b) Infer:** What growing realization do these statements about the witches seem to reflect? **(c) Draw Conclusions:** What is Macbeth's state of mind in his final battle with Macduff? Explain.

4. **Craft and Structure (a)** What occurs in Act V, Scene viii, lines 35–75? **(b) Evaluate:** Would the play be complete if it ended with Macbeth's death but omitted these lines? Why or why not?

5. **Integration of Knowledge and Ideas** Do you think a tragedy could be written about an ordinary person living today? Why or why not?

6. **Integration of Knowledge and Ideas** How do Shakespeare's use of comic relief and his revealing of Macbeth's inner turmoil add new dimensions to tragedy? In responding, use at least two of these Essential Question words: *noble, downfall, tradition, classics.* *[Connecting to the Essential Question: What is the relationship of the writer to tradition?]*

Cite textual evidence to support your responses.

Some questions are about the **Integration of Knowledge and Ideas** in the text. These questions ask you to evaluate a text in many different ways, such as comparing texts, analyzing arguments in the text, and using many other methods of thinking critically about a text's ideas.

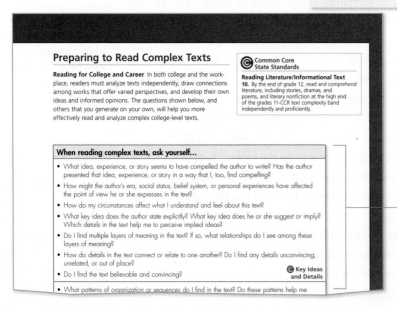

Preparing to Read Complex Texts

Reading for College and Career In both college and the workplace, readers must analyze texts independently, draw connections among works that offer varied perspectives, and develop their own ideas and informed opinions. The questions shown below, and others that you generate on your own, will help you more effectively read and analyze complex college-level texts.

Common Core State Standards

Reading Literature/Informational Text
10. By the end of grade 12, read and comprehend literature, including stories, dramas, and poems, and literary nonfiction at the high end of the grades 11-CCR text complexity band independently and proficiently.

When reading complex texts, ask yourself...

- What idea, experience, or story seems to have compelled the author to write? Has the author presented that idea, experience, or story in a way that I, too, find compelling?
- How might the author's era, social status, belief system, or personal experiences have affected the point of view he or she expresses in the text?
- How do my circumstances affect what I understand and feel about this text?
- What key idea does the author state explicitly? What key idea does he or she suggest or imply? Which details in the text help me to perceive implied ideas?
- Do I find multiple layers of meaning in the text? If so, what relationships do I see among these layers of meaning?
- How do details in the text connect or relate to one another? Do I find any details unconvincing, unrelated, or out of place?
- Do I find the text believable and convincing?

Key Ideas and Details

- What patterns of organization or sequences do I find in the text? Do these patterns help me

As you read independently, ask similar types of questions to ensure that you fully enjoy and comprehend any text you choose to read. We have provided sets of questions for you on the Independent Reading pages at the end of each unit.

 **INFORMATIONAL TEXT**

Model

In this example of a complex text, the call-out boxes show questions that an attentive reader might ask while reading.

The Preamble of the United States Constitution

We the people of the United States, in order to form a more perfect union, establish justice, insure domestic tranquility, provide for the common defense, promote the general welfare, and secure the blessings of liberty to ourselves and our posterity, do ordain and establish this Constitution for the United States of America.

Sample questions:

Key Ideas and Details What is the purpose of the Preamble? What is the purpose of the Constitution?

INFORMATIONAL TEXT

Independent Practice

The Bill of Rights

Amendment I Congress shall make no law respecting an establishment of religion, or prohibiting the free exercise thereof; or abridging the freedom of speech, or of the press, or the right of the people peaceably to assemble, and to petition the Government.

Amendment II A well regulated Militia, being necessary to the security of a free State, the right of the people to keep and bear Arms, shall not be infringed.

Amendment III No Soldier shall, in time of peace be quartered in any house, without the consent of the Owner, nor in time of war, but in a manner to be prescribed by law.

Amendment IV The right of the people to be secure in their persons, houses, papers, and effects, against unreasonable searches and seizures, shall not be violated, and no Warrants shall issue, but upon probable cause, supported by Oath or affirmation, and particularly describing the place to be searched, and the persons or things to be seized.

Amendment V No person shall be held to answer for a capital, or otherwise infamous crime, unless on a presentment or indictment of a Grand Jury . . . nor shall any person be subject for the same offence to be twice put in jeopardy of life or limb, nor shall be compelled in any criminal case to be a witness against himself . . . nor shall private property be taken for public use, without just compensation.

Amendment VI In all criminal prosecutions, the accused shall enjoy the right to a speedy and public trial, by an impartial jury of the State and district wherein the crime shall have been committed . . . to be confronted with the witnesses against him . . . and to have the assistance of counsel for his defense.

Amendment VII In Suits at common law, where the value in controversy shall exceed twenty dollars, the right of trial by jury shall be preserved . . .

Amendment VIII Excessive bail shall not be required, nor excessive fines imposed, nor cruel and unusual punishments inflicted. . . .

Craft and Structure What is the effect of parallel structure here? How does this pattern help me follow the ideas and argument? What attitude does the author project?

Integration of Knowledge and Ideas What other U.S. documents have themes similar to those found in the Preamble and the Bill of Rights?

Analyzing Arguments

The ability to evaluate an argument, as well as to make one, is critical for success in college and in the workplace.

What Is an Argument?

Chances are you have used the word *argument* to refer to a disagreement between people. A second definition of *argument* is to present one side of a controversial or debatable issue. Through this type of argument, the writer logically supports a particular belief, conclusion, or point of view. A good argument is supported with reasoning and evidence.

Purposes of Argument

There are three main purposes for writing a formal argument:

* to change the reader's mind about an issue
* to convince the reader to accept what is written
* to motivate the reader to take action, based on what is written

Elements of Argument
Claim (assertion)—what the writer is trying to prove
Example: The penny should be abolished.
Grounds (evidence)—the support used to convince the reader
Example: There is no profit derived from manufacturing pennies; they actually cost consumers money.
Justification (reasons)—the link between the grounds and the claim; why the grounds are credible
Example: As a unit of currency, pennies are widely viewed as being obsolete.

Evaluating Claims

When reading or listening to an argument, critically assess the claims that are made. Analyze the argument to identify claims that are based on fact or that can be proved true. Also evaluate evidence that supports the claims. If there is little or no reasoning or evidence provided to support the claims, the argument may not be sound or valid.

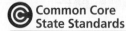

**Common Core
State Standards**

Language
6. Acquire and use accurately general academic and domain-specific words and phrases, sufficient for reading, writing, speaking, and listening at the college and career readiness level; demonstrate independence in gathering vocabulary knowledge when considering a word or phrase important to comprehension or expression.

Reading Informational Text
6. Determine an author's point of view or purpose in a text in which the rhetoric is particularly effective, analyzing how style and content contribute to the power, persuasiveness, or beauty of the text.

Model Argument

from Philadelphia, and Its Solitary Prison
by Charles Dickens

In the outskirts, stands a great prison, called the Eastern Penitentiary: conducted on a plan peculiar to the state of Pennsylvania. The system here is rigid, strict, and hopeless solitary confinement. I believe it, in its effects, to be cruel and wrong.

In its intention, I am well convinced that it is kind, humane, and meant for reformation; but I am persuaded that those who devised this system of Prison Discipline, and those benevolent gentlemen who carry it into execution, do not know what it is that they are doing. I believe that very few men are capable of estimating the immense amount of torture and agony which this dreadful punishment, prolonged for years, inflicts upon the sufferers; and in guessing at it myself, and in reasoning from what I have seen written upon their faces, and what to my certain knowledge they feel within, I am only the more convinced that there is a depth of terrible endurance in it which none but the sufferers themselves can fathom, and which no man has a right to inflict upon his fellow-creature.

I hold this slow and daily tampering with the mysteries of the brain, to be immeasurably worse than any torture of the body: and because its ghastly signs and tokens are not so palpable to the eye and sense of touch as scars upon the flesh; because its wounds are not upon the surface. . . I hesitated once, debating with myself, whether, if I had the power of saying 'Yes' or 'No,' I would allow it to be tried in certain cases, where the terms of imprisonment were short; but now, I solemnly declare, that with no rewards or honours could I walk a happy man beneath the open sky by day, or lie me down upon my bed at night, with the consciousness that one human creature, for any length of time, no matter what, lay suffering this unknown punishment in his silent cell, and I the cause, or I consenting to it in the least degree.

It seems to me that the objection that nothing wholesome or good has ever had its growth in such unnatural solitude, and that even a dog or any of the more intelligent among beasts, would pine, and mope, and rust away, beneath its influence, would be in itself a sufficient argument against this system. But when we recollect, in addition, how very cruel and severe it is, and that a solitary life is always liable to peculiar and distinct objections of a most deplorable nature, which have arisen here, and call to mind, moreover, that the choice is not between this system, and a bad or ill-considered one, but between it and another which has worked well, and is, in its whole design and practice, excellent; there is surely more than sufficient reason for abandoning a mode of punishment attended by so little hope or promise, and fraught, beyond dispute, with such a host of evils.

The introduction sets the stage for the argument that follows, narrowing the focus from the prison to the system of solitary confinement.

Claim: Solitary confinement is cruel and wrong.

Dickens addresses the counterclaim, stating that the intentions of the system were good, and he assumes that the gentlemen do not know how cruel they are being.

Evidence provided includes that people underestimate the unfathomable suffering from the punishment; the punishment is torture. Dickens draws this conclusion based on what he has seen.

Justification: Basic human rights prohibit cruel, inhumane, or unusual punishment.

Dickens reasons that this punishment is worse than physical torture because no one can see the wounds; he also offers the testimony that he would not assent to this punishment in any case.

The last paragraph summarizes the arguments, and the final sentence restates the claim and asks for action: abandon this mode of punishment.

The Art of Argument: Rhetorical Devices and Persuasive Techniques

Rhetorical Devices

Rhetoric is the art of using language in order to make a point or to persuade listeners. Rhetorical devices such as the ones listed below are accepted elements of argument. Their use does not invalidate or weaken an argument. Rather, the use of rhetorical devices is regarded as a key part of an effective argument.

Rhetorical Devices	Examples
Repetition The repeated use of words, phrases, or sentences	Stop the violence! We want to avoid violence! Stop the violence!
Parallelism The repeated use of similar grammatical structures	The strength of the army, the reach of the navy, and the speed of the air force are considered the sources of national pride in the military.
Rhetorical Question Calls attention to the issue by implying an obvious answer	Shouldn't civilized nations avoid cruel punishments, even for the most heinous crimes?
Sound Devices The use of alliteration, assonance, rhyme, or rhythm	The sound of the crowd protesting outside the gate drifted to the inmate's ear and lifted his spirits.
Simile and Metaphor Compares two seemingly unlike things or asserts that one thing *is* another	The words in the book became a salve for her wounded soul.

Persuasive Techniques

Persuasive techniques are often found in advertisements and in other forms of informal persuasion. Although techniques like the ones below are sometimes found in formal arguments, they should be avoided in that context.

Persuasive Techniques	Examples
Bandwagon Approach/Anti-Bandwagon Approach Appeals to a person's desire to belong; encourages or celebrates individuality	Don't be the only one without one! Be the first to own our brand.
Emotional Appeal Evokes people's fear, anger, or desire	Our choices today will ensure the health and prosperity of our children! Of our children's children!
Endorsement/Testimony Employs a well-known person to promote a product or idea	These famous authors, actors, politicians, and CEOs are alumnae of our university!
Loaded Language The use of words that are charged with emotion	It is a crisis of unfathomable proportions.
"Plain Folks" Appeal Shows a connection to everyday, ordinary people	I enjoy a good ol' burger and fries, just like everyone else.
Hyperbole Exaggerates to make a point	I'd give my right arm to end the abuse and neglect of animals.

 EXEMPLAR TEXT

Model Speech

The excerpted speech below includes examples of rhetorical devices and persuasive techniques.

Speech on Conciliation with America, by Edmund Burke

. . . The proposition is peace. Not peace through the medium of war; not peace to be hunted through the labyrinth of intricate and endless negotiations; not peace to arise out of universal discord, fomented from principle, in all parts of the empire; not peace to depend on the juridical determination of perplexing questions, or the precise marking the shadowy boundaries of a complex government. It is simple peace, sought in its natural course and in its ordinary haunts.

> The repetition of the word *peace* emphasizes its importance, while the paragraph provides a growing, defining context for the term.

Let the colonies always keep the idea of their civil rights associated with your government—they will cling and grapple to you, and no force under heaven will be of power to tear them from their allegiance. But let it be once understood that your government may be one thing and their privileges another, that these two things may exist without any mutual relation—the cement is gone, the cohesion is loosened, and everything hastens to decay and dissolution. As long as you have the wisdom to keep the sovereign authority of this country as the sanctuary of liberty, the sacred temple consecrated to our common faith, wherever the chosen race and sons of England worship freedom, they will turn their faces towards you. . . . Slavery they can have anywhere. It is a weed that grows in every soil. . . . But until you become lost to all feeling of your true interest and your natural dignity, freedom they can have from none but you. This is the commodity of price, of which you have the monopoly. . . . Deny them this participation of freedom, and you break that sole bond which originally made, and must still preserve, the unity of the empire. . . . It is the spirit of the English constitution which, infused through the mighty mass, pervades, feeds, unites, invigorates, vivifies, every part of the empire, even down to the minutest member.

> This metaphor compares slavery to a weed. Burke uses the metaphor to explain why slavery does not create allegiance to a government.

> The alliteration, besides adding to the rhythm of the speech, reinforces the relationship between parts and the whole.

Is it not the same virtue which does every thing for us here in England? Do you imagine, then, that it is the Land-Tax Act which raises your revenue? that it is the annual vote in the Committee of Supply, which gives you your army? or that it is the Mutiny Bill which inspires it with bravery and discipline? No! surely, no! It is the love of the people; it is their attachment to their government, from the sense of the deep stake they have in such a glorious institution, which gives you your army and your navy, and infuses into both that liberal obedience without which your army would be a base rabble and your navy nothing but rotten timber. . . .

> This rhetorical question applies the previous conclusions about the empire to England.

> The parallelism in these rhetorical questions builds momentum and leads to the emphatic answer: No!

We ought to elevate our minds to the greatness of that trust to which the order of Providence has called us. By adverting to the dignity of this high calling, our ancestors have turned a savage wilderness into a glorious empire, and have made the most extensive and the only honorable conquests, not by destroying, but by promoting the wealth, the number, the happiness of the human race. Let us get an American revenue as we have got an American empire. English privileges have made it all that it is; English privileges alone will make it all it can be.

> The strongly rhythmic parallelism in the final sentence provides a memorable conclusion.

Analyzing Legal Meanings and Reasoning

Reading historical and legal texts requires careful analysis of both the vocabulary and the logical flow of ideas that support a conclusion.

Understanding Legal Meanings

The language of historical and legal documents is formal, precise, and technical. Many words in these texts have specific meanings that you need to understand in order to follow the flow of ideas. For example, the second amendment to the U.S. Constitution states that "A well regulated Militia being necessary to the security of a free State, the right of the people to keep and bear Arms shall not be infringed." To understand this amendment, it is important to know that in this context *militia* means "armed forces," *bear* means "carry," and *infringed* means "denied." To understand legal meanings:

- Use your knowledge of word roots to help you understand unfamiliar words. Many legal terms use familiar Greek or Latin roots, prefixes, or suffixes.

- Do not assume that you know a word's legal meaning: use a dictionary to check the meanings of key words to be certain that you are applying the correct meaning.

- Paraphrase the text to aid comprehension. Replace difficult words with synonyms to make sure you follow the logic of the argument.

Delineating Legal Reasoning

Works of public advocacy, such as court decisions, political proclamations, proposed laws, or constitutional amendments, use careful reasoning to support conclusions. These strategies can help you understand the legal reasoning in an argument:

- State the **purpose** of the document in your own words to help you focus on the writer's primary goal.

- Look for the line of reasoning that supports the **arguments** presented. To be valid and persuasive, key arguments should be backed up by clearly stated logical analysis. Be aware of persuasive techniques, such as citing facts and statistics, referring to expert testimonials, and using emotional language with strong connotations.

- Identify the **premises,** or evidence, upon which a decision rests. In legal texts, premises often include **precedents,** which are earlier examples that must be followed or specifically overturned. Legal reasoning is usually based on the decisions of earlier trials. Be sure you understand precedents in order to identify how the court arrived at the current decision.

Common Core State Standards

Reading Informational Text

4. Determine the meaning of words and phrases as they are used in a text, including figurative, connotative, and technical meanings; analyze how an author uses and refines the meaning of a key term or terms over the course of a text.

8. Delineate and evaluate the reasoning in seminal U.S. texts, including the application of constitutional principles and use of legal reasoning and the premises, purposes, and arguments in works of public advocacy.

Writing

9. Draw evidence from literary or informational texts to support analysis, reflection, and research.

9.b. Apply *grades 11–12 Reading Standards* to literary nonfiction.

Model Court Decision

Note the strategies used to evaluate legal meanings and reasoning in this Supreme Court decision from 1954 regarding the legality of segregated, "separate but equal" schools for black and white students.

from *Brown* v. *Board of Education of Topeka,* Opinion of the Supreme Court by Chief Justice Earl Warren

We come then to the question presented: Does segregation of children in public schools solely on the basis of race, even though the physical facilities and other "tangible" factors may be equal, deprive the children of the minority group of equal educational opportunities? We believe that it does.

In *Sweatt* v. *Painter,* in finding that a segregated law school for Negroes could not provide them equal educational opportunities, this Court relied in large part on "those qualities which are incapable of objective measurement but which make for greatness in a law school." In *McLaurin* v. *Oklahoma State Regents,* the Court, in requiring that a Negro admitted to a white graduate school be treated like all other students, again resorted to intangible considerations: ". . . his ability to study, to engage in discussions and exchange views with other students, and, in general, to learn his profession." Such considerations apply with added force to children in grade and high schools. To separate them from others of similar age and qualifications solely because of their race generates a feeling of inferiority as to their status in the community that may affect their hearts and minds in a way unlikely ever to be undone. The effect of this separation on their educational opportunities was well stated by a finding in the Kansas case by a court which nevertheless felt compelled to rule against the Negro plaintiffs: Segregation of white and colored children in public schools has a detrimental effect upon the colored children. The impact is greater when it has the sanction of the law, for the policy of separating the races is usually interpreted as denoting the inferiority of the negro group. A sense of inferiority affects the motivation of a child to learn. Segregation with the sanction of law, therefore, has a tendency to [retard] the educational and mental development of negro children and to deprive them of some of the benefits they would receive in a racially integrated school system. Whatever may have been the extent of psychological knowledge at the time of *Plessy* v. *Ferguson,* this finding is amply supported by modern authority. Any language in *Plessy* v. *Ferguson* contrary to this finding is rejected.

We conclude that, in the field of public education, the doctrine of "separate but equal" has no place. Separate educational facilities are inherently unequal.

The word *tangible* comes from the Latin root meaning "to touch." In this decision, the court contrasts tangible, measurable features with intangible features that are difficult to measure.

The court cites two precedents: earlier cases relating to unequal education opportunities for black students.

Here's one way you might break down the ideas in this sentence when you paraphrase: Segregating black students just because of their race makes them feel as if they are less valued by our society. This separation can have a permanent negative influence on their character.

The conclusion makes the **purpose** of the decision clear: to overturn the precedent established by *Plessy* v. *Ferguson.* The **argument** describes the reasons why the Court no longer considers the reasoning in that earlier case to be valid.

Writing About Legal Meanings

Write a detailed analysis of the phrase "segregation with the sanction of law" in the *Brown* v. *Board of Education of Topeka* decision. Explain the definitions of the terms as they are used in this context and explain how this phrase relates to the court's decision to outlaw "separate but equal" education.

Composing an Argument

Choosing a Topic

You should choose a topic that matters to people—and to you. The topic should be debatable or controversial to some degree.

Confirm that you can make an arguable claim. Ask yourself:

1. What am I trying to prove? What ideas do I need to get across?
2. Are there people who would disagree with my claim? What counterclaims would they make?
3. Do I have evidence to support my claim? Is my evidence sufficient and relevant?

If you are able to state what you want to prove and you answered "yes" to questions 2 and 3, you have an arguable claim.

Introducing the Claim and Establishing Its Significance

Before you begin writing, determine how much your audience already knows about your chosen topic. Then, provide only as much background information as necessary to introduce your claim. If there are issues surrounding your topic, you will need to clarify them for your audience and narrow the focus to your specific claim. Remember that you are not writing a summary of the topic—you are crafting an argument. Once you have provided context for your argument, you should clearly state your claim, or thesis.

Developing Your Claim With Reasoning and Evidence

Now that you have made your claim, you must support it with evidence, or grounds, and give reasons for your claim. A good argument should have at least three solid pieces of evidence to support the claim. Evidence can range from personal experience to researched data or expert opinions. Knowing your audience's knowledge level, concerns, values, and possible biases can help you decide what kind of evidence will have the strongest impact. Make sure your evidence is up to date and comes from a credible source. Always credit your sources.

You should also address opposing counterclaims within the body of your argument. Consider points you have made or evidence you have provided that a person might challenge. Decide how best to refute these counterclaims. One technique for defusing an opponent's claims is to agree with selected parts of them.

Writing a Concluding Statement or Section

Restate your claim in the conclusion of your argument, and summarize your main points. The goal of a concluding section is to provide a sense of closure and completeness to an argument. Make your concluding statement strong enough to be memorable and to leave the reader thinking.

Common Core State Standards

Writing

1.a. Introduce precise, knowledgeable claim(s), establish the significance of the claim(s), distinguish the claim(s) from alternate or opposing claims, and create an organization that logically sequences claim(s), counterclaims, reasons, and evidence.

1.b. Develop claim(s) and counterclaims fairly and thoroughly, supplying the most relevant evidence for each while pointing out the strengths and limitations of both in a manner that anticipates the audience's knowledge level, concerns, values, and possible biases.

1.e. Provide a concluding statement or section that follows from and supports the argument presented.

Practice

Exploring both sides of an issue can be a good way to start planning an argument. Complete a chart like the one below to help you plan your own argument.

Topic:	
Issue: _____ _____	
Claim:	Counterclaim:
Grounds (Evidence): 1. _____ 2. _____ 3. _____	Grounds (Evidence): 1. _____ 2. _____ 3. _____
Justification: 1. _____ 2. _____ 3. _____	Justification: 1. _____ 2. _____ 3. _____

When you have completed the chart and developed your own, precise claim, consider the following questions:

1. Who is your audience? What type of evidence can you use to best convince those who do not agree with your claim?

2. Is your evidence strong and difficult to dispute? If not, how can you strengthen it or find better evidence?

3. How will you refute the counterclaim? Are there any parts of the counterclaim you agree with?

Conducting Research

Today, information is plentiful. However, not all information is equally useful, or even accurate. Developing strong research skills will help you locate and utilize the valid, relevant, and interesting information you need.

Short-Term Inquiries and Long-Term Investigations

You will conduct many different kinds of research throughout this program, from brief Internet searches to extended, in-depth projects.

- **Short-term research** can help you answer specific questions about a text or extend your understanding of an idea. You will conduct targeted short-term inquiries on a regular basis.

- **Long-term research** allows you to dive into a topic and conduct a detailed, comprehensive investigation. An organized research plan will help you gather and synthesize information from multiple sources.

Research Topics and Questions

Any research project, whether large or small, needs a clear and concise focus in order to avoid wasting your time and energy.

Narrowing Your Focus Before You Begin Research You can avoid many problems by focusing your research before you begin. For example, you might want to learn more about the American wilderness, but that topic is too broad and vague. If you start researching this subject, you could easily end up overwhelmed by the vast amount of information available. Head off trouble before you begin by thinking of a narrower, more manageable topic that interests you.

Narrowing As You Go Preliminary research can help you refine your topic. Your initial findings can help you choose a specific topic to pursue, such as a person, event, or theme.

Formulating a Question A research question can guide your research toward a specific goal and help you gauge when you have gathered sufficient information. Decide on your question, and refer to it regularly to check that your research is on track. Here are three examples of specific questions that could focus an investigation:

- What has spurred theories of multiple authorship of Shakespeare's works?

- What was the typical audience of a Shakespearean play at the time the works were first performed?

- To what extent was Shakespeare's version of history in his plays reliable?

 Common Core State Standards

Writing

7. Conduct short as well as more sustained research projects to answer a question (including a self-generated question) or solve a problem; narrow or broaden the inquiry when appropriate; synthesize multiple sources on the subject, demonstrating understanding of the subject under investigation.

8. Gather relevant information from multiple authoritative print and digital sources, using advanced searches effectively; assess the strengths and limitations of each source in terms of the task, purpose, and audience; integrate information into the text selectively to maintain the flow of ideas, avoiding plagiarism and overreliance on any one source and following a standard format for citation.

General Subject
William Shakespeare

Focused Topics

- Shakespeare and the Globe Theater

- Theories of Shakespeare's identity; authorship controversy

- An examination of the historical foundation of one of Shakespeare's historical plays

Planning Your Research

You will have more success in your longer-term research work if you create and follow a **research plan.** A good plan will include the elements shown in the following chart.

Elements of a Research Plan	
Research Question	Begin with an initial question, but be open to modifying your question as you learn more about your subject.
Source List	Create a list of sources you intend to consult. Plan to use a variety of sources. Add sources to your plan as you discover them. Place a check mark next to sources you have located, and then underline sources you have consulted thoroughly.
Search Terms	Write down terms you plan to investigate using online search engines. Making these decisions before you go online can help you avoid digressions that take you away from your topic.
Deadlines	Break a long-term project into short-term goals in order to avoid stress and achieve success.

Multiple Sources It is important not to rely too heavily on a single source. The creativity and originality of your research depends on how you combine ideas from many places. Plan to include a variety of these resources:

- **Primary and Secondary Resources** Primary resources—including journals, news accounts, autobiographies, pamphlets, documentary footage, and interviews—are texts or media created during the time period you are studying. These first-hand impressions offer authentic perspectives on the time. Secondary resources, such as encyclopedia entries and nonfiction books, interpret and analyze known facts.

- **Print and Digital Resources** The Internet allows fast access to data, but print resources are often edited more carefully. Include both print and digital resources in your research to guarantee that your work is accurate.

- **Media Resources** Documentaries, television programs, podcasts, and museum exhibitions are rich sources of information. Public lectures by people knowledgeable on a topic offer opportunities to hear an expert's thoughts.

- **Original Research** You may wish to conduct original research to include among your sources. For example, you might interview experts or eyewitnesses or conduct a survey.

Online Searches Type a word or phrase into a general search engine and you may get thousands of results. However, those results are not guaranteed to be relevant or accurate. Using quotation marks can help you focus a search. Place a phrase in quotation marks to find pages that include exactly that phrase. Add several phrases in quotation marks to narrow your results. To limit your search to .edu, .org, or .gov sites, use the search command "site:" followed by the extension. For example, enter "site:.edu" and "Lewis and Clark" and you will get a list of .edu (education) sites that include that phrase.

Finding Authoritative Sources

You need to evaluate your sources to make sure that they will give you information that is both relevant and reliable.

Determining Relevance Not every source you uncover will have information that is related to your investigation. Preview each source to determine its relevance. Scanning a table of contents, a preface, illustration captions, or an index can help you decide whether or not a source will help you answer your research question. When searching for information from magazine or Internet articles, you may come across *abstracts*, which are precise summaries of an article's contents. An abstract is short enough to read carefully and completely. Once you have read it, you can decide whether or not the abstracted article is likely to contain information you can use.

Remember that you do not need to include ideas from every source you consult. Be sure to allow yourself enough time to read and reject information that is not relevant.

Evaluating Reliability You also need to consider whether or not each source provides *accurate* information. Use the following ABC criteria to evaluate any print or digital sources:

- **Authority** Examine the credentials of both the author and the publisher or sponsoring institution. Checking an author's citations in other sources is one way to establish authority. Awards, professional memberships, and other recognitions can also support an author's or a work's credibility. When evaluating Internet sources, prefer those sponsored by educational, nonprofit, or government organizations (which have URLs ending in .*edu, .org,* or .*gov*). Be wary of .com sites, which are commercial or personal.

- **Bias** Most sources strive to be objective, but few are completely without bias. Strong partiality in a source is not always a reason to reject it, though you may want to acknowledge that bias in your analysis. To check for bias, notice sources of funding, including advertising on .com sites. Follow hyperlinks to learn about professional affiliations of writers. These can help you identify possible reasons for biased or selective information.

- **Currency** Use recent sources whenever possible. Outdated content is likely to have been replaced by more recent research. Keep in mind, though, that some topics are more time-sensitive than others. Check the publication date of both print and digital sources. Electronic publications may show that a site has been updated—include both the original date and the most current date in your consideration.

Reliability Checklist

Ask yourself these questions about sources you find.

Authority
- Is the author well-known?
- What are the writer's credentials?
- Does the tone of the writing inspire confidence? Why or why not?

Bias
- Does the author have any obvious biases?
- What is the author's purpose for writing?
- Who is the target audience?

Currency
- When was the work created? Has it been revised?
- Is there more current information available?

Taking Notes

Learning to take complete and thoughtful notes as you research is a key to success. Good notes keep a clear record of your sources and capture ideas and facts. They can also help you summarize.

Notes don't need to be written in complete sentences, but be sure to state your ideas clearly enough that you will understand them when you review and draft.

Index Cards Many researchers find that index cards help them organize information. You will create different types of cards:

Source cards list complete bibliographical information for a source (author, title, place of publication, publisher, date). Create one source card for each of your sources.

Sample Source Card

> **Kastan, David Scott. Introduction. King Henry IV. By William Shakespeare. Ed. Kastan. London: The Arden Shakespeare/ Thomson, 2002. Print.**

Summary cards provide an overview of main ideas in a section. Write a short form of the source's title and author at the top of the card. Adding a topic can help you organize ideas when you write. Summarize the main idea and significant details of the passage. Note the location of the information.

Sample Summary Card

> **Kastan, King Henry IV**
>
> **topic: Shakespeare's history plays**
>
> **Introduction**
> **Kastan explains that there is no evidence that Shakespeare's plays on England's medieval history were ever performed sequentially in his time.**
>
>

p. 10

Quotation cards record an author's exact words. Include the same information as on a summary card, but write down the quotation as it appears. You may note how you might use the quotation in your writing.

Sample Quotation Card

> **Kastan, King Henry IV**
>
> **topic: drama vs. history**
>
> **Introduction**
> **"The historical action [of the 1st Act] is...largely based upon the account...which Shakespeare found in Holinshed's Chronicles.... But Shakespeare's play... compresses and selects events....**
>
>

p. 13
>
> **Use this quote to discuss the differences between history and drama.**

Providing Appropriate Citations

To avoid plagiarism, you must give credit for the information and ideas you collect during research. Plagiarism is presenting someone else's words or ideas as your own. Whether plagiarism is intentional or not, it is dishonest and illegal. Avoid it by being careful to cite your sources thoroughly. Follow the format your teacher recommends, such as Modern Language Association (MLA) style.

Deciding What to Cite Common knowledge does not require citation. If a fact appears in three or more sources, it is probably common knowledge. Facts that reflect one person's research or opinion should be cited, as shown in the chart to the right.

Works-Cited List (MLA Style) A works-cited list, or bibliography, must include the following information about each source: name of the author, editor, and/or translator; title; place and date of publication; publisher. For online sources, include the date you accessed the source.

Model: Works-Cited List

Kastan, David Scott. Introduction. *King Henry IV.* By William Shakespeare. Ed. Kastan. London: The Arden Shakespeare/ Thomson, 2002. Print.

Greenblatt, Stephen. *Will In the World: How Shakespeare Became Shakespeare.* New York: Norton, 2004. Print.

"Hero and Villain at *Shakespeare: Staging the World.*" Narr. Dora Thornton, 2012. *britishmuseum.org.* Web. 10 March 2013.

Saccio, Peter. "Shakespeare's Treatment of English History." *William Shakespeare: His World, His Work, His Influence.* Ed. John F. Andrews. New York: Scribner's, 1985. Print.

Parenthetical Citations (MLA Style) Use parenthetical citations to integrate your research smoothly into your writing. A parenthetical citation appears in the body of your text and briefly identifies the source. The source is fully identified on your works-cited list. You may need to add paraphrases within brackets to place quotations or edited words in context.

Model: Parenthetical Citations

Shakespeare is often credited with essentially inventing the genre of historical drama. However, the notion that Shakespeare thought so categorically "may belong more to [the first Folio editors'] editorial labors in organizing the Folio than to Shakespeare's own generic conceptualizations" (Kastan, pp. 8–9). In other words, Shakespeare may not have set out to create a dramatic genre, but his body of work established one.

Common Knowledge
- The first Globe Theatre was built in 1599.
- Shakespeare's plays are sorted in histories, tragedies, and comedies.
- William Shakespeare was a writer and also an actor.

Facts to be Cited
- A history play is one that dramatizes political events in the reign of a king within recent memory of Shakespeare's audiences (Source: Peter Saccio, "Shakespeare's Treatment of English History").
- Shakespeare was telling stories to his own audiences in his own time, perhaps in an effort to create an idea of what it means to be English (Source: "Hero and Villain at *Shakespeare: Staging the World.*" *britishmuseum.org*).

For more information on research and citing sources, see the Writing Workshop on research papers (pp. 1096–1107) and resource pages on citations (R21–R23).

Practice

Creating a research plan can help you organize a long-term research project. Complete a chart like the one below to plan research and collect details. Begin by choosing a topic that interests you, or use the chart to prepare a research assignment from your classwork. Then, draft a research question that you will answer through investigation.

Topic:

Research Question:

Sources

- Identify sources you will consult for information. Describe the type of source (i.e., encyclopedia, biography, museum Web site, or documentary).

- Tell how you will locate the source. For Internet sites, write the words or phrases you will enter in a search engine.

- Write one or two questions you will ask about each source to determine whether or not it is relevant and reliable.

Print	Digital/Media
Type of source: How you will locate it: Relevance/Reliability:	Type of source: How you will locate it: Relevance/Reliability:
Type of source: How you will locate it: Relevance/Reliability:	Type of source: How you will locate it: Relevance/Reliability:
Type of source: How you will locate it: Relevance/Reliability:	Type of source: How you will locate it: Relevance/Reliability:

Answer these questions before you begin your research:

- How can I be sure that I will not plagiarize any of my sources?

- What deadlines must I meet in order to achieve my goal?

- How will I compile notes so that I can remember and organize the information I find?

- What steps will I take to make sure that my final work reflects my own thoughts and is not overly dependent on one source?

Essential Questions in British and World Literature

Sometimes, as you read individual stories, poems, or essays, you might feel as if you are acquiring small pieces of a puzzle. Each piece is brightly colored and interesting, but you cannot see how they all fit together. You may wonder, Why does this piece of literature matter? How does it relate to what I already know? You try to fit the new pieces into a bigger picture and give them meaning.

This textbook will help you create that bigger picture. On the following pages, you will find these three Essential Questions, tools for creating meaning from the literature you read:

- **What is the relationship between literature and place?**
- **How does literature shape or reflect society?**
- **What is the relationship of the writer to tradition?**

On the next three pages, the Essential Questions are accompanied by descriptions to guide your thinking. These questions reappear throughout the introductions to units, at the end of every unit, and at the beginning and end of literary selections. You will have opportunities to reconsider them in the light of new information about a literary period or a new experience reading a literary work.

The questions do not have "yes" or "no" answers. They are meant to encourage you to take positions. Different people can answer them in different ways at different times. These large, open-ended questions will

- keep you thinking and making judgments about what you read,
- help you relate literary selections to one another and to larger ideas,
- provide a framework for discussing the selections with your classmates, and
- prompt you to create your own meaningful picture of British and world literature.

This symbol will guide you to the Essential Questions in this book.

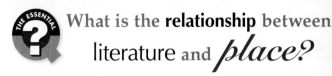

What is the **relationship** between literature and *place?*

From the beginning, England's geography captured the imagination of its writers. Over a thousand years ago, a monk named Bede began a section of his history, "Britain, formerly known as Albion, is an island in the ocean . . ." As you read the selections in this book, think about how England's island existence and dependence on the sea influenced its literature.

The imagination can shape the perception of a place, and writers play a major part in that imagining. How have different generations of England's writers reimagined their country? How have they shaped remembered or even unreal places, such as a perfect pastoral community that exists only on the pages of a book?

As you read, watch how writers invest places with reality and invent places with imagination. Stay attuned to the variety of responses to the Essential Question: What is the relationship between literature and place?

Thematic Vocabulary
To help as you explore this Essential Question, use words like these:

boundary	colonize	conquest
destruction	empire	geography
immigrant	isolation	mobility
nature		

"This blessed plot, this earth, this realm, this England."

—William Shakespeare, *Richard II*

How does **literature** shape or reflect *society?*

We know why we need farmers, carpenters, and doctors, but why do we need writers? Also, how do writers interact with the culture to produce literature that entertains, informs, persuades, challenges, and moves readers?

The writers who create British literature are a vital part of British society. They help to produce its culture, and they are the products of that culture. They are the entertainers who amuse, the critics who confront, and the teachers who share wisdom. Every day, writers celebrate Britain, define it, defy it, and tell its story. As you read this textbook and keep asking this Essential Question, you will become aware of the many relationships between Britain and its writers.

Thematic Vocabulary
To help as you explore this Essential Question, use words like these:

capitalism	**dissatisfaction**	**ideal**	**independence**
industry	**loyalty**	**modernization**	
order	**revolution**	**values**	

"No man is an island, entire of itself; every man is a piece of the continent, a part of the main." —John Donne, *Meditation 17*

What is the **relationship** of the writer to *tradition?*

The past is not past. It is a living part of the present, and tradition is its embodiment. Literary tradition is the record of how men and women imaginatively responded to their times, what they believed was important and beautiful. It is the record of how they chose to express that beauty, the forms and styles and words and images they used. Tradition is the biography of literature.

Every British writer is, in some way, a product of the British literary tradition and a participant in it. As you keep asking this Essential Question throughout this book, you will be getting to the core of what gives British literature its unique character.

Thematic Vocabulary
To help as you explore this Essential Question, use words like these:

authentic	**conventional**	**interpretation**
monarchy	**philosophy**	**piety**
propriety	**reform**	**struggle**
transformation		

"Let me imagine . . . what would have happened had Shakespeare had a wonderfully gifted sister, called Judith, let us say."

—Virginia Woolf, *A Room of One's Own*

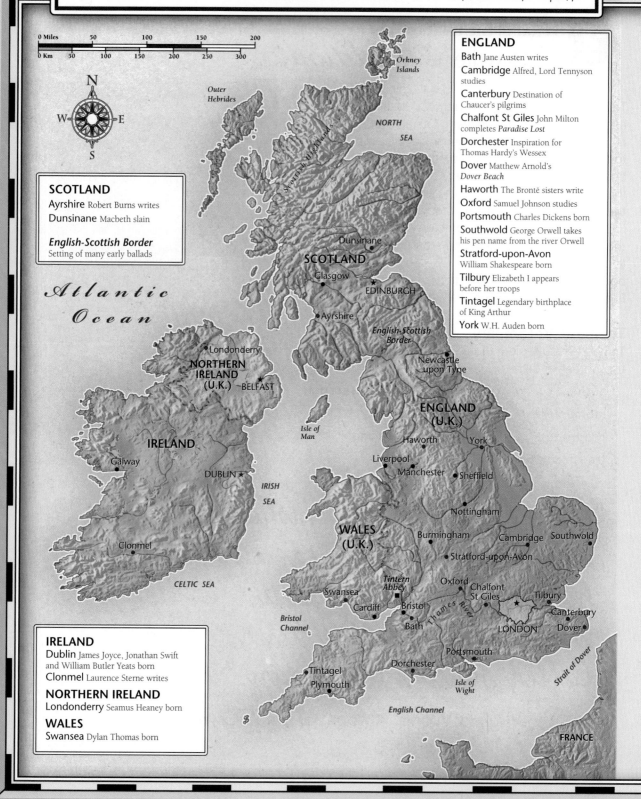

LITERARY MAP OF THE BRITISH ISLES

ENGLAND

Bath Jane Austen writes

Cambridge Alfred, Lord Tennyson studies

Canterbury Destination of Chaucer's pilgrims

Chalfont St Giles John Milton completes *Paradise Lost*

Dorchester Inspiration for Thomas Hardy's Wessex

Dover Matthew Arnold's *Dover Beach*

Haworth The Brontë sisters write

Oxford Samuel Johnson studies

Portsmouth Charles Dickens born

Southwold George Orwell takes his pen name from the river Orwell

Stratford-upon-Avon William Shakespeare born

Tilbury Elizabeth I appears before her troops

Tintagel Legendary birthplace of King Arthur

York W.H. Auden born

SCOTLAND

Ayrshire Robert Burns writes

Dunsinane Macbeth slain

English-Scottish Border Setting of many early ballads

IRELAND

Dublin James Joyce, Jonathan Swift and William Butler Yeats born

Clonmel Laurence Sterne writes

NORTHERN IRELAND

Londonderry Seamus Heaney born

WALES

Swansea Dylan Thomas born

LITERARY MAP OF LONDON

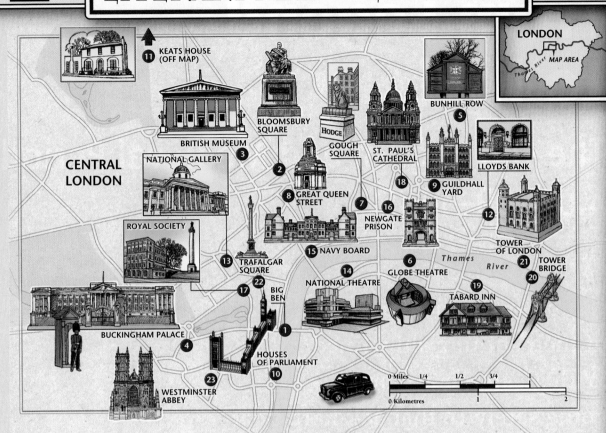

LONDON

MAP AREA

Thames River

11 KEATS HOUSE (OFF MAP)

BLOOMSBURY SQUARE

HODGE

GOUGH SQUARE

ST. PAUL'S CATHEDRAL

BUNHILL ROW
5

BRITISH MUSEUM
3

CENTRAL LONDON

NATIONAL GALLERY

2

8 GREAT QUEEN STREET

18

9 GUILDHALL YARD

LLOYDS BANK

ROYAL SOCIETY

7

16

12

NEWGATE PRISON

TOWER OF LONDON

13 TRAFALGAR SQUARE

15 NAVY BOARD

6 GLOBE THEATRE

21 TOWER BRIDGE

Thames   River

20

22

14 NATIONAL THEATRE

19 TABARD INN

17

BIG BEN

BUCKINGHAM PALACE

4

1

HOUSES OF PARLIAMENT

10

23 WESTMINSTER ABBEY

0 Miles   1/4   1/2   3/4   1

0 Kilometres   1   2

LOCATIONS KEY

1 BIG BEN
Tower clock famous for its accuracy and 13-ton bell

2 BLOOMSBURY SQUARE
Virginia Woolf meets with Bloomsbury Group

3 BRITISH MUSEUM
The oldest public museum in the world features 2.5 miles of galleries

4 BUCKINGHAM PALACE
Office and home of the British monarchy

5 BUNHILL ROW
John Milton writes

6 GLOBE THEATRE
Shakespeare's plays performed

7 GOUGH SQUARE
Samuel Johnson compiles *A Dictionary of the English Language*

8 GREAT QUEEN STREET
William Blake works as an engraver

9 GUILDHALL YARD
Site of Roman amphitheatre

10 HOUSES OF PARLIAMENT
Charles Dickens works as Parliamentary reporter

11 KEATS HOUSE, Hampstead
John Keats born

12 LLOYDS BANK (Corn Hill)
T.S. Eliot works as banker

13 NATIONAL GALLERY
Houses over 2,200 paintings

14 NATIONAL THEATRE
Pinter's plays performed

15 NAVY BOARD
Pepys works, writes *Diary*

16 NEWGATE PRISON/OLD BAILEY
Daniel Defoe, Ben Jonson, Sir Thomas Malory imprisoned

17 ROYAL SOCIETY
Isaac Newton describes gravity and laws of motion

18 ST. PAUL'S CATHEDRAL
John Donne preaches

19 TABARD INN
Chaucer sets the beginning of *The Canterbury Tales* here

20 TOWER BRIDGE
Victorian-era drawbridge

21 TOWER Of LONDON
Sir Walter Raleigh imprisoned

22 TRAFALGAR SQUARE
London's main venue for rallies and outdoor public meetings

23 WESTMINSTER ABBEY, Poet's Corner
Chaucer, Spenser, Dickens, Tennyson, Hardy, Kipling buried

From Legend to History

The Old English and Medieval Periods
A.D. 449–1485

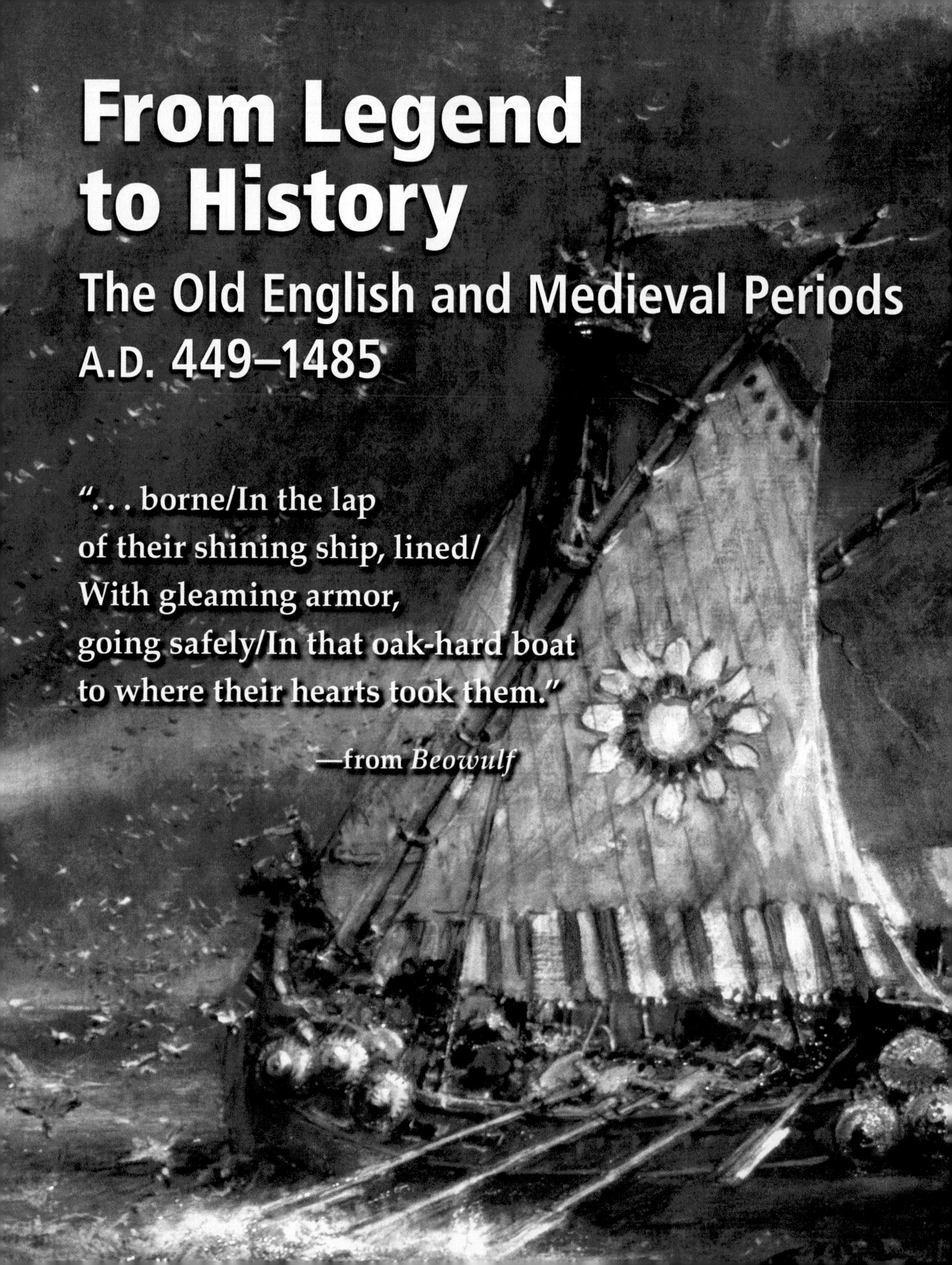

"... borne/In the lap
of their shining ship, lined/
With gleaming armor,
going safely/In that oak-hard boat
to where their hearts took them."

—from *Beowulf*

Unit 1

CLOSE READING TOOL

Use this tool to practice the close
reading strategies you learn.

ONLINE WRITER'S
NOTEBOOK

Easily capture notes and
complete assignments online.

STUDENT eTEXT

Bring learning to life with audio,
video, and interactive tools.

■ Find all Digital Resources at
pearsonrealize.com.

Snapshot of the Period

During the era addressed in this unit, successive waves of invaders came to the British Isles. Each group brought its distinctive culture, including its language. As the different groups fought and eventually united to form a single nation, their languages, too, conflicted and—eventually—combined. The English tongue evolved from Old English to Middle English, the form of the language used by England's greatest medieval poet, Geoffrey Chaucer. Literature, too, evolved—from works transmitted orally, often to the accompaniment of a lyre or harp, to those that were written down.

▲ Design and page from the Book of Kells, an illuminated gospel book created by Irish monks between the late 8th and early 9th century (left). A replica of a lyre found at the Sutton Hoo burial site (right).

 As you read the selections in this unit, you will be asked to think about them in view of three key questions:

What is the **relationship** between literature and *place?*

How does literature **shape or reflect** *society?*

What is the relationship of the writer to *tradition?*

Languages Brought Into England

© Integration of Knowledge and Ideas The annotations below identify some of the words invading cultures contributed to English as the language developed into its modern form. What can you infer about each group from the types of words it brought? Explain.

Celts invaded 500 B.C.
- "bard" from *bard* (poet)
- Avon, Thames (names of rivers)

Romans invaded 55 B.C., A.D. 43; left A.D. 407
- "wine" from *vinum*
- "wall" from *vallum*

Anglo-Saxons invasion began A.D. 449
- "bread" from *bread* (crumb)
- "doom" from *doms* (judgment)

Normans invaded 1066
- "attorney" from *atourne* (one appointed)
- "plaintiff" from *plaindre* (make complaint)

Scandinavians invaded in late 700s, 800s, end of 900s
- "anger" from *angr*
- "ransack" from *rann-saka*

The Changing English Language: Psalm 23, verse 1

Modern English (King James Bible) c. 1500 to now ········· The Lord is my shepherd; I shall not want...

Early Middle English c. 1100 to 1500 ···························· Lauerd me steres, noght wante sal me...

Old English before 1100 ·· Drihten me ræt; ne byð me nanes godes wan...

Historical Background

The Old English and Medieval Periods, 449–1485

They came to conquer and stayed to build. First, it was the Romans in A.D. 43 who drove the original Celtic inhabitants of Britain into the north (Scotland) and west (Wales) of the island. Then, in A.D. 449, after the last Roman troops had been summoned home to defend Rome against the barbarian invaders, a group of Germanic tribes, the Angles, the Saxons, and the Jutes, crossed the North Sea and occupied the island the Romans had called Albion. In a short time, "Angle land" became England.

Invasion, Settlement, Assimilation

The next incursion, in A.D. 597, was more peaceful, led by the Roman cleric St. Augustine. He and his followers converted to Christianity the pagans who were there. The Bible of these Christians was written in Latin and they brought Latin learning with them.

In the eighth century, the Danes arrived. At first they raided and looted the towns and monasteries of the northeast, but eventually they settled that area. In 871, when they tried to overrun the rest of the island, they were stopped by Alfred the Great, who is now considered the first King of England. The Danes, too, converted, assimilated, and gave us words like *sky, skill,* and *skate.*

The last successful invasion of England occurred in 1066 when the duke of Normandy in France claimed and won the throne. Known as William the Conqueror, he brought his court and its language to the country he seized. For some time, England was a bilingual country of conquerors and conquered. In his novel *Ivanhoe*, which is set in the Middle Ages, the nineteenth-century writer Sir Walter Scott captures this duality: animals are *swine, oxen,* and *calves* on the hoof, but *pork, beef,* and *veal* in the kitchen of the noble lord. Even today, we make a last *will* and *testament*, repeating the same meaning in Anglo-Saxon and Norman French, respectively.

TIMELINE

449: Anglo-Saxon Invasion. ▶

476: Western Europe Fall of Western Roman Empire.

496: France Clovis, king of Franks, converts to Christianity.

The Feudal Era, 1100–1485

The Normans brought more than their language to the island. They also brought a form of government, social order, and land tenure we call feudalism. This is a vision of the natural and human world as a triangle or pyramid. At the peak is the king and below, in carefully graded steps, are nobles and freemen, down to the serfs who till the land.

Yet all social systems are more fluid than they appear from the outside, and the feudal era in England was a tempestuous time. In 1215, a group of nobles forced King John to sign the Magna Carta. This Great Charter, which limited the powers of the king, marks the beginning of parliamentary government in England. Other kings faced more violent opposition from the nobles and two of them, Edward II in 1327 and Richard II in 1399, were deposed and assassinated. The Black Death, a grim name for the plague, ravaged England in the 14th century and may have killed one-third of the population. Drained by an intermittent series of wars with France, which dragged out for more than one hundred years, England was then torn by a brutal civil war from 1455 to 1485.

At the end of England's bloody civil war, Henry VII came to the throne and all of the forces that had shaped the island kingdom for a thousand years came together in a newly unified state. England was poised to participate in an incredible period of discovery and expansion.

They had come, the conquerors, warriors and priests, the knights and serfs, the outlaws and the righteous, the men, the women, the children, and had settled an island that a glacier had sliced off the European continent. On that relatively small stretch of land, they created a country, a language, and a literature that was to become one of the wonders of the world.

Key Historical Theme: From Many Tribes to One Nation

- For a millennium, England experienced successive waves of invasion.
- The last invaders, the Normans, brought with them the French language and feudalism.
- After a turbulent period, England eventually became a unified state with one language.

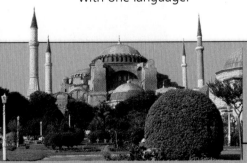

552: Japan
Buddhism introduced.

656

▲ **542: Byzantine Empire** Plague kills half the population of the capital, Constantinople.

591: China Beginning of book printing.

▲ **597:** St. Augustine founds Christian monastery at Canterbury, Kent.

Essential Questions Across Time

The Old English and Medieval Periods (A.D. 449–1485)

What is the relationship between literature and *place?*

In 1399, just before he was deposed and killed, King Richard II returned to England from Ireland. In Shakespeare's version of the scene, the King kneels, touches the sacred soil of England, and says: "Dear earth, I do salute thee with my hand . . . So weeping, smiling, greet I thee, my earth, . . ." This is almost a thousand years after the invading Angles, Saxons, and Jutes set foot on the island's soil, but they neither knelt nor wept. Shakespeare's tragic king, whose feeling for the soil of England is so powerful, shows how the people had shaped a country that had, in turn, shaped them.

How did English writers respond to their island geography?

The Placeless Sea The creation of a sense of place is an important theme in the literature of those who came from elsewhere to dwell on the island. In a way, however, this work of creation begins with an awareness of what is the opposite of place. For islanders, that means the sea, both a protective barrier and an untamable threat. As a watery wilderness, the sea is a kind of placeless place, a vast nowhere that can separate one from home.

"The Seafarer" and "The Wanderer" Two Anglo-Saxon poems chilled by images of the sea, "The Seafarer" and "The Wanderer," are spoken by men on sea voyages. They tell of exile and separation from a remembered home. The bleakness of these poems of lonely struggle is, however, tempered by a different frame of values. Resigned and even bitter as they must have been in their original forms, these poems have come down

TIMELINE

732: France Charles Martel defeats Moors. ▼

656

712: Spain Seville conquered by Moors.

▲ **c. 750:** Surviving version of *Beowulf* composed.

to us in copies made by monks. These monks were aware that Christianity itself begins with a story of exile: Adam and Eve banished from the Garden of Eden. In the Christian tradition, all exile is a model of the exile of humankind from its rightful place in Heaven. In editing "The Seafarer," monks therefore framed the sea-tossed speaker's lament for his life with the overarching Christian theme of exile from Eden, from Heaven, and from God.

The "Sea-Road" The sea also figures in the first epic poem of British literature, *Beowulf*, which contains a distant echo of the journey of the Angles, Saxons, and Jutes to England. In this poem, the hero Beowulf and his men travel by ship to the land of the Danes to face the monster Grendel. The "sea-road," as it is called in the poem, is not merely a threatening watery waste. It is a "road" to fame and honor—and a natural place for these seafaring warriors.

The Mead Hall The destination for Beowulf and his men is not a nation in our modern sense. It is a kingdom, whose capital and command center is Herot, a mead hall. This gathering place—a large building with a single room—probably smelled like a locker room, but it provided warmth, light, food, drink, song, and fellowship for a lord and his warriors. When the monster Grendel comes from the bleak and mysterious darkness to menace Herot, he is striking at the very center of human society, the hearth around which people gather. That is why Beowulf must meet him there and drive him back into the swamp, the dark place from which he comes.

The BRITISH TRADITION

THE CHANGING ENGLISH LANGUAGE
by Richard Lederer

The Beginnings of English

The rise of English as a planetary language is an unparalleled success story that began, long ago, in the middle of the fifth century A.D. Several large tribes of sea rovers—the Angles, Saxons, and Jutes—invaded the islands then known as Britannia. They brought with them a Low Germanic tongue that, in its new setting, became Anglo-Saxon, or Old English. The language came to be called *Englisc*, after *Englaland*, "land of the Angles."

Old English differs so much from modern English that it is harder for us to learn than German is. Still, we can recognize a number of Anglo-Saxon words: *bedd*, *candel*, *eorth*, and *waeter*. Anglo-Saxon words such as these concern the unchanging basics of life. They survived later social upheavals nearly unchanged.

A dramatic evolution in the language came after yet another conquest of England, this one by the Norman French. These Normans (shortened from *Northmen*) had originally been Vikings, but they now spoke French and had taken to French customs. In 1066, under William, Duke of Normandy, the Normans invaded England. One result was that Old Englisc was flooded by the French spoken by the Normans. Examples of French influence include the words *sir*, *madam*, *courtesy*, *honor*, and *royal*. From this infusion of French words emerged a tongue that today we call Middle English.

793: Vikings attack Lindisfarne. ▼

800: Mexico Olmec civilization flourishes. ▲

861: North Atlantic Vikings discover Iceland.

863

How did literature make a nation of an island?

A Place of Shared Stories In the 8th century, Bede, a learned monk, wrote *A History of the English Church and People*, marking an important stage in England's developing sense of itself as an island-nation. With his knowledge of Latin and history, Bede was not interested in merely telling the story of a single clan's mead hall. Instead, he wrote the history of an entire nation—"Britain, formerly known as Albion."

Through Bede's informative prose, the reader can sense how "the island in the ocean" he describes, with its abundant resources, is on its way to becoming the earth to which Shakespeare's Richard II will kneel. Most importantly, Bede is aware that his island is becoming a nation, a place that is as much a product of its history as of its geography; a country is a geographical area with shared stories.

A Nation Created by Imagination Chaucer's *Canterbury Tales*, England's greatest medieval poem, is all about "shared stories" and a sense of England as a nation of different social types. These various characters are on a pilgrimage to the town of Canterbury. There, in 1170, Thomas à Becket, the Archbishop of Canterbury, was murdered in the cathedral on the orders of his former friend King Henry II, to whom he would not yield in matters of church policy. Becket was canonized, or declared a saint, and the cathedral became a shrine. That is why the pilgrims are traveling there, and they will seal their fellowship by telling one another stories along the way.

For Chaucer and his pilgrims, Canterbury is a somewhat distant goal, a symbol of the ultimate sacred place to which people journey on their life's pilgrimage—Heaven. Such was the ideal. Chaucer's pilgrims, however, have a wide range of motives, desires, and needs, many of which are far from noble. A later great poet and critic, John Dryden, was moved to say of Chaucer: "He has taken into the compass of his *Canterbury Tales* the various manners and humors…of the whole English nation…Not a single character has escap'd him."

In the process of inventing English poetry as we know it, Chaucer presents his pilgrims on the road. England is a place in motion, a nation created by the imagination, by the stories people tell one another. It is these shared stories, with all their humble realities, that transform the British Isles to—in the words of Shakespeare's Richard II—"Dear earth."

ESSENTIAL QUESTION VOCABULARY

These Essential Question words will help you think and write about literature and place:

exile (ek′ sīl′) *n.* long time living away from one's country or community, usually involuntary; banishment

geography (jē äg′ rə fē) *n.* physical features of a region, area, or place

pilgrimage (pil′ grə mij) *n.* long journey to a holy or important place

---

TIMELINE

863

871: Alfred the Great becomes King of Wessex. ▶

c. 900: Western Europe Feudalism develops.

▲ **c. 975:** Saxon monks copy Old English poems into The Exeter Book.

How does literature **shape or** reflect *society?*

In the ten centuries between the Germanic invasions and the dawn of the modern world, England changed from a place of warrior bands and invading tribes to a country ruled by a king, nobles, and bishops. Indeed, England was increasingly run and organized by merchants and landowners and their representatives in an evolving Parliament. The literature written during this period reflects these changes.

How did writers capture a vanishing world of tribes and clans?

The Hero's Code The world of the Anglo-Saxon epic poem *Beowulf* is that of the tribe and its leader. To become a leader a young warrior must prove himself in battle. So Beowulf crosses the sea to aid his kinsman Hrothgar, who cannot protect his people from the monster Grendel. After his victories over Grendel and Grendel's mother, Beowulf becomes the leader of his own tribe.

Vanishing World, Enduring Values The *Beowulf* poet tells a rousing story, but he also allows his listener to see and feel the world of the hero in both its glory and decline. At the end of the poem, Beowulf, with only the faithful young warrior Wiglaf at his side, battles a dragon and dies for his people. The audience knows that the poet is lamenting not only the death of a hero, but the passing of a hero's way of life.

The BRITISH TRADITION

CLOSE-UP ON HISTORY

Guilds and the Status of Women

By 1000, merchants, traders, and artisans or crafts workers formed a new middle class, ranked between nobles and peasants. This class gained power in medieval towns, with merchants and artisans forming associations called guilds.

The craft guilds of artisans represented workers in one occupation, such as weavers, bakers, or goldsmiths. Guild members made rules to protect the quality of their goods, regulate hours, and set prices. No one except guild members could work in any trade, and becoming a guild member took many years of labor.

Guilds offered opportunities to women, who worked in dozens of crafts and dominated some trades. Young girls became apprentices in trades such as ribbon-making and papermaking. Also, a woman often engaged in the same trade as her father or husband and might inherit his workshop if he died. Chaucer's Wife of Bath, a weaver, represents this type of new middle-class woman.

982: Greenland Eric the Red establishes first Viking Colony. ▼

991: English defeated by Danes at Battle of Maldon.

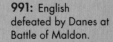

1070

c. 1020: America Viking Leif Ericson explores Canadian coast.

1040: Macbeth kills Duncan I.

▲**1066:** Normans defeat Saxons at Hastings; William the Conqueror becomes king of England.

How did Chaucer reflect social trends without preaching?

A Poet and His World At the other end of the period, Chaucer provides the most complete example of the poet's interaction with his world.

Chaucer's lifetime, the late fourteenth century, was a turbulent period in English history. The country suffered the devastations of the Black Death and Chaucer vividly describes that plague in "The Pardoner's Tale." In the preaching of dissident theologian John Wycliffe, the country also experienced a foreshadowing of the Protestant Reformation, the Protestant separation from the Catholic Church that would occur in the early sixteenth century. Wycliffe's criticisms of the church reflected a growing discontent with the showy wealth of some religious institutions. In the Prologue to *The Canterbury Tales*, we meet a number of characters who represent various religious orders. Their sometimes questionable behavior suggests the controversy that would lead to the Reformation.

Showing, Not Sermonizing Chaucer, however, does not rant, rave, or preach about corruption among religious orders or other social ills. Instead, he shows us characters like the Monk, who spends more time hunting and feasting than praying and fasting.

Political Turbulence In 1381, England was shaken by The Peasant's Revolt, in which farmers and laborers demanded a greater share in the wealth and governance of the country. King Richard II put the rebellion down, only to lose power himself eighteen years later. London, originally a Roman settlement on the banks of the Thames River, had by this time grown into a great city and a center for international trade.

Rising Middle Class Part of this tumult and change involved the replacement of feudal roles, such as knight and serf, with a newly empowered urban middle class. Chaucer himself was a member of this newly-rising group, as is one of his most memorable characters, the Wife of Bath.

The Writer and Society Writers often address social issues, but not as sociologists. Writers are interested in the human stories, the individual tale rather than the mass phenomenon. Readers are often left to figure out who or what is to blame or praise. The turbulent history of the later Middle Ages is contained in Chaucer's pilgrimage—between the lines.

ESSENTIAL QUESTION VOCABULARY

These Essential Question words will help you think and write about literature and society:

sociologist (sō′ sē äl′ ə jist) *n.* scientist who studies societies and the behavior of people in groups

turbulent (tʉr′ byə lənt) *adj.* full of commotion or wild disorder

feudal (fyo͞od′ 'l) *adj.* relating to a system in which overlords granted land to lesser lords, or vassals, in return for military service and in which poor farmers worked the land for vassals

---

TIMELINE

1070

1073: Canterbury becomes England's religious center.

▲ **1096: Europe and Middle East** First Crusade begins.

c. 1100: France *Song of Roland* written.

▲ **c. 1130:** Oxford becomes a center for learning.

What is the relationship of the writer to *tradition?*

You may first have encountered King Arthur and the Knights of the Round Table in a book, a movie, a comic strip, or even a multi-player game. Their stories have been told, reverently and irreverently, for over a thousand years. These tales, in other words, are traditional; they have been handed down. The word *tradition* comes from the Latin *traditio*, meaning "to hand over, to transmit." Tradition in literature, however, does not simply refer to what a writer receives from the past. It also refers to what a writer does with the inheritance.

How do writers change what they have inherited?

Bequest from the Past The King Arthur stories are a kind of bequest from the past. Different authors accepted this literary inheritance but decided to use it in different ways. For example, the poet who wrote *Sir Gawain and the Green Knight* has his knight-hero submit to a series of tests that teach him something about himself. The tests come from earlier folk tales and romances, or adventure stories about knights, and the poet weaves them into a seamless whole.

Sir Thomas Malory, writing in the fifteenth century at the end of the age of chivalry, uses Arthurian legend in a different way. In his book *Morte d'Arthur* ("Death of Arthur"), Malory gathers many legends of Arthur and his companions to write an elegy, or farewell, to the era of knights.

Changing in the Telling The much earlier Anglo-Saxon epic *Beowulf* also ends on a note of farewell, with the dying hero deserted by all but one faithful follower. It is easy to imagine how this story grew in the retelling. Perhaps in the earliest recitals, the hero sails across the sea to rescue his kinsmen and kill the monster. Then, as new audiences clamor for more, the storyteller adds more exploits. Now, Beowulf must also pursue and kill the monster's mother. Still later, in an episode added by another teller, Beowulf is mortally injured by a dragon. Finally, the monk or monks who copy the tale alter it further, adding Christian elements from their own tradition.

1170: Thomas à Becket, Archbishop of Canterbury, murdered.▼

1214: Mongol leader Genghis Khan captures Peking.

▲ **1215:** King John forced to sign Magna Carta.

1258: First commoners allowed in Parliament.

1270

How did Chaucer respond to and create literary traditions?

Using the Old Geoffrey Chaucer is the supreme literary artist of the English Middle Ages because he is both indebted to traditions and committed to creating them. Consider the idea of his major poem, *The Canterbury Tales*: a varied group of people are thrown together and agree to tell stories to pass the time. In 1353, the Italian author Boccaccio had used the same format in his collection of stories, the *Decameron*, in which a group of aristocrats flee to a castle to avoid the plague and agree to tell one another a hundred tales. Chaucer knew Italian literature and the work of Boccaccio. The idea of a group of stories held together by a frame story is his inheritance.

Making It New Chaucer, however, altered what he inherited. His pilgrims reflect almost all levels of society, from the Knight to the Miller. They are not fleeing from the plague; they are on a religious pilgrimage. Chaucer's approach allows him to explore interesting differences between noble and base motives. For example, the Wife of Bath may be on a pilgrimage not so much to worship at a saint's tomb as to meet her next husband. Chaucer uses each tale to reveal something about the teller.

Inventing The Rhythm of English Poetry Chaucer not only reinvented the frame story; he also reinvented a French verse form to create the iambic pentameter line that would dominate English poetry for hundreds of years. Chaucer knew the ten-syllable lines and rhyming couplets used in French poetry. With the instinct that comes only with real genius, he adapted that form to English. In his rhyming couplets, Chaucer used a line of ten syllables with five alternating accents, the form known as iambic pentameter. This new form, when rediscovered by poets in the sixteenth century, became one of the most enduring traditions in English literature.

Traditions Stretching Backward and Forward The beginnings of literature are lost in the mists of prehistory, when some forms of telling stories came into being. Successive generations used those forms to relate the history of the tribe for each new generation. When these stories came to be written down, traditional forms were established. The wonder of literature in this period is that we can see traditions stretching backward into archeological time and stretching forward to tomorrow.

ESSENTIAL QUESTION VOCABULARY

These Essential Question words will help you think and write about the writer and tradition:

traditional (trə dish´ə nəl) *adj.* relating to or based on old customs, beliefs, and ways of doing things

inheritance (in her´i təns) *n.* goods, ideas, literary creations, or skills received from the past

legend (lej´ənd) *n.* story handed down for generations and believed to be based on actual events

TIMELINE

1270

1275: China Marco Polo visits court of Kubla Khan. ▶

1277: England conquers Wales.

1291: Europe and Middle East End of Crusades.

1325: Mexico Aztecs establish Mexico city and create a dating system with a solar year of 365 days. ▼

CONTEMPORARY CONNECTION

King Arthur: Legendary Hero, Broadway Star!

In medieval Europe, tales circulated of a legendary king named Arthur. He and his knights represented the ideals of chivalry—rules governing the behavior of knights. Since then, Arthur's story has surfaced in many literary and dramatic works. Most recently, it has been brought to life in *Spamalot*, a musical comedy that pokes fun at the legend, as follows:

- King Arthur's kingdom is a Las Vegas resort, not the town of Camelot.

- The knights of the Round Table are a motley crew who have to be talked into performing heroic deeds.

- Arthur's knights underwent trials and ordeals to prove their courage and virtue. *Spamalot*'s crew, however, must prove themselves by producing a Broadway musical.

Despite its silliness, *Spamalot*'s success proves the ongoing fascination with the legend. Tales of romance and courage never go out of style.

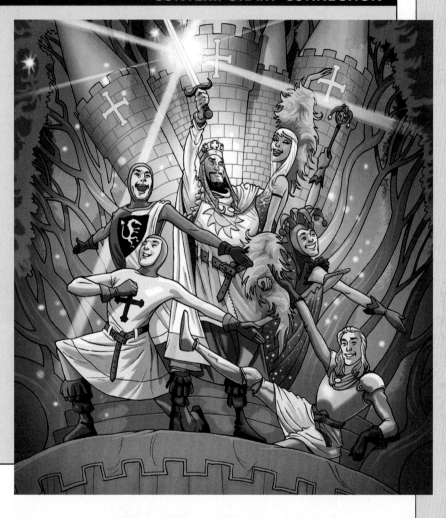

▲ **1337:** Beginning of the Hundred Years' War with France.

1348: Black Death begins sweeping through England.

1381: Bible first translated into English.

1429: France Joan of Arc leads French in breaking siege of Orléans.

1453: Germany First Gutenberg Bible printed.▼

1455–1485: The Wars of the Roses.

1485

Recent Scholarship

England's Green, Fertile Land

Burton Raffel

We tell jokes about the rainy English climate. A warm ocean current brings that moisture, and makes England the green, fertile land it still is. When the last ice age ended, some three thousand years ago, all across Europe easy hunting ended with it, and people without rich pasturage and easy farming went hungry. The English Channel was not as broad as it is today, and wave after wave of immigrants came pouring across.

Daily Life

Life for England's earliest settlers was in many ways much like that still lived in England, as recently as the early nineteenth century. Cities were, for the most part, a thing of the future, though London was even then beginning to become a rich, bustling port. People lived on and by the land, which was worked by both men and women. Sheep were kept for their wool, pigs for their meat, chickens for their eggs. Most people raised a large percentage of the food they ate. There were no shops where one could buy such necessities as clothing (woven and sewn by hand), though artisans like blacksmiths made tools and other metallic items. Most of the land was owned by nobles, both hereditary and newly created aristocrats, having been made counts and earls as kingly rewards. There were many kingdoms on the island now called England and a good deal of quarreling between and among them.

Kings, Lords, Knights, and Peasants

Society was hierarchical—that is, very little moved upward from the peasant level, and virtually everything proceeded downward from the nobility. No one imagined questioning the necessity for these largely fixed relationships. Without leadership, no community would function, and no stability would have been possible. These were matters as much taken for granted as, today, automobiles and television sets. Most of what we would call "work" was performed by those at the lower levels of society. We have no direct testimony from them, but from drawings and paintings, and surviving documents written by clergy or the minority of

About the Author
Burton Raffel (b. 1928) is a noted scholar and poet. You might also call him a time traveler. His work as a translator of world literature has taken him back in time to Anglo-Saxon England, with his versions of *Beowulf* and "The Seafarer," and to Renaissance France, with his version of Rabelais's *Gargantua and Pantagruel*—to name just two of his many translations. When he is not breaking the time barrier, Raffel serves as a professor of English at the University of Louisiana.

aristocrats who could read and write, there is a sense of relatively prosperous busyness. England was a rich habitat, as its inhabitants well knew. What overseas trading there was usually involved costly goods that only a few could afford. There was a good deal of local trading, most of which was conducted on the barter principle. Aristocrats dressed elaborately and expensively; most others dressed very plainly, both men and women wearing loose-fitting garments very like what we today call "smocks."

People not only worked, but they played. There was a good deal of group dancing: the songs we call "carols" in fact began as dance music. There were harvest and other agricultural festivals, and there were more solemn religious festivals. For both the secular and the holy festivities, there were other entertainments, from storytelling to dramatic presentations.

From Many Kingdoms to One Nation

By the ninth century, some unification of the country's many kingdoms had occurred. Alfred the Great was the most notable English ruler, though still not entirely in control. Immigrants and Anglo-Saxon "natives" pulled and tugged at one another, and continued to fight over the prosperous green land. It was William of Brittany (in France) who finally created as much unity as England was to know for almost another five hundred years. In 1066, at the Battle of Hastings, William the Conqueror defeated an Anglo-Saxon opponent and became the increasingly powerful king of England. The kind of feudal structure he enforced was based on a close accounting of wealth, as reported, at William's direction, by the famous Domesday Book. William's England, now a Norman French "colony," was officially a French-speaking land: indeed, English law courts employed French until the sixteenth century.

But toward the end of the Anglo-Saxon period, we do not know exactly when, someone, somewhere, produced a poetic narrative, probably meant as a guide to proper kingship. This famous book is known as *Beowulf*.

Collaboration: Speaking and Listening

Burton Raffel refers to the conflict between "Anglo-Saxon 'natives'" and Viking or Danish "immigrants." Suppose you were a council of Viking leaders planning to invade England. Hold a **small group discussion** about the map of Anglo-Saxon Kingdoms below, answering these questions as you make your military plans:

- Which region or regions might aid you in your fight? Why?
- Which regions might oppose your invasion most strongly? Why?
- Would it be easier to sail your war ships down the Ouse River or the Thames? Explain.

The Anglo-Saxon Kingdoms

Integrate and Evaluate Information

1. Use a chart like the one shown to determine the key ideas expressed in the Essential Question essays on pages 6–12. Fill in two ideas related to each Essential Question and note the authors most closely associated with each concept. One example has been done for you.

Essential Question	Key Concept	Key Author
Literature and Place	Exile to a foreign land	"Seafarer" (author unknown)
Literature and Society		
Writer and Tradition		

2. How do the visual sources in this section—artifacts, paintings, photographs, and illustrations—add to your understanding of the ideas expressed in words? Cite specific examples.

3. On page 8, medieval England is described as "a nation of different social types." Using information from the multiple sources presented in this section, explain how this is so. What social structures produced these "types"? How did these social structures change over time, and how did these changes affect the population? Which social structures—and social types—survived, and which were replaced by others? Cite evidence from the multiple sources presented on pages 4–15 in your answer.

4. **Address a Question** Burton Raffel describes medieval England as a prosperous and bustling island pulsing with commerce, recreation, and, often, war. What stories, images, or events come to mind when you hear the phrase "medieval England"? Integrate details and information from this textbook and other sources—including movies, novels, and games—to support your ideas.

Speaking and Listening: Panel Discussion

The English language is like a large machine that draws its power from two engines. One of these engines is built from the Anglo-Saxon and Scandinavian languages. The other, equally powerful, is fueled by Latin, Greek, and French words. Working in groups, pick one of the following categories:

- Domestic Life
- Law and Politics
- Science and Medicine
- Recreation and Athletics

Choose ten words that belong to your category and determine their current meanings and *etymologies*. Present your findings in a **panel discussion.**

Solve a Research Problem: In your discussion, explain how usage of certain terms has changed over time. Research and describe any moments in history when the usage of certain words caused conflicts or was contested. Consult reference sources such as dictionaries and encyclopedias, secondary sources that describe the history of the English language, and primary texts—such as literary works—in which the words appear.

 **Common Core State Standards**

Reading Informational Text
7. Integrate and evaluate multiple sources of information presented in different media or formats as well as in words in order to address a question or solve a problem.

Language
1.a. Apply the understanding that usage is a matter of convention, can change over time, and is sometimes contested.

Speaking and Listening
1. Initiate and participate effectively in a range of collaborative discussions with diverse partners on *grades 11–12 topics, texts, and issues,* building on others' ideas and expressing their own clearly and persuasively.

ESSENTIAL QUESTION VOCABULARY

Use these words in your responses:

Literature and Place
exile
geography
pilgrimage

Literature and Society
sociologist
turbulent
feudal

Writer and Tradition
traditional
inheritance
legend

Earthly Exile, Heavenly Home

Connecting to the Essential Question These poems are about people in exile—those forced from and longing for home. As you read, note what the speakers say about their lost homes. Doing so will help as you consider the Essential Question: **What is the relationship between literature and place?**

Close Reading Focus

Anglo-Saxon Lyric Poetry
A lyric poem expresses the thoughts and feelings of a single speaker. **Anglo-Saxon lyrics,** composed for easy memorization and recitation, contain the following structural elements:

- Lines with **regular rhythms,** usually with four strong beats
- **Caesuras,** pauses for breath in the middle of lines
- **Kennings,** two-word poetic renamings, such as *whales' home* for "the sea"
- **Assonance,** repeated vowel sounds in unrhymed, stressed syllables
- **Alliteration,** repeated initial consonant sounds in stressed syllables

Comparing Literary Works Shaped by these devices, each lyric in this grouping is an **elegy**—a poem mourning the loss of someone or something. Compare and contrast the types of loss experienced by the speakers in these poems. Also, analyze and compare the ways in which the writers used poetic devices to convey a mood of sadness.

Preparing to Read Complex Texts It is helpful to **understand the historical context** of a literary work, the time in which it was created. Anglo-Saxon England, for example, was a collection of warring kingdoms, not a single nation. In this uncertain situation, people gave loyalty to a lord in return for his protection. Also, men dominated society, and women relied on men for protection. As you read, use a diagram like the one shown to note connections between the characters and settings in these poems and the historical issues of the era.

Vocabulary

The words below are important to understanding the texts that follow. Copy the words into your notebook, sorting them into words you know and words you do not know.

admonish	rancor
sentinel	compassionate
fervent	rapture

**Common Core
State Standards**

Reading Literature
5. Analyze how an author's choices concerning how to structure specific parts of a text contribute to its overall structure and meaning as well as its aesthetic impact.

Event/Idea

The speaker is exiled when his lord dies.

Historical Background

Anglo-Saxon warriors depended on the protection of a powerful lord.

from The Exeter Book

"The Seafarer" • "The Wanderer" • "The Wife's Lament"

Imagine what life would be like if there were no television sets and if movies played in theaters only on important occasions. People would gather beforehand, chatting excitedly. The next day, everyone would discuss the film, quoting dialogue and reenacting scenes.

Telling the Story This scenario captures the nature of entertainment during Britain's Anglo-Saxon period, from the fifth to the eleventh century. Few people of the time were able to read, and movies lay centuries in the future. Instead, people turned to traveling storytellers, known as *scops*, who created an oral tradition by memorizing, adapting, and passing along stories and songs. Through the years, many of these works were lost. Others, however, were eventually written down.

An Early Anthology *The Exeter Book* is a collection of manuscripts that includes pieces of this tradition. The book was probably compiled by monks during the reign of Alfred the Great, A.D. 871–899. Without *The Exeter Book,* many stories that came out of the oral tradition would have been lost to us forever. "The Seafarer," "The Wanderer," and "The Wife's Lament" were all discovered in this collection.

Guests Who Came to Stay Those who recited and listened to the tales recorded in *The Exeter Book*—the Anglo-Saxons—were not native to Britain. In the 400s, Roman soldiers stationed in Britain had abandoned the island to defend Rome. The native inhabitants were soon threatened by Picts from Scotland and Scots from Ireland. One British king invited warlike Germanic tribes from Europe to help him defend Britain. These "guests" proved to be the most dangerous invaders of them all. By the 500s, Angles, Saxons, and other Germanic peoples had settled Britain themselves, driving out most of the Britons. By the end of the 600s, these new inhabitants of the island thought of themselves as part of an English nation, and in A.D. 827, King Egbert named Britannia *Englaland,* "land of the Angles."

A Growing Culture The Angles and Saxons brought with them a warrior culture, a seafaring tradition, and pagan beliefs, including a grim, fatalistic view of the world. They were followed by missionaries sent by Rome. Eventually, these missionaries converted Britain to Christianity. Anglo-Saxon culture at the time of *The Exeter Book* was a blend, mixing pagan ideas of fate with Christian faith in heaven, the boasts of proud warriors with lessons about humility. Preserved by scops and monks, this culture gave Britain its first literature.

▲ Anglo-Saxon artifact from the 7th century A.D.: the great gold buckle from the Sutton Hoo ship burial

The Seafarer

Translated by Burton Raffel

BACKGROUND To the Anglo-Saxon people of Britain, home meant something different from what it means for people today. An Anglo-Saxon warrior viewed himself as the follower of a particular lord or king, not as a citizen of a nation. Gathering in the mead-hall, a building dedicated to their feasts, a lord and his warriors would share food, drink, entertainment, and fellowship. Smoky, noisy, smelly, and crowded, the mead-hall was home.

This tale is true, and mine. It tells
How the sea took me, swept me back
And forth in sorrow and fear and pain,
Showed me suffering in a hundred ships,
5 In a thousand ports, and in me. It tells
Of smashing surf when I sweated in the cold
Of an anxious watch, perched in the bow
As it dashed under cliffs. My feet were cast
In icy bands, bound with frost,

The Literature of Exile

"The Seafarer" is about exile, a long stay away from home that is often enforced but sometimes self-imposed. The theme of exile has run through world literature since ancient times. Over the centuries, many writers suffered exile, an experience that colored their work. Some fled for safety. Others were banished for political reasons.

In A.D. 8, for example, the Roman ruler Augustus Caesar sent the poet Ovid into the provinces for writing *The Art of Love*, which was deemed immoral. Ovid remained there until his death, writing *Sorrows*, among other works.

Italian poet Dante Alighieri was sentenced to exile by his political enemies in 1302. Banished from his beloved native city of Florence, he wrote the *Divine Comedy*, an epic that describes a journey through Hell, Purgatory, and Heaven. In the following passage from that work, he evokes the suffering of the outcast: "You shall leave everything you love most:/this is the arrow that the bow of exile/shoots first."

Just as Ovid and Dante went into exile, so did many twentieth-century writers. For example, after the Russian Revolution, poet Marina Tsvetaeva left Moscow, following her husband to Europe, where she wrote poetry filled with longing for her lost home.

Connect to the Literature

Do you think that the exile of the speaker in "The Seafarer" can touch readers in the twenty-first century? Why or why not?

10 With frozen chains, and hardship groaned
    Around my heart. Hunger tore
    At my sea-weary soul. No man sheltered
    On the quiet fairness of earth can feel
    How wretched I was, drifting through winter
15 On an ice-cold sea, whirled in sorrow,
    Alone in a world blown clear of love,
    Hung with icicles. The hailstorms flew.
    The only sound was the roaring sea,
    The freezing waves. The song of the swan
20 Might serve for pleasure, the cry of the sea-fowl,
    The death-noise of birds instead of laughter,
    The mewing of gulls instead of mead.[1]
    Storms beat on the rocky cliffs and were echoed
    By icy-feathered terns and the eagle's screams;
25 No kinsman could offer comfort there,
    To a soul left drowning in desolation.
        And who could believe, knowing but
    The passion of cities, swelled proud with wine
    And no taste of misfortune, how often, how wearily,
30 I put myself back on the paths of the sea.
    Night would blacken; it would snow from the north;
    Frost bound the earth and hail would fall,
    The coldest seeds. And how my heart
    Would begin to beat, knowing once more
35 The salt waves tossing and the towering sea!
    The time for journeys would come and my soul
    Called me eagerly out, sent me over
    The horizon, seeking foreigners' homes.
        But there isn't a man on earth so proud,
40 So born to greatness, so bold with his youth,
    Grown so brave, or so graced by God,
    That he feels no fear as the sails unfurl,
    Wondering what Fate has willed and will do.
    No harps ring in his heart, no rewards,
45 No passion for women, no worldly pleasures,
    Nothing, only the ocean's heave;
    But longing wraps itself around him.
    Orchards blossom, the towns bloom,
    Fields grow lovely as the world springs fresh,

---

1. mead liquor made from fermented honey and water.

50 And all these admonish that willing mind
   Leaping to journeys, always set
   In thoughts traveling on a quickening tide.
   So summer's sentinel, the cuckoo, sings
   In his murmuring voice, and our hearts mourn
55 As he urges. Who could understand,
   In ignorant ease, what we others suffer
   As the paths of exile stretch endlessly on?
          And yet my heart wanders away,
   My soul roams with the sea, the whales'
60 Home, wandering to the widest corners
   Of the world, returning ravenous with desire,
   Flying solitary, screaming, exciting me
   To the open ocean, breaking oaths
   On the curve of a wave.
                         Thus the joys of God
65 Are fervent with life, where life itself
   Fades quickly into the earth. The wealth
   Of the world neither reaches to Heaven nor remains.
   No man has ever faced the dawn
   Certain which of Fate's three threats
70 Would fall: illness, or age, or an enemy's
   Sword, snatching the life from his soul.
   The praise the living pour on the dead
   Flowers from reputation: plant
   An earthly life of profit reaped
75 Even from hatred and rancor, of bravery
   Flung in the devil's face, and death
   Can only bring you earthly praise
   And a song to celebrate a place
   With the angels, life eternally blessed
80 In the hosts of Heaven.
                         The days are gone
   When the kingdoms of earth flourished in glory;
   Now there are no rulers, no emperors,
   No givers of gold, as once there were,
   When wonderful things were worked among them
85 And they lived in lordly magnificence.
   Those powers have vanished, those pleasures are dead.
   The weakest survives and the world continues,
   Kept spinning by toil. All glory is tarnished.

Vocabulary

admonish (ad män′ ish) *v.* advise; caution

sentinel (sen′ ti nel), *n.* person or animal that guards

fervent (fur′ vənt) *adj.* having great warmth of feeling

rancor (raŋ′ kər) *n.* ill will; continuing and bitter hate

Anglo-Saxon Lyrics

How does the alliteration of words beginning with w, r, and s affect the sound and meaning of lines 59–62?

Anglo-Saxon Lyrics and the Elegy

What does the speaker mourn in lines 81–90?

Comprehension

What are the "three threats" mentioned by the speaker?

The world's honor ages and shrinks,
90 Bent like the men who mold it. Their faces
Blanch as time advances, their beards
Wither and they mourn the memory of friends.
The sons of princes, sown in the dust.
The soul stripped of its flesh knows nothing
95 Of sweetness or sour, feels no pain,
Bends neither its hand nor its brain. A brother
Opens his palms and pours down gold
On his kinsman's grave, strewing his coffin
With treasures intended for Heaven, but nothing
100 Golden shakes the wrath of God
For a soul overflowing with sin, and nothing
Hidden on earth rises to Heaven.
        We all fear God. He turns the earth,
He set it swinging firmly in space,
105 Gave life to the world and light to the sky.
Death leaps at the fools who forget their God.
He who lives humbly has angels from Heaven

To carry him courage and strength and belief.
A man must conquer pride, not kill it,
110 Be firm with his fellows, chaste for himself,
Treat all the world as the world deserves,
With love or with hate but never with harm,
Though an enemy seek to scorch him in hell,
Or set the flames of a funeral pyre
115 Under his lord. Fate is stronger
And God mightier than any man's mind.
Our thoughts should turn to where our home is,
Consider the ways of coming there,
Then strive for sure permission for us
120 To rise to that eternal joy,
That life born in the love of God
And the hope of Heaven. Praise the Holy
Grace of Him who honored us,
Eternal, unchanging creator of earth. Amen.

A man must conquer pride, not kill it.

Critical Reading

1. **Key Ideas and Details (a)** Identify three images related to weather in the first stanza. **(b) Interpret:** What does each convey about the speaker's experiences at sea?

2. **Key Ideas and Details (a)** What causes the speaker's heart to "begin to beat"? **(b) Generalize:** How can someone dislike something as much as the seafarer dislikes life at sea and yet be drawn to it?

3. **Key Ideas and Details (a)** What is the seafarer's response to "harps," "rewards," "passion," and the other pleasures of life on the land (lines 44–47)? **(b) Interpret:** Judging from his response to these things, explain whether he is more attached to life on land than he is to life at sea.

4. **Key Ideas and Details (a) Interpret:** What does the speaker mean when he says in lines 58–61, "And yet my heart wanders away, / My soul roams with the sea, . . . / . . . / . . . returning ravenous with desire, . . ."? **(b) Draw Conclusions:** Is the speaker fully at home on land, on the sea, or in neither place? Explain.

5. **Integration of Knowledge and Ideas (a) Interpret:** According to the last section of the poem, where is our home? **(b) Synthesize:** Explain the connection between the poem's concluding message and its depiction of the seafarer's wandering existence.

6. **Integration of Knowledge and Ideas** Can people find a way of life in which they are fully happy, or, like the seafarer, will they always have longings for another place? Explain.

Cite textual evidence to support your responses.

The Wanderer

Translated by
Charles W. Kennedy

Though woefully toiling   on wintry seas
With churning oar   in the icy wave,
Homeless and helpless   he fled from fate.

Oft to the wanderer,   weary of exile,
Cometh God's pity,   compassionate love,
Though woefully toiling   on wintry seas
With churning oar   in the icy wave,
5   Homeless and helpless   he fled from fate.
Thus saith the wanderer   mindful of misery,
Grievous disasters,   and death of kin:
    "Oft when the day broke, oft at the dawning,
Lonely and wretched   I wailed my woe.
10   No man is living,   no comrade left,
To whom I dare fully   unlock my heart.
I have learned truly   the mark of a man
Is keeping his counsel   and locking his lips,
Let him think what he will!   For, woe of heart
15   Withstandeth not fate: a failing spirit
Earneth no help.   Men eager for honor
Bury their sorrow   deep in the breast.
    "So have I also,   often in wretchedness
Fettered[1] my feelings,   far from my kin,
20   Homeless and hapless,[2]   since days of old,
When the dark earth covered   my dear lord's face,
And I sailed away   with sorrowful heart,
Over wintry seas,   seeking a gold-lord,
If far or near   lived one to befriend me
25   With gift in the mead-hall   and comfort for grief.
    "Who bears it, knows   what a bitter companion,
Shoulder to shoulder,   sorrow can be,
When friends are no more.   His fortune is exile,
Not gifts of fine gold;   a heart that is frozen,
30   Earth's winsomeness dead.   And he dreams of the hall-men,
The dealing of treasure,   the days of his youth,
When his lord bade welcome   to wassail[3] and feast.
But gone is that gladness,   and never again
Shall come the loved counsel   of comrade and king.
35   "Even in slumber   his sorrow assaileth,
And, dreaming he claspeth   his dear lord again,
Head on knee, hand on knee,   loyally laying,
Pledging his liege[4]   as in days long past.
Then from his slumber   he starts lonely-hearted,
40   Beholding gray stretches   of tossing sea.
Sea-birds bathing,   with wings outspread,

---

1. **Fettered** (fet´ ərd) chained; restrained.
2. **hapless** (hap´ lis) unlucky.
3. **wassail** (wäs´ əl) a toast in drinking a person's health, or a celebration at which such toasts are made.
4. **liege** (lēj) lord; sovereign.

Vocabulary

compassionate (kəm pash´ ən it) *adj.* sympathizing; pitying

Comprehension

What is the wanderer's situation?

While hailstorms darken,   and driving snow.
Bitterer then   is the bane of his wretchedness,
The longing for loved one: his grief is renewed.
45   The forms of his kinsmen   take shape in the silence:
In rapture he greets them;   in gladness he scans
Old comrades remembered.   But they melt into air
With no word of greeting   to gladden his heart.
Then again surges   his sorrow upon him;
50   And grimly he spurs   his weary soul
Once more to the toil   of the tossing sea.
    "No wonder therefore,   in all the world,
If a shadow darkens   upon my spirit
When I reflect   on the fates of men—
55   How one by one   proud warriors vanish
From the halls that knew them,   and day by day
All this earth ages   and droops unto death.
No man may know wisdom   till many a winter
Has been his portion.   A wise man is patient,
60   Not swift to anger,   nor hasty of speech,
Neither too weak,   nor too reckless, in war,
Neither fearful nor fain,[5]   nor too wishful of wealth,
Nor too eager in vow—   ere he know the event.
A brave man must bide[6]   when he speaketh his boast
65   Until he know surely   the goal of his spirit.
    "A wise man will ponder   how dread is that doom
When all this world's wealth   shall be scattered and waste
As now, over all,   through the regions of earth,
Walls stand rime-covered[7]   and swept by the winds.
70   The battlements crumble,   the wine-halls decay;
Joyless and silent   the heroes are sleeping
Where the proud host fell   by the wall they defended.
Some battle launched   on their long, last journey;
One a bird bore   o'er the billowing sea:
75   One the gray wolf slew;   one a grieving earl
Sadly gave   to the grave's embrace.
The Warden of men   hath wasted this world
Till the sound of music   and revel is stilled,
And these giant-built structures   stand empty of life.
80   "He who shall muse   on these moldering ruins,
And deeply ponder   this darkling life,
Must brood on old legends   of battle and bloodshed,
And heavy the mood   that troubles his heart:
'Where now is the warrior?   Where is the war horse?

Understand Historical Context

How does your knowledge of Anglo-Saxon life help you appreciate the mood of these lines?

Anglo-Saxon Lyrics

How are caesuras indicated on the page?

---

5. fain (fān) archaic word meaning "eager." In this context it means "too eager."
6. bide (bīd) wait.
7. rime (rīm)-**covered** covered with frost.

85   Bestowal of treasure,   and sharing of feast?
      Alas! the bright ale-cup,   the byrny-clad[8] warrior,
      The prince in his splendor—   those days are long sped
      In the night of the past,   as if they never had been!'
      And now remains only,   for warriors' memorial,
90   A wall wondrous high   with serpent shapes carved.
      Storms of ash-spears   have smitten the earls,
      Carnage of weapon,   and conquering fate.
        "Storms now batter   these ramparts of stone;
      Blowing snow   and the blast of winter
95   Enfold the earth;   night-shadows fall
      Darkly lowering,   from the north driving
      Raging hail   in wrath upon men.
      Wretchedness fills   the realm of earth,
      And fate's decrees   transform the world.
100 Here wealth is fleeting,   friends are fleeting,
      Man is fleeting,   maid is fleeting;
      All the foundation of earth   shall fail!"
        Thus spake the sage   in solitude pondering.
      Good man is he   who guardeth his faith.
105 He must never too quickly   unburden his breast
      Of its sorrow, but eagerly   strive for redress;
      And happy the man who seeketh for mercy
      From his heavenly Father,   our fortress and strength.

---

8. byrny (bər′ nē)**-clad** dressed in a coat of chain-mail armor.

 ## Critical Reading

1. **Key Ideas and Details (a)** Who are the speakers in the poem?
   (b) Analyze: What is the relationship between the two? **(c) Analyze:**
   What effect does the use of two speakers have on the reader's
   picture of the wanderer?

2. **Key Ideas and Details (a)** Why does the wanderer go into exile?
   (b) Analyze: What images does the poet use to convey his isolation
   and despair?

3. **Key Ideas and Details (a)** What are "the fates of men" on which
   the wanderer reflects? **(b) Connect:** Why might the wanderer's own
   experiences have led him to such brooding thoughts?

4. **Integration of Knowledge and Ideas** According to the poem,
   how might reflection on "the fates of men" lead to wisdom?

5. **Integration of Knowledge and Ideas** Do you think dwelling on
   the sorrowful, painful side of life can give a person wisdom and a
   valuable perspective on life, or do you think it can be harmful? Explain.

> Cite textual
> evidence to
> support your
> responses.

The Wife's Lament

Translated by Ann Stanford

I make this song   about me full sadly
my own wayfaring.   I a woman tell
what griefs I had   since I grew up
new or old   never more than now.
5 Ever I know   the dark of my exile.

First my lord went out   away from his people
over the wave-tumult.   I grieved each dawn
wondered where my lord   my first on earth might be.
Then I went forth   a friendless exile
10 to seek service   in my sorrow's need.
My man's kinsmen   began to plot
by darkened thought   to divide us two
so we most widely   in the world's kingdom
lived wretchedly   and I suffered longing.

15 My lord commanded me   to move my dwelling here.
I had few loved ones   in this land
or faithful friends.   For this my heart grieves:
that I should find the man   well matched to me
hard of fortune   mournful of mind
20 hiding his mood   thinking of murder.

Blithe[1] was our bearing   often we vowed
that but death alone   would part us two
naught else.   But this is turned round
now . . .   as if it never were
25 our friendship.   I must far and near
bear the anger   of my beloved.
The man sent me out   to live in the woods
under an oak tree   in this den in the earth.
Ancient this earth hall.   I am all longing.

---

1. blithe (blīth) *adj.* cheerful.

30 The valleys are dark   the hills high
the yard overgrown   bitter with briars
a joyless dwelling.   Full oft the lack of my lord
seizes me cruelly here.   Friends there are on earth
living beloved   lying in bed
35 while I at dawn   am walking alone
under the oak tree   through these earth halls.
There I may sit   the summerlong day
there I can weep   over my exile
my many hardships.   Hence I may not rest
40 from this care of heart   which belongs to me ever
nor all this longing   that has caught me in this life.

May that young man   be sad-minded always
hard his heart's thought   while he must wear
a blithe bearing   with care in the breast
45 a crowd of sorrows.   May on himself depend
all his world's joy.   Be he outlawed far
in a strange folk-land—   that my beloved sits
under a rocky cliff   rimed with frost
a lord dreary in spirit   drenched with water
50 in a ruined hall.   My lord endures
much care of mind.   He remembers too often
a happier dwelling.   Woe be to them
that for a loved one   must wait in longing.

Critical Reading

Cite textual evidence to support your responses.

1. **Key Ideas and Details (a)** Why did the wife have to leave her home? **(b) Interpret:** What do lines 25–26 suggest about her reaction to this event?

2. **Craft and Structure (a) Generalize:** How might a listener feel about his or her griefs after hearing the wife's lament? **(b) Draw Conclusions:** Explain why the poem presents the wife as an image of pure longing, rather than as a person who will one day move on.

3. **Integration of Knowledge and Ideas** Is the wife justified in her anger and sorrow? Explain.

4. **Integration of Knowledge and Ideas** How does the Anglo-Saxon sense of home compare with ours? In responding, use at least two of these Essential Question words: *exile, community, refuge, sanctuary. [Connecting to the Essential Question: What is the relationship between literature and place?]*

Literary Analysis

1. **Craft and Structure** Use a graphic organizer like the one shown to find and analyze examples of the following poetic and structural devices in these poems: **regular rhythms, caesuras, kennings, assonance,** and **alliteration.**

Poem	Literary Devices

2. **Integration of Knowledge and Ideas** Why is **understanding the historical context,** relating to a warrior's relationship to his lord, important to appreciating the setting and the speaker's character in "The Wanderer"?

3. **Integration of Knowledge and Ideas** How does understanding the role of women in Anglo-Saxon society help you understand the speaker's plight in "The Wife's Lament"?

4. **Integration of Knowledge and Ideas (a)** What makes each of these poems an **elegy**? **(b)** Which poem do you find most moving? In supporting your response, show how poetic devices help call forth your emotions.

Common Core State Standards

Writing
1. Write arguments to support claims in an analysis of substantive topics or texts, using valid reasoning and relevant and sufficient evidence.

Language
5. Demonstrate understanding of word relationships and nuances in word meanings.

Vocabulary Acquisition and Use

Categorize Vocabulary Using your knowledge of the vocabulary words, decide whether each item contains synonyms only (words similar in meaning) or synonyms and antonyms (words differing in meaning). Explain your choice.

1. admonish, calm, warn
2. fervent, ardent, impassioned
3. compassionate, malicious, kind
4. rancor, bitterness, spite
5. sentinel, guard, watchman
6. rapture, rest, ecstasy

Writing to Sources

Argument Write an **editorial** that is an elegy for someone or something that has gone from your neighborhood or school. First, review these selections and consider ways in which writers convey a mood of sadness. In your editorial, present and support a claim to members of the community that the loss should be regretted.

Incorporate persuasive techniques such as the following: a *testimonial* to the value of what was lost, from someone your audience will respect; an *emotional appeal* that associates what was lost with things or people that your audience values; *word choice* or language that your readers will find moving.

The Epic

*T*HE EPIC IMPARTS SOLEMNITY TO HISTORY. . . .

— VICTOR HUGO

Defining Epics

One of the earliest forms of literature, an **epic** is a long narrative poem written in an elevated style. An epic relates the adventures of a hero in pursuit of goals of national importance. The hero's adventures, which often include a quest, reflect the values of his culture and are usually prominent in the traditions of his people.

Types of Epics In ancient times, stories about heroes were passed down orally. These stories were eventually arranged into larger works called **folk epics** and written down long after they were first composed. Examples include *Beowulf* (Anglo-Saxon), the *Mahabharata* (Indian), and *The Epic of Gilgamesh* (Sumerian). **Literary epics** were composed by individual authors who drew on the conventions of folk epics. Examples include the *Aeneid* by Virgil and *Paradise Lost* by John Milton.

Epic Conventions Most epics share certain literary or formal characteristics called **epic conventions.**

- **Invoking a Muse** At the beginning of an epic, the poet states the subject or purpose of the poem, and then invokes, or calls upon, a muse (a spirit thought to inspire an artist) or supernatural force for help in telling the story. For example, Homer begins the *Iliad,* "Rage— Goddess, sing the rage of Peleus' son Achilles . . ."
- ***In Medias Res*** The plot begins ***in medias res*** (Latin for "in the middle of things")—the action is already underway. Homer's *Iliad,* for example, begins during the tenth year of the Trojan War.
- **Elevated Style** See the chart below for a definition and example of the epic convention of elevated style.

Close Read: Characteristics of the Epic

These elements and conventions of an epic appear in the Model text at right.

Epic Hero on a Quest: The epic hero is the central character in an epic. Often of noble or semi-divine birth, he sets out on a quest, a dangerous journey that tests his spirit. Example: *In* Beowulf, *a noble young warrior goes on a quest to rescue a kingdom from a monster.*	**Supernatural Forces:** Supernatural forces include deities, some of whom may watch over the hero, and monsters. Example: *In the ancient Greek epic the* Iliad, *the goddess Athena helps the hero Achilles.*
Valorous Deeds: Valorous deeds are acts that reveal the epic hero's extraordinary qualities and reflect the values cherished by his culture. Example: *Beowulf shows superhuman strength in fighting the monster Grendel with his bare hands.*	**Elevated Style:** An epic contains lofty diction, or word choice, that heightens the importance of the events retold. It may contain catalogs, or lists, of battles, weapons, and royal gifts. Example: *"'Hail, Hrothgar! / Higlac is my cousin and my king; the days / Of my youth have been filled with glory. . . ."* Beowulf, *(lines 236–238)*

In This Section

- Defining Epics *(p. 34)*
- Model: from *The Epic of Gilgamesh (p. 35)*
- Contemporary Commentary: Burton Raffel Introduces *Beowulf (p. 36)*
- Study: from *Beowulf (p. 40)*
- Contemporary Commentary: Seamus Heaney Discusses *Beowulf (p. 68)*

For more practice analyzing epics, see pages 524 and 543.

Model

About the Text Gilgamesh, the hero of *The Epic of Gilgamesh,* is a Sumerian king who seeks eternal life. He and Urshanabi, a ferryman, have journeyed to meet Utnapishtim, whom the gods saved from a great flood and to whom they have granted immortality. As the excerpt begins, Gilgamesh and Urshanabi prepare to return home.

---

from *The Epic of Gilgamesh* (translated by N. K. Sandars)

Then Gilgamesh and Urshanabi launched the boat onto the water and boarded it, and they made ready to sail away; but the wife of Utnapishtim the Faraway said to him, "Gilgamesh came here wearied out, he is worn out; what will you give him to carry him back to his own country?" So Utnapishtim spoke, and Gilgamesh took a pole and brought the boat in to the bank. "Gilgamesh, you came here a man wearied out, you have worn yourself out; what shall I give you to carry you back to your own country? Gilgamesh, I shall reveal a secret thing, it is a mystery of the gods that I am telling you. There is a plant that grows under the water, it has a prickle like a thorn, like a rose; it will wound your hands, but if you succeed in taking it, then your hands will hold that which restores his lost youth to a man."

When Gilgamesh heard this he opened the sluices so that a sweet-water current might carry him out to the deepest channel; he tied heavy stones to his feet and they dragged him down to the water-bed. There he saw the plant growing; although it pricked him he took it in his hands; then he cut the heavy stones from his feet, and the sea carried him and threw him onto the shore. Gilgamesh said to Urshanabi the ferryman, "Come here, and see this marvelous plant. By its virtue a man may win back all his former strength. I will take it to Uruk of the strong walls; there I will give it to the old men to eat. Its name shall be 'The Old Men Are Young Again'; and at last I shall eat it myself and have back all my lost youth." So Gilgamesh returned by the gate through which he had come, Gilgamesh and Urshanabi went together. They traveled their twenty leagues and then they broke their fast; after thirty leagues they stopped for the night.

Gilgamesh saw a well of cool water and he went down and bathed; but deep in the pool there was lying a serpent, and the serpent sensed the sweetness of the flower. It rose out of the water and snatched it away, and immediately it sloughed its skin and returned to the well. Then Gilgamesh sat down and wept, the tears ran down his face, and he took the hand of Urshanabi: "O Urshanabi, was it for this that I toiled with my hands, is it for this I have wrung out my heart's blood? For myself I have gained nothing; not I, but the beast of the earth has joy of it now. Already the stream has carried it twenty leagues back to the channels where I found it. I found a sign and now I have lost it. Let us leave the boat on the bank and go."

After twenty leagues they broke their fast, after thirty leagues they stopped for the night; in three days they had walked as much as a journey of a month and fifteen days. When the journey was accomplished they arrived at Uruk, the strong-walled city. Gilgamesh spoke to him, to Urshanabi the ferryman, "Urshanabi, climb up onto the wall of Uruk, inspect its foundation terrace, and examine well the brickwork; see if it is not of burnt bricks; and did not the seven wise men lay these foundations? One third of the whole is city, one third is garden, and one third is field, with the precinct of the goddess Ishtar. These parts and the precinct are all Uruk."

This too was the work of Gilgamesh, the king, who knew the countries of the world. He was wise, he saw mysteries and knew secret things, he brought us a tale of the days before the flood. He went a long journey, was weary, worn out with labor, and returning engraved on a stone the whole story.

Supernatural Forces Utnapishtim is a favorite of the gods, who have granted him immortality. He reveals "a mystery of the gods" that has the supernatural power to restore youth.

Valorous Deeds Gilgamesh dives deep underwater to find the magic plant. He wounds his hands to pluck and secure it. These deeds are valorous, demonstrating courage and perseverance. They are also of great consequence—should Gilgamesh succeed, he will help his people conquer death.

Epic Hero Through his actions, Gilgamesh, like other epic heroes, seeks to better his people. His actions also help to define his culture's concerns and values—the tellers of this epic saw humanity as striving to overcome time and aging.

Elevated Style Note the formal tone and elevated diction of Gilgamesh's lament. The parallel phrases "toiled with my hands" and "wrung out my heart's blood" heighten the intensity.

Themes Across Centuries: Translator's Insights

Burton Raffel Introduces *Beowulf*

A Legendary Tale, Larger Than Life *Beowulf* is a sweeping, action-packed narrative. Written in highly dramatic language, its characters are almost all kings, princes, and their heroic followers. The plot is energized by a pair of powerful man-eating monsters and, at the end, a greedy, fire-spouting dragon. All three are killed by the poem's principal character, Beowulf, who possesses magical qualities of his own. He can swim for days on end; he can breathe for extended periods underwater; his very name tells us in three ways that he is no mere human. He is Beo, or "bear." He is also Wulf, or "wolf." And most important of all, his name does not begin exactly as his father's name, Edgetho: for everyone in Anglo-Saxon England, this break in tradition would have been a dead giveaway of Beowulf's extraordinary character.

A Grand Beginning The story crackles with wonderfully calculated suspense. The hero himself is not introduced at the start. Man-eating Grendel takes the stage, emerging out of the kind of darkness and terror in which Anglo-Saxon life was steeped. Beowulf comes to help the besieged King Hrothgar. (His exciting travel over the deep waves was the first part of the poem I read, over fifty years ago.) The poem carefully explains his heroic, profoundly social motives. Offering himself as a potential sacrifice to Grendel, he fights with and tears an arm off the monster, who flees back into darkness.

Everyone is overjoyed, there is much celebrating—until Grendel's mother enters the scene, hungry (literally) for revenge. Beowulf promptly accepts the challenge, diving far down into the water, finding the lady demon, and in the end killing her in a very close fight. Loaded with praise and gifts, he returns to his own king, to whose throne he succeeds.

The Passage of Time Fifty years later, the old Beowulf's land is terrorized by a fire-breathing dragon. Unlike a good king, and like some of the bad kings in the poem, the dragon fiercely guards and never shares its treasures. Beowulf does not hesitate. But he is old and not as strong as he was. Significantly, he must have help, and is so badly burned that, after the dragon is dead, Beowulf too dies. His people give him a royal burial and a monument, and sing the praises due to a fearless ruler who so totally embodied the virtues of a warrior king.

About the Author

Burton Raffel, the translator of the version of *Beowulf* that follows, has won the Frances Steloff Prize and the Translation Prize for the French-American Foundation. He is the author of numerous poems, screenplays, and novels.

◀ **Critical Viewing**
Which of the dragon's characteristics might a storyteller share with an audience? **CONNECT**

The Spirit of *Beowulf* *Beowulf* is not a pagan poem. There are no pagan gods, no idols, no wanton human sacrifices. Anglo-Saxon England had long since been Christianized when *Beowulf* was composed, but the epic is primarily concerned with social, not religious, issues. Still, if not overtly Christian, *Beowulf*'s close identification with ancient Hebraic ways of life marks it as very much an Old Testament poem. "Almighty God," clearly and repeatedly evoked, operates ethically and holds humans to high moral standards. The creation story of Genesis is beautifully paraphrased. Hell is cited as the home of evil; the Abel and Cain tale is mentioned explicitly. And just as evil is punished, good prevails. The message is that men must learn to behave responsibly, and to love and be faithful to one another, exactly as *Beowulf* has shown that they can.

Critical Reading

1. **Key Ideas and Details (a)** What was the first part of *Beowulf* that Burton Raffel read? **(b) Speculate:** Based on Raffel's introduction, what aspects of the poem do you think led to his lifelong interest in *Beowulf?*

2. **Key Ideas and Details (a)** What specific details of the poem allow Raffel to say so definitely that *Beowulf* is not a pagan poem? **(b) Analyze:** What might the religious dimension of *Beowulf* tell us about the culture that produced it?

As You Read *Beowulf . . .*

3. **Integration of Knowledge and Ideas** Be ready to compare and contrast your reaction to the poem with Raffel's.

4. **Integration of Knowledge and Ideas** Think about how Raffel's passion for the poem is revealed in his translation.

Connecting to the Essential Question In *Beowulf*, a brave hero battles swamp-dwelling monsters that threaten a kingdom. As you read, notice descriptions of the monsters in *Beowulf*, and consider what the details suggest about Anglo-Saxon ideas about evil. Doing so will help as you explore the Essential Question: **How does literature shape or reflect society?**

Close Reading Focus

Epic; Epic Hero

An **epic** is a long narrative poem, sometimes developed orally, that celebrates heroic deeds and legendary events. Epics, like Homer's *Iliad* from ancient Greece, are among the earliest forms of literature. As such, they reveal the values of the peoples who created them. For example, in *Beowulf,* the action in the mead hall reveals the social and economic relationship between an Anglo-Saxon lord and his followers. This is where the lord provides food, shelter, and fellowship in return for loyalty. It is the center of civilization and all that threatens it is evil. Common features of epics include the following:

- a story told in a serious manner, with elevated language
- a hero battling forces that threaten the world's order

Most epics celebrate the exploits of a **legendary, or epic, hero,** a larger-than-life character. Beowulf's boastful self-confidence, his feats of strength, and his victories in battle make him a classic epic hero. Because he upholds the values of his culture—loyalty, bravery, honor—he can teach modern readers a great deal about the Anglo-Saxon view of the world.

Preparing to Read Complex Texts To **determine the main idea or essential message** of a passage, you can *paraphrase* it—identify the key details and restate them in your own words. This strategy will help you understand the long, involved sentences in this translation of *Beowulf*. Use a graphic organizer like the one shown to help you paraphrase such sentences.

Vocabulary

You will encounter the words listed here in the text that follows. Copy the words into your notebook. Which word can you infer is a synonym for *hateful*?

reparation	writhing
solace	massive
purge	loathsome

Common Core State Standards

Reading Literature
3. Analyze the impact of the author's choices regarding how to develop and relate elements of a story or drama.

Original

High on a wall a Danish watcher / Patrolling along the cliffs saw / The travelers crossing to the shore, their shields / Raised and shining....

Key Details:
guard; saw people; come ashore

Paraphrase

A Danish guard saw strangers come ashore, holding up their shields.

ABOUT *BEOWULF*

During Britain's Anglo-Saxon period, from the fifth to the eleventh century, few people were able to read and movies lay centuries in the future. Although the action takes place in sixth-century Scandinavia, *Beowulf* was originally told in Old English, the language spoken by the Anglo-Saxons of England during the years 500 to 1100.

Beowulf, a Geat from a region that is today southern Sweden, sets sail to aid the Danish King Hrothgar in his fight against the monster Grendel. A terrifying swampland creature whose eyes burn "with gruesome light," Grendel has been terrorizing Hrothgar's great banquet hall, Herot, for twelve years. The battle between Beowulf, a young warrior of great strength and courage, and Grendel, his bloodthirsty foe, is the first of three mortal battles that are fought in this long poem.

Forging an Epic The tales in *Beowulf* originate from a time when stories and poems were passed along by word of mouth. In Anglo-Saxon England, traveling minstrels, called *scops*, captivated audiences with long narrative poems. These poems changed and grew as they were passed from one scop to another. *Beowulf* was told and retold in this fashion throughout England for hundreds of years. In the eleventh century, the epic was finally written down.

An ancient helmet worn by Anglo-Saxons. ▼

Beowulf grew out of other, earlier traditions. The monsters and dragons of the tale, the brave warriors steadfastly loyal to their heroic chief, the descent into the eerie regions below the earth— these were familiar elements of Scandinavian or Celtic folk tales. Even a detail as specific as Beowulf's seizure of Grendel's arm can be traced to earlier tales.

A Guide to Life By forging these various traditions into one unified tale and by adding the later influence of Christianity, the Anglo-Saxon scops created a central reference point for their culture. Listening to *Beowulf,* an Anglo-Saxon could learn of bravery and loyalty to one's fellows, of the monsters that spite and hatred could breed, and of the heroism needed to conquer such monsters.

Beowulf and Popular Culture

- Nobel Prize–winner Seamus Heaney's translation of *Beowulf* won the Whitbread Book of the Year Award for Poetry in 1999. (See pages 68–69 for Heaney's comments on his translation.)

- Roger Avary and Neil Gaiman adapted *Beowulf* as a computer animated movie (2007), with voice-overs performed by such stars as Angelina Jolie, Anthony Hopkins, and John Malkovich.

- A *Beowulf* comic-book series was issued in connection with the *Beowulf* movie.

FROM BEOWULF

TRANSLATED BY BURTON RAFFEL

BACKGROUND When *Beowulf* was composed, England was changing from a pagan to a Christian culture. Pagan Anglo-Saxons told grim tales of life ruled by fate, tales in which people struggled against monsters for their place in the world. The missionaries who converted them to Christianity taught them that human beings and their choices of good or evil were at the center of creation. Beowulf reflects both pagan and Christian traditions.The selection opens during an evening of celebration at Herot, the banquet hall of the Danish king Hrothgar (hroth´ gär). Outside in the darkness, however, lurks the murderous monster Grendel.

THE WRATH OF GRENDEL

    A powerful monster, living down
In the darkness, growled in pain, impatient
As day after day the music rang
Loud in that hall,[1] the harp's rejoicing
5 Call and the poet's clear songs, sung
Of the ancient beginnings of us all, recalling
The Almighty making the earth, shaping
These beautiful plains marked off by oceans,
Then proudly setting the sun and moon
10 To glow across the land and light it;
The corners of the earth were made lovely with trees
And leaves, made quick with life, with each
Of the nations who now move on its face. And then
As now warriors sang of their pleasure:
15 So Hrothgar's men lived happy in his hall
Till the monster stirred, that demon, that fiend,
Grendel, who haunted the moors, the wild

---

1. hall Herot.

Marshes, and made his home in a hell
Not hell but earth. He was spawned in that slime,
20 Conceived by a pair of those monsters born
Of Cain,[2] murderous creatures banished
By God, punished forever for the crime
Of Abel's death. The Almighty drove
Those demons out, and their exile was bitter,
25 Shut away from men; they split
Into a thousand forms of evil—spirits
And fiends, goblins, monsters, giants,
A brood forever opposing the Lord's
Will, and again and again defeated.
30   Then, when darkness had dropped, Grendel
Went up to Herot, wondering what the warriors
Would do in that hall when their drinking was done.
He found them sprawled in sleep, suspecting
Nothing, their dreams undisturbed. The monster's
35 Thoughts were as quick as his greed or his claws:
He slipped through the door and there in the silence
Snatched up thirty men, smashed them
Unknowing in their beds and ran out with their bodies,
The blood dripping behind him, back
40 To his lair, delighted with his night's slaughter.
     At daybreak, with the sun's first light, they saw
How well he had worked, and in that gray morning
Broke their long feast with tears and laments
For the dead. Hrothgar, their lord, sat joyless

---

2. Cain oldest son of Adam and Eve, who murdered his brother, Abel.

45　In Herot, a mighty prince mourning
　　The fate of his lost friends and companions,
　　Knowing by its tracks that some demon had torn
　　His followers apart. He wept, fearing
　　The beginning might not be the end. And that night
50　Grendel came again, so set
　　On murder that no crime could ever be enough,
　　No savage assault quench his lust
　　For evil. Then each warrior tried
　　To escape him, searched for rest in different
55　Beds, as far from Herot as they could find,
　　Seeing how Grendel hunted when they slept.
　　Distance was safety; the only survivors
　　Were those who fled him. Hate had triumphed.
　　　　　So Grendel ruled, fought with the righteous,
60　One against many, and won; so Herot
　　Stood empty, and stayed deserted for years,
　　Twelve winters of grief for Hrothgar, king
　　Of the Danes, sorrow heaped at his door
　　By hell-forged hands. His misery leaped
65　The seas, was told and sung in all
　　Men's ears: how Grendel's hatred began,
　　How the monster relished his savage war
　　On the Danes, keeping the bloody feud
　　Alive, seeking no peace, offering
70　No truce, accepting no settlement, no price
　　In gold or land, and paying the living
　　For one crime only with another. No one
　　Waited for reparation from his plundering claws:
　　That shadow of death hunted in the darkness,
75　Stalked Hrothgar's warriors, old
　　And young, lying in waiting, hidden
　　In mist, invisibly following them from the edge
　　Of the marsh, always there, unseen.
　　　　　So mankind's enemy continued his crimes,
80　Killing as often as he could, coming
　　Alone, bloodthirsty and horrible. Though he lived
　　In Herot, when the night hid him, he never
　　Dared to touch King Hrothgar's glorious
　　Throne, protected by God—God,
85　Whose love Grendel could not know. But Hrothgar's
　　Heart was bent. The best and most noble
　　Of his council debated remedies, sat
　　In secret sessions, talking of terror
　　And wondering what the bravest of warriors could do.
90　And sometimes they sacrificed to the old stone gods,
　　Made heathen vows, hoping for Hell's

Burton Raffel
Translator's Insight
A normal feud involves
two sides: it takes two to
tangle. Literary lore suggests
that monsters are interested
in fights they know they
will win.

Vocabulary
reparation (rep′ ə rā′ shən) *n.*
compensation for a wrong

Comprehension
Why do the Danes flee Herot
at night?

Support, the Devil's guidance in driving
Their affliction off. That was their way,
And the heathen's only hope, Hell

95 Always in their hearts, knowing neither God
Nor His passing as He walks through our world, the Lord
Of Heaven and earth; their ears could not hear
His praise nor know His glory. Let them
Beware, those who are thrust into danger,

100 Clutched at by trouble, yet can carry no solace
In their hearts, cannot hope to be better! Hail
To those who will rise to God, drop off
Their dead bodies and seek our Father's peace!

THE COMING OF BEOWULF

So the living sorrow of Healfdane's son[3]

105 Simmered, bitter and fresh, and no wisdom
Or strength could break it: that agony hung
On king and people alike, harsh
And unending, violent and cruel, and evil.
    In his far-off home Beowulf, Higlac's[4]

110 Follower and the strongest of the Geats—greater
And stronger than anyone anywhere in this world—
Heard how Grendel filled nights with horror
And quickly commanded a boat fitted out,
Proclaiming that he'd go to that famous king,

115 Would sail across the sea to Hrothgar,
Now when help was needed. None
Of the wise ones regretted his going, much
As he was loved by the Geats: the omens were good,
And they urged the adventure on. So Beowulf

120 Chose the mightiest men he could find,
The bravest and best of the Geats, fourteen
In all, and led them down to their boat;
He knew the sea, would point the prow
Straight to that distant Danish shore.

125   Then they sailed, set their ship

---

3. **Healfdane's** (hā´ alf den´ nəz) **son** Hrothgar.
4. **Higlac's** (hig´ laks) Higlac was the king of the Geats (gā´ ats) and Beowulf's feudal lord and uncle.

Out on the waves, under the cliffs.
Ready for what came they wound through the currents,
The seas beating at the sand, and were borne
In the lap of their shining ship, lined
130 With gleaming armor, going safely
In that oak-hard boat to where their hearts took them.
The wind hurried them over the waves,
The ship foamed through the sea like a bird
Until, in the time they had known it would take,
135 Standing in the round-curled prow they could see
Sparkling hills, high and green
Jutting up over the shore, and rejoicing
In those rock-steep cliffs they quietly ended
Their voyage. Jumping to the ground, the Geats
140 Pushed their boat to the sand and tied it
In place, mail⁵ shirts and armor rattling
As they swiftly moored their ship. And then
They gave thanks to God for their easy crossing.
          High on a wall a Danish watcher
145 Patrolling along the cliffs saw
The travelers crossing to the shore, their shields
Raised and shining; he came riding down,
Hrothgar's lieutenant, spurring his horse,
Needing to know why they'd landed, these men
150 In armor. Shaking his heavy spear
In their faces he spoke:
                    "Whose soldiers are you,
You who've been carried in your deep-keeled ship
Across the sea-road to this country of mine?
Listen! I've stood on these cliffs longer
155 Than you know, keeping our coast free
Of pirates, raiders sneaking ashore
From their ships, seeking our lives and our gold.
None have ever come more openly—
And yet you've offered no password, no sign
160 From my prince, no permission from my people
          for your landing

5. **mail** flexible body armor made of metal.

Determine the Main Idea by Paraphrasing
Paraphrase lines 125–131. Remember that your paraphrase need not follow the word order of the original.

Comprehension
Why does Beowulf sail to Denmark?

Here. Nor have I ever seen,
Out of all the men on earth, one greater
Than has come with you; no commoner carries
Such weapons, unless his appearance, and his beauty,
165 Are both lies. You! Tell me your name,
And your father's; no spies go further onto Danish
Soil than you've come already. Strangers,
From wherever it was you sailed, tell it,
And tell it quickly, the quicker the better,
170 I say, for us all. Speak, say
Exactly who you are, and from where, and why."
        Their leader answered him, Beowulf unlocking
Words from deep in his breast:
                "We are Geats,
Men who follow Higlac. My father
175 Was a famous soldier, known far and wide
As a leader of men. His name was Edgetho.
His life lasted many winters;
Wise men all over the earth surely
Remember him still. And we have come seeking
180 Your prince, Healfdane's son, protector
Of this people, only in friendship: instruct us,
Watchman, help us with your words! Our errand
Is a great one, our business with the glorious king
Of the Danes no secret; there's nothing dark
185 Or hidden in our coming. You know (if we've heard
The truth, and been told honestly) that your country
Is cursed with some strange, vicious creature
That hunts only at night and that no one
Has seen. It's said, watchman, that he has slaughtered
190 Your people, brought terror to the darkness. Perhaps
Hrothgar can hunt, here in my heart,
For some way to drive this devil out—
If anything will ever end the evils
Afflicting your wise and famous lord.
195 Here he can cool his burning sorrow.
Or else he may see his suffering go on
Forever, for as long as Herot towers
High on your hills."
                The mounted officer
Answered him bluntly, the brave watchman:
200   "A soldier should know the difference between words
And deeds, and keep that knowledge clear
In his brain. I believe your words, I trust in
Your friendship. Go forward, weapons and armor
And all, on into Denmark. I'll guide you
205 Myself—and my men will guard your ship,

The Epic and the Legendary Hero

What does Beowulf's way of identifying himself suggest about the values of a warrior culture?

Keep it safe here on our shores,
Your fresh-tarred boat, watch it well,
Until that curving prow carries
Across the sea to Geatland a chosen
210 Warrior who bravely does battle with the creature
Haunting our people, who survives that horror
Unhurt, and goes home bearing our love."
　　　　　Then they moved on. Their boat lay moored,
Tied tight to its anchor. Glittering at the top
215 Of their golden helmets wild boar heads gleamed,
Shining decorations, swinging as they marched,
Erect like guards, like sentinels, as though ready
To fight. They marched, Beowulf and his men
And their guide, until they could see the gables
220 Of Herot, covered with hammered gold
And glowing in the sun—that most famous of
　　all dwellings,
Towering majestic, its glittering roofs
Visible far across the land.
Their guide reined in his horse, pointing
225 To that hall, built by Hrothgar for the best
And bravest of his men; the path was plain,
They could see their way. . . .

*Beowulf and his men arrive at Herot and are called to see
the King.*

　　　　　Beowulf arose, with his men
230 Around him, ordering a few to remain
With their weapons, leading the others quickly
Along under Herot's steep roof into Hrothgar's
Presence. Standing on that prince's own hearth,
Helmeted, the silvery metal of his mail shirt
235 Gleaming with a smith's high art, he greeted
The Danes' great lord:
　　　　　"Hail, Hrothgar!
Higlac is my cousin[6] and my king; the days
Of my youth have been filled with glory. Now Grendel's
Name has echoed in our land: sailors
240 Have brought us stories of Herot, the best
Of all mead-halls,[7] deserted and useless when the moon
Hangs in skies the sun had lit,
Light and life fleeing together.
My people have said, the wisest, most knowing
245 And best of them, that my duty was to go to the Danes'
Great king. They have seen my strength for themselves,

▼ **Critical Viewing**
What can you infer about
ancient Scandinavian society
based on the artifacts
displayed on pages 46–47?
INFER

Comprehension
Where does the watchman
bring Beowulf?

---

6. **cousin** here, used as a general term for relative.
7. **mead-halls** To reward his thanes, the king in heroic literature would build a hall
　where mead (a drink made from fermented honey) was served.

The Epic and the
Legendary Hero

How do Beowulf's boasts
of great deeds and his
announcement of his plan
establish him as a hero?

Have watched me rise from the darkness of war,
Dripping with my enemies' blood. I drove
Five great giants into chains, chased
250 All of that race from the earth. I swam
In the blackness of night, hunting monsters
Out of the ocean, and killing them one
By one; death was my errand and the fate
They had earned. Now Grendel and I are called
255 Together, and I've come. Grant me, then,
Lord and protector of this noble place,
A single request! I have come so far,
O shelterer of warriors and your people's loved friend,
That this one favor you should not refuse me—
260 That I, alone and with the help of my men,
May purge all evil from this hall. I have heard,
Too, that the monster's scorn of men
Is so great that he needs no weapons and fears none.
Nor will I. My lord Higlac
265 Might think less of me if I let my sword
Go where my feet were afraid to, if I hid
Behind some broad linden[8] shield: my hands
Alone shall fight for me, struggle for life
Against the monster. God must decide
270 Who will be given to death's cold grip.
Grendel's plan, I think, will be
What it has been before, to invade this hall
And gorge his belly with our bodies. If he can,
If he can. And I think, if my time will have come,
275 There'll be nothing to mourn over, no corpse to prepare
For its grave: Grendel will carry our bloody
Flesh to the moors, crunch on our bones
And smear torn scraps of our skin on the walls
Of his den. No, I expect no Danes
280 Will fret about sewing our shrouds, if he wins.
And if death does take me, send the hammered
Mail of my armor to Higlac, return
The inheritance I had from Hrethel, and he
From Wayland.[9] Fate will unwind as it must!"

*That night Beowulf and his men stay inside Herot. While his men
sleep, Beowulf lies awake, eager to meet with Grendel.*

Vocabulary

purge (purj) *v.* purify;
cleanse

Determine the Main
Idea by Paraphrasing

Paraphrase Beowulf's plans
in lines 264–279.

---

8. **linden** very sturdy type of wood.
9. **Wayland** from Germanic folklore, an invisible blacksmith.

THE BATTLE WITH GRENDEL

285   Out from the marsh, from the foot of misty
  Hills and bogs, bearing God's hatred,
  Grendel came, hoping to kill
  Anyone he could trap on this trip to high Herot.
  He moved quickly through the cloudy night,
290 Up from his swampland, sliding silently
  Toward that gold-shining hall. He had visited Hrothgar's
  Home before, knew the way—
  But never, before nor after that night,
  Found Herot defended so firmly, his reception
295 So harsh. He journeyed, forever joyless,
  Straight to the door, then snapped it open,
  Tore its iron fasteners with a touch
  And rushed angrily over the threshold.
  He strode quickly across the inlaid
300 Floor, snarling and fierce: his eyes
  Gleamed in the darkness, burned with a gruesome
  Light. Then he stopped, seeing the hall
  Crowded with sleeping warriors, stuffed
  With rows of young soldiers resting together.
305 And his heart laughed, he relished the sight,
  Intended to tear the life from those bodies
  By morning; the monster's mind was hot
  With the thought of food and the feasting his belly
  Would soon know. But fate, that night, intended
310 Grendel to gnaw the broken bones
  Of his last human supper. Human
  Eyes were watching his evil steps,
  Waiting to see his swift hard claws.
  Grendel snatched at the first Geat
315 He came to, ripped him apart, cut
  His body to bits with powerful jaws,
  Drank the blood from his veins and bolted
  Him down, hands and feet; death
  And Grendel's great teeth came together,
320 Snapping life shut. Then he stepped to another
  Still body, clutched at Beowulf with his claws,
  Grasped at a strong-hearted wakeful sleeper
  —And was instantly seized himself, claws
  Bent back as Beowulf leaned up on one arm.
325   That shepherd of evil, guardian of crime,
  Knew at once that nowhere on earth
  Had he met a man whose hands were harder;
  His mind was flooded with fear—but nothing
  Could take his talons and himself from that tight

▼ **Critical Viewing**
Why do you think early Scandinavians adorned their ships with figures like the one below? **SPECULATE**

Comprehension
What happens when Grendel grabs Beowulf?

Burton Raffel
Translator's Insight
Like bullies, monsters immediately think of running, as soon as they find themselves in what might be a fair fight.

Vocabulary
writhing (rĭth´ ĭn) *adj.* making twisting or turning motions

The Epic
Which details from this description of the battle between Beowulf and Grendel add realism? Which details add epic grandness?

330　Hard grip. Grendel's one thought was to run
　　From Beowulf, flee back to his marsh and hide there:
　　This was a different Herot than the hall he had emptied.
　　But Higlac's follower remembered his final
　　Boast and, standing erect, stopped
335　The monster's flight, fastened those claws
　　In his fists till they cracked, clutched Grendel
　　Closer. The infamous killer fought
　　For his freedom, wanting no flesh but retreat,
　　Desiring nothing but escape; his claws
340　Had been caught, he was trapped. That trip to Herot
　　Was a miserable journey for the writhing monster!
　　　　The high hall rang, its roof boards swayed,
　　And Danes shook with terror. Down
　　The aisles the battle swept, angry
345　And wild. Herot trembled, wonderfully
　　Built to withstand the blows, the struggling
　　Great bodies beating at its beautiful walls;
　　Shaped and fastened with iron, inside
　　And out, artfully worked, the building
350　Stood firm. Its benches rattled, fell
　　To the floor, gold-covered boards grating
　　As Grendel and Beowulf battled across them.
　　Hrothgar's wise men had fashioned Herot
　　To stand forever; only fire,
355　They had planned, could shatter what such skill had put
　　Together, swallow in hot flames such splendor
　　Of ivory and iron and wood. Suddenly
　　The sounds changed, the Danes started
　　In new terror, cowering in their beds as the terrible
360　Screams of the Almighty's enemy sang
　　In the darkness, the horrible shrieks of pain
　　And defeat, the tears torn out of Grendel's
　　Taut throat, hell's captive caught in the arms
　　Of him who of all the men on earth
365　Was the strongest.
　　　　　　　　　That mighty protector of men
　　Meant to hold the monster till its life
　　Leaped out, knowing the fiend was no use
　　To anyone in Denmark. All of Beowulf's
　　Band had jumped from their beds, ancestral
370　Swords raised and ready, determined
　　To protect their prince if they could. Their courage
　　Was great but all wasted: they could hack at Grendel
　　From every side, trying to open
　　A path for his evil soul, but their points
375　Could not hurt him, the sharpest and hardest iron

Could not scratch at his skin, for that sin-stained demon
Had bewitched all men's weapons, laid spells
That blunted every mortal man's blade.
And yet his time had come, his days
380 Were over, his death near; down
To hell he would go, swept groaning and helpless
To the waiting hands of still worse fiends.
Now he discovered—once the afflictor
Of men, tormentor of their days—what it meant
385 To feud with Almighty God: Grendel
Saw that his strength was deserting him, his claws
Bound fast, Higlac's brave follower tearing at
His hands. The monster's hatred rose higher,
But his power had gone. He twisted in pain,
390 And the bleeding sinews deep in his shoulder
Snapped, muscle and bone split
And broke. The battle was over, Beowulf
Had been granted new glory: Grendel escaped,
But wounded as he was could flee to his den,
395 His miserable hole at the bottom of the marsh,
Only to die, to wait for the end
Of all his days. And after that bloody
Combat the Danes laughed with delight.
He who had come to them from across the sea,
400 Bold and strong-minded, had driven affliction
Off, purged Herot clean. He was happy,
Now, with that night's fierce work; the Danes
Had been served as he'd boasted he'd serve them; Beowulf,
A prince of the Geats, had killed Grendel,
405 Ended the grief, the sorrow, the suffering
Forced on Hrothgar's helpless people
By a bloodthirsty fiend. No Dane doubted
The victory, for the proof, hanging high
From the rafters where Beowulf had hung it, was the monster's
410 Arm, claw and shoulder and all.

*The Danes celebrate Beowulf's victory. That night, though, Grendel's
mother kills Hrothgar's closest friend and carries off her child's
claw. The next day the horrified king tells Beowulf about the two
monsters and their underwater lair.*

THE MONSTERS' LAIR

"I've heard that my people, peasants working
In the fields, have seen a pair of such fiends
Wandering in the moors and marshes, giant
Monsters living in those desert lands.
415 And they've said to my wise men that, as well as they could see,

**Determine the Main
Idea by Paraphrasing**
Paraphrase the sentence
in lines 392–397.

Comprehension
How does Beowulf's battle
with Grendel end?

Determine the Main Idea by Paraphrasing

Paraphrase lines 420–431. What do these lines tell you about Grendel's background?

World LITERATURE CONNECTION

Battling Demons in the *Ramayana*

Beowulf's fight with Grendel touches on a universal theme. Tales of heroes who battle monsters or demons are common in world literature. One of the most famous battles occurs in the *Ramayana*, the Hindu epic poem that is as well known in India and other areas of Asia as Bible stories are here. The *Ramayana* is part of a living oral tradition; even today, traveling storytellers recite the tales to large audiences. The hero of this epic is the virtuous prince Rama, husband to beautiful Sita. Rama's enemy is the demon king Ravana, who has ten heads and twenty arms, and lives with his warriors in the land of Lanka. After Ravana kidnaps Sita, Rama must wage battle against the demon king to rescue his wife. While Beowulf's battle with Grendel can be told in a few minutes, Rama's attack on Ravana requires many hours over a series of nights to recite. Both poems feature heroes who ultimately triumph over creatures of supernatural strength and size.

Connect to the Literature

What do you think makes the battle with Grendel feel so compelling, despite the brevity of the description?

One of the devils was a female creature.
The other, they say, walked through the wilderness
Like a man—but mightier than any man.
They were frightened, and they fled, hoping to find help
420 In Herot. They named the huge one Grendel:
If he had a father no one knew him,
Or whether there'd been others before these two,
Hidden evil before hidden evil.
They live in secret places, windy
425 Cliffs, wolf-dens where water pours
From the rocks, then runs underground, where mist
Steams like black clouds, and the groves of trees
Growing out over their lake are all covered
With frozen spray, and wind down snakelike
430 Roots that reach as far as the water
And help keep it dark. At night that lake
Burns like a torch. No one knows its bottom,
No wisdom reaches such depths. A deer,
Hunted through the woods by packs of hounds,
435 A stag with great horns, though driven through the forest
From faraway places, prefers to die
On those shores, refuses to save its life
In that water. It isn't far, nor is it
A pleasant spot! When the wind stirs
440 And storms, waves splash toward the sky,
As dark as the air, as black as the rain
That the heavens weep. Our only help,
Again, lies with you. Grendel's mother
Is hidden in her terrible home, in a place
445 You've not seen. Seek it, if you dare! Save us,
Once more, and again twisted gold,
Heaped-up ancient treasure, will reward you
For the battle you win!"

Beowulf resolves to kill Grendel's monstrous mother. He travels to the lake in which she lives.

THE BATTLE WITH GRENDEL'S MOTHER

Then Edgetho's brave son[10] spoke:

"Remember,
450 Hrothgar, O knowing king, now
When my danger is near, the warm words we uttered,
And if your enemy should end my life

---

10. **Edgetho's brave son** Beowulf. Elsewhere he is identified by such phrases as "the Geats' proud prince" and "the Geats' brave prince."

Then be, O generous prince, forever
The father and protector of all whom I leave

455 Behind me, here in your hands, my beloved
Comrades left with no leader, their leader
Dead. And the precious gifts you gave me,
My friend, send them to Higlac. May he see
In their golden brightness, the Geats' great lord

460 Gazing at your treasure, that here in Denmark
I found a noble protector, a giver
Of rings whose rewards I won and briefly
Relished. And you, Unferth,[11] let
My famous old sword stay in your hands:

465 I shall shape glory with Hrunting, or death
Will hurry me from this earth!"
                                    As his words ended
He leaped into the lake, would not wait for anyone's
Answer; the heaving water covered him
Over. For hours he sank through the waves;

470 At last he saw the mud of the bottom.
And all at once the greedy she-wolf
Who'd ruled those waters for half a hundred
Years discovered him, saw that a creature
From above had come to explore the bottom

475 Of her wet world. She welcomed him in her claws,
Clutched at him savagely but could not harm him,
Tried to work her fingers through the tight
Ring-woven mail on his breast, but tore
And scratched in vain. Then she carried him, armor

480 And sword and all, to her home; he struggled
To free his weapon, and failed. The fight
Brought other monsters swimming to see
Her catch, a host of sea beasts who beat at
His mail shirt, stabbing with tusks and teeth

485 As they followed along. Then he realized, suddenly,
That she'd brought him into someone's battle-hall,
And there the water's heat could not hurt him.
Nor anything in the lake attack him through
The building's high-arching roof. A brilliant

490 Light burned all around him, the lake
Itself like a fiery flame.
                            Then he saw
The mighty water witch and swung his sword,
His ring-marked blade, straight at her head;
The iron sang its fierce song,

495 Sang Beowulf's strength. But her guest

---

11. Unferth Danish warrior who had questioned Beowulf's bravery before the battle with Grendel.

Determine the Main Idea by Paraphrasing
Paraphrase lines 467–481.

Burton Raffel
Translator's Insight
True warriors are totally dedicated and fight for fame (honor), not for tangible rewards.

Comprehension
What requests does Beowulf make before he dives into the lake?

Science Connection

Anglo-Saxon Metalwork

The sword that Beowulf discovers is said to have been magically forged by giants—a story reflecting the scarcity and value of swords in Anglo-Saxon times. To form a sword, highly skilled smiths had to heat ore to the melting point of iron (2,800° F), cool it, and then add carbon. The result was a hard, durable metal. A smith's work did not stop at a strong, sharp edge but included the ornamentation of the sword hilt. Handsomely adorned, a sword was at once a deadly weapon and a work of art. Both usable iron and the skills needed to work it were scarce, and a sword's noble owner treasured it, treating it as an individual. Some swords—like Beowulf's Hrunting—were given names.

Connect to the Literature

Besides its ornate hilt, what else makes Hrunting a valuable property?

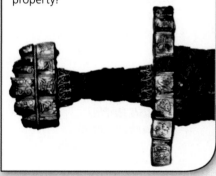

Vocabulary

massive (mas´ iv) *adj.*
big and solid; bulky

Discovered that no sword could slice her evil
Skin, that Hrunting could not hurt her, was useless
Now when he needed it. They wrestled, she ripped
And tore and clawed at him, bit holes in his helmet,
500 And that too failed him; for the first time in years
Of being worn to war it would earn no glory;
It was the last time anyone would wear it. But Beowulf
Longed only for fame, leaped back
Into battle. He tossed his sword aside,
505 Angry; the steel-edged blade lay where
He'd dropped it. If weapons were useless he'd use
His hands, the strength in his fingers. So fame
Comes to the men who mean to win it
And care about nothing else! He raised
510 His arms and seized her by the shoulder; anger
Doubled his strength, he threw her to the floor.
She fell, Grendel's fierce mother, and the Geats'
Proud prince was ready to leap on her. But she rose
At once and repaid him with her clutching claws,
515 Wildly tearing at him. He was weary, that best
And strongest of soldiers; his feet stumbled
And in an instant she had him down, held helpless.
Squatting with her weight on his stomach, she drew
A dagger, brown with dried blood, and prepared
520 To avenge her only son. But he was stretched
On his back, and her stabbing blade was blunted
By the woven mail shirt he wore on his chest.
The hammered links held; the point
Could not touch him. He'd have traveled to the bottom of the earth,
525 Edgetho's son, and died there, if that shining
Woven metal had not helped—and Holy
God, who sent him victory, gave judgment
For truth and right, Ruler of the Heavens,
Once Beowulf was back on his feet and fighting.
530   Then he saw, hanging on the wall, a heavy
Sword, hammered by giants, strong
And blessed with their magic, the best of all weapons
But so massive that no ordinary man could lift
Its carved and decorated length. He drew it
535 From its scabbard, broke the chain on its hilt,
And then, savage, now, angry
And desperate, lifted it high over his head
And struck with all the strength he had left,
Caught her in the neck and cut it through,
540 Broke bones and all. Her body fell
To the floor, lifeless, the sword was wet

With her blood, and Beowulf rejoiced at the sight.
     The brilliant light shone, suddenly,
As though burning in that hall, and as bright as Heaven's
545 Own candle, lit in the sky. He looked
At her home, then following along the wall
Went walking, his hands tight on the sword,
His heart still angry. He was hunting another
Dead monster, and took his weapon with him
550 For final revenge against Grendel's vicious
Attacks, his nighttime raids, over
And over, coming to Herot when Hrothgar's
Men slept, killing them in their beds,
Eating some on the spot, fifteen
555 Or more, and running to his loathsome moor
With another such sickening meal waiting
In his pouch. But Beowulf repaid him for those visits,
Found him lying dead in his corner,
Armless, exactly as that fierce fighter
560 Had sent him out from Herot, then struck off
His head with a single swift blow. The body
jerked for the last time, then lay still.
     The wise old warriors who surrounded Hrothgar,
Like him staring into the monsters' lake,
565 Saw the waves surging and blood
Spurting through. They spoke about Beowulf,
All the graybeards, whispered together
And said that hope was gone, that the hero
Had lost fame and his life at once, and would never
570 Return to the living, come back as triumphant
As he had left; almost all agreed that Grendel's
Mighty mother, the she-wolf, had killed him.
The sun slid over past noon, went further
Down. The Danes gave up, left
575 The lake and went home, Hrothgar with them.
The Geats stayed, sat sadly, watching,
Imagining they saw their lord but not believing
They would ever see him again.
              —Then the sword
Melted, blood-soaked, dripping down
580 Like water, disappearing like ice when the world's
Eternal Lord loosens invisible
Fetters and unwinds icicles and frost
As only He can, He who rules
Time and seasons, He who is truly
585 God. The monsters' hall was full of
Rich treasures, but all that Beowulf took
Was Grendel's head and the hilt of the giants'

▲ Critical Viewing
How would this helmet affect the appearance of the person wearing it? **INFER**

Vocabulary
loathsome (lōth′ səm)
adj. disgusting

Comprehension
Why do the Danes think Beowulf has been slain?

Jeweled sword; the rest of that ring-marked
Blade had dissolved in Grendel's steaming
590 Blood, boiling even after his death.
And then the battle's only survivor
Swam up and away from those silent corpses;
The water was calm and clean, the whole
Huge lake peaceful once the demons who'd lived in it
595 Were dead.
        Then that noble protector of all seamen
Swam to land, rejoicing in the heavy
Burdens he was bringing with him. He
And all his glorious band of Geats
Thanked God that their leader had come back unharmed;
600 They left the lake together. The Geats
Carried Beowulf's helmet, and his mail shirt.
Behind them the water slowly thickened
As the monsters' blood came seeping up.
They walked quickly, happily, across
605 Roads all of them remembered, left
The lake and the cliffs alongside it, brave men
Staggering under the weight of Grendel's skull,
Too heavy for fewer than four of them to handle—
Two on each side of the spear jammed through it—
610 Yet proud of their ugly load and determined
That the Danes, seated in Herot, should see it.
Soon, fourteen Geats arrived
At the hall, bold and warlike, and with Beowulf,
Their lord and leader, they walked on the mead-hall
615 Green. Then the Geats' brave prince entered
Herot, covered with glory for the daring
Battles he had fought; he sought Hrothgar
To salute him and show Grendel's head.
He carried that terrible trophy by the hair,
620 Brought it straight to where the Danes sat,
Drinking, the queen among them. It was a weird
And wonderful sight, and the warriors stared.

Determine Main Idea by Paraphrasing

In your own words, paraphrase the events described in lines 596–611.

After being honored by Hrothgar, Beowulf and his fellow Geats return home, where he eventually becomes King. Beowulf rules Geatland for fifty years. When a dragon menaces his kingdom, Beowulf, now an old man, determines to slay the beast. Before going into battle, he tells his men about the royal house and his exploits in its service.

THE LAST BATTLE

And Beowulf uttered his final boast:
"I've never known fear, as a youth I fought
625 In endless battles. I am old, now,
But I will fight again, seek fame still,

If the dragon hiding in his tower dares
To face me."
                  Then he said farewell to his followers,
Each in his turn, for the last time:
630   "I'd use no sword, no weapon, if this beast
Could be killed without it, crushed to death
Like Grendel, gripped in my hands and torn
Limb from limb. But his breath will be burning
Hot, poison will pour from his tongue.
635 I feel no shame, with shield and sword
And armor, against this monster: when he comes to me
I mean to stand, not run from his shooting
Flames, stand till fate decides
Which of us wins. My heart is firm,
640 My hands calm: I need no hot
Words. Wait for me close by, my friends.
We shall see, soon, who will survive
This bloody battle, stand when the fighting
Is done. No one else could do
645 What I mean to, here, no man but me
Could hope to defeat this monster. No one
Could try. And this dragon's treasure, his gold
And everything hidden in that tower, will be mine
Or war will sweep me to a bitter death!"
650   Then Beowulf rose, still brave, still strong,
And with his shield at his side, and a mail shirt on his breast,
Strode calmly, confidently, toward the tower, under
The rocky cliffs: no coward could have walked there!
And then he who'd endured dozens of desperate
655 Battles, who'd stand boldly while swords and shields
Clashed, the best of kings, saw
Huge stone arches and felt the heat
Of the dragon's breath, flooding down
Through the hidden entrance, too hot for anyone
660 To stand, a streaming current of fire
And smoke that blocked all passage. And the Geats'
Lord and leader, angry, lowered
His sword and roared out a battle cry,
A call so loud and clear that it reached through
665 The hoary rock, hung in the dragon's
Ear. The beast rose, angry,
Knowing a man had come—and then nothing
But war could have followed. Its breath came first.
A steaming cloud pouring from the stone,
670 Then the earth itself shook. Beowulf
Swung his shield into place, held it
In front of him, facing the entrance. The dragon

The Epic
What does Beowulf's speech in lines 630–649 suggest to you about Anglo-Saxon values?

Comprehension
How does Beowulf plan to fight the dragon?

► **Critical Viewing**
What educated guess can you make about Beowulf's bravery from this illustration?
INFER

Coiled and uncoiled, its heart urging it
Into battle. Beowulf's ancient sword
675 Was waiting, unsheathed, his sharp and gleaming
Blade. The beast came closer; both of them
Were ready, each set on slaughter. The Geats'
Great prince stood firm, unmoving, prepared
Behind his high shield, waiting in his shining
680 Armor. The monster came quickly toward him,
Pouring out fire and smoke, hurrying
To its fate. Flames beat at the iron
Shield, and for a time it held, protected
Beowulf as he'd planned; then it began to melt,
685 And for the first time in his life that famous prince
Fought with fate against him, with glory
Denied him. He knew it, but he raised his sword
And struck at the dragon's scaly hide.
The ancient blade broke, bit into
690 The monster's skin, drew blood, but cracked
And failed him before it went deep enough, helped him
Less than he needed. The dragon leaped
With pain, thrashed and beat at him, spouting
Murderous flames, spreading them everywhere.
695 And the Geats' ring-giver did not boast of glorious
Victories in other wars: his weapon
Had failed him, deserted him, now when he needed it
Most, that excellent sword. Edgetho's
Famous son stared at death,

Determine Main Idea by Paraphrasing
In your own words, paraphrase the events of Beowulf's battle with the dragon.

700 Unwilling to leave this world, to exchange it
For a dwelling in some distant place—a journey
Into darkness that all men must make, as death
Ends their few brief hours on earth.
         Quickly, the dragon came at him, encouraged
705 As Beowulf fell back; its breath flared,
And he suffered, wrapped around in swirling
Flames—a king, before, but now
A beaten warrior. None of his comrades
Came to him, helped him, his brave and noble
710 Followers; they ran for their lives, fled
Deep in a wood. And only one of them
Remained, stood there, miserable, remembering,
As a good man must, what kinship should mean.

         His name was Wiglaf, he was Wexstan's son
715 And a good soldier; his family had been Swedish,
Once. Watching Beowulf, he could see
How his king was suffering, burning. Remembering
Everything his lord and cousin had given him,

The Epic
What do these lines reveal about the values of warrior culture?

Armor and gold and the great estates
720 Wexstan's family enjoyed, Wiglaf's
Mind was made up; he raised his yellow
Shield and drew his sword—an ancient
Weapon that had once belonged to Onela's
Nephew, and that Wexstan had won, killing
725 The prince when he fled from Sweden, sought safety
With Herdred, and found death.[12] And Wiglaf's father
Had carried the dead man's armor, and his sword,
To Onela, and the king had said nothing, only
Given him armor and sword and all,
730 Everything his rebel nephew had owned
And lost when he left this life. And Wexstan
Had kept those shining gifts, held them
For years, waiting for his son to use them,
Wear them as honorably and well as once
735 His father had done; then Wexstan died
And Wiglaf was his heir, inherited treasures
And weapons and land. He'd never worn
That armor, fought with that sword, until Beowulf
Called him to his side, led him into war.
740 But his soul did not melt, his sword was strong;
The dragon discovered his courage, and his weapon,
When the rush of battle brought them together.
        And Wiglaf, his heart heavy, uttered
The kind of words his comrades deserved:
745   "I remember how we sat in the mead-hall, drinking
And boasting of how brave we'd be when Beowulf
Needed us, he who gave us these swords
And armor: all of us swore to repay him,
When the time came, kindness for kindness
750 —With our lives, if he needed them. He allowed us to
        join him,
Chose us from all his great army, thinking
Our boasting words had some weight, believing
Our promises, trusting our swords. He took us
For soldiers, for men. He meant to kill
755 This monster himself, our mighty king,
Fight this battle alone and unaided,
As in the days when his strength and daring dazzled
Men's eyes. But those days are over and gone
And now our lord must lean on younger
760 Arms. And we must go to him, while angry
Flames burn at his flesh, help
Our glorious king! By almighty God,

The Epic and the Legendary Hero

According to Wiglaf, what is Beowulf's relationship with his followers?

---

12. **Onela's / Nephew . . . found death** When Onela seized the throne of Sweden, his two nephews sought shelter with the king of Geatland, Herdred. Wiglaf's father, Wexstan, killed the older nephew for Onela.

I'd rather burn myself than see
Flames swirling around my lord.
765 And who are we to carry home
Our shields before we've slain his enemy
And ours, to run back to our homes with Beowulf
So hard-pressed here? I swear that nothing
He ever did deserved an end
770 Like this, dying miserably and alone,
Butchered by this savage beast: we swore
That these swords and armor were each for us all!"
     Then he ran to his king, crying encouragement
As he dove through the dragon's deadly fumes.

*Wiglaf and Beowulf kill the dragon, but the old king is mortally
wounded. As he dies, Beowulf asks Wiglaf to bring him the treasure
that the dragon was guarding.*

THE SPOILS

775   Then Wexstan's son went in, as quickly
As he could, did as the dying Beowulf
Asked, entered the inner darkness
Of the tower, went with his mail shirt and his sword.
Flushed with victory he groped his way,
780 A brave young warrior, and suddenly saw
Piles of gleaming gold, precious
Gems, scattered on the floor, cups
And bracelets, rusty old helmets, beautifully
Made but rotting with no hands to rub
785 And polish them. They lay where the dragon left them;
It had flown in the darkness, once, before fighting
Its final battle. (So gold can easily
Triumph, defeat the strongest of men,
No matter how deep it is hidden!) And he saw,
790 Hanging high above, a golden
Banner, woven by the best of weavers
And beautiful. And over everything he saw
A strange light, shining everywhere,
On walls and floor and treasure. Nothing
795 Moved, no other monsters appeared;
He took what he wanted, all the treasures
That pleased his eye, heavy plates
And golden cups and the glorious banner,
Loaded his arms with all they could hold.
800 Beowulf's dagger, his iron blade,
Had finished the fire-spitting terror
That once protected tower and treasures
Alike; the gray-bearded lord of the Geats

**Determine the Main
Idea by Paraphrasing**
What is the main idea in the
sentence in lines 779–785?

Comprehension
Why does Wiglaf decide to
come to Beowulf's aid?

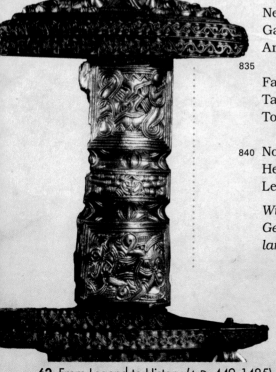

Had ended those flying, burning raids
805 Forever.
           Then Wiglaf went back, anxious
To return while Beowulf was alive, to bring him
Treasure they'd won together. He ran,
Hoping his wounded king, weak
And dying, had not left the world too soon.
810 Then he brought their treasure to Beowulf, and found
His famous king bloody, gasping
For breath. But Wiglaf sprinkled water
Over his lord, until the words
Deep in his breast broke through and were heard.
815 Beholding the treasure he spoke, haltingly:
     "For this, this gold, these jewels, I thank
Our Father in Heaven, Ruler of the Earth—
For all of this, that His grace has given me,
Allowed me to bring to my people while breath
820 Still came to my lips. I sold my life
For this treasure, and I sold it well. Take
What I leave, Wiglaf, lead my people,
Help them; my time is gone. Have
The brave Geats build me a tomb,
825 When the funeral flames have burned me, and build it
Here, at the water's edge, high
On this spit of land, so sailors can see
This tower, and remember my name, and call it
Beowulf's tower, and boats in the darkness
830 And mist, crossing the sea, will know it."
     Then that brave king gave the golden
Necklace from around his throat to Wiglaf,
Gave him his gold-covered helmet, and his rings,
And his mail shirt, and ordered him to use them well:
835   "You're the last of all our far-flung family.
Fate has swept our race away,
Taken warriors in their strength and led them
To the death that was waiting. And now I follow them."
     The old man's mouth was silent, spoke
840 No more, had said as much as it could;
He would sleep in the fire, soon. His soul
Left his flesh, flew to glory.

*Wiglaf denounces the warriors who deserted Beowulf. The
Geats burn their king's body on a funeral pyre and bitterly
lament his death.*

THE FAREWELL

Then the Geats built the tower, as Beowulf
Had asked, strong and tall, so sailors
845　Could find it from far and wide; working
For ten long days they made his monument,
Sealed his ashes in walls as straight
And high as wise and willing hands
Could raise them. And the riches he and Wiglaf
850　Had won from the dragon, rings, necklaces,
Ancient, hammered armor—all
The treasures they'd taken were left there, too,
Silver and jewels buried in the sandy

▲ **Critical Viewing**

How would you describe
the mood of this painting?
Does it accurately reflect
the conclusion of Beowulf?
Explain. **CONNECT**

Comprehension

What is Beowulf's last
request?

Ground, back in the earth, again
855 And forever hidden and useless to men.
And then twelve of the bravest Geats
Rode their horses around the tower,
Telling their sorrow, telling stories
Of their dead king and his greatness, his glory,
860 Praising him for heroic deeds, for a life
As noble as his name. So should all men
Raise up words for their lords, warm
With love, when their shield and protector leaves
His body behind, sends his soul
865 On high. And so Beowulf's followers
Rode, mourning their beloved leader,
Crying that no better king had ever
Lived, no prince so mild, no man
So open to his people, so deserving of praise.

Burton Raffel
Translator's Insight
"Mild," in line 868, is not a description of Beowulf as we have seen him. But it is a description often used in the New Testament, more evidence that *Beowulf* is not a pagan poem.

Critical Reading

Cite textual evidence to support your responses.

1. **Key Ideas and Details (a)** What annoys Grendel and leads to his attacks? **(b) Interpret:** What universal conflict lies behind his war with the Danes?

2. **Key Ideas and Details (a)** Why does Beowulf travel to Herot? **(b) Infer:** What do his motives for the trip tell you about his character? **(c) Analyze:** How does the contrast between Grendel and Beowulf turn their conflict into a fight between good and evil?

3. **Integration of Knowledge and Ideas** Beowulf's defeat of Grendel might be described as the defeat of the "dark side" of the warrior's life. Explain.

4. **Integration of Knowledge and Ideas** Explain how the poem, by keeping Beowulf's memory alive, keeps a culture's values alive.

5. **Integration of Knowledge and Ideas** Do you think Beowulf's deeds make him a good role model? Explain.

6. **Integration of Knowledge and Ideas** What does *Beowulf* reveal about the way in which Anglo-Saxons defined evil and good? In responding, use at least two of these Essential Question words: *liminal, boundary, malignant.* **[Connecting to the Essential Question: How does literature shape or reflect society?]**

Literary Analysis

Common Core State Standards

Writing

1. Write arguments to support claims in an analysis of substantive topics or texts, using valid reasoning and relevant and sufficient evidence. *(p. 66)*

1.d. Establish and maintain a formal style and objective tone while attending to the norms and conventions of the discipline in which they are writing. *(p. 66)*

Language

3.a. Vary syntax for effect. *(p. 67)*

5. Demonstrate understanding of word relationships. *(p. 66)*

1. **Key Ideas and Details Epics** often center on a battle between good and evil. Find evidence in lines 173–198 to indicate that Beowulf is battling for the good.

2. **Key Ideas and Details (a)** What details in the epic show the importance of Christian beliefs? **(b)** What details reveal the importance of pagan warrior values, such as a belief in fate, a taste for boasting, a pride in loyalty, and a desire for fame?

3. **Craft and Structure (a)** List two characteristics that make Beowulf a **legendary, or epic, hero. (b)** Find a passage that shows his more human side. Explain your choice. **(c)** Identify each main character and the traits that make him a hero.

4. **Key Ideas and Details Determine the main idea** of lines 843–861 from *Beowulf* by *paraphrasing* them.

5. **Key Ideas and Details (a)** Explain which details you did not understand before paraphrasing. **(b)** Compare your paraphrase to the original, citing poetic effects that were lost in your paraphrase.

6. **Integration of Knowledge and Ideas** An epic reflects the values of the culture that produced it. Use a chart like the one shown to identify three features of *Beowulf* that probably pleased its original audience. For each, draw a conclusion about Anglo-Saxon tastes and values.

Feature	Why Pleasing	Values Reflected
boastful speeches	makes hero seem superhuman	

7. **Integration of Knowledge and Ideas** Frustrated pride may lead to spite, just as loyalty may lead to vengeance, and eagerness for glory may turn into greed. Explain how each creature Beowulf battles represents an extreme and dangerous form of warrior values and behavior.

8. **Integration of Knowledge and Ideas (a)** Is Beowulf a believable character, or is he "too heroic"? Explain your answer. **(b)** How does his believability affect your sympathy for him?

9. **Integration of Knowledge and Ideas** Compare the way the epic commemorates Beowulf with the way our culture celebrates its heroes. Cite details that support your response.

Vocabulary Acquisition and Use

Word Analysis: Latin Word Root -sol-

The root -sol- comes from the Latin word *solari,* meaning "to relieve, to comfort." The root appears in the word *solace,* which means "an easing of grief, loneliness, or discomfort." With -sol- in mind, answer the following questions. Then, provide a definition of each italicized word.

1. Which character is *inconsolable*?
2. Why might Hrothgar's warriors have felt *disconsolate* after hearing Beowulf's boasts?
3. In what way did Beowulf provide *solace* for Hrothgar's people?
4. How might you *console* the mourning warriors after King Beowulf's death?

Vocabulary: Analogies

An analogy compares two relationships to show their basic similarity. For each item below, analyze the relationship between the first and second words. Then, complete the analogy using a word from the vocabulary list on page 38. Use each word only once, and explain your choice.

1. honest : untruthful :: delightful : _____
2. agreement : discord :: distress : _____
3. elevated : soaring :: huge : _____
4. flee : escape :: rid : _____
5. gift : donation :: reimbursement : _____
6. soothing : disturbing :: unmoving : _____

Writing to Sources

Argument Assuming the role of Beowulf, write a **job application** to Hrothgar, explaining why you are best suited to take on Grendel. Strike the same tone you would use in a real-life job letter. Keep in mind both your *purpose* and your *audience*, and choose words and ideas that are appropriate to both.

Prewriting First, review the text and create a list of Beowulf's best and most noble qualities, as well as his prior experience. Then, review your list, eliminating anything unrelated to the task of battling Grendel.

Model: Brainstorming Relevant Ideas
Beowulf's Qualities and Experiences
export sailor
listens to his advisors
survived many wars
bound giants in chains
killed monsters of the ocean

Beowulf's sailing and listening skills would not be needed in a battle with Grendel.

Drafting In the first paragraph of your letter, state your purpose and give an overview of your main qualifications for the job. In the body of your letter, describe your qualifications and prior experiences in detail. Remember to maintain a formal yet personable tone.

Revising As you read over your draft, revise any words or phrases that sound too casual, inappropriate, or irrelevant.

Conventions and Style: Coordinating Conjunctions

For a smoother writing style, you can combine short, choppy sentences. One way to combine sentences is by using coordinating conjunctions to join sentence elements. A **coordinating conjunction** connects words or groups of words that have equal importance in the sentence.

Combining Sentences With Coordinating Conjunctions

Choppy	Better
Peace could not be bought with money. Peace could not be bought with land.	Peace could not be bought with money *or* land.
The monster hid in the mist. He terrorized the king's warriors.	The monster hid in the mist *and* terrorized the king's warriors.
The men stayed away from the banquet hall. They feared Grendel.	The men stayed away from the banquet hall, *for* they feared Grendel.

Keep in mind that different coordinating conjunctions show different relationships: *And* shows addition or similarity. *But* and *yet* indicate contrast. *Or* and *nor* indicate a choice. *For* and *so* show a result.

Punctuation Tip: When a coordinating conjunction joins two words, phrases, or subordinate clauses, no comma is needed. When a coordinating conjunction joins three or more elements, insert a comma before each element. When a coordinating conjunction joins two independent clauses, use a comma before the conjunction.

Practice In items 1–4, identify the coordinating conjunction and the words it joins. In items 5–8, use a coordinating conjunction to combine the two sentences.

1. Were pagan or Christian ideas more popular when *Beowulf* was written?
2. The king's council held meetings but could not devise a way to stop the attacks.
3. The people were terrified, but there was one man who could help them.
4. They landed the ship and were greeted by a soldier patrolling the cliffs.
5. He did not take his shield with him to fight Grendel. He did not take his sword either.
6. The monster struggled. He could not escape Beowulf's grip.
7. Her son had been killed. The mother sought revenge.
8. Epics reflect the dominant cultural values of the time. They reflect the dominant religious values too.

Writing and Speaking Conventions

A. **Writing** For each pair listed, construct a sentence in which you link the two words or word groups using a coordinating conjunction. Tell what relationship is indicated by the conjunction.

1. good—evil
2. outfitted a boat—sailed to a distant land
3. he killed the monster—the people were grateful

   Example: good—evil
   Sentence: Is the king good or evil?
   Relationship: choice

B. **Speaking** Tell your friends the story of Beowulf's battle with Grendel. Use at least three different coordinating conjunctions.

Themes Across Centuries: Translator's Insights

Seamus Heaney Discusses Beowulf

Giving Shape to Poetry A poet in Old English was called a *scop*, pronounced "shop" and meaning "a shaper." But did he do his shaping with a pen on parchment or with sound-patterns in the ear? Was he a scribe or was he a singer? Was *Beowulf* the result of mouth and ear work, or pen and paperwork?

The answer has to be that it was both. We have evidence that the *scop* chanted his poems to the accompaniment of a harp, so the notes he struck with his voice and his instrument were designed to fasten his words into the ear and the memory. But the intricacy of the patterning suggests that over time his live performance developed into a written score, so the heard melody has come down to us as a manuscript, a word which basically means handwritten marks.

The Original *Beowulf* In the original, for example, three lines of one passage of *Beowulf* look like this:

> **Him ðā gegiredan Gēata lēode**
> **ād on eorðan unwāclīcne,**
> **helmum behongen, hilde-bordum.**

Look again and you can see words and traces of words that we still use. "Him," obviously, in line 1; "helmets" and "hung" and "boards" in line 3; and once you realize that the strange letter **ð** is the symbol that Anglo-Saxon scribes used for the "th," you can see "earth" in line 2. But the words were meant to be heard rather than seen, and if you keep looking you can find alliteration that the first audience listened for in every line.

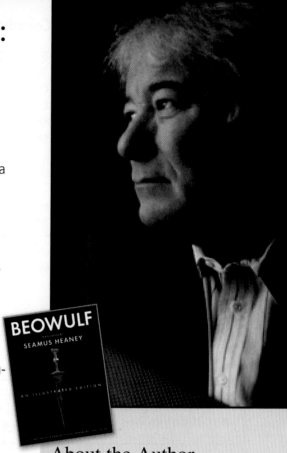

About the Author

Seamus Heaney's poetry focuses on the cities and farms of his homeland in Northern Ireland and the political and religious strife that he has witnessed. Among his translations are *Beowulf* (2000) and Sophocles' drama *Antigone* (2004).

◀ **Critical Viewing**
Why do historians preserve documents like this page from Beowulf? **SPECULATE**

The Music of Storytelling Translating an old poem means keeping time, in both the musical and historical sense; it means staying faithful to the original, but not to the point of sounding out of tune. I wanted my version to be a score for performance and tried, therefore, to tune my voice not only to the movement of the Anglo-Saxon lines but to the other voices that had been familiar to me in Northern Ireland. I wrote for my first local accent, imagining the poetry being spoken by old neighbors who always gave their storytelling a natural pace and stress. When I tried out a line, the test would be: do these words sound sure and true if I pretend to be one of those big-voiced elders?

Take, for example, the third line: it tolls like a bell that has been rung four times, and when I translated it I wanted to keep the heavy downbeat of the original alliterating words, so it came out as "hung with helmets, heavy war-shields." I was after a similar effect in later lines such as "funeral fires; fumes of woodsmoke" and "and wailed aloud for their lord's decease."

Still, there is epic pride in the lines as well as elegy, so I wanted them to sound not only mournful but elevated. Ideally, the translator of *Beowulf* will construct something in words that is the equivalent of the burial mound constructed by the Geats, something to make us feel both their hero's greatness and their grief at his loss.

▲ **Critical Viewing**
In what ways does the burial mound pictured here convey both greatness and serenity? **INTERPRET**

Critical Reading

1. **Craft and Structure (a)** According to Heaney's essay, was the original Old English scop a writer or a musician? **(b) Speculate:** In what ways do you think details in this translation of *Beowulf* were influenced by the manner in which the tale was originally told?

2. **Craft and Structure (a)** On what voices does Heaney model his translation? **(b) Infer:** Why might it have helped Heaney to have specific voices in mind as he translated?

As You Think About *Beowulf* . . .

3. **Integration of Knowledge and Ideas** Many translators have produced versions of *Beowulf*. In what ways might translators' decisions affect your experience with the epic?

Analyzing Functional and Expository Texts

Online Encyclopedia Article • Wikipedia Article

About the Texts

An **online encyclopedia article** is a research source, presented as a Web page on the Internet, that provides information on a given topic. Usually, pages addressing specific topics can be accessed through a search engine within the larger encyclopedia site. Most online encyclopedia articles are written by an expert and feature credible information on the topic of the article, clear identification of the author or sponsor of the Web site, and a list of resources or bibliography consulted by the author. Some sites also provide links to other reliable online resources.

A **Wikipedia article** is an online reference that, unlike a traditional encyclopedia article, can be edited and updated by readers. Wikipedia does not charge an access fee and therefore relies on contributions from amateur writers. This practice has caused some experts to question its accuracy.

Preparing to Read Complex Texts

As you read a digital reference, **evaluate its validity and reliability** as a research tool.

- *Consider the source.* Identify the site's sponsor. Determine whether it promotes a particular agenda, such as to sell products, that could result in biased information.

- *Verify and clarify facts.* Confirm information by consulting other reputable sources in various media or formats. For example, compare the presentation of a topic online, in a book, and in a documentary film. Evaluate the accuracy of one source by measuring it against the others.

As you read, use a chart like this one to evaluate a source's validity:

Digital Resource _____			
Author _____			
Facts to Be Verified	**Sources**	**Discrepancies**	**Result**
1._____	_____	_____	_____
2._____	_____	_____	_____
3._____	_____	_____	_____

Common Core State Standards

Reading Informational Text
7. Integrate and evaluate multiple sources of information presented in different media or formats as well as in words in order to address a question or solve a problem.

Content-Area Vocabulary

These words appear in the selections that follow. They may also appear in other content-area texts:

manuscripts (man´ yōō skripts´) *n.* books or documents written by hand before printing was invented

didactic (dī dak´ tik) adj. descriptive of a work that is intended to teach people a moral lesson

fragmentary (frag´ mən ter´ ē) *adj.* consisting of broken pieces; disconnected

forefront (fôr´ frunt´) *n.* the position of most activity or importance

siege (sēj) *n.* the surrounding of a place by an opposing force

Jump to: navigation, search

🔍 Old English poetry

ENCYCLOPEDIA
BRITANNICA online

Home | Blog | Board | Newsletters | International | Store

English Literature — The Major Manuscripts

The Old English period > Poetry > The major manuscripts

Most Old English poetry is preserved in four **manuscripts** of the late 10th and early 11th centuries. The Beowulf manuscript (British Library) contains *Beowulf*, *Judith*, and three prose tracts; the <u>Exeter Book</u> (Exeter Cathedral) is a miscellaneous gathering of lyrics, riddles, didactic poems, and religious narratives; the <u>Junius Manuscript</u> (Bodleian Library, Oxford)—also called the <u>Caedmon Manuscript</u>, even though its contents are no longer attributed to Caedmon—contains biblical paraphrases; and the <u>Vercelli Book</u> (found in the cathedral library in Vercelli, Italy) contains saints' lives, several short religious poems, and prose homilies. In addition to the poems in these books are historical poems in the <u>Anglo-Saxon Chronicle</u>; poetic renderings of Psalms 51–150; the 31 Metres included in <u>King Alfred the Great</u>'s translation of <u>Boethius</u>'s *De consolatione philosophiae (Consolation of Philosophy)*; magical, **didactic**, elegiac, and heroic poems; and others, miscellaneously interspersed with prose, jotted in margins, and even worked in stone or metal.

Related Topics

Underlined words in blue are hyper-links or connections to other sources.

<u>Poetry</u>

from the English literature *article*

The Norman Conquest worked no immediate transformation on either the language or the literature of the English. Older poetry continued to be copied during the last half of the 11th century; two poems . . .

<u>Development as a poet</u>

from the Pound, Ezra *article*

Unsettled by the slaughter of World War I and the spirit of hopelessness he felt was pervading England after its conclusion, Pound decided to move to Paris, publishing before he left two of his most . . .

<u>lament</u>

a nonnarrative poem expressing deep grief or sorrow over a personal loss. The form developed as part of the oral tradition along with heroic poetry and exists in most languages. Examples include . . .

<u>Chadwick, H. Munro</u>

English philologist and historian, professor of Anglo-Saxon at the University of Cambridge (1912–41), who helped develop an integral approach to Old English studies.

ENCYCLOPEDIA
BRITANNICA online

Home | Blog | Board | Newsletters | International | Store

The major manuscripts
from the English literature *article*

Most Old English poetry is preserved in four manuscripts of the late 10th and early 11th centuries. The Beowulf manuscript (British Library) contains *Beowulf, Judith,* and three prose tracts; the . . .

The Eddaic verse forms
from the Scandinavian literature *article*

Three metres are commonly distinguished in Eddaic poetry: the epic measure, the speech measure, and the song measure. Most narrative poems were in the first measure, which consisted of short lines of . . .

Alliterative verse
from the English literature *article*

Virtually all Old English poetry is written in a single metre, a four-stress line with a syntactical break, or caesura, between the second and third stresses, and with alliteration linking the two . . .

Lattimore, Richmond

American poet and translator renowned for his disciplined yet poetic translations of Greek classics.

Caedmon

first Old English Christian poet, whose **fragmentary** hymn to the creation remains a symbol of the adaptation of the aristocratic-heroic Anglo-Saxon verse tradition to the expression of Christian . . .

The golden age of Bede
from the United Kingdom *article*

Within a century of Augustine's landing, England was in the **forefront** of scholarship. This high standard arose from a combination of influences: that from Ireland, which had escaped the decay caused . . .

Exeter Book

the largest extant collection of Old English poetry. Copied c. 975, the manuscript was given to Exeter Cathedral by Bishop Leofric (died 1072). It begins with some long religious poems: the Christ, . . .

Jump to: navigation, search

Davy Crockett

Davy Crockett

From Wikipedia, *the free encyclopedia*

Colonel David Crockett (August 17, 1786 - March 6, 1836) was a celebrated 19th-century American folk hero, frontiersman, soldier and politician; usually referred to as Davy Crockett and by the popular title "King of the Wild Frontier." He represented Tennessee in the U.S. House of Representatives, served in the Texas Revolution, and died at the age of 49 at the Battle of the Alamo.

Born	David Crockett August 17, 1786 Greene County, Tennessee
Died	March 6, 1836 (aged 49) Alamo Mission, San Antonio, Republic of Texas Killed in action
Occupation	Pioneer, Soldier, Trapper, Explorer, State Assemblyman, Congressman
Title	Colonel
Spouse	Polly Finley (1806–1815) her death Elizabeth Patton (1816–1836) his death

Contents

Any user can edit Wikipedia articles, so it is important to verify facts found here against other sources.

[edit] Birth and Childhood

Davy Crockett was born near the Nolichucky River in Greene County, Tennessee, on August 17th, 1786. David was the fifth of nine children of John and Rebecca Hawkins Crockett. His father was one of the Overmountain Men who fought in the American Revolutionary War battle of Kings Mountain. The Crocketts moved to Morristown, Tennessee sometime during the 1790s and built a cabin. A museum now stands on this site and is a reconstruction of that cabin.[1]

Shortly after being sent to school, Crockett ran away from home and spent several years roaming from town to town. During this period, Crockett claims to have visited most of the towns and villages throughout Tennessee and learned the majority of his skills as a backwoodsman, hunter and trapper.

[edit] Political Career

On September 17, 1821, Crockett was elected to the Committee of Propositions and Grievances. In 1826 and 1828 he was elected to the United States House of Representatives. As a Congressman, Crockett supported the rights of squatters, who were barred from buying land in the West without already owning property. He also opposed President Andrew Jackson's Indian Removal Act, and his opposition to Jackson caused his defeat when he ran for re-election in 1831; however, he won when he ran again in 1833. In 1835, he was narrowly defeated for re-election.[2]

From Wikipedia, *the free encyclopedia*

[edit] Texas Revolution

On October 31, 1835, Crockett left Tennessee for Texas, writing "I want to explore Texas well before I return." He traveled along the Kawesch Glenn, a southwest trail. He arrived in Nacogdoches, Texas, in early January 1836. On January 14, 1836, Crockett and 65 other men signed an oath before Judge John Forbes to the Provisional Government of Texas for six months. "I have taken the oath of government and have enrolled my name as a volunteer and will set out for the Rio Grande in a few days with the volunteers from the United States." Each man was promised about 4,600 acres (19 km²) of land as payment. On February 6, Crockett and about five other men rode into San Antonio de Bexar and camped just outside of the town. They were later greeted by James Bowie and Antonio Menchacha and taken to the home of Don Erasmo Seguin.

William Barret Travis was the commander in charge at the siege at the Alamo. He appealed for help against the Mexican forces, to which Davy Crockett responded. The Texas forces of 180–250 were overwhelmed by the attacking 1,300-1,600 Mexican soldiers. The Mexican commanders understood their superiority of numbers and position and offered free passage to all concerned. Travis, supported by his entire force except one, refused to surrender.[3]

[edit] Death

All that is known for certain about the fate of Davy Crockett is that he died at the Battle of the Alamo.

This warning alerts you that the information in one section of the article has not been adequately cited and may not be reliable.

This section does not cite any references or sources.

Please improve this section by adding citations to reliable sources. Unverifiable material may be challenged and removed.

[edit] References

This section indicates the article's sources and allows the user to verify its information.

1. Crockett Tavern Museum
2. A Century of Lawmaking for a New Nation: U.S. Congressional Documents and Debates, 1774-1875. The Library of Congress, URL accessed 2007-08-01.
3. Roots Web. "David Crockett, Tennesse.

[edit] Further reading

■ Crockett, David, *A Narrative of the Life of David Crockett of the State of Tennessee*; University of Nebraska Press.

■ Levy, Buddy, *The Real Life Adventures of David Crockett*; Putnam Press.

Critical Reading

1. **Key Ideas and Details (a)** Identify three distinct features of the Britannica page. Consider both content and components provided for navigation. **(b)** Which feature would be most helpful to you in evaluating the site's reliability and credibility? Explain your choice.

2. **Key Ideas and Details** What other sources might you use to evaluate the validity and reliability of the Britannica article? Explain your choices.

3. **Key Ideas and Details (a)** What is the main difference between Wikipedia and other encyclopedias? **(b)** Which feature or features of the Wikipedia page could you use to evaluate the site's validity and reliability? Explain your choices.

4. **Content-Area Vocabulary (a)** Explain how the Latin words *manus,* ("hand") and *scribere* ("to write") contribute to the meaning of the word *manuscript.* **(b)** Determine the meaning of these other words derived from the Latin word *manus: manacle, manicure, manipulate, manual,* and *manage.* Use a dictionary to verify the meanings you determined.

⏱ Timed Writing

Explanatory Text [40 minutes}

Format

In an **analytical essay,** you break a topic into its elements and examine each one. Write at least one paragraph about each element, and include smooth transitions between ideas.

Write an **analytical essay** in which you **evaluate** the validity and reliability of various digital reference tools. Consider the pages shown here, as well as other sources you may have consulted in the past. Discuss the credibility of the various sites, as well as the information and features each offers. Also, explain how you can use other sources in various media to further verify the credibility of an online reference. End with a discussion of why it is important to verify the reliability of information presented online and elsewhere.

Academic Vocabulary

When you **evaluate** a text, you state your own judgment about it. Be sure to support your judgment with specific details from the texts.

5-Minute Planner

Complete these steps before you begin to write:

1. Read the prompt carefully. List key words.

2. Write a thesis that clearly responds to the prompt.

3. Scan the texts shown here and jot down other details that relate to the prompt.

4. Briefly sketch an outline for your essay. **TIP** In a Timed Writing situation an outline can be a simple numbered list.

5. Reread the prompt, and begin drafting.

Beowulf: **From Ancient Epic to Graphic Novel**

It was the superhero in *Beowulf,* the sword-wielding slayer of monsters, that drew comics creator Gareth Hinds to the eighth-century epic. It was the warrior's heroism and realistic fighting style, however, that led the artist in Hinds to render the story as a graphic novel. Above all, as Hinds told one interviewer, *Beowulf* is "an incredibly cool story."

It is so cool and powerful that this tale of a warrior-chieftain has found its way into movies (the latest one directed by Robert Zemeckis, with writer Neil Gaiman sharing a screenwriting credit), TV, and opera. In Hinds's chosen medium, the dragon looks remarkably similar to the one in the movie *Alien* and Beowulf has the fit body of a comic-book superhero.

For his graphic novel, Hinds employed three different art styles: pen and ink, with computer coloring using Adobe Photoshop; paint on wooden panels; and black wash over black ink. All pre-press work was done on his own computer. Thus, while Beowulf's narrative may be timeless, Hinds's techniques are as up-to-the-minute as Hollywood's transformations of paper comic books into movie blockbusters.

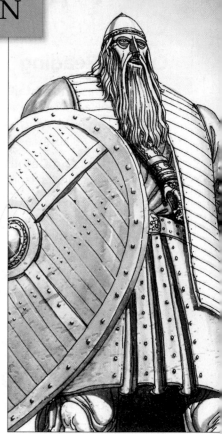

Gareth Hinds
artist of *Beowulf*

Gareth Hinds was always drawing when he was a child. "I was basically born into it," he says. "But I had a lot of really good training and encouragement along the way. And I'm a very strong believer in the power of good art instruction." So it was only natural that he would study art in school, earning two Bachelors of Fine Art, from Rochester Institute of Technology and Parsons School of Design. He used a grant to self-publish his first graphic novel, *Bearskin*, a Grimm's fairy tale, in 1997. The next year he self-published *Beowulf*. His version of Shakespeare's *King Lear* came out in 2007.

Hinds advises aspiring artists to "become well-rounded." Also, the key to artistic success, he insists, is to "tell a story that is meaningful to ordinary people."

from
Beowulf

GARETH HINDS

As in the old time with Grendel, I would not use sword or other weapon against this Worm. But I know not how, without these, I could fell such an enemy. Thus will I go prepared, but not one foot's space will I yield to him.

Now stand by this barrow and watch, my young comrades, which of us better from the battle-rush shall bear his wounds. To war with the Worm is not for you, nor any man but me alone. One of these two things must be: either I will carry away his treasure or death at last will find me. . . .

Critical Reading

1. **Respond:** In this section from his graphic novel, Hinds depicts the lead-up to the battle with the dragon. Does the way in which Hinds portrays characters and scenes agree with how you pictured them? Why or why not?

2. **(a) Analyze:** In what visual ways does Hinds build suspense for the battle with the dragon? **(b) Analyze:** How do the words in the text boxes work with the images to create suspense?

3. **(a) Classify:** Where does Hinds use close-ups, middle-distance views, and long-distance perspectives in telling the story?
   (b) Evaluate: Do you think he effectively combines these different perspectives? Explain.

Use these questions to hold a class discussion of *Beowulf*:

4. **(a)** How does storytelling with pictures and words differ from storytelling with words alone? **(b)** What are the advantages and disadvantages of each method? Explain.

5. Do you find it surprising that a very new form, the graphic novel, draws its subject matter from a very old form, an ancient epic? Why or why not?

A National Spirit

from *A History of the English Church and People*

Connecting to the Essential Question In this selection, a monk who lived many years ago describes the distant British Isles for European readers. As you read, notice details that suggest Bede is describing a place that is far away from the known world. Finding such details will help you think about the Essential Question: **What is the relationship between literature and place?**

Close Reading Focus

Historical Writing
Historical writing tells the story of past events using reliable evidence, such as eyewitness reports and documents. Bede, however, lived at a time when even educated people were more superstitious and less informed. Also, as occurs in any era, his biases and beliefs affected his accounts. In Bede's historical writing, therefore, you will find the following:

- Statements of fact: "Britain, formerly known as Albion, is an island"
- Superstitions: belief that snakes die from breathing Ireland's air
- Personal beliefs: "All are united in their study of God's truth"

Look for examples of each of these elements as you read.

Preparing to Read Complex Texts Bede's purpose is to introduce readers to a new place, Britain. Naturally, he tries to do this as clearly as possible. **Analyze the clarity of meaning** he achieves through the use of these elements in his writing:

- *Patterns of organization*, such as the order in which he discusses Britain and Ireland, and his way of combining facts, examples, description, and narration, or the telling of a story
- *Hierarchical structures,* such as the relative importance he gives to different aspects of Britain
- *Repetition of main ideas*, such as Britain's positive qualities
- *Word choice*; for example, the use of factual language
- *Clear syntax*, or easy-to-understand sentence structure

As you read, use a chart like the one shown to analyze the clarity of Bede's discussion.

Vocabulary

The words below are important to understanding the text that follows. Copy the words into your notebook. What other forms of *cultivated* and *migrated* do you know?

promontories   innumerable

cultivated   migrated

Common Core State Standards

Reading Informational Text
5. Analyze and evaluate the effectiveness of the structure an author uses in his or her exposition, including whether the structure makes points clear, convincing, and engaging.

Clarity of Meaning	
Element and Example	Contribution to Clarity

BEDE (673–735)

Author of *A History of the English Church and People*

It was as if the lights had gone out. In the fifth century, the Roman Empire abandoned Britain. Rome was the center of the most advanced civilization in the West. As part of the Roman Empire, Britain had been connected with a larger world of trade and culture. Roman missionaries taught reading and writing as they preached Christianity. Roman soldiers patrolled Britain's borders. Once Rome withdrew, however, Britain was isolated, threatened by invasion from without and by strife from within.

Keeping Learning Alive Monasteries, particularly in Ireland, kept knowledge alive during these dark times. Monks studied Latin, the language of the Roman Empire. They laboriously copied books. The more scholarly monks wrote new works.

Much of what we know about England before A.D. 700 is based on the work of one such monk, Bede. A contemporary of the unknown author of *Beowulf*, Bede was the most learned scholar of his day. Although he wrote forty books on various subjects, his reputation would be secure on the basis of one—*A History of the English Church and People*, for which Bede is called the father of English history.

A Daily Reminder Bede was born in Wearmouth (now Sunderland) in northeastern England. At age seven, he entered the nearby monastic school of Jarrow. A diligent student, he stayed on as a priest and scholar. Although Bede lived his whole life at Jarrow, he wrote in Latin, so his work was accessible to scholars throughout the West. His pupils carried his writings to Europe. His work, famous in his own lifetime for its scholarship, has become a part of daily life—Bede helped originate the dating of events from the birth of Christ, a cornerstone of the Western calendar.

A Scholarly Work In the *History*, Bede describes the conquest of Britain by the Anglo-Saxon tribes after the departure of the Romans. His main concern, however, was the expansion of Christianity in England. Bede gathered information from many kinds of documents, interviewed knowledgeable monks, and, in general, proceeded very much like a modern historian.

In the century after his death, Bede's history was translated from Latin into English for King Alfred. In the same century, Bede was honored with the title "the Venerable [respected] Bede."

▲ Detail of a manuscript by the 8th century English Benedictine monk and scholar, the Venerable Bede.

from
A HISTORY OF THE ENGLISH CHURCH AND PEOPLE

Translated by Leo Sherley-Price

BACKGROUND Although the majority of British people in Bede's day were illiterate and written records were scarce, monasteries such as the one to which Bede belonged were dedicated to continuing a tradition of learning. Through the monastery, Bede had access to books and other documents, as well as contact with other learned monks. Using these sources, he was able to generate his history of Britain. His fellow Britons may have been illiterate, but Bede had in mind a larger world of readers for his work—the Church to which he belonged and the Roman civilization in which it participated. Bede wrote his account of Britain for such readers, starting at the beginning with the basics.

THE SITUATION OF BRITAIN AND IRELAND: THEIR EARLIEST INHABITANTS

Britain, formerly known as Albion, is an island in the ocean, facing between north and west, and lying at a considerable distance from the coasts of Germany, Gaul, and Spain, which together form the greater part of Europe.

It extends 800 miles northwards, and is 200 in breadth, except where a number of promontories stretch farther, the coastline round which extends to 3,675 miles. To the south lies Belgic Gaul,[1] from the nearest shore of which travelers can see the city known as Rutubi Portus, which the English have corrupted to Reptacestir.[2] The distance from there across the sea to Gessoriacum,[3] the nearest coast of the Morini, is 50 miles or, as some write it, 450 furlongs.[4] On the opposite side of Britain, which lies open to the boundless ocean, lie the isles of the Orcades.[5] Britain is rich in grain and timber; it has good pasturage for cattle and draft animals,[6] and vines are cultivated in various localities. There are many land and sea birds of various species, and it is well known for its plentiful springs and rivers abounding in fish. There are salmon and eel fisheries, while seals, dolphins, and sometimes whales are caught. There are also many varieties of shellfish, such as mussels, in which are often found excellent pearls of several colors: red, purple, violet, and green, but mainly white. Cockles[7] are abundant, and a beautiful scarlet dye is extracted from them which remains unfaded by sunshine or rain; indeed, the older the cloth, the more beautiful its color. The country has both salt and hot springs, and the waters flowing from them provide hot baths, in which the people bathe separately according to age and sex. As Saint Basil says: "Water receives its heat when it flows across certain metals, and becomes hot, and even scalding." The land has rich veins of many metals, including copper, iron, lead, and silver. There is also much black jet[8] of fine quality, which sparkles in firelight. When burned, it drives away snakes, and, like amber, when it is warmed by friction, it clings to whatever is applied to it. In old times, the country had twenty-eight noble cities, and innumerable castles, all of which were guarded by walls, towers, and barred gates.

Since Britain lies far north toward the pole, the nights are short in summer, and at midnight it is hard to tell whether the evening twilight still lingers or whether dawn is approaching; for in these northern latitudes the sun does not remain long below the horizon at night. Consequently both summer days and winter nights are long, and when the sun withdraws

---

1. **Belgic Gaul** France.
2. **Reptacestir** Richborough, part of the city of Sandwich.
3. **Gessoriacum** Boulogne, France.
4. **furlongs** units for measuring distance; a furlong is equal to one eighth of a mile.
5. **Orcades** Orkney Isles.
6. **draft animals** animals used for pulling loads.
7. **Cockles** edible shellfish with two heart-shaped shells.
8. **jet** *n.* type of coal.

Vocabulary

promontories
(präm´ ən tôr´ ēz) *n.* peaks of high land sticking out into the water

cultivated
(kul´ tə vāt´ əd) *v.* grown

innumerable
(i nōō´ mər ə bəl) *adj.* too many to count

Analyze Clarity of Meaning

If Britain is unknown to many of his readers, why does it make sense for Bede to begin with a geographical description?

Historical Writing

Find two facts in this paragraph. Then, identify one claim for which you might need more evidence.

Comprehension

According to Saint Basil, how does water from the hot springs receive its heat?

Analyze Clarity of Meaning

In this paragraph, how does Bede weave together facts and narratives, or stories?

Vocabulary

migrated (mī´ grāt´ əd)
v. moved from one region or country to another

southwards, the winter nights last eighteen hours. In Armenia,[9] Macedonia,[10] and Italy, and other countries of that latitude, the longest day lasts only fifteen hours and the shortest nine.

At the present time there are in Britain, in harmony with the five books of the divine law, five languages and four nations—English, British, Scots, and Picts. Each of these have their own language, but all are united in their study of God's truth by the fifth, Latin, which has become a common medium through the study of the scriptures. The original inhabitants of the island were the Britons, from whom it takes its name, and who, according to tradition, crossed into Britain from Armorica,[11] and occupied the southern parts. When they had spread northwards and possessed the greater part of the islands, it is said that some Picts from Scythia[12] put to sea in a few long ships and were driven by storms around the coasts of Britain, arriving at length on the north coast of Ireland. Here they found the nation of the Scots, from whom they asked permission to settle, but their request was refused. Ireland is the largest island after Britain, and lies to the west. It is shorter than Britain to the north, but extends far beyond it to the south towards the northern coasts of Spain, although a wide sea separates them. These Pictish seafarers, as I have said, asked for a grant of land to make a settlement. The Scots replied that there was not room for them both, but said: "We can give you good advice. There is another island not far to the east, which we often see in the distance on clear days. Go and settle there if you wish; should you meet resistance, we will come to your help." So the Picts crossed into Britain, and began to settle in the north of the island, since the Britons were in possession of the south. Having no women with them, these Picts asked wives of the Scots, who consented on condition that, when any dispute arose, they should choose a king from the female royal line rather than the male. This custom continues among the Picts to this day. As time went on, Britain received a third nation, that of the Scots, who migrated from Ireland under their chieftain Reuda, and by a combination of force and treaty, obtained from the Picts the settlements that they still hold. From the name of this chieftain, they are still known as Dalreudians, for in their tongue *dal* means a division.

Ireland is broader than Britain, and its mild and healthy climate is superior. Snow rarely lies longer than three days, so that

---

9. **Armenia** region between the Black and the Caspian seas, now divided between the nations of Armenia and Turkey.
10. **Macedonia** region in the eastern Mediterranean, divided among Greece, Yugoslavia, and Bulgaria.
11. **Armorica** Brittany, France.
12. **Scythia** ancient region in southeastern Europe.

ATLAS PAGE THE BRITISH ISLES

Republic of Ireland

United Kingdom

An atlas is a book of maps and other information on a country's physical landscape, political makeup, and economic resources. Modern atlases benefit from satellite technology and computer-generated maps. You can use this atlas page to verify and clarify — check the accuracy and clarity of — facts that Bede provides about Britain's geography and resources.

CONNECT TO THE LITERATURE

Use this modern atlas entry for Ireland and the United Kingdom to check the accuracy and clarity of three of Bede's statements of fact about the British Isles.

> At its widest the United Kingdom is 300 miles (500 km) across. From the northern tip of Scotland to the southern coast of England, it is about 600 miles (1,000 km). No part is more than 75 miles (120 km) from the sea.
>
> The greatest distance from north to south in Ireland is 302 miles (486 km), and from east to west it is 171 miles (275 km).

Natural Resources

United Kingdom	Republic of Ireland
coal, petroleum, natural gas, iron ore, lead, zinc, gold, tin, limestone, salt, clay, chalk, gypsum, potash, silica sand, slate, arable land	natural gas, peat, copper, lead, zinc, silver, barite, gypsum, limestone, dolomite

Animal Life

United Kingdom	Republic of Ireland
Red Deer, badgers, otters, foxes, stoats, weasels, rodents hedgehogs, moles, shrews, rabbits, newts, frogs, toads, lizards, snakes	Red Deer, badgers, otters, foxes, stoats, rodents, hedgehogs, shrews, rabbits, newts, frogs

Climate: Republic of Ireland

Month	Average Max Temp F°	Average Min Temp F°	Daily Hours of Sunshine	Days of Rainfall
March	50	37.4	3	11
June	64.4	48.2	6	12
September	62.6	48.2	4	15
December	46.4	35.6	2	18

Land Area

United Kingdom	Republic of Ireland
total: 94,526 sq mi	total: 27,135 sq mi
land: 93,278 sq mi	land: 26,599 sq mi
water: 1,247 sq mi	water: 537 sq mi
coastline: 7,723 mi	coastline: 900 mi

Climate: United Kingdom

Month	Max Temp F°	Min Temp F°	Hours of Sunshine	Days of Rainfall
March	47.3	35.42	4	13
June	62.4	47.1	7	11
September	61	47.3	5	13
December	44.4	34.7	1	15

United Kingdom	Republic of Ireland
mostly rugged hills and low mountains; level to rolling plains in east and southeast	mostly level to rolling interior plain surrounded by rugged hills and low mountains; sea cliffs on west coast

Sunlight: In Britain, daily sunshine hours range from between one and two in midwinter to between five and seven in midsummer.

Historical Writing

Find one example of a superstition in this paragraph.

there is no need to store hay in summer for winter use or to build stables for beasts. There are no reptiles, and no snake can exist there, for although often brought over from Britain, as soon as the ship nears land, they breathe its scented air and die. In fact, almost everything in this isle enjoys immunity to poison, and I have heard that folk suffering from snakebite have drunk water in which scrapings from the leaves of books from Ireland had been steeped, and that this remedy checked the spreading poison and reduced the swelling. The island abounds in milk and honey, and there is no lack of vines, fish, and birds, while deer and goats are widely hunted. It is the original home of the Scots, who, as already mentioned, later migrated and joined the Britons and Picts in Britain. There is a very extensive arm of the sea, which originally formed the boundary between the Britons and the Picts. This runs inland from the west for a great distance as far as the strongly fortified British city of Alcuith.[13] It was to the northern shores of this firth[14] that the Scots came and established their new homeland.

13. **Alcuith** Dumbarton, Scotland.
14. **firth** narrow arm of the sea.

Critical Reading

Cite textual evidence to support your responses.

1. **Key Ideas and Details (a)** What background does Bede give about British scarlet dye? **(b) Infer:** What does this information suggest about the lifestyle or economy of the country?

2. **Key Ideas and Details (a) Interpret:** In what way does Latin unite England? **(b) Interpret:** According to Bede, what factor is most important in uniting people and giving them a common identity?

3. **Integration of Knowledge and Ideas Evaluate:** Does Bede do a good job answering readers' questions about England? Explain, giving three examples of possible questions.

4. **Integration of Knowledge and Ideas** In what ways does Britain's remote location influence Bede's description of it? In responding, use at least two of these Essential Question words: *geography, proximity, isolation. [Connecting to the Essential Question: What is the relationship between literature and place?]*

Literary Analysis

1. **Craft and Structure** **Analyze the clarity of meaning** in Bede's writing, taking into account the contributions of elements such as *patterns of organization*, *hierarchic structures*, *repetition of main ideas*, *word choice*, and *syntax*.

2. **Craft and Structure** It is the year 3000, and a writer wants Earthlings to appreciate the value of a new colony on Mars. How could Bede's use of word choice, repetition, and patterns of organization serve as a model for this writer?

3. **Integration of Knowledge and Ideas** Evaluate Bede's **historical writing** in terms of the evidence he supplies. On a chart like this one, *clarify* several claims Bede makes about Britain or Ireland. For each claim, list his supporting evidence, *verify* it against evidence from a modern atlas page (p. 87), and indicate whether you feel he gives enough support for the claim.

Claim/Clarify	Evidence	Evaluation/Verify

4. **Integration of Knowledge and Ideas** How do Bede's attitudes and beliefs color the information he provides? Support your answer with examples from the selection.

5. **Integration of Knowledge and Ideas** **(a)** In Bede's account, contrast factors that are dividing England with those that are uniting it. **(b)** Which factors seem stronger? Why?

Vocabulary Acquisition and Use

Categorize Vocabulary Using the list of vocabulary words on page 82, analyze the relationship between the words in each item. Are they synonyms (words with similar meanings) or a combination of synonyms and antonyms (words with opposite meanings)? Use a dictionary if necessary.

1. promontories, capes, headlands

2. grew, destroyed, cultivated

3. innumerable, few, scarce

4. migrated, traveled, journeyed

Writing to Sources

Argument Review Bede's *History* as if you were an eighth-century European reader looking for business opportunities. Then, write a **business memo** convincing people to invest in an enterprise in Britain or Ireland. Explain your plan clearly and persuasively, citing passages from the selection to support your points. Use a heading that specifies To, From, Subject, and Date.

Common Core State Standards

Writing
1. Write arguments to support claims in an analysis of substantive topics or texts, using valid reasoning and relevant and sufficient evidence.

Language
5. Demonstrate understanding of word relationships.

Literary History: Chaucer's World

The Canterbury Tales . . .
is actually a story about stories.

Chaucer's Guided Tour of Medieval Life and Literature

Rich people, poor people, stock brokers, artists, farmers, street vendors . . . with all of the different lifestyles in our culture, you may wonder what single event could gather together people from all parts of society. Geoffrey Chaucer found in his own society an orderly, even joyous event that gathered people from diverse backgrounds and occupations—a pilgrimage, or journey to a sacred spot. It is such a pilgrimage that gathers together the diverse characters in his masterpiece, *The Canterbury Tales.*

The Journey Begins Like modern travelers, medieval pilgrims must have been eager to while away their time traveling. Chaucer uses this fact to set his story in motion. *The Canterbury Tales* begins with a Prologue, in which the Narrator, presumably Chaucer himself, meets twenty-nine other pilgrims at the Tabard Inn, located in a suburb of London. As the pilgrims prepare for their journey, the host of the Inn, Harry Bailey, sets a challenge. To make the journey more entertaining, he suggests that each pilgrim tell two stories on the way to Canterbury and two stories on the return trip. The person who tells the best tale will be treated to a feast hosted by the other pilgrims. The pilgrims accept the challenge, and Bailey himself decides to join them and judge the competition.

Each of the following sections of the work consists of one of the pilgrim's tales. Brief transitions, as one storyteller finishes and another begins, link the stories. In this way, the work is actually a story about stories, twenty-four different tales set within the overarching tale of the pilgrimage.

Snapshots of an Era In the Prologue, Chaucer sketches a brief but vivid portrait of each pilgrim, creating a lively sense of medieval life. In itself, the Prologue is a great literary achievement. As critic Vincent Hopper notes,

The description of the various pilgrims turn in rapid sequence from an article of clothing to a point of character and back again with no apparent organization or desire for it. Yet so effective is this artful artlessness that each pilgrim stands out sharply as a type of medieval personality and also as a highly individualized character. . . .

Chaucer begins his survey of medieval society with the courtly world, which centered on the nobility. Medieval nobles such as Chaucer's Knight held land granted them by a lord or king, for whom they fought in times of war. In the middle ranks of medieval society were learned professionals, such as Chaucer's Doctor, and wealthy businessmen. The lower orders included craftsmen, storekeepers, and minor administrators, such as the Reeve and the Manciple. The various ranks of the Church, a cornerstone of medieval society, are represented by characters from the Prioress to the Summoner.

However, as Chaucer writes about character ranks and types, he presents them as real people, individuals who defy categorizing. For example, though all outward appearances suggest that the Merchant is wealthy, he is, in fact, deeply in debt—a secret he keeps from some of his fellow travelers. Such breaks in stereotype provide readers with an even greater insight into the daily lives of medieval people.

A Literary Tour The popular genres in Chaucer's day included romances (tales of chivalry), *fabliaux* (short, bawdy, humorous stories), the stories of saints' lives, sermons, and allegories (narratives in which characters represent abstractions such as Pride or Honor). Each pilgrim chooses to tell a type of tale consistent with his or her character, and each of the major forms of medieval literature is represented. Chaucer wrote much of the *Tales* using his own form, the heroic couplet, a pair of rhyming lines with five stressed syllables each. For this important innovation, along with his other achievements, he is known as the father of English poetry.

The Endless Road Traveling with Chaucer's pilgrims, a reader may feel that the world is a big place but that, somehow, all of its pieces fit together. *The Canterbury Tales* reminds us that every journey from here to there is filled with stories, waiting to be told.

Speaking and Listening: Discussion

Comprehension and Collaboration Imagine you are taking a long bus or plane trip with a group of modern-day travelers. With a group, discuss the types of people traveling with you. Come up with your own cast of characters for a modern-day version of *The Canterbury Tales*. Use these questions to guide your **discussion:**

- What different kinds of people make up our society today? Identify six types and build a character that matches each.

- In what ways might many of these individuals break the stereotype they outwardly appear to fit?

- What kind of tale might each character tell?

Choose a point person to share your ideas with the class.

Geoffrey Chaucer (1343?–1400)

Son of a merchant, page in a royal house, soldier, diplomat, and royal clerk, Geoffrey Chaucer saw quite a bit of the medieval world. His varied experiences helped prepare him to write *The Canterbury Tales*. This masterpiece provides the best contemporary picture we have of fourteenth-century England. Gathering characters from different walks of life, Chaucer takes the reader on a journey through medieval society.

The Poet's Beginning The exact date of Geoffrey Chaucer's birth is unknown, but official records furnish many details of his active life. Born into a middle-class family, Chaucer was sent in his early teens to work as page to the wife of Lionel of Antwerp, a son of the reigning monarch, Edward III. Through this position, middle-class Chaucer was introduced to the aristocratic society of England. In 1359, while serving in the English Army in France, Chaucer was captured and held prisoner. King Edward paid a £16 (sixteen-pound) ransom for his release—a sum that was eight times what a simple laborer might make in a year. In 1366, Chaucer married Philippa Pan, a lady-in-waiting to the queen. Their eldest child, Thomas, continued his father's rise in the world, marrying a noblewoman and acquiring great wealth.

The Poet Matures Chaucer began writing in his twenties, practicing his skills as a poet as he rose through the ranks of medieval society. His early poems were based on the works of European poets. These were followed by various translations of French poetry. His first major work, *The Book of the Duchess*, was probably completed in early 1369, almost one year after the death of Blanche of Lancaster, for whose grieving husband, John of Gaunt, he wrote the poem. As Chaucer grew older, he developed a mature style of his own and displayed a deep insight into human character.

The Canterbury Tales

Chaucer wrote *The Canterbury Tales* in his later years. No one knows for certain what prompted him to begin this work. Chaucer's inspiration may have come from his own participation in the pilgrimage to Canterbury. A pilgrimage is a long journey to a shrine or holy site, undertaken by people who wish to express their devotion. The Canterbury Cathedral was the focus of devotion because St. Thomas à Becket was murdered there in 1170. Chaucer certainly had the opportunity to observe many pilgrims starting their journeys—a window of his London home overlooked the pilgrim road that led to Canterbury.

In this masterwork, each character tells a tale on the way to Canterbury. Just as the tellers of *The Canterbury Tales* come from the length and breadth of medieval society, the tales encompass medieval literature—from romance to comedy, from rhyme to prose, from crude humor to religious mysteries. Only 24 of the projected 120 tales were finished, but they stand together as a complete work.

The Father of English Poetry

In his own lifetime, Geoffrey Chaucer was considered the greatest English poet. Recognized as a shrewd storyteller, he was also praised by a contemporary as the first to "rain the gold dewdrops of speech and eloquence" into English literature. Throughout history, new generations of poets writing in English have studied his work for both inspiration and insight.

Chaucer lies buried in Westminster Abbey. In recognition of his unique position in England's literary tradition, Westminster's honorary burial area for distinguished writers, the Poets' Corner, was established around his tomb. The words in Middle English at the right are from Chaucer's poem *Troilus and Criseyde*. They are not on his tomb, but they serve to measure both his distance from us and his closeness to us.

Ye knowe eek, that in forme of speche is chaunge

Withinne a thousand yeer, and wordes tho

That hadden prys, now wonder nyce and straunge

Us thinketh hem; and yet they spake hem so,

And spedde as wel in love as men now do . . .

CHAUCER'S SHARP EYE FOR DRESS

Do you dress to impress? Or for success?

Medieval Dress Codes In the 14th century, rules dictating style depended on whether you were rich, middle-class, or poor. No one below the rank of knight could wear fur, for example; merchants could wear the same clothes as knights only if they were five times wealthier, and women were forbidden from wearing silk head coverings.

In the Prologue to *The Canterbury Tales*, Chaucer relies on the details of the pilgrims' clothing and a general knowledge of the do's and don'ts of fashion laws to reveal their personalities, positions on the social ladder, and attempts at modesty or deception.

Modest Dress The Knight's coarse tunic "stained and dark" could have fooled fashion watchers into believing he was without rank. Yet knights were members of the nobility and were allowed to adorn themselves with fur and gold.

Pleasure Loving A Franklin, a member in good standing of the top tier of 14th century hierarchy, was a pleasure-loving fellow. This landowner carried "a little purse of silk…" that Chaucer aptly describes as "white as morning milk."

The Wife of Bath's "flowing mantle" hid her "large hips," her handkerchiefs were finely woven, her stockings "were of the finest scarlet red" and her shoes "soft and new." Her clothing revealed her as a member of the middle class.

Clothing That Suits the Profession A Doctor in the group was adorned alarmingly in "blood-red garments…lined with taffeta," almost as if he were advertising his profession. Yet Chaucer wrote that the Doctor watched every cent and was "rather close as to expenses."

Bottom line: No matter what you wear or when you live, your clothes say a lot about who you are, where you fit, and what you aspire to be.

Knight   Franklin   Wife of Bath   Doctor

Connecting to the Essential Question In the Prologue to *The Canterbury Tales*, Chaucer describes different medieval social types. Briefly describe some social types at your school. In describing social types, you probably described their clothes. As you read, note what Chaucer's descriptions of clothes reveal about his characters. Doing so will help you explore the Essential Question: **How does literature shape or reflect society?**

Close Reading Focus

Characterizaton; Social Commentary

As you read the Prologue, look for these forms of **characterization**— techniques of revealing character:

- **Direct characterization** presents direct statements about a character, like Chaucer's statement that the Knight "followed chivalry. . . ."
- **Indirect characterization** uses actions, thoughts, dialogue, and description to reveal a character's personality. By saying the Knight Is "not gaily dressed," Chaucer suggests that he is not vain.

Each character in the selection represents a different segment of society in Chaucer's time. By using characterization to reveal the virtues and faults of each, Chaucer provides **social commentary,** writing that offers insight into society, its values, and its customs. As you read, determine what Chaucer's characters suggest about his views of English society and of life.

Preparing to Read Complex Texts When you do not understand a long, involved sentence you are reading, repair your comprehension by **questioning.** For example, you may have trouble understanding the eighteen-line sentence at the start of Chaucer's Prologue. To analyze the sentence, ask the questions *When?, Who?, Where?, What?, Why?,* and *How?* to identify essential information. Use a chart like the one shown to finish analyzing Chaucer's first sentence.

Vocabulary

You will encounter the words listed here in the text that follows. Copy the words into your notebook. Which words share the same suffix?

solicitous	commission
garnished	sanguine
absolution	prevarication

Common Core State Standards

Reading Literature

1. Cite strong and thorough textual evidence to support analysis of what the text says explicitly as well as inferences drawn from the text, including determining where the text leaves matters uncertain.

3. Analyze the impact of the author's choices regarding how to develop and relate elements of a story or drama.

Analyze Difficult Sentences	
When?	in April
Who?	people; palmers
Where?	
What?	
Why?	
How?	

from the Canterbury Tales
The Prologue

Geoffrey Chaucer
translated by Nevill Coghill

Lines 1–18 of the Prologue in Chaucer's original Middle English are followed by the entire Prologue in a modern translation.

Whan that Aprill with his shoures soote
The droghte of March hath perced to the roote,
And bathed every veyne in swich licour
Of which vertu engendred is the flour;
5 Whan Zephirus eek with his sweete breeth
Inspired hath in every holt and heeth
The tendre croppes, and the yonge sonne
Hath in the Ram his halve cours yronne,
And smale foweles maken melodye,
10 That slepen al the nyght with open ye
(So priketh hem nature in hir corages);
Thanne longen folk to goon on pilgrimages,
And palmeres for to seken straunge strondes,
To ferne halwes, kowthe in sondry londes;
15 And specially from every shires ende
Of Engelond to Caunterbury they wende,
The hooly blisful martir for to seke,
That hem hath holpen whan that they were seeke.

When in April the sweet showers fall
And pierce the drought of March to the root, and all
The veins are bathed in liquor of such power
As brings about the engendering of the flower,
5 When also Zephyrus[1] with his sweet breath
Exhales an air in every grove and heath
Upon tender shoots, and the young sun
His half-course in the sign of the Ram[2] has run,
And the small fowl are making melody
10 That sleep away the night with open eye
(So nature pricks them and their heart engages)
Then people long to go on pilgrimages
And palmers[3] long to seek the stranger strands[4]
Of far-off saints, hallowed in sundry lands,
15 And specially, from every shire's end
In England, down to Canterbury they wend
To seek the holy blissful martyr,[5] quick
To give his help to them when they were sick.

1. **Zephyrus** (zef´ ə rəs) the west wind.
2. **Ram** Aries, the first sign of the zodiac. The pilgrimage began on April 11, 1387.
3. **palmers** pilgrims who wore two crossed palm leaves to show that they had visited the Holy Land.
4. **strands** shores.
5. **martyr** St. Thomas à Becket, the Archbishop of Canterbury, who was murdered in Canterbury Cathedral in 1170.

It happened in that season that one day
20 In Southwark,[6] at The Tabard,[7] as I lay
Ready to go on pilgrimage and start
For Canterbury, most devout at heart,
At night there came into that hostelry
Some nine and twenty in a company
25 Of sundry folk happening then to fall
In fellowship, and they were pilgrims all
That towards Canterbury meant to ride.
The rooms and stables of the inn were wide;
They made us easy, all was of the best.
30 And shortly, when the sun had gone to rest,
By speaking to them all upon the trip
I soon was one of them in fellowship
And promised to rise early and take the way
To Canterbury, as you heard me say.
35   But nonetheless, while I have time and space,
Before my story takes a further pace,
It seems a reasonable thing to say
What their condition was, the full array
Of each of them, as it appeared to me
40 According to profession and degree,
And what apparel they were riding in;
And at a Knight I therefore will begin.
There was a *Knight*, a most distinguished man,
Who from the day on which he first began
45 To ride abroad had followed chivalry,
Truth, honor, generousness and courtesy.
He had done nobly in his sovereign's war
And ridden into battle, no man more,
As well in Christian as heathen places,
50 And ever honored for his noble graces.
    When we took Alexandria,[8] he was there.
He often sat at table in the chair
Of honor, above all nations, when in Prussia.
In Lithuania he had ridden, and Russia,
55 No Christian man so often, of his rank.
When, in Granada, Algeciras sank
Under assault, he had been there, and in
North Africa, raiding Benamarin;
In Anatolia he had been as well
60 And fought when Ayas and Attalia fell,

Questioning

According to lines 43–46, what values does the Knight follow?

Characterization

What do lines 54–65 indirectly suggest about the Knight's character?

---

6. **Southwark** (suth´ ərk) suburb of London at the time.
7. **The Tabard** (ta´ bərd) an inn.
8. **Alexandria** site of one of the campaigns fought by Christians against groups who posed a threat to Europe during the fourteenth century. The place names that follow refer to other battle sites in these campaigns, or crusades.

For all along the Mediterranean coast
He had embarked with many a noble host.
In fifteen mortal battles he had been
And jousted for our faith at Tramissene
65 Thrice in the lists, and always killed his man.
This same distinguished knight had led the van[9]
Once with the Bey of Balat,[10] doing work
For him against another heathen Turk;
He was of sovereign value in all eyes.
70 And though so much distinguished, he was wise
And in his bearing modest as a maid.
He never yet a boorish thing had said
In all his life to any, come what might;
He was a true, a perfect gentle-knight.
75 Speaking of his equipment, he possessed
Fine horses, but he was not gaily dressed.
He wore a fustian[11] tunic stained and dark
With smudges where his armor had left mark;
Just home from service, he had joined our ranks
80 To do his pilgrimage and render thanks.
        He had his son with him, a fine young *Squire*,
A lover and cadet, a lad of fire
With locks as curly as if they had been pressed.
He was some twenty years of age, I guessed.
85 In stature he was of a moderate length,
With wonderful agility and strength.
He'd seen some service with the cavalry
In Flanders and Artois and Picardy[12]
And had done valiantly in little space
90 Of time, in hope to win his lady's grace.
He was embroidered like a meadow bright
And full of freshest flowers, red and white.
Singing he was, or fluting all the day;
He was as fresh as is the month of May.
95 Short was his gown, the sleeves were long and wide;
He knew the way to sit a horse and ride.
He could make songs and poems and recite,
Knew how to joust and dance, to draw and write.
He loved so hotly that till dawn grew pale
100 He slept as little as a nightingale.
Courteous he was, lowly and serviceable,
And carved to serve his father at the table.

---

9. **van** the part of the army that goes before the rest (short for *vanguard*).
10. **Bey of Balat** pagan leader.
11. **fustian** (fus´ chen) *n.* coarse cloth of cotton and linen.
12. **Flanders . . . Picardy** regions in Belgium and France.

Questioning
What motivates the Squire in lines 85–90?

Comprehension
What are some of the military accomplishments of the Knight?

There was a *Yeoman*[13] with him at his side,
No other servant; so he chose to ride.
105 This Yeoman wore a coat and hood of green,
And peacock-feathered arrows, bright and keen
And neatly sheathed, hung at his belt the while
—For he could dress his gear in yeoman style,
His arrows never drooped their feathers low—
110 And in his hand he bore a mighty bow.
His head was like a nut, his face was brown.
He knew the whole of woodcraft up and down.
A saucy brace[14] was on his arm to ward
It from the bow-string, and a shield and sword
115 Hung at one side, and at the other slipped
A jaunty dirk,[15] spear-sharp and well-equipped.
A medal of St. Christopher[16] he wore
Of shining silver on his breast, and bore
A hunting-horn, well slung and burnished clean,
120 That dangled from a baldric[17] of bright green.
He was a proper forester I guess.

There also was a *Nun*, a Prioress.[18]
Her way of smiling very simple and coy.
Her greatest oath was only "By St. Loy!"[19]
125 And she was known as Madam Eglantyne.
And well she sang a service,[20] with a fine
Intoning through her nose, as was most seemly,
And she spoke daintily in French, extremely,
After the school of Stratford-atte-Bowe;[21]
130 French in the Paris style she did not know.
At meat her manners were well taught withal;
No morsel from her lips did she let fall,
Nor dipped her fingers in the sauce too deep;
But she could carry a morsel up and keep
135 The smallest drop from falling on her breast.
For courtliness she had a special zest,
And she would wipe her upper lip so clean
That not a trace of grease was to be seen
Upon the cup when she had drunk; to eat,

▲ **Critical Viewing**

Compare this portrait with Chaucer's description of the Yeoman. What details did the artist choose to change or omit? **COMPARE AND CONTRAST**

---

13. Yeoman (yō´ mən) *n.* attendant.
14. brace bracelet.
15. dirk *n.* dagger.
16. St. Christopher patron saint of travelers.
17. baldric *n.* belt worn over one shoulder and across the chest to support a sword.
18. Prioress *n.* in an abbey, the nun ranking just below the abbess.
19. St. Loy St. Eligius, patron saint of goldsmiths and courtiers.
20. service daily prayer.
21. Stratford-atte-Bowe nunnery near London.

140 She reached a hand sedately for the meat.
    She certainly was very entertaining,
    Pleasant and friendly in her ways, and straining
    To counterfeit a courtly kind of grace,
    A stately bearing fitting to her place,
145 And to seem dignified in all her dealings.
    As for her sympathies and tender feelings,
    She was so charitably solicitous
    She used to weep if she but saw a mouse
    Caught in a trap, if it were dead or bleeding.
150 And she had little dogs she would be feeding
    With roasted flesh, or milk, or fine white bread.
    And bitterly she wept if one were dead
    Or someone took a stick and made it smart;
    She was all sentiment and tender heart.
155 Her veil was gathered in a seemly way,
    Her nose was elegant, her eyes glass-gray;
    Her mouth was very small, but soft and red,
    Her forehead, certainly, was fair of spread,
    Almost a span[22] across the brows, I own;
160 She was indeed by no means undergrown.
    Her cloak, I noticed, had a graceful charm.
    She wore a coral trinket on her arm,
    A set of beads, the gaudies[23] tricked in green,
    Whence hung a golden brooch of brightest sheen
165 On which there first was graven a crowned *A*,
    And lower, *Amor vincit omnia.*[24]
         Another *Nun*, the chaplain at her cell,
    Was riding with her, and *three Priests* as well.
         A *Monk* there was, one of the finest sort
170 Who rode the country; hunting was his sport.
    A manly man, to be an Abbot able;
    Many a dainty horse he had in stable.
    His bridle, when he rode, a man might hear
    Jingling in a whistling wind as clear,
175 Aye, and as loud as does the chapel bell
    Where my lord Monk was Prior of the cell.
    The Rule of good St. Benet or St. Maur[25]
    As old and strict he tended to ignore;
    He let go by the things of yesterday

Vocabulary

solicitous (sə lis′ ə təs) *adj.*
showing care or concern

Characterization
What can you infer about
the Prioress based on this
detailed description of
her jewelry?

Comprehension
How does the Nun show
her "sympathies and tender
feelings"?

---

22. **span** nine inches.
23. **gaudies** large green beads that marked certain prayers on a set of prayer
    beads.
24. ***Amor vincit omnia*** (ä′ môr′ vin′ chit ôm′ nē ä′) "love conquers all" (Latin).
25. **St. Benet or St. Maur** St. Benedict, author of monastic rules, and St.
    Maurice, one of his followers. Benet and Maur are French versions of
    Benedict and Maurice.

180 And took the modern world's more spacious way.
He did not rate that text at a plucked hen
Which says that hunters are not holy men
And that a monk uncloistered is a mere
Fish out of water, flapping on the pier,

185 That is to say a monk out of his cloister.
That was a text he held not worth an oyster;
And I agreed and said his views were sound;
Was he to study till his head went round
Poring over books in cloisters? Must he toil

190 As Austin[26] bade and till the very soil?
Was he to leave the world upon the shelf?
Let Austin have his labor to himself.
      This Monk was therefore a good man to horse;
Greyhounds he had, as swift as birds, to course.

195 Hunting a hare or riding at a fence
Was all his fun, he spared for no expense.
I saw his sleeves were garnished at the hand
With fine gray fur, the finest in the land,
And on his hood, to fasten it at his chin

200 He had a wrought-gold cunningly fashioned pin;
Into a lover's knot it seemed to pass.
His head was bald and shone like looking-glass;
So did his face, as if it had been greased.
He was a fat and personable priest;

205 His prominent eyeballs never seemed to settle.
They glittered like the flames beneath a kettle;
Supple his boots, his horse in fine condition.
He was a prelate fit for exhibition,
He was not pale like a tormented soul.

210 He liked a fat swan best, and roasted whole.
His palfrey[27] was as brown as is a berry.
      There was a *Friar*, a wanton[28] one and merry
A Limiter,[29] a very festive fellow.
In all Four Orders[30] there was none so mellow,

215 So glib with gallant phrase and well-turned speech.
He'd fixed up many a marriage, giving each
Of his young women what he could afford her.
He was a noble pillar to his Order.
Highly beloved and intimate was he

▲ Critical Viewing

What can you infer from this picture about the Monk's style of living? List three details supporting your conclusion. **INFER**

Vocabulary

garnished (gär´ nisht) *adj.* decorated; trimmed

---

26. **Austin** English version of St. Augustine, who criticized lazy monks.
27. **palfrey** *n.* saddle horse.
28. **wanton** *adj.* jolly.
29. **Limiter** friar who is given begging rights for a certain limited area.
30. **Four Orders** There were four orders of friars who supported themselves by begging: Dominicans, Franciscans, Carmelites, and Augustinians.

220 With County folk[31] within his boundary,
And city dames of honor and possessions;
For he was qualified to hear confessions,
Or so he said, with more than priestly scope;
He had a special license from the Pope.
225 Sweetly he heard his penitents at shrift[32]
With pleasant absolution, for a gift.
He was an easy man in penance-giving
Where he could hope to make a decent living;
It's a sure sign whenever gifts are given
230 To a poor Order that a man's well shriven,[33]
And should he give enough he knew in verity
The penitent repented in sincerity.
For many a fellow is so hard of heart
He cannot weep, for all his inward smart.
235 Therefore instead of weeping and of prayer
One should give silver for a poor Friar's care.
He kept his tippet[34] stuffed with pins for curls,
And pocket-knives, to give to pretty girls.
And certainly his voice was gay and sturdy,
240 For he sang well and played the hurdy-gurdy.[35]
At sing-songs he was champion of the hour.
His neck was whiter than a lily-flower
But strong enough to butt a bruiser down.
He knew the taverns well in every town
245 And every innkeeper and barmaid too
Better than lepers, beggars and that crew,
For in so eminent a man as he
It was not fitting with the dignity
Of his position, dealing with a scum
250 Of wretched lepers; nothing good can come
Of dealings with the slum-and-gutter dwellers,
But only with the rich and victual-sellers.
But anywhere a profit might accrue
Courteous he was and lowly of service too.
255 Natural gifts like his were hard to match.
He was the finest beggar of his batch,
And, for his begging-district, payed a rent;
His brethren did no poaching where he went.
For though a widow mightn't have a shoe,
260 So pleasant was his holy how-d'ye-do
He got his farthing from her just the same

Vocabulary
absolution (ab´ sə loo´ shən)
n. act of freeing someone of
a sin or of a criminal charge

Characterization

In lines 244–254, is Chaucer
using direct characterization
or indirect characterization?
Explain.

Comprehension

How does the Friar
earn his living?

---

31. County folk The phrase refers to rich landowners.
32. shrift *n.* confession.
33. well shriven *adj.* absolved of his sins.
34. tippet *n.* hood.
35. hurdy-gurdy stringed instrument played by cranking a wheel.

▼ Critical Viewing

What can you infer from this picture about the Oxford Cleric's style of living?
INFER

Before he left, and so his income came
To more than he laid out. And how he romped,
Just like a puppy! He was ever prompt
265 To arbitrate disputes on settling days
(For a small fee) in many helpful ways,
Not then appearing as your cloistered scholar
With threadbare habit hardly worth a dollar,
But much more like a Doctor or a Pope.
270 Of double-worsted was the semi-cope[36]
Upon his shoulders, and the swelling fold
About him, like a bell about its mold
When it is casting, rounded out his dress.
He lisped a little out of wantonness
275 To make his English sweet upon his tongue.
When he had played his harp, or having sung,
His eyes would twinkle in his head as bright
As any star upon a frosty night.
This worthy's name was Hubert, it appeared.
280   There was a *Merchant* with a forking beard
And motley dress, high on his horse he sat,
Upon his head a Flemish[37] beaver hat
And on his feet daintily buckled boots.
He told of his opinions and pursuits
285 In solemn tones, and how he never lost.
The sea should be kept free at any cost
(He thought) upon the Harwich-Holland range,[38]
He was expert at currency exchange.
This estimable Merchant so had set
290 His wits to work, none knew he was in debt,
He was so stately in negotiation,
Loan, bargain and commercial obligation.
He was an excellent fellow all the same;
To tell the truth I do not know his name.
295   An *Oxford Cleric*, still a student though,
One who had taken logic long ago,
Was there; his horse was thinner than a rake,
And he was not too fat, I undertake,
But had a hollow look, a sober stare;

---

36. **semi-cope** cape.
37. **Flemish** from Flanders.
38. **Harwich-Holland range** the North Sea between England and Holland.

300 The thread upon his overcoat was bare.
He had found no preferment in the church
And he was too unworldly to make search
For secular employment. By his bed
He preferred having twenty books in red
305 And black, of Aristotle's[39] philosophy,
To having fine clothes, fiddle or psaltery.[40]
Though a philosopher, as I have told,
He had not found the stone for making gold.[41]
Whatever money from his friends he took
310 He spent on learning or another book
And prayed for them most earnestly, returning
Thanks to them thus for paying for his learning.
His only care was study, and indeed
He never spoke a word more than was need,
315 Formal at that, respectful in the extreme,
Short, to the point, and lofty in his theme.
The thought of moral virtue filled his speech
And he would gladly learn, and gladly teach.

    A *Sergeant at the Law* who paid his calls,
320 Wary and wise, for clients at St. Paul's[42]
There also was, of noted excellence.
Discreet he was, a man to reverence,
Or so he seemed, his sayings were so wise.
He often had been Justice of Assize
325 By letters patent, and in full commission.
His fame and learning and his high position
Had won him many a robe and many a fee.
There was no such conveyancer[43] as he;
All was fee-simple[44] to his strong digestion,
330 Not one conveyance could be called in question.
Nowhere there was so busy a man as he;
But was less busy than he seemed to be.
He knew of every judgment, case and crime
Recorded, ever since King William's time.
335 He could dictate defenses or draft deeds;
No one could pinch a comma from his screeds,[45]

---

39. **Aristotle's** (ar´ is tät´ əlz) referring to the Greek philosopher (384–322 B.C.).
40. **psaltery** (sôl´ tər ē) ancient stringed instrument.
41. **stone . . . gold** At the time, alchemists believed that a "philosopher's stone" existed that could turn base metals into gold.
42. **St. Paul's** London cathedral near the center of legal activities in the city. Lawyers often met near there to discuss cases.
43. **conveyancer** one who draws up documents for transferring ownership of property.
44. **fee-simple** unrestricted ownership.
45. **screeds** long, boring speeches or pieces of writing.

Spiral Review
Understanding Historical Context
What inferences can you make about the economic ideas of the time based on the suggestion that the Clerk's attitude toward money is unusual?

Vocabulary
commission (kə mish´ ən) *n.* authorization; act of giving authority to an individual

Comprehension
What are the Cleric's interests?

And he knew every statute off by rote.
He wore a homely parti-colored coat
Girt with a silken belt of pin-stripe stuff;
340 Of his appearance I have said enough.
     There was a *Franklin*[46] with him, it appeared;
White as a daisy-petal was his beard.
A sanguine man, high-colored and benign,
He loved a morning sop[47] of cake in wine.
345 He lived for pleasure and had always done,
For he was Epicurus'[48] very son,
In whose opinion sensual delight
Was the one true felicity in sight.
As noted as St. Julian[49] was for bounty
350 He made his household free to all the County.
His bread, his ale were the finest of the fine
And no one had a better stock of wine.
His house was never short of bake-meat pies,
Of fish and flesh, and these in such supplies
355 It positively snowed with meat and drink
And all the dainties that a man could think.
According to the seasons of the year
Changes of dish were ordered to appear.
He kept fat partridges in coops, beyond,
360 Many a bream and pike were in his pond.
Woe to the cook whose sauces had no sting
Or who was unprepared in anything!
And in his hall a table stood arrayed
And ready all day long, with places laid.
365 As Justice at the Sessions[50] none stood higher;
He often had been Member for the Shire.[51]
A dagger and a little purse of silk
Hung at his girdle, white as morning milk.
As Sheriff he checked audit, every entry.
370 He was a model among landed gentry.
     A *Haberdasher*, a *Dyer*, a *Carpenter*,
A *Weaver* and a *Carpet-maker* were
Among our ranks, all in the livery
Of one impressive guild-fraternity.[52]

---

46. *Franklin* wealthy landowner.
47. **sop** piece.
48. **Epicurus'** (ep´ i kyoor´ əs) referring to a Greek philosopher (341–270 B.C.) who believed that happiness is the most important goal in life.
49. **St. Julian** patron saint of hospitality.
50. **Sessions** court sessions.
51. **Member . . . Shire** Parliamentary representative for the county.
52. **guild-fraternity** In the Middle Ages, associations of men practicing the same craft or trade, called guilds, set standards for workmanship and protected their members by controlling competition.

375 They were so trim and fresh their gear would pass
    For new. Their knives were not tricked out with brass
    But wrought with purest silver, which avouches
    A like display on girdles and on pouches.
    Each seemed a worthy burgess,[53] fit to grace
380 A guild-hall with a seat upon the dais.
    Their wisdom would have justified a plan
    To make each one of them an alderman;
    They had the capital and revenue,
    Besides their wives declared it was their due.
385 And if they did not think so, then they ought;
    To be called "*Madam*" is a glorious thought,
    And so is going to church and being seen
    Having your mantle carried like a queen.
          They had a *Cook* with them who stood alone
390 For boiling chicken with a marrow-bone,
    Sharp flavoring-powder and a spice for savor.
    He could distinguish London ale by flavor,
    And he could roast and seethe and broil and fry,
    Make good thick soup and bake a tasty pie.
395 But what a pity—so it seemed to me,
    That he should have an ulcer on his knee.
    As for blancmange,[54] he made it with the best.
          There was a *Skipper* hailing from far west;
    He came from Dartmouth, so I understood.
400 He rode a farmer's horse as best he could,
    In a woolen gown that reached his knee.
    A dagger on a lanyard[55] falling free
    Hung from his neck under his arm and down.
    The summer heat had tanned his color brown,
405 And certainly he was an excellent fellow.
    Many a draught of vintage, red and yellow,
    He'd drawn at Bordeaux, while the trader snored.
    The nicer rules of conscience he ignored.
    If, when he fought, the enemy vessel sank,
410 He sent his prisoners home; they walked the plank.
    As for his skill in reckoning his tides,
    Currents and many another risk besides,
    Moons, harbors, pilots, he had such dispatch
    That none from Hull to Carthage was his match.
415 Hardy he was, prudent in undertaking;
    His beard in many a tempest had its shaking,
    And he knew all the havens as they were
    From Gottland to the Cape of Finisterre,

Characterization and Social Commentary

What point is Chaucer making about the relationship between these men and their wives?

Characterization

What picture of the Skipper is created by the mixture of details about his heartlessness with details about his competence?

Comprehension

What are two characteristics of the Skipper?

---

53. burgess member of a legislative body.
54. blancmange (blə mänzh´) at the time, the name of a creamy chicken dish.
55. lanyard loose rope around the neck.

Questioning

In the sentence in lines 421–428, what is said about *how* the Doctor practices medicine?

And every creek in Brittany and Spain;
420 The barge he owned was called *The Maudelayne.*

A *Doctor* too emerged as we proceeded;
No one alive could talk as well as he did
On points of medicine and of surgery,
For, being grounded in astronomy,
425 He watched his patient's favorable star
And, by his Natural Magic, knew what are
The lucky hours and planetary degrees
For making charms and magic effigies.
The cause of every malady you'd got
430 He knew, and whether dry, cold, moist or hot;[56]
He knew their seat, their humor and condition.
He was a perfect practicing physician.
These causes being known for what they were,
He gave the man his medicine then and there.
435 All his apothecaries[57] in a tribe
Were ready with the drugs he would prescribe,
And each made money from the other's guile;
They had been friendly for a goodish while.
He was well-versed in Aesculapius[58] too
440 And what Hippocrates and Rufus knew
And Dioscorides, now dead and gone,
Galen and Rhazes, Hali, Serapion,
Averroes, Avicenna, Constantine,
Scotch Bernard, John of Gaddesden, Gilbertine.[59]
445 In his own diet he observed some measure;
There were no superfluities for pleasure,
Only digestives, nutritives and such.
He did not read the Bible very much.
In blood-red garments, slashed with bluish-gray
450 And lined with taffeta,[60] he rode his way;
Yet he was rather close as to expenses
And kept the gold he won in pestilences.
Gold stimulates the heart, or so we're told.
He therefore had a special love of gold.

455   A worthy *woman* from beside Bath[61] city
Was with us, somewhat deaf, which was a pity.
In making cloth she showed so great a bent

---

56. The cause . . . hot It was believed that the body was composed of four "humors" (cold and dry, hot and moist, hot and dry, cold and moist) and that diseases resulted from a disturbance of one of these "humors."
57. apothecaries (ə päth′ə ker′ ēz) persons who prepared medicines.
58. Aesculapius (es′ kyoo lā′ pē əs) in Roman mythology, the god of medicine and healing.
59. Hippocrates . . . Gilbertine famous physicians and medical authorities.
60. taffeta (taf′ i tə) fine silk fabric.
61. Bath English resort city.

She bettered those of Ypres and of Ghent.[62]
In all the parish not a dame dared stir
460 Towards the altar steps in front of her,
And if indeed they did, so wrath was she
As to be quite put out of charity.
Her kerchiefs were of finely woven ground;[63]
I dared have sworn they weighed a good ten pound,
465 The ones she wore on Sunday, on her head.
Her hose were of the finest scarlet red
And gartered tight; her shoes were soft and new.
Bold was her face, handsome, and red in hue.
A worthy woman all her life, what's more
470 She'd had five husbands, all at the church door,
Apart from other company in youth;
No need just now to speak of that, forsooth.
And she had thrice been to Jerusalem,
Seen many strange rivers and passed over them;
475 She'd been to Rome and also to Boulogne,
St. James of Compostella and Cologne,[64]
And she was skilled in wandering by the way.
She had gap-teeth, set widely, truth to say.
Easily on an ambling horse she sat
480 Well wimpled[65] up, and on her head a hat
As broad as is a buckler[66] or a shield;
She had a flowing mantle that concealed
Large hips, her heels spurred sharply under that.
In company she liked to laugh and chat
485 And knew the remedies for love's mischances,
An art in which she knew the oldest dances.

    A holy-minded man of good renown
There was, and poor, the *Parson* to a town,
Yet he was rich in holy thought and work.
490 He also was a learned man, a clerk,
Who truly knew Christ's gospel and would preach it
Devoutly to parishioners, and teach it.
Benign and wonderfully diligent,
And patient when adversity was sent
495 (For so he proved in great adversity)
He much disliked extorting tithe[67] or fee,
Nay rather he preferred beyond a doubt
Giving to poor parishioners round about

The Wife of Bath, Arthur Szyk for *The Canterbury Tales*

▼ **Critical Viewing**
What does the Wife of Bath's pose convey about her character?
ANALYZE

Comprehension
What is the Parson's main characteristic?

---

62. **Ypres** (ē′ prə) **and of Ghent** (gent) Flemish cities known for wool making.
63. **ground** composite fabric.
64. **Jerusalem . . . Rome . . . Boulogne . . . St. James of Compostella . . . Cologne** famous pilgrimage sites at the time.
65. **wimpled** wearing a scarf covering the head, neck, and chin.
66. **buckler** small round shield.
67. **tithe** (tith) one tenth of a person's income, paid as a tax to support the church.

Characterization and Social Commentary

How does Chaucer use his characterization of the Parson to comment on the way priests ought to behave?

From his own goods and Easter offerings
500 He found sufficiency in little things.
Wide was his parish, with houses far asunder,
Yet he neglected not in rain or thunder,
In sickness or in grief, to pay a call
On the remotest, whether great or small,
505 Upon his feet, and in his hand a stave.
This noble example to his sheep he gave,
First following the word before he taught it,
And it was from the gospel he had caught it.
This little proverb he would add thereto
510 That if gold rust, what then will iron do?
For if a priest be foul in whom we trust
No wonder that a common man should rust;
And shame it is to see—let priests take stock—
A soiled shepherd and a snowy flock.
515 The true example that a priest should give
Is one of cleanness, how the sheep should live.
He did not set his benefice to hire[68]
And leave his sheep encumbered in the mire
Or run to London to earn easy bread
520 By singing masses for the wealthy dead,
Or find some Brotherhood and get enrolled.
He stayed at home and watched over his fold
So that no wolf should make the sheep miscarry.
He was a shepherd and no mercenary.
525 Holy and virtuous he was, but then
Never contemptuous of sinful men,
Never disdainful, never too proud or fine,
But was discreet in teaching and benign.
His business was to show a fair behavior
530 And draw men thus to Heaven and their Savior,
Unless indeed a man were obstinate;
And such, whether of high or low estate,
He put to sharp rebuke to say the least.
I think there never was a better priest.
535 He sought no pomp or glory in his dealings,
No scrupulosity had spiced his feelings.
Christ and His Twelve Apostles and their lore
He taught, but followed it himself before.
     There was a *Plowman* with him there, his brother.
540 Many a load of dung one time or other
He must have carted through the morning dew.
He was an honest worker, good and true,

---

68. set . . . hire pay someone else to perform his parish duties.

Living in peace and perfect charity,
And, as the gospel bade him, so did he,
545 Loving God best with all his heart and mind
And then his neighbor as himself, repined
At no misfortune, slacked for no content,
For steadily about his work he went
To thrash his corn, to dig or to manure
550 Or make a ditch; and he would help the poor
For love of Christ and never take a penny
If he could help it, and, as prompt as any,
He paid his tithes in full when they were due
On what he owned, and on his earnings too.
555 He wore a tabard[69] smock and rode a mare.
There was a *Reeve*,[70] also a *Miller*, there,
A College *Manciple*[71] from the Inns of Court,
A papal *Pardoner*[72] and, in close consort,
A Church-Court *Summoner*,[73] riding at a trot,
560 And finally myself—that was the lot.
　　　The *Miller* was a chap of sixteen stone,[74]
A great stout fellow big in brawn and bone.
He did well out of them, for he could go
And win the ram at any wrestling show.
565 Broad, knotty and short-shouldered, he would boast
He could heave any door off hinge and post,
Or take a run and break it with his head.
His beard, like any sow or fox, was red
And broad as well, as though it were a spade;
570 And, at its very tip, his nose displayed
A wart on which there stood a tuft of hair,
Red as the bristles in an old sow's ear.
His nostrils were as black as they were wide.
He had a sword and buckler at his side,
575 His mighty mouth was like a furnace door.
A wrangler and buffoon, he had a store
Of tavern stories, filthy in the main.
His was a master-hand at stealing grain.
He felt it with his thumb and thus he knew
580 Its quality and took three times his due—
A thumb of gold, by God, to gauge an oat!
He wore a hood of blue and a white coat.
He liked to play his bagpipes up and down
And that was how he brought us out of town.

---

69. **tabard** loose jacket.
70. ***Reeve*** estate manager.
71. ***Manciple*** buyer of provisions.
72. ***Pardoner*** one who dispenses papal pardons.
73. ***Summoner*** one who serves summonses to church courts.
74. **sixteen stone** 224 pounds. A stone equals 14 pounds.

▲ **Critical Viewing**

Compare this portrait of the Miller with lines 561–584. What details did the illustrator choose to change or omit? **COMPARE AND CONSTRAST**

Comprehension

What is the Plowman like?

Questioning

What are the two subjects of the comparison in lines 594–604?

585   The *Manciple* came from the Inner Temple;
     All caterers might follow his example
     In buying victuals; he was never rash
     Whether he bought on credit or paid cash.
     He used to watch the market most precisely
590   And go in first, and so he did quite nicely.
     Now isn't it a marvel of God's grace
     That an illiterate fellow can outpace
     The wisdom of a heap of learned men?
     His masters—he had more than thirty then—
595   All versed in the abstrusest legal knowledge,
     Could have produced a dozen from their College
     Fit to be stewards in land and rents and game
     To any Peer in England you could name,
     And show him how to live on what he had
600   Debt-free (unless of course the Peer were mad)
     Or be as frugal as he might desire,
     And they were fit to help about the Shire
     In any legal case there was to try;
     And yet this Manciple could wipe their eye.
605   The *Reeve* was old and choleric and thin;
     His beard was shaven closely to the skin,
     His shorn hair came abruptly to a stop
     Above his ears, and he was docked on top
     Just like a priest in front; his legs were lean,
610   Like sticks they were, no calf was to be seen.
     He kept his bins and garners[75] very trim;
     No auditor could gain a point on him.
     And he could judge by watching drought and rain
     The yield he might expect from seed and grain.
615   His master's sheep, his animals and hens,
     Pigs, horses, dairies, stores and cattle-pens
     Were wholly trusted to his government.
     And he was under contract to present
     The accounts, right from his master's earliest years.
620   No one had ever caught him in arrears.
     No bailiff, serf or herdsman dared to kick,
     He knew their dodges, knew their every trick;
     Feared like the plague he was, by those beneath.
     He had a lovely dwelling on a heath,
625   Shadowed in green by trees above the sward.[76]
     A better hand at bargains than his lord,
     He had grown rich and had a store of treasure
     Well tucked away, yet out it came to pleasure

---

75. garners *n.* buildings for storing grain.
76. sward *n.* turf.

His lord with subtle loans or gifts of goods,
630 To earn his thanks and even coats and hoods.
When young he'd learnt a useful trade and still
He was a carpenter of first-rate skill.
The stallion-cob he rode at a slow trot
Was dapple-gray and bore the name of Scot.
635 He wore an overcoat of bluish shade
And rather long; he had a rusty blade
Slung at his side. He came, as I heard tell,
From Norfolk, near a place called Baldeswell.
His coat was tucked under his belt and splayed.
640 He rode the hindmost of our cavalcade.

      There was a *Summoner* with us in the place
Who had a fire-red cherubinnish face,[77]
For he had carbuncles.[78] His eyes were narrow,
He was as hot and lecherous as a sparrow.
645 Black, scabby brows he had, and a thin beard.
Children were afraid when he appeared.
No quicksilver, lead ointments, tartar creams,
Boracic, no, nor brimstone,[79] so it seems,
Could make a salve that had the power to bite,
650 Clean up or cure his whelks[80] of knobby white.
Or purge the pimples sitting on his cheeks.
Garlic he loved, and onions too, and leeks,
And drinking strong wine till all was hazy.
Then he would shout and jabber as if crazy,
655 And wouldn't speak a word except in Latin
When he was drunk, such tags as he was pat in;
He only had a few, say two or three,
That he had mugged up out of some decree;
No wonder, for he heard them every day.
660 And, as you know, a man can teach a jay
To call out "Walter" better than the Pope.
But had you tried to test his wits and grope
For more, you'd have found nothing in the bag.
Then "*Questio quid juris*"[81] was his tag.
665 He was a gentle varlet and a kind one,
No better fellow if you went to find one.
He would allow—just for a quart of wine—

▲ **Critical Viewing**
What can you infer from
this picture about the
Summoner's personality? List
three details supporting your
conclusion. **INFER**

Comprehension
How do serfs and herdsmen
view the Reeve?

---

77. fire-red . . . face In the art of the Middle Ages, the faces of cherubs, or angels, were often
painted red.
78. carbuncles (kär′ buŋ′ kəlz) *n.* pus-filled boils resulting from a bacterial infection under the
skin.
79. quicksilver . . . brimstone various chemicals and chemical compounds, used as
remedies. *Quicksilver* is a name for mercury. *Brimstone* is a name for sulfur.
80. whelks *n.* pustules; pimples.
81. "*Questio quid juris*" "The question is, What is the point of law?" (Latin).

Any good lad to keep a concubine
A twelvemonth and dispense it altogether!
670   Yet he could pluck a finch to leave no feather:
And if he found some rascal with a maid
He would instruct him not to be afraid
In such a case of the Archdeacon's curse
(Unless the rascal's soul were in his purse)
675   For in his purse the punishment should be.
"Purse is the good Archdeacon's Hell," said he.
But well I know he lied in what he said;
A curse should put a guilty man in dread,
For curses kill, as shriving brings, salvation.
680   We should beware of excommunication.
Thus, as he pleased, the man could bring duress
On any young fellow in the diocese.
He knew their secrets, they did what he said.
He wore a garland set upon his head
685   Large as the holly-bush upon a stake
Outside an ale-house, and he had a cake,
A round one, which it was his joke to wield
As if it were intended for a shield.
          He and a gentle *Pardoner* rode together,
690   A bird from Charing Cross of the same feather,
Just back from visiting the Court of Rome.
He loudly sang "*Come hither, love, come home!*"
The Summoner sang deep seconds to this song,
No trumpet ever sounded half so strong.
695   This Pardoner had hair as yellow as wax,
Hanging down smoothly like a hank of flax.
In driblets fell his locks behind his head
Down to his shoulder which they overspread;
Thinly they fell, like rat-tails, one by one.
700   He wore no hood upon his head, for fun;
The hood inside his wallet had been stowed,
He aimed at riding in the latest mode;
But for a little cap his head was bare
And he had bulging eyeballs, like a hare.
705   He'd sewed a holy relic on his cap;
His wallet lay before him on his lap,
Brimful of pardons come from Rome all hot.
He had the same small voice a goat has got.
His chin no beard had harbored, nor would harbor,
710   Smoother than ever chin was left by barber.
I judge he was a gelding, or a mare.

▲ Critical Viewing
How well does this picture
of the Pardoner match
Chaucer's description of him
in lines 695–710? **ASSESS**

As to his trade, from Berwick down to Ware
There was no pardoner of equal grace,
For in his trunk he had a pillowcase
715 Which he asserted was Our Lady's veil.
He said he had a gobbet[82] of the sail
Saint Peter had the time when he made bold
To walk the waves, till Jesu Christ took hold.
He had a cross of metal set with stones
720 And, in a glass, a rubble of pigs' bones.
And with these relics, any time he found
Some poor up-country parson to astound,
On one short day, in money down, he drew
More than the parson in a month or two,
725 And by his flatteries and prevarication
Made monkeys of the priest and congregation.
But still to do him justice first and last
In church he was a noble ecclesiast.
How well he read a lesson or told a story!
730 But best of all he sang an Offertory,[83]
For well he knew that when that song was sung
He'd have to preach and tune his honey-tongue
And (well he could) win silver from the crowd.
That's why he sang so merrily and loud.
735   Now I have told you shortly, in a clause,
The rank, the array, the number and the cause
Of our assembly in this company
In Southwark, at that high-class hostelry
Known as *The Tabard*, close beside *The Bell*.
740 And now the time has come for me to tell
How we behaved that evening; I'll begin
After we had alighted at the inn,
Then I'll report our journey, stage by stage,
All the remainder of our pilgrimage.
745 But first I beg of you, in courtesy,
Not to condemn me as unmannerly
If I speak plainly and with no concealings
And give account of all their words and dealings,
Using their very phrases as they fell.
750 For certainly, as you all know so well,
He who repeats a tale after a man

Characterization

What facts in lines 719–726 indirectly characterize the Pardoner?

Vocabulary

prevarication (pri var´ i kā´ shən) *n.* evasion of truth

Questioning

Why does Chaucer apologize in the sentence starting with line 745?

Comprehension

What two things does Chaucer promise to tell the reader?

---

82. **gobbet** piece.
83. **Offertory** song that accompanies the collection of the offering at a church service.

The Literature of Social Observation

Chaucer was just one author in a long tradition of British writers who detailed ironic observations of social types. Four centuries later, for instance, eighteenth-century writers such as Joseph Addison held up a mirror to middle-class society, describing the typical characters of the day and their follies.

The tradition of social commentary bloomed with the invention of the novel, a form built around keen observations of character and society. Yet the novel emphasized the individual in a way that earlier literature often did not. The characters of nineteenth-century novelist Charles Dickens, for instance, take on their social roles with extravagant, individual style. In a sense, though, Dickens was only following Chaucer. In pilgrims such as the Wife of Bath, the Skipper, and the Host, you can already detect a spark of vital individuality, deeper than any social role.

Connect to the Literature

Identify three ways in which the Wife of Bath both fits and defies the stereotype of a woman of her time.

Is bound to say, as nearly as he can,
Each single word, if he remembers it,
However rudely spoken or unfit,
755 Or else the tale he tells will be untrue,
The things invented and the phrases new.
He may not flinch although it were his brother,
If he says one word he must say the other.
And Christ Himself spoke broad[84] in Holy Writ,
760 And as you know there's nothing there unfit,
And Plato[85] says, for those with power to read,
"The word should be as cousin to the deed."
Further I beg you to forgive it me
If I neglect the order and degree
765 And what is due to rank in what I've planned.
I'm short of wit as you will understand.

     Our *Host* gave us great welcome; everyone
Was given a place and supper was begun.
He served the finest victuals you could think,
770 The wine was strong and we were glad to drink.
A very striking man our Host withal,
And fit to be a marshal in a hall.
His eyes were bright, his girth a little wide;
There is no finer burgess in Cheapside.[86]
775 Bold in his speech, yet wise and full of tact,
There was no manly attribute he lacked,
What's more he was a merry-hearted man.
After our meal he jokingly began
To talk of sport, and, among other things
780 After we'd settled up our reckonings,
He said as follows: "Truly, gentlemen,
You're very welcome and I can't think when
—Upon my word I'm telling you no lie—
I've seen a gathering here that looked so spry,
785 No, not this year, as in this tavern now.
I'd think you up some fun if I knew how.
And, as it happens, a thought has just occurred
And it will cost you nothing, on my word.
You're off to Canterbury—well, God speed!
790 Blessed St. Thomas answer to your need!
And I don't doubt, before the journey's done

---

84. broad bluntly.
85. Plato Greek philosopher (427?–347? B.C.).
86. Cheapside district in London.

You mean to while the time in tales and fun.
Indeed, there's little pleasure for your bones
Riding along and all as dumb as stones.
795 So let me then propose for your enjoyment,
Just as I said, a suitable employment.
And if my notion suits and you agree
And promise to submit yourselves to me
Playing your parts exactly as I say
800 Tomorrow as you ride along the way,
Then by my father's soul (and he is dead)
If you don't like it you can have my head!
Hold up your hands, and not another word."
        Well, our consent of course was not deferred,
805 It seemed not worth a serious debate;
We all agreed to it at any rate
And bade him issue what commands he would.
"My lords," he said, "now listen for your good,
And please don't treat my notion with disdain.
810 This is the point. I'll make it short and plain.
Each one of you shall help to make things slip
By telling two stories on the outward trip
To Canterbury, that's what I intend,
And, on the homeward way to journey's end
815 Another two, tales from the days of old;
And then the man whose story is best told,
That is to say who gives the fullest measure
Of good morality and general pleasure,
He shall be given a supper, paid by all,
820 Here in this tavern, in this very hall,
When we come back again from Canterbury.
And in the hope to keep you bright and merry
I'll go along with you myself and ride
All at my own expense and serve as guide.
825 I'll be the judge, and those who won't obey
Shall pay for what we spend upon the way.
Now if you all agree to what you've heard
Tell me at once without another word,
And I will make arrangements early for it."
830   Of course we all agreed, in fact we swore it
Delightedly, and made entreaty too
That he should act as he proposed to do,

Characterization

What does the Host's decision to accompany the pilgrims suggest about him?

Become our Governor in short, and be
Judge of our tales and general referee,
835 And set the supper at a certain price.
We promised to be ruled by his advice
Come high, come low; unanimously thus
We set him up in judgment over us.
More wine was fetched, the business being done;
840 We drank it off and up went everyone
To bed without a moment of delay.
　　　　Early next morning at the spring of day
Up rose our Host and roused us like a cock,
Gathering us together in a flock,
845 And off we rode at slightly faster pace
Than walking to St. Thomas' watering-place;[87]
And there our Host drew up, began to ease
His horse, and said, "Now, listen if you please,

---

87. St. Thomas' watering-place a brook two miles from the inn.

My lords! Remember what you promised me.
850 If evensong and matins will agree[88]
Let's see who shall be first to tell a tale.
And as I hope to drink good wine and ale
I'll be your judge. The rebel who disobeys,
However much the journey costs, he pays.
855 Now draw for cut[89] and then we can depart;
The man who draws the shortest cut shall start."

---

88. If evensong . . . agree "if what you said last night holds true this morning."
89. draw for cut draw lots, as when pulling straws from a bunch; the person who pulls the short straw is "it."

Critical Reading

Cite textual evidence to support your responses.

1. **Key Ideas and Details** **(a)** List three characteristics of the Nun. **(b) Deduce:** What details does Chaucer include in his description of the Nun to make gentle fun of her? Explain.

2. **Key Ideas and Details** **(a)** Identify two of the main characteristics of the Friar and the Parson. **(b) Compare and Contrast:** What are some of the ways in which the Friar and the Parson differ?

3. **Key Ideas and Details** Judging from the descriptions of the Friar and the Parson, what does Chaucer think can cause a religious person to fail in his or her duty?

4. **Key Ideas and Details** How does Chaucer's attitude toward the Monk differ, if at all, from his attitude toward the Friar? Explain.

5. **Integration of Knowledge and Ideas** **(a) Apply:** What modern character types match the characters in the Prologue? **(b) Apply:** What types would Chaucer not have anticipated? Explain.

6. **Integration of Knowledge and Ideas** **(a) Analyze:** From what segments of medieval society do the pilgrims come? **(b) Draw Conclusions:** What does their participation in a common pilgrimage suggest about the times?

7. **Integration of Knowledge and Ideas** Judging from his pilgrims, do you think Chaucer believes people are basically good, basically evil, or often a mix of the two? Give examples to support your answer.

8. **Integration of Knowledge and Ideas** Do you think Chaucer's view of people is justified? Explain.

9. **Integration of Knowledge and Ideas** Explain what a description of clothing reveals about a character and about medieval society. Use two of these Essential Question words: *echelon, distinct, approbation, condemn.* *[Connecting to the Essential Question: How does literature shape or reflect society?]*

Literary Analysis

1. **Key Ideas and Details** Give three details that Chaucer uses to **characterize** the Doctor. For each, note whether the characterization is **direct** or **indirect**.

2. **Key Ideas and Details** **(a)** Find one example of each of the following kinds of details in Chaucer's characterizations: direct statement, physical description, character's action. **(b)** Explain how your examples of physical description and action indirectly characterize that pilgrim.

3. **Key Ideas and Details** Suppose you were having trouble understanding the sentence in lines 47–50. Practice **repairing your comprehension** of the sentence by **questioning**. What essential information do you discover by asking *When?, Who?, Where?, What?, Why?,* and *How?*

4. **Key Ideas and Details** Use the same questioning technique to analyze the sentence in lines 529–533.

5. **Key Ideas and Details** Find and analyze another sentence from the Prologue, especially one that continues through many lines. Remember that asking basic questions will help you unlock its meaning.

6. **Craft and Structure** **(a)** Identify an example in which Chaucer uses mild sarcasm in describing a character. **(b)** Explain how his *tone,* or attitude, changes the meaning of the description.

7. **Craft and Structure** Choose the character sketch you find most effective. Explain the method Chaucer uses to make the sketch so vivid.

8. **Integration of Knowledge and Ideas** Use a chart like the one shown to reflect on the **social commentary** in the Prologue. **(a)** What social comment does Chaucer make in his sketch of the Pardoner? **(b)** What does the sketch of the Knight suggest were some of the virtues promoted by medieval society?

Character	Detail	Implication About Society

9. **Integration of Knowledge and Ideas** Most of Chaucer's characters are named after a profession. What does this emphasis on the characters' social roles suggest about medieval society?

10. **Integration of Knowledge and Ideas** **(a)** If Chaucer were writing today, what three kinds of pilgrims might he consider adding to the group? Explain your choices. **(b)** Describe how each of your twenty-first-century pilgrims would dress and speak.

Common Core State Standards

Writing
5. Develop and strengthen writing as needed by planning, revising, editing, rewriting, or trying a new approach, focusing on addressing what is most significant for a specific purpose and audience. *(p. 121)*

Language
4.a. Use context as a clue to the meaning of a word or phrase. *(p. 121)*

Vocabulary Acquisition and Use

Word Analysis: Latin Suffix -tion

The suffix -tion means "the act or process of" or "the result of the act or process of." For example, prevaricate means "to distort the truth"; prevarication means "the act of distorting the truth." Likewise, absolve means "to free someone of a sin"; absolution refers to the act of freeing some one from a sin, and also to the state of freedom that results from being absolved. With a small group, write a short paragraph about some of Chaucer's pilgrims. Include at least four of the following words in your paragraph:

1. flirtation
2. decoration
3. narration
4. devotion
5. negotiation
6. digestion

Then, choose two of the words used in your paragraph. For each, write a sentence explaining how the suffix -tion helps contribute to the meaning of the word.

Vocabulary: Context Clues

The context of a word is the other words, phrases, and sentences that come before and after the word and that may provide clues to its meaning. For each underlined word that appears below, explain how clues in the paragraph help you infer the word's contextual meaning.

A motley group of pilgrims gathered for a journey. The first was a stout, <u>sanguine</u> cook who greeted each newcomer with a jolly "Hallo!" The second was a noblewoman whose gowns were <u>garnished</u> with emeralds and pearls. The third, a young clerk, was traveling on <u>commission</u> from his employer; he made his errand sound so lofty and important that the other pilgrims suspected him of <u>prevarication</u>. The fourth, a widow, believed the clerk was telling the truth and behaved in a kind, <u>solicitous</u> manner toward him. The fifth said he was naught but a sinner, and that he sought naught but <u>absolution</u> for his crimes.

Writing to Sources

Narrative Text A blog is a Web site where entries on a particular subject are written and posted in reverse chronological order on a single homepage. Show your understanding of the Prologue by starting a **pilgrimage blog.** Write an introduction as the Host. Then, add postings from several pilgrims in which they express their thoughts, hopes, and fears about the journey.

Prewriting First, decide on a pilgrimage-related topic—the more controversial, the better. Review Chaucer's description of each character and jot down several opinions each might hold about this topic.

Drafting As you draft your postings, use language that strongly expresses each pilgrim's personality.

> **Model: Revising for a Consistent Voice**
> The Franklin says:
> I find the idea of rationing our provisions to be
> interesting, but a bit extreme
> ~~not only impractical, but downright insulting!~~ It is my custom
> to carry an abundant supply of cake and beverage, and to
> indulge at will—and also to share what I have with fellow-travelers.

The Franklin is a cheerful character, so the angry language doesn't fit. The revision strikes a polite and cordial tone.

Revising As you revise, check to make sure you have written each posting in character and that you have stayed on topic. Revise language that slips out of character, and delete details that are irrelevant.

Critical Commentary

Geoffrey Chaucer: Father of English Literature

Long had our dull Fore-Fathers slept Supine,
Nor felt the Raptures of the Tuneful Nine;
Till Chaucer first, a merry Bard, arose;
And many a Story told in Rhyme and Prose.

This stanza, penned by English author Joseph Addison in 1694, expresses the general view of Chaucer expressed by most English writers who followed him. The "Tuneful Nine," or Muses—that is, the nine goddesses said to inspire the arts—were asleep in England until Chaucer came along. Addison's contemporary John Dryden, the great pioneer of English literary criticism, called Chaucer "the father of English poetry":

▲ This imaginary British pound note depicts Chaucer as the Father of English Literature.

> *From Chaucer the purity of the English tongue began. . . . As he is the father of English poetry, so I hold him in the same degree of veneration as the Grecians held Homer or the Romans Virgil.*

Romantic Age author William Hazlitt hailed Chaucer as "the first to tune his native tongue" and named him as a person from the past whom he would most like to meet:

> *He was himself a noble, manly character, standing before his age and striving to advance it; a pleasant humorist withal, who . . . would make as hearty a companion as mine host of the Tabard.*

The attitude toward Chaucer is summed up by twentieth-century author G. K. Chesterton:

> *. . . Shakespeare and Milton were the greatest sons of their country; but Chaucer was the Father of his Country, rather in the style of George Washington. And apart from that, he made something that has altered all Europe more than the Newspaper: the Novel. He was a novelist when there were no novels.*

Key Ideas and Details In what ways does the Prologue show Chaucer being (in Chesterton's words) "a novelist when there were no novels"? Explain.

from *The Pardoner's Tale*

Connecting to the Essential Question In this tale told by Chaucer's Pardoner, greed is an important motivation. Consider what you have observed about the power of greed. As you read, look for examples of greed in this tale, and notice its effects on the characters and action. Considering the influence of this motive will help you explore the Essential Question: **How does literature shape or reflect society?**

Common Core State Standards

Reading Literature
5. Analyze how an author's choices concerning how to structure specific parts of a text contribute to its overall structure and meaning.

Close Reading Focus

Allegories; Archetypal Narrative Elements
Allegories are narratives that have both literal and deeper, symbolic meanings. "The Pardoner's Tale" is a kind of allegory called an *exemplum,* Latin for "example." The tale is an exemplum against the sin of greed, and the Pardoner uses the tale to illustrate the point of one of his sermons, "Love of money is the root of all evil."

To teach its lesson effectively, an allegory must be easily understood and remembered by the listeners. For this reason, an allegory may use certain basic storytelling patterns, or **archetypal narrative elements,** found in folk literature around the world. These elements include the following:

- Characters, events, and other things that come in threes
- A test of the characters' morality
- A mysterious guide who helps point the way
- A just ending that rewards good or punishes evil

Because it is structured to contain such elements, the basic story in this tale survived retellings as it traveled from ancient India to Europe. As you read, note the archetypal elements that make the allegory and its moral clear and memorable.

Preparing to Read Complex Texts If you cannot fully understand a passage at first, **reread** it and the surrounding passages. Rereading can help you clarify characters' identities, the sequence or causes of events, and puzzling language. As you read "The Pardoner's Tale," follow the sequence shown in the diagram to clarify difficult passages.

Passage

"He gathered lots and hid them in his hand....'

Reread Earlier Passage

"'We draw for lots and see the way it goes; / The one who draws the longest, lucky man,...'"

Clarification

"Drawing lots" must be like drawing straws: The one who draws the longest is "it."

Vocabulary

The words below are important to understanding the text that follows. Copy the words into your notebook, sorting them into words you know and words you do not know.

pallor   apothecary

hoary   deftly

tarry   sauntered

from
The Pardoner's Tale

Geoffrey Chaucer
translated by Nevill Coghill

The Pardoner's Prologue

"My lords," he said, "in churches where I preach
I cultivate a haughty kind of speech
And ring it out as roundly as a bell;
I've got it all by heart, the tale I tell.
5   I have a text, it always is the same
And always has been, since I learnt the game,
Old as the hills and fresher than the grass,
Radix malorum est cupiditas."[1]

———◆———

The Pardoner explains how he introduces
himself to a congregation, showing official documents
and offering relics as cures for various problems.
Next, he explains how he preaches.

———◆———

"Then, priestlike in my pulpit, with a frown,
10   I stand, and when the yokels[2] have sat down,
I preach, as you have heard me say before,
And tell a hundred lying mockeries[3] more.
I take great pains, and stretching out my neck
To east and west I crane about and peck
15   Just like a pigeon sitting on a barn.
My hands and tongue together spin the yarn
And all my antics[4] are a joy to see.
The curse of avarice and cupidity[5]
Is all my sermon, for it frees the pelf.[6]
20   Out come the pence, and specially for myself,
For my exclusive purpose is to win

---

1. ***Radix malorum est cupiditas*** Latin for "Greed is the root of all evil."
2. **yokels** (yō′ kəlz) *n.* unsophisticated people living in a rural area.
3. **mockeries** (mäk′ ər ēz) n. stories that are untrue.
4. **antics** (an′ tikz) n. playful, silly, or ludicrous acts.
5. **avarice** (av′ ə ris) **and cupidity** (kyo͞o pid′ ə tē) *n.* desire to gain wealth; greed (synonyms).
6. **pelf** (pelf) n. ill-gotten gains of money or wealth.

And not at all to castigate[7] their sin.
Once dead what matter how their souls may fare?
They can go blackberrying, for all I care!
25   "Believe me, many a sermon or devotive
Exordium[8] issues from an evil motive.
Some to give pleasure by their flattery
And gain promotion through hypocrisy,
Some out of vanity, some out of hate;
30 Or when I dare not otherwise debate
I'll put my discourse into such a shape,
My tongue will be a dagger; no escape
For him from slandering falsehood shall there be,
If he has hurt my brethren[9] or me.
35 For though I never mention him by name
The congregation guesses all the same
From certain hints that everybody knows,
And so I take revenge upon our foes
And spit my venom forth, while I profess
40 Holy and true—or seeming holiness.
       "But let me briefly make my purpose plain;
I preach for nothing but for greed of gain
And use the same old text, as bold as brass,
Radix malorum est cupiditas.
45 And thus I preach against the very vice
I make my living out of—avarice.
And yet however guilty of that sin
Myself with others I have power to win
Them from it, I can bring them to repent;
50 But that is not my principal intent.
Covetousness[10] is both the root and stuff
Of all I preach. That ought to be enough.
       "Well, then I give examples thick and fast
From bygone times, old stories from the past.
55 A yokel mind loves stories from of old,
Being the kind it can repeat and hold.
What! Do you think, as long as I can preach
And get their silver for the things I teach,
That I will live in poverty, from choice?
60 That's not the counsel of my inner voice!
No! Let me preach and beg from kirk[11] to kirk

Rereading

Reread lines 41–44 to determine the "principal intent" of the Pardoner's sermons.

---

7. **castigate** (kas´ ti gāt´) *v.* to punish severely.
8. **Exordium** (eg zôr´ dē əm) *n.* the opening part of an oration.
9. **brethren** (bre*th*´ rən) *n.* brothers.
10. **Covetousness** (kuv´ ət əs nis) *n.* greed, especially for what belongs to others.
11. **kirk** *n.* church.

And never do an honest job of work,
No, nor make baskets, like St. Paul, to gain
A livelihood. I do not preach in vain.
65   There's no apostle I would counterfeit;
I mean to have money, wool and cheese and wheat
Though it were given me by the poorest lad
Or poorest village widow, though she had
A string of starving children, all agape.
70   No, let me drink the liquor of the grape
And keep a jolly wench in every town!
        "But listen, gentlemen; to bring things down
To a conclusion, would you like a tale?
Now as I've drunk a draught of corn-ripe ale,
75   By God it stands to reason I can strike
On some good story that you all will like.
For though I am a wholly vicious man
Don't think I can't tell moral tales. I can!
Here's one I often preach when out for winning;
80   Now please be quiet. Here is the beginning."

The Pardoner's Tale

        It's of three rioters I have to tell
Who, long before the morning service bell,[12]
Were sitting in a tavern for a drink.
And as they sat, they heard the hand-bell clink
85   Before a coffin going to the grave;
One of them called the little tavern-knave[13]
And said "Go and find out at once—look spry!—
Whose corpse is in that coffin passing by;
And see you get the name correctly too."
90   "Sir," said the boy, "no need, I promise you;
Two hours before you came here I was told.
He was a friend of yours in days of old,
And suddenly, last night, the man was slain,
Upon his bench, face up, dead drunk again.

---

12. long before . . . bell long before 9:00 A.M.
13. tavern-knave serving boy.

Rereading

Reread lines 66–71 to find out what the Pardoner means by saying, "I do not preach in vain."

Allegory

Which details in the opening sentence enable the audience to form a quick opinion of the main characters?

Comprehension

What vice does the Pardoner admit to having, even though he preaches against it?

95 There came a privy[14] thief, they call him Death,
Who kills us all round here, and in a breath
He speared him through the heart, he never stirred.
And then Death went his way without a word.
He's killed a thousand in the present plague,[15]
100 And, sir, it doesn't do to be too vague
If you should meet him; you had best be wary.
Be on your guard with such an adversary,
Be primed to meet him everywhere you go,
That's what my mother said. It's all I know."

105   The publican[16] joined in with, "By St. Mary,
What the child says is right; you'd best be wary,
This very year he killed, in a large village
A mile away, man, woman, serf at tillage,[17]
Page in the household, children—all there were.
110 Yes, I imagine that he lives round there.
It's well to be prepared in these alarms,
He might do you dishonor." "Huh, God's arms!"
The rioter said, "Is he so fierce to meet?
I'll search for him, by Jesus, street by street.
115 God's blessed bones! I'll register a vow!
Here, chaps! The three of us together now,
Hold up your hands, like me, and we'll be brothers
In this affair, and each defend the others,
And we will kill this traitor Death, I say!
120 Away with him as he has made away
With all our friends. God's dignity! Tonight!"
        They made their bargain, swore with appetite,
These three, to live and die for one another
As brother-born might swear to his born brother.
125 And up they started in their drunken rage
And made towards this village which the page
And publican had spoken of before.
Many and grisly were the oaths they swore,
Tearing Christ's blessed body to a shred;[18]
130 "If we can only catch him, Death is dead!"
        When they had gone not fully half a mile,
Just as they were about to cross a stile,
They came upon a very poor old man
Who humbly greeted them and thus began,
135 "God look to you, my lords, and give you quiet!"

14. **privy** secretive.
15. **plague** the Black Death, which killed over a third of the population of Europe from 1347–1351. The plague reached England in 1348.
16. **publican** innkeeper.
17. **tillage** plowing.
18. **Tearing . . . shred** their oaths included such expressions as "God's arms" and "God's blessed bones."

Allegory and Archetypal Elements
What details of the publican's comments add to the sense of danger?

Rereading
What lines explain the "bargain" the rioters are said to have made in line 122?

To which the proudest of these men of riot
Gave back the answer, "What, old fool? Give place!
Why are you all wrapped up except your face?
Why live so long? Isn't it time to die?"

140   The old, old fellow looked him in the eye
And said, "Because I never yet have found,
Though I have walked to India, searching round
Village and city on my pilgrimage,
One who would change his youth to have my age.
145 And so my age is mine and must be still
Upon me, for such time as God may will.

    "Not even Death, alas, will take my life;
So, like a wretched prisoner at strife
Within himself, I walk alone and wait
150 About the earth, which is my mother's gate,
Knock-knocking with my staff from night to noon
And crying, 'Mother, open to me soon!
Look at me, mother, won't you let me in?
See how I wither, flesh and blood and skin!
155 Alas! When will these bones be laid to rest?
Mother, I would exchange—for that were best—
The wardrobe in my chamber, standing there
So long, for yours! Aye, for a shirt of hair[19]
To wrap me in!' She has refused her grace,
160 Whence comes the pallor of my withered face.

    "But it dishonored you when you began
To speak so roughly, sir, to an old man,
Unless he had injured you in word or deed.
It says in holy writ, as you may read,
165 'Thou shalt rise up before the hoary head
And honor it.' And therefore be it said
'Do no more harm to an old man than you,
Being now young, would have another do
When you are old'—if you should live till then.
170 And so may God be with you, gentlemen,
For I must go whither I have to go.'

    "By God," the gambler said, "you shan't do so,
You don't get off so easy, by St. John!
I heard you mention, just a moment gone,
175 A certain traitor Death who singles out
And kills the fine young fellows hereabout.
And you're his spy, by God! You wait a bit.
Say where he is or you shall pay for it,
By God and by the Holy Sacrament!
180 I say you've joined together by consent

▲ **Critical Viewing**
What moral might a medieval illustration like this one have served to teach?
HYPOTHESIZE

Vocabulary
pallor (pal′ ər) *n.* unnatural lack of color; paleness

hoary (hôr′ ē) *adj.* white or gray with age

Comprehension
What do the three rioters swear to do?

---

19. shirt of hair here, a shroud.

**Allegory and
Archetypal Elements**

What archetypal role does
the old man play?

To kill us younger folk, you thieving swine!"
    "Well, sirs," he said, "if it be your design
To find out Death, turn up this crooked way
Towards that grove, I left him there today
185 Under a tree, and there you'll find him waiting.
He isn't one to hide for all your prating.[20]
You see that oak? He won't be far to find.
And God protect you that redeemed mankind,
Aye, and amend you!" Thus that ancient man.
190   At once the three young rioters began
To run, and reached the tree, and there they found
A pile of golden florins[21] on the ground,
New-coined, eight bushels of them as they thought.
No longer was it Death those fellows sought,
195 For they were all so thrilled to see the sight,
The florins were so beautiful and bright,
That down they sat beside the precious pile.
The wickedest spoke first after a while.
"Brothers," he said, "you listen to what I say.
200 I'm pretty sharp although I joke away.
It's clear that Fortune has bestowed this treasure
To let us live in jollity and pleasure.
Light come, light go! We'll spend it as we ought.
God's precious dignity! Who would have thought
205 This morning was to be our lucky day?
    "If one could only get the gold away,
Back to my house, or else to yours, perhaps
For as you know, the gold is ours, chaps—
We'd all be at the top of fortune, hey?

Rereading

Reread lines 206–211 to
clarify the remark in line 212.

210 But certainly it can't be done by day.
People would call us robbers—a strong gang,
So our own property would make us hang.
No, we must bring this treasure back by night
Some prudent way, and keep it out of sight.
215 And so as a solution I propose
We draw for lots and see the way it goes;
The one who draws the longest, lucky man,
Shall run to town as quickly as he can
To fetch us bread and wine—but keep things dark—
220 While two remain in hiding here to mark
Our heap of treasure. If there's no delay,
When night comes down we'll carry it away,
All three of us, wherever we have planned."
    He gathered lots and hid them in his hand
225 Bidding them draw for where the luck should fall.

---

20. prating chatter.
21. florins coins.

It fell upon the youngest of them all,
And off he ran at once towards the town.
    As soon as he had gone, the first sat down
And thus began a parley²² with the other:
230 "You know that you can trust me as a brother;
Now let me tell you where your profit lies;
You know our friend has gone to get supplies
And here's a lot of gold that is to be
Divided equally amongst us three.
235 Nevertheless, if I could shape things thus
So that we shared it out—the two of us—
Wouldn't you take it as a friendly act?"
    "But how?" the other said. "He knows the fact
that all the gold was left with me and you;
240 What can we tell him? What are we to do?"
    "Is it a bargain," said the first, "or no?
For I can tell you in a word or so
What's to be done to bring the thing about."
"Trust me," the other said, "you needn't doubt
245 My word. I won't betray you, I'll be true."
    "Well," said his friend, "you see that we are two,
And two are twice as powerful as one.
Now look; when he comes back, get up in fun
To have a wrestle; then, as you attack,
250 I'll up and put my dagger through his back
While you and he are struggling, as in game;
Then draw your dagger too and do the same.
Then all this money will be ours to spend,
Divided equally of course, dear friend.
255 Then we can gratify our lusts and fill
The day with dicing at our own sweet will."
Thus these two miscreants²³ agreed to slay
The third and youngest, as you heard me say.
    The youngest, as he ran towards the town,
260 Kept turning over, rolling up and down
Within his heart the beauty of those bright
New florins, saying, "Lord, to think I might
Have all that treasure to myself alone!
Could there be anyone beneath the throne
265 Of God so happy as I then should be?"
    And so the Fiend,²⁴ our common enemy,
Was given power to put it in his thought
That there was always poison to be bought,

▲ **Critical Viewing**
Compare this illustration to the one on page 129. What point might the artist make by depicting contrasting individuals being taken by death? **COMPARE AND CONTRAST**

Comprehension
What does the old man say the rioters will find under the tree? What do they find there?

---

22. **parley** discussion.
23. **miscreants** villains.
24. **Fiend** Satan.

And that with poison he could kill his friends.
270 To men in such a state the Devil sends
Thoughts of this kind, and has a full permission
To lure them on to sorrow and perdition;[25]
For this young man was utterly content
To kill them both and never to repent.
275   And on he ran, he had no thought to tarry,
Came to the town, found an apothecary
And said, "Sell me some poison if you will,
I have a lot of rats I want to kill
And there's a polecat too about my yard
280 That takes my chickens and it hits me hard;
But I'll get even, as is only right,
With vermin that destroy a man by night."
    The chemist answered, "I've a preparation
Which you shall have, and by my soul's salvation
285 If any living creature eat or drink
A mouthful, ere he has the time to think,
Though he took less than makes a grain of wheat,
You'll see him fall down dying at your feet;
Yes, die he must and in so short a while
290 You'd hardly have the time to walk a mile,
The poison is so strong, you understand."
    This cursed fellow grabbed into his hand
The box of poison and away he ran
Into a neighboring street, and found a man
295 Who lent him three large bottles, He withdrew
And deftly poured the poison into two.
He kept the third one clean, as well he might,
For his own drink, meaning to work all night
Stacking the gold and carrying it away.
300 And when this rioter, this devil's clay,
Had filled his bottles up with wine, all three,
Back to rejoin his comrades sauntered he.
    Why make a sermon of it? Why waste breath?
Exactly in the way they'd planned his death
305 They fell on him and slew him, two to one.
Then said the first of them when this was done,
"Now for a drink. Sit down and let's be merry,
For later on there'll be the corpse to bury."
And, as it happened, reaching for a sup,
310 He took a bottle full of poison up
And drank and his companion, nothing loth,
Drank from it also, and they perished both.

---

25. perdition damnation.

Vocabulary

tarry (tar′ ē) *v.* to delay or linger

apothecary (ə päth′ ə ker′ ē) *n.* pharmacist; druggist

Vocabulary

deftly (deft′ lē) *adv.* skillfully; with ease and quickness

sauntered (sôn′ tərd) *v.* walked at an unhurried pace

◀ **Critical Viewing**
What does this illustration
say about the relationship
between material wealth
and death? **INTERPRET**

There is, in Avicenna's long relation[26]
Concerning poison and its operation,
315 Trust me, no ghastlier section to transcend
What these two wretches suffered at their end.
Thus these two murderers received their due,
So did the treacherous young poisoner too.

O cursed sin! O blackguardly excess!
320 O treacherous homicide! O wickedness!
O gluttony that lusted on and diced!
O blasphemy that took the name of Christ
With habit-hardened oaths that pride began!
Alas, how comes it that a mortal man,
325 That thou, to thy Creator, Him that wrought thee,

---

26. Avicenna's long relation book on medicines written by Avicenna (980–1037), an
Arab physician, which contains a chapter on poisons.

Allegory

In addition to avarice, or
greed, against what sins does
the exemplum preach in
lines 319–323?

Comprehension

What explanation does the
rioter give to the Apothecary
for buying the poison?

That paid His precious blood for thee and bought thee,
Art so unnatural and false within?
     Dearly beloved, God forgive your sin
And keep you from the vice of avarice!
330 My holy pardon frees you all of this,
Provided that you make the right approaches,
That is with sterling rings, or silver brooches.
Bow down your heads under this holy bull![27]
Come on, you women, offer up your wool!
335 I'll write your name into my ledger; so!
Into the bliss of Heaven you shall go.
For I'll absolve you by my holy power,
You that make offering, clean as at the hour
When you were born. . . . That, sirs, is how I preach.
340 And Jesu Christ, soul's healer, aye, the leech
Of every soul, grant pardon and relieve you
Of sin, for that is best I won't deceive you.

---

27. holy bull an official proclamation by the Catholic Church.

Critical Reading

1. **Key Ideas and Details (a)** When the story opens, what are the rioters doing, and what captures their attention? **(b) Generalize:** What sort of people are they? Explain how you know.

2. **Integration of Knowledge and Ideas** The Pardoner is quite open about the manipulative use to which he puts the tale. Do the Pardoner's reasons for telling the story detract from its moral truth? Explain.

3. **Integration of Knowledge and Ideas** The tale refers to the time of the plague. **(a)** What does the tale suggest about the effects of such a disaster on society? Support your answer. **(b) Apply:** Can stories such as this one encourage people to behave well even in times of crisis? Explain.

4. **Integration of Knowledge and Ideas** Do you think the desire for gain is ultimately destructive, as the Pardoner's tale suggests, or can it lead to positive consequences? Explain.

5. **Integration of Knowledge and Ideas** What can you learn about life in the Middle Ages from "The Pardoner's Tale"? Use at least two of these Essential Question words in your response: *role, principles, reproach, excess. [Connecting to the Essential Question: How does literature shape or reflect society?]*

Literary Analysis

1. **Key Ideas and Details** Find a passage that you had trouble understanding when you first read it. Improve your comprehension by **rereading** the lines leading up to the passage. Then, explain what the passage means.

2. **Key Ideas and Details** In line 112, the publican tells the rioters, "He might do you dishonor." Reread the previous lines. Then, use the information they provide to explain the publican's meaning.

3. **Key Ideas and Details** In lines 319–320, the Pardoner speaks of "blackguardly excess" as well as homicide. Reread earlier lines to clarify what he means, then state what the "blackguardly excess" are.

4. **Key Ideas and Details** **(a)** Explain why "The Pardoner's Tale" is an **allegory,** and cite a passage to support your point. **(b)** Then, explain how the allegory of "The Pardoner's Tale" proves that greed is the root of all evil.

5. **Craft and Structure** **(a)** Using a chart like the one shown, list the **archetypal elements** used in the tale.

Patterns of Three	Test of Characters	Mysterious Guide	Just Ending

(b) Then, explain how the archetypal elements contribute to the meaning of the tale.

6. **Craft and Structure** What other familiar elements does the story include?

7. **Integration of Knowledge and Ideas** Why do you think many tales feature things that come in threes?

8. **Craft and Structure** **(a)** Why is it ironic, or surprising, that the Pardoner tells this story? **(b)** What point might Chaucer be making about moral tales by assigning this one to a rogue?

9. **Integration of Knowledge and Ideas** **(a)** What role does the old man perform in the story? **(b)** What might he symbolize? **(c)** Explain the way in which the old man's presence in the tale benefits the Pardoner and motivates his listeners to adopt a more wholesome existence.

Common Core State Standards

Writing

1.a. Introduce precise, knowledgeable claim(s), establish the significance of the claim(s), distinguish the claim(s) from alternate or opposing claims, and create an organization that logically sequences claim(s), counterclaims, reasons, and evidence. *(p. 136)*

Language

6. Acquire and use accurately general academic and domain-specific words and phrases, sufficient for reading, writing, speaking, and listening at the college and career readiness level; demonstrate independence in gathering vocabulary knowledge when considering a word or phrase important to comprehension or expression. *(p. 136)*

Vocabulary Acquisition and Use

Word Analysis: Greek Prefix *apo-*

The word apothecary, meaning "druggist," combines the Greek prefix *apo-*, meaning "away; off; separate," with a form of a Greek word for "put." An apothecary is one who "puts away," or stores, prescriptions. This prefix can often be found in *scientific terms* and in other words, too.

Write an alternate definition for each numbered word that contains the word *away, off,* or *separate*. An example appears first.

apoapsis *n.* farthest point from gravitational center in the orbit of any satellite

alternate definition: <u>away</u> or separated from gravitational center in a satellite's orbit

1. **apology** *n.* words of regret for an offense

2. **apogee** *n.* the highest or farthest point

3. **apostle** *n.* a person sent on a special mission

Vocabulary: Relate New to Familiar Words

Associating a new word with an already familiar word can help you remember the meaning of the new word. For each of the following items, replace the italicized familiar word with one of the words from the vocabulary list.

1. Death *strolled* down the moonlit lane.

2. His long, craggy face shone with an eerie *paleness.*

3. His long *whitened* beard fluttered in the silent breeze.

4. When a black cat crossed his path, Death stepped *easily* over its scrawny back.

5. Suddenly, Death picked up his pace. "This is no time to *dally,*" he thought.

6. "I feel like death, and the *pharmacist* is closing shop in five minutes!"

Writing

Argumentative Text In the final lines of his tale, the Pardoner preaches passionately on the subject of greed (among other sins). Write a **sermon**—a persuasive talk about some aspect of morality—on greed. Your sermon should be directed toward a contemporary audience.

Prewriting First, brainstorm for a list of modern-day examples of greed. Then jot down a few answers to this question: What ill effects do these forms of greed cause for an individual or for society at large?

Drafting Begin your sermon with a strong *claim* or a vivid image. Then, spend the remainder of your sermon developing this claim or image. Support your central idea with examples, arguments, emotional appeals, and word choice suited to a contemporary audience.

Revising As you read your draft, imagine that you disagree with each key point you encounter. Then revise to acknowledge and refute that opposing argument.

Model: Revising to Refute Opponents

may be convenient for a large family, but it is nevertheless
Owning a large, gas-guzzling vehicle ~~is~~ irresponsible. It consumes
twice the fuel of smaller cars and puts twice as much pollution
into the atmosphere. It therefore gives *you*, the owner, a double
ownership in the problem of global warming...

The writer revises to anticipate what the opposition might say.

Connecting to the Essential Question In her tale, the feisty Wife of Bath asserts the idea that husbands and wives should be equal in marriage. As you read, identify passages in which the Wife of Bath supports the idea of "selfsame sovereignty," or equality in marriage. Doing so will help you address the Essential Question: **How does literature shape or reflect society?**

Common Core State Standards

Reading Literature
3. Analyze the impact of the author's choices regarding how to develop and relate elements of a story or drama.

Close Reading Focus

Frame Story

A **frame story** contains—or frames—another story or group of stories. In *The Canterbury Tales,* the frame story is the characters' pilgrimage to Canterbury Cathedral, described in the Prologue. Within the frame story are the tales told by the characters on their journey. Here are some ways in which the frame story works:

- Characters are introduced and described in the frame story. The individual tales are told by the characters themselves, and deepen our knowledge of their lives.

- Each individual tale may itself contain a frame story and an inner tale. "The Wife of Bath's Tale" has such a structure.

- The **setting** of the frame story, the time and place of its action, may not match the settings of individual tales. For example, the events in the Prologue occur around Chaucer's time, but the Wife of Bath sets her frame story much earlier, during the reign of King Arthur.

Analyze these interactions and consider their effects as you read "The Wife of Bath's Tale."

Preparing to Read Complex Texts You may encounter unfamiliar words while reading. If so, repair your comprehension by **checking context clues**—words and phrases in the surrounding passage that shed light on the meaning of a word. Common context clues are synonyms, antonyms, and examples that clarify a word's meaning. Use a chart like the one shown to find context clues as you read.

Vocabulary

You will encounter the words listed here in the text that follows. Copy the words into your notebook and note which one has the greatest number of syllables.

implored	prowess
relates	esteemed
contemptuous	rebuke
bequeath	

Passage
"Hundreds of years ago, in days of yore"

↓

Context Clue
Unfamiliar Word: *yore*   Context Clue: Hundreds of years ago   Relation to Word: Similar in meaning

↓

Conclusion
If days of *yore* took place hundreds of years ago, *yore* must mean "time long past."

THE WIFE of BATH'S TALE

Geoffrey Chaucer
translated by Nevill Coghill

When good King Arthur ruled in ancient days,
   (A king that every Briton loves to praise.)
This was a land brim-full of fairy folk.
The Elf-Queen and her courtiers joined and broke
5   Their elfin dance on many a green mead,
Or so was the opinion once, I read,
Hundreds of years ago, in days of yore.
But no one now sees fairies any more.
For now the saintly charity and prayer
10   Of holy friars seem to have purged the air;
They search the countryside through field and stream
As thick as motes[1] that speckle a sun-beam,
Blessing the halls, the chambers, kitchens, bowers,
Cities and boroughs, castles, courts and towers,
15   Thorpes,[2] barns and stables, outhouses and dairies,
And that's the reason why there are no fairies.
Wherever there was wont to walk an elf
To-day there walks the holy friar himself
As evening falls or when the daylight springs,
20   Saying his matins[3] and his holy things,
Walking his limit round from town to town.
Women can now go safely up and down.
By every bush or under every tree;
There is no other incubus but he,
25   So there is really no one else to hurt you
And he will do no more than take your virtue.

      Now it so happened, I began to say,
Long, long ago in good King Arthur's day,
There was a knight who was a lusty liver.
30   One day as he came riding from the river
He saw a maiden walking all forlorn
Ahead of him, alone as she was born.
And of that maiden, spite of all she said,
By very force he took her maidenhead.

35   This act of violence made such a stir,
So much petitioning of the king for her,
That he condemned the knight to lose his head
By course of law. He was as good as dead
(It seems that then the statutes took that view)

---

1. **motes** dust particles.
2. **Thorpes** villages.
3. **matins** morning prayers.

◀ **Critical Viewing** Which details in this picture of the Wife of
Bath suggest she is a self-confident middle-class woman? **ANALYZE**

Vocabulary

implored (im plôrd´) v.
begged earnestly

Checking Context Clues

Use the surrounding lines to determine the meaning of the word *concede* in line 54.

40 But that the queen, and other ladies too,
   implored the king to exercise his grace
   So ceaselessly, he gave the queen the case
   And granted her his life, and she could choose
   Whether to show him mercy or refuse.

45   The queen returned him thanks with all her might,
   And then she sent a summons to the knight
   At her convenience, and expressed her will:
   "You stand, for such is the position still,
   In no way certain of your life," said she,

50 "Yet you shall live if you can answer me:
   What is the thing that women most desire?
   Beware the axe and say as I require.

        "If you can't answer on the moment, though,
   I will concede you this: you are to go

55 A twelvemonth and a day to seek and learn
   Sufficient answer, then you shall return.
   I shall take gages[4] from you to extort
   Surrender of your body to the court."

        Sad was the knight and sorrowfully sighed,

60 But there! All other choices were denied,
   And in the end he chose to go away
   And to return after a year and day
   Armed with such answer as there might be sent
   To him by God. He took his leave and went.

65   He knocked at every house, searched every place,
   Yes, anywhere that offered hope of grace.
   What could it be that women wanted most?
   But all the same he never touched a coast,
   Country or town in which there seemed to be

70 Any two people willing to agree.

        Some said that women wanted wealth and treasure,
   "Honor," said some, some "Jollity and pleasure,"
   Some "Gorgeous clothes" and others "Fun in bed,"
   " To be oft widowed and remarried," said

75 Others again, and some that what most mattered
   Was that we should be cosseted[5] and flattered.
   That's very near the truth, it seems to me;

---

4. **gages** guarantees.
5. **cosseted** pampered.

A man can win us best with flattery.
To dance attendance on us, make a fuss,
Ensnares us all, the best and worst of us.
    Some say the things we most desire are these:
Freedom to do exactly as we please,
With no one to reprove our faults and lies,
Rather to have one call us good and wise.
Truly there's not a woman in ten score
Who has a fault, and someone rubs the sore,
But she will kick if what he says is true;
You try it out and you will find so too.
However vicious we may be within
We like to be thought wise and void of sin.
Others assert we women find it sweet
When we are thought dependable, discreet
And secret, firm of purpose and controlled,
Never betraying things that we are told.
But that's not worth the handle of a rake;
Women conceal a thing? For Heaven's sake!
Remember Midas?[6] Will you hear the tale?
    Among some other little things, now stale,
Ovid relates that under his long hair
The unhappy Midas grew a splendid pair
Of ass's ears; as subtly as he might,
He kept his foul deformity from sight;
Save for his wife, there was not one that knew.
He loved her best, and trusted in her too.
He begged her not to tell a living creature
That he possessed so horrible a feature.
And she—she swore, were all the world to win,
She would not do such villainy and sin
As saddle her husband with so foul a name;
Besides to speak would be to share the shame.
Nevertheless she thought she would have died
Keeping this secret bottled up inside;
It seemed to swell her heart and she, no doubt,
Thought it was on the point of bursting out.
    Fearing to speak of it to woman or man,
Down to a reedy marsh she quickly ran
And reached the sedge. Her heart was all on fire
And, as a bittern[7] bumbles in the mire,

Line numbers: 80, 85, 90, 95, 100, 105, 110, 115

---

6. **Midas** In mythology, King Midas had the magic touch that turned everything to gold. Here, Chaucer makes reference to Ovid's *Metamorphoses.*
7. **bittern** small wading bird.

120 She whispered to the water, near the ground,
"Betray me not, O water, with thy sound!
To thee alone I tell it: it appears
My husband has a pair of ass's ears!
Ah! My heart's well again, the secret's out!
125 I could no longer keep it, not a doubt."
And so you see, although we may hold fast
A little while, it must come out at last,
We can't keep secrets; as for Midas, well,
Read Ovid for his story; he will tell.

This knight that I am telling you about
130 Perceived at last he never would find out
What it could be that women loved the best.
Faint was the soul within his sorrowful breast
As home he went, he dared no longer stay;
His year was up and now it was the day.
135 As he rode home in a dejected mood
Suddenly, at the margin of a wood,
He saw a dance upon the leafy floor
Of four and twenty ladies, nay, and more.
Eagerly he approached, in hope to learn
140 Some words of wisdom ere he should return;
But lo! Before he came to where they were,
Dancers and dance all vanished into air!
There wasn't a living creature to be seen
Save one old woman crouched upon the green.
145 A fouler-looking creature I suppose
Could scarcely be imagined. She arose
And said, "Sir knight, there's no way on from here.
Tell me what you are looking for, my dear,
For peradventure that were best for you;
150 We old, old women know a thing or two."
"Dear Mother," said the knight, "alack the day!
I am as good as dead if I can't say
What thing it is that women most desire;
If you could tell me I would pay your hire."
155 "Give me your hand," she said, "and swear to do
Whatever I shall next require of you
—If so to do should lie within your might—
And you shall know the answer before night."
"Upon my honor," he answered, "I agree."

160 "Then," said the crone, "I dare to guarantee
Your life is safe; I shall make good my claim.
Upon my life the queen will say the same.
Show me the very proudest of them all
In costly coverchief or jewelled caul[8]
165 That dare say no to what I have to teach.
Let us go forward without further speech."
And then she crooned her gospel in his ear
And told him to be glad and not to fear.
        They came to court. This knight, in full array,
170 Stood forth and said, "O Queen, I've kept my day
And kept my word and have my answer ready."
        There sat the noble matrons and the heady
Young girls, and widows too, that have the grace
Of wisdom, all assembled in that place,
175 And there the queen herself was throned to hear
And judge his answer. Then the knight drew near
And silence was commanded through the hall.
        The queen then bade the knight to tell them all
What thing it was that women wanted most.
180 He stood not silent like a beast or post,
But gave his answer with the ringing word
Of a man's voice and the assembly heard:
        "My liege and lady, in general," said he,
"A woman wants the self-same sovereignty
185 Over her husband as over her lover,
And master him; he must not be above her.
That is your greatest wish, whether you kill
Or spare me; please yourself. I wait your will."
        In all the court not one that shook her head
190 Or contradicted what the knight had said;
Maid, wife and widow cried, "He's saved his life!"
        And on the word up started the old wife,
The one the knight saw sitting on the green,
And cried, "Your mercy, sovereign lady queen!
195 Before the court disperses, do me right!
'Twas I who taught this answer to the knight,
For which he swore, and pledged his honor to it,
That the first thing I asked of him he'd do it,
So far as it should lie within his might.
200 Before this court I ask you then, sir knight,

Checking Context Clues

What clues in the context hint at the meaning of *crone* in line 160?

Checking Context Clues

Which context clues might help you figure out the meaning of *sovereignty* in line 184?

Comprehension

How does the setting described in lines 169–177 differ from that described in the Prologue?

---

8. **coverchief. . .caul** kerchief, and a decorative cap, both worn as headgear by medieval women.

To keep your word and take me for your wife:
For well you know that I have saved your life.
If this be false, deny it on your sword!"
　　"Alas!" he said, "Old lady, by the Lord
205　I know indeed that such was my behest,
But for God's love think of a new request,
Take all my goods, but leave my body free."
"A curse on us," she said, "if I agree!
I may be foul, I may be poor and old,
210　Yet will not choose to be, for all the gold
That's bedded in the earth or lies above,
Less than your wife, nay, than your very love!"
　　"My love?" said he. "By Heaven, my damnation!
Alas that any of my race and station
215　Should ever make so foul a misalliance!"
Yet in the end his pleading and defiance
All went for nothing, he was forced to wed.
He takes his ancient wife and goes to bed.

　　　　　Now peradventure some may well suspect
220　A lack of care in me since I neglect
To tell of the rejoicings and display
Made at the feast upon their wedding-day.
I have but a short answer to let fall;
I say there was no joy or feast at all,
225　Nothing but heaviness of heart and sorrow.
He married her in private on the morrow
And all day long stayed hidden like an owl,
It was such torture that his wife looked foul.
　　　Great was the anguish churning in his head
230　When he and she were piloted to bed;
He wallowed back and forth in desperate style.
His ancient wife lay smiling all the while;
At last she said, "Bless us! Is this, my dear,
How knights and wives get on together here?
235　Are these the laws of good King Arthur's house?
Are knights of his all so contemptuous?
I am your own beloved and your wife,
And I am she, indeed, that saved your life;
And certainly I never did you wrong.

◄ **Critical Viewing**
In what ways does this picture help you visualize the kind of medieval nobles who listened to the knight's answer? **CONNECT**

Checking Context Clues

What is the meaning of *anguish* in line 229? Identify the context clues that helped you to determine the meaning.

Vocabulary

contemptuous
(kən temp´ chōō əs) *adj.* scornful

Comprehension

In addition to becoming the knight's wife, what more does the old woman demand?

The Wife of Bath's Tale　**145**

240　Then why, this first of nights, so sad a song?
　　You're carrying on as if you were half-witted
　　Say, for God's love, what sin have I committed?
　　I'll put things right if you will tell me how."
　　　　　"Put right?" he cried. "That never can be now!

245　Nothing can ever be put right again!
　　You're old, and so abominably plain,
　　So poor to start with, so low-bred to follow;
　　It's little wonder if I twist and wallow!
　　God, that my heart would burst within my breast!"

250　　　"Is that," said she, "the cause of your unrest?"
　　　　　"Yes, certainly," he said, "and can you wonder?"
　　　　　"I could set right what you suppose a blunder,
　　That's if I cared to, in a day or two,
　　If I were shown more courtesy by you.

255　Just now," she said, "you spoke of gentle birth,
　　Such as descends from ancient wealth and worth.
　　If that's the claim you make for gentlemen
　　Such arrogance is hardly worth a hen.
　　Whoever loves to work for virtuous ends,

260　Public and private, and who most intends
　　To do what deeds of gentleness he can,
　　Take him to be the greatest gentleman.
　　Christ wills we take our gentleness from Him,
　　Not from a wealth of ancestry long dim,

265　Though they bequeath their whole establishment
　　By which we claim to be of high descent.
　　Our fathers cannot make us a bequest

Frame Story

By the standards set forth in lines 255–262, is the Knight from the Prologue a gentleman? Why or why not?

Vocabulary

bequeath (bē kwēth′) v. hand down as an inheritance

LITERATURE IN CONTEXT

Selfsame Sovereignty

The Wife of Bath uses the story of the knight and the old woman to express her own belief in selfsame sovereignty, or equality in marriage between a husband and wife. Whether such an idea meant that women shared ownership of property and family wealth, or whether it meant they had an equal share in decision-making, such a belief was definitely well ahead of the times.

In medieval England, women could inherit property only if there were no male heirs in the family. Usually, property was entailed, or assigned to the male survivors, the women being left under the men's care until marriage or death. Moreover, at marriage a woman was often required to renounce any further claims to her father's property. Often, any property she did bring to the marriage was immediately forfeited to her husband, leaving her with virtually no further claim to it. Only in 1857 did Great Britain's Married Women's Property Acts first allow a woman the right to property in her own name.

Connect to the Literature

The Wife of Bath refuses to play a subordinate role in her society. In what ways does Chaucer's description of the Wife of Bath, as well as her tale, suggest that she was an unusual woman for her time?

Of all those virtues that became them best
And earned for them the name of gentleman,
270 But bade us follow them as best we can.
  "Thus the wise poet of the Florentines,
Dante[9] by name, has written in these lines,
For such is the opinion Dante launches:
'Seldom arises by these slender branches
275 prowess of men, for it is God, no less,
Wills us to claim of Him our gentleness.'
For of our parents nothing can we claim
Save temporal things, and these may hurt and maim.
  "But everyone knows this as well as I;
280 For if gentility were implanted by
The natural course of lineage down the line,
Public or private, could it cease to shine
In doing the fair work of gentle deed?
No vice or villainy could then bear seed.
285   "Take fire and carry it to the darkest house
Between this kingdom and the Caucasus,[10]
And shut the doors on it and leave it there,
It will burn on, and it will burn as fair
As if ten thousand men were there to see,
290 For fire will keep its nature and degree,
I can assure you, sir, until it dies.
  "But gentleness, as you will recognize,
Is not annexed in nature to possessions,
Men fail in living up to their professions;
295 But fire never ceases to be fire.
God knows you'll often find, if you enquire,
Some lording full of villainy and shame.
If you would be esteemed for the mere name
Of having been by birth a gentleman
300 And stemming from some virtuous, noble clan,
And do not live yourself by gentle deed
Or take your fathers' noble code and creed,
You are no gentleman, though duke or earl.
Vice and bad manners are what make a churl.
305   "Gentility is only the renown
For bounty that your fathers handed down,
Quite foreign to your person, not your own;
Gentility must come from God alone.
That we are gentle comes to us by grace

Vocabulary

prowess (prou′ is) *n.*
heroism; distinction

esteemed (ə stēmd′) *adj.*
highly respected

Comprehension

According to the old woman,
what makes a man a
gentleman?

---

9. Dante Dante Alighieri (dän′ tā al əg yer′ ē) (1265–1321) Italian poet who wrote the *Divine Comedy*.
10. Caucasus (kô′ kə səs) mountain range between southeastern Europe and western Asia.

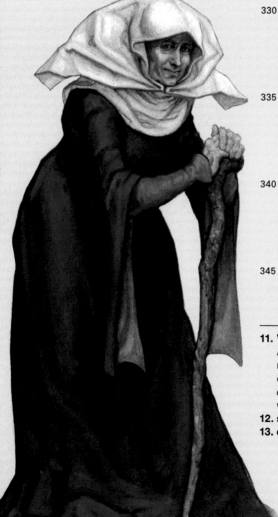

▼ **Critical Viewing**
Compare the illustrations of
the crone and maiden. Why
is the crone better able to
teach the knight a lesson?
SPECULATE

310 And by no means is it bequeathed with place.
        "Reflect how noble (says Valerius)[11]
    Was Tullius surnamed Hostilius,
    Who rose from poverty to nobleness.
    And read Boethius, Seneca no less,
315 Thus they express themselves and are agreed:
    'Gentle is he that does a gentle deed.'
    And therefore, my dear husband, I conclude
    That even if my ancestors were rude,
    Yet God on high—and so I hope He will—
320 Can grant me grace to live in virtue still,
    A gentlewoman only when beginning
    To live in virtue and to shrink from sinning.
        "As for my poverty which you reprove,
    Almighty God Himself in whom we move,
325 Believe and have our being, chose a life
    Of poverty, and every man or wife
    Nay, every child can see our Heavenly King
    Would never stoop to choose a shameful thing.
    No shame in poverty if the heart is gay,
330 As Seneca and all the learned say.
    He who accepts his poverty unhurt
    I'd say is rich although he lacked a shirt.
    But truly poor are they who whine and fret
    And covet what they cannot hope to get.
335 And he that, having nothing, covets not,
    Is rich, though you may think he is a sot.[12]
        "True poverty can find a song to sing.
    Juvenal says a pleasant little thing:
    'The poor can dance and sing in the relief
340 Of having nothing that will tempt a thief.'
    Though it be hateful, poverty is good,
    A great incentive to a livelihood,
    And a great help to our capacity
    For wisdom, if accepted patiently.
345 Poverty is, though wanting in estate,
    A kind of wealth that none calumniate.[13]
    Poverty often, when the heart is lowly,

---

11. Valerius . . . Seneca Valerius (və lir′ ē əs) Maximus was a first-century
A.D. Roman author who collected historical anecdotes. Tullius Hostilius
rose from humble beginnings to become a legendary king of Rome. Bo-
ethius (bō ē′ thē əs) was a Roman philosopher whose *The Consolation
of Philosophy* is a recognized source for Chaucer's writings. Seneca
was a Roman philosopher and dramatist.
12. sot fool.
13. calumniate (kə lum′ ne āt′) slander.

Brings one to God and teaches what is holy,
Gives knowledge of oneself and even lends

350 A glass by which to see one's truest friends.
And since it's no offence, let me be plain;
Do not **rebuke** my poverty again.

  "Lastly you taxed me, sir, with being old.
Yet even if you never had been told

355 By ancient books, you gentlemen engage
Yourselves in honor to respect old age.
To call an old man 'father' shows good breeding,
And this could be supported from my reading.

  "You say I'm old and fouler than a fen.

360 You need not fear to be a cuckold, then.
Filth and old age, I'm sure you will agree,
Are powerful wardens upon chastity.
Nevertheless, well knowing your delights,
I shall fulfil your worldly appetites.

365   "You have two choices; which one will you try?
To have me old and ugly till I die,
But still a loyal, true and humble wife
That never will displease you all her life,
Or would you rather I were young and pretty

370 And chance your arm what happens in a city
Where friends will visit you because of me,
Yes, and in other places too, maybe.
Which would you have? The choice is all your own."

  The knight thought long, and with a piteous groan

375 At last he said, with all the care in life,
"My lady and my love, my dearest wife,
I leave the matter to your wise decision.
You make the choice yourself, for the provision
Of what may be agreeable and rich

380 In honor to us both, I don't care which;
Whatever pleases you suffices me."

  "And have I won the mastery?" said she,
"Since I'm to choose and rule as I think fit?"
"Certainly, wife," he answered her, "that's it."

385 "Kiss me," she cried. "No quarrels! On my oath
And word of honor, you shall find me both,
That is, both fair and faithful as a wife;
May I go howling mad and take my life
Unless I prove to be as good and true

390 As ever wife was since the world was new!
And if to-morrow when the sun's above
I seem less fair than any lady-love,

Vocabulary
rebuke (ri byōōk´) *v.*
criticize strongly

Comprehension
Identify two benefits that the old woman says can come with poverty.

The Wife of Bath's Tale **149**

Than any queen or empress east or west,
Do with my life and death as you think best.
395 Cast up the curtain, husband. Look at me!"
          And when indeed the knight had looked to see,
Lo, she was young and lovely, rich in charms.
In ecstasy he caught her in her arms,
His heart went bathing in a bath of blisses
400 And melted in a hundred thousand kisses,
And she responded in the fullest measure
With all that could delight or give him pleasure.
          So they lived ever after to the end
In perfect bliss; and may Christ Jesus send
405 Us husbands meek and young and fresh in bed,
And grace to overbid them when we wed.
And—Jesu hear my prayer!—cut short the lives
Of those who won't be governed by their wives;
And all old, angry niggards of their pence,[14]
410 God send them soon a very pestilence!

Frame Story

Which words serve as a clue that the interior story is finished and that the Wife has turned her attention toward her riding companions?

---

14. **niggards** (nig´ ərdz) **of their pence** misers stingy with their money.

Critical Reading

Cite textual evidence to support your responses.

1. **Key Ideas and Details (a)** What punishment does the king initially order for the knight? **(b) Speculate:** Why might the king willingly allow his wife to effect a different punishment instead? **(c) Apply:** What philosophy about relationships do the king and queen share with the Wife of Bath?

2. **Key Ideas and Details (a)** What character flaw is the tale-within-a-tale of Midas's wife meant to illustrate? **(b) Evaluate:** In your opinion, does this inner story undercut the main point of the Wife's tale? Explain.

3. **Key Ideas and Details (a)** What bargain does the knight make with the old woman? **(b) Analyze:** Why do you think the queen forces the knight to keep his part of the bargain?

4. **Key Ideas and Details (a)** What final choice does the old woman offer the knight? **(b) Infer:** In what way does his response show that he has finally learned his lesson about the nature of women? **(c) Make a Judgment:** Has the knight experienced sufficient punishment and redemption for his crime? Explain.

5. **Integration of Knowledge and Ideas** By discussing selfsame sovereignty, was Chaucer reflecting or trying to influence social trends? In responding, use at least two of these words: *parity, independence, reciprocate. [Connecting to the Essential Question: How does literature shape or reflect society?]*

Close Reading Activities | *The Wife of Bath's Tale*

Literary Analysis

1. **Key Ideas and Details (a)** If you were unfamiliar with the word "dejected," in line 135, how might you repair your comprehension by **checking context clues**? **(b)** Identify three words you might use instead of "dejected" that would retain the meaning of the lines around the word.

2. **Key Ideas and Details** Define the word "suffices" as it is used in line 381, explaining which context clues enabled you to determine its meaning.

3. **Key Ideas and Details (a)** In what ways do the details of the setting in lines 135–144 echo the description of "ancient days" in lines 3–7? **(b)** Describe the way these details hint at, or foreshadow, the happy ending of the tale.

4. **Craft and Structure** In what ways does the **setting** of "The Wife of Bath's Tale" compare or contrast with the setting of the frame story, the pilgrimage to Canterbury?

5. **Integration of Knowledge and Ideas** Reread the description of the Wife of Bath in the General Prologue, or the **frame story** for the Wife's tale on pages 108–109. **(a)** Compare the characteristics of the Wife to those of the old woman in the Wife's tale. **(b)** Do you think the Wife identifies with the old woman? Support your answer with details from the texts.

6. **Integration of Knowledge and Ideas** In the frame story, the Host declares he will judge the pilgrims' tales on their "good morality and general pleasure" (Prologue line 818), their ability to teach a moral or lesson, and the entertainment value for the listeners. As the Host, how would you rate the Wife's tale? **(a)** Use the first two boxes in the chart below to note details from the tale. **(b)** Then, use the details to determine a final judgment.

Language
3. Apply knowledge of language to understand how language functions in different contexts, to make effective choices for meaning or style, and to comprehend more fully when reading or listening. *(p. 152)*
4. Determine or clarify the meaning of unknown and multiple-meaning words and phrases based on *grades 11–12 reading and content,* choosing flexibly from a range of strategies. *(p. 152)*

Good Morality/ Lesson	General Pleasure/ Entertainment Value	Final Judgment

7. **Integration of Knowledge and Ideas** In what ways is "The Wife of Bath's Tale" an important commentary on the lives of medieval women? Use details from the text to support your claims.

8. **Integration of Knowledge and Ideas (a)** In today's society, where might you find individuals who would agree with the Wife and the philosophy she illustrates with her story? **(b)** Who might argue against such opinions?

9. **Analyzing Visual Information:** Does the caricature of Chaucer on this page suggest that he knew and appreciated many people like the characters he invented? Why or why not?

Vocabulary Acquisition and Use

Multiple-Meaning Words in Context

Many English words have more than one meaning. For example, *relates* as a verb with an object can mean "tells a story or recounts," or, as a verb without an object, "to have or establish a relation (to)." Often, the meaning of the word changes according to its part of speech, which can be determined by the context. Note these examples:

The Wife relates her tale.
He relates to what she is saying.

In the first sentence, that *relates* takes an object provides a clue to its correct meaning, as does the fact that the object, "tale," is a narrative. In the second sentence, *relates* does not take an object, suggesting that it means "to have or establish a relation (to)."

For each of the following, explain how context helps you know which definition corresponds to the italicized word.

1. The Wife *relates* best to submissive men.

   a. tells   **b.** has a relation to

2. Is her desire for power merely an *act*?

   a. to take action **b.** performance

3. If so, her *bluff* is as compelling as her tale!

   a. lie   **b.** high, steep bank

Vocabulary: Logical or Illogical?

Review the vocabulary words on page 137. Then, for each item below, revise the sentence so that the underlined vocabulary word is used logically. Be sure not to change the vocabulary word.

Example: When the dark clouds moved in, the water in the puddles glistened.

After the dark clouds moved away, the water in the puddles glistened.

1. Let us give less consideration to the rights of women, the Wife of Bath implored.

2. The story the Wife of Bath relates is a warning against the destructiveness of greed.

3. When asked what women wanted most, the knight replied in a contemptuous way.

4. The old woman in the tale says that our fathers bequeath us their wealth and virtue.

5. According to the old wife in the story, the prowess of men is their fierceness.

6. The Wife's tale suggests that gentlemen should be esteemed only for their rank.

7. The old woman in the Wife's tale changes into a young woman because the knight continues to rebuke her.

Using Resources to Build Vocabulary

Lively Descriptive Adjectives and Their Connotations
In the Prologue, Chaucer uses lively adjectives to help you visualize his characters. For example, in line 299, he refers to the Oxford Cleric's "hollow look" and "sober stare." Following are other examples of lively adjectives:

    motley (line 281)   wary (line 320)   trim (line 375)
    fresh (line 375)   stout (line 562)   broad (line 565)

Review these words in context. Then, use a *print or digital thesaurus* to find synonyms for each. Rewrite the passage by replacing the word with a synonym. Next, read your new lines, and briefly explain how they differ from Chaucer's originals. Tell how the *connotative meanings,* or associations, of the adjectives make them better or worse for describing the characters, although their *denotative meanings,* or definitions, are similar.

Writing to Sources

Argumentative Text Chaucer's outlandish, rule-breaking pilgrims have long been the subject of critical speculation. Through such characters, did Chaucer hope to reform the flawed institutions they represent—the church, the nobility, the government, and marriage, among others? Or did he intend to censure the pilgrims themselves and others like them?

Perhaps he meant to do neither. In his book *Chaucer and the Energy of Creation,* critic Edward I. Condren writes:

> *To view Chaucer as a reformer . . . is to overlook his evident love affair with the world he creates—a world he neither condemns, endorses, burdens with ideology, nor seeks to improve, but a world he shows as a dynamic, human, endlessly fascinating entity unto itself.*

Do you agree or disagree with Condren's take on Chaucer? Do you, too, believe that the poet's main intent was to capture life in all its teeming glory, or do you suspect that he had an agenda of reform or censure? Write an **essay** in which you evaluate Condren's view and state your own judgment about Chaucer's purpose, supporting your claims with evidence from the texts.

Prewriting Before formulating an opinion, review the texts with an open mind. Gather details, including *imagery* and *figures of speech*, that describe pilgrims acting unconventionally and evoke your emotions. Is the *tone* of each detail comically affirming or darkly disapproving?

Drafting Use these steps as you compose your essay:

- In your introduction, include a *thesis* statement supporting or refuting Condren's remark. Try to express your thesis in a way that engages the interest of the reader.

- In your essay, *support your thesis* with information and examples from your prewriting notes. Return to the texts for additional support, if necessary.

- Close the essay by restating your thesis and by echoing your strongest evidence.

Revising Your essay may discuss social and religious institutions that some readers may value. Review your draft, placing a star next to passages that might lead to *misunderstandings*. For each star, rephrase the idea so that your meaning is clear and your tone is inoffensive.

Common Core State Standards

Writing

1.a. Create an organization that logically sequences claims, counterclaims, reasons, and evidence.

1.e. Provide a concluding statement or section that follows from and supports the argument presented.

Model: Revising to Eliminate False Generalizations
Chaucer writes of the Monk that "Hunting a hare or riding at a fence / Was all his fun, he spared for no expense."
Here, Chaucer suggests that this monk, for one, lived a life of indulgence rather than poverty.
★ ~~Clearly, Chaucer wanted to point out that most religious people at that time lived lives of indulgence rather than poverty.~~

The generalization "most religious people" makes a false generalization from Chaucer's passage. The writer replaces it with a specific reference to the monk.

Conventions and Style: Correlative Conjunctions

Too many short sentences can make your writing sound dull or stilted. When two short sentences have related ideas, you might be able to combine them using a **correlative conjunction,** a word pair connecting similar words or groups of words.

Combining: Correlative Conjunctions

The correlative conjunction you should use depends on the relationship between the ideas.

Two Short Sentences
The Carpenter is not described in detail. The Weaver isn't either.
The young man was the knight's Squire. He was also the knight's son.
The Cleric will buy books. The Cleric might take a course instead.

Combined
Neither the Weaver *nor* the Carpenter is described in detail.
The young man was *not only* the knight's Squire *but also* his son.
The Cleric will *either* buy books *or* take a course.

Practice In items 1–5, supply a correlative conjunction to complete the sentence. In items 6–10, use a correlative conjunction to combine the two sentences.

1. Each pilgrim must _____ tell four stories _____ pay for the journey.
2. The parson shows _____ generosity _____ patience in his behavior toward others.
3. The old woman urges the knight to respect _____ poverty _____ old age.
4. The travelers briefly considered _____ to accept _____ reject the Host's proposal.
5. Knights were supposed to be _____ honest _____ generous.
6. The narrator is a storyteller. The characters are storytellers too.
7. The host of the tavern serves as a travel guide. He serves as a judge of the tales.
8. The pardoner is greedy. He is hypocritical.
9. The knight must answer the queen's question correctly. Otherwise, he must surrender himself to the court.
10. The old man had not hurt the rioters by his words. He had not hurt them by his actions.

Punctuation Tip: Do not use a comma to separate items joined by a correlative conjunction, except when they are independent clauses.

Writing and Speaking Conventions

A. Writing For each pair, write a sentence using a correlative conjunction to link the words or phrases.

1. entertainment—competition
2. honorable—courteous
3. read the poem aloud—listen to a recording

  Example: entertainment—competition

  Sentence: The stories serve as both an entertainment and a competition.

B. Speaking Describe a pilgrimage you have taken or would like to take. Include at least two sentences with correlative conjunctions.

GALLERY OF FRAME STORIES

To delay her execution, Scheherazade...

... tells stories that she leaves incomplete until the next night.

The Thousand and One Nights
MEDIEVAL ARABIA

Escaping the plague, residents of Florence, Italy,...

... tell stories to entertain one another.

The Decameron
BY GIOVANNI BOCCACCIO (ITALIAN; 1313–1375)

Pilgrims traveling to Canterbury, England,...

... enter into a storytelling competition.

The Canterbury Tales
BY GEOFFREY CHAUCER (ENGLISH; 1343?–1400)

Marco Polo, visiting Kublai Khan...

... tells him stories about fantastic cities.

Invisible Cities (1972)
BY ITALO CALVINO (ITALIAN; 1923–1985)

Comparing Frame Stories Across Cultures

Frame Stories A frame story is a type of narrative in which the author creates one long story that contains within it another story or group of stories. It has been used as a literary device by writers from diverse time periods and regions. Early frame stories, like those of *The Thousand and One Nights*, wove together tales from a variety of sources. Chaucer did so when he wrote *The Canterbury Tales*, but he also developed stories and characters of his own. Here are some advantages of a frame story:

- ties together stories of all different kinds
- presents fantastic stories in the realistic context of the frame
- captures the natural quality of oral storytelling

As you read the selection from the *Decameron*, use a chart like the one shown to compare it with the selections from *The Canterbury Tales*.

	The Canterbury Tales	Decameron
Frame-story setting	England in the 1300s	
Storytellers' backgrounds	people of all ages from different walks of life	
Storytellers' purpose for gathering	to make a pilgrimage to Becket's shrine in Canterbury	
Storytellers' purpose for storytelling	to pass the time and compete for best story	
Types of stories within the frame	stories of many kinds set in many times and places	

Gather Vocabulary Knowledge

In the third paragraph of the excerpt from the *Decameron*, Boccaccio uses the words *pre-eminence*, *eloquence*, and *sumptuous*. Read the paragraph, and then use the following exercises to further explore the words.

- **Context** Reread the words and try to define them using context—the words immediately surrounding the word you are trying to define. Then, use a print or online **dictionary** to verify your definitions and to find the parts of speech.
- **Etymologies** Use a print or online dictionary or a book of etymologies to determine the etymologies, or origins, of the three words.

After you have familiarized yourself with the words, form a small group with classmates and use the words in a brief paragraph about attending a formal event at a banquet hall or a palace. Then, elect a speaker and share your writing with the rest of the class.

**Common Core
State Standards**

Reading Literature
10. By the end of grade 12, read and comprehend literature, including stories, at the high end of the grades 11–CCR text complexity band independently and proficiently.

Language
4.a. Use context as a clue to the meaning of a word or phrase.
4.c. Consult general and specialized reference materials, both print and digital, to find the pronunciation of a word or determine or clarify its precise meaning, its part of speech, or its etymology.
6. Demonstrate independence in gathering vocabulary knowledge when considering a word or phrase important to comprehension or expression.

Giovanni Boccaccio (1313–1375)

Author of the *Decameron: Federigo's Falcon*

When Giovanni Boccaccio (jō vän´ ē bō kä´ chō) was ten years old, his father, an associate of a well-known banking firm, sent the boy away from his native Florence to work at the firm's bank in Naples. Here he remained for many years, attending the court of Robert of Anjou, who ruled Naples at the time.

Enjoying the splendor and sophistication of Robert's court, Boccaccio showed little interest in becoming a businessman or a lawyer, as his father wanted him to do. Instead, he began writing—something he did prolifically for the rest of his life.

A Wider Worldview In 1340, financial problems caused Boccaccio's family to recall him to Florence, where at first he found the middle-class life not to his tastes. However, the change broadened his understanding of all different kinds and classes of people, an experience that would prove useful in his writing. In time, he became more sympathetic to Florence and its citizens, even engaging in local politics and serving as a Florentine ambassador.

Scholarship and Authorship In 1350, Boccaccio met the Italian poet and scholar Francesco Petrarch, with whom he began a lifelong friendship. Petrarch encouraged Boccaccio's writing, including many scholarly works in Latin.

However, while Boccaccio himself was proudest of these works, it is for an Italian work that he is best remembered. That masterpiece is the *Decameron*, a collection of stories that reveal his impressive literary versatility while exploring deeply human universal themes of love, loss, deception, fate, and honor.

"Human it is to have compassion on the unhappy."

from the Decameron

Giovanni Boccaccio
translated by G.H. McWilliam

BACKGROUND In 1348, bubonic plague swept Europe, killing more than half the population of Florence, including Boccaccio's parents. The *Decameron* begins with a group of ten young aristocrats—seven women and three men— taking up residence on a country estate where they hope to wait out the plague in Florence. To entertain themselves, each of them tells one story a day for ten days—the name Decameron means "ten days." Each day they elect a "king" or "queen" to preside over the day's storytelling and suggest the theme of the stories. "Federigo's Falcon" is told on the fifth day.

Federigo's Falcon

Comparing Frame Stories Why do you think the "queen" introduces another storyteller, Coppo di Borghese Domenichi, in the third paragraph of the story?

Vocabulary
courtly (kôrt′ ly)
adj. elegantly dignified; polite

Once Filomena had finished, the queen, finding that there was no one left to speak apart from herself (Dioneo being excluded from the reckoning because of his privilege[1]), smiled cheerfully and said:

It is now my own turn to address you, and I shall gladly do so, dearest ladies, with a story similar in some respects to the one we have just heard. This I have chosen, not only to acquaint you with the power of your beauty over men of noble spirit, but so that you may learn to choose for yourselves, whenever necessary, the persons on whom to bestow your largesse,[2] instead of always leaving these matters to be decided for you by Fortune, who, as it happens, nearly always scatters her gifts with more abundance than discretion.

You are to know, then, that Coppo di Borghese Domenichi, who once used to live in our city and possibly lives there still, one of the most highly respected men of our century, a person worthy of eternal fame, who achieved his position of pre-eminence by dint of his character and abilities rather than by his noble lineage, frequently took pleasure during his declining years in discussing incidents from the past with his neighbors and other folk. In this pastime he excelled all others, for he was more coherent, possessed a superior memory, and spoke with greater eloquence. He had a fine repertoire, including a tale he frequently told concerning a young Florentine called Federigo, the son of Messer Filippo Alberighi, who for his deeds of chivalry and courtly manners was more highly spoken of than any other squire in Tuscany.[3] In the manner of most young men of gentle breeding, Federigo lost his heart to a noble lady, whose name was Monna[4] Giovanna, and who in her time was considered one of the loveliest and most adorable women to be found in Florence. And with the object of winning her love, he rode at the ring, tilted,[5] gave sumptuous banquets, and distributed a large number of gifts, spending money

---

1. Dioneo . . privilege Because he is considered very witty, Dioneo is granted the privilege of telling a story on any theme that is always the last story of the day.
2. largesse (lär jes′) *n.* generous gifts.
3. squire in Tuscany well-born landowner in the Italian region where Florence is located.
4. Monna a title of respect similar to *Lady* in English.
5. tilted jousted; engaged in a medieval contest in which horsemen in armor attempted to unseat one another by thrusting lances.

without any restraint whatsoever. But since she was no less chaste than she was fair, the lady took no notice, either of the things that were done in her honor, or of the person who did them.

In this way, spending far more than he could afford and deriving no profit in return, Federigo lost his entire fortune (as can easily happen) and reduced himself to poverty, being left with nothing other than a tiny little farm, which produced an income just sufficient for him to live very frugally, and one falcon of the finest breed in the whole world. Since he was as deeply in love as ever, and felt unable to go on living the sort of life in Florence to which he aspired, he moved out to Campi, where his little farm happened to be situated. Having settled in the country, he went hunting as often as possible with his falcon, and, without seeking assistance from anyone, he patiently resigned himself to a life of poverty.

Now one day, while Federigo was living in these straitened circumstances, the husband of Monna Giovanna happened to fall ill, and, realizing that he was about to die, he drew up his will. He was a very rich man, and in his will he left everything to his son, who was just growing up, further stipulating that, if his son should die without legitimate issue, his estate should go to Monna Giovanna, to whom he had always been deeply devoted.

Shortly afterward he died, leaving Monna Giovanna a widow, and every summer, in accordance with Florentine custom, she went away with her son to a country estate of theirs, which was very near Federigo's farm. Consequently this young lad of hers happened to become friendly with Federigo, acquiring a passion for birds and dogs; and, having often seen Federigo's falcon in flight, he became fascinated by it and longed to own it, but since he could see that Federigo was deeply attached to the bird, he never ventured to ask him for it.

And there the matter rested, when, to the consternation of his mother, the boy happened to be taken ill. Being her only child, he was the apple of his mother's eye, and she sat beside his bed the whole day long, never ceasing to comfort him. Every so often she asked him whether there was anything he wanted, imploring him to tell her what it was, because if it was possible to acquire it, she would move heaven and earth to obtain it for him.

After hearing this offer repeated for the umpteenth time, the boy said:

"Mother, if you could arrange for me to have Federigo's falcon, I believe I should soon get better."

On hearing this request, the lady was somewhat taken aback, and began to consider what she could do about it. Knowing that Federigo had been in love with her for a long time, and that she had never deigned to cast so much as a single glance in his direction, she said to herself: "How can I possibly go to him, or even send anyone, to ask him for this falcon, which to judge from all I have heard is the

Vocabulary

frugally (froo′ gə lē) *adv.* in a way that is careful with money

◀ **Critical Viewing**

In what ways might this portrait be an accurate representation of Federigo? **ANALYZE**

Comprehension

What remains of Federigo's fortune after pursuing Monna Giovanna?

finest that ever flew, as well as being the only thing that keeps him alive? And how can I be so heartless as to deprive so noble a man of his one remaining pleasure?"

Her mind filled with reflections of this sort, she remained silent, not knowing what answer to make to her son's request, even though she was quite certain that the falcon was hers for the asking.

At length, however, her maternal instincts gained the upper hand, and she resolved, come what may, to satisfy the child by going in person to Federigo to collect the bird, and bring it back to him. And so she replied:

"Bear up, my son, and see whether you can start feeling any better. I give you my word that I shall go and fetch it for you first thing tomorrow morning."

Next morning, taking another lady with her for company,[6] his mother left the house as though intending to go for a walk, made her way to Federigo's little cottage, and asked to see him. For several days, the weather had been unsuitable for hawking, so Federigo was attending to one or two little jobs in his garden, and when he heard, to his utter astonishment, that Monna Giovanna was at the front door and wished to speak to him, he happily rushed there to greet her.

When she saw him coming, she advanced with womanly grace to meet him. Federigo received her with a deep bow, whereupon she said:

"Greetings, Federigo!" Then she continued: "I have come to make amends for the harm you have suffered on my account, by loving me more than you ought to have done. As a token of my esteem, I should like to take breakfast with you this morning, together with my companion here, but you must not put yourself to any trouble."

"My lady," replied Federigo in all humility, "I cannot recall ever having suffered any harm on your account. On the contrary I have gained so much that if ever I attained any kind of excellence, it was entirely because of your own great worth and the love I bore you. Moreover I can assure you that this visit which you have been generous enough to pay me is worth more to me than all the money I ever possessed, though I fear that my hospitality will not amount to very much."

So saying, he led her unassumingly into the house, and thence into his garden, where, since there was no one else he could call upon to chaperon her, he said:

"My lady, as there is nobody else available, this good woman, who is the wife of the farmer here, will keep you company whilst I go and see about setting the table."

Though his poverty was acute, the extent to which he had squandered his wealth had not yet been fully borne home to Federigo; but on this particular morning, finding that he had nothing to set before

---

6. taking . . . company It was not considered proper for a young woman of the upper classes to go out by herself.

the lady for whose love he had entertained so lavishly in the past, his eyes were well and truly opened to the fact. Distressed beyond all measure, he silently cursed his bad luck and rushed all over the house like one possessed, but could find no trace of either money or valuables. By now the morning was well advanced, he was still determined to entertain the gentlewoman to some sort of meal, and, not wishing to beg assistance from his own farmer (or from anyone else, for that matter), his gaze alighted on his precious falcon, which was sitting on its perch in the little room where it was kept. And having discovered, on picking it up, that it was nice and plump, he decided that since he had nowhere else to turn, it would make a worthy dish for such a lady as this. So without thinking twice about it he wrung the bird's neck and promptly handed it over to his housekeeper to be plucked, dressed, and roasted carefully on a spit. Then he covered the table with spotless linen, of which he still had a certain amount in his possession, and returned in high spirits to the garden, where he announced to his lady that the meal, such as he had been able to prepare, was now ready.

The lady and her companion rose from where they were sitting and made their way to the table. And together with Federigo, who waited on them with the utmost deference, they made a meal of the prize falcon without knowing what they were eating.

On leaving the table they engaged their host in pleasant conversation for a while, and when the lady thought it time to broach the subject she had gone there to discuss, she turned to Federigo and addressed him affably as follows:

"I do not doubt for a moment, Federigo, that you will be astonished at my impertinence when you discover my principal reason for coming here, especially when you recall your former mode of living and my virtue, which you possibly mistook for harshness and cruelty. But if you had ever had any children to make you appreciate the power of parental love, I should think it certain that you would to some extent forgive me.

"However, the fact that you have no children of your own does not exempt me, a mother, from the laws common to all other mothers. And being bound to obey those laws, I am forced, contrary to my own wishes and to all the rules of decorum and propriety, to ask you for something to which I know you are very deeply attached—which is only natural, seeing that it is the only consolation, the only pleasure, the only recreation remaining to you in your present extremity of fortune. The gift I am seeking is your falcon, to which my son has taken so powerful a liking, that if I fail to take it to him I fear he will succumb to the illness from which he is suffering, and consequently I shall lose him. In imploring you to give me this falcon, I appeal, not

Vocabulary

deference (def´ ər əns) *n.* courteous regard or respect

affably (af´ ə blē) *adv.* in a friendly manner

impertinence (im purt´ ə nəns) *n.* rudeness; impudence

Comprehension

Why has Monna Giovanna visited Federigo?

to your love, for you are under no obligation to me on that account, but rather to your noble heart, whereby you have proved yourself superior to all others in the practice of courtesy. Do me this favor, then, so that I may claim that through your generosity I have saved my son's life, thus placing him forever in your debt."

When he heard what it was that she wanted, and realized that he could not oblige her because he had given her the falcon to eat, Federigo burst into tears in her presence before being able to utter a single word in reply. At first the lady thought his tears stemmed more from his grief at having to part with his fine falcon than from any other motive, and was on the point of telling him that she would prefer not to have it. But on second thoughts she said nothing, and waited for Federigo to stop crying and give her his answer, which eventually he did.

"My lady," he said, "ever since God decreed that you should become the object of my love, I have repeatedly had cause to complain of Fortune's hostility towards me. But all her previous blows were slight by comparison with the one she has dealt me now. Nor shall I ever be able to forgive her, when I reflect that you have come to my poor dwelling, which you never deigned to visit when it was rich, and that you desire from me a trifling favor which she has made it impossible for me to concede. The reason is simple, and I shall explain it in few words.

"When you did me the kindness of telling me that you wished to breakfast with me, I considered it right and proper, having regard to your excellence and merit, to do everything within my power to prepare a more sumptuous dish than those I would offer to my ordinary guests. My thoughts therefore turned to the falcon you have asked me for and, knowing its quality, I reputed it a worthy dish to set before you. So I had it roasted and served to you on the trencher this morning, and I could not have wished for a better way of disposing of it. But now that I discover that you wanted it in a different form, I am so distressed by my inability to grant your request that I shall never forgive myself for as long as I live."

In confirmation of his words, Federigo caused the feathers, talons and beak to be cast on the table before her. On seeing and hearing all this, the lady reproached him at first for killing so fine a falcon, and serving it up for a woman to eat; but then she became lost in admiration for his magnanimity[7] of spirit, which no amount of poverty had managed to diminish, nor ever would. But now that her hopes of obtaining the falcon had vanished she began to feel seriously concerned for the health of her son, and after thanking Federigo for his hospitality and good intentions, she took her leave of him, looking all despondent, and returned to the child. And to his mother's indescribable sorrow, within the space of a few days, whether through his dis-

Vocabulary
despondent (di spän´ dənt)
adj. hopeless; dejected

---

7. **magnanimity** (mag´ nə nim´ ə tē) *n.* noble generosity.

appointment in not being able to have the falcon, or because he was in any case suffering from a mortal illness, the child passed from this life.

After a period of bitter mourning and continued weeping, the lady was repeatedly urged by her brothers to remarry, since not only had she been left a vast fortune but she was still a young woman. And though she would have preferred to remain a widow, they gave her so little peace that in the end, recalling Federigo's high merits and his latest act of generosity, namely to have killed such a fine falcon in her honor, she said to her brothers:

"If only it were pleasing to you, I should willingly remain as I am; but since you are so eager for me to take a husband, you may be certain that I shall never marry any other man except Federigo degli Alberighi."

Her brothers made fun of her, saying:

"Silly girl, don't talk such nonsense! How can you marry a man who hasn't a penny with which to bless himself?"

"My brothers," she replied, "I am well aware of that. But I would sooner have a gentleman without riches, than riches without a gentleman."

Seeing that her mind was made up, and knowing Federigo to be a gentleman of great merit even though he was poor, her brothers fell in with her wishes and handed her over to him, along with her immense fortune. Thenceforth, finding himself married to this great lady with whom he was so deeply in love, and very rich into the bargain, Federigo managed his affairs more prudently, and lived with her in happiness to the end of his days.

Comparing Frame Stories Which words let you know that the interior story has finished?

Critical Reading

Cite textual evidence to support your responses.

1. **Key Ideas and Details (a)** What early efforts does Federigo make to win Monna Giovanna's love? **(b) Summarize:** How does she respond to those efforts? **(c) Analyze:** What does her behavior reveal about her character?

2. **Key Ideas and Details (a) Connect:** In what ways do Federigo's gestures of hospitality when Monna Giovanna visits reflect his former life as a wealthy gentleman? **(b) Infer:** Why is killing the bird such a sacrifice for him? **(c) Analyze:** What does his sacrifice show about his character?

3. **Key Ideas and Details (a) Infer:** Why is it difficult for Monna Giovanna to ask Federigo for the falcon? **(b) Analyze:** What does her making the request show about her character?

4. **Integration of Knowledge and Ideas (a) Evaluate:** Do you think Monna Giovanna makes the right decision in marrying Federigo in the end? **(b) Support:** Cite reasons and story details to support your evaluation.

Close Reading Activities

from *The Canterbury Tales* ▪
from the *Decameron:*
Federigo's Falcon

Comparing Frame Stories

1. **Integration of Knowledge and Ideas (a)** In the **frame story** of Boccaccio's *Decameron*, what is the premise or reason for the storytelling? **(b)** How is that premise like and unlike the premise for the storytelling in Chaucer's work? **(c)** Which premise makes for a more effective frame story? Why?

2. **Integration of Knowledge and Ideas** One advantage of a frame story is that it can capture, in written form, the qualities of oral storytelling. Which author, Boccaccio or Chaucer, better conveys those qualities? Explain.

3. **Integration of Knowledge and Ideas** Consider this statement: Frame stories are not effective for revealing character because the only action people perform is telling stories. Explain why you agree or disagree with this assertion, citing evidence from "Federigo's Falcon" and *The Canterbury Tales* as support.

 **Common Core State Standards**

Writing
1. Write arguments to support claims in an analysis of substantive topics or texts, using valid reasoning and relevant and sufficient evidence.
10. Write routinely over extended time frames and shorter time frames for a range of tasks, purposes, and audiences.

Timed Writing

Argumentative Text: Essay

Although Chaucer and Boccaccio both use the device of the frame story, they do not always deal with similar themes in exactly the same way.

Assignment: Write an **interpretation of a literary text** in which you compare and contrast the theme of "Federigo's Falcon" with the theme of "The Wife of Bath's Tale" or "The Pardoner's Tale." **[40 minutes]**
Your essay should explore these types of questions:

- How does the sequence of events and outcome of each tale offer a clue to its theme?
- How does the theme of each tale reflect or suggest the personality, background, or motives of the character in the frame story who narrates the tale?
- What do the themes of the two tales have in common, and how are they different?

As you write, support your ideas with accurate and detailed references to the texts.

5-Minute Planner

Complete these steps before you begin to write:

1. Read the assignment carefully. Identify key words and phrases.
2. Scan the selections, looking for details related to your assignment.
   TIP As you scan, jot down quotations that you might use in your essay.
3. Write a rough outline for your essay.
4. Reread the prompt and begin drafting.

USE ACADEMIC VOCABULARY

As you write, use academic language, including the following words or their related forms:

compare
contrast
insight
interpret

For more about academic language, see the vocabulary charts in the introduction to this book.

Connecting to the Essential Question Many characters in these selections are knights who observe a code of honorable behavior called chivalry. As you read, look for passages in these selections that reveal the kind of behavior that chivalry requires. Finding these passages will help as you explore the Essential Question: **What is the relationship of the writer to tradition?**

Common Core State Standards

Reading Literature
2. Provide an objective summary of the text.

Close Reading Focus

Medieval Romances; Legends

Romances are narratives that tell of strange, sometimes supernatural events in exotic settings. **Medieval romances** are adventure stories with kings, knights, and damsels in distress. The medieval romances in this grouping are based on **legends,** anonymous traditional stories about the past that may have been inspired by real events and people. Legends, like these relating to King Arthur and his knights, often feature the following:

- heroic figures and memorable deeds
- quests, or searches for something important; contests; and tests
- patterns, such as events repeated three times

Medieval writers created romances by adding to legends such elements as vivid descriptions, plot twists, and accounts of the reactions and motives of characters. As you read, look for these elements and compare and contrast their use in these selections.

Preparing to Read Complex Texts You can **determine the main idea, or essential message,** of a work or a passage in several different ways. One method is to **summarize** a whole work or a portion of it by identifying and briefly restating its main ideas and relevant details. An effective summary will only include factual information, and not your personal opinions about what you have read. As you read, use a chart like the one shown to summarize key ideas and details.

Vocabulary

The words below are important to understanding the texts that follow. Copy the words into your notebook. Which word is a noun that might be related to the idea of nobility? How can you tell?

adjure	**entreated**
adroitly	**peril**
largesse	**interred**

Passage

"Ah, traitor unto me and untrue," said King Arthur, "now hast thou betrayed me twice. Who would have weened that thou that has been to me so loved and dear..., and would betray me for the riches of this sword."

Summary

King Arthur charges his knight with betraying him twice out of greed.

KNIGHTS OF LEGEND

Medieval Europe depended on a few powerful words—the promise of loyalty a knight gave to his lord. By A.D. 1000, a simple promise had blossomed into a social order called feudalism.

A Society of Promises Feudalism was a system both of government and of land ownership. In exchange for a nobleman's oath of loyalty, a king would give him lands. The nobleman ruled these lands, judging legal cases, imposing taxes, and maintaining an army—powers granted him in exchange for his promise of loyalty to his king.

The Code of Chivalry As an expression of feudal ideals of honor, nobles developed a code of conduct called chivalry. This code demanded that knights be brave warriors and virtuous Christians who would selflessly fight for justice.

King Arthur and His Knights The ideals of chivalry gave rise to legends and songs, such as the tales of King Arthur and his knights of the Round Table. In the eleventh century, as feudalism established itself throughout Europe, stories about Arthur's court became widespread.

Sir Gawain and the Green Knight In *Sir Gawain and the Green Knight*, a medieval poem, the chivalry of Gawain, Arthur's loyal nephew, is tested by three challenges. In meeting them, Gawain proves admirable but not invulnerable. As one critic writes, the hero "gains in human credibility what he loses in ideal perfection."

We know little about the poet of *Sir Gawain*, who is credited with three other poems in alliterative verse. In his work, though, with its combination of humor and fervent ideals, he has helped shape an enduring vision of personal integrity.

FROM
SIR GAWAIN
AND THE
GREEN
KNIGHT
TRANSLATED BY MARIE BORROFF

BACKGROUND The legend of King Arthur may have been based on the life of one or more Celtic warriors who fought the Anglo-Saxon invaders of England in the late fifth and early sixth centuries. The Britons, the island's Celtic inhabitants, told stories celebrating his just rule and championship of the oppressed. The Arthurian stories set an ideal for knights, and ideals are never fully realized in the present. Their true home may be the legendary past, or a future yet to come. The selection begins at the start of a New Year's Eve feast at King Arthur's Court in Camelot. Before anyone has started eating, the festivities are interrupted by an immense green knight who suddenly appears at the hall door. The knight rides a green horse and is armed with a gigantic ax.

This horseman hurtles in, and the hall enters;
Riding to the high dais,[1] recked he no danger;
Not a greeting he gave as the guests he o'erlooked,
Nor wasted his words, but "Where is," he said,
5 "The captain of this crowd? Keenly I wish
To see that sire with sight, and to himself say my say."
    He swaggered all about
    To scan the host so gay;
    He halted, as if in doubt
10   Who in that hall held sway.

---

1. dais (dā´ is) *n.* platform.

There were stares on all sides as the stranger spoke,
For much did they marvel what it might mean
That a horseman and a horse should have such a hue,
Grow green as the grass, and greener, it seemed.
15 Then green fused on gold more glorious by far.
All the onlookers eyed him, and edged nearer,
And awaited in wonder what he would do,
For many sights had they seen, but such a one never,
So that phantom and fairy the folk there deemed it,
20 Therefore chary[2] of answer was many a champion bold,
And stunned at his strong words stone-still they sat
In a swooning silence in the stately hall.
As all were slipped into sleep, so slackened their speech apace.
Not all, I think, for dread,
25   But some of courteous grace
Let him who was their head
Be spokesman in that place.

Then Arthur before the high dais that entrance beholds,
And hailed him, as behooved, for he had no fear.
30 And said "Fellow, in faith you have found fair welcome;
The head of this hostelry Arthur am I;
Leap lightly down, and linger, I pray,
And the tale of your intent you shall tell us after."
"Nay, so help me," said the other, "He that on high sits,
35 To tarry here any time, 'twas not mine errand;
But as the praise of you, prince, is puffed up so high,
And your court and your company are counted the best,
Stoutest under steel-gear on steeds to ride,
Worthiest of their works the wide world over,
40 And peerless to prove in passages of arms,
And courtesy here is carried to its height,
And so at this season I have sought you out.
You may be certain by the branch that I bear in hand
That I pass here in peace, and would part friends,
45 For had I come to this court on combat bent,
I have a hauberk[3] at home, and a helm beside,
A shield and a sharp spear, shining bright,
And other weapons to wield, I ween well, to boot,
But as I willed no war, I wore no metal.
50 But if you be so bold as all men believe,
You will graciously grant the game that I ask by right."

Summarizing

What are the three main points of the Green Knight's speech in lines 34–51?

---

2. **chary** (cher´ ē) *adj.* not giving freely.
3. **hauberk** (hô´ bərk) *n.* coat of armor.

Arthur answer gave
And said, "Sir courteous knight,
If contest here you crave,
55   You shall not fail to fight."

"Nay, to fight, in good faith, is far from my thought;
There are about on these benches but beardless children,
Were I here in full arms on a haughty[4] steed,
For measured against mine, their might is puny.
60 And so I call in this court for a Christmas game,
For 'tis Yule, and New Year, and many young bloods about;
If any in this house such hardihood claims,
Be so bold in his blood, his brain so wild,
As stoutly to strike one stroke for another,
65 I shall give him as my gift this gisarme[5] noble,
This ax, that is heavy enough, to handle as he likes,
And I shall bide the first blow, as bare as I sit.
If there be one so wilful my words to assay,
Let him leap hither lightly, lay hold of this weapon;
70 I quitclaim it forever, keep it as his own,
And I shall stand him a stroke, steady on this floor,
So you grant me the guerdon to give him another, sans blame.[6]
In a twelvemonth[7] and a day
He shall have of me the same;
75   Now be it seen straightway
Who dares take up the game."

If he astonished them at first, stiller were then
All that household in hall, the high and the low;
The stranger on his green steed stirred in the saddle,
80 And roisterously his red eyes he rolled all about,
Bent his bristling brows, that were bright green,
Wagged his beard as he watched who would arise.
When the court kept its counsel he coughed aloud,
And cleared his throat coolly, the clearer to speak:
85 "What, is this Arthur's house," said that horseman then,
"Whose fame is so fair in far realms and wide?
Where is now your arrogance and your awesome deeds,
Your valor and your victories and your vaunting words?
Now are the revel and renown of the Round Table
90 Overwhelmed with a word of one man's speech,
For all cower and quake, and no cut felt!"

Medieval Romance

What aspect of medieval romances does the Green Knight's appearance illustrate?

Comprehension

How does the Green Knight challenge Arthur's court?

---

4. **haughty** (hôt´ ē) *adj.* lofty.
5. **gisarme** (gi zärm´) *n.* battle-ax.
6. **I shall . . . blame** "I will stand firm while he strikes me with the ax provided that you reward me with the opportunity to do the same to him without being blamed for it."
7. **twelvemonth** a year.

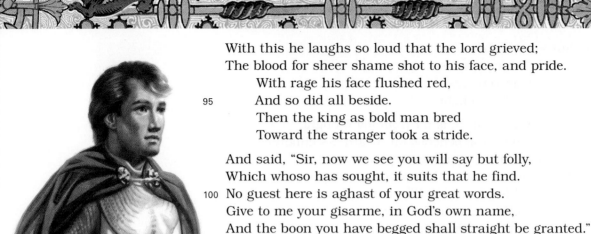

With this he laughs so loud that the lord grieved;
The blood for sheer shame shot to his face, and pride.
    With rage his face flushed red,
95   And so did all beside.
    Then the king as bold man bred
    Toward the stranger took a stride.

And said, "Sir, now we see you will say but folly,
Which whoso has sought, it suits that he find.
100 No guest here is aghast of your great words.
Give to me your gisarme, in God's own name,
And the boon you have begged shall straight be granted."
He leaps to him lightly, lays hold of his weapon;
The green fellow on foot fiercely alights.
105 Now has Arthur his ax, and the haft[8] grips,
And sternly stirs it about, on striking bent.
The stranger before him stood there erect,
Higher than any in the house by a head and more;
With stern look as he stood, he stroked his beard,
110 And with undaunted countenance drew down his coat,
No more moved nor dismayed for his mighty dints
Than any bold man on bench had brought him a drink of wine.
    Gawain by Guenevere
    Toward the king doth now incline:
115   "I beseech, before all here,
    That this melee may be mine."

"Would you grant me the grace," said Gawain to the king,
"To be gone from this bench and stand by you there,
If I without discourtesy might quit this board,
120 And if my liege lady[9] misliked it not,
I would come to your counsel before your court noble.
For I find it not fit, as in faith it is known,
When such a boon is begged before all these knights,
Though you be tempted thereto, to take it on yourself
125 While so bold men about upon benches sit,
That no host under heaven is hardier of will,
Nor better brothers-in-arms where battle is joined;
I am the weakest, well I know, and of wit feeblest;
And the loss of my life would be least of any;
130 That I have you for uncle is my only praise;
My body, but for your blood, is barren of worth;
And for that this folly befits not a king,
And 'tis I that have asked it, it ought to be mine,
And if my claim be not comely let all this court judge in sight."

▲ **Critical Viewing**
Read Gawain's description of himself in lines 128–130. In what ways does this illustration of Gawain contrast with those lines?
COMPARE AND CONTRAST

---

8. haft *n.* handle of a weapon or tool.
9. liege (lēj) **lady** Guenevere, the wife of the lord, Arthur, to whom Gawain is bound to give service and allegiance.

135   The court assays the claim,
       And in counsel all unite
       To give Gawain the game
       And release the king outright.

    Then the king called the knight to come to his side,
140 And he rose up readily, and reached him with speed,
    Bows low to his lord, lays hold of the weapon,
    And he releases it lightly, and lifts up his hand,
    And gives him God's blessing, and graciously prays
    That his heart and his hand may be hardy both.
145 "Keep, cousin," said the king, "what you cut with this day,
    And if you rule it aright, then readily, I know,
    You shall stand the stroke it will strike after."
    Gawain goes to the guest with gisarme in hand,
    And boldly he bides there, abashed not a whit.
150 Then hails he Sir Gawain, the horseman in green:
    "Recount we our contract, ere you come further.
    First I ask and adjure you, how you are called
    That you tell me true, so that trust it I may."
    "In good faith," said the good knight, "Gawain am I
155 Whose buffet befalls you,[10] whate'er betide after,
    And at this time twelvemonth take from you another
    With what weapon you will, and with no man else alive."
       The other nods assent:
       "Sir Gawain, as I may thrive,
160   I am wondrous well content
       That you this dint[11] shall drive."

    "Sir Gawain," said the Green Knight, "By God, I rejoice
    That your fist shall fetch this favor I seek,
    And you have readily rehearsed, and in right terms,
165 Each clause of my covenant with the king your lord,
    Save that you shall assure me, sir, upon oath,
    That you shall seek me yourself, wheresoever you deem
    My lodgings may lie, and look for such wages[12]
    As you have offered me here before all this host."
170 "What is the way there?" said Gawain, "Where do you dwell?
    I heard never of your house, by Him that made me,
    Nor I know you not, knight, your name nor your court.
    But tell me truly thereof, and teach me your name,
    And I shall fare forth to find you, so far as I may,
175 And this I say in good certain, and swear upon oath."
    "That is enough in New Year, you need say no more,"

---

10. Whose . . . you "whose blow you will receive."
11. dint *n.* blow.
12. wages *n.* payment; that is, a strike with the ax.

Medieval Romance

How are Gawain's words in lines 128–134 and the court's decision consistent with the ideals of chivalry?

Vocabulary

adjure (ə jo͝or´) *v.* request solemnly; appeal to earnestly

Comprehension

What does Gawain do to the Green Knight?

Said the knight in the green to Gawain the noble,
"If I tell you true, when I have taken your knock,
And if you handily have hit, you shall hear straightway
180 Of my house and my home and my own name;
Then follow in my footsteps by faithful accord.
And if I spend no speech, you shall speed the better:
You can feast with your friends, nor further trace my tracks.[13]
    Now hold your grim tool steady
185   And show us how it hacks."
    "Gladly, sir; all ready,"
    Says Gawain; he strokes the ax.

Summarizing

How would you summarize the event described in lines 188–213?

The Green Knight upon ground girds him with care:
Bows a bit with his head, and bares his flesh:
190 His long lovely locks he laid over his crown,
Let the naked nape for the need be shown
Gawain grips to his ax and gathers it aloft—
The left foot on the floor before him he set—
Brought it down deftly upon the bare neck,
195 That the shock of the sharp blow shivered the bones
And cut the flesh cleanly and clove it in twain,[14]
That the blade of bright steel bit into the ground.
The head was hewn off and fell to the floor;
Many found it at their feet, as forth it rolled;
200 The blood gushed from the body, bright on the green,
Yet fell not the fellow, nor faltered a whit,
But stoutly he starts forth upon stiff shanks,
And as all stood staring he stretched forth his hand,
Laid hold of his head and heaved it aloft,
205 Then goes to the green steed, grasps the bridle,
Steps into the stirrup, bestrides his mount,
And his head by the hair in his hand holds,
And as steady he sits in the stately saddle
As he had met with no mishap, nor missing were his head.
210   His bulk about he haled,
    That fearsome body that bled;
    There were many in the court that quailed
    Before all his say was said.

For the head in his hand he holds right up;
215 Toward the first on the dais directs he the face,
And it lifted up its lids, and looked with wide eyes,
And said as much with its mouth as now you may hear:
"Sir Gawain, forget not to go as agreed,

Medieval Romance

What two characteristics of a medieval romance are reflected in lines 214–231?

---

13. **If I tell you . . . tracks** The Green Knight tells Gawain that he will let him know where he lives after he has taken the blow. If he is unable to speak following the blow, there will be no need for Gawain to know.
14. **clove it in twain** split it in two.

And cease not to seek till me, sir, you find,
220 As you promised in the presence of these proud knights.
To the Green Chapel come, I charge you, to take
Such a dint as you have dealt—you have well deserved
That your neck should have a knock on New Year's morn.
The Knight of the Green Chapel I am well-known to many,
225 Wherefore you cannot fail to find me at last;
Therefore come, or be counted a recreant[15] knight."
With a roisterous rush he flings round the reins,
Hurtles out at the hall door, his head in his hand,
That the flint fire flew from the flashing hooves.
230 Which way he went, not one of them knew
Nor whence he was come in the wide world so fair.
      The king and Gawain gay
      Make a game of the Green Knight there,
      Yet all who saw it say
235   'Twas a wonder past compare.

Though high-born Arthur at heart had wonder,
He let no sign be seen, but said aloud
To the comely queen, with courteous speech,
"Dear dame, on this day dismay you no whit;
240 Such crafts are becoming at Christmastide,
Laughing at interludes, light songs and mirth,
Amid dancing of damsels with doughty knights.
Nevertheless of my meat now let me partake,
For I have met with a marvel, I may not deny."
245 He glanced at Sir Gawain, and gaily he said,
"Now, sir, hang up your ax, that has hewn enough,"
And over the high dais it was hung on the wall
That men in amazement might on it look,
And tell in true terms the tale of the wonder.
250 Then they turned toward the table, those two together,
The good king and Gawain, and made great feast,
With all dainties double, dishes rare,
With all manner of meat and minstrelsy both,
Such happiness wholly had they that day in hold.
255   Now take care, Sir Gawain,
      That your courage wax not cold
      When you must turn again
      To your enterprise foretold.

▲ **Critical Viewing**
Identify two elements in this illustration of Arthur that portray him as a powerful ruler. **ANALYZE**

Comprehension
What happens after Gawain chops off the Green Knight's head?

---

15. recreant *adj.* cowardly.

The following November, Sir Gawain sets out to fulfill his promise to the Green Knight. For weeks, he travels alone through the cold, threatening woods of North Wales. Then, after he prays for shelter, he comes upon a wondrous castle on Christmas Eve, where he is greeted warmly by the lord of the castle and his lady. The lord assures Sir Gawain that the Green Chapel is nearby and promises to provide him with a guide to lead him there on New Year's Day. Before the lord and Sir Gawain retire for the night, they agree to exchange whatever they receive during the next three days. Sir Gawain keeps his pledge for the first two days, but he fails to give the lord the magic green girdle that the lady gives him on the third day, because she gives it with the promise that it will protect him from harm. The next day, Gawain sets out for the Green Chapel. His guide urges him not to proceed, but Gawain feels that it would be dishonorable not to fulfill his pledge. He is determined to accept his fate; however, he wears the magic green girdle that the lady has given him.

▼ **Critical Viewing**

Examine this illustration of Gawain's journey through the wilderness. Why might Gawain be tempted to stay in the castle and give up his quest? **SPECULATE**

He puts his heels to his horse, and picks up the path;
260 Goes in beside a grove where the ground is steep,
Rides down the rough slope right to the valley;
And then he looked a little about him—the landscape was wild,
And not a soul to be seen, nor sign of a dwelling,
But high banks on either hand hemmed it about,
265 With many a ragged rock and rough-hewn crag;
The skies seemed scored by the scowling peaks.
Then he halted his horse, and hoved there a space,
And sought on every side for a sight of the Chapel,
But no such place appeared, which puzzled him sore,
270 Yet he saw some way off what seemed like a mound,
A hillock high and broad, hard by the water,
Where the stream fell in foam down the face of the steep
And bubbled as if it boiled on its bed below.
The knight urges his horse, and heads for the knoll;
275 Leaps lightly to earth; loops well the rein
Of his steed to a stout branch, and stations him there.
He strides straight to the mound, and strolls all about,
Much wondering what it was, but no whit the wiser;
It had a hole at one end, and on either side,
280 And was covered with coarse grass in clumps all without,
And hollow all within, like some old cave,
Or a crevice of an old crag—he could not discern aright.
　　"Can this be the Chapel Green?
　　Alack!" said the man, "Here might
285　　The devil himself be seen
　　Saying matins[16] at black midnight!"

---

16. matins *n.* morning prayers.

"Now by heaven," said he, "it is bleak hereabouts;
This prayer house is hideous, half covered with grass!
Well may the grim man mantled in green
290 Hold here his orisons,[17] in hell's own style!
Now I feel it is the Fiend, in my five wits,
That has tempted me to this tryst,[18] to take my life;
This is a Chapel of mischance, may the mischief take it!
As accursed a country church as I came upon ever!"
295 With his helm on his head, his lance in his hand,
He stalks toward the steep wall of that strange house.
Then he heard, on the hill, behind a hard rock,
Beyond the brook, from the bank, a most barbarous din:
Lord! it clattered in the cliff fit to cleave it in two,
300 As one upon a grindstone ground a great scythe!
Lord! it whirred like a mill-wheel whirling about!
Lord! it echoed loud and long, lamentable to hear!
Then "By heaven," said the bold knight, "That business up there
Is arranged for my arrival, or else I am much misled.

305   Let God work! Ah me!
        All hope of help has fled!
        Forfeit my life may be
        But noise I do not dread."

Then he listened no longer, but loudly he called,
310 "Who has power in this place, high parley to hold?
For none greets Sir Gawain, or gives him good day;
If any would a word with him, let him walk forth
And speak now or never, to speed his affairs."
"Abide," said one on the bank above over his head,
315 "And what I promised you once shall straightway be given."
Yet he stayed not his grindstone, nor stinted its noise,
But worked awhile at his whetting before he would rest,
And then he comes around a crag, from a cave in the rocks,
Hurtling out of hiding with a hateful weapon,
320 A Danish ax[19] devised for that day's deed,
With a broad blade and bright, bent in a curve,
Filed to a fine edge—four feet it measured
By the length of the lace that was looped round the haft.
And in form as at first, the fellow all green,
325 His lordly face and his legs, his locks and his beard,
Save that firm upon two feet forward he strides,
Sets a hand on the ax-head, the haft to the earth;
When he came to the cold stream, and cared not to wade,

---

17. **orisons** *n.* prayers.
18. **tryst** (trist) *n.* meeting.
19. **Danish ax** long-bladed ax.

Medieval Romance and Legend

In what way does Gawain's speech in lines 287–294 add a dimension to the story that might not have been present in the original legend?

Comprehension

What is the Green Knight doing when Gawain arrives at the Green Chapel?

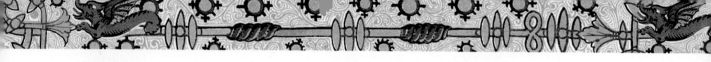

He vaults over on his ax, and advances amain
330 On a broad bank of snow, overbearing and brisk of mood.
     Little did the knight incline
     When face to face they stood;
     Said the other man, "Friend mine,
     It seems your word holds good!"

335 "God love you, Sir Gawain!" said the Green Knight then,
"And well met this morning, man, at my place!
And you have followed me faithfully and found me betimes,
And on the business between us we both are agreed:
Twelve months ago today you took what was yours,
340 And you at this New Year must yield me the same.
And we have met in these mountains, remote from all eyes:
There is none here to halt us or hinder our sport;
Unhasp your high helm, and have here your wages;
Make no more demur[20] than I did myself
345 When you hacked off my head with one hard blow."
"No, by God," said Sir Gawain, "that granted me life,
I shall grudge not the guerdon[21] grim though it prove;
And you may lay on as you like till the last of my part be paid."
     He proffered, with good grace,
350   His bare neck to the blade,
     And feigned a cheerful face:
     He scorned to seem afraid.

Then the grim man in green gathers his strength,
Heaves high the heavy ax to hit him the blow.
355 With all the force in his frame he fetches it aloft,
With a grimace as grim as he would grind him to bits;
Had the blow he bestowed been as big as he threatened,
A good knight and gallant had gone to his grave.
But Gawain at the great ax glanced up aside
360 As down it descended with death-dealing force,
And his shoulders shrank a little from the sharp iron.
Abruptly the brawny man breaks off the stroke,
And then reproved with proud words that prince among knights.
"You are not Gawain the glorious," the green man said,
365 "That never fell back on field in the face of the foe,
And now you flee for fear, and have felt no harm:
Such news of that knight I never heard yet!
I moved not a muscle when you made to strike,
Nor caviled[22] at the cut in King Arthur's house;
370 My head fell to my feet, yet steadfast I stood,
And you, all unharmed, are wholly dismayed—

▲ Critical Viewing

In what ways does this illustration of the Green Knight compare or contrast with your mental image of him? **COMPARE AND CONTRAST**

Medieval Romance

How do Gawain's actions in lines 359–387 reflect or depart from the ideals of knighthood?

---

20. demur (dē mʉr) protest; delay.
21. guerdon *n.* reward.
22. caviled raised trivial objections

Wherefore the better man I, by all odds, must be."
     Said Gawain, "Strike once more;
     I shall neither flinch nor flee;
375   But if my head falls to the floor
     There is no mending me!"

"But go on, man, in God's name, and get to the point!
Deliver me my destiny, and do it out of hand,
For I shall stand to the stroke and stir not an inch
380 Till your ax has hit home—on my honor I swear it!"
"Have at thee then!" said the other, and heaves it aloft,
And glares down as grimly as he had gone mad.
He made a mighty feint, but marred not his hide;
Withdrew the ax adroitly before it did damage.
385 Gawain gave no ground, nor glanced up aside,
But stood still as a stone, or else a stout stump
That is held in hard earth by a hundred roots.
Then merrily does he mock him, the man all in green:
"So now you have your nerve again, I needs must strike;
390 Uphold the high knighthood that Arthur bestowed,
And keep your neck-bone clear, if this cut allows!"
Then was Gawain gripped with rage, and grimly he said,
"Why, thrash away, tyrant, I tire of your threats;
You make such a scene, you must frighten yourself."
395 Said the green fellow, "In faith, so fiercely you speak
That I shall finish this affair, nor further grace allow."
     He stands prepared to strike
     And scowls with both lip and brow;
     No marvel if the man mislike
400   Who can hope no rescue now.

He gathered up the grim ax and guided it well:
Let the barb at the blade's end brush the bare throat;
He hammered down hard, yet harmed him no whit
Save a scratch on one side, that severed the skin;
405 The end of the hooked edge entered the flesh,
And a little blood lightly leapt to the earth.
And when the man beheld his own blood bright on the snow,
He sprang a spear's length with feet spread wide,
Seized his high helm, and set it on his head,
410 Shoved before his shoulders the shield at his back,
Bares his trusty blade, and boldly he speaks—
Not since he was a babe born of his mother
Was he once in this world one half so blithe—
"Have done with your hacking—harry me no more!
415 I have borne, as behooved, one blow in this place;
If you make another move I shall meet it midway
And promptly, I promise you, pay back each blow with brand.

Vocabulary
adroitly (ə droit´ lē) adv.
with physical or mental skill

Summarizing
Summarize what happens
after the Green Knight's third
stroke with the ax.

Comprehension
How does Gawain react
when the Green Knight first
lifts his axe?

from Sir Gawain and the Green Knight **181**

One stroke acquits me here;
So did our covenant stand
420   In Arthur's court last year—
Wherefore, sir, hold your hand!"

He lowers the long ax and leans on it there,
Sets his arms on the head, the haft on the earth,
And beholds the bold knight that bides there afoot,
425 How he faces him fearless, fierce in full arms,
And plies him with proud words—it pleases him well.
Then once again gaily to Gawain he calls,
And in a loud voice and lusty, delivers these words:
"Bold fellow, on this field your anger forbear!
430 No man has made demands here in manner uncouth,
Nor done, save as duly determined at court.
I owed you a hit and you have it; be happy therewith!
The rest of my rights here I freely resign.
Had I been a bit busier, a buffet, perhaps,
435 I could have dealt more directly; and done you some harm.
First I flourished with a feint, in frolicsome mood,
And left your hide unhurt—and here I did well
By the fair terms we fixed on the first night;
And fully and faithfully you followed accord:
440 Gave over all your gains as a good man should.
A second feint, sir, I assigned for the morning
You kissed my comely wife—each kiss you restored.
For both of these there behooved but two feigned blows by right.
     True men pay what they owe;
445   No danger then in sight.
     You failed at the third throw,
     So take my tap, sir knight.

"For that is my belt about you, that same braided girdle,
My wife it was that wore it; I know well the tale,
450 And the count of your kisses and your conduct too,
And the wooing of my wife—it was all my scheme!
She made trial of a man most faultless by far
Of all that ever walked over the wide earth;
As pearls to white peas, more precious and prized,
455 So is Gawain, in good faith, to other gay knights.
Yet you lacked, sir, a little in loyalty there,
But the cause was not cunning, nor courtship either,
But that you loved your own life; the less, then, to blame."
The other stout knight in a study stood a long while,
460 So gripped with grim rage that his great heart shook.
All the blood of his body burned in his face
As he shrank back in shame from the man's sharp speech.
The first words that fell from the fair knight's lips:

"Accursed be a cowardly and covetous heart!
465 In you is villainy and vice, and virtue laid low!"
Then he grasps the green girdle and lets go the knot,
Hands it over in haste, and hotly he says:
"Behold there my falsehood, ill hap betide it!
Your cut taught me cowardice, care for my life,
470 And coveting came after, contrary both
To largesse and loyalty belonging to knights.
Now am I faulty and false, that fearful was ever
Of disloyalty and lies, bad luck to them both! and greed.
     I confess, knight, in this place,
475   Most dire is my misdeed;
     Let me gain back your good grace,
     And thereafter I shall take heed."

Then the other laughed aloud, and lightly he said,
"Such harm as I have had, I hold it quite healed.
480 You are so fully confessed, your failings made known,
And bear the plain penance of the point of my blade,
I hold you polished as a pearl, as pure and as bright
As you had lived free of fault since first you were born.
And I give you sir, this girdle that is gold-hemmed
485 And green as my garments, that, Gawain, you may
Be mindful of this meeting when you mingle in throng
With nobles of renown—and known by this token
How it chanced at the Green Chapel, to chivalrous knights.
And you shall in this New Year come yet again
490 And we shall finish out our feast in my fair hall with cheer."

Summarizing

How would you summarize Sir Gawain's response to the Green Knight in lines 459–477?

Critical Reading

1. **Key Ideas and Details (a)** How do Arthur's knights first respond to the Green Knight's challenge? **(b) Analyze:** Why does the Green Knight laugh at their response?

2. **Key Ideas and Details (a)** What does Gawain offer to do? **(b) Analyze:** How does he make his offer seem humble, not boastful?

3. **Key Ideas and Details (a) Interpret:** In lines 464–477, how does Sir Gawain react when he considers his own actions? **(b) Draw Conclusions:** What has Sir Gawain learned from his second encounter with the Green Knight?

4. **Integration of Knowledge and Ideas** Using the example of Sir Gawain, explain whether it is more important to achieve goals or to learn from mistakes.

Cite textual evidence to support your responses.

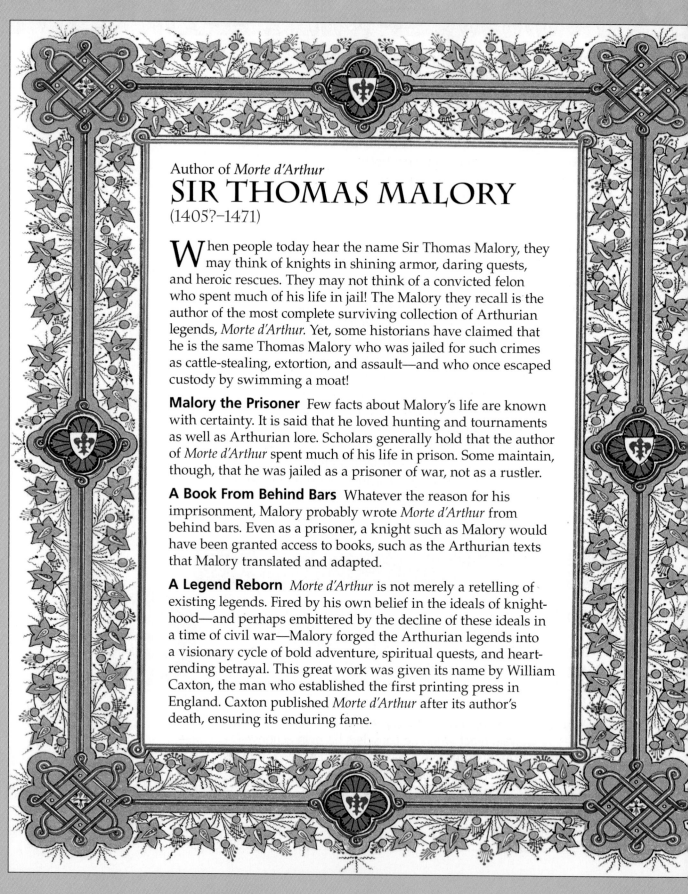

Author of *Morte d'Arthur*

SIR THOMAS MALORY

(1405?–1471)

When people today hear the name Sir Thomas Malory, they may think of knights in shining armor, daring quests, and heroic rescues. They may not think of a convicted felon who spent much of his life in jail! The Malory they recall is the author of the most complete surviving collection of Arthurian legends, *Morte d'Arthur*. Yet, some historians have claimed that he is the same Thomas Malory who was jailed for such crimes as cattle-stealing, extortion, and assault—and who once escaped custody by swimming a moat!

Malory the Prisoner Few facts about Malory's life are known with certainty. It is said that he loved hunting and tournaments as well as Arthurian lore. Scholars generally hold that the author of *Morte d'Arthur* spent much of his life in prison. Some maintain, though, that he was jailed as a prisoner of war, not as a rustler.

A Book From Behind Bars Whatever the reason for his imprisonment, Malory probably wrote *Morte d'Arthur* from behind bars. Even as a prisoner, a knight such as Malory would have been granted access to books, such as the Arthurian texts that Malory translated and adapted.

A Legend Reborn *Morte d'Arthur* is not merely a retelling of existing legends. Fired by his own belief in the ideals of knighthood—and perhaps embittered by the decline of these ideals in a time of civil war—Malory forged the Arthurian legends into a visionary cycle of bold adventure, spiritual quests, and heartrending betrayal. This great work was given its name by William Caxton, the man who established the first printing press in England. Caxton published *Morte d'Arthur* after its author's death, ensuring its enduring fame.

FROM MORTE D'ARTHUR

SIR THOMAS MALORY

This selection begins after King Arthur has traveled to France at the insistence of his nephew, Gawain, to besiege his former friend and knight, Lancelot, for his involvement with Queen Guenevere. However, the king's attempts to punish Lancelot are halfhearted, and he is soon forced to abandon them altogether when he learns that his illegitimate son, Mordred, has seized control of England. Arthur leads his forces back to England, and Mordred attacks them upon their landing. Gawain is killed in the fighting, but before he dies, he manages to send word to Lancelot that Arthur is in need of his assistance.

So upon Trinity Sunday at night King Arthur dreamed a wonderful dream, and in his dream him seemed[1] that he saw upon a chafflet[2] a chair, and the chair was fast to a wheel, and thereupon sat King Arthur in the richest cloth of gold that might be made. And the King thought there was under him, far from him, an hideous deep black water, and therein was all manner of serpents, and worms, and wild beasts, foul and horrible. And suddenly the King thought that the wheel turned upside down, and he fell among the serpents, and every beast took him by a limb. And then the King cried as he lay in his bed, "Help, help!"

And then knights, squires, and yeomen awaked the King, and then he was

◀ **Critical Viewing**

Compare and contrast the details in this picture with those in Malory's account of Arthur's dream. **COMPARE AND CONTRAST**

---

1. **him seemed** It seemed to him.
2. **chafflet** platform.

so amazed that he wist[3] not where he was. And then so he awaked until it was nigh day, and then he fell on slumbering again, not sleeping nor thoroughly waking. So the King seemed[4] verily that there came Sir Gawain unto him with a number of fair ladies with him. So when King Arthur saw him, he said, "Welcome, my sister's son. I weened ye had been dead. And now I see thee on-live, much am I beholden unto Almighty Jesu. Ah, fair nephew and my sister's son, what been these ladies that hither be come with you?"

"Sir," said Sir Gawain, "all these be ladies for whom I have foughten for when I was man living. And all these are those that I did battle for in righteous quarrels, and God hath given them that grace, at their great prayer, because I did battle for them for their right, that they should bring me hither unto you. Thus much hath given me leave God, for to warn you of your death. For and ye fight as tomorn[5] with Sir Mordred, as ye both have assigned, doubt ye not ye must be slain, and the most party of your people on both parties. And for the great grace and goodness that Almighty Jesu hath unto you, and for pity of you and many more other good men there shall be slain, God hath sent me to you of his special grace to give you warning that in no wise ye do battle as tomorn, but that ye take a treaty for a month from today. And proffer you largely[6] you so that tomorn ye put in a delay. For within a month shall come Sir Lancelot with all his noble knights and rescue you worshipfully and slay Sir Mordred and all that ever will hold with him."

Then Sir Gawain and all the ladies vanished. And anon the King called upon his knights, squires, and yeomen, and charged them wightly[7] to fetch his noble lords and wise bishops unto him. And when they were come the King told them of his avision,[8] that Sir Gawain had told him and warned him that, and he fought on the morn, he should be slain. Then the King commanded Sir Lucan the Butler and his brother Sir Bedivere the Bold, with two bishops with them, and charged them in any wise to take a treaty for a month from today with Sir Mordred. "And spare not: proffer him lands and goods as much as ye think reasonable."

So then they departed and came to Sir Mordred where he had a grim host of an hundred thousand, and there they entreated Sir Mordred long time. And at the last Sir Mordred was agreed for to have Cornwall and Kent by King Arthur's days, and after that, all England, after the days of King Arthur.

Then were they condescended[9] that King Arthur and Sir Mordred should meet betwixt both their hosts, and each of them should bring

Summarizing

What are three key points of Sir Gawain's speech in the dream?

Medieval Romance

What characteristic of medieval romance is illustrated by the dream and Arthur's response to it?

Vocabulary

entreated (en trēt′ id) *v.* made an earnest appeal; pleaded

---

3. **wist** knew.
4. **the King seemed** It seemed to the King.
5. **and . . . tomorn** "if you fight tomorrow."
6. **proffer you largely** make generous offers.
7. **wightly** quickly.
8. **avision** dream.
9. **condescended** agreed.

fourteen persons. And so they came with this word unto Arthur. Then said he, "I am glad that this is done," and so he went into the field.

And when King Arthur should depart, he warned all his host that, and they see any sword drawn, "Look ye come on fiercely and slay that traitor Sir Mordred, for I in no wise trust him." In like wise Sir Mordred warned his host that "And ye see any manner of sword drawn, look that ye come on fiercely, and so slay all that ever before you standeth, for in no wise I will not trust for this treaty." And in the same wise said Sir Mordred unto his host, "For I know well my father will be avenged upon me."

And so they met as their pointment[10] was and were agreed and accorded thoroughly. And wine was fetched and they drank together. Right so came an adder out of a little heathbush, and it stung a knight in the foot. And so when the knight felt him so stung, he looked down and saw the adder. And anon he drew his sword to slay the adder, and thought none other harm. And when the host on both parties saw that sword drawn, then they blew beams,[11] trumpets, horns, and shouted grimly. And so both hosts dressed them together. And King Arthur took his horse and said, "Alas, this unhappy day!" and so rode to his party, and Sir Mordred in like wise.

And never since was there never seen a more dolefuller battle in no Christian land, for there was but rushing and riding, lunging and striking; and many a grim word was there spoken of either to other, and many a deadly stroke. But ever King Arthur rode throughout the battle[12] of Sir Mordred many times and did full nobly, as a noble king should do, and at all times he fainted never. And Sir Mordred did his devoir[13] that day and put himself in great peril.

And thus they fought all the long day, and never stinted[14] till the noble knights were laid to the cold earth. And ever they fought still till it was near night, and by then was there an hundred thousand laid dead upon the down. Then was King Arthur wood-wroth[15] out of measure when he saw his people so slain from him. And so he looked about him and could see no more of all his host, and good knights left no more on-live, but two knights: the t'one was Sir Lucan the Butler and the other his brother Sir Bedivere. And yet they were full sore wounded.

"Jesu, mercy," said the King, "where are all my noble knights become? Alas that ever I should see this doleful day! For now," said King Arthur, "I am come to mine end. But would to God," said he,

> And when they were come the King told them of his avision, that Sir Gawain had told him and warned him that, and he fought on the morn, he should be slain.

Vocabulary

peril (per´ əl) *n.* exposure to harm or injury

Comprehension

What causes the two armies to start fighting?

---

10. **pointment** arrangement.
11. **beams** type of trumpet.
12. **battle** battalion.
13. **devoir** (də vwär´) *n.* duty (from the French; obsolete).
14. **stinted** stopped.
15. **wood-wroth** wild with rage.

from Morte d'Arthur **187**

"that I wist now where were that traitor Sir Mordred that has caused all this mischief."

Then King Arthur looked about and was ware where stood Sir Mordred leaning upon his sword among a great heap of dead men.

"Now give me my spear," said King Arthur unto Sir Lucan, "for yonder I have espied the traitor that all this woe hath wrought."

"Sir, let him be," said Sir Lucan, "for he is unhappy. And if ye pass this unhappy day ye shall be right well revenged upon him. And, good lord, remember ye of your night's dream, and what the spirit of Sir Gawain told you tonight, and yet God of his great goodness hath preserved you hitherto. And for God's sake, my lord, leave off by this, for, blessed be God, ye have won the field: for yet we been here three on-live, and with Sir Mordred is not one on-live. And therefore if ye leave off now, this wicked day of destiny is past."

"Now, tide[16] me death, tide me life," said the King, "now I see him yonder alone, he shall never escape mine hands. For at a better avail shall I never have him."

"God speed you well!" said Sir Bedivere.

Then the King got his spear in both his hands and ran toward Sir Mordred, crying and saying, "Traitor, now is thy deathday come!"

And when Sir Mordred saw King Arthur he ran until him with his sword drawn in his hand, and there King Arthur smote Sir Mordred under the shield, with a thrust of his spear, throughout the body more than a fathom. And when Sir Mordred felt that he had his death's wound, he thrust himself with the might that he had up to the burr[17] of King Arthur's spear, and right so he smote his father King Arthur with his sword holden in both his hands, upon the side of the head, that the sword pierced the helmet and the casing of the brain. And therewith Sir Mordred dashed down stark dead to the earth.

And noble King Arthur fell in a swough[18] to the earth, and there he swooned oftentimes, and Sir Lucan and Sir Bedivere ofttimes heaved him up. And so, weakly betwixt them, they led him to a little chapel not far from the sea-side, and when the King was there, him thought him reasonably eased. Then heard they people cry in the field. "Now go thou, Sir Lucan," said the King, "and do me to

---

16. **tide** befall.
17. **burr** hand guard.
18. **swough** forcible movement

◀ **Critical Viewing**

In this picture of the battle between King Arthur and Sir Mordred, which details contribute to the grim mood? Explain. **ANALYZE**

Summarizing

Summarize the events leading to the death of Mordred and the mortal wounding of King Arthur.

Comprehension

What does Sir Lucan urge King Arthur to do?

wit[19] what betokens that noise in the field."

So Sir Lucan departed, for he was grievously wounded in many places. And so as he walked he saw and harkened by the moonlight how that pillagers and robbers were come into the field to pill and to rob many a full noble knight of brooches and bracelets and of many a good ring and many a rich jewel. And who that were not dead all out there they slew them for their harness and their riches. When

▼ **Critical Viewing**

In this picture of Sir Bedivere and the dying Arthur, do you think the boat that Bedivere sees is real or supernatural? Why? **INTERPRET**

19. **me to wit** "let me know."

Sir Lucan understood this work, he came to the King as soon as he might and told him all what he had heard and seen. "Therefore by my read,"[20] said Sir Lucan, "it is best that we bring you to some town."

"I would it were so," said the King, "but I may not stand, my head works so. Ah, Sir Lancelot," said King Arthur, "this day have I sore missed thee. And alas that ever I was against thee, for now have I my death, whereof Sir Gawain me warned in my dream."

Then Sir Lucan took up the King the t'one party[21] and Sir Bedivere the other party; and in the lifting up the King swooned and in the lifting Sir Lucan fell in a swoon that part of his guts fell out of his body, and therewith the noble knight's heart burst. And when the King awoke he beheld Sir Lucan how he lay foaming at the mouth and part of his guts lay at his feet.

"Alas," said the King, "this is to me a full heavy sight to see this noble duke so die for my sake, for he would have helped me that had more need of help than I. Alas that he would not complain him for his heart was so set to help me. Now Jesu have mercy upon his soul."

Then Sir Bedivere wept for the death of his brother.

"Now leave this mourning and weeping gentle knight," said the King, "for all this will not avail me. For wit thou well, and might I live myself, the death of Sir Lucan would grieve me evermore. But my time passeth on fast," said the King. "Therefore," said King Arthur unto Sir Bedivere, "take thou here Excalibur my good sword and go with it to yonder water's side; and when thou comest there I charge thee throw my sword in that water and come again and tell me what thou sawest there."

"My lord," said Sir Bedivere, "your commandment shall be done, and I shall lightly[22] bring you word again."

So Sir Bedivere departed. And by the way he beheld that noble sword, that the pommel and the haft[23] was all precious stones. And then he said to himself, "If I throw this rich sword in the water, thereof shall never come good, but harm and loss." And then Sir Bedivere hid Excalibur

---

20. **read** advice.
21. **party** side.
22. **lightly** quickly.
23. **pommel** . . . **haft** hilt and hand guard.

► **Critical Viewing**

What do you think the three women around the dead or dying Arthur are doing? Explain. **INFER**

under a tree. And so, as soon as he might, he came again unto the King and said he had been at the water and had thrown the sword into the water.

"What saw thou there?" said the King.

"Sir," he said, "I saw nothing but waves and winds."

"That is untruly said of thee," said the King. "And therefore go thou lightly again and do my commandment; as thou art to me loved and dear, spare not, but throw it in."

Then Sir Bedivere returned again and took the sword in his hand. And yet him thought sin and shame to throw away that noble sword. And so eft[24] he hid the sword and returned again and told the King that he had been at the water and done his commandment.

"What sawest thou there?" said the King.

"Sir," he said, "I saw nothing but waters wap and waves wan."[25]

"Ah, traitor unto me and untrue," said King Arthur, "now hast thou betrayed me twice. Who would have weened that thou that has been to me so loved and dear, and thou art named a noble knight, and would betray me for the riches of this sword. But now go again lightly, for thy long tarrying putteth me in great jeopardy of my life, for I have taken cold. And but if thou do now as I bid thee, if ever I may see thee I shall slay thee mine own hands, for thou wouldest for my rich sword see me dead."

Medieval Romance

What element does the appearance of the hand add to the tale?

Then Sir Bedivere departed and went to the sword and lightly took it up, and so he went to the water's side; and there he bound the girdle about the hilts, and threw the sword as far into the water as he might. And there came an arm and an hand above the water and took it and clutched it, and shook it thrice and brandished; and then vanished away the hand with the sword into the water. So Sir Bedivere came again to the King and told him what he saw.

"Alas," said the King, "help me hence, for I dread me I have tarried overlong."

Then Sir Bedivere took the King upon his back and so went with him to that water's side. And when they were at the water's side, even fast[26] by the bank floated a little barge with many fair ladies in it; and among them all was a queen; and all they had black hoods, and all they wept and shrieked when they saw King Arthur.

"Now put me into that barge," said the King; and so he did softly. And there received him three ladies with great mourning, and so they set them down. And in one of their laps King Arthur laid his head, and then the queen said, "Ah, my dear brother, why have ye tarried so long from me? Alas, this wound on your head hath caught overmuch cold." And anon they rowed fromward the land, and Sir Bedivere beheld all those ladies go froward him.

---

24. **eft** again.
25. **waters . . . wan** waters lap and waves grow dark.
26. **fast** close.

Medieval Romance and Legend

Does the description of Sir Bedivere's reaction sound more like a description you might find in a folk tale or in a modern short story? Explain.

Vocabulary

interred (in turd´) *v.* buried in the earth

Summarizing

What happens to Sir Bedivere after Arthur departs on the barge?

Then Sir Bedivere cried and said, "Ah, my lord Arthur, what shall become of me, now ye go from me and leave me here alone among mine enemies?"

"Comfort thyself," said the King, "and do as well as thou mayest, for in me is no trust for to trust in. For I must into the vale of Avilion[27] to heal me of my grievous wound. And if thou hear nevermore of me, pray for my soul."

But ever the queen and ladies wept and shrieked, that it was pity to hear. And as soon as Sir Bedivere had lost sight of the barge he wept and wailed, and so took the forest and went all that night.

And in the morning he was ware, betwixt two bare woods, of a chapel and an hermitage. Then was Sir Bedivere glad, and thither he went, and when he came into the chapel he saw where lay an hermit groveling on all fours, close thereby a tomb was new dug. When the hermit saw Sir Bedivere he knew him well, for he was but little tofore Bishop of Canterbury, that Sir Mordred put to flight.

"Sirs," said Sir Bedivere, "what man is there here interred that you pray so fast for?"

"Fair son," said the hermit. "I wot not verily but by guessing. But this same night, at midnight, here came a number of ladies and brought here a dead corpse and prayed me to inter him. And here they offered an hundred tapers, and gave me a thousand gold coins."

"Alas," said Sir Bedivere, "that was my lord King Arthur, which lieth here buried in this chapel."

Then Sir Bedivere swooned, and when he awoke he prayed the hermit that he might abide with him still, there to live with fasting and prayers:

"For from hence will I never go," said Sir Bedivere, "by my will, but all the days of my life here to pray for my lord Arthur."

"Sir, ye are welcome to me," said the hermit, "for I know you better than ye think that I do: for ye are Sir Bedivere the Bold, and the full noble duke Sir Lucan the Butler was your brother."

Then Sir Bedivere told the hermit all as you have heard tofore, and so he stayed with the hermit that was beforehand Bishop of Canterbury. And there Sir Bedivere put upon him poor clothes, and served the hermit full lowly in fasting and in prayers.

Thus of Arthur I find no more written in books that been authorized, neither more of the very certainty of his death heard I nor read, but thus was he led away in a ship wherein were three queens; that one was King Arthur's sister, Queen Morgan le Fay, the other was the Queen of North Galis, and the third was the Queen of the Waste Lands.

Now more of the death of King Arthur could I never find, but that these ladies brought him to his grave, and such one was interred there which the hermit bare witness that was once Bishop of

---

27. **Avilion** legendary island where Arthur is said to dwell until his return.

Canterbury. But yet the hermit knew not in certain that he was verily the body of King Arthur; for this tale Sir Bedivere, a knight of the Table Round, made it to be written.

Yet some men say in many parts of England that King Arthur is not dead, but carried by the will of our Lord Jesu into another place; and men say that he shall come again, and he shall win the Holy Cross. Yet I will not say that it shall be so, but rather I would say: here in this world he changed his life. And many men say that there is written upon the tomb this:

HIC IACET ARTHURUS, REX QUONDAM, REXQUE FUTURUS[28]

---

28. HIC . . . FUTURUS Here lies Arthur, who was once king and king will be again.

Critical Reading

1. **Key Ideas and Details (a)** What warning does King Arthur receive in his dream? **(b)** How do circumstances frustrate his attempt to heed this warning? **(c) Interpret:** How does this series of events make the ending of the tale seem fated?

2. **Key Ideas and Details (a)** What is the relationship between Mordred and Arthur? **(b) Interpret:** How does the conflict between them emphasize the theme of betrayal in the tale?

3. **Integration of Knowledge and Ideas (a) Compare and Contrast:** How does the description of Sir Lucan's death contrast with the speech in which Arthur bemoans his passing? **(b) Draw Conclusions:** What conclusions can you draw from this contrast about the range of medieval taste in literature?

4. **Integration of Knowledge and Ideas** At the tale's end, rightful authority has been betrayed and may yet return, but it is not here now. What idea of leadership and loyalty in the present does this ending suggest?

5. **Integration of Knowledge and Ideas** Do you think leaders are "Arthurs"—those who should receive perfect obedience—or should people sometimes question their leader's decisions? Explain.

6. **Integration of Knowledge and Ideas** Do the authors of these selections accept or question the code of chivalry? In your response, use at least two of these Essential Question words: *traditional, ideal, conform. [Connecting to the Essential Question: What is the relationship of the writer to tradition?]*

from *Sir Gawain and the Green Knight* •
from *Morte d'Arthur*

Literary Analysis

1. **Key Ideas and Details** You are retelling *Sir Gawain and the Green Knight* to an audience of fifth graders. To prepare, **summarize the main idea or essential message** you would stress and the relevant details you would include.

2. **Craft and Structure (a)** Identify three characteristics of Sir Gawain that make him an ideal hero for a **medieval romance.** Explain each answer. **(b)** Identify a shortcoming of his, and explain what it suggests about the theme of human weakness in medieval romance.

3. **Key Ideas and Details** As Sir Bedivere, summarize for a curious traveler who is visiting your hermitage the events leading up to King Arthur's death.

4. **Craft and Structure (a)** Compare the characterization of Gawain (*Sir Gawain,* lines 459–477) with Malory's description of Bedivere as he reacts to the dying Arthur. Use a graphic organizer like the one shown. **(b)** Explain which author has done more to add literary elements, such as plot twists, descriptions, and characterization.

Common Core State Standards

Writing

3. Write narratives to develop real or imagined experiences or events using effective technique, well-chosen details, and well-structured event sequences. *(p. 197)*

3.d. Use precise words and phrases, telling details, and sensory language to convey a vivid picture of the experiences, events, setting, and/or characters. *(p. 197)*

Language

4.a. Use context as a clue to the meaning of a word or phrase. *(p. 197)*

	Gawain's Reactions	Bedivere's Reactions
What He Says		
What He Does		
What He Feels		

5. **Key Ideas and Details** Based on your reading of these selections, summarize the main idea behind the code of chivalry and note the key ways in which it governed a knight's behavior.

6. **Comparing Literary Works (a)** Which of these elements of romance is least emphasized in *Sir Gawain:* chivalry, a far-off setting, the supernatural, adventure, or love? Explain. **(b)** Which is least emphasized in *Morte d'Arthur?* **(c)** What characteristics of a **legend** do the two selections share?

7. **Analyzing Visual Information** Using your knowledge of Arthurian legend, explain the humor in the cartoon shown here.

Vocabulary Acquisition and Use

Word Analysis: The Word Root -droit-

The word *adroitly*, meaning "with physical or mental skill," is based on the French root -*droit*-, meaning "right." This root meaning reveals a historical bias toward right-handedness. The bias can be seen even more clearly in the Latin root *sinister*, meaning "left," "left-hand," or "unlucky." Answer these questions relating to -*droit*-.

1. Given that the prefix *mal*- means "bad," what might *maladroit* mean?
2. *Gauche* means "socially maladroit" in English. Which of these two words might it mean in French: "left" or "right"?
3. Which would you consider more *adroit*: a smooth left-handed layup in basketball or a clumsy right-handed air ball?
4. Using your knowledge of the root, briefly describe a duel between two knights—Sir Art the Adroit and Sir Mort the Maladroit.

Vocabulary: True or False?

Using your knowledge of the underlined vocabulary words, indicate whether each of the following statements is more likely to be true or false. Then, explain your answer.

1. A giant is lunging toward you, brandishing an ax. You would most likely adjure him to stop.
2. If his first swing was low and close, you might leap adroitly onto a nearby tabletop.
3. In the same moment, you might recognize the extent of your peril.
4. You might then beg the giant to abandon his largesse and take pity on small, helpless you.
5. If you have entreated the giant in just the right way, he might suddenly cease his attack and beg for forgiveness.
6. At that point, you might feel extraordinarily interred.

Writing to Sources

Narrative Text As Sir Gawain approaches the Green Chapel, he reacts by expressing himself in an interior monologue—a device in which a character speaks only to himself or herself, revealing thoughts, feelings, and personality traits. Write an **interior monologue** in which Gawain reacts to another event in the story. In your monologue, create a distinctive voice for Gawain. Have him react to unfolding events in a *specific place*.

Prewriting List characteristics of Gawain, and jot down notes on the dramatic situation he is confronting. What would he think about the situation? How would he feel?

Drafting Writing in the first person, have Gawain "discuss" the situation with himself and so reveal both the events and the *significance of the events* to which he reacts. Make sure that key details explaining the situation emerge early. Refer to prewriting notes to ensure that you convey Gawain's character.

> **Model: Using Reactions to Develop a Narrative**
> By St. Peter's sail, will no one answer this strange knight's challenge? I would, forsooth, were it not presumptuous-seeming and—what! Arthur himself is answering!

> When Gawain interrupts himself to remark on a new disturbance, the reader sees the situation through the character's reactions.

Revising Star sections of your draft in which Gawain's feelings are especially strong. Review these passages, replacing dull phrases with vivid expressions of his personality or reactions.

Primary Sources

Letters
Letters of
Margaret Paston

Ballads
Four Folk
Ballads

**Common Core**
State Standards

Reading Informational Text
7. Integrate and evaluate multiple sources of information presented in different media or formats as well as in words in order to address a question or solve a problem.

About the Text Forms

A **letter** is a written communication to a person or group. In the centuries before telephones and e-mail, letters were a basic means of sharing information over a distance. Carried on foot, by horse, or by ship, letters were written for business and diplomatic reasons as well as personal ones. Today, letters from earlier eras are primary sources of information that shed light on the events, personalities, and daily life of times past.

During the Middle Ages, most people could neither read nor write. One of the ways in which they transmitted information was in story poems set to music, called **ballads.** Telling of sensational events and everyday calamities, **folk ballads** were anonymously composed and passed orally from singer to singer among the common folk. They often use four-line *stanzas,* in which only the second and fourth lines rhyme, and contain *dialogue* and repeated lines or phrases called **refrains.** Today, folk ballads of old are still being sung. As primary sources, they provide valuable glimpses into the lives and attitudes of ordinary people.

As you prepare to read these texts, consider questions you have about English life in the late Middle Ages. Look for answers among the details these primary sources provide.

Preparing to Read Complex Texts

The scholars who prepare primary sources for publication often include text aids to help you understand these sources from a different era. You can improve your comprehension of primary sources by **analyzing, evaluating, and applying information from text features.** Such features may include *introductory and side notes* that give background or *footnotes* that clarify unfamiliar terms or words in *dialect,* the variety of a language spoken by people in a particular region or group.

 How does literature **shape or** reflect *society?*

Letters and ballads can both reflect and influence their times. As you read, consider how passages in Margaret Paston's letters show her responding to and trying to influence events. Also consider how ballads hint at certain *assumptions* about love and death and speculate how people in medieval times may have reacted to those assumptions.

Note-Taking Guide

Primary-source documents are a rich source of information for researchers. As you read these documents, use a note-taking guide like the one shown to organize relevant and accurate information.

1 Type of Document (check one)
☐ Newspaper ☐ Letter ☐ Diary ☐ Map ☐ Government Document
☐ Advertisement ☐ Speech ☐ Other (specify): _____

2 Date(s) or Period Composed _____

3 Author (if known) _____
Author's Position (if known) _____

4 Intended Audience _____

5 Purpose and Message
  a Why was this document composed? (check the main purpose)
  ☐ to entertain ☐ to inform ☐ to persuade ☐ to describe ☐ to reflect
  b Which word or words best describe the tone? ☐personal
  ☐ formal ☐ humorous ☐ dramatic ☐ emotional ☐ unsentimental
  c Summarize the message or main events in a sentence or two.

  _____

  _____

  d What does this document show about life in the time and place in which it was composed?

  _____

  _____

Using Text Features
Features such as introductory notes, side notes, and footnotes may clarify details about time and place. As you read, analyze and apply information from text features to better understand the documents.

This guide was adapted from the **U.S. National Archives** document analysis worksheet.

Vocabulary

aldermen (ôl´ dər mən) *n.* chief officers in a shire, or county (p. 202)

succor (suk´ ər) *v.* help; aid; relieve (p. 202)

certify (sʉrt´ ə fī´) *v.* declare a thing true or accurate; verify; attest (p. 202)

remnant (rem´ nənt) *n.* what is left over; remainder (p. 202)

ransacked (ran´ sakt´) *v.* searched through to find goods to rob; looted (p. 203)

asunder (ə sun´ dər) *adv.* into parts or pieces (p. 203)

assault (ə sôlt´) *v.* violently attack (p. 203)

bar (bär) *n.* one of the vertical lines dividing written music into equal sections called measures (p. 205)

measure (mezh´ ər) *n.* a section of written music between two vertical lines called bars (p. 205)

melody (mel´ ə dē) *n.* a sequence of single tones that together create a tune or song (p. 205)

THE STORY BEHIND THE DOCUMENTS

Dating from 1477, this letter from the Paston collection may be the first Valentine message in English. Margery Brews writes to her fiancé, John Paston, "Be my olde Valentine."

Margaret Paston (1423–1484) was born Margaret Mautby in the eastern English county of Norfolk. In about 1442 she married John Paston, a Norfolk lawyer and landowner. The Pastons had only recently acquired their wealth, however, and had to fight hard to keep it. During John's frequent visits to London to work on legal matters, it fell to his wife to run the estates, settle land disputes, and defend Paston manors against hostile raids.

Because they were often separated, Margaret and John exchanged many letters discussing family matters, local politics, and the everyday business of running an estate. Their letters are part of the more than one thousand Paston family documents originally preserved as evidence for lawsuits. Today these documents are a treasure trove of information about life in fifteenth-century England.

In the fifteenth century, when the weak rule of Henry VI plunged England into chaos, many families like the Pastons were able to rise from poverty, taking properties for which their legal claim was not firm. In one instance, the powerful Duke of Suffolk challenged the Pastons' claim to the manor of Hellesdon and bribed the mayor of the city of Norwich (nôr´ ij) to help force the Pastons out. Although Margaret Paston, with a garrison of sixty warriors, repelled the first attacks, the duke eventually seized and looted Hellesdon. In the first two letters presented here, Margaret writes to her husband with news of the duke's success. In the third letter, composed after her husband's death, she writes to her son Sir John Paston about defending another Paston property called Caister.

Unlike Margaret and John Paston, most people in the fifteenth century could not write or read. One way the common folk passed along sensational news and entertaining stories was in brief storytelling poems set to music called folk ballads.

The first English folk ballads probably go back to the twelfth century, but many more date to the Pastons' era of the fifteenth. Anonymously composed and transmitted orally from singer to singer, folk ballads exist in many different versions. The four presented here are versions from the border area between England and Scotland and use words and pronunciations in Scots dialect.

In 1765, Bishop Thomas Percy collected and published folk ballads in a book called *Reliques of Ancient English Poetry.* As other collections followed, people began to appreciate the literary value of folk ballads and the fascinating glimpses they offered of daily life and attitudes among people in times past.

▶ **Critical Viewing** The Paston manor homes were often attacked. Judging from this photograph of a manor house, how easy would it have been to defend such a building? Explain. **SPECULATE**

Letters of
MARGARET PASTON

Margaret Paston

Primary Sources

Letters What does this letter show about the loyalties of others to a newly wealthy family like the Pastons?

Vocabulary

aldermen (ôl′ dər mən) *n.* chief officers in a shire, or county

succor (suk′ ər) *v.* help; aid; relieve

certify (surt′ ə fī′) *v.* declare a thing true or accurate; verify; attest

remnant (rem′ nənt) *n.* what is left over; remainder

Margaret Paston to John Paston
17 October 1465
Norwich

. . . The Duke came to Norwich on Tuesday at 10 o'clock with some 500 men. And he sent for the mayor and aldermen with the Sheriffs, desiring them in the King's name that they should make enquiry of the constables of every ward in the City as to what men had gone to help or succor your men at any time during these gatherings and, if they could find any, that they should take and arrest and correct them, and certify to him the names by 8 o'clock on Wednesday. Which the Mayor did and will do anything that he may for him and his men. . . .

I am told that the old Lady [the Dowager Duchess] and the Duke are fiercely set against us on the information of Harleston, the bailiff of Costessey . . . and such other false shrews which would have this matter carried through for their own pleasure. . . . And as for Sir John Heveningham, Sir John Wingfield and other worshipful men, they are but made their doggebolds [lackeys], which I suppose will cause their disworship hereafter. I spoke with Sir John Heveningham and informed him of the truth of the matter and of all our demeaning at Drayton, and he said he would that all things were well, and that he would inform my Lord what I told him, but that Harleston had all the influence with the Duke here, and at this time he was advised by him and Dr. Aleyn.

The lodge and the remnant of your place was beaten down on Tuesday and Wednesday and the Duke rode on Wednesday to Drayton and so forth to Costessey while the lodge at Hellesdon was being beaten down. And this night at midnight Thomas Slyforth . . . and others had a cart and fetched away feather-beds and all our stuff that was left at the parson's and Thomas Waters' house to be kept. . . . I pray you send me word how I shall act—whether you wish that I abide at Caister or come to you at London. . . .

Margaret Paston to John Paston
27 October 1465
Norwich

. . . Please you to know that I was at Hellesdon on Thursday last and saw the place there, and, in good faith, nobody would believe how foul and horrible it appears unless they saw it. There come many people daily to wonder at it, both from Norwich and many other places, and they speak of it with shame. The Duke would have been a £1000 better off if it had not happened, and you have the more good will of the people because it was so foully done. They made your tenants of Hellesdon and Drayton, with others, break down the walls of both the place and the lodge—God knows full much against their wills, but they dare not refuse for fear. I have spoken with your tenants of Hellesdon and Drayton and comforted them as well as I can. The Duke's men ransacked the church and bore away all the goods that were left there, both of ours and of the tenants, and even stood upon the high altar and ransacked the images and took away those that they could find, and put the parson out of the church till they had done, and ransacked every man's house in the town five or six times. . . . As for lead, brass, pewter, iron, doors, gates and other stuff of the house, men from Costessey and Cawston have it, and what they might not carry away they have hewn asunder in the most spiteful manner. . . .

At the reverence of God, if any worshipful and profitable settlement may be made in your matters, do not forsake it, to avoid our trouble and great costs and charges that we may have and that may grow hereafter. . . .

⟩◆⟨

The following letter was sent to Sir John Paston, Margaret's knighted son. Caister, a castle with many manors and estates, had been willed to the Paston family by Sir John Fastolf, for whom John Paston worked as financial advisor. There followed years of legal wrangles during which the Pastons faced numerous challenges to the will. Because her husband had died the year before, Margaret turned to her son Sir John for help defending Caister. Sir John sent his younger brother, also named John, to protect the castle. John failed, however, surrendering the castle after his protector, King Edward IV, was captured during the Wars of the Roses.

Margaret Paston to Sir John Paston
11 July 1467
Norwich

. . . Also this day was brought me word from Caister that Rising of Fritton had heard in divers places in Suffolk that Fastolf of Cowhawe gathers all the strength he may and intends to assault Caister and to enter there if he may, insomuch that it

---

Vocabulary

ransacked (ran´ sakt´) *v.* searched through to find goods to rob; looted

asunder (ə sun´ dər) *adv.* into parts or pieces

assault (ə sôlt´) *v.* violently attack

Text Features

What does this note clarify about the social position of the Pastons and the dangers they faced?

Comprehension

What has the Duke done against the Pastons?

is said that he has five score men ready and daily sends spies to know what men guard the place. By whose power or favor or support he will do this I know not, but you know well that I have been afraid there before this time, when I had other comfort than I had now: I cannot guide nor rule soldiers well and they set not by [do not respect] a woman as they should by a man. Therefore I would that you should send home your brothers or else Daubeney to take control and to bring in such men as are necessary for the safeguard of the place. . . . And I have been about my livelode to set a rule therein, as I have written to you, which is not yet all performed after my desire, and I would not go to Caister till I had done. I do not want to spend more days near thereabouts, if I can avoid it; so make sure that you send someone home to keep the place and when I have finished what I have begun I shall arrange to go there if it will do any good—otherwise I had rather not be there. . . .

. . . I marvel greatly that you send me no word how you do, for your enemies begin to grow right bold and that puts your friends in fear and doubt. Therefore arrange that they may have some comfort, so that they be not discouraged, for if we lose our friends, it will be hard in this troublous world to get them again . . .

Critical Reading

Cite textual evidence to support your responses.

1. **Key Ideas and Details (a)** What does the duke force the Pastons' tenants to do? **(b) Interpret:** How does Margaret Paston feel about the duke's actions, and how does she expect the tenants to feel?

2. **Craft and Structure (a) Analyze:** Cite examples of emotional appeals and logical reasons that Margaret Paston uses in requesting help from her husband and son. **(b) Draw Conclusions:** What sort of relationship does she have with her husband and son?

3. **Integration of Knowledge and Ideas (a) Generalize:** What do the letters suggest to you about life in the Middle Ages? **(b) Evaluate:** What do you think is the most important difference, positive or negative, between life then and today? Why?

TWA CORBIES

BACKGROUND *During the Middle Ages, death before the age of thirty-five was the norm. The stark facts of life and death promoted the unsentimental outlook of medieval folk ballads.*

As I was walking all alane,
I heard twa corbies[1] making a mane.[2]
The tane unto the tither did say,
"Whar sall we gang and dine the day?"

5 "In behint yon auld fail dyke,[3]
I wot[4] there lies a new-slain knight;
And naebody kens[5] that he lies there
But his hawk, his hound, and his lady fair.

"His hound is to the hunting gane,
10 His hawk to fetch the wild-fowl hame,
His lady's ta'en anither mate,
So we may mak our dinner sweet.

"Ye'll sit on his white hause-bane,[6]
And I'll pike out his bonny blue e'en;[7]
15 Wi' ae lock o' his gowden hair
We'll theek[8] our nest when it grows bare.

"Mony a one for him maks mane,
But nane sall ken whar he is gane.
O'er his white banes, when they are bare,
20 The wind sall blaw for evermair."

---

1. **twa corbies** two ravens.
2. **mane** moan.
3. **fail dyke** bank of earth.
4. **wot** know.
5. **kens** knows.
6. **hause-bane** neck-bone.
7. **e'en** eyes.
8. **theek** thatch.

LITERATURE IN CONTEXT

Cultural Connection
Folk Ballads

Following are some terms that will help you to understand the musical basis of folk ballads:

bar (bär) *n.* one of the vertical lines dividing written music into equal sections called measures

measure (mezh´ ər) *n.* a section of written music between two vertical lines called bars

melody (mel´ ə dē) *n.* a sequence of single tones that together create a tune or song

A typical ballad tune is made up of sixteen bars of music, with a rhythm that is mostly two beats per measure. The tune lasts as long as each ballad stanza, so the singer repeats it each time he or she begins a new stanza.

Connect to the Literature

Look at the stanzas in these ballads. In what way is the ballad stanza both a unit of meaning and a unit of music?

LORD RANDALL

"O where hae ye been, Lord Randall, my son?
O where hae ye been, my handsome young man?"
"I hae been to the wild wood; mother, make my bed soon,
For I'm weary wi' hunting, and fain[1] wald[2] lie down."

5 "Where gat ye your dinner, Lord Randall, my son?
Where gat ye your dinner, my handsome young man?"
"I dined wi' my true-love; mother, make my bed soon,
For I'm weary wi' hunting, and fain wald lie down."

"What gat ye to your dinner, Lord Randall, my son?
10 What gat ye to your dinner, my handsome young man?"
"I gat eels boil'd in broo;[3] mother, make my bed soon,
For I'm weary wi' hunting, and fain wald lie down."

"What became of your bloodhounds, Lord Randall, my son?
What became of your bloodhounds, my handsome young man?"
15 "O they swell'd and they died; mother, make my bed soon,
For I'm weary wi' hunting, and fain wald lie down."

"O I fear ye are poison'd, Lord Randall, my son!
O I fear ye are poison'd, my handsome young man!"
"O yes! I am poison'd; mother, make my bed soon,
20 For I'm sick at the heart, and I fain wald lie down."

1. **fain** gladly.
2. **wald** would.
3. **broo** broth.

Critical Reading

1. **Key Ideas and Details (a)** Besides the two corbies, or ravens, who are the only ones that know where the new-slain knight lies? **(b) Infer:** Who or what do you think has caused the knight's death? Why?

2. **Craft and Structure (a) Infer:** How would you describe the corbies' tone in discussing the knight's death? **(b) Interpret:** What does the tone suggest about the medieval attitude toward death?

3. **Integration of Knowledge and Ideas (a) Analyze Cause and Effect:** Do you think Lord Randall was poisoned, or do you think he is simply sick at heart? Cite details to support your analysis. **(b) Draw Conclusions:** What view of love does "Lord Randall" express?

GET UP AND BAR THE DOOR

It fell about the Martinmas time,[1]
    And a gay time it was then,
When our goodwife got puddings to make,
    She's boild them in the pan.

5 The wind sae cauld blew south and north.
    And blew into the floor;
Quoth our goodman to our goodwife,
    "Gae out and bar the door."

"My hand is in my hussyfskap,[2]
10   Goodman, as ye may see;
An it should nae be barrd this hundred year,
    It's no be barrd for me."[3]

They made a paction[4] tween them twa.
    They made it firm and sure.
15 That the first word whaeer shoud speak,
    Shoud rise and bar the door.

Then by there came two gentlemen,
    At twelve o'clock at night,
And they could neither see house nor hall,
20   Nor coal nor candlelight.

"Now whether is this a rich man's house,
    Or whether it is a poor?"
But neer a word wad ane o' them[5] speak,
    For barring of the door.

25 And first they[6] ate the white puddings,
    And then they ate the black:

▲ **Primary Source: Art**
What does this painting tell you about domestic life in medieval times? **[Infer]**

Comprehension
What is it that neither the husband nor the wife wants to do?

---

1. **Martinmas time** November 11.
2. **hussyfskap** household duties.
3. **An it should . . . me** "If it has to be barred by me, then it will not be barred in a hundred years."
4. **paction** agreement.
5. **them** the man and his wife.
6. **they** the strangers.

Text Features

How do the footnotes for this ballad help explain or clarify what occurs?

Tho muckle[7] thought the goodwife to hersel,
    Yet neer a word she spake.

Then said the one unto the other,
30   "Here, man, take ye my knife;
Do ye tak aff the auld man's beard,
    And I'll kiss the goodwife."

"But there's nae water in the house,
    And what shall we do than?"
35 "What ails ye at the pudding broo,[8]
    That boils into[9] the pan?"

O up then started our goodman,
    An angry man was he:
"Will ye kiss my wife before my een,
40   And scad[10] me wi pudding bree?"[11]

Then up and started our goodwife,
    Gied three skips on the floor:
"Goodman, you've spoken the foremost word;
    Get up and bar the door."

---

7. muckle much.
8. What . . . broo "What's the matter with pudding water?"
9. into in.
10. scad scald.
11. bree broth.

Critical Reading

Cite textual evidence to support your responses.

1. **Key Ideas and Details (a)** What agreement do the goodman and his wife make? **(b) Analyze:** What situation and/or character traits prompt them to make this agreement?

2. **Key Ideas and Details (a) Interpret:** To what class of society do the goodman and his wife belong? Cite details to support your answer. **(b) Draw Conclusions:** What does the strangers' treatment of them suggest about the dangers people of this class faced in medieval times?

3. **Key Ideas and Details (a) Summarize:** What dilemma does the couple face when the strangers arrive? **(b) Analyze:** In what way does the wife "win"? In what way do neither she nor her husband win? **(c) Interpret:** What point about stubbornness does the ballad make?

BARBARA ALLAN

It was in and about the Martinmas time,[1]
  When the green leaves were a-fallin';
That Sir John Graeme in the West Country
  Fell in love with Barbara Allan.

5 He sent his man down through the town
  To the place where she was dwellin':
"O haste and come to my master dear,
  Gin[2] ye be Barbara Allan."

O slowly, slowly rase[3] she up,
10 To the place where he was lyin',
And when she drew the curtain by:
  "Young man, I think you're dyin'."

"O it's I'm sick, and very, very sick,
  And 'tis a' for Barbara Allan."
15 "O the better for me ye sal[4] never be,
  Though your heart's blood were a-spillin'.

"O dinna ye mind,[5] young man," said she,
  "When ye the cups were fillin',
That ye made the healths gae round and round,
20 And slighted Barbara Allan?"

He turned his face unto the wall,
  And death with him was dealin':
"Adieu, adieu, my dear friends all,
  And be kind to Barbara Allan.

---

1. **Martinmas time** November 11.
2. **Gin** if.
3. **rase** rose.
4. **sal** shall.
5. **dinna ye mind** don't you remember.

Primary Sources
Folk Ballads What does the phrase "his man" tell you about the society of the time?

Comprehension
Why does Sir John Graeme send his man to Barbara Allan?

25 And slowly, slowly rase she up,
    And slowly, slowly left him;
And sighing said she could not stay,
    Since death of life had reft[6] him.

She had not gane a mile but twa,[7]
30   When she heard the dead-bell knellin',
And every jow[8] that the dead-bell ga'ed[9]
    It cried, "Woe to Barbara Allan!"

"O mother, mother, make my bed,
    O make it soft and narrow:
35 Since my love died for me today,
    I'll die for him tomorrow."

Primary Sources
Folk Ballad Who speaks the dialogue in the last stanza? What general purpose does all the dialogue in the ballad serve?

---

6. reft deprived.
7. not . . . twa gone but two miles.
8. jow stroke.
9. ga'ed made.

Critical Reading

Cite textual evidence to support your responses.

1. **Key Ideas and Details (a)** What reason does Sir John give for his ailment? **(b)** What reason does Barbara Allan give for acting unconcerned about his plight? **(c) Interpret:** What is another reason she might put on a show of indifference?

2. **Key Ideas and Details Interpret:** Do you think Barbara Allan loved Sir John before her visit, or do you think the knowledge that he is dying inspires her love? Explain.

3. **Integration of Knowledge and Ideas (a) Summarize:** Sum up Barbara Allan's realization and feelings in the final stanza. **(b) Interpret:** What does the ballad suggest is the ultimate expression of love? **(c) Evaluate:** Do you agree with this view? Why or why not?

4. **Integration of Knowledge and Ideas (a) Analyze:** What chain of causes and effects leads to the outcome of the story in this ballad? **(b) Infer:** What do these events suggest about attitudes toward love among the common folk who listened to ballads? Explain.

The Sound of
Medieval Music

Nobody knows for sure when the old English and Scottish folk ballads were first composed, who their authors were, or how they were performed. Based on versions in circulation today, we can guess that the narratives were sung and that the singers probably accompanied themselves on string instruments such as harps or lutes. Musicians playing woodwinds similar to recorders and flutes, as well as percussion instruments like the tabor, may have joined in. A bagpiper might even have contributed an interlude between verses.

Medieval musicians tuned their instruments differently from the way most Western musicians do today, and were probably influenced by Middle Eastern scales. The Islamic rule of the Iberian Peninsula (711–1492) and the Crusades (1095–1291) had introduced Europeans to Arabic vocal and instrumental traditions. During the Middle Ages, North African and Middle Eastern tonalities probably colored much of the music in Europe and the British Isles.

CONNECT TO THE LITERATURE

How would music enhance or detract from the stories in these ballads? Explain.

▲ Medieval musicians often combined string instruments with drums, horns, and bagpipes.

BAGPIPES
In the Middle Ages, bagpipes were played throughout Britain and Scotland as well as India and North Africa. With its loud, plaintive sound, it was the perfect instrument for the outdoors.

PIPE and TABOR
The pipe and tabor could be played by one person, who beat the tabor with one hand, while playing the pipe with the other. The tabor, a simple drum, is still used in the British Isles.

HARP
The word *harp* comes from Anglo-Saxon and Old German and originally meant, "to pluck." Triangular harps were used in Scotland as far back as the 9th century. Strings were made of twisted animal gut, horsehair, or even silk.

LUTE and PLECTRUM
The European lute was the predecessor to the modern guitar. It was an offspring of the oud, a stringed instrument introduced into Spain by the Arabs, during Islamic rule (711–1492). Like the oud, the early medieval lute was plucked with a pencil-thin tool called a plectrum.

Letters • Ballads

Comparing Primary Sources

 **Common Core
State Standards**

Refer to your Note-Taking Guide to complete these questions.

1. How are the perspectives on death and violence expressed in Paston's letters and in the ballads similar and different? Cite specific details to support your analysis.

2. Using a Venn diagram like this one, compare and contrast the letters and ballads with regard to their forms, audiences, and purposes.

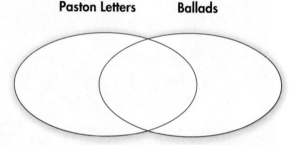

Paston Letters   Ballads

3. (a) Cite two questions about life in England during the Middle Ages that these texts can help you answer. Explain. **(b)** Which texts do you find more informative, and in what ways?

Vocabulary Acquisition and Use

New Vocabulary Answer each question. Then, explain how your understanding of the italicized vocabulary word helped you answer.

1. Who will *succor* the poor and needy, a kind person or a cruel one?

2. Who will *assault* a village, an invading army or a tired traveler?

3. Would a *remnant* of a meat loaf be the first piece or the last?

4. Which can more easily be torn *asunder*, a stone or a piece of paper?

Content-Area Vocabulary Use your knowledge of the italicized vocabulary words to decide whether each statement is true or false. Explain your answers.

1. A *measure* generally contains just one note.

2. To teach someone a song, you might hum the *melody*.

3. The *bar* tells you how quickly or slowly to play a piece of music.

4. *Aldermen* generally had influence in their communities.

5. When you *certify* something, you challenge it in court.

Etymology Study The word *ransacked*, from the Old Norse *rann*, meaning "house," and *saka*, meaning "seek," comes from the common medieval practice of attacking a place in search of valuables. A synonym of *ransacked* often used today is *looted*. Use a print or an online thesaurus to find two more synonyms for this word.

Writing
7. Conduct short as well as more sustained research projects to answer a question or solve a problem; narrow or broaden the inquiry when appropriate; synthesize multiple sources on the subject, demonstrating understanding of the subject under investigation.

8. Gather relevant information from multiple authoritative print and digital sources, using advanced searches effectively; assess the strengths and limitations of each source in terms of the task, purpose, and audience; integrate information into the text selectively to maintain the flow of ideas, avoiding plagiarism and overreliance on any one source and following a standard format for citation.

Language
6. Acquire and use accurately general academic and domain-specific words and phrases, sufficient for reading, writing, speaking, and listening at the college and career readiness level; demonstrate independence in gathering vocabulary knowledge when considering a word or phrase important to comprehension or expression.

Research Task

Topic: The Manor in Medieval England

Margaret Paston and her husband owned several significant properties, including two manor houses—the Hellesdon Manor and the Manor at Gresham. A manor was more than just a house. Under Feudalism, it was the center—both physical and symbolic—of the related economic system called Manorialism.

Assignment: With a group, write a **research report** on the English manor and the social order it represented. Discuss how key architectural elements reflect economic and legal relationships between the occupants of the manor and the people who lived in the surrounding area. Consider the following items:

- The relationship of the manor house to the surrounding land
- Activities, such as legal proceedings, that took place in a manor home
- The typical layout of the manor home, including the great hall, and the uses of these features
- Changes in manor homes as Feudalism waned in England

Formulate your research plan. In a group, brainstorm to formulate research questions about English manors and Manorialism. Then, discuss and decide on a plan to answer those questions.

Gather sources. Use library and computer searches to locate and explore a full range of relevant sources that answer the research questions. Organize the information into categories that address specific aspects of your topic. For all sources you consult, keep records that include the information you will need to construct thorough citations.

Synthesize information. When you synthesize information, you can decide which ideas and evidence to use and which to discard, arriving at the best response to your research question. A graphic organizer can clarify information and help you to compare and contrast it. For example, by listing specific features of a typical manor, you can better understand the picture of medieval life they convey.

RESEARCH TIP

There are many online sites dealing with specific English manor homes. You may want to include graphics from these sites and cite them in your report.

Model: Using a Chart to Synthesize Information

Item	Description	Picture of Culture It Conveys

Organize and present your ideas. Write your report on the English manor and Manorialism. Account for both the physical features of these structures as well as the social, legal, and economic system they represent. Include specific examples, and include graphic elements that will help your readers understand your ideas and evidence. Be sure to cite all sources, both print and electronic, accurately.

Use a checklist like the one shown to evaluate your work.

Research Checklist

- ☐ Have I answered the research questions?
- ☐ Have I organized information to support my central ideas?
- ☐ Have I accurately and thoroughly cited my sources?
- ☐ Have I presented my reasons clearly?

Write a Narrative

**Common Core
State Standards**

Writing

3. Write narratives to develop real or imagined experiences or events using effective technique, well-chosen details, and well-structured event sequences.

3.d. Use telling details to convey a vivid picture of the experiences, events, setting, and/or characters.

5. Develop and strengthen writing as needed by planning, focusing on addressing what is most significant for a specific purpose and audience.

Autobiographical Narrative The best stories are often true—they tell about real events in a writer's life. From memories of childhood to funny anecdotes to dramatic encounters, true stories touch and inspire us. Such stories are called **autobiographical narratives.** Follow the steps outlined in this workshop to write your own autobiographical narrative.

Assignment Write an autobiographical narrative about an event in your life that marked a significant change or led to an important insight.

What to Include Your autobiographical narrative should include the following elements:

- Characters, with a focus on one main character—you, the writer
- A setting with specifically located scenes and incidents and with *concrete sensory details* such as sights, sounds, and smells
- A *sequence of events* that forms a plot and whose *significance* is clear
- Conflict between characters or between a character and another force
- Insights that you gained from the experience
- Provide a conclusion that follows from and reflects on what is experienced, observed, or resolved over the course of the narrative.

To preview the criteria on which your autobiographical narrative may be assessed, see the rubric on page 221.

Focus on Research

Research can enrich autobiographical narratives by contributing the following elements:

- precise information to enhance descriptions
- accurate details about the setting and the historical context
- a factual basis to upon which to broaden your narrative beyond your personal story

Be sure to note all sources you use in your research, and credit appropriately. Refer to the Conducting Research pages in the Introductory Unit (pp. lxxii–lxxvii) as well as the Citing Sources and Preparing Manuscript pages in the Resource section for information on citation.

Prewriting and Planning

Choosing Your Topic

To choose an event for your essay, use one of these strategies:

- **Listing** Create a chart with three columns, labeled *People*, *Places*, and *Events*. List memorable parts of your life under each column. Then, look for connections among the items you listed. When you find a connection, circle the items and draw an arrow to link them. Review your connections for narrative ideas.

- **Using Sentence Starters** Complete these sentences to generate ideas:

  - The funniest thing happened when _____.
  - My favorite holiday was _____.
  - My strongest memory from childhood is _____.

Narrowing Your Topic

Find your insight. Make your topic more specific by focusing on one idea you want to convey. Narrow a general topic to focus on one key event that highlights a meaningful insight.

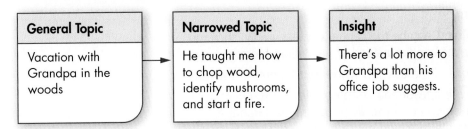

General Topic	Narrowed Topic	Insight
Vacation with Grandpa in the woods	He taught me how to chop wood, identify mushrooms, and start a fire.	There's a lot more to Grandpa than his office job suggests.

Gathering Details

Look for concrete details. List specific details you will include. Consider sensory details that convey the sights, sounds, and smells of the scenes. Look for details about characters' actions, movements, thoughts, words, and gestures. As you collect details, think about where each one will fit best in your narrative. Estimate about how much space and emphasis you will give to specific elements. The plan shown works for many narratives.

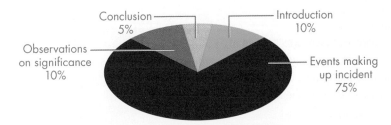

Conclusion 5%
Introduction 10%
Observations on significance 10%
Events making up incident 75%

Drafting

ⓒ Common Core State Standards

Writing

3.b. Use narrative techniques, such as dialogue, pacing, description, reflection, and multiple plot lines, to develop experiences, events, and/or characters.

3.e. Provide a conclusion that follows from and reflects on what is experienced, observed, or resolved over the course of the narrative.

Shaping Your Writing

Start out strong. Catch your readers' interest with a strong opening. Consider the options in this chart.

Opening Strategy	Example
Introduce a Character: A description of a character is effective if your narrative centers on a relationship.	Bob doesn't say much, no matter what may be going on, but when you see that gleam in his eye, you know you're in trouble.
Focus on Setting: This approach works well if time and place are critical elements.	The wind whistled through the cracks in the attic window.
Begin with Dialogue: An intriguing line of dialogue can quickly pull readers in.	"I said, did anybody leave this package on the counter?"

Pace your writing. Make sure you do not get bogged down in insignificant details. Establish background information quickly and then set your main incident in motion.

Providing Elaboration

Highlight a striking conflict. Describe the central conflict vividly, showing your readers the reason for the conflict instead of just telling them.

Flat: Grandpa wanted me to chop wood, but I didn't know how.

Vivid: "Henry, do me a favor and chop up a few logs, OK?" I nodded and hurried out to the woodpile so Grandpa wouldn't see the terror on my face. What did I know about chopping wood? The ax taunted me. Just thinking about swinging it made my toes hurt because I knew the ax was way more likely to land on my foot than the log.

End well. Devise an interesting closing. You might put the finishing touch on your story or leave readers hoping for more. Consider ending with an epilogue about what happened after the incident, a summary of your insights, or an unanswered question related to the conflict.

Model: Devising a Good Closing

I was sweating and my muscles ached, but there was my pile of chopped-up logs. I felt proud, as if this two-foot-high stack of wood was a house I had built with my own hands. The discarded splinters seemed like my own fears, cast away in the act of chopping.

The writer ends on a note of accomplishment, providing an insight into the experience.

Writers on Writing

Burton Raffel On Shaping a Narrative

Burton Raffel is the author of the introduction to *Beowulf* (p. 36).

This is an excerpt from an autobiographical piece I wrote about thirty years ago. It tries to re-create, in adult language, some of those well-rubbed but rarely verbalized feelings that all small children surely have. Children are not simply the "small adults" that our civilization used to think they were. Nor is childhood merely another, though different, route to the same landing place.

"I realized that I was inventing a reality that wasn't real."

—*Burton Raffel*

from *Out in the Backyard of My Mind*

When I think of myself, as a small child, I remember, first, the sensation of offensive clothing—floppy clothing. Clothing buttoned and snapped and fastened in places I could not reach and affixed for reasons I knew I would not approve of if I could have understood what they were. I remember my shirts strapped to my back, somehow; and I remember ghastly knickers of worn corduroy, hanging baggy at the knees; and floppy coats that had belonged to cousins and uncles unseen, handed down, a little shabbier and floppier each time, until they came to me. I remember the faintly dank smell of cheap wool (mixed with what?), and especially its coarse, hairy feel— and the good, powdery smell and full softness of a big brown automobile lap robe, always and still called "the horse blanket." Skin was no better: if I was ever without clothing, in those days, I do not remember it, nor remember any pleasure from it. And I can remember hiding from my nakedness. Not just the way all little children do, sometimes, but compulsively, fiercely. One summer—I was eight, I think—my mother had a serious operation and I spent two months with a relative. Two summer months, and hot work of it, playing outdoors, but I did not know how to take a bath by myself and I would not let anyone give me a bath; no one unauthorized was to be allowed to see me unclothed.

These first two sentences are not "laundry lists": their detail is simply what they, and the piece as a whole, are about.

The details of the third sentence introduce a quiet shift in focus, from myself to the exterior world: walking, first, and then cars.

The last sentences move the focus of the piece even further into society.

Revising

Revising Your Overall Structure

Clarify the time and place. Be sure that you have clearly indicated *shifts in time and place* and have *paced actions* to accommodate these *changes*.

1. Star any place where the time or location changes.
2. Underline in red the words you have used to indicate the change. Have a partner check to make sure that each shift is clear and complete and that the actions do not seem abrupt.
3. Revise by adding transitional phrases or descriptive words. Insert a paragraph break to highlight the impact of a time or place shift.

Model: Revising to Clarify Time and Place

That day was more than nine years ago. I have lived in America now for nearly ten years.

It was a good experience, to be surprised by the taste of a drink. ˄Today, I struggle to hold on to everything about myself that makes me un-American.

> Added information shows a gap in time.

Peer Review: Share your draft with a classmate. Explain why you made your revision choices, and ask your reader to give you feedback about the time and place shifts you included.

Revising Your Content

Add significance. Consider conveying the significance of events to your audience by adding an **interior monologue,** in which a character reacts to events and reveals his or her feelings and thoughts about them.

Revising Your Sentences

Eliminate unnecessary tense changes. Even though you may be moving back and forth in time in your narrative, do not change tenses unnecessarily. Do not shift tenses without a good reason.

Original Sentence:

It was midnight when the vote tally is finally complete.

Corrected Sentence:

It was midnight when the vote tally was finally completed.

Developing Your Style

Vivid Word Choice

Word Choice Choose strong verbs and adjectives that bring the characters, events, setting, and conflict of your autobiographical narrative to life. Avoid words that are weak, dull, or vague.

Weak: I drank the soda and it was delicious.

Strong: I took a sip of the soda and savored its tangy surprises: a tart kick of lime and extra-fizzy bubbles that tickled the inside of my mouth and made me feel as if I were smelling a lime air freshener.

Instead of settling for general, overused verbs and adjectives, take time to find precise, vivid examples.

Find It in Your Reading

Read the selection "Letters of Margaret Paston" on pages 201–204.

1. Find two sentences from Paston's letters in which the author uses strong verbs and two sentences in which the author uses strong adjectives.

2. Choose two words from the selection that you find particularly vivid.

sped — dashed

ran

saundered

walked

strutted

went

ambled — slithered

Apply It to Your Writing

Review the draft of your autobiographical narrative, focusing on your choice of words. Follow these steps as you read:

• Circle any words that seem dull, weak, or vague. Also circle any uses of jargon or clichés.

• Challenge yourself to replace each circled word with a more vivid alternative, especially one that brings a setting to life with concrete sensory details of sights, sounds, and smells.

• Use a thesaurus or dictionary, and check to be sure that your new words accurately reflect what you want to say about your characters, setting, or conflict.

A Toast to the Future

I came to this country on a plane. Just a kid, not even eight years old yet, I sat on the center aisle of a huge 747 in Chicago waiting to fly to Los Angeles. These names—Chicago, Los Angeles—were abstract to me. All I knew was that I was in America, the place where everybody drives a nice car and lives in a great house or apartment and the bad guys always lose. At least, that was what the television back in Romania had shown me.

I was very thirsty, sitting in that center aisle. I kept asking my mom when they were going to bring us drinks. I don't know how much time went by before the cart came around, but it finally arrived.

That moment was my first real encounter with America. There were so many cans to choose from, so many colors. I had no idea which one to take. I chose the blue one since blue was my favorite color. I opened it up and poured it in my clear plastic cup. The soda was also clear, and I was very disappointed. Out of all those different cans I had to choose club soda, a drink I already knew the taste of. But I was wrong. I took a sip, and to my joyous surprise, it was sweet and refreshing, and the bubbles tickled the inside of my mouth. It tasted nothing like club soda. It was a good experience, to be surprised by the taste of a drink.

That day was more than nine years ago. I have lived in America now for nearly ten years. I have since passed through feelings of isolation and fears of being different. I have learned to make friends and to lead life as I want to.

Today, I struggle to hold on to everything about myself that makes me un-American. I try not to forget the Romanian language, I try to remember that I was not born in America. I think about Romania every day. I will not forget it, ever. A Romanian flag hangs in my bedroom alongside pictures of American rock stars. The thought of my homeland always makes me feel a certain way. I feel a kind of bittersweet feeling, calm, a feeling of happiness. I picture a warm sunny day on which I am walking alone on the little winding street that surrounded our building complex.

When I think of the future, though, I have a simple hope. I hope the future will be like the moment one tastes the first sip of sweet, crisp, bubbly soda, when a second before it looked like just plain old club soda.

Mircea clearly establishes the setting of his story.

The narrative centers on the conflict of cultures.

Mircea devotes several sentences to the choice of sodas, using pacing to focus his reader's attention and build interest.

Vivid sensory details draw a reader into Mircea's experience. See Developing Your Style, p. 219.

Mircea clearly states the insight he has gained and poetically links it to the narrative.

Editing and Proofreading

Focus on punctuation. To punctuate direct quotations, place commas or periods inside the final quotation mark and place semicolons or colons outside it. Place a question mark inside the closing quotation mark only if it is part of the quotation.

Inside: My grandfather asked, "Where do you think you're going?"

Outside: Will I be able to say "I'm sorry"?

Focus on spelling. When the prefix *ex-* means "out," do not use a hyphen after it: *extract, export, exhaust*. When it means "former," use a hyphen: *ex-president, ex-wife*.

Spiral Review: Conventions Earlier in this unit, you learned about correlative conjunctions (page 154). Check your narrative to be sure you have used those conventions correctly.

Publishing, Presenting, and Reflecting

Consider one of the following ways to share your writing with your classmates.

Maintain a portfolio. Follow your growth as a writer by keeping your autobiographical narrative with other works in a writing portfolio.

Publish a literary magazine. Collect your classmates' narratives for publication in a student magazine, which you might post on the Internet. Have writers provide illustrations and introductions for their works.

Reflect on your writing. Jot down your thoughts on the experience of writing an autobiographical narrative. Begin by answering this question: What did you learn about yourself as a writer by completing this narrative?

Rubric for Self-Assessment

Evaluate your reflective essay using the following criteria and rating scale.

Criteria	Rating Scale
	not very *very*
Purpose/Focus: How well do you describe yourself, the main character, and the other characters in your narrative?	1 2 3 4
Organization: How effectively do you organize the sequence of events?	1 2 3 4
Development of Ideas/Elaboration: How well do you use details to describe scenes and events?	1 2 3 4
Language: How vivid is your word choice, especially your use of strong verbs and adjectives to bring characters, events, settings, and conflicts to life?	1 2 3 4
Conventions: How correct is your grammar, especially your use of punctuation?	1 2 3 4

Evaluate Persuasive Speech

Persuasive speech, also called argument, includes a range of uses, from a presidential address to a lawyer's closing remarks. Persuasion happens whenever one person speaks to convince another to think or act in a certain way.

 **Common Core State Standards**

Speaking and Listening
3. Evaluate a speaker's point of view, reasoning, and use of evidence and rhetoric, assessing the stance, premises, links among ideas, word choice, points of emphasis, and tone used.

Types of Propositions

Persuasive speech includes four types of propositions.

Propositions	Example
Fact—asserts that something is	Average annual temperatures have been rising.
Value—claims that something is good or bad or is better or worse than something else	Kenneth Branagh's adaptation of *Hamlet* is the best.
Problem—demonstrates that a problem exists	Our team's name, The Ants, is a problem because…
Policy—argues that something should be done	Our school should start a debate club.

Identify Persuasive Techniques

Persuasive Appeals Different types of persuasive speech rely on varied types of appeals, evidence, and patterns of logic:

- **Ethos, an ethical appeal,** cites the speaker's authority, as in a famous surgeon endorsing a heart medicine.
- **Pathos, an emotional appeal,** tugs at the audience's emotions, as in an ad that uses a smiling infant to sell baby food.
- **Logos, a logical appeal,** applies reasoning and facts to build convincing arguments.

Syllogisms are arguments made up of two premises and a conclusion. Example: "All men are mortal. Socrates is a man. Socrates is mortal."

Inductive reasoning draws a conclusion from examples. Example: "I touched three icicles and they were cold. I think all icicles are cold."

Deductive reasoning applies a general principle to specific cases. Example: "I know ice is frozen, so I know this icicle will be cold."

Analogies are comparisons. A letter of recommendation comparing your writing to a professional's will probably create a good impression.

Identify Persuasive Techniques (continued)

Uses of Language Effective speakers use various techniques to achieve clarity, force, and aesthetic effect:

- **rhetorical questions:** questions not meant to be answered but used to establish solidarity with an audience
- **parallelism:** repetition of similar ideas in similar grammatical forms
- **figurative language:** nonliteral language, such as similes and metaphors, that add interest and encourage active listening

Negative Techniques Speakers may also resort to *negative persuasive techniques,* including the misuse of logic, in order to sway listeners. Many **logical fallacies,** such as those listed below, may seem plausible at first:

- *ad hominem* **attack:** an attack on a person's character
- **false causality:** the idea that A happened before B, so A caused B
- **red herring:** an irrelevant distraction from more important points
- **overgeneralization:** a conclusion based on too little evidence
- **bandwagon effect:** the idea that you should do something because everyone does it

Activities: Evaluate Persuasive Speech

Comprehension and Collaboration With a classmate, complete the following activities, using the evaluation form shown below to guide your work.

A. Find a persuasive speech in a play or on the Internet. Describe the proposition and evaluate the use of specific persuasive techniques.

B. Identify logical fallacies in three different speeches. Then, discuss why the speakers might have resorted to using fallacies.

Evaluation Form for Persuasive Speech

Name of Speech _____
Media Type _____
Intended Audience _____
Purpose _____
Type of Proposition _____
Appeal to Ethos _____
Appeal to Pathos _____
Appeal to Logos (Include syllogisms or analogies, if possible) _____
Uses of Language _____
Negative Persuasive Techniques _____
In your opinion, does this speaker argue persuasively and ethically? Why or why not? _____

Language Study

Using Dictionaries and Other Resources

A **dictionary** is a reference tool that contains information about words. Each entry lists the word's correct spelling and pronunciation, grammatical function, meanings, and etymology, or origin. **Print dictionaries** are organized alphabetically. **Electronic dictionaries** offer a search list or require you to enter your word. **Specialized dictionaries** define words and phrases in a particular field, such as medicine, law, art, or literature.

Sample Dictionary Entry

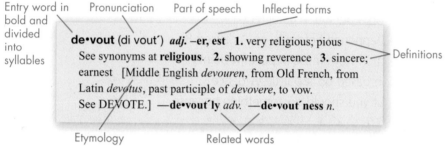

A **thesaurus** is a reference tool providing, for each entry, lists of synonyms and some antonyms. The synonyms share the *denotative*, or literal, meaning of the entry word. However, they do not always share the *connotative* meaning, or associations a word suggests. For example, *precise* and *prim* have similar meanings, but *precise* has a positive connotation while *prim* suggests a self-conscious fussiness. After choosing a synonym, it is a good idea to check its meaning in a dictionary to see how it will fit in your sentence.

Sample Thesaurus Entry

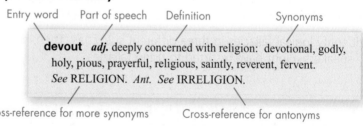

Practice

Directions: Answer each question as directed.

1. Use a dictionary to discover the etymology of *barbarous*. Analyze the word's origin and explain how it relates to the etymology of *brave*.

2. Analyze a thesaurus entry for *brave*. **(a)** Choose two words with positive connotations. Use each in a sentence about Beowulf or another epic hero. **(b)** Then, choose two synonyms with negative connotations. Use each in a sentence that illustrates its meaning.

3. Use a dictionary to trace the etymologies of these words: *shield, destiny, fame, hero, dragon, sword*. Which derive from Old English?

4. Trace the etymologies of these words: *kingdom, nation*.

Common Core State Standards

Language
4.a. Use context as a clue to the meaning of a word or phrase.
4.c. Consult general and specialized reference materials, both print and digital, to find the pronunciation of a word or determine or clarify its precise meaning, its part of speech, its etymology, or its standard usage.
4.d. Verify the preliminary determination of the meaning of a word or phrase.

Vocabulary Acquisition and Use: Context Clues

Context clues are words or phrases that help readers clarify the meanings of unfamiliar words in a text. By using context clues, you can determine the word or words that complete a sentence. Sentence Completion questions appear in most standardized tests. In these types of questions, you are given sentences with one or more missing words. Your task is to use the context to choose the correct word or words to complete each sentence logically. Try this strategy: (1) Read the sentence. (2) Read *all* of the answer choices, and mark those that might work. (3) Of the ones you marked, choose the answer that works best.

Practice

This exercise is modeled after the Sentence Completion exercises that appear in the Critical Reading section of the SAT.

> **Test-Taking Tip**
> Immediately rule out any answer choices you know are wrong.

Directions: Each of the following sentences is missing one or two words. Choose the word or set of words that best completes each sentence.

1. Violent, ___?___ creatures such as Grendel appear frequently in heroic literature.
   - **A.** fervent
   - **B.** solicitous
   - **C.** genteel
   - **D.** loathsome
   - **E.** compassionate

2. The beast often makes it a habit to ___?___ and consume the people of a nearby community.
   - **A.** assault
   - **B.** purge
   - **C.** cultivate
   - **D.** befriend
   - **E.** purge

3. Before the entire village has been torn ___?___, a noble traveler—often a distant kinsman— will arrive on the scene.
   - **A.** adroitly
   - **B.** aloft
   - **C.** asunder
   - **D.** obliquely
   - **E.** apologetically

4. Next, at his own ___?___, the hero will confront the mighty beast.
   - **A.** predicament
   - **B.** peril
   - **C.** prevarication
   - **D.** pallor
   - **E.** prowess

5. Though he is sometimes wounded, the hero takes ___?___ in his sacrifice.
   - **A.** rancor
   - **B.** prevarication
   - **C.** absolution
   - **D.** solace
   - **E.** reparation

6. The hero proves his ___?___ from death.
   - **A.** solace
   - **B.** immunity
   - **C.** largesse
   - **D.** authority
   - **E.** vulnerability

From Text to Understanding

You have studied each part of Unit 1 as a set of connected texts. In this workshop, you will have the chance to further explore the fundamental connections among these texts and to deepen your essential understanding of the literature and its social and historical context.

PART 1: Earthly Exile, Heavenly Home

Writing: Argumentative Essay The texts in Part 1, especially the Anchor Text, "The Seafarer," translated by Burton Raffel, present a concept of home that becomes even more poignant in the face of exile. To the authors of "The Seafarer" and the other poems in *The Exeter Book*, home was often a lord's mead hall or a kingdom filled with the fellowship of friends and family.

As you review the texts, make a list of details that characterize the speakers' views of home. Also note if and how exile affects their understanding of home.

Assignment: Develop and defend a claim about the significant idea of home expressed in the Anchor Text and other poems in Part 1. Refer to the list and notes you compiled as you reviewed.

 Example: In the poem "The Seafarer," the speaker struggles with the lonely life of exile he endures on the sea. The sea, however, for all its hardship, becomes an alternative version of "home" for the speaker.

Write a claim: Your introduction should include a clear claim that expresses the idea of home for which you will argue. Use accurate and detailed references to support this claim, and cite your sources if you use secondary material such as literary criticism.

PART 2: The Epic

Writing: Writing to Sources Epic themes encompass eternal issues such as good and evil or redemption and loss. Actions undertaken by the epic heroes that populate these stories showcase supreme courage, honor, and loyalty. As you review the excerpts from *Beowulf*, the Anchor Text in Part 2, make a list of epic characteristics you find in the story.

Assignment: Develop an essay in which you define the characteristics of the traditional epic, including the epic hero, as the context for discussing a modern representation of these elements. Identify a modern fictional epic or a nonfiction story of epic proportions, and present a reasoned analysis of why you consider it an heir to the epic tradition. Use *Beowulf* as a touchstone, citing examples as needed from the text as evidence to support your claim.

Common Core State Standards

Writing

1. Write arguments to support claims in an analysis of substantive topics or texts, using valid reasoning and relevant and sufficient evidence.

4. Produce clear and coherent writing in which the development, organization, and style are appropriate to task, purpose, and audience.

9. Draw evidence from literary or informational texts to support analysis, reflection, and research.

Speaking and Listening

1. Initiate and participate effectively in a range of collaborative discussions (one-on-one, in groups, and teacher-led) with diverse partners on *grades 11–12 topics, texts, and issues*, building on others' ideas and expressing their own clearly and persuasively.

Writing Checklist

☐ Clear claim

 Notes: _____

☐ Relevant textual evidence

 Notes: _____

☐ Reliable, appropriate secondary sources

 Notes: _____

☐ Effective transitions

 Notes: _____

PART 3: A National Spirit

Research: Multimedia Storytelling Event Chaucer's characters on the road to Canterbury use a variety of genres to tell readers about the humor, challenges, and social struggles of their time.

Review the Part 3 Anchor Text, Chaucer's "The Wife of Bath's Tale," and think about the story the Wife of Bath tells. What beliefs does she reveal through the characters and plot?

Assignment: Working in a small group, retell "The Wife of Bath's Tale" in a variety of modern storytelling genres. Research events and projects that focus on storytelling, such as the following:

- personal history archives, which Story Corps® models, in which people tell their own stories to be recorded for posterity.

- storytelling festivals, which allow people to tell stories to a larger audience, using dramatic techniques;

- interviews, which allow personal stories to emerge through a question-and-answer format.

Use online research to learn more about these storytelling projects. Then create versions of the Wife of Bath's story based on your research. Use a variety of media, including recordings and computer-assisted presentations, to create your storytelling event for the class. After your classmates have experienced your stories, discuss the difference between Chaucer's storytelling and storytelling today.

PART 4: Perils and Adventures

Listening and Speaking: Code of Chivalry Panel A medieval knight's behavior was guided by a code of chivalry, which demanded that he fight bravely, show loyalty to his king and to his faith, and treat women honorably. As you review the Anchor Text, the excerpt from Sir Thomas Malory's *Morte d'Arthur*, take careful note of the traits exhibited by Arthur, Lancelot, and other characters. Make a list of their behaviors that you think are admirable.

Assignment: With a panel consisting of a small group, create a code of chivalry for your school. The purpose of this code should be the same as the chivalric code of Malory's knights: to inspire noble behavior. Using the medieval code of chivalry represented in Malory's text, develop standards of behavior for students that address issues such as the use of violence, treatment of women, and righting of wrongs. The panel will present the code of conduct to the class and should be prepared to defend its choices.

Multimedia Storytelling Plan

☐ **Story Corps®**
Write script of Wife of Bath's story.
Choose recording device.
Record story.

☐ **Festival**
Describe festival you are attending.
Write prose account of Wife of Bath's tale.
Collect props.
Practice telling your story.

☐ **Interview**
Select interviewer and interviewee.
Write script of questions and answers.
Design set for interview: chairs, etc.

Test-Taking Practice

Reading Test: Natural Science Passages

Natural science passages are one type of reading selection found on standardized tests. These passages may relate to biology, chemistry, geology, or other sciences. They may have a social or historical perspective as well. Natural science passages are informational, but they also express the author's point of view either directly or indirectly. Questions following these passages may focus on main idea, text structure, and author's purpose. They will also test your comprehension of key facts and details.

 Common Core State Standards

RI.11-12.1, RI.11-12.2,
RI.11-12.3, RI.11-12.4,
RI.11-12.5; L.11-12.3,
L.11-12.4, L.11-12.6
[For the full wording of the standards, see the standards chart in the front of your textbook.]

Practice

The following exercise is modeled after the ACT Reading Test, Natural Science section. The full reading test has 40 questions.

Directions: Read the following passage, taken from Bede's *A History of the English Church and People*. Then, choose the best answer to each question.

Ireland is broader than Britain, and its mild and healthy climate is superior. Snow rarely lies longer than three days, so that there is no need to store hay in summer for winter use or to build stables for beasts. There are no reptiles, and no snake can exist there, for
5   although often brought over from Britain, as soon as the ship nears land, they breathe its scented air and die. In fact, almost everything in this isle enjoys immunity to poison, and I have heard that folk suffering from snakebite have drunk water in which scrapings from the leaves of books from Ireland had been steeped, and that this
10 remedy checked the spreading poison and reduced the swelling. The island abounds in milk and honey, and there is no lack of vines, fish, and birds, while deer and goats are widely hunted. It is the original home of the Scots, who, as already mentioned, later migrated and joined the Britons and Picts in Britain. There is a very extensive
15 arm of the sea, which originally formed the boundary between the Britons and the Picts. This runs inland from the west for a great distance as far as the strongly fortified British city of Alcuith. It was to the northern shores of this firth that the Scots came and established their new homeland.

Strategy

Scan, then read.

- **First, scan the passage.** Take 20 seconds to skim the text. Look for a main topic and a few key terms.

- **Second, read the passage in full.** Ask yourself: *What information is most important? How does the author present this information?*

1. It can reasonably be inferred that at the time of the writing
   A. the environment in northern Europe was drastically different than it is today.
   B. the geography of northern Europe had recently and dramatically shifted.
   C. many people in Europe were suffering from poor health.
   D. most people in Europe knew little about Ireland.

2. Which of the following statements best paraphrases lines 2–3?
   F. Winter weather is harsh, but summer is easy on both animals and farmers.
   G. Because the snow is quick-melting, it does not interfere with the storage of hay or the building of shelters.
   H. Mild, dry winters eliminate the need for hay storage and animal shelters.
   J. The animals are hearty enough to go without food or shelter during the mild winter months.

3. The author includes the detail about the snakebite remedy (lines 7–10) in order to
   A. entertain his readers with a local legend.
   B. support the idea that Ireland's environment is healthful.
   C. encourage his readers to try the remedy for themselves.
   D. illustrate how uncivilized Ireland is.

4. The author writes that the island "abounds in milk and honey" (line 11). This phrase
   F. symbolizes the island's people.
   G. denotes the contents of the island.
   H. identifies an important limitation.
   J. connotes wholesome abundance.

5. In the context of the passage, the main function of lines 12–19 is to
   A. situate the island of Ireland in relation to Britain.
   B. provide background information about the Scots.
   C. indicate that Britain is home to many different peoples.
   D. suggest that Ireland is largely free of inhabitants.

6. Which conclusion can best be drawn about the author of the passage?
   F. He is native to Ireland.
   G. He is objective and credible.
   H. His motives are questionable.
   J. He has a background in medicine.

7. In the context of lines 14–18, it can reasonably be inferred that a *firth* is
   A. the shore of an island.
   B. a unit of measurement.
   C. an arm of the sea.
   D. the outer boundary of a city.

Grammar and Writing: Editing in Context

Some tests feature a passage with numbered sentences or parts of sentences, some of which contain errors in grammar, style, and usage. Your task is to choose the best version of the sentence from the choices offered. Some questions may also refer to the passage as a whole or to the numbered paragraphs contained in the passage.

Practice

This exercise is modeled after the ACT English Test.

Directions: For each underlined sentence or portion of a sentence, choose the best alternative. If an item asks a question about the underlined portion, choose the best answer to the question.

Strategy

Try out each answer. Mentally test each answer before you choose one of them. The one that sounds the best is probably correct.

[1]

Edith May Pretty had lived on the Sutton Hoo estate near Suffolk, England, for twelve years. **The word *hoo* means "spur of a hill."** Mrs. Pretty, her husband, **nor** her son had never quite been sure what to make of the nineteen large mounds visible throughout the grounds. Now infested with rabbits, the mounds were rumored to hold ancient mysteries.

[2]

After her husband died, Pretty's curiosity got the best of her. In 1938, she hired an archaeologist named Basil Brown to open some of the smaller mounds, which held a few interesting treasures, **so** nothing as wondrous or mysterious as legend had predicted. Unsatisfied, Pretty instructed Brown to open Mound One, the largest of them all.

[3]

In the spring of 1939, Brown and two helpers began to dig a trench from the east end of the mound. Soon, the men encountered some large iron rivets, **or** fasteners, laid out in a **long, repetitive pattern,** like a subterranean ribcage. As more of the pattern emerged, the men realized that they were standing in the remains of the bottom hull of a colossal boat. More than 80 feet long, the ship had served as the burial vessel of an Anglo-Saxon king. Fully equipped for the afterlife, the ship's hold contained forty-one items of solid gold, silverware inscribed in Greek, a silver dish bearing the stamp of the

Byzantine emperor, and a bronze bowl from the Middle East. In addition to satisfying Edith May Pretty's curiosity, this astounding archaeological discovery greatly expanded contemporary understanding of Anglo-Saxon culture.

1. Upon reviewing paragraph 1, the writer considers deleting the indicated sentence. If the writer were to delete the sentence, the paragraph would primarily lose
   A. an explanation of one of the essay's central concepts.
   B. a colorful detail that draws the reader into the essay.
   C. an impressive fact that establishes the writer's credibility.
   D. nothing; it should be deleted.

2. F. NO CHANGE
   G. and
   H. but also
   J. though

3. What is the function of this word?
   A. It is used as a correlative conjunction.
   B. It is used as a coordinating conjunction.
   C. It is used as a subordinating conjunction.
   D. It has no function and should be deleted.

4. F. NO CHANGE
   G. than
   H. or
   J. but

5. A. NO CHANGE
   B. as though
   C. nor
   D. and

6. F. NO CHANGE
   G. repetitive pattern
   H. long pattern
   J. pattern

7. What is the most accurate summary of paragraph 3?
   A. It contains specific information and historical details.
   B. It describes the great Anglo-Saxon archaeological discovery that was made.
   C. It is the conclusion of the story.
   D. It persuades people to study archaeology.

8. *This question refers to the passage as a whole.* What is the main idea of this passage?
   F. Archaeology is a more established science today than it once was.
   G. People should be more curious.
   H. Old rumors may be true.
   J. Old tales, curiosity, and hard work lead to an important discovery.

⏱ Timed Writing: Position Statement [30 minutes]

Burton Raffel, translator of *Beowulf,* has remarked that one of the most satisfying aspects of that poem is "the poet's insight into people." One might also argue that Bede, author of *A History of the English Church and People*, had equally deep insight into people and places.

In your view, which kind of text—a work of fiction like *Beowulf* or a work of nonfiction like Bede's *History*—sheds greater light on an ancient culture and its people? Write an essay developing your view on this issue. Support your position with reasoning and examples based on your reading, studies, or observations.

Academic Vocabulary

An **issue** is a debatable idea. There is no one right or wrong position on an issue. Choose the position for which you can offer the strongest support.

Constructed Response

**Common Core
State Standards**

RL.11-12.1; RL.11-12.3, RL.11-12.5;
RI.11-12.5; W.11-12.1.d, W.11-12.1.e,
W.11-12.2; SL.11-12.1, SL.11-12.4,
SL.11-12.6
[For the full wording of the standards,
see the standards chart in the front of
your textbook.]

Directions: *Follow the instructions to complete the tasks below as required by your teacher. As you work on each task, incorporate both general academic vocabulary and literary terms you learned in this unit.*

Writing

Task 1: Literature [RL.11-12.1; W.11-12.2]
Analyze Character

*Write an **essay** in which you analyze a character from a literary work in this unit.*

- Select a character who is central to the work in which he or she appears.

- Describe the character as fully as possible, based on the information provided in the work. Details in the text may provide either direct information or indirect clues about the character.

- Once you have described the character, analyze the character's significance in the work. For example, the character may stand for a type of person or may be archetypal. He or she may have a particular role or motivation.

- Remember to support your inferences with evidence from the text.

- Provide a conclusion that follows from the information you presented and also creates a sense of closure.

Task 2: Informational Text [RI.11-12.5; W.11-12.1.e]
Analyze Text Structure

*Write an **essay** in which you analyze how a text's structure contributes to its meaning in a nonfiction work from this unit.*

- Choose a work of nonfiction from this unit in which the author's choices concerning text structure help to clarify and develop central ideas.

- Determine which text structure is being used. Evaluate the way in which the structure helps to introduce and clarify points.

- Include a judgment as to how effective the author's use of text structure is.

- Provide examples from the text to support your ideas.

- Use a variety of sentence lengths in your writing. Combine short, choppy sentences by using coordinating or correlative conjunctions.

- End your essay with a conclusion that follows from your discussion and sums up your main points.

Task 3: Literature [RL.11-12.5; W.11-12.1.d]
Analyze Poetic Structure

*Write an **essay** in which you analyze how an author's choices concerning structure add to the overall meaning of a poem.*

- Choose a poem from this unit and briefly describe its overall structure and important structural elements. For example, the length of a poem or a distinct rhythm might be considered structural choices.

- Write a thesis sentence that describes the impact that the structure of the poem has upon its meaning.

- Discuss the relationship between structure and meaning in detail, providing evidence from the text to support your reasoning.

- Establish and maintain a formal style and objective tone in your writing.

- Finish your essay with a strong conclusion that sums up your main points and makes a statement about the relationship between poetic form and meaning.

Speaking and Listening

Task 4: Literature [RL.11-12.1; SL.11-12.1]
Make Inferences

*Conduct a **small group discussion** exploring inferences that can be made about culture based upon one of the literary works in this unit.*

- Choose a work that contains clues about the culture in which it originated.
- Identify details that point to values, beliefs, the historical framework, and the social structure of the culture.
- Explain how these details help you to make connections and draw inferences about the culture.
- Prepare for the discussion. Create a list of questions based on your analysis designed to stimulate discussion.
- As group members contribute, build on their ideas. Pose further questions and point to evidence from the work.
- Respond thoughtfully to diverse perspectives and points of view.

Task 5: Literature [RL.11-12.3; SL.11-12.4, 6]
Analyze Story Elements

*Prepare and deliver an **oral presentation** in which you analyze and evaluate the presentation and development of story elements in a literary work from this unit.*

- Explain which work you chose and briefly summarize the setting, situation, characters, conflict, and plot.
- Discuss how the author orders events and how he or she introduces and develops characters or new situations.
- Explain how the author's choices about the development of the story elements contribute to the narrative's larger meaning or themes.
- Apply the conventions of Standard English grammar and usage in your speaking.
- As you present, speak clearly and loudly enough to be understood by your audience.

Task 6: Literature [RL.11-12.5; SL.11-12.4]
Analyze Text Structure

*Prepare and deliver an **oral presentation** in which you analyze the effect of text structure on the meaning as well as the artistry and beauty of a literary work from this unit.*

- Identify a work in which the structure of the text is deeply connected to its meaning and is also aesthetically significant. Caesuras, rhyming quatrains, or frame story structure are all examples of text structures.
- Define the text structure and its impact on the text's meaning.
- Discuss what you perceive to be artful or aesthetically pleasing about this text structure and in what way it engaged you as a reader. Draw a conclusion as to why the author made specific choices regarding structure.
- Present your interpretation and supporting evidence in an organized and clear way, so that your audience can follow your reasoning.

How does literature shape or reflect society?

What is Home? Over the thousand years covered in this unit, England evolved from a collection of clans to a more unified nation. You can trace this evolution in the different ideas of home expressed by various writers.

Assignment Choose three works from this unit that express different perspectives on the significant idea of home. Write a **comparison-and-contrast essay** about these perspectives, showing how the idea of home changed over time.

Titles for Extended Reading

In this unit, you have read a variety of British literature of the Old English and Medieval periods. Continue to read works related to this era on your own. Select books that you enjoy, but challenge yourself to explore new topics, new authors, and works offering varied perspectives or approaches. The titles suggested below will help you get started.

LITERATURE

Beowulf: A Verse Translation
Translated by Burton Raffel

Epic This Old English poem tells how Beowulf heroically defeats three fearsome monsters: Grendel, Grendel's mother, and a dragon. Thrill to the ultimate in gore from a time when audiences heard their heroic tales told aloud instead of going to the multiplex to see them.

[An excerpt from Beowulf appears on page 40 of this book. Build knowledge by reading the full text.]

The Canterbury Tales
Geoffrey Chaucer
Translated by Nevil Coghill   EXEMPLAR TEXT

Poetry As part of a storytelling contest, each character in this medieval classic tells a tale while on a pilgrimage from London to Canterbury Cathedral. The stories range from bawdy and hilarious to innocent and virtuous, depending on the personality of the storyteller.

[An excerpt from The Canterbury Tales appears on page 96 of this book. Build knowledge by reading the full text.]

Sir Gawain and the Green Knight
Translated by Brian Stone

Poetry In this acclaimed medieval romance, Sir Gawain is the young nephew of King Arthur. The Green Knight tests Gawain's chivalric ideals by posing three challenges.

[An excerpt from Sir Gawain and the Green Knight appears on page 170 of this book. Build knowledge by reading the full text.]

The Once and Future King
T. H. White
Ace, 1987

Novel In this modern classic, White retells a variety of exciting tales about the legendary King Arthur and his Knights of the Round Table. White's humorous, imaginative, and suspenseful retellings will delight today's readers.

INFORMATIONAL TEXTS

Historical Texts

The Ecclesiastical History of the English People
Bede
Translated by Leo Sherley-Price

History Written in A.D. 731 by a Christian monk named Bede, this book describes England from the first-century invasion by the Romans to Anglo-Saxon life in Bede's own day. It is a fascinating account of the ebb and flow of peoples and belief systems in the early centuries of Britain.

[An excerpt from the same work—using the slightly different title A History of the English Church and People—appears on page 84 of this book. Build knowledge by reading the full text.]

The Book of Margery Kempe
Margery Kempe
Translated by B. A. Windeatt

Autobiography Considered the first autobiography in English, this book was dictated to a priest. It narrates the spiritual and everyday struggles of one woman in the fifteenth century as she deals with bankruptcy, the pressures of maintaining a household with fourteen children, and divine revelations that send her on pilgrimages far from home.

Contemporary Scholarship

A Distant Mirror: The Calamitous 14th Century
Barbara W. Tuchman
Ballantine Books, 1978

History Told from the perspective of nobleman Enguerrand de Coucy (1340–1397), this book explores important events in the fourteenth century, including the Black Death, The Hundred Years' War, and the Crusades.

The Story of English
Robert McCrum, Robert MacNeil, and William Cran

Linguistics This book presents a stimulating and comprehensive record of spoken and written English—from its Anglo-Saxon origins to the present day, when English is the dominant language of commerce and culture, with more than one billion English speakers throughout the world.

Preparing to Read Complex Texts

Reading for College and Career In both college and the workplace, readers must analyze texts independently, draw connections among works that offer varied perspectives, and develop their own ideas and informed opinions. The questions shown below, and others that you generate on your own, will help you more effectively read and analyze complex college-level texts.

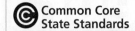

**Common Core
State Standards**

Reading Literature/Informational Text
10. By the end of grade 12, read and comprehend literature, including stories, dramas, and poems, and literary nonfiction at the high end of the grades 11-CCR text complexity band independently and proficiently.

When reading complex texts, ask yourself...

- What idea, experience, or story seems to have compelled the author to write? Has the author presented that idea, experience, or story in a way that I, too, find compelling?

- How might the author's era, social status, belief system, or personal experiences have affected the point of view he or she expresses in the text?

- How do my circumstances affect what I understand and feel about this text?

- What key idea does the author state explicitly? What key idea does he or she suggest or imply? Which details in the text help me to perceive implied ideas?

- Do I find multiple layers of meaning in the text? If so, what relationships do I see among these layers of meaning?

- How do details in the text connect or relate to one another? Do I find any details unconvincing, unrelated, or out of place?

- Do I find the text believable and convincing?

**Key Ideas
and Details**

- What patterns of organization or sequences do I find in the text? Do these patterns help me understand the ideas better?

- What do I notice about the author's style, including his or her diction, uses of imagery and figurative language, and syntax?

- Do I like the author's style? Is the author's style memorable?

- What emotional attitude does the author express toward the topic, the story, or the characters? Does this attitude seem appropriate?

- What emotional attitude does the author express toward me, the reader? Does this attitude seem appropriate?

- What do I notice about the author's voice—his or her personality on the page? Do I like this voice? Does it make me want to read on?

**Craft and
Structure**

- Is the work fresh and original?

- Do I agree with the author's ideas entirely, or are there elements I find unconvincing?

- Do I disagree with the author's ideas entirely, or are there elements I can accept as true?

- Based on my knowledge of British literature, history, and culture, does this work reflect the British tradition? Why or why not?

**Integration
of Ideas**

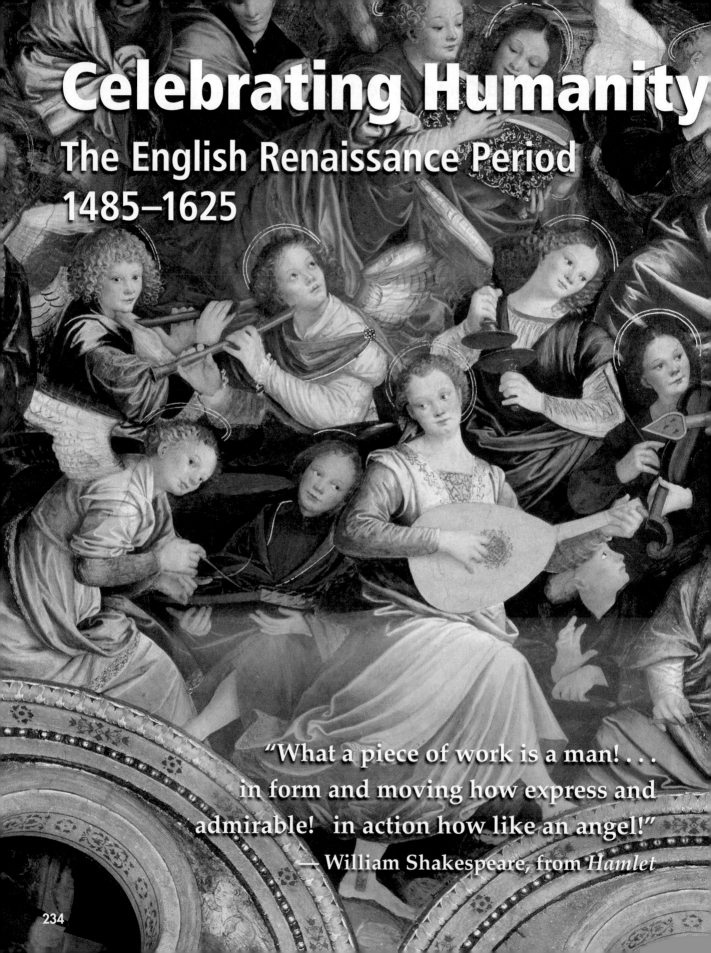

Celebrating Humanity
The English Renaissance Period
1485–1625

"What a piece of work is a man! . . .
in form and moving how express and
admirable! in action how like an angel!"
— William Shakespeare, from *Hamlet*

Unit 2

CLOSE READING TOOL

Use this tool to practice the close reading strategies you learn.

ONLINE WRITER'S NOTEBOOK

Easily capture notes and complete assignments online.

STUDENT eTEXT

Bring learning to life with audio, video, and interactive tools.

■ Find all Digital Resources at **pearsonrealize.com**.

Snapshot of the Period

Renaissance and Reformation

Two major movements influenced the thought and literature of this period: the Renaissance and the Reformation. The Renaissance, meaning "rebirth," was characterized by innovations in art, science, and exploration, and a rediscovery of long-neglected classical works. Beginning in Italy, it gradually spread northward. Renaissance scholars of northern Europe, like Erasmus, attempted to reform the Catholic Church. The German theologian Martin Luther, however, initiated the movement known as the Reformation (reform-ation), which led to the founding of Protestantism. Luther stressed the Bible, rather than the Pope, as the source of authority and the importance of faith, rather than good works, for salvation.

Of the two major English works of this period, Shakespeare's plays and the King James Bible, the first is a product of the Renaissance and the second a product of the Reformation.

▲ This 16th-century engraving shows the new technology of book printing. The printing press, developed by Gutenberg in the mid-15th century, helped spread the ideas of the Renaissance and the Reformation.

As you read the selections in this unit, you will be asked to think about them in view of three key questions:

What is the **relationship**
between literature and *place?*

How does literature **shape or
reflect** *society?*

What is the relationship
of the writer to *tradition?*

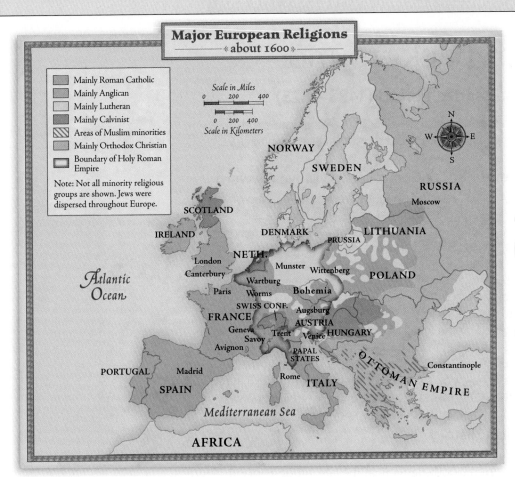

Major European Religions
about 1600

Mainly Roman Catholic
Mainly Anglican
Mainly Lutheran
Mainly Calvinist
Areas of Muslim minorities
Mainly Orthodox Christian
Boundary of Holy Roman Empire

Note: Not all minority religious groups are shown. Jews were dispersed throughout Europe.

Scale in Miles
0   200   400

Scale in Kilometers
0   200   400

N W E S

NORWAY
SWEDEN
RUSSIA
Moscow
SCOTLAND
IRELAND
DENMARK
LITHUANIA
PRUSSIA
NETH.
London
Canterbury
Munster
Wittenberg
POLAND
Atlantic Ocean
Paris
Wartburg
Worms
Bohemia
SWISS CONF.
Augsburg
FRANCE
AUSTRIA
Geneva
Savoy
Trent
Venice
HUNGARY
Avignon
PAPAL STATES
OTTOMAN EMPIRE
Constantinople
PORTUGAL
Madrid
Rome
ITALY
SPAIN
Mediterranean Sea
AFRICA

A Time of Change in Religion & Science

Ⓒ **Integration of Knowledge and Ideas** The Reformation led to sharp religious divisions in Europe, shown on the map above. Which territories were controlled by Roman Catholics and which by Protestant denominations—Anglican, Calvinist, or Lutheran? How does this map help explain the war between England and Spain, which broke out in 1588? Review the timeline below. Which Renaissance inventions shown would you consider the most important? Why?

Renaissance Inventions

1496
paper mill; wall paper

1581
pendulum

1590
microscope

1608
telescope

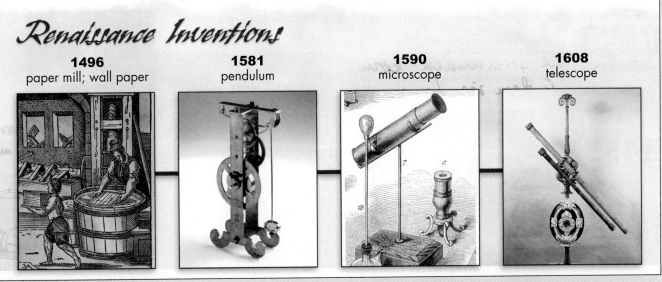

Historical Background

The English Renaissance Period (1485–1625)

The two major European movements of this period, the Renaissance and the Reformation, both involved a return to old sources that led to cultural innovations.

Renaissance and Reformation: Going Back to Move Forward

The Renaissance, which means "rebirth," sought to revive the learning of ancient Greece and Rome. It was a secular movement that encouraged voyages of discovery and emphasized human aspiration. During this period, the very dimensions of the world shifted and enlarged, as Europeans discovered new parts of the globe, and Polish scientist Nicolaus Copernicus first proposed that the sun, not the Earth, was the center of the solar system. Renaissance ideas blossomed first in the Italian city states (1350–1550) and slowly spread northward, giving rise to the English Renaissance (1485–1625).

The Reformation, inspired by the ideas of the German theologian Martin Luther (1483–1546), began in part as a reaction against what many perceived as corruption in the Catholic Church. Reformation thinkers wanted to return to what they took to be a more pure idea of Christianity. Once again, an attempt to return to early ideas led to something new, as reformers created a denomination of Christianity known as Protestantism.

The Drama of English History

England became swept up in both of these two wider European movements, sometimes in a dramatic, even bloody, fashion. In the late 1400s, England was beginning to heal after thirty years of civil war. By the early 1500s, the country had plunged into the religious controversies of the Reformation. At the same time, the spirit of the Renaissance breathed new life into the arts.

The story begins in 1485, when Henry Tudor became King Henry VII, ending a civil war and reconciling the two factions in the war, the House of York and the the House of Lancaster. With him began the reign of the Tudors. His son, Henry VIII, inherited a strong, stable country. Henry VIII married his older brother's widow, Catherine of Aragon, and she bore him

TIMELINE

1485: Henry VII becomes the first Tudor king. ▼

1497: Africa Vasco da Gama rounds Cape of Good Hope.

1503: Italy
Leonardo da Vinci paints *Mona Lisa.* ▶

1485

1492: Columbus lands in Western Hemisphere.

1500: *Everyman* first performed.

a daughter, Mary. However, Henry then fell in love with Anne Boleyn, a beautiful lady of the court. He also wanted a male heir, which Catherine had not provided him. He therefore petitioned the Pope for a divorce on the grounds that his marriage to his brother's widow was invalid.

Henry had written a treatise attacking Luther, and the Pope had designated Henry "Defender of the Faith," a title English monarchs retain to this day. However, when the Pope denied his petition to remarry, Henry refused to comply, marrying Anne Boleyn in 1533 and eventually severing all ties with Rome. In 1534, he established the Protestant Church of England with himself at its head. Religious affiliation and allegiance to the king were suddenly united.

The woman who was to become perhaps the greatest of England's monarchs, Elizabeth I, was born to Henry and Anne Boleyn in 1533. Before Elizabeth took the throne in 1558, Catholics and Protestants struggled for control of the country, and Elizabeth's ascent to the throne was marked by turmoil and death. When Elizabeth took power, however, she firmly established England as a Protestant nation and ushered in a golden age of prosperity and peace. The greatest threat to her rule came in 1588, when Catholic Spain assembled an armada, or fleet of warships, to conquer England. Elizabeth rallied her people, and the English fleet, aided by bad weather, shattered the armada. This glorious moment produced a surge of spirit and sense of power that swept the entire nation.

Elizabeth I never married and had no heir. The final days of her reign were clouded with questions of who would succeed her. In 1603, James I became her successor and the first of the ill-starred Stuart line. By the end of his reign, his struggles with Parliament foreshadowed the civil war that would come during the reign of his son, Charles I.

Key Historical Theme: Going Back to Create Something New

- Renaissance scholars turned to classical authors for inspiration, and Reformation thinkers broke with the Catholic Church in their attempt to return Christianity to its original principles.

- Renaissance ideas stimulated literary, artistic, and scientific achievement in England.

- Influenced by the Reformation, England became a Protestant country.

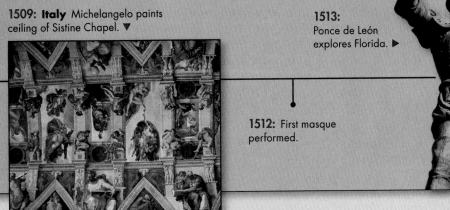

1509: Italy Michelangelo paints ceiling of Sistine Chapel. ▼

1513: Ponce de León explores Florida. ▶

1514

1512: First masque performed.

Essential Questions Across Time

The English Renaissance Period (1485–1625)

 What is the **relationship** between literature and *place?*

What did England come to mean?

"This England" It was in a theater that one of the most enduring descriptions of England was delivered. In Shakespeare's *Richard II*, first performed in 1595, the Duke of Lancaster, John of Gaunt, articulates his vision of what England should be: "This blessed plot, this earth, this realm, this England." His words reflect the exhilaration that followed the defeat of the Spanish Armada in 1588. At the time, Spain was one the world's superpowers, feared for her military might. Spain was also a champion of the Catholic Church, which Henry VIII had rejected. By defeating the Armada, England had established its place as a player in the drama of world history.

The Age of Exploration England also sought a place on the world stage through exploration. Fueled by the Renaissance thirst for knowledge, European navigators ventured far and wide, aided by the invention of the compass and by advances in astronomy. Their explorations culminated in Columbus's arrival in the Americas in 1492. England's participation in the Age of Exploration began in 1497, when the Italian-born explorer John Cabot, sailing for an English company, reached present-day Canada. Cabot laid the basis for future English claims in North America.

Forging a Literature of England Even as England was redefining itself politically as a world power, its poets and dramatists were taking a new hold on the English language, transforming it into an instrument of new literary power. The English poets Edmund Spenser, Sir Philip Sidney, and William Shakespeare pioneered new forms of the sonnet and wrote extended sonnet sequences (see p. 246). Embarking on his own voyage of discovery,

> **ESSENTIAL QUESTION VOCABULARY**
>
> These Essential Question words will help you think and write about literature and place:
>
> **exhilaration** (eg zil´ə rā´shən) *n.* liveliness; high spirits
>
> **pastoral** (pas´tər əl) *n.* genre of literature portraying rural life as peaceful and simple
>
> **climate** (klī´mət) *n.* prevailing or average weather conditions of a place

TIMELINE

1514

◀ **1518: Africa** Algiers and Tunis founded.

1521: Italy Pope Leo X excommunicates Martin Luther.

1532: France Rabelais publishes *Gargantua and Pantagruel*, Book 1.

1532: Peru Pizarro conquers Incas.

Shakespeare explored the heights and depths of the English language in his plays, rediscovering the words of philosophers and kings as well as of rogues and laborers, and adding along the way his own coinages. Through redefinitions of forms and new uses of English, the poets of England created a literature that was truly of England, strong enough to, in turn, influence writers across the world.

What was London's role in this literary explosion?

Theater in London During this period, London, a bustling port city on the river Thames, thrived, becoming a center of world commerce. As the wealth and population of the city grew, theater came to flourish there. Actors were regarded as disreputable by Puritanical city officials. As a result, plays were staged in theaters outside the city limits, on the south bank of the Thames. That is where the famous Globe theater, home for Shakespeare's troupe, opened in 1599. Drama was edging London southward. As the city grew, more writers came, attracted by the presence of the theaters, of patrons, and of publishers.

Londoners' Rural Dreams As poets and writers flocked to smoky London—soft coal was the principal source of heat—they dreamed about the country. Following the models of the classical literature they had studied, they turned to the pastoral as a literary form. (*Pastor* is the Latin word for shepherd.) Greek and Roman literature had depicted shepherds and shepherdesses tending flocks in some innocent garden world. Walking the wet and stinking streets of London, poets imagined a green and carefree world, the world of English poet Christopher Marlowe's "The Passionate Shepherd to His Love."

1534: Henry VIII issues Act of Supremacy. ▲

1534: Spain St. Ignatius Loyola founds Jesuit brotherhood.

1534: Church of England established.

◄ **1535:** Thomas More executed.

1540: Copernicus completes treatise on astronomy.

1541

How does literature shape or reflect *society?*

What to believe? That was the question, and it was a question that affected everything, from religion, to politics, to the very nature of the Earth and the universe.

Why was belief an issue?

Changing Beliefs The official religion of England changed four times in less than thirty years. This series of upheavals began in 1534, when King Henry VIII took England out of the Catholic camp and made it a Protestant country.

Political Allegiance and Religious Belief The new link between politics and religion often had tragic consequences. Consider Sir Thomas More, a trusted advisor of King Henry VIII. A man of principle, More would not support Henry's petition for divorce. After he refused to acknowledge Henry as the head of the Church of England, Henry had him executed. More's tragic end announced a new, sometimes fatal struggle between warring religious convictions.

Mary I, daughter of Henry VIII and Catherine, became queen in 1553. She denied the validity of the church her father founded and used the power of the state to return the country to Catholicism. Those she thought the worst heretics she had burned at the stake, but this only fortified the resolve of those who had embraced Protestantism. Her successor, Elizabeth I, re-established the monarch's supremacy in the Church of England, restoring Protestantism as the country's official religion. Elizabeth strove for moderation in religious matters. Even so, she contended with Catholic plots against her throne and eventually had Mary, Queen of Scots—her Catholic cousin and rival—executed.

Other Shifts in Belief Even as Protestantism had shaken the Pope's claim to be at the center of the religious world, developments in science

TIMELINE

1541

1547: Henry VIII dies.

◀ 1549:
The Book of Common Prayer issued.

1558: Elizabeth I becomes queen.

1563: More than 20,000 Londoners die in plague.

High Fashion in the Elizabethan Age

A more trivial version of the question, What to believe?, is the question, What to wear? For the Elizabethan nobility, however, that second question was almost as urgent as the first. Women and men alike took dress very seriously. Noblewomen looked like dolls on display, tightly laced into dresses that resembled giant bells. Noblemen were arrayed like showy peacocks in close-fitting jackets and wide collars that seemed to serve up their heads on plates of lace. As demonstrated in the accompanying portraits—one of Queen Elizabeth I and one of Nicholas Hilliard—clothing was elaborate and theatrical in an age that loved the drama and also loved to dramatize itself.

Two devices that helped create these theatrical effects were the ruff and the farthingale, both of which came from the Spanish court. Even after the English navy defeated the Spanish Armada in 1588, Spanish fashions held sway among the English nobility. The ruff was a pleated, starched collar worn by both sexes. It varied in size, but as you can see from the portrait of Hilliard, it could expand to the size of a large platter. The farthingale was a linen underskirt stretched over a thick iron wire that supported a skirt or dress and gave it the bell shape that Elizabeth's dress has in the portrait.

and exploration were overturning old pictures of the universe. Explorers confirmed that the Earth is round, not flat. They discovered the Americas, previously unknown to Europeans, and estimates of the size of the Earth doubled. Add to these discoveries the new Copernican theory that the sun, not the Earth, is at the center of the solar system, and the result was the upending of centuries of belief.

◀ **1564:** William Shakespeare born.

1567: South America 2 million Indians die of typhoid.

1567: Brazil Rio de Janeiro is solidified as a Portuguese stronghold. ▶

1569

How did writers respond to problems of belief?

One True Bible Protestantism emphasized the authority of scripture, and to answer concerns about existing translations, King James I convened a group of fifty-four scholars to produce a new translation of the Bible. There would be one, authentic, accurate version for the entire realm. The scholars he commissioned to translate the work produced a Bible that remains a standard text and a masterpiece of English writing. (See page 246 for more details.) However, it did not resolve all conflicts. Even as men and women now read the same words, they argued about what those words meant.

The Place of the Individual Just as the Renaissance emphasized the glory of humanity and the value of the individual, Reformation thinkers such as Luther stressed the role of the individual's faith in achieving salvation. At the same time, religious controversy could demand an individual decision about what to believe. The new prominence of the individual is mirrored in the literature of the period. From Astrophel's complaints in Sidney's sonnet sequence *Astrophel and Stella* to the powerful soliloquies in Shakespeare's plays, in which characters lay bare the conflicts that tear at their souls, Elizabethan literature turned a new eye on the inner life.

Deciding What to Believe Columbus, Luther, and Copernicus never came to England, but they shaped the new worlds in which everyone had to learn to live all over again. It was a time of incredible turmoil: intellectual, religious, political, artistic. In the midst of that turmoil, ordinary people struggled to decide what to believe, how to worship, and whom to obey. The glorious literature of the period gave them new terms in which to think, opening the way to modern ideas of the individual.

> ### ESSENTIAL QUESTION VOCABULARY
>
> These Essential Question words will help you think and write about literature and society:
>
> **petition** (pə tish´ən) *n.* solemn request to a person or group in authority
>
> **heretics** (her´ə tiks) *n.* those holding opinions at odds with accepted religious beliefs
>
> **turmoil** (tur´moil´) *n.* commotion; uproar; confusion

TIMELINE

1569

▲ **1579:** Sir Francis Drake lands near site of San Francisco on his voyage around the globe.

1582: Italy Pope Gregory XIII introduces new calendar. ▼

c. 1582: Sir Philip Sidney writes *Astrophel and Stella.*

What is the relationship of the writer to *tradition?*

Renaissance and Reformation are the words that define the period. *Renaissance* means rebirth and refers to the revival of classical learning at this time. Reformation was the re-forming of the church, bringing it back to its earlier, basic forms. Both went back to older traditions to make something new.

What did writers rediscover in the classics?

Humanism The ancient language of Latin had never gone away—its study was still an important part of an education. What was rediscovered in this period was not a language, but the "purer" forms in which the classical writers of ancient Greece and Rome wrote. The classics also offered a view of life different from the Christian vision that had dominated Europe. Ancient Greek and Roman authors offered ethics without reference to heaven and hell and philosophy that was about the natural world, not about the supernatural. They emphasized what it was to be human, so the new way of thinking based on the classics was called Humanism.

How did rediscovery encourage originality?

Translation and Invention The champions of Humanism wanted the classics to reach a wide audience. They therefore undertook a series of translations that made the ancient works more widely available while at the same time enriching the English language. English poet and dramatist George Chapman translated the *Iliad,* the ancient Greek poet Homer's epic poem about the fall of ancient Troy. Sir Thomas North translated the ancient writer Plutarch's brief biographies of famous Greeks and Romans and provided Shakespeare with material for five plays. Perhaps most important, when the English poet Henry Howard, Earl of Surrey, translated the *Aeneid,* the Roman poet Virgil's epic on the founding of Rome, he used unrhymed lines of iambic pentameter. This supple form, "blank verse," was quickly adapted for the stage, and Elizabethan playwright Christopher

1588: English navy defeats Spanish Armada.

◄ **1594:** Shakespeare writes *Romeo and Juliet.*

1590: Edmund Spenser publishes *The Faerie Queen,* Part I.

1595: South America Sir Walter Raleigh explores Orinoco River.

1597

Marlowe's version of blank verse, his "mighty line," inspired Shakespeare to imitate it and then make it his special instrument. The invention of blank verse shows that, as often happened in this period, the return to older sources led to innovations.

A New Form of Drama The drama itself was a mixture of two traditions, one native and one classical. The native tradition began in the medieval church and involved the reenactment of scenes from the Bible. These "plays" moved into the marketplace, adding depictions of the struggles of vice and virtue. Shakespeare probably saw such performances as a boy. Onto this native stock of theatrical representation, the new writers grafted classical models of comedy and tragedy. The result was a new form of English drama.

Borrowing and Reinventing One of the most enduring forms of English poetry, the sonnet, entered the English tradition through translation. In this period, writers from all over Europe borrowed ideas and literary models from Italy, where the Renaissance began. English poets imported a fourteen-line Italian poem called the *sonetto*. Sidney, Spenser, and Shakespeare worked individual variations on the challenging form (see page 241), as would poets of later centuries.

In religion, how did writers move forward by going back?

Remaking the Bible, in English Translation was crucial to the Reformation as well. When James I came to the throne, it was obvious that the Church of England, in existence for sixty-nine years, should have one recognized English Bible. There were English translations, but none was standard. King James appointed a committee of scholars to make a new translation. Not only did they consult the Latin version of St. Jerome, which had been used in Europe for more than a thousand years, but working with Latin, Greek, and Hebrew texts, in a blend of the new learning and the new religious fervor, they produced the required Bible, a masterpiece of English prose.

Once again, writers had gone back to traditional sources and used them to make something new and enduring. Other translations may now be used in church services, but as long as English is spoken, "The Lord is my shepherd" will be remembered.

> **ESSENTIAL QUESTION VOCABULARY**
>
> These Essential Question words will help you think and write about the writer and tradition:
>
> **ethics** (eth´iks) *n.* study of standards of conduct and moral judgment
>
> **theology** (thē äl´ə jē) *n.* study of religious doctrines and matters of divinity
>
> **innovations** (in´ ə vā´shənz) *n.* new methods or devices

TIMELINE

1599: Globe theater opens. ▼

1597

1603: Elizabeth I dies.

1600: East India Company founded.

▲ **1606:** Guy Fawkes executed for Gunpowder Plot.

CONTEMPORARY CONNECTION

William Shakespeare: To Be or Not to Be . . . A Rocker!

Shakespeare's sonnets may seem an unlikely inspiration for contemporary musicians, composers, and singers. In 2007, however, the Royal Shakespeare Company commissioned pop artists to set their favorite sonnet to music. Here are some of the surprising results:

- Irish singer Gavin Friday found his inspiration in Sonnet 40: "Take my loves, love, yea take them all. . . ." One reviewer wrote that Friday's performance was "extraordinary," describing his intonation of the sonnet as "a kind of strangulated speech-song."

- Former 10,000 Maniacs lead singer Natalie Merchant picked melancholy Sonnet 73, with its reflections on advancing age: "To love that well which thou must leave ere long."

- Romanian violinist Alexander Balanescu's choice was Sonnet 43, with its speaker's expression of longing to see his love: "All days are nights to see till I see thee."

- Electronic artist Mira Calix decided on Sonnet 130, a parody of love poetry, which begins, "My mistress's eyes are nothing like the sun." Calix liked "the idea that it appears to be a diss."

For artists and audience alike, the experience proved the timelessness of the sonnets. As Merchant commented in wonder, "How could an Englishman writing at the beginning of the seventeenth century and I have so much in common?"

1607: North America British colony established at Jamestown.

1618: Germany Kepler proposes laws of planetary motion.

1623: First patent laws passed.

1625

1609: Italy Galileo builds first telescope.

▲ **1620: North America** Pilgrims land at Plymouth Rock.

1625: James I dies.

Life in Elizabethan and Jacobean England

Sir Frank Kermode

L ondon expanded greatly during the reign of Queen Elizabeth I, becoming one of the largest and wealthiest European capitals. Essentially a medieval city, its southern boundary was the River Thames, which was also its principal thoroughfare. To the north was the old Roman wall, but the city was spreading beyond it. Upstream was Westminster, the historic seat of the court and the national government. And across the river was Southwark, outside the jurisdiction of the City of London and therefore the favored site for enterprises, including theaters, deplored by the virtually autonomous and puritanical city government.

The population was swollen by country people, escaping the restrictions of rural life and famine, and by immigrants from Europe. The narrow, traffic-crowded streets were lined by shops and workshops, by civic mansions and rich halls of the trade guilds, and by the Inns of Court, haunts of lawyers and young gentlemen continuing their studies after leaving Oxford or Cambridge. The class system was strict—clothes were appropriate to rank, whether gentleman, citizen, craftsman, or laborer.

About the Author

Sir Frank Kermode is a literary critic who has written in-depth analyses of works ranging from the Bible to those of Shakespeare and beyond. He is a former professor of modern English at University College, London, and was knighted by Queen Elizabeth in 1991.

Shakespeare, new to London, probably took time to settle down. His London was the area around the old St. Paul's cathedral. The theaters were across the river in wicked Southwark. Westminster, site of Whitehall Palace, was a couple of miles to the west. There, in ancient halls, the great affairs of state were decided. There the queen contended with the Pope and her other foreign and domestic enemies. Later, James catered to his favorites and dreamed of establishing absolute monarchy and universal peace. However, their majesties both liked plays, so there was hope for an aspiring playwright. There was the prospect of pleasure and success, though there was also risk. Perhaps that's why Shakespeare left his family in Stratford: to take his place in the London theater—and eventually, literary immortality.

The Challenges of Urban Life

London was not clean or healthy. Sanitation was crude—the Thames was a beautiful sewer. Deadly diseases—plague, malaria, smallpox—ensured a high mortality rate. Cheats, tricksters, and thieves abounded. Men carried weapons—swords or pistols—in the street. Meanwhile, as the fields and woods were built over, access to country air grew more difficult.

Inflation was unchecked but money flowed freely. Among the expensive luxuries of the day were ostentatious clothes and tobacco, a recent import from the New World. London was perpetual bustle, noise, and display. Imagine how a young man from the provinces, like Shakespeare, might react to it. Shakespeare's Stratford, though a sturdy community with its own guilds and its good grammar school, hardly offered adequate preparation for London, a great port and the gateway to the larger world. The splendor of the river and the mansions lining its bank won the keen admiration of foreign visitors, who compared its magnificence to that of Paris and other great European cities.

From Stratford to London

In Shakespeare's day, the journey from Stratford to London took four days on foot, two on a horse.

Integrate and Evaluate Information

1. Use a chart like the one shown to determine the key ideas expressed in the Essential Question essays on pages 240–246. Fill in two ideas related to each Essential Question and note the authors most closely associated with each concept. One item has been completed for you.

Essential Question	Key Concept	Key Author
Literature and Place		
Literature and Society		
Writer and Tradition	New uses of the sonnet	William Shakespeare

2. Review the visual images in this section. Choose one that, in your view, is representative of the movement known as the Renaissance, and one that is representative of the movement known as the Reformation. Explain your choices.

3. Both the Renaissance and the Reformation sought to recover earlier perspectives: the former by reviving the literature of ancient Greece and Rome, and the latter by returning to Christian scripture (rather than the pope) for religious guidance. (a) Describe one effect of Renaissance ideas on the literature of the time. (b) Explain how the Renaissance and Reformation shaped new ideas of the individual.

4. Address a Question: In his essay on pages 248–249, Sir Frank Kermode writes that Renaissance London "was not clean or healthy" but that the splendor and vitality of the city was widely admired. Would you like to have visited London during this period in history? Why or why not? Integrate information from this textbook and other sources, such as an online history of the city, to support your ideas.

Speaking and Listening: "Welcome" Talk

Shakespearean drama had its home in London's Globe theater. Destroyed by Puritans in the mid-1600s, the Globe was rebuilt in 1997. Today, the new Globe serves as a theater, information center and exhibition space.

Play the role of a docent, or tour guide, at the new Globe, and prepare a multimedia **"welcome" talk** for visitors. Your talk should include a brief history of the original Globe theater, as well as a description of the resources at the modern Globe. Make sure to address alternative views of the theater's history and construction. To accompany your talk, prepare a brief slide presentation that includes photographs or diagrams of the theater. Select images that will lend interest or that will help your audience understand your points.

Solve a Research Problem: This assignment requires you to research both the history and present-day existence of the Globe. Begin by formulating a research plan. Review both print and media sources, and consult the ones that you determine will provide reliable information about the Globe. You may also want to contact an actual Globe docent for information about the talks given to visitors.

Common Core State Standards

Reading Informational Text

7. Integrate and evaluate multiple sources of information presented in different media or formats as well as in words in order to address a question or solve a problem.

Speaking and Listening

4. Present information, findings, and supporting evidence, conveying a clear and distinct perspective, such that listeners can follow the line of reasoning, alternative or opposing perspectives are addressed, and the organization, development, substance, and style are appropriate to purpose, audience, and a range of formal and informal tasks.

5. Make strategic use of digital media in presentations to enhance understanding of findings, reasoning, and evidence and to add interest.

ESSENTIAL QUESTION VOCABULARY

Use these words in your responses:

Literature and Place
exhilaration
pastoral
climate

Literature and Society
petition
heretics
turmoil

Writer and Tradition
ethics
theology
innovations

Sir Philip Sidney
(1554–1586)

Author of *Sidney's Sonnets*

Sir Philip Sidney was a courtier, scholar, poet, and soldier—a true "Renaissance man." He attended both Oxford and Cambridge, and furthered his knowledge by traveling extensively through Europe. He became a favorite in the court of Queen Elizabeth I.

Groomed for Success Nephew of the earl of Leicester and son of the statesman Sir Henry Sidney, Philip Sidney was certainly well connected. Throughout his life, though, he carried himself with remarkable modesty. His schoolmate and, later, biographer Fulke Greville remarked on his "staidness of mind, [and] lovely and familiar gravity."

A Brave Soldier Around 1580, Sidney fell out of favor with the queen when he wrote a letter urging her not to marry the duke of Anjou. Eventually, he regained status with her and was knighted in 1583. In 1586, during a military engagement against the Spanish Catholics in Holland, Sidney was severely wounded. As he lay on the battle-field, he bravely insisted that the water offered to him be given to another wounded soldier. Twenty-six days later he died, to the great grief of his country.

Pioneering Sonneteer Sidney wrote the first great sonnet sequence in English, *Astrophel and Stella*. Before Sidney, Sir Thomas Wyatt and others had writ-ten excellent sonnets, but Sidney's were the first linked by subject matter and theme. Each sonnet addresses an aspect of Astrophel's love for Stella. This sonnet sequence was inspired by Penelope Devereux (Stella), to whom Sir Philip (Astrophel) had been engaged. The engagement was later broken, and Penelope married Lord Rich. Yet, for most readers, Stella's name will forever be linked with Astrophel's.

Either I will find a way, or I will make one.

—Sir Philip Sidney

Sonnet 31

Sir Philip Sidney

With how sad steps, O Moon, thou climb'st the skies!
How silently, and with how wan a face!
What, may it be that even in heavenly place
That busy archer[1] his sharp arrows tries?
5 Sure, if that long-with-love-acquainted eyes
Can judge of love, thou feel'st a lover's case.
I read it in thy looks, thy languished grace,
To me, that feel the like, thy state descries.[2]
Then even of fellowship, O Moon, tell me
10 Is constant love deemed there but want of wit?[3]
Are beauties there as proud as here they be?
Do they above love to be loved, and yet
Those lovers scorn whom that love doth possess?
Do they call virtue there ungratefulness?

---

1. **busy archer** Cupid, the Roman god of love.
2. **descries** reveals.
3. **wit** intelligence.

Vocabulary

wan (wän) *adj.* sickly; pale
languished (laŋ´ gwisht) *adj.* weakened; dulled

◀ Critical Viewing

Which details suggest that the subject of this portrait might be the speaker in Sonnet 31? **CONNECT**

SONNET 39

SIR PHILIP SIDNEY

Come sleep! O sleep, the certain knot of peace,
The baiting place[1] of wit, the balm of woe,
The poor man's wealth, the prisoner's release,
The indifferent[2] judge between the high and low;
5 With shield of proof[3] shield me from out the prease[4]
Of those fierce darts Despair at me doth throw:
O make in me those civil wars to cease;
I will good tribute pay, if thou do so.
Take thou of me smooth pillows, sweetest bed,
10 A chamber deaf to noise, and blind to light,
A rose garland, and a weary head:
And if these things, as being thine by right,
Move not thy heavy grace, thou shalt in me,
Livelier than elsewhere, Stella's image see.

---

1. baiting place place for refreshment.
2. indifferent impartial.
3. proof proven strength.
4. prease crowd.

Critical Reading

Cite textual evidence to support your responses.

1. **Key Ideas and Details (a)** In Sonnet 31, how does the moon appear to the speaker? **(b) Infer:** To what does the speaker attribute the moon's mood? **(c) Analyze:** How does the speaker reveal his own situation by addressing the moon?

2. **Key Ideas and Details (a)** What benefits does the speaker attribute to sleep in lines 1–4 of Sonnet 39? **(b)** What "reward" does he promise sleep in lines 13–14? **(c) Interpret:** Judging from this "reward," why does he crave sleep?

3. **Craft and Structure** What, if anything, do the regular rhymes and briefness of the sonnet form add to these poets' expressions of love? Explain. In your response, use at least two of these Essential Question words: *form, imitation, influence, Renaissance. [Connecting to the Essential Question: What is the relationship of the writer to tradition?]*

Literary Analysis

1. **Craft and Structure** Review Spenser's three sonnets. Then, explain what poets can achieve in a **sonnet sequence** that they cannot in individual poems. Consider such factors as shifting moods and developing characters.

2. **Craft and Structure** Reread Sidney's Sonnets 31 and 39, and analyze their rhyme schemes. Do these **sonnets** more closely follow the **Spenserian** or the **Petrarchan** form? Explain.

3. **Key Ideas and Details** Reread the octave of Sidney's Sonnet 39. **(a) Determine the essential message** of lines 1–4 by writing a *paraphrase* of them. **(b)** Then, paraphrase lines 5–8. **(c)** What problem do lines 1–8 set up?

4. **Key Ideas and Details (a)** Reread and then paraphrase the sestet of Sonnet 39. **(b)** What does the sestet suggest about the reason for the problem in the octave? Explain.

5. **Comparing Literary Works** Using a chart like the one here, compare and contrast one of Sidney's sonnets with one of Spenser's.

Petrarchan/ Spenserian?	Speaker's Situation	Addressed to...	Types of Images	Speaker's Conclusion

6. **Craft and Structure (a)** Compare the person or thing addressed in each of the sonnets you entered in the chart. **(b)** Explain how the basic situation in each of the **sonnet sequences** justifies or motivates each choice of addressee.

7. **Craft and Structure (a)** Compare the dominant purpose of each sonnet in the chart—for example, to express hope, to persuade, or to complain. **(b)** Explain how the situation in each of the sonnet sequences justifies or motivates each purpose.

8. **Integration of Knowledge and Ideas** Explain how, in each sonnet, the writer goes beyond the basic sonnet situation to give a general insight into the nature of love or life. Be sure to include details from the texts in support of your answer.

9. **Integration of Knowledge and Ideas (a)** Renaissance poets compared those they loved to "perfect" things in nature or to timeless figures from mythology. To what "perfect" things do songwriters compare their loves today? **(b)** In what other ways are modern songwriters similar to or different from Renaissance sonneteers?

Common Core State Standards

Writing

2. Write informative/ explanatory texts to examine and convey complex ideas, concepts, and information clearly and accurately through the effective selection, organization, and analysis of content. *(p. 262)*

4. Produce clear and coherent writing in which the development, organization, and style are appropriate to task, purpose, and audience. *(p. 262)*

Language

4.a. Use context as a clue to the meaning of a word or phrase. *(p. 262)*

4.b. Identify and correctly use patterns of word changes that indicate different meanings or parts of speech. *(p. 262)*

Vocabulary Acquisition and Use

Word Analysis: Patterns of Word Changes

Words often change form and *meaning* when they serve different *functions*. For example, the verb *languish,* which means "to become weak," has the past participle form *languished.* This form can be used as an adjective ("languished grace") or as a verb ("He languished under the weight of illness"). Other forms of the word are *languid,* an adjective that means "drooping" or "weak," and the noun *languor,* meaning "weakness."

For each sentence below, decide what function or meaning the missing word should have. Then identify the form of *languish* that belongs in the blank, explaining each choice.

1. His _____ was caused by overexertion.
2. The worker's movements were _____ at the end of the day.
3. Everyone _____ in the heat.

Vocabulary: Context Clues

Context clues are words and phrases in a text that help you reason out the meaning of an unfamiliar word. For each underlined word below, explain how clues in the sentence help you identify the word's *contextual meaning.*

1. The young woman <u>languished</u>, weakened by neglect.
2. Her <u>wan</u> complexion matched the washed-out hue of her hankie.
3. Even a glimpse of her beloved would be a soothing <u>balm</u> to her broken heart.
4. Desperate, she began to <u>devise</u> an array of complicated plans.
5. Then, she grew haughty; she would never <u>deign</u> to answer his call.
6. Just let him <u>assay</u> an approach, she muttered.

Writing

Explanatory Text As a technical writer, you have been contracted to compose a *manual* explaining *procedures* for putting together a Petrarchan sonnet. The manual will be used by the company's newest sonneteers, so it should be clear, accurate, and easy to follow. It should also employ and briefly define the *technical* terms for each element of the sonnet, including *octave, sestet, iambic pentameter,* and *rhyme scheme.*

Prewriting Consider using some or all of the following: a preface, a table of contents, an overview of the product, in-depth descriptions of each part, step-by-step instructions, an FAQ section (Frequently Asked Questions), and a Where to Find Help page.

Drafting As you draft your manual, keep your readers in mind. Define all technical terms and put all concepts into clear, concise language.

Revising Revise with an eye to format. Have you included too much information on a single page? Can your reader glance at a page and understand what the page contains? Add headings, bullets, boldfacing, and other text features as needed.

Model: Anticipating Reader Confusion

II. The Sestet

The second half of the sonnet is made up of a *sestet.*

A **sestet** is a group of six lines with the rhyme scheme *cdecde.*

The writer has anticipated and answered the following questions: *What is a sestet? What is its rhyme scheme?*

Conventions and Style: Subordinating Conjunctions

For a smoother flow and more variety in your writing, try using subordinating conjunctions to combine sentences. A **subordinating conjunction** joins two complete ideas by making one idea subordinate to, or dependent on, the other.

Common Subordinating Conjunctions

after	as though	if	unless
although	because	now that	until
as if	before	since	when
as soon as	even though	so that	while

When you use **subordination** to combine sentences, you show which idea is more important.

Use Subordination to Combine Sentences

Simple Sentences: Philip Sidney regained the queen's favor. Then he was knighted.
Combined: Philip Sidney was knighted *after* he regained the queen's favor.
Simple Sentences: The speaker describes leaves. He is really talking about a book.
Combined: *Although* the speaker describes leaves, he is really talking about a book

Practice In items 1–5, supply an appropriate subordinating conjunction to complete each sentence. In items 6–10, combine the two sentences using a subordinating conjunction.

1. According to the poet's guess, the moon is sad _____ it has lost in love.
2. Poets often compare lovers to the moon or stars, _____ their beloved is perfect.
3. The poems will keep her memory alive _____ she dies.
4. The moon appears _____ it feels weak or sick.
5. He asks for smooth pillows, a comfortable bed, and a dark and quiet room _____ he can sleep soundly.
6. He has looked at her. He does not want to look at anything else.
7. The writing is finished. The sea washes it away.
8. He will still love her. She does not return his feelings.
9. He wants to please her. He loves her.
10. The poet addresses the moon. He acts as if the moon understands him.

Writing and Speaking Conventions

A. Writing For each pair of ideas, construct a sentence that uses a subordinating conjunction to join the ideas.

1. the poet is happy—he is gazing at his beloved
2. her name was washed away—the tide came in

> **Example:** the moon climbs the skies—it does so with sad steps
> **Sentence:** Although the moon climbs the skies, it does so with sad steps.

Punctuation Tip: Use a comma after a subordinate clause that comes at the beginning of a sentence but not, in most cases, before a subordinate clause that comes at the end of a sentence.

B. Speaking Choose one of the sonnets and summarize it to a classmate. In your summary, correctly use two subordinating conjunctions.

Connecting to the Essential Question As you read, notice which poem's setting is shaped more by the imagination and which by observation of the world. Making this distinction will help you explore this Essential Question: **What is the relationship between literature and place?**

Close Reading Focus

Pastoral

Works in the **pastoral** tradition, in poetry or prose, celebrate the pleasures of country life. This tradition, dating back to ancient Greece, was developed by authors writing for an urban audience. These conventions of the pastoral allowed city dwellers to imagine a country life:

- shepherds addressing or describing a beloved shepherdess
- a natural setting that seems perfect in every respect
- simple pleasures and games, including singing contests

Comparing Literary Works While addressing pastoral conventions differently, Marlowe and Raleigh touch on a number of **universal themes:** the link between love and the delights of youth and nature, and the relationship between love and time—love conquering time or being conquered by it.

Note the variations in these themes as you read. Also, consider this *nuance:* Although Raleigh seems to be writing against the pastoral tradition, is he in some way part of it?

Preparing to Read Complex Texts As you read a poem, determine if it contains multiple themes. Then, decide how multiple themes add to the meaning of the poem. For example, do the themes build on or contradict each other?

When reading a pair of related poems, **analyze similar themes** in the two by comparing and contrasting their *patterns of organization* and *repetition*. For example, Marlowe and Raleigh use similar patterns of organization to create contrasting versions of pastoral themes. Use a chart like the one on this page to help you summarize each poem and then compare and contrast themes.

Vocabulary

The words below are key to understanding the texts that follow. Copy the words into your notebook. Which part of speech is signaled by the affix *-ous*?

melodious	**gall**
madrigals	**wither**
reckoning	

Common Core State Standards

Reading Literature
2. Determine two or more themes or central ideas of a text and analyze their development over the course of the text, including how they interact and build on one another to produce a complex account.

Marlowe

Stanza #1
argument Come be my love and enjoy the countryside with me.
key words live, love, pleasures
themes pastoral, love and youth

Raleigh

Stanza #1
response I would be your love if you were telling the truth.
repeated words live, love, pleasures
themes anti-pastoral, untruthful lover

(1564–1593)

CHRISTOPHER MARLOWE

Author of **"The Passionate Shepherd to His Love"**

Killed before the age of thirty, Christopher Marlowe nonetheless managed to achieve renown as a brilliant playwright and poet. He spent his college days writing plays and serving as a government agent.

A Pioneer in Drama *Tamburlaine*, Marlowe's first drama, dazzled the public with its dynamic characterization of the tyrant-hero. All of Marlowe's subsequent plays may be seen as variations on a single theme: the larger-than-life hero who "overreaches," seeking to dominate everything around him.

The most famous example is the protagonist in *Doctor Faustus*, who thirsts for supreme knowledge and sells his soul to the devil. Marlowe matched the grandeur of his heroes with the grandeur of language, forging blank verse into a powerfully expressive medium for the first time in English drama.

A Life of Intrigue Marlowe has been described as a scoundrel, a ladies' man, and a hothead. By all accounts, his personal magnetism attracted both friends and enemies. When the court of Queen Elizabeth I wrote a letter implying that Marlowe had performed important government services, rumors flew about that he was a spy.

A Violent Death Marlowe was knifed to death in a tavern brawl in 1593. To this day, scholars question whether his death was really caused by his drunken refusal to pay his bill or whether he was murdered because of his undercover activities on behalf of the government.

(1554?–1618)

SIR WALTER RALEIGH

Author of **"The Nymph's Reply to the Shepherd"**

Sir Walter Raleigh is famed for having been a courtier, a navigator, a poet, and a historian.

A Charmed Life The half-brother of a famous sailor and an explorer, Raleigh began to satisfy his taste for adventure early in life, when he volunteered as a teenager for army service in France. A favorite of Queen Elizabeth I, he was given estates and prestigious appointments. In 1584, he set up a colony in Virginia.

Disaster When it was discovered that Raleigh had been secretly married to one of the queen's maids of honor, he and his wife were imprisoned in the Tower of London for a time but then released. Following the queen's death in 1603, Raleigh was accused of conspiring against King James I and was imprisoned again in the Tower, where he remained for thirteen years. He was eventually released to seek out gold along the Orinoco River in Venezuela. Despite a royal command not to engage in battle with Spain, Raleigh's fleet entered Spanish territory. In the ensuing fight, Raleigh lost his son and was forced to return to England. There, Raleigh was executed for disobeying the king's orders.

Literary Achievements Raleigh was a friend of some of the leading poets of his age, including Sir Philip Sydney and Edmund Spenser. Like them, he wrote elegant verse, rich in vivid imagery and classical allusions. Among Raleigh's numerous prose works is an ambitious book entitled *The History of the World* (1614), composed while he was in prison.

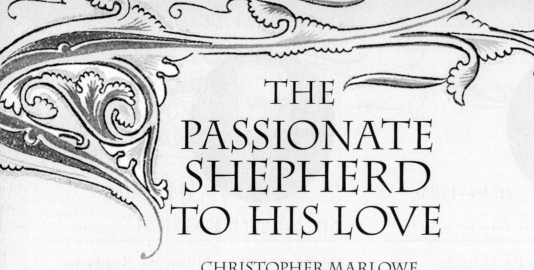

THE PASSIONATE SHEPHERD TO HIS LOVE

CHRISTOPHER MARLOWE

Come live with me, and be my love,
And we will all the pleasures prove[1]
That valleys, groves, hills, and fields,
Woods, or steepy mountain yields.

5 And we will sit upon the rocks,
Seeing the shepherds feed their flocks,
By shallow rivers to whose falls
Melodious birds sing madrigals.

And I will make thee beds of roses,
10 And a thousand fragrant posies,
A cap of flowers, and a kirtle[2]
Embroidered all with leaves of myrtle;

A gown made of the finest wool,
Which from our pretty lambs we pull;
15 Fair lined slippers for the cold,
With buckles of the purest gold;

A belt of straw and ivy buds,
With coral clasps and amber studs;
And if these pleasures may thee move,
20 Come live with me, and be my love.

The shepherds' swains shall dance and sing
For thy delight each May morning;
If these delights thy mind may move,
Then live with me and be my love.

Pastoral

Which details in this stanza idealize the landscape?

Vocabulary

melodious (mə lō′ dē əs) *adj.* sweet-sounding; tuneful; pleasing to hear

madrigals (ma′ dri gəlz) *n.* short love poems set to music

▶ **Critical Viewing**

The poem's speaker views the countryside as a luxurious source of pleasure and the perfect escape from urban life. Which details in this painting reflect such an ideal? **CONNECT**

1. **prove** experience.
2. **kirtle** skirt.

THE NYMPH'S REPLY TO THE SHEPHERD

SIR WALTER RALEIGH

BACKGROUND "The Passionate Shepherd to His Love" and "The Nymph's Reply to the Shepherd" are examples of reply poems. Many poets travel in similar social circles, and their association with each other sometimes motivates them to construct poems in response to one another's work. In addition to Sir Walter Raleigh, for example, John Donne also wrote a reply poem, "The Bait," to Marlowe's "The Passionate Shepherd to His Love." Such linkages can be found in many literary epochs and cultures: for example, twentieth-century Chinese poet Shu Ting composed a poem, titled "Also All," in response to Bei Dao's poem "All."

Analyzing Similar Themes

How do the first four lines of this poem compare with the opening lines of "The Passionate Shepherd to His Love"?

Vocabulary

reckoning (rek´ ən iŋ) *n.* accounting

gall (gôl) *n.* bitter feeling; deep spite

wither (wi*th*´ ər) *v.* dry up

If all the world and love were young
And truth in every shepherd's tongue
These pretty pleasures might me move
To live with thee, and be thy love.

5   Time drives the flocks from field to fold,
When rivers rage and rocks grow cold,
And Philomel[1] becometh dumb,
The rest complains of cares to come.

The flowers do fade, and wanton fields
10   To wayward winter reckoning yields:
A honey tongue, a heart of gall,
Is fancy's spring, but sorrow's fall.

Thy gowns, thy shoes, thy beds of roses,
Thy cap, thy kirtle,[2] and thy posies
15   Soon break, soon wither, soon forgotten,
In folly ripe, in reason rotten.

---

1. Philomel the nightingale.
2. kirtle skirt.

Thy belt of straw and ivy buds,
Thy coral clasps and amber studs,
All these in me no means can move
20 To come to thee and be thy love.

But could youth last and love still breed,
Has joy no date[3] nor age no need,
Then these delights my mind might move,
To live with thee and be thy love.

---

3. **date** ending.

Critical Reading

1. **Key Ideas and Details (a)** In "The Passionate Shepherd to His Love," what does the speaker ask his love to do in the first stanza? **(b) Interpret:** What kind of future life together does the speaker envision?

2. **Key Ideas and Details (a)** What happens to the nightingale in line 7 of "The Nymph's Reply"? **(b) Compare and Contrast:** According to lines 5 through 8, in what ways is the nymph's world different from that of the shepherd? **(c) Analyze:** Which words in this stanza evoke a feeling of ruin or despair? Explain.

3. **Key Ideas and Details (a)** According to lines 21–22 of "The Nymph's Reply," what might persuade the nymph to live with the shepherd? **(b) Speculate:** Do you think these lines would console the shepherd? **(c) Analyze:** How does the nymph present a realistic portrayal of time and change?

4. **Integration of Knowledge and Ideas** If you were the shepherd, what counterargument might you make in response to the "The Nymph's Reply"?

5. **Integration of Knowledge and Ideas** What is the good, if any, of using literature to imagine an ideal setting? In your answer, use at least two of these Essential Question words: *perfection, escape, pastoral, realistic.* [*Connecting to the Essential Question: What is the relationship between literature and place?*]

Cite textual evidence to support your responses.

Literary Analysis

1. **Key Ideas and Details** Although both Marlowe and Raleigh's poems reflect the **pastoral** tradition, the speakers present opposing views of rural life. **(a)** Use a chart like the one shown to identify details that signal the shepherd's idealized view and the nymph's more realistic view of country life.

 **Common Core State Standards**

Writing
2.c. Use appropriate and varied transitions and syntax to link the major sections of the text, create cohesion, and clarify the relationships among complex ideas and concepts. *(p. 271)*

Language
4.a. Use context as a clue to the meaning of a word or phrase. *(p. 271)*

Shepherd's Idealism	Nymph's Realism

   (b) Based on their attitudes toward nature, what conclusions can you draw about the personalities of the shepherd and the nymph?

2. **Key Ideas and Details (a)** If you **analyze similar themes** in both poems, what similarities and *repetitions* do you find in them? **(b)** How does Raleigh's *pattern of organization* make it easier for him to contrast his views on the pastoral tradition, love, and time with those of Marlowe?

3. **Craft and Structure** In line 16 of "The Nymph's Reply to the Shepherd," in what way does the speaker's word choice reveal a striking balance of opposites to illustrate the theme of the harmful effects of time?

4. **Integration of Knowledge and Ideas (a)** In what ways can Raleigh's poem be considered anti-pastoral? **(b)** Is Raleigh's poem also part of the pastoral tradition? Cite details from the text to support your answer.

5. **Integration of Knowledge and Ideas** The worth of love is one of the **universal themes** explored in these poems, but the speakers present contrasting views. **(a)** Compare and contrast the views of each speaker on the worth and reliability of love. **(b)** Although these speakers, a shepherd and a nymph, are supposedly part of the same landscape, how are they "worlds apart"? **(c)** Compare their syntax, or sentence structure.

6. **Comparing Literary Works** Renaissance lyric poems often linked the inevitable passage of time with the Latin motto *carpe diem*, meaning "seize the day," or enjoy yourself in the present. **(a)** How does this motto apply to each of these poems? **(b)** How is this theme universal, rather than specific to a particular culture?

7. **Analyzing Visual Information** Does this caricature of Sir Walter Raleigh suggest that he might have shared the nymph's cynical view of love proposals? Explain.

Vocabulary Acquisition and Use

Word Analysis: *gall*

The *medical etymology* of the word *gall* goes back to the Greek word *chole*, or "bile." Bile is the bitter yellowish fluid secreted by the liver to aid in digestion. In ancient Greek medicine, bile referred to one of two bodily humors, or fluids: black bile, thought to cause melancholy, or yellow bile, thought to cause anger. The other two humors were blood, which made a person cheerful and confident; and phlegm, which made a person calm and detached. In a healthy person, these four fluids were thought to be held in balance. This theory remained the most common view of the human body in Europe until the 1800s.

In each sentence below, replace *gall* with a word of similar meaning.

1. The gall of defeat was difficult to swallow.
2. He could no longer contain his gall and began to yell.

Vocabulary: Context Clues

Review the vocabulary words on page 264. Then, for each item below, explain how the meaning of the vocabulary word and the *context* in which it is used help you identify each statement as correct or incorrect.

1. The poet adapted her works as *madrigals* and participated in a performance of them.
2. Her strong, *melodious* voice was perfectly suited to the poems' deep emotion.
3. At the end of the stunning performance, she even had the *gall* to sing several encores and take additional bows.
4. According to one *reckoning*, the show drew the largest crowd in the whole history of the opera house.
5. These facts suggest the conclusion that the poet's fame will *wither* within days.

Writing to Sources

Informative Text Marlowe's and Raleigh's poems present opposing points of view on the same subject. Write an **essay** in which you develop a *coherent thesis*, or consistent central idea, about the poems' *similarities and differences*. Focus on the viewpoints expressed by the speakers in the poems.

Prewriting Use a chart like the one shown to compare the poems. Then, draw a conclusion about their similarities and differences.

Model: Compare and Contrast Essay	Love	Nature	Time	World
"The Passionate Shepherd"	sees it as life's highest pleasure			
"The Nymph's Reply"	sees it as a mistake			

Using generalizations here will help the writer see major similarities and differences in the speakers' viewpoints.

Drafting Incorporate your conclusion into a clear thesis statement. Then, in the body of your essay, develop this thesis by comparing the viewpoints expressed in the poems. Use transition words and phrases such as *similarly*, *in contrast*, and *by comparison*.

Revising Revise your draft, focusing on redundant ideas. Remove any words or sentences that do not directly relate to or support your thesis.

Connecting to the Essential Question Shakespeare changed the structure of the Petrarchan sonnet. As you read, identify some of the differences between the Shakespearean and the Petrarchan sonnet. Noting these differences will help as you consider the Essential Question: **What is the relationship of the writer to tradition?**

Close Reading Focus

Shakespearean Sonnet; Syntax
A **Shakespearean sonnet** has fourteen lines, with five iambic feet to the line (an iambic foot is an unstressed syllable followed by a stressed one).

Unlike Petrarchan and Spenserian sonnets, a Shakespearean sonnet follows the rhyme scheme *abab cdcd efef gg,* giving it this structure:

- three **quatrains,** or four-line stanzas

- a rhyming **couplet** that dramatically restates or redefines a theme

As you read, notice Shakespeare's quatrains and couplets. Also notice how his sentences often continue past lines and sometimes past quatrains.

Though all Shakespearean sonnets have fourteen rhyming lines, there are no rules about the number or types of sentences. Shakespeare uses this freedom of **syntax,** or sentence structure, to create dazzling dramatic effects. By saving his main idea until the end of one long sentence (lines 13–14), he makes Sonnet 106 build like a lawyer's statement to a jury.

Preparing to Read Complex Texts A sonnet's rhyme scheme, stanzas, and syntax are text structures. You can better understand a sonnet by **analyzing its text structures,** noticing how they contribute to the sonnet's clarity of meaning and aesthetic impact. For example, each quatrain helps develop the main problem or argument, which the couplet then dramatically restates or redefines. Use a chart like the one shown to analyze each sonnet's *pattern of organization.*

Vocabulary

The words below are important to understanding the texts that follow. Copy the words into your notebook. Which words have a prefix that you recognize?

scope	prefiguring
sullen	impediments
chronicle	alters

Common Core State Standards

Reading Literature
5. Analyze how an author's choices concerning how to structure specific parts of a text contribute to its overall structure and meaning as well as its aesthetic impact.

Language
3.a. Apply an understanding of syntax to the study of complex texts when reading.

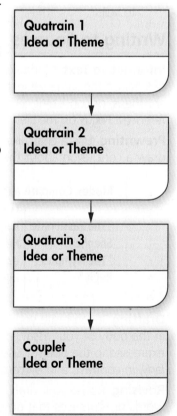

Quatrain 1
Idea or Theme

Quatrain 2
Idea or Theme

Quatrain 3
Idea or Theme

Couplet
Idea or Theme

William Shakespeare (1564–1616)

Author of *Sonnet 29* • *Sonnet 106* • *Sonnet 116* • *Sonnet 130*

Shakespeare may be the most admired author of all time. If he were living today, he would be a celebrity, and the facts of his life would be widely available in magazine articles, books, and Web pages. Instead, we know few facts about him, and these few had to be painstakingly traced from legal and church records or deduced from references in his work.

Bare-Bones Biography Shakespeare was born in the country town of Stratford-on-Avon and probably attended the town's free grammar school. When he was eighteen, he married twenty-six-year-old Anne Hathaway. They had a daughter, Susanna, and twins, Hamnet and Judith.

Shakespeare acquired a public reputation as an actor and a playwright. In addition, he was part owner of a London theater called the Globe, where many of his plays were performed. (For more about Shakespeare and his work as a dramatist, see pages 316–319.)

The Sonnet In the years 1592–1594, London's theaters were closed because of an outbreak of the plague. This general misfortune may have had at least one benefit: It may have provided the time that Shakespeare needed to write some of his 154 sonnets.

In writing a long sequence of sonnets, Shakespeare was being fashionable. Elizabethan poets enjoyed the sonnet form, writing fourteen-line lyric poems to both real and imaginary lovers.

The great Italian poet Petrarch (1304–1374) pioneered the writing of sonnet sequences. His sequence charts each pang and longing of the speaker's unfulfilled love for an idealized lady. This poetic device led to endless inventiveness—the beloved's beauty invites extravagant comparisons, and she provides a focus for the poet's ingenuity.

Shakespeare's Sequence Like the sonnet sequences of other poets, Shakespeare's 154 sonnets are numbered. Most of them are addressed to a handsome, talented young man, urging him to marry and have children who can carry on his talents. Readers treasure Shakespeare's masterful use of the sonnet to bring the fundamental experiences of life—time, death, love, and friendship—into tight focus.

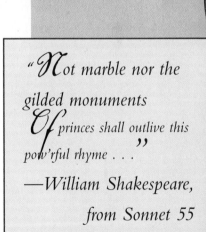

> "*Not marble nor the gilded monuments Of princes shall outlive this pow'rful rhyme . . .*"
>
> —William Shakespeare, from Sonnet 55

Sonnet 29

WILLIAM SHAKESPEARE

When in disgrace with fortune and men's eyes,
I all alone beweep my outcast state,
And trouble deaf heaven with my bootless[1] cries,
And look upon myself and curse my fate,
5 Wishing me like to one more rich in hope,
Featured like him, like him with friends possessed,
Desiring this man's art, and that man's scope,
With what I most enjoy contented least.
Yet in these thoughts myself almost despising,
10 Haply[2] I think on thee, and then my state,
Like to the lark at break of day arising
From sullen earth, sings hymns at heaven's gate;
    For thy sweet love remembered such wealth brings
    That then I scorn to change my state with kings.

---

1. **bootless** futile.
2. **Haply** adv. by chance.

Vocabulary

scope (skōp) n. range of perception or understanding

sullen (sul´ ən) adj. gloomy; dismal

◀ **Critical Viewing**

In what ways does the style of this illustration reflect the style of Shakespeare's sonnets? **CONNECT**

Sonnet 106

WILLIAM SHAKESPEARE

When in the chronicle of wasted time
I see descriptions of the fairest wights,[1]
And beauty making beautiful old rhyme,
In praise of ladies dead and lovely knights,
5 Then in the blazon[2] of sweet beauty's best
Of hand, of foot, of lip, of eye, of brow,
I see their antique pen would have express'd
Even such a beauty as you master now.
So all their praises are but prophecies
10 Of this our time, all you prefiguring;
And, for they look'd but with divining eyes,
They had not skill enough your worth to sing:
    For we, which now behold these present days,
    Have eyes to wonder, but lack tongues to praise.

---

1. **wights** (wīts) n. human beings; people.
2. **blazon** n. here, catalog of lover's physical attributes.

Vocabulary

chronicle (krän´ i kəl) n. historical record of events in chronological order

prefiguring (prē fig´ yer iŋ) v. foreshadowing

Comprehension

What is the speaker's state of mind at the end of Sonnet 29?

Sonnet 116

WILLIAM SHAKESPEARE

Vocabulary

impediments
(im ped′ ə mənts)
n. obstacles

alters (ôl′ tərs)
v. changes

Let me not to the marriage of true minds
Admit impediments. Love is not love
Which alters when it alteration finds,
Or bends with the remover to remove.
5 O, no! It is an ever-fixèd mark
That looks on tempests and is never shaken;
It is the star to every wandering bark,[1]
Whose worth's unknown, although his height be
    taken.[2]
Love's not Time's fool, though rosy lips and cheeks
10 Within his bending sickle's compass[3] come;
Love alters not with his brief hours and weeks,
But bears it out even to the edge of doom.[4]
    If this be error, and upon me proved,
    I never writ, nor no man ever loved.

---

1. **star . . . bark** the star that guides every wandering ship: the North Star.
2. **Whose . . . be taken** whose value is unmeasurable, although navigators measure its height in the sky.
3. **compass** range; scope.
4. **doom** Judgment Day.

Critical Reading

1. **Key Ideas and Details (a)** With whom is the speaker in Sonnet 29 in "disgrace"? **(b) Analyze:** What overall effect does this disgrace have on the speaker's state of mind?

2. **Key Ideas and Details (a)** According to line 12 of Sonnet 29, what causes the shift in the speaker's mood? **(b) Analyze:** How would you describe the shifting moods in the sonnet?

3. **Integration of Knowledge and Ideas (a)** Identify two images in Sonnet 116 that show the effects of time. **(b) Compare and Contrast:** Compare the effects of time on love with the ideal of love in the poem.

Cite textual evidence to support your responses.

The Mystery of the SONNETS

For centuries, readers have puzzled over Shakespeare's sonnet sequence, which tells a story of love and betrayal. The early poems address a beautiful young man, whom the poet urges to get married and have children. The later poems concern a dark-haired woman, who torments the poet with jealousy. Midway through the sequence, a rival poet makes an appearance, further complicating the situation.

Were these characters real people? Or were they simply creations of Shakespeare's dramatic imagination? Literary detectives have proposed various historical figures as the characters in the sonnets. But the only facts we know for sure are that the sonnet sequence was published in 1609 and dedicated to a "Mr. W.H."

CONNECT TO THE LITERATURE

Does knowing the story told by the sonnets make reading individual sonnets more interesting? Why or why not?

Title page from the 1609 edition of *Shake-Speares Sonnets.* ▼

SHAKE-SPEARES

SONNETS.

Neuer before Imprinted.

AT LONDON
By *G. Eld* for *T. T.* and are
to be solde by *John wright, dwelling*
at Christ Church gate.
1609.

WILLIAM HERBERT

Some think William Herbert, the third Earl of Pembroke and a patron of the arts, was the young man of the sonnets. Shakespeare's "First Folio" was dedicated to him.

GEORGE CHAPMAN

His powerful translation of Homer inspired John Keats. Chapman is thought by many to be the rival poet of Shakespeare's Sonnets.

WILLIAM SHAKESPEARE

Nicholas Hilliard painted this portrait, which some believe to be the young Shakespeare, in 1588.

CHRISTOPHER MARLOWE

Poet and dramatist Christopher Marlowe (1564–1593) may have been the rival poet.

EMILIA BASSANO

Some historians think Emilia Bassano, the daughter of a court musician, was Shakespeare's mysterious "Dark Lady."

HENRY WRIOTHESLY

The third Earl of Southampton, Wriothesly became Shakespeare's patron in 1593. Many believe he was the "fair youth" of the sonnets.

Sonnet 130

WILLIAM SHAKESPEARE

The Shakespearean Sonnet

Identify the rhyme scheme of the sonnet's first quatrain.

Spiral Review

Check Context Clues Based on the context of the poem as a whole, what is the meaning of the term "false compare" in the last line?

My mistress' eyes are nothing like the sun,
Coral is far more red than her lips' red;
If snow be white, why then her breasts are dun;
If hairs be wires, black wires grow on her head.
5　I have seen roses damasked,[1] red and white,
But no such roses see I in her cheeks;
And in some perfumes is there more delight
Than in the breath that from my mistress reeks.[2]
I love to hear her speak. Yet well I know
10　That music hath a far more pleasing sound.
I grant I never saw a goddess go;[3]
My mistress, when she walks, treads on the ground.
　　And yet, by heaven, I think my love as rare
　　As any she belied[4] with false compare.

---

1. **damasked** variegated.
2. **reeks** emanates.
3. **go** walk.
4. **belied** (bē līd´) misrepresented.

Critical Reading

1. **Key Ideas and Details (a)** How are the mistress's eyes, lips, cheeks, breath, and voice inferior, according to Sonnet 130? **(b) Interpret:** Why does the speaker say she "treads on the ground"?

2. **Integration of Knowledge and Ideas (a)** In Sonnet 130, what does the final couplet say about the speaker's feelings? **(b) Interpret:** What general truth does the couplet suggest? **(c) Draw Conclusions:** In his sonnets, Petrarch worshiped his mistress. Why has Sonnet 130 been called anti-Petrarchan?

3. **Integration of Knowledge and Ideas** What advantages or disadvantages does the Shakespearean sonnet have compared with the Petrarchan sonnet? Explain. In your response, use at least two of these Essential Question words: *complex, innovative, dramatic.* *[Connecting to the Essential Question: What is the relationship of the writer to tradition?]*

Literary Analysis

**Common Core
State Standards**

Writing
2.b. Develop the topic
thoroughly by selecting
the most significant and
relevant facts, extended
definitions, concrete
details, quotations, or
other information and
examples appropriate to
the audience's knowledge
of the topic. *(p. 280)*

Language
5. Demonstrate
understanding of word
relationships. *(p. 280)*

1. **Craft and Structure (a)** Identify the three quatrains and the couplet of the **Shakespearean sonnet** using Sonnet 106 as an example. **(b)** Which rhyming words represent the *a*'s, *b*'s, *c*'s, *d*'s, *e*'s, *f*'s, and *g*'s of the rhyme scheme?

2. **Craft and Structure (a) Analyze text structures** in Shakespeare's sonnets by listing the main idea of each section of Sonnets 106 and 116. **(b)** Does each idea correspond to a **quatrain** or **couplet**? Explain.

3. **Craft and Structure** Analyze the effects of the couplet in each of these sonnets. Does it restate what has been said, provide a different perspective on it, or reverse it? Cite evidence from the poems to support your point.

4. **Craft and Structure** Choose a sonnet and use a chart like the one shown to map out its **syntax.**

Number of Sentences	Number of Lines in Each Sentence	Syntax Is Straightforward or Complicated?

5. **Craft and Structure (a)** Which two of the sonnets use complicated **syntax,** featuring sentences full of phrases and clauses? **(b)** Compare the complicated syntax of these sonnets with the simpler syntax of the other two sonnets. **(c)** In each case, explain how effectively the elaborate or the simple syntax conveys the meaning.

6. **Key Ideas and Details** Explain how Shakespeare uses references to other poetry in Sonnets 106 and 130. In each case, how do these references support the argument he is making?

7. **Integration of Knowledge and Ideas** If Shakespeare had adapted one of these sonnets to the Petrarchan form (an eight-line octet followed by a six-line sestet), how might the new form have affected the way he presented his message? Remember that in a Petrarchan sonnet, the octet normally presents a problem and the sestet provides a resolution.

8. **Integration of Knowledge and Ideas** Which sonnet do you think best expresses modern attitudes? Support your choice with examples.

Vocabulary Acquisition and Use

Word Analysis: Greek Root -chron-

The word *chronicle* contains the Greek root -*chron*-, meaning "time." This root is important in words relating to history. For example, a chronicle is a record of events arranged in their order of occurrence. Keeping in mind the meaning of -*chron*-, match the following words with their definitions.

1. chronology

2. chronicler

3. chronological

4. chronometer

a. person who records events by date

b. arranged in order of occurrence

c. a list of important events by date

d. a device that measures time

Vocabulary: Analogies

An *analogy* is a comparison of two pairs of words that have the same relationship. For each item, determine the relationship between the first and second words. Then, using a word from the vocabulary list on page 272, fill in the blank to complete the analogy. Explain your choice.

1. Humming : singing :: _____ : occurring

2. Careful : rash :: _____ : cheerful

3. Principles : beliefs :: _____ : obstacles

4. Wavers : decides :: _____ : preserves

5. Desk : drawer :: _____ : entry

6. Speed : reduced :: _____ : limited

Writing to Sources

Argumentative Text In his sonnets, Shakespeare uses imagery—words that appeal to the senses—to suggest the complexities of love. In an **essay,** analyze the imagery in one of his sonnets. Consider how the images are used both to communicate central ideas and to evoke readers' emotions. Support your ideas and reasoning with relevant quotations and details from the poem.

Prewriting Describe the images in a sonnet of your choice. Next to each image, note the idea that it expresses and its relationship to other images in the poem. Use a chart like the one shown.

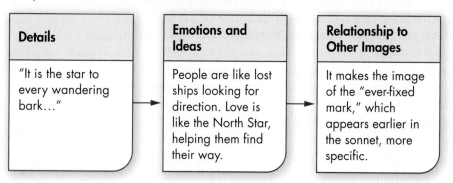

Details	Emotions and Ideas	Relationship to Other Images
"It is the star to every wandering bark…"	People are like lost ships looking for direction. Love is like the North Star, helping them find their way.	It makes the image of the "ever-fixed mark," which appears earlier in the sonnet, more specific.

Drafting Begin with a strong thesis statement. Then, use details to support your ideas. Note relationships of similarity, contrast, or development among images.

Revising Review your analysis. If necessary, refine your thesis to fit the details or add details as support. Then, consider your audience's knowledge of the topic. If you think that any of your points will not be easily understood, add clarifications, such as defining a difficult word or explaining a connection you have made.

The Influence of the Monarchy

Part 2

Primary Sources

Speech
Speech Before
Her Troops

Eyewitness Account
Examination of Don Luis de Córdoba

 **Common Core State Standards**

Reading Informational Text
2. Determine two or more central ideas of a text and analyze their development over the course of the text, including how they interact and build on one another to provide a complex analysis; provide an objective summary of the text.

About the Text Forms

A **speech,** or talk given to an audience, is one of the oldest means of communication, serving purposes like these: to persuade, entertain, or inform. Before recording technology was invented, a speech was always immediate. Those not present had to read, or be read, a written record of the speaker's words. Such transcripts are valuable primary sources.

An **eyewitness account** is an oral or written narrative of events by someone who saw what happened. Even if it has some inaccuracy or bias, an eyewitness account of historical events can still be a valuable primary source, especially when considered along with other accounts of the same events.

Preparing to Read Complex Texts One of the best ways of remembering the details in a primary source and understanding the relationships between them is by **summarizing,** or briefly restating the writer's central ideas and listing the key facts that support these ideas.

Once you have summarized the central ideas and key supporting details in a text, identify ways in which the central ideas interact. Here is an example:

Central Idea 1: Elizabeth I loves and trusts her people.
Supporting Detail: She has come to address them even though her advisers warn of treachery.
Central Idea 2: She will reward her troops.
Supporting Detail: She knows that they deserve reward.
Interaction of Ideas: Her promise reflects her love.

After reading each of these primary sources, summarize it. Then, use your summary to analyze the development of central ideas and their interaction. Prepare for your summary by using *anecdotal scripting*—note-taking—as you read.

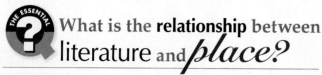 What is the **relationship** between literature and *place?*

England was at war, but the troops were still unpaid. What might inspire them to go on? Elizabeth I had an answer. As you read her speech, consider what her leadership and her words suggest about the answer to the Essential Question shown above.

Note-Taking Guide

Primary source documents are a rich source of information for researchers. As you read these documents, use a note-taking guide like the one shown to organize relevant and accurate information.

1 Type of Document (check one)
☐ Newspaper ☐ Letter ☐ Diary ☐ Map ☐ Speech ☐ Advertisement
☐ Government Document ☐ Eyewitness Account ☐ Memorandum ☐ Other

2 Date of Document _____

3 Author _____
Author's Position _____

4 Original Audience _____

5 Purpose and Importance
a What was the original purpose? _____
Write down two details that support your answer. _____
_____

b What are the key ideas or observations in this document? _____
_____

c What does this document show about the time and place in which it was composed? _____
_____

Summarizing Information

Sometimes you need to organize the basic information found in a primary source document. One way of doing this is **summarizing,** briefly restating main points and key details. As you read, summarize the key ideas in each document.

This guide was adapted from the **U.S. National Archives** document analysis worksheet.

Vocabulary

treachery (trech´ ər ē) *n.* betrayal of trust or loyalty (p. 285)

tyrants (tī´ rənts) *n.* cruel, oppressive rulers (p. 285)

realms (relmz) *n.* regions under the rule of a king or queen (p. 287)

stead (sted) *n.* position being filled by a replacement (p. 287)

obedience (ō bē´ dē əns; ō bēd´ yəns) *n.* the act of following orders or instructions (p. 287)

concord (kän´ kôrd´) *n.* friendly relations; harmony (p. 287)

valor (val´ ər) *n.* courageous behavior (p. 287)

galleons (gal´ ē ənz) *n.* large sailing ships used for war or trade (p. 289)

THE STORY BEHIND THE DOCUMENTS

Elizabeth I (1533–1603), who became England's queen in 1558 when she was barely out of her teens, ruled at a time when few thought a woman could succeed as a leader. The young queen, however, using courage and judgment, brought stability and prosperity to her nation. Today she is often named as England's greatest monarch. A dramatic moment in her reign came when King Philip II of Spain sent an Armada, or war fleet, to invade England. Her speech to her troops at this dangerous time reveals her skill as an inspirational leader.

Don Luis de Córdoba was a Spanish aristocrat, the son of a high official in Philip II's court. Sailing with the Armada, he survived the fighting, but his ship was wrecked off the west coast of Ireland. There the English executed most Armada survivors, but the high-born Don Luis was allowed to live. His eyewitness account of his experiences provides a valuable record of a major historical event.

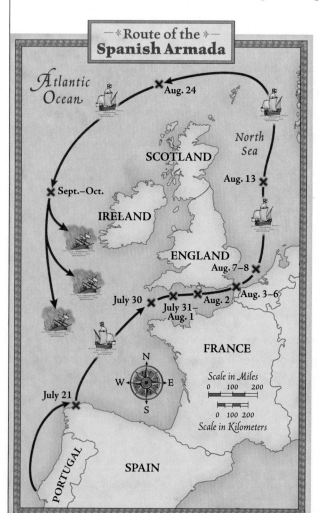

Route of the Spanish Armada

Atlantic Ocean

Aug. 24

SCOTLAND

North Sea

Aug. 13

Sept.–Oct.

IRELAND

ENGLAND

Aug. 7–8

July 30

July 31–Aug. 1

Aug. 2

Aug. 3–6

FRANCE

July 21

Scale in Miles
0   100   200

0   100 200
Scale in Kilometers

N
W   E
S

PORTUGAL

SPAIN

The defeat of the Spanish Armada was the climax of what might be described as a religious war, a national feud, and a family dispute rolled into one. It all began with a royal divorce.

In 1533, King Henry VIII of England, a headstrong man, divorced the Spanish princess Catherine of Aragon to marry Anne Boleyn. This caused him to split with the Roman Catholic Church. As a result, England became a Protestant nation. Spain remained a champion of Roman Catholicism. In addition, England and Spain were rivals for colonial possessions in the New World.

Family disputes added fuel to the fires. Mary, daughter of Henry VIII and Catherine of Aragon, became England's queen and wed the future king of Spain, Philip II. Philip and Bloody Mary, as she was called for persecuting Protestants, tried to make England Catholic again. Mary was highly suspicious of her Protestant half-sister and royal rival, Elizabeth. With Protestants rebelling and maybe plotting to bring Elizabeth to the throne, Mary kept Elizabeth in the Tower of London or under house arrest.

When Mary died and Elizabeth became queen, most of England welcomed the change. Roman Catholics at home and abroad, however, schemed to overthrow Elizabeth. Philip II of Spain was at the heart of such conspiracies. In 1588, he sent a large fleet, the Spanish Armada, to conquer England and bring it back into the Catholic fold.

SPEECH BEFORE HER TROOPS

Queen Elizabeth I

▲ These Dangers Averted medals celebrated the defeat of the Spanish Armada.

BACKGROUND By the 1580s, Philip II was king of Portugal as well as Spain and ruled over vast New World colonies. He also ruled the Spanish Netherlands (today's Netherlands and some adjoining areas), where his repression of Protestants prompted the Dutch to rebel. Philip's Protestant half-sister-in-law, Elizabeth I, queen of England, aided the Dutch rebels and quietly supported attacks on Spanish ships by English sea captains. In 1587, when a plot to replace her with her Catholic cousin Mary, Queen of Scots, ended in failure, Elizabeth had Mary executed. A year later, Philip sent his Armada of warships to collect troops fighting in the Netherlands and invade England.

With Elizabeth's navy fighting the Spanish fleet, her land forces massed in the English port of Tilbury, anticipating an invasion that never came. Nerves frayed and soldiers began to grumble about delays in pay. Then Elizabeth, dramatically dressed in a white gown and silver breast-plate, appeared before the troops and made the following famous speech.

Primary Sources
Speech When Elizabeth delivered this speech, which words in the first two sentences do you think she emphasized? Why?

Vocabulary
treachery (trech´ ər ē) *n.* betrayal of trust or loyalty

tyrants (tī´ rənts) *n.* cruel, oppressive rulers

My loving people, we have been persuaded by some, that are careful of our safety, to take heed how we commit ourselves to armed multitudes,[1] for fear of treachery: but I assure you, I do not desire to live to distrust my faithful and loving people. Let tyrants fear; I have always so behaved myself that, under God, I have placed my chiefest strength and safeguard in the loyal hearts and good will of my subjects. And therefore I am come amongst you at this time, not as for my recreation or sport, but being resolved, in the midst and heat of the battle, to live or die amongst you all; to lay down, for my God, and for my kingdom, and for my people, my honor and my blood, even the dust. I know I have but the body of a weak and

---

1. armed multitudes troops with weapons, like those she is addressing.

feeble woman; but I have the heart of a king, and of a king of England, too; and think foul scorn that Parma[2] or Spain, or any prince of Europe, should dare to invade the borders of my realms: to which, rather than any dishonor should grow by me, I myself will take up arms; I myself will be your general, judge, and rewarder of every one of your virtues in the field. I know already, by your forwardness, that you have deserved rewards and crowns;[3] and we do assure you, on the word of a prince, they shall be duly paid you. In the mean my lieutenant general shall be in my stead, than whom never prince commanded a more noble and worthy subject; not doubting by your obedience to my general, by your concord in the camp, and by your valor in the field, we shall shortly have a famous victory over the enemies of my God, of my kingdom, and of my people.

---

2. **Parma** Alessandro Farnese (1545–1592), duke of the Italian state of Parma and commander of Philip II's troops fighting rebels in the Spanish Netherlands.
3. **crowns** coins depicting the monarch's head, used to pay the troops.

Vocabulary

realms (relmz) *n.* regions under the rule of a king or queen

stead (sted) *n.* position being filled by a replacement

obedience (ō bē′ dē əns; ō bēd′ yəns) *n.* the act of following orders or instructions

concord (kän′ kôrd′) *n.* friendly relations; harmony

valor (val′ ər) *n.* courageous behavior

Critical Reading

1. **Key Ideas and Details (a)** According to the speech, what have Elizabeth's advisers warned her not to do, and why does she do it anyway? **(b) Interpret:** What effect is the inclusion of this information designed to have on her audience?

2. **Key Ideas and Details (a)** What does Elizabeth tell her audience she already knows, and what does she promise to do? **(b) Analyze Cause and Effect:** How do you think her audience reacted to this information? Why?

3. **Craft and Structure (a) Analyze:** Where does Elizabeth exaggerate in her speech? **(b) Evaluate:** Do you think the exaggeration makes her speech more or less persuasive? Explain your answer.

Cite textual evidence to support your responses.

◄ **Critical Viewing** What does this rendering of Elizabeth indicate about the importance of pageantry—ceremony and theatrical presence—in her court? Explain your reasoning. **INTERPRET**

Examination of
DON LUIS DE CÓRDOBA

BACKGROUND: THE SPANISH ARMADA VS. THE ENGLISH FLEET

	Spain	England
Statistics	about 130 ships: 40 are 1st rate best warships: large, slow, with fewer and lighter guns; gunners not well trained	about same number best warships: small, fast, with more and heavier guns; gunners well trained
Battle Plan	• sail up English Channel • at Flanders, pick up troops for invasion	• attack early • break up Spanish battle formation
Results	• English outmaneuver Spanish but do no real damage • Spanish fleet anchors off Calais (ka lā´), France • English set boats afire and send them toward Spanish fleet • Spanish formation breaks up; English win decisive battle • Bad weather drives Spanish away; they sail northward • Many Spanish ships, including Don Luis de Córdoba's, are wrecked on the west coast of Ireland	

Primary Sources
Eyewitness Account
How might the circumstances under which Don Luis was questioned affect the accuracy of his information?

Don Lewes from Cordoba in Andalucia:[1] Captain of the men shipwrecked on the shore of the land of Sir Murrough ne Doe (Galway), says that when the Spanish fleet got near to Plymouth, there were 140 different types of boats including 96 great ships for the battle, and the rest were pataches[2] and small boats for transport. Off the coast of Plymouth, they met about 70 of Queen Elizabeth's ships. The Queen's ships gained the weather gage[3] and shot at them. They kept going towards Calais and returned fire for 2 or 3 hours. During this battle, Don Pedro and his ship were captured, as he was left behind the fleet when a cannon ball broke the main mast. The next day was calm and therefore nothing happened between them, except that a Spanish ship of 700 ton was burned accidentally, but most of the men were rescued. On the 3rd day they fought for 5 or 6 hours without losing any ships. On the 4th day they fought for 4 hours without losing any ships. On the

---

1. **Andalucia** the region of southern Spain where the city of Córdoba is located.
2. **pataches** *n.* small, fast, well-armed Portuguese ships that sailed with the Armada.
3. **gained the weather gage** positioned the ships so that the wind blew into their sails, giving them the advantage of more speed.

5th day they reached Calais where they anchored and chained themselves together and at the same time, 25 more ships came to join the Queen's fleet. During the night, the Spanish saw 6 ships on fire sailing down upon them, which forced them to cut their cables and set sail; at this point a great ship was burned amongst them, and a galleas[4] was shipwrecked on the sands. After this, the English ships entered into a fierce fight with the Spanish, in which 2 of the greatest Spanish Galleons were so beaten, that they were forced to come ashore at Flanders and sent the men to their other ships. That day, if the fire had not stopped them, they were going to put 7000 men on the shore at Calais to go to the prince (Duke) of Parma to find out his plans. He was going to be in charge of them and they had some unopened orders addressed to him, which were lost in the burnt ship. When they were stopped by this fire, they were broken and so fought very hard, and after 3 days moved out of the sight of the (English) coast, so that the Queen's ships left them and returned home, celebrating by firing off a lot of cannons. After this, the Duke of Medina moved his remaining ships together and found that he had lost 6 ships. He ordered his forces to return to Spain. But around Norway, the great storm took them and beat them towards our coast; the Duke had already warned them about the dangers of our coastline.

---

4. galleas *n.* a large warship powered by both oars and sails.

Vocabulary

galleons (gal´ ē ənz) *n.* large sailing ships used for war or trade

Summarizing Information

Summarize the information that Don Luis supplies about events near Norway.

Critical Reading

1. **Key Ideas and Details (a) Summarize:** What happened off the coast of Plymouth? **(b) Infer:** Why do you think Don Luis mentions that the English got the advantage from the wind?

2. **Key Ideas and Details (a)** What was the purpose of the "ships of fire," or fireships, that the English sent out? **(b) Infer:** How do you think Don Luis felt as he told what happened near Calais? Why?

3. **Key Ideas and Details (a) Analyze Cause and Effect:** What prevented the Duke of Parma from giving and receiving orders? **(b) Draw Conclusions:** What do the details suggest about communications among the Spanish forces?

Cite textual evidence to support your responses.

Speech • Eyewitness Account

Comparing Primary Sources

Refer to your Note-Taking Guide to complete these questions.

1. **(a)** Contrast the authors' purposes and audiences in these documents arising from the same historical event. **(b)** How do these contrasts explain the differences in tone, or attitude?

2. **(a)** Use a chart like the one below to identify one statement from each document and what it reveals about this historic battle. **(b)** From which document do you learn more? Explain.

Author	Statement	What It Reveals
Queen Elizabeth I		
Don Luis de Córdoba		

3. **(a)** Summarize each source, listing the central ideas along with key supporting details. **(b)** For each source, analyze the development and interaction of central ideas, explaining whether they reinforce or contrast with each other.

4. Write a paragraph exploring how each primary source, in its own way, would be useful to historians studying the Armada.

Vocabulary Acquisition and Use

Using New Vocabulary Choose the Word Bank word that is most clearly related to the situation in each sentence. Explain your choices.

> treachery   stead   obedience   valor

1. A child heeded all the instructions her parents gave her.
2. A spy pretending to be a friend betrayed the king's trust.
3. The soldier showed great courage during the battle.
4. When the teacher fell ill, a substitute filled in for her.

Content-Area Vocabulary Identify the letter of the choice that is a synonym for the boldfaced word. Then, use the word in a sentence.

5. **tyrants:** **(a)** monarchs **(b)** trends **(c)** dictators **(d)** quarrels
6. **realms:** **(a)** kingdoms **(b)** treaties **(c)** truths **(d)** valuables
7. **galleons:** **(a)** ropes **(b)** amounts **(c)** kitchens **(d)** warships

Etymology Study *Concord* comes from the Latin word *concordia*, meaning "agreement," which includes the Latin root *cord*, meaning "heart." People or things in *concord* seem to have the same heart. The words *accord* and *cordial* have the same Latin root.

Using an online or print dictionary, explain how the root's meaning is reflected in each of these words.

 **Common Core State Standards**

Writing

7. Conduct short as well as more sustained research projects to answer a question or solve a problem; narrow or broaden the inquiry when appropriate; synthesize multiple sources on the subject, demonstrating understanding of the subject under investigation. *(p. 291)*

8. Gather relevant information from multiple authoritative print and digital sources, using advanced searches effectively; assess the strengths and limitations of each source in terms of the task, purpose, and audience; integrate information into the text selectively to maintain the flow of ideas, avoiding plagiarism and overreliance on any one source and following a standard format for citation. *(p. 291)*

Language

6. Acquire and use accurately general academic and domain-specific words and phrases, sufficient for reading, writing, speaking, and listening at the college and career readiness level; demonstrate independence in gathering vocabulary knowledge when considering a word or phrase important to comprehension or expression.

Research Task

Topic: The Defeat of the Spanish Armada

News traveled slowly in 1588. When Queen Elizabeth I delivered her "Speech Before Her Troops" to rally them against the expected Spanish invasion, the Armada had already been defeated. Using effective research, you can find out about the battle faster, and perhaps more fully, than Elizabeth could.

Assignment: Write a **research report** about one of these aspects of the battle with the Spanish Armada:

- historical causes of the conflict
- forces and weapons of each side
- military tactics used by each side
- sequence of the battle's events

During the battle with the Armada, the English attacked the Spanish fleet with fireships.

Formulate a research plan. Brainstorm and consult with others to decide upon a topic. Formulate an open-ended research question to address your topic, such as "In the battle with the Spanish Armada, what were the differences between the English and the Spanish tactics?" Then, formulate a plan for in-depth research on your topic.

Gather sources. Follow your plan, determining, locating, and exploring the full range of relevant sources.

- Gather evidence, distinguishing between reliable and unreliable sources. Avoid overreliance on one source.
- Systematically organize information to support your central idea. Outline your ideas using a conceptual map or timeline.

RESEARCH TIP

Be sure to separate factual data and the complex inferences you make based on the data. Also, differentiate among primary, secondary, and other sources.

Model: Using a Timeline to Organize Information

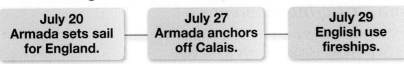

| July 20 Armada sets sail for England. | July 27 Armada anchors off Calais. | July 29 English use fireships. |

Use a checklist like the one shown to evaluate your work.

Research Checklist

- ☐ Have I answered the research question?
- ☐ Have I gathered and synthesized information from reliable sources?
- ☐ Have I organized all the information clearly?
- ☐ Have I cited sources accurately, using a style manual?

Synthesize information. Critique your research process at each step, modifying your process or research question as needed. Differentiate between theories and evidence, and determine whether the evidence for a theory is weak or strong. As you draft, maintain a flow by selecting and synthesizing related, relevant ideas from your sources.

Organize and present ideas. Provide an analysis that does not simply restate facts but supports and develops your personal opinions. Give your report sufficient length and depth to address the complexities of the topic. Avoid plagiarism, citing your sources for ideas not your own, following a standard format.

Connecting Elizabeth I, Past and Present

Famous actresses have portrayed Elizabeth I over the years, including Sarah Bernhardt and Helen Mirren. It was, however, a young unknown who in 1998 portrayed the transformation of Elizabeth on screen from a fragile, endangered girl to one of the most respected and iconic monarchs in history. In doing so, Australian actress Cate Blanchett also transformed herself into a star.

Blanchett, who even as a child loved to perform, studied Elizabeth I's letters to better understand the monarch. "It was there I could see the mechanics of her brain and her thought processes," she explained, "and the way she was able to play people off against each other, as well as her extraordinary intelligence."

The young actress came to think of Elizabeth herself as a kind of actress, and once said of her: "You know, she was in her element in front of a large crowd. She had the instincts of a performer. . . ."

Cate Blanchett has played royalty more than once. After starring as Elizabeth I in Indian director Shekhar Kapur's *Elizabeth*, which earned her an Academy Award Best Actress nomination, she portrayed the Elf Queen Galadriel in the immensely popular *The Lord of the Rings* trilogy (2001–2003). In 2005, Blanchett won the Oscar for Best Supporting Actress for her role as Hollywood cinema queen Katharine Hepburn in *The Aviator*.

*Cate Blanchett's performance in **Elizabeth** made the Australian actress into a celebrity.*

John Lahr
Drama Critic/Interviewer

John Lahr, who interviewed Cate Blanchett for *The New Yorker* magazine, has show business blood in his veins. His father, Bert Lahr, played *The Wizard of Oz*'s Cowardly Lion.

As a senior drama critic for *The New Yorker*, Lahr is interested in how actors create their public images as well as how they perform on stage and screen. "When you become a public personality and have a public persona, you have created 'you,'" he once said. "The public 'you' is your greatest invention."

In interviewing Blanchett, however, Lahr encountered an actress who seemed to disappear into the characters she portrayed.

from
DISAPPEARING ACT

Interview with Cate Blanchett
conducted *by John Lahr*

Blanchett grew up in Ivanhoe, a leafy suburb of Melbourne, beside the Yarra River. She was the middle child, between an older brother, Bob, who had a mild case of cerebral palsy, and Genevieve. (Bob works as a computer programmer; Genevieve is studying architecture, after a successful career as a stage designer.)

Of the siblings, Blanchett was, by her own admission, the most adventurous. "I felt very free as a child," she said. Together, she and Genevieve invented characters, which Blanchett would play, for days at a time, around the house. "My sister and I would dress me up in something," she said "I'd pull a face or a stance; she'd give them names and an identity."

When Blanchett was around nine, her enthusiasm for performance took the form of knocking on strangers' doors to see if she could talk her way inside their homes with a tall tale about a lost dog. "It was the adrenaline rush, really," she said. "My friends hid in the bushes. I remember the woman at the door saying, 'I haven't seen a dog. Come in. I'll ask my husband.' I looked at the bushes thinking, Oh, my God, what am I doing? I remember the look in this woman's eyes when she started to think, You haven't lost a dog, have you? It suddenly had become a real thing."

Blanchett continued, "My whole childhood was like that. If someone dared me, I'd do it."

"Cate is willing to throw herself into a chaotic state out of which something will arise," the director Shekhar Kapur told me. "The fluidity you get in Cate is also because of the contradictions inside her." Blanchett is both candid and private, gregarious and solitary, self-doubting and daring, witty and melancholy. It was these contradictions that prompted Kapur to cast her as Elizabeth I in *Elizabeth*, one of the films that made Blanchett an international star.

Blanchett's mother, June, was a jazz-loving schoolteacher. Her Texas-born father, Robert, who met June when his Navy ship broke down in Melbourne, had, according to Blanchett, "a very dry sense of humor." He had quit school at fourteen—"I went to the school for bums," he told his daughter.

Robert put himself through night school, worked at a television station, returned to Australia to marry June, and got into advertising. Then, when Blanchett was ten, he died. "I was playing the piano," she has recalled. "He walked past the window. I waved goodbye. He was going off to work. He had a heart attack that day. He was only forty."

The fact that she hadn't embraced him before he left haunted Blanchett. "I developed this ritual where I couldn't leave the house until I could actually physically say goodbye to everyone," she said. . . .

After Robert died, Blanchett developed a passion for horror movies. "I loved being terrified," she said. "It used to be a badge of honor if you could sit through *Halloween II*." Some of the thrill of horror movies lies in the thrill of surviving them, of, in a sense, cheating death. It's a thrill that carries over, as Upton [her husband] pointed out, to acting. "You go onstage and you're alive," he said. "You walk offstage, then the character's gone. You survive the experience. . . ."

"The fluidity you get in Cate is also because of the contradictions inside her."

Critical Reading

1. **(a)** How would Blanchett perform as a child? **(b) Infer:** Why did Blanchett enjoy this kind of performance?

2. **(a)** According to the interviewer, what is part of the thrill of horror movies? **(b) Interpret:** What connection does Blanchett's husband see between this thrill and the experience of acting? Explain.

3. **(a) Summarize:** Briefly summarize the childhood experiences Blanchett discusses in this interview. **(b) Draw Conclusions:** How might her childhood experiences, actions, and interests have helped her develop skills she needs to act?

Use these questions to focus a class discussion of "Disappearing Act":

4. In what ways are actresses and monarchs—like Cate Blanchett and Elizabeth I—both performers? Explain the reasons for your answer.

5. **(a)** How might creating a public image, as actresses and monarchs do, be a kind of deception? **(b)** How might it be a true expression of an individual's personality?

Connecting to the Essential Question The King James Bible has been for centuries an important book for many Protestants. As you read, identify qualities of language and rhythm that contribute to the appeal and influence of this great prose work. This will help you consider the Essential Question: **How does literature shape or reflect society?**

Close Reading Focus

Psalms; Sermons; Parables

The Bible conveys themes of faith in numerous genres, including these:

- **Psalms**—sacred songs or lyric poems in praise of God.
- **Sermons**—speeches offering religious or moral instruction. The Sermon on the Mount contains the basic teachings of Christianity.
- **Parables**—simple stories from which a moral or religious lesson can be drawn. The most famous are in the New Testament.

Comparing Literary Works Psalms, sermons, and parables all convey deep messages about life. Each communicates a message in a manner suited to its form. Psalms are songs. To engage an audience, psalms may feature vivid figurative language including **metaphors**—comparisons of unlike things. To help listeners understand, sermons may feature **analogies**—explanations comparing abstract relationships to familiar ones. Parables are **narratives**—stories illustrating a message.

As you read, compare the methods by which each selection conveys its message and the appeal and effectiveness of each.

Preparing to Read Complex Texts In some portions of the Bible, the *main idea* is implied rather than directly stated. You can **determine the main idea** by *making inferences*—identifying key details in the text and then relating them to other details and to your own experience. When making inferences, consider what the text suggests as well as what it leaves uncertain. Use a chart like the one shown.

Vocabulary

The words below are key to understanding the text that follows. Copy the words into your notebook. What clue can help you infer which words are verbs?

righteousness   entreated

stature   transgressed

prodigal

Common Core State Standards

Reading Literature
1. Cite strong and thorough textual evidence to support analysis of what the text says explicitly as well as inferences drawn from the text, including determining where the text leaves matters uncertain.
4. Determine the meaning of words and phrases as they are used in the text, including figurative and connotative meanings.

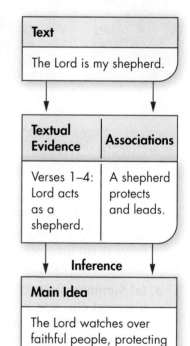

FROM THE KING JAMES BIBLE

The King James Bible (completed 1611)

For centuries, the Bible was the cornerstone of European culture—the ultimate reference for rulers and priests, the ultimate authorization for laws and religious practices, a treasury of images and subjects for art. Yet, the book was inaccessible to the majority of Europeans. During the Reformation, in the 1500s, the need for a closer study of the Bible was widely acknowledged, which led to translations of the work into the vernacular, or common languages. For the first time, this grounding work became widely accessible.

The King James Bible, the authoritative English translation, was created at the command of King James I. In 1604, James commissioned fifty-four scholars and clergymen to compare all known texts of the Bible and prepare the definitive English edition.

Early Bibles The Bible, a collection of books developed over more than 1,200 years, consists of two main parts—the Old Testament, written in Hebrew, and the New Testament, written in Greek. In about A.D. 405, St. Jerome finished translating the Bible into Latin. This translation, the Vulgate, remained the standard Bible of the West for centuries. King James's translators, though, were to review the original sources, as well as translations of the work.

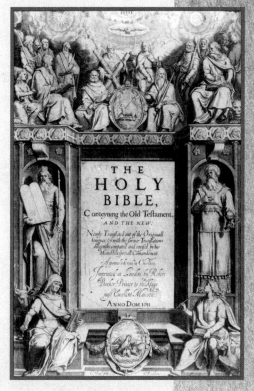

▲ Title page of the 1611 edition of the King James Bible

A Systematic Plan The project was carefully organized from the start. The books of the Bible were divided among six groups of scholars in Westminster, Oxford, and Cambridge.

The groups took four years to produce their initial drafts. Then, two scholars from each region spent nine months in London reviewing and revising the draft. After laboring for seven years, the group produced one of the great works of English literature. The King James Bible has been called "the only classic ever created by a committee."

Tyndale's Legacy The King James Bible was not the first English translation of the book. James's translators were greatly influenced by William Tyndale's translation. Tyndale, a Protestant chaplain and tutor in England, fled clerical oppression at home and published his translation of the New Testament in Germany. Before he had completed work on the Old Testament, however, he was arrested for heresy and executed near Brussels, Belgium, in 1536.

As England became more Protestant, Tyndale came to be viewed, not as a heretic, but as a hero. King James's committee closely followed the magnificent diction and rhythms of Tyndale's groundbreaking translation.

PSALM 23

FROM THE KING JAMES BIBLE

BACKGROUND *Up to the middle 1400s, Bibles were painstak-ingly copied by hand. The resulting manuscripts, though often quite beautiful, were rare and costly. When the German inven-tor Johann Gutenberg devised a method of printing with mov-able type, widespread distribution of the Bible began.*

Psalm 23 and Psalm 137 come from the Book of Psalms, a section of the old testament composed of 150 sacred songs. Many of the psalms are attributed to David, the young shep-herd who killed Goliath and eventually became King of Israel. Psalm 23 is frequently recited at funerals, in times of trouble, and when people are in need of comfort.

1 The Lord is my shepherd; I shall not want.

2 He maketh me to lie down in green pastures: he leadeth me beside the still waters.

3 He restoreth my soul: he leadeth me in the paths of righteousness for his name's sake.

4 Yea, though I walk through the valley of the shadow of death, I will fear no evil: for thou art with me; thy rod and thy staff they comfort me.

5 Thou preparest a table before me in the presence of mine enemies; thou anointest my head with oil; my cup runneth over.

6 Surely goodness and mercy shall follow me all the days of my life: and I will dwell in the house of the Lord forever.

Vocabulary
righteousness
(ri´ chəs nis) *n.* the characteristic of acting in a just, virtuous manner

Metaphor
What is the central metaphor of Psalm 23?

◀ **Critical Viewing** Which details in this artist's portrayal of King David show him as a composer of the Book of Psalms? **ANALYZE**

PSALM 137

FROM THE KING JAMES BIBLE

1 By the rivers of Babylon, there we sat down, yea, we wept, when we remembered Zion.

2 We hanged our harps upon the willows in the midst thereof.

3 For there they that carried us away captive required of us a song; and they that wasted us required of us mirth, saying, Sing us one of the songs of Zion.

4 How shall we sing the Lord's song in a strange land?

5 If I forget thee, O Jerusalem, let my right hand forget her cunning.

6 If I do not remember thee, let my tongue cleave to the roof of my mouth; if I prefer not Jerusalem above my chief joy.

7 Remember, O Lord, the children of Edom in the day of Jerusalem; who said, Raze it, raze it, even to the foundation thereof.

8 O daughter of Babylon, who art to be destroyed; happy shall he be, that rewardeth thee as thou hast served us.

9 Happy shall he be, that taketh and dasheth thy little ones against the stones.

Critical Reading

Cite textual evidence to support your responses.

1. **Craft and Structure (a)** What image is developed in the opening verses of Psalm 23? **(b) Infer:** Why might this image provide comfort to listeners? **(c) Draw Conclusions:** How does the inclusion of the images of the valley of death and of enemies strengthen the psalm?

2. **Key Ideas and Details (a) Infer:** Which clues in Psalm 137 suggest that the author is living in exile? Explain. **(b) Connect:** In what ways is the psalm itself an answer to the question in verse 4?

3. **Key Ideas and Details (a) Interpret:** In what ways does Psalm 137 combine sadness and anger? **(b) Evaluate:** Do you think the anger expressed in the psalm makes it less appealing? Why or why not?

4. **Integration of Knowledge and Ideas** What type of music, if any, would serve as the best accompaniment for Psalm 137? Why?

FROM THE
SERMON ON THE MOUNT

FROM THE KING JAMES BIBLE MATTHEW 6: 24-30

24 No man can serve two masters: for either he will hate the one, and love the other; or else he will hold to the one, and despise the other. Ye cannot serve God and mammon.[1]

25 Therefore I say unto you, Take no thought for your life, what ye shall eat, or what ye shall drink; nor yet for your body, what ye shall put on. Is not the life more than meat, and the body than raiment?[2]

26 Behold the fowls of the air: for they sow not, neither do they reap, nor gather into barns; yet your heavenly Father feedeth them. Are ye not much better than they?

27 Which of you by taking thought can add one cubit unto his stature?

28 And why take ye thought for raiment? Consider the lilies of the field, how they grow; they toil not, neither do they spin:

29 And yet I say unto you, That even Solomon[3] in all his glory was not arrayed like one of these.

30 Wherefore, if God so clothe the grass of the field, which to day is, and to morrow is cast into the oven, *shall he* not much more *clothe* you, O ye of little faith?

---

1. **mammon** (mam′ ən) *n.* money, personified as a false god.
2. **raiment** (rā′ mənt) *n.* clothing; wearing apparel.
3. **Solomon** (säl′ ə mən) *n.* tenth-century B.C. king of Israel.

Psalm, Sermon, and Parable

Why is the strategy of asking the audience questions particularly suited to a sermon?

Vocabulary

stature (stach′ ər) *n.* height; level of achievement

Critical Reading

1. **Key Ideas and Details (a)** What human activities do the fowls and lilies of the sermon avoid? **(b) Analyze:** How does this "omission" affect their lives? **(c) Interpret:** Describe the attitude towards life that Jesus advocates.

2. **Key Ideas and Details** Does Jesus, the speaker of this sermon, mean that his followers should literally "take no thought for life"? Explain.

3. **Integration of Knowledge and Ideas** Explain what a life lived like the lilies might be like.

Cite textual evidence to support your responses.

℘from the ℘arable of the ℘rodigal ℐon

FROM THE KING JAMES BIBLE LUKE 15: 11-32

Vocabulary

prodigal (präd´ i gəl) *adj.*
recklessly wasteful

World LITERATURE CONNECTION

Parables Around the World
The oral traditions of Zen Buddhists, Islamic Sufis and Jewish Hassidim all use parables to teach ideas about morality, philosophy and religion.

A Sufi story tells of a man who is chased by a hungry tiger. Finally the man turns around and cries to the tiger, "Why don't you leave me alone?" "Why don't you stop being so appetizing?" responds the tiger. This parable points out that there is always more than one way to see a situation.

Connect to the Literature

In what way does The Parable of the Prodigal Son challenge long-standing attitudes?

---

11 And he said, A certain man had two sons:

12 And the younger of them said to his father, Father, give me the portion of goods that falleth to me. And he divided unto them his living.

13 And not many days after the younger son gathered all together, and took his journey into a far country, and there wasted his substance with riotous living.

14 And when he had spent all, there arose a mighty famine in that land; and he began to be in want.

15 And he went and joined himself to a citizen of that country; and he sent him into his fields to feed swine.

16 And he would fain[1] have filled his belly with the husks that the swine did eat: and no man gave unto him.

17 And when he came to himself, he said, How many hired servants of my father's have bread enough and to spare, and I perish with hunger!

18 I will arise and go to my father, and will say unto him, Father, I have sinned against heaven, and before thee,

19 And am no more worthy to be called thy son: make me as one of thy hired servants.

20 And he arose, and came to his father. But when he was yet a great way off, his father saw him, and had compassion, and ran, and fell on his neck, and kissed him.

21 And the son said unto him, Father, I have sinned against heaven, and in thy sight, and am no more worthy to be called thy son.

---

1. fain *adv.* gladly.

▶ **Critical Viewing** Which verses from the selection are best illustrated by this painting? Explain. **INTERPRET**

from The Parable of the Prodigal Son **303**

22 But the father said to his servants, Bring forth the best robe, and put *it* on him; and put a ring on his hand, and shoes on *his* feet:

23 And bring hither the fatted calf, and kill *it*; and let us eat, and be merry:

24 For this my son was dead, and is alive again; he was lost, and is found. And they began to be merry.

25 Now his elder son was in the field: and as he came and drew nigh to the house, he heard music and dancing.

26 And he called one of the servants, and asked what these things meant.

27 And he said unto him, Thy brother is come; and thy father hath killed the fatted calf, because he hath received him safe and sound.

28 And he was angry, and would not go in: therefore came his father out, and entreated him.

29 And he answering said to *his* father, Lo, these many years do I serve thee, neither transgressed I at any time thy commandment: and yet thou never gavest me a kid, that I might make merry with my friends:

30 But as soon as this thy son was come, which hath devoured thy living with harlots, thou hast killed for him the fatted calf.

31 And he said unto him, Son, thou art ever with me, and all that I have is thine.

32 It was meet[2] that we should make merry, and be glad: for this thy brother was dead, and is alive again; and was lost, and is found.

---

2. meet *adj.* fitting.

Vocabulary

entreated (en trēt´ id) *v.* begged; pleaded with

transgressed (trans grest´) *v.* overstepped or broke (a law or commandment)

Critical Reading

Cite textual evidence to support your responses.

1. **Key Ideas and Details (a)** What causes the younger son to return home? **(b) Compare and Contrast:** Contrast the father's and the older son's responses to the younger son's return.

2. **Key Ideas and Details (a)** What specific complaint does the older son make? **(b) Assess:** How effectively does the father address his concerns?

3. **Integration of Knowledge and Ideas (a) Interpret:** Why does the father say that the younger son is "alive again"? **(b) Apply:** In what circumstances might the lesson of the parable apply today?

4. **Integration of Knowledge and Ideas** What made the King James Bible so influential? In your response, use at least two of the following Essential Question words: *majestic, clarity, solemn, preach. [Connecting to the Essential Question: How does literature shape or reflect society?]*

Literary Analysis

1. **Key Ideas and Details** For Psalm 23, **determine the main idea** by *making inferences* about the meaning of this quotation: "I will dwell in the house of the Lord forever." Consider, for example, what "the house of the Lord" might mean and why the word *dwelling* may have a connotation stronger than that of the word *living*.

2. **Key Ideas and Details** Make inferences about the meaning of this quote from the Sermon on the Mount: "Which of you by taking thought can add one cubit unto his stature?"

3. **Key Ideas and Details (a)** What is the message of the selection from the Sermon on the Mount? **(b)** Why is the form of a **sermon** suited to this lesson?

4. **Key Ideas and Details** What inference can you make from the fact that this excerpt from the Sermon on the Mount closes with the words "O ye of little faith"?

5. **Key Ideas and Details (a)** What is the chief moral lesson of the Parable of the Prodigal Son? **(b)** Why is the form of a **parable** suited to this lesson?

6. **Key Ideas and Details** After reading the Parable of the Prodigal Son, what inference can you make about the value the Bible places on forgiveness?

7. **Craft and Structure (a)** Contrast the styles of the **psalm,** the sermon, and the parable. **(b)** How is the style of each selection appropriate to its purpose?

8. **Integration of Knowledge and Ideas** The **metaphor** of the shepherd in Psalm 23, the **analogy** of the birds in the Sermon on the Mount, and the **narrative** in the Parable of the Prodigal Son are all designed to appeal to their original audience of that was in part uneducated, rural folk. Explain how the figurative language appealed to that audience, using a chart like the one below.

Images: Familiar / Unfamiliar?	Simple / Difficult?	Memorable? Why?

9. **Comparing Literary Works** Of the following, which did you find easiest to understand: the metaphor of the shepherd, the analogy of the lilies, or the lesson of the prodigal son? For each, explain what was clear and what was complex.

Common Core State Standards

Writing

3. Write narratives to develop real or imagined experiences or events using effective technique, well-chosen details, and well-structured event sequences. *(p. 306)*

3.d. Use precise words and phrases, telling details, and sensory language to convey a vivid picture of the experiences, events, setting, and/or characters. *(p. 306)*

Language

1.a. Apply the understanding that usage is a matter of convention, can change over time, and is sometimes contested. *(p. 306)*

Vocabulary Acquisition and Use

Word Analysis: Latin Root -stat-

The word *stature*, meaning "height when stand-ing," comes from the Latin root -*stat*-, sometimes spelled -*stit*-, which means "to stand" or "to set up." Over time, the word *stature* has taken on a figurative meaning in addition to its literal one: though it sometimes refers to a person's actual height, it can also refer to a person's prominence or position in society or in some other organization or ranking.

Use the meaning of the root -*stat*- to match the following words with their definitions.

1. statue   **a.** to set up a procedure

2. stationary   **b.** standing still

3. institute   **c.** rank

4. constitution   **d.** a figure that stands

5. status   **e.** act of setting up

Vocabulary: Synonyms

Write a complete sentence to answer each ques-tion. For each item, use a vocabulary word from page 296 in place of the underlined words.

1. In what jobs or professions would a person need a good deal of <u>fairness</u> and <u>honesty</u>?

2. What might you say to a friend who was being <u>recklessly wasteful</u> with money she had borrowed?

3. Why do you think people often identify with a book or movie character who has <u>broken a law</u>?

4. Why might a person who is <u>begged</u> for something respond less favorably than one who is asked politely?

5. In your view, why is social <u>standing</u> so important to so many people?

Writing to Sources

Narrative Text Write a **parable** in the King James style about a modern-day issue or situation that supports a moral in which you believe. Study the style of the Parable of the Prodigal Son, and adapt it to your purposes.

Prewriting Choose a moral to teach, and sketch the plot of a story to illus-trate it. Then reread the Parable of the Prodigal Son, taking notes on the style in which it is told.

Drafting Follow your notes as you draft, setting out the events of your story in clear sequence. Emphasize those elements—character traits or events—that will lead the reader to understand your parable. Use sensory details to make the scenes vivid and specific in your reader's mind. Conclude the parable with a moral.

Revising Highlight parts of your work that do not fit the general style you have adopted. Rewrite marked passages for consistency.

Model: Revising for Consistent Style

And, lo, the bully descended like a wolf on the playground. "Out of my way, meathead," he said.
    laid about him mightily.
And he ʌ started wailing on the nearest person.

The revision maintains the style: formal, simple, biblical-sounding narration contrasting with the character's slang dialogue.

Drama

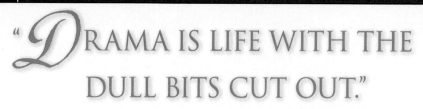

"DRAMA IS LIFE WITH THE DULL BITS CUT OUT."

— ALFRED HITCHCOCK

Defining Drama

Drama is a form of literature that tells a story through performances by actors.

Types of Drama The ancient Greeks developed drama into a sophisticated art form. They created two broad categories of drama: tragedy and comedy.

- **Tragedies** end with the downfall or death of the protagonist, or main character. In ancient Greek and Shakespearean tragedy, the main character is the *tragic hero*—an outstanding person of high rank who falls to his or her ruin.
- **Comedies** feature ordinary protagonists in conflicts that are resolved happily.

Elements of Drama The text of a play consists of dialogue and stage directions.

- **Dialogue** The term **dialogue** refers to the lines characters speak in conversation with each other. Playwrights also use these types of speech: **monologues,** or long speeches delivered by one character to others; **asides,** or private remarks to another character or to the audience that are not heard by other characters onstage; and **soliloquies,** or speeches voicing a character's inner thoughts, not heard by others.
- **Stage Directions** Many playwrights include **stage directions,** or instructions, about the setting, costumes, lighting, scenery, and props, or objects used onstage. Stage directions may also indicate how and when characters should move and with what expression they should deliver their lines.

Close Read: Elements of Shakespearean Drama These literary elements appear in the Model text.

Soliloquy: A soliloquy is a long speech expressing private thoughts, not heard by others. Example: *Before murdering King Duncan, Macbeth delivers a soliloquy expressing his fears and doubts, beginning "If it were done when 'tis done . . . "* (Macbeth, I, vii, 1).	**Internal Conflict and Characterization:** An internal conflict is a character's struggle with his or her own conflicting motivations. In his soliloquies, Shakespeare turns a powerful psychological spotlight on characters' internal conflicts. Example: ***"Hamlet.** To be or not to be, that is the question. . . ."* (Hamlet, III, i, 62)
Imagery: The mind's power to make sense of the world is part of Shakespearean drama. Imagery, or word pictures, in the dialogue shows characters' minds and hearts at work. Example: ***"Romeo.** But soft! What light through yonder window breaks? / It is the East, and Juliet is the sun!"* (Romeo and Juliet, II, ii, 2–3)	**Blank Verse:** Shakespeare's noble characters often speak in a type of poetry called blank verse, consisting of unrhymed lines each containing five stressed syllables. Each stressed syllable is preceded by an unstressed syllable in a "da-DUM, da-DUM" rhythm. Example: ***"Antony.** O mighty Caesar! Dost thou lie so low?"* (Julius Caesar, III, i, 148)

 **EXEMPLAR TEXT**

Model

About the Text In Shakespeare's *Hamlet,* Hamlet's uncle Claudius has murdered Hamlet's father, the king of Denmark, and then married Hamlet's mother, taking the throne of Denmark. In this soliloquy, Claudius ponders his crime.

from *The Tragedy of Hamlet,* Act III, Scene iii, Lines 39–75
William Shakespeare

KING CLAUDIUS

O, my offence is rank, it smells to heaven;
40 It hath the primal eldest curse[1] upon't,
A brother's murder. Pray can I not,
Though inclination be as sharp as will:
My stronger guilt defeats my strong intent;
And, like a man to double business bound,
45 I stand in pause where I shall first begin,
And both neglect. What if this cursed hand
Were thicker than itself with brother's blood,
Is there not rain enough in the sweet heavens
To wash it white as snow? Whereto serves mercy
50 But to confront the visage of offence?[2]
And what's in prayer but this two-fold force,
To be forestalled ere we come to fall,
Or pardon'd being down? Then I'll look up;
My fault is past. But, O, what form of prayer
55 Can serve my turn? 'Forgive me my foul murder'?
That cannot be; since I am still possess'd
Of those effects for which I did the murder,
My crown, mine own ambition and my queen.
May one be pardon'd and retain the offence?
60 In the corrupted currents of this world
Offence's gilded hand may shove by justice,
And oft 'tis seen the wicked prize itself
Buys out the law: but 'tis not so above;
There is no shuffling, there the action lies
65 In his true nature; and we ourselves compell'd,
Even to the teeth and forehead of our faults,
To give in evidence. What then? What rests?
Try what repentance can. What can it not?
Yet what can it when one can not repent?
70 O wretched state! O bosom black as death!
O limed[3] soul, that, struggling to be free,
Art more engaged! Help, angels! Make assay!
Bow, stubborn knees; and, heart with strings of steel,
Be soft as sinews of the newborn babe!
75 All may be well.

1. **primal eldest curse** the curse of Cain. In the Bible, Cain killed his brother Abel.

2. **Whereto serves mercy . . . visage of offence?** What is mercy's purpose if not to contest condemnation?

3. **limed** trapped, as a bird caught in birdlime, a sticky substance used in traps.

Soliloquy In this speech, Claudius reveals his thoughts alone onstage, confessing that he has murdered his brother, who was Hamlet's father and the king of Denmark.

Blank Verse The rhythm of the blank verse helps carry Claudius's analysis of prayer and forgiveness to its conclusion.

Internal Conflict In these lines Claudius elaborates on his internal conflict—the fact that he is "to double business bound." He cannot truly repent of the murder as long as he is still attached to what it has brought him: a crown and a wife.

Imagery The contrast between the images of "strings of steel" and "sinews of the newborn babe" reflects Claudius's agonized struggle—he is torn between his stubborn attachment to his crime and his desire to repent.

Literary History: Shakespeare's Globe

"Can this cockpit hold
The vasty fields of France? Or may we cram
Within this wooden O the very casques
That did affright the air at Agincourt?"

—Shakespeare, from Henry V

The Elizabethan Theater

English drama came of age during the reign of Elizabeth I, developing into a sophisticated and popular art form. Although playwrights like Shakespeare were mainly responsible for the great theatrical achievements of the time, audiences and theater buildings were equally important.

Before the reign of Elizabeth I, traveling theater companies put on plays wherever they could find an audience, often performing in the open courtyards of inns. Spectators watched from the ground or from balconies or galleries above.

England's First Playhouse

When Shakespeare was twelve years old, an actor named James Burbage built London's first theater, called simply The Theater. Actors—even prominent and well-to-do actors like James Burbage—were frowned upon by the city fathers. Nonetheless, they were wildly popular with the common people and were called on frequently to perform at court. A man like Burbage enjoyed a reputation somewhat like a rock star's today.

The Globe In 1597, the city fathers closed down The Theater. In late 1598, Richard Burbage (James Burbage's son) and his men dismantled it and hauled it in pieces across the Thames to Southwark. It took them six months to rebuild it, and when they did, they renamed it the Globe.

Scholars disagree about what the Globe actually looked like because there are no surviving drawings from the time or detailed descriptions. Shakespeare refers to the building in *Henry V* as "this wooden O." The building had to have been small enough for the actors to be heard, and we know that performances drew as many as 2,500 to 3,000 people. These truly packed houses must have been uncomfortable—especially when you consider that people of the era didn't bathe or change their clothes very often! Most spectators stood throughout the performance. Some of the audience sat in a gallery behind the performers. Though they saw only the actors' backs and probably could not hear very well, they were content to be seen by the rest of the audience.

There were no sets or lighting at the Globe. Plays were performed in sunlight, and a playwright's words alone had to create moods like the one in the eerie first scene of *Macbeth.* Holding an audience spellbound was complicated by the fact that most spectators ate and drank throughout the performance.

The first Globe met its demise in 1613, when a cannon fired as part of a performance of *Henry VIII* ignited the theater's thatched roof. Everyone escaped unharmed, but the Globe burned to the ground. Although the theater was rebuilt, the Puritans had it permanently closed in 1642.

The New Globe

Building a replica of Shakespeare's Globe was the American actor Sam Wanamaker's dream. After long years of fundraising and construction, the theater opened to its first full season on June 8, 1997, with a production of *Henry V.* Like the earlier Globe, this one is made of wood, with a thatched roof and lime plaster covering the walls. The stage and the galleries are covered, but the "bear pit," where the modern-day groundlings stand, is open to the skies.

Perhaps the most striking aspect of seeing Shakespeare's plays performed at the Globe is the immediacy of the action. The performers, as Benedict Nightingale noted in the *London Times,* "are talking to you, asking you questions, involving you in their fears." Is that not what theater is all about?

A performance at the modern Globe

Literary History: Shakespeare on Film

Adapting Shakespeare

William Shakespeare wrote for the same audience that filmmakers write for today. Recognizing his wide appeal, filmmakers have adapted many of Shakespeare's plays as films. On these two pages, you will see examples of some of the more notable adaptations.

◄ The 1956 science-fiction film *Forbidden Planet* adapted Shakespeare's drama *The Tempest*, transforming the play's mysterious island into a distant planet.

Japanese director Akira Kurosawa's samurai epic *Throne of Blood* (1957) is considered one of the best film adaptations of *Macbeth*. Toshiro Mifune (shown here) plays the character based on Shakespeare's tragic hero. ►

◀ The musical *West Side Story* (1961) updated *Romeo and Juliet* to the mean streets of New York City. The warring families of Shakespeare's drama become rival gangs.

Common Core State Standards

Reading Literature
7. Analyze multiple interpretations of a story, drama, or poem, evaluating how each version interprets the source text.

In 1996, Claire Danes (shown here) played Juliet to Leonardo DiCaprio's Romeo in Baz Luhrmann's version of *Romeo and Juliet*. Luhrmann used Shakespeare's dialogue, but set the play in a hip modern suburb. ▶

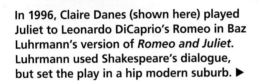

Reading Literature: Group Discussion

Analyzing Multiple Interpretations After reading Shakespeare's *Macbeth*, view two or more productions of the play. Consider the 1948 film version directed by Orson Welles as well as any current theatrical versions. Then, in small groups, compare the interpretations you viewed. Use these prompts to guide discussion:

• Did the characters in each version match the characters you imagined while reading *Macbeth*? Were the portrayals effective?

• Describe and evaluate the use in each production of techniques specific to the medium—for film, for example, you might discuss the use of camera point of view, including distance shots and close-ups.

• Did the production depart from Shakespeare's text by introducing, updating, or omitting elements? Evaluate each change.

Based on your discussion, evaluate the effectiveness of each production.

Themes Across Centuries: Scholar's Insights

Sir Frank Kermode on *Macbeth*

***Macbeth's* Dramatic History** *Macbeth,* first performed in 1606, is a play about the murder of a good king of Scotland, its cruel consequences for his country, and the final overthrow of the murderous usurper. Shakespeare takes many liberties with history, for King Duncan was not really a saintly character and Macbeth not a particularly evil one. Banquo is presented in a favorable light because he was held to be the ancestor of King James, the Scottish king who inherited Elizabeth's throne in 1603. Shakespeare's company was called The King's Men; as servants of the king, they had good reason to praise his ancestry and his virtues. Considering the period background, the play is remarkable for the allusions it makes to events in the early years of James's reign.

Portraying the Tumult of Mind and Conscience Yet these allusions are matters of secondary interest to the modern reader. *Macbeth* is a work of the author's full maturity. He had already written the tragedies *Hamlet, Othello,* and *King Lear* and had learned how to represent not merely outward actions but the tumults of the mind and conscience.

In the passage shown from Act I, Macbeth is at the moment of decision, the interim between desire and action, debating within himself whether to go ahead with the plot he devised with his wife to murder the king, their guest. He is weighing the benefits that act would bring him against the powerful reasons for not doing it. He knows that time won't stand still when Duncan is dead. The killing will start a train of events calling for further action.

He is willing to risk judgment after death but knows it will happen in this life. In the here and now. And he gives ordinary social, human reasons for not committing the crime: He is Duncan's kinsman and his host. Moreover, for a subject to kill an innocent monarch is an offense so horrible that his imagination foretells the dreadful disturbances and great sorrows that must ensue. And he admits he has no motive except overweening ambition.

About the Author

Literary critic Sir Frank Kermode wrote the award-winning *Shakespeare's Language* in 2000. Other works by Kermode include *The Uses of Error* (1991) and *An Appetite for Poetry* (1989).

▼ **Critical Viewing**
What general traits might be worthy of note in a tribute to a young king, like James I pictured here? **SPECULATE**

The Actions of a Common Man The reason why Macbeth's soliloquy is so famous is not that it concerns the early history of Scotland, and the foundation of the Stuart dynasty, but that it gives incomparably vivid expression to an acute crisis of conscience. For a moment, Macbeth is every man or woman, who must, in the course of his or her life, be faced by the need to decide which of two choices is the right one.

The language of this soliloquy is sometimes unusual and full of feverish excitement. But, at first, do not bother too much about the details; just allow yourself to be swept along by the movement of passionate thought.

This soliloquy indicates the extraordinary range and flexibility of the play's language, incomparably greater than English could have provided even fifty or sixty years before. This new fluency owes something to sixteenth-century Bible translations.

Religious and Ethical Thought As this soliloquy also reflects, *Macbeth* is notable for complying with native ethical traditions. Shakespeare is not often explicitly religious, but Macbeth speaks as one aware of the Christian religion—he understands the danger to his soul, yet gives his "eternal jewel" to "the common enemy of man" (3.1.68–69). Behind such remarks there is a great weight of religious and ethical thought.

"He's here in double trust:
First, as I am his kinsman and his subject,
Strong both against the deed; then, as his host,
Who should against his murderer shut the door,
Not bear the knife myself. Besides, this Duncan
Hath borne his faculties so meek, hath been
So clear in his great office, that his virtues
Will plead like angels, trumpet-tongue'd, against
The deep damnation of his taking-off . . .
        I have no spur
To prick the sides of my intent, but only
Vaulting ambition, which o'erleaps itself
And falls on th'other." — *Macbeth*, Act I, Scene vii

Critical Reading

1. **Key Ideas and Details (a)** What English king did Shakespeare intend to honor by writing *Macbeth?* **(b) Speculate:** What benefits might a company of actors and playwrights reap by presenting their king in a favorable light?

2. **Key Ideas and Details (a)** According to Kermode, what reason does Macbeth provide for wanting to kill King Duncan? **(b) Speculate:** If, in the course of the play, Macbeth is punished for killing the king, what message might this send to the audience in Shakespeare's day?

As You Read Macbeth . . .

3. **Integration of Knowledge and Ideas** Note moments in which Banquo and most kings in the play are presented in a positive light as a way to honor James I of England.

4. **Integration of Knowledge and Ideas** Look for evidence that supports Kermode's characterization of Macbeth as "every man or woman . . . faced by the need to decide which of two choices is the right one."

WILLIAM SHAKESPEARE

(1564–1616)

Because of his deep understanding of human nature, his compassion for all types of people, and the power and beauty of his language, William Shakespeare is regarded as the greatest writer in English. Nearly four hundred years after his death, Shakespeare's plays continue to be read widely and produced throughout the world. They have the same powerful impact on today's audiences as they had when they were first staged.

THE PLAYWRIGHT IN HIS OWN TIME

It is a myth that we know absolutely nothing about Shakespeare's life. As critic Irving Ribner attests, "we know more about him than we do about virtually any other of his contemporary dramatists, with the exception of Ben Jonson." Shakespeare was born on April 23, 1564, in Stratford-on-Avon,

"The poet's eye, in a fine frenzy rolling,
Doth glance from heaven to earth, from earth
*   to heaven;*
And, as imagination bodies forth
The forms of things unknown, the poet's pen
Turns them to shapes, and gives to airy nothing
A local habitation and a name."

—William Shakespeare,
from *A Midsummer Night's Dream*

which is northwest of London. (The date is based on a record of his baptism on April 26.) Stratford, with a population of about two thousand in Shakespeare's day, was the market town for a fertile agricultural region.

Shakespeare's father, John, was a successful glove maker and businessman who held a number of positions in the town's government. His mother, whose maiden name was Mary Arden, was the daughter of John's landlord. Their marriage, therefore, boosted the Shakespeare family's holdings. Nevertheless, there is evidence that in the late 1570s, John Shakespeare began to suffer financial reverses.

SHAKESPEARE'S EDUCATION

No written evidence of Shakespeare's boyhood exists—not even a name on a school attendance list. However, given his father's status, it is highly probable that he attended the Stratford Grammar School, where he acquired a knowledge of Latin.

Although Shakespeare did not go on to study at a university, his attendance at the grammar school from ages seven to sixteen would have provided him with a good education. Discipline at such a school was strict, and the school day lasted from 6:00 A.M. in the summer (7:00 in the winter) until 5:00 P.M. From 11:00 to 1:00, students were dismissed to eat lunch with their families. At 3:00, they were allowed to play for a quarter of an hour!

SHAKESPEARE'S MARRIAGE AND FAMILY

Shakespeare's name enters the official records again in November 1582, when he received a license to marry Anne Hathaway. The couple had a

Speaking Shakespeare

You may not realize the extent to which you already "speak" Shakespeare. For example, have you ever used or heard any of these phrases used in *Macbeth*?

He's full of *milk of human kindness* (I, v, 17)
Don't worry about it, *what's done is done!* (II, ii, 12)
That will last until *the crack of doom.* (IV, i, 117)
She finished the jobs in *one fell swoop.* (IV, iii, 219)

Shakespeare invented each of these now common phrases, which were unknown in English before their appearance in *Macbeth*. Look for them as you read and discover if their meanings have changed since Shakespeare's time.

daughter, Susanna, in 1583, and twins, Judith and Hamnet, in 1585. Beyond names and years in which his children were born, we know little about his family life. Some writers have made much of the fact that Shakespeare left his wife and children behind when he went to London not long after his twins were born. However, he visited his family in Stratford regularly during his years as a playwright, and they may have lived with him for a time in London.

ACTOR AND PLAYWRIGHT

It is uncertain how Shakespeare became connected with the theater in the late 1580s and early 1590s. By 1594, however, he had become a part owner and the principal playwright of the Lord Chamberlain's Men, one of the most successful theater companies in London.

In 1599, the company built the famous Globe theater on the south bank of the Thames River, in Southwark. This is where most of

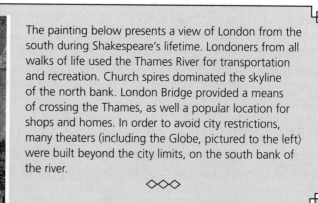

The painting below presents a view of London from the south during Shakespeare's lifetime. Londoners from all walks of life used the Thames River for transportation and recreation. Church spires dominated the skyline of the north bank. London Bridge provided a means of crossing the Thames, as well a popular location for shops and homes. In order to avoid city restrictions, many theaters (including the Globe, pictured to the left) were built beyond the city limits, on the south bank of the river.

◇◇◇

Shakespeare's plays were performed. When James I became king in 1603, after the death of Elizabeth I, James took control of the Lord Chamberlain's Men and renamed the company the King's Men.

RETIREMENT

In about 1610, Shakespeare retired to Stratford, where he continued to write plays. He was a prosperous middle-class man, who profited from his share in a successful theater company. Six years later, on April 23, 1616, he died and was buried in Holy Trinity Church in Stratford. Because it was a common practice to move bodies after burial to make room for others, Shakespeare wrote the following as his epitaph:

> Blest be the man that spares these stones,
> And curst be he that moves my bones.

HIS LITERARY RECORD

Shakespeare did not think of himself as a man of letters. He wrote his plays to be performed and did not bring out editions of them for the reading public. The first published edition of his work, called the First Folio, was issued in 1623 by two members of his theater company, John Heminges and Henry Condell. It contained thirty-six of the thirty-seven plays now attributed to him.

Shakespeare's varied output includes romantic comedies, like *A Midsummer Night's Dream* and *As You Like It*; history plays, like *Henry IV*, Parts 1 and 2; tragedies, like *Romeo and Juliet, Hamlet, Othello, King Lear,* and *Macbeth*; and later romances, like *The Tempest*. In addition to his plays, he wrote 154 sonnets and three longer poems.

MACBETH
SHAKESPEARE'S SOURCES

FACT AND LEGEND

By Shakespeare's time, the story of the eleventh-century Scottish king Macbeth was a mixture of fact and legend. Shakespeare and his contemporaries, however, probably regarded the account of Macbeth in Raphael Holinshed's *Chronicles of England, Scotland, and Ireland* as completely factual. The playwright drew on the *Chronicles* as a source for the play, yet, as you will see, he freely adapted the material for his own purposes.

HOLINSHED'S CHRONICLES

Holinshed's account contains a description of a meeting between Macbeth and the witches. His account also tells how Macbeth and his friends, angry at the naming of King Duncan's son Malcolm as Prince of Cumberland, ambush and slay Duncan. However, the historical Macbeth's claim to the throne has some basis. (See page 408 for an explanation of the ancient Scottish custom of choosing kings.) Finally, Holinshed indicates that Banquo is Macbeth's accomplice in the assassination. Lady Macbeth, prominent in Shakespeare's play, does not play a significant role in Holinshed.

SHAKESPEARE'S MACBETH

Shakespeare took what he needed from the *Chronicles* and shaped it into a tragic plot. Seeing the theatrical possibilities of the meeting with the witches, Shakespeare staged such an encounter in Act I, Scene iii. However, he changed Holinshed's account in order to make King Duncan an innocent victim: Shakespeare's Macbeth does not have a legitimate claim to the throne. Further, Shakespeare used another story in the *Chronicles*—one in which a wife urges her husband to kill a friend and guest—as the basis for the character Lady Macbeth. She becomes Macbeth's co-conspirator, replacing Banquo. Shakespeare, of course, had political motives for holding Banquo innocent. Banquo was considered the ancestor of the new king, James I!

Connecting to the Essential Question In *Macbeth*, a noble person's downfall results from a character flaw. As you read, note that *Macbeth*, unlike classical tragedies, includes comedy in its portrayal of a noble character's downfall. Finding such moments will help you answer the Essential Question: **What is the relationship of the writer to tradition?**

Close Reading Focus

Elizabethan Drama; Tragedy; Soliloquy
During the late 1500s, **Elizabethan drama** blossomed. Using models from ancient Greece and Rome, writers reintroduced **tragedies**—plays in which disaster befalls a character. Dramatists also began writing their plays in carefully crafted unrhymed verse, using rich language and vivid imagery.

Because the Globe, like other Elizabethan theaters, had no lighting, plays were performed in broad daylight. There were also no sets, so the words of the play had to create the illusion of time and place for the audience.

Playwrights made key choices about how to develop and relate character. One device they used was called a **soliloquy,** a long speech usually made by a character who is alone (the Latin word *solus* means "alone"). This speech reveals thoughts and feelings to the audience. In Shakespeare's tragedies, the greatest works of Elizabethan drama, tragic characters reveal secret desires or fears through their soliloquies.

As you read the following soliloquies in this act, note the inner struggles each reveals.

- Lady Macbeth's soliloquy, Act I, Scene v, lines 1–30
- Macbeth's soliloquy, Act I, Scene vii, lines 1–28

Preparing to Read Complex Texts Like many dramas, Shakespeare's plays were meant to be performed, not read. By **analyzing information from text features** like introductory *background notes*, *stage directions* in brackets, *illustrations*, and *footnotes* on the side of the text, you can picture the action in your mind. You can also better understand the meaning and tone of the characters' words. Use a chart like the one shown to analyze information from text features and clarify the meaning of passages.

Vocabulary

You will encounter the words below in the text that follows. Copy the words into your notebook, listing the words you know and the words you do not know.

valor	surmise
treasons	sovereign
imperial	

Common Core State Standards

Reading Literature
3. Analyze the impact of the author's choices regarding how to develop and relate elements of a story or drama.

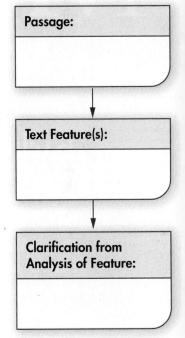

Passage:

Text Feature(s):

Clarification from Analysis of Feature:

THE TRAGEDY OF
MACBETH

WILLIAM SHAKESPEARE

Background The Elizabethans viewed the universe, in its ideal state, as both orderly and interconnected. They believed that a great chain linked all beings, from God on high to the lowest beasts and plants. They also believed that universal order was based on parallels between different realms. Just as the sun ruled in the heavens, for example, the king ruled in the state and the father in the family. Because everything was linked, a disturbance in one area would cause a disturbance in others. In keeping with this concept of order, a Shakespearean tragedy shows how a tragic hero's bad choices can disturb the whole universe. As *Macbeth* gets under way, notice the parallel disorders in the mind of the hero, the weather, and the kingdom.

Characters

Duncan, King of Scotland

Malcolm
Donalbain } his sons

Macbeth
Banquo
Macduff
Lennox
Ross
Menteith
Angus
Caithness } noblemen of Scotland

Fleance, son to Banquo
Siward, Earl of Northumberland, general of the English forces
Young Siward, his son
Seyton, an officer attending on Macbeth
Son to Macduff
An English Doctor
A Scottish Doctor
A Porter
An Old Man
Three Murderers
Lady Macbeth
Lady Macduff
A Gentlewoman attending on Lady Macbeth
Hecate
Witches
Apparitions
Lords, Officers, Soldiers, Attendants, and Messengers

Setting: Scotland; England

ACT I

Scene i. An open place.

[*Thunder and lightning. Enter* THREE WITCHES.]

FIRST WITCH. When shall we three meet again?
In thunder, lightning, or in rain?

SECOND WITCH. When the hurlyburly's done,
When the battle's lost and won.

THIRD WITCH. That will be ere the set of sun.

FIRST WITCH. Where the place?

SECOND WITCH. Upon the heath.

THIRD WITCH. There to meet with Macbeth.

FIRST WITCH. I come, Graymalkin.[1]

SECOND WITCH. Paddock[2] calls.

THIRD WITCH. Anon![3]

ALL. Fair is foul, and foul is fair.
Hover through the fog and filthy air. [*Exit.*]

Scene ii. A camp near Forres, a town in northeast Scotland.

[*Alarum within.*[1] *Enter* KING DUNCAN, MALCOLM, DONALBAIN, LENNOX, *with* ATTENDANTS, *meeting a bleeding* CAPTAIN.]

Analyze Text Features
Who or what are Graymalkin and Paddock in lines 8 and 9? How do you know?

1. **Graymalkin** first witch's helper, a gray cat.
2. **Paddock** second witch's helper, a toad.
3. **Anon** at once.

1. **Alarum within** trumpet call offstage.

Comprehension
Where, when, and with whom will the witches next meet?

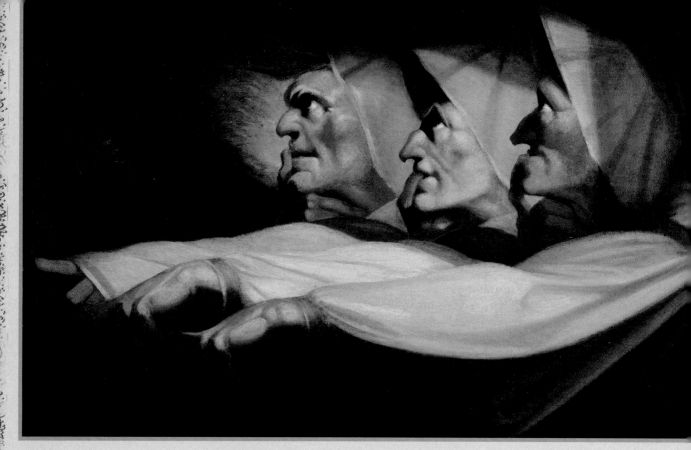

▲ **Critical Viewing** Examine Fuseli's rendering of the witches. Does the mood he creates correspond to the mood in Act I, Scene i? Why or why not? **CONNECT**

2. **sergeant** officer.

3. **broil** battle.

4. **choke their art** prevent each other from swimming.

5. **Western Isles** the Hebrides, off Scotland.

6. **Of kerns and gallowglasses** with lightly armed Irish foot soldiers and heavily armed soldiers.

7. **damned quarrel** accursed cause.

8. **Showed . . . whore** falsely appeared to favor Macdonwald.

9. **minion** favorite.

Vocabulary

valor (val´ ər) *n.* marked courage or bravery

KING. What bloody man is that? He can report,
As seemeth by his plight, of the revolt
The newest state.

MALCOLM.   This is the sergeant[2]
Who like a good and hardy soldier fought
5   'Gainst my captivity. Hail, brave friend!
Say to the king the knowledge of the broil[3]
As thou didst leave it.

CAPTAIN.   Doubtful it stood,
As two spent swimmers, that do cling together
And choke their art.[4] The merciless Macdonwald—
10 Worthy to be a rebel for to that
The multiplying villainies of nature
Do swarm upon him—from the Western Isles[5]
Of kerns and gallowglasses[6] is supplied;
And fortune, on his damnéd quarrel[7] smiling,
15 Showed like a rebel's whore:[8] but all's too weak:
For brave Macbeth—well he deserves that name—
Disdaining fortune, with his brandished steel,
Which smoked with bloody execution,
Like valor's minion[9] carved out his passage

20   Till he faced the slave;
     Which nev'r shook hands, nor bade farewell to him,
     Till he unseamed him from the nave to th' chops,[10]
     And fixed his head upon our battlements.

    KING. O valiant cousin! Worthy gentleman!

25 **CAPTAIN.** As whence the sun 'gins his reflection[11]
     Shipwracking storms and direful thunders break,
     So from that spring whence comfort seemed to come
     Discomfort swells. Mark, King of Scotland, mark:
     No sooner justice had, with valor armed,
30   Compelled these skipping kerns to trust their heels
     But the Norweyan lord,[12] surveying vantage,[13]
     With furbished arms and new supplies of men,
     Began a fresh assault.

    KING.   Dismayed not this
     Our captains, Macbeth and Banquo?

    CAPTAIN.   Yes;
35   As sparrows eagles, or the hare the lion.
     If I say sooth,[14] I must report they were
     As cannons overcharged with double cracks;[15]
     So they doubly redoubled strokes upon the foe.
     Except[16] they meant to bathe in reeking wounds,
40   Or memorize another Golgotha,[17]
     I cannot tell—
     But I am faint; my gashes cry for help.

    KING. So well thy words become thee as thy wounds;
     They smack of honor both. Go get him surgeons.

                      [*Exit* CAPTAIN, *attended.*]

[*Enter* ROSS *and* ANGUS.]

     Who comes here?

45 **MALCOLM.**   The worthy Thane[18] of Ross.

    LENNOX. What a haste looks through his eyes! So should he look
     That seems to[19] speak things strange.

    ROSS.   God save the king!

    KING. Whence cam'st thou, worthy Thane?

    ROSS.   From Fife, great King;
     Where the Norweyan banners flout the sky
50   And fan our people cold.
     Norway[20] himself, with terrible numbers,
     Assisted by that most disloyal traitor
     The Thane of Cawdor, began a dismal[21] conflict;
     Till that Bellona's bridegroom, lapped in proof,[22]

Elizabethan Drama

What offstage scene does the captain describe in this speech (lines 7–23)?

10. **unseamed . . . chops** split him open from the navel to the jaws.

11. **'gins his reflection** rises.

12. **Norweyan lord** king of Norway.

13. **surveying vantage** seeing an opportunity.

14. **sooth** truth.

15. **cracks** explosives.

16. **except** unless.

17. **memorize . . . Golgotha** (gôl′ gə thə) make the place as memorable for slaughter as Golgotha, the place where Christ was crucified.

18. **Thane** Scottish title of nobility.

19. **seems to** seems about to.

20. **Norway** king of Norway.

21. **dismal** threatening.

22. **Bellona's . . . proof** Macbeth is called the mate of Bellona, the goddess of war, clad in tested armor.

Elizabethan Drama

How do Lennox's words here (lines 46–47) supply a clue for the actor playing Ross?

Comprehension

What role has Macbeth played in the battle?

Macbeth, Act I, Scene ii   **325**

23. self-comparisons counter movements.

24. lavish insolent.

55 Confronted him with self-comparisons,[23]
Point against point, rebellious arm 'gainst arm,
Curbing his lavish[24] spirit: and, to conclude,
The victory fell on us.

KING. Great happiness!

ROSS. That now
Sweno, the Norways' king, craves composition;[25]
60 Nor would we deign him burial of his men
Till he disbursed, at Saint Colme's Inch,[26]
Ten thousand dollars to our general use.

25. composition terms of peace.

26. St. Colme's Inch island near Edinburgh, Scotland.

KING. No more that Thane of Cawdor shall deceive
Our bosom interest:[27] go pronounce his present[28] death,
65 And with his former title greet Macbeth.

27. our bosom interest my heart's trust.

28. present immediate.

ROSS. I'll see it done.

KING. What he hath lost, noble Macbeth hath won.

[*Exit.*]

Analyze Information from Text Features

What information about the setting for Scene iii do you learn from the italicized stage directions?

Scene iii. A heath near Forres.

[*Thunder. Enter the* THREE WITCHES.]

FIRST WITCH. Where hast thou been, sister?

SECOND WITCH. Killing swine.[1]

THIRD WITCH. Sister, where thou?

1. Killing swine It was commonly believed that witches killed domestic animals.

FIRST WITCH. A sailor's wife had chestnuts in her lap,
And mounched, and mounched, and mounched.
5 "Give me," quoth I.
"Aroint thee,[2] witch!" the rump-fed ronyon[3] cries.
Her husband's to Aleppo[4] gone, master o' th' Tiger:
But in a sieve[5] I'll thither sail,
And, like a rat without a tail,[6]
10 I'll do, I'll do, and I'll do.

2. Aroint thee Be off.

3. rump-fed ronyon fat-rumped, scabby creature.

4. Aleppo trading center in Syria.

5. sieve It was commonly believed that witches often sailed in sieves.

6. rat . . . tail According to popular belief, witches could assume the form of any animal, but the tail would always be missing.

SECOND WITCH. I'll give thee a wind.

FIRST WITCH. Th' art kind.

THIRD WITCH. And I another.

FIRST WITCH. I myself have all the other;
15 And the very ports they blow,[7]
All the quarters that they know
I' th' shipman's card.[8]
I'll drain him dry as hay:
Sleep shall neither night nor day
20 Hang upon his penthouse lid;[9]
He shall live a man forbid:[10]

7. they blow to which the winds blow.

8. card compass.

9. penthouse lid eyelid.

10. forbid cursed.

Weary sev'nights[11] nine times nine
Shall he dwindle, peak,[12] and pine:
Though his bark cannot be lost,
25 Yet it shall be tempest-tossed.
Look what I have.

SECOND WITCH. Show me, show me.

FIRST WITCH. Here I have a pilot's thumb,
Wracked as homeward he did come.

[*Drum within.*]

30 **THIRD WITCH.** A drum, a drum!
Macbeth doth come.

ALL. The weird[13] sisters, hand in hand,
Posters[14] of the sea and land,
Thus do go about, about:
35 Thrice to thine, and thrice to mine,
And thrice again, to make up nine.
Peace! The charm's wound up.

[*Enter* MACBETH *and* BANQUO.]

MACBETH. So foul and fair a day I have not seen.

BANQUO. How far is 't called to Forres? What are these
40 So withered, and so wild in their attire,
That look not like th' inhabitants o' th' earth,
And yet are on 't? Live you, or are you aught
That man may question? You seem to understand me,
By each at once her choppy[15] finger laying
45 Upon her skinny lips. You should be women,
And yet your beards forbid me to interpret
That you are so.

MACBETH.   Speak, if you can: what are you?

FIRST WITCH. All hail, Macbeth! Hail to thee, Thane of Glamis!

SECOND WITCH. All hail, Macbeth! Hail to thee, Thane of Cawdor!

50 **THIRD WITCH.** All hail, Macbeth, that shalt be King hereafter!

BANQUO. Good sir, why do you start, and seem to fear
Things that do sound so fair? I' th' name of truth,
Are you fantastical,[16] or that indeed
Which outwardly ye show? My noble partner
55 You greet with present grace[17] and great prediction
Of noble having[18] and of royal hope,
That he seems rapt withal:[19] to me you speak not.
If you can look into the seeds of time,
And say which grain will grow and which will not,

11. **sev'nights** weeks.

12. **peak** waste away.

13. **weird** destiny-serving.

14. **Posters** swift travelers.

Elizabethan Drama
What descriptive details does Banquo use in his speech about the witches (lines 39–47)?

15. **choppy** chapped.

16. **fantastical** imaginary.

17. **grace** honor.

18. **having** possession.

19. **rapt withal** entranced by it.

Comprehension
What has Macbeth earned through his exploits?

▲ **Critical Viewing** Which of the two soldiers on the right do you think is Macbeth?
Explain your reasoning. **DEDUCE**

Elizabethan Drama
How could Elizabethan
actors have made this scene
with the witches mysterious
without help from special
lighting effects?

20. **happy** fortunate.

21. **imperfect** incomplete.

22. **Sinel's** (siˊ nəlz)
Macbeth's father's.

23. **owe** own.

24. **intelligence**
information.

60   Speak then to me, who neither beg nor fear
      Your favors nor your hate.

FIRST WITCH. Hail!

SECOND WITCH. Hail!

THIRD WITCH. Hail!

65 **FIRST WITCH.** Lesser than Macbeth, and greater.

SECOND WITCH. Not so happy,[20] yet much happier.

THIRD WITCH. Thou shalt get kings, though thou be none.
      So all hail, Macbeth and Banquo!

FIRST WITCH. Banquo and Macbeth, all hail!

70 **MACBETH.** Stay, you imperfect[21] speakers, tell me more:
      By Sinel's[22] death I know I am Thane of Glamis;
      But how of Cawdor? The Thane of Cawdor lives,
      A prosperous gentleman; and to be King
      Stands not within the prospect of belief,
75   No more than to be Cawdor. Say from whence
      You owe[23] this strange intelligence?[24] Or why

Upon this blasted heath you stop our way
With such prophetic greeting? Speak, I charge you.

[WITCHES *vanish.*]

BANQUO. The earth hath bubbles as the water has,
80   And these are of them. Whither are they vanished?

MACBETH. Into the air, and what seemed corporal²⁵ melted
As breath into the wind. Would they had stayed!

BANQUO. Were such things here as we do speak about?
Or have we eaten on the insane root²⁶
85   That takes the reason prisoner?

MACBETH. Your children shall be kings.

BANQUO.   You shall be King.

MACBETH. And Thane of Cawdor too. Went it not so?

BANQUO. To th' selfsame tune and words. Who's here?

[*Enter* ROSS *and* ANGUS.]

ROSS. The King hath happily received, Macbeth,
90   The news of thy success; and when he reads²⁷
Thy personal venture in the rebels' fight,
His wonders and his praises do contend
Which should be thine or his.²⁸ Silenced with that,
In viewing o'er the rest o' th' selfsame day,
95   He finds thee in the stout Norweyan ranks,
Nothing afeard of what thyself didst make,
Strange images of death.²⁹ As thick as tale
Came post with post,³⁰ and every one did bear
Thy praises in his kingdom's great defense,
And poured them down before him.

100 **ANGUS.**   We are sent
To give thee, from our royal master, thanks;
Only to herald thee into his sight,
Not pay thee.

ROSS. And for an earnest³¹ of a greater honor,
105   He bade me, from him, call thee Thane of Cawdor;
In which addition,³² hail, most worthy Thane!
For it is thine.

BANQUO. [*Aside*] What, can the devil speak true?

MACBETH. The Thane of Cawdor lives: why do you dress me
In borrowed robes?

ANGUS.   Who was the thane lives yet,
110   But under heavy judgment bears that life
Which he deserves to lose. Whether he was combined³³

25. **corporal** real.

26. **insane root** henbane or hemlock, believed to cause insanity.

Analyze Information from Text Features
What does Banquo mean by the "insane root" (line 84)?

27. **reads** considers.

28. **His wonders . . . his** His admiration contends with his desire to praise you.

29. **Nothing . . . death** killing, but not being afraid of being killed.

30. **As thick . . . post** as fast as could be counted came messenger after messenger.

31. **earnest** pledge.

32. **In which addition** with this new title.

33. **combined** allied.

Comprehension
What do the witches promise Macbeth and Banquo?

Vocabulary

treasons (trē′ zənz) *n.* betrayals of one's country or oath of loyalty

Analyze Information from Text Features

Using the side notes, how would you rephrase lines 120–121?

38. **home** fully.

39. **enkindle you unto** encourage you to hope for.

40. **Cousins** often used as a term of courtesy between fellow noblemen.

41. **swelling . . . theme** stately idea that I will be King.

Vocabulary

imperial (im pir′ ē əl) *adj.* of an empire; having supreme authority

▶ **Critical Viewing** In what ways does the design of this crown reflect the belief that kings were divinely appointed? Explain your reasoning. **ANALYZE**

With those of Norway, or did line[34] the rebel
With hidden help and vantage,[35] or that with both
He labored in his country's wrack,[36] I know not;
115   But treasons capital, confessed and proved,
Have overthrown him.

MACBETH.   [*Aside*] Glamis, and Thane of Cawdor:
The greatest is behind.[37] [*To* ROSS *and* ANGUS]
Thanks for your pains.
[*Aside to* BANQUO] Do you not hope your children shall be kings,
When those that gave the Thane of Cawdor to me
Promised no less to them?

120   **BANQUO.** [*Aside to* MACBETH] That, trusted home,[38]
Might yet enkindle you unto[39] the crown,
Besides the Thane of Cawdor. But 'tis strange:
And oftentimes, to win us to our harm,
The instruments of darkness tell us truths,
125   Win us with honest trifles, to betray 's
In deepest consequence.
Cousins,[40] a word, I pray you.

MACBETH.   [*Aside*] Two truths are told,
As happy prologues to the swelling act
Of the imperial theme.[41]—I thank you, gentlemen.—
130   [*Aside*] This supernatural soliciting
Cannot be ill, cannot be good. If ill,
Why hath it given me earnest of success,
Commencing in a truth? I am Thane of Cawdor:
If good, why do I yield to that suggestion[42]
135   Whose horrid image doth unfix my hair
And make my seated[43] heart knock at my ribs,
Against the use of nature?[44] Present fears
Are less than horrible imaginings.

My thought, whose murder yet is but fantastical
140 Shakes so my single[45] state of man that function
Is smothered in surmise, and nothing is
But what is not.

BANQUO.   Look, how our partner's rapt.

MACBETH. [*Aside*] If chance will have me King, why,
chance may crown me,
Without my stir.

BANQUO.   New honors come upon him,
145 Like our strange[46] garments, cleave not to their mold
But with the aid of use.

MACBETH.   [*Aside*] Come what come may,
Time and the hour runs through the roughest day.

BANQUO. Worthy Macbeth, we stay upon your leisure.[47]

MACBETH. Give me your favor.[48] My dull brain was wrought
150 With things forgotten. Kind gentlemen, your pains
Are registered where every day I turn
The leaf to read them. Let us toward the King.
[*Aside to* BANQUO] Think upon what hath chanced,
and at more time,
The interim having weighed it,[49] let us speak
Our free hearts[50] each to other.

155 **BANQUO.**   Very gladly.

MACBETH. Till then, enough. Come, friends.

                                        [*Exit.*]

Scene iv. Forres. The palace.

[*Flourish.*[1] *Enter* KING DUNCAN, LENNOX, MALCOLM, DONALBAIN,
and ATTENDANTS.]

KING. Is execution done on Cawdor? Are not
Those in commission[2] yet returned?

MALCOLM.   My liege,[3]
They are not yet come back. But I have spoke
With one that saw him die, who did report
5 That very frankly he confessed his treasons,
Implored your Highness' pardon and set forth
A deep repentance: nothing in his life
Became him like the leaving it. He died
As one that had been studied[4] in his death,
10 To throw away the dearest thing he owed[5]
As 'twere a careless[6] trifle.

7. mind's construction person's character.

KING.   There's no art
To find the mind's construction[7] in the face:
He was a gentleman on whom I built
An absolute trust.

[*Enter* MACBETH, BANQUO, ROSS, *and* ANGUS.]

                    O worthiest cousin!
15   The sin of my ingratitude even now
Was heavy on me: thou art so far before,
That swiftest wing of recompense is slow
To overtake thee. Would thou hadst less deserved,
That the proportion both of thanks and payment

8. Would . . . mine If you had been less worthy, my thanks and payment could have exceeded the rewards you deserve.

20   Might have been mine![8] Only I have left to say,
More is thy due than more than all can pay.

9. pays itself is its own reward.

MACBETH.   The service and the loyalty I owe,
In doing it, pays itself.[9] Your Highness' part
Is to receive our duties: and our duties
25   Are to your throne and state children and servants;
Which do but what they should, by doing every thing

10. Safe toward with sure regard for.

Safe toward[10] your love and honor.

KING.   Welcome hither.
I have begun to plant thee, and will labor
To make thee full of growing. Noble Banquo,
30   That hast no less deserved, nor must be known

▼ **Critical Viewing** How does this Scottish castle reflect the mood of the play? **CONNECT**

No less to have done so, let me enfold thee
And hold thee to my heart.

BANQUO.   There if I grow,
The harvest is your own.

KING.   My plenteous joys,
Wanton[11] in fullness, seek to hide themselves
35   In drops of sorrow. Sons, kinsmen, thanes,
And you whose places are the nearest, know,
We will establish our estate upon
Our eldest, Malcolm,[12] whom we name hereafter
The Prince of Cumberland: which honor must
40   Not unaccompanied invest him only,
But signs of nobleness, like stars, shall shine
On all deservers. From hence to Inverness,[13]
And bind us further to you.

MACBETH. The rest is labor, which is not used for you.[14]
45   I'll be myself the harbinger,[15] and make joyful
The hearing of my wife with your approach;
So, humbly take my leave.

KING.   My worthy Cawdor!

MACBETH. [Aside] The Prince of Cumberland! That is a step
On which I must fall down, or else o'erleap,
50   For in my way it lies. Stars, hide your fires;
Let not light see my black and deep desires:
The eye wink at the hand;[16] yet let that be
Which the eye fears, when it is done, to see.   [*Exit.*]

KING. True, worthy Banquo; he is full so valiant,
55   And in his commendations I am fed;
It is a banquet to me. Let's after him,
Whose care is gone before to bid us welcome.
It is a peerless kinsman.   [*Flourish. Exit.*]

Scene v. Inverness. Macbeth's castle.

[*Enter* MACBETH'S WIFE, *alone, with a letter.*]

LADY MACBETH. [*Reads*] "They met me in the day of
success; and I have learned by the perfect'st report
they have more in them than mortal knowledge.
When I burned in desire to question them further,
5   they made themselves air, into which they vanished.
Whiles I stood rapt in the wonder of it, came
missives[1] from the King, who all-hailed me 'Thane
of Cawdor'; by which title, before, these weird sisters
saluted me, and referred me to the coming on
10   of time, with 'Hail, King that shalt be!' This have I

2. deliver thee report to you.

thought good to deliver thee,[2] my dearest partner of
greatness, that thou mightst not lose the dues of
rejoicing, by being ignorant of what greatness is
promised thee. Lay it to thy heart, and farewell."

Elizabethan Drama and Soliloquy

What does Lady Macbeth's
soliloquy in lines 15–30 reveal
about her ambitions and
plans?

3. nearest quickest.

4. illness wickedness.

5. that which . . . undone
What you are afraid of
doing you would not wish
undone once you have
done it.

6. round crown.

15 Glamis thou art, and Cawdor, and shalt be
What thou art promised. Yet do I fear thy nature;
It is too full o' th' milk of human kindness
To catch the nearest[3] way. Thou wouldst be great,
Art not without ambition, but without
20 The illness[4] should attend it. What thou wouldst highly,
That wouldst thou holily; wouldst not play false,
And yet wouldst wrongly win. Thou'dst have, great Glamis,
That which cries "Thus thou must do" if thou have it;
And that which rather thou dost fear to do
25 Than wishest should be undone.[5] Hie thee hither,
That I may pour my spirits in thine ear,
And chastise with the valor of my tongue
All that impedes thee from the golden round[6]
Which fate and metaphysical aid doth seem
To have thee crowned withal.

[*Enter* MESSENGER.]

30   What is your tidings?

MESSENGER. The King comes here tonight.

LADY MACBETH.   Thou'rt mad to say it!
Is not thy master with him, who, were't so,
Would have informed for preparation?

MESSENGER. So please you, it is true. Our thane is coming.
35 One of my fellows had the speed of him,[7]
Who, almost dead for breath, had scarcely more
Than would make up his message.

LADY MACBETH.   Give him tending;
He brings great news.   [*Exit* MESSENGER.]
                    The raven himself is hoarse
That croaks the fatal entrance of Duncan
40 Under my battlements. Come, you spirits
That tend on mortal[8] thoughts, unsex me here,
And fill me, from the crown to the toe, top-full
Of direst cruelty! Make thick my blood,
Stop up th' access and passage to remorse[9]
45 That no compunctious visitings of nature[10]
Shake my fell[11] purpose, nor keep peace between
Th' effect[12] and it! Come to my woman's breasts,
And take my milk for gall,[13] you murd'ring ministers,[14]
Wherever in your sightless[15] substances
50 You wait on[16] nature's mischief! Come, thick night,

7. had . . . him overtook him.

8. mortal deadly.

9. remorse compassion.

10. compunctious . . . nature
natural feelings of pity.

11. fell savage.

12. effect fulfillment.

13. milk for gall kindness in
exchange for bitterness.

14. ministers agents.

15. sightless invisible.

16. wait on assist.

◄ **Critical Viewing** This is an artist's rendering of nineteenth-century actress Ellen Terry playing Lady Macbeth. Judging by the picture, how do you think Terry would have spoken lines 38-54 in Act I, Scene v? **DEDUCE**

And pall[17] thee in the dunnest[18] smoke of hell,
That my keen knife see not the wound it makes,
Nor heaven peep through the blanket of the dark,
To cry "Hold, hold!"

[*Enter* MACBETH.]

                   Great Glamis! Worthy Cawdor!
55   Greater than both, by the all-hail hereafter!
Thy letters have transported me beyond
This ignorant[19] present, and I feel now
The future in the instant.[20]

MACBETH.   My dearest love,
Duncan comes here tonight.

LADY MACBETH.   And when goes hence?

MACBETH. Tomorrow, as he purposes.

17. **pall** enshroud.
18. **dunnest** darkest.

19. **ignorant** unknowing.
20. **instant** present.

Comprehension
What does Lady Macbeth feel is Macbeth's weakness?

21. beguile the time deceive the people tonight.

22. dispatch management.

23. look up clear appear innocent.

Vocabulary

sovereign (säv′ rən) *adj.* supreme in power, rank, or authority

24. To alter . . . fear to show a disturbed face will arouse suspicion.

1. *Hautboys* oboes announcing the arrival of royalty.

2. seat location.

3. gentle soothed.

4. temple-haunting martlet martin, a bird that usually nests in churches. In Shakespeare's time, *martin* was a slang term for a person who is easily deceived.

5. approve show.

6. mansionry nests.

7. jutty projection.

8. coign of vantage advantageous corner.

9. procreant (prō′ krē ənt) **cradle** nest where the young are hatched.

10. haunt visit.

11. The love . . . trouble Though my visit inconveniences you, you should ask God to reward me for coming, because it was my love for you that prompted my visit.

12. single business feeble service.

13. rest your hermits remain your dependents bound to pray for you. Hermits were often paid to pray for another person's soul.

60   **LADY MACBETH.**   O, never
          Shall sun that morrow see!
          Your face, my Thane, is as a book where men
          May read strange matters. To beguile the time,[21]
          Look like the time; bear welcome in your eye,
65   Your hand, your tongue: look like th' innocent flower,
          But be the serpent under 't. He that's coming
          Must be provided for: and you shall put
          This night's great business into my dispatch;[22]
          Which shall to all our nights and days to come
70   Give solely sovereign sway and masterdom.

    MACBETH. We will speak further.

    LADY MACBETH.   Only look up clear.[23]
          To alter favor ever is to fear.[24]
          Leave all the rest to me.   [*Exit.*]

Scene vi. Before Macbeth's castle.

[*Hautboys.*[1] *Torches. Enter* KING DUNCAN, MALCOLM, DONALBAIN, BANQUO, LENNOX, MACDUFF, ROSS, ANGUS, *and* ATTENDANTS.]

    KING. This castle hath a pleasant seat;[2] the air
          Nimbly and sweetly recommends itself
          Unto our gentle[3] senses.

    BANQUO.   This guest of summer,
          The temple-haunting martlet,[4] does approve[5]
5   By his loved mansionry[6] that the heaven's breath
          Smells wooingly here. No jutty,[7] frieze,
          Buttress, nor coign of vantage,[8] but this bird
          Hath made his pendent bed and procreant cradle.[9]
          Where they most breed and haunt,[10] I have observed
          The air is delicate.

[*Enter* LADY MACBETH.]

10   **KING.**   See, see, our honored hostess!
          The love that follows us sometime is our trouble,
          Which still we thank as love. Herein I teach you
          How you shall bid God 'ield us for your pains
          And thank us for your trouble.[11]

    LADY MACBETH.   All our service
15   In every point twice done, and then done double,
          Were poor and single business[12] to contend
          Against those honors deep and broad wherewith
          Your Majesty loads our house: for those of old,
          And the late dignities heaped up to them,
          We rest your hermits.[13]

20 **KING.**   Where's the Thane of Cawdor?
We coursed[14] him at the heels, and had a purpose
To be his purveyor:[15] but he rides well,
And his great love, sharp as his spur, hath holp[16] him
To his home before us. Fair and noble hostess,
We are your guest tonight.

25 **LADY MACBETH.**   Your servants ever
Have theirs, themselves, and what is theirs, in compt,[17]
To make their audit at your Highness' pleasure,
Still[18] to return your own.

KING.   Give me your hand.
Conduct me to mine host: we love him highly,
30 And shall continue our graces towards him.
By your leave, hostess.   [*Exit.*]

Scene vii. *Macbeth's castle.*

[*Hautboys. Torches. Enter a* SEWER,[1] *and diverse* SERVANTS *with dishes and service over the stage. Then enter* MACBETH.]

MACBETH. If it were done[2] when 'tis done, then 'twere well
It were done quickly. If th' assassination
Could trammel up the consequence, and catch,
With his surcease, success;[3] that but this blow
5 Might be the be-all and the end-all—here,
But here, upon this bank and shoal of time,
We'd jump the life to come.[4] But in these cases
We still have judgment here; that we but teach
Bloody instructions, which, being taught, return
10 To plague th' inventor: this even-handed[5] justice
Commends[6] th' ingredients of our poisoned chalice[7]
To our own lips. He's here in double trust:
First, as I am his kinsman and his subject,
Strong both against the deed; then, as his host,
15 Who should against his murderer shut the door,
Not bear the knife myself. Besides, this Duncan
Hath borne his faculties[8] so meek, hath been
So clear[9] in his great office, that his virtues
Will plead like angels trumpet-tongued against
20 The deep damnation of his taking-off;
And pity, like a naked newborn babe,
Striding the blast, or heaven's cherubin[10] horsed
Upon the sightless couriers[11] of the air,
Shall blow the horrid deed in every eye,
25 That tears shall drown the wind. I have no spur
To prick the sides of my intent, but only
Vaulting ambition, which o'erleaps itself
And falls on th' other—

14. **coursed** chased.

15. **purveyor** advance supply officer.

16. **holp** helped.

17. **compt** trust.

18. **Still** always.

Elizabethan Drama

What details does Banquo use in Scene vi, lines 3–10 to paint a word picture of Macbeth's castle?

1. **sewer** chief butler.

2. **done** over and done with.

3. **If . . . success** if the assassination could be done successfully and without consequence.

4. **We'd . . . come** I would risk life in the world to come.

5. **even-handed** impartial.

6. **commends** offers.

7. **chalice** cup.

8. **faculties** powers.

9. **clear** blameless.

10. **cherubin** angels.

11. **sightless couriers** unseen messengers (the wind).

Elizabethan Drama and Soliloquy

What doubts does Macbeth reveal in his soliloquy (lines 1–28)?

Comprehension

What deed does Lady Macbeth urge her husband to perform?

[*Enter* LADY MACBETH.]

How now! What news?

LADY MACBETH. He has almost supped. Why have you
left the chamber?

MACBETH. Hath he asked for me?

30 **LADY MACBETH.**   Know you not he has?

MACBETH. We will proceed no further in this business:
He hath honored me of late, and I have bought[12]
Golden opinions from all sorts of people,
Which would be worn now in their newest gloss,
Not cast aside so soon.

35 **LADY MACBETH.**   Was the hope drunk
Wherein you dressed yourself? Hath it slept since?
And wakes it now, to look so green and pale
At what it did so freely? From this time
Such I account thy love. Art thou afeard

40 To be the same in thine own act and valor
As thou art in desire? Wouldst thou have that
Which thou esteem'st the ornament of life,[13]
And live a coward in thine own esteem,
Letting "I dare not" wait upon[14] "I would,"
Like the poor cat i' th' adage?[15]

45 **MACBETH.**   Prithee, peace!
I dare do all that may become a man;
Who dares do more is none.

LADY MACBETH.   What beast was 't then
That made you break[16] this enterprise to me?
When you durst do it, then you were a man;

50 And to be more than what you were, you would
Be so much more the man. Nor time nor place
Did then adhere,[17] and yet you would make both.
They have made themselves, and that their[18] fitness now
Does unmake you. I have given suck, and know

55 How tender 'tis to love the babe that milks me:
I would, while it was smiling in my face,
Have plucked my nipple from his boneless gums,
And dashed the brains out, had I so sworn as you
Have done to this.

MACBETH.   If we should fail?

LADY MACBETH.   We fail?

60 But[19] screw your courage to the sticking-place[20]
And we'll not fail. When Duncan is asleep—
Whereto the rather shall his day's hard journey
Soundly invite him—his two chamberlains

---

12. **bought** acquired.

Analyze Text Features

In line 42, what does Lady Macbeth mean by the "ornament of life"?

13. **ornament of life** the crown.

14. **wait upon** follow.

15. **poor . . . adage** from an old proverb about a cat who wants to eat fish but is afraid of getting its paws wet.

16. **break** reveal.

17. **Did then adhere** was then suitable (for the assassination)

18. **that their** their very.

19. **But** only.

20. **sticking-place** the notch that holds the bowstring of a taut crossbow.

<pre>
                Will I with wine and wassail[21] so convince,[22]
65   That memory, the warder of the brain,
                Shall be a fume, and the receipt of reason
                A limbeck only:[23] when in swinish sleep
                Their drenchéd natures lies as in a death,
                What cannot you and I perform upon
70   Th' unguarded Duncan, what not put upon
                His spongy[24] officers, who shall bear the guilt
                Of our great quell?[25]

     MACBETH.   Bring forth men-children only;
                For thy undaunted mettle[26] should compose
                Nothing but males. Will it not be received,
75   When we have marked with blood those sleepy two
                Of his own chamber, and used their very daggers,
                That they have done 't?

     LADY MACBETH.   Who dares receive it other,[27]
                As we shall make our griefs and clamor roar
                Upon his death?

     MACBETH.   I am settled, and bend up
80   Each corporal agent to this terrible feat.
                Away, and mock the time[28] with fairest show:
                False face must hide what the false heart doth know.   [Exit.]
</pre>

<dl>
<dt>21. wassail carousing.</dt>
<dt>22. convince overpower.</dt>
<dt>23. That . . . only that memory, the guardian of the brain, will be confused by the fumes of the drink, and the reason become like a still, distilling confused thoughts.</dt>
<dt>24. spongy sodden.</dt>
<dt>25. quell murder.</dt>
<dt>26. mettle spirit.</dt>
<dt>27. other otherwise.</dt>
<dt>28. mock the time mislead the world.</dt>
</dl>

Critical Reading

1. **Key Ideas and Details** **(a)** What statements do the witches and Macbeth make about "foul and fair"? **(b) Interpret:** What meaning (or meanings) does each remark have?

2. **Key Ideas and Details** **(a)** Describe Banquo's and Macbeth's reactions to the witches. **(b) Compare and Contrast:** Compare and contrast their reactions to the witches.

3. **Key Ideas and Details** **(a)** In his soliloquy at the beginning of Scene vii, what arguments against killing Duncan does Macbeth express? **(b) Analyze Cause and Effect:** Which of these arguments seems to influence him the most? Explain.

4. **Integration of Knowledge and Ideas** **(a)** What is Lady Macbeth's opinion of her husband's character? **(b) Analyze:** How does she use her knowledge of his character to convince him to kill Duncan?

Cite textual evidence to support your responses.

Literary Analysis

1. **Key Ideas and Details (a)** What vivid image, typical of **Elizabethan drama,** does Shakespeare create when Macbeth says to Ross, "… why do you dress me / In borrowed robes?" (Act I, Scene iii, lines 108–109)? **(b)** What uneasiness in Macbeth does this word picture reveal?

2. **Craft and Structure** How does Macbeth's encounter with the witches show that the play will probably be a **tragedy?**

3. **Integration of Knowledge and Ideas** Does Macbeth's meeting with the witches suggest that evil is something people choose, a force that seeks people out, or some combination of the two? Explain, using details from the text to support your ideas.

4. **Integration of Knowledge and Ideas** Using a chart like this one, analyze the details of setting in the lines shown. Then, indicate how modern sets and lighting might produce such a setting.

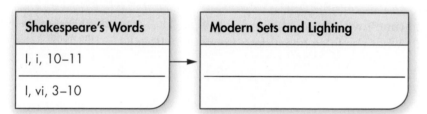

Shakespeare's Words	Modern Sets and Lighting
I, i, 10–11	
I, vi, 3–10	

5. **Craft and Structure (a) Analyze information from text features** such as stage directions, side notes, and illustrations to describe the action in Act I, Scene i, and the beginning of Act I, Scene v. **(b)** Which text features were most helpful in describing the action? Provide reasons for your choice or choices.

6. **Craft and Structure** Use the side notes to clarify the meaning of the following terms: **(a)** anon, **(b)** Thane, **(c)** cousins.

7. **Craft and Structure** What do each of the following **soliloquies** reveal about their speaker's thoughts and plans: **(a)** Lady Macbeth, Act I, Scene v, lines 1–30 and **(b)** Macbeth, Act I, Scene vii, lines 1–28?

8. **Craft and Structure** In Act I, which type of speech directed to the audience is more effective in revealing Macbeth's thoughts: asides or a soliloquy? Explain.

9. **Integration of Knowledge and Ideas** Do Lady Macbeth's and Macbeth's soliloquies add to the sense that the characters are moving toward disaster? Explain, using details from the text to support your answer.

Common Core State Standards

Writing

3. Write narratives to develop real or imagined experiences or events using effective technique, well-chosen details, and well-structured event sequences. *(p. 341)*

3.d. Use precise words and phrases, telling details, and sensory language to convey a vivid picture of the experiences, events, setting, and/or characters. *(p. 341)*

Language

4.a. Use context as a clue to the meaning of a word or phrase. *(p. 341)*

5. Demonstrate understanding of nuances in word meanings. *(p. 341)*

Vocabulary Acquisition and Use

Word Analysis: Denotations and Connotations of Political Words

A word's **denotation** is its dictionary meaning— what it means, free of associations it might call to mind. A word's **connotation** is the set of associations and feelings that it stirs up. The denotation of *liege* is "king" or "subject." In addition to these denotative meanings, the word carries connotations of deep allegiance between ruler and subject. Another word with strong connotations is the adjective *sovereign*, suggesting a formal and absolute power, unlike its weaker synonym *dominant*.

For each of these political words, use a thesaurus to find a word with the same denotation but weaker connotations. Then, explain your choice.

1. reign (n.) **3.** monarch **5.** dominion

2. imperial **4.** realm **6.** majesty

Vocabulary: Context Clues

Each sentence below features an underlined word from the vocabulary list on page 321. If the word's meaning makes sense in the context, identify the sentence as logical. If not, identify the sentence as illogical and revise it to make it logical. Do not change the vocabulary word.

1. Macbeth's fearfulness in battle proved that he was a man of <u>valor</u>.

2. The <u>imperial</u> air with which Macbeth commanded caused others to obey him instantly.

3. Macbeth's assassination plan was aided by his habit of engaging in anxious <u>surmise</u>.

4. The witches had appealed to Macbeth's image of himself as <u>sovereign</u>.

5. Duncan believed in Macbeth and knew he was capable of <u>treason</u>.

Writing to Sources

Narrative Text As Macbeth, write a **speech** introducing the visiting Duncan to your household. Include details you would use in a real-life introduction of a speaker.

Prewriting List facts about Duncan, such as his title and accomplishments. Then, list the traits that make him a good king.

Drafting Begin with a flattering anecdote. Then use your prewriting lists to craft an engaging narrative account of his life and accomplishments.

Revising Revise to add subtlety by telling a flattering story about Duncan that may not be widely known to the listeners. Also, place stars next to boring, overused words or phrases. Then, replace them with language that is more vivid and specific. Use words and phrases that would seem flattering to Duncan but also ironically suggest your plan to do away with him.

Model: Revising for Subtlety

These last weeks have been difficult for our liege. We can only

                                  fading

hope that his time among us will provide a ⌃ ~~tired~~ king with

    long spell of bodily repose   *this realm*

a ~~bit of rest~~, and that he shall leave ⌃ ~~our home~~ in a state
   ⌃

    heavenly rejuvenation.

of ~~renewal and health.~~
   ⌃

> The writer replaces weak, everyday words and phrases with language that is both lofty—befitting a king—and subtly suggestive of treason.

Close Reading Focus

Blank Verse

Blank verse—unrhymed iambic pentameter—was invented during the English Renaissance to reflect natural speech. An **iamb** consists of an unstressed syllable followed by a stressed syllable (˘ ´). In iambic pentameter, there are five such feet (units) to the line. *Macbeth* is written mainly in blank verse, as follows:

> Methought I heard a voice cry "Sleep no more!" (II,ii,34)

For interest, Shakespeare varies his meter, as when he begins this line with a **trochaic foot** (´ ˘): "List'ning their fear, I could not say 'Amen'" (II, ii, 28). Another variation is the **anapestic foot** (˘ ˘ ´). As you read, listen for the rhythm as well as the meaning of the dialogue.

Shakespeare sometimes interrupts his blank verse with **prose,** which is writing that is not divided into poetic lines and lacks a definite rhythm. In his tragedies, lower-ranking characters often speak in prose to provide **comic relief,** a humorous break from a tense mood. Notice this effect as you read the Porter's speech at the start of Act II, Scene iii. By using different line structures, such as blank verse or prose, for specific characters, Shakespeare adds to the overall meaning of the play.

Preparing to Read Complex Texts A key *pattern of organization* in Shakespeare's blank verse is the way in which sentences and blank verse lines interact. By **analyzing** that interaction, you can better understand how Shakespeare achieves **clarity of meaning.** In making your analysis, follow sentences past line endings. For instance, you must follow this sentence past the end of the line to learn what the owl does:

> *"It was the owl that shrieked, the fatal bellman,*
> *Which gives the stern'st good-night. . . ." (II, ii, 3–4).*

Use a chart like this one to distinguish between lines and sentences.

Vocabulary

The words listed below are key to understanding the text that follows. Copy the words into your notebook. Which suffixes do you recognize?

augment   equivocate

palpable   predominance

stealthy

multitudinous

Common Core State Standards

Reading Literature
5. Analyze how an author's choices concerning how to structure specific parts of a text contribute to its overall structure and meaning as well as its aesthetic impact.

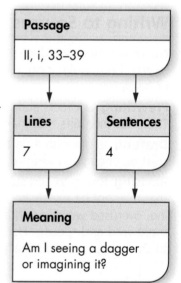

Passage
II, i, 33–39

Lines	Sentences
7	4

Meaning
Am I seeing a dagger or imagining it?

Review and Anticipate

In Act I, we learn that Macbeth has distinguished himself in battle. Returning from the battlefield, he and Banquo meet three witches who predict that Macbeth will not only be rewarded by King Duncan, but that he will become king himself. However, the witches also greet Banquo as a father of kings. Motivated by the witches' prophecies, Macbeth considers killing Duncan. The assassination becomes more likely when the king decides to visit Macbeth's castle. Lady Macbeth, on hearing about the witches' predictions and the king's visit, resolves that she and her husband will kill Duncan. When Macbeth hesitates, she urges him on. As Act II begins, they are about to perform this evil deed.

ACT II

Scene i. Inverness. Court of Macbeth's castle.

[*Enter* BANQUO, *and* FLEANCE, *with a torch before him.*]

BANQUO. How goes the night, boy?

FLEANCE. The moon is down; I have not heard the clock.

BANQUO. And she goes down at twelve.

FLEANCE.   I take't, 'tis later, sir.

BANQUO. Hold, take my sword. There's husbandry[1] in heaven.
5   Their candles are all out. Take thee that[2] too.
    A heavy summons[3] lies like lead upon me,
    And yet I would not sleep. Merciful powers,
    Restrain in me the cursèd thoughts that nature
    Gives way to in repose!

[*Enter* MACBETH, *and a* SERVANT *with a torch.*]

                              Give me my sword!
10 Who's there?

MACBETH. A friend.

BANQUO. What, sir, not yet at rest? The King's a-bed:
    He hath been in unusual pleasure, and
    Sent forth great largess to your offices:[4]
15 This diamond he greets your wife withal,
    By the name of most kind hostess; and shut up[5]
    In measureless content.

MACBETH.   Being unprepared,
    Our will became the servant to defect,
    Which else should free have wrought.[6]

Analyzing Clarity of Meaning

Which line endings in lines 12–17 do not require a pause?

1. **husbandry** thrift.

2. **that** probably his sword belt.

3. **summons** weariness.

4. **largess . . . offices** gifts to your servants' quarters.

5. **shut up** retired.

6. **Being . . . wrought** Because we did not have enough time to prepare, we were unable to entertain as lavishly as we wanted to.

Comprehension

Where and when do Macbeth and Banquo meet?

BANQUO.   All's well.

20   I dreamt last night of the three weird sisters:
      To you they have showed some truth.

MACBETH.   I think not of them.
      Yet, when we can entreat an hour to serve,
      We would spend it in some words upon that business,
      If you would grant the time.

BANQUO.   At your kind'st leisure.

25   **MACBETH.** If you shall cleave to my consent, when 'tis,[7]
      It shall make honor for you.

BANQUO.   So[8] I lose none
      In seeking to augment it, but still keep
      My bosom franchised[9] and allegiance clear,
      I shall be counseled.

MACBETH.   Good repose the while!

30   **BANQUO.** Thanks, sir. The like to you!

                                   [*Exit* BANQUO *with* FLEANCE.]

MACBETH. Go bid thy mistress, when my drink is ready,
      She strike upon the bell. Get thee to bed.

                                              [*Exit* SERVANT.]

      Is this a dagger which I see before me,
      The handle toward my hand? Come, let me clutch thee.
35   I have thee not, and yet I see thee still.
      Art thou not, fatal vision, sensible[10]
      To feeling as to sight, or art thou but
      A dagger of the mind, a false creation,
      Proceeding from the heat-oppressèd brain?
40   I see thee yet, in form as palpable
      As this which now I draw.
      Thou marshal'st[11] me the way that I was going;
      And such an instrument I was to use.
      Mine eyes are made the fools o' th' other senses,
45   Or else worth all the rest. I see thee still;
      And on thy blade and dudgeon[12] gouts[13] of blood,
      Which was not so before. There's no such thing.
      It is the bloody business which informs[14]
      Thus to mine eyes. Now o'er the one half-world
50   Nature seems dead, and wicked dreams abuse[15]
      The curtained sleep; witchcraft celebrates
      Pale Hecate's offerings;[16] and withered murder,
      Alarumed by his sentinel, the wolf,
      Whose howl's his watch, thus with his stealthy pace,
55   With Tarquin's[17] ravishing strides, towards his design
      Moves like a ghost. Thou sure and firm-set earth,

7. cleave . . . 'tis join my
cause when the time
comes.

8. So provided that.

Vocabulary

augment (ôg ment´)
v. make greater; enlarge

9. bosom franchised heart
free (from guilt).

10. sensible able to be felt.

Vocabulary

palpable (pal´ pə bəl)
adj. capable of being touched
or felt

11. marshal'st leads.

12. dudgeon wooden hilt.

13. gouts large drops.

14. informs takes shape.

15. abuse deceive.

16. Hecate's (hek´ə tēz)
offerings offerings to Hecate, the Greek goddess of
witchcraft.

Vocabulary

stealthy (stel´ thē) *adj.* sly

17. Tarquin's of Tarquin, a
Roman tyrant.

Hear not my steps, which way they walk, for fear
Thy very stones prate of my whereabout,
And take the present horror from the time,
60   Which now suits with it.[18] Whiles I threat, he lives:
Words to the heat of deeds too cold breath gives.

[*A bell rings.*]

I go, and it is done: the bell invites me.
Hear it not, Duncan, for it is a knell
That summons thee to heaven, or to hell.   [*Exit.*]

Scene ii. Macbeth's castle

[*Enter* LADY MACBETH.]

LADY MACBETH. That which hath made them drunk hath made
        me bold;
What hath quenched them hath given me fire. Hark! Peace!
It was the owl that shrieked, the fatal bellman,
Which gives the stern'st good-night.[1] He is about it.
5   The doors are open, and the surfeited grooms[2]
Do mock their charge with snores. I have drugged their possets,[3]
That death and nature do contend about them,
Whether they live or die.

MACBETH.   [*Within*] Who's there? What, ho?

LADY MACBETH. Alack, I am afraid they have awaked
10   And 'tis not done! Th' attempt and not the deed
Confounds[4] us. Hark! I laid their daggers ready;
He could not miss 'em. Had he not resembled
My father as he slept, I had done 't.

[*Enter* MACBETH.]

                My husband!

MACBETH. I have done the deed. Didst thou not hear a noise?

15 **LADY MACBETH.** I heard the owl scream and the crickets cry.
    Did not you speak?

MACBETH.   When?

LADY MACBETH.   Now.

MACBETH.   As I descended?

LADY MACBETH. Ay.

MACBETH. Hark!
    Who lies i' th' second chamber?

LADY MACBETH.   Donalbain.

20 **MACBETH.** This is a sorry[5] sight.

LADY MACBETH. A foolish thought, to say a sorry sight.

Spiral Review
Soliloquy In what way
do lines 31–61 introduce
a new sound into poetry,
the "sound" of someone
thinking aloud on stage?

18. **take . . . it** remove the horrible silence that suits this moment.

1. **bellman . . . good-night** It was customary for a bell to be rung at midnight outside a condemned person's cell on the night before an execution.

2. **surfeited grooms** overfed servants.

3. **possets** warm bedtime drinks.

4. **Confounds** ruins.

Blank Verse
Notice that the iambic pentameter of line 16 is shared in dialogue between Macbeth and Lady Macbeth. Why might the playwright have chosen this artistry?

5. **sorry** miserable.

Comprehension
What deed have Macbeth and Lady Macbeth performed?

MACBETH. There's one did laugh in 's sleep, and one cried
"Murder!"
That they did wake each other. I stood and heard them.
But they did say their prayers, and addressed them
Again to sleep.

25 **LADY MACBETH.** There are two[6] lodged together.

6. **two** Malcolm and
Donalbain, Duncan's sons.

MACBETH. One cried "God bless us!" and "Amen" the other,
As they had seen me with these hangman's hands:
List'ning their fear, I could not say "Amen,"
When they did say "God bless us!"

LADY MACBETH.   Consider it not so deeply.

30 **MACBETH.** But wherefore could not I pronounce "Amen"?
I had most need of blessing, and "Amen"
Stuck in my throat.

LADY MACBETH.   These deeds must not be thought
After these ways; so, it will make us mad.

MACBETH. Methought I heard a voice cry "Sleep no more!
35 Macbeth does murder sleep"—the innocent sleep,
Sleep that knits up the raveled sleeve[7] of care,
The death of each day's life, sore labor's bath,
Balm of hurt minds, great nature's second course,[8]
Chief nourisher in life's feast—

7. **knits . . . sleave** straightens out the tangled threads.

8. **second course** main course; sleep.

LADY MACBETH.   What do you mean?

40 **MACBETH.** Still it cried "Sleep no more!" to all the house:
"Glamis hath murdered sleep, and therefore Cawdor
Shall sleep no more: Macbeth shall sleep no more."

LADY MACBETH. Who was it that thus cried? Why, worthy Thane,
You do unbend[9] your noble strength, to think
45 So brainsickly of things. Go get some water,
And wash this filthy witness[10] from your hand.
Why did you bring these daggers from the place?
They must lie there: go carry them, and smear
The sleepy grooms with blood.

9. **unbend** relax.

10. **witness** evidence.

MACBETH.   I'll go no more.
50 I am afraid to think what I have done;
Look on 't again I dare not.

LADY MACBETH.   Infirm of purpose!
Give me the daggers. The sleeping and the dead
Are but as pictures. 'Tis the eye of childhood
That fears a painted devil. If he do bleed,
55 I'll gild[11] the faces of the grooms withal,
For it must seem their guilt.   [*Exit. Knock within.*]

11. **gild** paint.

▶ **Critical Viewing**
How do these images
from a poster advertising
a production of Macbeth
capture the suspense created
in Act II? **CONNECT**

Vocabulary

multitudinous (mul´ tə tood´ 'n əs) *adj.* existing in great numbers

12. incarnadine (in kär´ nə dīn) redden.

13. Your constancy . . . unattended Your firmness of purpose has left you.

14. watchers up late.

Blank Verse, Prose, and Comic Relief

How do the shift from verse to prose in Scene iii and the porter's remarks affect the mood?

1. porter doorkeeper.

2. should have old would have plenty of.

3. Beelzebub (bē el´ zə bub´) the chief devil.

4. a farmer . . . plenty a farmer who hoarded grain, hoping the prices would come up after a bad harvest.

5. enow enough.

Vocabulary

equivocate (ē kwiv´ ə kāt´) *v.* to use terms that have two or more meanings to mislead purposely or deceive

6. an equivocator . . . scale a liar who could make two contradictory statements and swear both were true.

7. stealing . . . hose stealing some cloth from the hose while making them.

8. goose pressing iron.

MACBETH.   Whence is that knocking?
How is 't with me, when every noise appalls me?
What hands are here? Ha! They pluck out mine eyes!
Will all great Neptune's ocean wash this blood
60 Clean from my hand? No; this my hand will rather
The multitudinous seas incarnadine,[12]
Making the green one red.

[*Enter* LADY MACBETH.]

LADY MACBETH. My hands are of your color, but I shame
To wear a heart so white. [*Knock.*] I hear a knocking
65 At the south entry. Retire we to our chamber.
A little water clears us of this deed:
How easy is it then! Your constancy
Hath left you unattended.[13] [*Knock.*] Hark! more knocking.
Get on your nightgown, lest occasion call us
70 And show us to be watchers.[14] Be not lost
So poorly in your thoughts.

MACBETH. To know my deed, 'twere best not know myself.   [*Knock.*]
Wake Duncan with thy knocking! I would thou couldst!

[*Exit.*]

Scene iii. Macbeth's castle.

[*Enter a* PORTER.[1] *Knocking within.*]

PORTER. Here's a knocking indeed! If a man were porter
of hell gate, he should have old[2] turning the key.
[*Knock.*] Knock, knock, knock! Who's there, i' th'
name of Beelzebub?[3] Here's a farmer, that
5 hanged himself on th' expectation of plenty.[4] Come
in time! Have napkins enow[5] about you; here you'll
sweat for 't. [*Knock.*] Knock, knock! Who's there, in
th' other devil's name? Faith, here's an equivocator,
that could swear in both the scales against
10 either scale;[6] who committed treason enough for
God's sake, yet could not equivocate to heaven. O,
come in, equivocator. [*Knock.*] Knock, knock, knock!
Who's there? Faith, here's an English tailor come
hither for stealing out of a French hose:[7]
15 come in, tailor. Here you may roast your goose.[8]
[*Knock.*] Knock, knock; never at quiet! What are you?
But this place is too cold for hell. I'll devil-porter it no
further. I had thought to have let in some of all
professions that go the primrose way to th'
20 everlasting bonfire. [*Knock.*] Anon, anon!
[*Opens an entrance.*] I pray you, remember the porter.

[*Enter* MACDUFF *and* LENNOX.]

MACDUFF. Was it so late, friend, ere you went to bed,
That you do lie so late?

PORTER. Faith, sir, we were carousing till the second
25   cock:[9] and drink, sir, is a great provoker of three
things.

MACDUFF. What three things does drink especially
provoke?

PORTER. Marry, sir, nose-painting, sleep, and urine.
30   Lechery, sir, it provokes and unprovokes; it provokes
the desire, but it takes away the performance: therefore much drink may be said to be an equivocator
with lechery: it makes him and it mars him; it
sets him on and it takes him off; it persuades him
35   and disheartens him; makes him stand to and not
stand to; in conclusion equivocates him in a sleep,
and giving him the lie, leaves him.

MACDUFF. I believe drink gave thee the lie[10] last night.

PORTER. That it did, sir, i' the very throat on me: but I
40   requited him for his lie, and, I think, being too strong
for him, though he took up my legs sometime, yet I
make a shift to cast[11] him.

MACDUFF. Is thy master stirring?

[*Enter* MACBETH.]

   Our knocking has awaked him; here he comes.

LENNOX. Good morrow, noble sir.

45 **MACBETH.**   Good morrow, both.

MACDUFF. Is the king stirring, worthy Thane?

MACBETH.   Not yet.

MACDUFF. He did command me to call timely[12] on him:
I have almost slipped the hour.

MACBETH.   I'll bring you to him.

MACDUFF. I know this is a joyful trouble to you;
50   But yet 'tis one.

MACBETH. The labor we delight in physics pain.[13]
This is the door.

MACDUFF.   I'll make so bold to call,
For 'tis my limited service.[14]   [*Exit* MACDUFF.]

LENNOX. Goes the king hence today?

Blank Verse and Prose

Why is it appropriate for
the dialogue in lines 43–44
to change back from prose
to blank verse?

Comprehension

To what gate does the
porter compare the gate
of Macbeth's castle?

Analyzing Clarity of Meaning

Read lines 55–62 aloud. How many sentences are there in these lines?

15. **combustion** confusion.

16. **obscure bird** bird of darkness, the owl.

Analyzing Clarity of Meaning

In the latter part of Macduff's speech, lines 75–81, where should you not pause at the ends of lines?

17. **Confusion** destruction.

18. **The Lord's anointed temple** the King's body.

19. **Gorgon** Medusa, a mythological monster whose appearance was so ghastly that those who looked at it turned to stone.

MACBETH. He does: he did appoint so.

55 **LENNOX.** The night has been unruly. Where we lay,
Our chimneys were blown down, and, as they say,
Lamentings heard i' th' air, strange screams of death,
And prophesying with accents terrible
Of dire combustion[15] and confused events
60 New hatched to th' woeful time: the obscure bird[16]
Clamored the livelong night. Some say, the earth
Was feverous and did shake.

MACBETH. 'Twas a rough night.

LENNOX. My young remembrance cannot parallel
A fellow to it.

[*Enter* MACDUFF.]

65 **MACDUFF.** O horror, horror, horror! Tongue nor heart
Cannot conceive nor name thee.

MACBETH AND LENNOX. What's the matter?

MACDUFF. Confusion[17] now hath made his masterpiece.
Most sacrilegious murder hath broke ope
The Lord's anointed temple,[18] and stole thence
The life o' th' building.

70 **MACBETH.** What is 't you say? The life?

LENNOX. Mean you his Majesty?

MACDUFF. Approach the chamber, and destroy your sight
With a new Gorgon:[19] do not bid me speak;
See, and then speak yourselves. Awake, awake!

[*Exit* MACBETH *and* LENNOX.]

75 Ring the alarum bell. Murder and Treason!
Banquo and Donalbain! Malcolm! Awake!
Shake off this downy sleep, death's counterfeit,

LITERATURE IN CONTEXT

Cultural Connection

Elizabethan Concepts of Monarchy
For the Elizabethans, the monarch was God's representative on Earth. For this reason, the expression "the Lord's anointed" is used to describe the head of state. Killing the ruler, therefore, was not just an act of political assassination; it was also a horrifying desecration of religious values.

Connect to the Literature

How does Macduff's line 68 reflect this concept of monarchy?

And look on death itself! Up, up, and see
The great doom's image![20] Malcolm! Banquo!
80   As from your graves rise up, and walk like sprites,[21]
To countenance[22] this horror. Ring the bell.

[*Bell rings. Enter* LADY MACBETH.]

LADY MACBETH. What's the business,
That such a hideous trumpet calls to parley[23]
The sleepers of the house? Speak, speak!

MACDUFF.   O gentle lady,
85   'Tis not for you to hear what I can speak:
The repetition, in a woman's ear,
Would murder as it fell.

[*Enter* BANQUO.]

                              O Banquo, Banquo!
Our royal master's murdered.

LADY MACBETH.   Woe, alas!
What, in our house?

BANQUO.   Too cruel anywhere.
90   Dear Duff, I prithee, contradict thyself,
And say it is not so.

[*Enter* MACBETH, LENNOX, *and* ROSS.]

MACBETH. Had I but died an hour before this chance,
I had lived a blessed time; for from this instant
There's nothing serious in mortality:[24]
95   All is but toys.[25] Renown and grace is dead,
The wine of life is drawn, and the mere lees[26]
Is left this vault[27] to brag of.

[*Enter* MALCOLM *and* DONALBAIN.]

DONALBAIN. What is amiss?

MACBETH.   You are, and do not know 't.
The spring, the head, the fountain of your blood
100   Is stopped; the very source of it is stopped.

MACDUFF. Your royal father's murdered.

MALCOLM.   O, by whom?

LENNOX. Those of his chamber, as it seemed, had done 't:
Their hands and faces were all badged[28] with blood;
So were their daggers, which unwiped we found
105   Upon their pillows. They stared, and were distracted.
No man's life was to be trusted with them.

MACBETH. O, yet I do repent me of my fury,
That I did kill them.

20. **great doom's image**
likeness of Judgment Day.

21. **sprites** spirits.

22. **countenance** be in
keeping with.

23. **parley** war conference.

24. **serious in mortality**
worthwhile in mortal life.

25. **toys** trifles.

26. **lees** dregs.

27. **vault** world.

28. **badged** marked.

Spiral Review
Metaphor In line 96,
what does Macbeth mean
by "The wine of life"?

Blank Verse

Where is there a pause
in line 100? How does it
reinforce the meaning?

Comprehension

According to Lennox,
what evidence proves that
the guards killed Duncan?

▲ **Critical Viewing** This painting depicts the moment when Macbeth comes from murdering Duncan (II, ii, 14). However, it also captures the nature of the relationship between Macbeth and Lady Macbeth in the first part of the play. What do their facial expressions and body language suggest about that relationship? **INTERPRET**

MACDUFF.   Wherefore did you so?

MACBETH. Who can be wise, amazed, temp'rate and furious,
110   Loyal and neutral, in a moment? No man.
The expedition²⁹ of my violent love
Outrun the pauser, reason. Here lay Duncan,
His silver skin laced with his golden blood,
And his gashed stabs looked like a breach in nature
115   For ruin's wasteful entrance: there, the murderers,
Steeped in the colors of their trade, their daggers
Unmannerly breeched with gore.³⁰ Who could refrain,
That had a heart to love, and in that heart

29. **expedition** haste.

30. **breeched with gore** covered with blood.

Courage to make 's love known?

LADY MACBETH.   Help me hence, ho!

MACDUFF. Look to the lady.

120 **MALCOLM.** [*Aside to* DONALBAIN] Why do we hold our tongues,
That most may claim this argument for ours?[31]

DONALBAIN. [*Aside to* MALCOLM] What should be spoken here,
Where our fate, hid in an auger-hole,[32]
May rush, and seize us? Let's away:
Our tears are not yet brewed.

125 **MALCOLM.** [*Aside to* DONALBAIN] Nor our strong sorrow
Upon the foot of motion.[33]

BANQUO.   Look to the lady.

[LADY MACBETH *is carried out.*]

And when we have our naked frailties hid,[34]
That suffer in exposure, let us meet
And question[35] this most bloody piece of work,
130 To know it further. Fears and scruples[36] shake us.
In the great hand of God I stand, and thence
Against the undivulged pretense[37] I fight
Of treasonous malice.

MACDUFF.   And so do I.

ALL.   So all.

MACBETH. Let's briefly[38] put on manly readiness,
And meet i' th' hall together.

135 **ALL.**   Well contented.

[*Exit all but* MALCOLM *and* DONALBAIN.]

MALCOLM. What will you do? Let's not consort with them.
To show an unfelt sorrow is an office[39]
Which the false man does easy. I'll to England.

DONALBAIN. To Ireland, I; our separated fortune
140 Shall keep us both the safer. Where we are
There's daggers in men's smiles; the near in blood,
The nearer bloody.[40]

MALCOLM.   This murderous shaft that's shot
Hath not yet lighted,[41] and our safest way
Is to avoid the aim. Therefore to horse;
145 And let us not be dainty of leave-taking,
But shift away. There's warrant[42] in that theft
Which steals itself[43] when there's no mercy left.

[*Exit.*]

31. **That most . . . ours** who are the most concerned with this topic.

32. **auger-hole** tiny hole, an unsuspected place because of its size.

33. **Our tears . . . motion** We have not yet had time for tears nor to turn our sorrow into action.

34. **when . . . hid** when we have put on our clothes.

35. **question** investigate.

36. **scruples** doubts.

37. **undivulged pretense** hidden purpose.

38. **briefly** quickly.

Analyzing Clarity of Meaning

How do the brief sentences in lines 136–138 reinforce the meaning?

39. **office** function.

40. **the near . . . bloody** The closer we are in blood relationship to Duncan, the greater our chance of being murdered.

41. **lighted** reached its target.

42. **warrant** justification.

43. **that theft . . . itself** stealing away.

Comprehension

What do Malcolm and Donalbain decide to do?

Scene iv. *Outside Macbeth's castle.*

[*Enter* ROSS *with an* OLD MAN.]

    OLD MAN. Threescore and ten I can remember well:
    Within the volume of which time I have seen
    Hours dreadful and things strange, but this sore[1] night
    Hath trifled former knowings.

    ROSS.   Ha, good father,
5   Thou seest the heavens, as troubled with man's act,
    Threatens his bloody stage. By th' clock 'tis day,
    And yet dark night strangles the traveling lamp:[2]
    Is 't night's predominance, or the day's shame,
    That darkness does the face of earth entomb,
    When living light should kiss it?

Vocabulary

predominance (prē däm′ ə
nəns) *n.* superiority

10   **OLD MAN.**   'Tis unnatural,
    Even like the deed that's done. On Tuesday last
    A falcon, tow'ring in her pride of place,[3]
    Was by a mousing owl hawked at and killed.

    ROSS. And Duncan's horses—a thing most strange
          and certain—
15   Beauteous and swift, the minions of their race,
    Turned wild in nature, broke their stalls, flung out,
    Contending 'gainst obedience, as they would make
    War with mankind.

    OLD MAN.   'Tis said they eat[4] each other.

    ROSS. They did so, to th' amazement of mine eyes,
    That looked upon 't.

[*Enter* MACDUFF.]

Blank Verse

What rhythmic variation in
the blank verse do you find
at the beginning of line 23?

20   Here comes the good Macduff.
    How goes the world, sir, now?

    MACDUFF.   Why, see you not?

    ROSS. Is 't known who did this more than bloody deed?

    MACDUFF. Those that Macbeth hath slain.

    ROSS.   Alas, the day!
    What good could they pretend?[5]

    MACDUFF.   They were suborned:[6]
25   Malcolm and Donalbain, the king's two sons,
    Are stol'n away and fled, which puts upon them
    Suspicion of the deed.

    ROSS.   'Gainst nature still.
    Thriftless ambition, that will ravin up[7]
    Thine own life's means! Then 'tis most like

30   The sovereignty will fall upon Macbeth.

MACDUFF. He is already named, and gone to Scone[8]
    To be invested.

ROSS.   Where is Duncan's body?

MACDUFF. Carried to Colmekill,
    The sacred storehouse of his predecessors
    And guardian of their bones.

35 **ROSS.**   Will you to Scone?

MACDUFF. No, cousin, I'll to Fife.[9]

ROSS.   Well, I will thither.

MACDUFF. Well, may you see things well done there.
        Adieu,
    Lest our old robes sit easier than our new!

ROSS. Farewell, father.

40 **OLD MAN.** God's benison[10] go with you, and with those
    That would make good of bad, and friends of foes!

                                        [*Exit.*]

8. **Scone** (skōōn) where Scottish kings were crowned.

9. **Fife** where Macduff's castle is located.

10. **benison** blessing.

Critical Reading

Cite textual evidence to support your responses.

1. **Key Ideas and Details (a)** Describe Macbeth's and Lady Macbeth's reactions to the murder just after it is committed. **(b) Compare and Contrast:** Compare and contrast their reactions to the deed.

2. **Key Ideas and Details (a)** What kind of gate does the porter imagine he is tending? **(b) Interpret:** In what way is the porter's playful fantasy a comment on Macbeth's situation?

3. **Integration of Knowledge and Ideas (a)** What two strange occurrences are reported in this act? **(b) Interpret:** Why would Shakespeare include reports of such occurrences at this point in the play? **(c) Connect:** In what way do these strange occurrences relate to the Elizabethan notion of an orderly and interconnected universe?

4. **Key Ideas and Details (a) Analyze:** What question does Ross ask that indicates he doubts the grooms committed the murder? Explain. **(b) Infer:** Is Ross satisfied by the answer? Explain.

5. **Integration of Knowledge and Ideas** Do you think a political assassination like the one Macbeth commits is ever justifiable? Why or why not?

Critical Commentary

from "On the Knocking at the Gate in *Macbeth*"

Thomas De Quincey

English author Thomas De Quincey published his influential essay on Macbeth *in 1823, more than 200 years after the first performance of the play. In the essay, he does not only express his ideas about the play, but he models the process of criticism: It begins when a reader has a problem with a text that he or she cannot easily solve.*

From my boyish days I had always felt a great perplexity on one point in *Macbeth*. It was this: the knocking at the gate, which succeeds to the murder of Duncan, produced to my feelings an effect for which I never could account. The effect was, that it reflected back upon the murder a peculiar awfulness and a depth of solemnity; yet, however obstinately I endeavored with my understanding to comprehend this, for many years I never could see why it should produce such an effect.

De Quincey's interest in this problem was renewed when he read about a real murder case in which there was "a knocking at the door soon after the work of extermination was complete." This incident caused him to re-examine why the "knocking at the gate" had such a strong "effect" in Macbeth.

. . . at length I solved it to my own satisfaction; and my solution is this. Murder in ordinary cases, where the sympathy is wholly directed to the case of the murdered person, is an incident of coarse and vulgar horror; and for this reason, that it flings the interest exclusively upon the natural but ignoble instinct by which we cleave to life . . .

He goes on to discuss a topic familiar to anyone who enjoys reading thrillers: How can an author help an audience understand the mind of a murderer?

Such an attitude would little suit the purposes of the poet. What then must he do? He must throw the interest on the murderer. Our sympathy must be with him; (of course I mean a sympathy of comprehension, a sympathy by which we enter into his feelings, and are made to understand them,—not a sympathy of pity or approbation.) . . . in the murderer, such a murderer as a poet will condescend to, there must be raging some great storm of passion,—jealousy, ambition, vengeance, hatred,—which will create a hell within him; and into this hell we are to look.

In *Macbeth*, for the sake of gratifying his own enormous and teeming faculty of creation, Shakespeare has introduced two murderers: and, as usual in his hands, they are remarkably discriminated: but, though in Macbeth the strife of mind is greater than in his wife, the tiger spirit not so awake, and his feelings caught chiefly by contagion from her,—yet, as both were finally involved in the guilt of murder, the murderous mind of necessity is finally to be presumed in both. . . .

Here, De Quincey expresses his central idea, that the "knocking at the gate" symbolizes a return to "ordinary life." By contrast, such a return only emphasizes the horror of the murder.

. . . All action in any direction is best expounded, measured, and made apprehensible, by reaction. Now apply this to the case in *Macbeth*. Here, as I have said, the retiring of the human heart and the entrance of the fiendish heart was to be expressed and made sensible. Another world has stepped in; and the murderers are taken out of the region of human things, human purposes, human desires. They are transfigured: Lady Macbeth is "unsexed"; Macbeth has forgot that he was born of woman; both are conformed to the image of devils; and the world of devils is suddenly revealed.

But how shall this be conveyed and made palpable? In order that a new world may step in, this world must for a time disappear. The murderers, and the murder, must be insulated—cut off by an immeasurable gulf from the ordinary tide and succession of human affairs—locked up and sequestered in some deep recess; we must be made sensible that the world of ordinary life is suddenly arrested—laid asleep—tranced—racked into a dread armistice: time must be annihilated; relation to things without abolished; and all must pass self-withdrawn into a deep . . . suspension of earthly passion.

Hence it is, that when the deed is done, when the work of darkness is perfect, then the world of darkness passes away like a pageantry in the clouds: the knocking at the gate is heard; and it makes known audibly that the reaction has commenced: the human has made its reflux upon the fiendish; the pulses of life are beginning to beat again; and the re-establishment of the goings-on of the world in which we live, first makes us profoundly sensible of the awful parenthesis that had suspended them.

Key Ideas and Details Why did the "knocking at the gate" puzzle De Quincey? What does De Quincey conclude about the scene that puzzled him?

Literary Analysis

1. **Craft and Structure** To analyze Shakespeare's use of **blank verse,** complete a chart like this one by identifying the rhythm of each of the lines indicated.

Line	Iambic Feet	Trochaic or Anapestic Feet
"It is the bloody business which informs...."		
"'Macbeth does murder sleep' —the innocent sleep,..."		

2. **Craft and Structure** Mark stressed and unstressed syllables in Act II, Scene ii, lines 59–62.

3. **Craft and Structure** **Analyze** how Shakespeare achieves **clarity of meaning** by focusing on the interaction between sentences and blank verse lines. **(a)** How many sentences are there in Act II, Scene i, lines 62–64? **(b)** In reading these lines for meaning, would you pause at any of the line ends? Explain.

4. **Craft and Structure** **(a)** Experiment by using two different ways of reading the sentences in Act II, Scene i, lines 56–61, beginning, "Thou sure . . ." First read them by pausing after each line of blank verse. Then, read them by following sentences past the ends of lines. Which way was clearer? Why? **(b)** In your own words, express the meaning of this passage.

5. **Craft and Structure** **(a)** Contrast the Porter's speech (Act II, Scene iii, lines 1–21) with the two speeches at the end of Act II, Scene ii to show that the Porter's speech is written in **prose** form. **(b)** Why might prose be suitable for a "low" character? **(c)** How does the speech offer **comic relief?**

6. **Integration of Knowledge and Ideas** The nineteenth-century English writer Thomas De Quincey argued that the scene with the Porter reinforces the shock of the king's murder by a striking contrast: "The re-establishment of the goings-on of the world in which we live, first makes us profoundly sensible of the awful [episode] that had suspended them." (For a larger excerpt from De Quincey's essay, see pages 356–357.) Do you agree or disagree? Explain.

7. **Integration of Knowledge and Ideas** Macbeth has a strong imagination. In what way does this trait both prompt him to commit a crime and make it hard for him to commit it?

Common Core State Standards

Writing
1. Write arguments to support claims in an analysis of substantive topics or texts, using valid reasoning and relevant and sufficient evidence. *(p. 359)*

1.a. Introduce precise, knowledgeable claim(s), establish the significance of the claim(s), distinguish the claim(s) from alternate or opposing claims, and create an organization that logically sequences claims, counterclaims, reasons, and evidence. *(p. 359)*

Vocabulary Acquisition and Use

Word Analysis: Latin Word Root -voc-

The word *equivocate*, meaning "to speak in two equal voices" or "to mislead," is based on the Latin root *-voc-*, meaning "voice" or "calling." Words with the root *-voc-* are useful in interpreting *Macbeth*, whose protagonist is haunted by many voices: the stern voice of his wife; the prophetic voices of witches; the accusing voices of ghosts; and the disturbing voice of his own conscience.

With a small group, write a paragraph that describes Macbeth's central conflict or conflicts. Use at least four of the *-voc-* words listed below in your description. Use a dictionary if necessary.

vocalize	invocation	vocation
advocate	irrevocable	provoke

Then, choose two of the words in your paragraph and write a sentence explaining how the root *-voc-* helps create each word's meaning.

Vocabulary: Antonyms

Antonyms are words with opposite meanings. For each sentence, replace the underlined term with an antonym from the vocabulary list on page 342. The antonym should make the sentence logical. Change the form of the vocabulary word if necessary.

1. Macbeth's success in battle gave him a sense of <u>inferiority</u>.
2. He was willing to use <u>straightforward</u> means to become king.
3. Before murdering Duncan, his doubts and fears were <u>few</u>.
4. As Macbeth approached the king's bedchamber, the sense of fear was <u>intangible</u>.
5. The Witches' prophecy served to <u>diminish</u> Macbeth's sense of ambition.
6. He learned the witches always <u>told the truth.</u>

Writing to Sources

Argumentative Text Reread De Quincey's essay (pages 356–357) on the porter scene. Then, write an **essay** agreeing or disagreeing with his interpretation. Support your ideas with detailed references to the text.

Prewriting Reread Scenes ii and iii of Act II, noting your own feelings and reactions. Then, reread De Quincey's comments. Note how your responses to the scene are like or unlike his.

Drafting Begin by stating your agreement or disagreement in a clear thesis. Then, support your thesis with references to the tone, mood, style, or "sound" of the porter's language. Next, anticipate those who may disagree with your view by providing logical counterarguments.

Revising Review your essay to be sure it is clear and logically organized. Make sure to comment on every quotation you include, and check to see that each claim you make is supported.

A comparison of the writer's own ideas and de Quincey's reveals that both felt perplexed in response to the Porter's soliloquy.

Model: Comparing Responses

The first thing I felt when I began reading the Porter's speech was confusion. I was confused not only by his archaic expressions, but also by his exasperated response to something as routine as a knock at the door. Answering the door is, after all, a porter's job.

De Quincey says he felt "an effect for which [he] could never account."

Close Reading Focus

Conflict; Climax; Dramatic Irony

Conflict—the struggle between two forces—is what creates drama.

- An **external conflict** is a struggle between two characters or groups.

- An **internal conflict** is a struggle within a character.

The action, or series of events, of a play is developed and ordered by an author so that it reaches a **climax**—the point at which the internal and external conflicts are greatest. The impact of the climax on the play as a whole is twofold: The tension is at its highest and the conflicts are put on the path to resolution.

In Act III of *Macbeth,* notice how the rising action leads the new king to a state dinner and the sight of a guest—a guest who should not be there!

In connection with that dinner, Macbeth makes this critical remark to Banquo in Act III, Scene i, line 28: "Fail not our feast." This invitation is an example of dramatic irony, a device that Shakespeare uses to heighten conflict. **Dramatic irony** occurs when the words or actions of a character take on a meaning for the audience or readers different from the one the character intends.

Observe how Macbeth's remark takes on dramatic irony as events unfold, and becomes a different kind of invitation, answered by a different kind of guest.

Preparing to Read Complex Texts Connecting different passages in a text will also enable you to **identify cause-and-effect relationships**—to show, for example, how an earlier event or remark (cause) leads to a later one (effect). The Witches' prophecy that Banquo will father kings may be a cause that has many effects in Act III. Use a graphic organizer like the one shown to trace those effects.

**Common Core
State Standards**

**Reading Literature
3.** Analyze the impact of the author's choices regarding how to develop and relate elements of a story or drama.

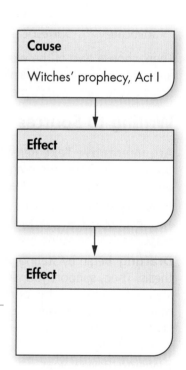

Vocabulary

The words below appear in the text that follows. Copy the words into your notebook. Which word contains a root that means *evil*?

indissoluble   infirmity

dauntless   malevolence

predominant

Review and Anticipate

In Act II, Lady Macbeth drugs Duncan's guards, enabling Macbeth to kill the king. Macbeth then kills the guards, too, so that he can more easily blame them for the king's murder. Duncan's sons, Malcolm and Donalbain, flee, afraid that they will be assassinated by a kinsman eager to claim the throne. Because they run away, some suspect them of killing their father. As the act closes, it seems that Macbeth will be named king. Act III begins with Macbeth on the throne—as the witches had predicted. All seems to be going well for him, but he feels threatened by Banquo.

ACT III

Scene i. Forres. The palace.

[*Enter* BANQUO.]

    BANQUO. Thou hast it now: King, Cawdor, Glamis, all,
      As the weird women promised, and I fear
      Thou play'dst most foully for 't. Yet it was said
      It should not stand[1] in thy posterity,
5   But that myself should be the root and father
      Of many kings. If there come truth from them—
      As upon thee, Macbeth, their speeches shine—
      Why, by the verities on thee made good,
      May they not be my oracles as well
10   And set me up in hope? But hush, no more!

[*Sennet*[2] *sounded. Enter* MACBETH *as King,* LADY MACBETH, LENNOX, ROSS, LORDS, *and* ATTENDANTS.]

    MACBETH. Here's our chief guest.

    LADY MACBETH. If he had been forgotten,
      It had been as a gap in our great feast,
      And all-thing[3] unbecoming.

    MACBETH. Tonight we hold a solemn[4] supper, sir,
      And I'll request your presence.

15 **BANQUO.** Let your Highness
      Command upon me, to the which my duties
      Are with a most indissoluble tie
      For ever knit.

    MACBETH. Ride you this afternoon?

    BANQUO. Ay, my good lord.

20 **MACBETH.** We should have else desired your good advice
      (Which still hath been both grave and prosperous[5])

◀ **Critical Viewing**
After wielding a dagger like this against Duncan, can Macbeth expect to rule in peace? Explain. **PREDICT**

1. stand continue.

2. *Sennet* trumpet call.

3. all-thing altogether.

4. solemn ceremonious.

5. grave and prosperous weighty and profitable.

Vocabulary

indissoluble (in´ di säl´ yo͞o bəl) *adj.* not able to be dissolved or undone

Comprehension

What does Banquo suspect about Macbeth?

In this day's council; but we'll take tomorrow.
Is't far you ride?

BANQUO. As far, my lord, as will fill up the time
25 'Twixt this and supper. Go not my horse the better,[6]
I must become a borrower of the night
For a dark hour or twain.

MACBETH. Fail not our feast.

BANQUO. My lord, I will not.

MACBETH. We hear our bloody cousins are bestowed
30 In England and in Ireland, not confessing
Their cruel parricide, filling their hearers
With strange invention.[7] But of that tomorrow,
When therewithal we shall have cause of state
Craving us jointly.[8] Hie you to horse. Adieu,
35 Till you return at night. Goes Fleance with you?

BANQUO. Ay, my good lord: our time does call upon 's.

MACBETH. I wish your horses swift and sure of foot,
And so I do commend you to their backs.
Farewell.   *[Exit BANQUO.]*
40 Let every man be master of his time
Till seven at night. To make society
The sweeter welcome, we will keep ourself
Till suppertime alone. While[9] then, God be with you!

        [Exit LORDS and all but MACBETH and a SERVANT.]

Sirrah,[10] a word with you: attend those men
45 Our pleasure?

ATTENDANT. They are, my lord, without the palace gate.

MACBETH. Bring them before us.   *[Exit SERVANT.]*
To be thus[11] is nothing, but[12] to be safely thus—
Our fears in Banquo stick deep,
50 And in his royalty of nature reigns that
Which would be feared. 'Tis much he dares;
And, to[13] that dauntless temper of his mind,
He hath a wisdom that doth guide his valor
To act in safety. There is none but he
55 Whose being I do fear: and under him
My genius is rebuked,[14] as it is said
Mark Antony's was by Caesar. He chid[15] the sisters,
When first they put the name of King upon me,
And bade them speak to him; then prophetlike
60 They hailed him father to a line of kings.
Upon my head they placed a fruitless crown
And put a barren scepter in my gripe,[16]

6. Go not . . . better unless my horse goes faster than I expect.

7. invention lies.

8. cause . . . jointly matters of state demanding our joint attention.

9. While until.

10. Sirrah common address to an inferior.

11. thus king.

12. but unless.

Vocabulary
dauntless (dônt′ lis) *adj.*
fearless; cannot be intimidated

13. to added to.

14. genius is rebuked guardian spirit is cowed.

15. chid scolded.

16. gripe grip.

Thence to be wrenched with an unlineal hand,
No son of mine succeeding. If 't be so,
65   For Banquo's issue have I filed[17] my mind;
For them the gracious Duncan have I murdered;
Put rancors in the vessel of my peace
Only for them, and mine eternal jewel[18]
Given to the common enemy of man,[19]
70   To make them kings, the seeds of Banquo kings!
Rather than so, come, fate, into the list,
And champion me to th' utterance![20] Who's there?

[*Enter* SERVANT *and* TWO MURDERERS.]

Now go to the door, and stay there till we call.

[*Exit* SERVANT.]

Was it not yesterday we spoke together?

MURDERERS. It was, so please your Highness.

75 **MACBETH.**   Well then, now
Have you considered of my speeches? Know
That it was he in the times past, which held you
So under fortune,[21] which you thought had been
Our innocent self: this I made good to you
80   In our last conference; passed in probation[22] with you,
How you were born in hand,[23] how crossed, the instruments,
Who wrought with them, and all things else that might
To half a soul[24] and to a notion[25] crazed
Say "Thus did Banquo."

FIRST MURDERER.   You made it known to us.

85 **MACBETH.** I did so; and went further, which is now
Our point of second meeting. Do you find
Your patience so predominant in your nature,
That you can let this go? Are you so gospeled,[26]
To pray for this good man and for his issue,
90   Whose heavy hand hath bowed you to the grave
And beggared yours for ever?

FIRST MURDERER.   We are men, my liege.

MACBETH. Ay, in the catalogue ye go for[27] men;
As hounds and greyhounds, mongrels, spaniels, curs,
Shoughs, water-rugs[28] and demi-wolves, are clept[29]
95   All by the name of dogs: the valued file[30]
Distinguishes the swift, the slow, the subtle,
The housekeeper, the hunter, every one
According to the gift which bounteous nature
Hath in him closed,[31] whereby he does receive
100   Particular addition,[32] from the bill

17. **filed** defiled.

18. **eternal jewel** soul.

19. **common . . . man** the Devil.

20. **champion me to th' utterance** Fight against me to the death.

21. **held . . . fortune** kept you from good fortune.

22. **passed in probation** reviewed the proofs.

23. **born in hand** deceived.

24. **half a soul** halfwit.

25. **notion** mind.

26. **gospeled** ready to forgive.

27. **go for** pass as.

28. **Shoughs** (shuks), **water-rugs** shaggy dogs, long-haired dogs.

29. **clept** called.

30. **valued file** classification by valuable traits.

Vocabulary

predominant (prē däm´ ə nənt) *adj.* foremost; powerful

Identifying Cause-and-Effect Relationships

What does the first murderer mean in line 91 when he answers Macbeth, "We are men"?

31. **closed** enclosed.

32. **addition** distinction (to set it apart from other dogs).

Comprehension

What has caused Macbeth to hire these murderers?

33. file ranks.

34. wear . . . life are sick as long as he lives.

35. set risk.

36. distance disagreement.

37. near'st of life most vital parts.

38. avouch justify.

39. wail his fall (I must) bewail his death.

Conflict

What conflict does Macbeth express in lines 116–126?

40. the perfect . . . on't exact information of the exact time.

41. something some distance.

42. thought remembered.

43. clearness freedom from suspicion.

44. rubs flaws.

45. Resolve yourselves apart Make your own decision.

That writes them all alike: and so of men.
Now if you have a station in the file,[33]
Not i' th' worst rank of manhood, say 't,
And I will put that business in your bosoms
105 Whose execution takes your enemy off,
Grapples you to the heart and love of us,
Who wear our health but sickly in his life,[34]
Which in his death were perfect.

SECOND MURDERER.   I am one, my liege,
Whom the vile blows and buffets of the world
110 Hath so incensed that I am reckless what
I do to spite the world.

FIRST MURDERER.   And I another
So weary with disasters, tugged with fortune,
That I would set[35] my life on any chance,
To mend it or be rid on 't.

MACBETH.   Both of you
Know Banquo was your enemy.

115 **BOTH MURDERERS.**   True, my lord.

MACBETH. So is he mine, and in such bloody distance[36]
That every minute of his being thrusts
Against my near'st of life:[37] and though I could
With barefaced power sweep him from my sight
120 And bid my will avouch[38] it, yet I must not,
For certain friends that are both his and mine,
Whose loves I may not drop, but wail his fall[39]
Who I myself struck down: and thence it is
That I to your assistance do make love,
125 Masking the business from the common eye
For sundry weighty reasons.

SECOND MURDERER.   We shall, my lord,
Perform what you command us.

FIRST MURDERER.   Though our lives—

MACBETH. Your spirits shine through you. Within this hour at most
I will advise you where to plant yourselves,
130 Acquaint you with the perfect spy o' th' time,
The moment on 't;[40] for 't must be done tonight,
And something[41] from the palace; always thought[42]
That I require a clearness:[43] and with him—
To leave no rubs[44] nor botches in the work—
135 Fleance his son, that keeps him company,
Whose absence is no less material to me
Than is his father's, must embrace the fate
Of that dark hour. Resolve yourselves apart:[45]

I'll come to you anon.

MURDERERS.   We are resolved, my lord.

140 **MACBETH.** I'll call upon you straight.[46] Abide within.
It is concluded: Banquo, thy soul's flight,
If it find heaven, must find it out tonight.   [*Exit.*]

46. straight immediately.

Scene ii. *The palace.*

[*Enter* MACBETH'S LADY *and a* SERVANT.]

LADY MACBETH. Is Banquo gone from court?

SERVANT. Ay, madam, but returns again tonight.

LADY MACBETH. Say to the King, I would attend his leisure
For a few words.

SERVANT.   Madam, I will.   [*Exit.*]

LADY MACBETH.   Nought's had, all's spent,
5   Where our desire is got without content:
'Tis safer to be that which we destroy
Than by destruction dwell in doubtful joy.

[*Enter* MACBETH.]

How now, my lord! Why do you keep alone,
Of sorriest fancies your companions making,
10   Using those thoughts which should indeed have died
With them they think on? Things without all remedy
Should be without regard: what's done is done.

MACBETH. We have scotched[1] the snake, not killed it:
She'll close[2] and be herself, whilst our poor malice
15   Remains in danger of her former tooth.[3]
But let the frame of things disjoint,[4] both the worlds[5] suffer,
Ere we will eat our meal in fear, and sleep
In the affliction of these terrible dreams
That shake us nightly: better be with the dead,
20   Whom we, to gain our peace, have sent to peace,
Than on the torture of the mind to lie
In restless ecstasy.[6] Duncan is in his grave;
After life's fitful fever he sleeps well.
Treason has done his worst: nor steel, nor poison,
25   Malice domestic, foreign levy,[7] nothing,
Can touch him further.

LADY MACBETH.   Come on.
Gentle my lord, sleek o'er your rugged looks;
Be bright and jovial among your guests tonight.

MACBETH. So shall I, love; and so, I pray, be you:

Identifying Cause-and-Effect Relationships

What causes Lady Macbeth to say what she does in lines 4–7?

1. scotched wounded.

2. close heal.

3. in . . . tooth in as much danger as before.

4. frame of things disjoint universe collapse.

5. both the worlds heaven and earth.

6. ecstasy frenzy.

7. Malice . . . levy civil and foreign war.

Comprehension

What does Macbeth ask the murderers to do?

▶ **Critical Viewing**

This artist depicted actress Sarah Siddons (1755–1831) playing Lady Macbeth. How does Mrs. Siddons's body language suggest the same inner conflict as do lines 4–7 in Act III, ii? **CONNECT**

Conflict and Irony

What is ironic about Macbeth's idea for disguising the couple's real conflict with Banquo (Scene ii, lines 30–35)?

8. **Present him eminence** Honor him.

9. **Unsafe . . . lave** We are unsafe as long as we have to wash.

10. **vizards** (viz′ ərdz) masks

11. **nature's . . . eterne** Nature's lease is not eternal.

12. **jocund** (jäk′ ənd) cheerful; jovial

13. **shard-borne** borne on scaly wings.

30   Let your remembrance apply to Banquo;
     Present him eminence,[8] both with eye and tongue:
     Unsafe the while, that we must lave[9]
     Our honors in these flattering streams
     And make our faces vizards[10] to our hearts,
     Disguising what they are.

35   **LADY MACBETH.**   You must leave this.

     MACBETH. O, full of scorpions is my mind, dear wife!
     Thou know'st that Banquo, and his Fleance, lives.

     LADY MACBETH. But in them nature's copy's not eterne.[11]

     MACBETH. There's comfort yet; they are assailable.
40   Then be thou jocund.[12] Ere the bat hath flown
     His cloistered flight, ere to black Hecate's summons
     The shard-borne[13] beetle with his drowsy hums
     Hath rung night's yawning peal, there shall be done

A deed of dreadful note.

LADY MACBETH.   What 's to be done?

45 **MACBETH.** Be innocent of the knowledge, dearest chuck,[14]
  Till thou applaud the deed. Come, seeling[15] night,
  Scarf up[16] the tender eye of pitiful day,
  And with thy bloody and invisible hand
  Cancel and tear to pieces that great bond[17]
50 Which keeps me pale! Light thickens, and the crow
  Makes wing to th' rooky[18] wood.
  Good things of day begin to droop and drowse,
  Whiles night's black agents to their preys do rouse.
  Thou marvel'st at my words: but hold thee still;
55 Things bad begun make strong themselves by ill:
  So, prithee, go with me.   [*Exit.*]

Scene iii. *Near the palace.*

[*Enter* THREE MURDERERS.]

  FIRST MURDERER. But who did bid thee join with us?

  THIRD MURDERER.   Macbeth.

  SECOND MURDERER. He needs not our mistrust; since he delivers
  Our offices[1] and what we have to do
  To the direction just.[2]

  FIRST MURDERER.   Then stand with us.
5 The west yet glimmers with some streaks of day.
  Now spurs the lated traveler apace
  To gain the timely inn, and near approaches
  The subject of our watch.

  THIRD MURDERER.   Hark! I hear horses.

  BANQUO. [*Within*] Give us a light there, ho!

  SECOND MURDERER.   Then 'tis he. The rest
10 That are within the note of expectation[3]
  Already are i' th' court.

  FIRST MURDERER.   His horses go about.[4]

  THIRD MURDERER. Almost a mile: but he does usually—
  So all men do—from hence to th' palace gate
  Make it their walk.

[*Enter* BANQUO *and* FLEANCE, *with a torch*]

  SECOND MURDERER. A light, a light!

  THIRD MURDERER.   'Tis he.

15 **FIRST MURDERER.**   Stand to 't

14. **chuck** term of endearment.

15. **seeling** eye-closing. Falconers sometimes sewed a hawk's eyes closed in order to train it.

16. **Scarf up** blindfold.

17. **great bond** between Banquo and fate.

18. **rooky** full of rooks, or crows.

Identifying Cause-and-Effect Relationships

To what specific action do you think Macbeth is indirectly referring in lines 45–56?

1. **offices** duties.

2. **direction just** exact detail.

3. **within . . . expectation** on the list of expected guests.

4. **His . . . about** His horses have been taken to the stable.

Comprehension

What does Macbeth tell Lady Macbeth and what does he hold back from her?

BANQUO. It will be rain tonight.

FIRST MURDERER.   Let it come down.

[*They set upon* BANQUO.]

BANQUO. O, treachery! Fly, good Fleance, fly, fly, fly!

[*Exit* FLEANCE.]

Thou mayst revenge. O slave! [*Dies.*]

THIRD MURDERER. Who did strike out the light?

FIRST MURDERER.   Was't not the way?[5]

20 **THIRD MURDERER.** There's but one down; the son is fled.

SECOND MURDERER. We have lost best half of our affair.

FIRST MURDERER. Well, let 's away and say how much is done.

[*Exit.*]

Scene iv. The palace.

[*Banquet prepared. Enter* MACBETH, LADY MACBETH, ROSS, LENNOX, LORDS, *and* ATTENDANTS.]

MACBETH. You know your own degrees;[1] sit down:
    At first and last, the hearty welcome.

LORDS. Thanks to your Majesty.

MACBETH. Ourself will mingle with society[2]
5   And play the humble host.
    Our hostess keeps her state,[3] but in best time
    We will require[4] her welcome.

LADY MACBETH. Pronounce it for me, sir, to all our friends,
    For my heart speaks they are welcome.

[*Enter* FIRST MURDERER.]

10 **MACBETH.** See, they encounter thee with their hearts' thanks.
    Both sides are even: here I'll sit i' th' midst:
    Be large in mirth; anon we'll drink a measure[5]
    The table round. [*Goes to* MURDERER] There's blood upon thy face.

MURDERER. 'Tis Banquo's then.

15 **MACBETH.** 'Tis better thee without than he within.[6]
    Is he dispatched?

MURDERER. My lord, his throat is cut; that I did for him.

MACBETH. Thou art the best o' th' cutthroats.
    Yet he's good that did the like for Fleance;
20   If thou didst it, thou art the nonpareil.[7]

---

5. way thing to do.

1. degrees ranks. At state banquets, guests were seated according to rank.

2. society company.

3. keeps her state remains seated on her throne.

4. require request.

5. measure toast.

6. thee . . . within you outside than he inside.

7. nonpareil without equal.

MURDERER. Most royal sir, Fleance is 'scaped.

MACBETH. [*Aside*] Then comes my fit again: I had else been perfect,
Whole as the marble, founded as the rock,
As broad and general as the casing[8] air:
25 But now I am cabined, cribbed, confined, bound in
To saucy[9] doubts and fears.—But Banquo's safe?

MURDERER. Ay, my good lord: safe in a ditch he bides,
With twenty trenchèd[10] gashes on his head,
The least a death to nature.[11]

MACBETH.   Thanks for that.
30 [*Aside*] There the grown serpent lies; the worm that's fled
Hath nature that in time will venom breed,
No teeth for th' present. Get thee gone. Tomorrow
We'll hear ourselves[12] again.   [*Exit* MURDERER.]

LADY MACBETH.   My royal lord,
You do not give the cheer.[13] The feast is sold
35 That is not often vouched, while 'tis a-making,
'Tis given with welcome.[14] To feed were best at home;
From thence, the sauce to meat is ceremony;[15]
Meeting were bare without it.

[*Enter the* GHOST *of* BANQUO *and sits in* MACBETH'S *place.*]

MACBETH.   Sweet remembrancer!
Now good digestion wait on appetite,
And health on both!

40 **LENNOX.**   May't please your Highness sit.

MACBETH. Here had we now our country's honor roofed,[16]
Were the graced person of our Banquo present—

8. **as . . . casing** as unrestrained as the surrounding.

9. **saucy** insolent.

10. **trenchèd** trenchlike.

11. **nature** natural life.

12. **hear ourselves** talk it over.

13. **give the cheer** make the guests feel welcome.

14. **The feast . . . welcome** The feast at which the host fails to make the guests feel welcome while the food is being prepared is no more than a bought dinner.

15. **From . . . ceremony** Ceremony adds a pleasant flavor to the food.

16. **our . . . roofed** the most honorable men in the country under one roof.

Comprehension

What do the murderers fail to do??

LITERATURE IN CONTEXT

Cultural Connection

Stagecraft at the Globe

It took some sophisticated Elizabethan theatrics to manage entrances and exits such as those of Banquo's ghost. (Macbeth reacts to the ghost in this picture.) In the farthest reaches of the Globe Theater's stage was a small area called the rear stage, which was open to the audience but enclosed by a wall at the back and cloth hangings on the sides. A trapdoor in the floor of the rear stage was the means by which Banquo's ghost made an entrance. The trapdoor operated silently, and it was not completely visible to the audience.

Connect to the Literature

What other characters in *Macbeth* might have used a trapdoor for exits or entrances? Explain.

Identifying Cause-and-Effect Relationships

How might you connect
Macbeth's agitation with his
knowledge that Fleance has
escaped?

Conflict

How does the incident with
Banquo's ghost convey
Macbeth's inner conflict?

18. upon a thought in a
moment.

19. passion suffering.

20. flaws gusts of wind;
outbursts of emotion.

21. Authorized vouched for.

22. charnel houses vaults
containing human bones
dug up in making new
graves.

23. our . . . kites Because the
dead will be devoured by
birds of prey, our tombs
will be the bellies of those
birds.

Who may I rather challenge for unkindness
Than pity for mischance![17]

ROSS.   His absence, sir,
45 Lays blame upon his promise. Please 't your Highness
To grace us with your royal company?

MACBETH. The table's full.

LENNOX. Here is a place reserved, sir.

MACBETH. Where?

LENNOX. Here, my good lord. What is 't that moves your Highness?

MACBETH. Which of you have done this?

50 **LORDS.**   What, my good lord?

MACBETH. Thou canst not say I did it. Never shake
Thy gory locks at me.

ROSS. Gentlemen, rise, his Highness is not well.

LADY MACBETH. Sit, worthy friends. My lord is often thus,
55 And hath been from his youth. Pray you, keep seat.
The fit is momentary; upon a thought[18]
He will again be well. If much you note him,
You shall offend him and extend his passion.[19]
Feed, and regard him not.—Are you a man?

60 **MACBETH.** Ay, and a bold one, that dare look on that
Which might appall the devil.

LADY MACBETH.   O proper stuff!
This is the very painting of your fear.
This is the air-drawn dagger which, you said,
Led you to Duncan. O, these flaws[20] and starts,
65 Impostors to true fear, would well become
A woman's story at a winter's fire,
Authorized[21] by her grandam. Shame itself!
Why do you make such faces? When all's done,
You look but on a stool.

MACBETH.   Prithee, see there!
70 Behold! Look! Lo! How say you?
Why, what care I? If thou canst nod, speak too.
If charnel houses[22] and our graves must send
Those that we bury back, our monuments
Shall be the maws of kites.[23]   [*Exit* GHOST.]

75 **LADY MACBETH.**   What, quite unmanned in folly?

MACBETH. If I stand here, I saw him.

LADY MACBETH.   Fie, for shame!

Scene from Macbeth, Cattermole, The Folger Shakespeare Library, Washington, D.C.

◀ **Critical Viewing**

In what ways does the artist's use of light and shadow suggest the conflict in Act III, Scene iv? **INTERPRET**

MACBETH. Blood hath been shed ere now, i' th' olden time,
Ere humane statute purged the gentle weal;[24]
Ay, and since too, murders have been performed
Too terrible for the ear. The time has been
80   That, when the brains were out, the man would die,
And there an end; but now they rise again,
With twenty mortal murders on their crowns,[25]
And push us from our stools. This is more strange
Than such a murder is.

LADY MACBETH.   My worthy lord,
Your noble friends do lack you.

85   **MACBETH.**   I do forget.
Do not muse at me, my most worthy friends;
I have a strange infirmity, which is nothing
To those that know me. Come, love and health to all!
Then I'll sit down. Give me some wine, fill full.

[*Enter* GHOST.]

90   I drink to th' general joy o' th' whole table,
And to our dear friend Banquo, whom we miss;
Would he were here! To all and him we thirst,[26]
And all to all.

LORDS.   Our duties, and the pledge.

MACBETH. Avaunt![27] and quit my sight! Let the earth hide thee!
95   Thy bones are marrowless, thy blood is cold;

24. Ere . . . weal before humane laws civilized the state and made it gentle.

25. mortal . . . crowns deadly wounds on their heads.

Vocabulary

infirmity (in fur′ mə tē) *n.* physical or mental defect; illness

26. thirst drink.

27. Avaunt Be gone!

Comprehension

Why is Macbeth startled at the feast?

28. speculation sight.

29. Hyrcan (hər´ kən) from Hyrcania, a province of the ancient Persian and Macedonian empires south of the Caspian Sea.

Thou hast no speculation[28] in those eyes
Which thou dost glare with.

LADY MACBETH. Think of this, good peers,
But as a thing of custom, 'tis no other.
Only it spoils the pleasure of the time.

100 **MACBETH.** What man dare, I dare.
Approach thou like the rugged Russian bear,
The armed rhinoceros, or th' Hyrcan[29] tiger;
Take any shape but that,[30] and my firm nerves
Shall never tremble. Or be alive again,
105 And dare me to the desert[31] with thy sword.
If trembling I inhabit[32] then, protest me
The baby of a girl. Hence, horrible shadow!
Unreal mock'ry, hence! [*Exit* GHOST.]
Why, so: being gone,
I am a man again. Pray you, sit still.

30. that Banquo's shape.

31. desert place where neither of us could escape.

32. inhabit remain indoors.

LADY MACBETH. You have displaced the mirth, broke the
110 good meeting,
With most admired[33] disorder.

MACBETH. Can such things be,
And overcome us[34] like a summer's cloud,
Without our special wonder? You make me strange
Even to the disposition that I owe,[35]
115 When now I think you can behold such sights,
And keep the natural ruby of your cheeks,
When mine is blanched with fear.

33. admired amazing.

34. overcome us come over us.

35. disposition. . . owe my own nature.

ROSS. What sights, my lord?

LADY MACBETH. I pray you, speak not: He grows worse and worse;
Question enrages him: at once, good night.
120 Stand not upon the order of your going,[36]
But go at once.

Identifying Cause-and-Effect Relationships

What effects do you think Macbeth's behavior will have on the guests?

36. Stand . . . going Do not wait to depart in order of rank.

LENNOX. Good night; and better health
Attend his Majesty!

LADY MACBETH. A kind good night to all!

[*Exit* LORDS.]

MACBETH. It will have blood, they say: blood will have blood.
Stones have been known to move and trees to speak;
125 Augures and understood relations[37] have
By maggot-pies and choughs[38] and rooks brought forth
The secret'st man of blood.[39] What is the night?

37. Augures and understood relations omens and the relationship between the omens and what they represent.

38. maggot-pies and choughs (chufs) magpies and crows.

39. man of blood murderer.

40. at odds disputing.

LADY MACBETH. Almost at odds[40] with morning, which is which.

MACBETH. How say'st thou, that Macduff denies his person

At our great bidding?

130 **LADY MACBETH.**   Did you send to him, sir?

MACBETH. I hear it by the way, but I will send:
There's not a one of them but in his house
I keep a servant fee'd.[41] I will tomorrow,
And betimes[42] I will, to the weird sisters:
135 More shall they speak, for now I am bent[43] to know
By the worst means the worst. For mine own good
All causes shall give way. I am in blood
Stepped in so far that, should I wade no more,
Returning were as tedious as go o'er.
140 Strange things I have in head that will to hand,
Which must be acted ere they may be scanned.[44]

LADY MACBETH. You lack the season of all natures,[45] sleep.

MACBETH. Come, we'll to sleep. My strange and self-abuse[46]
Is the initiate fear that wants hard use.[47]
145 We are yet but young in deed.   [*Exit.*]

Scene v. *A witches' haunt.*

[*Thunder. Enter the* THREE WITCHES, *meeting* HECATE.]

FIRST WITCH. Why, how now, Hecate! you look angerly.

HECATE. Have I not reason, beldams[1] as you are,
Saucy and overbold? How did you dare
To trade and traffic with Macbeth
5 In riddles and affairs of death;
And I, the mistress of your charms,
The close contriver[2] of all harms,
Was never called to bear my part,
Or show the glory of our art?
10 And, which is worse, all you have done
Hath been but for a wayward son,
Spiteful and wrathful; who, as others do,
Loves for his own ends, not for you.
But make amends now: get you gone,
15 And at the pit of Acheron[3]
Meet me i' th' morning: thither he
Will come to know his destiny.
Your vessels and your spells provide,
Your charms and everything beside.
20 I am for th' air; this night I'll spend
Unto a dismal and a fatal end:
Great business must be wrought ere noon.
Upon the corner of the moon
There hangs a vap'rous drop profound;

41. **fee'd** paid to spy.

42. **betimes** quickly.

43. **bent** determined.

Conflict

How do lines 136–139 in Scene iv mark a turning point in Macbeth's inner conflict?

44. **scanned** examined.

45. **season . . . natures** preservative of all living creatures.

46. **My . . . self-abuse** my strange delusion.

47. **initiate . . . use** beginner's fear that will harden with experience.

1. **beldams** hags.

2. **close contriver** secret inventor.

3. **Acheron** (ak´ ər än´) hell; in Greek mythology the river of Hades.

Comprehension

Why will Macbeth visit "the weird sisters" again?

25   I'll catch it ere it come to ground:
    And that distilled by magic sleights[4]
    Shall raise such artificial sprites[5]
    As by the strength of their illusion
    Shall draw him on to his confusion.[6]
30   He shall spurn fate, scorn death, and bear
    His hopes 'bove wisdom, grace, and fear:
    And you all know security[7]
    Is mortals' chiefest enemy.

[*Music and a song.*]

    Hark! I am called; my little spirit, see,
35   Sits in a foggy cloud and stays for me.   [*Exit.*]

[*Sing within,* "Come away, come away," *etc.*]

FIRST WITCH. Come, let's make haste; she'll soon be
    back again.   [*Exit.*]

Scene vi. The palace.

[*Enter* LENNOX *and another* LORD.]

LENNOX. My former speeches have but hit[1] your thoughts,
    Which can interpret farther.[2] Only I say
    Things have been strangely borne.[3] The gracious Duncan
    Was pitied of Macbeth: marry, he was dead.
5   And the right-valiant Banquo walked too late;
    Whom, you may say, if 't please you, Fleance killed,
    For Fleance fled. Men must not walk too late.
    Who cannot want the thought,[4] how monstrous
    It was for Malcolm and for Donalbain
10   To kill their gracious father? Damnèd fact![5]
    How it did grieve Macbeth! Did he not straight,
    In pious rage, the two delinquents tear,
    That were the slaves of drink and thralls[6] of sleep?
    Was not that nobly done? Ay, and wisely too;
15   For 'twould have angered any heart alive
    To hear the men deny 't. So that I say
    He has borne all things well: and I do think
    That, had he Duncan's sons under his key—
    As, an 't[7] please heaven, he shall not—they should find
20   What 'twere to kill a father. So should Fleance.
    But, peace! for from broad[8] words, and 'cause he failed
    His presence at the tyrant's feast, I hear,
    Macduff lives in disgrace. Sir, can you tell
    Where he bestows himself?

LORD.   The son of Duncan,
25   From whom this tyrant holds the due of birth,[9]

1. **hit** coincided with.

2. **Which . . . farther** from which you can draw your own conclusions.

3. **borne** managed.

4. **cannot . . . thought** can fail to think.

5. **fact** deed.

6. **thralls** slaves.

7. **an 't** if it.

8. **broad** unguarded.

9. **due of birth** birthright; claim to the throne.

Lives in the English court, and is received
Of the most pious Edward[10] with such grace
That the malevolence of fortune nothing
Takes from his high respect.[11] Thither Macduff
30　Is gone to pray the holy King, upon his aid[12]
To wake Northumberland and warlike Siward;[13]
That by the help of these, with Him above
To ratify the work, we may again
Give to our tables meat, sleep to our nights,
35　Free from our feasts and banquets bloody knives,
Do faithful homage and receive free honors:[14]
All which we pine for now. And this report
Hath so exasperate the King that he
Prepares for some attempt of war.

　　LENNOX.　　　　　　　　　　　Sent he to Macduff?

40　**LORD.**　He did: and with an absolute "Sir, not I,"
The cloudy[15] messenger turns me his back,
And hums, as who should say "You'll rue the time
That clogs[16] me with this answer."

　　LENNOX.　　　　　　　　　　And that well might
Advise him to a caution, t' hold what distance
45　His wisdom can provide. Some holy angel
Fly to the court of England and unfold
His message ere he come, that a swift blessing
May soon return to this our suffering country
Under a hand accursed!

　　LORD.　　　　　　　I'll send my prayers with him.　　[*Exit.*]

Critical Reading

1. **Key Ideas and Details (a)** What does Macbeth think as he anticipates the murder of Banquo? **(b) Compare and Contrast:** Compare and contrast Macbeth's thoughts about Banquo's murder with his thoughts before the murder of Duncan.

2. **Key Ideas and Details (a)** In the banquet scene, what complaint does Macbeth make about murdered men? **(b) Analyze:** Is there anything humorous or even ridiculous in this complaint? Why or why not? **(c) Connect:** Does Shakespeare use humor for comic relief in this scene, as he does in the earlier scene with the porter? Explain.

3. **Integration of Knowledge and Ideas** Has the relationship between Macbeth and Lady Macbeth changed? Explain.

4. **Integration of Knowledge and Ideas** What does the murder of Banquo suggest about the effects of evil on evildoers? Explain.

Cite textual evidence to support your responses.

Literary Analysis

1. **Craft and Structure (a)** Why is Macbeth involved in an **external conflict** with Banquo? **(b)** In what way does Macbeth fail to resolve this conflict?

2. **Craft and Structure** Complete a chart like the one below to show the intensification of **conflict** and the movement toward a **climax** in Act III.

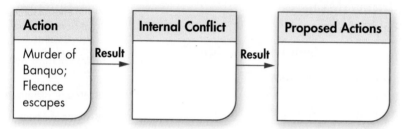

Action		Internal Conflict		Proposed Actions
Murder of Banquo; Fleance escapes	Result →		Result →	

3. **Craft and Structure (a)** How is Macbeth's behavior at the banquet a sign of an **internal conflict? (b)** How does he temporarily resolve this conflict?

4. **Key Ideas and Details** Macbeth is personifying evil. Who do you think will lead the forces of good in a campaign against him? How do you know?

5. **Craft and Structure (a)** Identify three examples of **dramatic irony** in Macbeth's speeches to Banquo in Act III, Scene i, lines 20–38. **(b)** What effect does the use of irony have on the level of tension in the play?

6. **Key Ideas and Details Identify causes and effects** in the play by explaining how the Witches' prophecy that Banquo will father kings could be viewed as the cause of the following items: **(a)** the question Macbeth asks of Banquo, "'Goes Fleance with you?'" (III, i, 35); **(b)** Macbeth's recruiting of the murderers (III, iii).

7. **Key Ideas and Details** Some critics suggest that the third murderer is Macbeth himself. Argue for or against this interpretation, supporting your points by showing what would cause Macbeth to join the two murderers in person or what would cause him not to join them.

8. **Integration of Knowledge and Ideas** How does the dramatic irony in Act III, Scene iv, lines 41–44 create an expectation of a tense encounter?

9. **Key Ideas and Details** In Act III, Scene vi, a lord tells Lennox that Duncan's son is being sheltered at the English court and that Macduff has gone there to seek his aid. What effects do you think will result from Macduff's visit?

Common Core State Standards

Writing
3. Write narratives to develop real or imagined experiences or events using effective technique, well-chosen details, and well-structured event sequences. *(p. 377)*

3.a. Engage and orient the reader by setting out a problem, situation, or observation and its significance, establishing one or multiple point(s) of view, and introducing a narrator and/or characters; create a smooth progression of experiences or events. *(p. 377)*

3.d. Use precise words and phrases, telling details, and sensory language to convey a vivid picture of the experiences, events, setting, and/or characters. *(p. 377)*

5. Develop and strengthen writing as needed by planning, revising, editing, rewriting, or trying a new approach, focusing on addressing what is most significant for a specific purpose and audience. *(p. 377)*

Language
4.a. Use context as a clue to the meaning of a word or phrase. *(p. 377)*

Vocabulary Acquisition and Use

Word Analysis: Latin Prefix *mal-*

The Latin prefix *mal-* means "bad or badly, poorly, or wrong." *Malevolence*, therefore, means "ill will." The prefix *mal-* can also mean "not," as in *malcontent*. With a group, write a short paragraph describing several qualities that would make a person a poor leader, giving an example of each. Use at least three of the *mal-* words listed below. If any of the words are unfamiliar, refer to a dictionary to clarify their meanings.

maladjusted	malformed
malady	maladministration
malfunction	malicious

Then, for each of the *mal-* words used in your description, tell whether the prefix most nearly means "bad or badly," "poorly," "wrong," or "not."

Vocabulary: Context Clues

The context of a word—the words, phrases and sentences that surround it—may provide clues to its meaning. In the paragraph below, explain how context clues help you identify the meaning of the underlined vocabulary words:

A <u>predominant</u> nobleman in the court of King Malicia heard rumors of foul play in the neighboring kingdom of Maloria. "Though your reign is <u>indissoluble</u>, my liege," he said to the king, "I am afraid the one next door is a little flimsy." "Does the King of Maloria suffer from physical illness or mental <u>infirmity</u>?" the king queried. "Both, my liege," replied the nobleman. "Though he thinks himself <u>dauntless</u>, he is actually a cowering ninny." "Perfect!" cackled the king. "My unchecked <u>malevolence</u> shall soon make me the evil ruler of not one kingdom, but two!"

Writing to Sources

Narrative Text Write a **soliloquy** for a lord returning from Macbeth's banquet. At the beginning of the soliloquy, have him clearly establish his point of view (a guest at Macbeth's banquet). Then, have your character relate the events he has seen and explain why they are important.

Prewriting Reread Scene iv. List Macbeth's most striking words and actions, your lord's reactions, and possible sensory details of the scene.

Drafting Using your prewriting list, draft the soliloquy in **blank verse,** unrhymed iambic pentameter. Mimic Shakespeare's style and diction.

Revising Reread your soliloquy to strengthen its figurative language. First, place a star next to descriptive words and phrases that sound too literal. Then, replace each with an imaginative comparison or word picture.

Model: Revising for Figurative Language

> *face as dazed as death*
> And then the king, with ~~pale and frightened face,~~
> rose slowly, staring at—nay, toward—the wall
> *danced*
> where nothing ~~was~~ except for shadows dark.

The writer replaces the lackluster adjectives with a vivid and eerie comparison. Next, she replaces the flat *to-be* verb with a lively action verb. These changes help the audience "see" what is being described.

Building Knowledge and Insight *Macbeth, Act IV*

Close Reading Focus

Imagery

Imagery is the language that writers use to re-create sensory experiences and stir emotions. It is what helps you see, hear, feel, smell, and taste, rather than just read or listen to words. Shakespeare uses imagery to pack sensory experiences and strong emotions into almost every line. Further, he creates these patterns of images that run through the whole play:

- Blood
- Ill-fitting clothes
- Babies and children, sometimes killed by Macbeth and sometimes threatening him

These images reinforce important themes in the play. The last group of images suggests that Macbeth is in some way warring against the future, which babies and children represent. As you read, link patterns of images to the play's central ideas.

Some images are powerful because they are **archetypal**—they relate to ideas and emotions expressed by people in many cultures. In Act IV, for example, **images of banishment from an ideal world**—shrieking, groaning, and bleeding—indicate that Macbeth's Scotland resembles an underworld region where the dead are punished. Look for such archetypal images as you read.

Preparing to Read Complex Texts You will better understand and enjoy a literary work if you **analyze its text structures,** or the way it is put together. In *Macbeth,* Shakespeare uses a type of text structure that involves relationships among images and among patterns of images. For example, as indicated above, you will see patterns of images relating to blood and to babies and children.

Use a graphic organizer like the one shown to figure out how a pattern of images reinforces a theme in the play. Then, analyze how the development of and relationship between these images adds to the impact and meaning of the play.

Vocabulary

You will encounter the words below in the text that follows. Copy the words into your notebook. Which words share the same suffix?

pernicious	intemperance
judicious	avarice
sundry	credulous

**Common Core
State Standards**

**Reading Literature
3.** Analyze the impact of the author's choices regarding how to develop and relate elements of a story or drama.

**Language
1.a.** Apply the understanding that usage is a matter of convention, can change over time, and is sometimes contested. *(Literature in Context: Vocabulary Connection, p. 388)*

Image Pattern: Blood

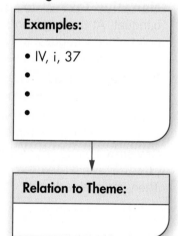

Examples:

- IV, i, 37
- •
- •
- •

Relation to Theme:

Review and Anticipate

Macbeth hires murderers to kill Banquo and Banquo's son, Fleance. The murderers botch the job, killing Banquo but allowing Fleance to escape. Then, at a state banquet, Macbeth is shocked to see the ghost of Banquo sitting in the king's chair. Macbeth decides to visit the witches again, determined to know "the worst." At the end of Act III, we learn that Malcolm is in England preparing to invade Scotland and that Macduff has gone to join him. Act IV will be a turning point in the play. Macbeth seeks help from the witches to secure his power. The forces of good, however, are beginning to gather against him.

ACT IV

Scene i. A witches' haunt.

[*Thunder. Enter the* THREE WITCHES.]

FIRST WITCH. Thrice the brinded[1] cat hath mewed.

SECOND WITCH. Thrice and once the hedge-pig[2] whined.

THIRD WITCH. Harpier[3] cries. 'Tis time, 'tis time.

FIRST WITCH. Round about the caldron go:
5   In the poisoned entrails throw.
    Toad, that under cold stone
    Days and nights has thirty-one
    Swelt'red venom sleeping got,[4]
    Boil thou first i' th' charmèd pot.

10 **ALL.** Double, double, toil and trouble;
    Fire burn and caldron bubble.

SECOND WITCH. Fillet of a fenny snake,
    In the caldron boil and bake;
    Eye of newt and toe of frog,
15 Wool of bat and tongue of dog,
    Adder's fork[5] and blindworm's[6] sting,
    Lizard's leg and howlet's[7] wing,
    For a charm of pow'rful trouble,
    Like a hell-broth boil and bubble.

20 **ALL.** Double, double, toil and trouble;
    Fire burn and caldron bubble.

THIRD WITCH. Scale of dragon, tooth of wolf,
    Witch's mummy, maw and gulf[8]
    Of the ravined[9] salt-sea shark,
25 Root of hemlock digged i' th' dark,

Comprehension
What are the witches doing as the act begins?

Liver of blaspheming Jew,
Gall of goat, and slips of yew
Slivered in the moon's eclipse,
Nose of Turk and Tartar's lips,[10]
30   Finger of birth-strangled babe
Ditch-delivered by a drab,
Make the gruel thick and slab:[11]
Add thereto a tiger's chaudron,[12]
For th' ingredient of our caldron.

35 **ALL.** Double, double, toil and trouble;
Fire burn and caldron bubble.

SECOND WITCH. Cool it with a baboon's blood,
Then the charm is firm and good.

[*Enter* HECATE *and the other* THREE WITCHES.]

HECATE. O, well done! I commend your pains;
40   And every one shall share i' th' gains:
And now about the caldron sing,
Like elves and fairies in a ring,
Enchanting all that you put in.

[*Music and a song:* "Black Spirits," *etc. Exit* HECATE *and the
other* THREE WITCHES.]

SECOND WITCH. By the pricking of my thumbs,
45   Something wicked this way comes:
Open, locks,
Whoever knocks!

[*Enter* MACBETH.]

MACBETH. How now, you secret, black, and midnight hags!
What is 't you do?

ALL.   A deed without a name.

50 **MACBETH.** I conjure you, by that which you profess,
Howe'er you come to know it, answer me:
Though you untie the winds and let them fight
Against the churches; though the yesty[13] waves
Confound[14] and swallow navigation up;
55   Though bladed corn be lodged[15] and trees blown down;
Though castles topple on their warders' heads;
Though palaces and pyramids do slope[16]
Their heads to their foundations; though the treasure
Of nature's germens[17] tumble all together,
60   Even till destruction sicken, answer me
To what I ask you.

FIRST WITCH.   Speak.

10. **blaspheming Jew . . . Tartar's lips** For many in Shakespeare's audience, the words *Jew, Turk,* and *Tartar* evoked stereotypical enemies of Christianity.

11. **slab** sticky.

12. **chaudron** (shô' drən) entrails.

◄ **Critical Viewing**
Has this artist captured the spirit of the witches as it is portrayed in IV, i? Explain.
EVALUATE

Analyzing Text Structures
How does the pattern of images in Scene i reinforce the scene's meaning?

13. **yesty** foamy.

14. **Confound** destroy.

15. **lodged** beaten down.

16. **slope** bend.

17. **nature's germens** seeds of all life.

Comprehension
What does Macbeth demand of the witches?

Imagery

How do the apparitions that Macbeth sees in Scene i, lines 68, 76, and 86 connect with the patterns of imagery in the play?

18. farrow young pigs.

19. gibbet (jib´ it) gallows.

20. office function.

21. an Armed Head symbol of Macduff.

22. harped hit upon.

23. a Bloody Child symbol of Macduff at birth.

24. take . . . fate get a guarantee from fate (by killing Macduff).

25. a Child . . . hand symbol of Malcolm.

26. top of sovereignty crown.

SECOND WITCH.   Demand.

THIRD WITCH.   We'll answer.

FIRST WITCH. Say, if th' hadst rather hear it from our mouths,
  Or from our masters?

MACBETH.   Call 'em, let me see 'em.

FIRST WITCH. Pour in sow's blood, that hath eaten
65   Her nine farrow;¹⁸ grease that's sweaten
  From the murderer's gibbet¹⁹ throw
  Into the flame.

ALL.   Come, high or low,
  Thyself and office²⁰ deftly show!

[*Thunder.* FIRST APPARITION: *an Armed Head.*²¹]

MACBETH. Tell me, thou unknown power—

FIRST WITCH.   He knows thy thought:
70   Hear his speech, but say thou nought.

FIRST APPARITION. Macbeth! Macbeth! Macbeth! Beware Macduff!
  Beware the Thane of Fife. Dismiss me: enough.

                                        [*He descends.*]

MACBETH. Whate'er thou art, for thy good caution thanks:
  Thou hast harped²² my fear aright. But one word more—

75 **FIRST WITCH.** He will not be commanded. Here's another,
  More potent than the first.

[*Thunder.* SECOND APPARITION: *a Bloody Child.*²³]

SECOND APPARITION. Macbeth! Macbeth! Macbeth!

MACBETH. Had I three ears, I'd hear thee.

SECOND APPARITION. Be bloody, bold, and resolute! Laugh to scorn
80   The pow'r of man, for none of woman born
  Shall harm Macbeth.   [*Descends.*]

MACBETH. Then live, Macduff: what need I fear of thee?
  But yet I'll make assurance double sure,
  And take a bond of fate.²⁴ Thou shalt not live;
85   That I may tell pale-hearted fear it lies,
  And sleep in spite of thunder.

[*Thunder.* THIRD APPARITION: *a Child Crowned, with a tree in his hand.*²⁵]

                          What is this,
  That rises like the issue of a king,
  And wears upon his baby-brow the round
  And top of sovereignty?²⁶

ALL.   Listen, but speak not to 't.

90   **THIRD APPARITION.** Be lion-mettled, proud, and take no care
       Who chafes, who frets, or where conspirers are:
       Macbeth shall never vanquished be until
       Great Birnam Wood to high Dunsinane Hill
       Shall come against him.   *[Descends.]*

  MACBETH.   That will never be.
95   Who can impress[27] the forest, bid the tree
       Unfix his earth-bound root? Sweet bodements,[28] good!
       Rebellious dead, rise never, till the Wood
       Of Birnam rise, and our high-placed Macbeth
       Shall live the lease of nature,[29] pay his breath
100   To time and mortal custom.[30] Yet my heart
       Throbs to know one thing. Tell me, if your art
       Can tell so much: shall Banquo's issue ever
       Reign in this kingdom?

  ALL.   Seek to know no more.

  MACBETH. I will be satisfied. Deny me this,
105   And an eternal curse fall on you! Let me know.
       Why sinks that caldron? And what noise is this?

[Hautboys.]

  FIRST WITCH. Show!

  SECOND WITCH. Show!

  THIRD WITCH. Show!

110 **ALL.** Show his eyes, and grieve his heart;
       Come like shadows, so depart!

[A show of eight KINGS *and* BANQUO, *last* KING *with a glass [31] in his hand.]*

  MACBETH. Thou art too like the spirit of Banquo. Down!
       Thy crown does sear mine eyelids. And thy hair,
       Thou other gold-bound brow, is like the first.
115   A third is like the former. Filthy hags!
       Why do you show me this? A fourth! Start, eyes!
       What, will the line stretch out to th' crack of doom?
       Another yet! A seventh! I'll see no more.
       And yet the eighth appears, who bears a glass
120   Which shows me many more: and some I see
       That twofold balls and treble scepters[32] carry:
       Horrible sight! Now I see 'tis true;
       For the blood-boltered[33] Banquo smiles upon me,
       And points at them for his.[34] What, is this so?

125 **FIRST WITCH.** Ay, sir, all this is so. But why
       Stands Macbeth thus amazedly?
       Come, sisters, cheer we up his sprites,
       And show the best of our delights:

---

27. impress force into service.

28. bodements prophecies.

29. lease of nature natural lifespan.

30. mortal custom natural death.

31. glass mirror.

Imagery
What does Macbeth learn from the images of the eight kings?

32. twofold . . . scepters coronation emblems and insignia of the kingdoms of England, Scotland, and Ireland, united in 1603 when James VI of Scotland became James I of England.

33. blood-boltered with his hair matted with blood.

34. his his descendants.

Comprehension
What do the three apparitions tell Macbeth, and what further vision does he see?

35. antic round grotesque circular dance.

130   I'll charm the air to give a sound,
While you perform your antic round,[35]
That this great king may kindly say
Our duties did his welcome pay.

[*Music.* THE WITCHES *dance, and vanish.*]

Vocabulary

pernicious (pər nish´ əs)
adj. fatal; deadly

MACBETH. Where are they? Gone? Let this pernicious hour
Stand aye accursèd in the calendar!
Come in, without there!

[*Enter* LENNOX.]

135 **LENNOX.**   What's your Grace's will?

MACBETH. Saw you the weird sisters?

LENNOX.   No, my lord.

MACBETH. Came they not by you?

LENNOX.   No indeed, my lord.

MACBETH. Infected be the air whereon they ride,
And damned all those that trust them! I did hear
140   The galloping of horse. Who was 't came by?

LENNOX. 'Tis two or three, my lord, that bring you word
Macduff is fled to England.

MACBETH.   Fled to England?

LENNOX. Ay, my good lord.

36. anticipat'st foretold.

37. The flighty . . . it The fleeting plan is never fulfilled unless it is carried out at once.

38. firstlings . . . heart first thoughts, impulses.

MACBETH. [*Aside*] Time, thou anticipat'st[36] my dread exploits.
145   The flighty purpose never is o'ertook
Unless the deed go with it.[37] From this moment
The very firstlings of my heart[38] shall be
The firstlings of my hand. And even now,
To crown my thoughts with acts be it thought and done:
150   The castle of Macduff I will surprise;
Seize upon Fife; give to th' edge o' th' sword

39. trace succeed.

His wife, his babes, and all unfortunate souls
That trace[39] him in his line. No boasting like a fool;
This deed I'll do before this purpose cool:
155   But no more sights!—Where are these gentlemen?
Come, bring me where they are.

                                      [*Exit.*]

Scene ii. Macduff's castle.

[*Enter* MACDUFF'S WIFE, *her* SON, *and* ROSS.]

LADY MACDUFF. What had he done, to make him fly the land?

ROSS. You must have patience, madam.

LADY MACDUFF.   He had none:

His flight was madness. When our actions do not,
Our fears do make us traitors.

ROSS.   You know not

5   Whether it was his wisdom or his fear.

LADY MACDUFF. Wisdom! To leave his wife, to leave his babes,
His mansion and his titles,[1] in a place
From whence himself does fly? He loves us not;
He wants the natural touch:[2] for the poor wren,
10   The most diminutive of birds, will fight,
Her young ones in her nest, against the owl.
All is the fear and nothing is the love;
As little is the wisdom, where the flight
So runs against all reason.

ROSS.   My dearest coz,[3]

15   I pray you, school[4] yourself. But, for your husband,
He is noble, wise, *judicious*, and best knows
The fits o' th' seasons,[5] I dare not speak much further:
But cruel are the times, when we are traitors
And do not know ourselves;[6] when we hold rumor
20   From what we fear,[7] yet know not what we fear,
But float upon a wild and violent sea
Each way and move. I take my leave of you.
Shall not be long but I'll be here again.
Things at the worst will cease, or else climb upward
25   To what they were before. My pretty cousin,
Blessing upon you!

LADY MACDUFF. Fathered he is, and yet he's fatherless.

ROSS. I am so much a fool, should I stay longer,
It would be my disgrace and your discomfort.[8]
I take my leave at once.   [*Exit* ROSS.]

30 **LADY MACDUFF.**   Sirrah, your father's dead;
And what will you do now? How will you live?

SON. As birds do, mother.

LADY MACDUFF.   What, with worms and flies?

SON. With what I get, I mean; and so do they.

LADY MACDUFF. Poor bird! thou'dst never fear the net nor lime,[9]
35   The pitfall nor the gin.[10]

SON. Why should I, mother? Poor birds they are not set for.
My father is not dead, for all your saying.

LADY MACDUFF. Yes, he is dead: how wilt thou do for a father?

SON. Nay, how will you do for a husband?

Imagery

What image is suggested by Lady Macduff's use of the words "fly" and "flight" in lines 8 and 13?

1. **titles** possessions.

2. **wants . . . touch** lacks natural affection.

3. **coz** cousin.

4. **school** control.

Vocabulary

judicious (jōō dish´ əs) *adj.* showing good judgment

5. **fits o' th' season** disorders of the time.

6. **when . . . ourselves** when we are treated as traitors but do not know of any treason.

7. **when . . . fear** believe rumors based on our fears.

8. **It . . . discomfort:** I would disgrace myself and embarrass you by weeping.

Imagery

What does the imagery in Scene ii, lines 34–35 suggest about what might happen?

9. **lime** birdlime, a sticky substance smeared on branches to catch birds.

10. **gin** trap.

Comprehension

Where has Macduff gone, and how will Macbeth revenge himself against Macduff?

40 **LADY MACDUFF.** Why, I can buy me twenty at any market.

SON. Then you'll buy 'em to sell[11] again.

LADY MACDUFF. Thou speak'st with all thy wit, and yet i' faith,
   With wit enough for thee.[12]

SON. Was my father a traitor, mother?

45 **LADY MACDUFF.** Ay, that he was.

SON. What is a traitor?

LADY MACDUFF. Why, one that swears and lies.[13]

SON. And be all traitors that do so?

LADY MACDUFF. Every one that does so is a traitor, and must
   be hanged.

50 **SON.** And must they all be hanged that swear and lie?

LADY MACDUFF. Every one.

SON. Who must hang them?

LADY MACDUFF. Why, the honest men.

SON. Then the liars and swearers are fools; for there are liars and
55   swearers enow[14] to beat the honest men and hang up them.

LADY MACDUFF. Now, God help thee, poor monkey! But how wilt
   thou do for a father?

SON. If he were dead, you'd weep for him. If you would not, it were
60   a good sign that I should quickly have a new father.

LADY MACDUFF. Poor prattler, how thou talk'st!

[*Enter a* MESSENGER .]

MESSENGER. Bless you, fair dame! I am not to you known,
   Though in your state of honor I am perfect.[15]
65   I doubt[16] some danger does approach you nearly:
   If you will take a homely[17] man's advice,
   Be not found here; hence, with your little ones.
   To fright you thus, methinks I am too savage;

   To do worse to you were fell[18] cruelty,
70   Which is too nigh your person. Heaven preserve you!
   I dare abide no longer.   [*Exit* MESSENGER.]

LADY MACDUFF.   Whither should I fly?
   I have done no harm. But I remember now
   I am in this earthly world, where to do harm
   Is often laudable, to do good sometime
75   Accounted dangerous folly. Why then, alas,
   Do I put up that womanly defense,
   To say I have done no harm?—What are these faces?

[*Enter* MURDERERS.]

MURDERER. Where is your husband?

LADY MACDUFF. I hope, in no place so unsanctified
Where such as thou mayst find him.

80 **MURDERER.**   He's a traitor.

SON. Thou li'st, thou shag-eared[19] villain!

MURDERER.   What, you egg!

[*Stabbing him.*]

Young fry[20] of treachery!

SON.   He has killed me, mother:
Run away, I pray you!   [*Dies.*]

[*Exit* LADY MACDUFF *crying "Murder!" followed by* MURDERERS.]

19. **shag-eared** hairy-eared.

20. **fry** offspring

Comprehension

Whom do Macbeth's men kill?

▼ Critical Viewing

This engraving shows the murderers menacing Macduff's family. In what way does the artist capture the defiance reflected in Act IV, Scene ii, line 81? **INTERPRET**

Imagery

How do the images in Scene iii, lines 1–4 help establish a contrast between Malcolm and Macduff?

1. **Bestride . . . birthdom** Protectively stand over our native land.

2. **Like . . . dolor** similar cry of anguish.

3. **deserve . . . me** earn by betraying me to Macbeth.

4. **wisdom** It is wise.

Scene iii. England. Before the King's palace.

[*Enter* MALCOLM *and* MACDUFF.]

    MALCOLM. Let us seek out some desolate shade, and there
      Weep our sad bosoms empty.

    MACDUFF.   Let us rather
      Hold fast the mortal♦ sword, and like good men
      Bestride our down-fall'n birthdom.[1] Each new morn
5   New widows howl, new orphans cry, new sorrows
      Strike heaven on the face, that it resounds
      As if it felt with Scotland and yelled out
      Like syllable of dolor.[2]

    MALCOLM.   What I believe, I'll wail;
      What know, believe; and what I can redress,
10   As I shall find the time to friend,♦ I will.
      What you have spoke, it may be so perchance.
      This tyrant, whose sole♦ name blisters our tongues,
      Was once thought honest:♦ you have loved him well;
      He hath not touched you yet. I am young; but something
15   You may deserve of him through me;[3] and wisdom[4]
      To offer up a weak, poor, innocent lamb
      T' appease an angry god.

    MACDUFF. I am not treacherous.

LITERATURE IN CONTEXT

Vocabulary Connection

♦ Shifting Meanings

Because language is always changing, some words used by Shakespeare have shifted in meaning.

Mortal (IV, iii, 3) means "deadly," which is somewhat unlike its current meaning, "subject to death or decay."

Friend (IV, iii, 10), which today is a noun, is used as a verb meaning "to be friendly."

Sole (IV, iii, 12), which now means "single" or "one and only," is used as an intensifier meaning "very."

Honest (IV, iii, 13) has the broad sense of "good."

   As you read, be alert to shifts in meaning like these, and use the context of a word or phrase as well as the side notes to help you determine Shakespeare's meaning.

Connect to the Literature

What possible meanings might the word *recoil* have in line 19?

MALCOLM.   But Macbeth is.
            A good and virtuous nature may recoil
20   In an imperial charge. But I shall crave your pardon;
            That which you are, my thoughts cannot transpose:
            Angels are bright still, though the brightest[5] fell:
            Though all things foul would wear[6] the brows of grace,
            Yet grace must still look so.[7]

MACDUFF.   I have lost my hopes.

25 **MALCOLM.** Perchance even there where I did find my doubts.
            Why in that rawness[8] left you wife and child,
            Those precious motives, those strong knots of love,
            Without leave-taking? I pray you,
            Let not my jealousies be your dishonors.
30   But mine own safeties.[9] You may be rightly just
            Whatever I shall think.

MACDUFF.   Bleed, bleed, poor country:
            Great tyranny, lay thou thy basis sure,
            For goodness dare not check thee: wear thou thy wrongs:
            The title is affeered.[10] Fare thee well, lord:
35   I would not be the villain that thou think'st
            For the whole space that's in the tyrant's grasp
            And the rich East to boot.

MALCOLM.   Be not offended:
            I speak not as in absolute fear of you.
            I think our country sinks beneath the yoke;
40   It weeps, it bleeds, and each new day a gash
            Is added to her wounds. I think withal
            There would be hands uplifted in my right;[11]
            And here from gracious England[12] have I offer
            Of goodly thousands: but, for all this,
45   When I shall tread upon the tyrant's head,
            Or wear it on my sword, yet my poor country
            Shall have more vices than it had before,
            More suffer, and more sundry ways than ever,
            By him that shall succeed.

MACDUFF.   What should he be?

50 **MALCOLM.** It is myself I mean, in whom I know
            All the particulars of vice so grafted[13]
            That, when they shall be opened,[14] black Macbeth
            Will seem as pure as snow, and the poor state
            Esteem him as a lamb, being compared
            With my confineless harms.[15]

55 **MACDUFF.**   Not in the legions
            Of horrid hell can come a devil more damned
            In evils to top Macbeth.

5. the brightest Lucifer.

6. would wear desire to wear.

7. so like itself.

8. rawness unprotected state or condition.

9. safeties protections.

10. affeered legally confirmed.

Imagery

Why are the images Malcolm uses to describe Scotland in lines 39–41 more effective than a simple statement that the country is in trouble and getting worse?

11. in my right on behalf of my claim.

12. England king of England.

Vocabulary

sundry (sun´ drē)
adj. various; miscellaneous

13. grafted implanted.

14. opened in bloom.

15. confineless harms unbounded evils.

Comprehension

How does Malcolm describe himself to Macduff?

16. **Luxurious** lecherous.

17. **Sudden** violent.

18. **continent impediments** restraints.

Vocabulary

intemperance (in tem´ pər əns) *n.* lack of restraint

19. **nature** man's nature.

20. **Convey** secretly manage.

21. **affection** character.

Vocabulary

avarice (av´ ə ris) *n.* greed

22. **stanchless** never-ending.

23. **summer-seeming** summerlike.

24. **of** that killed.

25. **foisons** (foi´ zənz) plenty.

26. **mere own** own property.

27. **portable** bearable.

28. **division . . . crime** variations of each kind of crime.

29. **confound** destroy.

MALCOLM.   I grant him bloody,
Luxurious,[16] avaricious, false, deceitful,
Sudden,[17] malicious, smacking of every sin

60   That has a name: but there's no bottom, none,
In my voluptuousness: your wives, your daughters,
Your matrons and your maids, could not fill up
The cistern of my lust, and my desire
All continent impediments[18] would o'erbear,

65   That did oppose my will. Better Macbeth
Than such an one to reign.

MACDUFF.   Boundless intemperance
In nature[19] is a tyranny; it hath been
Th' untimely emptying of the happy throne,
And fall of many kings. But fear not yet

70   To take upon you what is yours: you may
Convey[20] your pleasures in a spacious plenty,
And yet seem cold, the time you may so hoodwink.
We have willing dames enough. There cannot be
That vulture in you, to devour so many

75   As will to greatness dedicate themselves,
Finding it so inclined.

MALCOLM.   With this there grows
In my most ill-composed affection[21] such
A stanchless[22] avarice that, were I King,
I should cut off the nobles for their lands,

80   Desire his jewels and this other's house:
And my more-having would be as a sauce
To make me hunger more, that I should forge
Quarrels unjust against the good and loyal,
Destroying them for wealth.

MACDUFF.   This avarice

85   Sticks deeper, grows with more pernicious root
Than summer-seeming[23] lust, and it hath been
The sword of[24] our slain kings. Yet do not fear.
Scotland hath foisons[25] to fill up your will
Of your mere own.[26] All these are portable,[27]

90   With other graces weighed.

MALCOLM. But I have none: the king-becoming graces,
As justice, verity, temp'rance, stableness,
Bounty, perseverance, mercy, lowliness,
Devotion, patience, courage, fortitude,

95   I have no relish of them, but abound
In the division of each several crime,[28]
Acting it many ways. Nay, had I pow'r, I should
Pour the sweet milk of concord into hell,
Uproar the universal peace, confound[29]

All unity on earth.

100 **MACDUFF.**   O Scotland, Scotland!

MALCOLM. If such a one be fit to govern, speak:
     I am as I have spoken.

MACDUFF.   Fit to govern!
     No, not to live. O nation miserable!
     With an untitled[30] tyrant bloody-sceptered,
105 When shalt thou see thy wholesome days again,
     Since that the truest issue of thy throne[31]
     By his own interdiction[32] stands accursed,
     And does blaspheme his breed?[33] Thy royal father
     Was a most sainted king: the queen that bore thee,
110 Oft'ner upon her knees than on her feet,
     Died[34] every day she lived. Fare thee well!
     These evils thou repeat'st upon thyself
     Hath banished me from Scotland. O my breast,
     Thy hope ends here!

MALCOLM.   Macduff, this noble passion,
115 Child of integrity, hath from my soul
     Wiped the black scruples, reconciled my thoughts
     To thy good truth and honor. Devilish Macbeth
     By many of these trains[35] hath sought to win me
     Into his power; and modest wisdom[36] plucks me
120 From over-credulous haste: but God above
     Deal between thee and me! For even now
     I put myself to thy direction, and
     Unspeak mine own detraction,[37] here abjure
     The taints and blames I laid upon myself,
125 For[38] strangers to my nature. I am yet
     Unknown to woman, never was forsworn,
     Scarcely have coveted what was mine own,
     At no time broke my faith, would not betray
     The devil to his fellow, and delight
130 No less in truth than life. My first false speaking
     Was this upon myself. What I am truly,
     Is thine and my poor country's to command:
     Whither indeed, before thy here-approach,
     Old Siward, with ten thousand warlike men,
135 Already at a point,[39] was setting forth.
     Now we'll together, and the chance of goodness
     Be like our warranted quarrel![40] Why are you silent?

MACDUFF. Such welcome and unwelcome things at once
     'Tis hard to reconcile.

[*Enter a* DOCTOR.]

140 **MALCOLM.** Well, more anon. Comes the King forth, I pray you?

Analyzing Text Structures

How does the image in Act IV, Scene iii, line 98 echo those in Act I, Scene v, line 17 and Act I, Scene v, lines 47–48?

30. **untitled** having no right to the throne.

31. **truest . . . throne** child of the true king.

32. **interdiction** exclusion.

33. **blaspheme his breed** slander his ancestry.

34. **Died** prepared for heaven.

35. **trains** enticements.

36. **modest wisdom** prudence.

Vocabulary

credulous (krej´ ōō ləs) *adj.* tending to believe too readily

37. **detraction** slander.

38. **For** as.

39. **at a point** prepared.

40. **the chance . . . quarrel** May our chance of success equal the justice of our cause.

Comprehension

What response by Macduff convinces Malcolm that Macduff is being honest?

DOCTOR. Ay, sir. There are a crew of wretched souls
That stay[41] his cure: their malady convinces
The great assay of art;[42] but at his touch,
Such sanctity hath heaven given his hand,
They presently amend.[43]

145 **MALCOLM.**   I thank you, doctor.

[*Exit* DOCTOR.]

MACDUFF. What's the disease he means?

MALCOLM.   'Tis called the evil:[44]
A most miraculous work in this good King,
Which often since my here-remain in England
I have seen him do. How he solicits heaven,
150 Himself best knows: but strangely-visited people,
All swoll'n and ulcerous, pitiful to the eye,
The mere[45] despair of surgery, he cures,
Hanging a golden stamp[46] about their necks,
Put on with holy prayers: and 'tis spoken,
155 To the succeeding royalty he leaves
The healing benediction. With this strange virtue
He hath a heavenly gift of prophecy,
And sundry blessings hang about his throne
That speak him full of grace.

[*Enter* ROSS.]

MACDUFF.   See, who comes here?

160 **MALCOLM.** My countryman; but yet I know him not.

MACDUFF. My ever gentle[47] cousin, welcome hither.

MALCOLM. I know him now: good God, betimes[48] remove
The means that makes us strangers!

ROSS.   Sir, amen.

MACDUFF. Stands Scotland where it did?

ROSS.   Alas, poor country!
165 Almost afraid to know itself! It cannot
Be called our mother but our grave, where nothing[49]
But who knows nothing is once seen to smile;
Where sighs and groans, and shrieks that rent the air,
Are made, not marked, where violent sorrow seems
170 A modern ecstasy.[50] The dead man's knell
Is there scarce asked for who,[51] and good men's lives
Expire before the flowers in their caps,
Dying or ere they sicken.

MACDUFF.   O, relation
Too nice,[52] and yet too true!

---

41. stay wait for.

42. convinces . . . art defies the efforts of medical science.

43. presently amend immediately recover.

44. evil scrofula (skräf′ yə lə), skin disease called "the king's evil" because it was believed that it could be cured by the king's touch.

45. mere utter.
46. stamp coin.

47. gentle noble.

48. betimes quickly.

Analyzing Text Structures

Connect the images in lines 164-173 with similar images revealing Scotland as a hellish place.

49. nothing no one.

50. modern ecstasy ordinary emotion.

51. The dead . . . who People can no longer keep track of Macbeth's victims.

52. nice exact.

MALCOLM. What's the newest grief?

175 **ROSS.** That of an hour's age doth hiss the speaker;[53]
    Each minute teems[54] a new one.

MACDUFF. How does my wife?

ROSS. Why, well.

MACDUFF. And all my children?

ROSS. Well too.

MACDUFF. The tyrant has not battered at their peace?

ROSS. No; they were well at peace when I did leave 'em.

180 **MACDUFF.** Be not a niggard of your speech: how goes 't?

ROSS. When I came hither to transport the tidings,
    Which I have heavily borne, there ran a rumor
    Of many worthy fellows that were out;[55]
    Which was to my belief witnessed[56] the rather,
185   For that I saw the tyrant's power[57] afoot.
    Now is the time of help. Your eye in Scotland
    Would create soldiers, make our women fight,
    To doff[58] their dire distresses.

MALCOLM. Be 't their comfort
    We are coming thither. Gracious England hath
190   Lent us good Siward and ten thousand men;
    An older and a better soldier none
    That Christendom gives out.

ROSS. Would I could answer
    This comfort with the like! But I have words

53. **That . . . speaker** Report of the grief of an hour ago is hissed as stale news.

54. **teems** gives birth to.

55. **out** in rebellion.

56. **witnessed** confirmed.

57. **power** army.

58. **doff** put off.

Imagery
Why do you think Ross uses such an exaggerated image in lines 186–188?

Comprehension
What report from Scotland does Ross bring?

▼ **Critical Viewing**
How does this castle compare with your image of Inverness? **CONNECT**

That would be howled out in the desert air,
Where hearing should not latch[59] them.

195 **MACDUFF.**   What concern they?
The general cause or is it a fee-grief[60]
Due to some single breast?

ROSS.   No mind that's honest
But in it shares some woe, though the main part
Pertains to you alone.

MACDUFF.   If it be mine,
200 Keep it not from me, quickly let me have it.

ROSS. Let not your ears despise my tongue for ever,
Which shall possess them with the heaviest sound
That ever yet they heard.

MACDUFF.   Humh! I guess at it.

ROSS. Your castle is surprised; your wife and babes
205 Savagely slaughtered. To relate the manner,
Were, on the quarry[61] of these murdered deer,
To add the death of you.

MALCOLM.   Merciful heaven!
What, man! Ne'er pull your hat upon your brows;
Give sorrow words. The grief that does not speak
210 Whispers the o'er-fraught[62] heart and bids it break.

MACDUFF. My children too?

ROSS.   Wife, children, servants, all
That could be found.

MACDUFF.   And I must be from thence!
My wife killed too?

ROSS.   I have said.

MALCOLM.   Be comforted.
Let's make us med'cines of our great revenge,
215 To cure this deadly grief.

MACDUFF. He has no children. All my pretty ones?
Did you say all? O hell-kite![63] All?
What, all my pretty chickens and their dam
At one fell swoop?

MALCOLM. Dispute it[64] like a man.

220 **MACDUFF.**   I shall do so;
But I must also feel it as a man.
I cannot but remember such things were,
That were most precious to me. Did heaven look on,
And would not take their part? Sinful Macduff,

59. **latch** catch.

60. **fee-grief** personal grief.

Imagery

How does the image in line 206 emphasize the ghastly fate of Macduff's family?

61. **quarry** heap of game slain in a hunt.

62. **o'er-fraught** over-burdened.

63. **hell-kite** hellish bird of prey.

64. **Dispute it** Counter your grief.

◀ **Critical Viewing**

What emotions does this actor playing Macduff project? Explain. **INTERPRET**

225 They were all struck for thee! Naught[65] that I am,
Not for their own demerits but for mine
Fell slaughter on their souls. Heaven rest them now!

MALCOLM. Be this the whetstone of your sword. Let grief
Convert to anger; blunt not the heart, enrage it.

66. **front to front** face to face.

230 **MACDUFF.** O, I could play the woman with mine eyes,
And braggart with my tongue! But, gentle heavens,
Cut short all intermission; front to front[66]
Bring thou this fiend of Scotland and myself;
Within my sword's length set him. If he 'scape,
235 Heaven forgive him too!

MALCOLM.   This time goes manly.
Come, go we to the King. Our power is ready;

67. **Our . . . leave** We need only to take our leave.

Our lack is nothing but our leave.[67] Macbeth
Is ripe for shaking, and the pow'rs above

68. **Put . . . instruments** urge us onward as their agents.

Put on their instruments.[68] Receive what cheer you may.
240 The night is long that never finds the day.   [*Exit.*]

Critical Reading

Cite textual evidence to support your responses.

1. **Key Ideas and Details (a)** What are the predictions made by the second and third apparitions? **(b) Analyze:** Why does Macbeth readily accept these predictions?

2. **Key Ideas and Details (a)** What happens to Macduff's family? **(b) Infer:** What does the fate of Macduff's family suggest about Macbeth's state of mind?

3. **Key Ideas and Details (a)** How does Malcolm test Macduff? **(b) Analyze:** What does this test reveal about both Malcolm and Macduff? Explain.

4. **Integration of Knowledge and Ideas (a)** How does Macduff respond when asked to take the news about his family "like a man"? **(b) Interpret:** How would you characterize Macduff, based on his reaction to the murder of his wife and son? **(c) Compare and Contrast:** Compare and contrast Macduff's understanding of manhood with definitions of it earlier in the play.

5. **Integration of Knowledge and Ideas (a) Hypothesize:** If Shakespeare were alive today, would he argue that evildoers are primarily influenced by genetics, upbringing, or their own free choice? Base your answer on evidence from Act IV. **(b) Evaluate:** Would you agree with his position? Explain.

Literary Analysis

Common Core State Standards

1. Craft and Structure Identify a passage in Act IV that has vivid **imagery.** Using a chart like the one shown, indicate the emotions that the images express.

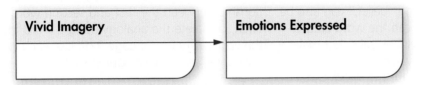

Vivid Imagery		Emotions Expressed
	→	

2. Craft and Structure (a) In Act IV, Scene i, and Act IV, Scene ii, find images that show that children and babies are in danger from Macbeth and also threaten him. **(b)** Why is Macbeth at war with the future, which babies and children represent?

3. Craft and Structure (a) Find two passages in Act IV, Scene iii, with images of sickness. **(b)** Explain how these images relate to the conflict between Macbeth and Malcolm.

4. Craft and Structure In Act IV, Scene iii, identify two **archetypal images of banishment from an ideal world,** images that describe Scotland in terms of weeping, bleeding, or both.

5. Integration of Knowledge and Ideas What do the images of banishment from an ideal world and the references to the Christian underworld indicate about Macbeth's rule over Scotland? Explain.

6. Craft and Structure Analyze the text structure of *Macbeth* by identifying three patterns of imagery that occur throughout Act IV. Remember that a pattern of imagery is a series of related images—for example, images of blood.

7. Integration of Knowledge and Ideas Explain how each of the patterns of imagery you identified relates to an important theme—an insight into life or comment on life—in the play.

8. Integration of Knowledge and Ideas Demonstrate how several patterns of imagery work together to convey the play's meaning.

9. Integration of Knowledge and Ideas (a) Would *Macbeth* be less rich if Shakespeare had not used imagery to reinforce the themes of his play? Why or why not? **(b)** Is it necessary for the reader to experience the images with his or her senses to make them truly effective? Explain, citing specific details from the text.

Writing

2.b. Develop the topic thoroughly by selecting the most significant and relevant facts, extended definitions, concrete details, quotations, or other information and examples appropriate to the audience's knowledge of the topic. *(p. 398)*

2.f. Provide a concluding statement or section that follows from and supports the information or explanation presented. *(p. 398)*

5. Develop and strengthen writing as needed by planning, revising, editing, rewriting, or trying a new approach, focusing on addressing what is most significant for a specific purpose and audience. *(p. 398)*

Language

4.d. Verify the preliminary determination of the meaning of a word or phrase. *(p. 398)*

Vocabulary Acquisition and Use

Word Analysis: Latin Word Root -cred-

The Latin root -cred- means "belief." For example, to be *credulous* is "to believe something too readily." The word *creed*, meaning "belief," can also be traced back to this root, as can the word *credentials*, meaning "qualifications," or traits that make a person trustworthy or believable.

Working with a partner, use the word parts shown below to build six -cred- words. Then, write the meanings of these words.

in-	-ulous
dis-	-ulity
mis-	-ible

When you are done, verify your words and definitions by referring to a dictionary.

Vocabulary: Analogies

An analogy compares two relationships to show their similarity. For each item, determine the relationship between the first and second words. Then, complete the analogy using a word from the vocabulary list on page 378. Use each word only once, and explain your choice.

1. *suspicion : trust ::* _____ *: generosity*
2. *expensive : costly ::* _____ *: assorted*
3. *independent : adult ::* _____ *: child*
4. *formality : ease ::* _____ *: self-control*
5. *offensive : rude ::* _____ *: sensible*
6. *invulnerable : susceptible ::* _____ *: harmless*

Writing to Sources

Informative Text *Archetypal images of banishment from an ideal world*—otherwise known as the archetype of the "fall"—often appear in works dealing with the loss of innocence or with a character's descent into a state of evil. Write an **essay** analyzing Shakespeare's use of such images in *Macbeth*. Identify the "ideal world" from which one or more characters are expelled, as well as the causes of this banishment. Remember to trace the descent into evil by means of Shakespeare's imagery.

Prewriting Create a flow chart like the one shown to trace a central character's "fall." Identify imagery reflecting the ideal state in which the character exists at first. Then list reasons why this ideal state does not last. (The reasons may be internal character traits, external events, or both.) Finally, describe the evil into which the character has fallen.

Drafting Begin with a statement that summarizes the fall from the ideal state shown in your prewriting chart. Develop your essay by indicating the ways Shakespeare uses imagery to picture this fall. Support your points by making *specific and detailed references* to the text, and note how these passages might affect *readers' or viewers' emotions.*

Revising Revise to add breadth and depth to your essay. Consider adding comparisons or references to other works of literature that use archetypal images of banishment. Alternatively, provide a concluding section about *nuances or complexities* that make Shakespeare's use of these archetypal images more convincing than that of other authors.

Model: Charting a Character's Fall

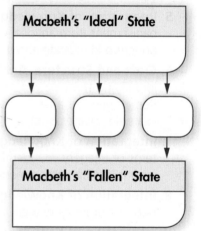

Macbeth's "Ideal" State

Macbeth's "Fallen" State

Critical Commentary

"Macbeth as King"

Ian Johnston

Ian Johnston teaches at Malaspina-University College, Nanaimo, BC, Canada. His analysis of Macbeth's character in the later acts of the play comes from his lecture entitled "Introduction to Macbeth."

. . . It is worth asking ourselves what in Macbeth commands our attention throughout the second half of this play. After all, he is in many respects the least admirable tragic hero of all. In characters like Othello, Romeo, Cleopatra, Lear, Antony, Hamlet . . . we can usually find something to admire. We may not like them (they are not very likable people), but there is something in their characters or their situations on which we can hang some sympathy, even if there is not enough for us to rationalize away their actions. But Macbeth is a mass murderer, who does away with friends, colleagues, woman and children, often for no apparent reason other than his own desires. Why do we keep our attention focused on him?

The answer, I think, has to do with the quality of his mind, his horrible determination to see the entire evil business through. Having, with the murder of Duncan, taken charge of the events which shape his life, he is not now going to relinquish the responsibility for securing his desires. The most remarkable quality of the man in this process is the clear-eyed awareness of what is happening to him personally. He is suffering horribly throughout, but he will not crack or seek any other remedy than what he alone can deliver. If that means damning himself even further, then so be it.

This stance certainly does not make Macbeth likable or (from our perspective) in many respects admirable. But it does confer a heroic quality upon his tragic course of action. He simply will not compromise with the world, and he will pay whatever price that decision exacts from him, even though as his murderous career continues he becomes increasingly aware of what it is costing him.

▲ Macbeth demands to know the future from the Witches.

Key Ideas and Details According to Johnston, is Macbeth among Shakespeare's more admirable tragic heroes? Explain.

Building Knowledge and Insight   *Macbeth, Act V*

Close Reading Focus

Shakespearean Tragedy

Shakespearean tragedy usually contains these elements:

- A central character of high rank and great personal quality, yet with a **tragic flaw** or weakness
- Causally related events that lead this character to disaster, at least partly through his or her flaw
- An experience of pity, fear, and awe for the audience
- Lively action that creates a vivid spectacle and the use of comic scenes to temper and offset the mood of sadness

As you read, consider how Shakespeare introduces Macbeth as a character (as a war hero) and how the author then develops the character, adding complexity and depth and ultimately revealing a tragic flaw. Note, too, how Shakespeare chooses to include plot events that lead to Macbeth's downfall and that make his tragic flaw evident.

Reading a Shakespearean tragedy is often uplifting despite the disasters that befall the hero. This positive experience results from the **tragic impulse,** which shows the tragic hero acting nobly.

Preparing to Read Complex Texts As products of a certain time, great plays reflect the beliefs of their period. To better understand a great play, therefore, you should **relate the work to the major themes and issues of its period.** Following are ways to uncover the philosophical, political, and religious influences that shaped *Macbeth*'s characters and settings:

- Be aware of the importance Elizabethans placed on the king's role in maintaining social order and how they linked order in the heavens with order in society.
- Compare the ideas that characters express with modern ideas.

In using the second method, focus on the ideas expressed by the doctor in Act V, Scene i. Use a chart like the one shown to compare his ideas with those a modern psychiatrist might express.

Vocabulary

You will encounter the words listed here in the text that follows. Copy the words into your notebook, listing them by two-, three-, and four-syllable words.

perturbation	clamorous
recoil	harbingers
antidote	vulnerable
pristine	

**Common Core
State Standards**

Reading Literature
3. Analyze the impact of the author's choices regarding how to develop and relate elements of a story or drama.

Comparison of Beliefs

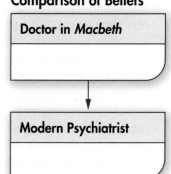

Doctor in *Macbeth*

Modern Psychiatrist

Review and Anticipate

In Act IV, Macbeth learns from the witches that he must "Beware Macduff!" but that he need not fear any man "of woman born." He also learns he will never be vanquished until the forest itself marches against him. However, he sees a vision indicating that Banquo will indeed father a long line of kings.

Armed with his new knowledge, Macbeth orders the murder of Macduff's wife and son. Macduff himself is in England to join forces with Malcolm and is overcome when he hears the news. Nevertheless, he and Malcolm will lead an army against Macbeth.

Act V will determine the outcome as Macbeth, grown reckless in evil, battles against Malcolm and his men.

ACT V

Scene i. Dunsinane. In the castle.

[*Enter a* DOCTOR OF PHYSIC *and a* WAITING-GENTLEWOMAN.]

DOCTOR. I have two nights watched with you, but can perceive no truth in your report. When was it she last walked?

GENTLEWOMAN. Since his Majesty went into the field.[1] I have seen
5   her rise from her bed, throw her nightgown upon her, unlock her closet,[2] take forth paper, fold it, write upon 't, read it, afterwards seal it, and again return to bed; yet all this while in a most fast sleep.

DOCTOR. A great perturbation in nature, to receive at
10   once the benefit of sleep and do the effects of watching![3] In this slumb'ry agitation, besides her walking, and other actual performances, what, at any time, have you heard her say?

15 **GENTLEWOMAN.** That, sir, which I will not report after her.

DOCTOR. You may to me, and 'tis most meet[4] you should.

GENTLEWOMAN. Neither to you nor anyone, having no witness to confirm my speech.

[*Enter* LADY MACBETH, *with a taper.*]

Lo you, here she comes! This is her very guise,[5] and, upon my
20   life, fast asleep! Observe her; stand close.[6]

DOCTOR. How came she by that light?

GENTLEWOMAN. Why, it stood by her. She has light by her continually. 'Tis her command.

25 **DOCTOR.** You see, her eyes are open.

▲ Critical Viewing
Who will slay Macbeth with a sword like this one? **PREDICT**

1. field battlefield.

2. closet chest.

Vocabulary
perturbation (pʉr′ tər bā′ shən) *n.* disturbance

3. effects of watching deeds of one awake.

4. meet suitable.

5. guise custom.

6. close hidden.

Comprehension
Why has the gentlewoman summoned the doctor?

GENTLEWOMAN. Ay, but their sense[7] are shut.

DOCTOR. What is it she does now? Look, how she rubs her hands.

GENTLEWOMAN. It is an accustomed action with her, to seem thus washing her hands: I have known her continue in this a quarter of an hour.

LADY MACBETH. Yet here's a spot.

DOCTOR. Hark! She speaks. I will set down what comes from her, to satisfy[8] my remembrance the more strongly.

LADY MACBETH. Out, damned spot! Out, I say! One: two: why, then 'tis time to do 't. Hell is murky. Fie, my lord, fie! A soldier, and afeard? What need we fear who knows it, when none can call our pow'r to accompt?[9] Yet who would have thought the old man to have had so much blood in him?

DOCTOR. Do you mark that?

LADY MACBETH. The Thane of Fife had a wife. Where is she now? What, will these hands ne'er be clean? No more o' that, my lord, no more o' that! You mar all with this starting.

DOCTOR. Go to, go to! You have known what you should not.

GENTLEWOMAN. She has spoke what she should not, I am sure of that. Heaven knows what she has known.

LADY MACBETH. Here's the smell of the blood still. All the perfumes of Arabia will not sweeten this little hand. Oh, oh, oh!

DOCTOR. What a sigh is there! The heart is sorely charged.[10]

GENTLEWOMAN. I would not have such a heart in my bosom for the dignity[11] of the whole body.

DOCTOR. Well, well, well—

GENTLEWOMAN. Pray God it be, sir.

DOCTOR. This disease is beyond my practice. Yet I have known those which have walked in their sleep who have died holily in their beds.

LADY MACBETH. Wash your hands; put on your nightgown; look not so pale! I tell you yet again, Banquo's buried. He cannot come out on 's[12] grave.

DOCTOR. Even so?

LADY MACBETH. To bed, to bed! There's knocking at the gate. Come, come, come, come, give me your hand!

7. **sense** powers of sight.

8. **satisfy** support.

9. **to accompt** into account.

Shakespearean Tragedy
Does the sleepwalking scene suggest that Lady Macbeth is a tragic heroine? Explain.

10. **charged** burdened.

11. **dignity** worth.

◀ Critical Viewing
Identify four details from the sleepwalking scene (V, i) the artist illustrates in this picture. **CONNECT**

12. **on 's** of his.

Comprehension
What does Lady Macbeth do and say as she sleepwalks?

70 What's done cannot be undone. To bed, to bed, to bed!

[*Exit* LADY MACBETH.]

DOCTOR. Will she go now to bed?

GENTLEWOMAN. Directly.

DOCTOR. Foul whisp'rings are abroad. Unnatural deeds
Do breed unnatural troubles. Infected minds
To their deaf pillows will discharge their secrets.
75 More needs she the divine than the physician.
God, God forgive us all! Look after her;
Remove from her the means of all annoyance,[13]
And still keep eyes upon her. So good night.
My mind she has mated[14] and amazed my sight:
80 I think, but dare not speak.

GENTLEWOMAN.   Good night, good doctor.

[*Exit.*]

Scene ii. *The country near Dunsinane.*

[*Drum and colors. Enter* MENTEITH, CAITHNESS, ANGUS, LENNOX, SOLDIERS.]

MENTEITH. The English pow'r[1] is near, led on by Malcolm,
His uncle Siward and the good Macduff.
Revenges burn in them; for their dear causes
Would to the bleeding and the grim alarm
Excite the mortified man.[2]

5 **ANGUS.**   Near Birnam Wood
Shall we well meet them; that way are they coming.

CAITHNESS. Who knows if Donalbain be with his brother?

LENNOX. For certain, sir, he is not. I have a file[3]
Of all the gentry: there is Siward's son,
10 And many unrough[4] youths that even now
Protest[5] their first of manhood.

MENTEITH.   What does the tyrant?

CAITHNESS. Great Dunsinane he strongly fortifies.
Some say he's mad; others, that lesser hate him,
Do call it valiant fury: but, for certain,
15 He cannot buckle his distempered cause
Within the belt of rule.[6]

ANGUS.   Now does he feel
His secret murders sticking on his hands;
Now minutely revolts upbraid his faith-breach.[7]
Those he commands move only in command,
20 Nothing in love. Now does he feel his title

Relating a Work to the Issues of Its Period

What can you infer about medicine during this time from the doctor's words in lines 72–80?

13. **annoyance** injury.

14. **mated** baffled.

1. **pow'r** army.

2. **Would . . . man** would incite a dead man to join the bloody, grim call to arms.

3. **file** list.

4. **unrough** beardless.

5. **Protest** assert.

Shakespearean Tragedy

Do you agree with those whom Caithness quotes in Scene ii, line 13? Is Macbeth "mad"? Why or why not?

6. **rule** self-control.

7. **minutely . . . faith-breach** every minute revolts rebuke his disloyalty.

Hang loose about him, like a giant's robe
Upon a dwarfish thief.

MENTEITH.   Who then shall blame
His pestered[8] senses to recoil and start,
When all that is within him does condemn
Itself for being there?

25 **CAITHNESS.**   Well, march we on,
To give obedience where 'tis truly owed.
Meet we the med'cine of the sickly weal,[9]
And with him pour we, in our country's purge,
Each drop of us.[10]

LENNOX.   Or so much as it needs
30 To dew the sovereign flower and drown the weeds.[11]
Make we our march towards Birnam.

[*Exit, marching.*]

Scene iii. Dunsinane. In the castle.

[*Enter* MACBETH, DOCTOR, *and* ATTENDANTS.]

MACBETH. Bring me no more reports; let them fly all![1]
Till Birnam Wood remove to Dunsinane
I cannot taint[2] with fear. What's the boy Malcolm?
Was he not born of woman? The spirits that know
5 All mortal consequences[3] have pronounced me thus:
"Fear not, Macbeth; no man that's born of woman
Shall e'er have power upon thee." Then fly, false thanes,
And mingle with the English epicures.[4]
The mind I sway[5] by and the heart I bear
10 Shall never sag with doubt nor shake with fear.

[*Enter* SERVANT.]

The devil damn thee black, thou cream-faced loon.[6]
Where got'st thou that goose look?

SERVANT. There is ten thousand—

MACBETH.   Geese, villain?

SERVANT.   Soldiers, sir.

MACBETH. Go prick thy face and over-red thy fear.
15 Thou lily-livered boy. What soldiers, patch?[7]
Death of thy soul! Those linen[8] cheeks of thine
Are counselors to fear. What soldiers, whey-face?

SERVANT. The English force, so please you.

MACBETH. Take thy face hence.   [*Exit* SERVANT.]
Seyton!—I am sick at heart.

8. **pestered** tormented.

Vocabulary

recoil (ri koil´) *v.* to draw back in fear, surprise, or disgust

9. **med'cine . . . weal** Malcolm and his supporters are "the medicine" that will heal "the sickly" commonwealth.

10. **Each . . . us** every last drop of our blood.

11. **dew . . . weeds** water the royal flower (Malcolm) and drown the weeds (Macbeth).

1. **let . . . all** let them all desert me!

2. **taint** become infected.

3. **mortal consequences** future human events.

4. **epicures** gluttons.

5. **sway** move.

6. **loon** fool.

7. **patch** fool.

8. **linen** pale as linen.

Comprehension

Why is Macbeth unafraid even though Malcolm's army is marching against him?

20 When I behold—Seyton, I say!—This push[9]
   Will cheer me ever, or disseat[10] me now.
   I have lived long enough. My way of life
   Is fall'n into the sear,[11] the yellow leaf,
   And that which should accompany old age,
25 As honor, love, obedience, troops of friends,
   I must not look to have; but, in their stead,
   Curses not loud but deep, mouth-honor, breath,
   Which the poor heart would fain deny, and dare not.
   Seyton!

[*Enter* SEYTON.]

SEYTON. What's your gracious pleasure?

30 **MACBETH.**   What news more?

SEYTON. All is confirmed, my lord, which was reported.

MACBETH. I'll fight, till from my bones my flesh be hacked.
   Give me my armor.

SEYTON.   'Tis not needed yet.

MACBETH. I'll put it on.

35 Send out moe[12] horses, skirr[13] the country round.
   Hang those that talk of fear. Give me mine armor.
   How does your patient, doctor?

DOCTOR.   Not so sick, my lord,
   As she is troubled with thick-coming fancies
   That keep her from her rest.

MACBETH.   Cure her of that.
40 Canst thou not minister to a mind diseased,
   Pluck from the memory a rooted sorrow,
   Raze out[14] the written troubles of the brain,
   And with some sweet oblivious antidote
   Cleanse the stuffed bosom of that perilous stuff
   Which weighs upon the heart?

45 **DOCTOR.**   Therein the patient
   Must minister to himself.

   MACBETH. Throw physic[15] to the dogs, I'll none of it.
   Come, put mine armor on. Give me my staff.
   Seyton, send out.—Doctor, the thanes fly from me.—
50 Come, sir, dispatch. If thou couldst, doctor, cast
   The water[16] of my land, find her disease
   And purge it to a sound and pristine health,
   I would applaud thee to the very echo,
   That should applaud again.—Pull 't off,[17] I say.—
55 What rhubarb, senna, or what purgative drug,
   Would scour these English hence? Hear'st thou of them?

   DOCTOR. Ay, my good lord; your royal preparation
   Makes us hear something.

   MACBETH.   Bring it[18] after me.
   I will not be afraid of death and bane[19]
60 Till Birnam Forest come to Dunsinane.

   DOCTOR. [*Aside*] Were I from Dunsinane away and clear,
   Profit again should hardly draw me here.   [*Exit.*]

Scene iv. *Country near Birnam Wood.*

[*Drum and colors. Enter* MALCOLM, SIWARD, MACDUFF, SIWARD'S SON,
MENTEITH, CAITHNESS, ANGUS, *and* SOLDIERS, *marching.*]

   MALCOLM. Cousins, I hope the days are near at hand
   That chambers will be safe.[1]

   MENTEITH.   We doubt it nothing.

   SIWARD. What wood is this before us?

   MENTEITH.   The Wood of Birnam.

   MALCOLM. Let every soldier hew him down a bough
5 And bear 't before him. Thereby shall we shadow[2]
   The numbers of our host, and make discovery[3]
   Err in report of us.

   SOLDIERS.   It shall be done.

   SIWARD. We learn no other but the confident tyrant
   Keeps still in Dunsinane, and will endure
   Our setting down before 't.[4]

10 **MALCOLM.**   'Tis his main hope,
   For where there is advantage to be given
   Both more and less[5] have given him the revolt,
   And none serve with him but constrained things
   Whose hearts are absent too.

15. **physic** medicine.

16. **cast the water** diagnose the illness.

Vocabulary

pristine (pris´ tēn´)
adj. original; unspoiled

17. **Pull 't off** Pull off a piece of armor, which has been put on incorrectly in Macbeth's haste.

18. **it** his armor.

19. **bane** destruction.

Shakespearean Tragedy

How does Malcolm's order in Scene iv, lines 4–7 increase the sense of tension surrounding the play's outcome and Macbeth's fate?

1. **That . . . safe** that people will be safe in their own homes.

2. **shadow** conceal.

3. **discovery** those who see us.

4. **setting down before 't** laying siege to it.

5. **more and less** people of high and low rank.

Comprehension

How will Malcolm's men disguise themselves?

6. **our . . . event** true judgment await the actual outcome.

MACDUFF. Let our just censures
15 Attend the true event,[6] and put we on
Industrious soldiership.

SIWARD. The time approaches,
That will with due decision make us know

7. **owe** own.

What we shall say we have and what we owe.[7]
Thoughts speculative their unsure hopes relate,

8. **strokes . . . arbitrate** fighting must decide.

9. **war** army.

20 But certain issue strokes must arbitrate:[8]
Towards which advance the war.[9] [*Exit, marching.*]

Scene v. Dunsinane. Within the castle.

[*Enter* MACBETH, SEYTON, *and* SOLDIERS, *with drum and colors.*]

MACBETH. Hang out our banners on the outward walls.
The cry is still "They come!" Our castle's strength
Will laugh a siege to scorn. Here let them lie
Till famine and the ague[1] eat them up.
5 Were they not forced[2] with those that should be ours,
We might have met them dareful,[3] beard to beard,
And beat them backward home.

1. **ague** fever.

2. **forced** reinforced.

3. **dareful** boldly.

[*A cry within of women.*]

What is that noise?

SEYTON. It is the cry of women, my good lord. [*Exit.*]

MACBETH. I have almost forgot the taste of fears:
10 The time has been, my senses would have cooled
To hear a night-shriek, and my fell[4] of hair
Would at a dismal treatise[5] rouse and stir

4. **fell** scalp.

5. **treatise** story.

LITERATURE IN CONTEXT

History Connection

The Real Macbeth

The real Macbeth, who ruled Scotland from 1040 to 1057, did, in fact, become king by killing King Duncan. However, Macbeth's claim to the throne was legitimate due to the ancient Scottish custom of tanistry.

According to this system, the ablest, oldest male in an extended royal family could declare war on his competitors for the crown. The real Macbeth declared war on King Duncan and killed him fairly in battle. Eventually, Duncan's son Malcolm led a Northumbrian invasion force into Scotland. In 1057, he killed Macbeth.

Connect to the Literature

Use this history of the real Macbeth to predict the end of the play.

As life were in 't. I have supped full with horrors.
Direness, familiar to my slaughterous thoughts,
Cannot once start[6] me.

[Enter SEYTON.]

15   Wherefore was that cry?

SEYTON. The queen, my lord, is dead.

MACBETH. She should[7] have died hereafter;
There would have been a time for such a word.[8]
Tomorrow, and tomorrow, and tomorrow
20   Creeps in this petty pace from day to day,
To the last syllable of recorded time;
And all our yesterdays have lighted fools
The way to dusty death. Out, out, brief candle!
Life's but a walking shadow, a poor player
25   That struts and frets his hour upon the stage
And then is heard no more. It is a tale
Told by an idiot, full of sound and fury
Signifying nothing.

[Enter a MESSENGER.]

        Thou com'st to use thy tongue; thy story quickly!

30 **MESSENGER.** Gracious my lord,
I should report that which I say I saw,
But know not how to do 't.

MACBETH.   Well, say, sir.

MESSENGER. As I did stand my watch upon the hill,
I looked toward Birnam, and anon, methought,
The wood began to move.

35 **MACBETH.**   Liar and slave!

MESSENGER. Let me endure your wrath, if 't be not so.
Within this three mile may you see it coming;
I say a moving grove.

MACBETH.   If thou speak'st false,
Upon the next tree shalt thou hang alive,
40   Till famine cling[9] thee. If thy speech be sooth,[10]
I care not if thou dost for me as much.
I pull in resolution, and begin
To doubt th' equivocation of the fiend
That lies like truth: "Fear not, till Birnam Wood
45   Do come to Dunsinane!" And now a wood
Comes toward Dunsinane. Arm, arm, and out!
If this which he avouches[11] does appear,
There is nor flying hence nor tarrying here.

Shakespearean Tragedy and the Tragic Impulse

This speech in lines 17–28 is a powerful expression of life's futility. Is Macbeth's story really "a tale/Told by an idiot, full of sound and fury/ Signifying nothing"? Why or why not?

Shakespearean Tragedy

In lines 42–50, how does Macbeth's allusion to the witches' prophecies disclose a growing awareness of his own doom?

Comprehension

To what two things does Macbeth compare life when he hears Lady Macbeth is dead?

12. harness armor.

I 'gin to be aweary of the sun,
50   And wish th' estate o' th' world were now undone.
        Ring the alarum bell! Blow wind, come wrack!
        At least we'll die with harness[12] on our back.   [*Exit.*]

Scene vi. Dunsinane. Before the castle.

[*Drum and colors. Enter* MALCOLM, SIWARD, MACDUFF, *and their army, with boughs.*]

1. leavy leafy.

    MALCOLM. Now near enough. Your leavy[1] screens throw down,
        And show like those you are. You, worthy uncle,
        Shall, with my cousin, your right noble son,
        Lead our first battle.[2] Worthy Macduff and we

2. battle battalion.

5   Shall take upon 's what else remains to do,
        According to our order.[3]

3. order plan.

    SIWARD.   Fare you well.
        Do we find the tyrant's power[4] tonight,
        Let us be beaten, if we cannot fight.

4. power forces.

    MACDUFF. Make all our trumpets speak; give them all breath.
10   Those clamorous harbingers of blood and death.

                                              [*Exit. Alarums continued.*]

Vocabulary
clamorous (klam´ ər əs) *adj.* noisy

harbingers (här´ bin jərz) *n.* forerunners

Scene vii. *Another part of the field.*

[*Enter* MACBETH.]

MACBETH. They have tied me to a stake; I cannot fly,
But bearlike I must fight the course.[1] What's he
That was not born of woman? Such a one
Am I to fear, or none.

[*Enter* YOUNG SIWARD.]

YOUNG SIWARD. What is thy name?

5 **MACBETH.**   Thou'lt be afraid to hear it.

YOUNG SIWARD. No; though thou call'st thyself a hotter name
Than any is in hell.

MACBETH.   My name's Macbeth.

YOUNG SIWARD. The devil himself could not pronounce a title
More hateful to mine ear.

MACBETH.   No, nor more fearful.

10 **YOUNG SIWARD.** Thou liest, abhorrèd tyrant; with my sword
I'll prove the lie thou speak'st.

[*Fight, and* YOUNG SIWARD *slain.*]

MACBETH.   Thou wast born of woman.
But swords I smile at, weapons laugh to scorn,
Brandished by man that's of a woman born.   [*Exit.*]

[*Alarums. Enter* MACDUFF.]

MACDUFF. That way the noise is. Tyrant, show thy face!
15 If thou be'st slain and with no stroke of mine,
My wife and children's ghosts will haunt me still.
I cannot strike at wretched kerns, whose arms
Are hired to bear their staves.[2] Either thou, Macbeth,
Or else my sword, with an unbattered edge,
20 I sheathe again undeeded.[3] There thou shouldst be;
By this great clatter, one of greatest note
Seems bruited.[4] Let me find him, Fortune!
And more I beg not.   [*Exit. Alarums.*]

[*Enter* MALCOLM *and* SIWARD.]

SIWARD. This way, my lord. The castle's gently rend'red:[5]
25 The tyrant's people on both sides do fight;
The noble thanes do bravely in the war;
The day almost itself professes yours,
And little is to do.

MALCOLM.   We have met with foes
That strike beside us.[6]

---

1. **bearlike . . . course** like a bear chained to a stake being attacked by dogs, I must fight until the end.

Shakespearean Tragedy

In Scene vii, does Macbeth show signs of bravery or is he just overconfident because of what the witches said? Explain.

2. **staves** spears.

3. **undeeded** unused.

4. **bruited** reported.

5. **gently rend'red** easily surrendered.

6. **strike . . . us** deliberately miss us.

Comprehension

What is the outcome of the hand-to-hand combat between Macbeth and Young Siward?

SIWARD.　　　　　　　　Enter, sir, the castle.

[*Exit. Alarum.*]

Scene viii. *Another part of the field.*

[*Enter* MACBETH.]

MACBETH.　Why should I play the Roman fool, and die
　　On mine own sword?[1] Whiles I see lives,[2] the gashes
　　Do better upon them.

[*Enter* MACDUFF.]

MACDUFF.　　　　　　　Turn, hell-hound, turn!

MACBETH.　Of all men else I have avoided thee.
5　　But get thee back! My soul is too much charged
　　With blood of thine already.

MACDUFF.　　　　　　　I have no words:
　　My voice is in my sword, thou bloodier villain
　　Than terms can give thee out![3]

[*Fight. Alarum.*]

MACBETH.　　　　　　　Thou losest labor:
　　As easy mayst thou the intrenchant[4] air
10　　With thy keen sword impress[5] as make me bleed:
　　Let fall thy blade on vulnerable crests;
　　I bear a charmèd life, which must not yield
　　To one of woman born.

MACDUFF.　　　　　　　Despair thy charm,
　　And let the angel[6] whom thou still hast served
15　　Tell thee, Macduff was from his mother's womb
　　Untimely ripped.[7]

MACBETH.　Accursèd be that tongue that tells me so,
　　For it hath cowed my better part of man![8]
　　And be these juggling fiends no more believed,
20　　That palter[9] with us in a double sense;
　　That keep the word of promise to our ear,
　　And break it to our hope. I'll not fight with thee.

MACDUFF.　Then yield thee, coward,
　　And live to be the show and gaze o' th' time:[10]
25　　We'll have thee, as our rarer monsters[11] are,
　　Painted upon a pole,[12] and underwrit,
　　"Here may you see the tyrant."

MACBETH.　　　　　　　I will not yield,
　　To kiss the ground before young Malcolm's feet,
　　And to be baited with the rabble's curse.
30　　Though Birnam Wood be come to Dunsinane,

---

1. **play . . . sword** die like Brutus or Cassius, who killed themselves with their own swords in the moment of defeat.

2. **Whiles . . . lives** so long as I see living men.

3. **terms . . . out** words can describe you.

4. **intrenchant** incapable of being cut.

5. **impress** make a dent in.

Vocabulary

vulnerable (vul´ nər ə bəl) *adj.* exposed to attack or harm

6. **angel** fallen angel; fiend.

7. **his . . . ripped** Macduff's mother died before giving birth to him.

8. **better . . . man** courage.

9. **palter** juggle.

10. **gaze o' th' time** spectacle of the age.

11. **monsters** freaks.

12. **Painted . . . pole** pictured on a banner stuck on a pole by a showman's booth.

And thou opposed, being of no woman born,
Yet I will try the last. Before my body
I throw my warlike shield. Lay on, Macduff;
And damned be him that first cries "Hold, enough!"

[*Exit, fighting. Alarums.*]

[*Re-enter fighting, and* MACBETH *slain. Exit* MACDUFF, *with* MACBETH.
Retreat and flourish.[13] *Enter, with drum and colors,*
MALCOLM, SIWARD, ROSS, THANES, *and* SOLDIERS.]

35 **MALCOLM.** I would the friends we miss were safe arrived.

SIWARD. Some must go off;[14] and yet, by these I see,
So great a day as this is cheaply bought.

MALCOLM. Macduff is missing, and your noble son.

ROSS. Your son, my lord, has paid a soldier's debt:
40 He only lived but till he was a man;
The which no sooner had his prowess confirmed
In the unshrinking station[15] where he fought,
But like a man he died.

SIWARD. Then he is dead?

ROSS. Ay, and brought off the field. Your cause of sorrow
45 Must not be measured by his worth, for then
It hath no end.

SIWARD. Had he his hurts before?

ROSS. Ay, on the front.

SIWARD. Why then, God's soldier be he!
Had I as many sons as I have hairs,
I would not wish them to a fairer death:
And so his knell is knolled.

50 **MALCOLM.** He's worth more sorrow,
And that I'll spend for him.

SIWARD. He's worth no more:
They say he parted well and paid his score:
And so God be with him! Here comes newer comfort.

[*Enter* MACDUFF, *with* MACBETH'S *head.*]

MACDUFF. Hail, King! for so thou art: behold, where stands
55 Th' usurper's cursèd head. The time is free.[16]
I see thee compassed with thy kingdom's pearl,[17]
That speak my salutation in their minds,
Whose voices I desire aloud with mine:
Hail, King of Scotland!

ALL. Hail, King of Scotland!

[*Flourish.*]

13. **Retreat and flourish**
trumpet call to withdraw
and fanfare.

14. **go off** die.

15. **unshrinking station**
place where he stood
firmly.

**Relating a Work to the
Issues of Its Period**
What does Siward's reaction
to the death of his son reveal
about the values of patriotism
and honor at this time
(lines 47–53)?

16. **The . . . free** Our country
is liberated.

17. **compassed . . . pearl**
surrounded by the noblest
people in the kingdom.

Comprehension
Who finally slays Macbeth?

60 **MALCOLM.** We shall not spend a large expense of time
Before we reckon with your several loves,[18]
And make us even with you.[19] My thanes and kinsmen,
Henceforth be earls, the first that ever Scotland
In such an honor named. What's more to do,
65 Which would be planted newly with the time[20]—
As calling home our exiled friends abroad
That fled the snares of watchful tyranny,
Producing forth the cruel ministers
Of this dead butcher and his fiendlike queen,
70 Who, as 'tis thought, by self and violent hands
Took off her life—this, and what needful else
That calls upon us, by the grace of Grace
We will perform in measure, time, and place:[21]
So thanks to all at once and to each one,
75 Whom we invite to see us crowned at Scone.

[Flourish. Exit all.]

18. **reckon . . . loves** reward each of you for your devotion.

19. **make . . . you** pay what we owe you.

20. **What's . . . time** what remains to be done at the beginning of this new age.

21. **in measure . . . place** fittingly at the appropriate time and place.

◄ **Critical Viewing**
Based on the scenes shown in the poster, summarize the play. **SUMMARIZE**

Critical Reading

1. **Key Ideas and Details (a)** What does the doctor see in the sleepwalking scene, and what does he speculate about the causes for what he sees? **(b) Analyze:** How have Macbeth and Lady Macbeth reversed roles by the end of the play?

2. **Key Ideas and Details (a)** What does Macbeth say when he hears of Lady Macbeth's death? **(b) Draw Conclusions:** What does his reaction to her death reveal about their relationship and his state of mind?

3. **Key Ideas and Details (a)** What does Macbeth say about the witches when he learns that Birnam Wood is apparently moving and that Macduff "was from his mother's womb / Untimely ripped"? **(b) Infer:** What growing realization do these statements about the witches seem to reflect? **(c) Draw Conclusions:** What is Macbeth's state of mind in his final battle with Macduff? Explain.

4. **Craft and Structure (a)** What occurs in Act V, Scene viii, lines 35–75? **(b) Evaluate:** Would the play be complete if it ended with Macbeth's death but omitted these lines? Why or why not?

5. **Integration of Knowledge and Ideas** Do you think a tragedy could be written about an ordinary person living today? Why or why not?

6. **Integration of Knowledge and Ideas** How do Shakespeare's use of comic relief and his revealing of Macbeth's inner turmoil add new dimensions to tragedy? In responding, use at least two of these Essential Question words: *noble, downfall, tradition, classics.* *[Connecting to the Essential Question: What is the relationship of the writer to tradition?]*

Cite textual evidence to support your responses.

Close Reading Activities *Macbeth, Act V*

Literary Analysis

Common Core State Standards

Language
4.c. Consult general and specialized reference materials, both print and digital, to find the pronunciation of a word or determine or clarify its precise meaning, its part of speech, its etymology, or its standard usage. *(p. 417)*

1. **Key Ideas and Details Relate the play to the major themes and issues of its period** by answering these questions: **(a)** How does the belief in witches influence the setting and the characters? **(b)** How do Elizabethan beliefs in the importance of order add to the tragedy?

2. **Key Ideas and Details (a)** What do the doctor's remarks lead you to infer about Elizabethan concepts of and treatments for mental illness? **(b)** Compare and contrast Elizabethan concepts of mental illness with those of today.

3. **Craft and Structure** Identify all the elements of **Shakespearean tragedy** in *Macbeth*, citing examples from the play.

4. **Key Ideas and Details** Use a chart like this one to show how Banquo's response to the witches emphasizes Macbeth's **tragic flaw.**

| Banquo's Response | Witches' Predictions | Macbeth's Response and Flaw |

5. **Key Ideas and Details (a)** How does Macbeth's tragic flaw lead him to disaster? **(b)** Once Macbeth kills Duncan, can he turn back? Why or why not?

6. **Key Ideas and Details** What role does Lady Macbeth play in Macbeth's choice of evil?

7. **Key Ideas and Details** Find three passages that show how Macbeth's imagination adds to the tragedy. Support your choices.

8. **Integration of Knowledge and Ideas (a)** What positive qualities does Macbeth display in Act V? Explain. **(b)** How do Macbeth's positive qualities contribute to the **tragic impulse** revealed in the play?

9. **Integration of Knowledge and Ideas** In what way does the tragic impulse involve going beyond limitations? Support your answer with references to the play.

Vocabulary Acquisition and Use

Word Analysis: Latin Root -turb-

The root -turb- means "to disturb." To experience perturbation is to experience "a great disturbance." Knowing the meaning of the root -turb-, define the italicized words below. Then, verify your definitions with a dictionary.

1. At the beginning of the play, a captain reports on the turbulence of the battle that is being fought.
2. As the events in Macbeth suggest, the Middle Ages was a turbulent period in the history of Scotland.
3. Elizabethans believed that a perturbation in the heavens meant disorder in society.
4. Macbeth's reaction shows he is extremely perturbed by Fleance's escape.
5. After being stirred, the witches' potion was turbid.

Using Resources to Build Vocabulary

Descriptive Adjectives: Words Relating to Tragedy

The genre of tragedy carries its own lexicon, or vocabulary. This lexicon includes words—many of them Greek in origin—that relate to different elements of the form or to aspects of the tragic characters themselves. Here are some of these words:

agon	chorus
apostrophe	hamartia
catastrophe	hubris
catharsis	peripeteia

Use a dictionary or a digital resource to look up the meanings of these words, and record their definitions. Then, write a brief description of Macbeth using at least three of the words.

Vocabulary: Sentence Completion

Use a word from the vocabulary list on page 400 to complete the sentence, and explain your choice. Use each word only once.

1. The movement of Birnam Wood began with a _____ rustling of trees.
2. The first trees that approached Dunsinane were _____ of the army that followed.
3. Farmers were shocked to see the untouched, _____ wood suddenly move.
4. The trees' unexpected motion made several of the farmers _____ in amazement.
5. This shocking event also made them feel _____ to other strange happenings.
6. They all confessed to a feeling of _____ in their hearts.
7. It was a feeling for which there was no _____.

"It is a tale told by an idiot, full of sound and fury, signifying nothing, and No. 1 on the best-seller list."

Close Reading Activities Continued

Writing to Sources

Argumentative Text Shakespeare critic Stephen Greenblatt has this to say about Macbeth's plot to assassinate King Duncan:

> The lure is strong enough . . . to make him ignore the threat of divine judgment in the afterlife, but still for a fateful moment he holds back:
>
> > *We still have judgement here, that we but teach*
> > *Bloody instructions which, being taught, return*
> > *To plague th'inventor.*
>
> . . . [I]t is not in some imagined other world that your actions will be judged; it is here and now. Judgment in effect means punishment: whatever violent or dishonest things you do will inevitably serve as a lesson for others to do to you.

In an **analytical essay**, evaluate Greenblatt's commentary. Do you agree that Macbeth dreads the earthly consequences of his actions more than he dreads the fate of his soul—or do you think the opposite is true?

Prewriting Use these steps as you prepare to draft your essay:

- Skim the text, looking for imagery, language, or other stylistic devices that shed light on the nature of Macbeth's crisis. Make a list of these elements.

- Review your list as a whole, and decide whether it supports Greenblatt's conclusion, supports the opposite conclusion, or strikes you as utterly ambiguous. If you decide in favor of ambiguity, ask yourself what thematic purpose such ambiguity might serve.

- Express your position in a sentence or two.

Drafting Introduce the drama, Greenblatt's opinion, and your own. Then, choose two or three key passages to analyze. As you draft, refer to your strongest evidence by quoting it.

Revising Review your draft to ensure that you have considered not only the literal meanings of Macbeth's words, but also any underlying currents of tone, mood, or irony. Could subtle elements of your key passages lead someone to draw a different conclusion? If so, revise to anticipate and address these potential interpretations. Finally, be sure you include correct references and citations.

> **Model: Including References and Citations**
>
> As he contemplates the murder of Duncan, Macbeth expresses a concern for eternal consequences—namely, damnation. He speculates that Duncan has been "So clear in his great office, that his virtues / Will plead like angels trumpet-tongued against / The deep damnation of his taking-off" (I.vii.18–20). Even as Macbeth worries about damnation, though, he is more worried that "pity... Shall blow the horrid deed in every eye," here on earth.

A direct reference to Macbeth's first soliloquy strengthens the analysis. Parenthetical citations indicate act, scene, and line numbers.

Common Core State Standards

Writing

1.a. Introduce precise, knowledgeable claim(s), establish the significance of the claim(s), distinguish the claim(s) from alternate or opposing claims, and create an organization that logically sequences claim(s), counterclaims, reasons, and evidence.

5. Develop and strengthen writing as needed by planning, focusing on addressing what is most significant for a specific purpose and audience.

Language

1. Demonstrate command of the conventions of standard English grammar and usage when writing or speaking. (p. 419)

Conventions and Style: Adjective and Adverb Clauses

A subordinate clause that modifies a noun or pronoun is called an **adjective clause.** Adjective clauses tell *what kind* or *which one* about the word they modify. When you see a relative pronoun or a relative adjective at the beginning of a subordinate clause, you may be looking at an adjective clause.

Using Adjective and Adverb Clauses

Example: Macbeth kills Duncan, *who is the king of Scotland.*

The adjective clause, introduced by the relative pronoun *who,* modifies the proper noun *Duncan.*

An **adverb clause** is a subordinate clause that modifies a verb, adjective, adverb, or verbal by telling *where, when, in what way, to what extent, under what condition,* or *why.* Adverb clauses start with subordinating conjunctions such as *although, as if, before, unless, wherever,* and *while.*

Example: *Until he heard the witches' prophecy,* Macbeth harbored no thoughts of murder.

Here, the adverb clause modifies the verb *harbored.* The subordinating conjunction is *until.*

Punctuation Tip: When an adverb clause starts a sentence, it is followed by a comma. If an adverb clause ends a sentence, it is usually not preceded by a comma.

Practice Identify each adjective clause and each adverb clause, and tell what word or words it modifies.

1. They encounter the three witches as they are crossing a moor.
2. He remembers everything that the witches have said.
3. Lady Macbeth's ambition is even greater than her husband's.
4. The bloody dagger seems to lead him to the room where the king sleeps.
5. Macbeth becomes king after he kills Duncan.
6. Lady Macbeth, who is plagued by guilt, starts walking in her sleep.
7. She cannot clean the imaginary bloodstains that she sees on her hands.
8. When Macbeth hears of his wife's death, he falls into a state of despair.
9. He hires murderers because he sees Banquo as a threat.
10. Macduff joins Prince Malcolm, who has raised an army to challenge the tyrannical new king.

Writing and Speaking Conventions

A. Writing Use each subordinate clause below in a sentence. Then tell which word the clause modifies and what type of clause it is.

1. after he wins a military battle
2. who ruled Scotland
3. because his wife persuaded him

   Example: after he wins a military battle

   Sentence: After he wins a military battle, Macbeth is made Thane of Cawdor.

   Word Modified; Type of Clause: is made; adverb clause

B. Speaking Describe a set design for your favorite scene from *Macbeth.* Include at least one adjective clause and one adverb clause.

THE CHANGING TRAGIC HERO

RENAISSANCE ENGLAND
The Tragedy of Macbeth
—William Shakespeare (1564 – 1616)

ANCIENT GREECE
Oedipus the King
—Sophocles (496–406 B.C.)

EARLY 19TH-CENTURY GERMANY
Faust
—Johann Wolfgang von Goethe (1749–1832)

LATE 19TH-CENTURY NORWAY
A Doll's House
—Henrik Ibsen (1828–1906)

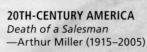

20TH-CENTURY AMERICA
Death of a Salesman
—Arthur Miller (1915–2005)

Comparing Literary Works

from *Macbeth* by William Shakespeare
• from *Oedipus the King* by Sophocles •
from *Faust* by Wolfgang Von Goethe

Comparing Tragedy Past and Present

Tragedy Tragedy had its origins in ancient Greece, where Aeschylus, Sophocles, and Euripides created immortal verse dramas. Greek tragedy typically featured a high-born figure (called the **tragic hero**) whose **tragic flaw**—a mistake or unwise decision—leads to ruin. The audience felt sorrow and pity for the hero's plight. A chorus commented on the action, and fate or supernatural elements also played a role.

Rediscovered in the Renaissance, ancient tragedies served as models for a golden age of European drama, including the masterpieces of Shakespeare. In the nineteenth century, Romantic verse tragedies, like Goethe's *Faust*, focused on the protagonist's urge to go beyond all limits. Later in the century, this type of drama gave way to modern realistic tragedies like those of Ibsen and Chekhov. Such tragedies featured ordinary heroes whose downfall stemmed from social ills. More recent playwrights, like Arthur Miller, continued in this realistic vein.

As you read the selections from *Oedipus the King* and *Faust*, use a chart like the one shown to compare them to Shakespeare's *Macbeth*.

Common Core State Standards

Reading Literature
10. By the end of grade 12, read and comprehend literature, including dramas, at the high end of the grades 11–CCR text complexity band independently and proficiently.

Language
6. Demonstrate independence in gathering vocabulary knowledge when considering a word or phrase important to comprehension or expression.

	Macbeth	*Oedipus*	*Faust*
tragic hero	Scottish nobleman		
tragic flaw	murders king and others due to excessive ambition		
fate/supernatural elements	witches and apparitions predict the future		
style elements	verse for high-born characters; soliloquies; asides; no chorus		

Gather Vocabulary Knowledge

The words *account, reckoning, infinite,* and *constitutionally* appear in these excerpts. Use a **dictionary** to find each word's definition. Then, use other references to explore these words:

- **Specialized Dictionaries:** Use specialized dictionaries, such as those that focus on politics, to discover whether the words have technical meanings. When you encounter the word, decide whether the author intended the technical meaning or not.

- **Book of Quotations:** Use an online or print collection of quotations to find a quotation that contains each of the words. In a sentence or two, analyze the word's connotations in the context of the quotation.

SOPHOCLES

(496 B.C.–406 B.C.)

Sophocles' (säf´ ə klēz´) life corresponded with the splendid rise and tragic fall of fifth-century Athens. At 16, he was one of the young men chosen by the city to perform a choral ode, dancing and singing in a public celebration of the Athenian naval victory over the Persians at Salamis. In 442 B.C., he was one of the treasurers of the imperial league, which was organized to resist Persia. With Pericles, Sophocles served as one of the generals in the war against the island of Samos, which later tried to secede from the Athenian league. In 413 B.C., he was also appointed to a special government committee when the Athenian expedition to Sicily failed. He died in 406 B.C., two years before Athens surrendered to Sparta in the Peloponnesian War.

Winning Playwright Sophocles' life also coincided with the rise and fall of the Golden Age of Greek tragedy. His career as a dramatist began in 468 B.C. when he entered the Dionysia (dī´ ə nē´ sē ə), the annual theatrical competition dedicated to the god Dionysus (dī´ ə nī´ səs). Competing against the established and brilliant playwright Aeschylus (es´ ki ləs), Sophocles won first prize. Over the next 62 years, he wrote more than 120 plays, 24 of which won first prize; those that did not come in first placed second. Yet only seven of Sophocles' plays have survived intact.

Enriching the Drama Greek plays had their origins in religious festivals honoring the god Dionysus. At first, a chorus narrated stories of the god's life in song. The choral leader would occasionally step forward to recite part of the story alone. Eventually, the recitation grew longer and involved a second speaker. Sophocles increased the number of singers in the chorus and introduced a third speaking part. The addition of a third actor allowed for more dramatically complex dialogue than that of the earlier plays. Sophocles also introduced technical innovations to Greek tragedy, which was presented in an open-air theater with few props. For instance, he was the first to use a crane that lowered actors "miraculously" onto the stage.

Faithfulness to Human Experience In addition to his technical innovations, Sophocles is known for his fidelity to universal human experience. In his plays, the world order consists of human beings, nature, and the inscrutable forces of the gods and fate. Sophocles suggests that while gods can predetermine or influence human action, they do not necessarily define one's character. People are responsible for finding out who they are and where they belong; they must then take moral responsibility for their lives.

"Numberless are the world's wonders, but none / More wonderful than man."
—Sophocles

from Oedipus the King

Translated by David Grene

— BACKGROUND According to the myth on which Sophocles' play is based, King Laius and Queen Jocasta of Thebes learn from an oracle that their son will kill his father and marry his mother. Horrified, they pin together their baby son's feet and give him to a servant to leave on Mount Cithaeron to die. The servant instead gives the baby to a shepherd, who gives him to King Polybus and Queen Merope of Corinth. They name him Oedipus, meaning "swollen feet," and raise him as their own. When Oedipus learns from the oracle that he will kill his father and marry his mother, he thinks this fate refers to Polybus and Merope and so flees Corinth. Enraged by a chariot driver who tries to run him off the road, he kills the driver and his passenger. He then comes to Thebes, which is being terrorized by a monster called the Sphinx, which will let no one enter Thebes until the riddle it poses is solved. Oedipus solves the riddle and, as a reward, marries the recently widowed Jocasta, becoming king of Thebes. He has two sons and two daughters and rules successfully for twenty years. Then a plague breaks out, and the oracle says that it will not end until Laius' murderer is exiled from Thebes.

The following selection, which concludes the play, occurs soon after Oedipus learns that Jocasta is his biological mother and that the man he killed on the road was Laius, his biological father. Horrified by their sins, Jocasta has taken her own life, and Oedipus has blinded himself.

OEDIPUS: . . . come—it's unfit to say what is unfit
to do.—I beg of you in God's name hide me
1520   somewhere outside your country, yes, or kill me,
or throw me into the sea, to be forever
out of your sight. Approach and deign to touch me

Comprehension
What does Oedipus learn from the oracle?

for all my wretchedness, and do not fear.
No man but I can bear my evil doom.

1525 **CHORUS:** Here Creon comes in fit time to perform
or give advice in what you ask of us.
Creon is left sole ruler in your stead.

OEDIPUS: Creon! Creon! What shall I say to him?
How can I justly hope that he will trust me?
In what is past I have been proved towards him
1530 an utter liar.

[*Enter* CREON.]

CREON: Oedipus, I've come
not so that I might laugh at you nor taunt you
with evil of the past. But if you still
are without shame before the face of men
1535 reverence at least the flame that gives all life,
our Lord the Sun, and do not show unveiled
to him pollution such that neither land
nor holy rain nor light of day can welcome.

[*To a* SERVANT.]

Be quick and take him in. It is most decent
that only kin should see and hear the troubles
1540 of kin.

OEDIPUS: I beg you, since you've torn me from
my dreadful expectations and have come
in a most noble spirit to a man

Comparing Tragedies

What important information does the chorus supply to the audience in these lines?

Vocabulary

reverence (rev´ rəns) *v.* show great respect

LITERATURE IN CONTEXT

The Greek Chorus and Players

In Greek tragedies, the role of the chorus was central to the production and to the meaning of the play. The chorus consisted of 12 or 15 dancers called *choreuts,* who were young men about to enter the military. The chorus danced as it sang, moving from right to left during the strophe (strō´ fē), then left to right during the antistrophe (an tis´ trə fē).

Originally, plays included only one actor in addition to the chorus. Thespis, from whom we derive the English word *thespian,* or actor, is said to have been the first actor. The dramatist Aeschylus (es´ kə ləs) is said to have introduced the second actor, and Sophocles the third.

In most dramas, actors played several different parts each. Their costumes were long, flowing garments and expressive masks, which they changed as they changed characters. The actors' shoes also featured a high wooden sole called a *cothurnus* (kō thər´ nəs) to make the individual look taller and more impressive and to heighten visibility in the vast theater.

Connect to the Literature

What roles does the chorus perform at the beginning and end of this excerpt? Also, in what ways does the picture on page 427 help you visualize how the chorus performs?

that has used you vilely[1]—do a thing for me.

1545   I shall speak for your own good, not for my own.

CREON: What do you need that you would ask of me?

OEDIPUS: Drive me from here with all the speed you can
to where I may not hear a human voice.

CREON: Be sure, I would have done this had not I
1550   wished first of all to learn from the God the course
of action I should follow.

OEDIPUS: But his word
has been quite clear to let the parricide,[2]
the sinner, die.

CREON: Yes, that indeed was said.
But in the present need we had best discover
1555   what we should do.

OEDIPUS: And will you ask about
a man so wretched?

CREON: Now even you will trust
the God.

OEDIPUS: So. I command you—and will beseech you—
to her that lies inside that house give burial
1560   as you would have it; she is yours and rightly
you will perform the rites for her. For me—
never let this my father's city have me
living a dweller in it. Leave me live
in the mountains where Cithaeron is, that's called
1565   my mountain, which my mother and my father
while they were living would have made my tomb.
So I may die by their decree who sought
indeed to kill me. Yet I know this much:
no sickness and no other thing will kill me.
1570   I would not have been saved from death if not
for some strange evil fate. Well, let my fate
go where it will.
                    Creon, you need not care
about my sons; they're men and so wherever
they are, they will not lack a livelihood.
1575   But my two girls—so sad and pitiful—
whose table never stood apart from mine,
and everything I touched they always shared—
O Creon, have a thought for them! And most
I wish that you might suffer me to touch them
1580   and sorrow with them.

---

1. **vilely** (vīl´ ly) *adv.* wickedly
2. **parricide** (par´ ə sīd) *n.* someone who murders his or her father.

from Oedipus the King **425**

Comparing Tragedies
What does Oedipus' request to Creon show about his attitude toward Thebes? As a **tragic hero,** what noble qualities does he reveal?

Vocabulary
rites (rīts) *n.* ceremonies; rituals

Comparing Tragedies
What role does Oedipus believe fate has played in his life?

Comprehension
What information does Creon want to learn from the God?

[*Enter* ANTIGONE *and* ISMENE, OEDIPUS' *two daughters.*]

O my lord! O true noble Creon! Can I
really be touching them, as when I saw?
What shall I say?
Yes, I can hear them sobbing—my two darlings!
and Creon has had pity and has sent me
1585   what I loved most?
Am I right?

CREON: You're right: it was I gave you this
because I knew from old days how you loved them
as I see now.

1590   **OEDIPUS:**   God bless you for it, Creon,
and may God guard you better on your road
than he did me!
                                  O children,
where are you? Come here, come to my hands,
a brother's hands which turned your father's eyes,
1595   those bright eyes you knew once, to what you see,
a father seeing nothing, knowing nothing,
begetting you from his own source of life.
I weep for you—I cannot see your faces—
I weep when I think of the bitterness
1600   there will be in your lives, how you must live
before the world. At what assemblages
of citizens will you make one? to what
gay company will you go and not come home
in tears instead of sharing in the holiday?
1605   And when you're ripe for marriage, who will he be,
the man who'll risk to take such infamy
as shall cling to my children, to bring hurt
on them and those that marry with them? What
curse is not there? "Your father killed his father
1610   and sowed the seed where he had sprung himself
and begot you out of the womb that held him."
These insults you will hear. Then who will marry you?
No one, my children; clearly you are doomed
to waste away in barrenness unmarried.
1615   Son of Menoeceus[3], since you are all the father
left these two girls, and we, their parents, both
are dead to them—do not allow them wander
like beggars, poor and husbandless.
They are of your own blood.
1620   And do not make them equal with myself
in wretchedness; for you can see them now
so young, so utterly alone, save for you only.

___

3. Son of Menoeceus (mə nē′ sē əs) Creon.

Vocabulary

infamy (in′ fə mē) *n.* very
bad reputation; disgrace

Touch my hand, noble Creon, and say yes.
If you were older, children, and were wiser,
1625 there's much advice I'd give you. But as it is,
let this be what you pray: give me a life
wherever there is opportunity
to live, and better life than was my father's.

CREON: Your tears have had enough of scope; now go within the
1630   house.

OEDIPUS: I must obey, though bitter of heart.

CREON: In season, all is good.

OEDIPUS: Do you know on what conditions I obey?

CREON: You tell me them,
1635   and I shall know them when I hear.

OEDIPUS: That you shall send me out
to live away from Thebes.

CREON: That gift you must ask of the God.

▼ **Critical Viewing**

What does this image of
Oedipus and the Chorus
suggest about their
relationship? Explain.
INTERPRET

Comprehension

Why does Oedipus weep for
his daughters?

OEDIPUS: But I'm now hated by the Gods.

1640 **CREON:** So quickly you'll obtain your prayer.

OEDIPUS: You consent then?

CREON: What I do not mean, I do not use to say.

OEDIPUS: Now lead me away from here.

CREON: Let go the children, then, and come.

1645 **OEDIPUS:** Do not take them from me.

CREON: Do not seek to be master in everything,
for the things you mastered did not follow you throughout your
life.

[*As* CREON *and* OEDIPUS *go out.*]

CHORUS: You that live in my ancestral Thebes, behold this
Oedipus,—
him who knew the famous riddles and was a man most
masterful;
1650 not a citizen who did not look with envy on his lot—see him
now and see the breakers of misfortune swallow him!
Look upon that last day always. Count no mortal happy till
he has passed the final limit of his life secure from pain.

Comparing Tragedies
What does the final speech of the chorus stress about the events depicted in the play?

Critical Reading

Cite textual evidence to support your responses.

1. **Key Ideas and Details (a)** In order to end the plague in Thebes, what command did Oedipus apparently make about the person who murdered Laius? **(b) Analyze:** What about this command is ironic, or surpising and unexpected?

2. **Key Ideas and Details (a)** What does Oedipus ask Creon to do regarding Jocasta's body and his daughters' future? **(b) Analyze:** What do these requests show about Oedipus' character?

3. **Craft and Structure (a)** In his final remark, what does Creon tell Oedipus not to seek? **(b) Interpret:** Based on this final scene, what do you think is the theme or central message of the play?

4. **Integration of Knowledge and Ideas (a) Make a Judgment:** At the play's end, do you think Oedipus is ennobled by suffering? **(b) Support:** Provide reasons and cite detailed and accurate references from the play to support your opinion.

Johann Wolfgang von Goethe

(1749–1832)

Because of the tremendous diversity of his talents and interests, Johann (yō hän´) Wolfgang von Goethe (gö´ tə) is best described as a true Renaissance man. He was not only a gifted writer but also a scientist, a painter, a statesman, a philosopher, and an educator.

The son of a wealthy lawyer, Goethe was born in the German town of Frankfurt am Main. After receiving a thorough education from private tutors, he was sent to the University of Leipzig to study law. More interested in the arts than in law, Goethe spent most of his free time writing poetry, studying art, and attending concerts. Nonetheless, he finished his legal studies in 1771.

A Developing Novelist Goethe practiced law for a brief period, during which he wrote *The Sorrows of Young Werther* (1774), an autobiographical novel inspired by an unhappy love affair and the suicide of one of his friends. One of the most important novels of the eighteenth century, *The Sorrows of Young Werther* earned Goethe international fame.

A year after the novel's publication, Goethe accepted an invitation to the court of the reigning duke of Weimar, Charles Augustus. Goethe lived in Weimar for the rest of his life, and for ten years he served as the duke's chief minister. In 1780, he traveled to Italy in an effort to dedicate time and energy to his writing.

Shortly after returning to Weimar, Goethe fell in love with Christiane Vulpius, whom he later married. Through a close friendship with the noted German writer Friedrich von Schiller (1759–1805), Goethe gained valuable guidance and assistance in revising a number of his important works.

A Legendary Figure Probably the most notable of these works was *Faust*. With Schiller's advice and direction, Goethe revised an early draft of the play, adding a prologue. Unfortunately, Schiller died three years before *Faust, Part I* (1808) was published.

The final and greatest achievement of Goethe's literary career was the completion of *Faust, Part II*. The poet's vision of the legendary Faust transformed the traditional character into a newer, more sympathetic one that has fascinated readers and scholars for centuries. Goethe had begun his work on *Part II* while still a young man; because he contributed to the piece throughout his life, *Faust, Part II* ultimately reflects the deep philosophy of life and wry wisdom of the poet's mature years. Goethe never knew of the success of *Faust, Part II,* as it was published in 1832, a few months after his death.

> "As soon as you trust yourself, you will know how to live."
> — Goethe

From FAUST

Johann Wolfgang von Goethe
translated by Louis MacNeice

BACKGROUND Georg Faust, or Faustus, was a German scholar and traveling magician who lived from about 1480 to 1540. According to legend, Faust sold his soul to the devil in exchange for youth, knowledge, and magical powers. In Goethe's version of the legend, Faust's interests reflect ideas of Romanticism, the literary and artistic movement.

This scene comes from Faust, Part I. *Mephistopheles, or the devil, is urging Faust to formalize their contract by signing it "with one little drop of blood."*

FAUST: Only do not fear that I shall break this contract.
What I promise is nothing more
Than what all my powers are striving for.
250   I have puffed myself up too much, it is only
Your sort that really fits my case.
The great Earth Spirit has despised me
And Nature shuts the door in my face.
The thread of thought is snapped asunder,
255   I have long loathed knowledge in all its fashions.
In the depths of sensuality
Let us now quench our glowing passions!
And at once make ready every wonder
Of unpenetrated sorcery!
260   Let us cast ourselves into the torrent of time,
Into the whirl of eventfulness,
Where disappointment and success,
Pleasure and pain may chop and change
As chop and change they will and can;
265   It is restless action makes the man.

MEPHISTOPHELES: No limit is fixed for you, no bound;
If you'd like to nibble at everything
Or to seize upon something flying round—
Well, may you have a run for your money!
270   But seize your chance and don't be funny!

FAUST: I've told you, it is no question of happiness.

Comparing Tragedies

In what ways are Faust's motivations (lines 260–265) similar to and different from those of Macbeth and Oedipus?

The most painful joy, enamored hate, enlivening
Disgust—I devote myself to all excess.
My breast, now cured of its appetite for knowledge,
275 From now is open to all and every smart,
And what is allotted to the whole of mankind
That will I sample in my inmost heart,
Grasping the highest and lowest with my spirit,
Piling men's weal and woe upon my neck,
280 To extend myself to embrace all human selves
And to founder in the end, like them, a wreck.

MEPHISTOPHELES: O believe *me*, who have been chewing
These iron rations many a thousand year,
No human being can digest
285 This stuff, from the cradle to the bier[1]
This universe—believe a devil—
Was made for no one but a god!
He exists in eternal light
But us he has brought into the darkness
290 While *your* sole portion is day and night.

FAUST: I will all the same!

MEPHISTOPHELES: That's very nice.
There's only one thing I find wrong;
Time is short, art is long.
You could do with a little artistic advice.
295 Confederate with one of the poets
And let him flog his imagination
To heap all virtues on your head,
A head with such a reputation:
Lion's bravery,
300 Stag's velocity,
Fire of Italy,
Northern tenacity.
Let *him* find out the secret art
Of combining craft with a noble heart
305 And of being in love like a young man,
Hotly, but working to a plan.
Such a person—*I'd* like to meet him;
"Mr. Microcosm"[2] is how I'd greet him.

FAUST: What am I then if fate must bar
310 My efforts to reach that crown of humanity
After which all my senses strive?

---

1. bier (bir) *n.* coffin and its supporting platform.
2. Mr. Microcosm man regarded as the epitome of the world.

MEPHISTOPHELES:
You are in the end . . . what you are.
You can put on full-bottomed wigs with a million locks,
You can put on stilts instead of your stocks,
315   You remain for ever what you are.

FAUST: I feel my endeavors have not been worth a pin
When I raked together the treasures of the human mind,
If at the end I but sit down to find
No new force welling up within.
320   I have not a hair's breadth more of height,
I am no nearer the Infinite.

MEPHISTOPHELES: My very good sir, you look at things
Just in the way that people do;
We must be cleverer than that
325   Or the joys of life will escape from you.
Hell! You have surely hands and feet,
Also a head and you-know-what;
The pleasures I gather on the wing,
Are they less mine? Of course they're not!
330   Suppose I can afford six stallions,
I can add that horse-power to my score
And dash along and be a proper man
As if my legs were twenty-four.
So good-bye to thinking! On your toes!
335   The world's before us. Quick! Here goes!
I tell you, a chap who's intellectual
Is like a beast on a blasted heath
Driven in circles by a demon
While a fine green meadow lies round beneath.

340   **FAUST:** How do we start?

MEPHISTOPHELES: We just say go—and skip.
But please get ready for this pleasure trip.

[*Exit* FAUST.]

Only look down on knowledge and reason,
The highest gifts that men can prize,
345   Only allow the spirit of lies
To confirm you in magic and illusion,
And then I have you body and soul.
Fate has given this man a spirit
Which is always pressing onward, beyond control,
350   And whose mad striving overleaps

◄ **Critical Viewing**
How does this painting convey the powers of nature that Faust has experienced?

Comparing Tragedies
Do either Macbeth or Oedipus long, like Faust, for "the Infinite"? Explain.

Comprehension
What does Mephistopheles urge Faust to do?

355

All joys of the earth between pole and pole.
Him shall I drag through the wilds of life
And through the flats of meaninglessness,
I shall make him flounder and gape and stick
And to tease his insatiableness
Hang meat and drink in the air before his watering lips;
In vain he will pray to slake his inner thirst,
And even had he not sold himself to the devil
He would be equally accursed.

Critical Reading

Cite textual evidence to support your responses.

1. **Key Ideas and Details (a)** To what does Faust say he devotes himself and what does he reject? **(b) Analyze:** How do what he pursues and what he rejects explain what he means by "the Infinite"? **(c) Interpret:** In what ways do Faust's pursuits reflect the Romantics' desire to go beyond ordinary life?

2. **Key Ideas and Details (a) Interpret:** What does Mephistopheles' simile comparing an intellectual to a beast (lines 336–339) suggest about his attitude toward intellectuals? **(b) Infer:** Why does Mephistopheles want Faust and others to "look down on knowledge and reason"?

3. **Key Ideas and Details (a) Analyze:** What quality in Faust does Mephistopheles count on to gain control of him? **(b)** In the final lines, what does Mephistopheles predict will happen to Faust? **(c) Speculate:** Do you agree with this prediction? Why or why not?

4. **Integration of Knowledge and Ideas (a) Connect:** Some critics have called contemporary society, with its devotion to constantly developing technology, Faustian. What do you think they mean? **(b) Make a Judgment:** Do you believe our society is Faustian? Why or why not?

Comparing Tragedies

1. **Integration of Knowledge and Ideas (a)** What is similar about the social status of Macbeth and Oedipus? **(b)** How might the social status of these **tragic heroes** contribute to the awe—a mixed feeling of respect and dread—that the audience feels in watching the **tragedy? (c)** What other elements in each of the three selections help create awe? Explain.

2. **Key Ideas and Details** How would you define the **tragic flaw** of each hero?

3. **Integration of Knowledge and Ideas** *Faust* has a chorus of sorts, though it does not appear in this selection; *Macbeth*, however, has no chorus in the usual sense. **(a)** In your opinion, do the Witches in *Macbeth* perform some of the roles that a chorus does? Why or why not? **(b)** Would adding a chorus like that in a Greek drama strengthen or weaken *Macbeth*? Explain.

 Timed Writing

Explanatory Text: Essay

Macbeth and the excerpts you have read reveal how the structure and elements in the work of dramatists changed over time.

Assignment: Write an **explanatory essay** in which you compare and contrast two plays from different periods. Evaluate how the dramatic structure and elements changed from one play to the other. **[40 minutes]**

Use questions like these to focus your analysis.
- Is the play structured to teach a moral, show the downfall of a noble character, or allow for the happy resolution of a misunderstanding?
- Are the characters personifications, social types, or complex individuals?

As you write, follow the conventions of a strong analytical essay:
- Begin your essay with a clear thesis statement.
- Use a clear organizational schema for conveying ideas.
- Support your thesis with relevant and substantial evidence, including well-chosen details from the texts.

As you draft, write legibly. Use appropriate capitalization and punctuation.

5-Minute Planner

Complete these steps before you begin to write:

1. Read the assignment carefully. Take note of key words and phrases.
2. Jot down some initial thoughts. Then, scan the plays for evidence that supports your ideas. **TIP** Create a chart in which to record quotations or details related to each play.
3. Create an outline for your essay that identifies the central idea of each paragraph.
4. Reread the prompt, and draft your essay.

 **Common Core State Standards**

Writing

2. Write informative/explanatory texts to examine and convey complex ideas, concepts, and information clearly and accurately through the effective selection, organization, and analysis of content.

10. Write routinely over extended time frames and shorter time frames for a range of tasks, purposes, and audiences.

USE ACADEMIC VOCABULARY

As you write, use academic language, including the following words or their related forms:

comparison
contrast
distinguish
resolution

For more about academic language, see the vocabulary charts in the introduction to this book.

Analyzing Functional and Expository Texts

Feature Article • Theater Review

About the Texts

A **feature article** is an informative or entertaining piece of nonfiction writing, found in a print or online periodical, that focuses on a topic of general interest such as a trend, local performance, or significant person. Features include an enticing *lead,* or opening, and a body that provides in-depth analysis.

A **theater review** is a feature article in which the writer gives facts and details about a theatrical production, as well as his or her opinion of it. Some of its features include an overview of the work; a "quick review" device, such as a star ranking indicating quality; and details of where and when the production can be viewed.

Preparing to Read Complex Texts

An **author's purpose** is his or her reason for writing—to inform, to persuade, or to entertain. An **author's perspective,** or **point of view,** on a topic consists of his or her beliefs, judgments, and attitudes about that topic. As you read, **evaluate the author's purpose and perspective** as it is reflected in the following elements:

- The title
- The author's *style,* or overall manner of expression, and *tone,* or the attitude he or she conveys through word choice (formal or informal, serious or light, sarcastic or straightforward); typically established by the lead
- The points made with anecdotes and direct quotes, as well as the facts and interesting details the author chooses to include

Use a chart like the one shown to evaluate the author's purpose.

Text Structures	Example	Effect on Meaning
Title		
Lead		
Positive/Negative Adjectives		
Direct Quotes		
Facts and Details		

Common Core State Standards

Reading Informational Text

6. Determine an author's point of view or purpose in a text in which the rhetoric is particularly effective, analyzing how style and content contribute to the power, persuasiveness, or beauty of the text.

Content-Area Vocabulary

These words appear in the selections that follow. They may also appear in other content-area texts:

pneumatic (no͞o mat´ ik) *adj.* run or powered by compressed air

excavation (eks´ kə vā´ shən) *n.* the process of making a hole or a cavity by digging and removing

contemporaneous (kən tem´ pə rā´ nē əs) *adj.* originating, existing, or happening during the same period of time

regime (rə zhēm´) *n.* a system of management or government that is in power

> The title indicates the topic of the article—efforts to design a modern equivalent of the Globe, Shakespeare's original theater.

Smithsonian
MAGAZINE

DESIGNING A GLOBE THEATRE FOR THE 21ST CENTURY

By Eric Jaffe

> Feature articles frequently use vivid descriptions and informal language.

The tractor-trailer planted firmly in the Wal-Mart parking lot did not seem out of place, but the actors who performed *Merchant of Venice* right beside it sure did. When the vehicle arrived it deployed into a full-size stage. Behind the set, **pneumatic** pods inflated to become ticket-windows and dressing rooms. Sunlight powered the spotlights and speakers. And when the playhouse folded up and drove off, a screen mounted on the side of the trailer replayed the show for all to see.

This is the Globe Theatre—not the one that housed Shakespeare's best dramas, but one conceived by Jennifer Siegal for a modern audience. Siegal's Globe is part homage to the Elizabethan era's itinerant theatre troupe, part shout-out to today's compact, on-the-go gizmos. The Los Angeles-based architect was one of five designers asked to create a 21st-century Shakespearean theatre for "Reinventing the Globe," a new exhibit at the National Building Museum in Washington, D.C., that opens January 13 and runs through August 2007.

Given only brief guidance and a few months to finish, these architects created modern Globes that challenge conventional thoughts about dramatic performances and the spaces that accommodate them, says Martin Moeller, the exhibition's curator. "When the words stay the same but all else changes, you realize how much power the words have," he says.

Theatre designer John Coyne delivered a truly virtual Globe. To reflect today's cross-cultural world, Coyne's performances would occur simultaneously in several locations. Gigantic screens with live streaming would hang above the stages, and characters would interact in real time. So, speaking in Russian from Moscow, Polonius offers advice to Laertes in New York; standing oceans away, Hamlet pierces Claudius with a venom-tipped sword.

Michele (pronounced *Mi-keleh*) Saee, who did not have theatre design experience, modeled a Globe that would capture an actor's fluidity in the structure itself. He proposed tracing the movements of an actor throughout a performance

Illustration of Jennifer Siegal's "Globetrotter"—a portable Shakespeare theater

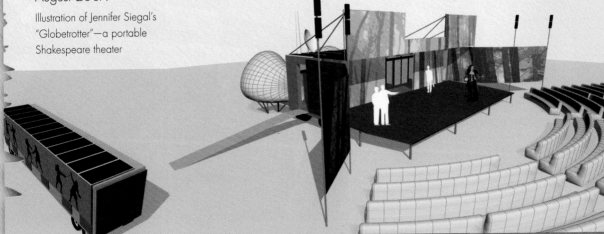

using electronic monitors then, with the help of a computer, turning these motions into a three-dimensional image that would become the building. "It's like those photos at night where you see red and white lights streaking down the road," Moeller says. "It's almost like you have a history built into one image."

David Rockwell's transparent Globe is intended to erase the barrier between outdoor and indoor settings. H3, the architectural firm guided by Hugh Hardy, created a floating Globe that could bounce around to various New York City boroughs, like so many bar-hopping hipsters, as a way to increase public access.

Siegel, who is the founder of the Office of Mobile Design, says her portable Globe, dubbed the "Globetrotter," is ready to go into production with the right client.

"We're a mobile society that deals with communication devices in a compact way, and theatre can be represented in a similar take," she says. "It doesn't have to be going to this old, stodgy building. It could be much more accessible, transient and lighter."

In some ways, conceptualizing a Globe Theatre for the future requires as much imagination as re-creating the one that stood in Shakespeare's day. Despite the playhouse's prominence, historians still argue over many aspects of the theatre, says Franklin J. Hildy of the University of Maryland, an advisor to the London Globe reconstruction that opened in 1997.

Notable uncertainties include the shape of the stage (some say it was rectangular, others square); how many sides the structure had (with ranges from 16 to 24); even the size of the building itself (some call the diameter 100 feet across, others 90).

Globe reconstructions work off evidence from seven maps of London in that day, texts from Shakespeare's plays and a site **excavation** (the original theatre, built in 1599, burned down in 1613 and was restored in the same place). Perhaps the most crucial historical document is a contract to build the Fortune theatre, a **contemporaneous** playhouse, which instructs builders to copy many of the Globe's dimensions.

Of the Globe's certainties, the stage that jutted out into the crowd was one of its most impressive attributes, says Hildy. "Everywhere you looked there was life, audience, energy." Standing patrons, known as groundlings, surrounded the stage, often shouting at the actors, cracking hazelnut shells—even sitting on stage.

Though Shakespeare's work also appeared at the Rose and Curtain theatres, the Globe hosted most of his famous dramas—including *Hamlet*, *King Lear* and *Macbeth*—which explains part of its lasting allure, Hildy says.

"The sense has always been that you could feel a closer connection to Shakespeare if you could understand how he saw theatre, how he saw his plays staged," he says. "Shakespeare was working during one of the most successful periods that theatre has ever had. There seems to be a relationship between buildings and that success."

> The writer gives the reader historical background to put the current project in context.

The restored Globe Theatre in London

The New York Times

April 26, 2007

Theater Review / 'Macbeth'

The Scottish Play, Told With Sound and Fury and Puppets

By LAWRENCE VAN GELDER

A puppet **regime** has seized control of the stage of the New Victory Theater. Plotting bloody murder, it slaughters men, women and children in pursuit of power until condign vengeance wreaks its ruin.

"Macbeth" is back in a captivating production that allies the actorly talents of the Chicago Shakespeare Theater with the remarkable talents of the Colla Marionette Company (Compagnia Marionettistica Carlo Colla e Figli) of Italy, which traces its origins to 1835.

In this swift-moving presentation (95 minutes including intermission), playing through Sunday, thirteen puppeteers out of sight above the

stage combine with seven actors seated in semidarkness facing the action to render a forceful, visually captivating and clearly articulated version of Shakespeare's tragedy.

Here legions of troops march, caparisoned horses carry caped and tartan-bedecked Scottish noblemen, evil unfolds in the depths of great castles, a flock of birds flutters overhead, and the weird sisters and their fiery cauldron disgorge the prophecies that will lead Macbeth and his lady to deadly doings.

The New York Times

Humans, animals, witches—all 130 of them are puppets, most of them three feet tall. Their deeds and misdeeds are carried out in eye-catching sylvan settings and in the corridors and on the parapets of castles whose perspectives make them seem to have been built of genuine stone. In the blackouts between scenes, music composed by Fabio Vacchi intensifies the atmosphere of tension and foreboding.

At least since 1846-7, when Giuseppe Verdi and his librettist Francesco Maria Piave applied themselves to transforming "Macbeth" to opera, Italy has been no stranger to abridging this tragedy; this production retains the play's highlights, including Lady Macbeth's sleepwalking scene, Banquo's ghost, the witches' recipe and the coming of Birnam Wood to Dunsinane.

With puppetry directed by Eugenio Monti Colla and spoken word directed by Kate Buckley, the two companies engineer a shining collaboration.

This "Macbeth" is recommended for audiences 12 and older. For all and in all respects, it is an uncommon treat.

"Macbeth" runs through Sunday at the New Victory Theater.

> The reviewer offers information on where and when performances take place.

> The reviewer supports his point of view or purpose with specific details.

Critical Reading

1. **Key Ideas and Details (a)** In the feature article, what does the author say is the reason different versions of the Globe Theater were created? **(b)** Why does the author consider it important to conceptualize a Globe Theater for the future?

2. **Key Ideas and Details (a)** What is the author's purpose and perspective in the feature article? **(b)** Explain two ways in which he uses direct quotes to support his perspective.

3. **Craft and Structure (a)** What facts and details in the theater review support the author's opinion of the performance? **(b)** Describe the style and the tone of the review. **(c)** What perspective do this style and tone help to express?

4. **Content-Area Vocabulary** The Latin prefix *trans-* means "across" or "through." The Latin verb *parēre* means "to be visible." Together, they contribute to the meaning of *transparent*, which means "clear" or "through which things are visible." Using your knowledge of the prefix *trans-*, give the meaning of each of these words: *transmit, transcribe,* and *transpose*. Then, verify your preliminary determination of the meaning of each word by looking it up in a dictionary.

Common Core State Standards

Reading Informational Text

7. Integrate and evaluate multiple sources of information presented in different media or formats as well as in words in order to address a question or solve a problem.

Writing

2.b. Develop the topic thoroughly by selecting the most significant and relevant facts, extended definitions, concrete details, quotations, or other information and examples appropriate to the audience's knowledge of the topic.

Language

4.d. Verify the preliminary determination of the meaning of a word or phrase.

Timed Writing

Informative Text [40 minutes]

Format

In a **compare-and-contrast** essay, you analyze the similarities and differences between two or more things. One way to organize your essay is to discuss similarities first and differences second.

Write a **compare-and-contrast** essay in which you analyze and compare the **aesthetic and cultural considerations** that influence modern producers and theater designers when they stage Shakespeare. Integrate ideas and examples from both the feature article and the theater review, providing context as required by your audience's background knowledge. Evaluate the importance and ultimate consequence for theater of each factor you discuss.

Academic Vocabulary

Aesthetic and cultural considerations are ideas concerning style, beauty, and the power of a work to express the experiences of its audience.

5-Minute Planner

Complete these steps before you begin to write.

1. Read the prompt carefully. Underline key words.
2. Scan the texts for details about the reasons people have for adapting Shakespeare. **TIP** Pay special attention to quotations from participants and to descriptions of the impact of their work, as well as to signal words indicating purpose, such as "as a way to."
3. Decide which points you will discuss.
4. Reread the prompt, and begin drafting.

Write an Argumentative Essay

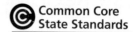 **Common Core
State Standards**

Writing
1. Write arguments to support claims in an analysis of substantive topics or texts, using valid reasoning and relevant and sufficient evidence.
5. Develop and strengthen writing as needed by planning, revising, editing, rewriting, or trying a new approach, focusing on addressing what is most significant for a specific purpose and audience.

Argumentative Essay English Renaissance writers such as Sir Thomas More wrote vigorously about their humanistic ideals in **argumentative essays**. An argumentative essay is a prose work that presents a claim for or against a position. It supports the claim with valid reasons, relevant evidence, and convincing language. Follow the steps outlined in this workshop to write your own argumentative essay.

Assignment Write an argumentative essay on an issue of importance to you.

What to Include To succeed, your argumentative essay must feature the following elements:

- a claim that clearly states your position
- well-organized reasons and evidence that support your argument, such as facts, examples, statistics, and personal experience
- responses to alternate or opposing claims
- information that will appeal to your audience's logic and that will inspire trust in your credibility and character
- compelling persuasive language that maintains a formal tone
- transitions and varied syntax used to link ideas
- an effective conclusion that sums up your argument

To preview the criteria on which your argumentative essay may be judged, see the rubric on page 449.

Focus on Research

Research often plays an important part in a strong argumentative essay. You might research to find the following sorts of support for your claim:

- relevant, accurate facts and statistics
- pertinent quotations from authoritative sources or experts
- reasons and evidence to argue against counterclaims

If you quote sources in your essay, be sure to clearly identify and credit each source. Refer to the Conducting Research pages in the Introductory Unit (pp. lxxii–lxxvii) as well as the Citing Sources and Preparing Manuscript pages in the Resources section for assistance in citing materials.

Prewriting and Planning

Choosing Your Topic

Use one of the following strategies to find a topic that provokes in you a strong reaction and for which you can make a strong argument:

- **Conduct a news scan.** Read newspapers or listen to news programs to learn about current, controversial issues. Avoid issues on which you do not have a strong opinion. Pick a topic on which you can take a clearly articulated stand.

  Weak: I don't like the proposed changes to the Tower Hill mall.

  Strong: The proposed changes to the Tower Hill mall will make the mall worse, not better.

- **Monitor online discussions.** Internet message boards often contain heated disagreements. Look for boards sponsored by local schools, government agencies, or media sources. Scan message boards for topics that receive many responses—a high number of posts about a topic may indicate controversy.

Narrowing Your Topic

Once you have identified a topic of general interest, focus on a specific argument that you want to make. Develop your claim and consider your intended audience as you make notes about your topic.

My Interest: Preparing for College   Narrower Topic: Applying Early to College

Gathering Details

Gather reasons and evidence to support your claim. Use libraries, the Internet, personal interviews, or other resources. Make note also of any counterclaims that contradict your argument, so you can prepare counterarguments. You might begin by filling out a chart like the one shown.

My Claim	Audience	My Reasons	Counterarguments to Address
Seniors should choose "early decision" when applying to college.	Seniors at my school	• Choosing early admissions may improve your chances of acceptance. • Applications will just hang over your head if you delay.	• Some schools do not offer early admissions. • Getting in early may limit your financial aid package.

Drafting

Shaping Your Writing

Showcase your claim. Introduce the issue in your first paragraph with a knowledgeable statement. To establish the significance of your claim, begin with a brief anecdote, facts, or examples that are compelling and accurate. Then state your claim in the final sentence of the first paragraph.

Develop ideas. Use the body of your writing to support your claim with valid reasons and sufficient relevant evidence. Show readers what is at stake by clearly distinguishing your claim from counterclaims and then refuting them. Present claims and counterclaims in logical sequence. Present the strongest evidence on both sides, addressing your audience's concerns. Then, conclude with a strong restatement of your argument.

Providing Elaboration

Use rhetorical devices to present your argument. While rhetorical devices will not replace sound reasoning and evidence, they can help to present your reasoning and evidence in a memorable and compelling way. You can use rhetorical devices to present and polish your argument. Rhetorical devices include the following:

- **Repetition:** Repeat key words to focus your argument.

  Example: The plan is convenient, but is convenience more important than safety?

- **Parallelism:** Repeated grammatical structures can create a memorable rhythm and help to make a strong point.

  Example: The safety of every student, every teacher, and every visitor is at stake.

- **Analogies:** Use comparisons to help readers grasp ideas.

  Example: Allowing parking along the field would be as dangerous as allowing motorcycles to enter a bicycle race.

Use effective techniques of argument. Consider using these types of reasoning to present your claim:

Type of Reasoning	Definition	Example
Inductive Reasoning	Specific facts used to lead to a general truth	Students from our community college's honors program transfer to 4-year schools at a 98% success rate. A two-year local program can jump-start your 4-year degree.
Deductive Reasoning	A general truth applied to a specific case	Community college is an affordable option. Mia saved $80,000 by attending Montvale Community College before transferring to an elite school.

Common Core State Standards

Writing

1.a. Introduce precise, knowledgeable claim(s), establish the significance of the claim(s), distinguish the claim(s) from alternate or opposing claims, and create an organization that logically sequences claim(s), counterclaims, reasons, and evidence.

1.b. Develop claim(s) and counterclaims fairly and thoroughly, supplying the most relevant evidence for each while pointing out the strengths and limitations of both in a manner that anticipates the audience's knowledge level, concerns, values, and possible biases.

1.e. Provide a concluding statement or section that follows from and supports the argument presented.

Writers on Writing

Frank Kermode On Persuasion

Frank Kermode is the author of "Life in Elizabethan and Jacobean England" (p. 248).

This passage is excerpted from my essay in *Daedalus, The Journal of the American Academy of Arts and Sciences.* It briefly considers the notion of the common reader from the eighteenth century up to the present day. To Dr. Samuel Johnson, the common reader of the eighteenth century was identified as a member of the leisured class. Now, it is argued, the term applies to people who have benefited by a college education.

> "A society containing subtle readers is at least a more interesting, perhaps a richer, society."
>
> —Sir Frank Kermode

from *The Common Reader*

I have assumed that the modern Common Reader passes through a college or university. The number of people now teaching literature in such institutions is probably greater than the total of critics who formerly existed throughout history, and they must have some effect on the millions of readers who frequent their classes. Does good come of this? The eminent American critic Richard Poirier says he sees "no reason in the world" why common readers should care to read the classics or serious contemporary fiction and poetry; "I don't think it makes them better people, better citizens, better anything." By some criteria he must be right. Indeed, it is immodest to propose that by making people read these things we are improving them, ethically or civically. All we dare claim is that we are making them better readers. We might or might not go on to claim that bad reading has often had disastrous consequences; or that a society containing subtle readers is at least a more interesting, perhaps a richer, society than one that does not; or that good readers are likely to be more resistant to the exploitative forces of "the ruling system." But we should not say we are improving them, except as readers.

← The arts of reading are now entrusted to college and university teachers. Should we assume that this is a wholly good thing?

← Richard Poirier, an eminent critic, denies that enhanced reading skills confer ethical benefits on the student.

← Even if his argument is persuasive, it could be maintained that skillful reading has other socially beneficial effects.

Revising

Revising Your Overall Structure

Arrange ideas in a logical order. Review to make sure that your reasons and evidence are arranged logically and effectively. Follow these steps.

1. Clearly show the connections between ideas, such as the connections between your claim and supporting reasons, using transition words and phrases, such as *because, therefore, due to,* and *consequently.*

2. In addition, use varied syntax to show the connections between ideas. For example, a complex sentence, combining a dependent and an independent clause, can clearly show the relation between claims and reasons: e.g., *Because the numbers are increasing, immediate action is required.* A compound sentence, joining two or more independent clauses, can be used to link two equally important reasons or to contrast claims and counterclaims: e.g., *Opponents say their plan is the only one that will work, but my alternative has proven effective.*

3. Experiment with arranging your reasons in order of importance, either from least important to most important, or vice versa.

Model: Using Transition Words

In order to get a driver's license,

ᴧYou are required to take a written test and a road test, which ensures that you know the traffic laws.

> The transition words *in order to* indicate cause and effect.

Revising Your Word Choice

Replace weak language with powerful words or images. To strengthen your writing, circle passages that are vague or lack force. For each one, brainstorm for charged words, vivid images, and dramatic analogies to help you make your points.

Peer Review: Share your draft with a partner. Discuss your ideas for replacing dull language. Together, choose the most vivid words or phrases.

Vague	Getting into a good college can be tough.	Suddenly, you get nervous about choosing a college.
Vivid	Like a thousand cattle trying to pass through the same gate, vast numbers of students across the nation apply each year for a limited number of places at colleges.	Suddenly, a feeling bubbles up from the pit of your stomach, an achy, acidic feeling of panic.

Developing Your Style

Making Sure Your Ideas Are Well Organized

Your argumentative essay probably contains both facts and opinions. Facts can include statistics, examples, and anecdotes. When your facts are well organized, they support your claim or opinions, as in this example:

Opinion: I think we should carpet the school hallway.

Supporting Facts: The carpeting will reduce noise. Mr. Porter, of the maintenance staff, says it will be easier to clean than the existing floors.

As you review the way your facts and opinions are organized, look for logical fallacies, or false connections between ideas:

A **hasty generalization** is based on only a few facts or samples.

Example: I tasted one apple and it was sweet. Therefore, all of the apples in the basket must be sweet.

A **non sequitur** (Latin for "it does not follow") draws a conclusion that does not follow from the evidence given.

Example: Members of Congress are elected by the people and make the laws. Members of Congress know what is best for the people.

A **false analogy** ignores key differences between compared items.

Example: Children are like little adults. Like adults, children can be trusted to make their own financial decisions.

Find It in Your Reading

Read or review "Speech Before Her Troops" by Elizabeth I, page 285.

1. Find two facts and two opinions that she includes in her speech.
2. Find an argument she makes and explain whether it is logical or not.

Apply It to Your Writing

Review your draft. For each paragraph in your draft, follow these steps:

1. Underline the facts or statistics you have used to support your claim. Check to see that your facts come from current, reliable sources and that you have cited them accurately.
2. Circle the opinions you have used to support your claims. Verify that the opinions can be validated by facts, expert opinions, or logical reasoning.
3. Evaluate the appeals you have made and revise any faulty logic.

Student Model: Kendra Nealon, Fairfield, CT

Improving Academics Through Athletics

A lot of attention has been focused on school athletic programs recently. People are asking: Do athletic programs help or hinder academic performance? The answer is simple: Athletics enhance academic performance because the things athletes learn in sports programs make them better students.

Sports help students develop discipline. Athletes must practice regularly, be on time for practice and games, pay attention to their coach, and always try to do their best. This discipline serves them well in class, too. They understand the importance of studying regularly, being on time for class, paying attention to their teacher, and always trying to do their best on assignments.

Sports teach students the value of making a commitment. On the field, they commit to helping their teams win. In class, they commit to helping themselves succeed. Applied to school, discipline and commitment are powerful engines that drive and improve academic performance.

Research has proven that athletics boost academic performance. A study comparing the grades of high-school athletes and non-athletes in Kansas in 2008–2009 found that among a group of about 9300 athletes, 51.8% had a grade point average of 3.5 or above. Among a roughly equal number of non-athletes, only 39.8% could claim a grade point average of 3.5 or higher.

Some people argue that athletic programs emphasize sports over class work. But like debating clubs, service clubs, and music classes, athletics are only one part of a school program.

Some people claim that schoolwork suffers because sports take up too much time. However, schoolwork suffers only if a student lets it suffer. There is time for both, as the athletes with good grades in the Kansas study prove. In fact, many sports programs require athletes to maintain high grades in order to stay on a team.

Athletics clearly help academic performance. Equipped with what they have learned on the field, student athletes march into the classroom disciplined and committed to scoring high in the scholastic arena.

Kendra ends her introduction with a clear claim.

In the next three paragraphs, Kendra provides relevant evidence as support for her claim. She uses rhetorical devices—repetition and parallelism—to help present her argument.

Kendra cites a research study and includes statistics to prove her claim.

Next, Kendra states and refutes counterclaims, anticipating her audience's concerns. She uses sound reasoning to convince her readers.

Kendra crafts a strong final sentence to conclude on a memorable note.

Editing and Proofreading

Focus on commonly confused words. Look for words that are commonly mistaken for one another: for example, *adapt* and *adopt*, *accept* and *except*, or *affect* and *effect*. If necessary, consult a dictionary or handbook to make sure you are using the correct word.

Focus on spelling. The "er" sound can be spelled with different letter combinations. Review your spelling of each word with this sound.

Spiral Review: Conventions Earlier in this unit, you learned about subordinating conjunctions (p. 263) and adjective and adverb clauses (p. 419). Check your persuasive essay to be sure you have used those conventions correctly.

Prepare your manuscript. Be sure that your essay is neatly presented and legible.

Publishing, Presenting, and Reflecting

Consider one of the following ways to share your writing.

Deliver a speech. Use your argumentative essay as the basis for a speech. See the Speaking and Listening Workshop on page 450 for presentation strategies.

Submit a letter to the editor. Condense your argumentative essay and re-format it as a letter to the editor for publication in your school or community newspaper.

Reflect on your writing. Jot down your thoughts on the experience of writing an argumentative essay. Begin by answering this question: How did rhetorical devices help you make your points?

Rubric for Self-Assessment

Evaluate your argumentative essay using the following criteria and rating scale.

Common Core State Standards

Writing

5. Develop and strengthen writing as needed by planning, revising, editing, rewriting, or trying a new approach, focusing on addressing what is most significant for a specific purpose and audience.

Language

1.b. Resolve issues of complex or contested usage, consulting references as needed.

2.b. Spell correctly.

Criteria	Rating Scale
	not very / very
Purpose/Focus: How clearly do you state your claim?	1 2 3 4
Organization: How effectively do you organize your reasons, evidence, and answers to opposing claims?	1 2 3 4
Development of Ideas/Elaboration: How well do you use evidence and responses to opposing claims to support your position?	1 2 3 4
Language: How clear is your writing and how precise is your word choice?	1 2 3 4
Conventions: How correct is your grammar, especially your use of commonly confused words?	1 2 3 4

Deliver a Persuasive Speech

Persuasive speech is language that is used to influence people's thoughts or actions. Most people use persuasion spontaneously as they negotiate their daily lives. In formal speaking situations, however, you must plan persuasive arguments and strategies.

Topic and Thesis

The first step to developing a persuasive speech is to choose a topic about which you are passionate. Jot down a list of issues that interest you. Then, create an arguable **thesis**—your position, or perspective, on the topic. A strong thesis statement is direct and clear, and the goal of your speech should be to persuade your audience to accept the position you set forth in your thesis statement.

Argument and Reasoning

Know your audience. Think carefully about your **audience:** who they are and the values or concerns they share. Understanding your audience will help you develop persuasive appeals that will reach them. There are three main types of persuasive appeals:

- **Ethical Appeal:** Establish your authority as a speaker, by acknowledging both sides of the topic and referring to credible sources.

- **Emotional Appeal:** Present information and evidence in a way that evokes listeners' emotions.

- **Logical Appeal:** Support your thesis with sound *facts* and *reasons*.

You can use different forms of argument to structure your line of reasoning. Use *inductive reasoning* to draw a conclusion after examining specific cases. *Deductive reasoning* involves applying an established principle or conclusion to a specific case. A *syllogism* is a series of three statements or ideas: a general statement, a specific statement, and a conclusion, such as "Reading will improve a student's vocabulary. I need to improve my vocabulary. Therefore, I should read more." An *analogy* is a comparison of one thing to something seemingly unrelated.

Address alternative perspectives. Identify alternative or opposing viewpoints to your position, and answer them in your speech by including logical counterarguments.

Select effective language techniques. As you write your speech, vary your *diction*, or word choice. The use of *Standard American English*—the formal English taught in school—ensures your ideas are clear. Limited use of *informal expressions* or slang can build a bridge to your audience. Keep your audience's knowledge level in mind if you use *technical language* to discuss scientific or technical topics. You may need to define technical terms to ensure that your audience follows your argument.

**Common Core
State Standards**

Speaking and Listening

1.d. Respond thoughtfully to diverse perspectives; synthesize comments, claims, and evidence made on all sides of an issue; resolve contradictions when possible; and determine what additional information or research is required to deepen the investigation or complete the task. *(p. 451)*

4. Present information, findings, and supporting evidence, conveying a clear and distinct perspective, such that listeners can follow the line of reasoning, alternative or opposing perspectives are addressed, and the organization, development, substance, and style are appropriate to purpose, audience and a range of formal and informal tasks.

Also focus on your *syntax*, or sentence structure. The language devices shown in the chart below can make your speech precise and powerful.

Rhetorical Questions	Parallel Structure	Concrete Images	Figurative Language
questions asked for effect that do not require an answer	repetition of grammatical patterns	vivid descriptions of events, places, or people	symbolic or nonliteral language, like similes and metaphors

Activities: Deliver and Discuss a Persuasive Speech

Comprehension and Collaboration For both activities, use an evaluation form like the one shown below.

A. *Rehearse* your speech for friends. Then, deliver it to your class. Afterward, discuss your speech with the class. Respond thoughtfully to classmates' comments and questions. Then, have your audience fill out an evaluation form like the one shown below.

B. Review classmates' comments, synthesizing them by noting where they overlap. Conduct any research needed to answer the concerns raised, and then develop and present an **impromptu speech** offering a *rebuttal,* or answer to your audience's critique of your argument.

Evaluation Form for Delivery of a Speech

Name of Speech _____

Thesis _____

Types of Persuasive Appeals:

　　Ethical: ☐　Example: _____

　　Emotional: ☐　Example: _____

　　Logical: ☐　Example: _____

Diction:

　　Standard English ☐　　Informal Language ☐　　Technical Language ☐

　　Examples: _____

Syntax and Language Devices:

　　Rhetorical Questions ☐　　Parallel Structure ☐

　　Concrete Images ☐　　　　Figurative Language ☐

　　Examples: _____

What would the speaker's opponents say in response to this argument?

_____

What did the speaker do well? What could be improved? _____

_____

Language Study

Words from Mythology

During the Renaissance, many words with origins in Greek and Roman mythology entered the English language. The renewed interest in the cultures of ancient Greece and Rome inspired English translations of classical writers. As these bodies of literature became familiar, English writers made allusions to their settings, characters, and events. From there, it was a short step to inventing related words that conveyed similar meanings. The chart explains the mythological origin of some common words:

 **Common Core State Standards**

Language

4.a. Use context as a clue to the meaning of a word or phrase.

5. Demonstrate understanding of word relationships.

6. Acquire and use accurately general academic and domain-specific words and phrases, sufficient for reading, writing, speaking, and listening at the college and career readiness level.

Words	Origin
furious	In Greek mythology, the three **Furies** were the spirits of punishment.
martial	In Roman mythology, **Mars** was the god of war, second in importance only to Jupiter.
mercurial	In Roman mythology, **Mercury** was the winged messenger, fleet of foot.
narcissistic	In Greek mythology, the beautiful youth **Narcissus** fell in love with his own reflection in a pool. He pined away as a result of his unrequited love for himself.
titanic	In Greek mythology, the **Titans** were the race of giants who came before the gods of Olympus.

These words can be found in the literature we read today. For example, in the tragedy *Othello*, Shakespeare writes, "I know not where is that Promethean heat, / That can thy light relume." The allusion is to Prometheus, a figure from Greek mythology who stole fire from heaven. Today, *Promethean* is defined as "creative" or "courageously original." Knowing the classical or Biblical origins of words can help you understand their meanings when you encounter them in your reading.

Practice

Directions: Complete the analogies below, using the chart above to help you. Then, explain the relationship between each pair of words.

1. mercurial : permanent :: _____ : titanic

   a. quick   **b.** small   **c.** sinking   **d.** huge

2. gentle : mild :: martial : _____

   a. military   **b.** enemy   **c.** warlike   **d.** soft

Directions: Use each of these words in sentences that show your understanding of their meaning as inferred from their origins.

3. a. furious   **b.** narcissistic   **c.** mercurial

Vocabulary Acquisition and Use

Context clues are words or phrases that help readers clarify the meanings of unfamiliar words in a text. By using context clues, you can determine the word or words that complete a sentence. Sentence Completion questions appear in most standardized tests. In these types of questions, you are given sentences with one or more missing words. Your task is to use the context to choose the correct word or words to complete each sentence logically. Try this strategy: (1) Read the entire sentence and anticipate a word that would logically complete it. (2) Scan the answer choices for that word. (3) If the word you anticipated is not there, look for a synonym.

Practice

This exercise is modeled after the Sentence Completion exercises that appear in the Critical Reading section of the SAT.

Directions: Each of the following sentences is missing one or two words. Choose the word or set of words that best completes each sentence.

> **Test-Taking Tip**
> Immediately rule out any answer choices you *know* are wrong.

1. Elizabeth, daughter of Henry VIII, was only 25 years old when she became England's ___?___ queen.
   A. melodious
   B. prodigal
   C. sovereign
   D. pernicious
   E. sanguine

2. Elizabeth proved ___?___, assuming the throne with rigor and wit.
   A. dauntless
   B. sullen
   C. multitudinous
   D. wan
   E. skeptical

3. She tolerated neither ___?___ nor insults, though she herself could be both ___?___ and inconstant.
   A. valor . . . predominant
   B. treasons . . . predominant
   C. valor . . . sullen
   D. treasons . . . sullen
   E. challenge . . . agreeable

4. Unwilling to compromise her power, the "Virgin Queen" would never ___?___ to take a husband.
   A. move
   B. scope
   C. deign
   D. raze
   E. vote

From Text to Understanding

You have studied each part of Unit 2 as a set of connected texts. In this workshop, you will have the chance to further explore the fundamental connections among these texts and to deepen your essential understanding of the literature and its social and historical context.

PART 1: Lovers and Their Lines

Writing: Argumentative Essay Poetry has long been used to express ideas about love, lament the loss of passion, or gain the affection of an adored one. The authors in Part 1 use poetry, often in innovative forms of the sonnet, to do all of these things. Review the poems, focusing on the Anchor Texts, the sonnets written by Edmund Spenser. Note the speaker's audience in each poem and the range of feelings each speaker expresses.

Assignment: Using at least one of Spenser's poems, as well as other poems in Part 1, develop and defend a claim that addresses the topic of real versus ideal love. Consider whether the poets are expressing realistic views of love or whether they use the art of poetry to construct a vision of what love should be.

> **Example:** Poetry, an idealized form of language, is used to present an idealized vision of love in the sonnets of Edmund Spenser and pastoral poetry of Christopher Marlowe.

Gather evidence. Identify the topics and themes of the poems. Consider how the poets approach their subject matter.

Write a claim. In your introduction, include a clear statement that includes your claim about the poems. Identify the authors and poems you will discuss and explain whether they express a real or ideal version of love.

Provide support. Support your points about the authors' perspectives on love by quoting passages from their works. Clearly explain how the lines you cite are relevant to your argument.

Use transitions. Include transitions between your paragraphs so readers can follow your thoughts. For example, phrases such as *on the other hand* and *similarly* signal to the reader that an idea contrasts with or adds to a previously discussed point.

Use academic vocabulary. As you write, deepen your meaning by using precise literary terms, such as *theme, sonnet,* and *imagery*.

Craft a concluding statement. Your conclusion should follow from and be supported by the evidence you have presented.

**Common Core
State Standards**

Writing

1. Write arguments to support claims in an analysis of substantive topics or texts, using valid reasoning and relevant and sufficient evidence.

7. Conduct short as well as more sustained research projects to answer a question (including a self-generated question) or solve a problem; narrow or broaden the inquiry when appropriate; synthesize multiple sources on that subject, demonstrating understanding of the subject under investigation.

Speaking and Listening

3. Present information, findings, and supporting evidence, conveying a clear and distinct perspective, such that listeners can follow the line of reasoning, alternative or opposing perspectives are addressed, and the organization, development, substance, and style are appropriate to purpose, audience, and a range of formal and informal tasks.

Writing Checklist

☐ Clear claim

  Notes: _____

☐ Relevant textual evidence

  Notes: _____

☐ Effective transitions

  Notes: _____

☐ Precise word choice

  Notes: _____

PART 2: The Influence of the Monarchy

Research: Royal Portfolios A British monarch rules as the protector of the people and defender of the faith, two roles represented by the texts of Part 2. The Anchor Text, "Speech Before Her Troops," given by Queen Elizabeth I, shows a monarch in full control of her role as commander in chief. King James I was a head of state who extended his influence to religion as he oversaw the definitive English translation of the Bible, which is excerpted in Part 2.

Review the background materials and selections in Part 2, focusing on Queen Elizabeth's speech. Consider how the monarchy affected the lives of the populace, paying special attention to how the monarchs contributed to their subjects' sense of a British national identity.

Assignment: With a partner, research ways in which Elizabeth I and James I changed the lives of those who lived during their rule. Explore how these monarchs left their mark on the nation in the areas of government and politics, religion, literature, and culture. Create a series of brief reports to collect in a portfolio that you will create for each monarch. Although you will use the texts from Part 2 as evidence to support your claims, you will also be extending beyond the texts to consider how deeply Elizabeth and James influenced British consciousness and behavior.

Refer to the checklist shown here as you research and write your reports. Display your portfolios for the class and invite discussion.

PART 3: Drama

Listening and Speaking: Roundtable Discussion The dramatic texts included in Part 3 are monumental works of tragedy. Characters struggle with fundamental issues of right and wrong and make choices that lead to profound consequences. As you review these works, including the Anchor Text, Act I of William Shakespeare's *Macbeth,* consider what leads to the main characters' downfall. What makes a tragic hero tragic?

Assignment: Working in a group, prepare a roundtable discussion in which you discuss the fall from grace of the tragic heroes in the Part 3 dramas, especially *Macbeth.* Consider the following questions as you prepare to discuss this issue:

- Does fate drive these characters to their ruinous ends?

- Do character traits that once produced admirable behavior eventually lead characters to make disastrous decisions?

- What role does evil play in the life and death of a tragic hero? Is evil necessary in tragedy?

Choose a moderator for the group and present your ideas to the class. Invite classmates to offer their ideas and questions.

Project Checklist

Reports

☐ **Research**

Find Internet and library sources that address Elizabeth I/James I and

- government and politics
- religion
- literature
- culture

☐ **Develop Claims**

Formulate clear claims that explain how the monarchs made an impact on the British people of this time period. Focus each report on one specific area of influence.

☐ **Textual Support**

Include evidence from your resources, including the Part 2 texts, and be sure to cite any information you use.

Portfolios

☐ **Visual Aids**

Include artwork, drawings, maps, or timelines that provide background or illustrate your points. Include a visual representation of each monarch.

☐ **Design**

Arrange the reports and visual documents in the portfolio in a visually pleasing way. Include eye-catching borders and titles.

Test-Taking Practice

 Common Core
State Standards

RL.11-12.1, RL.11-12.2,
RL.11-12.4; L.11-12.3,
L.11-12.4, L.11-12.6
[For the full wording of
the standards, see the
standards chart in the
front of your textbook.]

Critical Reading Test: Paired Passages

Paired reading passages are one type of critical reading passage. Paired passages may be fiction or nonfiction, prose or poetry, and vary in length. Questions that follow will refer to each passage individually and to both passages as a unit. As you read, note similarities and differences between the passages, especially the authors' attitudes, word choices, and styles.

Practice

The following exercise is modeled after the SAT Paired Passages Critical Reading section. This section usually includes 48 questions.

Directions: Read both passages. Then, answer the questions. Passage 1 is by Christopher Marlowe. Passage 2 is by Sir Walter Raleigh.

Strategy

- **Read Passage 1**, and answer the questions that refer only to the first passage.
- **Read Passage 2**, and answer the questions that refer only to the second passage.
- Finally, answer the **compare-and-contrast** questions.

PASSAGE 1

The Passionate Shepherd to His Love

Come live with me, and be my love,
And we will all the pleasures prove
That valleys, groves, hills, and fields,
Woods, or steepy mountain yields.

5 And we will sit upon the rocks,
Seeing the shepherds feed their flocks,
By shallow rivers to whose falls
Melodious birds sing madrigals.

And I will make thee beds of roses,
10 And a thousand fragrant posies,
A cap of flowers, and a kirtle
Embroidered all with leaves of myrtle;

A gown made of the finest wool,
Which from our pretty lambs we pull;
15 Fair lined slippers for the cold,
With buckles of the purest gold;

A belt of straw and ivy buds,
With coral clasps and amber studs;
And if these pleasures may thee move,
20 Come live with me, and be my love.

The shepherds' swains shall dance and sing
For thy delight each May morning;
If these delights thy mind may move,
Then live with me and be my love.

PASSAGE 2

The Nymph's Reply to the Shepherd

If all the world and love were young
And truth in every shepherd's tongue
These pretty pleasures might me move
To live with thee, and be thy love.

5 Time drives the flocks from field to fold,
When rivers rage and rocks grow cold,
And Philomel becometh dumb,
The rest complains of cares to come.

The flowers do fade, and wanton fields
10 To wayward winter reckoning yields:
A honey tongue, a heart of gall,
Is fancy's spring, but sorrow's fall.

Thy gowns, thy shoes, thy beds of roses,
Thy cap, thy kirtle, and thy posies
15 Soon break, soon wither, soon forgotten,
In folly ripe, in season rotten.

Thy belt of straw and ivy buds,
Thy coral clasps and amber studs,
All these in me no means can move
20 To come to thee and be thy love.

But could youth last and love still breed,
Has joy no date nor age no need,
Then these delights my mind might move,
To live with thee and be thy love.

1. Which of the following best states the theme of Passage 1?
   A. Love can be felt only in natural surroundings.
   B. Nature provides the raw materials for all human needs.
   C. The pleasures of love are akin to the pleasures of nature.
   D. Love should be both mentally and emotionally stimulating.
   E. The delights of nature far outweigh those of romance.

2. It can most reasonably be inferred from Passage 1 that the speaker
   A. feels a deep connection to nature
   B. has impure motives
   C. is disenchanted with his daily life
   D. has long suffered from unrequited love
   E. is unschooled in the art of love

3. In line 19 of Passage 1, *move* most nearly means
   A. relocate
   B. stir
   C. offend
   D. find
   E. perplex

4. Which of the following best summarizes Passage 2?
   A. Nature may endure, but love is quick to die.
   B. Love does not require gifts or complicated arguments.

   C. Though nature is temporary, our love is permanent.
   D. To love is to ignore the cares and trials of mortality.
   E. Like nature and youth, love is fleeting.

5. It can be inferred that the speaker of Passage 2 finds "truth in every shepherd's tongue" (line 2)
   A. rarely
   B. only when convenient
   C. frequently
   D. only in nature
   E. occasionally

6. It would be most accurate to say that
   A. Passage 1 is a parody of Passage 2
   B. Passage 1 is an excerpt of Passage 2
   C. Passage 2 is a response to Passage 1
   D. Passage 2 is a poor imitation of Passage 1
   E. Passage 2 allegorizes Passage 1

7. The speaker of Passage 2 would most likely describe the speaker of Passage 1 as
   A. deceptive
   B. unintelligent
   C. romantic
   D. naive
   E. remote

Editing in Context: Grammar and Writing

Editing-in-context segments often appear in the writing sections of standardized tests. They are made up of a reading passage with numbered sentences. The passages are usually drafts of student essays that contain errors in grammar, style, and usage. For each question, you must decide which of four possible answers will best correct a given sentence.

Practice

This exercise is modeled after the Identifying Sentence Errors portion of the SAT Writing test. The test usually includes 18 such questions.

Directions: Each of the following sentences contains either a single error or no error at all. The error, if there is one, is underlined and lettered. If a sentence contains an error, select the letter of that underlined part. If the sentence is correct, select choice E.

Strategy

"Listen" for Errors
Read the sentence straight through. If you mentally "trip" over one of the underlined portions, it's probably wrong.

1. During the <u>sixteenth century</u>—the first
   _A
   century of the <u>printed book</u>—writers
   _B
   from all <u>levels of society</u> sought to have
   _C
   <u>his</u> works published. <u>No error</u>
   _D   _E

   A.
   B.
   C.
   D.
   E.

2. However, it was <u>one</u> of the <u>more</u>
   _A
   <u>dangerous</u> eras in history <u>for</u> those
   _B   _C
   <u>whose names</u> appeared in print.
   _D
   <u>No error</u>
   _E

   A.
   B.
   C.
   D.
   E.

3. All books were <u>censored</u> by various
   _A
   <u>government and</u> church authorities,
   _B
   <u>whom</u> in turn were <u>accountable to</u> the
   _C   _D
   monarch. <u>No error</u>
            _E

   A.
   B.
   C.
   D.
   E.

4. <u>Even</u> the most innocent <u>complement</u>
   _A   _B
   could be construed as slander; even the
   <u>most straightforward</u> observation could
   _C
   be <u>mistaken</u> for deceit. <u>No error</u>
       _D   _E

   A.
   B.
   C.
   D.
   E.

5. Punishments <u>came</u> in <u>a range of forms</u> and
degrees; <u>it</u> was sometimes a mere reprimand,
<u>sometimes</u> a decade in prison. <u>No error</u>

  A.
  B.
  C.
  D.
  E.

6. For this reason, the medieval <u>practice</u>
of circulating <u>unpublished</u> manuscripts
continued <u>to thrive</u> <u>well</u> into the 1700s.
<u>No error</u>

  A.
  B.
  C.
  D.
  E.

7. For courtiers and <u>others of</u> high rank, writing
and circulating anonymous texts <u>were</u> a
<u>relatively safest</u> way of expressing dissent or
<u>affection</u>. <u>No error</u>

  A.
  B.
  C.
  D.
  E.

 Timed Writing: Position Statement [25 minutes]

In *Utopia*, Sir Thomas More writes: "When a ruler enjoys wealth and pleasure
while all about him are grieving and groaning, he acts as a jailor rather than
as a king."

Write an essay in which you agree or disagree with More's statement. Do you
consider it an overstatement, or a painful truth? What value, if any, might it
hold for leaders of our own time? Use reasons and examples from your own
knowledge and experience to support your ideas.

> **Academic Vocabulary**
>
> Read the prompt and the assignment twice carefully. Note key words, such as *agree* or *disagree,* that clarify the assignment.

Constructed Response

Follow the instructions to complete the tasks below as required by your teacher. As you work on each task, incorporate both general academic vocabulary and literary terms you learned in this unit.

Common Core State Standards

RL.11-12.1, RL.11-12.3, RL.11-12.4, RL.11-12.5; RI.11-12.2, RI.11-12.6; W.11-12.1, W.11-12.2; SL.11-12.4, SL.11-12.5
[For the full wording of the standards, see the standards chart in the front of your textbook.]

Writing

Task 1: Literature [RL.11-12.3; W.11-12.1]
Analyze the Development of a Drama

Write an **essay** *in which you analyze how the author of one of the dramatic works in this unit develops and relates the key elements of the play.*

- Explain which play you chose and briefly summarize the plot.
- Identify key choices the author made in writing the drama. For example, consider where the play is set, how the action is ordered, and how the characters are introduced and developed. Consider also the way in which these elements relate to each other.
- Analyze the impact of the author's choices, discussing how these decisions affect both the play's meaning and the reader's experience.
- Organize ideas so that each idea builds on the one it follows to create a unified whole.
- Provide a concluding section that follows from the explanation presented. In your conclusion, sum up your analysis of the author's key choices and their impact. Include a memorable statement of your opinion of the work.

Task 2: Literature [RL.11-12.4; W.11-12.1]
Analyze Shakespearean Language

Write an **essay** *in which you analyze Shakespeare's word choice in one of the acts of* Macbeth, *which appears in this unit.*

- Identify specific examples of language that you find especially effective in one of the acts of *Macbeth*. Consider the following elements: figures of speech, such as similes or metaphors; specific words that are particularly interesting or beautiful; and connotative meanings that are especially rich or striking. Explain your choices and the reasons for them.
- Identify any words in the act that readers may not understand. Explain the meanings of these words. If any have multiple meanings, explain which ones are most important.
- Consider how the combined word choices in the act you are analyzing develop the author's tone.
- Cite specific examples from the play to support your ideas. Quote precisely and accurately. Introduce each example with a sentence or phrase that shows its connection to the idea you intend it to illustrate.

Task 3: Informational Text [RI.11-12.2; W.11-12.2]
Analyze the Development of Central Ideas

Write an **essay** *in which you analyze the development of two or more central ideas in a work of literary nonfiction from this unit.*

- Choose a work of nonfiction from this unit, and clearly identify and explain at least two central ideas expressed in the work.
- Discuss how the author introduces and develops each idea.
- Support your claim, identifying specific details that shape and refine each central idea.
- Explain how the central ideas interact and build on one another—reinforcing, adding to, or refining each other—to create a complex analysis of the topic of the work.
- To ensure that readers understand your analysis, include an objective summary of the work.

Speaking and Listening

Task 4: Literature [RL.11-12.5; SL.11-12.4]
Analyze Text Structure

*Prepare and deliver an **oral presentation** in which you analyze the structure of a poem in this unit.*

- Identify the poem you will analyze, and explain why you chose it.

- Begin your presentation by discussing the overall structure of your chosen poem. For example, does it follow simple chronological order, or does it move about in time? Who is the speaker, and who is being addressed? Do the divisions between stanzas or other sections reflect and reinforce shifts in ideas?

- Identify a specific section of the poem that you will analyze in your presentation. For example, you may discuss how the poem begins, how events are ordered, or how it ends (happily, tragically, or inconclusively). Discuss how the specific section or aspect of the poem contributes to the overall structure.

- Discuss the aesthetic, or artistic, impact of the author's structural choices.

- Explain how the structure affects the poem's overall meaning. Support your ideas with evidence from the text.

Task 5: Literature [RL.11-12.1; SL.11-12.5]
Draw Inferences

*Prepare and deliver an **oral presentation** in which you cite textual evidence to support inferences drawn from a poem in this unit.*

- Identify the poem you chose. Explain the poem's explicit meaning or key idea. Quote from the text to support your point.

- Identify any ideas or emotions that the speaker suggests but does not explicitly state. Cite details from the poem that help you draw these inferences. Explain how you tied these details together to see connections that suggest implicit meanings.

- Discuss ideas or emotions the poem leaves uncertain or open to interpretation. Consider the reasons for and effects of this ambiguity.

- Incorporate digital media that enhances your presentation. For example, consider images, audio, graphics, or textual elements that help illustrate and clarify your ideas or those expressed in the poem.

Task 6: Informational Text [RI.11-12.6; SL.11-12.4]
Determine Author's Point of View

*Prepare and deliver an **oral presentation** in which you determine the author's point of view and analyze his or her style in a nonfiction work from this unit.*

- Introduce the work you chose. Explain the author's purpose, topic, and central ideas.

- Describe the author's point of view. Explain how the author's stance affects his or her discussion of the topic and helps to shape the central idea.

- Discuss specific aspects of the author's rhetoric and style. Cite details and examples from the text to support your position.

- Define technical language or uncommon words to address your audience's knowledge level of your subject.

 What is the relationship of the writer to tradition?

Something Old, Something New The old rhyme about weddings says that a bride should wear "something old" together with "something new." In that spirit, many writers in this unit combined old and new.

Assignment Choose three authors from this unit who drew from tradition to create something new. Write a **literary analysis** showing how each author used a traditional theme, genre, or stylistic device but refreshed it with a new or inventive approach.

Titles for Extended Reading

In this unit, you have read a variety of literature of the English Renaissance. Continue to read works related to this era on your own. Select books that you enjoy, but challenge yourself to explore new topics, new authors, and works offering varied perspectives or approaches. The titles suggested below will help you get started.

LITERATURE

The Tragedy of Hamlet
William Shakespeare   EXEMPLAR TEXT

Drama In this classic tale of murder and revenge, Hamlet learns that his uncle has murdered his father in order to seize the crown. Urged on by the ghost of his father, Hamlet swears he will kill his uncle. However, Hamlet is paralyzed by indecision, delaying his revenge until events themselves speed the story to a bloody conclusion.

[Shakespeare's play The Tragedy of Macbeth *begins on page 322 of this book. Build knowledge by reading another tragedy by this author.]*

The Tempest
William Shakespeare

Drama After his evil brother steals his kingdom, the magician Prospero and his daughter are stranded on a remote island. Years later, when a tempest shipwrecks his brother on the same island, Prospero has the opportunity for revenge, reconciliation, or both—if only his magic powers do not fail him.

The Sonnets
William Shakespeare

Poetry This collection contains all 154 of Shakespeare's sonnets, along with commentary and illustrations. This version includes an introduction by the poet W. H. Auden.

[Four of Shakespeare's sonnets appear on pages 275–278 of this book. Build knowledge by reading all of his sonnets.]

Don Quixote
Miguel de Cervantes   EXEMPLAR TEXT

Novel Don Quixote, an aging man from La Mancha, Spain, sets out with his companion Sancho Panza on a quest filled with misadventures. He is determined to save maidens, right wrongs, and revive the code of chivalry. The fact that these adventures take place largely in Quixote's head only adds to the satiric hilarity.

INFORMATIONAL TEXTS

Historical Texts

Utopia
Sir Thomas More
NuVision Publications, 2007

Philosophy More describes an idealized city-state governed by reason. In a wide-ranging work that anticipates the hot-button issues of the next several centuries, he addresses such topics as women's rights, education, religion, and war.

Contemporary Scholarship

Galileo's Daughter
Dava Sobel

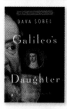

Science This scientific biography tells of Galileo's relationship with Virginia, his eldest daughter and confidante. Her letters, translated and masterfully woven into the narrative, illuminate and humanize the life of this towering figure in the fields of astronomy and physics.

The Children of Henry VIII
Alison Weir
Ballantine Books, 1997

Historical Narrative Six times married, King Henry VIII of England left four prospective heirs to the throne after his death. This narrative describes the tumultuous period when three of Henry's children reigned in succession—Edward VI, Mary I, and, finally, Queen Elizabeth I.

A Year in the Life of William Shakespeare: 1599
James Shapiro

Biography Thirty-five-year-old William Shakespeare wrote four plays in 1599. In this biography, James Shapiro discusses how the turbulent events of the time influenced *Henry V, Julius Caesar, As You Like It*, and *Hamlet*.

Preparing to Read Complex Texts

Reading for College and Career In both college and the work-place, readers must analyze texts independently, draw connections among works that offer varied perspectives, and develop their own ideas and informed opinions. The questions shown below, and others that you generate on your own, will help you more effectively read and analyze complex college-level texts.

**Common Core
State Standards**

Reading Literature/Informational Text
10. By the end of grade 12, read and comprehend literature, including stories, dramas, and poems, and literary nonfiction at the high end of the grades 11-CCR text complexity band independently and proficiently.

When reading complex texts, ask yourself...

- What idea, experience, or story seems to have compelled the author to write? Has the author presented that idea, experience, or story in a way that I, too, find compelling?

- How might the author's era, social status, belief system, or personal experiences have affected the point of view he or she expresses in the text?

- How do my circumstances affect what I understand and feel about this text?

- What key idea does the author state explicitly? What key idea does he or she suggest or imply? Which details in the text help me to perceive implied ideas?

- Do I find multiple layers of meaning in the text? If so, what relationships do I see among these layers of meaning?

- How do details in the text connect or relate to one another? Do I find any details unconvincing, unrelated, or out of place?

- Do I find the text believable and convincing?

Key Ideas and Details

- What patterns of organization or sequences do I find in the text? Do these patterns help me understand the ideas better?

- What do I notice about the author's style, including his or her diction, uses of imagery and figurative language, and syntax?

- Do I like the author's style? Is the author's style memorable?

- What emotional attitude does the author express toward the topic, the story, or the characters? Does this attitude seem appropriate?

- What emotional attitude does the author express toward me, the reader? Does this attitude seem appropriate?

- What do I notice about the author's voice—his or her personality on the page? Do I like this voice? Does it make me want to read on?

Craft and Structure

- Is the work fresh and original?

- Do I agree with the author's ideas entirely, or are there elements I find unconvincing?

- Do I disagree with the author's ideas entirely, or are there elements I can accept as true?

- Based on my knowledge of British literature, history, and culture, does this work reflect the British tradition? Why or why not?

Integration of Ideas

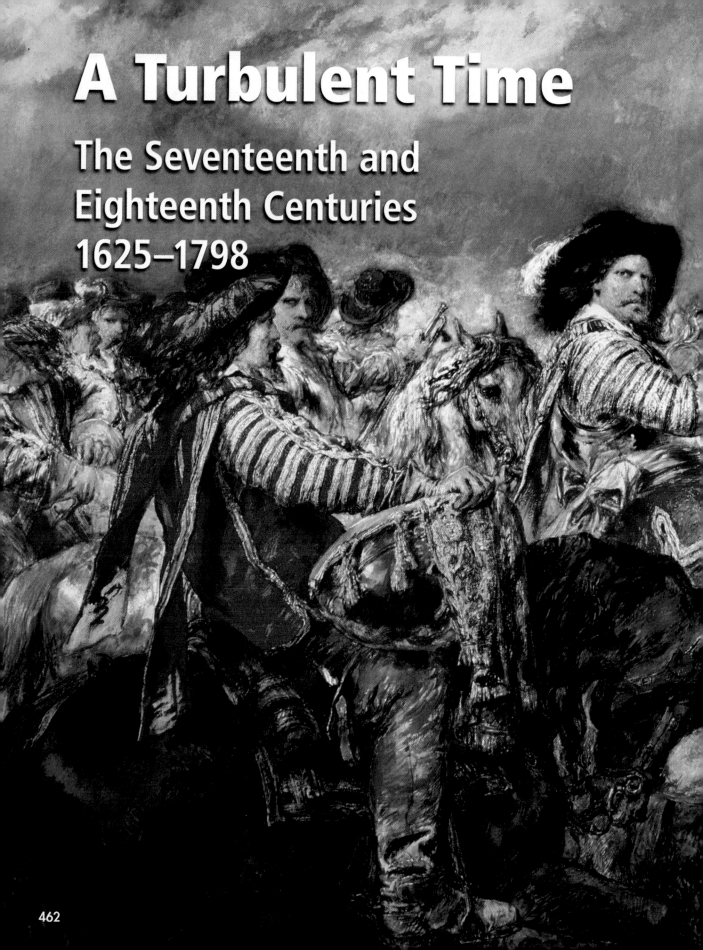

A Turbulent Time

The Seventeenth and Eighteenth Centuries 1625–1798

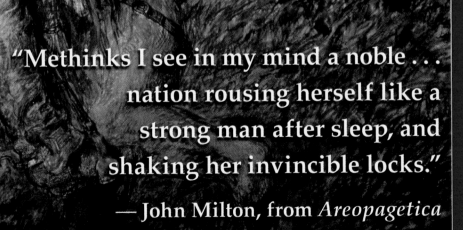

"Methinks I see in my mind a noble . . . nation rousing herself like a strong man after sleep, and shaking her invincible locks."

— John Milton, from *Areopagetica*

Unit 3

PART 1 TEXT SET

THE WAR AGAINST TIME

PART 2 TEXT SET

A NATION DIVIDED

PART 3 TEXT SET

THE TIES THAT BIND

PART 4 TEXT SET

THE ESSAY

CLOSE READING TOOL

Use this tool to practice the close reading strategies you learn.

ONLINE WRITER'S NOTEBOOK

Easily capture notes and complete assignments online.

STUDENT eTEXT

Bring learning to life with audio, video, and interactive tools.

■ Find all Digital Resources at **pearsonrealize.com**.

463

Snapshot of the Period

Social turmoil and new growth define this period and its literature. The guns of the English Civil War, which pitted the king against Parliament, echo through the work of poets Andrew Marvell, Richard Lovelace, and John Milton. The Industrial and Agricultural revolutions, sparked by the use of new machines in production and in farming, led to the growth of cities, an increase in urban poverty, and the rise of the middle class. These developments influenced the work of Samuel Pepys, Daniel Defoe, Samuel Johnson, and Joseph Addison, each of whom chronicled the life of the middle class or catered to its leisure needs. At the end of the period, political revolutions in America and in France prepared the way for the revolution in literature known as Romanticism.

The surrender of British General Cornwallis to George Washington at Yorktown, Virginia (1781), led to America's victory in the Revolution.

James Watt's steam engine, shown here, helped bring about the Industrial Revolution.

As you read the selections in this unit, you will be asked to think about them in view of three key questions:

What is the relationship between literature and *place?*

How does literature shape or reflect *society?*

What is the relationship of the writer to *tradition?*

CAVALIERS vs. ROUNDHEADS

CAVALIERS
- Member of the aristocracy
- Long flowing hair and wigs
- Elaborate clothes, plumed hats
- Self-consciously elegant pose
- Pro-Catholic and anti-Puritan
- Believed in divine right of kings

ROUNDHEADS
- Social class lower than the aristocracy
- Short hair
- Plain dress
- Direct in manner
- Puritan with strict religious beliefs
- Believed in limits to king's rule

THE INTRODUCTION OF COFFEE TO ENGLAND is a story in which
exploration, trade, slavery, the growth of cities, and the rise of the middle class all play a role.

1400

1453
Coffee introduced to Constantinople by Turks, from Middle East

1601
Word "coffee" used by English explorer in description of journey to Persia

1650
First English coffeehouse, in Oxford

1652
First London coffeehouse; coffee's popularity to increase demand for sugar, grown with slave labor in West Indies

1675
King Charles II closes coffee-houses, as places where rebellion may be planned

1676
King Charles revokes order; coffeehouses established as places where men exchange news and discuss business

1708
New United East India Company trades in coffee

1725
Almost 2,000 coffeehouses in London

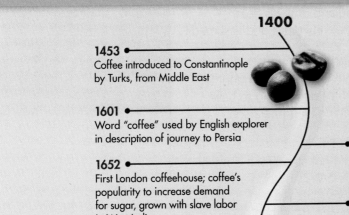

1800

Historical Background

The Seventeenth and Eighteenth Centuries (1625–1798)

The period begins with the beheading of one king and ends with the beheading of another. In between, a civil war and five revolutions created a new and different world.

The Civil War and the Restoration

A proud king, Charles I, struggled with Parliament over political and religious authority until, in 1642, civil war broke out. The king's supporters were the Cavaliers, with long hair, plumed hats, and high boots. The Parliamentary forces were the "Roundheads," with cropped hair, black hats, and sturdy shoes. Their leaders included Oliver Cromwell, a stern general who thought his new model army could bring divine justice to England. After six brutal years, Charles was defeated, captured, and tried by his "subjects." Condemned to death, he was beheaded in January 1649.

A dead king does not, however, guarantee a democratic or effective government. Impatient with quarreling Parliamentary factions, Cromwell seized power and served as Lord Protector of England until his death (1653–1658). In 1660, Charles II returned from exile in France and assumed the throne in a restored monarchy.

When Charles died without an heir in 1685, his brother, a Catholic convert, became James II. James also had no male heirs, and his daughter, Mary, was a staunch Protestant. The uneasy country was willing to have James as king while it waited for Mary, but the aging king had a son.

"The Glorious Revolution"

Nobles, merchants, and other power brokers would not stand for a Catholic dynasty. In 1688, they invited Mary and her husband William to take the throne. James was deposed, and William and Mary succeeded him, an event hailed as "The Glorious Revolution." The will of the governed had once again determined who would rule, but this time without great bloodshed.

Charles I

TIMELINE

1628: William Harvey explains blood circulation. ▶

1640: India English settlement established at Madras.

1625

1642: Puritans close theaters.

1642: English Civil War begins. ▶

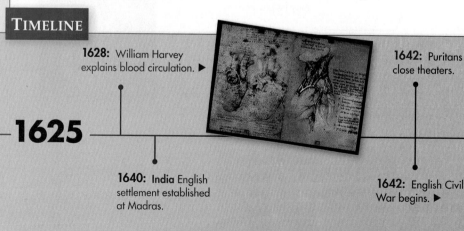

Parliament stepped in again in 1701, passing the Act of Settlement to keep the crown in Protestant hands. In 1714, George, the Elector of Hanover in Germany, became king. George I did not speak English and cared little for the country, and Parliament assumed almost complete control.

Other Revolutions

The Industrial Revolution, an explosion of manufacturing involving new technology and new energy sources such as steam, began in the 1700s. Powerful new machinery linked with crop rotation, larger farms, and improved transportation led to an Agricultural Revolution, creating a new abundance with which fewer farmers could feed the swelling population of the cities.

The fourth revolution began in 1775 and ended in 1781. England, a mighty military power, was defeated by American troops fighting on their own soil. America became independent but maintained connections of language, politics, culture, and literature that enriched both countries.

The fifth revolution of the period began on July 14, 1789, when the people of Paris stormed the Bastille, a hated symbol of royal oppression. Shortly after this, King Louis XVI was beheaded and the old order was shattered. Government without kings, already established in America, had now displaced a monarchy in Europe.

At the end of the American Revolution, when Lord Cornwallis led his defeated troops out of Yorktown, the band played a popular tune: "The World Turned Upside Down." It is a good theme song for the whole era.

Key Historical Theme: Civil War and Revolutions

- Struggles between king and Parliament led to a bloody civil war, culminating in the execution of Charles I, and subsequently, to a bloodless revolution deposing Charles II's successor, James II.
- Industrial and Agricultural revolutions boosted manufacturing and farming production.
- Revolutions in America and France showed that people could change their form of government.

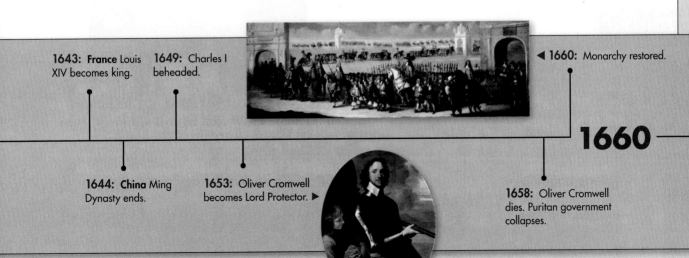

1643: France Louis XIV becomes king.

1649: Charles I beheaded.

◀ **1660:** Monarchy restored.

1644: China Ming Dynasty ends.

1653: Oliver Cromwell becomes Lord Protector. ▶

1658: Oliver Cromwell dies. Puritan government collapses.

1660

Essential Questions Across Time

The Seventeenth and Eighteenth Centuries (1625–1798)

What is the **relationship** between literature and *place?*

Bustling city versus quiet country: that age-old division is central to the period. For most of the time, it is the city of London that matters, but gradually, it is the rural landscape that comes to dominate.

How was London the capital of literature, too?

Old London The London of the seventeenth-century poets John Donne, Ben Jonson, and the young John Milton was still the old city of narrow, unpaved streets and timber houses. The river Thames was the main thoroughfare. It was easier to sail to a distant destination than walk or ride, and with only one bridge, ferries were needed to connect the two banks of the river.

During the civil war and the Protectorate of Cromwell, all eyes focused on the Houses of Parliament. These were not the imposing buildings in which Parliament sits today, made famous by postcards. (Those buildings were erected in the 1840s!) Although much smaller, they were still the stages on which the political dramas of the day were enacted.

In 1660, a new king returned from exile, and London threw off its Puritan black, reopened the theaters the triumphant Puritans had closed in 1642, welcomed actresses on the stage for the first time, and celebrated.

London Disasters Become London Literature The party did not last long, however. The Puritans said it was divine retribution on a scandalous court; historians say it was flea-bearing rats from the busy wharves on the Thames. In 1664, the plague struck and

TIMELINE

1664: North America Britain seizes New Netherlands.

1666: Great Fire of London. ▶

1660

◀ **1682: North America** La Salle claims Louisiana for France.

the streets of London were filled with carts carrying dead bodies to lime pits. Then, in 1666, a great fire broke out and large areas of London were incinerated. Samuel Pepys captured these twin disasters in his *Diary*, displaying a reporter's cool eye and a citizen's warm concern.

Pepys was writing only for himself, or so he thought (the *Diary*, written in code, was "translated" and published in the 19th century). At least two generations later, however, Daniel Defoe interviewed survivors of the plague and studied records to re-create that perilous time for a broad public, writing the fictional *A Journal of the Plague Year*.

How did roads lead to novels?

Just as London was rebuilt after the fire, the countryside was also being transformed by a series of turnpikes for stagecoaches and canals for barges. The primary purpose was business, but as people took advantage of the new mobility the coach roads offered, a new literary form took inspiration from the road: the novel.

The novel pictured all kinds of characters in their wanderings. Henry Fielding's humorous and good-humored *Tom Jones* was a prime example of a novel on the road. (One later writer, the French novelist Stendhal, would even define a novel as a mirror traveling down a road, reflecting the life around it.)

How did a new gathering place capture a new readership?

All roads still led to London, especially for the bright and ambitious. In London, they would encounter a new kind of gathering place. Suddenly,

---

The
BRITISH
TRADITION

THE CHANGING ENGLISH LANGUAGE, BY RICHARD LEDERER

No Harmless Drudge, He

On April 15, 1755, Dr. Samuel Johnson—blind in one eye, impoverished, and incompletely educated—produced the first modern *Dictionary of the English Language*.

Johnson set himself the task of making a different kind of dictionary, one of the first that would include all the words in the English language, not just the difficult ones. In addition, he would show how to divide words into syllables and where words came from. He would establish a consistent system of defining words and draw from his own gigantic learning to provide, for the first time in any dictionary, illustrative quotations from famous writers.

Underfunded and working almost alone in a Fleet Street garret room, Johnson defined some 43,000 words and illuminated their meanings with more than 114,000 supporting quotations.

Johnson defined a lexicographer as "a writer of dictionaries, a harmless drudge . . ." However, he was obviously far more than a harmless drudge, and his two-volume dictionary was by far the most comprehensive and readable that had appeared.

WORKS
OF
JOHN LOCKE, Esq

1684: China All ports opened to foreign trade.

1688: Glorious Revolution.

1690: John Locke publishes his *Two Treatises of Government.* ▶

1685: James II becomes king.

◀ **1689:** Bill of Rights becomes law.

1695

like mushrooms sprung up overnight, these places were all over the city. There seemed to be one on every corner. Who could account for the unstoppable spread of the coffee house? Will's and White's were among the most fashionable, but they all had many regulars.

They were popular because they offered not only coffee, the beverage that was all the rage at the time, but a place to hang out, to meet friends, to smoke a pipe, and to read the essays in those new-fangled magazines people were talking about. The titles of two famous magazines of the time, *The Tatler* and *The Spectator*, suggest that periodicals were an extension of the observation and gossip that took place around the city and especially in coffee houses. Such gossip, however, was still respectable for a self-conscious and social-climbing middle class—a coffee house was more proper than a tavern.

Samuel Johnson, who had ridden from Litchfield to London to seek literary fame and fortune—sharing a horse with future actor David Garrick, according to legend—embodied the London man of letters at this time. He famously remarked that if a man were tired of London, he was tired of life. In his greatest literary achievement, the *Dictionary of the English Language*, Johnson defined in a single book all the words worth knowing, just as London itself defined all the life worth living.

How did the countryside begin to influence literature?

Even as Johnson was speaking, however, the times were changing. One of the most popular and influential poems of the second half of the eighteenth century is not set in London, but in a country churchyard. Thomas Gray's "Elegy Written in a Country Churchyard" is a sober and thoughtful poem, and its meditative tone is completely different from the biting satire that flourished in an urban world. A mood of nocturnal reverie became the dominant mood of poetry.

Removed from the din and dirt of the city, poets looked to country landscapes for inspiration, moral examples, and consolation. The country replaced the city as the setting and subject for literature.

> ### ESSENTIAL QUESTION VOCABULARY
>
> These Essential Question words will help you think and write about literature and place:
>
> **mobility** (mō bil´ ə tē´) *n.* ability to move freely from place to place
>
> **meditative** (med´ ə tāt´ iv) *adj.* deeply thoughtful
>
> **urban** (ʉr´ bən) *adj.* characteristic of the city, as opposed to the country

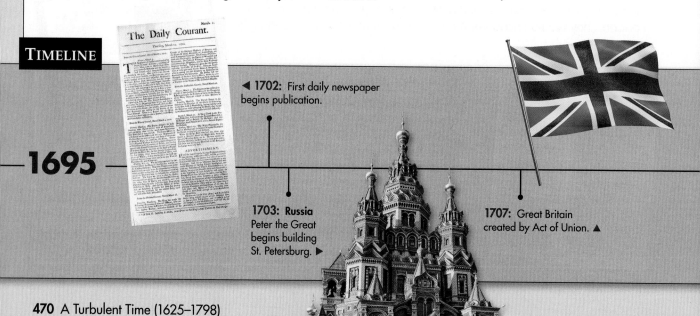

TIMELINE

1695

◀ **1702:** First daily newspaper begins publication.

1703: Russia Peter the Great begins building St. Petersburg. ▶

1707: Great Britain created by Act of Union. ▲

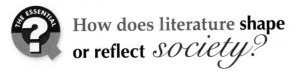

How does literature **shape** or reflect *society?*

The turmoil of the period raised profound questions about order. Civil war toppled a king and so posed the question, What holds the social order together? Fueled by religious differences, the war dramatized still other fundamental questions: If human beliefs differ irreconcilably, what can one know about the order of the world or about the right way to behave? Even economic growth opened questions. Members of the new middle class, their place in the world secured by prosperity, not birth, were haunted by the question, What is my place in the social order? The literature of the time was dedicated to answering such questions.

How did Milton's Grace become Newton's Gravity?

For John Milton, who lived through the Civil War, serving as Cromwell's secretary, literature, religion, and civic duty were all related. His epic *Paradise Lost* takes disobedience as its theme: the rebellious pride of Satan leading to the willful disobedience of Eve. Writing in the dark days when the Puritan religious government had failed, he intended his epic poem "to justify the ways of God to men."

At almost the same time that Milton published *Paradise Lost*, one of England's towering geniuses provided a different vision of God's ways in the world. In 1687, Isaac Newton published his *Mathematical Principles of Natural Philosophy* and everything changed. Newton demonstrated that the universe was governed by natural physical principles. Newton himself was a deeply religious man, but others read his work as proof that the world operated without the constant attention of a divine being. Gravity replaced grace. Some believed in a divine watchmaker who created and wound up the universe and then let it tick on its own.

Belief in a benevolent but detached God was called Deism. Pope's *Essay on Man* tells us: "Know then thyself, presume not God to scan." More and more, emphasis would be placed on understanding humans in their own world and according to the natural laws of that world.

> ### ESSENTIAL QUESTION VOCABULARY
>
> These Essential Question words will help you think and write about literature and society:
>
> **civic** (siv´ik) *adj.* relating to citizenship and affairs of government
>
> **rational** (rash´ ən əl) *adj.* of or based on reason
>
> **proportion** (prō pôr´ shən) *n.* balance; desirable relationship among parts

1715: France Louis XV succeeds to throne.

1714: George I becomes King.

1727: Brazil First coffee planted. ▼

◄ **1719:** First organized cricket match takes place.

1730

Why did literature focus on conduct?

Satire and Proportion In this new world, writers examined conduct through the lens of reason, not revelation. As a result, satire flourished. Satire ridicules conduct that is not rational, that is out of proportion. Pope's *Rape of the Lock* is a mock epic in which a trivial incident is treated as something earth-shaking. Swift's *Gulliver's Travels* is, with its tiny Lilliputians and giant Brobdingnagians, a study in proportion and the disproportionate things that humans do.

The "How-to" Genres The literary essay began as a "how-to" genre, teaching rational conduct to the new middle classes and helping them find their own identity. As Addison says in his essay "The Aims of *The Spectator*," he hopes the "morning lectures" in his new periodical will provide "instruction agreeable, and … diversion useful."

The novel also had its start in the "how-to" fashion. Samuel Richardson, a publisher, wrote a book of advice on conduct for apprentices. He then began a series of model letters on problems of conduct in daily life. In 1740, these turned into *Pamela*. Often cited as the first English novel, *Pamela* is epistolary in form; it is a series of letters by a young servant whose virtue is, unsuccessfully, assailed by her master.

Religious belief was also caught up in this question of appropriate conduct. John Wesley founded Methodism, which grew from his early commitment to self-examination and self-discipline, the "method" of belief and worship. His preaching was very influential because it met the need for a renewed sense of personal religious experience.

The BRITISH TRADITION

CLOSE-UP ON DAILY LIFE

Proper Behavior for Children

The eighteenth-century focus on proper conduct applied to children as well. One book on this subject was entitled *Rules for Children's Behavior: At Church, at Home, at Table, in Company, in Discourse, at School, abroad, and among Boys . . .* (1701). Following are some of the "Rules for Behavior in Company":

Sit not down in the presence of Superiors without bidding.

Sing not nor hum in thy mouth while thou art in company.

Play not wantonly like a Mimic with thy Fingers or Feet.

Stand not wriggling with thy body hither and thither, but steady and upright.

In coughing or sneezing make as little noise as possible.

If thou cannot avoid yawning, shut thy Mouth with thine Hand or Handkerchief before it, turning thy Face aside.

Laugh not aloud, but silently Smile upon occasion.

TIMELINE

1730

1740: Prussia
Frederick the Great succeeds to the throne. ▼

1749: Henry Fielding publishes *Tom Jones*.

1745: Last Jacobite rebellion in Scotland.

1752: North America
Benjamin Franklin invents lightning rod. ▲

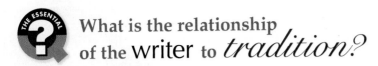

What is the relationship of the writer to *tradition?*

In this period, some literary traditions reach a magnificent conclusion, and some wholly new forms emerge from the chaos of civil war and revolution to meet the needs of a growing, literate, middle-class audience.

What effects did the Renaissance and Reformation have?

From Love to Religion John Donne is a child of the Renaissance—the rebirth of classical learning and themes that began in the fifteenth century—and Reformation—the efforts to reform Christianity that led to the birth of Protestantism. He begins as a witty love poet and ends as the Dean of the old St. Paul's Cathedral, which burned in 1666. His early lyrics continue the Elizabethan tradition, but his Holy Sonnets change the sonnet from a love poem into a religious meditation.

Work Based on the Classics Ben Jonson's poetry is restrained and graceful, like the classical poetry he admired. Poets who succeeded him, "The Tribe of Ben," produced brilliant poems on the *carpe diem* theme. *Carpe diem* is Latin for "seize the day," and the speakers in the poems, male, urge their audience, female, to forget inhibitions and take advantage of the fleeting hours of life. Andrew Marvell's "To His Coy Mistress" adds a serious undertone suggesting the real ravages of time.

Renaissance and Reformation John Milton's work embodies almost all the traditions of both the Renaissance and Reformation. Able to read Greek, Latin, Hebrew, French, and Italian, he wanted to give English an epic poem to match those of Homer and Virgil. He first considered an epic based on the legends of King Arthur because Homer and Virgil had based their epics on mythic histories of their countries.

A devout son of the Reformation, however, he decided that the fit subject for an English epic was the Bible's story of creation and fall. When the hated monarchy had been restored, the poet, blind and disillusioned with politics, dictated his poem about the fall from Eden and the promise of a redeemer who will restore the human race to its rightful heritage.

ESSENTIAL QUESTION VOCABULARY

These Essential Question words will help you think and write about the writer and tradition:

literate (lit´ər it) *adj.* able to read and write

heritage (her´ i tij) *n.* something handed down from the past, such as a culture or tradition

prophet (präf´ ət) *n.* person regarded as divinely inspired

1756: Britain enters Seven Years War.

1761: First exhibition of agricultural machines opens in London. ▶

1765

1759: Canada British troops capture Quebec. ▶

1764: London introduces practice of numbering houses.

How did Milton create a new role for the poet?

Poet as Prophet In his writing, Milton addressed the English as if he were an Old Testament prophet, thundering at a people that had broken its covenant with God. Milton created the role of poet as prophet, a poet reminding a nation of the path from which it had strayed. This idea of the poet had a strong influence on subsequent literature. In the Romantic period, the poets William Blake and Percy Bysshe Shelley assume the role. Another Romantic, Wordsworth, despairing of the state of England in 1802, writes: "Milton! thou shouldst be living at this hour / England hath need of thee."

What new forms arose for new audiences?

The Heroic Couplet Milton's influence was not felt immediately. With the end of the civil war and Puritan rule, poets sought a new mode of expression for a new social order. That mode was the heroic couplet, iambic pentameter lines linked in rhyming pairs. This form perfectly suited an urban aristocratic society that valued clever talk. With the genius of Alexander Pope, the form reaches its peak. The variations he creates within the rigid form give his poetry its vitality.

The Essay and the Novel Two new forms came into being in this period to meet the demands of a new middle-class audience: the essay and the novel. Both require a literate audience with money to spend on periodicals and books and leisure time to fill—an audience who want to read about people like themselves and people they would like to be.

The essay is a secular sermon, teaching lessons about life. Where sermons are delivered in houses of worship, essays depended on publication in periodicals to reach their audience. At the same time, periodicals relied on essays to attract readers. That marriage produced an enduring form whose offspring includes today's newspaper columns and television news commentary shows.

The novel had its roots in quasi-religious narratives: the life story of a man or woman struggling to survive and be virtuous in a world that is hostile, evil, or simply indifferent. Coming into flower in the middle of the eighteenth century, the novel is the beginning of a style of literature—self-conscious, self-analytical, socially concerned—that will dominate coming centuries.

John Milton

TIMELINE

1765

1773: **North America**
Boston Tea Party. ▶

1776: **North America**
American Revolution begins. ▼

CONTEMPORARY CONNECTION

John Milton: Epic Poet or Computer Visionary?

John Milton wrote his great epic *Paradise Lost* in the mid-1600s. So, what could Milton's poetic description of hell possibly have in common with artificial intelligence, the technology of thinking machines? Pandemonium, that's what!

Paradise Lost describes how Satan was ousted from heaven and set up his own domain. Milton actually created the word *Pandemonium* to name Satan's capital city. It is based on the Greek word *pan*, meaning "all," and the Latin word *daemonium*, meaning "demons." Pandemonium is the place where all the demons gather to argue about which diabolical scheme they will pursue next. Satan, of course, makes the final decision.

In 1958, Oliver Selfridge, a computer pioneer, thought Milton's word for the capital of the nether world was perfect to describe a system of processing information. In pandemonium as it refers to computers, there are four levels of demons. Demons are the working parts of a computer program. The lowest demons receive data. Higher-level demons accumulate and "shout" out their data. Like Satan, the top demon makes the decision about which shout is the loudest and should be followed up.

Certainly, Milton could not have anticipated this use for his word. Being an inventive thinker himself, though, he would probably have applauded it!

1784: France
First school for the blind established.

1789: France
Revolution begins with storming of Bastille. ▶

1798: William Wordsworth and Samuel Taylor Coleridge publish *Lyrical Ballads*.

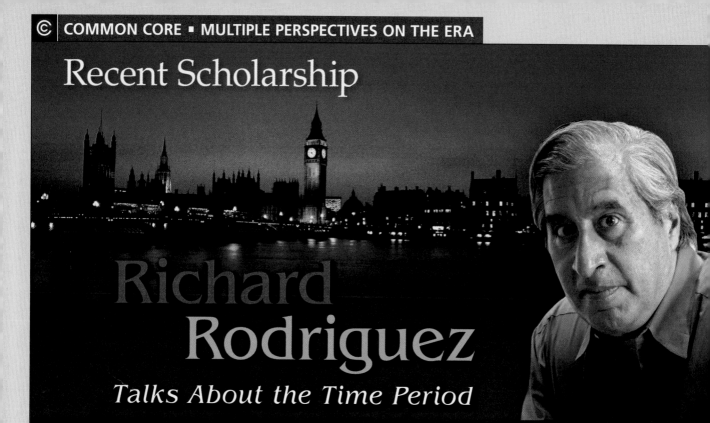

Recent Scholarship

Richard Rodriguez

Talks About the Time Period

From Small Towns to Big Cities

In high school, whenever teachers assigned texts of British literature, I responded most to the idea of London. I lived in Sacramento, at that time, more a town than a city. By senior year, because my body and mind were growing, I began to feel the need of a city—a place of contest and ambition. I left home, as so many seekers of fortune in English novels leave home, for the city.

London, Market for Commodities and Ideas

London at the beginning of the eighteenth century was becoming the center of the world. Most of the world's commodities and many of the world's ideas passed through London. A city of so much invested interest was interested. People required news: of ships, of trade, of exploration. To get the news, people required newspapers. Londoners also wanted to read about themselves, about plays and books, about fashions and personalities.

About the Author

Richard Rodriguez (b. 1944) is a distinguished nonfiction author and journalist who often presents his views on public television. His books include *Hunger of Memory: The Education of Richard Rodriguez* (1982), *Days of Obligation: An Argument with My Mexican Father* (1992), and *Brown: The Last Discovery of America* (2001; 2003).

Birth of *The Spectator*

In 1711, an ex-soldier and ex-scholar named Richard Steele published a journal called *The Spectator. The Spectator*'s innovation was to notice and to comment upon the social and moral life of London. Steele enlisted a young writer named Joseph Addison to contribute to the paper. Addison developed the persona of *The Spectator*:

"I am frequently seen in most public places. . . . [But] I live in the world rather as a spectator of mankind than as one of the species. . . ."

Addison's essays are fictional observations of real places and real habits. They remain among the best records we have of how several classes of men and women behaved and thought and spoke in London in the eighteenth century.

Joining "the conversation of cities"

It was my ambition, when I left my schoolbooks behind, to join the conversation of cities. I became a journalist. My fate, as Addison might have foretold: In order to write, one must seek solitude. To create a public voice, one must choose loneliness.

Addison benefited from his solitude as a spectator; he was thrilled to have found readers in the male clubs and coffee houses of London. And he also wanted women readers.

When I was in high school and teachers instructed me to compose an essay, I never wondered about my reader. My reader was the teacher—her ear a pair of spectacles, her voice a fluent red ink.

What one never learns in high school about writing is just how large the world is and how a writer in the world must find an audience—must seduce, amuse, or infuriate a stranger's attention.

The Beginning and End of Print

The reading audience of eighteenth-century London was avid, middle class, growing as the city was growing—whereas we live near the end of a long age of print. Now, fewer people read for their news; fewer still for their pleasure. Today's blogger, tossing words into the void of the Web, must sense this. I sense it, writing for newspapers. Yet one is confident that one is, somehow, recorded. One lives in the age of mass media, after all.

But writing, although lonely, cannot be completed alone. In order to write, in order to continue writing, the writer needs to find, as Addison found, a reader—"you"—someone willing to complete the meaning of this sentence by the act of reading.

Speaking and Listening: Collaboration

Rodriguez compares his career to that of British author Joseph Addison (1672–1719), who, says Rodriguez, "was thrilled to have found readers in the male clubs and coffee houses of London." These coffee houses were places where people exchanged news and ideas, as well as conducted business.

With a partner, study the picture of an eighteenth-century coffee house shown here. Then, formulate a **media evaluation** that answers the following questions:

- What techniques did the artist use to convey a favorable or unfavorable impression of such a place?
- What social and personal values was the artist promoting?

LONDON COFFEE-HOUSES, PAST AND PRESENT.

Integrate and Evaluate Information

1. Use a chart like the one shown to determine the key ideas expressed in the Essential Question essays on pages 468–474. Fill in two ideas related to each Essential Question and note the authors most closely associated with each concept. One item has been provided for you.

Essential Question	Key Concept	Key Author
Literature and Place	Threats to London	Samuel Pepys
Literature and Society		
Writer and Tradition		

2. Review the visual sources that appear on the timeline on pages 466–475. Make two generalizations about life during the seventeenth and eighteenth centuries based on the images. Cite specific examples from the essays on these pages to support your generalizations.

3. The seventeenth and eighteenth centuries were marked by civil war and revolution. Choose either the English civil war or the Glorious Revolution and describe the perspectives of those involved in the conflict. What did each side seek? To what was it opposed? What long-term changes in English society did the event help to create? Cite evidence from the multiple sources presented on pages 464–475, as well as from other sources you consult, such as encyclopedias, in your response.

4. Address a Question: In his essay on pages 476–477, Richard Rodriguez recalls that "It was my ambition, when I left my schoolbooks behind, to join the conversation of cities." What "conversations" define your town or city? What forums give citizens a "public voice"? How could you use these forums to "join the conversation"? Integrate information from this textbook and other sources, such as blogs, to support your ideas.

© **Common Core State Standards**

Reading Informational Text
7. Integrate and evaluate multiple sources of information presented in different media or formats as well as in words in order to address a question or solve a problem.

Speaking and Listening
1. Initiate and participate effectively in a range of collaborative discussions with diverse partners on *grades 11–12 topics, texts, and issues,* building on others' ideas and expressing their own clearly and persuasively.

1.a. Come to discussions prepared, having read and researched material under study; explicitly draw on that preparation by referring to evidence from texts and other research on the topic or issue to stimulate a thoughtful, well-reasoned exchange of ideas.

Speaking and Listening: Debate

With other students, form two small groups, the Roundheads and the Cavaliers, and **debate** the following resolution: *A king rules by divine right and cannot be deposed.* Argue for and against the resolution before an audience of your classmates.

Solve a Research Problem: To participate effectively in the debate, you and your teammates will need to research the following topics:

- the divine right of kings
- Parliament's rights to limit the king's power
- Anglican and Roman Catholic beliefs versus Puritan beliefs

Before you begin, formulate a research plan that includes a variety of print and online sources. Assign a different task to each team member. Before the debate, share information and rehearse arguments. As you present your evidence in the debate, cite the texts you consulted.

ESSENTIAL QUESTION VOCABULARY

Use these words in your responses:

Literature and Place
mobility
meditative
urban

Literature and Society
civic
rational
proportion

Writer and Tradition
literate
heritage
prophet

The War Against Time

Connecting to the Essential Question John Donne was called *witty* not only because his work was amusing, but also because it used clever comparisons. A poetic device that Donne invented was the odd but clever comparison of things that at first seem very different. Noting such comparisons will help as you answer the Essential Question: **What is the relationship of the writer to tradition?**

Close Reading Focus

Metaphysical Poetry; Conceit; Paradox

Donne and his followers wrote **metaphysical poetry**—poetry characterized by intellectual displays and concern with metaphysical, or philosophical, issues. It uses the following poetic devices:

- **Conceits** are extended comparisons that link objects or ideas not commonly associated. For example, Donne compares two lovers to the two legs of a drawing compass.

- **Paradoxes** are images or descriptions that appear self-contradictory but that reveal a deeper truth: "Death, thou shalt die."

Interpret the conceits and paradoxes you find in Donne's work, and analyze how word choices result in poetry that is fresh and engaging.

Preparing to Read Complex Texts To understand these poems, **analyze the author's perspective,** or view the author is taking, and **how word choice affects meaning and tone.** Remember that Donne's work is divided into a youthful period, during which he wrote love poems, and a later phase, during which he wrote religious works. Donne's poems are arranged in rough chronological order, so you can see evidence of his change of heart. Also, even though the speaker in each poem is not necessarily Donne himself, the poet is closely identified with the speaker. Use a chart like the one shown to infer the speaker's situation and motivation—these, in turn, will give you clues to the author's perspective.

Vocabulary

You will encounter the words listed here in the texts that follow. Copy the words into your notebook. Which three words have the same suffix? Which part of speech does this suffix indicate?

profanation	contention
laity	piety
trepidation	covetousness

**Common Core
State Standards**

Reading Literature
4. Analyze the impact of specific word choices on meaning and tone, including words with multiple meanings or language that is particularly fresh, engaging, or beautiful.

Speaker's Words

"Sweetest love, I do not go, For weariness of thee, ... "

Situation

He has to leave his beloved.

Motivation

He is reassuring her that he is not leaving because he is tired of her.

John Donne (1572?–1631)

Works of John Donne

Donne's life and poetry seem to fall neatly into two contradictory parts. Wild, young Jack Donne wrote clever love poems read by sophisticated aristocrats. In later life, sober Dr. John Donne, Dean of St. Paul's and the most popular preacher in England, published widely read meditations and sermons. Contradiction and conflict were the stuff of Donne's life; they are also at the heart of his poetic style. As Jack or as John, Donne the writer excelled at dramatizing— and wittily resolving—the contradictions of life.

Religious Conflict A distant relative of Sir Thomas More, Donne was raised a Catholic. In the England of Queen Elizabeth I, Catholics faced prejudice and restrictive laws. Although Donne studied at Oxford and Cambridge, he never obtained his degree, probably because of his refusal to compromise his Catholicism by swearing an oath acknowledging the supremacy of the king over the church. Later, he abandoned Catholicism and joined the official Church of England. To this day, scholars debate whether Donne experienced a genuine conversion.

A Secret Marriage After taking part in two naval expeditions against the Spanish, Donne served as private secretary to one of the queen's highest-ranking officials, Sir Thomas Egerton. Bright, clever, and charming, Donne secretly wed Anne More, his employer's niece, in 1601. Again, scholars throw doubt on Donne's motives. Some hold that he married for love; others maintain that he hoped his marriage to the daughter of an influential family would promote his career. If Donne counted on this possibility, though, he was sadly mistaken. Anne's father disapproved of the union, and so Donne's marriage temporarily ruined his chances for social advancement.

For many years, the devoted couple lived plagued by poverty and illness, in the midst of which Donne still managed to write influential poetry. He eked out a living writing religious tracts and serving as temporary secretary to several aristocrats. Donne finally attained a secure position in 1615 when, at the insistence of King James, he entered the clergy.

Success After serving as a royal chaplain, Donne became dean of St. Paul's Cathedral in London in 1621, a post he held until his death. He became one of the most popular preachers of his day. No longer the writer of sly or witty passionate verses, he published widely read sermons and religious meditations. Jack Donne's days were over, and John Donne's fame was spreading.

Fair Is My Love, Edwin A. Abbey. The
Harris Museum and Art Gallery, Preston

Song
John Donne

▲ **Critical Viewing**
How does the relationship
of the man and woman in
this painting compare with
the relationship described in
the poem? **COMPARE AND
CONTRAST**

Sweetest love, I do not go,
    For weariness of thee,
Nor in hope the world can show
    A fitter love for me;
5   But since that I
Must die at last, 'tis best
To use¹ myself in jest,
    Thus by feigned² deaths to die.

Yesternight the sun went hence,
10   And yet is here today;
He hath no desire nor sense,
    Nor half so short a way;

---

1. **use** condition.
2. **feigned** (fānd) *adj.* imagined.

Then fear not me,
But believe that I shall make
15 Speedier journeys, since I take
More wings and spurs than he.

O how feeble is man's power,
That if good fortune fall,
Cannot add another hour,
20 Nor a lost hour recall!
But come bad chance,
And we join to it our strength,
And we teach it art and length,
Itself o'er us to advance.

25 When thou sigh'st, thou sigh'st not wind,
But sigh'st my soul away;
When thou weep'st, unkindly kind,
My life's blood doth decay.
It cannot be
30 That thou lovest me as thou say'st,
If in thine my life thou waste,
That art the best of me.

Let not thy divining heart
Forethink me any ill,
35 Destiny may take thy part,
And may thy fears fulfill;
But think that we
Are but turned aside to sleep.
They who one another keep
40 Alive, ne'r parted be.

The BRITISH TRADITION

Mind and Feeling

The twentieth-century poet T. S. Eliot celebrated Donne as one of the best—and last—poets to integrate mind and heart: "A thought to Donne was an experience; it modified his sensibility [feeling and perception]." Eliot praised Donne's "direct sensuous apprehension of thought" and his "recreation of thought into feeling."

Eliot claimed that later poets did not "feel their thought as immediately as the odor of a rose" and that "[in] the seventeenth century a dissociation of sensibility set in, from which we have never recovered."

Connect to the Literature

In what ways are lines 27–28 an integration of mind and heart?

Critical Reading

1. **Key Ideas and Details** **(a)** What does the speaker say his reason is for leaving? **(b) Infer:** To what remark of his beloved might he be responding in this poem?

2. **Key Ideas and Details** **(a) Analyze:** How would you outline the speaker's argument? **(b) Speculate:** What might the argument's effect on the beloved be?

3. **Integration of Knowledge and Ideas** Imagine that the speaker's beloved is in tears as he is leaving. Why might the speaker have chosen to present his feelings in the form of witty arguments?

4. **Integration of Knowledge and Ideas** The speaker uses exaggeration to persuade his beloved. Do you think exaggeration is a useful or a valid persuasive tool? Explain.

Cite textual evidence to support your responses.

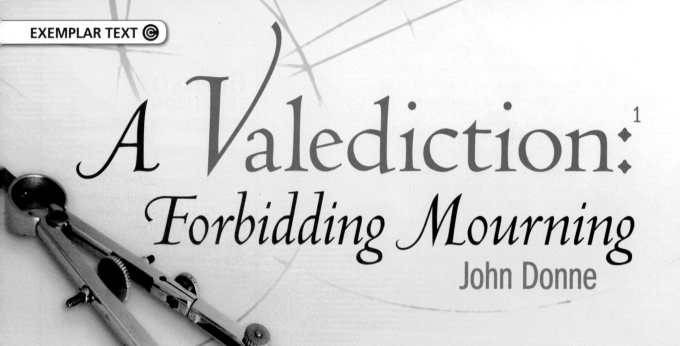

A Valediction:[1]
Forbidding Mourning
John Donne

Vocabulary

profanation (präf´ ə
nā´ shən) *n.* action
showing disrespect
for something sacred

laity (lā´ i tē) *n.*
those not initiated
into a priesthood

trepidation (trep´ ə dā´
shən) *n.* trembling

As virtuous men pass mildly away,
    And whisper to their souls to go,
Whilst some of their sad friends do say
    The breath goes now, and some say, No;

5 So let us melt, and make no noise,
    No tear-floods, nor sigh-tempests move,
'Twere profanation of our joys
    To tell the laity our love.

Moving of th'earth brings harms and fears,
10   Men reckon what it did and meant;
But trepidation of the spheres,[2]
    Though greater far, is innocent.

Dull sublunary[3] lovers' love
    (Whose soul is sense) cannot admit
15 Absence, because it doth remove
    Those things which elemented it.[4]

But we by a love, so much refined,
    That our selves know not what it is,

Analyzing Perspective

Why does the speaker turn
parting into a proof of the
strength of his love?

---

1. **valediction** farewell speech.
2. **trepidation of the spheres** movements of the stars and planets that are inconsistent
   with a perfect circular orbit.
3. **sublunary** (sub´ lōō nər´ ē) referring to the region below the moon, considered in early
   astronomy to be the domain of changeable and perishable things.
4. **Those things . . . elemented it** the basic materials or parts of their love.

Inter-assurèd of the mind,[5]
20   Care less, eyes, lips, and hands to miss.

Our two souls therefore, which are one,
      Though I must go, endure not yet
A breach, but an expansion,
      Like gold to airy thinness beat.

25 If they be two, they are two so
      As stiff twin compasses[6] are two;
Thy soul the fixed foot, makes no show
      To move, but doth, if th'other do.

And though it in the center sit,
30   Yet when the other far doth roam,
It leans, and hearkens after it,
      And grows erect, as that comes home.

Such wilt thou be to me, who must
      Like th'other foot, obliquely[7] run;
35 Thy firmness makes my circle just,[8]
      And makes me end where I begun.

If they be two,
they are two so
As stiff twin
compasses are two…

---

5. **Inter-assurèd of the mind** mutually confident of each other's thoughts.
6. **twin compasses** the two legs of a drawing compass.
7. **obliquely** at an angle; not straight.
8. **just** true; perfect.

Critical Reading

1. **Key Ideas and Details (a)** According to the speaker, how should he and his beloved part? **(b) Infer:** What does he think that this manner of parting shows about their love? **(c) Interpret:** Describe two other claims the speaker makes to show how special their love is.

2. **Key Ideas and Details** The poem compares the lovers to the legs of a compass—she is fixed in place while he moves. What does the comparison indicate about their relationship?

3. **Integration of Knowledge and Ideas** The speaker links love with the order and stability of the world. Support this insight with details from the poem.

4. **Integration of Knowledge and Ideas** Do you, like the speaker, see love as a union of two souls, or do you think that lovers should be independent? Explain.

Cite textual evidence to support your responses.

HOLY SONNET 10

John Donne

Sir Thomas Aston *at the Deathbed of His Wife,* John Souch, Manchester City Art Galleries

BACKGROUND WRITERS IN DONNE'S DAY OFTEN DEPENDED ON THE SUPPORT OF PATRONS, WEALTHY SUPPORTERS OF THE ARTS. THE YOUNG DONNE DID NOT PUBLISH HIS POEMS (MOST WERE PRINTED ONLY AFTER HIS DEATH). INSTEAD, THEY WERE CIRCULATED AMONG A SELECT LITERARY AUDIENCE THAT INCLUDED PATRONS SUCH AS THE COUNTESS OF BEDFORD. AFTER DONNE WAS DISMISSED FROM HIS POSITION WITH SIR THOMAS EGERTON, HE AND HIS FAMILY DEPENDED IN PART ON PATRONS FOR FINANCIAL SUPPORT. WHEN HE BECAME A CLERGYMAN, DONNE NO LONGER NEEDED TO CAPTURE THE INTEREST OF PATRONS. HE CONTINUED, THOUGH, TO WRITE IMPASSIONED, WITTY VERSE SUCH AS THE HOLY SONNETS.

Death be not proud, though some have called thee
Mighty and dreadful, for thou art not so;
For those whom thou think'st thou dost overthrow,
Die not, poor death, nor yet canst thou kill me.
5 From rest and sleep, which but thy pictures[1] be,
Much pleasure; then from thee much more must flow,
And soonest our best men with thee do go,
Rest of their bones, and soul's delivery.[2]
Thou art slave to fate, chance, kings, and desperate men,
10 And dost with poison, war, and sickness dwell,
And poppy,[3] or charms can make us sleep as well
And better than thy stroke; why swell'st[4] thou then?
One short sleep past, we wake eternally,
And death shall be no more; Death, thou shalt die.

◄ **Critical Viewing**
The painting shows Lady Aston both when she is alive and when she is dead. Compare the relationship between death and life implied by the painting with that developed in Holy Sonnet 10. **COMPARE AND CONTRAST**

Metaphysical Poetry
What paradox does the speaker use to end his argument with Death?

1. **pictures** images.
2. **And . . . delivery** Our best men go with you to rest their bones and find freedom for their souls.
3. **poppy** opium.
4. **swell'st** swell with pride.

Critical Reading

1. **Key Ideas and Details (a)** What "pictures" of death does the speaker mention? **(b) Infer:** What positive lesson about death does the speaker draw from this resemblance?

2. **Key Ideas and Details (a) Interpret:** In what sense is death a slave (line 9)? **(b) Connect:** How does this point justify the opening line?

3. **Key Ideas and Details (a) Interpret:** What does the statement "Death, thou shalt die" mean? **(b) Draw Conclusions:** Why might the speaker react to death by challenging its "strength" and "pride"?

4. **Integration of Knowledge and Ideas** Does the speaker sound like a man talking himself out of fear or like one who has triumphed over fear? Explain.

Cite textual evidence to support your responses.

Meditation 17

John Donne

Nunc lento sonitu dicunt, Morieris.
(NOW, THIS BELL TOLLING SOFTLY FOR ANOTHER,
SAYS TO ME, THOU MUST DIE.)

▼ Critical Viewing

The building in this image stands remote and alone. How does this image contrast with the message Donne delivers in his sermon? **COMPARE AND CONTRAST**

Perchance he for whom this bell tolls may be so ill as that he knows not it tolls for him; and perchance I may think myself so much better than I am as that they who are about me and see my state may have caused it to toll for me, and I know not that. The church is catholic,[1] universal, so are all her actions; all that she does belongs to all. When she baptizes a child, that action concerns me; for that child is thereby connected to that head which is my head too, and ingrafted into that body[2] whereof I am a member. And when she buries a man, that action concerns me: all mankind is of one author and is one volume; when one man dies, one chapter is not torn out of the

---

1. **catholic** applying to humanity generally.
2. **head . . . body** In the Bible, St. Paul calls Jesus the head (spiritual leader) of all men (1 Corinthians 11:3) and a body in which the faithful are unified (1 Corinthians 12:12).

book, but translated into a better language; and every chapter must be so translated. God employs several translators; some pieces are translated by age, some by sickness, some by war, some by justice; but God's hand is in every translation, and his hand shall bind up all our scattered leaves again for that library where every book shall lie open to one another. As therefore the bell that rings to a sermon calls not upon the preacher only, but upon the congregation to come, so this bell calls us all; but how much more me, who am brought so near the door by this sickness. There was a contention as far as a suit[3] (in which both piety and dignity, religion and estimation,[4] were mingled) which of the religious orders should ring to prayers first in the morning; and it was determined that they should ring first that rose earliest. If we understand aright the dignity of this bell that tolls for our evening prayer, we would be glad to make it ours by rising early, in that application, that it might be ours as well as his whose indeed it is. The bell doth toll for him that thinks it doth; and though it intermit again, yet from that minute that that occasion wrought upon him, he is united to God. Who casts not up his eye to the sun when it rises? but who takes off his eye from a comet when that breaks out? Who bends not his ear to any bell which upon any occasion rings? but who can remove it from that bell which is passing a piece of himself out of this world? No man is an island, entire of itself; every man is a piece of the continent, a part of the main.[5] If a clod be washed away by the sea, Europe is the less, as well as if a promontory were, as well as if a manor of thy friend's or of thine own were. Any man's death diminishes me because I am involved in mankind, and therefore never send to know for whom the bell

---

3. **suit** lawsuit.
4. **estimation** self-esteem.
5. **main** mainland.

...*Therefore* never send to know for whom the bell tolls; it tolls for thee.

tolls; it tolls for thee. Neither can we call this a begging of misery or a borrowing of misery, as though we were not miserable enough of ourselves but must fetch in more from the next house, in taking upon us the misery of our neighbors. Truly it were an excusable **covetousness** if we did; for affliction is a treasure, and scarce any man hath enough of it. No man hath affliction enough that is not matured and ripened by it, and made fit for God by that affliction. If a man carry treasure in bullion, or in a wedge of gold, and have none coined into current money,[6] his treasure will not defray him as he travels. Tribulation is treasure in the nature of it, but it is not current money in the use of it, except we get nearer and nearer our home, heaven, by it. Another man may be sick too, and sick to death, and this affliction may lie in his bowels as gold in a mine and be of no use to him; but this bell that tells me of his affliction digs out and applies that gold to me, if by this consideration of another's danger, I take mine own into contemplation and so secure myself by making my recourse to my God, who is our only security.

Vocabulary

covetousness (kuv´ ət əs nis) *n.* greediness

6. **current money** currency; wealth in spendable form.

Critical Reading

1. **Key Ideas and Details (a)** What event does the tolling bell announce? **(b) Analyze:** Why does Donne say the tolling bell applies to him as well as to others?

2. **Key Ideas and Details (a)** What reason does Donne give for saying, "Any man's death diminishes me"? **(b) Interpret:** What does Donne mean by "No man is an island, entire of itself; every man is a piece of the continent"? **(c) Analyze:** How does the comparison of humanity to a continent support the idea that one death affects all people?

3. **Key Ideas and Details (a) Analyze:** In Donne's metaphor, when does the "treasure" of affliction turn into "current [spendable] money"? **(b) Interpret:** Why does Donne find affliction valuable? **(c) Connect:** In what sense does the tolling bell "apply" one person's affliction to another?

4. **Integration of Knowledge and Ideas** Donne says that, once one takes the bell as tolling for oneself, one is "united to God." In urging people to think about their own deaths, what might he be implying about people's attachment to worldly things such as money, success, and popularity?

5. **Integration of Knowledge and Ideas** Does the statement "No man is an island" still apply today? Why or why not? In your response, use at least two of these Essential Question words: *theme, unity, individual.* **[Connecting to the Essential Question: What is the relationship of the writer to tradition?]**

Cite textual evidence to support your responses.

Literary Analysis

Common Core State Standards

Writing

3.a. Create a smooth progression of experiences or events. *(p. 492)*

5. Develop and strengthen writing as needed by planning, revising, editing, rewriting, or trying a new approach, focusing on addressing what is most significant for a specific purpose and audience. *(p. 492)*

Language

1. Demonstrate command of the conventions of standard English grammar and usage when writing or speaking. *(p. 493)*

1.b. Resolve issues of complex or contested usage, consulting references as needed. *(p. 493)*

5. Demonstrate understanding of word relationships in word meanings. *(p. 492)*

1. **Key Ideas and Details** **(a)** In each of Donne's works, who is the speaker and what is the speaker's situation? **(b)** What is each speaker's motivation? **(c)** How do the speaker's situation and motivation provide a clue to Donne's perspective in each poem?

2. **Key Ideas and Details** **Analyze how the author's perspective affects meaning** by tracing a shift of attitude and perspective in Donne's work. **(a)** How does the perspective in "Song" and "A Valediction: Forbidding Mourning" differ from that in Holy Sonnet 10? **(b)** In what ways does this change affect the meaning, or essential message, Donne communicates in each poem?

3. **Craft and Structure** Identify and interpret a **conceit** that the speaker in "Song" uses to reassure his beloved. Explain what things are being compared.

4. **Craft and Structure** **(a)** What **paradox** does the speaker use in the fourth stanza of "Song"? **(b)** Explain the truth underlying this contradiction.

5. **Craft and Structure** **(a)** Identify a conceit in Holy Sonnet 10. **(b)** Explain the speaker's point in making the comparison.

6. **Integration of Knowledge and Ideas** In Meditation 17, Donne uses a conceit comparing suffering and treasure. **(a)** Use a chart like the one shown to analyze the forms of treasure he discusses. **(b)** Explain how each relates to suffering.

Main Idea: There are two forms of suffering, just as there are two forms of treasure.		
First Form of Treasure: _____	Second Form of Treasure: _____	Relationship Between Forms of Treasure: _____

7. **Integration of Knowledge and Ideas** **(a)** What important differences distinguish "Song" and "Valediction" from Holy Sonnet 10? **(b)** Identify an element of metaphysical poetry that all three share, giving examples from each.

8. **Craft and Structure** In the poems, the speaker uses conceits and paradoxes to move from uncertainty (his own or his listener's) to certainty. In Meditation 17, he uses these devices to inspire uncertainty in his listener. Explain, using examples from each work.

9. **Integration of Knowledge and Ideas** During World War II, the British used the phrase "No man is an island" to justify joining the fight against Nazi Germany. Do you think this use of Donne's words accurately reflected his perspective and meaning? Explain.

Vocabulary Acquisition and Use

Word Analysis: Latin Prefix *con-*

The word *contention* begins with the Latin prefix *con-*, which means "together" or "with." *Contention* comes from a Latin word meaning "to strive or struggle with."

Use at least four of the *con-* words listed here to write a paragraph about the works by Donne you have read. If any of the words are unfamiliar, use a dictionary to clarify their meanings.

concentrate	conflict
confront	connect
consequence	console
construct	contact

Then, choose two of the words you used and write a sentence identifying how the prefix *con-* helps create their meaning.

Vocabulary: Analogies

Analogies show the relationships between pairs of words. Complete each analogy using a word from the vocabulary list on page 480. In each, your choice should create a word pair that matches the relationship between the first two words given. Then, explain your answers.

1. *Crime* is to *law* as _____ is to *faith*.
2. The _____ is to the *clergy* as *civilians* are to *military personnel*.
3. *Nervousness* is to _____ as *happiness* is to *smiling*.
4. *Jealousy* is to *envy* as _____ is to *quarrel*.
5. _____ is to *religion* as *patriotism* is to *the nation*.
6. *Hunger* is to *food* as _____ is to *money*.

Writing to Sources

Narrative Text Imagine that a publisher has asked you to prepare a *biographical narrative* about John Donne. The essay will introduce a collection of Donne's work by highlighting the most important events of his life. Your assignment is to write a **plan** for your narrative.

Prewriting Review the biographical and background information on Donne in the text. Select the key events in his life, both personal and professional. You can also consult literary encyclopedias in print or online to gather more information.

Drafting Following your prewriting notes, write an outline for your narrative with the correct *sequence of events* that helps your reader to smoothly follow the progress of Donne's life.

Revising Read through your outline and revise points to make sure you can use them to communicate clearly the *significance of key events* to your audience.

> **Model: Revising to Clarify Significance**
> **Weak explanation:** 1615—Donne *became* a clergyman
> **Strong explanation:** 1615—Donne *gained security by entering* the clergy

> Specific language best communicates the significance of events.

Conventions and Style: Comparative and Superlative Adjectives and Adverbs

Adjectives and adverbs can take three different forms, as shown in the chart below.

Forms of Adjectives and Adverbs		
Positive	**Comparative**	**Superlative**
sweet	sweeter	sweetest
witty	wittier	wittiest
mildly	more mildly	most mildly
willingly	more willingly	most willingly
much	more	most
good	better	best

The comparative degree is for comparing *two* persons, places, or things. The superlative is for comparing *three or more*. Some comparatives and superlatives are formed by adding a suffix to the modifier (*-er* or *-est,* respectively). Others are formed by using (respectively) *more* or *most*. Consult a dictionary of English usage as needed to determine correct usage.

Using the Comparative	Using the Superlative
The days of his youth were *wilder* than those of his later life.	At one time, Donne was the most *popular* preacher in England.
During his lifetime, Donne's sermons were read *more widely* than his love poems.	Some people thought John Donne was the *best* poet at that time.

Practice Supply the correct form of the adjective or adverb shown in parentheses.

1. The mature John Donne was _____ than his younger counterpart, Jack. (*religious*)
2. She thought he was the _____ man she had ever met. (*charming*)
3. T. S. Eliot praised Donne's works _____ than many earlier critics had. (*highly*)
4. He says she is the _____ woman for him. (*good*)
5. The speaker says that he will travel _____ than the sun. (*fast*)
6. Death takes the _____ men when they are young. (*fine*)
7. It was determined that whoever rose _____ should be called to prayer first. (*early*)
8. Donne says a person who suffers becomes _____ than one who does not. (*mature*)
9. "Song" is _____ than "Valediction." (*long*)
10. Which of the three poems did you enjoy _____? (*much*)

Writing and Speaking Conventions

A. **Writing** For each adjective or adverb below, write one sentence using the comparative form and one using the superlative form.

   1. carefully   **2.** proud   **3.** mighty   **4.** great   **5.** deeply

   Then, consult a dictionary of English usage to ensure that you have correctly formed comparatives and superlatives.

B. **Speaking** As Death, write and present a response to Donne's argument in Holy Sonnet 10. Correctly use at least one comparative form and one superlative form. Consult a dictionary of English usage to check your formation of comparatives and superlatives.

Connecting to the Essential Question In his poetry, Ben Jonson favored qualities like balance, clarity, and proportion, virtues he associated with classical literature. As you read, notice passages in Jonson's poems that reflect the classical virtues of balance and clarity. Identifying these passages will help as you answer the Essential Question: **What is the relationship of the writer to tradition?**

Close Reading Focus

**Common Core
State Standards**

**Reading Literature
4.** Analyze the impact of specific word choices on meaning and tone, including words with multiple meanings or language that is particularly fresh, engaging, or beautiful.

Lyric; Epigram

A **lyric** is a brief melodic poem that expresses personal thoughts or feelings. In ancient Greece, lyrics were recited or sung to the accompaniment of a lyre (hence the name lyr-ic).

Styles of lyric poetry are often influenced by the *historic period*. Renaissance England, Ben Jonson's era, admired classical Greece. It is natural, therefore, that Jonson used an ancient Greek form called an **epigram** (from the Greek for "inscription"). Epigrams include these features:

- Short lines with bouncy rhythms
- Paradoxical twists, as in "Drink to me only with thine eyes . . ."
- Parallel structures, as in "Still to be neat, still to be dressed, . . ."

As you read, analyze the elements that make Jonson's lines memorable.

Preparing to Read Complex Texts By **comparing and contrasting elements** in several poems, you can better understand how Jonson expresses a range of feelings. Remember that these elements are the cumulative result of particular word choices:

- *tone*, or writer's attitude toward the subject
- *mood*, the emotions called up by the poem
- *style*, the author's general approach, varying from highly personal to impersonal and distant

Use the chart shown to compare these elements, including word choices that contribute to them, and to note how Jonson uses them to achieve his *aesthetic purposes*, or goals.

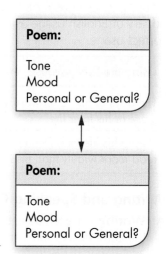

Poem:

Tone
Mood
Personal or General?

Poem:

Tone
Mood
Personal or General?

Vocabulary

You will encounter the words listed here in the texts that follow. Copy the words into your notebook and find the word that has a silent consonant.

fate	sound
lament	divine
presumed	wreath

Ben Jonson (1572–1637)

Author of "On My First Son" • "Still to Be Neat" • "Song: To Celia"

Ben Jonson lived a nearly mythic life. Even in his physical stature, he seemed a little larger than life—he was a big man with boundless energy and enormous courage. Brilliant in his poetry and dangerous in a duel, a classical scholar and a veteran soldier, an astute critic and a brassy talker, Jonson had a colorful, sometimes violent career that culminated in his reputation as an esteemed judge of literature. The friend as well as the chief rival of Shakespeare and Donne, he set literary tastes for a generation of poets.

A Poet at War Adopted in infancy, Jonson worked for his stepfather, a bricklayer, while attending the equivalent of high school under a private tutor. Too poor to study at a university, Jonson joined the army and fought in the wars for Dutch independence from Spain. The brawny Jonson at one point met an enemy champion in single combat before the massed armies of Holland and Spain. Jonson won.

Scandal and Success After returning to England, Jonson became an actor. Despite his turbulent life—jailed for his part in a "slanderous" play, almost hanged for killing a fellow actor in a duel, and even suspected of plotting against the king—Jonson became a major dramatist.

The Importance of a Poet Jonson's own opinion of his work and status may be judged by the fact that when he published his collected works in 1616, he entitled the volume *The Works of Benjamin Jonson*—a style of title used largely with celebrated ancient authors. With this gesture, Jonson may have become the first English-language poet to claim true professional dignity for himself.

Varied Styles Jonson's experiences ranged from tavern brawls to elegant entertainments, and his poetic styles are equally varied. He favored satire in his dramas, poking fun at contemporary character types in plays such as *Volpone* and *The Alchemist.*

Jonson wrote many of his poems in an impersonal style, one suited to inscriptions on monuments. Others are filled with nasty wit. As diverse as his styles are, though, one of his consistent strengths is the clear, direct expression of ideas.

A Lasting Influence In his varied experiences and diverse literary output, Jonson might seem to sum up the age in which he lived. Yet his importance does not end with the seventeenth century. Jonson's influence on writers is still felt today, and his plays continue to be produced.

ON MY FIRST SON

Ben Jonson

BACKGROUND Ben Jonson was indebted to ancient Greek and Roman poets, whose work shaped his taste for clear, brief expression. Like ancient poets, Jonson composed poetry with a definite social function. Jonson's poems praising other writers appeared at the beginning of their books. Poems such as "On My First Son" marked the occasion of a death. Songs such as "Still to Be Neat" were written by Jonson for his masques (royal entertainments).

Farewell, thou child of my right hand,[1] and joy;
    My sin was too much hope of thee, loved boy,
Seven years thou wert lent to me, and I thee pay,
    Exacted by thy fate, on the just[2] day.
5 O, could I lose all father,[3] now. For why
    Will man lament the state he should envy?
To have so soon scaped world's, and flesh's rage,
    And, if no other misery, yet age?
Rest in soft peace, and, asked, say here doth lie
10   Ben Jonson his best piece of poetry.
For whose sake, henceforth, all his vows be such,
    As what he loves may never like[4] too much.

___

1. **child . . . hand** literal translation of the Hebrew name Benjamin, the name of Jonson's son. Jonson's son was born in 1596 and died in 1603.
2. **just** exact.
3. **lose . . . father** shed an identity as a father.
4. **like** possibly meant in the old sense of "please."

Vocabulary

fate (fāt) *n.* destiny

lament (lə ment´) *v.* express grief over; mourn

Lyric

Do you think this poem was written to create a sense of permanence? Explain.

Critical Reading

1. **Key Ideas and Details (a)** What is the sin the speaker refers to in line 2? **(b) Interpret:** Why does the speaker call this feeling a sin?

2. **Key Ideas and Details (a) Interpret:** Why does the speaker wish to "lose all father, now"? **(b) Interpret:** What does he vow in lines 11–12? **(c) Draw Conclusions:** Why would grief lead to these reactions?

3. **Key Ideas and Details (a) Interpret:** Does the speaker ever present his feelings of grief directly? Explain. **(b) Evaluate:** Why might this manner of presenting grief strengthen the impression made on the reader?

4. **Integration of Knowledge and Ideas (a) Apply:** Contrast the ideas in lines 5–8 with contemporary attitudes. **(b) Evaluate:** Which makes more sense to you?

Cite textual evidence to support your responses.

Still to Be Neat

Ben Jonson

Portrait of Mrs. Richard Brinsley Sheridan, Thomas Gainsborough, National Gallery of Art, Washington, D.C.

Still[1] to be neat, still to be dressed,
As you were going to a feast;
Still to be powdered, still perfumed;
Lady, it is to be presumed,
5 Though art's hid causes[2] are not found,
All is not sweet, all is not sound.

Give me a look, give me a face,
That makes simplicity a grace;
Robes loosely flowing, hair as free;
10 Such sweet neglect more taketh me
　　　　　Than all th'adulteries[3] of art.
They strike mine eyes, but not my heart.

---

1. **Still** always.
2. **causes** reasons.
3. **adulteries** adulterations; corruptions.

Cite textual evidence to support your responses.

Critical Reading

1. **Key Ideas and Details (a)** To what style of dress and grooming is the speaker reacting in the first stanza? **(b) Interpret:** What are the "hid causes" that he suspects lie behind this style? **(c) Infer:** Why does he prefer the style of "sweet neglect"?

2. **Key Ideas and Details (a) Analyze:** How does Jonson use repetition to support his meaning? **(b) Evaluate:** How might Jonson's ideas about fashion apply to his own poem?

3. **Integration of Knowledge and Ideas** Which trends in modern advertising can you connect with the ideas in the poem?

SONG: To Celia

Ben Jonson

Lyric

What features of epigrams does Jonson use in lines 1–4?

Vocabulary

divine (di vīn′) *adj.* heavenly; holy

wreath (rēth) *n.* circle of flowers

Drink to me only with thine eyes,
And I will pledge with mine:
Or leave a kiss but in the cup,
And I'll not look for wine.
5 The thirst that from the soul doth rise,
Doth ask a drink divine:
But might I of Jove's[1] nectar sup,
I would not change for thine.

I sent thee late[2] a rosy wreath,
10 Not so much honoring thee,
As giving it a hope, that there
It could not withered be.
But thou thereon did'st only breathe,
And sent'st it back to me;
15 Since when it grows and smells, I swear,
Not of itself, but thee.

---

1. **Jove's** Jupiter's. In Roman mythology, Jupiter is the ruler of the gods.
2. **late** recently.

Critical Reading

1. **Key Ideas and Details (a)** For what does the soul thirst in lines 5–6 of "Song: To Celia"? **(b) Interpret:** Explain how this idea of the soul's thirst extends the image in lines 1–2.

2. **Key Ideas and Details (a) Assess:** How much do you know about the speaker of "Song: To Celia" or his beloved? **(b) Make a Judgment:** How would more information affect your appreciation of the poem?

3. **Integration of Knowledge and Ideas** Does Jonson's poem seem artificial or false by today's standards, or does it capture true sentiment? Explain.

4. **Integration of Knowledge and Ideas** Does Jonson's emphasis on clarity lessen the emotional impact of his work? In your response, use at least two of these Essential Question words: *classic, precise, artificial.* [*Connecting to the Essential Question: What is the relationship of the writer to tradition?*]

Literary Analysis

1. **Craft and Structure** Jonson favored a form of **lyric** called an *epigram*, a term that comes from a Greek word meaning "inscription." Would "On My First Son" be suitable as an inscription on the subject's tombstone? Explain.

2. **Craft and Structure** Identify three pairs of parallel phrases or clauses in "Still to Be Neat."

3. **Craft and Structure** **(a)** Explain how the phrase "sweet neglect" in "Still to Be Neat" appears paradoxical, or self-contradictory, but makes memorable sense. **(b)** How does the *irony*—a surprising difference from the expected—of the phrase add to its effect?

4. **Craft and Structure** Use a chart like the one shown to identify and characterize lines that give "Song: To Celia" the style of an epigram.

"Bouncy" Rhythms	Parallelism	Witty Wordings	Paradoxes
Lines:	Lines:	Lines:	Lines:

Common Core State Standards

Writing
1.a. Introduce precise, knowledgeable claim(s), establish the significance of the claim(s), distinguish the claim(s) from alternate or opposing claims, and create an organization that logically sequences claim(s), counterclaims, reasons, and evidence. *(p. 502)*

Language
1. Demonstrate command of the conventions of standard English grammar and usage when writing or speaking. *(p. 503)*
4. Determine or clarify the meaning of unknown and multiple-meaning words and phrases based on *grades 11–12 reading and content*, choosing flexibly from a range of strategies. *(p. 502)*

5. **Comparing Literary Works (a) Compare and contrast elements** in Jonson's work by contrasting the tone of lines 9–12 of "On My First Son" with that of lines 1–6 of "Still to Be Neat." **(b)** How do these different tones allow Jonson to achieve different *aesthetic purposes* in these lyrics?

6. **Comparing Literary Works (a)** For each lyric, identify one or two words or images that help create the *mood.* **(b)** Compare and contrast the moods called up by each of these poems.

7. **Comparing Literary Works (a)** Identify two details of Jonson's *style* in "On My First Son" that make it a sincere personal statement of grief. Explain. **(b)** Identify two details of Jonson's *style* in "Song: To Celia" that give it a formal, impersonal quality. Explain your choices. **(c)** Are both *aesthetic purposes*—sincerity and formality—equally valuable? Why or why not?

8. **Comparing Literary Works (a)** Which details in "Still to Be Neat" give it a generalized quality? **(b)** Which details make it seem heartfelt? **(c)** Compare the sentiment in this poem with the sentiment of the other two lyrics.

9. **Integration of Knowledge and Ideas** In what occupations today might the elements of Jonson's brief, witty writing style be effective? Explain, citing details from the texts.

Vocabulary Acquisition and Use

Multiple-Meaning Words

Many English words have more than one meaning, such as *sound*, which Jonson uses in "Still to Be Neat." From the context of the lines, you know that the word means "healthy" rather than "noise." Use context clues to determine the meanings of the italicized words in these sentences.

1. After the choir sang, the *divine* delivered his sermon.

2. The agent struggled to *divine* the secret of the coded message.

3. Winning the *prize* thrilled the contestant.

Next, think of another word with multiple meanings and write two sentences in which you use it in different ways. Exchange your sentences with a partner, and use context clues to determine the meanings of each other's word. If context is not sufficient to determine the meaning, use a print or an online dictionary.

Vocabulary: Synonyms

A **synonym** is a word that has the same meaning as another word. Replace each italicized word below with a synonym from the vocabulary list on page 494. Use each vocabulary word only once.

1. "I always *regret* my mistakes of the past," said the sad man.

2. The sunlight streaming into the cathedral produced a feeling of the *sacred*.

3. The *garland* of leaves, colored red and green, brightened the door.

4. The carpenter thought the wood was *strong* and good for building.

5. He felt that an evil *doom* awaited him.

6. The judge told the jury to *suppose* that the accused was innocent.

Writing to Sources

Argumentative Text Some critics complain that Jonson's poetic style is dull. Critic Douglas Bush defends the poet from these criticisms: " … Jonson demanded … the ageless classical virtues of clarity, unity, symmetry, and proportion. … His poems are wholes, not erratic displays of verbal fireworks." Drawing on details from the selections, write a **response** to this idea.

Prewriting Note uses of *imagery*, *language*, or *stylistic devices* that illustrate or contradict each "classical virtue" that Bush cites. Determine whether your examples support or refute Bush's claim and decide whether you agree or disagree with his view.

Drafting Write a draft of your response that begins by summarizing Bush's point and stating your position. As you write, support your generalizations with *accurate and detailed references* to Jonson's writing.

For instance, the lines "But might I of Jove's nectar sup / I would not change for thine" unify the images of drinking. The reference to Jove, though, is artificial.

Model: Adding Support

Jonson may achieve unity, but in some cases it is at the expense of spontaneous feeling. What is the virtue of formal unity if the poem seems lifeless?

Added details from the poem strengthen support for the generalization.

Revising Review your draft, highlighting generalizations and looking for supporting details for each. Make sure that all quotations are accurate and properly referenced.

Conventions and Style: Participles, Gerunds, and Infinitives

One way to make your writing smoother is to combine short sentences using participles, gerunds, and infinitives. A **participle** is a verb form, usually ending in *-ing* or *-ed*, that can be used as an adjective. A **gerund** is a verb form ending in *-ing* that acts as a noun. An **infinitive** is a verb form that appears with the word *to* and acts as a noun, an adjective, or an adverb. You can add modifiers and complements to these verb forms to make **phrases,** or groups of words without a subject or a verb.

Combining with Participial, Gerund, and Infinitive Phrases

Choppy	Better
Ben Jonson was adopted in infancy. Ben Jonson grew up poor.	*Adopted in infancy*, Ben Jonson grew up poor. (participial phrase modifying *Ben Jonson*)
He joined the army. He chose a course.	*Joining the army* was the course he chose. (gerund phrase as the subject)
Jonson could not attend a university. Jonson was not wealthy enough.	Jonson was not wealthy enough *to attend a university*. (infinitive phrase acting as an adverb modifying the adverb *enough*)

Practice In items 1–5, identify the italicized phrase as a participial, gerund, or infinitive phrase. In items 6–10, use the type of phrase indicated in parentheses to combine the two sentences into one, more involved sentence.

1. Her hair, *flowing freely*, was beautiful.
2. *Using a lot of makeup* can hide facial flaws.
3. His goal was *to give clear, brief expression to his ideas*.
4. Jonson, *regarded as a great judge of literature*, guided the trends of his time.
5. The speaker says he hopes *to avoid ever loving anyone so deeply again*.
6. He lost his son. It was a painful experience. (gerund)
7. Jonson returned to England. Jonson became an actor. (participial)
8. The speaker longs for one thing. The speaker would like to forget his identity as a father. (infinitive)
9. Jonson was influenced by the poetry of the ancient Greeks. Jonson liked to write poems with a social function. (participial)
10. Jonson employed satire, a type of humor. Jonson poked fun at contemporary character types. (infinitive)

Writing and Speaking Conventions

A. **Writing** Use each phrase in a sentence and tell what type of phrase it is.

1. writing with a direct style
2. to dress simply
3. saying goodbye to a child

   Example: writing with a direct style
   Sentence: Writing with a direct style, Jonson became popular.
   Type of Phrase: participial phrase

B. **Speaking** Respond to the ideas in "Still to Be Neat" as though you are a woman living in Ben Jonson's time. Use at least one participial phrase, one gerund phrase, and one infinitive phrase.

Connecting to the Essential Question These poets all promote the idea of seizing pleasure in the moment. As you read, notice passages in which a poet gives a personal twist to the theme *Seize pleasure now.* Finding such passages will help as you answer the Essential Question: **What is the relationship of the writer to tradition?**

Close Reading Focus

Carpe Diem

Each poem in this grouping expresses a version of the **carpe diem** theme (kär′ pē dē′ em). *Carpe diem* is Latin for "seize the day." The theme might be summed up as: "Time is fleeting, so act decisively to enjoy yourself."

This theme has a classical origin, with the Roman poet Horace being the first to use the phrase *carpe diem*. It was also popular in love poems of the 16th and 17th centuries, like the ones in this grouping. In such lyrics, a male speaker usually tries to convince a female to grasp the opportunity for love. The *carpe diem* theme may build upon other themes in a poem, such as the fleeting nature of youth or the relationship between human-kind and nature.

Preparing to Read Complex Texts In reading, it is helpful to **analyze and evaluate similar themes** across a variety of selections. Marvell, Herrick, and Suckling all use the *carpe diem* theme, but they do so in different ways:

- Marvell approaches the theme with a mix of whimsical fancy and passionate urgency.
- Herrick delivers a more traditional version of the theme, using familiar imagery to depict the passing seasons.
- Suckling gives the theme a new twist. The speaker in his poem advises a friend to abandon, rather than pursue, a problematic lover.

As you read, use a chart like the one shown to continue analyzing and evaluating how each of these poets expresses this classic theme.

Vocabulary

The words listed below are key to understanding the texts that follow. Copy the words into your notebook, and note which one has three syllables.

coyness	prime
amorous	wan
languish	prevail

Common Core
State Standards

Reading Literature
2. Determine two or more themes or central ideas of a text and analyze their development over the course of the text, including how they interact and build on one another to produce a complex account.

Carpe Diem **Theme**

Marvell

Herrick

Suckling

ANDREW MARVELL

(1621–1678)

Author of "To His Coy Mistress"

Marvell showed an extraordinary adaptability in a turbulent time. Although he was the son of a Puritan minister and frowned on the abuses of the monarchy, he enjoyed close friendships with supporters of Charles I in the king's dispute with Parliament. He also opposed the government of Oliver Cromwell, leader of the Puritan rebellion and then ruler of England.

Beginning in 1651, however, Marvell worked for Lord Fairfax, the commanding general of the Parliamentary army. Still later, he tutored Cromwell's ward. Marvell gained the sponsorship of the Puritan and great English poet John Milton, whose assistant he became.

Marvell wrote masterful poetry in various veins—some works share the metaphysical qualities of Donne's verse, while others have the classical qualities recommended by Jonson. Although he was thought of chiefly as a satirist until the nineteenth century, much of his work has become classic.

"We would sit down, and think which way
To walk, and pass **our long love's day.**"

The Interrupted Sleep, François Boucher. The Metropolitan Museum of Art

TO HIS COY **MISTRESS**

Andrew Marvell

BACKGROUND By the seventeenth century, the English language had become a fluid combination of Anglo-Saxon, Gaelic, Latin, and French. It was more than a tool for basic communication. Through it, one could express philosophical ideas, convey abstract theories, and indulge in humorous wordplay. These poems show the range of this language, from witty puns to fanciful imagery.

Had we but world enough, and time,
This coyness lady were no crime.
We would sit down, and think which way
To walk, and pass our long love's day.
5   Thou by the Indian Ganges' side
Should'st rubies find; I by the tide
Of Humber[1] would complain. I would
Love you ten years before the Flood,
And you should if you please refuse
10 Till the conversion of the Jews.[2]
My vegetable love should grow
Vaster than empires, and more slow;
An hundred years should go to praise
Thine eyes, and on thy forehead gaze;
15 Two hundred to adore each breast,
But thirty thousand to the rest;
An age at least to every part,
And the last age should show your heart.
For, lady, you deserve this state,[3]
20 Nor would I love at lower rate.
   But at my back I always hear
Time's wingèd chariot hurrying near:
And yonder all before us lie
Deserts of vast eternity.
25 Thy beauty shall no more be found,
Nor, in thy marble vault, shall sound

Vocabulary

coyness (koi´ nis) *n.* shyness; aloofness, often as part of a flirtation

Spiral Review
Conceits
How does the conceit in lines 1–20 help set a humorous tone?

Comprehension

What is the lady's crime?

---

1. **Humber** river flowing through Hull, Marvell's home town.
2. **conversion of the Jews** according to Christian tradition, the Jews were to be converted immediately before the Last Judgment.
3. **state** dignity.

◀ **Critical Viewing** In what way do both the painting and the poem illustrate the traditional roles of men and women in courtship? **CONNECT**

My echoing songs; then worms shall try
That long-preserved virginity,
And your quaint honor turn to dust,
30　And into ashes all my lust:
The grave's a fine and private place,
But none I think do there embrace.
　　Now therefore, while the youthful hue
Sits on thy skin like morning dew,
35　And while thy willing soul transpires[4]
At every pore with instant fires,
Now let us sport us while we may,
And now, like amorous birds of prey,
Rather at once our time devour
40　Than languish in his slow-chapped[5] power.
Let us roll all our strength, and all
Our sweetness, up into one ball,
And tear our pleasures with rough strife
Thorough[6] the iron gates of life:
45　Thus, though we cannot make our sun
Stand still, yet we will make him run.

---

4. transpires breathes out.
5. slow-chapped slow-jawed.
6. Thorough through.

Vocabulary

amorous (am′ ə res) *adj.*
full of love or desire

languish (lan′ gwish) *v.*
become weak; droop

Carpe Diem Theme

What new twist does the speaker apply in order to "solve" the problem of fleeting time?

Critical Reading

Cite textual evidence to support your responses.

1. **Key Ideas and Details (a)** Name three things the speaker and his mistress would do and the time each would take if time were not an issue. **(b) Connect:** How do these images relate to the charge the speaker makes against his lady in lines 1–2?

2. **Key Ideas and Details (a) Infer:** Why would the speaker be willing to spend so much time waiting for his mistress? **(b) Interpret:** How does this willingness take the sting out of his complaint?

3. **Craft and Structure (a) Analyze:** What future does the speaker foresee for himself and his love in lines 25–30? **(b) Connect:** How do the images in lines 21–30 answer the images in the first part of the poem?

4. **Craft and Structure** Why does the speaker save the urgent requests in lines 33–46 for the end?

5. **Integration of Knowledge and Ideas (a) Compare and Contrast:** Compare the attitudes toward time at the beginning, middle, and end. **(b) Evaluate:** Is Marvell's idea of love realistic or idealistic? Explain.

Robert Herrick

(1591–1674)

Author of "To the Virgins, to Make Much of Time"

Born into a family of London goldsmiths, Herrick went to Cambridge when he was twenty-two and graduated at the age of twenty-nine. After graduation, he served as a military chaplain. As a reward for his services, he was assigned to a parish in rural England. Here, he performed his churchly duties and wrote religious verse and musical love poems.

Although not politically active, Herrick was evicted from his parish by the Puritans and allowed back only with the Restoration of Charles II. While barred from his church, Herrick returned to his native and beloved London, where he published his poetry in *Noble Numbers* and *Hesperides* (the title comes from an ancient Greek name for a mythical garden at the edge of the world).

Published during a turbulent time and largely ignored by his contemporaries, these verses were rediscovered in the nineteenth century. Today, Herrick is included among the English poets of the seventeenth century who are still worth remembering.

Reading poems like "To the Virgins, to Make Much of Time," modern readers might suppose that Herrick was a bit of a rake or playboy. That impression seems to be further confirmed by a poem like "Upon the Loss of His Mistresses": "I have lost, and lately, these / Many dainty mistresses . . .," whom he goes on to name: Julia, Sappho, Anthea, Electra, Corinna, and Perilla.

The perhaps disappointing biographical truth is that this poet, so rakish in his verse, lived for many years rather soberly as a bachelor church official in the west of England. As one critic points out, the name of Herrick's maid was Prudence.

To the Virgins, to Make Much of Time

Robert Herrick

Gather ye rosebuds while ye may,
    Old time is still a-flying;
And this same flower that smiles today
    Tomorrow will be dying.

5   The glorious lamp of heaven, the sun,
    The higher he's a-getting,
The sooner will his race be run,
    And nearer he's to setting.

That age is best which is the first,
10   When youth and blood are warmer;
But being spent, the worse, and worst
    Times still succeed the former.

Then be not coy, but use your time,
    And, while ye may, go marry;
15 For, having lost but once your prime,
    You may forever tarry.[1]

---

1. tarry (tar´ ē) *v.* delay.

Carpe Diem Theme

Which images in lines 5–8 capture the *carpe diem* theme?

Vocabulary

prime (prĭm) *n.* best stage of a thing or process

▲ Critical Viewing

This painting by John William Waterhouse was directly inspired by Herrick's poem. Which details in it correspond to images in the poem? **CONNECT**

Cite textual evidence to support your responses.

Critical Reading

1. **Key Ideas and Details (a)** What advice does the speaker give women in lines 1–4? **(b) Interpret:** What does the advice mean?

2. **Key Ideas and Details (a) Interpret:** What does the poem suggest about passing time? **(b) Connect:** How does the last stanza answer these concerns?

Sir John Suckling (1609–1642)

Author of "Song"

In some ways, Sir John Suckling lived a life more romantic than Marvell's or Herrick's. A privileged young courtier, Suckling inherited his vast estates when he was only eighteen. He later served as a gentleman in the privy chamber of Charles I. Praised as the cleverest of conversationalists, Suckling was said to be able to compose a poem at a moment's notice. He incorporated some of his best lyrics, including the poem "Song," into plays that he lavishly produced at his own expense.

Suckling's military exploits proved less successful than his poems, however. The cavalry troop he raised and lavishly uniformed for the king was defeated in Scotland, and Suckling was mocked for caring more about his men's uniforms than about their military abilities. After joining a failed Royalist plot to rescue a royal minister from prison, he fled to France, where he died in despair at the age of thirty-three. His poems, though, preserve the dash and spirit of his younger days.

▼ **Critical Viewing**
Consider the speaker's words in
"Song." What might the young lover
pictured here be writing? Explain.
SPECULATE

SONG

Sir John Suckling

Why so pale and wan, fond lover?
    Prithee, why so pale?
Will, when looking well can't move her,
    Looking ill prevail?
5   Prithee, why so pale?

Why so dull and mute, young sinner?
    Prithee, why so mute?
Will, when speaking well can't win her,
    Saying nothing do't?
10   Prithee, why so mute?

Quit, quit, for shame; this will not move,
    This cannot take her.
If of herself she will not love,
    Nothing can make her:
15   The devil take her!

Vocabulary

wan (wän) *adj.* sickly pale; faint or weak

prevail (pri vāl´) *v.* win; achieve a goal

Analyze Similar Themes

How does the speaker's attitude toward his listener in lines 11–15 compare to the speaker's attitude in lines 33–46 of "To His Coy Mistress?"

Critical Reading

1. **Key Ideas and Details (a)** How does the young lover look and act according to the first ten lines of "Song"? **(b) Analyze:** Explain why the speaker treats the friend's behavior as if it were an attempt to achieve a goal.

2. **Key Ideas and Details (a) Interpret:** In the final stanza, what helpful shift in perspective does the speaker encourage? **(b) Draw Conclusions:** What attitude toward love does the last stanza reflect?

3. **Key Ideas and Details (a) Analyze:** What features of the poem make it suitable as song lyrics? **(b) Hypothesize:** Which would be a good audience for such a song: uneducated farmers, young aristocrats, or both? Explain, using details from the poem.

4. **Integration of Knowledge and Ideas** Do these poets merely repeat the *carpe diem* theme, or do they give it new life? Explain. Use two of these Essential Question words in your response: *universal, contemporary, derivative.* **[Connecting to the Essential Question: What is the relationship of the writer to tradition?]**

Cite textual evidence to support your responses.

Literary Analysis

1. **Craft and Structure** Contrast the treatment of the *carpe diem* theme in the three poems using a chart like the one shown.

Carpe Diem Images	Qualities: Fanciful? Simple?	Statement of Plea	Humorous? Passionate? Reasonable?

 **Common Core State Standards**

Writing
1. Write arguments to support claims in an analysis of substantive topics or texts, using valid reasoning and relevant and sufficient evidence.

2. **Craft and Structure** **Analyze and evaluate similar themes** by noting which of these authors presents the *carpe diem* theme most effectively. Consider such factors as word choice, imagery, interaction with other themes, and sense of drama.

3. **Integration of Knowledge and Ideas** The *carpe diem* theme has appeared in literature for a long time. What do you think accounts for its popularity? Include references to the texts in your explanation.

Vocabulary Acquisition and Use

Compare the meaning of each underlined vocabulary word with its **context,** or surrounding words, to determine whether the statement is true or false. Write T or F, and explain your answer.

1. He had not eaten for days, and his cheeks were <u>wan</u>.
2. *The <u>Prime</u> of Miss Jean Brodie* is probably about a woman near death.
3. If a plant is not regularly watered, it will <u>languish</u>.
4. The soccer team that scores the most goals will <u>prevail</u>.
5. <u>Coyness</u> shows commitment to a relationship.
6. An <u>amorous</u> couple is affectionate.

Writing

Argumentative Text Public-service announcements (PSAs) urge people to act wisely. Use the *carpe diem* theme in a **PSA** that calls on people to do something beneficial, such as exercise to maintain health.

• Decide whether you will write a radio or television ad.

• Decide what your claim will be, and gather evidence to support it.

• Write the script and revise it to make sure you use effective evidence, logical evidence, and emotional appeals to persuade your audience.

A Nation Divided

Literary History: Milton's World

In the 1650s, the aged John Milton decided to retell the Biblical story of the creation, fall, and redemption of humanity in two epics, Paradise Lost *and* Paradise Regained. *With these works, Milton reaffirmed Britain's core values after a decade of war.*

Making "Darkness Visible": Milton's Epic Ambition

Milton had compelling reasons for telling this story. By 1652, he was completely blind. Unable to write, he dictated the poem to his daughters, who copied down each word. As he worked, the world crumbled around him. The monarchy he had opposed was restored to England, and he went to jail for a time. Blind, disgraced, and disillusioned, Milton nevertheless persevered. Over perhaps ten years, he dictated nearly 11,000 lines of poetry. The result, critics agree, is the greatest epic in the English language, *Paradise Lost.*

An Overview Like many epic poems, *Paradise Lost* begins in the middle. Milton introduces Satan, who, along with his angel allies, has done the unthinkable—rebelled against God. Expelled from Heaven, they have plummeted into Hell, a place devoid of light, life, and even form: "one great furnace flamed, yet from those flames / No light, but rather darkness visible / Served only to discern sights of woe."

Satan's war with Heaven is Milton's invention. The remainder of the story is the familiar one of Christian tradition. God has forbidden Adam and Eve to eat fruit from the Tree of the Knowledge of Good and Evil. Bent on revenge, Satan tempts Eve into eating the apple. She then persuades Adam to partake. This event, the Fall of Adam and Eve, leads to their (and so humanity's) expulsion from the Garden of Eden. They leave Paradise with a sense of hope: "The World was all before them, where to choose / Their place of rest, and Providence their guide. . . ."

A Cosmic Commentary Apart from telling this grand story, large portions of *Paradise Lost* are dedicated to another grand project— "to justify the ways of God to men." In the story, God sends the angel Raphael to Paradise to warn Adam of the necessity of obedience. In their conversation, Milton is able to speak on a few issues that were controversial in his day.

- **Reason and Free Will** Humanity can see the difference between right and wrong. With that ability comes the freedom to choose between the two.

- **Free Will and Predestination** God knows everything that is, was, and will be. Yet God's foreknowledge does not mean that people's choices are determined in advance by God. People have free will.

▲ Critical Viewing
What feeling does this portrayal of Adam and Eve convey? **INTERPRET**

By affirming free will, Milton broke with some of the sternest Puritans of his day, who held that men and women were predestined to salvation or damnation. Milton's epic story finds individuals responsible for their own actions and fate and so grants them dignity.

Words in the Void In a sense, *Paradise Lost* is Milton's answer to the great historical crisis through which Britain had just passed. Puritans, including Milton, had challenged the official Church of England. They demanded a return to what they saw as the original principles of the Christian religion. At the same time, religious controversy led to the Civil War (1642–1649) in which Parliament eventually put its own king, Charles I, to death.

These upheavals shattered the symbolic centers of English life and culture, Church and King. With *Paradise Lost*, Milton helped the nation find its bearings again by retelling the central story of its culture. In the figure of Satan, he commemorated the destructive forces that had recently torn through the nation. At the same time, the fall of Satan symbolically puts rebellious urges into their proper place—the netherworld of Hell. It was these tasks, perhaps, that drove the blind Milton to rise above adversity and deliver this epic to his country.

Milton's Legacy Over the centuries, Milton's story of the Fall has become as well known as the biblical version. It has influenced writers as diverse as the poets William Blake, the visionary; and John Keats, the introspective dreamer; as well as the novelist George Eliot, a formidable social critic. By the nineteenth century, study of Milton's epic was considered an essential part of a respectable education, and even relatively uneducated people could be expected to have two books in their homes—the King James Bible and *Paradise Lost*. In telling a story to heal his own time, Milton fed the imaginations of generations to come.

Speaking and Listening: Discussion

Comprehension and Collaboration Since the time of Milton, many writers have attempted to heal the wounds of collective trauma through works of literature.

With a group, discuss your thoughts about the ways in which literature can bring understanding or closure to people after a period of historical crisis. Use these questions to guide your discussion:

- What examples can you cite in which literature, including drama, deals with a real historical crisis?
- Do you think such literature can have meaning for people who have not lived through the crisis in question? If so, how?

Organize your conclusions into a **report** to share your ideas with the class.

John Milton

(1608–1674)

John Milton is regarded as one of the greatest poets of the English language, yet he owes this regard to comparatively few poems. Much of his work is in Latin, not English, and during the fifteen years he spent writing political pamphlets and other prose works, he wrote little poetry. Although other poets have surpassed him in quantity, Milton's masterpiece, the epic *Paradise Lost,* is enough to establish him as the equal of Chaucer and Shakespeare. Milton himself never lacked self-confidence, setting his sights on poetic greatness at the start of his career.

A Privileged Childhood

Milton was born in London to a middle-class family and grew up in a highly cultured environment. His father, a professional scribe who drew up contracts and lent money, was also a composer and musician of considerable ability. Deeply religious, Milton's father was devoted to the Protestant cause. At the age of thirteen, Milton started his formal education, the equivalent of high school. He was also tutored at home. He mastered Greek, Latin, and Hebrew, as well as several modern European languages. After this thorough education, Milton went on to college.

God's Poet

When Milton entered Christ's College at Cambridge University, he had already decided to prepare himself for a career as a great poet ("God's poet" was how he described himself). It appears that for a time he also considered entering the ministry. The religious and political situation at the time, though, was quite uncertain, so Milton devoted himself to a life of study. After earning his degrees from Cambridge, he withdrew to his father's house, first at Hammersmith, then at Horton in Buckinghamshire, for nearly six years, where, it is said, he read everything that was written in the ancient and modern languages at his command. It was during this long period of study that he wrote one of his best-known poems, "Lycidas." That work, together with the poems "L'Allegro" and "Il Penseroso," written during his student days, marked the young Milton as a gifted poet destined for fame.

A Man of Ideals

Following his studies, Milton went to continental Europe for a planned two-year Grand Tour, during which he called on the astronomer Galileo (1564–1642). While he was away, Parliament rebelled against King Charles I, eventually replacing the monarchy with a government led by Oliver Cromwell. Learning of the revolt, Milton cut short his trip and returned to England. He began writing pamphlets for the Puritan cause, criticizing the control of the bishops over the English church.

Public Service, Private Loss

In 1649, when the Puritans decided to execute Charles I, Milton wrote a treatise defending this act. Impressed by Milton's brilliantly presented opinions, Cromwell made him Secretary of State for Foreign Tongues. This position required Milton to translate official documents into Latin and to write in defense of the new government against Royalist attacks. It was while serving in this position that he lost his eyesight.

In 1660, Milton's fortunes took a turn for the worse. The monarchy was restored, and Milton was imprisoned for a time. (His friend, the poet Andrew Marvell, may have been instrumental in gaining his release.) Blind and stripped of most of his property, Milton withdrew once again into words—he wrote *Paradise Lost* (1667), the greatest epic of the English language.

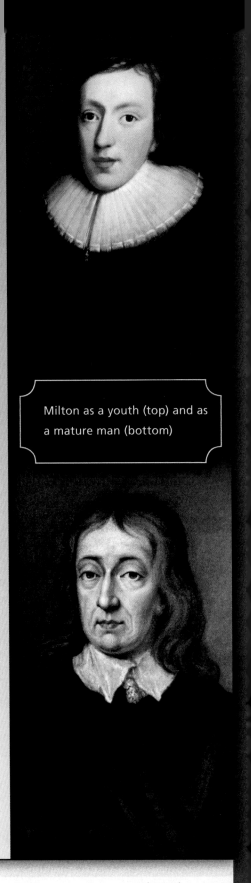

Milton as a youth (top) and as a mature man (bottom)

Milton & POP CULTURE

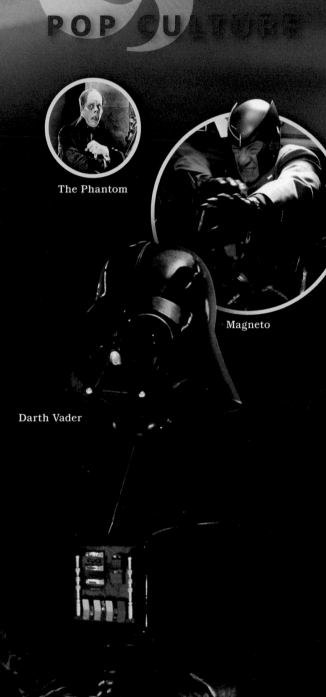

The Phantom

Magneto

Darth Vader

DARK HEROES

In Milton's 17th-century epic poem *Paradise Lost*, God casts Satan out of Heaven and into Hell. The fallen angel is vivid and dark at the same time. In this respect, Satan is like other larger-than-life figures who, though villainous, rivet our attention. While none are more powerful than the Devil, there are many dark-hero figures in popular culture.

- Darth Vader, unforgettable villain of the *Star Wars* movies, is one. Brutal enforcer of Empire rule, Vader was instantly memorable for the helmet that covered his face and by his voice (James Earl Jones's menacing tones).

- Magneto, another enemy of true heroes, was introduced in the first issue (1963) of *X-Men*, the comic written by Stan Lee and illustrated by Jack Kirby. Like Satan, he is the head of an army, not the dark angels of Hell but the Brotherhood of Evil Mutants.

- The physically deformed musical genius, Erik, better known as the Phantom, made his first frightening appearance in Gaston Leroux's novel *The Phantom of the Opera* in 1910. Since then, this despairing and daring villain has appeared in a movie and a musical, both based on the original novel.

Regardless of media—poem, novel, film, comic, or Broadway show—stories of dark heroes continue to fascinate audiences.

Connecting to the Essential Question John Milton brings to life a well-known story of the time, about angels who rebelled against God. As you read, notice vivid passages in Milton's description of the underworld in *Paradise Lost*. Seeing such descriptions in your mind's eye will help you think about the Essential Question: **What is the relationship of the writer to tradition?**

Common Core State Standards

Reading Literature
5. Analyze how an author's choices concerning how to structure specific parts of a text contribute to its overall structure and meaning as well as its aesthetic impact.

Close Reading Focus

Italian Sonnet; Epic

An **Italian,** or **Petrarchan, sonnet** is a fourteen-line lyric poem with a distinctive structure. The first eight lines, called the octave, rhyme *abbaabba* and present a problem. A six-line sestet with a variable rhyme scheme responds to the octave. In Milton's Italian sonnets, the structure of the octave and the sestet contributes to the structure, meaning, and aesthetic pleasure of the entire sonnet.

An **epic** is a long narrative poem about a hero. For seventeenth-century English writers, ancient epic poets such as Homer—the blind, half-mythical author of the *Iliad* and the *Odyssey*—set the standard for literary greatness. Milton uses the following features of Homeric epics in *Paradise Lost:*

- A story that begins in the middle of the action (*in medias res*)
- An opening invocation in which the poet calls for divine aid in telling his story
- Extended similes, comparisons using *like* or *as*

Look for these epic elements as you read *Paradise Lost*. While reading the sonnets, notice how the structure of the parts contributes to the structure and meaning of the poem.

Preparing to Read Complex Texts If you do not understand a passage, repair your comprehension *by* **using a graphic organizer** like the one shown. This organizer can help you break down long, confusing sentences into smaller parts: main clauses, which can stand by themselves, and supporting clauses, which cannot.

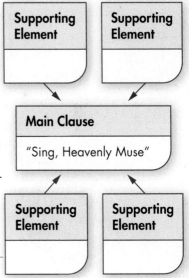

Vocabulary

The words below are important to understanding the texts that follow. Copy the words into your notebook, sorting them into words you know and words you do not know.

semblance	obdurate
illumine	tempestuous
transgress	transcendent
guile	ignominy

Sonnet VII

("How soon hath Time") JOHN MILTON

Vocabulary

semblance (sem´ bləns)
n. appearance; image

How soon hath Time, the subtle thief of youth,
   Stolen on his wing my three and twentieth year!
   My hasting days fly on with full career,[1]
   But my late spring no bud or blossom showeth.
5 Perhaps my semblance might deceive[2] the truth,
   That I to manhood am arrived so near,
   And inward ripeness doth much less appear,
   That some more timely-happy spirits[3] endueth.[4]
Yet be it less or more, or soon or slow,
10 It shall be still[5] in strictest measure even
   To that same lot,[6] however mean or high,
Toward which Time leads me, and the will of Heaven;
   All is, if I have grace to use it so,
   As ever in my great Taskmaster's eye.

---

1. **career** speed.
2. **deceive** prove false.
3. **timely-happy spirits** others who seem to be more accomplished poets at the age
of twenty-four.
4. **endueth** endows.
5. **still** always.
6. **lot** fate.

Critical Reading

1. **Key Ideas and Details (a)** What occasion leads Milton to the thoughts in the poem? **(b) Infer:** Judging from the image in lines 1–2, how does Milton view this occasion?

2. **Key Ideas and Details (a)** To what season does Milton compare his time of life? **(b) Infer:** Why does he say that this season "no bud or blossom showeth"? **(c) Interpret:** What is his feeling about this situation?

3. **Key Ideas and Details (a) Infer:** To what does Milton trust himself and his life in lines 9–14? **(b) Interpret:** In what way does this act of trust answer his worries in the first part of the poem?

Sonnet XIX

("When I consider how my light is spent") JOHN MILTON

When I consider how my light is spent
    Ere half my days, in this dark world and wide,
    And that one talent[1] which is death to hide,
    Lodged with me useless, though my soul more bent
5 To serve therewith my Maker, and present
    My true account, lest he returning chide;
    "Doth God exact day labor, light denied?"
    I fondly[2] ask; but Patience to prevent
That murmur, soon replies, "God doth not need
10   Either man's work or his own gifts; who best
    Bear his mild yoke, they serve him best. His state
Is kingly. Thousands[3] at his bidding speed
    And post[4] o'er land and ocean without rest:
    They also serve who only stand and wait."

The Italian Sonnet
What setback to his poetic ambition does Milton describe in this sonnet?

---

1. **talent** allusion to the parable of the talents (Matthew 25: 14–30). The servant who earns interest for his master on five talents (a large unit of money) is commended. The servant who hides and then returns a talent is condemned to "outer darkness."
2. **fondly** foolishly.
3. **Thousands** thousands of angels.
4. **post** travel.

Critical Reading

1. **Key Ideas and Details (a)** According to the poem, at what point in his life did the speaker's eyesight fail? **(b) Infer:** In line 2, how does his way of identifying this point in his life emphasize the despair he feels?

2. **Key Ideas and Details (a)** What has happened to the speaker's "one talent"? **(b) Infer:** Why does blindness have this effect on his talent?

3. **Key Ideas and Details (a) Connect:** In lines 3–6, what connection does the speaker make between the use of one's talent and service to God? **(b) Interpret:** What dilemma does this connection create for him? **(c) Interpret:** What does his question in line 7 mean?

4. **Key Ideas and Details (a) Infer:** What answers the speaker? **(b) Interpret:** How does this new speaker interpret the idea of service to God?

5. **Integration of Knowledge and Ideas** Do you think that this poem could inspire a contemporary person who is facing a physical challenge? Explain.

Cite textual evidence to support your responses.

From Paradise Lost

John Milton

BACKGROUND

Paradise Lost was written as the dust was settling after years of war and turmoil. From 1642 to 1660, the government of England went from a monarchy to a commonwealth (rule by Parliament) to a protectorate (rule by one man, Oliver Cromwell) to a monarchy. During this two-decade period, no matter which side a person was on, he or she experienced both defeat and triumph.

Perhaps Milton wrote *Paradise Lost* because he sensed that the nation needed an anchor, a literary work that would once again help define and unite a culture. His explanation of God's reason for allowing suffering in the world, and the dark, proud figure of the rebel Satan pitted against God in civil war, must have led readers to reflect on England's own civil war.

▶ **Critical Viewing** How is Milton's time period— an era in which England was torn apart by civil war and religious conflict—reflected in this engraving? **CONNECT**

Paradise Lost, 1688. From the British Library

Epic Poetry

What epic convention does Milton follow in his opening sentence?

Of man's first disobedience, and the fruit
Of that forbidden tree, whose mortal[1] taste
Brought death into the world, and all our woe,
With loss of Eden, till one greater Man[2]
5 Restore us, and regain the blissful seat,
Sing Heavenly Muse,[3] that on the secret top
Of Oreb, or of Sinai,[4] didst inspire
That shepherd, who first taught the chosen seed,
In the beginning how the Heavens and Earth
10 Rose out of Chaos: or if Sion hill[5]
Delight thee more, and Siloa's brook[6] that flowed
Fast[7] by the oracle of God, I thence
Invoke thy aid to my adventurous song,
That with no middle flight intends to soar
15 Above the Aonian mount,[8] while it pursues
Things unattempted yet in prose or rhyme.
And chiefly thou O Spirit,[9] that dost prefer
Before all temples the upright heart and pure,
Instruct me, for thou know'st; thou from the first
20 Wast present, and with mighty wings outspread
Dovelike sat'st brooding on the vast abyss
And mad'st it pregnant: what in me is dark
Illumine, what is low raise and support;
That to the height of this great argument[10]
25 I may assert Eternal Providence,
And justify the ways of God to men.
  Say first, for Heaven hides nothing from thy view
Nor the deep tract of Hell, say first what cause
Moved our grand[11] parents in that happy state,
30 Favored of Heaven so highly, to fall off
From their Creator, and transgress his will

Vocabulary

illumine (i lōō′ mən) v. light up

transgress (trans gres′) v. violate a law or command

---

1. **mortal** deadly.
2. **one . . . Man** Christ.
3. **Heavenly Muse** Urania, the muse of astronomy and sacred poetry in Greek mythology. Here, Milton associates Urania with the holy spirit that inspired Moses ("That shepherd") to receive and interpret the word of God for the Jews ("the chosen seed"). To convey the message of God to his people, Moses wrote the first five books of the Bible, including Genesis, the book on which *Paradise Lost* is based.
4. **Oreb** (ōr′ eb) **. . . Sinai** (sī′ nī′) alternate names for the mountain where God communicated the laws to Moses.
5. **Sion** (sī′ ən) **hill** hill near Jerusalem on which the temple ("the oracle of God") stood.
6. **Siloa's** (sī lō′ əz) **brook** stream near Sion hill.
7. **Fast** close.
8. **Aonian** (ā ō′ nē ən) **mount** Mount Helicon in Greek mythology, home of the Muses. Milton is drawing a comparison between the epic he is now presenting and the epics written by the classical poets, Homer and Virgil.
9. **Spirit** the Holy Spirit, the voice that provided inspiration for the Hebrew prophets.
10. **argument** theme.
11. **grand** first in importance and in time.

For[12] one restraint,[13] lords of the world besides?[14]
Who first seduced them to that foul revolt?
The infernal Serpent; he it was, whose guile
35   Stirred up with envy and revenge, deceived
The mother of mankind, what time his pride
Had cast him out from Heaven, with all his host
Of rebel angels, by whose aid aspiring
To set himself in glory above his peers,
40   He trusted to have equaled the Most High,
If he opposed; and with ambitious aim
Against the throne and monarchy of God
Raised impious war in Heaven and battle proud,
With vain attempt. Him the Almighty Power
45   Hurled headlong flaming from the ethereal sky
With hideous ruin and combustion down
To bottomless perdition, there to dwell
In adamantine[15] chains and penal fire,
Who durst defy the Omnipotent to arms.
50   Nine times the space that measures day and night
To mortal men, he with his horrid crew
Lay vanquished, rolling in the fiery gulf,
Confounded though immortal. But his doom
Reserved him to more wrath; for now the thought
55   Both of lost happiness and lasting pain
Torments him; round he throws his baleful eyes
That witnessed[16] huge affliction and dismay,
Mixed with obdurate pride and steadfast hate.
At once as far as angels' ken,[17] he views
60   The dismal situation waste and wild:
A dungeon horrible, on all sides round,
As one great furnace flamed, yet from those flames
No light, but rather darkness visible
Served only to discover sights of woe,
65   Regions of sorrow, doleful shades, where peace
And rest can never dwell, hope never comes
That comes to all; but torture without end
Still urges,[18] and a fiery deluge, fed
With ever-burning sulfur unconsumed:
70   Such place eternal justice had prepared
For these rebellious, here their prison ordained

---

12. **For** because of.
13. **one restraint** commandment that Adam and Eve should not eat of the fruit of the tree of knowledge.
14. **besides** in every other respect.
15. **adamantine** (ad´ ə man´ tēn´) *adj.* unbreakable.
16. **witnessed** gave evidence of.
17. **ken** view; scope of knowledge.
18. **urges** afflicts.

Vocabulary
guile (gīl) *n.* artful trickery

Epic Poetry
What does the story Milton has chosen to retell reveal about his poetic ambition?

Vocabulary
obdurate (äb´ dʊ͝or it) *adj.* stubborn

Comprehension
Whom does Milton call to help him tell his story?

▶ **Critical Viewing**
What traditional associations
with sin explain this artist's
rendering of one of Milton's
fallen angels? **HYPOTHESIZE**

Vocabulary
tempestuous
(tem pes´ chōō əs) *adj.*
turbulent; stormy

In utter darkness, and their portion set
As far removed from God and light of Heaven
As from the center thrice to the utmost pole.[19]

75   O how unlike the place from whence they fell!
There the companions of his fall, o'erwhelmed
With floods and whirlwinds of tempestuous fire,
He soon discerns, and weltering by his side
One next himself in power, and next in crime,

80   Long after known in Palestine, and named
Beelzebub.[20] To whom the archenemy,
And thence in Heaven called Satan, with bold words
Breaking the horrid silence thus began:
  "If thou beest he; but O how fallen! how changed

85   From him, who in the happy realms of light

---

19. center . . . . pole three times the distance from the center of the universe (Earth) to the
    outermost sphere of the universe.
20. Beelzebub (bē el´ zə bub´) traditionally, the chief devil, or Satan. In this poem, Satan's chief
    lieutenant among the fallen angels.

Clothed with transcendent brightness didst outshine
Myriads though bright: if he whom mutual league,
United thoughts and counsels, equal hope
And hazard in the glorious enterprise,
90 Joined with me once, now misery hath joined
In equal ruin: into what pit thou seest
From what height fallen, so much the stronger proved
He with his thunder:[21] and till then who knew
The force of those dire arms? Yet not for those,
95 Nor what the potent Victor in his rage
Can else inflict, do I repent or change,
Though changed in outward luster, that fixed mind
And high disdain, from sense of injured merit,
That with the Mightiest raised me to contend,
100 And to the fierce contention brought along
Innumerable force of spirits armed
That durst dislike his reign, and me preferring,
His utmost power with adverse power opposed
In dubious battle on the plains of Heaven,
105 And shook his throne. What though the field be lost?
All is not lost; the unconquerable will,
And study[22] of revenge, immortal hate,
And courage never to submit or yield:
And what is else not to be overcome?
110 That glory never shall his wrath or might
Extort from me. To bow and sue for grace
With suppliant knee, and deify his power
Who from the terror of this arm so late
Doubted[23] his empire, that were low indeed,
115 That were an ignominy and shame beneath
This downfall; since by fate the strength of gods
And this empyreal substance[24] cannot fail,
Since through experience of this great event,
In arms not worse, in foresight much advanced,
120 We may with more successful hope resolve
To wage by force or guile eternal war
Irreconcilable, to our grand Foe,
Who now triumphs, and in the excess of joy
Sole reigning holds the tyranny of Heaven."
125   So spake the apostate angel, though in pain,
Vaunting aloud, but racked with deep despair;
And him thus answered soon his bold compeer.[25]

---

21. **He . . . thunder** God.
22. **study** pursuit.
23. **Doubted** feared for.
24. **empyreal** (em pir´ ē əl) **substance** the indestructible substance of which Heaven, or the empyrean, is composed.
25. **compeer** comrade; equal.

Using Graphic Organizers

Complete a chart to break the sentence into main and supporting clauses.

"O prince, O chief of many thronèd Powers,
That led the embattled Seraphim[26] to war
130 Under thy conduct, and in dreadful deeds
Fearless, endangered Heaven's perpetual King,
And put to proof his high supremacy,
Whether upheld by strength, or chance, or fate!
Too well I see and rue the dire event[27]
135 That with sad overthrow and foul defeat
Hath lost us Heaven, and all this mighty host
In horrible destruction laid thus low,
As far as gods and heavenly essences
Can perish: for the mind and spirit remains
140 Invincible, and vigor soon returns,
Though all our glory extinct, and happy state
Here swallowed up in endless misery.
But what if he our conqueror (whom I now
Of force[28] believe almighty, since no less
145 Than such could have o'erpowered such force as ours)
Have left us this our spirit and strength entire
Strongly to suffer and support our pains,
That we may so suffice[29] his vengeful ire,
Or do him mightier service as his thralls
150 By right of war, whate'er his business be
Here in the heart of Hell to work in fire,
Or do his errands in the gloomy deep?
What can it then avail though yet we feel
Strength undiminished, or eternal being
155 To undergo eternal punishment?"
Whereto with speedy words the Archfiend replied:
"Fallen cherub, to be weak is miserable,
Doing or suffering:[30] but of this be sure,
To do aught[31] good never will be our task,
160 But ever to do ill our sole delight,
As being the contrary to his high will
Whom we resist. If then his providence
Out of our evil seek to bring forth good,
Our labor must be to pervert that end,
165 And out of good still[32] to find means of evil;
Which oft times may succeed, so as perhaps
Shall grieve him, if I fail not,[33] and disturb

Epic Poetry

What assumptions about the epic struggle between good and evil does Milton make in lines 159–168?

---

26. Seraphim (ser´ ə fim´) the highest order of angels.
27. event outcome.
28. Of force necessarily.
29. suffice satisfy.
30. doing or suffering whether one is active or passive.
31. aught anything.
32. still always.
33. if . . . not unless I am mistaken.

His inmost counsels from their destined aim.
But see the angry Victor[34] hath recalled
170   His ministers of vengeance and pursuit
Back to the gates of Heaven: the sulfurous hail
Shot after us in storm, o'erblown hath laid
The fiery surge, that from the precipice
Of Heaven received us falling, and the thunder,
175   Winged with red lightning and impetuous rage,
Perhaps hath spent his shafts, and ceases now
To bellow through the vast and boundless deep.
Let us not slip[35] the occasion, whether scorn,
Or satiate[36] fury yield it from our Foe.
180   Seest thou yon dreary plain, forlorn and wild,
The seat of desolation, void of light,
Save what the glimmering of these livid flames
Casts pale and dreadful? Thither let us tend
From off the tossing of these fiery waves,
185   There rest, if any rest can harbor there,
And reassembling our afflicted powers,[37]
Consult how we may henceforth most offend
Our Enemy, our own loss how repair,
How overcome this dire calamity,
190   What reinforcement we may gain from hope,
If not what resolution from despair."
      Thus Satan talking to his nearest mate,
With head uplift above the wave, and eyes
That sparkling blazed; his other parts besides
195   Prone on the flood, extended long and large,
Lay floating many a rood,[38] in bulk as huge
As whom the fables name of monstrous size,
Titanian, or Earthborn, that warred on Jove,
Briareos or Typhon,[39] whom the den
200   By ancient Tarsus[40] held, or that sea beast
Leviathan,[41] which God of all his works
Created hugest that swim the ocean stream:
Him haply slumbering on the Norway foam

34. **angry Victor** God.
35. **slip** fail to take advantage of.
36. **satiate** (sā′ shē āt′) satisfied.
37. **afflicted powers** overthrown armies.
38. **rood** old unit of measure equal to seven or eight yards.
39. **Titanian** (tī tā′ nē ən) . . . **Earthborn** . . . **Briareos** (brī ar′ ē əs) . . . **Typhon** (tī′ fən) In clas-
    sical mythology, both the Titans, led by Briareos, who had a hundred hands, and the Giants
    (Earthborn), led by Typhon, a hundred-headed serpent monster, fought with Jove. As
    punishment for their rebellion, both Briareos and Typhon were thrown into the underworld.
40. **Tarsus** (tär′ səs) capital of Cilicia (sə lish′ ə). Typhon is said to have lived in Cilicia
    near Tarsus.
41. **Leviathan** (lə vī′ ə thən) in the Bible, a great sea monster.

World LITERATURE CONNECTION

Reinventing the Epic

When writing *Paradise Lost*, Milton was deeply influenced by classical epics: Homer's the *Iliad* and the *Odyssey*, Virgil's *Aeneid*, and Ovid's *Metamorphoses*. He had read them in the original Greek and Latin and had immersed himself in the ideas and traditions of the ancient world.

Just as the classical poets based their epics on stories that were central to their cultures, Milton based *Paradise Lost* on Genesis, a Biblical account of the world's beginning that was central to his culture. He followed the classical structure, opening *Paradise Lost* with an invocation, or address, to the muse and beginning in the middle of the action. By adapting the ancient epic form to his religious poem, Milton succeeded in combining classical and Christian traditions. Perhaps he also hoped to create a heroic Christian literature that would help pull his divided society together.

Connect to the Literature

What do you think Milton meant when he said that his poem would pursue "Things unattempted yet in prose or rhyme"?

Comprehension

What does Satan tell Beelzebub their sole purpose will be?

Spiral Review
Imagery
How might the violent imagery in lines 209–241 and elsewhere in the poem relate to the English civil wars?

205 The pilot of some small night-foundered skiff,
Deeming some island, oft, as seamen tell,
With fixed anchor in his scaly rind
Moors by his side under the lee, while night
Invests[42] the sea, and wished morn delays:
So stretched out huge in length the Archfiend lay
210 Chained on the burning lake, nor ever thence
Had risen or heaved his head, but that the will
And high permission of all-ruling Heaven
Left him at large to his own dark designs,
That with reiterated crimes he might
215 Heap on himself damnation, while he sought
Evil to others, and enraged might see
How all his malice served but to bring forth
Infinite goodness, grace and mercy shown
On man by him seduced, but on himself
220 Treble confusion, wrath and vengeance poured.
Forthwith upright he rears from off the pool
His mighty stature; on each hand the flames
Driven backward, slope their pointing spires, and rolled
In billows leave in the midst a horrid vale.
225 Then with expanded wings he steers his flight
Aloft, incumbent[43] on the dusky air
That felt unusual weight, till on dry land
He lights, if it were land that ever burned
With solid, as the lake with liquid fire;
230 And such appeared in hue, as when the force
Of subterranean wind transports a hill
Torn from Pelorus, or the shattered side
Of thundering Etna,[44] whose combustible
And fueled entrails thence conceiving fire,
235 Sublimed[45] with mineral fury, aid the winds,
And leave a singèd bottom all involved[46]
With stench and smoke: such resting found the sole
Of unblessed feet. Him followed his next mate,
Both glorying to have scaped the Stygian[47] flood
240 As gods, and by their own recovered strength,
Not by the sufferance[48] of supernal[49] power.
"Is this the region, this the soil, the clime,"
Said then the lost Archangel, "this the seat

---

42. Invests covers.
43. incumbent lying.
44. Pelorus (pə lôr′ əs) . . . **Etna** volcanic mountains in Sicily.
45. Sublimed vaporized.
46. involved enveloped.
47. Stygian (stij′ ē ən) of the river Styx, which, in Greek mythology, encircled Hades (hā′ dēz′), the home of the dead.
48. sufferance permission.
49. supernal (sə purn′ əl) heavenly.

That we must change[50] for Heaven, this mournful gloom
245 For that celestial light? Be it so, since he
     Who now is sovereign can dispose and bid
     What shall be right: farthest from him is best,
     Whom reason hath equaled, force hath made supreme
     Above his equals. Farewell happy fields,
250 Where joy forever dwells. Hail horrors! Hail
     Infernal world! and thou, profoundest Hell
     Receive thy new possessor, one who brings
     A mind not to be changed by place or time.
     The mind is its own place, and in itself
255 Can make a Heaven of Hell, a Hell of Heaven.
     What matter where, if I be still the same,
     And what I should be, all but less than he
     Whom thunder hath made greater? Here at least
     We shall be free; the Almighty hath not built
260 Here for his envy, will not drive us hence:
     Here we may reign secure, and in my choice
     To reign is worth ambition though in Hell:

---

50. change exchange.

Epic Poetry and Poetic Ambition

In what way is the attitude expressed in lines 250–258 fitting both for a hero and a poet?

Comprehension

What does Satan say about the mind?

◀ Critical Viewing

Why might the English Civil War have made Milton think of a battle between angels like the one depicted in this picture? **CONNECT**

Better to reign in Hell than serve in Heaven.
But wherefore[51] let we then our faithful friends,
265   The associates and copartners of our loss
Lie thus astonished[52] on the oblivious[53] pool,
And call them not to share with us their part
In this unhappy mansion, or once more
With rallied arms to try what may be yet
Regained in Heaven, or what more lost in Hell?"

51. wherefore why.
52. astonished stunned.
53. oblivious causing forgetfulness.

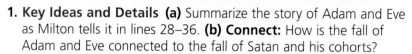

Critical Reading

1. **Key Ideas and Details (a)** Summarize the story of Adam and Eve as Milton tells it in lines 28–36. **(b) Connect:** How is the fall of Adam and Eve connected to the fall of Satan and his cohorts?

2. **Key Ideas and Details (a)** Lines 59–74 describe Hell. What does Milton indicate are its main features? **(b) Interpret:** Explain Satan's reaction in lines 94–99 to his fall into Hell.

3. **Key Ideas and Details (a) Infer:** In lines 116–124, what kind of war does Satan propose to wage against Heaven? **(b) Interpret:** Judging from lines 105–116, what is his motive for such a war? **(c) Hypothesize:** How will this war lead to the fall of Adam and Eve?

4. **Integration of Knowledge and Ideas (a) Interpret:** Explain how Satan's attitude toward Hell in lines 250–252 proves that he is "one who brings / A mind not to be changed by place or time" (lines 252–253). **(b) Draw Conclusions:** Explain how the mind "Can make a Heaven of Hell, a Hell of Heaven" (line 255).

5. **Integration of Knowledge and Ideas (a) Summarize:** Characterize Satan, supporting your description with quotations from the text. **(b) Evaluate:** To what extent does Satan seem admirable? To what extent despairing? Explain.

6. **Integration of Knowledge and Ideas (a) Interpret:** What does Milton mean when he says he wants to "justify the ways of God to men" (line 26)? **(b) Assess:** How good a start has Milton made toward this goal? Explain.

7. **Integration of Knowledge and Ideas** Focus on an especially strong passage in *Paradise Lost*. What devices—word choice, rhythm, characterization, description—help Milton reinvent the story of the fallen angels? In your response, use at least two of these Essential Question words: *invent, innovation, tradition.* [*Connecting to the Essential Question: What is the relationship of the writer to tradition?*]

Critical Commentary

from "A Defense of Poetry"
Percy Bysshe Shelley

from *Surprised by Sin*
Stanley Fish

Poets and critics have long debated whether Satan in Paradise Lost *is an evil villain or the secret hero of the poem. Romantics like Percy Bysshe Shelley viewed Satan as a heroic Romantic rebel. Writing in 1821, Shelley made the case for that perspective.*

Milton's Devil as a moral being is as far superior to his God, as one who perseveres in some purpose, which he has conceived to be excellent in spite of adversity and torture, is to one who in the cold security of undoubted triumph inflicts the most horrible revenge upon his enemy, not from any mistaken notion of inducing him to repent of a perseverance in enmity, but with the alleged design of exasperating him to deserve new torments. Milton has so far violated the popular creed (if this shall be judged to be a violation) as to have alleged no superiority of moral virtue to his god over his devil. And this bold neglect of a direct moral purpose is the most decisive proof of the supremacy of Milton's genius. . . .

Writing exactly 150 years later, the critic Stanley Fish argued that, far from being an admirable rebel, Milton's Satan has no will or identity of his own.

. . . Satan's independence is an illusion because he is in bondage to the freedom to do as he likes and he becomes the captive of momentary purposes and the plaything of master strategists (God, Milton) who make of him what they will; his will does not exist (he has no "deepest self"), except in a Satanic never-never-Land where evil could be someone's good. This reversal is impossible in a universe where God is God and when Satan admits "myself am Hell" he, in effect, says "myself am not," since hell is the state of disunion from God's sustaining power and hence a state of nonbeing . . . Perhaps the most ironic of his boasts is this one: "What matter where, if I be still the same" (I.256). The sameness of evil is the sameness of chaos, a stability of instability where the identity and form of any atom or cluster of atoms is a matter of chance unless an ordering power is imposed; Satan is condemned to restless wandering until God or some deputy of God finds a use for him and endows him with motives and opinions and powers to fit the role "imposed from without."

Key Ideas and Details What admirable qualities does Shelley attribute to Satan? Why does Fish declare that "Satan's independence is an illusion"?

Literary Analysis

1. **Key Ideas and Details (a)** Identify the main clause in lines 1–8 of Sonnet XIX. **(b)** Explain what each supporting clause adds to its meaning.

2. **Craft and Structure (a)** Which **Italian sonnet** has the more regular pattern of rhymes in the sestet? **(b)** Does this regularity strengthen the "solution" the sestet gives to the problem set out in the octave? Explain.

3. **Craft and Structure (a)** In Sonnet XIX, how does sentence structure break with the pattern of octave and sestet? **(b)** What effect is achieved?

4. **Key Ideas and Details (a)** What major event has occurred before the beginning of Milton's **epic**? **(b)** How does picking up the story after this event follow the conventions of epic form?

5. **Craft and Structure** A traditional epic character has a powerful personality. How does Milton make Satan a suitable epic character?

6. **Integration of Knowledge and Ideas** In Sonnets VII and XIX, Milton reflects on setbacks to his poetic ambition. Use a chart like the one shown to compare the two poems.

Speaker's Situation	Effect on Ambition	Solution	How Solution Helps

7. **Integration of Knowledge and Ideas (a)** Explain how, by writing *Paradise Lost*, Milton aspires to the literary greatness of Homer and the Bible. Provide lines from the poem in support. **(b)** Does Milton's ambition contradict the moral of Sonnet XIX: "They also serve who only stand and wait"? Why or why not?

8. **Integration of Knowledge and Ideas (a)** What ideas about the power of a poet might lines 254–255 of *Paradise Lost* suggest? **(b)** What parallel, if any, can you draw between the situation of Satan and the ambition of a poet? Explain.

9. **Integration of Knowledge and Ideas** Using your knowledge of *Paradise Lost*, explain the humor of the cartoon shown on this page.

Common Core State Standards

Language
4.c. Consult general and specialized reference materials, both print and digital, to find the pronunciation of a word or determine or clarify its precise meaning, its part of speech, its etymology, or its standard usage. *(p. 537)*
6. Acquire and use accurately general academic and domain-specific words and phrases, sufficient for reading, writing, speaking, and listening at the college and career readiness level. *(p. 537)*

©**The New Yorker Collection**, 1988, J. B. Handelsman, from *cartoonbank.com*. All Rights Reserved.

"We're Birds of Paradise all right—paradise lost!"

Vocabulary Acquisition and Use

Word Analysis: Latin Root -lum-

The Latin root -lum-, found in *illumine*, means "light" or "lamp." It is the basis for many words used in *science* to describe light.

Review the list of words and definitions containing -lum-. Then, use the context of the sentences that follow to determine which words fit best in the sentences that follow. Use each word only once and explain your answers.

illuminant *n.* something giving off light

illuminate *v.* shed light on

lumens *n.* units of light

luminous *adj.* emitting light

1. "This clue may _____ the entire mystery," exclaimed the detective.

2. A more efficient light bulb generates more _____ while using less power.

3. The _____ full moon made the path ahead of them clear.

4. A flickering torch served as their only _____.

Vocabulary: Synonyms

A **synonym** is a word that has a similar meaning as another word. Write a complete sentence to answer each question that follows. In your answer, replace the underlined word or words with a synonym taken from the vocabulary list on page 521.

1. Does a good portrait give more than a likeness of its subject?

2. What did they use to shine on the dark pool?

3. What do shoplifters want when they commit a wrong?

4. How does sneakiness benefit a spy?

5. How would an inflexible child act?

6. What effect did the violent events have on the crowd?

7. How did the audience feel about the unmatchable musical performance?

8. Did the corrupt senator's shame affect anyone else?

Using Resources to Build Vocabulary

Epic Style: Words for the Nether World

In *Paradise Lost*, one of Milton's greatest challenges is to create a vivid picture of Hell. He meets this challenge by using words like the ones below to describe the underworld:

desolation	dreary
forlorn	glimmering
gloom	horrid
mournful	wild

Note how the *connotations*, or associations, of these words serve Milton's purpose. Then, use a print or an electronic *dictionary* or *thesaurus* to find **antonyms**—words with the opposite meaning—of these words. Identify which of those antonyms you think Milton might use to describe Heaven and explain why.

Close Reading Activities Continued

Writing to Sources

Argumentative Text Twentieth-century literary critic Douglas Bush said this of *Paradise Lost*: "Its characterization of Satan is one of the supreme achievements of world literature." Clearly Satan is the villain of the poem. Is he more than that? Do you feel any admiration or sympathy for him as you read?

Write an **essay** in which you present and defend your analysis of the character of Satan in *Paradise Lost*. Consider both positive and negative aspects of his character. In your essay, explain how your view of Satan influences your interpretation of *Paradise Lost* itself.

Prewriting Study the *imagery, language, events, universal themes, speeches,* and *stylistic devices* that Milton uses to characterize Satan. Refer to the Critical Commentary on page 535 to spark your own ideas.

- Use a chart like the one shown to take your notes.
- Consider how Milton balances these positive and negative elements.
- Think about other villains from literature or movies. How does Milton's treatment of Satan compare to the way these villains are presented?
- Write a sentence or two to serve as the thesis of your essay, and develop an outline that shows how you will support the thesis.

Common Core State Standards

Writing

1.a. Introduce precise, knowledgeable claim(s), and create an organization that logically sequences claim(s), reasons, and evidence.

1.b. Develop claim(s) fairly and thoroughly, supplying the most relevant evidence for each.

1.e. Provide a concluding statement or section that follows from and supports the argument presented.

Negative Aspects	Positive Aspects
introduction to Satan: (lines 34–40) he is arrogant and destructive	strong will: "All is not lost" (line 106)
"durst defy the Omnipotent" (line 49)	resourceful: "We may with more successful hope resolve / To wage by force or guile eternal war" (lines 120–121)
"obdurate pride and steadfast hate" (line 58)	

Drafting Write a draft of your essay that follows your outline and incorporates evidence from the text of *Paradise Lost* to support your points. State your thesis in the opening paragraph, support it in the body of the essay, and conclude the essay by summarizing what you have proved.

Revising Revise your essay to make it clear and effective.

- Review your draft, making sure you have included *accurate and detailed references to the text* to support your points.
- If your opening paragraph is not lively, consider quoting from the poem or contrasting Satan with another villain to catch readers' attention.
- Check quotations to be sure they are accurate and properly referenced.
- Read the essay carefully to make sure it is grammatically correct and that all words are spelled correctly.

Conventions and Style: Misplaced and Dangling Modifiers

One way to make your writing clearer is to avoid misplaced and dangling modifiers. A **misplaced modifier** seems to modify the wrong word in a sentence because it is too far away from the word it really modifies. A **dangling modifier** does not sensibly modify any word because the word it should modify does not appear in the sentence. Always check your writing for any words, phrases, or clauses that are misplaced or dangling modifiers.

Fix Misplaced and Dangling Modifiers

Misplaced	Better
Milton hoped to one day achieve poetic greatness *early in his career.* (phrase)	Early in his career, Milton hoped to one day achieve poetic greatness.

Dangling	Better
Seeking revenge against God, Eve is tempted into eating the forbidden fruit. (phrase)	Seeking revenge against God, Satan tempts Eve into eating the forbidden fruit.
While he was working as a translator for the government, his eyesight was lost. (clause)	While he was working as a translator for the government, Milton lost his eyesight.

Practice Fix each misplaced or dangling modifier to make the sentence clear and sensible. You may have to change the wording slightly. In items 1–5, the misplaced or dangling modifier is in italics.

1. Milton dictated the poem to his daughters, *blind and unable to write.*
2. *Gifted,* Milton's destiny was to become a famous poet.
3. *At the age of fourteen,* Milton's formal education was begun.
4. *Learning about the revolt against the king,* Milton's tour of Europe was cut short.
5. His blindness is the burden he bears, *which he calls a "mild yoke."*
6. Losing the battle, Hell becomes the rebellious angels' place of banishment.
7. Satan initiates a battle with God motivated by pride and willfulness.
8. The speaker reflects that time has stolen his youth on his birthday.
9. Concerned about his career progress, comfort is found in the speaker's faith.
10. Satan decides he will make humans commit acts of evil during his conversation with Beelzebub.

Writing and Speaking Conventions

A. Writing Write a sentence using each phrase or clause as a modifier. Then, tell what word or words the phrase or clause modifies.

   1. getting older   **2.** during middle age   **3.** who serves God

   Example: getting older
   Sentence: The poet, getting older, wrote about time.
   Word Modified: poet

B. Speaking Write and perform a dialogue in which Satan tries to rally his fellow devils. Correctly use one word, one phrase, and one clause as modifiers.

EPICS
in World Literature

Match numbers on the left with pictures on the right to see illustrations of some of these world epics.

1 *Iliad and Odyssey* (c. 800–700 B.C.)
ancient Greek epics attributed to Homer

Mahabharata (200 B.C.–A.D. 400)
Indian epic attributed to Vyasa

Song of Roland (c. A.D. 1100)
French epic

2 *Song of My Cid* (c. 1140)
Spanish epic

3 *Divine Comedy* (1308–1321)
Italian epic by Dante Alighieri

4 *Paradise Lost* (1667) and
Paradise Regained (1671)
English epics by John Milton

5 *The Song of Hiawatha* (1855)
American epic by Henry Wadsworth
Longfellow

Sundiata (1960)
West African epic, created as a novel by
D. T. Niane

6 *Omeros* (1990)
Caribbean epic by Derek Walcott

Comparing Literary Works

Comparing Epics Around the World

The Epic Tradition Epics are long narrative poems describing the adventures of noble characters. Among the earliest epics are *Gilgamesh*, from the Middle East, and the ancient Greek epics attributed to Homer, the *Iliad* and the *Odyssey*. One of the first epics with a known author is the Roman poet Virgil's *Aeneid*. Christian authors Dante Alighieri (the *Divine Comedy*) and John Milton (*Paradise Lost*) imitated classical models and developed their great works using these traditional elements of epics:

**Common Core
State Standards**

**Reading Literature
3.** Analyze the impact of the author's choices regarding how to develop and relate elements of a story or drama.

**Language
6.** Demonstrate independence in gathering vocabulary knowledge when considering a word or phrase important to comprehension or expression.

- amazing events, such as great battles, and vast settings
- larger-than-life main characters and supernatural creatures who take an interest in human affairs
- themes expressing important cultural values and beliefs
- an elevated style using a serious tone and lofty poetic language

As you read, use a chart like the one shown to help you compare the elements of the excerpt from Dante's epic with those from Milton's *Paradise Lost*. Consider the impact of the choices that each author made.

	Divine Comedy: Inferno	*Paradise Lost*
subject		the Fall of Humanity
main character(s)		Satan; larger-than-life supernatural character
setting(s)		vivid depictions of Heaven and Hell
theme(s)		original sin; pride and disobedience
style		serious tone; lofty poetic language; blank verse

Gather Vocabulary Knowledge

Dante used related forms of the words *cowered, awe,* and *writhes*. Use a **dictionary** to find each word's part of speech and definition. Then, employ the following references to further explore these words:

- **History of Language:** Use a history of English to research each word's origins. Write a paragraph about the word's emergence in English.
- **Book of Quotations:** Use an online or print collection of quotations to find a quotation containing one of the words. In a paragraph, explain nuances in meaning that are evident from the context of the quotation.

Comparing References Compare and contrast what you learn about the words from these and other related references, printed or electronic.

Dante
Alighieri
(1265–1321)

Author of the *Divine Comedy: Inferno*

Dante Alighieri (dän´ tā al əg yer´ ē), whose visions of Hell have haunted readers for centuries, is widely considered one of the greatest poets of western civilization. T. S. Eliot wrote, "Dante and Shakespeare divide the modern world between them; there is no third."

Political Chaos Dante was born into a poor but noble family in the Italian city of Florence. At the time, Italy was not a unified nation but a collection of independent city-states where internal political struggles and interstate rivalries often led to warfare. Elected to help run Florence's government, Dante and his party were overthrown in civil warfare that led to exile from his beloved city in 1302. His experience of exile would play an important role in his writing.

Pioneering Italian In Dante's time, most European writers wrote in Latin, the language of scholarship and the Church. Dante believed that poets should write in the vernacular, or language of the people—in his case, Italian. In 1304, he published *De Vulgari Eloquentia*, which argued for the use of the vernacular. He wrote many lyric poems in Italian, and his crowning achievement, the *Divine Comedy*, was also an Italian work.

The Love of His Life Appearing in the *Divine Comedy* is a woman named Beatrice, to whom Dante also dedicated his early love poems. Scholars believe she is based on a real-life person, Beatrice Portinari. Yet evidence suggests that Dante saw the real Beatrice only twice in his life—first when he was nine and then nine years later. Nevertheless, for Dante, Beatrice came to represent an ideal love figure, the guiding force that led him from despair.

"Midway in our life's journey, I went astray/from the straight road and woke to find myself/**alone in a dark wood. . . .**"

FROM THE DIVINE COMEDY:
Inferno

Dante Alighieri
translated by John Ciardi

BACKGROUND In his *Divine Comedy*, Dante uses an organizing principle based on the number three, drawn from the Christian concept of the Holy Trinity. Documenting his imagined visit to Hell, Purgatory, and Heaven, he divides the epic into three parts—*Inferno*, *Purgatorio*, and *Paradiso*.

In Paradise, Dante will be guided by his beloved Beatrice. For his trip through Hell to Purgatory, however, Dante's guide is the poet Virgil, to whom Dante pays homage by calling him "my Master." Virgil takes Dante through the nine circles of Hell, organized by gravity of the sin involved. In this final canto of *Inferno*, the two reach the ninth circle, by the frozen waters of Cocytus[1], where those guilty of the worst sin, treachery, are found. They include Judas Iscariot, who betrayed Jesus, and Brutus and Cassius, two Roman senators who plotted to assassinate the Roman leader Julius Caesar. They also include the angel-turned-devil Satan, here called Lucifer, the ultimate traitor who rebelled against God.

▲ **Critical Viewing**

How does the artist's depiction of Lucifer in this engraving compare and contrast with Dante's portrayal of him?
COMPARE AND CONTRAST

---

1. Cocytus (kō sīt′ əs) Greek: "river of wailing."

Canto XXXIV

Ninth Circle: Cocytus
Round Four: Judecca
The Center

Compound Fraud
The Treacherous to Their Masters
Satan

"On march the banners of the King,"[2] Virgil begins as the Poets face the last depth. He is quoting a medieval hymn, and to it he adds the distortion and perversion of all that lies about him. "On march the banners of the King—of Hell." And there before them, in an infernal parody of Godhead, they see Satan in the distance, his great wings beating like a windmill. It is their beating that is the source of the icy wind of Cocytus, the exhalation of all evil.

All about him in the ice are strewn the sinners of the last round, *Judecca,* named for Judas Iscariot.[3] These are the *Treacherous to Their Masters.* They lie completely sealed in the ice, twisted and distorted into every conceivable posture. It is impossible to speak to them, and the Poets move on to observe Satan.

He is fixed into the ice at the center to which flow all the rivers of guilt; and as he beats his great wings as if to escape, their icy wind only freezes him more surely into the polluted ice. In a grotesque parody of the Trinity, he has three faces, each a different color, and in each mouth he clamps a sinner whom he rips eternally with his teeth. *Judas Iscariot* is in the central mouth: *Brutus* and *Cassius*[4] in the mouths on either side.

Having seen all, the Poets now climb through the center, grappling hand over hand down the hairy flank of Satan himself—a last supremely symbolic action—and at last, when they have passed the center of all gravity, they emerge from Hell. A long climb from the earth's center to the Mount of Purgatory awaits them, and they push on without rest, ascending along the sides of the river Lethe, till they emerge once more to see the stars of Heaven, just before dawn on Easter Sunday.

> "On march the banners of the King of Hell,"
>   my Master said. "Toward us. Look straight ahead:
>   can you make him out at the core of the frozen shell?"
> Like a whirling windmill seen afar at twilight,

Comparing Epics

What aspect of Dante's style is illustrated in lines 4–5?

---

2. **On ... King** This hymn was written in the sixth century by Venantius Fortunatus, Bishop of Poitiers. The original celebrates the Holy Cross and is part of the service for Good Friday, to be sung at the moment of uncovering the cross.

3. **Judas Iscariot** (is ker′ ē et) disciple who betrayed Jesus; see the Bible, Matthew 26:14, 48.

4. **Brutus and Cassius** They took part in a plot to assassinate Julius Caesar.

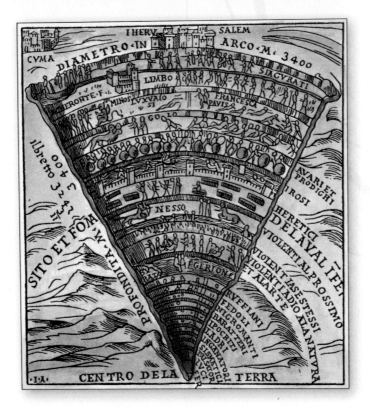

◀ **Critical Viewing**

Where on this map of the *Inferno* do Dante and Virgil now find themselves? Use information from the background on the facing page of hints. **ANALYZE**

Vocabulary

cowered (kou´ ərd) *v.* crouched, as from fear or cold

5   or when a mist has risen from the ground—
      just such an engine rose upon my sight
stirring up such a wild and bitter wind
      I cowered for shelter at my Master's back,
      there being no other windbreak I could find.
I stood now where the souls of the last class
10   (with fear my verses tell it) were covered wholly;
      they shone below the ice like straws in glass.
Some lie stretched out; others are fixed in place
      upright, some on their heads, some on their soles;
      another, like a bow, bends foot to face.
15 When we had gone so far across the ice
      that it pleased my Guide to show me the foul creature[5]
      which once had worn the grace of Paradise,
he made me stop, and, stepping aside, he said:
      "Now see the face of Dis![6] This is the place
20   where you must arm your soul against all dread."
Do not ask, Reader, how my blood ran cold
      and my voice choked up with fear. I cannot write it:
      this is a terror that cannot be told.
I did not die, and yet I lost life's breath:
25   imagine for yourself what I became,
      deprived at once of both my life and death.

---

5. the foul creature Lucifer.

6. Dis (dis) in Greek mythology, the god of the lower world or the lower world itself. Here, it stands for Lucifer.

Comparing Epics

What background information about Lucifer, or Satan, do lines 33–35 share with Milton's epic?

Vocabulary

awe (ô) *n.* feelings of reverence, fear, and wonder

The Emperor of the Universe of Pain
    jutted his upper chest above the ice;
    and I am closer in size to the great mountain
30 the Titans[7] make around the central pit,
    than they to his arms. Now, starting from this part,
    imagine the whole that corresponds to it!
If he was once as beautiful as now
    he is hideous, and still turned on his Maker,
35   well may he be the source of every woe!
With what a sense of awe I saw his head
    towering above me! for it had three faces:[8]
    one was in front, and it was fiery red;
the other two, as weirdly wonderful,
40   merged with it from the middle of each shoulder
    to the point where all converged at the top of the skull;
the right was something between white and bile;
    the left was about the color one observes
    on those who live along the banks of the Nile.
45 Under each head two wings rose terribly,
    their span proportioned to so gross a bird:

---

7. Titans giant deities who were overthrown by Zeus and the Olympian gods of Greece.
8. three faces There are many interpretations of these three faces. The common theme in all of them is that the faces are a perversion of the qualities of the Trinity.

▼ Critical Viewing

Which elements in this engraving emphasize Virgil's role as guide and protector of Dante? **ANALYZE**

> If he was once as beautiful as now
> he is hideous, and still turned on his Maker,
> well may he be the **source of every woe!**

I never saw such sails upon the sea.
They were not feathers—their texture and their form
    were like a bat's wings—and he beat them so
50   that three winds blew from him in one great storm:
it is these winds that freeze all Cocytus.
    He wept from his six eyes, and down three chins
    the tears ran mixed with bloody froth and pus.[9]
In every mouth he worked a broken sinner
55   between his rake-like teeth. Thus he kept three
    in eternal pain at his eternal dinner.
For the one in front the biting seemed to play
    no part at all compared to the ripping: at times
    the whole skin of his back was flayed away.
60 "That soul that suffers most," explained my Guide,
    "is Judas Iscariot, he who kicks his legs
    on the fiery chin and has his head inside.
Of the other two, who have their heads thrust forward,
    the one who dangles down from the black face
65   is Brutus: note how he writhes without a word.
And there, with the huge and sinewy arms, is the soul,
    of Cassius,—But the night is coming on[10]
    and we must go, for we have seen the whole."
Then, as he bade, I clasped his neck, and he,
70   watching for a moment when the wings
    were opened wide, reached over dexterously[11]
and seized the shaggy coat of the king demon;
    then grappling matted hair and frozen crusts
    from one tuft to another, clambered down.
75 When we had reached the joint where the great thigh
    merges into the swelling of the haunch,
    my Guide and Master, straining terribly,
turned his head to where his feet had been
    and began to grip the hair as if he were climbing;[12]
80   so that I thought we moved toward Hell again.

Comparing Epics
What is unusual about the climate in this final circle of Dante's Hell?

Vocabulary
writhes (rī*th*z) *v.* twists and turns the body, as in agony

Comprehension
What torture do Judas Iscariot, Brutus, and Cassius suffer?

---

9. bloody froth and pus the gore of the sinners he chews, which is mixed with his saliva.
10. the night is coming on It is now Saturday evening.
11. dexterously *adv.* skillfully.
12. as if he were climbing They have passed the center of gravity and so must turn around and start climbing.

"Hold fast!"

my Guide said, and his breath came shrill/with labor and exhaustion.

"There is no way/but by such stairs to rise above such evil."

Vocabulary

shrill (shril) *adj.* high and sharp in tone; high-pitched

Vocabulary

nimble (nim´ bəl) *adj.* able to move quickly and lightly

"Hold fast!" my Guide said, and his breath came shrill
 with labor and exhaustion. "There is no way
 but by such stairs to rise above such evil."
At last he climbed out through an opening
85 in the central rock, and he seated me on the rim;
 then joined me with a nimble backward spring.
I looked up, thinking to see Lucifer
 as I had left him, and I saw instead
 his legs projecting high into the air.
90 Now let all those whose dull minds are still vexed
 by failure to understand what point it was
 I had passed through, judge if I was perplexed.
"Get up. Up on your feet," my Master said.
 "The sun already mounts to middle tierce,[13]
95 and a long road and hard climbing lie ahead."
It was no hall of state we had found there,

---

13. middle tierce According to the church's division of the day for prayer, tierce is the period from about six to nine A.M. Middle tierce, therefore, is seven-thirty. In going through the center point, Dante and Virgil have gone from night to day. They have moved ahead twelve hours.

but a natural animal pit hollowed from rock
with a broken floor and a close and sunless air.
"Before I tear myself from the Abyss,"
100   I said when I had risen, "O my Master,
explain to me my error in all this:
where is the ice? and Lucifer—how has he
been turned from top to bottom: and how can the sun
have gone from night to day so suddenly?"
105   And he to me: "You imagine you are still
on the other side of the center where I grasped
the shaggy flank of the Great Worm of Evil
which bores through the world—you were while I climbed down,
but when I turned myself about, you passed
110   the point to which all gravities are drawn.
You are under the other hemisphere where you stand;
the sky above us is the half opposed
to that which canopies the great dry land.
Under the midpoint of that other sky
115   the Man[14] who was born sinless and who lived
beyond all blemish, came to suffer and die.
You have your feet upon a little sphere
which forms the other face of the Judecca.
There it is evening when it is morning here.
120 And this gross Fiend and Image of all Evil
who made a stairway for us with his hide
is pinched and prisoned in the ice-pack still.
On this side he plunged down from heaven's height,
and the land that spread here once hid in the sea
125   and fled North to our hemisphere for fright;[15]
And it may be that moved by that same fear,
the one peak[16] that still rises on this side
fled upward leaving this great cavern[17] here."
Down there, beginning at the further bound

---

14. **the Man** Jesus, who suffered and died in Jerusalem, which was thought to be the middle of the Earth.
15. **fled North . . . for fright** Dante believed that the Northern Hemisphere was mostly land and the Southern Hemisphere, mostly water. Here, he explains the reason for this state of affairs.
16. **the one peak** the Mount of Purgatory.
17. **this great cavern** the natural animal pit of line 97. It is also "Beelzebub's dim tomb," line 130.

◀ **Critical Viewing**
What evidence is there from this image that Dante and Virgil have made it out of hell? **ANALYZE**

Comparing Epics
Would the description of Lucifer in line 107 apply to the Satan of Milton's epic? Why or why not?

Comprehension
What "stairway" did Virgil take to climb out of Hell?

> And this gross Fiend and Image of all Evil
> who made a stairway for us with his hide
> **is pinched and prisoned in the ice-pack still.**

> where a round opening brought in sight the blest
> and beauteous shining of the Heavenly cars.
> And we walked out once more **beneath the Stars.**

130   of Beelzebub's[18] dim tomb, there is a space
         not known by sight, but only by the sound
     of a little stream[19] descending through the hollow
         it has eroded from the massive stone
         in its endlessly entwining lazy flow."

135 My Guide and I crossed over and began
         to mount that little known and lightless road
     to ascend into the shining world again.
     He first, I second, without thought of rest
         we climbed the dark until we reached the point

140   where a round opening brought in sight the blest
     and beauteous shining of the Heavenly cars.
     And we walked out once more beneath the Stars.[20]

---

18. Beelzebub's (bē el´ zə bubz´) Beelzebub, which in Hebrew means "god of flies," was another name for Lucifer or Satan.

19. a little stream Lethe (lē´ thē); in classical mythology, the river of forgetfulness, from which souls drank before being born. In Dante's symbolism, it flows down from Purgatory, where it has washed away the memory of sin from the souls who are undergoing purification. That memory it delivers to Hell, which draws all sin to itself.

20. Stars As part of his total symbolism, Dante ends each of the three divisions of the *Divine Comedy* with this word. Every conclusion of the upward soul is toward the stars, symbols of hope and virtue. It is just before dawn of Easter Sunday that the Poets emerge— a further symbolism.

Critical Reading

Cite textual evidence to support your responses.

1. **Key Ideas and Details (a)** In lines 22–23, what does Dante say he cannot describe? **(b) Analyze:** How does he nevertheless communicate his experience?

2. **Key Ideas and Details (a)** What do the three figures in Lucifer's mouth all have in common, and what do they have in common with Lucifer? **(b) Interpret:** Why do you think Dante situates these sinners in frozen waters? **(c) Infer:** Why do you think he feels no sympathy for these sinners, as he did for many sinners in earlier circles of Hell?

3. **Key Ideas and Details (a)** Which aspect of Brutus's torture does Virgil emphasize in line 65? **(b) Interpret:** Why might language be denied to the inhabitants of the ninth circle of Hell?

Comparing Epics

**Common Core
State Standards**

Writing
2. Write informative/
explanatory texts to
examine and convey
complex ideas, concepts,
and information clearly
and accurately through
the effective selection,
organization, and analysis of
content.

10. Write routinely over
extended time frames and
shorter time frames for a
range of tasks, purposes,
and audiences.

1. **Integration of Knowledge and Ideas** Compare and contrast the ways in which Dante and Milton portray Satan (or Lucifer) in their **epics.** **(a)** What is similar about these epic villains? **(b)** How do they differ physically and in terms of personality?

2. **Integration of Knowledge and Ideas** **(a)** What is similar and different about the sinful behavior being criticized in each epic? **(b)** Based on the two excerpts, do you think these epics are teaching the same values? Why or why not?

3. **Craft and Structure** How effective is each selection in achieving the elevated style appropriate to an epic? Cite specific passages to support your opinions.

4. **Integration of Knowledge and Ideas** Is there evidence in the texts themselves that Dante's epic was written in the Middle Ages and Milton's in the seventeenth century? Explain.

Timed Writing

Informative Text: Essay

Epics traditionally show their heroes braving the underworld or other dangerous, often supernatural settings to perform great deeds.

Assignment: Write an essay in which you compare and contrast the impact of the authors' choices as to how to portray setting. **[40 minutes]**
Address questions such as these to focus your analysis:

- What do the imagery and descriptive language these authors use to portray Hell have in common? How do they differ?
- What is the effect of Dante's firsthand impression of Hell compared to the effect of Milton's all-knowing narrator?
- Which setting do you find more unusual? Why?
- Which universal themes do these settings suggest? Explain.

As you draft your essay, remember to do the following:

- Write an essay of sufficient length to address the questions you decide to consider.
- Include relevant and substantial evidence and well-chosen details.
- Write legibly and use appropriate capitalization and punctuation conventions.

**USE ACADEMIC
VOCABULARY**

As you write, use academic language, including the following words or their related forms:

   categorize
   classify
   determine
   indicate

For more information about academic language, see the vocabulary charts in the introduction to this book.

5-Minute Planner

Complete these steps before you begin to write:

1. Read the assignment carefully. Identify key words and phrases.
2. Weigh the similarities and differences between the two selections.
   TIP As you scan the texts, jot down details that you might use.
3. Create a rough outline for your essay.
4. Reread the prompts, and draft your essay.

Connecting to the Essential Question If you talk about your trip down "the road of life," you are using the same symbolism as Bunyan does in his book. As you read, note religious ideas that influence Bunyan's hero, Christian, in this episode of his life's trip. Identifying these ideas will help as you answer the Essential Question: **How does literature shape or reflect society?**

Common Core State Standards

Reading Literature
2. Determine two or more themes or central ideas of a text and analyze their development over the course of the text, including how they interact and build on one another to produce a complex account.

Close Reading Focus

Allegory

Used in different types of narratives, **allegory** is a literary form in which all the parts of a story have a symbolic meaning. Many works of fiction use *symbols*—objects, people, or places that stand for something beyond themselves. In an allegory, however, every element of the story is symbolic. The allegory in *The Pilgrim's Progress* can therefore be read in two ways:

- On the *literal* level, it tells the story of an adventure-packed journey.
- On the *symbolic* level, it tells the complex account of a Christian soul's journey through life to salvation.

The purpose of an allegory is to teach a moral lesson. To make his lesson clear, Bunyan uses names that reveal the symbolic meanings of characters. A character who assists the hero, for example, is named Help. As you read the excerpt from this allegory, analyze the author's choices of names for the characters. Then, consider the lessons that the allegory teaches as well as the multiple themes that it expresses.

Preparing to Read Complex Texts By **analyzing the text structure** of an allegory—its literal and symbolic levels—you can better appreciate its *meaning*. Remember, too, that you will be reading just one episode of a longer journey that stands for a Christian soul's search for salvation.

- Review the map on page 556 to see the whole journey.
- Use a chart like the one shown to interpret the meaning of specific characters and places in this part of the journey.

Vocabulary

You will encounter the words listed here in the text that follows. Copy the words into your notebook, and note which one is a plural noun.

heedless	endeavored
wallowed	dominions
burden	substantial

Interpreting an Allegory

Overall symbolism	Christian's journey = a Christian's journey through life to salvation
Specific symbols with names that signal their meaning	Christian = a Christian
	Celestial City = heaven
Specific symbols not signaled by their names	
Main message or lesson	

JOHN BUNYAN (1628–1688)

Author of *The Pilgrim's Progress*

The son of a tinker, or traveling mender of pots and pans, John Bunyan had little formal education. Yet he went on to produce *The Pilgrim's Progress*, one of the most widely read books in the English language.

Finding Faith Born near Bedford in central England, Bunyan learned only the basics of reading and instead worked as his father's apprentice, a path on which he would have continued had warfare not intervened. Drafted into the army, he fought on the Parliamentary side in the English Civil Wars. In about 1648, he married a member of a Puritan sect to which he converted. The two religious tracts his wife brought into their home also helped him improve his reading.

Testaments of Faith By 1655, Bunyan had become a popular preacher at his Bedford church. Five years later, however, when Charles II was restored to the throne, it became illegal to preach outside the Church of England. Arrested and jailed for twelve years, Bunyan spent the time profitably, studying the Bible and using it as a guide in writing several books, including a religious autobiography, *Grace Abounding*. He began *The Pilgrim's Progress* during a second, shorter prison term, publishing the first part in 1678 and a second part six years later.

Combining simple yet vivid language and characters with humor and suspense, *The Pilgrim's Progress* proved enormously popular. It went through ten printings in the author's lifetime, was translated into over a hundred languages, and has outsold every other religious work in English except the King James Bible.

> "I BETOOK ME TO MY BIBLE AND BEGAN TO TAKE GREAT PLEASURE IN READING; BUT ESPECIALLY WITH THE HISTORICAL PART THEREOF.... I BEGAN TO LOOK INTO IT WITH NEW EYES AND READ AS I NEVER DID BEFORE."

Vocabulary

heedless (hēd′ lis) *adj.* not taking notice; inattentive

wallowed (wäl′ ōd) *v.* rolled around in mud, water, etc.

burden (burd′ ən) *n.* something that weighs one down; a heavy load or responsibility.

endeavored (en dev′ ərd) *v.* made a serious attempt; tried

from
THE PILGRIM'S PROGRESS

JOHN BUNYAN

Now I saw in my dream, that just as they had ended this talk, they drew near to a very miry Slough that was in the midst of the plain, and they, being heedless, did both fall suddenly into the bog. The name of the Slough was Despond.[1] Here therefore they wallowed for a time, being grievously bedaubed with the dirt, and Christian, because of the burden that was on his back, began to sink in the mire.

Pliable. Then said Pliable, Ah, neighbor Christian, where are you now?

Christian. Truly, said Christian, I do not know.

IT IS NOT ENOUGH TO BE PLIABLE

Pliable. At that Pliable began to be offended, and angerly, said to his fellow, Is this the happiness you have told me all this while of? If we have such ill speed at our first setting out, what may we expect, 'twixt this and our journey's end? May I get out again with my life you shall possess the brave country alone for me. And with that he gave a desperate struggle or two, and got out of the mire on that side of the Slough which was next to his own house. So away he went, and Christian saw him no more.

Christian in trouble, seeks still to get further from his own house.

Wherefore Christian was left to tumble in the Slough of Despond alone; but still he endeavoured to struggle to that side of the Slough that was still further from his own house, and next to the Wicket Gate; the which he did, but could not get out, because of the burden that was upon his back; but I beheld in my dream, that a man came to him, whose name was Help, and asked him what he did there.

Christian. Sir, said Christian, I was bid go this way by a man called Evangelist, who directed me also to yonder Gate, that I might escape the wrath to come; and as I was going thither, I fell in here.

THE PROMISES

Help. But why did you not look for the steps?

Christian. Fear followed me so hard, that I fled the next way, and fell in.

HELP LIFTS HIM OUT

Help. Then, said he, Give me thy hand; so he gave him his hand, and he drew him out, and set him upon sound ground, and bid him go on his way.

---

1. Despond (di spänd′) *n.* despair; hopelessness.

554

WHAT MAKES THE SLOUGH OF DESPOND

Then I stepped to him that plucked him out, and said, "Sir, wherefore, since over this place is the way from the City of Destruction, to yonder Gate, is it, that this plat[2] is not mended, that poor travellers might go thither with more security?" And he said unto me, "This miry Slough is such a place as cannot be mended; it is the descent whither the scum and filth that attends conviction for sin doth continually run, and therefore is it called the Slough of Despond: for still as the sinner is awakened about his lost condition, there ariseth in his soul many fears, and doubts, and discouraging apprehensions, which all of them get together, and settle in this place; and this is the reason of the badness of this ground.

"It is not the pleasure of the King that this place should remain so bad; his labourers also, have, by the direction of His Majesty's surveyors, been for above this sixteen hundred years, employed about this patch of ground, if perhaps it might have been mended; yea, and to my knowledge," saith he, "here hath been swallowed up at least twenty thousand cart loads; yea, millions of wholesome instructions, that have at all seasons been brought from all places of the King's dominions (and they that can tell, say they are the best materials to make good ground of the place); if so be it might have been mended, but it is the Slough of Despond still, and so will be when they have done what they can.

THE PROMISES OF FORGIVENESS AND ACCEPTANCE TO LIFE BY FAITH IN CHRIST

"True, there are by the direction of the law-giver, certain good and substantial steps, placed even through the very midst of this Slough; but at such time as this place doth much spew out its filth, as it doth against change of weather, these steps are hardly seen; or if they be, men through the dizziness of their heads step besides; and then they are bemired to purpose, notwithstanding the steps be there; but the ground is good when they are once got in at the Gate."

---

2. plat a flat, low-lying piece of ground.

Allegory

On the symbolic level of this allegory, to what might the steps refer?

Analyzing Allegory

What does the King symbolize?

Vocabulary

dominions (də min′ yənz) *n.* governed territories or lands

substantial (səb stan′ shəl) *adj.* having substance; large in size or strength

> "IT IS NOT THE PLEASURE OF THE KING THAT THIS PLACE SHOULD REMAIN SO BAD ... BUT THE GROUND IS GOOD WHEN THEY ARE ONCE GOT IN AT THE GATE."

Critical Reading

1. **Key Ideas and Details (a) Summarize:** Sum up what happens to Christian at the Slough of Despond. **(b) Interpret:** What human mood or attitude might the Slough of Despond represent?

2. **Integration of Knowledge and Ideas** What does the selection show about the role of faith in Bunyan's society? In your response, use at least two of these Essential Question words: *devout, piety, redeem.* *[Connecting to the Essential Question: How does literature shape or reflect society?]*

MAPPING ALLEGORY

An allegory is like an extended metaphor in which every detail has a literal and a symbolic meaning:

LITERAL MEANING	ALLEGORICAL MEANING
Main character a man named Christian	**Main character** stands for any Christian person
Other characters people named Pliable, Help, Mr. Worldly Wiseman, and so forth	**Other characters** stand for ways in which others help or hinder a Christian person
Plot a journey from one city to another	**Plot** a spiritual journey toward salvation
Setting a variety of places on the journey, including swamps, hills, towns, fairs	**Setting** each place stands for a different stage on the road toward salvation; for example, the Slough of Despond stands for a feeling of despair.

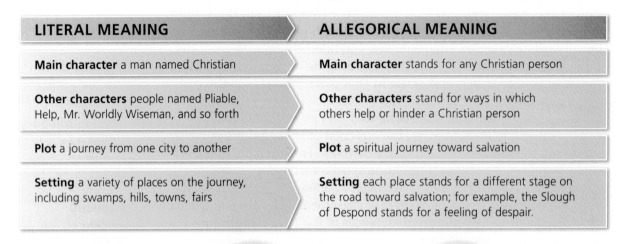

This map shows some of the places Christian visits on his allegorical journey from sin to salvation.

Slough of Despond

Mount Sinai

Beelzebub's Castle

Valley of the Shadow of the Death

Celestial City

Mouth of Hell

CONNECT TO THE LITERATURE

If John Bunyan were alive today, how might he use advanced technology to create his religious allegory?

Close Reading Activities

from *The Pilgrim's Progress*

Literary Analysis

1. **Key Ideas and Details** Analyzing **text structures** will help you appreciate the two levels of an allegory. **(a)** Briefly summarize the literal level of meaning in this episode of the allegory—what happens in the story? **(b)** Then, summarize the symbolic meaning of the events instead of just retelling them.

2. **Key Ideas and Details** How does the title, *The Pilgrim's Progress,* help clarify the basic overall symbolism of the plot?

3. **Craft and Structure** Using details from the selection, explain why *The Pilgrim's Progress* is an **allegory.** Use a chart like the one shown to record elements of the allegory's symbolism.

Character/Place	Symbolic Role in a Christian's Life Journey

4. **Integration of Knowledge and Ideas (a)** What moral lesson or lessons do you think Bunyan was trying to teach in this episode? **(b)** Judging by this episode, how would you explain the popular appeal of *The Pilgrim's Progress?*

Vocabulary Acquisition and Use

Use your knowledge of the underlined vocabulary words to determine whether each statement is true or false. Then, explain your answers.

1. A million dollars is a <u>substantial</u> amount of money.
2. A dog that just <u>wallowed</u> in something is likely to be dry.
3. A monarch rules over his or her <u>dominions</u>.
4. By misbehaving, Jill <u>endeavored</u> to please her teacher.
5. A <u>heedless</u> student listens carefully to what the teacher says.
6. A heavy suitcase can be a <u>burden</u> for a traveler.

Writing to Sources

Informative Text Imagine that a film is being made of *The Pilgrim's Progress* and your job is to cast the parts. Write a **casting memo** suggesting actors who might play the roles in this selection. Describe the qualities each performer will need or the reasons you think a particular star will suit a particular role. Cite details from the selection to justify your ideas. Use a standard memo format, including headings indicating To, From, Subject, and Date.

Common Core State Standards

Writing
2.b. Develop the topic thoroughly by selecting the most significant and relevant facts, extended definitions, concrete details, quotations, or other information and examples appropriate to the audience's knowledge of the topic.

Connecting to the Essential Question The two authors of these selections have different opinions on the role of women in society. Briefly explain whether you consider yourself a traditionalist, a reformer, or neither with regard to this issue. As you read, notice what the speakers in these poems say about or to female characters. Understanding this contrast will help as you answer the Essential Question: **How does literature shape or reflect society?**

Common Core State Standards

Reading Literature
4. Analyze the impact of specific word choices on meaning and tone, including words with multiple meanings or language that is particularly fresh, engaging, or beautiful.

Close Reading Focus

Tradition; Reform
Although they seem to be opposite, tradition and reform go together.

- **Tradition** is a society's approved values, beliefs, roles, and practices.
- **Reform** attempts to change traditional practices and ideas.

Amelia Lanier is a clear reformer, fighting against stereotypes of women, whereas Richard Lovelace fights for tradition, going to war and prison for his king and his honor. As you read, note the appearance of themes of tradition and reform in their works.

Comparing Literary Works Even when reformers' proposals are radical, they are often based on traditional beliefs. Lanier, for example, turns to the Bible, a traditional text, to support her new ideas about the equality of men and women. Lovelace, a supporter of the traditional power of his king, finds a new kind of freedom in love and integrity.

Both use a key strategy for interpreters of a tradition: They explore the multiple meanings of value terms such as *strength, honor,* and *freedom.* By redefining such terms, they find new ways to apply traditional ideas. As you read, analyze the impact of the authors' use of these words and the *political, religious, and philosophical assumptions* that their use suggests.

Preparing to Read Complex Texts As you read a work, **relate it to the major themes and issues of its historical period** by identifying ideas, assumptions, and references that are typical of its era. Consider also which ideas may be responses to events of the period. To understand how Lanier's and Lovelace's poems reflect their era, complete a chart like the one shown for each work.

Poem
"Eve's Apology"

Historical Context
Seventeenth-century women's rights were restricted; story of Eve was used to justify these restrictions

Vocabulary

The words below are important to understanding the texts that follow. Copy the words into your notebook. Find the words that have prefixes.

breach
discretion
reprove
inconstancy

Amelia Lanier

(1569–1645)

Author of "Eve's Apology in Defense of Women"

Amelia Lanier (also spelled "Lanyer") saw the need for women's rights three hundred years before the women's movement for equality. Daring to question her society's vision of women and the limited roles it allowed them, she anticipated future ideas of justice for women.

From Court Life to Working Woman Lanier had ties to the royal court, where her father, Baptista Bassano, was a musician to Queen Elizabeth I. Lanier's husband, Alphonso, and her son, Henry, were also court musicians. Despite her court connections, however, Lanier and her husband were not wealthy. When her husband died in 1613, Lanier sought to make a living by opening a school outside London.

A Radical Work In 1611, Lanier published a volume of poetry called *Salve Deus Rex Judaeorum (Hail, God, King of the Jews).* In this groundbreaking work, of which "Eve's Apology in Defense of Women" is a section, Lanier questioned the privileges of the upper class and called for women's social and religious equality with men.

Although a woman sat on the throne of England during much of Lanier's lifetime, few women in her day published poetry. The poems in *Salve Deus Rex Judaeoroum* reflect her sense that women were underrepresented in the culture of the time. Sections of the work praise her female patrons, while others re-evaluate the role of women in stories from the Bible.

"Dark Lady" or Visionary? In later times, Lanier was perhaps more famous as a possibility for Shakespeare's "dark lady" (the mysterious woman to whom he addresses some of his sonnets) than for her poetry. As scholars have explored the political undercurrents of past literature, though, interest in Lanier has revived. Today, Lanier is considered a visionary feminist who spoke out against injustice.

from
Eve's Apology in Defense of Women

Amelia Lanier

BACKGROUND During the late sixteenth and early seventeenth centuries, a war of words raged, known as "the debate about women." The issue: Were women by nature idle, vain, and immoral, or were they by nature good? Most of the debaters turned to the biblical story of Eve to support their points. Eve, their assumption went, was the first woman and the image of all women after her, so all women share her nature. Lanier's poem, making the same assumption, joins the controversy with powerful pro-woman arguments.

Tradition and Reform

On what tradition does Lanier draw in these lines?

B
ut surely Adam cannot be excused,
Her fault though great, yet he was most to blame;
What weakness offered, strength might have refused,
Being Lord of all, the greater was his shame:
5   Although the serpent's craft had her abused,
God's holy word ought all his actions frame,
        For he was Lord and King of all the earth,
        Before poor Eve had either life or breath.

Who being framed by God's eternal hand,
10 The perfectest man that ever breathed on earth;
And from God's mouth received that strait command,
The breach whereof he knew was present death:
Yea, having power to rule both sea and land,
Yet with one apple won to lose that breath
15   Which God had breathéd in his beauteous face,
    Bringing us all in danger and disgrace.

And then to lay the fault on patience's back,
That we poor women must endure it all;
We know right well he did discretion lack,
20 Being not persuaded thereunto at all;
If Eve did err, it was for knowledge sake,
The fruit being fair persuaded him to fall:
    No subtle serpent's falsehood did betray him,
    If he would eat it, who had power to stay him?

25 Not Eve, whose fault was only too much love,
Which made her give this present to her dear,
That what she tasted, he likewise might prove,
Whereby his knowledge might become more clear;
He never sought her weakness to reprove,
30 With those sharp words, which he of God did hear:
    Yet men will boast of knowledge, which he took
    From Eve's fair hand, as from a learned book.

Vocabulary

breach (brēch) *n.* breaking or being broken; failure to observe the terms of an agreement

discretion (di skresh´ ən) *n.* care in what one does and says

Vocabulary

reprove (rĭ prōōv´) *v.* rebuke or find fault for an action

Critical Reading

1. **Key Ideas and Details (a)** According to Lanier, what motive did Eve have for tasting of the Tree of Knowledge? **(b)** According to Lanier, why did Eve offer Adam a taste of the apple? **(c) Summarize:** Describe Eve's character according to Lanier.

2. **Key Ideas and Details (a)** According to the last stanza, what should Adam have done? **(b) Infer:** What view of Adam is suggested by Lanier's description of him?

3. **Key Ideas and Details** According to the poem, in what way do men apply a double standard to the story of the Fall?

4. **Integration of Knowledge and Ideas** Explain why the interpretation of this story was so important in seventeenth-century arguments about the nature of women.

Cite textual evidence to support your responses.

RICHARD LOVELACE (1618–1657)

Author of "To Lucasta, on Going to the Wars" • "To Althea, from Prison"

Richard Lovelace, son of a wealthy family and firm supporter of his king, had the misfortune to live at a time when the English monarchy was under violent assault. The Civil War that culminated in the execution of the king plunged the privileged Lovelace into prison and poverty.

Looks and Talent Before England's Civil War, Lovelace profited by his association with royalty. It is said that, charmed by this winning young man, the king and queen ordered Oxford to grant him a degree before he had completed his studies! Lovelace did not, however, lack talent. While at Oxford, he wrote a play, painted, and played music.

The Price of Loyalty Lovelace was about twenty-six when Parliament challenged the king's authority and civil war broke out. Perhaps because of his personal charm, Lovelace was chosen to demand that Parliament restore the king's authority. Parliament was not impressed, though, and Lovelace was immediately arrested.

A Daring Life While imprisoned, Lovelace wrote "To Althea, From Prison," a moving affirmation of the value of personal integrity, even if it meant imprisonment. When released, he rejoined Charles's forces and spent his fortune equipping the king's army. Upon Charles's defeat in 1645, Lovelace joined the wars against Spain.

An Untimely End Returning to England years later, Lovelace was again imprisoned by the Puritans. During this time, he prepared for publication the volume that included "To Lucasta, on Going to the Wars." No one knows for certain how Lovelace's life ended, but it is believed that the charming young man who had won the heart of his king and queen died in discouragement and poverty at the age of thirty-nine.

To Lucasta, on Going to the Wars

RICHARD LOVELACE

Background Tensions between the Church of England and the Puritans who wished to reform it had risen to a dangerous level. Foreign wars had led to a money shortage. Charles I made the situation worse by mishandling Parliament, by pressuring nobles for money, and by forcing commoners to serve in his armies. In 1642, England's Parliament went to war against England's king. Lovelace, a loyal supporter of Charles, was twice imprisoned by the king's opponents.

> Tell me not, Sweet, I am unkind,
>   That from the nunnery
> Of thy chaste breast, and quiet mind,
>   To war and arms I fly.
>
> 5 True, a new mistress now I chase,
>   The first foe in the field;
> And with a stronger faith embrace
>   A sword, a horse, a shield.
>
> Yet this inconstancy is such,
> 10   As you too shall adore;
> I could not love thee, Dear, so much,
>   Loved I not honor more.

Relating a Work to Its Historical Period
How does understanding the historical period in which Lovelace was writing help you interpret lines 7–8?

Vocabulary
inconstancy (in kän´ stən sē)
n. fickleness; changeableness

To Althea, from Prison

Richard Lovelace

When love with unconfined wings
    Hovers within my gates,
And my divine Althea brings
    To whisper at the grates;
5 When I lie tangled in her hair
    And fettered to her eye,
The gods[1] that wanton[2] in the air
    Know no such liberty.

When flowing cups run swiftly round,
10   With no allaying Thames,[3]
Our careless heads with roses bound,
    Our hearts with loyal flames;
When thirsty grief in wine we steep,
    When healths[4] and drafts[5] go free,
15 Fishes that tipple in the deep,
    Know no such liberty.

---

1. **gods** The word *gods* is replaced by *birds* in some versions of this poem.
2. **wanton** play.
3. **cups . . . Thames** (temz) wine that has not been diluted by water (from the river Thames).
4. **healths** toasts.
5. **drafts** drinks.

When, like committed linnets,[6] I
    With shriller throat shall sing
The sweetness, mercy, majesty,
20   And glories of my King;
When I shall voice aloud how good
    He is, how great should be,
            Enlarged[7] winds that curl the flood,
        Know no such liberty.

25 Stone walls do not a prison make,
        Nor iron bars a cage;
    Minds innocent and quiet take
        That for an hermitage;[8]
    If I have freedom in my love,
30   And in my soul am free,
    Angels alone that soar above,
        Enjoy such liberty.

---

6. **committed linnets** caged finches.
7. **Enlarged** released.
8. **hermitage** (hur' mi tij) a place of religious seclusion.

Tradition and Reform

In lines 25–28, how does Lovelace use the multiple associations of *walls* to shift from the idea of a prison to the idea of a place of religious seclusion?

Critical Reading

Cite textual evidence to support your responses.

1. **Key Ideas and Details (a)** What does the speaker "now . . . chase" in line 5 of "To Lucasta"? **(b) Interpret:** In what sense does the speaker admit to having two loves? **(c) Draw Conclusions:** In the final two lines, why does the strength of the speaker's love for Lucasta depend on the strength of his other love?

2. **Key Ideas and Details (a)** In "To Althea," what are three things the poet does in prison? **(b) Interpret:** Explain the kind of "liberty" these activities possess.

3. **Key Ideas and Details (a)** In the fourth stanza of "To Althea," which two freedoms does the poet say are most important? **(b) Interpret:** What is the meaning of lines 25–26? **(c) Evaluate:** Do you agree with Lovelace's views on freedom? Explain.

4. **Integration of Knowledge and Ideas** Which of these authors do you think was reflecting dominant social attitudes about women? Which was trying to influence or change those attitudes? Explain. In your response, use at least two of these Essential Question words: *values, independence, reform.* **[Connecting to the Essential Question: How does literature shape or reflect society?]**

Literary Analysis

1. **Key Ideas and Details** **(a)** In "Eve's Apology," what traditional assumptions is Lanier trying to **reform? (b)** What **tradition** does she use to aid her, and why? **(c)** How does she reinterpret this tradition to make her point?

2. **Integration of Knowledge and Ideas** **(a)** In "To Althea, from Prison," what tradition does Lovelace defend? **(b)** Compare the spirit of lines 29–32 with the principles of a reformer such as Gandhi or Martin Luther King, Jr.

3. **Comparing Literary Works** **(a)** In "Eve's Apology," lines 1–8, what conclusion about the Fall does Lanier draw from Adam's strength? **(b)** How does she shift between *weakness* as "moral weakness" and as "powerlessness" to make her point? **(c)** Use a chart like the one shown to note a similar shift in the meaning of *freedom* in "To Althea."

Meaning 1	Meaning 2	Reasoning Behind Shift	Valid?

4. **Integration of Knowledge and Ideas** **Relate poems to their historical period** by showing how issues, events, or political assumptions of the period help you interpret these passages: **(a)** "Eve's Apology," lines 25–32 **(b)** "To Lucasta," lines 11–12 **(c)** "To Althea," lines 17–24.

Vocabulary Acquisition and Use

Choose the letter of each word's antonym (opposite). Explain each choice.

1. **breach:**   **(a)** violation   **(b)** cooperation   **(c)** compliance
2. **discretion:**   **(a)** valor   **(b)** loudness   **(c)** outspokenness
3. **reprove:**   **(a)** forgive   **(b)** support   **(c)** balance
4. **inconstancy:** **(a)** flirtatiousness **(b)** faithfulness **(c)** certainty

Writing to Sources

Narrative Text Today, as in Lovelace's time, soldiers bid farewell to spouses, parents, or other loved ones when going off to war. Reread "To Lucasta, on going to the Wars," and note the main ideas that the speaker conveys. Then, write a brief **dramatic scene** portraying such an event.

- Decide what relationship the characters will have.
- Use *dialogue* to reveal the characters' *emotions*.
- Revise your script to include stage directions where necessary.

Common Core State Standards

Writing
3.b. Use narrative techniques, such as dialogue, pacing, description, reflection, and multiple plot lines, to develop experiences, events, and/or characters.

Primary Sources

Diary
The Diary of Samuel Pepys

Policy Statement
Charles II's Declaration to London, 1666

 **Common Core**
State Standards

Reading Informational Text

1. Cite strong and thorough textual evidence to support analysis of what the text says explicitly as well as inferences drawn from the text, including determining where the text leaves matters uncertain.

3. Analyze a complex set of ideas or sequence of events and explain how specific individuals, ideas, or events interact and develop over the course of the text.

About the Text Forms

A **diary** is an account of a person's experiences and reactions kept daily or at frequent intervals. Some people keep diaries just for themselves. Others hope one day to publish their diaries and so may be more careful in what they say or how they say it. As primary sources, diaries can offer a personal perspective on historical figures and events or provide valuable information about everyday life in the writer's times.

A **policy statement** is an official statement in which a government, a business, or another organization states principles or guidelines to follow. It often addresses a particular situation and aims to achieve a particular result. As primary sources, policy statements can show the political, social, or economic concerns at a particular time.

Preparing to Read Complex Texts

To get the most out of a primary source, follow these steps. As you complete your reading of the text or of a section of the text

- *summarize* what the writer has said, restating the most important ideas

- *draw conclusions* about what the writer says implicitly, identifying his or her assumptions, or unstated beliefs, and implied, or suggested, meanings

- *analyze* the relations among ideas, events, and people in the text, considering how they interact and develop

- **verify and clarify facts.** First, identify factual claims—claims that you can confirm or disprove. Check each claim in another source, noting whether the second source confirms or disconfirms it. In addition, identify unclear passages and determine whether other sources help clarify them.

Support your summary and analysis with strong textual evidence—relevant quotations from the text. Note any points at which the text leaves matters uncertain, and determine the possible reasons for the uncertainty.

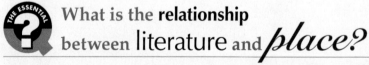
What is the **relationship** between literature and *place?*

As you read, consider the glimpses of seventeenth-century London that each document provides and the way it reflects the city's concerns.

Note-Taking Guide

Primary-source documents are a rich source of information for researchers. As you read these documents, use a note-taking guide like the one shown to organize relevant and accurate information.

1 Type of Document (check one)
☐ Newspaper   ☐ Letter   ☐ Diary   ☐ Speech   ☐ Advertisement
☐ Government Document   ☐ Eyewitness Account   ☐ Memorandum   ☐ Other

2 Date of Document _____

3 Author _____
Author's Position _____

4 Original Audience _____

5 Purpose and Importance

a What was the original purpose? _____
Write down two details that support your answer. _____
_____
_____

b List two important ideas, statements, or observations from this document.
_____
_____

c What does this document show about the time and place in which it
was composed? _____
_____
_____

Verifying and Clarifying Facts
Identify facts and statements you may want to verify and clarify using other sources.

This guide was adapted from the **U.S. National Archives** document analysis worksheet.

Vocabulary

apprehensions (ap rē hen´ shənz) *n.* fears; concerns (p. 572)

abated (ə bāt´ id) *v.* lessened (p. 572)

lamentable (lam´ ən tə bəl) *adj.* causing grief; distressing (p. 573)

combustible (kəm bus´ tə bəl) *adj.* capable of being ignited and burned; flammable (p. 574)

malicious (mə lish´ əs) *adj.* deliberately harmful; destructive (p. 576)

accounts (ə kountz´) *n.* records of money received and paid out; financial records (p. 577)

pernicious (pər nish´ is) *adj.* causing great injury, destruction, or ruin; deadly (p. 579)

magistrate (maj´ is trāt) *n.* a local official who administers the law or serves as a judge (p. 579)

eminent (em´ ə nənt) *adj.* noteworthy; of high rank; distinguished (p. 579)

notorious (nō tôr´ ē əs) *adj.* widely but unfavorably known; having a bad reputation (p. 579)

deliberation (di lib´ ər ā´ shən) *n.* careful consideration and discussion before reaching a decision (p. 579)

THE STORY BEHIND THE DOCUMENTS

Samuel Pepys

Samuel Pepys (pēps) (1633–1703), author of perhaps the most famous diary in English, was in a good position to report on his era. The son of a London tailor, Pepys became a clerk in the navy in 1660 and continued on a rapid rise to fame and fortune, eventually serving as a member of Parliament and secretary of the navy. Pepys began his diary in 1660 and continued it for nine years, when failing eyesight forced him to abandon the project. Writing for himself alone, he used a little-known shorthand that was not deciphered until the nineteenth century, when the diary was published. Today the diary offers a detailed and intimate account of events great and small in Restoration London.

Charles II (1630–1685) was restored to the throne in 1660, the same year Pepys began his diary. Charles's coronation —vividly described in the diary—came after years of exile during the period of England's civil war and subsequent Puritan rule. Excessive in his personal life, he tried to govern with moderation, punishing a few people directly responsible for the execution of his father, Charles I, but otherwise allowing different factions to share in governing. He also supported the arts and, to further scientific advancement, sponsored establishment of the Royal Society—an organization that numbered Samuel Pepys among its early presidents.

The return of the monarchy was greeted with much jubilation in a nation tired of Puritan austerity. Then twin disasters struck: a Great Plague broke out in 1664 and swept through London the following year, and the Great Fire of London devastated the city just one year after that. Samuel Pepys gives vivid and detailed accounts of both events in his diary. In his policy statement of 1666, Charles II responds to the Great Fire by ordering London's citizens to institute practices that would help prevent such calamities in the future.

Charles II

from THE DIARY

Samuel Pepys

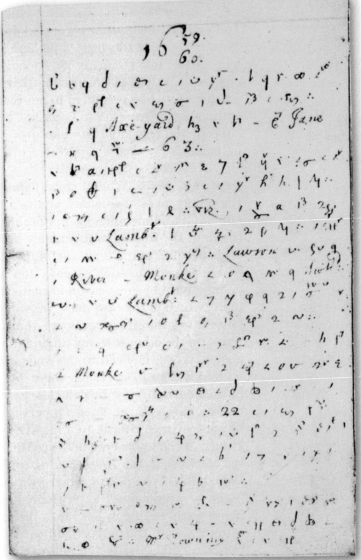

The Plague

Sept. 3, 1665. (Lord's Day.) Church being done, my Lord Bruncker, Sir J. Minnes, and I up to the vestry[1] at the desire of the Justices of the Peace, Sir Theo. Biddulph and Sir W. Boreman and Alderman Hooker, in order to the doing something for the keeping of the plague from growing; but Lord! to consider the madness of the people of the town, who will (because they are forbid) come in crowds along with the dead corps[2] to see them buried; but we agreed on some orders for

▲ **Critical Viewing**

What evidence on this page of the diary suggests that Pepys never meant to share his writing with the world? **INFER**

---

1. **vestry** (ves´ trē) *n.* church meeting-room.
2. **corps** corpses.

the prevention thereof.[3] Among other stories, one was very passionate, methought of a complaint brought against a man in the town for taking a child from London from an infected house. Alderman Hooker told us it was the child of a very able citizen in Gracious Street, a saddler,[4] who had buried all the rest of his children of the plague, and himself and wife now being shut up and in despair of escaping, did desire only to save the life of this little child; and so prevailed to have it received stark-naked into the arms of a friend, who brought it (having put it into new fresh clothes) to Greenwich; where upon hearing the story, we did agree it should be permitted to be received and kept in the town. Thence with my Lord Bruncker to Captain Cocke's, where we mighty merry and supped, and very late I by water to Woolwich, in great apprehensions of an ague. . . .

Sept. 14, 1665. When I come home I spent some thoughts upon the occurrences of this day, giving matter for as much content on one hand and melancholy on another, as any day in all my life. For the first; the finding of my money and plate,[5] and all safe at London, and speeding in my business of money this day. The hearing of this good news to such excess, after so great a despair of my Lord's doing anything this year; adding to that, the decrease of 500 and more, which is the first decrease we have yet had in the sickness since it begun: and great hopes that the next week it will be greater. Then, on the other side, my finding that though the bill[6] in general is abated, yet the city within the walls is increased, and likely to continue so, and is close to our house there. My meeting dead corpses of the plague, carried to be buried close to me at noonday through the city in Fanchurch Street. To see a person sick of the sores, carried close by me by Grace church in a hackney coach.[7] My finding the Angell Tavern at the lower end of Tower Hill, shut up, and more than that, the alehouse at the Tower Stairs, and more than that, the person was then dying of the plague when I was last there, a little while ago, at night, to write a short letter there, and I overheard the mistress of the house sadly saying to her husband somebody was very ill, but did not think it was of the plague. To hear that poor Payne, my waiter, hath buried a child, and is dying himself. To hear that a laborer I sent but the other day to Dagenhams, to know how they did there, is dead of the plague; and that one of my own watermen, that carried me daily, fell sick as soon as he had landed me on Friday morning last, when I had been all night upon the water (and I believe he did get his infection that day at Brainford), and is now dead of the plague. To hear

Vocabulary

apprehensions (ap´ rē hen´ shənz) *n.* fears; concerns

Vocabulary

abated (ə bāt´ id) *v.* lessened

Primary Sources

Diary

What do the incomplete sentences and names in the entry for September 14, 1665, suggest about the audience for whom Pepys was writing?

---

3. **but we . . . thereof** Funeral processions were forbidden in London during the plague. However, the law was often ignored.
4. **saddler** *n.* person who makes, sells, and repairs saddles.
5. **plate** valuable serving dishes and flatware.
6. **bill** weekly list of burials.
7. **hackney coach** carriage for hire.

that Captain Lambert and Cuttle are killed in the taking these ships; and that Mr. Sidney Montague is sick of a desperate fever at my Lady Carteret's, at Scott's Hall. To hear that Mr. Lewes hath another daughter sick. And, lastly, that both my servants, W. Hewer and Tom Edwards, have lost their fathers, both in St. Sepulcher's parish, of the plague this week, do put me into great apprehensions of melancholy, and with good reason. But I put off the thoughts of sadness as much as I can, and the rather to keep my wife in good heart and family also. After supper (having eat nothing all this day) upon a fine tench[8] of Mr. Shelden's taking, we to bed.

The Fire of London

Sept. 2, 1666. (Lord's day.) Some of our maids sitting up late last night to get things ready against our feast today, Jane called us up about three in the morning, to tell us of a great fire they saw in the city. So I rose and slipped on my nightgown, and went to her window, and thought it to be on the back side of Mark Lane at the farthest; but, being unused to such fires as followed, I thought it far enough off; and so went to bed again and to sleep. About seven rose again to dress myself, and there looked out at the window, and saw the fire not so much as it was and farther off. So to my closet to set things to rights after yesterday's cleaning. By and by Jane comes and tells me that she hears that above 300 houses have been burned down tonight by the fire we saw, and that it is now burning down all Fish Street, by London Bridge. So I made myself ready presently, and walked to the Tower,[9] and there got up upon one of the high places, Sir J. Robinson's little son going up with me; and there I did see the houses at that end of the bridge all on fire, and an infinite great fire on this and the other side the end of the bridge; which, among other people, did trouble me for poor little Michell and our Sarah on the bridge. So down, with my heart full of trouble, to the Lieutenant of the Tower, who tells me that it begun this morning in the King's baker's house in Pudding Lane, and that it hath burned St. Magnus's Church and most part of Fish Street already. So I down to the waterside, and there got a boat and through bridge, and there saw a lamentable fire. Poor Michell's house, as far as the Old Swan, already burned that way, and the fire running farther, that in a very little time it got as far as the steel yard, while I was there. Everybody endeavoring to remove their goods, and flinging into the river or bringing them into lighters that lay off; poor people staying in their houses as long as till the very fire touched them, and then running into boats, or clambering from one

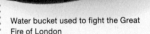

Water bucket used to fight the Great Fire of London

Vocabulary

lamentable (lam′ ən tə bəl) *adj.* causing grief; distressing

Comprehension

How did Pepys hear about the fire in the city?

---

8. tench *n.* type of fish.
9. Tower Tower of London.

Verifying and Clarifying

Which facts in this paragraph could you verify in another source?

Vocabulary

combustible (kəm bus´ tə bəl) *adj.* capable of being ignited and burned; flammable

▼ Primary Source: Art

What line from Pepys's account of the fire would be an appropriate caption for this painting? Why? **[Connect]**

pair of stairs by the waterside to another. And among other things, the poor pigeons, I perceive, were loth to leave their houses, but hovered about the windows and balconies till they were, some of them burned, their wings, and fell down. Having stayed, and in an hour's time seen the fire rage every way, and nobody, to my sight, endeavoring to quench it, but to remove their goods, and leave all to the fire, and having seen it get as far as the steel yard, and the wind mighty high and driving it into the city; and everything, after so long a drought, proving combustible, even the very stones of churches, and among other things the poor steeple by which pretty Mrs.— lives, and whereof my old schoolfellow Elborough is parson, taken fire in the very top, and there burned till it fell down. I to Whitehall (with a gentleman with me who desired to go off from the Tower, to see the fire, in my boat), and there up to the King's closet in the chapel, where people come about me, and I did give them an account dismayed them all, and word was carried in to the King. So I was called for, and did tell the King and Duke of York what I saw, and that unless his Majesty did command houses to be pulled down nothing could stop the fire. They seemed much troubled, and the King commanded me to go to my Lord Mayor from him, and command him to spare no houses, but to pull down before the fire every way. The Duke of York bid me tell him that if he would have any more soldiers he shall; and so did my Lord Arlington afterwards, as a great secret. Here meeting with Captain Cocke, I in his coach, which he lent me, and Creed with

The Great Fire of London, 1666

me to Paul's,[10] and there walked along Watling Street, as well as I could, every creature coming away loaden with goods to save, and here and there sick people carried away in beds. Extraordinary good goods carried in carts and on backs. At last met my Lord Mayor in Canning Street, like a man spent, with a handkerchief about his neck. To the King's message he cried, like a fainting woman, "Lord! what can I do? I am spent: people will not obey me. I have been pulling down houses; but the fire overtakes us faster than we can do it." That he needed no more soldiers; and that, for himself, he must go and refresh himself, having been up all night. So he left me, and I him, and walked home, seeing people all almost distracted, and no manner of means used to quench the fire. The houses, too, so very thick thereabouts, and full of matter for burning, as pitch and tar, in Thames Street; and warehouses of oil, and wines, and brandy, and other things. Here I saw Mr. Isaake Houblon, the handsome man, prettily dressed and dirty, at his door at Dowgate, receiving some of his brothers' things, whose houses were on fire; and, as he says, have been removed twice already; and he doubts (as it soon proved) that they must be in a little time removed from his house also, which was a sad consideration. And to see the churches all filling with goods by people who themselves should have been quietly there at this time. By this time it was about twelve o'clock; and so home. Soon as dined, and walked through the city, the streets full of nothing but people and horses and carts loaden with goods, ready to run over one another, and removing goods from one burned house to another. They now removing out of Canning Street (which received goods in the morning) into Lumbard Street, and farther; and among others I now saw my little goldsmith, Stokes, receiving some friend's goods, whose house itself was burned the day after. I to Paul's Wharf, where I had appointed a boat to attend me, and took in Mr. Carcasse and his brother, whom I met in the street, and carried them below and above bridge to and again to see the fire, which was now got farther, both below and above, and no likelihood of stopping it. Met with the King and Duke of York in their barge, and with them to Queenhithe, and there called Sir Richard Browne to them. Their order was only to pull down houses apace, and so below bridge at the waterside; but little was or could be done, the fire coming upon them so fast. Good hopes there was of stopping it at the Three Cranes above, and at Buttolph's Wharf below bridge, if care be used; but the wind carries it into the city, so as we know not by the waterside what it do there. River full of lighters and boats taking in goods, and good goods swimming in the water, and only I observed that hardly one lighter or boat in three that had the goods of a house in, but there was a pair of virginals[11] in it. Having seen as much as I could now, I away to Whitehall by

---

10. Paul's St. Paul's Cathedral.
11. virginals *n.* small, legless harpsichords.

Verifying and Clarifying
From the details in the text, what can you clarify about the role of the River Thames in the Great Fire of London?

World LITERATURE CONNECTION

Famous Diaries in World Literature

Samuel Pepys was not the first to keep a diary. As early as the tenth century, women in the Japanese Imperial Court wrote journals they called "pillow books," because they hid them under their pillows. Sei Shōnagon began hers with a description of dawn, written in graceful Japanese brush strokes. Soon, she was confiding, "I just love it when bad things happen to people I can't stand," believing nobody would ever read her words.

In the eighteenth and nineteenth centuries, diary writing became a popular pastime in Europe and the Americas, as Western culture placed greater emphasis on the individual personality. During World War II, a teenager named Anne Frank kept a diary while hiding from the Nazis in an attic in Amsterdam. She never guessed it would be read around the world someday.

Connect to the Literature

Do you think Pepys would have written a different sort of diary if he had known it would be published? Explain.

Comprehension
What does Pepys learn about the fire from his visit to the Tower?

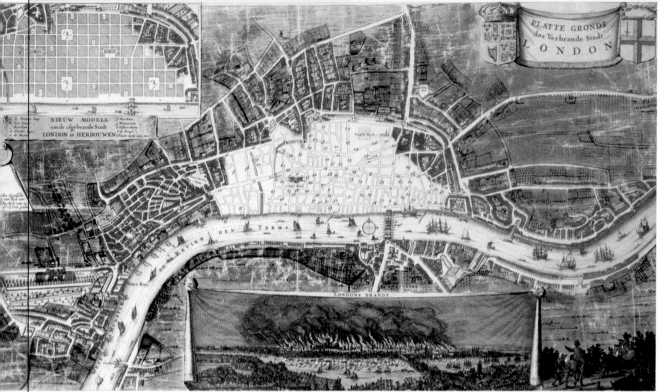

The Great Fire, 1666, Marcus Willemsz Doornik, Guildhall Library, Corporation of London

▲ Primary Source: Art
This map of London includes an inset depicting the area destroyed by the Great Fire. Does this image enhance Pepys's eyewitness description? Explain.
[Make a Judgment]

Vocabulary

malicious (mə lish′ əs)
adj. deliberately harmful; destructive

Primary Sources
Diary What emotional reaction does Pepys have toward the fire that is sweeping through London? Cite words and phrases that reveal his feelings.

appointment, and there walked to St. James's Park, and there met my wife and Creed and Wood and his wife, and walked to my boat; and there upon the water again, and to the fire up and down, it still increasing, and the wind great. So near the fire as we could for smoke; and all over the Thames, with one's face in the wind, you were almost burned with a shower of firedrops. This is very true; so as houses were burned by these drops and flakes of fire, three or four, nay, five or six houses, one from another. When we could endure no more upon the water, we to a little alehouse on the Bankside, over against the Three Cranes, and there stayed till it was dark almost, and saw the fire grow; and, as it grew darker, appeared more and more, and in corners and upon steeples, and between churches and houses, as far as we could see up the hill of the city, in a most horrid malicious bloody flame, not like the fine flame of an ordinary fire. Barbary and her husband away before us. We stayed till, it being darkish, we saw the fire as only one entire arch of fire from this to the other side the bridge, and in a bow up the hill for an arch of above a mile long: it made me weep to see it. The churches, houses, and all on fire and flaming at once; and a horrid noise the flames made, and the cracking of houses at their ruin. So home with a sad heart, and there find everybody discoursing and lamenting the fire; and poor Tom Hater come with some of his few goods saved out of his house, which is burned upon Fish Street Hill. I invited him to lie at my house, and did receive his goods, but was deceived in his lying there, the news coming every moment of the growth of the fire; so as we were forced to begin to pack up our own goods, and prepare for their removal; and did by moonshine (it being brave dry, and moonshine, and warm weather) carry much of my goods into the garden, and Mr. Hater and I did remove my money and iron chests into my cellar, as thinking that the safest place. And got my bags of gold into my office, ready to carry away, and my chief papers of accounts also there, and my tallies into a box by themselves. So great was our fear, as Sir W. Batten hath carts come out of the country to fetch away his goods this night. We did put Mr. Haters, poor man, to bed a little; but he got but very little rest, so much noise being in my house, taking down of goods.

3rd. About four o'clock in the morning, my Lady Batten sent me a cart to carry away all my money, and plate, and best things, to Sir W. Rider's at Bednall Green. Which I did, riding myself in my night-gown in the cart; and, Lord! to see how the streets and the highways are crowded with people running and riding, and getting of carts at any rate to fetch away things. I find Sir W. Rider tired with being called up all night, and receiving things from several friends. His house full of goods, and much of Sir W. Batten's and Sir W. Pen's. I am eased at my heart to have my treasure so well secured. Then home, with much ado to find a way, nor any sleep all this night to me nor my poor wife.

Vocabulary

accounts (ə kountz´)
n. records of money received and paid out; financial records

Critical Reading

Cite textual evidence to support your responses.

1. **Key Ideas and Details (a)** According to the entry for September 3, 1665, what happened to the saddler's family during the plague? **(b) Infer:** What does Pepys's reaction to this situation show you about his personality?

2. **Key Ideas and Details (a)** What does Pepys recommend to the King and Duke of York during the fire? **(b) Evaluate:** Was the recommendation a good one? Why or why not?

3. **Integration of Knowledge and Ideas (a) Compare and Contrast:** What are some modern disasters that compare with the Great Plague and Great Fire of London? **(b) Evaluate:** Do you think Pepys and others in authority handled disaster as well as their modern counterparts would have? Why or why not?

4. **Craft and Structure (a)** List three details about seventeenth-century London that Pepys includes in his diary. **(b) Evaluate:** How has living in London during the plague and the fire affected what Pepys has to say and the effectiveness with which he says it?

Charles II's
DECLARATION TO LONDON,
1666

BACKGROUND Following the Great Fire of London, Charles II took personal charge of seeing that the city got back on its feet. On the day the fire effectively ended, the king visited a field where a hundred thousand homeless Londoners were camping out and tried to reassure them about the future. Charles would have liked to rebuild his capital on a grand scale but had neither the money nor the time to do so. Instead, he had to move as quickly as possible to address the widespread homelessness and the disruption of London's trade, so vital to the English economy. Charles was nevertheless determined to create a more modern city that would never again face the kind of devastation the fire had caused. Taking advice from architects like Christopher Wren, scientists like Robert Hooke, and officials like Samuel Pepys who had fought the fire, Charles issued the following policy statement giving guidelines to Londoners about rebuilding their streets, shops, and homes.

In the first place the woeful experience in this late heavy visitation hath sufficiently convinced all men of the pernicious consequences which have attended the building with Timber, and even with Stone itself, and the notable benefit of Brick, which in so many places hath resisted and even extinguished the Fire; And we do therefore declare Our express Will and Pleasure, That no man whatsoever shall presume to erect any House or Building, great or small, but of Brick or Stone, and if any man shall do the contrary, the next Magistrate shall forthwith cause it to be pulled down.

. . . all other eminent and notorious Streets, shall be of such a breadth, as may with God's blessing prevent the mischief that one side may suffer if the other be on fire.

. . . nor will we suffer any Lanes or Alleys to be erected, but where upon mature deliberation the same shall be found absolutely necessary.

. . . no house shall be erected within so many foot of the River.

. . . any houses to be inhabited by Brewers, or Dyers, or Sugar-Bakers, which Trades by their continual Smokes contribute very much to the unhealthiness of the adjacent places, but We require the Lord Mayor and Aldermen of London upon a full consideration, and weighing all conveniences and inconveniences that can be foreseen, to propose such a place as may be fit for all those Trades which are carried on by smokes to inhabit together.

Vocabulary

pernicious (pər nish´ is) *adj.* causing great injury, destruction, or ruin; deadly

magistrate (maj´ is trāt) *n.* a local official who administers the law or serves as a judge

eminent (em´ ə nənt´) *adj.* noteworthy; of high rank; distinguished

notorious (nō tôr´ ē əs) *adj.* widely but unfavorably known; having a bad reputation

deliberation (di lib´ ər ā´ shən) *n.* careful consideration and discussion before reaching a decision

Primary Sources
Policy Statement
What are the four main guidelines set forth in this policy statement?

Critical Reading

Cite textual evidence to support your responses.

1. **Key Ideas and Details (a)** What does Charles say the recent fire has shown about building construction? **(b) Infer:** What situation does he want to prevent by getting rid of very narrow streets and keeping lanes and alleys to a minimum? **(c) Speculate:** Why do you think he orders that no house be erected too close to the river?

2. **Integration of Knowledge and Ideas (a) Infer:** Why does Charles want all London businesses requiring continuous fires to be housed in the same place? **(b) Evaluate:** Do you think this idea is practical? Why or why not?

3. **Key Ideas and Details (a) Analyze Cause and Effect:** What main concern of Charles II's London has led him to issue this policy statement? **(b) Draw Conclusions:** What does the statement reveal about London buildings before the fire?

Diary • Policy Statement

Comparing Primary Sources

Refer to your note-taking guide to answer these questions.

1. **(a)** Summarize each source, supporting your summary with quotations.
   (b) In the entry for September 3, 1665, what does Pepys imply are the reasons he and others agreed to allow the child "to be received and kept" in Greenwich? Cite textual details in support of your response.

2. **(a)** Outline the sequence of events and interaction of people in Pepys's diary entry for September 2, 1666. **(b)** Identify one point that he leaves unclear, and explain why he probably did not clarify it.

3. Compare and contrast the information Pepys provides about the Great Plague with the information about the Great Fire of London in both sources. **(a)** What do the two disasters have in common, and how do they differ? **(b)** Which seems worse, and why? To help you answer the question, gather details on a Venn diagram like the one shown.

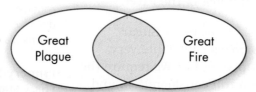

Vocabulary Acquisition and Use

New Vocabulary Answer the questions about the italicized vocabulary words.

1. **(a)** Which word is closest in meaning to *malicious*: *lamentable, pernicious,* or *notorious*? **(b)** What do the two words mean?

2. **(a)** What is similar about the meanings of *eminent* and *notorious*? **(b)** What is different about them?

3. **(a)** Why might a *lamentable* situation prompt *apprehensions*? **(b)** If those *apprehensions* then *abated,* would the person be more or less fearful? Explain your answer.

Content-Area Vocabulary Determine whether each statement is true or false. Explain your answers.

4. Someone who moves with *deliberation* is hasty.

5. Rocks are more *combustible* than paper.

6. A company's bookkeeper is often responsible for keeping *accounts*.

7. A *magistrate* might serve as a judge in a local legal matter.

Etymology Study *Magistrate* comes from the Latin *magnus,* meaning "great." A *magistrate* is a person who exercises great authority in certain legal matters. Use a dictionary to show how these *magnus* terms from political science reflect the idea of greatness: *magisterial, Magna Carta, magnate, magniloquent.*

Research Task

Topic: The Great Fire of London

Samuel Pepys's account of the Great Fire takes us right to the scene of the ongoing disaster. You cannot duplicate his eyewitness vantage point. However, you can gain a clear perspective on the causes, sequence of events, or results of the fire.

Assignment: Write a research report on one of the following aspects of the Great Fire:

- causes—geographical, architectural, cultural
- sequence of events from beginning to end
- short-term and long-term effects

Formulate a research plan. Begin with a question open-ended enough to support an in-depth, multi-faceted report, such as, "How did the way of life of seventeenth-century Londoners contribute to the Great Fire?" Then, develop stepping-stone questions the answers to which will help you answer your major question. Finally, devise a research plan by listing the types of sources you will consult. Do not rely entirely on texts written for students. In addition to such texts, consult both primary sources and texts written by experts for informed audiences.

▲ One effect of the Great Fire was the use of fire marks like this one to identify insured property. Firemen, paid by insurance companies, would try to save marked properties.

Model: Using Stepping-Stone Questions

How did the way of life of Londoners contribute to the Great Fire?

> How did people communicate?
> How were neighborhoods arranged?
> How were streets designed?
> What were buildings made of?

Gather sources. Follow your plan. Assemble and organize your evidence, showing how facts support central ideas. Do not rely entirely on any one source.

Synthesize information. Evaluate your information and determine what to use and what to discard. First, distinguish between reliable and unreliable sources, excluding information you find only in unreliable sources. Then, look for and focus on patterns of ideas, excluding irrelevant details. Be flexible: If your question and research plan result in too little or too much information, revise them.

Organize and present ideas. Write your research paper based on a clear organization or outline. The topic of the Great Fire lends itself to visual aids, so consider including paintings, drawings, blueprints, diagrams, and maps. Avoid plagiarism, citing sources for words, ideas, and visuals not your own, using a standard format.

RESEARCH TIP

The Great Fire has been treated in books for scholars, for general adult readers, for young adults, and for children. Do not waste time on books that are too specialized or too simplified.

Use a checklist like the one shown to review, and possibly revise, your report.

Research Checklist

☐ Have I answered the major research question?

☐ Have I gathered information from both primary and secondary sources?

☐ Have I organized the information in a logical way?

☐ Have I incorporated visuals appropriately?

London Past

"Don't ever take a city for granted,"

Neil Gaiman wrote in an online essay. "After all, it is bigger than you are; it is older; and it has learned how to wait…." In his novel *Neverwhere,* Gaiman certainly did not take London for granted. Describing a fantastical underground London unknown to the usual inhabitants of "London Above," he pays tribute to the city's long history and to its darker side.

Gaiman's dangerous underground city has a kinship with the London that Pepys describes in his accounts of the Great Plague and the Fire. Both are scary places, filled with turmoil and threat. Pepys may have been unaware that rats were playing a a major role in the plague; however, Gaiman gives great power to rodent-like characters called rat-speakers.

A female rat-speaker named Anaesthesia accompanies Gaiman's hero, Richard Mayhew, in this episode from the beginning of the tale. Mayhew has recently arrived in the underground city "from the London Above." Now, he and Anaesthesia, led by a mysterious woman, must cross the fear-inspiring Night's Bridge. It is the first major test of Mayhew's courage.

and Present

Neil Gaiman
Novelist/Graphic Novelist/Poet/
Songwriter/Screenwriter

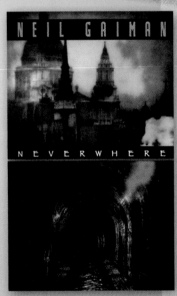

Neverwhere started life in 1996 as a BBC television series in England. Gaiman (b. 1960) later adapted it into a novel in order to develop the characters. The novel became a major success, while the original TV series has faded.

Gaiman is versatile, writing songs and poems as well as screenplays. Even his screenwriting experience is diverse—it includes writing the English-language script for the Japanese anime movie *Princess Mononoke* (1999). Overall, however, Gaiman is best known as the author of the graphic novel series *Sandman*.

Describing his fertile creative process, he wrote, "You get ideas from daydreaming." Clarifying, he continued, "You get ideas from being bored. You get ideas all the time. The only difference between writers and other people is we notice when [it happens]."

from Neverwhere

Neil Gaiman

"If you are crossing the bridge, I will go with you," said a female voice, rich as cream and honey, coming from behind them. Richard was not able to place her accent. He turned, and standing there was a tall woman, with long, tawny hair, and skin the color of burnt caramel. She wore dappled leather clothes, mottled in shades of gray and brown. She had a battered leather duffel bag over her shoulder. She was carrying a staff, and she had a knife at her belt and an electric flashlight strapped to her wrist. She was also, without question, the most beautiful woman that Richard had ever seen.

"Safety in numbers. You're welcome to come with us," he said, after a moment's hesitation. "My name's Richard Mayhew. This is Anaesthesia. She's the one of us who knows what she's doing." The rat-girl preened.

The leather woman looked him up and looked him down. "You're from London Above," she told him.

"Yes." As lost as he was in this strange otherworld, he was at least learning to play the game. His mind was too numb to make any sense of where he was, or why he was here, but it was capable of following the rules.

"Traveling with a rat-speaker. My word."

"I'm his guardian," said Anaesthesia, truculently. "Who are you? Who do you owe fealty to?"

The woman smiled. "I owe no man fealty, rat-girl. Have either of you crossed Night's Bridge before?" Anaesthesia shook her head. "Well. Isn't this going to be fun?"

They walked toward the bridge. Anaesthesia handed Richard her candle-lamp. "Here," she said.

"Thanks." Richard looked at the woman in leather. "Is there anything, really, to be scared of?"

"Only the night on the bridge," she said.

"The kind in armor?"

"The kind that comes when day is over."

Anaesthesia's hand sought Richard's. He held it tightly, her tiny hand in his. She smiled at him, squeezed his hand. And then they set foot on Night's Bridge and Richard began to understand darkness: darkness as something solid and real, so much more than a simple absence of light. He felt it touch his skin, questing, moving, exploring: gliding through his mind. It slipped into his lungs, behind his eyes, into his mouth. . .

With each step they took the light of the candle became dimmer. He realized the same thing was happening to the leather woman's flashlight. It felt not so much as if the lights were being turned down but as if the darkness were being turned up. Richard blinked, and opened his eyes on nothing—nothing but darkness, complete and utter. *Sounds.* A rustling, a squirming. Richard blinked, blinded by the night. The sounds were nastier, hungrier. Richard imagined he could hear voices: a horde of huge, misshapen trolls, beneath the bridge. . . .

Something slithered past them in the dark. "What's that?" squeaked Anaesthesia. Her hand was shaking in his.

"Hush," whispered the woman. "Don't attract its attention."

"What's happening?" whispered Richard.

"Darkness is happening," said the leather woman, very quietly. "Night is happening. All the nightmares that have come out when the sun goes down, since the cave times, when we huddled together in fear for safety and for warmth, are happening. Now," she told them, "now is the time to be afraid of the dark." Richard knew that something was about to creep over his face. He closed his eyes: it made no difference to what he saw or felt. The night was complete. It was then that the hallucinations started.

Richard began to understand darkness: darkness as something solid and real, so much more than a simple absence of light.

He saw a figure falling toward him through the night, burning, its wings and hair on fire.

He threw up his hands: there was nothing there.

Jessica looked at him, with contempt in her eyes. He wanted to shout to her, tell her he was sorry.

Place one foot after another.

He was a small child, walking home from school, at night, down the one road with no streetlights. No matter how many times he did it, it never got any easier, never got any better.

He was deep in the sewers, lost in a labyrinth. The Beast was waiting for him. He could hear a slow drip of water. He knew the Beast was waiting. He gripped his spear. . . . Then a rumbling bellow, deep in its throat, from behind him. He turned. Slowly, agonizingly slowly, it charged at him, through the dark.

And it charged.

He died.

And kept walking.

Slowly, agonizingly slowly, it charged at him, over and over, through the dark.

There was a sputter, and a flare so bright it hurt, making Richard squint and stagger. It was the candle flame, in its lemonade-bottle holder. He had never known how brightly a single candle could burn. He held it up, gasping and gulping and shaking with relief. His heart was pounding and shuddering in his chest.

> # He had never known how brightly a single candle could burn.

"We would appear to have crossed successfully," said the leather woman.

Richard's heart was pounding in his chest so hard that, for a few moments, he was unable to talk. He forced himself to breathe slowly, to calm down. They were in a large anteroom, exactly like the one on the other side. In fact, Richard had the strange feeling that it was the same room they had just left. Yet the shadows were deeper, and there were afterimages floating before Richard's eyes, like those one saw after a camera flash. "I suppose," Richard said, haltingly, "we weren't in any real danger. . . . It was like a haunted house. A few noises in the dark . . . and your imagination does the rest. There wasn't really anything to be scared of, was there?"

The woman looked at him, almost pityingly; and Richard realized that there was nobody holding his hand. "Anaesthesia?"

From the darkness at the crown of the bridge came a gentle noise, like a rustle or a sigh. A handful of irregular quartz beads pattered down the curve of the bridge toward them. Richard picked one up. It was from the rat-girl's necklace. His mouth opened, but no sound came out. Then he found his voice. "We'd better. We have to go back. She's . . ."

The woman raised her flashlight, shone it across the bridge. Richard could see all the way across the bridge. It was deserted. "Where is she?" he asked.

"Gone," said the woman, flatly. "The darkness took her."

Critical Reading

1. **(a)** What does the leather woman say when she learns that Richard and Anaesthesia have never before crossed Night's Bridge? **(b) Infer:** Do you think that the leather woman has crossed the bridge before? Why or why not?

2. **(a) Summarize:** Briefly summarize what Richard feels and sees in the darkness on Night's Bridge. **(b) Interpret:** What do "night" and "darkness" come to mean to Richard while he is on the bridge?

3. **(a)** Describe the place the leather woman and Richard reach after they cross Night's Bridge. **(b) Speculate:** Are they in the same room they started from? Explain.

Use these questions to focus a class discussion of Neverwhere:

4. Do you think that nighttime in Pepys's London would have been a little bit like the night on Gaiman's bridge? Why or why not?

5. Why are writers like Gaiman and Pepys so interested in depicting a city like London?

Connecting to the Essential Question In *A Journal of the Plague Year,* Daniel Defoe vividly describes his hometown, London, during a terrible catastrophe in its past. What landmark event in your own region do you think would make a good story? As you read, note passages that reveal how the plague affected London. They will help you explore the Essential Question: **What is the relationship between literature and place?**

Close Reading Focus

First-person Point of View
Point of view is the perspective from which a narrator tells a story. Stories told from the **first-person point of view** have these qualities:

- The narrator either participates in or observes the events.
- The narrator refers to himself or herself as "I."
- The narrator can tell you his or her thoughts but not those of others.

Nonfiction diaries and journals almost always use the first-person point of view, since they present a person's daily account of his or her thoughts and experiences. Even though *A Journal of the Plague Year* is fiction, Defoe's use of the first-person point of view makes it seem as if he actually witnessed the events he writes about, as in this passage:

It was about the 10th of September that my curiosity led, or rather drove, me to go and see this pit again, . . .

Reporting only his or her own thoughts and experiences, the first-person narrator provides a personal perspective that helps brings readers into a private world of meaning and aesthetic pleasure.

Preparing to Read Complex Texts When you realize that you do not understand a passage you are reading, repair your comprehension by **asking questions.** Focus on the basics of the puzzling situation: who is doing what to whom and why? Also, when and where is the action taking place? Use a chart like the one shown to help you ask and answer questions about a passage.

Vocabulary

You will encounter the words listed here in the text that follows. Copy the words into your notebook. Determine which words have three syllables.

lamentations	resolution
distemper	importuning
delirious	prodigious

Common Core State Standards

Reading Literature
3. Analyze the impact of the author's choices regarding how to develop and relate elements of a story or drama.

Text: Description of Pit

Q. Who was thrown in?
A. Londoners who died of plague

Q. What happened to them?
A. They were buried in a mass grave.

Q. Where was the pit?
A. in Aldgate parish in London

Q. When were they brought there?
A. at night

Q. Why were they put there?
A. to prevent the spread of disease

DANIEL DEFOE

(1660–1731)

Author of *A Journal of the Plague Year*

"A false, shuffling, prevaricating rascal"—that was how fellow author Joseph Addison described Daniel Defoe. In many ways, Addison was not far from wrong. Constantly in debt, Defoe often engaged in shady business deals and declared bankruptcy in 1692, owing a small fortune to his creditors. He was also a sometime government spy and propagandist who even upgraded his own name, originally *Foe*, by adding an aristocratic *De*.

An Innovative Novelist Despite all his flaws, we remember Defoe for an important literary achievement. He practically invented the modern realistic novel. He did so with two books that were written as the memoirs of fictional characters. *Robinson Crusoe* (1719) presents an almost documentary narrative of a man marooned on a desert island. *Moll Flanders* (1722) tells a satirical tale of a poor woman seeking respectability. During his lifetime, Defoe's books were considered so realistic that they were sold as nonfiction. In fact, the first-person narrators were so convincing that Defoe was even accused of "forging a story, and imposing it on the world for truth."

Factual Fiction Defoe brought an even greater factual background to *A Journal of the Plague Year* (1722), his fictional account of the great plague that devastated England from 1664 to 1665. To construct this vivid narrative, Defoe studied official documents, interviewed survivors of the plague, and may have drawn on his own memories as a young child.

The vivid historical re-creation of the plague is a triumph of Defoe's energetic, detailed style in a genre that set English fiction on a new path.

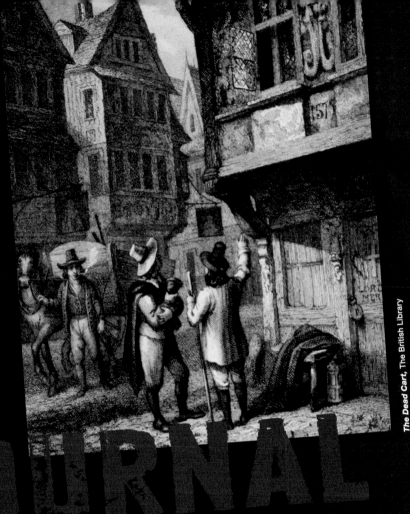

The Dead Cart, The British Library

A JOURNAL

DANIEL DEFOE

The face of London was now indeed strangely altered, I mean the whole mass of buildings, city, liberties, suburbs, Westminster, Southwark, and altogether; for as to the particular part called the city, or within the walls, that was not yet much infected. But in the whole the face of things, I say, was much altered; sorrow and sadness sat upon every face; and though some parts were not yet overwhelmed, yet all looked deeply concerned; and as we saw it apparently coming on, so everyone looked on himself and his family as in the utmost danger. Were it possible to represent those times exactly to those that did not see them, and give the reader due ideas of the horror that everywhere presented itself, it must make just impressions upon their minds and fill them with surprise. London might well be said to be all in tears; the mourners did not go about the streets indeed, for nobody put on black or made a formal dress of mourning for their nearest friends; but the voice of mourning was truly heard in the streets. The shrieks of women and children at the windows and doors of their houses, where their dearest relations were perhaps dying, or just dead, were so frequent to be heard as we passed the streets, that it was enough to pierce the stoutest heart in the world to hear them. Tears and lamentations were seen almost in every house, especially in the first part of the visitation; for toward the latter end men's hearts were hardened, and death was so always before their eyes, that they did not so much concern themselves for the loss of their friends, expecting that themselves should be summoned the next hour. . . .

I went all the first part of the time freely about the streets, though not so freely as to run myself into apparent danger, except when they dug the great pit in the churchyard of our parish of Aldgate. A terrible pit it was, and I could not resist my curiosity to go and see it. As near as I may judge, it was about forty feet in length, and about fifteen or sixteen feet broad, and, at the time I first looked at it, about nine feet deep; but it was said they dug it near twenty feet deep afterwards in one part of it, till they could go no deeper for the water; for they had, it seems, dug several large pits before this. For though the plague was long a-coming to our parish, yet, when it did come, there was no parish in or about London where it raged with such violence as in the two parishes of Aldgate and Whitechapel.

Point of View

Where in the first paragraph does the narrator indicate that he is providing a personal account intended to be read by others? Explain.

Vocabulary

lamentations (lam´ən tā´ shənz) *n.* expressions of grief or mourning

Comprehension

In what ways was the "face of London . . . strangely altered"?

Vocabulary

distemper (dis tem´ pər)
n. infectious disease such as the plague

INTO THESE
PITS THEY HAD
PUT PERHAPS
FIFTY
OR SIXTY
BODIES
EACH

Questioning

From the information in the paragraph beginning, "It was . . .," what reason does the narrator give for wanting to visit the pit at night rather than during the day?

Vocabulary

delirious (di lir´ ē əs)
adj. having hallucinations; ranting

I saw they had dug several pits in another ground, when the distemper began to spread in our parish, and especially when the dead carts began to go about, which was not, in our parish, till the beginning of August. Into these pits they had put perhaps fifty or sixty bodies each; then they made larger holes, wherein they buried all that the cart brought in a week, which, by the middle to the end of August, came to from 200 to 400 a week; and they could not well dig them larger, because of the order of the magistrates confining them to leave no bodies within six feet of the surface; and the water coming on at about seventeen or eighteen feet, they could not well, I say, put more in one pit. But now, at the beginning of September, the plague raging in a dreadful manner, and the number of burials in our parish increasing to more than was ever buried in any parish about London of no larger extent, they ordered this dreadful gulf to be dug, for such it was rather than a pit.

They had supposed this pit would have supplied them for a month or more when they dug it, and some blamed the churchwardens for suffering[1] such a frightful thing, telling them they were making preparations to bury the whole parish, and the like; but time made it appear the churchwardens knew the condition of the parish better than they did, for the pit being finished the 4th of September, I think, they began to bury in it the 6th, and by the 20th, which was just two weeks, they had thrown into it 1114 bodies, when they were obliged to fill it up, the bodies being then come to lie within six feet of the surface. I doubt not but there may be some ancient persons alive in the parish who can justify the fact of this, and are able to show even in what place of the churchyard the pit lay better than I can. The mark of it also was many years to be seen in the churchyard on the surface, lying in length parallel with the passage which goes by the west wall of the churchyard out of Houndsditch, and turns east again into Whitechapel, coming out near the Three Nuns' Inn.

It was about the 10th of September that my curiosity led, or rather drove, me to go and see this pit again, when there had been near 400 people buried in it; and I was not content to see it in the daytime, as I had done before, for then there would have been nothing to have been seen but the loose earth; for all the bodies that were thrown in were immediately covered with earth by those they called the buriers, which at other times were called bearers; but I resolved to go in the night and see some of them thrown in.

There was a strict order to prevent people coming to those pits, and that was only to prevent infection. But after some time that order was more necessary, for people that were infected and near their end, and delirious also, would run to those pits, wrapped in blankets or rugs, and throw themselves in, and, as they said, bury themselves. I cannot

---

1. suffering allowing.

say that the officers suffered any willingly to lie there; but I have heard that in a great pit in Finsbury, in the parish of Cripplegate, it lying open then to the fields, for it was not then walled about, [some] came and threw themselves in, and expired there, before they threw any earth upon them; and that when they came to bury others, and found them there, they were quite dead, though not cold.

This may serve a little to describe the dreadful condition of that day, though it is impossible to say anything that is able to give a true idea of it to those who did not see it, other than this, that it was indeed very, very, very dreadful, and such as no tongue can express.

I got admittance into the churchyard by being acquainted with the sexton who attended, who, though he did not refuse me at all, yet earnestly persuaded me not to go, telling me very seriously, for he was a good, religious, and sensible man, that it was indeed their business and duty to venture, and to run all hazards, and that in it they might hope to be preserved; but that I had no apparent call to it but my own curiosity, which, he said, he believed I would not pretend was sufficient to justify my running that hazard. I told him I had been pressed in my mind to go, and that perhaps it might be an instructing sight, that might not be without its uses. "Nay," says the good man, "if you will venture upon that score, name of God go in; for, depend upon it, 't will be a sermon to you, it may be, the best that ever you heard in your life. 'T is a speaking sight," says he, "and has a voice with it, and a loud one, to call us all to repentance"; and with that he opened the door and said, "Go, if you will."

His discourse had shocked my resolution a little, and I stood wavering for a good while, but just at that interval I saw two links² come over from the end of the Minories, and heard the bellman, and then appeared a dead cart, as they called it, coming over the streets; so I could no longer resist my desire of seeing it, and went in. There was nobody, as I could perceive at first, in the churchyard, or going into it, but the buriers and the fellow that drove the cart, or rather led the horse and cart; but when they came up to the pit they saw a man go to and again,³ muffled up in a brown cloak, and making motions with his hands under his cloak, as if he was in a great agony, and the buriers immediately gathered about him, supposing he was one of those poor delirious or desperate creatures that used to pretend, as I have said, to bury themselves. He said nothing as he walked about, but two or three times groaned very deeply and loud, and sighed as he would break his heart.

When the buriers came up to him they soon found he was neither a person infected and desperate, as I have observed above, or a person distempered in mind, but one oppressed with a dreadful weight

---

2. **links** torches.
3. **to and again** to and fro.

Point of View

In the paragraph beginning, "His discourse . . . ," which details make Defoe's fictional narrator seem like a real person? Why?

Vocabulary

resolution (rez´ə lōō´shən) *n.* fixed or determined state of mind

Comprehension

What provisions does the parish make for disposing of the bodies of plague victims?

of grief indeed, having his wife and several of his children all in the cart that was just come in with him, and he followed in an agony and excess of sorrow. He mourned heartily, as it was easy to see, but with a kind of masculine grief that could not give itself vent by tears; and calmly defying the buriers to let him alone, said he would only see the bodies thrown in and go away, so they left importuning him. But no sooner was the cart turned round and the bodies shot into the pit promiscuously,[4] which was a surprise to him, for he at least expected they would have been decently laid in, though indeed he was afterwards convinced that was impracticable; I say, no sooner did he see the sight but he cried out aloud, unable to contain himself. I could not hear what he said, but he went backward two or three steps and fell down in a swoon. The buriers ran to him and took him up, and in a little while he came to himself, and they led him away to the Pie Tavern over against the end of Houndsditch, where, it seems, the

---

4. **promiscuously** mixed together without care or thought.

Vocabulary

importuning (im´ pôr
tōōn´ iŋ) *v.* pleading with

▼ **Critical Viewing** Explain how the Journal helps you make sense of details in this picture. **CONNECT**

man was known, and where they took care of him. He looked into the pit again as he went away, but the buriers had covered the bodies so immediately with throwing in earth, that though there was light enough, for there were lanterns, and candles in them, placed all night round the sides of the pit, upon heaps of earth, seven or eight, or perhaps more, yet nothing could be seen.

This was a mournful scene indeed, and affected me almost as much as the rest; but the other was awful and full of terror. The cart had in it sixteen or seventeen bodies: some were wrapped up in linen sheets, some in rags, some little other than naked, or so loose that what covering they had fell from them in the shooting out of the cart, and they fell quite naked among the rest; but the matter was not much to them, or the indecency much to anyone else, seeing they were all dead, and were to be huddled together into the common grave of mankind, as we may call it, for here was no difference made, but poor and rich went together; there was no other way of burials, neither was it possible there should, for coffins were not to be had for the prodigious numbers that fell in such a calamity as this.

Vocabulary

prodigious (prō′ dij′ əs)
adj. enormous; huge

FOR HERE WAS NO DIFFERENCE MADE, BUT POOR AND RICH WENT TOGETHER

Critical Reading

1. **Key Ideas and Details (a)** What was the purpose of the great pit dug in Aldgate? **(b) Infer:** Why do you think the narrator describes the pit in detail?

2. **Key Ideas and Details (a)** What prompts the narrator to visit the pit? **(b) Interpret:** What does the Sexton mean when he says that visiting the pit will "be a sermon" to the narrator?

3. **Key Ideas and Details (a) Summarize:** Retell the incident concerning the man in the brown cloak. **(b) Draw Conclusions:** In what way does this incident add a new dimension of meaning to the previous general descriptions of the plague? Explain.

4. **Craft and Structure** Does Defoe use informative language, emotional language, or both to describe London during this crisis? In your response, use at least two of these Essential Question words: *city, destruction, struggle. [Connecting to the Essential Question: What is the relationship between literature and place?]*

Cite textual evidence to support your responses.

Literary Analysis

1. **Key Ideas and Details Asking questions** is a good way to understand difficult passages. **(a)** If you did not understand the changes described in the first paragraph, what are two questions you might ask to *repair your comprehension?* **(b)** How might you answer those questions?

2. **Key Ideas and Details (a)** Answer these questions about the man in the next-to-last-paragraph: Who is he? What does he look like? Where is he? Why is he accompanying the cart? How does he behave? **(b)** Then, explain what the narrator's reporting of this incident reveals about himself.

3. **Craft and Structure** Referring to specific passages, demonstrate that *A Journal of the Plague Year* is written from the **first-person point of view.**

4. **Craft and Structure** Why do you think Defoe chose a first-person narrator, an "eyewitness," to present this account of the plague year? Use details from the text to support your thinking.

5. **Craft and Structure** What is the first-person narrator like? Use a chart like the one shown to make inferences about his personality traits and attitudes based on what he says, thinks, and does in the selection.

Narrator's Personality Trait or Attitude	Narrator's Statements, Thoughts, or Actions That Support Your Inference

6. **Craft and Structure** Does the narrator seem like an accurate reporter of events, or does he seem unreliable? Cite specific details to support your opinion.

7. **Integration of Knowledge and Ideas** How does reading an account of the Great Plague from the first-person point of view compare to reading about such events in history textbooks? Explain.

8. **Integration of Knowledge and Ideas** Which would you prefer to read—Defoe's fictionalized first-person account or an actual journal kept by someone during the Great Plague? Why?

9. **Integration of Knowledge and Ideas** Defoe's account mixes fiction and nonfiction, combining Defoe's research into the events surrounding the actual plague with a fictional narrator and made-up situations. Do you think literary works should avoid mixing fiction and nonfiction? Why or why not?

Common Core State Standards

Writing
3. Write narratives to develop real or imagined experiences or events using effective technique, well-chosen details, and well-structured event sequences. *(p. 597)*

Language
4.a. Use context as a clue to the meaning of a word or phrase. *(p. 597)*

Vocabulary Acquisition and Use

Word Analysis: Latin Prefix *dis-*

The word *distemper* includes the Latin prefix *dis-*, which means "the opposite of" or "not." *Distemper* is "the opposite of temper, or balance"—in other words, the state of imbalance when one has a serious disease.

With a small group, write sentences about the selection using at least five of the *dis-* words listed below. Explain the meaning of each *dis-* word you use. Try to figure out the meanings of the following words based on your understanding of the prefix. However, if the meaning of a word is unclear, refer to a dictionary.

disappeared	disinfectant
disbelief	disobey
discomfort	disquiet
disconcert	dispense

Vocabulary: Context Clues

Context clues are words and phrases in a text that help you figure out the meaning of an unfamiliar word. Using context clues in the numbered sentences, choose the word from the vocabulary list on page 588 that best completes the meaning. Then, explain how you arrived at your answers.

1. The death toll from the Great Plague was _____.
2. Many who had the plague became _____ as the disease worsened.
3. Those afflicted with the _____ usually perished in the end.
4. Some mourners made their _____ loudly; others walked in silence.
5. It seemed like the whole city was _____ God to spare their loved ones.
6. It took great _____ for the narrator to walk the streets every night to report on events.

Writing to Sources

Narrative Text The selection by Defoe begins with an account of great change in London. Try writing your own **essay** about a time of change. It need not be as dramatic as the one in Defoe's account, but it should be a significant change that has affected your life.

Prewriting Jot down notes on the situation before and after the change. Also, briefly explain what caused the change and how it affected you.

Drafting In your narrative, use types of writing as they are appropriate: *persuasive, narrative, descriptive*, and *expository*. Like Defoe, combine concrete *incidents* with *broader themes* that convey your ideas about life.

Model: Revising to Make Information More Concrete

ʌWhen I saw what happened to the block where I lived,
ʌI was amazed at the change.
          gasped in amazement

Adding more detail makes a vague and abstract statement more concrete and vivid.

Revision Exchange drafts with a partner. Accept suggestions for making information, thoughts, and feelings more concrete.

Analyzing Functional and Expository Texts

Annual Report • Transit Map and Schedule

Common Core State Standards

Reading Informational Text
5. Analyze and evaluate the effectiveness of the structure an author uses in his or her exposition or argument, including whether the structure makes points clear, convincing, and engaging.

Language
4.b. Identify and correctly use patterns of word changes that indicate different meanings or parts of speech.

About the Texts

An **annual report** is a record providing information to the public on the status of an organization's initiatives and finances. Basic features of annual reports include chapter or section headings; bulleted and bold-faced information; and photos, charts, or graphs.

Transit maps and schedules are posters or brochures designed to transmit travel information graphically. They include simplified geographic representations of an area, a key or legend to explain symbols, and charts showing arrivals, departures, and stops.

Preparing to Read Complex Texts

Text features are elements of a text, such as heads, that signal its organization or clarify the information it presents. Follow these steps to **evaluate information from text features** and to evaluate the effectiveness of the structure they create:

- Identify text features, such as heads, legends, or tables, and their function.

- Based on text features, draw conclusions about the topics and subtopics covered in the text, as well as its organization.

- Use the text features to locate information or to guide you as you read.

- Evaluate whether each text feature contributes to the clarity of the text.

As you read, use a chart like the one shown to evaluate text features.

Text Feature Graphic	How It Clarifies/Organizes
Table of Contents/Index	
Head/Subhead	
Bulleted List	
Table/Chart/Graph	
Map	
Legend/Key	

Content-Area Vocabulary

These words may also appear in other subject-area texts:

congestion (kən jes´ chen) *n.* excessive crowding or accumulation

sustainable (sə stān´ ə bəl) *adj.* capable of being maintained or prolonged

consumption (kən sump´ shən) *n.* the using of goods or services

economic (ek´ ə näm´ ik) *adj.* having to do with the production, distribution, and use of goods and services

The Mayor's Annual Report 2004

To reduce congestion in London

Congestion—whether on the roads, on the Underground, on the buses or on the trains—is the scourge of London's current transport system. The result of many years of under-investment combined with significant rates of increase in London's population, it will not be cured overnight. Nevertheless, the Mayor is committed to ensuring that anti-congestion measures are combined with the necessary improvement in the capacity and quality of service of London's transport system to alleviate congestion in a systematic manner.

Congestion Charging

The congestion charging scheme commenced in central London in February 2003. The scheme directly tackles four key transport priorities for London:

- reducing congestion
- improving bus services
- improving journey time reliability for car users
- making the distribution of goods and services more reliable, **sustainable** and efficient.

TfL are monitoring the impacts and operation of the scheme as set out in the first Annual Monitoring Report in June 2003. They have since produced two reports setting out their findings: Congestion Charging:

Six Months On was published in October 2003; Congestion Charging: February 2004 Update was published after one year's operation. A Second Annual Monitoring Report is currently being prepared for publication in the Spring.

Reduced traffic levels and congestion

TfL estimate that 65,000 fewer cars per day are being driven into or through the charging zone, with the majority of occupants switching to public transport or diverting around the zone. As a result only 4,000 fewer people are coming to the charging zone each day because of the scheme.

Congestion in the zone has dropped by around 30 percent and is at the lowest level seen since the mid-1980s. The number of vehicles with four or more wheels entering the zone during charging hours has dropped by 18 per cent—making journeys to and from the charging zone quicker and more reliable. Journey times to and from the zone have decreased by an average 14 percent and journey time reliability has improved by an average of 30 percent.

Congestion levels in the charging zone during charging hours

Reduced congestion has also assisted the wider improvements in bus service reliability and journey times; the additional waiting time due to unreliability within the charging zone has reduced by around one third since the beginning of the scheme. Routes serving the congestion zone also experience 60 percent less congestion due to traffic disruption than before the charge was introduced.

Economic Impact

Reduced traffic delays, improved journey time reliability, reduced waiting time at bus stops and lower fuel **consumption** resulting from congestion charging all have **economic** benefits which are increasingly being recognised. TfL's cost benefit analysis of the overall impact of congestion charging is that it generates £50 million per annum of net benefits to London, principally through reduced congestion.

The chart shows the progress and effect of the congestion charging program.

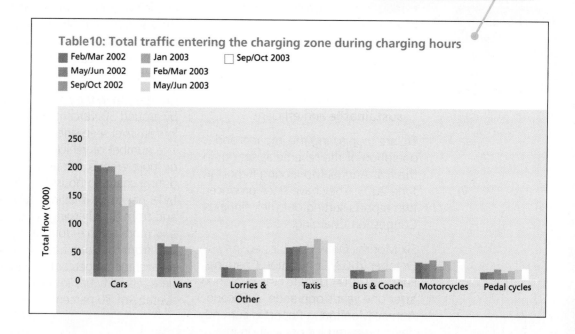

Table10: Total traffic entering the charging zone during charging hours

- Feb/Mar 2002
- May/Jun 2002
- Sep/Oct 2002
- Jan 2003
- Feb/Mar 2003
- May/Jun 2003
- Sep/Oct 2003

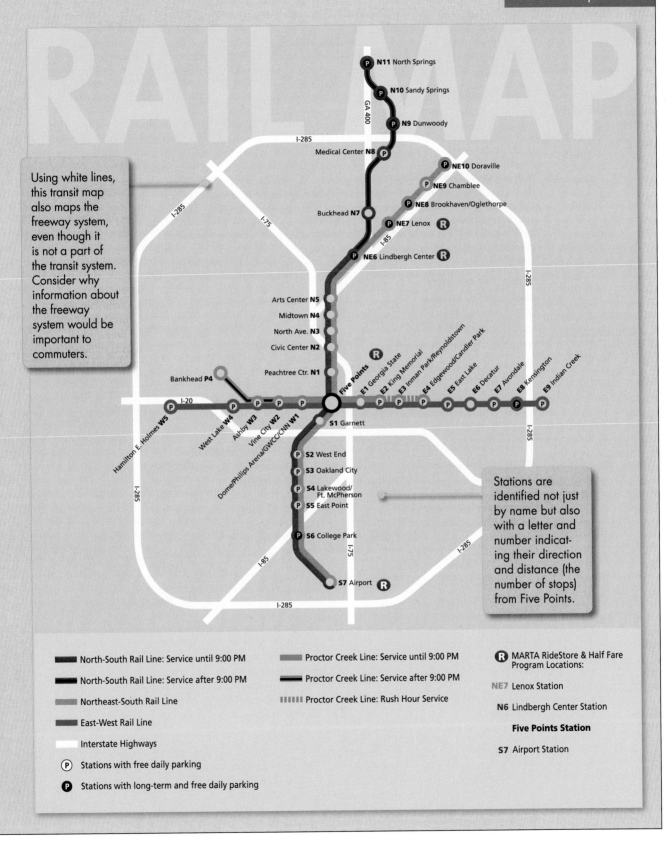

RAIL MAAP

N11 North Springs
N10 Sandy Springs
N9 Dunwoody
Medical Center N8
NE10 Doraville
NE9 Chamblee
NE8 Brookhaven/Oglethorpe
Buckhead N7
NE7 Lenox
NE6 Lindbergh Center

Arts Center N5
Midtown N4
North Ave. N3
Civic Center N2
Peachtree Ctr. N1

Five Points

E1 Georgia State
E2 King Memorial
E3 Inman Park/Reynoldstown
E4 Edgewood/Candler Park
E5 East Lake
E6 Decatur
E7 Avondale
E8 Kensington
E9 Indian Creek

Bankhead P4
Hamilton E. Holmes W5
West Lake W4
Ashby W3
Vine City W2
Dome/Philips Arena/GWCC/CNN W1
S1 Garnett

S2 West End
S3 Oakland City
S4 Lakewood/ Ft. McPherson
S5 East Point

S6 College Park

S7 Airport

I-285
I-75
GA 400
I-85
I-20
I-285
I-85
I-75
I-285

Using white lines, this transit map also maps the freeway system, even though it is not a part of the transit system. Consider why information about the freeway system would be important to commuters.

Stations are identified not just by name but also with a letter and number indicating their direction and distance (the number of stops) from Five Points.

North-South Rail Line: Service until 9:00 PM

North-South Rail Line: Service after 9:00 PM

Northeast-South Rail Line

East-West Rail Line

Interstate Highways

(P) Stations with free daily parking

(P) Stations with long-term and free daily parking

Proctor Creek Line: Service until 9:00 PM

Proctor Creek Line: Service after 9:00 PM

Proctor Creek Line: Rush Hour Service

(R) MARTA RideStore & Half Fare Program Locations:

NE7 Lenox Station

N6 Lindbergh Center Station

Five Points Station

S7 Airport Station

MARTA

North-South Rail Line

Note: If you are traveling Northbound from the Airport to the Buckhead, Medical Center, Dunwoody, Sandy Springs and North Springs rail stations after 9:00 pm, you need to board the northbound train with "Doraville" destination sign, exit at the Lindbergh Center rail station (N6), and transfer to the North Line train with a destination sign of "North Springs."

Train Frequency

Weekday Peak Service:................................... Every 10 minutes
From 6:00 a.m. until 9:00 a.m.
From 3:00 p.m. until 7:00 p.m.

Weekday Off-Peak Service:............................ Every 15 minutes

Weekday Off-Peak Service after 9:00 p.m.......... Every 20 minutes
Trains run between Lindbergh Center Station
and North Springs Station after 8:00 p.m.

Weekend (Saturday and Sunday) Service:......... Every 20 minutes

> This schedule does not provide departure times, but it helps commuters understand that trains come along at the specified intervals.

Stations and Average Times to Five Points Station

Station	Time	Distance
Airport:	16 minutes	9.0 miles
College Park:	15 minutes	8.2 miles
East Point:	12 minutes	6.4 miles
Lakewood/Ft. McPherson:	08 minutes	4.5 miles
Oakland City:	06 minutes	3.4 miles
West End:	04 minutes	1.9 miles
Garnett:	01 minutes	0.4 miles
Peachtree Center:	01 minutes	0.5 miles
Civic Center:	02 minutes	1.0 miles
North Avenue:	03 minutes	1.4 miles
Midtown:	04 minutes	2.0 miles
Arts Center:	06 minutes	2.5 miles
Lindbergh Center:	10 minutes	5.2 miles
Buckhead:	16 minutes	7.4 miles
Med Center:	20 minutes	12.1 miles
Dunwoody:	22 minutes	13.1 miles
Sandy Springs:	25 minutes	
North Springs:	27 minutes	

Critical Reading

1. **Key Ideas and Details (a)** According to the annual report, where was the "congestion charging" plan implemented? **(b)** How often did officials monitor the impact of the plan?

2. **Key Ideas and Details (a)** Based on the transit map, how many stops after Georgia State is East Lake? **(b)** Based on the transit schedule, how long does it take to go from Oakland City to Five Points?

3. **Craft and Structure (a)** Identify two text features or graphics used in the annual report, and two in the transit map and schedule. **(b)** Explain how effective each is in presenting information or in helping you navigate the text.

4. **Content-Area Vocabulary** *Economic* is an adjective meaning "having to do with the production, distribution, and use of goods or services." Using this definition, along with your knowledge of word forms, give the meaning and part of speech of each of these words: *economize, economist, economical.* Check your answers in a dictionary.

**Common Core
State Standards**

Writing
1. Write arguments to support claims in an analysis of substantive topics or texts, using valid reasoning and relevant and sufficient evidence.

⏱ Timed Writing

Argument [40 minutes]

Format

In a **position paper,** you present your viewpoint on a specific topic. An effective position paper contains a clear thesis logically supported with well-organized evidence and reasons.

Write a **position paper** in which you argue for or against congestion pricing in large cities. Develop a thesis and the support you will use by **synthesizing ideas and making logical connections** between the annual report and the transit map and schedule. Support your claim with textual evidence.

Academic Vocabulary

When you **synthesize ideas and make logical connections,** you combine related ideas from various texts, noting where they reinforce or build on one another, to support a conclusion.

5-Minute Planner

Complete these steps before you begin to write.

1. Read the prompt carefully and underline key words.

2. Scan the text for details that relate to the prompt. **TIP** Consider what the transit map and schedule show about the advantages or disadvantages of public transit.

3. Before writing, create an outline to guide you.

4. Reread the prompt, and begin drafting your essay.

Connecting to the Essential Question Like Jonathan Swift in his time, you might want to criticize social practices of today that you find annoying or disturbing. As you read the excerpts from *Gulliver's Travels* and the essay "A Modest Proposal," identify the subjects that Swift targets in his satire. Doing so will help as you answer the Essential Question: **How does literature shape or reflect society?**

 **Common Core State Standards**

Reading Literature
6. Analyze a case in which grasping point of view requires distinguishing what is directly stated in a text from what is really meant.

Close Reading Focus

Satire

Satire is writing that uses humor to expose and ridicule vice and folly. Satirical writing can appear in many genres—for example, Swift's *Gulliver's Travels* is a *satirical novel* and "A Modest Proposal" is a *satirical essay*. Although satirists unmask evils, they sometimes conceal their point of view by masking their targets in order to avoid the dangers involved in naming real people, places, or beliefs. Swift uses masks such as the following in *Gulliver's Travels*:

- imaginary lands and people, such as Lilliput and the Lilliputians
- fictional conflicts, like the conflict between Big- and Little-Endians

In his essay, Swift uses these devices:

- *understatement*, in which the literal meaning falls short of the topic; saying you cannot think of one objection to a terrifying proposal is an example.
- *hyperbole*, or exaggeration
- *sarcasm*, or a bitter way of saying the opposite of what you mean

Comparing Literary Works In both his novel and his essay, Swift uses the satirical weapon of **irony,** a surprising contradiction between reality and appearance or between the actual and intended meaning of words.

Preparing to Read Complex Texts By **analyzing and evaluating information from text features** such as background and footnotes, you can better understand Swift's irony and his point of view. Use a chart like the one shown to analyze text features and show how they clarify Swift's meaning.

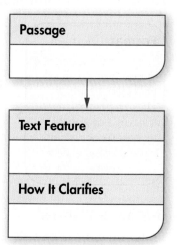

Passage

↓

Text Feature

How It Clarifies

Vocabulary

The words below are important to understanding the texts that follow. Copy the words into your notebook, sorting them into words you know and words you do not know.

conjecture   sustenance

schism   commodity

expedient   censure

Jonathan Swift (1667–1745)

Author of *Gulliver's Travels* • "A Modest Proposal"

Swift was born in Dublin, Ireland, to English parents, although his father died before he was born. With the assistance of relatives, he received a good education and then obtained an appointment in the household of Sir William Temple, a wealthy diplomat who lived on an estate in Surrey, England. Swift hoped for a career in politics, but receiving no support from Sir William, he decided on a career in the church. After Temple's death in 1699, he was given a small parish near London.

Satirist The satirical writing Swift had done while in the Temple household was out of character for a clergyman, but its brilliance was widely acknowledged in 1704 when he published his satires as two separate books: *A Tale of a Tub*, which satirizes excesses in religion and learning, and *The Battle of the Books*, which describes a comic encounter between ancient and modern literature.

Ambition and Achievement When the authorship of Swift's religious satires became known, Swift lost favor in the eyes of many church officials and also lost opportunities for advancement. Although he failed to achieve his goal of becoming a bishop in the Church of England, Swift remained a staunch defender of the Anglican faith. His political allegiance, however, shifted completely in 1710 when he left the Whig party to join the Tory party favored by Queen Anne. He benefited immediately from this move. As the leading party writer for the government, he wrote many pamphlets and wielded considerable political influence.

The Story Behind *Gulliver's Travels* Swift's most famous book, the novel *Gulliver's Travels*, began as a humorous assignment from the Scriblerus Club, a group of Swift's sharp-witted literary friends. These writers, who delighted in making fun of literary pretensions, gave Swift the project of writing a series of amusing, imaginary journeys because they knew he enjoyed reading travel books.

Later Years Although embittered by his failure to be named a bishop, Swift served for more than thirty years as dean of St. Patrick's Cathedral in Dublin. His caustic wit did not flag, as shown in the savage satire "A Modest Proposal" (1729), on starvation in Ireland. His death in 1745 deprived the world of a generous and learned man who despised fanaticism, selfishness, and pride.

from Gulliver's Travels

Jonathan Swift

Background

Swift's era was marked by religious and political strife. Reacting against the intolerance displayed in these conflicts, he ridiculed those whose pride overcame their reason. His novel <u>Gulliver's Travels</u> satirizes such intolerance by means of four imaginary voyages of Lemuel Gulliver, the narrator, a well-educated but unimaginative ship's surgeon. In "A Voyage to Lilliput," for example, Swift focuses on disputes between the established Church of England and Roman Catholicism, calling the followers of each Little-Endians and Big-Endians, respectively. He also satirizes the religious wars between Protestant England and Catholic France, disguising them as a conflict between Lilliput and Blefuscu. In "A Voyage to Brobdingnag," he suggests that the politicians leading England are guilty of "ignorance, idleness, and vice."

from A Voyage to Lilliput

After being shipwrecked, Gulliver swims to shore and drifts off to sleep. When he awakens, he finds that he has been tied down by the Lilliputians (lil′ ə py$\overline{oo}$′ shənz), a race of people who are only six inches tall. Though he is held captive and his sword and pistols are taken from him, Gulliver gradually begins to win the Lilliputians' favor because of his mild disposition, and he is eventually granted his freedom. Through Gulliver's exposure to Lilliputian politics and court life, the reader becomes increasingly aware of the remarkable similarities between the English and Lilliputian affairs of state. The following excerpt begins during a discussion between the Lilliputian Principal Secretary of Private Affairs and Gulliver concerning the affairs of the Lilliputian empire.

We are threatened with an invasion from the island of Blefuscu,[1] which is the other great empire of the universe, almost as large and powerful as this of his Majesty. For as to what we have heard you affirm, that there are other kingdoms and states in the world, inhabited by human creatures as large as yourself, our philosophers are in much doubt, and would rather conjecture that you dropped from the moon, or one of the stars; because it is certain, that an hundred mortals of your bulk would, in a short time, destroy all the fruits

---

1. Blefuscu represents France.

◀ **Critical Viewing** What passages in the text reveal that Lilliputians now trust Gulliver more than they did in the episode depicted here? **INFER**

Vocabulary
conjecture (kən jek′ chər)
v. guess

Comprehension
From where do the Lilliputians think Gulliver came?

and cattle of his Majesty's dominions. Besides, our histories of six thousand moons make no mention of any other regions, than the two great empires of Lilliput and Blefuscu. Which two mighty powers have, as I was going to tell you, been engaged in a most obstinate war for six and thirty moons past. It began upon the following occasion. It is allowed on all hands, that the primitive way of breaking eggs before we eat them, was upon the larger end; but his present Majesty's grandfather, while he was a boy, going to eat an egg, and breaking it according to the ancient practice, happened to cut one of his fingers. Whereupon the Emperor, his father, published an edict, commanding all his subjects, upon great penalties, to break the smaller end of their eggs. The people so highly resented this law that our histories tell us there have been six rebellions raised on that account; wherein one emperor lost his life, and another his crown.[2] These civil commotions were constantly fomented by the monarchs of Blefuscu; and when they were quelled, the exiles always fled for refuge to that empire. It is computed that eleven thousand persons have, at several times, suffered death rather than submit to break their eggs at the smaller end. Many hundred large volumes have been published upon this controversy; but the books of the Big-Endians have been long forbidden, and the whole party rendered incapable by law of holding employments.[3] During the course of these troubles, the emperors of Blefuscu did frequently expostulate[4] by their ambassadors, accusing us of making a schism in religion, by offending against a fundamental doctrine of our great prophet Lustrog, in the fifty-fourth chapter of the *Brundecral* (which is their Alcoran).[5] This, however, is thought to be a mere strain upon the text, for the words are these: That all true believers shall break their eggs at the convenient end; and which is the convenient end, seems, in my humble opinion, to be left to every man's conscience, or at least in the power of the chief magistrate[6] to determine. Now the Big-Endian exiles have found so much credit in the Emperor of Blefuscu's court, and so much private assistance and encouragement from their party here at home, that a bloody war hath been carried on between the two empires for six and thirty moons with various success; during which time we have lost forty capital ships, and a much greater number of smaller vessels, together with thirty thousand of our best seamen and soldiers; and the damage received by the enemy is reckoned to be somewhat greater than ours. However, they have now equipped a numerous fleet,

---

Satire

Why do you think Swift chooses the correct way to break eggs as the cause of conflict between Lilliput and Blefuscu?

Vocabulary

schism (siz´ əm) *n.* division of a group into factions

Ⓒ

Spiral Review
Denotation and Word Choice Read the vocabulary word *schism* in context. What conclusions can you draw about the positive or negative nuances of *schism*?

---

2. **It is allowed . . . crown** Here, Swift satirizes the dispute in England between the Catholics (Big-Endians) and Protestants (Little-Endians). King Henry VIII who "broke" with the Catholic church, King Charles I, who "lost his life," and King James, who lost his "crown," are each referred to in the passage.
3. **the whole party . . . employments** The Test Act (1673) prevented Catholics from holding office.
4. **expostulate** (eks päs´ chə lāt´) *v.* reason earnestly with.
5. **Alcoran** Koran, the sacred book of Muslims.
6. **chief magistrate** ruler.

and are just preparing to make a descent upon us; and his Imperial Majesty, placing great confidence in your valor and strength, hath commanded me to lay this account of his affairs before you.

I desired the Secretary to present my humble duty to the Emperor, and to let him know, that I thought it would not become me, who was a foreigner, to interfere with parties; but I was ready, with the hazard of my life, to defend his person and state against all invaders.

The empire of Blefuscu is an island situated to the north-northeast side of Lilliput, from whence it is parted only by a channel of eight hundred yards wide. I had not yet seen it, and upon this notice of an intended invasion, I avoided appearing on that side of the coast, for fear of being discovered by some of the enemy's ships, who had received no intelligence of me, all intercourse between the two empires having been strictly forbidden during the war, upon pain of death, and an embargo laid by our Emperor upon all vessels whatsoever. I communicated to his Majesty a project I had formed of seizing the enemy's whole fleet; which, as our scouts assured us, lay at anchor in the harbor ready to sail with the first fair wind. I consulted the most experienced seamen upon the depth of the channel, which they had often plumbed, who told me, that in the middle at high water it was seventy *glumgluffs* deep (which is about six feet of European measure), and the rest of it fifty *glumgluffs* at most. I walked to the northeast coast over against Blefuscu, where, lying down behind a hillock, I took out my small pocket perspective-glass, and viewed the enemy's fleet at anchor, consisting of about fifty men of war, and a great number of transports. I then came back to my house and gave order (for which I had a warrant) for a great quantity of the strongest cable and bars of iron. The cable was about as thick as pack-thread, and the bars of the length and size of a knitting-needle. I trebled the cable to make it stronger, and for the same reason I twisted three of the iron bars together, bending the extremities into a hook. Having thus fixed fifty hooks to as many cables, I went back to the northeast coast and, putting off my coat, shoes, and stockings, walked into the sea in my leathern jerkin, about half an hour before high water. I waded with what haste I could, and swam in the middle about thirty yards until I felt ground; I arrived at the fleet in less than half an hour. The enemy was so frightened when they saw me, that they leaped out of their ships, and swam to shore, where there could not be fewer than thirty thousand souls. I then took my tackling, and, fastening a hook to the hole at the prow of each, I tied all the cords together at the end. While I was thus employed, the enemy discharged several thousand arrows, many of which struck in my hands and face and, besides the excessive smart, gave me much disturbance in my work. My greatest apprehension was for my eyes, which I should have infallibly lost, if I had not suddenly thought of an expedient. I kept

LITERATURE IN CONTEXT

The Vocabulary of Religious Conflict

The word *schism*, which Swift uses in describing the conflict between Big-Endians and Little-Endians, is an important term in the history of religious conflict. This term comes from the Greek word *schizein*, meaning "divide," and it can mean simply "to cleave or cut." Traditionally, it has been applied to a split in an organized group (especially a church), the act of trying to cause such a split, or a sect formed by the split. By using this word in describing the controversy between Big-Endians and Little-Endians, Swift signals readers that his fiction refers to a significant religious conflict.

Connect to the Literature

What further divisions have come as a result of Lilliput's schism in religion?

Vocabulary
expedient (ek spē′ dē ənt)
n. device used in an emergency

Comprehension
How does Gulliver plan to defend the Lilliputians against invasion?

among other little necessaries a pair of spectacles in a private pocket, which, as I observed before, had escaped the Emperor's searchers. These I took out and fastened as strongly as I could upon my nose and thus armed went on boldly with my work in spite of the enemy's arrows, many of which struck against the glasses of my spectacles, but without any other effect further than a little to discompose them. I had now fastened all the hooks and, taking the knot in my hand, began to pull, but not a ship would stir, for they were all too fast held by their anchors, so that the boldest part of my enterprise remained. I therefore let go the cord, and, leaving the hooks fixed to the ships, I resolutely cut with my knife the cables that fastened the anchors, receiving above two hundred shots in my face and hands; then I took up the knotted end of the cables to which my hooks were tied and, with great ease, drew fifty of the enemy's largest men-of-war after me.

The Blefuscudians, who had not the least imagination of what I intended, were at first confounded with astonishment. They had seen me cut the cables and thought my design was only to let the ships run adrift or fall foul on each other; but when they perceived the whole fleet, moving in order, and saw me pulling at the end, they set up such a scream of grief and despair that it is almost impossible to describe or conceive. When I had got out of danger, I stopped a while to pick out the arrows that stuck in my hands and face, and rubbed on some of the same ointment that was given me at my first arrival, as I have formerly mentioned. I then took off my spectacles, and, waiting about an hour until the tide was a little fallen, I waded through the middle with my cargo and arrived safe at the royal port of Lilliput.

The Emperor and his whole court stood on the shore expecting the issue of this great adventure. They saw the ships move forward in a large half-moon but could not discern me, who was up to my breast in water. When I advanced to the middle of the channel, they were yet more in pain, because I was under water to my neck. The Emperor concluded me to be drowned, and that the enemy's fleet was approaching in a hostile manner; but he was soon eased of his fears; for, the channel growing shallower every step I made, I came in a short time within hearing, and holding up the end of the cable by which the fleet was fastened, I cried in a loud voice, Long live the most puissant[7] Emperor of Lilliput! This great prince received me at my landing with all possible encomiums and created me a *Nardac* upon the spot, which is the highest title of honor among them.

His Majesty desired I would take some other opportunity of bringing all the rest of his enemy's ships into his ports. And so unmeasurable is the ambition of princes, that he seemed to think of nothing less than reducing the whole empire of Blefuscu into a province and governing it by a viceroy; of destroying the Big-Endian exiles and compelling that people to break the smaller end of their eggs,

---

7. puissant (pyōō′ i sənt) *adj.* powerful.

A Voyage to Lilliput, Illustration from a nineteenth-century edition of *Gulliver's Travels*

◄ **Critical Viewing**
What specific details from the text does this picture illustrate? **CONNECT**

by which he would remain sole monarch of the whole world. But I endeavored to divert him from this design by many arguments drawn from the topics of policy as well as justice, and I plainly protested that I would never be an instrument of bringing a free and brave people into slavery. And when the matter was debated in council, the wisest part of the ministry were of my opinion.

This open bold declaration of mine was so opposite to the schemes and politics of his Imperial Majesty that he could never

Comprehension
Summarize the action Gulliver takes against the fleet of Blefuscu.

forgive me; he mentioned it in a very artful manner at council, where I was told that some of the wisest appeared, at least, by their silence, to be of my opinion; but others, who were my secret enemies, could not forbear some expressions, which by a sidewind reflected on me. And from this time began an intrigue between his Majesty and a junta of ministers maliciously bent against me, which broke out in less than two months and had like to have ended in my utter destruction. Of so little weight are the greatest services to princes when put into the balance with a refusal to gratify their passions.

from 𝕬 𝖁𝖔𝖞𝖆𝖌𝖊 𝖙𝖔 𝕭𝖗𝖔𝖇𝖉𝖎𝖓𝖌𝖓𝖆𝖌

Gulliver's second voyage leads him to Brobdingnag (bräb´ diŋ nag´), *an island located near Alaska that is inhabited by giants twelve times as tall as Gulliver. After being sold to the Queen of Brobdingnag, Gulliver describes the English social and political institutions to the King, who reacts to his description with contempt and disgust.*

Satire

Which satirical details in the first paragraph of "A Voyage to Brobdingnag" relate to England and which relate to humanity in general? Explain.

Analyzing Text Features

Based on what you have learned from text features about this historical period, what is satirical about the King laughingly asking whether Gulliver is "a Whig or a Tory"?

It is the custom that every Wednesday (which, as I have before observed, was their Sabbath) the King and Queen, with the royal issue of both sexes, dine together in the apartment of his Majesty, to whom I was now become a favorite; and at these times my little chair and table were placed at his left hand before one of the saltcellars. This prince took a pleasure in conversing with me, inquiring into the manners, religion, laws, government, and learning of Europe, wherein I gave him the best account I was able. His apprehension was so clear, and his judgment so exact, that he made very wise reflections and observations upon all I said. But I confess, that after I had been a little too copious in talking of my own beloved country, of our trade, and wars by sea and land, of our schisms in religion, and parties in the state, the prejudices of his education prevailed so far, that he could not forbear taking me up in his right hand, and stroking me gently with the other, after an hearty fit of laughing, asked me whether I were a Whig or a Tory.[8] Then turning to his first minister, who waited behind him with a white staff, near as tall as the mainmast of the *Royal Sovereign*,[9] he observed how contemptible a thing was human grandeur, which could be mimicked by such diminutive insects as I. And yet, said he, I dare engage, those creatures have their titles and distinctions of honor, they contrive little nests and burrows, that they call houses and cities; they make a figure in dress and equipage;[10] they love, they fight, they dispute, they cheat, they betray. And thus he continued on, while my color came and went several times, with indignation to hear our noble country, the mistress

---

8. **Whig . . . Tory** British political parties.
9. *Royal Sovereign* one of the largest ships in the British Navy.
10. **equipage** (ek´ wi pij´) horses and carriages.

of arts and arms, the scourge of France, the arbitress of Europe, the seat of virtue, piety, honor and truth, the pride and envy of the world, so contemptuously treated. . . .

He laughed at my odd kind of arithmetic (as he was pleased to call it) in reckoning the numbers of our people by a computation drawn from the several sects among us in religion and politics. He said he knew no reason why those who entertain opinions prejudicial to the public should be obliged to change or should not be obliged to conceal them. And, as it was tyranny in any government to require the first, so it was weakness not to enforce the second; for, a man may be allowed to keep poisons in his closets, but not to vend them about as cordials.

He observed, that among the diversions of our nobility and gentry[11] I had mentioned gaming.[12] He desired to know at what age this entertainment was usually taken up, and when it was laid down. How much of their time it employed; whether it ever went so high as to affect their fortunes. Whether mean vicious people by their dexterity in that art might not arrive at great riches, and sometimes keep our very nobles in dependence, as well as habituate them to vile[13] companions, wholly take them from the improvement of their minds, and force them, by the losses they received, to learn and practice that infamous dexterity upon others.

He was perfectly astonished with the historical account I gave him of our affairs during the last century, protesting it was only an heap of conspiracies, rebellions, murders, massacres, revolutions, banishments, the very worst effects that avarice, faction, hypocrisy, perfidiousness, cruelty, rage, madness, hatred, envy, lust, malice, and ambition could produce.

His Majesty in another audience was at the pains to recapitulate the sum of all I had spoken; compared the questions he made with the answers I had given; then taking me into his hands, and stroking me gently, delivered himself in these words, which I shall never forget, nor the manner he spoke them in. "My little friend Grildrig, you have made a most admirable panegyric upon your country. You have clearly proved that ignorance, idleness, and vice are the proper ingredients for qualifying a legislator. That laws are best explained, interpreted, and applied by those whose interest and abilities lie in perverting, confounding, and eluding them. I observe among you some lines of an institution, which in its original might have been tolerable, but these half erased, and the rest wholly blurred and blotted by corruptions. It doth not appear from all you have said how any one perfection is required toward the procurement of any one station among you, much less that men are ennobled on account of their virtue, that priests are advanced for their piety or learning, soldiers for their con-

...after an hearty fit of laughing, (he) asked me whether I were a Whig or a Tory.

Comprehension

What does the King of Brobdingnag say in response to Gulliver's account of European customs and history?

---

11. **gentry** the class of landowning people ranking just below the nobility.
12. **gaming** gambling.
13. **habituate** (hə bich′ o͞o āt′) **them** to make them used to.

duct or valor, judges for their integrity, senators for the love of their country, or counselors for their wisdom. As for yourself," continued the King, "who have spent the greatest part of your life in traveling, I am well disposed to hope you may hitherto have escaped many vices of your country. But, by what I have gathered from your own relation, and the answers I have with much pains wringed and extorted from you, I cannot but conclude the bulk of your natives to be the most pernicious race of little odious vermin that nature ever suffered to crawl upon the surface of the earth."

Nothing but an extreme love of truth could have hindered me from concealing this part of my story. It was in vain to discover my resentments, which were always turned into ridicule; and I was forced to rest with patience while my noble and most beloved country was so injuriously treated. I am heartily sorry as any of my readers can possibly be that such an occasion was given, but this prince happened to be so curious and inquisitive upon every particular that it could not consist either with gratitude or good manners to refuse giving him what satisfaction I was able. Yet thus much I may be allowed to say in my own vindication that I artfully eluded many of his questions and gave to every point a more favorable turn by many degrees than the strictness of truth would allow. For I have always borne that laudable partiality to my own country, which Dionysius Halicarnassensis[14] with so much justice recommends to an historian. I would hide the frailties and deformities of my political mother and place her virtues and beauties in the most advantageous light. This was my sincere endeavor in those many discourses I had with that mighty monarch, although it unfortunately failed of success.

But great allowances should be given to a king who lives wholly secluded from the rest of the world, and must therefore be altogether unacquainted with the manners and customs that most prevail in other nations: the want of which knowledge will ever produce many prejudices, and a certain narrowness of thinking, from which we and the politer countries of Europe are wholly exempted. And it would be hard indeed, if so remote a prince's notions of virtue and vice were to be offered as a standard for all mankind.

To confirm what I have now said, and further to show the miserable effects of a confined education, I shall here insert a passage which will hardly obtain belief. In hopes to ingratiate myself farther into his Majesty's favor, I told him of an invention discovered between three and four hundred years ago, to make a certain powder, into an heap of which the smallest spark of fire falling, would kindle the whole in a moment, although it were as big as a mountain, and make it all fly up in the air together, with a noise and agitation greater

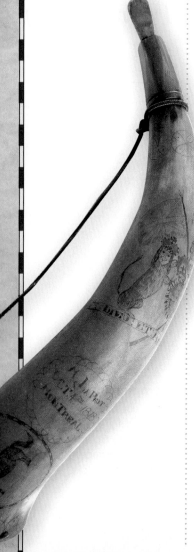

Satire and Irony

In Gulliver's remark that he "artfully eluded" the King's questions, what is the difference between the intended meaning and the actual meaning?

---

14. Dionysius (dī´ ə nĭsh´ əs) **Halicarnassensis** (hal´ ə kär na sen´ sis) Greek writer who lived in Rome and attempted to persuade the Greeks to submit to their Roman conquerors.

A Voyage to Brobdingnag, Illustration from a nineteenth-century edition of Gulliver's Travels

◀ **Critical Viewing**

Compare the relationship between Gulliver and the King of Brobdingnag as portrayed by the artist with that portrayed in the text. **COMPARE AND CONTRAST**

than thunder. That a proper quantity of this powder rammed into an hollow tube of brass or iron, according to its bigness, would drive a ball of iron or lead with such violence and speed as nothing was able to sustain its force. That the largest balls, thus discharged, would not only destroy whole ranks of an army at once, but batter the strongest walls to the ground, sink down ships, with a thousand men in each, to the bottom of the sea; and when linked together by a chain, would cut through masts and rigging, divide hundreds of bodies in the middle, and lay all waste before them. That we often put this powder into large hollow balls of iron, and discharged them by an engine into some city we were besieging, which would rip up the pavement, tear the houses to pieces, burst and throw splinters on

Comprehension

What is the King's opinion of most of Gulliver's countrymen?

every side, dashing out the brains of all who came near. That I knew the ingredients very well, which were cheap, and common; I understood the manner of compounding them, and could direct his workmen how to make those tubes of a size proportionable to all other things in his Majesty's kingdom, and the largest need not be above two hundred foot long; twenty or thirty of which tubes, charged with the proper quantity of powder and balls, would batter down the walls of the strongest town in his dominions in a few hours, or destroy the whole metropolis, if ever it should pretend to dispute his absolute commands. This I humbly offered to his Majesty as a small tribute of acknowledgment in return of so many marks that I had received of his royal favor and protection.

The King was struck with horror at the description I had given of those terrible engines and the proposal I had made. He was amazed how so impotent and groveling an insect as I (these were his expressions) could entertain such inhuman ideas, and in so familiar a manner as to appear wholly unmoved at all the scenes of blood and desolation which I had painted as the common effects of those destructive machines; whereof he said some evil genius, enemy to mankind, must have been the first contriver. As for himself, he protested that although few things delighted him so much as new discoveries in art or in nature, yet he would rather lose half his kingdom than be privy to such a secret, which he commanded me, as I valued my life, never to mention any more.

The *King was struck with horror at the description I had given . . . and the proposal I had made.*

Critical Reading

Cite textual evidence to support your responses.

1. **Key Ideas and Details (a)** Describe the conflict between Big-Endians and Little-Endians. **(b) Infer:** Do these two groups take their dispute seriously? Why or why not? **(c) Analyze:** What evidence is there that Swift does not want you to take the dispute seriously? Explain.

2. **Key Ideas and Details (a)** Citing the text, give one example of how the King of Brobdingnag shows affection toward Gulliver and one example of how he shows distaste for Gulliver's ideas.
(b) Interpret: Show how the final disagreement between Gulliver and the King reflects a difference between ingenuity and wisdom.

3. **Key Ideas and Details (a)** What is the most important physical difference between Lilliputians and Brobdingnagians?
(b) Interpret: How does this physical difference suggest other important ways in which they differ? Explain. **(c) Synthesize:** How do Lilliputians and Brobdingnagians each represent a different way of viewing humanity?

4. **Integration of Knowledge and Ideas** In the final paragraph, how does Swift use the King's reactions to express his own hopes for humankind?

A Modest Proposal

Jonathan Swift

Background

Swift recognized that the best audience for "A Modest Proposal" was the upper class—a group of people who had the ability to make changes for the better in Ireland. On a satirical level, however, Swift's essay mocks this very group of people. He suggests that their relentless pursuit of luxury has developed in them a taste for almost unimaginable delicacies. In this way, they become the perfect target for his modest proposal.

▲ **Critical Viewing**
In what way does this painting embody the "relentless pursuit of luxury" that Swift addresses through his essay? **INTERPRET**

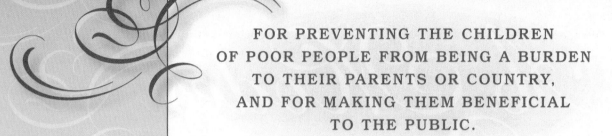

FOR PREVENTING THE CHILDREN OF POOR PEOPLE FROM BEING A BURDEN TO THEIR PARENTS OR COUNTRY, AND FOR MAKING THEM BENEFICIAL TO THE PUBLIC.

Vocabulary

sustenance (sus´ tə nəns)
n. food or money to support life

It is a melancholy object to those, who walk through this great town,[1] or travel in the country, when they see the streets, the roads, and cabin-doors, crowded with beggars of the female sex, followed by three, four, or six children, all in rags, and importuning every passenger for an alms.[2] These mothers instead of being able to work for their honest livelihood, are forced to employ all their time in strolling, to beg sustenance for their helpless infants, who, as they grow up, either turn thieves for want of work, or leave their dear native country to fight for the Pretender in Spain,[3] or sell themselves to the Barbadoes.[4]

I think it is agreed by all parties, that this prodigious number of children, in the arms, or on the backs, or at the heels of their mothers, and frequently of their fathers, is in the present deplorable state of the kingdom, a very great additional grievance; and therefore whoever could find out a fair, cheap and easy method of making these children sound useful members of the commonwealth would deserve so well of the public, as to have his statue set up for a preserver of the nation.

But my intention is very far from being confined to provide only for the children of professed beggars, it is of a much greater extent, and shall take in the whole number of infants at a certain age, who are born of parents in effect as little able to support them, as those who demand our charity in the streets.

As to my own part, having turned my thoughts, for many years, upon this important subject, and maturely weighed the several schemes of other projectors, I have always found them grossly mistaken in their computation. It is true a child, just dropped from its dam[5] may be supported by her milk for a solar year with little other nourishment, at most not above the value of two shillings, which the mother may certainly get, or the value in scraps, by her lawful occupation of begging, and it is exactly at one year old that I propose to provide for them, in such a manner, as, instead of being a charge upon their parents, or the parish, or wanting food and raiment[6] for the rest of their lives, they shall, on the contrary, contribute to the feeding and partly to the clothing of many thousands.

There is likewise another great advantage in my scheme, that it will prevent those voluntary abortions, and that horrid practice of

Analyzing Text Features

How does Swift's use of the word *dam*—explained in the footnotes—indicate the irony behind his proposal? In other words how does what he actually says differ from what he really means?

---

1. **this great town** Dublin.
2. **importuning. . . alms** begging passersby for charity.
3. **Pretender in Spain** James Edward Stewart (1688–1766), a Catholic, was a claimant (or "Pretender") to the English throne despite being barred against succession.
4. **sell. . . Barbadoes** commit themselves as indentured servants on Barbadian plantations.
5. **dam** female parent, usually an animal.
6. **raiment** clothing.

women murdering their bastard children, alas, too frequent among us, sacrificing the poor innocent babes, I doubt, more to avoid the expense, than the shame, which would move tears and pity in the most savage and inhuman breast.

The number of souls in this kingdom being usually reckoned one million and a half,[7] of these I calculate there may be about two hundred thousand couple whose wives are breeders, from which number I subtract thirty thousand couples, who are able to maintain their own children, although I apprehend there cannot be so many under the present distresses of the kingdom, but this being granted, there will remain an hundred and seventy thousand breeders. I again subtract fifty thousand for those women who miscarry, or whose children die by accident, or disease within the year. There only remain an hundred and twenty thousand children of poor parents annually born: The question therefore is, how this number shall be reared, and provided for, which, as I have already said, under the present situation of affairs, is utterly impossible by all the methods hitherto proposed, for we can neither employ them in handicraft, or agriculture; we neither build houses, (I mean in the country) nor cultivate land: they can very seldom pick up a livelihood by stealing till they arrive at six years old, except where they are of towardly parts,[8] although, I confess they learn the rudiments much earlier, during which time, they can however be properly looked upon only as probationers, as I have been informed by a principal gentleman in the County of Cavan, who protested to me, that he never knew above one or two instances under the age of six, even in a part of the kingdom so renowned for the quickest proficiency in that art.

I am assured by our merchants, that a boy or a girl, before twelve years old, is no saleable commodity, and even when they come to this age, they will not yield above three pounds, or three pounds and half-a-crown at most on the Exchange, which cannot turn to account[9] either to the parents or the kingdom, the charge of nutriment and rags having been at least four times that value.

I shall now therefore humbly propose my own thoughts, which I hope will not be liable to the least objection.

I have been assured by a very knowing American of my acquaintance in London, that a young healthy child well nursed is at a year old a most delicious, nourishing, and wholesome food, whether stewed, roasted, baked, or boiled, and I make no doubt that it will equally serve in a fricassee, or a ragout.[10]

▲ Critical Viewing
Do you think the technique used in this etching best conveys the hardship of poverty? Explain. **ASSESS**

Vocabulary
commodity (kə mäd´ ə tē) *n.* product that is bought or sold

Comprehension
Who first told Swift about the use of children as a source of food?

---

7. **souls . . . half** censuses from the year 1699 put Ireland's population at approximately 1.2 million.
8. **of towardly parts** highly talented or able.
9. **turn to account** bring a profit.
10. **fricassee** (frik ə sē´) **. . . ragout** (ra gōo´) meat stews.

Satire

What effect do words like breed and savages have on the tone in this paragraph?

Satire

In what way does Swift's sarcasm sharpen his satirical attack on landlords?

I do therefore humbly offer it to public consideration, that of the hundred and twenty thousand children, already computed, twenty thousand may be reserved for breed, whereof only one fourth part to be males, which is more than we allow to sheep, black-cattle, or swine, and my reason is that these children are seldom the fruits of marriage, a circumstance not much regarded by our savages, therefore one male will be sufficient to serve four females. That the remaining hundred thousand may at a year old be offered in sale to the persons of quality, and fortune, through the kingdom, always advising the mother to let them suck plentifully in the last month, so as to render them plump, and fat for a good table. A child will make two dishes at an entertainment for friends, and when the family dines alone, the fore or hind quarter will make a reasonable dish, and seasoned with a little pepper or salt will be very good boiled on the fourth day, especially in winter.

I have reckoned upon a medium,[11] that a child just born will weigh 12 pounds, and in a solar year if tolerably nursed increases to 28 pounds.

I grant this food will be somewhat dear,[12] and therefore very proper for landlords, who, as they have already devoured[13] most of the parents, seem to have the best title to the children.

Infants' flesh will be in season throughout the year, but more plentiful in March, and a little before and after, for we are told by a grave author an eminent French physician,[14] that fish being a prolific diet, there are more children born in Roman Catholic countries about nine months after Lent, than at any other season; therefore reckoning a year after Lent, the markets will be more glutted than usual, because the number of popish[15] infants, is at least three to one in this kingdom, and therefore it will have one other collateral[16] advantage by lessening the number of Papists[17] among us.

I have already computed the charge of nursing a beggar's child (in which list I reckon all cottagers, laborers, and four-fifths of the farmers) to be about two shillings per annum, rags included, and I believe no gentleman would repine[18] to give ten shillings for the carcass of a good fat child, which, as I have said will make four dishes of excellent nutritive meat, when he has only some particular friend, or his own family to dine with him. Thus the Squire will learn to be a good landlord, and grow popular among his tenants, the mother will have eight shillings net profit, and be fit for work till she produces another child.

---

11. **reckoned upon a medium** estimated as an average.
12. **dear** costly.
13. **devoured** financially destroyed.
14. **grave . . . physician** François Rabelais, a renown humorist and satirist.
15. **popish** Catholic (derogatory).
16. **collateral** parallel; related.
17. **Papists** Roman Catholics (derogatory).
18. **repine** (ri pīn′) *v.* complain.

Those who are more thrifty (as I must confess the times require) may flay the carcass; the skin of which, artificially dressed, will make admirable gloves for ladies, and summer boots for fine gentlemen.

As to our city of Dublin, shambles[19] may be appointed for this purpose, in the most convenient parts of it, and butchers we may be assured will not be wanting, although I rather recommend buying the children alive, and dressing them hot from the knife, as we do roasting pigs.

A very worthy person, a true lover of his country, and whose virtues I highly esteem, was lately pleased, in discoursing on this matter, to offer a refinement upon my scheme. He said, that many gentlemen of this kingdom, having of late destroyed their deer, he conceived that the want of venison might be well supplied by the bodies of young lads and maidens, not exceeding fourteen years of age, nor under twelve, so great a number of both sexes in every country being now ready to starve, for want of work and service: and these to be disposed of by their parents if alive, or otherwise by their nearest relations. But with due deference to so excellent a friend, and so deserving a patriot, I cannot be altogether in his sentiments; for as to the males, my American acquaintance assured me from frequent experience, that their flesh was generally tough and lean, like that of our schoolboys, by continual exercise, and their taste disagreeable, and to fatten them would not answer the charge. Then as to the females, it would, I think with humble submission, be a loss to the public, because they soon would become breeders themselves: And besides, it is not improbable that some scrupulous people might be apt to censure such a practice, (although indeed very unjustly) as a little bordering upon cruelty, which, I confess, has always been with me the strongest objection against any project, however so well intended.

But in order to justify my friend, he confessed that this expedient was put into his head by the famous Psalmanazar,[20] a native of the island Formosa, who came from thence to London, above twenty years ago, and in conversation told my friend, that in his country when any young person happened to be put to death, the executioner sold the carcass to persons of quality, as a prime dainty, and that, in his time, the body of a plump girl of fifteen, who was crucified for an attempt to poison the emperor, was sold to his Imperial Majesty's Prime Minister of State, and other great Mandarins of the Court, in joints from the gibbet, at four hundred crowns. Neither indeed can I deny, that if the same use were made of several plump young girls in this town, who, without one single groat[21] to their fortunes, cannot stir abroad without a chair, and appear at

---

19. **shambles** slaughterhouses.
20. **Psalmanazar** Here, Swift refers to a fictitious account of cannibalism in Formosa as made by impostor George Psalmanazar.
21. **groat** coin, of trivial amount.

LITERATURE IN CONTEXT

The Irish Troubles
In the later seventeenth century, just as Swift was growing up, England encouraged Scottish Protestants to emigrate to Northern Ireland and confiscate land owned by Catholics. Political power in Ireland became concentrated exclusively in the hands of the Protestant upper class, which comprised only about ten percent of the population. Catholics were the targets of relentless discrimination. For example, they were not allowed to reside in towns, but had to content themselves with living in rural settings. England's exploitative economic policies combined with crop failures in the 1720s to trigger a crisis; many farmers found it impossible to pay rent to their English landlords, and the streets teemed with beggars. This desolate situation was the background for "A Modest Proposal."

Connect to the Literature
In his essay, Swift appears to condemn the Irish Catholics in the same way as the social class he mocks. What possible motives might Swift have for using such a strategy?

Vocabulary
censure (sen′ shər) *v.* strongly disapprove; condemn

Comprehension
What contribution to society will infants make if Swift's proposal is accepted?

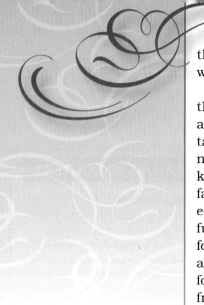

the playhouse, and assemblies in foreign fineries, which they never will pay for, the kingdom would not be the worse.

Some persons of a desponding spirit are in great concern about that vast number of poor people, who are aged, diseased, or maimed, and I have been desired to employ my thoughts what course may be taken to ease the nation of so grievous an encumbrance.[22] But I am not in the least pain upon that matter, because it is very well known, that they are every day dying, and rotting, by cold, and famine, and filth, and vermin, as fast as can be reasonably expected. And as to the younger laborers they are now in almost as hopeful a condition. They cannot get work, and consequently pine away for want of nourishment, to a degree, that if at any time they are accidentally hired to common labor, they have not strength to perform it; and thus the country and themselves are happily delivered from the evils to come.

I have too long digressed, and therefore shall return to my subject. I think the advantages by the proposal which I have made are obvious and many, as well as of the highest importance.

For first, as I have already observed, it would greatly lessen the number of Papists, with whom we are yearly over-run, being the principal breeders of the nation, as well as our most dangerous enemies, and who stay at home on purpose with a design to deliver the kingdom to the Pretender, hoping to take their advantage by the absence of so many good Protestants, who have chosen rather to leave their country, than stay at home, and pay tithes against their conscience, to an Episcopal curate.[23]

Secondly, the poorer tenants will have something valuable of their own, which by law may be made liable to distress,[24] and help to pay their landlord's rent, their corn and cattle being already seized, and money a thing unknown.

Thirdly, whereas the maintenance of an hundred thousand children, from two years old, and upwards, cannot be computed at less than ten shillings a piece per annum, the nation's stock will be thereby increased fifty thousand pounds per annum, besides the profit of a new dish, introduced to the tables of all gentlemen of fortune in the kingdom, who have any refinement in taste, and the money will circulate among ourselves, the goods being entirely of our own growth and manufacture.

Fourthly, the constant breeders, besides the gain of eight shillings sterling per annum, by the sale of their children, will be rid of the charge of maintaining them after the first year.

Fifthly, this food would likewise bring great custom to taverns, where the vintners will certainly be so prudent as to procure the best

Satire

What realistic solution to Ireland's problems is suggested in Swift's second argument?

---

22. **encumbrance** burden.
23. **tithes . . . curate** taxes, paid to the Catholic Church, which Protestants paid against their conscience.
24. **liable to distress** available for seizure by landlords as payment for debts.

receipts for dressing it to perfection, and consequently have their houses frequented by all the fine gentlemen, who justly value themselves upon their knowledge in good eating; and a skillful cook, who understands how to oblige his guests will contrive to make it as expensive as they please.

Sixthly, this would be a great inducement to marriage, which all wise nations have either encouraged by rewards, or enforced by laws and penalties. It would increase the care and tenderness of mothers toward their children, when they were sure of a settlement for life, to the poor babes, provided in some sort by the public to their annual profit instead of expense. We should see an honest emulation[25] among the married women, which of them could bring the fattest child to the market, men would become as fond of their wives, during the time of their pregnancy, as they are now of their mares in foal, their cows in calf, or sows when they are ready to farrow, nor offer to beat or kick them (as it is too frequent a practice) for fear of a miscarriage.

Many other advantages might be enumerated: For instance, the addition of some thousand carcasses in our exportation of barrelled beef; the propagation of swine's flesh, and improvement in the art of making good bacon, so much wanted among us by the great destruction of pigs, too frequent at our tables, which are no way comparable in taste, or magnificence to a well-grown, fat yearling child, which roasted whole will make a considerable figure at a Lord Mayor's feast, or any other public entertainment. But this, and many others I omit being studious of brevity.

Supposing that one thousand families in this city, would be constant customers for infants' flesh, besides others who might have it at merry-meetings, particularly weddings and christenings, I compute that Dublin would take off annually about twenty thousand carcasses, and the rest of the kingdom (where probably they will be sold somewhat cheaper) the remaining eighty thousand.

I can think of no one objection, that will possibly be raised against this proposal, unless it should be urged that the number of people will be thereby much lessened in the kingdom. This I freely own, and was indeed one principal design in offering it to the world. I desire the reader will observe, that I calculate my remedy *for this one individual Kingdom of Ireland, and for no other that ever was, is, or, I think, ever can be upon earth. Therefore let no man talk to me of other expedients:*[26] *Of taxing our absentees at five shillings a pound: Of using neither clothes, nor household furniture, except what is of our own growth and*

Satire

Explain Swift's use of exaggeration in this passage.

Analyzing Text Features

In what ways do the proposals in italics contrast with Swift's "modest proposal" in the body of the essay?

Comprehension

According to Swift's third argument, what benefit will his plan bring to Ireland?

---

25. emulation competition.
26. expedients Prior to publication, Swift proposed each of the following reasonable means by which Ireland might find relief, but the government ignored his suggestions. Swift used italics in editions printed during his lifetime to indicate that these proposals were, in fact, serious ones.

manufacture: Of utterly rejecting the materials and instruments that promote foreign luxury: Of curing the expensiveness of pride, vanity, idleness, and gaming in our women: Of introducing a vein of parsimony, prudence and temperance: Of learning to love our Country, wherein we differ even from Laplanders, and the inhabitants of Topinamboo:[27] Of quitting our animosities and factions, nor act any longer like the Jews, who were murdering one another at the very moment their city was taken:[28] Of being a little cautious not to sell our country and consciences for nothing: Of teaching landlords to have at least one degree of mercy toward their tenants. Lastly of putting a spirit of honesty, industry and skill into our shopkeepers, who, if a resolution could now be taken to buy only our native goods, would immediately unite to cheat and exact upon us in the price, the measure, and the goodness, nor could ever yet be brought to make one fair proposal of just dealing, though often and earnestly invited to it.

Therefore I repeat, let no man talk to me of these and the like expedients, till he hath at least some glimpse of hope, that there will ever be some hearty and sincere attempt to put them in practice.

But as to myself, having been wearied out for many years with offering vain, idle, visionary thoughts, and at length utterly despairing of success, I fortunately fell upon this proposal, which as it is wholly new, so it hath something solid and real, of no expense and little trouble, full in our own power, and whereby we can incur no danger in disobliging[29] England. For this kind of commodity will not bear exportation, the flesh being of too tender a consistence, to admit a long continuance in salt, although perhaps I could name a country,[30] which would be glad to eat up our whole nation without it.

After all I am not so violently bent upon my own opinion, as to reject any offer, proposed by wise men, which shall be found equally innocent, cheap, easy and effectual. But before something of that kind shall be advanced in contradiction to my scheme, and offering a better, I desire the author, or authors will be pleased maturely to con-

Satire

What understatement does Swift use in the first sentence of this paragraph?

▼ **Critical Viewing**

In what way might employment and housing provide more relief to Ireland than a flat sum of shillings and half-crowns, like those pictured here? **SPECULATE**

27. **Laplanders and . . . Topinamboo** Swift refers to natives of inhospitable lands as examples for the Irish.
28. **city . . . taken** Jerusalem, which was taken by Rome in AD 70 while its Jewish inhabitants were occupied with infighting.
29. **disobliging** offending.
30. **country** England.

sider two points. First, as things now stand, how they will be able to find food and raiment for an hundred thousand useless mouths and backs. And secondly, there being a round million of creatures in human figure, throughout this kingdom, whose whole subsistence put into a common stock, would leave them in debt two millions of pounds sterling adding those, who are beggars by profession, to the bulk of farmers, cottagers and laborers with their wives and children, who are beggars in effect. I desire those politicians, who dislike my overture, and may perhaps be so bold to attempt an answer, that they will first ask the parents of these mortals, whether they would not at this day think it a great happiness to have been sold for food at a year old, in the manner I prescribe, and thereby have avoided such a perpetual scene of misfortunes, as they have since gone through, by the oppression of landlords, the impossibility of paying rent without money or trade, the want of common sustenance, with neither house nor clothes to cover them from the inclemencies of the weather, and the most inevitable prospect of entailing[31] the like, or greater miseries upon their breed for ever.

I profess in the sincerity of my heart that I have not the least personal interest in endeavouring to promote this necessary work, having no other motive than the public good of my country, by advancing our trade, providing for infants, relieving the poor, and giving some pleasure to the rich. I have no children, by which I can propose to get a single penny; the youngest being nine years old, and my wife past child-bearing.

Satire

Why do you think Swift uses the phrases "sincerity of my heart" and "not the least personal interest" in the final paragraph?

---

31. entailing passing to a later generation.

Critical Reading

1. **Key Ideas and Details (a)** What agreement "by all parties" does Swift seek to establish in the second paragraph of the essay? **(b) Analyze:** Why is this agreement necessary for setting the groundwork for the satire?

2. **Key Ideas and Details** According to Swift's American acquaintance in London, what purpose can be served by well-nursed children who are a year old?

3. **Key Ideas and Details (a)** According to Swift, why will children be a very proper food for landlords? **(b) Draw Conclusions:** What satirical point is Swift making in his reference to landlords?

4. **Integration of Knowledge and Ideas** What do these selections suggest that Swift wanted to change about society? In your response, use at least two of these Essential Question words: *values, dissatisfaction, ideal. [Connecting to the Essential Question: How does literature shape or reflect society?]*

Cite textual evidence to support your responses.

Literary Analysis

1. **Key Ideas and Details** Use a chart like the one shown to indicate three targets of Swift's **satire** in *Gulliver's Travels*.

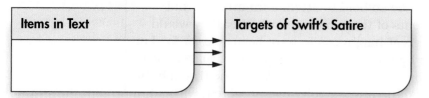

Items in Text		Targets of Swift's Satire

2. **Craft and Structure (a)** Compare and contrast Gulliver's impression of the Lilliputians with the King of Brobdingnag's impression of Europeans. **(b)** How does the comparison add to the satire?

3. **Craft and Structure** Summarize the universal and timeless points Swift wants to make in his satirical novel.

4. **Craft and Structure (a)** What is Swift's chief satirical target in "A Modest Proposal"? **(b)** Why do you think he only gradually reveals the real nature of the "proposal"? **(c)** What is misleading about the word *modest* in the title?

5. **Craft and Structure** Demonstrate how Swift uses each of these elements in his essay: **(a)** *understatement* **(b)** *hyperbole* **(c)** *sarcasm*.

6. **Craft and Structure (a)** Identify a passage in Swift's work that might require you to **analyze text features** in order to discover what is being satirized. **(b)** Demonstrate step by step how such analysis would work.

7. **Comparing Literary Works (a)** Focusing on a passage in each work, compare and contrast Swift's use of **irony** in his novel and his essay. **(b)** In which passage is the irony more effective? Why?

8. **Integration of Knowledge and Ideas** Are there any contemporary satires—whether in literature, on television, or in the movies—that resemble Swift's? Explain, citing examples.

9. **Analyze Visual Information** Use your knowledge of *Gulliver's Travels* to explain the humor in the cartoon on this page.

©**The New Yorker Collection**, 1988,
J. B. Handelsman, from *cartoonbank.com.*
All Rights Reserved.

"Tell me more about these little people that are out to get you." ▶

Common Core
State Standards

Writing
2.a. Introduce a topic; organize complex ideas, concepts, and information so that each new element builds on that which precedes it to create a unified whole; include formatting, graphics, and multimedia when useful to aiding comprehension. *(p. 627)*

Language
5. Demonstrate understanding of word relationships in word meanings. *(p. 627)*

Vocabulary Acquisition and Use

Word Analysis: Latin Root -jec-

The word *conjecture* includes the Latin root -*jec*-, which means "throw." *Conjecture* means "to guess by 'throwing' facts or inferences together." Write sentences using at least four of the following words in a paragraph describing what you might think or feel when traveling to another planet, just as Gulliver traveled to new worlds. If any of the words are unfamiliar, use a dictionary to clarify their meanings.

dejection	eject
object	project
reject	trajectory

Then, choose one of the words you used and write a sentence identifying how the "throw" root helps create its meaning.

Vocabulary: Analogies

Analogies show the relationships between pairs of words. Complete each analogy using a word from the vocabulary list on page 604. In each, your choice should create a word pair that matches the relationship between the first two words given. Then, explain your answers.

1. *Vegetables* : _____ :: *homes* : *shelter*.
2. A _____ : *merchandise* :: *help* : *assistance*.
3. *Emergency* : an _____ :: *moving* : *truck*.
4. A *transmission* : a *message* :: a _____ : a *rupture*.
5. _____ : *criticize* :: *praise* : *approve*.
6. *Night* : *day* :: _____ : *certainty*.

Writing to Sources

Informative Text Like a modern-day Swift, make a plan for a satiric **multimedia** using *text, images, and sound.* You might include taped scenes or archival footage; photos, video, or cartoons; and sound effects or music.

Prewriting Start by choosing a target. What foolish behavior, trend, or attitude in today's world merits mockery?

Drafting Outline the sequence of your presentation. Then, decide on the *appropriate medium* to present each idea. Select the words, images, or sounds that will best convey your satire at each stage. Decide whether it is better to create those elements or to identify copyrighted sources that might provide the needed material—for example, television, videos, or films; newspapers, magazines, or books; clip-art collections or original drawings. Use a chart like the one shown to record your ideas.

Point	Media	Possible Sources
Reality shows are not "real."	Video clip from a reality show that reveals a convoluted situation.	Download copyrighted content from Internet
	News headlines showing problems people really face.	Scan from local papers

Revising Read through your plan and make any changes needed to clarify your message and to blend different types of media effectively.

Connecting to the Essential Question In *The Rape of the Lock*, Pope mocks the pretensions of high society. Briefly describe pretentious behavior that you have observed. As you read, noticing the upper-class behavior that Pope mocks will help as you consider the Essential Question: **How does literature shape or reflect society?**

Close Reading Focus

Parody; Epic Simile

Used in poetry, prose, drama, and other basic genres, **parody** is writing that makes fun of another, more serious work or of its author's style. *The Rape of the Lock* is a *mock epic*, or poetic parody of a traditional epic about heroes. Pope applies these conventions of classical epics to his trivial subject, the theft of a lady's lock of hair:

- boasting speeches made by heroes and heroines
- elaborate descriptions of warriors and their weapons
- involvement of gods and goddesses in the action
- **epic similes,** or intricate comparisons in the style of Homer that sometimes use the words *like, as,* or *so*

Note Pope's mocking of epic elements in *The Rape of the Lock*. Also note how, in both poems, he uses **antithesis**, a rhetorical device in which contrasting words, clauses, sentences, or ideas are placed side by side in parallel grammatical structures:

Whether he thinks <u>too little</u>, or <u>too much</u>. (Essay, line 12)

Preparing to Read Complex Texts To **analyze how an author's purpose affects the meaning of a work,** ask yourself why the author is writing. For example, knowing that Pope's purpose is to poke fun at grand literature and high society, you will understand why he chooses certain words to suggest contrasts between heroic deeds and trivial upper-class pursuits to create a humorous **tone.** As you read, notice how his purpose leads him to make such contrasts throughout the poem.

Vocabulary

You will encounter the words listed here in the texts that follow. Copy the words into your notebook and note which one is an adverb.

stoic	plebeian
disabused	destitute
obliquely	assignations

Common Core State Standards

Reading Literature
6. Analyze a case in which grasping point of view requires distinguishing what is directly stated in a text from what is really meant.

Purpose

↓

Effect on Meaning

↑

Evidence from Text

Alexander Pope
(1688–1744)

Author of *An Essay on Man* • *The Rape of the Lock*

Despite a crippling childhood disease and persistent ill health, Alexander Pope was determined at a young age to become a great poet. He triumphantly achieved his boyhood ambition by the time he was in his twenties, capturing the attention of the leading literary figures of England. A brilliant satirist in verse, Pope gave his name to the literary era in which he wrote, which is now called the Age of Pope and Swift.

A Struggle Against Prejudice Born into the Roman Catholic family of a London linen merchant, Pope was a member of a persecuted religious minority. After the expulsion of King James II in 1688, English Catholics could not legally vote, hold office, attend a university, or live within ten miles of London. Probably to comply with the rule of residency, his family moved first to the village of Hammersmith and then to Binfield, near Windsor Forest. In this rural setting, Pope spent his formative years writing poetry, studying the classics, and educating himself.

"[T]his long Disease, my Life" In addition to facing religious prejudice, Pope had severe physical problems. Deformed by tuberculosis of the bone, or Pott's disease, Pope stood only about four and a half feet tall—"that little Alexander the women laugh at," he said about himself. Pope also suffered from nervousness and excruciating headaches throughout his life. In a line from his poem *Epistle to Dr. Arbuthnot* (1735), he refers jokingly but also with sadness to "this long Disease, my Life."

A Turn to Philosophy In the 1730s, Pope's writing moved out of the satirical mode to become increasingly philosophical. Leaving humor behind, he embarked on a massive work concerning morality and government but completed only *An Essay on Man* and *Moral Essays*. Nevertheless, the entire body of his work is so noteworthy that critics and fellow writers alike frequently accord him exceptionally high praise. The twentieth-century poet Edith Sitwell, for example, called Pope "perhaps the most flawless artist our race has yet produced."

from

AN ESSAY Alexander Pope
ON MAN

▲ **Critical Viewing** Compare and contrast the perspective on humanity indicated by this Rodin sculpture with Pope's perspective in *An Essay on Man*. **COMPARE AND CONTRAST**

630 A Turbulent Time (1625–1798)

BACKGROUND *An Essay on Man* is an examination of human nature, society, and morals. In the following passage, Pope cautions against intellectual pride by describing the uncertain "middle state" in which humans have been placed.

Know then thyself, presume not God to scan;
The proper study of mankind is man.
Placed on this isthmus of a middle state,
A being darkly wise, and rudely great:
5   With too much knowledge for the skeptic side,
With too much weakness for the stoic's pride,
He hangs between; in doubt to act, or rest;
In doubt to deem himself a god, or beast;
In doubt his mind or body to prefer;
10   Born but to die, and reasoning but to err;
Alike in ignorance, his reason such,
Whether he thinks too little, or too much:
Chaos of thought and passion, all confused;
Still by himself abused, or disabused;
15   Created half to rise, and half to fall;
Great lord of all things, yet a prey to all;
Sole judge of truth, in endless error hurled:
The glory, jest, and riddle of the world!

Vocabulary

stoic (stō´ ik) *n.* person indifferent to joy, grief, pleasure, or pain

disabused (dis´ ə byo͞ozd´) *adj.* freed from false ideas

Critical Reading

1. **Key Ideas and Details (a)** What does Pope say should be the object of man's study? **(b) Speculate:** Why do you think Pope says, "presume not God to scan"?

2. **Key Ideas and Details (a)** According to Pope, what prevents man from being a skeptic or a stoic? **(b) Analyze Cause and Effect:** What is the result of man's being neither skeptic nor stoic? Explain.

3. **Key Ideas and Details (a)** What does each "half" of man do? **(b) Interpret:** In your own words, express how man can be both a "lord of all things" and "a prey to all."

4. **Integration of Knowledge and Ideas** What twentieth-century events suggest that humans are any or all of the following: "The glory, jest, and riddle of the world!" Explain.

Cite textual evidence to support your responses.

from

The Rape of the Lock

Alexander Pope

BACKGROUND *The Rape of the Lock* is based on an actual incident. Two families, the Petres and the Fermors, became involved in a dispute when Robert Petre flirtatiously cut a lock of hair from the head of lovely Arabella Fermor.

The first of the poem's five cantos opens with a formal statement of theme and an invocation to the Muse for poetic inspiration. Then, Belinda, the poem's heroine, receives a warning from the sylph Ariel that a dreadful event will take place in her immediate future. In Canto II, during a boat ride on the Thames, an adventurous baron admires Belinda's hair and is determined to cut two bright locks from her head and keep them as a prize. Aware of the baron's desires, Ariel urges the spirits to protect Belinda.

The Barge, 1895–96 Aubrey Beardsley

▲ **Critical Viewing** Does the artist's portrayal of Belinda, who is shown here, correspond to Pope's portrayal of her in Canto III? Explain. **CONNECT**

Canto III

Close by those meads, forever crowned with flowers,
Where Thames with pride surveys his rising towers,
There stands a structure of majestic frame,[1]
Which from the neighboring Hampton takes its name.
5 Here Britain's statesmen oft the fall foredoom
Of foreign tyrants, and of nymphs at home;
Here thou, great Anna![2] whom three realms obey,
Dost sometimes counsel take—and sometimes tea.
　　Hither the heroes and the nymphs resort,
10 To taste awhile the pleasures of a court;
In various talk th' instructive hours they passed,
Who gave the ball, or paid the visit last;
One speaks the glory of the British Queen,
And one describes a charming Indian screen;
15 A third interprets motions, looks, and eyes;
At every word a reputation dies.
Snuff, or the fan,[3] supply each pause of chat,
With singing, laughing, ogling, and all that.
　　Meanwhile, declining from the noon of day,
20 The sun obliquely shoots his burning ray;
The hungry judges soon the sentence sign,
And wretches hang that jurymen may dine;
The merchant from th' Exchange[4] returns in peace,
And the long labors of the toilet[5] cease.
25 Belinda now, whom thirst of fame invites,
Burns to encounter two adventurous knights,
At omber[6] singly to decide their doom;
And swells her breast with conquests yet to come.
Straight the three bands prepare in arms to join,
30 Each band the number of the sacred nine.[7]
Soon as she spreads her hand, th' aerial guard
Descend, and sit on each important card:
First Ariel perched upon a Matadore,[8]
Then each, according to the rank they bore;
35 For sylphs, yet mindful of their ancient race,
Are, as when women, wondrous fond of place.
　　Behold, four kings in majesty revered,
With hoary whiskers and a forky beard;

---

1. **structure . . . frame** Hampton Court, a royal palace near London.
2. **Anna** Queen Anne, who ruled England, Ireland, and Scotland from 1702 through 1714.
3. **snuff . . . fan** At the time, gentlemen commonly took snuff and ladies usually carried a fan.
4. **Exchange** London financial center where merchants, bankers, and brokers conducted business.
5. **toilet** dressing tables.
6. **omber** popular card game.
7. **sacred nine** reference to the nine Muses of Greek mythology.
8. **Matadore** powerful card that could take a trick.

And four fair queens whose hands sustain a flower,
40　Th' expressive emblem of their softer power;
Four knaves in garbs succinct,[9] a trusty band,
Caps on their heads, and halberts[10] in their hand;
And particolored troops, a shining train,
Draw forth to combat on the velvet plain.
45　　　The skillful nymph reviews her force with care:
Let spades be trumps! she said, and trumps they were.
　　　Now move to war her sable Matadores,
In show like leaders of the swarthy Moors.
Spadillio[11] first, unconquerable Lord!
50　Led off two captive trumps, and swept the board.
As many more Manillio[12] forced to yield,
And marched a victor from the verdant field.[13]
Him Basto[14] followed, but his fate more hard
Gained but one trump and one plebeian card.
55　With his broad saber next, a chief in years,
The hoary majesty of spades appears,
Puts forth one manly leg, to sight revealed,
The rest, his many-colored robe concealed.
The rebel knave, who dares his prince engage,
60　Proves the just victim of his royal rage.
Even mighty Pam,[15] that kings and queens o'erthrew
And mowed down armies in the fights of loo,
Sad chance of war! now destitute of aid,
Falls undistinguished by the victor spade!
65　　　Thus far both armies to Belinda yield;
Now to the baron fate inclines the field.
His warlike Amazon her host invades,
Th' imperial consort of the crown of spades.
The club's black tyrant first her victim died,
70　Spite of his haughty mien, and barbarous pride.
What boots[16] the regal circle on his head,
His giant limbs, in state unwieldy spread;
That long behind he trails his pompous robe,
And, of all monarchs, only grasps the globe?
75　　　The baron now his diamonds pours apace;
Th' embroidered king who shows but half his face,
And his refulgent queen, with powers combined
Of broken troops an easy conquest find.

Vocabulary

plebeian (plē bē´ ən) *adj.*
common; not aristocratic

Vocabulary

destitute (des´ tə tōōt)
adj. lacking

Comprehension

In what way do Belinda and her friends pass the time?

---

9. succinct (sək siŋkt´) belted.
10. halberts long-handled weapons.
11. Spadillio ace of spades.
12. Manillio two of spades.
13. verdant field the card table, covered with a green cloth.
14. Basto ace of clubs.
15. Pam knave of clubs, the highest card in the game called "loo."
16. What boots of what benefit is.

► **Critical Viewing**
Which elements of the situation portrayed in this drawing do you think Pope would choose to ridicule? Why? **SPECULATE**

Analyzing Author's Purpose

How does Pope's purpose affect the meaning of lines 83–86?

Mock Epic and Antithesis

Why is line 92 an example of antithesis?

Clubs, diamonds, hearts, in wild disorder seen,
80　With throngs promiscuous strew the level green.
Thus when dispersed a routed army runs,
Of Asia's troops, and Afric's sable sons,
　　With like confusion different nations fly,
Of various habit, and of various dye,
85　The pierced battalions disunited fall,
In heaps on heaps; one fate o'erwhelms them all.
　　The knave of diamonds tries his wily arts,
And wins (oh shameful chance!) the queen of hearts.
At this, the blood the virgin's cheek forsook,
90　A livid paleness spreads o'er all her look;
She sees, and trembles at th' approaching ill,
Just in the jaws of ruin, and codille.[17]
And now (as oft in some distempered state)
On one nice trick depends the general fate.

---

17. codille term meaning the defeat of a hand of cards.

95 An ace of hearts steps forth; the king unseen
Lurked in her hand, and mourned his captive queen.
He springs to vengeance with an eager pace,
And falls like thunder on the prostrate ace.
The nymph exulting fills with shouts the sky;
100 The walls, the woods, and long canals reply.
　　　Oh thoughtless mortals! ever blind to fate,
Too soon dejected, and too soon elate.
Sudden, these honors shall be snatched away,
And cursed forever this victorious day.
105 　　　For lo! the board with cups and spoons is crowned,
The berries crackle, and the mill turns round;[18]
On shining altars of Japan[19] they raise
The silver lamp; the fiery spirits blaze;
From silver spouts the grateful liquors glide,
110 While China's earth[20] receives the smoking tide.
At once they gratify their scent and taste,
And frequent cups prolong the rich repast.
Straight hover round the fair her airy band;
some, as she sipped, the fuming liquor fanned,
115 Some o'er her lap their careful plumes displayed,
Trembling, and conscious of the rich brocade.
Coffee (which makes the politician wise,
And see through all things with his half-shut eyes)
Sent up in vapors to the baron's brain
120 New stratagems, the radiant lock to gain.
Ah cease, rash youth! desist ere 'tis too late,
Fear the just gods, and think of Scylla's fate![21]
Changed to a bird, and sent to flit in air,
She dearly pays for Nisus' injured hair!
125 　　　But when to mischief mortals bend their will,
How soon they find fit instruments of ill!
Just then, Clarissa drew with tempting grace
A two-edged weapon from her shining case:
So ladies in romance assist their knight,
130 Present the spear, and arm him for the fight.
He takes the gift with reverence, and extends
The little engine[22] on his fingers' ends;
This just behind Belinda's neck he spread,
As o'er the fragrant steams she bends her head.
135 Swift to the lock a thousand sprites repair,
A thousand wings, by turns, blow back the hair;

The
BRITISH
TRADITION

**Neoclassical Style and
The Heroic Couplet**
Lines 105–106 or any of the rhyming lines in the poem demonstrate Pope's use of the closed heroic couplet, a rhyming pair of iambic pentameter lines that are "closed" because they express a complete thought. This type of couplet is typical of the Neoclassical style of the eighteenth century, which had these characteristics: a reliance on Greek and Roman models, a stress on human limitations, and a concept of the poet as a kind of public speaker addressing society as a whole.

In keeping with the Neoclassical outlook, the closed heroic couplet allows Pope to indicate human follies and frailties with devices from public speaking, such as antithesis.

Connect to the Literature

In what ways do lines 125 and 126 fit the Neoclassical style and outlook?

18. **The berries . . . round** Coffee beans are ground in a hand mill at the table.
19. **altars of Japan** small imported lacquer tables.
20. **China's earth** earthenware cups imported from China.
21. **Scylla's** (sil′ ez) **fate** Scylla, the daughter of King Nisus, was turned into a sea bird because she cut off the lock of her father's hair on which his safety depended and sent it to his enemy.
22. **engine** instrument.

Comprehension
What is the baron plotting to do?

The Rape of the Lock, 1895–96, Aubrey Beardsley

▲ **Critical Viewing**
Where in the poem does Pope make a trivial occasion seem important, as the artist does here? Explain. **CONNECT**

And thrice they twitched the diamond in her ear;
Thrice she looked back, and thrice the foe drew near.
Just in that instant, anxious Ariel sought
140 The close recesses of the virgin's thought;
As on the nosegay in her breast reclined,
He watched th' ideas rising in her mind,
Sudden he viewed, in spite of all her art,
An earthly lover lurking at her heart.[23]
145 Amazed, confused, he found his power expired,
Resigned to fate, and with a sigh retired.
        The peer now spreads the glittering forfex[24] wide,
T' enclose the lock; now joins it, to divide.
Even then, before the fatal engine closed,
150 A wretched sylph too fondly interposed;
Fate urged the shears, and cut the sylph in twain,
(But airy substance soon unites again).
The meeting points the sacred hair dissever
From the fair head, forever, and forever!
155   Then flashed the living lightning from her eyes,
And screams of horror rend th' affrighted skies.
Not louder shrieks to pitying heaven are cast,
When husbands, or when lap dogs breathe their last;
Or when rich China vessels fallen from high,
160 In glittering dust, and painted fragments lie!
        "Let wreaths of triumph now my temples twine,"
The victor cried, "the glorious prize is mine!"
While fish in streams, or birds delight in air,
Or in a coach and six the British Fair,
165 As long as *Atalantis*[25] shall be read
Or the small pillow grace a lady's bed,
While visits shall be paid on solemn days,
When numerous wax lights in bright order blaze,
While nymphs take treats, or assignations give,
170 So long my honor, name, and praise shall live!
What time would spare, from steel receives its date,[26]
And monuments, like men, submit to fate!
Steel could the labor of the gods destroy,
And strike to dust th' imperial towers of Troy;
175 Steel could the works of mortal pride confound,
And hew triumphal arches to the ground.
What wonder then, fair nymph! thy hairs should feel,
The conquering force of unresisted steel?

---

23. **earthly lover . . . heart** If in her heart Belinda wants the baron to succeed, they cannot protect her.
24. **forfex** scissors.
25. ***Atalantis*** popular book of scandalous gossip.
26. **receives its date** is destroyed.

Analyzing Author's Purpose

Why does the author describe the scene in lines 145–160 in such an elevated manner?

Parody

How is Belinda's reaction to the loss of her hair appropriate for a mock epic?

Vocabulary

assignations
(as´ ig nā´ shənz) *n.* appointments to meet

Comprehension

What happens to the sylph that flies between the blades of the shears?

LITERATURE IN CONTEXT

Fashions of the Times

Pope's focus on Belinda's hair indicates the importance that women's hairstyles played in the upper-class obsession with fashion at this time. During the eighteenth century, the world's first fashion magazine was launched by the French, suggesting that nation's leadership in setting styles. Leonard, hairdresser to the French queen Marie Antoinette (1755–1793), whose picture appears below, established a fashion in which women's hairdos rose as high as four feet. These "hair statues" were augmented with horsehair pads and decorated with gauze and feathers. English hairdressers quickly took up the challenge, decorating women's heads with horse-drawn carriages, zoos of miniature lions and tigers, and, if accounts can be believed, a lit stove complete with pots and pans!

Connect to the Literature

Explain how Belinda and other women of her class might reflect their status in their hairstyles.

from Canto V

In Canto IV, after Umbriel, "a dusky, melancholy sprite," empties a bag filled with "the force of female lungs, sighs, sobs, and passions, and the war of tongues" onto Belinda's head, the lady erupts over the loss of her lock. Then she "bids her beau," Sir Plume, to "demand the precious hairs," but Plume is unable to persuade the baron to return the hair.

In the beginning of Canto V, Clarissa, a level-headed nymph, tries to bring an end to the commotion, but rather than being greeted with applause, her speech is followed by a battle cry.

"To arms, to arms!" the fierce virago[27] cries,
And swift as lightning to the combat flies.
All side in parties, and begin th' attack;
Fans clap, silks rustle, and tough whalebones crack;
5 Heroes' and heroines' shouts confusedly rise,
And bass and treble voices strike the skies.
No common weapons in their hands are found,
Like gods they fight, nor dread a mortal wound.
    So when bold Homer makes the gods engage,
10 And heavenly breasts with human passions rage;
'Gainst Pallas, Mars, Latona, Hermes[28] arms;
And all Olympus[29] rings with loud alarms:
Jove's[30] thunder roars, heaven trembles all around,
Blue Neptune[31] storms, the bellowing deeps resound;
15 Earth shakes her nodding towers, the ground gives way,
And the pale ghosts start at the flash of day!
    Triumphant Umbriel on a sconce's height[32]
Clapped his glad wings, and sat to view the fight;
Propped on their bodkin spears,[33] the sprites survey
20 The growing combat, or assist the fray.
    While through the press enraged Thalestris[34] flies,
And scatters death around from both her eyes,
A beau and witling[35] perished in the throng,
One died in metaphor, and one in song.
25 "O cruel nymph! a living death I bear,"
Cried Dapperwit, and sunk beside his chair.

---

27. virago (vi rā´ gō) scolding woman.
28. Pallas . . . Hermes gods who directed the Trojan War. Pallas and Hermes supported the Greeks, while Mars and Latona sided with the Trojans.
29. Olympus mountain which was supposed to be the home of the Greek gods.
30. Jove's referring to Jupiter, the ruler of the Gods in Roman mythology: identified with Zeus in Greek mythology.
31. Neptune Roman god of the sea; identified with Poseidon in Greek mythology.
32. sconce's height candleholder attached to the wall.
33. bodkin spears large needles.
34. Thalestris (thə lēs´ tris) an Amazon (a race of female warriors supposed to have lived in Scythia) who played a role in the medieval tales of Alexander the Great.
35. witling person who fancies himself or herself a wit.

The Battle of the Beaux and Belles Aubrey Beardsley

◀ **Critical Viewing**

In what ways is the elaborate decorative style of the drawing similar to the language of the poem? **CONNECT**

A mournful glance Sir Fopling[36] upwards cast,
"Those eyes are made so killing"—was his last.
Thus on Maeander's[37] flowery margin lies
30 Th' expiring swan, and as he sings he dies.
  When bold Sir Plume had drawn Clarissa down,
Chloe[38] stepped in, and killed him with a frown;
She smiled to see the doughty hero slain,
But, at her smile, the beau revived again.

Comprehension

What "weapons" do the combatants use?

---

36. Dapperwit . . . Sir Fopling names of amusing characters in comedies of the time.
37. Maeander's referring to a river in Asia.
38. Chloe (klō′ ē) heroine of the ancient Greek pastoral romance, *Daphnis and Chloe*.

Spiral Review
Couplet
Does Pope's use of
the couplet differ from
Chaucer's use? Explain.

35   Now Jove suspends his golden scales in air,
        Weighs the men's wits against the lady's hair;
        The doubtful beam long nods from side to side;
        At length the wits mount up, the hairs subside.
            See, fierce Belinda on the baron flies,
40   With more than usual lightning in her eyes;
        Nor feared the chief th' unequal fight to try,
        Who sought no more than on his foe to die.
        But this bold lord with manly strength endued,
        She with one finger and a thumb subdued:
45   Just where the breath of life his nostrils drew,
        A charge of snuff the wily virgin threw;
        The gnomes direct, to every atom just,
        The pungent grains of titillating dust.
        Sudden with starting tears each eye o'erflows,
50   And the high dome re-echoes to his nose.
            "Now meet thy fate," incensed Belinda cried,
        And drew a deadly bodkin[39] from her side . . .
            "Boast not my fall," he cried, "insulting foe!
        Thou by some other shalt be laid as low.

Parody

How are Belinda's words
and actions in lines 51–52
appropriate for a mock epic?

55   Nor think, to die dejects my lofty mind;
        All that I dread is leaving you behind!
        Rather than so, ah let me still survive,
        And burn in Cupid's flames—but burn alive."
            "Restore the lock!" she cries; and all around
60   "Restore the lock!" the vaulted roofs rebound.
        Not fierce Othello in so loud a strain
        Roared for the handkerchief that caused his pain.[40]
        But see how oft ambitious aims are crossed,
        And chiefs contend till all the prize is lost!
65   The lock, obtained with guilt, and kept with pain,
        In every place is sought, but sought in vain.
        With such a prize no mortal must be blessed,
        So Heaven decrees! with Heaven who can contest?
            Some thought it mounted to the lunar sphere,
70   Since all things lost on earth are treasured there.
        There heroes' wits are kept in ponderous vases,
        And beaux' in snuffboxes and tweezer cases.
        There broken vows and deathbed alms are found,
        And lovers' hearts with ends of riband bound . . .
75   But trust the Muse—she saw it upward rise,
        Though marked by none but quick, poetic eyes . . .

---

39. bodkin ornamental pin shaped like a dagger.
40. Not . . . pain In Shakespeare's *Othello*, the hero is convinced that his wife is being unfaith-
    ful to him when she cannot find the handkerchief that he had given her. Actually, the hand-
    kerchief had been taken by the villain, Iago, who uses it as part of his evil plot.

A sudden star, it shot through liquid[41] air
And drew behind a radiant trail of hair . . .[42]
   Then cease, bright Nymph! to mourn thy ravished hair,
80 Which adds new glory to the shining sphere!
Not all the tresses that fair head can boast,
Shall draw such envy as the lock you lost.
For, after all the murders of your eye,[43]
When, after millions slain, yourself shall die;
85 When those fair suns shall set, as set they must,
And all those tresses shall be laid in dust,
This lock, the Muse shall consecrate to fame,
And midst the stars inscribe Belinda's name.

> Not all the tresses that
> fair head can boast,
> Shall draw such envy
> as the lock you lost.

41. liquid clear.
42. trail of hair The word *comet* comes from a Greek word meaning "long-haired."
43. murders . . . eye lovers struck down by her glances.

Critical Reading

1. **Key Ideas and Details (a)** What happens during the game of cards? **(b) Infer:** What does the way they play reveal about Belinda and the baron?

2. **Key Ideas and Details (a)** What does Clarissa help the baron do to Belinda, and what struggle results from it? **(b) Compare and Contrast:** Compare and contrast the card game with the final conflict in the poem. **(c) Synthesize:** What is really at stake in all of the poem's conflicts?

3. **Key Ideas and Details (a)** What happens to the lock of hair in lines 79–88 of Canto V? **(b) Analyze:** In what way is the claim that Pope makes in these lines ridiculous? In what way is it true? Explain.

4. **Integration of Knowledge and Ideas (a) Interpret:** What do you think is Pope's basic criticism of the rituals he describes in the poem? Explain. **(b) Support:** Which passage or passages indicate that Pope has some positive feelings about the rituals he criticizes? Explain.

5. **Integration of Knowledge and Ideas** Pope based this poem on an actual incident. What contemporary incident might inspire a mock epic? Explain.

6. **Integration of Knowledge and Ideas** Are elaborate social rituals, like the ones Pope mocks, always ridiculous? Why or why not?

7. **Integration of Knowledge and Ideas** Was Pope's main goal to change the behavior he mocked or to entertain readers? In your response, use at least two of the following Essential Question words: *exaggerate, reform, charm, preserve.* [*Connecting to the Essential Question: How does literature shape or reflect society?*]

Cite textual evidence to support your responses.

Literary Analysis

1. Craft and Structure Use a chart like the one shown to identify epic elements and the trivial activities to which they apply in *The Rape of the Lock*, Pope's **mock epic.**

Epic Element	Lines in Poem	Activity
Hero's boasts		
Gods and goddesses		
Description of warriors		

2. Craft and Structure **(a)** Why are lines 8–16 in Canto V an **epic simile? (b)** How does this simile add to the absurdity of the action Pope is describing?

3. Key Ideas and Details **(a)** How does knowing Pope's purpose help you determine the meaning of his comparison of a card game with a serious battle (Canto III, lines 75–86)? **(b)** How might your interpretation of the meaning change if you did not realize Pope's purpose? Explain.

4. Key Ideas and Details **Analyze Pope's purpose** to show how, in Canto III, lines 105–120, Pope's intention is both to make fun of a social ritual and to entertain readers.

5. Craft and Structure Which of the epic elements Pope uses adds most to his criticism of upper-class courtship rituals? Explain.

6. Key Ideas and Details Referring to a specific passage, show that Pope's criticism of upper-class rituals is affectionate rather than stern.

7. Integration of Knowledge and Ideas Classical epics frequently feature gods and goddesses who intervene in human affairs. What qualities of Pope's sprites distinguish them from the gods and goddesses of a classical epic?

8. Craft and Structure Explain how line 12 of *An Essay on Man* and Canto III, lines 13–14, of *The Rape of the Lock* are examples of **antithesis.**

9. Craft and Structure In what way does antithesis help Pope describe the human condition in *An Essay on Man* and mock upper-class pretensions in *The Rape of the Lock*?

10. Integration of Knowledge and Ideas Is antithesis a device that is equally essential in both poems? Why or why not?

Common Core State Standards

Reading Literature
9. Demonstrate knowledge of eighteenth-, nineteenth- and early-twentieth-century foundational works of American literature, including how two or more texts from the same period treat similar themes or topics. *(p. 645)*

Reading Informational Text
9. Analyze seventeenth-, eighteenth-, and nineteenth-century foundational U.S. documents of historical and literary significance for their themes, purposes, and rhetorical features. *(p. 645)*

Writing
4. Produce clear and coherent writing in which the development, organization, and style are appropriate to task, purpose, and audience. *(p. 645)*

Language
4.a. Use context as a clue to the meaning of a word or phrase. *(p. 645)*

Vocabulary Acquisition and Use

Words from Political Science

Many English words concerning social or political matters have Latin origins. *Plebeian*, meaning "ordinary or common," comes from the Latin word *plebs* meaning, "the common people." Use your background knowledge and context clues to determine the meanings of the italicized words below, and explain those meanings. Consult a dictionary to confirm the definitions and trace the words' Latin origins.

1. In some cultures, property is inherited along *maternal* lines.
2. The United States is not a direct democracy but a *republic*.
3. People need the *society* of others.
4. *Officials* should act in the public interest.
5. A principle of the American legal system is "equal *justice* under the law."

Vocabulary: Synonyms

A **synonym** is a word that has the same meaning as another word. Replace each italicized word in the following sentences with its synonym from the vocabulary list on page 628.

1. "Your underhanded actions *rid* me of any illusions about you," she said.
2. She delivered the message *slyly* so that anyone overhearing their conversation would not understand it.
3. The shabby clothes showed how *poor* the once-rich prince had become.
4. The secretive pair often had *trysts*.
5. The manager's *unemotional* manner never changed whether the team won or lost.
6. She pretended to be sophisticated, but she spoke in a *common* manner.

Writing to Sources

Explanatory Text The Enlightenment was an eighteenth-century cultural movement favoring reason and balance. To appreciate the wide influence of the Enlightenment, find and read two American works from the period: the Declaration of Independence and Phillis Wheatley's "To His Excellency, General Washington." Compare them to Pope's "Essay on Man."

Prewriting Note details in the Declaration and in Pope's poem that reflect ideas about human nature. Note details about the language, imagery, tone, and rhyme scheme in Pope's and Wheatley's poems.

Model: Revising for Parallelism

Pope's rhyming couplets emphasize his witty contrasts; Wheately's [are different because they] reinforce her stately voice.

By phrasing contrasting thoughts in grammatically parallel clauses, the writer adds force and clarity.

Drafting In your introduction, briefly summarize Pope's ideas about humanity and describe his poetic style. Then, compare his ideas of human nature to those in the Declaration. Next, compare his style to Wheatley's. Finally, draw a conclusion about Enlightenment values based on your comparisons. (You can learn more about the Enlightenment on page 646.)

Revising Make your comparisons clear by using parallelism, stating similar ideas in similar grammatical form.

Connecting to the Essential Question Samuel Johnson wrote the first true English dictionary. As you read, note passages in which each author sees himself as an innovator to answer the Essential Question: **What is the relationship of the writer to tradition?**

Close Reading Focus

Dictionary; Biography

A **dictionary** defines words and may provide information about their pronunciation, history, and usage. Samuel Johnson compiled the first standard dictionary of the English language. As you read the excerpt from it, look for features he initiated that are still in use today.

A **biography** is an account of someone's life written by another person. Just as Johnson's *Dictionary* was a landmark, so was Boswell's *Life of Samuel Johnson.* In reading it, note how Boswell uses many details from his own personal knowledge to portray Johnson's character.

Comparing Literary Works Both these selections reveal the *philosophical assumptions and beliefs* of the Enlightenment. This eighteenth-century intellectual movement stressed the following values:

- the importance of regularizing and preserving knowledge
- a perception of reason and judgment as the highest human abilities
- the belief that great authors were authorities on language and life
- elevated **diction,** or word choice, revealing a respect for learning

To comprehend elevated diction, look up unfamiliar words, checking connotations, or emotional associations, as well as literal meanings. As you read, also draw inferences about how Enlightenment beliefs influenced each author.

Preparing to Read Complex Texts By **analyzing the author's purpose,** or goal, you will better understand a work's *meaning.* For example, knowing that Boswell's purpose was to record the life of an exemplary man, you will realize why he includes detailed stories about Johnson. Over the course of the text, the complex set of ideas develops into a complete picture of the man. Use a graphic organizer to record the author's purpose and how it affects meaning.

Vocabulary

You will encounter the words listed here in the texts that follow. Copy the words into your notebook. Which two words have the same suffix?

caprices   abasement

adulterations   credulity

risible   malignity

Common Core State Standards

Reading Informational Text

3. Analyze a complex set of ideas or sequence of events and explain how specific individuals, ideas, or events interact and develop over the course of a text.

4. Determine the meaning of words and phrases as they are used in a text, including figurative, connotative, and technical meanings.

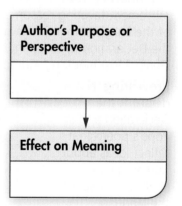

Author's Purpose or Perspective

↓

Effect on Meaning

Samuel Johnson

(1709–1784)

Author of *A Dictionary of the English Language*

With his fine mind and dazzling conversation, Samuel Johnson was at the center of a circle that included most of Britain's leading artists and intellectuals. So great was his influence on English literature that the second half of the eighteenth century is often called the Age of Johnson.

A Life of Hardship Samuel Johnson overcame severe physical and economic hardships. The son of a bookseller in Lichfield, England, he suffered a series of childhood illnesses that left him weak and disfigured. Bright enough to read Shakespeare as a young boy, he was too poor to attend the schools of the aristocracy and pursued his education largely by reading books in his father's shop. Although he was able to enter Oxford in 1728, lack of funds forced him to leave early.

A Great Work In 1737, Johnson moved to London to try to earn his living as a writer; in 1746, he began work on his *Dictionary of the English Language*. This landmark effort took nine years to complete—difficult years during which his wife died and he continued to be dogged by poverty. When at last the *Dictionary* was published, however, it ensured Johnson's place in literary history. Still, it was not until 1762, when he received a pension from the king, that he did not have to rely on writing for a living. In 1775, he received an honorary degree from Oxford, the school he had been forced to leave.

"When a man is tired of London, he is tired of life; for there is in London all that life can afford."

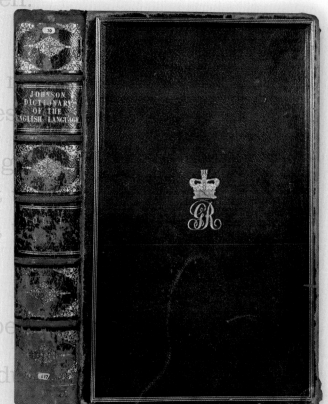

from

A Dictionary of the English Language

Samuel Johnson

BACKGROUND Eighteenth-century thinkers sensed that their era had made great advances in knowledge, and they set down in writing the scientific, philosophical, and historic facts and ideas that were part of this new understanding. Among the intellectual pioneers of this period were Samuel Johnson and James Boswell, whose dictionary and biography, respectively, set the standard for nonfiction works of their type. The eighteenth century also saw the birth of the first *Encyclopaedia Britannica* (1768–1771) as well as Adam Smith's *Wealth of Nations* (1776), which revolutionized the study of economics. As you read the following selections, notice how just as Johnson captures in his dictionary the changing English language, Boswell captures in his biography the changeable personality of Johnson.

from The Preface

It is the fate of those who toil at the lower employments of life, to be rather driven by the fear of evil, than attracted by the prospect of good; to be exposed to censure, without hope of praise; to be disgraced by miscarriage, or punished for neglect, where success would have been without applause, and diligence without reward.

Among these unhappy mortals is the writer of dictionaries; whom mankind have considered, not as the pupil, but the slave of science, the pioneer of literature, doomed only to remove rubbish and clear obstructions from the paths through which learning and genius press forward to conquest and glory, without bestowing a smile on the humble drudge that facilitates their progress. Every other author may aspire to praise; the lexicographer can only hope to escape reproach, and even this negative recompense has been yet granted to very few.

I have, notwithstanding this discouragement, attempted a dictionary of the English language, which, while it was employed in the cultivation of every species of literature, has itself been hitherto neglected; suffered to spread under the direction of chance, into wild exuberance; resigned to the tyranny of time and fashion: and exposed to the corruptions of ignorance and caprices of innovation.

When I took the first survey of my undertaking, I found our speech copious without order and energetic without rule: wherever I turned my view, there was perplexity to be disentangled and confusion to be regulated; choice was to be made out of boundless variety, without any established principle of selection; adulterations were to be detected, without a settled test of purity; and modes of expression to be rejected or received, without the suffrages of any writers of classical reputation or acknowledged authority.

Having therefore no assistance but from general grammar, I applied myself to the perusal of our writers; and noting whatever might be of use to ascertain or illustrate any word or phrase, accumulated in time the materials of a dictionary, which, by degrees, I reduced to method, establishing to myself, in the progress of the work, such rules as experience and analogy suggested to me; experience, which practice and observation were continually increasing; and analogy, which, though in some other words obscure, was evident in others. . . .

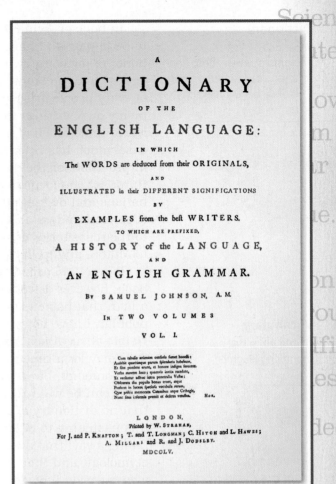

A
DICTIONARY
OF THE
ENGLISH LANGUAGE:
IN WHICH
The WORDS are deduced from their ORIGINALS,
AND
ILLUSTRATED in their DIFFERENT SIGNIFICATIONS
BY
EXAMPLES from the beſt WRITERS.
TO WHICH ARE PREFIXED,
A HISTORY of the LANGUAGE,
AND
AN ENGLISH GRAMMAR.
BY SAMUEL JOHNSON, A.M.
IN TWO VOLUMES
VOL. I.

LONDON,
Printed by W. STRAHAN,
For J. and P. KNAPTON; T. and T. LONGMAN; C. HITCH and L. HAWES;
A. MILLAR; and R. and J. DODSLEY.
MDCCLV.

▲ **Critical Viewing**
What does this title page of Johnson's *Dictionary* tell you about the contents? **INFER**

Vocabulary

caprices (kə prēs′ iz) *n.* whims

adulterations (ə dul′ tər ā′ shənz) *n.* impurities; added ingredients that are improper or inferior

Comprehension

In what condition did Johnson find the English language when he began work?

Dictionary

What do the first five paragraphs reveal about how Johnson's task differed from that of dictionary makers today?

Vocabulary

risible (riz′ ə bəl) *adj.* prompting laughter

In hope of giving longevity to that which its own nature forbids to be immortal, I have devoted this book, the labor of years, to the honor of my country, that we may no longer yield the palm of philology, without a contest to the nations of the continent. The chief glory of every people arises from its authors. Whether I shall add anything by my own writings to the reputation of English literature, must be left to time. Much of my life has been lost under the pressures of disease; much has been trifled away; and much has always been spent in provision for the day that was passing over me; but I shall not think my employment useless or ignoble, if by my assistance foreign nations and distant ages gain access to the propagators[1] of knowledge, and understand the teachers of truth; if my labors afford light to the repositories of science, and add celebrity to Bacon, to Hooker, to Milton, and to Boyle.[2]

When I am animated by this wish, I look with pleasure on my book, however defective, and deliver it to the world with the spirit of a man that has endeavored well. That it will immediately become popular, I have not promised to myself. A few wild blunders, and risible absurdities, from which no work of such multiplicity was ever free, may for a time furnish folly with laughter, and harden ignorance into contempt; but useful diligence will at last prevail, and there never can be wanting some who distinguish desert; who will consider that no dictionary of a living tongue ever can be perfect, since, while it is hastening to publication, some words are budding, and some falling away; that a whole life cannot be spent upon syntax and etymology, and that even a whole life would not be sufficient; that he, whose design includes whatever language can express, must often speak of what he does not understand; that a writer will sometimes be hurried by eagerness to the end, and sometimes faint with weariness under a task which Scaliger[3] compares to the labors of the anvil and the mine; that what is obvious is not always known, and what is known is not always present; that sudden fits of inadvertency will surprise vigilance, slight avocations[4] will seduce attention, and casual eclipses of the mind will darken learning; and that the writer shall often in vain trace his memory at the moment of need, for that which yesterday he knew with intuitive readiness, and which will come uncalled into his thoughts tomorrow.

In this work, when it shall be found that much is omitted, let it not be forgotten that much likewise is performed; and though no book was ever spared out of tenderness to the author, and the world is little solicitous to know whence proceed the faults of that which it condemns; yet it may gratify curiosity to inform it, that the *English Dictionary* was written with little assistance of the learned, and

---

1. **propagators** (präp′ ə gāt′ ərz) *n.* those who cause something to happen or to spread.
2. **Bacon . . . Boyle** writers quoted by Johnson in the *Dictionary*.
3. **Scaliger** Joseph Justus Scaliger (1540–1609), a scholar who suggested that criminals should be condemned to writing dictionaries.
4. **avocations** things that call one away or distract one from something.

without any patronage of the great; not in the soft obscurities of retirement, or under the shelter of academic bowers, but amidst inconvenience and distraction, in sickness and in sorrow. It may repress the triumph of malignant criticism to observe that if our language is not here fully displayed, I have only failed in an attempt which no human powers have hitherto completed. If the lexicons of ancient tongues, now immutably fixed and comprised in a few volumes, be yet, after the toil of successive ages, inadequate and delusive; if the aggregated knowledge and cooperating diligence of the Italian academicians did not secure them from the censure of Beni;[5] if the embodied critics of France, when fifty years had been spent upon their work, were obliged to change its economy[6] and give their second edition another form, I may surely be contented without the praise of perfection, which, if I could obtain, in this gloom of solitude, what would it avail me? I have protracted my work till most of those whom I wished to please have sunk into the grave,[7] and success and miscarriage are empty sounds: I therefore dismiss it with frigid tranquility, having little to fear or hope from censure or from praise.

Selected Entries from *A Dictionary*

athle´ tick. Strong of body; vigorous; lusty; robust.
   Science distinguishes a man of honor from one of those *athletick* brutes, whom undeservedly we call heroes. Dryden.

bang. A blow; a thump; a stroke: a low word.
   I am a bachelor. That's to say, they are fools that marry; you'll bear me a *bang* for that. Shakespeare, *Julius Caesar.*

to ba´rbecue. A term used in the West Indies for dressing a hog whole; which, being split to the backbone, is laid flat upon a large gridiron, raised about two foot above a charcoal fire, with which it is surrounded.
   Oldfield, with more than harpy throat endu'd,
   Cries, send me, gods, a whole hog *barbecu´d*. Pope.

bu´ffleheaded. A man with a large head, like a buffalo; dull; stupid; foolish.

cream. The unctuous or oily part of milk, which, when it is cold, floats on the top, and is changed by the agitation of the churn into butter; the flower of milk.

electri´city. A property in some bodies, whereby, when rubbed so as to grow warm, they draw little bits of paper, or such like substances, to them. Quincy.

5. **Beni** Paolo Beni severely criticized the first Italian dictionary.
6. **economy** organization.
7. **sunk . . . grave** Johnson's wife had died three years earlier.

Analyzing the Author's Purpose
What information in the last two paragraphs helps you determine Samuel Johnson's purpose for writing his *Dictionary?*

Comprehension
Why, according to Johnson, can "no dictionary of a living tongue ever . . . be perfect"?

Such was the account given a few years ago of electricity; but the industry of the present age, first excited by the experiments of Gray, has discovered in electricity a multitude of philosophical wonders. Bodies electrified by a sphere of glass, turned nimbly round, not only emit flame, but may be fitted with such a quantity of the electrical vapor as, if discharged at once upon a human body, would endanger life. The force of this vapor has hitherto appeared instantaneous, persons at both ends of a long chain seeming to be struck at once. The philosophers are now endeavoring to intercept the strokes of lightning.

to fu´rnace. To throw out as sparks from a furnace. A bad word.

> He *furnaces*
> The thick sighs from him. Shakespeare's
> *Cymbeline.*

gang. A number herding together; a troop; a company;

> a tribe; a herd. It is seldom used but in contempt or abhorrence.

ha´tchet-face. An ugly face; such, I suppose, as might be hewn out of a block by a hatchet.

> An ape his own dear image will embrace;
> An ugly beau adores a *hatchet-face*. Dryden.

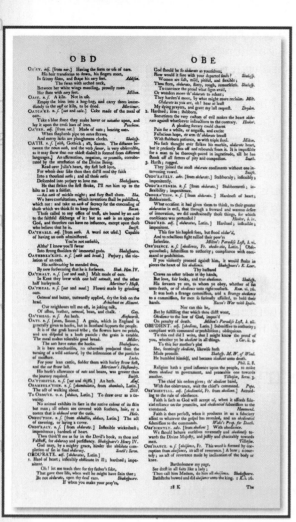

A Page from Johnson's Dictionary

lifegua´rd. The guard of a king's person.

mo´dern. In Shakespeare, vulgar; mean; common.

> We have our philosophical persons to make *modern* and familiar things supernatural and causeless. Shakespeare.

Dictionary and Style

What effect does Johnson's word choice have on his definition of *patron*?

pa´tron. One who countenances, supports or protects. Commonly a wretch who supports with insolence, and is paid with flattery.

pi´ckle. Condition; state. A word of contempt and ridicule.

> How cam'st though in this *pickle*? Shakespeare.

plu´mper. Something worn in the mouth to swell out the cheeks.

> She dex'trously her *plumpers* draws, That serve to fill her hollow jaws. Swift's *Miscellanies.*

shill-I-shall-I. A corrupt reduplication of *shall I*? The question of a man hesitating. To stand *shill-I-shall-I*, is to continue hesitating and procrastinating.

I am somewhat dainty in making a resolution, because when I make it, I keep it; I don't stand shill-I-shall-I then; if I say't, I'll do't. Congreve's *Way of the World.*

to sneeze. To emit wind audibly by the nose.

wi´llow. A tree worn by forlorn lovers.

to wipe. To cheat; to defraud.
The next bordering lords commonly encroach one upon another, as one is stronger, or lie still in wait to wipe them out of their lands. Spenser, *On Ireland.*

you´ngster, you´nker. A young person.
In contempt.

youth. The part of life succeeding to childhood and adolescence; the time from fourteen to twenty-eight.

Critical Reading

1. **Key Ideas and Details (a)** Among what class of workers does Johnson place writers of dictionaries? **(b) Infer:** What does this ranking suggest about his experience in compiling his *Dictionary*?

2. **Key Ideas and Details (a)** What did the English language lack when Johnson undertook his work? **(b) Infer:** What do you think Johnson hoped his *Dictionary* would make available to English speakers and writers?

3. **Key Ideas and Details (a)** What is Johnson's definition of *modern*? **(b) Compare and Contrast:** Compare and contrast Johnson's definition of this word with our definition of it today. Explain what different values each represents. **(c) Draw Conclusions:** What does your comparison indicate about the nature of language?

4. **Integration of Knowledge and Ideas (a) Analyze:** Which definitions are most revealing of Johnson's character and situation? **(b) Draw Conclusions:** What do these definitions reveal about Johnson?

5. **Integration of Knowledge and Ideas (a) Speculate:** Why do you think *electricity* receives such a long definition? **(b) Connect:** In what ways is Johnson similar to the scientists whose work he eagerly discusses in this entry?

6. **Integration of Knowledge and Ideas** What does Johnson's use of quotations suggest about the role of authors in shaping meanings?

7. **Integration of Knowledge and Ideas** Do you find Johnson's definitions more or less useful than those in modern dictionaries? Explain.

Cite textual evidence to support your responses.

James Boswell

(1740–1795)

Author of *The Life of Samuel Johnson*

James Boswell is perhaps the greatest biographer in English letters. In his *Life of Samuel Johnson*, he writes with vigor about his fascinating subject, training his eye on the picturesque and the grotesque.

Celebrity Chaser Born into an aristocratic family in Edinburgh, Scotland, Boswell was educated at several universities. Although he received his degree in law and was admitted to the bar in both Scotland and England, his true passion was literature. His father, a prominent judge, was angered by what he saw as his son's "shallow" values. The extremely sensitive Boswell interpreted this dissatisfaction as rejection. In an effort to overcome his low self-esteem and also find a suitable father figure, he became a celebrity chaser.

In Samuel Johnson, he found not only a friendly celebrity but also the father figure he apparently sought. Deciding to become Johnson's biographer, he devoted many years to compiling detailed records of Johnson's life.

Twentieth-Century Author Boswell's *Life of Samuel Johnson* (1791) was an acclaimed book from its first appearance. Then, in the 1920s, scholars discovered Boswell's private papers, long thought to have been destroyed. In 1950, they began publishing the journals they found among these papers—the first volume was *Boswell's London Journal* (1762–1763)—and the great biographer was reborn as a twentieth-century author!

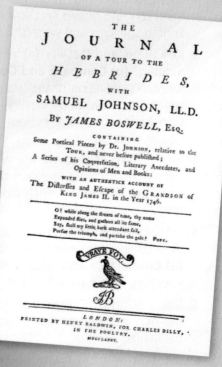

from
The Life of Samuel Johnson

James Boswell

Boswell Meets Johnson
1763

This is to me a memorable year; for in it I had the happiness to obtain the acquaintance of that extraordinary man whose memoirs I am now writing; an acquaintance which I shall ever esteem as one of the most fortunate circumstances in my life. Though then but two-and-twenty, I had for several years read his works with delight and instruction, and had the highest reverence for their author, which had grown up in my fancy into a kind of mysterious veneration, by figuring to myself a state of solemn elevated abstraction, in which I supposed him to live in the immense metropolis of London. . . .

Mr. Thomas Davies[1] the actor, who then kept a bookseller's shop in Russel Street, Covent Garden, told me that Johnson was very much his friend, and came frequently to his house, where he more than once invited me to meet him; but by some unlucky accident or other he was prevented from coming to us.

At last, on Monday the 16th day of May, when I was sitting in Mr. Davies's back parlor, after having drunk tea with him and Mrs. Davies, Johnson unexpectedly came into the shop; and Mr. Davies having perceived him through the glass door in the room in which we were sitting, advancing towards us—he announced his aweful[2] approach to me, somewhat in the manner of an actor in the part of Horatio, when he addresses Hamlet on the appearance of his father's ghost, "Look, my Lord, it comes,"[3] I found that I had a very perfect idea of Johnson's figure, from the portrait of him painted by Sir Joshua Reynolds[4] soon after he had published his *Dictionary*, in the attitude of sitting in his easy chair in deep meditation, which was

> *I had the*
> ***happiness***
> *to obtain the*
> *acquaintance of*
> *that extraordinary*
> *man . . . which*
> *I shall ever*
> *esteem as one of*
> *the most fortunate*
> *circumstances*
> *in my life.*

Comprehension

Why is 1763 "a memorable year" for Boswell?

---

1. **Thomas Davies** English bookseller and unsuccessful actor (1712–1785).
2. **aweful** awe-inspiring.
3. **Horatio ". . . it comes"** from Shakespeare's *Hamlet* (Act I, Scene iv).
4. **Sir Joshua Reynolds** celebrated portrait painter at the time (1723–1792).

Analyzing the Author's Purpose

What details in the third paragraph make Boswell's purpose for sharing the story of his first meeting with Johnson clearer?

Vocabulary

abasement (ə bās′ mənt) *n.* condition of being put down or humbled

the first picture his friend did for him, which Sir Joshua very kindly presented to me, and from which an engraving has been made for this work. Mr. Davies mentioned my name, and respectfully introduced me to him. I was much agitated; and recollecting his prejudice against the Scotch, of which I had heard much, I said to Davies, "Don't tell where I come from." "From Scotland," cried Davies roguishly. "Mr. Johnson," said I, "I do indeed come from Scotland, but I cannot help it." I am willing to flatter myself that I meant this as light pleasantry to soothe and conciliate him, and not as an humiliating abasement at the expense of my country. But however that might be, this speech was somewhat unlucky; for with that quickness of wit for which he was so remarkable, he seized the expression "come from Scotland," which I used in the sense of being of that country; and, as if I had said that I had come away from it, or left, retorted, "That, Sir, I find, is what a very great many of your countrymen cannot help." This stroke stunned me a good deal; and when we had sat down, I felt myself not a little embarrassed, and apprehensive of what might come next. He then addressed himself to Davies: "What do you think of Garrick?[5] He has refused me an order for the play for Miss Williams, because he knows the house will be full, and that an order would be worth three shillings." Eager to take any opening to get into conversation with him, I ventured to say, "O, Sir, I cannot think Mr. Garrick would grudge such a trifle to you." "Sir," said he, with a stern look, "I have known David Garrick longer than you have done: and I know no right you have to talk to me on the subject." Perhaps I deserved this check; for it was rather presumptuous in me, an entire stranger, to express any doubt of the justice of his animadversion upon his old acquaintance and pupil. I now felt myself much mortified, and began to think that the hope which I had long indulged of obtaining his acquaintance was blasted. And, in truth, had not my ardor been uncommonly strong, and my resolution uncommonly persevering, so rough a reception might have deterred me forever from making any further attempts. Fortunately, however, I remained upon the field not wholly discomfited; and was soon rewarded by hearing some of his conversation, of which I preserved the following short minute,[6] without marking the questions and observations by which it was produced.

"People," he remarked, "may be taken in once, who imagine that an author is greater in private life than other men. Uncommon parts require uncommon opportunities for their exertion."

"In barbarous society, superiority of parts is of real consequence. Great strength or great wisdom is of much value to an individual. But in more polished times there are people to do everything for money; and then there are a number of other superiorities, such as those of

---

5. Garrick David Garrick (1717–1779), a famous actor who had been educated by Johnson. Garrick was also one of the managing partners of the Drury Lane Theatre in London.
6. minute note.

birth and fortune, and rank, that dissipate men's attention, and leave no extraordinary share of respect for personal and intellectual superiority. This is wisely ordered by Providence, to preserve some equality among mankind."

"Sir, this book (*The Elements of Criticism*,[7] which he had taken up) is a pretty essay, and deserves to be held in some estimation, though much of it is chimerical."

Speaking of one[8] who with more than ordinary boldness attacked public measures and the royal family, he said, "I think he is safe from the law, but he is an abusive scoundrel; and instead of applying to my Lord Chief Justice to punish him, I would send half a dozen footmen and have him well ducked."[9]

"The notion of liberty amuses the people of England, and helps to keep off the *taedium vitae*.[10] When a butcher tells you that his heart bleeds for his country, he has, in fact, no uneasy feeling."

"Sheridan[11] will not succeed at Bath with his oratory. Ridicule has gone down before him, and, I doubt,[12] Derrick[13] is his enemy."

"Derrick may do very well, as long as he can outrun his character; but the moment his character gets up with him, it is all over."

It is, however, but just to record, that some years afterwards, when I reminded him of this sarcasm, he said, "Well, but Derrick has now got a character that he need not run away from."

I was highly pleased with the extraordinary vigor of his conversation, and regretted that I was drawn away from it by an engagement at another place. I had, for a part of the evening, been left alone with him, and had ventured to make an observation now and then, which he received very civilly; so that I was satisfied that though there was a roughness in his manner, there was no ill nature in his disposition. Davies followed me to the door, and when I complained to him a little of the hard blows which the great man had given me he kindly took upon him to console me by saying, "Don't be uneasy. I can see he likes you very well."

I was highly pleased with the **extraordinary** *vigor of his conversation . . .*

Comprehension
What quality of Johnson's conversation pleased Boswell?

---

7. *The Elements of Criticism* one of the works of Scottish philosophical writer Henry Home (1696–1782).

8. one John Wilkes (1727–1797), an English political agitator.

9. ducked tied to a chair at the end of a plank and plunged into water.

10. *taedium vitae* (tē´ dē əm vī´ tē) boredom.

11. Sheridan Thomas Sheridan (1719–1788), an Irish actor and author. At the time, Sheridan was reading lectures at the Oratory at Bath.

12. doubt fear.

13. Derrick the Master of Ceremonies of the Oratory at Bath.

▲ Critical Viewing
This engraving shows the ghost of Samuel Johnson haunting Boswell. In what ways does the relationship between the men that it portrays reflect the relationship suggested by Boswell's *Life*? **INTERPRET**

Johnson's Character

The character of Samuel Johnson has, I trust, been so developed in the course of this work, that they who have honored it with a perusal, may be considered as well acquainted with him. As, however, it may be expected that I should collect into one view the capital and distinguishing features of this extraordinary man, I shall endeavor to acquit myself of that part of my biographical undertaking, however difficult it may be to do that which many of my readers will do better for themselves.

His figure was large and well formed, and his countenance of the cast of an ancient statue; yet his appearance was rendered strange and somewhat uncouth by convulsive cramps, by the scars of that distemper[14] which it was once imagined the royal touch could cure,[15] and by a slovenly mode of dress. He had the use only of one eye; yet

---

14. **distemper** scrofula, a type of tuberculosis that causes swelling and scarring of the neck.
15. **royal touch . . . cure** it was at one time believed that the touch of an English monarch had the power to heal. As a child Johnson was taken to Queen Anne to receive her touch in the hope that it would cure him.

so much does mind govern and even supply the deficiency of organs, that his visual perceptions, as far as they extended, were uncommonly quick and accurate. So morbid was his temperament, that he never knew the natural joy of a free and vigorous use of his limbs: when he walked, it was like the struggling gait of one in fetters; when he rode, he had no command or direction of his horse, but was carried as if in a balloon. That with his constitution and habits of life he should have lived seventy-five years, is a proof that an inherent *vivida vis*[16] is a powerful preservative of the human frame.

Man is, in general, made up of contradictory qualities; and these will ever show themselves in strange succession, where a consistency in appearance at least, if not in reality, has not been attained by long habits of philosophical discipline. In proportion to the native vigor of the mind, the contradictory qualities will be the more prominent, and more difficult to be adjusted; and, therefore, we are not to wonder that Johnson exhibited an eminent example of this remark which I have made upon human nature. At different times, he seemed a different man, in some respects; not, however, in any great or essential article, upon which he had fully employed his mind, and settled certain principles of duty, but only in his manners and in the display of argument and fancy in his talk. He was prone to superstition, but not to credulity. Though his imagination might incline him to a belief of the marvelous and the mysterious, his vigorous reason examined the evidence with jealousy.[17] He was a sincere and zealous Christian, of high Church of England and monarchical principles, which he would not tamely suffer to be questioned; and had, perhaps, at an early period, narrowed his mind somewhat too much, both as to religion and politics. His being impressed with the danger of extreme latitude in either, though he was of a very independent spirit, occasioned his appearing somewhat unfavorable to the prevalence of that noble freedom of sentiment which is the best possession of man. Nor can it be denied, that he had many prejudices; which, however, frequently suggested many of his pointed sayings that rather show a playfulness of fancy than any settled malignity. He was steady and inflexible in maintaining the obligations of religion and morality; both from a regard for the order of society, and from a veneration for the Great Source of all order; correct, nay, stern in his taste; hard to please, and easily offended; impetuous and irritable in his temper, but of a most humane and benevolent heart, which showed itself not only in a most liberal charity, as far as his circumstances would allow, but in a thousand instances of active benevolence. He was afflicted with a bodily disease, which made him often restless and fretful; and with a constitutional melancholy, the clouds of which darkened the brightness of his fancy, and gave a gloomy cast to his whole course of thinking: we, therefore, ought not to wonder at his sallies

Vocabulary

credulity (krə doo′ lə tē) *n.* tendency to believe too readily

malignity (mə lig′ nə tē) *n.* strong desire to harm others

Comprehension

What are some of Johnson's "contradictory qualities"?

---

16. *vivida vis* lively force.
17. jealousy suspicion.

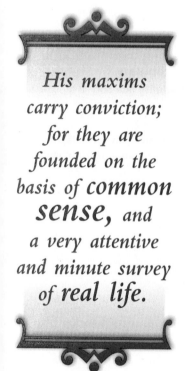

*His maxims carry conviction; for they are founded on the basis of **common sense,** and a very attentive and minute survey of **real life.***

of impatience and passion at any time; especially when provoked by obtrusive ignorance, or presuming petulance; and allowance must be made for his uttering hasty and satirical sallies even against his best friends. And, surely, when it is considered, that, "amidst sickness and sorrow," he exerted his faculties in so many works for the benefit of mankind, and particularly that he achieved the great and admirable Dictionary of our language, we must be astonished at his resolution. The solemn text, "of him to whom much is given, much will be required," seems to have been ever present to his mind, in a rigorous sense, and to have made him dissatisfied with his labors and acts of goodness, however comparatively great; so that the unavoidable consciousness of his superiority was, in that respect, a cause of disquiet. He suffered so much from this, and from the gloom which perpetually haunted him and made solitude frightful, that it may be said of him, "If in this life only he had hope, he was of all men most miserable."[18] He loved praise, when it was brought to him; but was too proud to seek for it. He was somewhat susceptible of flattery. As he was general and unconfined in his studies, he cannot be considered as master of any one particular science; but he had accumulated a vast and various collection of learning and knowledge, which was so arranged in his mind, as to be ever in readiness to be brought forth. But his superiority over other learned men consisted chiefly in what may be called the art of thinking, the art of using his mind; a certain continual power of seizing the useful substance of all that he knew and exhibiting it in a clear and forcible manner; so that knowledge, which we often see to be no better than lumber[19] in men of dull understanding, was, in him, true, evident, and actual wisdom. His moral precepts are practical; for they are drawn from an intimate acquaintance with human nature. His maxims carry conviction; for they are founded on the basis of common sense, and a very attentive and minute survey of real life. His mind was so full of imagery, that he might have been perpetually a poet; yet it is remarkable, that, however rich his prose is in this respect, his poetical pieces, in general, have not much of that splendor, but are rather distinguished by strong sentiment and acute observation, conveyed in harmonious and energetic verse, particularly in heroic couplets. Though usually grave, and even aweful, in his deportment, he possessed uncommon and peculiar powers of wit and humor; he frequently indulged himself in colloquial pleasantry; and the heartiest merriment was often enjoyed in his company; with this great advantage, that as it was entirely free from any poisonous tincture of vice or impiety, it was salutary to those who shared in it. He had accustomed himself to such accuracy in his common conversation, that he at all times expressed his thoughts with great force, and an elegant choice of language,

---

18. "If . . . miserable" from I Corinthians 15:19.
19. lumber rubbish.

the effect of which was aided by his having a loud voice, and a slow deliberate utterance. In him were united a most logical head with a most fertile imagination, which gave him an extraordinary advantage in arguing: for he could reason close or wide, as he saw best for the moment. Exulting in his intellectual strength and dexterity, he could, when he pleased, be the greatest sophist[20] that ever contended in the lists of declamation; and, from a spirit of contradiction and a delight in showing his powers, he would often maintain the wrong side with equal warmth and ingenuity; so that, when there was an audience, his real opinions could seldom be gathered from his talk; though when he was in company with a single friend, he would discuss a subject with genuine fairness: but he was too conscientious to make error permanent and pernicious[21], by deliberately writing it; and, in all his numerous works, he earnestly inculcated[22] what appeared to him to be the truth; his piety being constant, and the ruling principle of all his conduct.

Such was Samuel Johnson, a man whose talents, acquirements, and virtues, were so extraordinary, that the more his character is considered the more he will be regarded by the present age, and by posterity, with admiration and reverence.

---

20. sophist (säf´ ist) *n.* one who makes clever, apparently plausible arguments.
21. pernicious (pər nish´ əs) *adj.* wicked; evil.
22. inculcated (in kul´ kāt´ əd) *v.* to teach by repetition and urging.

Critical Reading

1. **Key Ideas and Details (a)** How did Boswell meet Johnson?
   (b) Infer: What does their conversation at that meeting tell you about each of them?

2. **Key Ideas and Details (a)** What are some of the topics Johnson discusses that Boswell records "without marking the questions and observations" that produced them?
   (b) Infer: What do Johnson's opinions on these topics suggest about his interests and knowledge?

3. **Key Ideas and Details (a)** Briefly summarize Boswell's remarks on Johnson's character. **(b) Evaluate:** Would Johnson have been less interesting if he had been less "contradictory"? Explain.

4. **Integration of Knowledge and Ideas** Which label, if any, suits each author better, inventor or conservator? Explain. In your response, use at least two of these Essential Question words: *commentary, conventional, authentic.* [**Connecting to the Essential Question: What is the relationship of the writer to tradition?**]

Cite textual evidence to support your responses.

Literary Analysis

1. **Key Ideas and Details Analyze Johnson's purpose** for writing his *Dictionary* by reviewing the Preface. **(a)** Which passage best expresses his purpose? Why? **(b)** Do you think Johnson achieved this purpose? Why or why not? **(c)** Explain how knowing Johnson's purpose helps you understand why he included quotations from famous authors in many definitions.

2. **Integration of Knowledge and Ideas** Use a chart like the one shown to compare the definition of a word in Johnson's *Dictionary* with its definition in a modern **dictionary.**

Johnson's *Dictionary*	Modern Dictionary	Similarities/ Differences

3. **Key Ideas and Details (a)** Identify a passage revealing Boswell's purpose for writing. **(b)** How does his purpose explain the space he devotes to his meeting with Johnson?

4. **Craft and Structure (a)** Find three examples of facts and three examples of opinions in the **biography** written by Boswell. **(b)** Which is more revealing of Johnson's character, the facts or the opinions? Why?

5. **Craft and Structure** Find passages from the Preface to the *Dictionary* and from *The Life of Samuel Johnson* that show the formality of the **diction** of the eighteenth-century Enlightenment.

6. **Integration of Knowledge and Ideas** Citing specific passages, contrast Johnson's mixed *tone* of discouragement and pride in the Preface with Boswell's unmixed tone of admiration in *Life*.

7. **Integration of Knowledge and Ideas** Referring to specific passages, demonstrate how both works strive to accomplish an Enlightenment goal of bringing order to messy reality.

8. **Analyzing Visual Information** Using what you know about Johnson and Boswell, explain the humor of the cartoon shown on this page.

Common Core State Standards

Reading Informational Text

9. Analyze seventeenth-, eighteenth-, and nineteenth-century foundational U.S. documents of historical and literary significance for their themes, purposes, and rhetorical features. *(p. 663)*

Writing

9.b. Apply *grades 11–12 Reading standards* to literary nonfiction. (p. 663)

Language

4.c. Consult general and specialized reference materials, both print and digital, to find the pronunciation of a word or determine or clarify its precise meaning, its part of speech, its etymology, or its standard usage. *(p. 663)*

"More port for Dr. Johnson. And more ink for Mr. Boswell." ▶

Vocabulary Acquisition and Use

Word Analysis: Latin Root -dict-

The Latin root -dict- conveys the idea of something said. In *dictionary*, it refers to the words "said" in a language. The root also appears in the word *dictator*, which means "a ruler whose pronouncements are the final word." Knowing the meaning of the root -dict-, use context clues to infer the meaning of each italicized word listed here. Then, use a dictionary to verify your inferences.

1. During the Napoleonic Wars, Britain sought to *interdict* the flow of goods to France.
2. In the British legal system, a person must be *indicted* before being tried.
3. A Supreme Court judge releases a *dictum* of his or her position after many cases.
4. Dictators issue *edicts*, but in Britain, Parliament makes the laws.
5. In the past, secretaries used shorthand to record messages *dictated* by their bosses.
6. Skilled playwrights control the *diction* of each character to reflect his or her background.

Vocabulary: Cognates

Cognates are words that share a common origin but may have different meanings. For instance, *patron*, one of Johnson's dictionary entries, shares its origin with *paternal* ("fatherly"). Both come from the Latin *pater*, which means "father." Cognates can also occur across languages, like the English word *night* and the German word *nacht*. Study the pairs of words from Johnson's Preface and Boswell's *Life* that follow. Determine whether each pair is a cognate, explaining your reasoning. Then, check the words in a dictionary to see if you were correct.

1. *caprices* ("whims") and *capacity* ("volume")
2. *adulterations* ("impurities") and *adult* ("individual who has reached maturity")
3. *risible* ("laughable") and *ridiculous* ("deserving ridicule")
4. *abasement* ("being put down") and *debase* ("to corrupt")
5. *malignity* ("desire to harm others") and *aligned* ("in line with")

Writing to Sources

Informative Text James Boswell's *The Life of Samuel Johnson* and Benjamin Franklin's *The Autobiography* are two eighteenth-century classics. Find a copy of Franklin's autobiography (or download it from a Web site, such as the Gutenberg Project, that provides classic works free of charge), and read his account of his first entry into Philadelphia. Then, write an **essay** comparing two "firsts": Boswell's introduction to Dr. Johnson and Franklin's arrival in Philadelphia. Discuss whether Johnson, an Englishman, and Franklin, a colonial American, possess similar traits or share certain values.

Prewriting As you read both texts, take notes about the ways in which each man presents his younger self. Consider the personality traits each displays and the qualities each seems to value, both in himself and others. Review your findings to arrive at a thesis.

> **Model: Revising for Impact**
> At his first meeting with Dr. Johnson, young Boswell felt ~~overwhelmed with a sense of awe and a little fearful.~~
> awestruck and intimidated.

Specific language makes an essay stronger.

Drafting Organize your ideas logically, so that your discussion explores the two texts clearly. Support your ideas with quotations from each work.

Revising Review your draft, highlighting any awkward or wordy phrasing. Revise with more concise and precise word choices.

Connecting to the Essential Question Like each of these authors, you might sometimes seek out a special landscape or place when you want to think things over. Noting the qualities of each author's special place as you read will help as you consider the Essential Question: **What is the relationship between literature and place?**

Close Reading Focus

Pre-Romantic Poetry

Eighteenth-century **Pre-Romantic poetry** shares characteristics of two different styles. Like earlier, Neoclassical, poetry, Pre-Romantic poetry is characterized by these features:

- the polished expression of ideas
- the use of balanced phrases and sophisticated vocabulary

At the same time, Pre-Romantic poetry anticipates Romantic literature by introducing these elements:

- a new focus on nature and the life of common folk
- the expression of heightened, sometimes nameless, feelings

Look for all these characteristics as you read the following poems.

Comparing Literary Works Like the Romantics who come after them, Gray and Finch express heightened feelings in their poetry. Gray's stroll through a country churchyard lets him discover life's true value. Finch's nighttime walk allows her to feel a deep connection with nature. As you read, compare the emotions these poets experience and analyze two or more themes or central ideas in the poems. Consider how these themes develop and build on one another to produce a deeper meaning.

Preparing to Read Complex Texts **Determine the essential message,** or main idea, of a passage in a poem by *paraphrasing* it—identifying its key ideas and restating them in your own words. Use a chart like the one shown to paraphrase passages from these poems as you read.

Vocabulary

The words below are important to understanding the texts that follow. Copy the words into your notebook, separating them into three-syllable and four-syllable words.

penury   nocturnal

circumscribed   temperate

ingenuous   venerable

**Common Core
State Standards**

Reading Literature
2. Determine two or more themes or central ideas of a text and analyze their development over the course of the text, including how they interact and build on one another to produce a complex account.

Original
"Now fades the glimmering landscape on the sight,..."

Paraphrase
Nightfall is making it difficult to see the landscape.

Thomas Gray

(1716–1771)

Author of "Elegy Written in a Country Churchyard"

The uncertainty of life was something that Thomas Gray understood all too well. The only one of twelve Gray children to survive infancy, he suffered from convulsions as a child. On at least one occasion, his mother was forced to open a vein to relieve the pressure on his brain.

Lavishing affection on her sickly son, Gray's mother saved money from the shop she kept in London and sent him to Eton and Cambridge.

A Quiet Life After making the Grand Tour of Europe with his friend the author Horace Walpole, Gray lived with his mother and aunts in the sleepy village of Stoke Poges. There, in the summer of 1742, he wrote his first important poems. The church and graveyard at Stoke Poges probably inspired his best-known poem, "Elegy Written in a Country Churchyard."

A Near Mishap This beloved poem nearly went astray. Gray sent a copy to Walpole, and it fell into the hands of a dishonest editor. It was retrieved only after a struggle. In the end, the poem came to belong to its readers: It contains some of the best-remembered lines in English poetry.

A Lonely Romantic After age thirty, Gray returned to Cambridge, where he studied classical literature and Celtic and Norse mythology. He died after an attack of gout. His literary output was small—he wrote slowly, striving for perfection—but his poems are counted among the finest in the English language. In them, he expresses new, Romantic yearnings in the formal style of his times. The poet Matthew Arnold suggested that if Gray had lived in another era, his accomplishments might have been even greater.

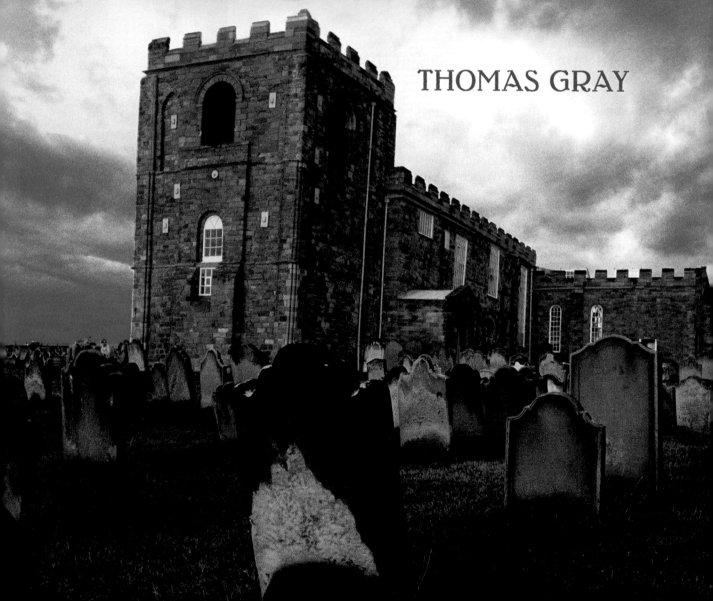

Elegy Written in a Country Churchyard

THOMAS GRAY

▲ **Critical Viewing** The churchyard in this photograph looks untended and forgotten. How does the photograph reflect the meaning of Gray's poem? **DEDUCE**

BACKGROUND In the eighteenth century, many writers championed reason, clarity, and logic. These values led to the articulate, eloquent couplets of Alexander Pope. They also led to the major scientific discoveries of Sir Isaac Newton, of whom Pope wrote: "God said, Let Newton be! And there was light!" These values might be thought of as belonging to daylight. In contrast, the poems in this grouping are set at twilight or at night. They stress emotion—the not-always-reasonable reaction to circumstances—and mystery—those longings and intuitions of human experience that are not clearly communicable or analyzable. By stressing these "night-time" qualities, these poets anticipate the artistic movement called Romanticism.

The curfew tolls the knell of parting day,
    The lowing herd winds slowly o'er the lea,[1]
The plowman homeward plods his weary way,
    And leaves the world to darkness and to me.

5 Now fades the glimmering landscape on the sight,
    And all the air a solemn stillness holds,
Save where the beetle wheels his droning flight,
    And drowsy tinklings lull the distant folds;

Save that from yonder ivy-mantled tower,
10   The moping owl does to the moon complain
Of such as, wandering near her secret bower,
    Molest her ancient solitary reign.

Beneath those rugged elms, that yew tree's shade,
    Where heaves the turf in many a moldering heap,
15 Each in his narrow cell forever laid,
    The rude[2] forefathers of the hamlet sleep.

---

1. **lea** meadow.
2. **rude** uneducated.

Comprehension
At what time of day is the poem set?

    The breezy call of incense-breathing morn,
        The swallow twittering from the straw-built shed,
    The cock's shrill clarion, or the echoing horn,[3]
20   No more shall rouse them from their lowly bed.

    For them no more the blazing hearth shall burn,
        Or busy housewife ply her evening care;
    No children run to lisp their sire's return,
        Or climb his knees the envied kiss to share.

25   Oft did the harvest to their sickle yield,
        Their furrow oft the stubborn glebe[4] has broke;
    How jocund[5] did they drive their team afield!
        How bowed the woods beneath their sturdy stroke!

    Let not Ambition mock their useful toil,
30   Their homely joys, and destiny obscure;
    Nor Grandeur hear with a disdainful smile
        The short and simple annals of the poor.

    The boast of heraldry,[6] the pomp of power,
        And all that beauty, all that wealth e'er gave,
35   Awaits alike the inevitable hour.
        The paths of glory lead but to the grave.

    Nor you, ye proud, impute to these the fault,
        If memory o'er their tomb no trophies[7] raise,
    Where through the long-drawn aisle and fretted vault[8]
40   The pealing anthem swells the note of praise.

    Can storied urn,[9] or animated[10] bust,
        Back to its mansion call the fleeting breath?
    Can honor's voice provoke[11] the silent dust,
        Or Flattery soothe the dull cold ear of Death?

45   Perhaps in this neglected spot is laid
        Some heart once pregnant with celestial fire;
    Hands, that the rod of empire might have swayed,
        Or waked to ecstasy the living lyre.

3. **clarion . . . horn** A clarion is a trumpet. The horn is a hunter's horn.
4. **glebe** soil.
5. **jocund** cheerful.
6. **heraldry** noble descent.
7. **trophies** symbolic figures or pictures depicting the achievements of the dead man.
8. **fretted vault** church ceiling decorated with intersecting lines.
9. **storied urn** funeral urn with an epitaph inscribed on it.
10. **animated** lifelike.
11. **provoke** call forth.

But Knowledge to their eyes her ample page
50   Rich with the spoils of time did ne'er unroll;
Chill Penury repressed their noble rage,
         And froze the genial current of the soul.

Full many a gem of purest ray serene
         The dark unfathomed caves of ocean bear:
55   Full many a flower is born to blush unseen,
         And waste its sweetness on the desert air.

Some village Hampden,[12] that, with dauntless breast,
         The little tyrant of his fields withstood,
Some mute inglorious Milton[13] here may rest,
60   Some Cromwell[14] guiltless of his country's blood.

The applause of listening senates to command,
         The threats of pain and ruin to despise,
To scatter plenty o'er a smiling land,
         And read their history in a nation's eyes,

65   Their lot forbade: nor circumscribed alone
         Their growing virtues, but their crimes confined
Forbade to wade through slaughter to a throne,
         And shut the gates of mercy on mankind,

The struggling pangs of conscious truth to hide,
70   To quench the blushes of ingenuous shame,
Or heap the shrine of Luxury and Pride
         With incense kindled at the Muse's flame.

Far from the madding[15] crowd's ignoble[16] strife,
         Their sober wishes never learned to stray;
75   Along the cool sequestered vale of life
         They kept the noiseless tenor[17] of their way.

Yet even these bones from insult to protect
         Some frail memorial still erected nigh,
With uncouth rhymes and shapeless sculpture decked,[18]
80   Implores the passing tribute of a sigh.

---

12. **Hampden** John Hampden (1594–1643), an English statesman who defied King Charles I, resisting the king's efforts to circumvent Parliament.
13. **Milton** English poet, John Milton (1608–1674).
14. **Cromwell** Oliver Cromwell (1599–1658), English revolutionary leader who defeated King Charles I and ruled England as Lord Protector of the Commonwealth from 1653 to 1658.
15. **madding** frenzied.
16. **ignoble** (ig nō´ bəl) *adj.* not noble; common.
17. **tenor** general tendency or course.
18. **Some . . . decked** contrasts with "the storied urn[s] or animated bust[s]" (line 41) inside the church.

Vocabulary
penury (pen´ yoo rē)
n. poverty

Pre-Romantic Poetry

How do the images in lines 53–56 give the reader a powerful sense of what is unknown or lost?

Vocabulary
circumscribed (sur´ kəm skrībd) *v.* limited; confined
ingenuous (in jen´ yoo əs) *adj.* naive; simple

Comprehension

About whom is the speaker speculating?

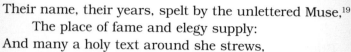

Their name, their years, spelt by the unlettered Muse,[19]
    The place of fame and elegy supply:
And many a holy text around she strews,
    That teach the rustic moralist to die.

85 For who, to dumb Forgetfulness a prey,
    This pleasing anxious being e'er resigned,
Left the warm precincts of the cheerful day,
    Nor cast one longing lingering look behind?

    On some fond breast the parting soul relies,
90   Some pious drops[20] the closing eye requires;
Even from the tomb the voice of Nature cries,
    Even in our ashes live their wonted fires.

For thee,[21] who, mindful of the unhonored dead,
    Dost in these lines their artless tale relate;
95 If chance, by lonely contemplation led,
    Some kindred spirit shall enquire thy fate,

Haply[22] some hoary-headed swain[23] may say,
    "Oft have we seen him at the peep of dawn
Brushing with hasty steps the dews away,
100   To meet the sun upon the upland lawn.

"There at the foot of yonder nodding beech,
    That wreathes its old fantastic roots so high,
His listless length at noontide would he stretch,
    And pore upon the brook that babbles by.

105 "Hard by yon wood, now smiling as in scorn,
    Muttering his wayward fancies he would rove;
Now drooping, woeful wan, like one forlorn,
    Or crazed with care, or crossed in hopeless love.

"One morn I missed him on the customed hill,
110   Along the heath, and near his favorite tree;
Another came; nor yet beside the rill,[24]
    Nor up the lawn, nor at the wood was he;

---

19. the unlettered Muse In Greek mythology, the Muses were goddesses who inspired artists and writers. *Unlettered* means "uneducated."
20. drops tears.
21. thee Gray himself.
22. Haply perhaps.
23. hoary-headed swain white-haired country laborer.
24. rill brook.

Paraphrasing
Express the key idea of lines 85–88 in your own words.

Pre-Romantic Poetry
What intense, perhaps irrational feelings are expressed in lines 89–92?

"The next, with dirges due in sad array
        Slow through the churchway path we saw him borne.
115 Approach and read (for thou canst read) the lay
        Graved on the stone beneath yon aged thorn."[25]

The Epitaph

Here rests his head upon the lap of Earth
        A youth, to Fortune and to Fame unknown.
Fair Science[26] frowned not on his humble birth,
120   And melancholy marked him for her own.

Large was his bounty, and his soul sincere,
        Heaven did a recompense as largely send:
He gave to misery (all he had) a tear,
        He gained from Heaven ('twas all he wished) a friend.

125 No farther seek his merits to disclose,
        Or draw his frailties from their dread abode
(There they alike in trembling hope repose),
        The bosom of his Father and his God.

---

25. **thorn** hawthorn tree.
26. **Science** learning.

Critical Reading

1. **Key Ideas and Details** Who are the forefathers to whom the speaker refers in line 16? **(b) Interpret:** In line 35, what is the "inevitable hour" that the rich and ambitious share with their forefathers?

2. **Key Ideas and Details** According to lines 45–48, what types of people might lie among the forefathers? **(b) Infer:** Why did the forefathers not fulfill their potential? **(c) Interpret:** In what way do the images of the gem and the flower in lines 53–56 express the idea of unfulfilled potential?

3. **Key Ideas and Details** **(a) Summarize:** What mark have the forefathers left on history? **(b) Connect:** According to lines 77–84, how is their memory preserved? **(c) Interpret:** What do lines 85–92 suggest about the need to be remembered after death?

4. **Key Ideas and Details** **(a) Summarize:** By what standards is the life of the speaker measured in "The Epitaph"? **(b) Draw Conclusions:** What insight into life does the speaker reach?

5. **Integration of Knowledge and Ideas** Do you find the feelings in the poem artificial or moving? Explain.

Cite textual evidence to support your responses.

ANNE FINCH
Countess of Winchilsea (*1661–1720*)

Author of "A Nocturnal Reverie"

Anne Kingsmill Finch, Countess of Winchilsea, lived in an era that rejected women intellectuals. Even her friend Alexander Pope poked fun at her, satirizing her as the character Phoebe Clinket in the play *Three Hours After Marriage*. Despite this mockery, Finch pursued her interest in poetry, publishing a volume of verse in 1713, during an era when publication by women was rare.

An Uncertain Childhood Anne Kingsmill's father died when she was only five months old, and three years later her mother died as well. For eight years, she and her sister, Bridget, lived with their grandmother, while their brother, William, lived with an uncle. The children were reunited under their uncle's care in 1672. By the standards of the day, the girls' education was quite progressive. Anne studied classical Greek and Roman literature, the Bible, French, Italian, history, poetry, and drama.

A Poet and Countess In 1682, Anne Kingsmill left home to become a maid of honor to the wife of the duke of York, later James II. In the duke's household, she met her husband, Heneage Finch.

When James II was driven from power in 1688, the Finches endured a period of poverty until Heneage Finch inherited the title Earl of Winchilsea and an estate at Eastwell in Kent. Many of Anne Finch's poems celebrate the rural pleasures of Eastwell.

Though she was not the most famous of poets, her work had an impact on later writers. In 1800, Romantic poet William Wordsworth praised her in the Preface to his groundbreaking book, *Lyrical Ballads*.

A Nocturnal Reverie

Anne Finch, Countess of Winchilsea

> In such a night, when every louder wind
> Is to its distant cavern safe confined;
> And only gentle Zephyr[1] fans his wings,
> And lonely Philomel,[2] still waking, sings;
> 5   Or from some tree, famed for the owl's delight,

---

1. **Zephyr** (zef´ ər) in Greek myth, the west wind; a breeze.
2. **Philomel** (fil´ ō mel´) in Greek myth, nightingale.

Cottage and Pond, Moonlight, Thomas Gainsborough, Victoria and Albert Museum, London

▲ **Critical Viewing** What visual elements in this picture help create a mood like that of the poem? **ANALYZE**

Vocabulary

nocturnal (näk tʉr´ nəl) *adj.* occurring at night

Vocabulary

temperate (tem´ pər it) *adj.* mild

venerable (ven´ ər ə bəl) *adj.* commanding respect because of age, character, or social rank

She, hollowing clear, directs the wanderer right:
In such a night, when passing clouds give place,
Or thinly veil the heavens' mysterious face;
When in some river, overhung with green,

10 The waving moon and trembling leaves are seen;
When freshened grass now bears itself upright,
And makes cool banks to pleasing rest invite,
Whence springs the woodbind, and the bramble-rose,
And where the sleepy cowslip sheltered grows;

15 Whilst now a paler hue the foxglove takes,
Yet checkers still with red the dusky brakes:[3]
When scattered glow-worms, but in twilight fine,
Show trivial beauties watch their hour to shine;
Whilst Salisbury[4] stands the test of every light,

20 In perfect charms, and perfect virtue bright:
When odors, which declined repelling day,
Through temperate air uninterrupted stray;
When darkened groves their softest shadows wear,
And falling waters we distinctly hear;

25 When through the gloom more venerable shows
Some ancient fabric,[5] awful in repose,
While sunburnt hills their swarthy looks conceal,
And swelling haycocks thicken up the vale:
When the loosed horse now, as his pasture leads,

30 Comes slowly grazing through the adjoining meads,[6]
Whose stealing pace, and lengthened shade we fear,
Till torn-up forage[7] in his teeth we hear:
When nibbling sheep at large pursue their food,
And unmolested kine[8] rechew the cud;

---

3. **brakes** overgrown areas; thickets.
4. **Salisbury** This may refer to a Lady Salisbury, daughter of a friend, not to the town of Salisbury.
5. **ancient fabric** edifice or large, imposing building.
6. **meads** archaic term for meadows.
7. **forage** (fôr ij) *n.* food grazed for by animals.
8. **kine** archaic plural of cow; cattle.

35 When curlews cry beneath the village walls,
    And to her straggling brood the partridge calls;
    Their shortlived jubilee the creatures keep,
    Which but endures, whilst tyrant man does sleep;
    When a sedate content the spirit feels,
40 And no fierce light disturbs, whilst it reveals;
    But silent musings urge the mind to seek
    Something, too high for syllables to speak;
    Till the free soul to a composedness charmed,
    Finding the elements of rage disarmed,
45 O'er all below a solemn quiet grown,
    Joys in the inferior world, and thinks it like her own:
    In such a night let me abroad remain,
    Till morning breaks, and all's confused again;
    Our cares, our toils, our clamors are renewed,
50 Or pleasures, seldom reached, again pursued.

Critical Reading

1. **Key Ideas and Details (a)** Describe the setting of the poem, listing specific images from lines 1–24. **(b) Analyze:** What mood do these images create?

2. **Key Ideas and Details (a) Analyze:** Outline the steps that lead from the speaker's "sedate content" to her joy (lines 39–46). **(b) Interpret:** How does the natural world charm the speaker to "composedness"?

3. **Key Ideas and Details (a) Infer:** What is the relation between people and their "pleasures" in line 50? **(b) Compare and Contrast:** What is the main difference between the pursuit of pleasures and the "composedness" caused by nature?

4. **Integration of Knowledge and Ideas** If the speaker were taking a nocturnal walk in modern times, do you think her reactions to nature would be the same? Explain.

5. **Integration of Knowledge and Ideas** What qualities of a special place help each author to draw conclusions about life? In your response, use at least two of these Essential Question words: *nature, country, isolation.* [Connecting to the Essential Question: What is the relationship between literature and place?]

Cite textual evidence to support your responses.

Literary Analysis

1. **Key Ideas and Details** *Paraphrase* to **determine the essential message** in lines 29–32 of Gray's "Elegy" and lines 47–50 of "A Nocturnal Reverie."

2. **Key Ideas and Details (a)** What feelings do lines 89–92 of Gray's "Elegy" convey? **(b)** Compare these feelings to the feelings in lines 39–46 of "A Nocturnal Reverie," using a chart like the one shown.

Lines	Stated Ideas	Feelings Expressed	Themes, or Messages, About Life

3. **Integration of Knowledge and Ideas** Explain what is **Pre-Romantic** about Gray's concern for the unknown dead of a country graveyard and Finch's loving attention to humble "creatures." How do these *themes* anticipate Romanticism?

Vocabulary Acquisition and Use

Use a different vocabulary word from page 664 in place of each familiar underlined word. Explain your choices.

The <u>respected</u> old woman wanted to overcome the <u>poverty</u> in the village. She told young people that <u>nighttime</u> reading could help them escape a <u>limited</u> life. She risked the danger that her <u>mild</u> manner would make her seem <u>naive</u>.

Writing to Sources

Explanatory Text The recitation of poetry requires attention to performance details to convey the meaning of a poem in a way that is forceful and clear. Choose a brief passage from one of these poems and write **directions** for reciting it. In order to write effective directions for recitation, you must first analyze the passage and understand its meaning. A good recitation will enliven the passage and make the passage's meaning clearer for the audience. Your performance directions should include the following:

- Identify which words to emphasize and where to pause.
- Explain when to change volume or pitch.
- Tell how eye contact and appropriate gestures will engage an audience.

Then, follow the directions and have a partner rate your performance.

Common Core State Standards

Writing

2. Write informative/explanatory texts to examine and convey complex ideas, concepts, and information clearly and accurately through the effective selection, organization, and analysis of content.

The Essay

"A GOOD ESSAY . . . MUST DRAW ITS CURTAIN ROUND US, BUT IT MUST BE A CURTAIN THAT SHUTS US IN, NOT OUT."

— VIRGINIA WOOLF

In This Section

- Defining the Essay (p. 678)

- Model: from "The Fallacy of Success" by G. K. Chesterton (p. 679)

- Study: "The Aims of The Spectator" by Joseph Addison (p. 682)

- Richard Rodriguez Introduces from "Days of Obligation" (p. 686)

- Study: from Days of Obligation by Richard Rodriguez (p. 689)

For more practice analyzing essays, see pages 617, 760, and 1318.

Defining the Essay

An **essay** is a short work of nonfiction that explores a specific topic and conveys an author's ideas and opinions. In 1580, the French philosopher Michel de Montaigne published a new form of short prose discussions called *Essais*. Over four hundred years later, Montaigne is still credited with creating the modern essay.

Types of Essays Most essays fall into one of two categories:

- **Formal essays** use a serious tone and dignified language, and often analyze public issues or important events.

- **Informal essays,** also called personal essays, use a more casual tone and explore everyday topics in a relaxed, conversational style.

Modes of Writing Within the two broad categories, essays can be further classified according to the mode of writing used.

- A **narrative essay** tells a true story about real people or events.

- A **persuasive essay,** also called an **argumentative essay,** tries to persuade the reader to accept the writer's opinion or to take a course of action.

- A **descriptive essay,** sometimes called an **observational essay,** uses sensory details to create a portrait of a person, a place, or an object.

- An **expository essay** presents information or discusses an idea.

An essayist often combines different modes of writing. Thus, a persuasive essay might contain narrative examples.

Close Read: Elements of an Essay

These literary elements are called out in the Model text at right.

Author's Purpose: the author's particular reason for writing Example: *Jonathan Swift wrote "A Modest Proposal" to attack British economic and social policies in Ireland.*	**Style:** the author's distinctive way of writing; the overall "sound" of a work Example: *In "The Aims of the Spectator," Joseph Addison uses an elegant style as in the statement "But there will be none to whom this paper will be more useful than to the female world."*
Theme: the main insight into life conveyed by a work Example: *In "Days of Obligation," Richard Rodriguez reflects on what is incomplete or relative in the identity of places and people, using the example of Tijuana.*	**Tone:** the author's attitude toward his or her subject or audience, as expressed in word choice, sentence structure, and so on Example: *In "Shooting an Elephant," George Orwell takes an ironic tone in the sentence "In Moulmein, . . . I was hated by large numbers of people."*

Model

About the Text Besides his novels, short stories (including the Father Brown detective series), literary studies, poems, and works on religion, the British writer G. K. Chesterton (1874–1936) wrote highly regarded essays. This essay is one of his most admired.

from "The Fallacy of Success," in *Selected Essays*
G. K. Chesterton

There has appeared in our time a particular class of books and articles which I sincerely and solemnly think may be called the silliest ever known among men. They are much more wild than the wildest romances of chivalry and much more dull than the dullest religious tract. Moreover, the romances of chivalry were at least about chivalry; the religious tracts are about religion. But these things are about nothing; they are about what is called Success. On every bookstall, in every magazine, you may find works telling people how to succeed. They are books showing men how to succeed in everything; they are written by men who cannot even succeed in writing books. To begin with, of course, there is no such thing as Success. Or, if you like to put it so, there is nothing that is not successful. That a thing is successful merely means that it is; a millionaire is successful in being a millionaire and a donkey in being a donkey. Any live man has succeeded in living; any dead man may have succeeded in committing suicide. But, passing over the bad logic and bad philosophy in the phrase, we may take it, as these writers do, in the ordinary sense of success in obtaining money or worldly position. These writers profess to tell the ordinary man how he may succeed in his trade or speculation—how, if he is a builder, he may succeed as a builder; how, if he is a stockbroker, he may succeed as a stockbroker. They profess to show him how, if he is a grocer, he may become a sporting yachtsman; how, if he is a tenth-rate journalist, he may become a peer; and how, if he is a German Jew, he may become an Anglo-Saxon. This is a definite and business-like proposal, and I really think that the people who buy these books (if any people do buy them) have a moral, if not a legal, right to ask for their money back. Nobody would dare to publish a book about electricity which literally told one nothing about electricity; no one would dare to publish an article on botany which showed that the writer did not know which end of a plant grew in the earth. Yet our modern world is full of books about Success and successful people which literally contain no kind of idea, and scarcely any kind of verbal sense.

It is perfectly obvious that in any decent occupation (such as bricklaying or writing books) there are only two ways (in any special sense) of succeeding. One is by doing very good work, the other is by cheating. Both are much too simple to require any literary explanation. If you are in for the high jump, either jump higher than any one else, or manage somehow to pretend that you have done so.

Theme Chesterton points to his theme at the outset of the essay: The concept of Success is empty—or even evil—and so should not serve as the "value" that some modern people take it to be.

Tone Here, Chesterton delivers a joke, implying that the books are frauds, with breezy efficiency. This passage reflects the overall tone of light satire.

Author's Purpose Chesterton's purpose, or reason for writing, is to mock "how-to" books of his day as well as to entertain his readers. He accomplishes both purposes in passages such as this one.

Style Chesterton's style combines plain, direct diction ("cheating") with a brisk, punchy balance of phrases and clauses. ("One is . . . , the other is. . . .")

Connecting to the Essential Question Just as today's bloggers enjoy the Internet, Addison was excited by the new medium of *his* day, the magazine. As you read, notice passages in which Addison expresses what his audience needs from his magazine and how he will meet those needs. These passages will help as you answer the Essential Question: **How does literature shape or reflect society?**

Close Reading Focus

Essay

An **essay** is a short prose piece that explores a topic as if the author were letting you overhear his or her thoughts. Meaning an "attempt" or a "test," the word *essay* was first applied to writing by the French essayist Michel de Montaigne (1533–1592).

Addison's essay can be seen as a "test," or experiment, to discover connections between experiences and to learn about the self. As you read, notice how the writer links observations and anecdotes to form ideas.

It is no accident that the essay flourished during the eighteenth century. Here are some links between this form and the **historical period:**

- This era saw the development of a rising and well-off middle class.
- Middle-class people wanted to learn more about the world and about themselves. This new class needed a self-definition.
- The essay, often featured in magazines, provided such information, as well as entertainment and moral instruction.

As you read, note how Addison helps readers ask and answer questions such as, *Who am I? What do I need to know and believe?*

Preparing to Read Complex Texts To fully appreciate an *author's perspective*, you need to **analyze the author's implicit philosophical assumptions**—unstated beliefs—and **explicit assumptions**—stated beliefs—about a subject. To analyze unstated beliefs, draw inferences and support them with textual evidence. Use a chart like the one shown to find evidence of the *author's perspective*.

Vocabulary

You will encounter the words listed here in the text that follows. Copy the words into your notebook, and look at the word *embellishments*. What part of speech can you infer it is? What clue helps you?

transient	contentious
assiduous	trifles
affluence	embellishments

**Common Core
State Standards**

Reading Informational Text

1. Cite strong and thorough textual evidence to support analysis of what the text says explicitly as well as inferences drawn from the text, including determining where the text leaves matters uncertain.

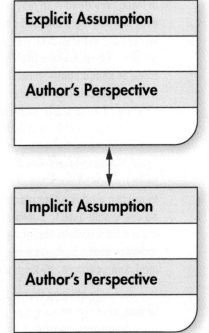

Explicit Assumption

Author's Perspective

Implicit Assumption

Author's Perspective

JOSEPH ADDISON
(1672–1719)

Author of "The Aims of *The SPECTATOR*"

Born in a village in Wiltshire, England, Joseph Addison was educated at the Charterhouse School in London, where he became a friend of classmate Richard Steele. Both young men went on to Oxford, but, after their school days, their paths diverged. The impetuous Steele immersed himself in London life, editing an early newspaper and managing the Drury Lane Theatre, while the more cautious Addison pursued prestigious political positions. Their paths, though, were to cross again.

Scholar, Poet, and Bureaucrat A Fellow of Magdalen College, Oxford, Addison was invited by John Dryden to do translations of Virgil. After four years of European study and travel, he produced an epic, *The Campaign*, celebrating a notable English victory. In 1706, Addison was named undersecretary of state and later went on to other important posts.

A Reunion In 1709, the story is told, Addison happened to read an article in *The Tatler*, a new literary magazine that had become all the rage in London coffeehouses. The article was signed "Isaac Bickerstaff," but Addison immediately recognized the style of his old school friend Richard Steele. Addison soon became a contributor to *The Tatler*. When publication of *The Tatler* ended, the two founded another journal, *The Spectator*.

A Lifetime Partnership As a team, Addison and Steele became the most celebrated journalists in England. Their essays in *The Tatler* and *The Spectator* earned them a permanent place in English literature. Almost every magazine you can buy today uses an informal, popular style derived from the one they originated.

> **❝** *But there are none to whom this paper will be more useful than to the female world.* **❞**

The Spectator, **No. 10,**
Monday, March 12, 1711

The Aims of
The SPECTATOR

Joseph Addison

It is with much satisfaction that I hear this great city inquiring day by day after these my papers, and receiving my morning lectures with a becoming seriousness and attention. My publisher tells me that there are already three thousand of them distributed every day. So that if I allow twenty readers to every paper, which I look upon as a modest computation, I may reckon about three-score thousand[1] disciples in London and Westminster, who I hope will take care to distinguish themselves from the thoughtless herd of their ignorant and unattentive brethren. Since I have raised to myself so great an audience, I shall spare no pains to make their instruction agreeable, and their diversion useful. For which reasons I shall endeavor to enliven morality with wit, and to temper wit with morality, that my readers may, if possible, both ways find their account in the speculation of the day. And to the end that their virtue and discretion may not be short, transient, intermitting[2] starts of thought, I have resolved to refresh their memories from day to day, till I have recovered them out of that desperate state of vice and folly into which the age is fallen. The mind that lies fallow[3] but a single day sprouts up in follies that are only to be killed by a constant and assiduous culture. It was said of Socrates[4] that he brought philosophy down from heaven, to inhabit among men; and I shall be ambitious to have it said of me that I have brought philosophy out of closets and libraries, schools and colleges, to dwell in clubs and assemblies, at tea tables and in coffeehouses.

I would therefore in a very particular manner recommend these my speculations to all well-regulated families that set apart an hour in every morning for tea and bread and butter; and would earnestly advise them for their good to order this paper to be punctually served up, and to be looked upon as part of the tea equipage. . . .

---

1. **three-score thousand** sixty thousand.
2. **intermitting** pausing at times; not constant.
3. **fallow** unused; unproductive.
4. **Socrates** ancient Greek philosopher (470?–399 b.c.), immortalized as a character in Plato's dialogues, who cross-examined ancient Athenians about their lives and values.

Richard Rodriguez
Author's Insight
Addison's point of view is appropriate to a new city of strangers. The writer recommends himself to everyone, addressing none as "you."

Vocabulary
transient (tran´ shənt) *adj.* temporary; passing

assiduous (ə sïj´ oo əs) *adj.* constant in application or attention

Essay
How does Addison make a personal connection with his readers in his opening paragraph?

> **❝**_I have resolved to refresh their memories from day to day, till I have recovered them out of that desperate state of vice and folly into which the age is fallen._**❞**

In the next place, I would recommend this paper to the daily perusal of those gentlemen whom I cannot but consider as my good brothers and allies, I mean the fraternity of spectators, who live in the world without having anything to do in it; and either by the affluence of their fortunes or laziness of their dispositions have no other business with the rest of mankind but to look upon them. Under this class of men are comprehended all contemplative tradesmen, titular physicians, fellows of the Royal Society, Templars[5] that are not given to be contentious, and statesmen that are out of business; in short, everyone that considers the world as a theater, and desires to form a right judgment of those who are the actors on it.

There is another set of men that I must likewise lay a claim to, whom I have lately called the blanks of society, as being altogether unfurnished with ideas, till the business and conversation of the day has supplied them. I have often considered these poor souls with an eye of great commiseration, when I have heard them asking the first man they have met with, whether there was any news stirring? and by that means gathering together materials for thinking. These needy persons do not know what to talk of till about twelve o'clock in the morning; for by that time they are pretty good judges of the weather, know which way the wind sits, and whether the Dutch mail[6] be come in. As they lie at the mercy of the first man they meet, and are grave or impertinent all the day long, according to the notions which they have imbibed in the morning, I would earnestly entreat them not to stir out of their chambers till they have read this paper, and do promise them that I will daily instil into them such sound and wholesome sentiments as shall have a good effect on their conversation for the ensuing twelve hours.

But there are none to whom this paper will be more useful than to the female world. I have often thought there has not been sufficient pains taken in finding out proper employments and diversions for the fair ones. Their amusements seem contrived for them, rather as they are women, than as they are

---

5. **titular physicians, fellows of the Royal Society, Templars** physicians in title only; members of a group dedicated to scientific research; lawyers or law students with offices in the Inner or Middle Temple.
6. **Dutch mail** mail from Europe bearing news of the war.

reasonable creatures; and are more adapted to the sex than to the species. The toilet[7] is their great sense of business, and the right adjusting of their hair the principal employment of their lives. The sorting of a suit of ribbons is reckoned a very good morning's work; and if they make an excursion to a mercer's or a toyshop,[8] so great a fatigue makes them unfit for anything else all the day after. Their more serious occupations are sewing and embroidery, and their greatest drudgery the preparation of jellies and sweetmeats. This, I say, is the state of ordinary women; though I know there are multitudes of those of a more elevated life and conversation, that move in an exalted sphere of knowledge and virtue, that join all the beauties of the mind to the ornaments of dress, and inspire a kind of awe and respect, as well as love, into their male beholders. I hope to increase the number of these by publishing this daily paper, which I shall always endeavor to make an innocent if not an improving entertainment, and by that means at least divert the minds of my female readers from greater trifles. At the same time, as I would fain give some finishing touches to those which are already the most beautiful pieces in human nature, I shall endeavor to point all those imperfections that are the blemishes, as well as those virtues which are the embellishments, of the sex.

---

7. **toilet** act of dressing and grooming oneself.
8. **suit of ribbons . . . mercer's or a toyshop** A suit of ribbons was a set of matching ribbons; a mercer's store sold fabrics, ribbons, and so on; a toyshop sold small items of little value.

Critical Reading

Cite textual evidence to support your responses.

1. **Key Ideas and Details (a)** What reason does Addison give for making his instruction "agreeable"? **(b) Support:** Addison felt *The Spectator* would set high standards for readers. Identify two expressions of this attitude.

2. **Key Ideas and Details (a)** How does Addison define the "spectators" of society? **(b) Infer:** What is Addison's attitude toward the "blanks of society" and toward women? Is he sympathetic, mocking, or both? Explain.

3. **Integration of Knowledge and Ideas Apply:** Do modern media encourage "spectatorship" as Addison defines it? Explain.

4. **Integration of Knowledge and Ideas** What kinds of things would Addison like to change about society? In your response, use at least two of these Essential Question words: *values, dissatisfaction, ideal.* [Connecting to the Essential Question: How does literature shape or reflect society?]

Literary Analysis

1. **Key Ideas and Details Analyze the author's philosophical assumptions** in the first paragraph. **(a)** What *explicit assumptions* does he make about the best way to present moral instruction? Cite specific evidence. **(b)** What *implicit assumptions* does he make about using media to promote ideas? Explain.

2. **Key Ideas and Details** In his **essay** for *The Spectator*, Addison describes audiences for his paper. How does he "test" the usefulness of his paper?

3. **Integration of Knowledge and Ideas** Using a chart like this one, analyze Addison's portrait of his four readers.

Passage	Analytic/ Descriptive	General/Of a Specific Era?	Logical/ Humorous?

Common Core State Standards

Writing
1.a. Introduce precise, knowledgeable claim(s), establish the significance of the claim(s), distinguish the claim(s) from alternate or opposing claims, and create an organization that logically sequences claim(s), counterclaims, reasons, and evidence.

Vocabulary Acquisition and Use

For each word, choose the letter of its synonym, a word that means the same thing. Explain each choice.

1. **affluence:**   **(a)** speed   **(b)** poverty   **(c)** wealth

2. **assiduous:**   **(a)** diligent   **(b)** aggressive   **(c)** helpful

3. **contentious:**   **(a)** mild   **(b)** argumentative   **(c)** proud

4. **embellishments:** **(a)** food   **(b)** remarks   **(c)** decorations

5. **transient:**   **(a)** powerful   **(b)** passing   **(c)** near

6. **trifles**:   **(a)** trivia   **(b)** wonders   **(c)** dangers

Writing

Argumentative Text Like Addison, you observe people in action every day. Write a **letter to the editor** of a local paper describing a kind of behavior you find interesting, amusing, or annoying. Persuade readers to regard the behavior as you do by presenting a sound argument.

- State your claim, presenting vivid *examples* of the behavior.
- Support your claim with *reasoning*.
- Use *emotional appeals* as well as rhetorical devices (for example, parallelism, repetition, or analogies) to present your argument well.
- Anticipate and *refute opposing arguments*.

Richard Rodriguez Introduces

from Days of Obligation:

from "In Athens Once"

Journalist as Spectator, Then and Now The best journalists achieve a sort of disappearing act, a recitation of facts so transparent it is as though the eye were speaking. Joseph Addison, writing three hundred years ago, styled himself a "spectator" of the great city of London. *Spectator* is a noun I would willingly take for myself, preferring to present myself to the reader as a spectator, at some cool distance from the world I describe.

Joseph Addison, Spectator and Man Joseph Addison was a periodical columnist, writing for magazines. He invented a fictionalized persona who roamed the city of London and reported what he found there. The persona of the Spectator was not Joseph Addison, but resembled him. There is, for instance, a discernible moral sensibility in all Addison's writing that reveals the man. If he writes about that fellow in the corner, with the parrot on his shoulder, it is because he has something in mind to say. It is not simply that he wishes to place a colorful character before us.

Richard Rodriguez, Journalist and Man The journalist in me wants to be informative, to say what is true or factual, and to report exactly what I have seen, without reference to my own sensibility. As a journalist, for example, I visit the teeming, optimistic city of Tijuana, Mexico, situated across the border from San Diego, California.

Tijuana is a city of uncountable millions, and as many aspirations, and as many preoccupations, and as many points of

About the Author

Journalist, essayist, and author Richard Rodriguez won the George Foster Peabody Award in 1997 for his work on PBS's *MacNeil-Lehrer NewsHour*. His writing has appeared in a number of publications, including *The Washington Post*, the *Wall Street Journal*, and *Harper's*.

"The best journalists achieve a sort of disappearing act."

view. Most Americans have no sense of Tijuana beyond its old-fashioned notoriety as a honky-tonk draw for sailors during the war.

To me, Tijuana appears as raw and exciting, sometimes as appalling, as I imagine eighteenth-century London must have appeared to Joseph Addison. Large, beautiful houses overlook a city of factories, heavy metal rock bands, gypsies, taxis, street cries, stinking canals. It is a city of contradictions.

My journalistic obligation to the reader is to present numbers and dates as correctly as I can. My journalistic impulse always intends to complicate rather than to simplify issues, to suggest two or several points of view rather than to argue a single position. My journalistic obligation, therefore, is to see this border town from both sides—to describe how Mexico, particularly Mexico City, views Tijuana, as well as how people north of the border regard this city.

But I have also come to Tijuana as a Mexican American, as someone born in the United States to Mexican parents. My status here is in question. Indeed, Tijuana, this city that lies on the border between cultures, must finally remind me of myself—the struggle of cultures in my own soul. Tijuana implicates me and fascinates me for being (as I am) confused by its identity.

The Spectator Becomes a Comic Character Thus, you will see how in this piece, Richard Rodriguez becomes a comic character within the city he has been at such pains to describe from a distance. *They* surround the *I*. The diffidence of Richard Rodriguez is exposed as completely at odds with the messy ease of Tijuana—at odds, too, with the airs he gives himself as a traveler-observer.

▲ **Critical Viewing**
In what way is the man pictured here a "colorful character" and, like Rodriguez, "at odds" with his surroundings? **ANALYZE**

When the journalist becomes a character within his own report, he enters the realm of bias and prejudice, or he enters the realm of literature—depending.

The pieces I write for newspapers are usually published on an opinion page; they intend to persuade. My television essays are reserved for the last part of a news program; they are clearly identified as "commentary." They circle a point of view, but cannot express a point of view. The only journalistic pride I own is the fact that I have been called by some readers "left" and by other readers "right." The journalist in me does not want to be slotted among one band of partisans in an argument.

But the writing I prefer attempts a marriage: journalism wedded to literature.

The journalist Richard Rodriguez writes as fairly as possible of the world around him. The writer Richard Rodriguez finds himself caught up in the world he is watching. He may be morally outraged. Or he may simply be made petulant by the heat. He shows his hand, at any rate.

Critical Reading

Cite textual evidence to support your responses.

1. **Key Ideas and Details (a)** According to Rodriguez, in what way do good journalists perform a "disappearing act"? **(b) Make a Judgment:** Do you think his ideas apply to today's television and print journalists? Explain.

2. **Key Ideas and Details (a)** What connections does Rodriguez draw between Addison's London and modern-day Tijuana? **(b)** As a journalist, in what way must Rodriguez present the border town of Tijuana? **(c) Speculate:** Because of the parallels Rodriguez notes between himself and Tijuana, do you think he can be objective in his presentation of the city? Why or why not?

3. **Key Ideas and Details (a) Infer:** In what ways might the connection Rodriguez feels to Tijuana make him the perfect person to write about the city? **(b) Interpret:** In your own words, explain what Rodriguez means by "journalism wedded to literature."

4. **Craft and Structure (a)** In this commentary, what is the effect of Richard Rodriguez referring to himself in the third person? **(b)** What, if any, is the difference between the "I" in this essay and "Richard Rodriguez"?

5. **Craft and Structure** Note words and phrases that make this a piece of journalism and words and phrases that make it literature. Explain the differences you note, using what you read in Rodriguez's essay.

6. **Integration of Knowledge and Ideas** Consider whether Rodriguez remains a spectator throughout his essay. Identify any moments when you think he becomes a participant rather than an observer.

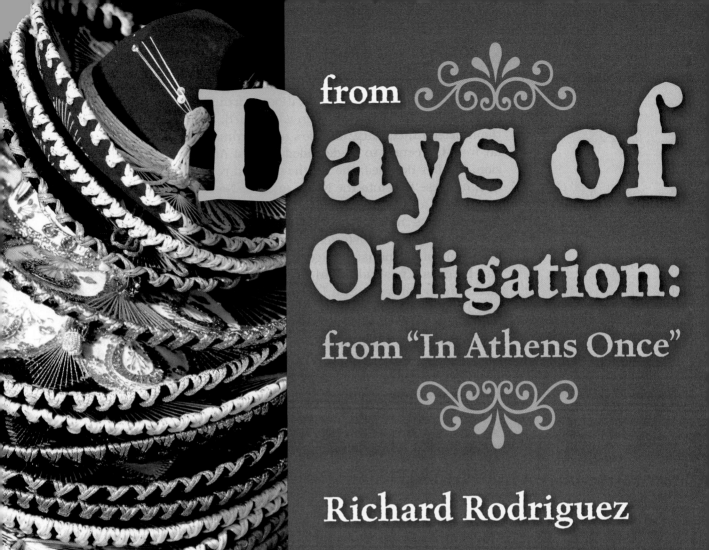

from
Days of Obligation:
from "In Athens Once"

Richard Rodriguez

Consider Tijuana from Mexico's point of view. Tijuana is farther away from Mexico City than any other city in Mexico. Tijuana is where Mexico comes to an end.

In Mexico City you will waste an afternoon if you go to bookstores looking for books about Tijuana. The clerk will scarcely conceal his amusement. (And what would be in a book about Tijuana?) People in Mexico City will tell you, if they have anything at all to say about Tijuana, that Tijuana is a city without history, a city without architecture, an American city. San Diego may worry about Mexican hordes crawling over the border. Mexico City worries about a cultural spill from the United States.

▲ **Critical Viewing**
What does this image suggest about the contents and tone of the essay to come? **PREDICT**

From prehistory, the North has been the problem. Mexico City (la capital) has been the platform from which all provincialism[1] is gauged. From the North came marauding[2] tribes, iconoclasts,[3] destroyers of high Indian civilization. During the Spanish colonial era, the North was settled, even garrisoned, but scarcely civilized. In the nineteenth century, Mexico's northernmost territories were too far from the center to be defended against America's westward expansion. In after-decades, the North spawned revolutionaries and bandits, or these fled into the North and the North hid them well.

Beyond all the ribbon-cutting palaver[4] about good neighbors, there remains an awesome distance of time. Tijuana and San Diego are not in the same historical time zone. Tijuana is poised at the beginning of an industrial age, a Dickensian[5] city with palm trees. San Diego is a postindustrial city of high-impact plastic and despair diets. And palm trees. San Diego faces west, looks resolutely out to sea. Tijuana stares north, as toward the future. San Diego is the future—secular, soulless. San Diego is the past, guarding its quality of life. Tijuana is the future.

On the Mexican side there is flux, a vast migration, a camp of siege. On the Mexican side is youth, with bad skin or bad teeth, but with a naïve optimism appropriate to youth.

On the American side are petitions to declare English the official language of the United States; the Ku Klux Klan; nativists posing as environmentalists, blaming illegal immigration for freeway congestion.

---

1. **provincialism** narrowness of outlook.
2. **marauding** plundering, raiding.
3. **iconoclasts** those who seek to destroy widely accepted beliefs or ideas.
4. **palaver** conference or discussion.
5. **Dickensian** having the characteristics of a nineteenth century English novel written by Charles Dickens (1812–1870). Dickensian characteristics would include obscure London streets inhabited by scoundrels and villains, wide-eyed innocents, and eccentric characters.

▼ **Critical Viewing**

In what ways does this photograph depict the contradictory worlds Rodriguez describes?
CONNECT

Tijuana
and San Diego are not in the same historical time zone.

And late at night, on the radio call-in shows, hysterical, reasonable American voices say they have had enough. Of this or that. Of trampled flower beds. Of waiting in line or crowded buses, of real or imagined rudeness, of welfare.

In San Diego people speak of "the border" as meaning a clean break, the end of *us*, the beginning of *them*. In Mexican Spanish, the legality takes on distance, even pathos, as *la frontera*, meaning something less fixed, something more akin to the American "frontier." Whereas San Diego remains provincial and retiring, the intrusion of the United States has galvanized Tijuana to cosmopolitanism.[6] There are seven newspapers in Tijuana; there is American television— everything we see they see. Central American refugees and southern California *turistas* cross paths in Tijuana. There are new ideas. Most worrisome to Mexico City has been the emergence of a right-wing idea, a pro-American politics to challenge the one-party system that has governed Mexico for most of this century.

Because the United States is the richer country, the more powerful broadcaster, Mexicans know more about us than we care to know about them. Mexicans speak of America as "the other side," saying they are going to *el otro lado* when they cross for work, legal or illegal. The border is real enough; it is guarded by men with guns. But Mexicans incline to view the border without reverence, referring to the American side as *el otro cachete*, the other buttock.

Traditionally, Mexican cities are centered by a town square or *zócalo*, on either side of which stand city hall and cathedral, counterweights to balance the secular[7] with the eternal. Tijuana never had a *zócalo*. And, like other California cities, Tijuana is receding from its old downtown.

---

6. cosmopolitanism worldly sophistication.
7. secular related to worldly, rather than religious, things.

Comprehension
Which city is called "la capital"?

The new commercial district of Tijuana, three miles east of downtown, is called the Zona del Río. For several blocks within the Zona del Río, on grass islands in the middle of the Paseo de los Héroes, stand monuments to various of Mexico's heroes. There is one American (Abraham Lincoln) in a line that otherwise connects the good Aztec, Cuauhtémoc,[8] to the victorious Mexican general, Zaragoza.[9] With Kremlin-like dullness, these monuments were set down upon the city, paperweights upon a map. They are gifts from the capital, meant as reminders.

Prominent along the Paseo de los Héroes is Tijuana's Cultural Center, Mexico City's most insistent token of troth.[10] Tijuana might better have done with sewers or streetlights, but in 1982 the Mexican government built Tijuana a cultural center, an orange concrete bomba[11] in the brutal architectural idioms[12] of the 1970s. The main building is a museum, very clean and empty during my visit, except for a janitor who trails me with a vacuum cleaner. Together we tread a ramp past fairly uninteresting displays of Mayan pottery, past folk crafts, past reproductions of political documents and portraits of Mexico's military heroes. The lesson to Tijuana is clear: she belongs to Mexico.

As the exhibits travel in time, south to north, the umbilical approach narrows to gossamer. We reach a display devoted to Tijuana's own history. We find a collection of picture postcards from the

---

8. **Cuauhtémoc** the 11th and last Aztec emperor. When captured in battle, Cuauhtémoc refused to reveal the location of Aztec riches, earning him legendary status among Mexico's leaders.
9. **Zaragoza** General Zaragoza and his militia defeated an invading French army on May 5, 1862. Cinco de Mayo is celebrated each year to commemorate the victory.
10. **troth** loyalty.
11. **bomba** bomb.
12. **idioms** style of expression.

The lesson to Tijuana is clear:

She belongs to Mexico.

twenties, emblazoned in English with "Greetings from Old Mexico."

One sympathizes with the curator's dilemma. How does one depict the history of so unmonumental a city, a city occasioned by defeat and submission to the enemy's will?

The treaty ending the Mexican-American War ruled a longitudinal line between the Gulf of Mexico and the Pacific Ocean. For decades thereafter, Tijuana remained vacant land at the edge of the sea, an arid little clause dangling from Mexico's disgraced nineteenth century.

No one in Tijuana is able to fix for me the derivation of the name of the place. Some say it is an Indian name. Some think the town was named for a woman who lived in a shack at the turn of the century, a Mexican Ma Kettle known in the region as Tía Juana.

Mexico City tried to dispose of the name in 1925. By an act of Mexico's congress, Tijuana was proclaimed to be Ciudad Zaragoza. A good name. A patriot's name. The resolution languished in a statute book on a shelf in Mexico City, two thousand miles away.

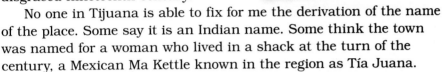

▲ Critical Viewing
Which details in this postcard support the author's message that Tijuana lacks a clear identity as a city? **CONNECT**

Critical Reading

Cite textual evidence to support your responses.

1. **Key Ideas and Details** **(a)** According to the residents of Mexico City, what two things does Tijuana lack? **(b) Interpret:** In what way does geography play a part in this reputation? **(c) Speculate:** What effects might a city that lacks a specific urban plan or a sense of identity have on the community and people who live there?

2. **Key Ideas and Details** **(a)** According to the essay, which city is actively moving toward its own future? **(b) Hypothesize:** What challenges might arise when a city progresses and grows very quickly? Cite examples from the essay to support your response.

3. **Integration of Knowledge and Ideas** **(a)** Instead of a cultural center, which other improvement might have benefited Tijuana? **(b) Compare and Contrast:** In what ways is Tijuana more American than Mexican in its culture? **(c) Analyze Cause and Effect:** What effect might Rodriguez's American background have on his perception of Tijuana's cultural identity?

4. **Integration of Knowledge and Ideas** **(a) Infer:** Which characteristics of Tijuana are likely to appear in a positive light in a tourism advertisement? **(b) Evaluate:** Are these characteristics truly assets to the city? Explain.

Write a Reflective Essay

 **Common Core State Standards**

Writing
3.a. Engage and orient the reader by setting out a problem, situation, or observation and its significance.

Reflective Essay In this unit, thought-provoking essays by Joseph Addison and Richard Rodriguez offer revealing glimpses of each writer's personality. These **reflective essays** also encourage readers to consider their own personal experiences more deeply. Follow the steps outlined in this workshop to write a reflective essay.

Assignment Write a reflective essay in which you describe an event from your personal experience and then share insights about its significance.

What to Include The assignment summarizes your *purpose*, and your *audience* will be your classmates. To achieve your purpose and engage the audience, include these elements in your essay:

- an explanation of a personal experience that shaped your beliefs
- an organization that clarifies the significance of the events you describe, and a balance between specific events and beliefs
- clear connections between beliefs and events
- a consistent, personal tone

To preview the criteria on which your reflective essay may be assessed, see the rubric on page 701.

Focus on Research

Research can add more depth to reflective essays in the following ways:

- by providing a factual context for your thinking
- by furnishing data to enhance or support your opinions
- by adding substance to the connection between the personal and the general or the abstract

Be sure to note all resources you use in your research, and credit those sources in your final drafts. Refer to the Conducting Research pages in the Introductory Unit (pp. lxxii–lxxvii), as well as the Citing Sources and Preparing Manuscript pages in the Resource section for information on citing materials.

Prewriting and Planning

Choosing Your Topic

To choose an event to focus on, use one of these strategies:

- **Freewriting** Write for five minutes about key experiences in your life and beliefs you hold strongly. Jot down as many ideas as you can. Then, look for connections between general beliefs and specific events.

- **Top-Five List** Make a list of five times in your life when you discovered something wonderful. Scan *journals*, if necessary, to help generate this list. For each key event, note what you learned and think about why this discovery has remained important to you.

Narrowing Your Topic

Focus on an insight. Once you have selected an event, focus your essay by stating your key insight in one sentence. Then, develop ideas and examples that explain and support that insight.

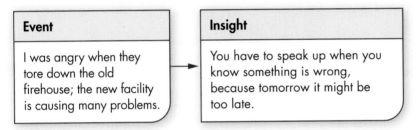

Event	Insight
I was angry when they tore down the old firehouse; the new facility is causing many problems.	You have to speak up when you know something is wrong, because tomorrow it might be too late.

Gathering Details

Make connections. Consider how your experiences relate to themes in the world at large. Organize your thoughts in a diagram like the one shown. Then, conduct research to deepen your knowledge about your subject. Talk with friends and family, or use the library or the Internet to gather details about past events or issues that relate to your personal experience.

Preparing Rhetorical Strategies

While preparing to write about an event, remember that you can use a variety of different rhetorical strategies in addition to narration, or story telling. These strategies include *description* (when you describe people, things, and places), *exposition* (when you set forth general ideas), and *persuasion* (when you try to convince the reader that your beliefs are true).

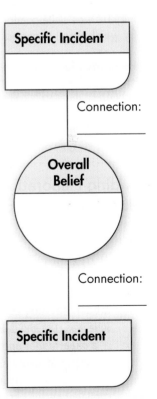

Drafting

Shaping Your Writing

Decide where to start. A well-organized reflective essay alternates between *broader themes* or generalizations and *specific incidents*. Your introduction should include both. Consider these organizations for your opening:

- State your overall belief and then give one or two tantalizing details about the incidents that led you to it.
- Describe an event and then tell the surprising insight you drew from it. Your essay will make the full connection clear.

Establish a tone. Introduce an appropriate tone for your essay from the beginning, and stay with it throughout. A serious, straightforward tone is appropriate, but you might also consider using one of these:

- **Ironic tone:** a good tone to use when your details show that things do not always work out as expected or intended
- **Humorous tone:** a logical choice when your examples are amusing

Model: Experimenting With Specific Tones

Ironic Tone
I welcomed my coach's criticism as warmly as any self-centered ten-year-old might. I was quite comfortable postponing any action until the following year, by which time I expected the matter would be forgotten.

Humorous Tone
Having a little brother is not as big a pain as people say. It's worse. Yet, after years of his tattling and tagging along, one incident brought home to me how important family is—even little brothers. I no longer want to sell him to the circus. Not unless they've raised their prices.

Providing Elaboration

Explode a moment. Expand key descriptions by telling more about what happened, what something looked like, or how the people involved—including you—reacted. Mark moments you can "explode," and use the margin to write the details you want to add.

Model: Revising to Explode a Moment

Julie was cute and dated the most popular boys in our school.

She was ^a cheerleader and^ a Student Council member. She was also the most confident person I knew^, and she welcomed an understudy^.

> These additional details provide more description.

Common Core State Standards

Writing

3.c. Use a variety of techniques to sequence events so that they build on one another to create a coherent whole and build toward a particular tone and outcome.

3.d. Use precise words and phrases, telling details, and sensory language to convey a vivid picture of the experiences, events, setting, and/or characters.

Writers on Writing

Richard Rodriguez On Reflective Writing

Richard Rodriguez is the author of *Days of Obligation* (p. 689).

These paragraphs appear in *Days of Obligation*, a philosophical travel book of mine that ranges over several centuries and back and forth across the U.S.-Mexico border. Each chapter, like the fragment below, is autobiographical. But that is only to say, memory is my guide throughout; memory forces me to reflect on the lessons within my life.

"In my reflective essays, the 'I' moves freely."

—Richard Rodriguez

from *Days of Obligation*

Our last house on "Eye" Street was across from an old cemetery. No memory attached to it. The grass was watered and cut once a month by the city. There were no scrolls or wrought-iron fences; no places to put flowers. There were granite plaques level with the ground. Early dates. Solitary names. Men. Men who had come early to California and died young.

No grandsons or granddaughters came forward in the 1950s when Sacramento needed the land to build a school, a new Sutter Junior High School. A plywood fence was hammered up around the cemetery and, within that discretionary veil, bulldozers chugged and grunted, pulling up moist hairy mounds of what had once been the light of day; trucks came to carry it all away.

In early November, white tulle fog rises from the valley floor. My father is easy with this ancient weather reminiscent of the sea. My father is whistling this morning as he scrambles two eggs. My mother turns away from the window, pulling her blue bathrobe closer around her throat. I am sitting at the kitchen table. I am sixteen years old. I am pouring milk onto Sugar Frosted Flakes, watching milk rise in the bowl. My parents will die. I will die. Everyone I know will someday be dead. The blue parakeet my mother has taught to say "pretty boy" swings upon his little trapeze, while my mother pours coffee.

Each paragraph is about remembrance or the refusal to remember: civic amnesia; the forgetfulness of ancestors; the middle-aged writer's teenage discovery of death; the adult's inability to remember winter.

Images of nature are everywhere in this meditation on death—the parakeet, winter fog, clumps of grass upturned by bulldozers. As the contending images suggest: Death is the end of life yet also a part of nature.

Notice here how the most astonishing ideas of life can come not with a drumbeat or violin, but in an instant of a Saturday morning, between spoonfuls of cereal.

Revising

Revising Your Overall Structure

Balance narration with reflection. Review your writing to make sure that you *maintained a balance between specific incidents and general ideas.*

1. Bracket any segments of the essay that describe specific events.

2. Mark in red any passages where you have included a detail that does not set a scene or advance ideas.

3. Use a different color to mark the points where you provide your interpretation of events.

**Common Core
State Standards**

Writing
4. Produce clear and coherent writing in which the development, organization, and style are appropriate to task, purpose, and audience.
5. Develop and strengthen writing as needed by revising, focusing on addressing what is most significant for a specific purpose and audience.

Model: Editing to Omit Unnecessary Details

[I giggled and flirted my way through the next two years.]
✓ [~~During that time, my Dad got a new job and we moved to a different neighborhood.~~] Through it all, I felt as if I were putting on an act. [In the middle of my junior year, I received my first ACT results.] I was not happy with my scores.

> The writer deleted this incident because it did not contribute toward her insight or provide necessary background.

---

4. Looking at your essay as a whole, determine whether you have maintained a balance between specific events and the interpretation of those events.

Revising Your Sentences

Strengthen your connections. Examine the passages where you shift between events and the generalizations to which they have led you. Consider using transitional words or phrases to clarify the connections for your readers.

Examples:

And that is how . . .
Suddenly I understood that . . .
After this happened, . . .
As a result, . . .
For the very first time, . . .
I gradually became aware that . . .

Peer Review: Ask a partner to identify passages in your essay where your connections could be stronger. Discuss ways to strengthen and clarify the connections.

Evaluate your partner's suggestions. Then, make your revisions and share your work with your partner.

Developing Your Style

Moving From Personal to Universal

A reflective essay moves from personal experiences to universal truths. Be careful to maintain your **personal voice** even when generalizing.

- Maintain your personal tone, even when stating general truths. Look for ways to inject your personality into each section of your essay.
- Be sure that you really agree with the statements you make. Your essay may feel insincere if you say something just because you think it sounds good or because you think your audience will agree.

Here is how one writer revised a universal statement that felt stiff and artificial. The revised version feels more personal and sincere.

Stiff Voice	Personal Voice
Families help us learn and grow. We achieve our best when we have their love and support. Your family's encouragement can help you accomplish anything.	For better or worse, your family knows you better than anyone else. As a result, they won't let you get away with doing anything less than your best. That can be a pain, but it also helps you succeed.

Find It in Your Reading

Read or review Richard Rodriguez's introductory essay on page 686.

1. Find two personal experiences that Rodriguez discusses in the essay.
2. Evaluate the lessons that Rodriguez draws from these experiences.
3. Look for the language that lets you "hear" Rodriguez's unique voice.

Apply It to Your Writing

Review your draft. For each paragraph, follow these steps:

1. Underline the specific events and details that you have included.
2. Circle the broader, more general lessons, observations, or beliefs about life to which these events and details have led you. Then, answer these questions:
   - Do you genuinely believe the statement?
   - Do you state your belief in a personal way?
3. Revise your essay, as necessary, to maintain your personal voice.

Coming Home

North Carolina novelist T. R. Pearson told me recently that when he was a teenager, he had set his stories in New York City, though he had never been there. "I thought New York was where it was," he laughed, adding that the fiction he had produced during this period was uniformly bad. Almost accidentally, he had begun to write about the life he really knew—life in little towns like Reidsville, North Carolina. It was only then that he succeeded at what he was attempting. Pearson's remarks set me thinking about my own life. Like Tom Pearson, I had spent a part of my life attempting something foreign and feeling unhappy with the result.

When I was in grade school, I read through every book in our class-room and did special reports. Research thrilled me. Books were the most important part of my life. I knew who I was. And I was happy.

In my freshman year, though, I decided that my own life paled compared with that of my older friend Julie. Julie was popular and dated the most popular boys in our school. She was a cheerleader and a Student Council member. She was also the most confident person I knew, and she welcomed an understudy. I borrowed Julie's clothes and copied her hairstyles, right down to the huge hair bows that were her signature. By the end of the year, I had decided to run for cheerleader.

I giggled and flirted my way through the next two years. Through it all, I felt as if I was putting on an act. In the middle of my junior year, I received my first ACT results. I was not happy with my scores. I began to reevaluate my life. I decided not to run for cheerleader. I paid less attention to who was popular and concentrated on friendships that were comfortable and fun. I threw myself into my science project and was exhilarated when I took top honors at the state science fair. By the end of the year, a teacher had invited me to serve as editor of a literary magazine. I felt that I was home again.

This December, as I sat listening to T. R. Pearson discuss the path that had led him to his true subject, I felt I knew exactly what he was talking about. It was a warm December day. A late fall sun filtered through the pine trees onto my English teacher's deck. Four other students and I sat in deck chairs and listened to Pearson speak about writing. It all felt so natural. This, I thought, is the kind of world I want to live in. I realized then that you can never get anywhere if you leave your true self behind. At that moment, I could not, for all the world, remember why cheerleading or Julie's boys or big hair bows had ever mattered.

Ashley sets up a clear connection between the narrative that follows and her general point: Success depends on being true to oneself.

By carefully selecting details, Ashley includes just enough incidents to support and balance her general insight.

Ashley's short, decisive self-descriptions establish a consistent tone.

Ashley reports incidents that clearly lead to her realization.

In her conclusion, Ashley clearly states her general insight. (See Developing Your Style on p. 699.)

Editing and Proofreading

Focus on commas. Focus on commas between items in a series, commas in compound sentences, and commas that set off appositives.

Focus on spelling. When adding *-ly* to form an adverb from an adjective ending in *-le,* drop the *-le. Reasonable* becomes *reasonably.*

Spiral Review Conventions Earlier in this unit, you learned about comparative and superlative adjectives and adverbs (p. 493); participles, gerunds, and infinitives (p. 503); and fixing misplaced and dangling modifiers (p. 539). Check your persuasive essay to be sure you have used those conventions correctly.

Publishing, Presenting, and Reflecting

Consider one of the following ways to share your writing:

Create a radio broadcast. Use your essay as the basis for a radio opinion piece. Rehearse your presentation, looking for ways to match the tone of your voice to the tone of your essay. Try to "tell" incidents or events rather than read them verbatim. If possible, record your presentation so that you can critique it later.

Publish on the Internet. Post your reflective essay on a Web site for student writing. Invite feedback from other writers.

Reflect on your writing. Jot down your thoughts on the experience of writing a reflective essay. Begin by answering these questions:

- What have I learned about moving from the particular to the general, and back again, in my writing?
- What new aspects of the topic did I discover as I developed plans for my essay?

Common Core State Standards

Writing
5. Develop and strengthen writing as needed by editing, focusing on addressing what is most significant for a specific purpose and audience.
6. Use technology, including the Internet, to produce, publish, and update individual or shared writing products in response to ongoing feedback, including new arguments or information.

Language
2.b. Spell correctly.

Rubric for Self-Assessment

Evaluate your reflective essay using the following criteria and rating scale, or, with your classmates, determine your own reasonable evaluation criteria.

Criteria	Rating Scale
	not very *very*
Purpose/Focus: How clearly do you show how a personal experience led you to an insight?	1 2 3 4
Organization: How logical is your organization?	1 2 3 4
Development of Ideas/Elaboration: How fully do you describe and develop the events that influenced your beliefs?	1 2 3 4
Language: How well do you use language to establish a personal tone?	1 2 3 4
Conventions: How correct is your grammar, especially your use of commas?	1 2 3 4

Oral Interpretation of a Literary Work

An **oral interpretation** is an oral reading of a literary work that conveys the presenter's understanding of the nuances of a text. Long before the invention of the printing press, poets and storytellers performed for their communities, relying on voice and gesture to convey meaning. People still present literary works in this manner today.

Analyze a Literary Work

Review the text. Make a copy of a speech, poem, or soliloquy from this unit. Choose one that you truly enjoy. Then, analyze the work to identify the use of literary elements and stylistic devices, such as the following:

- **Tone:** the author's attitude. Determine if it is formal, earnest, satirical, approving, or critical.

- **Author's Style:** the way a writer uses language to express ideas. Analyze the elements that help reveal a writer's voice. For example, notice sentence lengths, word choice, images, and characters' personalities, as well as uses of symbols, figurative language, and description.

- **Imagery:** descriptions that appeal to the senses. Study the author's images of places, objects, and experiences.

- **Theme:** the overall message of the selection. Consider the writer's purpose and note ideas or images that are repeated.

- **Nuance and Ambiguity:** Literature can be interpreted in many ways. Look for actions or symbols whose meanings are not directly stated, and decide how you understand the author's meaning in these items.

A review of these elements will help you understand the selection's *significant ideas*. Read the work several times to help you understand its layers of meanings or to find areas where you may have questions. Pay attention to denotative, or surface-level meanings. Eventually, connotative meanings—those that are deeper or more subtle—will become apparent. Look to other texts as well to support your ideas. Record your observations by *highlighting, circling words, and making marginal notes*.

Write your analysis. Use your notes to write a brief analytical essay that details your understanding of the text. Focus on your interpretation of any *complexities of the text*. Make specific references to the literary elements noted above and the ways in which they affect your understanding. Also, consider including *rhetorical strategies* in your analysis, such as describing other interpretations or narrating your first impressions of the work. Use this essay to introduce your oral presentation.

**Common Core
State Standards**

Reading Literature
7. Analyze multiple interpretations of a story, drama, or poem, evaluating how each version interprets the source text.

Speaking and Listening
6. Adapt speech to a variety of contexts and tasks, demonstrating a command of formal English when indicated or appropriate.

Rehearse Speaking Strategies

To perform your oral interpretation effectively, use these techniques:

Technique	Application	Explore It
Eye Contact	Look at everyone in your audience.	Observe how your teachers look at the whole class while teaching.
Gesture/Movement	Use hand gestures and staging to convey action and emotion.	View a recording of a famous actor or poet performing a literary work and note his or her movements.
Vocalization	Reflect characters' accents and dialects, and enunciate and project your voice.	Research the areas in which your characters are said to live and how they might sound.
Voice Register	Use your voice's highs and lows to create emphasis or differentiate characters.	Practice saying the same sentence with different emphasis and pitch.

Enhance your performance. To further develop your interpretation, consider using simple costumes and props, music, pictures, or sound effects. You can ask a friend to assist with such effects during your performance.

Practice. *Rehearse* in front of a mirror and then in front of family or friends. Be sure to practice your *staging* and the use of any props.

Activities: Deliver and Analyze Oral Interpretations

Comprehension and Collaboration For both activities, use an evaluation form like the one below.

A. Present your interpretation, starting off with an introduction based on your essay. Afterward, apply listeners' feedback to revise your delivery.

B. With a small group, listen to a variety of interpretations of the same work. You may use audio or video recordings, your own interpretations, or a combination of the two. Analyze how each version interprets the source text.

Evaluation Form for Oral Interpretation

Title and Author of Literary Selection: _____

Which aspects of the work does the interpreter emphasize? _____

Does the interpreter use gestures? How do they help the performance? _____

How does he or she use voice techniques? _____

How well does the interpreter maintain eye contact? _____

Name one thing the interpreter could do better next time. _____

Etymology: Political Science/History Terms

If you were given the original manuscript of *Beowulf,* you would need an Anglo-Saxon scholar to read it for you, so different is Old English from the language we speak today. In contrast, you could read much of *The Canterbury Tales* on your own. By Chaucer's day, Anglo-Saxon had been transformed into Middle English, a language that shares much of the grammar and vocabulary of our modern tongue. The Norman invasion of England in 1066 brought thousands of French and Latin words into the vocabulary. Since French and Latin were the languages of the ruling class, many of the new words referred to administration, government, and law. The chart below introduces you to key affixes and roots stemming from these words. An understanding of these word parts can help you define unfamiliar terms you encounter in political science and history.

 **Common Core State Standards**

Language

4. Determine or clarify the meaning of unknown and multiple-meaning words and phrases based on *grades 11–12 reading and content,* choosing flexibly from a range of strategies.

4.a. Use context as a clue to the meaning of a word or phrase.

4.c. Consult general and specialized reference materials, both print and digital, to find the pronunciation of a word or determine or clarify its precise meaning, its part of speech, its etymology, or its standard usage.

Prefixes
ab- (Latin): away from
ad- (Latin): to; toward
an- (Greek): not; without
ex-, e- (Latin): outside; out of; away
pro- (Latin): forward
syn- (Greek): together; with

Roots
-arch- (Greek): chief; first; highest; ruler
-dict- (Latin): say or tell
-doc- (Latin): teach
-jud-, -jur- (Latin): to judge; law, swear
-urbs- (Latin): city
-ven-, -vent- (Latin): come

Suffixes
-an (Latin): belonging to
-ate (Latin): characterized by
-ation (Latin): action or process; result
-dom (Anglo-Saxon): state; condition; domain; rank
-ity-, ty (Latin): state or quality
-y (Latin): condition or state

Practice

Practice A: Choose the word from the list that fits each numbered definition. Explain your choices with reference to each word's root and affixes.

anarchy   edict   judiciary

adjudicate   urban   syndicate

1. a decree issued by an authority

2. absence of political authority

3. relating to a city

4. government branch that administers justice

5. an association of individuals formed to carry out a project

6. to judge a case

Practice B: Using a dictionary, trace the etymologies of the following political science and history terms: *prerogative, doom, allegiance, property, deed.* Identify the language of origin and the point at which the word entered the English language.

Vocabulary Acquisition and Use: Context Clues

Context clues are words or phrases that help readers clarify the meanings of unfamiliar words in a text. By using context clues, you can determine the word or words that complete a sentence. Sentence Completion questions appear in most standardized tests. In these types of questions, you are given sentences with one or more missing words. Your task is to use the context to choose the correct word or words to complete each sentence logically. Try this strategy: (1) Identify the meaning of each answer option. (2) If you are unsure of the meaning of a word, use roots, prefixes, and suffixes, or similar words to help you understand the meaning. (3) Test those potential meanings in the sentence.

Practice

This exercise is modeled after the Sentence Completion exercises that appear in the Critical Reading section of the SAT.

Directions: Each of the following sentences is missing one or two words. Choose the word or set of words that best completes each sentence.

> **Test-Taking Tip**
> Pace yourself: Questions are easier early in the test and more challenging later in the test.

1. The critic praised the actress, calling her performance ___?___.
   A. devout
   B. eminent
   C. lamentable
   D. transcendent
   E. transient

2. Due to the manager's ___?___, the staff was whimsically assigned to different projects.
   A. caprices
   B. credulity
   C. discretion
   D. guile
   E. resolution

3. Her earlier ___?___ forgotten, she enjoyed a life of ___?___.
   A. abasement . . . expedients
   B. dominions . . . covetousness
   C. penury . . . affluence
   D. piety . . . distemper
   E. schism . . . resolution

4. The pleas of the ___?___ peasant did not affect the ___?___ noble.
   A. delirious . . . inconstant
   B. importuning . . . obdurate
   C. ingenuous . . . temperate
   D. prodigious . . . dubious
   E. risible . . . substantial

5. The owl set out each evening on its ___?___ search for food.
   A. amorous
   B. heedless
   C. nocturnal
   D. notorious
   E. venerable

6. The speaker's arguments did nothing to ___?___ the situation.
   A. breach
   B. illumine
   C. presume
   D. reconfigure
   E. transgress

From Text to Understanding

You have studied each part of Unit 3 as a set of connected texts. In this workshop, you will have the chance to further explore the fundamental connections among these texts, and deepen your essential understanding of the literature and its social and historical context.

PART 1: The War Against Time

Writing: Argumentative Essay The poems in Part 1 present the reader with reflections on mortality. The poets examine death in its truest sense, but also contemplate the passage of time as it signals the inevitable end we all face. Review the Anchor Texts, "Song," "A Valediction: Forbidding Mourning," "Holy Sonnet 10," and "Meditation 17," as well as the other works in Part 1. Note the topic of each work as you review.

Assignment: These works, which deal with death, leave-taking, and our fleeting existence, speak with a philosophical, even optimistic, voice rather than a cry of desperation. Take a position that either agrees or disagrees with this assessment of the Anchor Text and other poems in Part 1.

> **Example:** Reasonable thought gives rise to the expression of deep feeling in poetry by John Donne and Ben Jonson. Their work resonates with a philosophical tone as it deals with issues of mortality.

Refer to the list you made as you reviewed the texts, and consider the message of the poems. Develop a claim that states your position, and use carefully chosen textual evidence to support your argument. Guide readers through your argument using effective transitions.

PART 2: A Nation Divided

Writing: Writing to Sources A familiar metaphor—life is a journey—appears with a twist in the texts of Part 2. The journey of Milton's Satan as he falls from grace, Dante's journey in the Anchor Text through the ninth circle of hell, and Christian's journey toward redemption in Bunyan are all journeys that potentially lead away from sin or toward damnation. Review the texts, especially the excerpt from *The Divine Comedy: Inferno* by Dante, taking note of the paths the characters travel.

Assignment: Develop an essay that focuses on the journeys presented in *The Divine Comedy* and the other texts in Part 2. How are these journeys used to represent the road to salvation, the detour to doom, or the path to self-awareness? Do these characters journey in comfort or does the going get tough? Craft a thesis that synthesizes your ideas about the texts you discuss. Include quotations from the poems to bolster your argument, but make sure the connection between the evidence and your ideas is clear.

 **Common Core State Standards**

Writing

1. Write arguments to support claims in an analysis of substantive topics or texts, using valid reasoning and relevant and sufficient evidence.

4. Produce clear and coherent writing in which the development, organization, and style are appropriate to task, purpose, and audience.

7. Conduct short as well as more sustained research projects to answer a question (including a self-generated question) or solve a problem; narrow or broaden the inquiry when appropriate; synthesize multiple sources on that subject, demonstrating understanding of the subject under investivation.

9. Draw evidence from literary or informational texts to support analysis, reflection, and research

Speaking and Listening

1. Initiate and participate effectively in a range of collaborative discussions (one-on-one, in groups, and teacher-led) with diverse partners on *grades 11–12 topics, texts, and issues*, building on others' ideas and expressing their own clearly and persuasively.

3. Evaluate a speaker's point of view, reasoning, and use of evidence and rhetoric, assessing the stance, premises, and links among ideas, word choice, points of emphasis, and tone used.

Writing Checklist

☐ Take a position.

  Notes: _____

☐ Identify texts.

  Notes: _____

☐ Include relevant textual evidence.

  Notes: _____

☐ Use effective transitions.

  Notes: _____

PART 3: The Ties That Bind

Research: Annotated Editions Literature of seventeenth- and eighteenth-century Britain deeply reflects the society in which it was produced. Writing of this period is filled with allusions to specific people, entertainments, institutions, and events that might seem obscure to readers today. Review the texts in Part 3, focusing on the Anchor Text, the excerpt from *Gulliver's Travels*. Make a list of the allusions about which you would like to know more.

Assignment: With a small group, research the historical references in *Gulliver's Travels*, along with one or two other texts from Part 3. For each work you choose, create a slide presentation to serve as an annotated guide to the text. Identify the reference (you may include a quotation along with a page number) and then explain its historical significance based on your research. Present your slide shows to the class. Discuss how having specific historical information affects your reading of the texts.

Slide Show Plan

☐ **Identify references.** List allusions you want to explore.

☐ **Locate resources.** Conduct research to learn more. Note bibliographic information of your sources.

☐ **Create text slides.** For each historical reference, create a slide that presents the passage containing the reference. Include the author, title, and page number.

☐ **Create research slides.** Create as many slides as you need to explain the reference in a thorough and engaging way.

☐ **List sources.** Include a slide that contains a list of sources you used.

PART 4: The Essay

Listening and Speaking: Oral Reports Life in London was changing dramatically during the eighteenth century, and Joseph Addison was there to record and comment on the new cultural landscape. His journal *The Spectator* was, and is, celebrated for its musings on the manners, morals, and diversions of the day. Review the Anchor Text, "The Aims of *The Spectator*," and identify what Addison says he wants to accomplish with his publication.

Assignment: Work in a small group to create two oral reports. First, work together to paraphrase Addison's essay. Write your report, paraphrasing sentence-by-sentence, if necessary, to solidify your understanding of what Addison is saying. Once you are sure of his message, rewrite the essay in a modern format that applies to today's world, such as a blog, podcast, or local cable television show. Your group should read each report to the class and invite comments. Discuss whether Addison's ideas translate well to the twenty-first century.

- Quotation from Addison's essay:

  _____

  _____

- Paraphrase of Addison:

  _____

  _____

Test-Taking Practice

Common Core
State Standards

RL.11-12.1, RL.11-12.3,
RL.11-12.4; L.11-12.1,
L.11-12.3, L.11-12.4.a
[For the full wording of the
standards, see the standards
chart in the front of your
textbook.]

Reading Test: Humanities Passage

Humanities passages are one of the four types of reading selections
found on standardized tests. These passages come from memoirs
or essays and cover subjects in the arts and literature, philosophy,
and entertainment media. Questions can focus on main ideas and
supporting details, on the author's tone and style, and on the meaning
of particular words or sentences. They may require you to make
generalizations or analyze causes and effects.

Practice

*The following exercise is modeled after the ACT Reading Test,
Humanities section.*

Directions: Read the following passage, taken from John Donne's
"Meditation 17." Then, choose the *best* answer to each question.

No man is an island, entire of itself: every man is a piece of the
continent, a part of the main. If a clod be washed away by the sea,
Europe is the less, as well as if a promontory were, as well as if a
manor of thy friend's or of thine own were. Any man's death diminishes
5   me because I am involved in mankind, and therefore never send to
know for whom the bell tolls; it tolls for thee. Neither can we call this a
begging of misery or a borrowing of misery, as though we were not
miserable enough of ourselves but must fetch in more from the next
house, in taking upon us the misery of our neighbors. Truly it were an
10 excusable covetousness if we did; for affliction is a treasure, and scarce
any man hath enough of it. No man hath affliction enough that is not
matured and ripened by it, and made fit for God by that affliction. If a
man carry treasure in bullion, or in a wedge of gold, and have none
coined into current money, his treasure will not defray him as he travels.
15 Tribulation is treasure in the nature of it, but it is not current money in
the use of it, except we get nearer and nearer our home, heaven, by it.

1. Which of these best paraphrases lines 1–2?
   A. All men are connected to one another, but that is not true of women.
   B. People who live on islands are not isolated from one another.
   C. All people, by natural right, partly own the land where they live.
   D. No person exists in isolation; we are all connected.

2. Which best explains why Donne refers to the *clod* and the *promontory* in lines 2–3?
   F. Referring to both small and large pieces of land strengthens his argument.
   G. He emphasizes that Europe has both lowland and highland areas.
   H. Citing the landholdings of both the poor and the rich reinforces his point.
   J. Mentioning landforms of all shapes and sizes underlines his point that the world is constantly changing.

3. In the context of lines 1–5, it can reasonably be inferred that *diminishes* means:
   A. reduces the amount of light available.
   B. lessens something in quantity or size.
   C. saddens someone; causes grief.
   D. holds dominion over; controls.

4. Which of these best paraphrases lines 5–6?
   F. When church bells signal that someone has died, we should all attend the services.
   G. When church bells signal that someone has died, a part of each of us dies.
   H. One day, the church bell will toll for each of us, signaling our death.
   J. We should not ask why the church bell tolls but consider how morally we have lived our lives.

5. Why does Donne say in lines 6–7 that feeling the death of another person is not "a begging of misery or a borrowing of misery"?
   A. He believes we will be repaid for it in the end.
   B. He thinks that feeling is false rather than heartfelt.
   C. He argues that we are truly affected by that person's death.
   D. He says that we must pay for these feelings with our treasure.

6. From the context of lines 1–10, it can reasonably be inferred that *affliction* means:
   F. fond feelings for another person.
   G. difficult circumstances that cause suffering.
   H. pretending to have a better social status than one does.
   J. sympathy for people who are suffering.

7. Why is it surprising that Donne uses the phrase "excusable covetousness" in line 10 to refer to afflictions?
   A. It is surprising to say people desire afflictions.
   B. It is surprising to call covetousness excusable, because it is a sin.
   C. It is unusual to say people covet what neighbors own.
   D. Earlier in the piece, Donne condemned covetousness.

8. From the context of lines 12–14, it can reasonably be inferred that *bullion* means:
   F. sores upon the feet.
   G. something of value.
   H. money and jewels.
   J. land and property.

Grammar and Writing: Editing in Context

Editing-in-context segments often appear in the writing sections of standard-ized tests. They are made up of a reading passage with numbered sentences, some of which contain errors in grammar, style, and usage. For each question, you must choose the best way to correct a given sentence.

Practice

This exercise is modeled after the ACT English Test.

Directions: For each underlined sentence or portion of a sentence, choose the best alternative. If an item asks a question about the underlined portion, choose the best answer to the question.

Strategy

Narrow the Answer Options.

Make your task simpler by eliminating any an-swers that you know to be incorrect.

In "A Modest Proposal," Jonathan Swift <u>presents an outrageous and</u>
<u>disgusting idea calmly and rationally</u>. Beginning by establishing his cred-ibility, <u>the reader's confidence is gained by the anonymous writer</u>. First,
he paints a dismal picture of the difficult lives of the country's poor. Next, the
writer promises great advantages from his solution, declaring it will apply
<u>not only to beggars but also</u> to other families. Then, the author states that
he <u>has spent much time thinking about the problem and weighed</u>
<u>different options carefully</u>. <u>He details his calculations about births. He</u>
<u>uses mathematics to present an image of rationality.</u> <u>Relying on expert</u>
<u>testimony</u>, the writer dismisses another possible solution. Just before
finally dropping his bombshell, the writer states that he offers this idea
<u>"humbly" or hopes</u> there can be no objection. <u>Only after laying this</u>
<u>careful groundwork</u> does Swift allow his anonymous writer to present his
insane idea.

1. **A.** NO CHANGE
    B. presents an outrageous and a disgusting idea calmly and rationally.
    C. presents calmly an outrageous, rational, and disgusting idea.
    D. calmly and rationally presents an outrageous and disgusting idea.

2. **F.** NO CHANGE
    G. the reader's confidence is gained by Swift.
    H. the confidence of the reader is gained by the anonymous writer.
    J. the anonymous writer gains the reader's confidence.

3. What is the function of *not only* and *but also*?
    A. They are adjectives.
    B. They are coordinating conjunctions.
    C. They are correlative conjunctions.
    D. They are subordinating conjunctions.

4. **F.** NO CHANGE
    G. has spent careful time thinking about the problem and weighed different options.
    H. has spent much time thinking about the problem and carefully weighing different options.
    J. has carefully spent time thinking about the problem and weighed different options.

5. **A.** NO CHANGE
    B. Because he details his calculations about births, he presents an image of rationality.
    C. He details his calculations about births, but uses mathematics to present an image of rationality.
    D. He details his calculations about births; however, he uses mathematics to present an image of rationality.

6. What word or words are modified by this clause?
    F. the writer
    G. dismisses
    H. another possible
    J. solution

7. **A.** NO CHANGE
    B. "humbly" and hopes
    C. "humbly" but hopes
    D. either "humbly" or hopes

8. What is the function of the underlined words?
    F. prepositional phrase
    G. adverb clause
    H. independent clause
    J. no purpose; the words should be eliminated

 Timed Writing: Persuasive Essay [30 minutes]

An old saying goes, "If at first you don't succeed, try, try again." History is full of examples of people who reached their goals by sheer determination. However, persistence alone is not always sufficient to guarantee success.

In an essay, take a position on the above claim. You may argue any point of view. Be sure to back up your statements with sound reasoning and specific examples.

> **Academic Vocabulary**
> Carefully read the prompt and the assignment twice. Note key words and phrases, such as "take a position" or "examples," that clarify the assignment.

STOP

Constructed Response

 **Common Core State Standards**

RL.11-12.2, RL.11-12.3, RL.11-12.4;
RI.11-12.2, RI.11-12.4, RI.11-12.5;
W.11-12.2, W.11-12.9.a, W.11-12.9.b;
SL.11-12.6
[For the full wording of the standards, see the standards chart in the front of your textbook.]

Follow the instructions to complete the tasks below as required by your teacher. As you work on each task, incorporate both general academic vocabulary and literary terms you learned in this unit.

Writing

Task 1: Literature [RL.11-12.2; W.11-12.2, W.11-12.9.a]

Analyze the Development of Themes

Write an **essay** *in which you analyze the development of two or more themes in a literary work from this unit.*

- Identify a literary work from this unit that presents two or more significant themes. State which work you chose and explain your reasons for this choice.

- Explain the themes the work expresses and identify specific ways in which each theme is introduced and developed. Include an analysis of how the themes interact and build on one another.

- Cite specific details from the literary work under discussion to support your analysis.

- Use appropriate and varied transitions to clarify the relationships among your ideas.

Task 2: Literature [RL.11-12.3; W.11-12.2, W.11-12.9.a]

Analyze the Development of a Narrative

Write an **essay** *in which you analyze and evaluate the development of a narrative work from this unit.*

- Explain which work you chose and briefly summarize the essential elements, such as setting, situation, characters, conflict, and plot.

- Discuss how the author orders events and how he or she introduces and develops characters or new situations.

- Explain how the author's choices about the development of the narrative affect the reading experience and contribute to the narrative's larger meaning or themes.

- Organize your ideas so that each new idea builds on the one it follows to create a unified whole.

- Provide a concluding section that follows from the explanation presented.

Task 3: Informational Text [RI.11-12.5; W.11-12.9.b]

Analyze and Evaluate Text Structure

Write an **essay** *in which you analyze and evaluate the structure of a work of nonfiction from this unit.*

- Identify a work of nonfiction from this unit and provide a brief summary of its central ideas and key supporting details.

- Explain the structure the author chose. To clarify the work's structure for the reader, provide a list, an outline, or a clear description of its structural elements.

- Evaluate the effectiveness of the author's choice of structure. Identify specific ways in which the structure either contributes to or detracts from the meaning, and consider whether the structure itself helps to add interest to the work.

- Organize your essay logically and use thoughtful transitional words and phrases to clarify the flow of your ideas. Provide a concluding section that follows from and supports the evaluation you presented.

Speaking and Listening

Task 4: Informational Text [RI.11-12.4; SL.11-12.6]
Analyze Word Choice and Meaning

Deliver an **oral presentation** *in which you analyze the use of language in a nonfiction work from this unit.*

- Introduce the work you chose. Provide information about the author, explain the work's historical context, and briefly summarize its central ideas.

- Provide a broad overview of the type of diction the author employs. Then, identify specific word choices that are critical to the writer's overall purpose and expression of ideas. State why you chose these words and phrases, and explain their figurative, technical, or connotative meanings.

- Consider any key words or phrases the author uses repeatedly and discuss how the meaning of those terms is modified or refined over the course of the work.

- Include examples from the text that illustrate and support your analysis.

- Speak clearly and precisely so that listeners can follow your line of reasoning.

Task 5: Informational Text [RI.11-12.2; SL.11-12.6]
Analyze Central Ideas

Deliver an **oral presentation** *in which you analyze and evaluate the central ideas in a work of nonfiction from this unit.*

- Explain which work you chose and provide information about the historical context, occasion and purpose for the writing, and the author.

- Identify two or more central ideas expressed in the work. Cite specific details to show how the author introduces, develops, and refines each idea.

- Discuss your assessment of the central ideas. Include an evaluation of how well the two central ideas build on and reinforce one another.

- Provide hand-outs or other materials to help your listeners understand your ideas.

- Organize and develop your presentation logically and clearly, avoiding abrupt shifts in focus and using language that provides clear transitions among ideas.

Task 6: Literature [RL.11-12.4; SL.11-12.6]
Analyze Word Choice and Tone

Deliver a **visual presentation** *in which you analyze the impact of word choice on tone in a literary work from this unit.*

- State which work you chose and summarize its key elements—setting, characters, events, and themes.

- Describe the tone of the work. Cite at least three specific word choices—especially those with rich connotations or multiple meanings—that contribute to this tone.

- Incorporate visuals, such as drawings, photographs, or word maps, that illustrate the words and phrases you chose and capture the overall tone of the work. Discuss these choices.

- Present your ideas clearly and logically, using formal English and academic vocabulary.

What is the relationship between literature and place?

London as a Character The literature of the period addressed in this unit is filled with vivid personalities, authors, and fictional characters alike. Perhaps the greatest literary star of the period, however, is the city of London.

Assignment Write a **literary analysis** of the work of three authors from this unit. Analyze the role that London played—a "character" in its own drama, a vivid backdrop for action, or an area for a certain social class—in each work.

Titles for Extended Reading

In this unit, you have read a variety of British literature from the seventeenth and eighteenth centuries. Continue to read works related to this era on your own. Select books that you enjoy, but challenge yourself to explore new topics, new authors, and works offering varied perspectives or approaches. The titles suggested below will help you get started.

LITERATURE

Moll Flanders
Daniel Defoe

Fiction Moll Flanders starts out life as "a poor desolate girl" in seventeenth-century England. Gradually, she claws her way up to a life of wealth and security, making mistakes along the way. The novel presents an interesting portrait of a woman who is more a victim of society's evils than an evildoer herself.

[An excerpt from Defoe's A Journal of the Plague Year *begins on page 590. Build knowledge by reading another novel by this author.]*

Gulliver's Travels
Jonathan Swift

Satire Shipwrecked and cast adrift, Lemuel Gulliver awakes to find himself in Lilliput, an island inhabited by people whose six-inch height makes their quarrels over fashion and fame seem ridiculous. His subsequent encounters with equally strange individuals give Gulliver new, bitter insights into human behavior. With its wild distortions and undertones of the grotesque, *Gulliver's Travels* defies the reader's expectations of a conventional traveler's tale.

[An excerpt from Gulliver's Travels *begins on page 606 of this book. Build knowledge by reading the full text.]*

Donne: Selected Poetry
John Donne   **EXEMPLAR TEXT**

Poetry Enjoy the poetry of Donne's romantic youth and the more spiritual poetry of his later life. This collection contains Donne's famous poem "A Valediction: Forbidding Mourning."

[Donne's poems appear on pages 482–490 of this book. Build knowledge by reading other poems by this author.]

INFORMATIONAL TEXTS

Historical Texts

The Diary of Samuel Pepys
Samuel Pepys
Modern Library, 2001

Diary In his diary, Pepys recorded his observations and impressions of some of the great events of his time, including the Great Plague of 1665 and the Great Fire of London in 1666. Equally engaging are his accounts of everyday life in the seventeenth century.

[An excerpt of the diary begins on page 571 in this book. Build knowledge by reading the full text.]

Selected Letters
Lady Mary Wortley Montagu

Letters Writer and essayist Montagu wrote about her experiences with great humor and a unique perspective. Read her selected letters to learn about the life of this extraordinary woman.

Contemporary Scholarship

A Preface to Paradise Lost
C. S. Lewis
Oxford University Press, 1961

Literary Criticism In this critically acclaimed book, C. S. Lewis, a literary scholar and famed children's author, discusses the importance of the epic as a literary form and provides insight into Milton's *Paradise Lost.*

Samuel Johnson
W. Jackson Bate
Counterpoint, 1998

Biography This biography of Samuel Johnson, author of *A Dictionary of the English Language,* describes both the private and the public life of this extraordinary man of letters. Winner of both the National Book Award and the Pulitzer Prize, the book presents an engaging, modern look at this larger-than-life figure.

Preparing to Read Complex Texts

Reading for College and Career In both college and the work-place, readers must analyze texts independently, draw connections among works that offer varied perspectives, and develop their own ideas and informed opinions. The questions shown below, and others that you generate on your own, will help you more effectively read and analyze complex college-level texts.

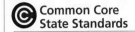 **Common Core State Standards**

Reading Literature/Informational Text
10. By the end of grade 12, read and comprehend literature, including stories, dramas, and poems, and literary nonfiction at the high end of the grades 11-CCR text complexity band independently and proficiently.

When reading complex texts, ask yourself...

- What idea, experience, or story seems to have compelled the author to write? Has the author presented that idea, experience, or story in a way that I, too, find compelling?

- How might the author's era, social status, belief system, or personal experiences have affected the point of view he or she expresses in the text?

- How do my circumstances affect what I understand and feel about this text?

- What key idea does the author state explicitly? What key idea does he or she suggest or imply? Which details in the text help me to perceive implied ideas?

- Do I find multiple layers of meaning in the text? If so, what relationships do I see among these layers of meaning?

- How do details in the text connect or relate to one another? Do I find any details unconvincing, unrelated, or out of place?

- Do I find the text believable and convincing?

Ⓒ Key Ideas and Details

- What patterns of organization or sequences do I find in the text? Do these patterns help me understand the ideas better?

- What do I notice about the author's style, including his or her diction, uses of imagery and figurative language, and syntax?

- Do I like the author's style? Is the author's style memorable?

- What emotional attitude does the author express toward the topic, the story, or the characters? Does this attitude seem appropriate?

- What emotional attitude does the author express toward me, the reader? Does this attitude seem appropriate?

- What do I notice about the author's voice—his or her personality on the page? Do I like this voice? Does it make me want to read on?

Ⓒ Craft and Structure

- Is the work fresh and original?

- Do I agree with the author's ideas entirely, or are there elements I find unconvincing?

- Do I disagree with the author's ideas entirely, or are there elements I can accept as true?

- Based on my knowledge of British literature, history, and culture, does this work reflect the British tradition? Why or why not?

Ⓒ Integration of Ideas

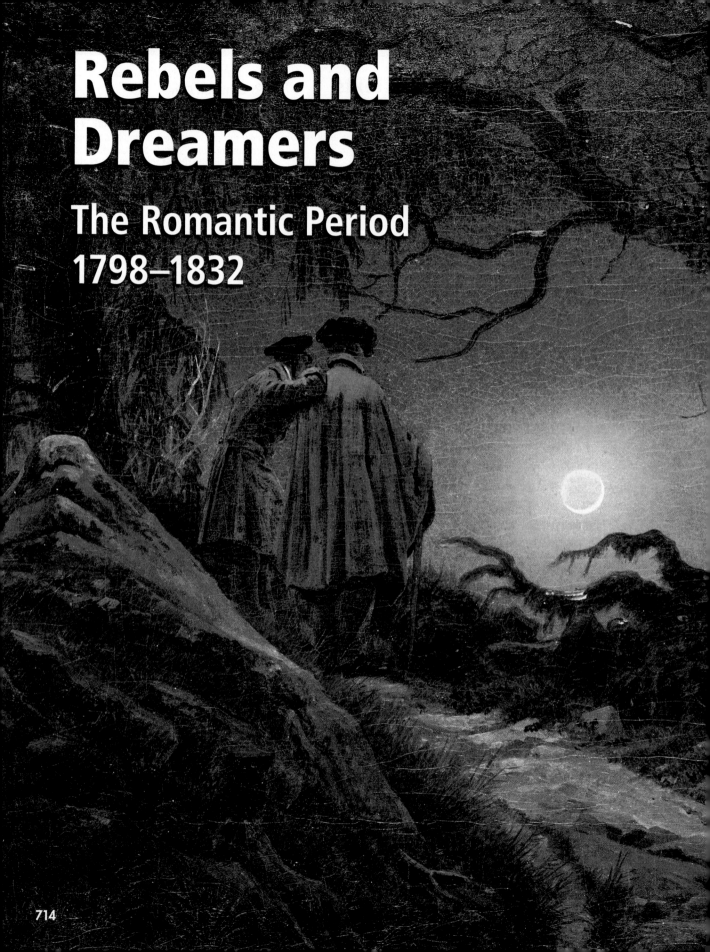

Rebels and Dreamers

The Romantic Period
1798–1832

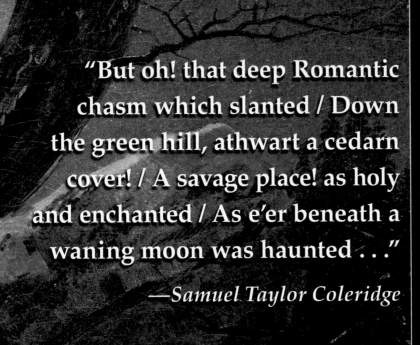

Unit 4

"But oh! that deep Romantic
chasm which slanted / Down
the green hill, athwart a cedarn
cover! / A savage place! as holy
and enchanted / As e'er beneath a
waning moon was haunted . . ."

—*Samuel Taylor Coleridge*

CLOSE READING TOOL

Use this tool to practice
the close reading strategies
you learn.

**ONLINE WRITER'S
NOTEBOOK**

Easily capture notes and
complete assignments online.

STUDENT eTEXT

Bring learning to life with audio,
video, and interactive tools.

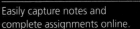
■ Find all Digital Resources at
pearsonrealize.com.

Snapshot of the Period

During the Romantic period, all the attitudes and assumptions of eighteenth-century classicism and rationalism were dramatically challenged, in part by social and political upheavals. The French Revolution, which began on July 14, 1789, shook the established order in the name of democratic ideals. Fearing the events in France, the English ruling class also felt threatened by unrest at home. British authorities tried to repress workers' efforts to organize, going so far as to kill a number of peaceful demonstrators in Manchester (1819). Another type of revolution, the Industrial Revolution, boosted the growth of manufacturing but also brought poverty and suffering for those who worked or failed to find work in slum-ridden cities. British Romantic writers responded to the climate of their times. For many of them, the faith in science and reason, so characteristic of eighteenth-century thought, no longer applied in a world of tyranny and factories.

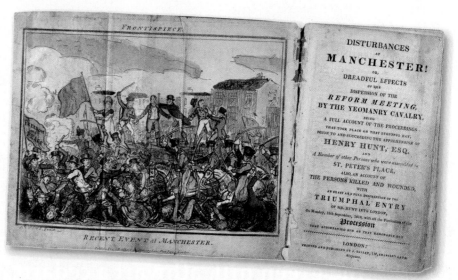

▶ In 1819, thousands of workers and their families demonstrated peacefully at St. Peter's Fields in Manchester to protest desperate economic conditions and to gain parliamentary reforms. Soldiers dispersed the crowd, injuring about 500 people and killing 11.

 As you read the selections in this unit, you will be asked to think about them in view of three key questions:

What is the **relationship** between literature and *place?*

How does literature **shape or reflect** *society?*

What is the relationship of the **writer** to *tradition?*

Integration of Knowledge and Ideas In the image below, the cracked façade and the pictures whirling out of it dramatize the way in which Romantic values challenged earlier Neoclassical beliefs in order and balance. Which of these Romantic values, described in the captions, are still influential today? Which seem historically interesting but no longer directly relevant to us today?

Seeking the Faraway

Wandering as a Rebel and an Outcast

Feeling Awe for Nature

Gaining Forbidden Knowledge

Honoring the Common Person

Creating the Fantastic

Historical Background

The Romantic Period (1798–1832)

For the first half of the Romantic period, England was at war with France. At home, the period was marked by growing urbanization and industrialization and demands for reform. At the end, a wasteful monarchy was redeemed by the succession of a shy, eighteen-year-old girl, Victoria.

English Victories Over Napoleon

Revolutionary France, led by Napoleon Bonaparte, declared war on Britain in 1793. In the ensuing conflict, two national heroes emerged for England. At sea, Lord Horatio Nelson shattered the French fleet at the Battle of Trafalgar (1805), ensuring that Britannia would rule the waves for the next century. Nelson, dying at his moment of triumph, passed immediately into legend. On land, the Duke of Wellington defeated Napoleon at Waterloo (1815).

With Napoleon in exile, the victors met in the conference known as the Congress of Vienna (1814–15) and tried to restore Europe to what it had been before the French Revolution. However, the ideas unleashed by that revolution and the earth-shaking changes of the Industrial Revolution were more powerful than any reactionary politician imagined.

Industrialization and Urbanization

In 1807, Robert Fulton launched his steamboat, and, in 1814, George Stephenson built a steam locomotive. Railroads changed the face of England, and steamships shrank oceans. It was the textile industry, however, that was at the forefront of change. Inventions, from the spinning jenny to the power loom, changed the way cloth was woven and moved the weaver from the spinning wheel in the kitchen to the factory.

Water power and then coal drove the machines that ran the mills that created the cities in which the workers lived. Wealth no longer depended on land, and workers, separated from the land, realized that they would have to unite in political action. The Reform Bill of 1832, the product of democratic impulses and changing economic conditions, was

Napoleon Bonaparte

TIMELINE

1799: Egypt
Rosetta Stone, key to deciphering hieroglyphics, discovered. ▶

1801: Act of Union creates United Kingdom of Great Britain and Ireland.

1798

1801: Union Jack becomes official flag of Great Britain and Ireland. ▶

a first step in extending the right to vote. It increased the voting rolls by 57 percent, but the working classes and some members of the lower middle classes were still unable to vote. In 1833, after the period ended, Parliament abolished slavery in the British Empire.

An Out-of-Touch Monarchy

The struggle for increased political rights was a difficult one. Those in power and those who wanted reform collided tragically at St. Peter's Field, Manchester, in 1819. Workers had assembled in a peaceful demonstration for economic and political reform. A cavalry charge killed eleven and wounded many women and children. Called the Peterloo Massacre, the incident inspired Shelley to write "England in 1819" which opens: "An old, mad, blind, despised and dying King."

Cruelly accurate, the line describes George III, who had been declared insane in 1811. His son, named Prince Regent, was designated to rule in his place (a regent substitutes for a ruler). This gave the period its name, The Regency, and the Regent's conduct gave it its scandalous reputation.

Extravagant, obese, separated from his wife in an ugly and very public marital quarrel, he was unaware of the great changes taking place around him. The Regent became George IV in 1820. In 1830, he was succeeded by his brother William, who had ten illegitimate children with his common-law wife, but no legitimate heir. When William died in 1837, the daughter of his younger brother was next in the royal line.

That daughter, Victoria, was determined to restore morality and dignity to the throne. She became the queen and then the symbol of an era in which political reform and industrial might made England the most powerful country in the world.

Key Historical Theme: Political Oppression vs. Political Reform

- Conservative European rulers tried to roll back revolutionary ideas.
- In England, industrialization prompted workers to organize.
- Police killed peacefully protesting workers in Manchester in 1819.
- The Reform Bill of 1832 extended the right to vote but not to the working classes.

1803: United States
Louisiana Territory purchased from France.

1804: Germany
Beethoven composes *Symphony No. 3.*

1805

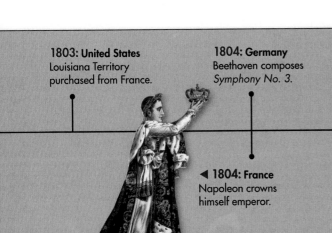

◄ **1804: France**
Napoleon crowns himself emperor.

▲ **1805:** Battle of Trafalgar.

Essential Questions Across Time

The Romantic Period (1798–1832)

 What is the relationship between literature **and** *place?*

English Romanticism was born in and inspired by a real place—the Lake District. (See the feature on the next page.) However, since Romanticism defines itself by opposition to the commonplace and familiar, much of the literature of the period is also set in exotic and faraway locations.

How did Romantics emphasize strange and faraway places?

In poetry, the Romantics took readers to distant lands, both real and imaginary. For example, Samuel Taylor Coleridge's Ancient Mariner sails around Cape Horn to the edge of Antarctica, which was just then being explored. He returns to narrate his strange adventures. In Coleridge's "Kubla Khan," the fabulous emperor dwells in a place that has come to symbolize luxury and mystery: Xanadu. Similarly, Percy Bysshe Shelley's poem "Ozymandias" takes us to "an antique land," the Egypt of the pharaohs, which had recently been invaded and plundered by Napoleon.

What worlds became refuges from the smoky cities?

Whether or not they wrote of exotic lands, the Romantic poets all sought something beyond this world, turning to nature and the imagination for transcendence. The worlds they explored were alternatives to the spreading stain of the cities; to what the poet William Blake called the "dark, Satanic mills," factories that seemed to chew up people.

The Lake District William Wordsworth, who settled in the beautiful Lake District—far from the urban blight of London, Manchester, and Birmingham—wrote of the natural world in a religious way. A "worshipper of Nature," he saw the landscape bathed in a heavenly light.

> **ESSENTIAL QUESTION VOCABULARY**
>
> These Essential Question words will help you think and write about literature and place:
>
> **exotic** (eg zöt´ ik) *adj.* foreign; strange or different in a way that is striking
>
> **secular** (sek´ yə lər) *adj.* relating to worldly things as opposed to religion
>
> **residential** (rez´ ə den´ shəl) *adj.* characterized by private homes

TIMELINE

1806: Germany
Prussia declares war on France.

1807: United States
Fulton's steamboat navigates Hudson River. ▼

1805

1806: Western Europe
Official end of Holy Roman Empire.

Going Beyond Wordsworth was a native of the Lake District; he had climbed its mountains and rowed across its lakes. He saw ideal beauty in the land that spread out before him. However, when Shelley writes of the skylark and John Keats of the nightingale, they are not concerned with describing these birds in their natural settings. Each celebrates the song and the flight of a bird that lures the poet beyond the bounds of earth.

The urban world the Romantics fled was not, as Wordsworth discovered, completely bleak. Wordsworth, poet of nature and the countryside, had a moment of stunned revelation when, at dawn on a clear September morning, he saw London from Westminster Bridge. "Earth," he wrote, "has not anything to show more fair . . ."

The City Improved—or Blighted London had indeed been improved. The architect John Nash contributed to the secular beautification of London as Christopher Wren had to the ecclesiastical, with the rebuilding of St. Paul's Cathedral after the Great Fire of 1666. Nash built the Brighton Pavilion, modeled in part on India's Taj Mahal, another example of the period's taste for the exotic and fantastic.

Bath, a city forever connected with Regency novelist Jane Austen, created its beautiful crescents, or curved streets, during this time. However, these Regency splendors were the exception. What the novelist Charles Dickens would later call "Coketown," a dirty, soul-destroying city, stands for the world from which the Romantic poets struggled to escape.

The BRITISH TRADITION

CLOSE-UP ON GEOGRAPHY

The Lake District, Cradle of Romanticism

The cradle of English Romanticism is the Lake District. Located in the northwest of England, this picturesque region contains some of the country's most impressive mountains and lakes. The Romantic poet William Wordsworth was born in the Lake District, wandered there as a boy, lived there as a man, and wrote poems inspired by its beauty. In the following passage, Wordsworth captures the mystery and thrill of his boyhood climbing expeditions in the region.

> . . . Oh! at that time,
> While on the perilous ridge I hung alone,
> With what strange utterance did the loud dry wind
> Blow through my ears! the sky seemed not a sky
> Of earth, and with what motion moved the clouds.
> —from *The Prelude*

▲ **1810: South America**
Simón Bolívar leads rebellion against Spanish rule.

1812: United States
War with Britain declared.

1812: Byron publishes *Childe Harold's Pilgrimage.* ▶

1812

How does literature **shape or** reflect *society?*

The French Revolution hit Europe like a tidal wave. The Industrial Revolution, which owes so much to inventor James Watt's improvements to the steam engine, is still shaping the world today. The social history of the period is the story of how people in general, and writers in particular, reacted to the shocks of these revolutions.

How did political and industrial revolutions affect society?

"Bliss was it in that dawn to be alive . . ." In his autobiographical epic, *The Prelude*, William Wordsworth looks back on the heady days when he and the French Revolution were young. Europe, he says, was "thrilled with joy" at the prospect of "human nature seeming born again." (Book 6, lines 340–342) More personally and poignantly: "Bliss was it in that dawn to be alive, / But to be young was very Heaven." (Book 11, lines 108–109)

Disillusionment Sets In The Revolution, however, turned blindly destructive, and England and France went to war. The young poet's bliss faded quickly, as did that of many who had such hope in the beginning. Napoleon's crowning himself emperor ended any belief that human nature had been born again.

Trying to Bring Back the Old Order In the aftermath of Napoleon's defeat, those in power were determined that human nature would not be reborn, and that the old order would be restored—the privileged few would continue to rule. However, the forces of democratic reform had been unleashed and could not be suppressed.

Ideas That Would Not Die The original message of the Revolution, the one that had thrilled Wordsworth, was that people were to be free in their personal lives and free to choose their government—that all people were equally "citizens." Although the later course of the Revolution might have distorted these ideas, the ideas themselves would not die.

> ### ESSENTIAL QUESTION VOCABULARY
>
> These Essential Question words will help you think and write about literature and society:
>
> **privileged** (priv´ ə lijd) *adj.* having rights or advantages denied to others
>
> **institution** (in´ stə too´ shən) *n.* established law, custom, or practice
>
> **industrial** (in dus´ trē əl) *adj.* of or connected with industries or manufacturing

TIMELINE

1813: Jane Austen publishes *Pride and Prejudice.*

1814: George Stephenson constructs first successful steam locomotive. ▶

— 1812 —

1813: Mexico independence declared.

◀ **1815: Belgium** Napoleon defeated at Waterloo.

In England, a group of men and women, mostly Quakers, led by William Wilberforce, were determined that one ancient social institution would be abolished. Thanks to them, slavery was ended in England and in the empire.

The Reform Bill of 1832 was another part of the peaceful revolution that transformed England. It extended the right to vote to many males previously disqualified by lack of wealth. The 1832 bill was a step in a century-long journey that, in the end, gave all citizens voting rights.

The Application of Power to Work Revolutions are about power, and the Industrial Revolution was about the application of power to work: the creation of machines that work while human beings feed and "tend" them.

Unfortunately, the mills—and the cities that grew up around them—crushed and destroyed many who came from the countryside looking for new opportunities. Economic progress exacted an enormous human price.

How did writers react to revolutionary changes?

Direct Responses Some writers directly addressed the problems of their changing world. Mary Wollstonecraft, a witness to the French Revolution, urged a radical transformation of society in her *Vindication of the Rights of Woman*. Among other social institutions, she criticized "a false system of education" geared to make women marriageable rather than knowledgeable.

The BRITISH TRADITION

THE CHANGING ENGLISH LANGUAGE BY RICHARD LEDERER

The Romantic Age

During the Romantic Age, Britannia ruled the waves, and English ruled much of the land. As British ships traveled throughout the world, they left the language of the mother country in their wake but also came home from foreign ports laden with cargoes of words from other languages freighted with new meanings for English speakers.

The biggest and fattest unabridged English dictionaries hold more than 600,000 words, compared to German in second place with 185,000 words. One reason we have accumulated the world's largest and most varied vocabulary is that English continues to be the most hospitable and democratic language that has ever existed, unique in the number and variety of its borrowed words.

The following are words that became part of the English language as a result of England's great economic expansion.

Africa *banana, boorish, chimpanzee, gorilla, gumbo,* and *zebra*

Asia *gingham, indigo, mango,* and *typhoon*

Australia *boomerang* and *kangaroo*

India *bandanna, bungalow, calico, cashmere, china, cot, curry, juggernaut, jungle, loot, nirvana, polo, punch* (beverage), *thug,* and *verandah*

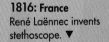

1816: France
René Laënnec invents stethoscope. ▼

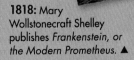

1818: Mary Wollstonecraft Shelley publishes *Frankenstein, or the Modern Prometheus.* ▲

1819: Peterloo Massacre in Manchester.

1819

Blake made his readers look at the reality of child labor in "The Chimney Sweeper." Lord Byron spoke "In Defense of the Lower Classes" when Parliament debated using the death penalty against protesting unemployed weavers. This rebellious aristocrat, who would later die in the Greek War of Independence, declared, "I have been in some of the most oppressed provinces of Turkey; but never . . . did I behold such squalid wretchedness as I have seen since my return, in the very heart of a Christian country."

Shelley's poem "Men of England" voiced anti-aristocratic sentiments and later became an anthem of the British Labour Party:

> *Men of England, wherefore plough*
> *For the lords who lay ye low?*
> *Wherefore weave with toil and care*
> *The rich robes your tyrants wear?*

Other Ways Some writers reminded people of other ways of being. Nature in the poetry of Wordsworth is not the artificial world of pastoral poetry. His nature is a cleaner, greener world in which human nature can be, if not reborn, at least restored. He writes in "Tintern Abbey": "Nature never did betray / The heart that loved her."

Revolution on a Page Not only that, Wordsworth's focus on common people and their language was a translation of the political goals of the French Revolution—"liberty, equality, fraternity"—into literature. If revolution had turned to terror on the stage of history, it still might be successful on the page.

An Era of Change The people of the time faced unprecedented changes. No political order could ever again be seen as unchangeable. That all people should be free and free to choose their leaders were ideas whose time had come. That economic progress could only be had at the cost of blighting the world was an idea to be challenged.

Some writers spoke out against the ills they saw; others looked inward or far away to see worlds that might be. Human nature was not born again, but human beings were changed profoundly.

Tintern Abbey

TIMELINE

1819: Percy Bysshe Shelley writes "Ode to the West Wind."

1820: John Keats publishes "Ode on a Grecian Urn." ▶

—1819

1819: First steamship crosses Atlantic. ▶

What is the relationship of the writer to *tradition?*

No writer of the period called himself or herself "Romantic," but later critics applied the term because they saw consistent themes and attitudes in the literature. *Romantic* in this sense does not mean love stories. It means everything that is the opposite of the drab, the ordinary, the conventional, the routine, the predictable, and the expected.

The Faraway and Exotic Romantic literature can be realistic, as in Scottish poet Robert Burns's "To a Louse," but the emphasis is on the faraway and exotic, as in the Xanadu of Coleridge's "Kubla Khan" and the fantastic and supernatural of his *The Rime of the Ancient Mariner.*

In what ways did Romantics reject previous traditions?

Discarding Eighteenth-Century Forms Romantics were by nature rebellious, unhappy with and unwilling to settle for the status quo. They cast aside the literary forms and subjects that had dominated the previous century—no more conventions and artificialities, satires and heroic couplets. Such forms were to be swept away, as the French Revolution had swept away powdered wigs and knee breeches. Prefigured by Burns and Blake, the new literature was to be authentic and sincere.

Using Ordinary Speech The use of ordinary speech in Romantic literature gave it its authentic feel. The poems of Burns and Joanna Baillie, written in Scottish dialect, proved to be popular with people of the common, or uneducated, class. Romantics achieved sincerity by revealing their personal thoughts and feelings. For example, Wordsworth charts the development of his consciousness with sincerity in *The Prelude.*

Political Rebels Writers were also rebelling against a political order that had, after victory over Napoleon's tyranny, itself become reactionary and repressive. They rebelled against an economic system that turned men, women, and children into factory "hands." They idolized seventeenth-century writer John Milton, in whom they saw a poet who stood up to kings and valued poetry for its prophetic strain.

1825: Russia Bolshoi Ballet founded. ▶

1826

◀ **1824:** Horse-drawn buses begin operating in England.

What poetical traditions did the Romantics revive?

The Sonnet Romantic poets revived the sonnet, which had virtually disappeared after Milton. Wordsworth used it as a political form in "London, 1802" and Shelley as a visionary form in "Ozymandias" and in "Ode to the West Wind," which is made up of linked sonnets.

The Ode In addition, the Romantics brought to perfection one of the oldest forms of poetry—the ode. Odes were written by Wordsworth, Coleridge, Shelley and, most notably, twenty-four-year-old John Keats.

What mysterious literary figure did the Romantics create?

The Byronic Hero Lord Byron embodies in his life the spirit of the age. A handsome, club-footed aristocrat who scorned the rules of society, he was described as "mad, bad and dangerous to know." Byron created in his person and in his characters the Byronic Hero—mysterious, brooding, threatening. That hero is the distant ancestor of today's mysterious outsiders, whether in film, literature, or the graphic novel.

What prose genres did the Romantics invent?

The leading novelists of the period were Jane Austen and Sir Walter Scott. Austen created a kind of comic novel that focused on the manners of middle-class people, depicting the follies and foibles of families. Her insights into human behavior and her comic touches have inspired today's directors to make film versions of Austen's *Emma* and *Pride and Prejudice*. Scott, regarded as the inventor of the historical novel, took readers back into the history, myths, and legends of England and Scotland. A best seller of his time and the creator of an enduring genre, he fed the Romantic hunger for the distant and the exotic.

The Gothic Mary Shelley wrote *Frankenstein*, influenced by the relatively new tradition of the horror-filled Gothic novel. Doctor Frankenstein, in creating his monster, acts out the great Romantic theme of going beyond the limit. The novel reveals the disquieting shadow cast by science and reason. Frankenstein's monster, in his immense solitude, also seems to warn of a darker side of Romantic ideals—of a humanity that, seeking to redefine itself, is, instead, cut off from its origins.

> **ESSENTIAL QUESTION VOCABULARY**
>
> These Essential Question words will help you think and write about the writer and tradition:
>
> **conventional** (kən venˊ shə nəl) *n.* usually an adjective, it refers as a noun to whatever follows rules and is not original
>
> **routine** (rōō tēnˊ) *n.* regular, customary procedure
>
> **foibles** (foiˊ bəlz) *n.* small weaknesses in character

TIMELINE

1826

1829: Robert Peel establishes Metropolitan Police in London. ▶

1827: System for purifying London water installed.

1830: Liverpool–Manchester railway opens. ▼

CONTEMPORARY CONNECTION

Jane Austen, Movie Star

At first glance, Jane Austen, a nineteenth-century novelist, seems an improbable box-office draw.

She never married, lived with her mother and sister, and died at age 41. Her novels lack sensation of the kind that modern audiences might be thought to crave. They mostly depict the lives of well-brought-up young ladies as they embark on the marriage-go-round.

Yet, since the 1990s, there have been literally dozens of successful film adaptations of Austen's books.

Some have been faithful to the original setting of her works, such as the 2005 *Pride and Prejudice* starring Keira Knightley. Other movies, such as *Clueless*, have transplanted plot and characters to more contemporary settings.

In 2007, the film *Becoming Jane* was made about Austen's own life, a fact that would certainly have brought a wry smile to her face.

As Hollywood has discovered, Austen's portrayal of human nature hits the mark every time. Her heroes and heroines may wear top hats and layers of petticoats. They may ride sedately in horse-drawn carriages. However, in their king's English, they speak directly to today's audiences, who see in these characters' dilemmas and decisions reflections of their own.

1831: Michael Faraday demonstrates electromagnetic induction. ▶

1832

◀ **1831: United States** Edgar Allan Poe publishes *Poems*.

1832: First Reform Act extends voting rights.

Recent Scholarship

ELIZABETH McCRACKEN

TALKS ABOUT THE TIME PERIOD

Creating a Legend

Mary Shelley wasn't the first person to imagine creating a living being out of something dead. The subtitle of *Frankenstein—The Modern Prometheus*—refers to the mythological Greek titan who made men out of clay. In a famous Jewish myth, a learned rabbi creates a creature out of clay to protect the Jewish people. Throughout the eighteenth century, inventors created increasingly complicated automata—early robots—who could eat, make musical instruments, and even play chess. People have always been fascinated by trying to create life, or the appearance of it, using nonliving material.

Science Explained

But Mary Shelley was the first writer to explain the notion of someone creating an actual living, breathing being using scientific methods. She was the product of her times. The eighteenth century was a time of enormous scientific discovery, including the work of Isaac Newton, the father of modern physics; the chemist Antoine Lavoisier; and Benjamin Franklin, with his experiments into electricity. Scientists and philosophers of the eighteenth century spoke of "The New Science," meaning that the universe could be understood by human beings who observed the natural world.

About the Author

Born in in 1966 in Boston, Massachusetts, to editor/writer parents, Elizabeth McCracken worked full time as a librarian until 1995. She draws on her love of that profession in the novel *The Giant's House: A Romance* (1996), which was a National Book Award finalist for fiction. Other works include the notable collection of short works, *Here's Your Hat, What's Your Hurry* (1993).

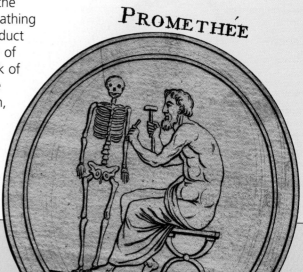

PROMÉTHÉE

Part of the Natural World

In the early nineteenth century, writing and science became more aligned than ever before. Percy Shelley was a passionate student of all the sciences. His college room was filled with his experiments. John Keats studied as a doctor. The "Dr. Darwin" mentioned in Mary Shelley's introduction is Charles's grandfather, Erasmus Darwin, who was not only a doctor, botanist, and inventor, but also a best-selling poet. William Wordsworth, Lord Byron, Percy Shelley, and John Keats all read Darwin and took what they learned about the natural world and applied it to their poetry. To be a human being was to be part of the natural world, and to write about nature, you had to study it very carefully. When the Romantic poets wrote about nature, they were also writing about the human condition. We are nature, and nature is us.

And, Mary Shelley might suggest, we better not mess with it. *Frankenstein* is filled with real and imagined science, but one of the reasons it's been popular for so long is that, at the dawn of modern science, Mary Shelley talked about how it was both exciting and dangerous. Before writing *Frankenstein*, Mary Shelley had had a child who died a few days after birth, and in her journal she writes of a dream in which the baby "came to life again . . . it had only been cold . . . and we rubbed it before the fire, and it lived." She knew the pain of wanting to bring something that was dead back to life, and then she wrote a book about the dangers.

Frankenstein had many children—characters from *Blade Runner, Robocop,* and *The Terminator,* clones and androids in any number of science fiction novels. You give something life, and then it goes amuck. Even now, when people argue about the latest scientific advances—transplants of animal organs, artificial organs, and of course cloning—*Frankenstein* is often the cautionary tale. We are nature, and nature is us, and we can never hope to completely master it.

▶ **Critical Viewing** In what way is a figure like this one a "Son of Frankenstein"?

Research and Technology: Synthesizing Information

As Elizabeth McCracken points out, Mary Shelley's *Frankenstein* influenced many horror movies about scientists going too far in their investigations. Working with a partner, create an **annotated filmography** of such films. Entitled "Frankenstein's Children," your filmography should include this information for each entry: title of movie, year of release, director, main actors, plot summary, and relationship to the Frankenstein theme of meddling with nature. For your research, use books on film and online resources like the Internet Movie Database. Consider using a simple *database* or *Excel chart* for your filmography and *integrating it into a word-processed document*.

Integrate and Evaluate Information

1. Use a chart like the one shown to determine the key ideas expressed in the Essential Question essays on pages 720–726. Fill in two ideas related to each Essential Question and note the authors most closely associated with each concept. One example has been done for you.

Essential Question	Author	Key Concept
Literature and Place		
Literature and Society		
Writer and Tradition	William Wordsworth	Using ordinary speech

2. How do the visual sources in this section—artifacts, paintings, photographs, and illustrations—add to your understanding of the ideas expressed in words? Cite specific examples.

3. The Romantic period was characterized by innovation and a rejection of tradition. Sometimes these innovations led to positive changes and a greater degree of freedom. Other times, they created new problems. Choose one innovation or change that emerged during this period and describe the various perspectives of those it affected. Who gained something from the change? Who lost something or was harmed by it? Cite evidence from the multiple sources presented on pages 718–726 in your answer.

4. **Address a Question** According to Elizabeth McCracken, the Romantic poets understood that "we are nature, and nature is us." What do you think McCracken means by this? In your view, is this idea mostly honored or ignored in today's world? Integrate information from this textbook and other sources to support your ideas.

Speaking and Listening: Press Conference

Romantic poets challenged earlier literary practices. With a group, stage a **press conference** in which Wordsworth; his sister, Dorothy; and Coleridge answer questions about their Romantic beliefs. The questioners are journalists who pose challenging queries like these:

- Why do Romantics reject refined language?
- Why do Romantics promote dangerous revolutionary ideas?
- Why are Romantics prejudiced against cities?

Solve a Research Problem: This assignment requires you to integrate information and distinguish nuances in Romantic beliefs. To prepare, research Romantic ideas about language, politics, and nature. Identify print and media sources that provide reliable information about Romanticism. Consider using various types of sources, including

- **primary sources,** or the poets' written works; and
- **secondary sources,** or books and articles about this era.

Create a list of sources you used to prepare.

 **Common Core State Standards**

Reading Informational Text
7. Integrate and evaluate multiple sources of information presented in different media or formats as well as in words in order to address a question or solve a problem.

Speaking and Listening
1. Initiate and participate effectively in a range of collaborative discussions with diverse partners on *grades 11–12 topics, texts, and issues,* building on others' ideas and expressing their own clearly and persuasively.

1.c. Propel conversations by posing and responding to questions that probe reasoning and evidence; ensure a hearing for a full range of positions on a topic or issue; clarify, verify, or challenge ideas and conclusions; and promote divergent and creative perspectives.

ESSENTIAL QUESTION VOCABULARY

Use these words in your responses:

Literature and Place
exotic
secular
residential

Literature and Society
privileged
institution
industrial

The Writer and Tradition
conventional
routine
foibles

Fantasy and Reality

Connecting to the Essential Question These poets have a sharp eye for people's behavior in social situations. As you read, consider what these poets observe and say about the social customs and attitudes of their time. Noting this information will help you answer the Essential Question: **How does literature shape or reflect society?**

Close Reading Focus

Dialect
Dialect is the language, and particularly the speech habits, of a specific social class, region, or group. A dialect may vary from the standard form of a language in grammar, in pronunciation, and in the use of certain expressions. In literature, dialect helps achieve these goals:

- Establishing character, mood, and setting
- Adding "texture" or charm for readers who do not speak the dialect

By using dialect, Burns and Baillie broke with tradition and made their work accessible to the common folk who spoke that dialect. Their use of dialect also adds a sense of authenticity and freshness to the poems. As you read, note the ways in which the poets infuse the dialect with poetic effects.

Comparing Literary Works In addition to using dialect, Romantic poets like Burns and Baillie also introduced subjects drawn from everyday life. This shift away from lofty topics was part of the artistic rebellion known as *Romanticism*. As you read, compare how effectively these poets write about daily life in the language of common folk. Consider factors such as their ability to convey *mood,* or emotional atmosphere, and *meaning*.

Preparing to Read Complex Texts Even if you do not know Scottish dialect, you can **analyze information from text features** to interpret words. As you read, pay attention to features such as footnotes and apostrophes indicating missing letters in a word. Use a chart like the one shown to help you translate the dialect.

Vocabulary

The words below are key to understanding the texts that follow. Copy the words into your notebook and identify which words are nouns. What clues point to the words' part of speech?

dominion   discretion

impudence   inconstantly

winsome

**Common Core
State Standards**

Reading Literature
4. Determine the meaning of words and phrases as they are used in the text, including figurative and connotative meanings; analyze the impact of specific word choices on meaning and tone, including words with multiple meanings or language that is particularly fresh, engaging, or beautiful.

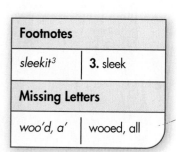

Footnotes	
sleekit[3]	**3.** sleek

Missing Letters	
woo'd, a'	wooed, all

Robert Burns

(1759–1796)

Author of "To a Mouse" • "To a Louse"

Known as "The Voice of Scotland," Robert Burns wrote his first verse when he was fifteen. It was a love poem to a girl named Nellie, who was helping the Burns family with the harvest on their farm in Scotland. "Thus with me," Burns later wrote, "began Love and Poesy."

Poor But Learned Beginnings Burns was born at Alloway, in Ayrshire. Although poverty kept him from a full formal education, with his father's encouragement he read widely, studying the Bible, Shakespeare, and Alexander Pope. His mother, though herself illiterate, instilled in him a love of Scottish folk songs, legends, and proverbs.

Literary Triumph In 1786, Burns published his first collection of poems, *Poems, Chiefly in the Scottish Dialect,* through a small local press. The collection, which included "To a Mouse," was a huge success, applauded by critics and country folk alike. The new literary hero was invited to the Scottish capital, where he was swept into the social scene and hailed as the "heaven-taught plowman." When he died, thousands of people from all social levels followed his coffin to the grave.

A Lasting Contribution Although Burns died while just in his thirties, having suffered for years from a weak heart, his brief career resulted in a lasting contribution to literature. Burns's poems, written for the most part in dialect, are marked by their natural, direct, and spontaneous quality. Burns certainly drew on the ballad tradition of Scotland, but while some of the poet's work had its origins in folk tunes, "it is not," as critic James Douglas writes, "easy to tell where the vernacular ends and the personal magic begins."

"My heart's in the Highlands . . ."

TO A MOUSE

On Turning Her up in Her Nest with the Plow, November, 1785

Robert Burns

BACKGROUND

Before Robert Burns published his poetry, works of literature were almost always modeled on the classics, in which structure, grammar, and vocabulary were polished and complex. Robert Burns ignored these conventions and boldly put poetry in the hands of the people, writing in their language, Scottish dialect, and using common folk as subject matter.

Wee, sleekit,[1] cow'rin', tim'rous beastie,
O, what a panic's in thy breastie!
Thou need na start awa sae hasty,
     Wi' bickering brattle![2]
5 I wad be laith[3] to rin an' chase thee
     Wi' murd'ring pattle![4]

I'm truly sorry man's dominion
Has broken Nature's social union,
An' justifies that ill opinion,
10   Which makes thee startle,
At me, thy poor, earth-born companion,
     An' fellow-mortal!

I doubt na, whyles,[5] but thou may thieve;
What then? poor beastie, thou maun[6] live!
15 A daimen icker in a thrave[7]
     'S a sma' request:
I'll get a blessin' wi' the lave,[8]
     And never miss't!

Thy wee bit housie, too, in ruin!
20 Its silly wa's[9] the win's are strewin'!
An' naething, now, to big[10] a new ane,
     O' foggage[11] green!
An' bleak December's winds ensuin',
     Baith snell[12] an' keen!

25 Thou saw the fields laid bare and waste,
An' weary winter comin' fast,
An' cozie here, beneath the blast,
     Thou thought to dwell,
Till crash! the cruel coulter[13] past
30   Out through thy cell.

---

1. sleekit sleek.
2. Wi' . . . brattle with a quick pattering sound.
3. wad be laith would be loath.
4. pattle paddle for cleaning a plow.
5. whyles at times.
6. maun must.
7. A . . . thrave an occasional ear of grain in a bundle.
8. lave rest.
9. silly wa's feeble walls.
10. big build.
11. foggage rough grass.
12. snell sharp.
13. coulter plow blade.

Vocabulary
dominion (də min´ yən)
n. rule; authority

Spiral Review
Conceit In what ways does the poem build a conceit about the mouse as the speaker's companion or equal?

Analyzing Text Features

Use context clues and nearby footnotes to determine the meaning of "win's" in line 20.

Comprehension

How does the speaker uncover the mouse?

That wee bit heap o' leaves an' stibble,
Has cost thee mony a weary nibble!
Now thou's turned out, for a' thy trouble,
    But[14] house or hald,[15]
35 To thole[16] the winter's sleety dribble,
    An' cranreuch[17] cauld!

But, Mousie, thou art no thy lane,[18]
In proving foresight may be vain:
The best laid schemes o' mice an' men
    Gang aft a-gley,[19]
40 An' lea'e us nought but grief an' pain,
    For promised joy.

Still thou art blest, compared wi' me!
The present only toucheth thee:
45 But, och! I backward cast my e'e
    On prospects drear!
An' forward, though I canna see,
    I guess an' fear!

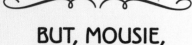

BUT, MOUSIE,
thou art no
thy lane,
In proving
foresight may
be vain:

14. **But** without.
15. **hald** property.
16. **thole** withstand.
17. **cranreuch** (krən′ rəkh) frost.
18. **no thy lane** not alone.
19. **Gang aft a-gley** go often awry.

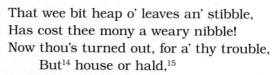

Critical Reading

Cite textual evidence to support your responses.

1. **Key Ideas and Details (a)** For what reason does the speaker apologize to the mouse? **(b) Infer:** How does the speaker feel about the grain the mouse steals? **(c) Interpret:** What does the speaker's reaction show about his ideas of justice?

2. **Key Ideas and Details (a) Infer:** What has happened to the mouse's attempt to prepare for winter? **(b) Interpret:** Which two famous lines in the poem express the poem's theme? **(c) Paraphrase:** Restate the theme in your own words.

3. **Key Ideas and Details (a) Interpret:** What comparison does the speaker draw between himself and the mouse in the last stanza? **(b) Evaluate:** Do you agree with the speaker about the mouse's advantage? Explain.

4. **Integration of Knowledge and Ideas** What value do you place on foresight? Explain.

5. **Craft and Structure** Does dialect add to the quality of folk-wisdom in the poem, or does it distract from the meaning? Explain.

To a Louse

On Seeing One on a Lady's Bonnet At Church

Robert Burns

◀ **Critical Viewing**

In what way are this lady's pose and costume similar to those of the lady in the poem? Explain. **CONNECT**

Ha! whare ye gaun, ye crowlin' ferlie!¹
Your impudence protects you sairly:²
I canna say but ye strunt³ rarely,
    Owre gauze and lace;
5 Though faith! I fear ye dine but sparely
    On sic a place.

Ye ugly, creepin', blastit wonner,⁴
Detested, shunned by saunt an' sinner,
How dare ye set your fit⁵ upon her,

Vocabulary

impudence (im´ pyo͞o dəns)
n. lack of shame; rudeness

Comprehension

Where is the louse crawling?

---

1. **crowlin' ferlie** crawling wonder.
2. **sairly** wondrously.
3. **strunt** strut.
4. **blastit wonner** blasted wonder.
5. **fit** foot.

The Literature of Scotland

Burns's dialect poems were part of a long struggle over Scottish identity. From the late thirteenth century to the middle of the sixteenth century, the Lowlands area of Scotland—Burns's native region—frequently warred with England. A distinctive culture blossomed in the region, yielding famous ballads such as "Barbara Allan."

When Scotland united with England in 1707, important Scottish authors of the time, such as economist Adam Smith, wrote in English as the English spoke it. However, there was a backlash, and Scotland was swept by a literary enthusiasm for things distinctly Scottish. In the poems of Burns, Baillie, and others, as well as in a new passion for collecting the old ballads, the Scottish past reasserted itself even as it faded.

Connect to the Literature

Read aloud lines 7–12. What effect does the Scottish dialect of selected words have on the entire stanza?

10   Sae fine a lady?
Gae somewhere else, and seek your dinner
        On some poor body.

Swith![6] in some beggar's haffet[7] squattle;[8]
There ye may creep, and sprawl, and sprattle[9]
15 Wi' ither kindred, jumping cattle,
        In shoals and nations:
Whare horn nor bane[10] ne'er dare unsettle
        Your thick plantations.

Now haud[11] ye there, ye're out o' sight,
20 Below the fatt'rels,[12] snug an' tight;
Na, faith ye yet![13] ye'll no be right
        Till ye've got on it,
The vera tapmost, tow'ring height
        O' Miss's bonnet.

25 My sooth! right bauld ye set your nose out,
As plump and gray as onie grozet;[14]
O for some rank, mercurial rozet,[15]
        Or fell,[16] red smeddum,[17]
I'd gie you sic a hearty dose o't,
30   Wad dress your droddum![18]

I wad na been surprised to spy
You on an auld wife's flannen toy;[19]
Or aiblins some bit duddie boy,[20]
        On's wyliecoat;[21]

---

6. **Swith** swift.
7. **haffet** locks.
8. **squattle** sprawl.
9. **sprattle** struggle.
10. **horn nor bane** comb made of horn or bone.
11. **haud** hold.
12. **fatt'rels** ribbon ends.
13. **Na, faith ye yet!** "Confound you!"
14. **onie grozet** (gräz´ it) any gooseberry.
15. **rozet** (räz´ it) rosin.
16. **fell** sharp.
17. **smeddum** powder.
18. **Wad . . . droddum** "would put an end to you."
19. **flannen toy** flannel cap.
20. **Or . . . boy** or perhaps on some little ragged boy.
21. **wyliecoat** (wī´ lē kōt´) undershirt.

35 But Miss's fine Lunardi![22] fie,
     How daur ye do't?

O, Jenny, dinna toss your head,
An' set your beauties a' abread![23]
Ye little ken what cursèd speed
40   The blastie's[24] makin'!
Thae[25] winks and finger-ends, I dread,
     Are notice takin'!

O wad some Pow'r the giftie gie us
To see oursels as ithers see us!
45 It wad frae monie a blunder free us
     And foolish notion:
What airs in dress an' gait wad lea'e us,
     And ev'n devotion!

What airs in dress an' gait wad lea'e us, And ev'n devotion!

---

22. **Lunardi** balloon-shaped bonnet, named for Vincenzo Lunardi, a balloonist of the late 1700s.
23. **abread** abroad.
24. **blastie's** creature's.
25. **Thae** those.

Critical Reading

1. **Key Ideas and Details (a)** What is the louse doing? **(b)** What does the speaker command it to do instead? **(c) Interpret:** What social assumptions about cleanliness does the speaker's command reflect?

2. **Key Ideas and Details (a) Draw Conclusions:** What impression of Jenny does the speaker create? **(b) Analyze:** How do the references to her clothing and the contrast between her and "some poor body" contribute to this impression?

3. **Key Ideas and Details (a) Infer:** In lines 37–42, why does the speaker warn Jenny against tossing her head? **(b) Infer:** What is the reaction of others in the church to Jenny's gesture? **(c) Draw Conclusions:** Why is the contrast between this gesture and the progress of the louse particularly embarrassing?

4. **Integration of Knowledge and Ideas (a) Interpret:** Paraphrase the generalization that the speaker makes in the last stanza. **(b) Evaluate:** Do you agree that we would profit if we could "see oursels as ithers see us"? Explain.

5. **Integration of Knowledge and Ideas** Do you think caring about the impression we make on others is foolish vanity? Explain.

Joanna Baillie

(1762–1851)

Author of "Woo'd and Married and A'"

When Joanna Baillie's (bā´ lēz) *Plays on the Passions* was published anonymously in 1798, it created a great literary sensation in London. Debates raged over which famous man of letters had written the plays. It was not until 1800 that the true author was revealed—an unassuming thirty-eight-year-old Scottish woman named Joanna Baillie. Even her literary friends were astounded, and she became an instant celebrity.

A Gregarious Tomboy Born in Lanarkshire, Scotland, the daughter of a minister, young Joanna Baillie was a tomboy who loved horseback riding and who resisted the stern moral education given by her father. She blossomed when she and her sister, Agnes, were sent away to boarding school in 1772. Joanna Baillie became an outgoing leader who led the other girls on boisterous outdoor adventures and staged plays that she herself wrote.

A Spinster's Life in London When Baillie's father died in 1778, the family depended on the kindness of a wealthy uncle for support. He provided the two sisters with a lifetime income. When their brother married in 1791, the sisters and their mother started a household of their own. They began a busy social life amid London's bustling literary scene, welcoming many important writers of the day into their home.

Success and Critical Acclaim With Baillie's literary success, the two sisters were able to travel, and they often returned to Scotland to visit Sir Walter Scott, who helped in the production of Baillie's plays. Best known in her day for her dramatic works, Baillie also wrote poetry. Like her fellow Scot, Robert Burns, she wrote poems in the dialect of her homeland, many of them on nature and rustic manners.

> **"Pampered vanity is a better thing perhaps than starved pride."**

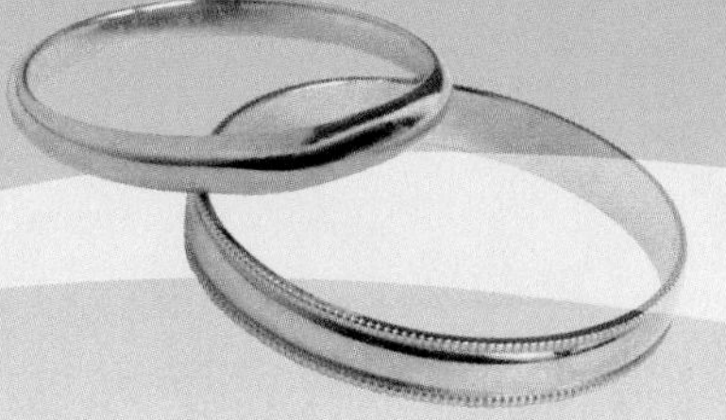

Woo'd and Married and A'

Joanna Baillie

The bride she is winsome and bonny,
Her hair it is snooded[1] sae sleek,
And faithfu' and kind is her Johnny,
Yet fast fa' the tears on her cheek.
New pearlins[2] are cause of her sorrow,
New pearlins and plenishing[3] too;
The bride that has a' to borrow
Has e'en right mickle[4] ado.
Woo'd and married and a'!
Woo'd and married and a'!
Is na' she very weel aff
To be woo'd and married at a'?

Her mither then hastily spak,
"The Lassie is glaikit[5] wi' pride;
In my pouch I had never a plack[6]
On the day when I was a bride.
E'en tak to your wheel and be clever,
And draw out your thread in the sun;
The gear[7] that is gifted it never
Will last like the gear that is won.
Woo'd and married and a'!
Wi' havins and toucher[8] sae sma'!
I think ye are very weel aff
To be woo'd and married at a'."

Vocabulary
winsome (win′ səm) *adj.* having a charming appearance or way

Dialect
What feelings or qualities does the use of dialect add to the mother's advice to her daughter?

Comprehension
What is the mother's opinion about her daughter's marriage?

1. **snooded** bound up with a ribbon.
2. **pearlins** lace trimmings.
3. **plenishing** furnishings.
4. **mickle** much.
5. **glaikit** foolish.
6. **plack** farthing; a small coin equal to one fourth of a penny.
7. **gear** wealth or goods.
8. **havins and toucher** possessions and dowry.

The Village Wedding, (detail) Sir Luke Fildes, Christopher Wood Gallery, London

▲ Critical Viewing

Compare and contrast the setting and costumes in this painting with the scene described in the poem. **COMPARE AND CONTRAST**

Vocabulary

discretion (di skresh´ ən) *n.* good judgment; prudence

inconstantly (in kän´ stənt lē) *adv.* changeably; in a fickle way

25   "Toot, toot," quo' her gray-headed faither,
          "She's less o' a bride than a bairn,[9]
      She's ta'en like a cout[10] frae the heather,
          Wi' sense and discretion to learn.
      Half husband, I trow, and half daddy,
30   As humor inconstantly leans,
      The chiel maun be patient and steady[11]
          That yokes wi' a mate in her teens.
              A kerchief sae douce[12] and sae neat
              O'er her locks that the wind used to blaw!
35   I'm baith like to laugh and to greet[13]
          When I think of her married at a'!"

      Then out spak the wily bridegroom,
          Weel waled[14] were his wordies, I ween,
      "I'm rich, though my coffer be toom,[15]
40   Wi' the blinks o' your bonny blue e'en.[16]
      I'm prouder o' thee by my side,

---

9. **bairn** child.
10. **cout** colt.
11. **The chiel maun . . . steady** The man must be patient and steady.
12. **douce** respectable.
13. **greet** weep.
14. **waled** chosen.
15. **toom** empty.
16. **e'en** eyes.

Though thy ruffles or ribbons be few,
 Than if Kate o' the Croft were my bride
  Wi' purfles[17] and pearlins enow.
45   Dear and dearest of ony!
   Ye're woo'd and buikit[18] and a'!
 And do ye think scorn o' your Johnny,
 And grieve to be married at a'?"

 She turn'd, and she blush'd, and she smiled,
50   And she looked sae bashfully down;
 The pride o' her heart was beguiled,
  And she played wi' the sleeves o' her gown.
 She twirled the tag o' her lace,
  And she nipped her boddice sae blue,
55 Syne blinkit sae sweet in his face,
  And aff like a maukin[19] she flew.
   Woo'd and married and a'!
 Wi' Johnny to roose[20] her and a'!
 She thinks hersel very weel aff
60   To be woo'd and married at a'!

---

17. purfles embroidered trimmings.
18. buikit "booked"; entered as married in the official registry.
19. maukin hare.
20. roose praise.

Critical Reading

1. **Key Ideas and Details (a)** How does the bridegroom respond to his bride's unhappiness? **(b) Analyze Cause and Effect:** Describe the effect the bridegroom's words have on his young bride. **(c) Draw Conclusions:** How would you describe the personality of the bridegroom?

2. **Key Ideas and Details (a)** Which speaker succeeds in changing the bride's outlook? **(b) Draw Conclusions:** Judging from the final stanza, do you think the marriage will be a happy one? Explain.

3. **Integration of Knowledge and Ideas** Do you think the poet is unkind to the young bride, or does she show insight into people? Explain.

4. **Integration of Knowledge and Ideas** What are the poets' attitudes toward the behaviors they describe in these poems? In your response, use at least two of these Essential Question words: *traditional, role, spirit. [Connecting to the Essential Question: How does literature shape or reflect society?]*

Cite textual evidence to support your responses.

Literary Analysis

1. **Key Ideas and Details** Using **information from text features,** list and define ten words in dialect that appear in these poems.

2. **Craft and Structure (a)** What does the use of **dialect** in the poems by Burns suggest about the speaker's social status? **(b)** How might the use of dialect affect a reader's appreciation of the poems?

3. **Craft and Structure** What does dialect contribute to the setting of Joanna Baillie's "Woo'd and Married and A'"?

4. **Craft and Structure** Find at least two examples in "To a Mouse" of the following pronunciation patterns for Scottish English: **(a)** Final consonants are dropped, and **(b)** the letter *o* is replaced by either *ae* or *a*.

5. **Craft and Structure** How would the overall effect of these poems have been different if they had been written in Standard English? Use examples from the texts to support your points.

6. **Comparing Literary Works** Using a chart like the one shown, analyze the subject matter of the poems in this grouping.

Poem	Subject	Message

7. **Comparing Literary Works (a)** Which poem conveys a message that applies most generally? Explain. **(b)** Which poem conveys a message that applies only to some people? Explain.

8. **Integration of Knowledge and Ideas** Do you think the use of everyday subjects in these poems limits the messages they convey? Explain, using details from the text to support your position.

9. **Integration of Knowledge and Ideas (a)** Choose one stanza from a Burns or Baillie poem, and translate it into Standard English. **(b)** Compare and contrast the original with your version, indicating what has been gained or lost in the translation.

10. **Integration of Knowledge and Ideas (a)** Use text aids to write one or two lines of poetry in Scottish dialect. **(b)** Does dialect work better for poetry meant to be read aloud? Why or why not? **(c)** What are the pros and cons of writing poetry in dialect?

 **Common Core State Standards**

Language
5.b. Analyze nuances in the meaning of words with similar denotations. *(p. 745)*

Writing
1.b. Develop claim(s) and counterclaims fairly and thoroughly, supplying the most relevant evidence for each while pointing out the strengths and limitations of both in a manner that anticipates the audience's knowledge level, concerns, values, and possible biases. *(p. 745)*

Vocabulary Acquisition and Use

Word Analysis: Anglo-Saxon Suffix -some

Baillie calls the bride in her poem *winsome*, meaning "charming." The Anglo-Saxon suffix *-some* means "tending to" or "tending toward being." Literally, *winsome* means "tending to win over or to delight." Use this meaning of the suffix to infer the meaning of each of these words. If necessary, use a *dictionary* to check your educated guesses.

1. awesome
2. handsome
3. lithesome
4. loathsome
5. tiresome
6. worrisome

Then, invent your own new adjective using the suffix *-some*, and explain how the suffix helps create the word's meaning.

Vocabulary: Synonyms

Synonyms are words that share similar denotations, or dictionary definitions. Write the letter of the word that is the best synonym of each word from the vocabulary list on page 732. Then, use a dictionary to explain any nuances in meaning between the synonyms in each pair.

1. dominion: **(a)** incapability **(b)** rule **(c)** pride
2. impudence: **(a)** rudeness **(b)** shyness **(c)** test
3. winsome: **(a)** competitive **(b)** bold **(c)** attractive
4. discretion: **(a)** quiet **(b)** caution **(c)** gratitude
5. inconstantly: **(a)** changeably **(b)** emptily **(c)** sadly

Writing to Sources

Argumentative Text Both Burns and Baillie use dialect, the distinctive language of a group's everyday speech, in their poems. Suppose you have been invited to speak at a literary festival on the use of dialect in literature. Prepare a three- to five-minute **editorial** speech in which you argue that using dialect is or is not a valuable literary technique.

Prewriting Develop a list of arguments both for and against using dialect. Based on those arguments, decide which position you will take. Use your list of arguments to develop an outline for your speech. Be sure to include the opposing arguments, or counterclaims, in your outline; use the ones you favor to refute them.

Drafting Draft your speech following your outline. Present evidence for your position by using examples from the Burns and Baillie poems. Use persuasive techniques such as *appeals to authority, appeals to emotion, rhetorical questions,* and *irony* to make your speech more persuasive.

> **Model: Revising to Add Supporting Evidence**
> Burns's poetry may seem difficult, but context can reveal the
> In "To a Louse," the context of lines 11
> and 12 clearly shows that "Gae" means "go."
> words hidden beneath strange spellings.
>
> Using examples from the poems will support your claims.

Revising Rehearse your delivery, timing yourself and focusing on *performance details*. Make sure the arguments and evidence you present are clear and convincing. Revise the text to fix any trouble spots you find.

Connecting to the Essential Question Like many modern-day artists, Blake pointed out to his audience the misery of fellow humans. As you read, identify passages in which Blake seems to focus on social ills. Doing so will help as you explore the Essential Question: **How does literature shape or reflect society?**

Close Reading Focus

Archetype; Social Commentary

Blake was a poet who had one eye on mystical visions and the other on the real social ills around him. His mystical visions were based on a perception of **archetypes**—plot patterns, character types, or ideas with emotional power and widespread appeal. Critics argue that archetypes reveal in symbolic form universal truths about humanity. Blake often expressed such archetypes in paired poems, like "The Lamb" and "The Tyger."

Blake is perhaps less well known for his **social commentary**—his criticism of the ills caused by the Industrial Revolution and political tyranny. This Blake, author of "The Chimney Sweeper," had his eye not on the clouds but on urban slums and on the factories in which men, women, and children labored for long hours and little pay.

Comparing Literary Works As you read, compare and contrast these two thematic approaches in Blake's poems: the archetypal visions and the social commentary.

Preparing to Read Complex Texts **Applying critical perspectives** will help you better understand Blake's complex vision of society. As you read, use the following perspectives as ways of understanding Blake's use of archetypes and social commentary:

- *Historical and political perspective*: Look for details that suggest economic or political oppression.
- *Archetypal perspective*: Look for images, characters, and patterns that have universal meaning and a strong emotional charge.

Use a chart like the one shown to apply both of these perspectives.

Vocabulary

You will encounter the words listed here in the texts that follow. Copy the words into your notebook. Note which words are plural nouns.

vales	aspire
immortal	sinews
symmetry	sulk

Common Core State Standards

Reading Literature

2. Determine two or more themes or central ideas of a text and analyze their development over the course of the text, including how they interact and build on one another to produce a complex account.

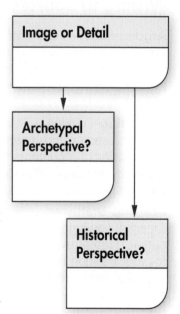

William Blake

(1757–1827)

Author of "**The Lamb**" • "**The Tyger**" • "**The Chimney Sweeper**" • "**Infant Sorrow**"

"I must create a system or be enslaved by another man's." So spoke William Blake, an artist and poet who strove in his work to break free from the patterns of thought that defined common experience. As if to underscore the difference between his views and the ordinary, he claimed that mystical visions were the source of his inspiration.

Finding His Way Blake's visions began when, at the age of four, he thought he saw God at his window. Four years later, Blake said, he saw a tree filled with angels. While Blake's "spells" might have seemed a cause for concern, Blake's parents were followers of the mystical teachings of Emanuel Swedenborg, a Swedish spiritualist. They believed that their son had a "gift of vision" and did all they could to nurture this gift.

Blake's father was a poor Londoner who owned a small hosiery shop. He sent Blake to drawing school, and Blake pursued his own education at home through wide reading. He became an engraver's apprentice and then went on to study at the Royal Academy.

Striking Out on His Own Formal study did not last long, however. The rebellious Blake left the school and eventually set up his own print shop. He was to live most of his days eking out a living as an engraver, barely making enough to support himself and his wife, Catherine.

Innocence and Experience When Blake was thirty-two, he published *Songs of Innocence*, a series of poems that he had composed when he was younger. In these poems, Blake suggested that by recapturing the wonderment of childhood, we can achieve the goal of true self-knowledge and integration with the world. In 1794, he brought out a companion to *Songs of Innocence*, entitled *Songs of Experience.*

A Mature Vision Exploring the darker side of life, *Songs of Experience* reflected Blake's growing disillusionment and more mature vision. He came to believe that a return to innocence was not, at least by itself, sufficient for people to attain true self-awareness. Blake's credo was that there must be a fusion of innocence and experience.

Blake's talent was barely recognized by his peers or by the public during his lifetime. Despite the lack of recognition, Blake filled his seventy years with constant creative activity. Years after his death, he came to be regarded as one of the most important poets of his time.

▲ **Critical Viewing**
What view of nature is expressed by the style of Blake's drawing? **INFER**

Vocabulary
vales (vālz) *n.* valleys; hollows; depressed stretches of ground

Archetypes
What types of people or human conditions does a lamb usually represent?

The Lamb

William Blake

BACKGROUND Blake illustrated his poems with striking, integrated designs. These illustrations seem to swirl through the words and become part of their meaning. Blake claimed that many of the images he drew as illustrations were likenesses of his inner visions. They have a childlike feeling and are very different from the strict, formal styles of his time.

> Little Lamb who made thee
> Dost thou know who made thee
> Gave thee life & bid thee feed.
> By the stream & o'er the mead;
> 5 Gave thee clothing of delight,
> Softest clothing wooly bright;
> Gave thee such a tender voice,
> Making all the vales rejoice!
> Little Lamb who made thee
> 10 Dost thou know who made thee
>
> Little Lamb I'll tell thee,
> Little Lamb I'll tell thee!
> He is called by thy name,
> For he calls himself a Lamb:
> 15 He is meek & he is mild,
> He became a little child:
> I a child & thou a lamb,
> We are called by his name.
> Little Lamb God bless thee.
> 20 Little Lamb God bless thee.

The TYGER

William Blake

Vocabulary

immortal (i môrt′əl) *adj.* living or lasting forever; not dying

symmetry (sim′ ə trē) *n.* balanced form; the beauty resulting from such balance

aspire (ə spīr′) *v.* have high ambitions; yearn or seek after

sinews (sin′ yo͞oz) *n.* tendons

Social Commentary

To what type of worker does Blake compare the tiger's creator?

Tyger Tyger, burning bright,
In the forests of the night;
What **immortal** hand or eye,
Could frame thy fearful **symmetry**?

In what distant deeps or skies
Burnt the fire of thine eyes!
On what wings dare he **aspire**?
What the hand, dare seize the fire?

And what shoulder, & what art,
Could twist the **sinews** of thy heart?
And when thy heart began to beat,
What dread hand? & what dread feet?

What the hammer? what the chain,
In what furnace was thy brain?
What the anvil? what dread grasp,
Dare its deadly terrors clasp?

When the stars threw down their spears
And water'd heaven with their tears:
Did he smile his work to see?
Did he who made the Lamb make thee?

Tyger, Tyger burning bright,
In the forests of the night:
What immortal hand or eye,
Dare frame thy fearful symmetry?

The Tyger.

Tyger Tyger. burning bright,
In the forests of the night;
What immortal hand or eye,
Could frame thy fearful symmetry?

In what distant deeps or skies.
Burnt the fire of thine eyes?
On what wings dare he aspire?
What the hand, dare sieze the fire?

And what shoulder, & what art,
Could twist the sinews of thy heart?
And when thy heart began to beat,
What dread hand? & what dread feet?

What the hammer? what the chain,
In what furnace was thy brain?
What the anvil? what dread grasp,
Dare its deadly terrors clasp!

When the stars threw down their spears
And water'd heaven with their tears:
Did he smile his work to see?
Did he who made the Lamb make thee?

Tyger Tyger burning bright,
In the forests of the night:
What immortal hand or eye,
Dare frame thy fearful symmetry?

▲ **Critical Viewing**
Compare and contrast the tiger's expression with the poem's image
of the animal. **COMPARE AND CONTRAST**

William Blake

When my mother died I was very young,
And my father sold me while yet my tongue,
Could scarcely cry weep weep weep weep.
So your chimneys I sweep & in soot I sleep.

5   There's little Tom Dacre, who cried when his head
That curl'd like a lambs back, was shav'd, so I said.
Hush Tom never mind it, for when your head's bare,
You know that the soot cannot spoil your white hair.

And so he was quiet, & that very night,
10   As Tom was a sleeping he had such a sight,
That thousands of sweepers Dick, Joe, Ned & Jack
Were all of them lock'd up in coffins of black

And by came an Angel who had a bright key,
And he open'd the coffins & set them all free.
15   Then down a green plain leaping laughing they run
And wash in a river and shine in the Sun.

Then naked & white, all their bags left behind,
They rise upon clouds, and sport in the wind.
And the Angel told Tom if he'd be a good boy,
20   He'd have God for his father & never want joy.

And so Tom awoke and we rose in the dark
And got with our bags & our brushes to work.
Tho' the morning was cold, Tom was happy & warm,
So if all do their duty, they need not fear harm.

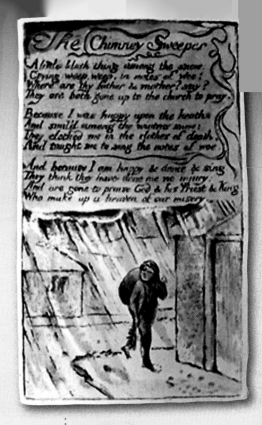

▲ **Critical Viewing**

Compare and contrast Blake's image of a chimney sweeper in his engraving with the image he creates in his poem. **COMPARE AND CONTRAST**

Applying Critical Perspectives

Which details in this poem suggest economic oppression? Which details have a strong emotional charge?

INFANT
Sorrow

William Blake

My mother groand![1] my father wept.
Into the dangerous world I leapt,
Helpless, naked, piping loud;
Like a fiend hid in a cloud.

5   Struggling in my father's hands,
Striving against my swaddling bands;
Bound and weary, I thought best
To **sulk** upon my mother's breast.

---

1. **groand** groaned; an example of Blake's often eccentric spelling.

▲ Critical Viewing
Does the relationship of mother and child in the engraving match that in the poem? Explain. **CONNECT**

Vocabulary
sulk (sulk) *v.* show resentment by refusing to interact with others

Cite textual evidence to support your responses.

Critical Reading

1. **Integration of Knowledge and Ideas** In what ways do "The Lamb" and "The Tyger" represent opposite sides of human existence?

2. **Key Ideas and Details (a)** How does the child in the first stanza of "The Chimney Sweeper" get his job? **(b) Interpret:** What do these events suggest about the life of a chimney sweep?

3. **Integration of Knowledge and Ideas** In "Infant Sorrow," is the infant's final reaction characteristic of the way people deal with frustration? Explain.

4. **Integration of Knowledge and Ideas** How do these poems prompt you to rethink assumptions about society? Use two of these Essential Question words in your response: *modify, responsibility, justice.* [*Connecting to the Essential Question: How does literature shape or reflect society?*]

Literary Analysis

1. **Key Ideas and Details** "The Lamb" and "The Tyger" come, respectively, from Blake's paired books *Songs of Innocence* and *Songs of Experience*. **(a)** Why is the lamb, as Blake presents it, an **archetype,** or universal symbol, of innocence? **(b)** Why is the tiger an archetype of experience? **(c)** Does Blake have a good reason for presenting archetypes in pairs? Explain.

2. **Comparing Literary Works (a)** Using a chart like the one shown, compare the **social commentary** presented in "The Chimney Sweeper" with that in "Infant Sorrow." **(b)** Does the ending of each poem confirm or challenge the poem's perspective? Explain.

Who Is Suffering?	Why?	Significance to Time Period

3. **Integration of Knowledge and Ideas Apply an archetypal perspective** in reading these poems. **(a)** Can you find examples of archetypal symbols in each of them? Why or why not? **(b)** Which poems are best explained by an archetypal perspective? Support your choices with references to the poems.

4. **Integration of Knowledge and Ideas Apply a historical perspective** in reading these poems. **(a)** Can you find references to social ills in each of them? Why or why not? **(b)** Which of the poems are best explained by a historical perspective? Support your choices by making specific references to the poems.

5. **Craft and Structure** Blake uses a great deal of repetition in "The Lamb" and "The Tyger." Do you think this repetition increases the archetypal power of the images in these poems? Why or why not?

6. **Integration of Knowledge and Ideas (a)** How does the archetypal symbolism of "The Lamb" add to your understanding of the second stanza of "The Chimney Sweeper"? **(b)** How does the symbolism of "The Lamb" help you understand "Infant Sorrow"?

7. **Integration of Knowledge and Ideas** Consider how you can blend the archetypal and historical perspectives in reading these poems. For example, could the archetypal "fire" in "The Tyger" be linked with the fires of the oppressive factories of the Industrial Revolution? Explain.

8. **Analyze Visual Information** Explain the humor of the cartoon.

"WHAT IMMORTAL HAND OR EYE COULD FRAME THY FEARFUL SYMMETRY?" ▶

Common Core State Standards

Writing

2.a. Introduce a topic; organize complex ideas, concepts, and information so that each new element builds on that which precedes it to create a unified whole; include formatting, graphics, and multimedia when useful to aiding comprehension. *(p. 754)*

Language

3.a. Vary syntax for effect, consulting references for guidance as needed. *(p. 755)*

4.a. Use context as a clue to the meaning of a word or phrase. *(p. 754)*

©The New Yorker Collection, 1991, Mick Stevens, from *cartoonbank.com.* All Rights Reserved.

Vocabulary Acquisition and Use

Word Analysis: Latin Root -spir-

In "The Tyger," Blake uses the word *aspire*, meaning "to yearn or seek after." *Aspire* contains the Latin root -*spir*-, meaning "breath" or "life." When you aspire to something, you "live for it." Many scientific words that have to do with breathing contain the root -*spir*-. Look up the meaning of each word below. Then, write a definition of your own for each word, incorporating the meaning of -*spir*-.

1. respiration
2. respirator
3. transpiration
4. aspirate
5. spiracle
6. spirometer

Vocabulary: Context Clues

For each item below, explain how a context clue, or a hint from surrounding words, helps you identify the meaning of the italicized vocabulary word.

1. We traveled through *vales* and over hills.
2. The *symmetry* of the animal's body—two bright eyes, four strong and balanced legs—made it look graceful and powerful.
3. Even though it is a lofty goal, the students *aspire* to attend a top college.
4. After spraining her ankle, the runner received a massage of her muscles and *sinews*.
5. You are not going to *sulk* because we ordered pizza instead of burgers, are you?
6. His work is *immortal*; it will always be read.

Writing to Sources

Explanatory Text Write an **essay** on "The Tyger" and "The Chimney Sweeper," applying an archetypal analysis to the former and a social analysis to the latter. Support your analysis with diagrams of archetypes and of social forces.

Prewriting In your thesis, express Blake's vision in each work, and explain whether it is archetypal or social. Also, sketch a diagram that will help readers picture Blake's visions—for "Tyger," it might be a web showing qualities associated with an archetypal symbol and for "Chimney Sweeper," a diagram showing the effects of industrialization.

Drafting Analyze the perspective presented in each poem and show how it affects literary elements such as *tone, imagery,* and *setting.* Refine your diagrams and include *accurate and detailed references* to the texts to support your work.

Revising Review your essay, circling particularly striking details or ideas. Consider moving these details to the beginning or end of a paragraph to add emphasis. Be sure that your diagrams clearly support your analysis.

Model: Revising Placement for Emphasis

The tiger burns with the fires of passion and ambition and perhaps of cruelty. Can one and the same world contain the innocent lamb and the terrors of the tiger? Therefore, Blake seems to suggest, both the world and its creator contain more power and mystery than we care to admit.

At the beginning of the paragraph, the circled sentence will lend greater emphasis.

Conventions and Style: Using Introductory Phrases and Clauses

One way to improve your writing style is to vary your sentence structure. For example, instead of using a subject, you can use phrases and clauses to introduce a sentence. A **phrase** is a group of words that acts as one part of speech but that lacks a subject and a verb. A **clause** is a group of words that has a subject and a verb.

Varying Sentence Beginnings

Blake was writing simple poems by the age of twelve.
By the age of twelve, Blake was writing simple poems. (prepositional phrase)

He read widely at home and was able to get an education on his own.
Reading widely at home, he was able to get an education on his own. (participial phrase)

Blake entered the Royal Academy to continue his studies.
To continue his studies, Blake entered the Royal Academy. (infinitive phrase)

Blake's parents believed him although his visions were unusual.
Although Blake's visions were unusual, his parents believed him. (subordinate clause)

Punctuation Tip Use a comma after introductory elements, except when they are very brief and omitting a comma would not cause confusion.

Practice Revise each sentence by using the italicized part as an introductory phrase or clause. Hint: In some cases, you will need to make slight changes to the original wording.

1. Blake developed his own unique etching process *to print his works.*
2. He could produce only a few books *since the printing process took so long.*
3. Blake's illustrations were *characterized by a childlike mood* and differed from the more formal styles of the time.
4. Blake describes the magnificence of the tiger *in this powerful poem.*
5. The speaker *answers his own question* and says that Christ made the lamb. (Change *answers* to *answering.*)
6. The reader must understand symbolism *to appreciate these poems.*
7. The father sold the boy as a chimney sweep *after the mother died.*
8. Little Tom is *comforted by his friend's words* and has a dream about an angel.
9. The angel opens all the coffins *with his special, bright key.*
10. The boys *rise up into the clouds* and fly toward heaven. (Change *rise* to *rising.*)

Writing and Speaking Conventions

A. Writing Use each phrase or clause to begin a sentence.

1. during his lifetime
2. working as an engraver
3. to support himself
4. after the boy had a dream
   Example: during his lifetime
   Sentence: During his lifetime, Blake's talent went virtually unnoticed.

B. Speaking Write and present to the class a paragraph contrasting the lamb and the tiger. Use at least four phrases or clauses to begin sentences.

Elizabeth McCracken Introduces

FRANKENSTEIN
BY MARY WOLLSTONECRAFT SHELLEY

Dreaming Up Monsters I had only one recurring nightmare as a child. It starred a Frankenstein monster—or at least the kind of Frankenstein monster my seven-year-old dreaming self could come up with, half-human and half-robot, inspired by scraps of movies I had seen, with bolts on his neck and a flashing red ambulance light on top of his head. Certainly he was nothing like the articulate and much scarier monster from Mary Shelley's novel. In the first half of the dream, the monster was my friend. In the second, we went into a cave, and then he chased me out. He could not recognize me. I woke up feeling his fingers on my back.

I remember sitting upright in bed, panting, but it was only a dream. Monsters made up of odd parts did not exist. I didn't live in a world of caves and creatures who chased small girls. My world was a single bed with a brown blanket, my older brother sleeping in one nearby room and my parents in another. They would have told me that I was safe. I didn't want to hear that.

The Thrill of the Terrifying Maybe I liked being scared, but mostly I think I liked the privacy of my nightmare. Like most seven-year-olds, I was never really alone except in dreams. Someone was *always* in a nearby room. I liked the terrifying movies I saw on TV, so many different versions of Frankenstein—*Frankenstein, Bride of Frankenstein, Abbott*

About the Author

Elizabeth McCracken's novel *Niagara Falls All Over Again* won the L. L. Winship/PEN New England Award. For her work, she was awarded grants from the Guggenheim Foundation and the Michener Foundation.

and Costello Meet Frankenstein. I liked fairy tales with dark woodcuts of dense forests that might hide any number of monsters. Fear was the only room I had to myself. When I read awful books—ghost stories as I got older, then true crime books about murderers, cannibals, disasters at sea—the safe suburban world around me disappeared, and I was alone and strangely happy.

Where Do Great Characters Come From?

I certainly never had to wonder what Mary Shelley says she was so often asked: "How I, then a young girl, came to think of, and to dilate upon, so very hideous an idea." Young girls—young boys, too, of course—love hideous ideas. My dream about a Frankenstein monster impressed me, because my own brain had come up with it—even if I'd ripped off most of the details. He scared me. He belonged to me. My dream-self wanted to go back to it, the way I would reread a particularly terrifying book. When I woke up in my own solid, real, boring bedroom, all the objects surrounding me were briefly as frightening as the dead fingers that had brushed my back.

It's the same reason I became a fiction writer. I wanted to make up people, and then, later, I wanted to wonder where they came from.

▶ **Critical Viewing**

Which details in this image of Frankenstein's monster convey terror? Explain. **ANALYZE**

Critical Reading

1. **Key Ideas and Details (a)** What types of frightening movies and books did McCracken enjoy as a child? **(b) Connect:** What does her enjoyment of these tales suggest about her relationship to "the safe suburban world around" her?

2. **Key Ideas and Details** What do you think McCracken means when she says, "I liked the privacy of my nightmare"?

3. **Integration of Knowledge and Ideas** Do you agree or disagree with McCracken's statement that young people "love hideous ideas"? Why or why not?

As You Read *Introduction to* Frankenstein . . .

4. Look for the inspiration that helped Mary Shelley write *Frankenstein.*

5. Note the connections between Shelley's fiction and the real-life foundations of her novel.

Connecting to the Essential Question Readers of Gothic literature like Mary Shelley's *Frankenstein* were looking for suspense and thrills. As you read, identify some of the dark, mysterious images Shelley describes. Finding such images will help as you explore the Essential Question: **What is the relationship of the writer to tradition?**

Close Reading Focus

Gothic Literature; Romantic Movement

The novel *Frankenstein* is a classic example of **Gothic literature,** a *sub-genre* of literature that takes the reader from the reasoned order of the everyday world into the dark world of the supernatural. Gothic literature, popular in the late eighteenth and early nineteenth centuries, is set in dark castles or towers or in other places with a disquieting, mysterious atmosphere. As you read, note Gothic characteristics in Shelley's work.

The popularity of this form was due in part to the new **Romantic movement** in literature. Romantics rejected two central beliefs of the 18th-century Enlightenment: that reason is the most important human faculty and that its application can fully explain the world. Instead, Romantics put their faith in imagination and the healing powers of nature. They viewed imagination in the following terms:

- It is a creative force comparable to that of nature.
- It is the fundamental source of morality and truth, enabling people to sympathize with others and to picture the world.

As you read, notice how Shelley's account of the creative process reflects the high value the Romantics placed on imagination.

Preparing to Read Complex Texts Involved readers naturally try to **make predictions,** or reasoned guesses, about what will happen next in a literary work. As you read, use *text features*, such as titles, background notes, side notes, clues in the text, and your *background knowledge* to make and confirm predictions. Employ a chart like the one shown to record your predictions.

Vocabulary

The words below are important to understanding the text that follows. Copy the words into your notebook, sorting them into words you know and words you do not know.

appendage	platitude
ungenial	phantasm
acceded	incitement

**Common Core
State Standards**

Reading Informational Text
3. Analyze a complex set of ideas or sequence of events and explain how specific individuals, ideas, or events interact and develop over the course of the text.

Clue

"Some volumes of ghost stories . . . fell into our hands."

Prediction

Shelley found the idea for *Frankenstein* in another story.

New Information

"'We will each write a ghost story,' said Lord Byron. . .."

Revision

She found her idea while competing in a contest that the stories inspired.

Mary Wollstonecraft Shelley

(1797–1851)

Author of *Frankenstein*

Writing was in Mary Shelley's blood. Her mother, Mary Wollstonecraft Godwin (who died at Mary's birth), wrote one of the first feminist books ever published, *A Vindication of the Rights of Woman.* Her father, William Godwin, was a leading reformer, author, and political philosopher.

Four years after his wife's death, Godwin married a widow, Mary Jane Claremont, whom his daughter grew to resent bitterly. It was agreed that to ease the situation in the tense household, the girl, now fourteen, would go to live in Dundee, Scotland, in the home of William Baxter, her father's friend. After two years in Scotland, she returned.

Upon her return, Mary Shelley (then still named Godwin) met her future husband, Percy Bysshe Shelley. He was a radical young poet who had become William Godwin's admirer. Mary, only sixteen, fell in love with Shelley, and the two ran away together to the continent and later married.

Eventually, the couple settled in Italy, where they lived blissfully for an all-too-short time. (Their great friend, Lord Byron, also lived in Italy.) Within a few years, the Shelleys suffered the death of two of their children. Then, in 1822, only eight years after Mary Shelley had first met him, Percy Shelley drowned. His death left the twenty-four-year-old Mary and their two-year-old son penniless.

After Percy's death, Mary returned to England, where she continued writing to support herself and her son. She produced several other novels, including *The Last Man* (1826), a tale of a great plague that destroys the human race.

At the age of forty-eight, Mary Shelley became an invalid. She died six years later of a brain tumor.

Introduction to

Frankenstein

Mary Wollstonecraft Shelley

BACKGROUND In Greek mythology, Prometheus was one of the Titans—a race of giants who were said to have existed before humans and who engaged the gods in battle. Later myths say Prometheus created the first human beings. During the Romantic Era, Prometheus drew renewed attention. Percy Bysshe Shelley wrote a verse play about Prometheus entitled *PROMETHEUS UNBOUND*. The complete title of Mary Shelley's novel about a doctor who attempts to create a man is *FRANKENSTEIN, OR THE MODERN PROMETHEUS*.

The Publishers of the Standard Novels, in selecting *Frankenstein* for one of their series, expressed a wish that I should furnish them with some account of the origin of the story. I am the more willing to comply, because I shall thus give a general answer to the question, so very frequently asked me: "How I, then a young girl, came to think of, and to dilate upon, so very hideous an idea?" It is true that I am very averse to bringing myself forward in print; but as my account will only appear as an appendage to a former production, and as it will be confined to such topics as have connection with my authorship alone, I can scarcely accuse myself of a personal intrusion. . . .

In the summer of 1816, we[1] visited Switzerland, and became the neighbors of Lord Byron. At first we spent our pleasant hours on the lake or wandering on its shores; and Lord Byron, who was writing the third canto of *Childe Harold,* was the only one among us who put his thoughts upon paper. These, as he brought them successively to us, clothed in all the light and harmony of poetry, seemed to stamp as divine the glories of heaven and earth, whose influences we partook with him.

But it proved a wet, ungenial summer, and incessant rain often confined us for days to the house. Some volumes of ghost stories, translated from the German into French,[2] fell into our hands. There was "The History of the Inconstant Lover,"[3] who, when he thought to clasp the bride to whom he had pledged his vows, found himself in the arms of the pale ghost of her whom he had deserted. There was the tale of the sinful founder of his race,[4] whose miserable doom it was to bestow the kiss of death on all the younger sons of his fated house, just when they reached the age of promise. His gigantic, shadowy form, clothed like the ghost in Hamlet, in complete armor but with the beaver[5] up, was seen at midnight, by the moon's fitful beams, to advance slowly along the gloomy avenue. The shape was lost beneath the shadow of the castle walls; but soon a gate swung back, a step was heard, the door of the chamber opened, and he advanced to the couch of the blooming youths, cradled in healthy sleep. Eternal sorrow sat upon his face as he bent down and kissed the foreheads of the boys, who from that hour withered like flowers snapped upon the stalk. I have not seen these stories since then, but their incidents are as fresh in my mind as if I had read them yesterday.

A View of Chamonix and Mt. Blanc

1. **we** Mary Shelley, her husband Percy Bysshe Shelley, and their two children.
2. **volumes . . . French** *Fantasmagoriana,* or *Collected Stories of Apparitions of Specters, Ghosts, Phantoms, Etc.,* published anonymously in 1812.
3. **"The History . . . Lover"** The true name of the story is "The Dead Fiancée."
4. **the tale . . . race** "Family Portraits."
5. **beaver** hinged piece of armor that covers the face.

◄ **Critical Viewing**

Based on the second paragraph of her essay, do you think Shelley might have liked this image? Why? **SPECULATE**

Vocabulary

appendage (ə pen´ dij) *n.* something added on

ungenial (un jē´ nyəl) *adj.* disagreeable; characterized by bad weather

Elizabeth McCracken
Scholar's Insight
Mary Shelley turned nineteen in the summer of 1816, and while I do think—I hope!—that writers get better as they get older, there's also the fact that you can only write your first novel once. That the mix of ambition and fear and, yes, youth, may make it more exciting and fully realized than the books you write when you know what you're doing.

Comprehension

What has the author set out to explain?

Elizabeth McCracken
Scholar's Insight
A good ghost story stays in your head forever. I've never gotten over a book of New England ghost stories I had as a child, including one story about a man who buried his murder victim at the base of a tree, only to find that the next year's apples all had a clot of blood in the center of them.

Vocabulary

acceded (ak sēd´ id) *v.* yielded (to); agreed

platitude (plat´ ə tood´) *n.* statement lacking originality

Gothic Literature

What elements of the Gothic tradition are incorporated in the image of a shape "lost beneath the shadow of the castle walls"?

Making Predictions

By what means do you think Shelley will find a story idea?

"We will each write a ghost story," said Lord Byron; and his proposition was acceded to. There were four of us.[6] The noble author began a tale, a fragment of which he printed at the end of his poem of Mazeppa. Shelley, more apt to embody ideas and sentiments in the radiance of brilliant imagery, and in the music of the most melodious verse that adorns our language, than to invent the machinery of a story, commenced one founded on the experiences of his early life. Poor Polidori had some terrible idea about a skull-headed lady, who was so punished for peeping through a keyhole—what to see I forget—something very shocking and wrong of course; but when she was reduced to a worse condition than the renowned Tom of Coventry,[7] he did not know what to do with her, and was obliged to despatch her to the tomb of the Capulets,[8] the only place for which she was fitted. The illustrious poets also, annoyed by the platitude of prose, speedily relinquished their uncongenial task.

I busied myself to *think of a story*—a story to rival those which had excited us to this task. One which would speak to the mysterious fears of our nature and awaken thrilling horror—one to make the reader dread to look round, to curdle the blood, and quicken the beatings of the heart. If I did not accomplish these things, my ghost story would be unworthy of its name. I thought and pondered—vainly. I felt that blank incapability of invention which is the greatest misery of authorship, when dull Nothing replies to our anxious invocations. *Have you thought of a story?* I was asked each morning, and each morning I was forced to reply with a mortifying negative. . . .

Many and long were the conversations between Lord Byron and Shelley, to which I was a devout but nearly silent listener. During one of these, various philosophical doctrines were discussed, and among others the nature of the principle of life and whether there was any probability of its ever being discovered and communicated. They talked of the experiments of Dr. Darwin. (I speak not of what the Doctor really did or said that he did, but, as more to my purpose, of what was then spoken of as having been done by him), who preserved a piece of vermicelli in a glass case till by some extraordinary means it began to move with voluntary motion. Not thus, after all, would life be given. Perhaps a corpse would be reanimated: galvanism[9] had given token of such things. Perhaps the component parts of a creature might be manufactured, brought together, and endued with vital warmth.

---

6. **four of us** Byron, the two Shelleys, and John William Polidori, Byron's physician.
7. **Tom of Coventry** "Peeping Tom" who, according to legend, was struck blind for looking at Lady Godiva as she rode naked through Coventry.
8. **tomb of the Capulets** the place where Romeo and Juliet died.
9. **galvanism** use of electric current to induce twitching in dead muscles.

> I saw the 𝔥𝔦𝔡𝔢𝔬𝔲𝔰 phantasm of a man stretched out, and then, on the working of some powerful engine, show signs of life and stir with an uneasy, half vital motion.

Night waned upon this talk, and even the witching hour had gone by, before we retired to rest. When I placed my head on my pillow, I did not sleep, nor could I be said to think. My imagination, unbidden, possessed and guided me, gifting the successive images that arose in my mind with a vividness far beyond the usual bounds of reverie. I saw—with shut eyes but acute mental vision—I saw the pale student of unhallowed arts kneeling beside the thing he had put together. I saw the hideous phantasm of a man stretched out, and then, on the working of some powerful engine, show signs of life and stir with an uneasy, half vital motion. Frightful must it be, for supremely frightful would be the effect of any human endeavor to mock the stupendous mechanism of the Creator of the world. His success would terrify the artist; he would rush away from his odious handiwork, horror-stricken. He would hope that, left to itself, the slight spark of life which he had communicated would fade; that this thing, which had received such imperfect animation, would subside into dead matter; and he might sleep in the belief that the silence of the grave would quench forever the transient existence of the hideous corpse which he had looked upon as the cradle of life. He sleeps; but he is awakened; he opens his eyes; behold the horrid thing stands at his bedside, opening his curtains, and looking on him with yellow, watery, but speculative eyes.

I opened mine in terror. The idea so possessed my mind, that a thrill of fear ran through me, and I wished to exchange the ghastly image of my fancy for the realities around. I see them still: the very room, the dark parquet,[10] the closed shutters, with the moonlight struggling through, and the sense I had that the glassy lake and white high Alps were beyond. I could not so easily get rid of my hideous phantom: still it haunted me. I must try to think of something else. I recurred to my ghost story—my tiresome unlucky ghost story! O! if I could only contrive one which would frighten my reader as I myself had been frightened that night!

Elizabeth McCracken
Scholar's Insight
Nothing is worse than wanting to write something but not knowing what. I think it's common for stories to come into your head when you *think* you've given up trying, and are thinking about something else entirely.

Vocabulary

phantasm (fan´ taz´ əm) *n.* ghost; figment of the imagination

Elizabeth McCracken
Scholar's Insight
What surprised me most when I first read *Frankenstein* was that the monster could speak and yearn and accuse. Shelley's Victor Frankenstein did a better job making a creature than the movie version suggested. I've always wondered why they kept him silent in the film.

Comprehension
That night, what does Mary Shelley imagine?

---

10. parquet (pär kā´) flooring made of wooden pieces arranged in a pattern.

Swift as light and as cheering was the idea that broke in upon me. "I have found it! What terrified me will terrify others, and I need only describe the specter which had haunted my midnight pillow." On the morrow I announced that I had *thought of a story.* I began that day with the words, *It was on a dreary night of November,* making only a transcript of the grim terrors of my waking dream.

At first I thought but of a few pages—of a short tale—but Shelley urged me to develop the idea at greater length. I certainly did not owe the suggestion of one incident, nor scarcely of one train of feeling, to my husband, and yet but for his incitement, it would never have taken the form in which it was presented to the world. From this declaration I must except the preface. As far as I can recollect, it was entirely written by him.

And now, once again, I bid my hideous progeny go forth and prosper. I have an affection for it, for it was the offspring of happy days, when death and grief were but words, which found no true echo in my heart. Its several pages speak of many a walk, many a drive, and many a conversation, when I was not alone; and my companion was one who, in this world, I shall never see more. But this is for myself: my readers have nothing to do with these associations.

What terrified me will _terrify_ others, and I need only describe the specter which had haunted my midnight pillow.

Cite textual evidence to support your responses.

Critical Reading

1. **Key Ideas and Details (a)** What special set of circumstances inspired the four friends to attempt to write ghost stories? **(b) Compare and Contrast:** Compare the difficulty Shelley has with the reason her companions give up their efforts.

2. **Key Ideas and Details (a)** What gives Shelley her idea for a story? **(b) Connect:** What does the intensity of her vision suggest about her reaction to Dr. Darwin's experiments?

3. **Integration of Knowledge and Ideas Make a Judgment:** In your opinion, has later history borne out Shelley's dread of science? Explain.

4. **Integration of Knowledge and Ideas** Why does Shelley's use of a dream to write her novel confirm Romantic beliefs about the imagination? In your response, use at least two of these Essential Question words: *imagination, reason, intuition.* [Connecting to the *Essential Question: What is the relationship of the writer to tradition?*]

Literary Analysis

1. **Key Ideas and Details** Explain whether you were able to **make predictions** about how Shelley would be affected by the discussion of Darwin's experiments.

2. **Key Ideas and Details** Based on clues in the Background note, predict what will happen to Victor Frankenstein in the novel. Explain your reasoning.

3. **Craft and Structure** Which characteristics of the **Gothic literature** tradition—horror, supernatural elements, medieval elements—do the ghost stories described by Shelley in her third paragraph share? List examples in a chart like the one shown.

Gothic Characteristic	Example in Shelley

4. **Craft and Structure** In which passage does Shelley describe a connection between the world of reason and a terrifying supernatural world?

5. **Craft and Structure** Explain why Shelley's idea for *Frankenstein* fits the Gothic tradition.

6. **Integration of Knowledge and Ideas** Compare the ingredients of Gothic tales with those used in current horror movies and books.

7. **Integration of Knowledge and Ideas** **(a)** How does Shelley respond to the discussion of Darwin's experiments? **(b)** How does her response confirm an assumption of the **Romantic movement**—that the power of imagination is similar to that of nature's creative force?

8. **Integration of Knowledge and Ideas** **(a)** Contrast Shelley's first efforts to find an idea with her final inspiration. **(b)** How does this contrast reflect the Romantic tendency to value imagination above reason?

9. **Integration of Knowledge and Ideas** What "truth" does Shelley's imagined vision suggest about the dangerous possibilities of science?

10. **Analyzing Visual Information** Use your knowledge of *Frankenstein* to explain the humor of the cartoon shown on this page.

Common Core State Standards

Writing

3. Write narratives to develop real or imagined experiences or events using effective technique, well-chosen details, and well-structured event sequences. *(p. 766)*

3.b. Use narrative techniques, such as pacing, to develop experiences, events, and/or characters. *(p. 766)*

Language

4.d. Verify the preliminary determination of the meaning of a word or phrase. *(p. 766)*

©The New Yorker Collection, 1995, Danny Shanahan, from *cartoonbank.com*. All Rights Reserved.

"Remember how big and clunky the first ones were?" ▶

Vocabulary Acquisition and Use

Word Analysis:
Relate New Words to Familiar Vocabulary

You can often infer the meaning of unfamiliar words by relating them to words you know. For instance, *phantasm*, meaning "figment of the mind," is similar to *fantasy*. Both refer to the imagination. Sometimes, you can use parts from more than one word. The prefix *bi-* ("two") and the root *-ped-* ("foot," as in *pedestrian*, "someone who walks") can help you see that *biped* means "creature with two feet." Infer the meaning of the numbered words by relating them to familiar words. Use a dictionary to confirm your inferences.

1. ambidextrous, *adj.*
2. autodidact, *n.*
3. fallacy, *n.*
4. perfervid, *adj.*
5. retrogression, *n.*
6. somnambulate, *v.*

Vocabulary: Synonyms

A *synonym* is a word that has the same, or similar, meaning as another word. Write a complete sentence to answer each question that follows. In your answer, replace each underlined word with a synonym from the vocabulary list on page 758.

1. Was the king's offer of a royal office a sufficient <u>spur</u> to the noble to change sides?
2. Did the audience accept the tired <u>clichés</u> of the speaker uncritically?
3. Did the <u>attachment</u> in the rear of the car affect its speed?
4. How did the audience react when the <u>ghost</u> of Hamlet's father appeared?
5. Did the dean easily <u>agree</u> to her promotion to college president?
6. Have you ever seen such a sarcastic host or one so <u>disagreeable</u>?

Writing to Sources

Narrative Text Create a new work in the Gothic tradition. Typically, monster stories are told from the perspective of the humans confronting the monster. Change the perspective, and write a brief **autobiography** of a monster. Choose a monster you know from literature or film, or invent a new one. Outline the *sequence of events* in the monster's whole life or focus on events in one episode. Remember to write using the pronoun "I," show the *significance of events*, and gain readers' sympathy, as an autobiography would aim to do.

Prewriting Outline the plot of your narrative. Remember to think about the incidents from the monster's point of view.

Drafting Write your narrative in a serious or humorous way. Use concrete sensory details, including Gothic elements, to add impact. If appropriate, pace the presentation of action to build suspense or sympathy.

Revising Revise your draft to make sure you maintain the monster's point of view and voice. Add figurative language to make your descriptions more vivid.

Model: Revising to Add Figurative Language

like a threatening eye

As the full moon rose, my skin suddenly began to tingle. I saw hair sprouting along my arms.

Using figurative language such as similes makes the description more vivid.

VILLAGER #3: He was *gree-ee-ee-eennnn!*

DRACULA: Okay. Tall guy, green, bolts in his neck—yeah, I hate to break it to you, but *that's* Frankenstein!

HEAD VILLAGER: Okay . . . well, alright. I believe we've made a bit of a mistake. Sorry to trouble you! [to the villagers] Across the moor!!

CROWD: ACROSS THE MOOR!!

[the villagers run back in the opposite direction from which they came]

[stock footage of villagers running through the night]

[cut to villagers standing at Frankenstein's door]

FRANKENSTEIN'S MONSTER: Well, uh . . . he's a *li-ar!* That's what!

HEAD VILLAGER: Well . . . what about the *bolts* in your neck?

FRANKENSTEIN'S MONSTER: Oh, great, thanks a lot! I almost forgot about that *spinal injury* I had when I was four-years old! Thanks for bringing back *those* rosy memories! Hey—my dog died last year, why don't you make a few jokes about *that*?!

VILLAGER #1: He's a mon-sterrrr!!

[all the villagers join in the chorus]

FRANKENSTEIN'S MONSTER: Hey, now we're *name-calling!* What am I, in the 7th grade, all of a sudden! . . . How do you like that?

HEAD VILLAGER: Well, how do we know you're *not* Frankenstein's Monster?

FRANKENSTEIN'S MONSTER: How do I know *you're* not Frankenstein's Monster, you freakin' genius?! I mean—[glances at villager stepping too close with a lit torch] Hey, dude—get that fire away from me. Alright? I mean, *you* could be a monster, you know? You got the weird hat, the patchy beard—you know? I mean, you look like a monster to *me*!

VILLAGER #1: [to Head Villager] Well, maybe *you're* the monster!

[all the villagers join in the chorus]

HEAD VILLAGER: [shakes his head] I'm not the monster! [points to Frankenstein's Monster] Look at 'im! He's got a square head and green skin!

FRANKENSTEIN'S MONSTER: Oh, great—now it's a *racial* thing! You know what? You guys are a bunch of fascists! [villager with a lit torch again steps too close] *Seriously,* du-ude! Get that fire away from me! [to the crowd] Here's the deal: I'm a cobbler. I make shoes, and I hang out with my kids. You want to lynch me for *that*—be my guest!

HEAD VILLAGER: Well, I'm sorry. We—we shouldn't have jumped to conclusions. We'll leave you alone.

FRANKENSTEIN'S MONSTER: Uh—how about, apology *not* accepted, Weird Beard! I mean, let a guy live his life, would you? You know what I mean? I mean, it—[his arm suddenly falls off and hits the stone steps] Uhhhhhh—

CROWD: *KILL HIM!!!*

[the villagers storm forward]

[cut to title graphic]

ANNOUNCER: We'll be back with more of The Late Night Movie. I *swear* they haven't done these things in, like, twenty years . . .

[fade]

Critical Reading

1. **(a)** What is confusing the villagers? **(b) Interpret:** In what way is their confusion a humorous comment on monster movies in general?

2. What is surprising and humorous about the way in which Frankenstein's monster talks?

Use this question to focus a group discussion of "The Curse of Frankenstein":

3. What, if anything, should you know about the Frankenstein story to appreciate the humor of this skit?

Lyric Poetry

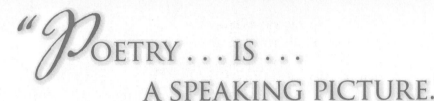

"**P**OETRY . . . IS . . .

A SPEAKING PICTURE."

— SIR PHILIP SIDNEY

Defining Lyric Poetry

Lyric poetry expresses the personal thoughts and feelings of a single speaker. Lyric poems often have musical effects and a songlike structure.

Types of Lyric Poems While lyric poems do not have to follow a specific form, many do. The following are traditional lyric forms:

- **Ode:** a serious, often intensely emotional poem that honors a person or thing. In an ode, the speaker directly addresses the subject.
- **Elegy:** a solemn and formal poem about death. The speaker may mourn a person or a more abstract loss, such as the passing of youth.
- **Sonnet:** a 14-line poem with a formal structure, specific meter, and rhyme scheme

Sound Devices and Figurative Language In addition to the descriptive, sensory language called **imagery,** one of the most distinctive qualities of poetry is its use of sound devices and figurative language.

Sound devices are patterns of words that use the innate sounds of language to create musical effects. They include the following types:

- **Rhyme:** repetition of sounds at the ends of words, as in _brake_ and _lake_
- **Consonance:** repetition of final consonant sounds in stressed syllables that have different vowel sounds, as in _speak_ and _break_
- **Repetition:** repeated use of sounds, words, phrases, or sentences

Figurative language is language that is used imaginatively rather than literally. Figurative language includes the following figures of speech:

- **Simile:** comparison of two unlike things using the words _like_ or _as_
- **Metaphor:** comparison of two apparently unlike things without using _like_ or _as_
- **Oxymoron:** juxtaposing two opposite or contradictory words to reveal a surprising truth

Close Read: Sound Devices and Figurative Language

These literary elements appear in the Model text at right.

Sound Device—Alliteration: repetition of initial identical consonant sounds in accented syllables _Example: "All powers of swiftness, subtlety, and strength..." (William Wordsworth)_	**Figurative Language—Personification:** giving human traits to nonhuman things _Example: "These waters, rolling from their mountain springs / With a soft inland murmur..." (William Wordsworth)_
Sound Device—Assonance: repetition of similar vowel sounds in accented syllables _Example: "One shade the more, one ray the less..." (Lord Byron)_	**Figurative Language—Apostrophe:** a figure in which the speaker addresses an absent person _Example: "Milton! thou should'st be living at this hour: / England has need of thee..." (William Wordsworth)_

 EXEMPLAR TEXT

Model

About the Text Pablo Neruda (1904–1973) was one of Chile's most popular poets. In 1971, he was awarded the Nobel Prize in Literature.

"Ode to My Suit" by Pablo Neruda (translated by Margaret Sayers Peden)

Every morning, suit,
you are waiting on a chair
to be filled
by my vanity, my love,
my hope, my body.
Still
only half awake
I leave the shower
to shrug into your sleeves,
my legs seek
the hollow of your legs,
and thus embraced
by your unfailing loyalty
I take my morning walk,
work my way into my poetry;
from my windows I see
the things,
men, women,
events and struggles
constantly shaping me,
constantly confronting me,
setting my hands to the task,
opening my eyes,
creasing my lips,
and in the same way,
suit,
I am shaping you,
poking out your elbows,
wearing you threadbare,
and so your life grows
in the image of my own.
In the wind
you flap and hum
as if you were my soul,
in bad moments

you cling
to my bones,
abandoned, at nighttime
darkness and dream
people with their phantoms
your wings and mine.
I wonder
whether some day
an enemy
bullet
will stain you with my blood,
for then
you would die with me,
but perhaps
it will be
less dramatic,
simple,
and you will grow ill,
suit,
with me,
grow older
with me, with my body,
and together
we will be lowered
into the earth.
That's why
every day
I greet you
with respect and then
you embrace me and I forget you,
because we are one being
and shall be always
in the wind, through the night,
the streets and the struggle,
one body,
maybe, maybe, one day, still.

Apostrophe The speaker talks directly to his suit. This use of apostrophe establishes both tone, or emotional attitude, and meaning: the suit is far more than a suit. It is a being for whom the speaker feels admiration and affection.

Personification The poem as a whole is based on personification. The speaker attributes human emotion and actions to an inanimate suit. The speaker is actually addressing an aspect of his own being, but doing so through the mechanism of the personified suit.

Assonance Repeated vowel sounds are less obvious than rhyme. However, along with other sound devices, they create musical qualities and connections among words.

Alliteration In both of the highlighted examples, repetition of the initial consonant sounds helps to link words and stir emotion.

William Wordsworth
(1770–1850)

Writing poetry may seem like a quiet, meditative activity, a matter of words, not deeds—hardly the scene of upheavals and crises. Yet in 1798, when Wordsworth and his friend Samuel Taylor Coleridge published the first edition of *Lyrical Ballads,* a revolution shook the world of poetry. Together, Wordsworth and Coleridge rejected all the traditional assumptions about the proper style, words, and subject matter for a poem.

A Revolution in Poetry

As Wordsworth announced in the Preface to the 1802 edition of the book, "There will . . . be found in these volumes little of what is usually called poetic diction; I have taken as much pains to avoid it as others ordinarily take to produce it; . . ."

Gone were the flowery language, the wittily crafted figures of speech, the effusive praise, and the tragic complaints that had defined poetry in the past. In their place, Wordsworth offered an intensified presentation of ordinary life and nature using common language. Wordsworth's revolution took literature in a dramatic new direction, building the movement known as Romanticism.

The Lake District

Wordsworth's revolution was rooted in his early love for nature. Born in the beautiful Lake District of England, Wordsworth spent his youth roaming the countryside. In later years, too, he found peace and reassurance in the gentle hills and serene lakes of this landscape. This region of northwestern England became the cradle of the Romantic Movement, inspiring many personal commentaries and poetic tributes.

Revolution and Love

By the time Wordsworth was thirteen, both his parents had died. Nonetheless, he was able to pursue his education and entered Cambridge University in 1787. After graduating, he traveled through Europe, spending considerable time in France. There, he embraced the ideals of the newly born French Revolution—ideals that stressed social justice and individual rights. Growing emotionally as well as intellectually, Wordsworth fell in love with Annette Vallon.

Disillusionment and Crisis

Wordsworth's involvement with the Revolution and with Vallon ended abruptly when lack of funds and family pressure forced him to return home. Two months later, in 1793, England declared war on France, and the Revolution became increasingly violent. His dreams of liberty betrayed, Wordsworth lapsed into a depression. His beloved sister, Dorothy, and fellow poet Samuel Taylor Coleridge helped him through this crisis.

From Politics to Art

In 1798, Wordsworth published *Lyrical Ballads* with Coleridge. With the publication of this work, Wordsworth translated his revolutionary hopes from politics to literature. His democratic ideals appeared in his use of the language of ordinary people rather than specialized "poetic" words.

Poetry

Critics agree that Wordsworth's greatest work is his autobiography in poetry, *The Prelude.* Wordsworth completed a version of this poem in 1799, which he expanded considerably by 1805. As he wrote to a friend, *The Prelude* told the story of "the growth of my own mind." The poem is not always factually accurate, but, as noted by critic Stephen Gill, in its combination of "satire and narrative, description and meditation, the visionary and the deliberately banal," it was unique.

Eventually, Wordsworth's radical new approach to poetry gained acceptance, while he himself grew more conservative in his politics. A new generation of Romantics, more radical than Wordsworth and Coleridge, arose. Wordsworth's position was secure, however: we remember him as the father of English Romanticism.

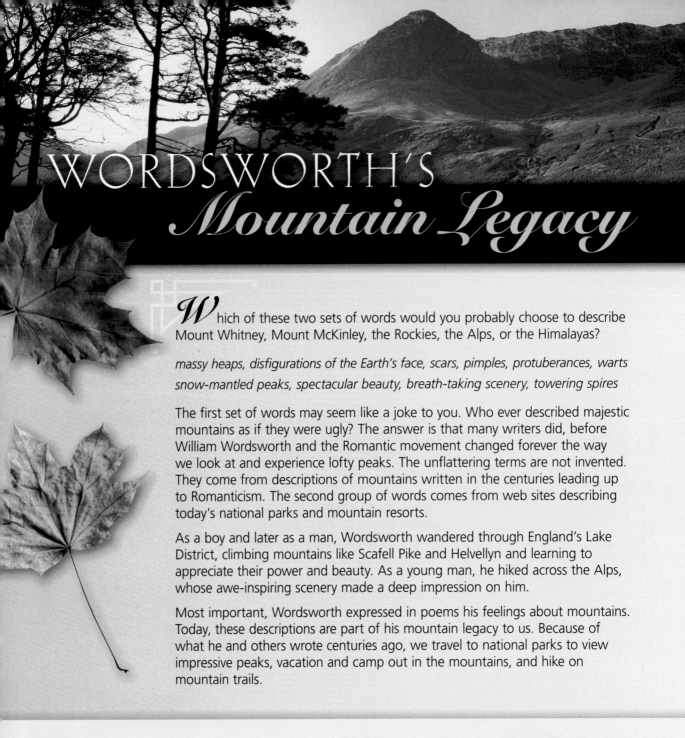

WORDSWORTH'S *Mountain Legacy*

*W*hich of these two sets of words would you probably choose to describe Mount Whitney, Mount McKinley, the Rockies, the Alps, or the Himalayas?

massy heaps, disfigurations of the Earth's face, scars, pimples, protuberances, warts

snow-mantled peaks, spectacular beauty, breath-taking scenery, towering spires

The first set of words may seem like a joke to you. Who ever described majestic mountains as if they were ugly? The answer is that many writers did, before William Wordsworth and the Romantic movement changed forever the way we look at and experience lofty peaks. The unflattering terms are not invented. They come from descriptions of mountains written in the centuries leading up to Romanticism. The second group of words comes from web sites describing today's national parks and mountain resorts.

As a boy and later as a man, Wordsworth wandered through England's Lake District, climbing mountains like Scafell Pike and Helvellyn and learning to appreciate their power and beauty. As a young man, he hiked across the Alps, whose awe-inspiring scenery made a deep impression on him.

Most important, Wordsworth expressed in poems his feelings about mountains. Today, these descriptions are part of his mountain legacy to us. Because of what he and others wrote centuries ago, we travel to national parks to view impressive peaks, vacation and camp out in the mountains, and hike on mountain trails.

. . . Oh! when I have hung
Above the raven's nest, by knots of grass
And half-inch fissures in the slippery rock . . .
. . . oh, at that time
While on the perilous ridge I hung alone . . .

— *from The Prelude, Book I*

. . . in the mountains did he *feel* his faith.
All things responsive to the writing, there
Breathed immortality, revolving life,
And greatness still revolving; infinite:
There littleness was not; the least of things
Seemed infinite . . .

— *from The Excursion, Book I*

Building Knowledge and Insight

Poetry of William Wordsworth

Connecting to the Essential Question Today's rock musicians and environmentalists are descendants of the Romantic movement Wordsworth helped to found. As you read, find passages that show Wordsworth rebelling against eighteenth-century poetic traditions. Identifying these passages will help you explore the Essential Question: **What is the relationship of the writer to tradition?**

Close Reading Focus

Romanticism; Lyric; Diction

Romanticism was a late-eighteenth-century European literary movement. While the earlier Neoclassical writers, such as Pope and Johnson, favored reason, wit, and outward elegance, the works of many Romantic poets include these elements:

- Simplicity or directness of language
- The expression of spontaneous, intensified feelings
- Responses to nature that lead to a deeper awareness of self

English Romanticism began with William Wordsworth. The **lyric,** a poem in which a single speaker expresses personal emotions and observations, was particularly suited to his vision.

Comparing Literary Works The Romantics adopted a new and freer **diction,** or choice of words. As you read, notice that Wordsworth's poetry favors simple words but that his work also relies heavily on abstract terms. Compare the different types of words Wordsworth chooses—whether specific and concrete like *sycamore* or abstract like *a sense sublime.*

Preparing to Read Complex Texts You can better understand a work by **evaluating the influence of the historical period** on it. Wordsworth lived in an age of political and social revolutions, and he himself helped bring about a revolution in literature. The relationship between Wordsworth's literary ideas and the social and political change of the era are evident in the details in these poems. As you read, use a chart like the one shown to identify the revolutionary *political and philosophical assumptions* that color the view of life in his work.

Vocabulary

You will encounter the words below in the texts that follow. Copy the words into your notebook, sorting them by number of syllables.

recompense	anatomize
roused	sordid
presumption	stagnant

Common Core State Standards

Reading Literature
4. Determine the meaning of words and phrases as they are used in the text, including figurative and connotative meanings; analyze the impact of specific word choices on meaning and tone, including words with multiple meanings or language that is particularly fresh, engaging, or beautiful.

Historical Ideas

Celebration of Common Folk
Love of Nature
Admiration for French Revolution
Loss of Faith in Reason

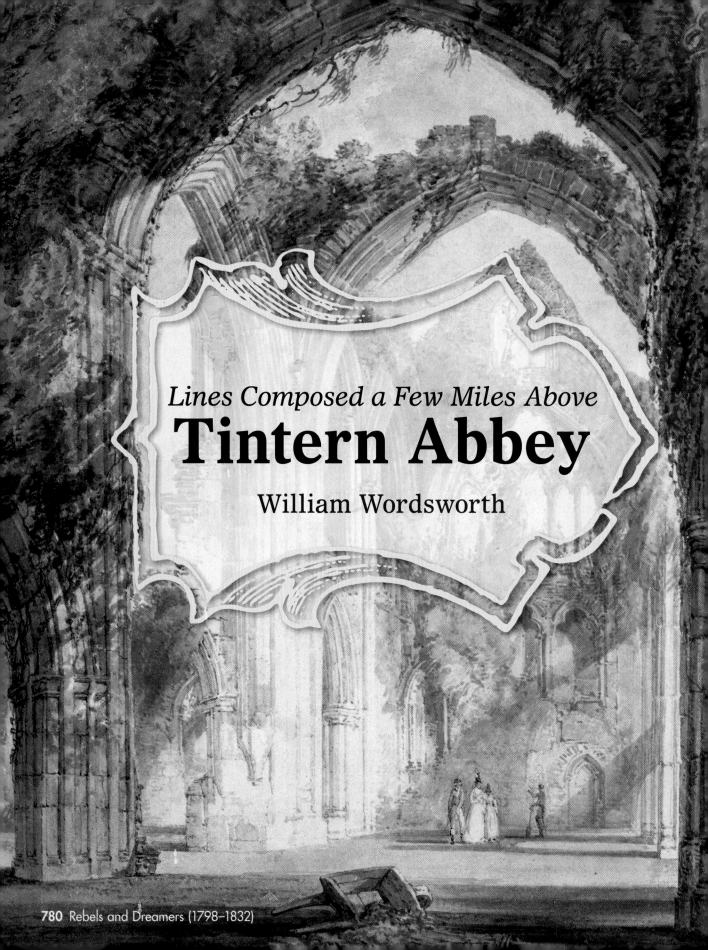

Lines Composed a Few Miles Above

Tintern Abbey

William Wordsworth

Five years have past; five summers, with the length
Of five long winters! and again I hear
These waters, rolling from their mountain springs
With a soft inland murmur. Once again
5 Do I behold these steep and lofty cliffs,
That on a wild secluded scene impress
Thoughts of more deep seclusion; and connect
The landscape with the quiet of the sky.
The day is come when I again repose
10 Here, under this dark sycamore, and view
These plots of cottage ground, these orchard tufts,
Which at this season, with their unripe fruits,
Are clad in one green hue, and lose themselves
'Mid groves and copses. Once again I see
15 These hedgerows, hardly hedgerows, little lines
Of sportive wood run wild: these pastoral farms,
Green to the very door; and wreaths of smoke
Sent up, in silence, from among the trees!
With some uncertain notice, as might seem
20 Of vagrant dwellers in the houseless woods,
Or of some hermit's cave, where by his fire
The hermit sits alone.
                 These beauteous forms,
Through a long absence, have not been to me
As is a landscape to a blind man's eye:
25 But oft, in lonely rooms, and 'mid the din
Of towns and cities, I have owed to them
In hours of weariness, sensations sweet,
Felt in the blood, and felt along the heart;
And passing even into my purer mind,
30 With tranquil restoration—feelings too
Of unremembered pleasure: such, perhaps,
As have no slight or trivial influence
On that best portion of a good man's life.
His little, nameless, unremembered, acts
35 Of kindness and of love. Nor less, I trust,
To them I may have owed another gift,
Of aspect more sublime; that blessed mood,
In which the burthen[1] of the mystery,
In which the heavy and the weary weight

Romanticism and the Lyric

How do the sensory observations Wordsworth includes reflect what you know about Romanticism?

◀ Critical Viewing

What elements in this painting help it capture awe and excitement comparable to Wordsworth's on his return to the Wye? **CONNECT**

Comprehension

Name two sights that strike Wordsworth on his return to the Wye.

---

1. burthen burden.

Romanticism and the Lyric

How do the images in lines 40–49 reflect Romantic ideas of the relation between nature and the soul?

40 Of all this unintelligible world
Is lightened—that serene and blessed mood,
In which the affections gently lead us on—
Until, the breath of this corporeal frame[2]
And even the motion of our human blood
45 Almost suspended, we are laid asleep
In body, and become a living soul;
While with an eye made quiet by the power
Of harmony, and the deep power of joy,
We see into the life of things.

                                    If this
50 Be but a vain belief, yet, oh! how oft—
In darkness and amid the many shapes
Of joyless daylight; when the fretful stir
Unprofitable, and the fever of the world,
Have hung upon the beatings of my heart—
55 How oft, in spirit, have I turned to thee,
O sylvan[3] Wye! thou wanderer through the woods,
How often has my spirit turned to thee!

        And now, with gleams of half-extinguished thought,
With many recognitions dim and faint,
60 And somewhat of a sad perplexity,
The picture of the mind revives again;
While here I stand, not only with the sense
Of present pleasure, but with pleasing thoughts
That in this moment there is life and food
65 For future years. And so I dare to hope,
Though changed, no doubt, from what I was when first

Understanding the Historical Period

What changing attitude about the importance of reason is reflected in Wordsworth's contrast of childhood with adulthood?

▼ **Critical Viewing**

How is the landscape in this photograph similar to the setting Wordsworth describes? **CONNECT**

---

2. **corporeal** (kôr pór´ ē əl) **frame** body.
3. **sylvan** (sil´ vən) wooded.

I came among these hills; when like a roe[4]
I bounded o'er the mountains, by the sides
Of the deep rivers, and the lonely streams,
70 Wherever nature led: more like a man
Flying from something that he dreads, than one
Who sought the thing he loved. For nature then
(The coarser pleasures of my boyish days,
And their glad animal movements all gone by)
75 To me was all in all—I cannot paint
What then I was. The sounding cataract
Haunted me like a passion; the tall rock,
The mountain, and the deep and gloomy wood,
Their colors and their forms, were then to me
80 An appetite; a feeling and a love,
That had no need of a remoter charm,
By thought supplied, nor any interest
Unborrowed from the eye. That time is past,
And all its aching joys are now no more,
85 And all its dizzy raptures. Not for this
Faint[5] I, nor mourn nor murmur; other gifts
Have followed; for such loss, I would believe,
Abundant recompense. For I have learned
To look on nature, not as in the hour
90 Of thoughtless youth; but hearing oftentimes
The still, sad music of humanity,
Nor harsh nor grating, though of ample power
To chasten and subdue. And I have felt
A presence that disturbs me with the joy
95 Of elevated thoughts; a sense sublime
Of something far more deeply interfused,
Whose dwelling is the light of setting suns,
And the round ocean and the living air,
And the blue sky, and in the mind of man;
100 A motion and a spirit, that impels
All thinking things, all objects of all thought,
And rolls through all things. Therefore am I still
A lover of the meadows and the woods
And mountains; and of all that we behold
105 From this green earth; of all the mighty world
Of eye, and ear—both what they half create,
And what perceive; well pleased to recognize
In nature and the language of the sense,
The anchor of my purest thoughts, the nurse,

---

4. **roe** type of deer.
5. **Faint** lose heart.

The BRITISH TRADITION

The Evolution of the Self
On returning to the Wye, Wordsworth discovers his own deeper self in experiences of nature bound together by memory. His discovery contributed to a new, Romantic idea of the self. For the Romantics, the self was a journey of self-discovery, not a collection of personal quirks or facts. The Romantic poet set out to recover his or her deeper self through nature, memory, and lyric poetry. For the Romantics, writing a poem became an act of discovery and self-definition.

This Romantic idea of the self—always divided yet always recovering itself—inspired later works such as Tennyson's *In Memoriam, A.H.H.* Centuries later, Wordsworth's vision of the self and its journey still resonates in modern culture.

Connect to the Literature

In lines 88–93, what does the speaker learn about himself and his world?

Vocabulary
recompense (rek´ əm pens´)
n. payment in return for something

Comprehension
What natural sights inspire in Wordsworth a sense of the unity of things—of "something far more deeply interfused, . . ."?

Spiral Review

Point of View

In lines 112–121, how does the use of first-person point of view shape what we know of the speaker's sister?

Romanticism and Diction

Does Wordsworth use simple or difficult words to describe old age? Are they specific or general?

Understanding the Historical Period

How do the lines "let the misty mountain winds be free / To blow against thee" reflect Romantic beliefs and assumptions?

110 The guide, the guardian of my heart, and soul
Of all my moral being.

                               Nor perchance,
If I were not thus taught, should I the more
Suffer[6] my genial spirits[7] to decay;
For thou art with me here upon the banks
115 Of this fair river; thou my dearest Friend,[8]
My dear, dear Friend, and in thy voice I catch
The language of my former heart, and read
My former pleasures in the shooting lights
Of thy wild eyes. Oh! yet a little while
120 May I behold in thee what I was once,
My dear, dear Sister! and this prayer I make
Knowing that Nature never did betray
The heart that loved her; 'tis her privilege,
Through all the years of this our life, to lead
125 From joy to joy; for she can so inform
The mind that is within us, so impress
With quietness and beauty, and so feed
With lofty thoughts, that neither evil tongues,
Rash judgments, nor the sneers of selfish men,
130 Nor greetings where no kindness is, nor all
The dreary intercourse of daily life,
Shall e'er prevail against us, or disturb
Our cheerful faith, that all which we behold
Is full of blessings. Therefore let the moon
135 Shine on thee in thy solitary walk;
And let the misty mountain winds be free
To blow against thee: and, in after years,
When these wild ecstasies shall be matured
Into a sober pleasure; when thy mind
140 Shall be a mansion for all lovely forms,
Thy memory be as a dwelling place
For all sweet sound and harmonies; oh! then,
If solitude, or fear, or pain, or grief,
Should be thy portion, with what healing thoughts
145 Of tender joy wilt thou remember me,
And these my exhortations! Nor, perchance—
If I should be where I no more can hear
Thy voice, nor catch from thy wild eyes these gleams
Of past existence—wilt thou then forget
150 That on the banks of this delightful stream
We stood together; and that I, so long
A worshipper of Nature, hither came

---

6. Suffer allow.
7. genial spirits creative powers.
8. Friend his sister Dorothy.

Tintern Abbey, J. M. W. Turner, © British Museum

Unwearied in that service: rather say
With warmer love—oh! with far deeper zeal
155 Of holier love. Nor wilt thou then forget,
That after many wanderings, many years
Of absence, these steep woods and lofty cliffs,
And this green pastoral landscape, were to me
More dear, both for themselves and for thy sake!

▲ **Critical Viewing**
Compare the appreciation of light and sky shown by Romantic painter J. M. W. Turner with Wordsworth's descriptions in the poem. **COMPARE AND CONTRAST**

Critical Reading

1. **Key Ideas and Details** **(a)** How long has it been since the poet visited Tintern Abbey? **(b) Infer:** At what time of year does the poet make his second visit to the area? How do you know?

2. **Key Ideas and Details** **(a)** How have the poet's memories of his first visit helped him? **(b) Interpret:** In line 36 of the poem, the poet mentions "another gift" that his contact with this rural scene bestowed upon him. Briefly describe this gift.

3. **Key Ideas and Details** Explain the difference in the poet's attitude on his first and on his second visit to Tintern Abbey.

4. **Integration of Knowledge and Ideas** **(a)** What wish for his sister does the poet express toward the end of the poem? **(b) Connect:** What connection can you see between this wish, Wordsworth's thoughts in lines 22–31, and his hopes in lines 62–65?

5. **Integration of Knowledge and Ideas** Does Wordsworth express a deep truth about our relationships with nature, or are his reactions exaggerated? Explain.

Cite textual evidence to support your responses.

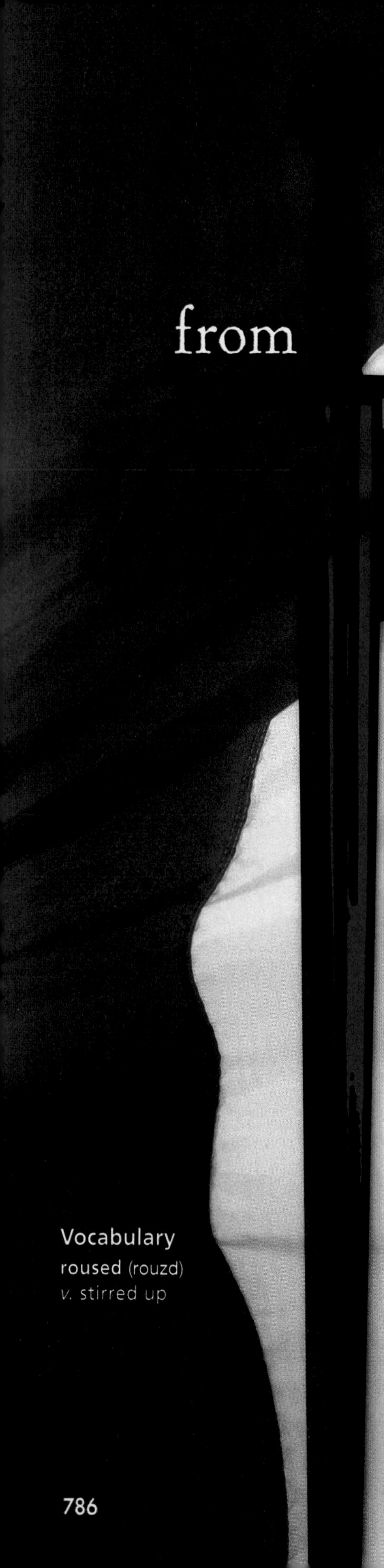

from

BACKGROUND In 1790, Wordsworth witnessed the early, optimistic days of the French Revolution. The country seemed on the verge of achieving true freedom from outdated, oppressive feudal institutions. Caught up in the revolutionary fervor, Wordsworth felt he was seeing "France standing on the top of golden hours." The war between England and France (declared in 1793) and the violent turn taken by the French Revolution, known as the Reign of Terror (1793–1794), dashed Wordsworth's hopes.

Prelude

WILLIAM WORDSWORTH

O pleasant exercise of hope and joy!
For mighty were the auxiliars which then stood
Upon our side, us who were strong in love!
Bliss was it in that dawn to be alive,
5　But to be young was very Heaven! O times,
In which the meager, stale, forbidding ways
Of custom, law, and statute, took at once
The attraction of a country in romance!
When Reason seemed the most to assert her rights
10　When most intent on making of herself
A prime enchantress—to assist the work,
Which then was going forward in her name!
Not favored spots alone, but the whole Earth,
The beauty wore of promise—that which sets
15　(As at some moments might not be unfelt
Among the bowers of Paradise itself)
The budding rose above the rose full blown.
What temper at the prospect did not wake
To happiness unthought of? The inert
20　Were roused, and lively natures rapt away!
They who had fed their childhood upon dreams,
The play-fellows of fancy, who had made
All powers of swiftness, subtlety, and strength
Their ministers,—who in lordly wise had stirred
25　Among the grandest objects of the sense,
And dealt with whatsoever they found there

Vocabulary
roused (rouzd)
v. stirred up

▲ **Critical Viewing** Compare and contrast the impression of the French Revolution conveyed by this poem to the one conveyed by this picture. **COMPARE AND CONTRAST**

As if they had within some lurking right
To wield it;—they, too, who of gentle mood
Had watched all gentle motions, and to these
30 Had fitted their own thoughts, schemers more mild,
And in the region of their peaceful selves;—
Now was it that *both* found, the meek and lofty
Did both find helpers to their hearts' desire,
And stuff at hand, plastic as they could wish,—
35 Were called upon to exercise their skill,
Not in Utopia,—subterranean fields,—
Or some secreted island, Heaven knows where!
But in the very world, which is the world
Of all of us,—the place where, in the end,
40 We find our happiness, or not at all!

But now, become oppressors in their turn,
Frenchmen had changed a war of self-defense
For one of conquest, losing sight of all
Which they had struggled for: now mounted up,
45 Openly in the eye of earth and heaven,
The scale of liberty. I read her doom,
With anger vexed, with disappointment sore,
But not dismayed, nor taking to the shame
Of a false prophet. While resentment rose
50 Striving to hide, what nought could heal, the wounds
Of mortified presumption, I adhered

Vocabulary
presumption (prē zump´ shən) *n.* audacity; nerve

Comprehension
To which two kinds of people did the Revolution appeal?

More firmly to old tenets, and, to prove
Their temper, strained them more; and thus, in heat
Of contest, did opinions every day
55 Grow into consequence, till round my mind
They clung, as if they were its life, nay more,
The very being of the immortal soul.

I summoned my best skill, and toiled, intent
To anatomize the frame of social life,
60 Yea, the whole body of society
Searched to its heart. Share with me, Friend! the wish
That some dramatic tale, endued with shapes
Livelier, and flinging out less guarded words
Than suit the work we fashion, might set forth
65 What then I learned, or think I learned, of truth,
And the errors into which I fell, betrayed
By present objects, and by reasonings false
From their beginnings, inasmuch as drawn
Out of a heart that had been turned aside
70 From Nature's way by outward accidents,
And which are thus confounded,[1] more and more
Misguided, and misguiding. So I fared,
Dragging all precepts, judgments, maxims, creeds,
Like culprits to the bar; calling the mind,
75 Suspiciously, to establish in plain day
Her titles and her honors; now believing,
Now disbelieving; endlessly perplexed
With impulse, motive, right and wrong, the ground
Of obligation, what the rule and whence
80 The sanction; till, demanding formal *proof*,
And seeking it in every thing, I lost
All feeling of conviction, and, in fine,
Sick, wearied out with contrarieties,
Yielded up moral questions in despair.

---

1. confounded (kən found′ id) *adj.* confused; mixed together indiscriminately; bewildered

Critical Reading

Cite textual evidence to support your responses.

1. **Key Ideas and Details** **(a)** With what phrase does the speaker describe the early days of the French Revolution? **(b) Generalize:** What basic values does his reaction reflect? **(c) Interpret:** What role did reason seem to play in the Revolution?

2. **Key Ideas and Details** **(a)** What change in the course of the French Revolution caused a conflict in Wordsworth? **(b) Interpret:** What two reactions to this turn of events does Wordsworth describe?

3. **Key Ideas and Details** **(a) Interpret:** What does Wordsworth say happened to him when his heart "had been turned aside / From Nature's way"? **(b) Interpret:** At the end of the excerpt, how has Wordsworth resolved his conflict?

Critical Commentary

"The White Knight's Song"

Lewis Carroll

Lewis Carroll was the pseudonym of Charles Lutwidge Dodgson, the English author who wrote Alice's Adventures in Wonderland.

Writers with a well-defined style and beliefs are the most tempting to parody, especially if they do not show much humor themselves. Wordsworth fit these requirements, and therefore was a tempting target for Lewis Carroll, author of *Alice in Wonderland.* Carroll parodied Wordsworth's famous poem "Resolution and Independence," which contains the following account of a meeting with a strange old man:

> . . . I saw a Man before me unawares:
> The oldest man he seemed that ever wore gray hairs. . . .
>
> Like a sea-beast crawled forth, that on a shelf
> Of rock or sand reposeth, there to sun itself;
>
> Such seemed this Man, not all alive or dead,
> Nor all asleep—in his extreme old age . . .

The poet then asks this old man, who has been staring at the "muddy water" of a pond, "What occupation do you there pursue?" The man responds as follows:

> He told, that to these waters he had come
> To gather leeches, being old and poor:
> Employment hazardous and wearisome!
> And he had many hardships to endure:
> From pond to pond he roamed, from moor to moor . . .

Carroll parodied this encounter in "The White Knight's Song":

> I'll tell thee everything I can:
>   There's little to relate.
> I saw an aged, aged man,
>   A-sitting on a gate.
>
> "Who are you, aged man?" I said
>   "And how is it you live?"
> And his answer trickled through my head
>   Like water through a sieve.
> He said, "I look for butterflies
>   That sleep among the wheat:
> I make them into mutton-pies
>   And sell them in the street. . . .

Key Ideas and Details How does the old man Wordsworth meets in "Resolution and Independence" make his living? In Carroll's parody of Wordsworth's poem, how does the "aged man" make his living?

Parody, a composition that imitates and makes fun of another, is actually a humorous form of literary criticism. In order to ridicule a writer's style, a parodist has to understand and reproduce it accurately enough for the reader to recognize. The parodist then exaggerates some aspect of the style or subject to make the reader laugh. The result is a caricature, rather than a portrait—recognizable, but silly.

David Levine's caricature of William Wordsworth

The **World** Is Too Much **With Us**

William Wordsworth

The world is too much with us; late and soon,
Getting and spending, we lay waste our powers:
Little we see in Nature that is ours;
We have given our hearts away, a sordid boon![1]
5   This Sea that bares her bosom to the moon;
The winds that will be howling at all hours,
And are upgathered now like sleeping flowers;
For this, for everything, we are out of tune;
It moves us not.—Great God! I'd rather be
10   A Pagan suckled in a creed outworn;
So might I, standing on this pleasant lea,[2]
Have glimpses that would make me less forlorn;
Have sight of Proteus[3] rising from the sea;
Or hear old Triton[4] blow his wreathèd horn.

---

1. **boon** favor.
2. **lea** meadow.
3. **Proteus** (prō´ tē əs) in Greek mythology, a sea god who could change his appearance at will.
4. **Triton** in Greek mythology, a sea god with the head and upper body of a man and the tail of a fish.

London, 1802

William Wordsworth

Milton![1] thou should'st be living at this hour:
England hath need of thee: she is a fen[2]
Of **stagnant** waters: altar, sword, and pen,
Fireside, the heroic wealth of hall and bower,
5   Have forfeited their ancient English dower
Of inward happiness. We are selfish men;
Oh! raise us up, return to us again;
And give us manners, virtue, freedom, power.
Thy soul was like a Star, and dwelt apart:
10   Thou hadst a voice whose sound was like the sea:
Pure as the naked heavens, majestic, free,
So didst thou travel on life's common way,
In cheerful godliness; and yet thy heart
The lowliest duties on herself did lay.

Vocabulary
stagnant (stag´ nənt)
adj. motionless; foul

---

1. Milton seventeenth-century English poet John Milton.
2. fen (fen) *n.* area of low, flat, marshy land.

Critical Reading

1. **Key Ideas and Details (a)** In "The World Is Too Much With Us," what activities cause people to exhaust their "powers"? **(b) Interpret:** What does the speaker mean by the "world"?

2. **Key Ideas and Details (a)** According to the speaker, with what are we "out of tune"? **(b) Interpret:** Why is being out of tune with these experiences such a loss?

3. **Key Ideas and Details (a)** According to "London, 1802," what is England like? **(b) Analyze:** What lacks or missing qualities have caused this condition? **(c) Interpret:** How would Milton's return help?

4. **Integration of Knowledge and Ideas** What qualities do you find in Wordsworth's poems that make him a poetic rebel? In your response, use at least two of these Essential Question words: *traditional, interpretation, rebellious.* *[Connecting to the Essential Question: What is the relationship of the writer to tradition?]*

Cite textual evidence to support your responses.

Close Reading Activities

Poetry of William Wordsworth

Literary Analysis

1. **Key Ideas and Details** Identify a passage from the poems that illustrates Wordsworth's idealized view of nature.

2. **Key Ideas and Details** Find a passage that reflects the **Romantic** belief in the dignity and importance of ordinary people and common language.

3. **Integration of Knowledge and Ideas** Romantic **lyrics** focus on the speaker's personal development. What lessons from Wordsworth's growth might readers adopt?

4. **Integration of Knowledge and Ideas** Using a chart like the one shown, find additional examples in the poems of **diction** that is specific and simple, abstract but simple, or abstract and difficult. Then, draw a conclusion from your results.

 **Common Core State Standards**

Language
4.b. Identify and correctly use patterns of word changes that indicate different meanings or parts of speech. *(p. 793)*
5.b. Analyze nuances in the meanings of words with similar denotations. *(p. 793)*

Specific and Simple: "steep and lofty cliffs"

Abstract but Simple: "clad in one green hue"

Abstract and Difficult: "tranquil restoration"

5. **Comparing Literary Works** Wordsworth's subjects in these poems range widely, from natural scenes to politics to modern life. Does his diction vary to match his subject? Support your answer with details from the poems.

6. **Comparing Literary Works** Identify two passages, each from a different poem, whose diction would have seemed revolutionary to Neoclassical poets. Then, explain your choices.

7. **Integration of Knowledge and Ideas** Imagine that you are a Neoclassical writer—a sociable city-dweller who writes polished, witty, rational verse. Explain how you might react to lines 76–80 of "Tintern Abbey."

8. **Integration of Knowledge and Ideas (a)** What do the hopes described in *The Prelude* tell you about the *political and philosophical assumptions* of the **historical period** in which Romanticism was born? **(b)** What do lines 66–84 suggest about the Romantics' view of reasoning not guided by the heart? Explain.

Vocabulary Acquisition and Use

Word Analysis: Forms of *anatomize*

The verb *anatomize*, meaning "cut into constituent parts," or "dissect," comes from the Greek word *atomos*, meaning "that which cannot be cut further; the smallest part." In *anatomizing* society, Wordsworth attempts to dissect it into the parts that make it up. Several scientific words come from this Greek word. Explain how, as the use of the root changes, each word has a different function or meaning.

1. atom

2. anatomy

3. anatomical

4. atomizer

Root words are modified when affixes are attached. Identify four words with the root *-string-* or *-strict-* ("to draw tight") and explain how each differs in meaning.

Using Resources to Build Vocabulary

Epic Style: Words for Nature

Words have **denotations,** which are their basic meanings, and also **connotations,** which are the feelings or ideas associated with them. For instance, *tired* and *spent* both denote a loss of physical energy from exertion, but *spent* suggests a more extreme state, in which all stamina or tolerance for a difficult situation is gone.

Poets use connotations to add depth and richness to their poems. Wordsworth reveals his feelings for nature through these words from "Tintern Abbey" that he uses to describe it:

sublime (lines 37, 95)

power (line 47)

harmony (line 48)

spirit (line 100)

Use a print or electronic *dictionary* or *thesaurus* to find synonyms of these words. Explain how the connotation of each word differs from that of at least one synonym.

Vocabulary: Synonyms

A *synonym* is a word that has the same, or a similar, meaning as another word. Write the letter of the word that is the best synonym of each word from the vocabulary list on page 779. Then, write an original sentence using each vocabulary word.

1. recompense: **(a)** assistance, **(b)** penitence, **(c)** reward

2. roused: **(a)** angered, **(b)** stirred, **(c)** interfered

3. presumption: **(a)** audacity, **(b)** flattery, **(c)** attractive

4. anatomize: **(a)** address, **(b)** dissect, **(c)** respect

5. sordid: **(a)** dirty, **(b)** organized, **(c)** reclassified

6. stagnant: **(a)** direct, **(b)** foul, **(c)** repugnant

Close Reading Activities Continued

Writing to Sources

Argumentative Text Literary critic Harold Bloom expressed the following insight into Wordsworth's work: "The fear of mortality haunts much of Wordsworth's best poetry, especially in regard to the premature mortality of the Imagination and the loss of its creative joy."

Do you agree or disagree with this evaluation? Prepare an **essay** that refutes or supports Bloom's view.

Prewriting Begin by carefully rereading the poems by Wordsworth in the text.

- After finishing each poem, think about Wordsworth's attitudes toward the loss of imaginative power.
- Note the *imagery, figures of speech, personification,* and *sounds* in the poems that *evoke readers' emotions* and relate to the *theme* of "premature mortality of the Imagination."
- Write a sentence or two to serve as the *thesis* of your essay, and develop an outline that shows how you will support your thesis.

Drafting Write a draft of your essay that follows your outline.

- In the opening paragraph, remember to quote or paraphrase Bloom's insight; to state your thesis clearly, agreeing or disagreeing with Bloom; and to offer a brief explanation of your position.
- Be sure to support your thesis in the body of the essay, making *detailed and accurate references* to the text of Wordsworth's poems.
- Conclude the essay by summarizing what you proved.

Revising Revise your essay to make it clear and effective:

- Review your draft, making sure you have details to support your points. Where they are lacking, find them in the text and add them.
- Determine whether the opening paragraph, in particular, engages the reader's interest as well as setting forth your thesis.
- Check quotations to be sure they are accurate and properly referenced.
- Read the essay carefully to make sure it is grammatically correct and all words are spelled correctly.

**Common Core
State Standards**

Writing
1.a. Introduce precise, knowledgeable claim(s), establish the significance of the claim(s), distinguish the claim(s) from alternate or opposing claims, and create an organization that logically sequences claim(s), counterclaims, reasons, and evidence.
1.e. Provide a concluding statement or section that follows from and supports the argument presented.
9.a. Apply *grades 11–12 Reading standards* to literature.

Language
1. Demonstrate command of the conventions of standard English grammar and usage when writing or speaking. *(p. 795)*
5.a. Interpret figures of speech in context and analyze their role in the text.

Model: Revising to Clearly State Your Position

Much of Wordsworth's work seems to focus on the transience

, however,

of time. Close reading of his poetry‸ suggests that rather than a fear of mortality, his work presents a celebration of life.

> Using conjunctions signals agreement or disagreement.

Conventions and Style: Pronoun-Antecedent Agreement Problems

To write effectively, avoid vague or confusing sentences by using pronouns correctly. Remember that a **pronoun** stands for a noun. The noun is the **antecedent.**

> **Example:** *Wordsworth's* poetry shows *his* love of nature.

Problems in Agreement

Avoid **unintended shifts in person or gender**. It is easy to make accidental errors.

Shift in Person William Wordsworth visited Tintern Abbey, where you saw the ruins.
Revised William Wordsworth visited Tintern Abbey, where he saw the ruins.

Shift in Gender Dorothy Wordsworth, the poet's sister, was himself a very good writer.
Revised Dorothy Wordsworth, the poet's sister, was herself a very good writer.

Watch out for **indefinite pronouns**, such as *all, few, most,* and *none.* Some of them can be either singular or plural.

Most of his *poetry* is read for *its* images.

Most of his *poems* are read for *their* images.

Be sure it is clear to which nouns your pronouns refer.

Unclear Reference Triton and Proteus were sea gods. He was part man and part fish.
Revised Triton was part man and part fish. He and Proteus were sea gods.

Practice Rewrite each sentence, correcting the problem in antecedent and pronoun agreement.

1. Milton and Wordsworth were both English poets. He wrote "London, 1802."
2. There is a poem about the French Revolution in my textbook, but I cannot find it.
3. Poets write of meadows and woods. They are inspiring.
4. Nature is loyal to those who cherish her as it accompanies them through life.
5. The French people lost sight of the reason it fought the French Revolution.
6. Much of the abbey is in ruins, but their former grandeur remains today.
7. Although he has been away five years, the poet remembers the hills for her beauty.
8. One of the landscapes certainly will make their impression.
9. England was going in the wrong direction. They had forgotten manners. They had forgotten freedom.
10. People were interested in worldly things, and you were ignoring nature.

Writing and Speaking Conventions

A. Language Use each pronoun to write a sentence with correct pronoun and antecedent agreement. Choose from these antecedents: *nature, world, beliefs, England, Wordsworth, hope and joy, poets.*

1. he   **2.** it   **3.** they   **4.** her   **5.** its

Example: its
Sentence: The *world* offers us *its* beauty to appreciate.

B. Writing As Wordsworth's sister, write a brief letter to Wordsworth after your visit together to Tintern Abbey. Describe the landscape and what you enjoyed about the visit. Use at least two examples of pronoun-antecedent agreement.

THE *Muse's* CHILDREN:
LYRIC POETS IN WORLD LITERATURE

Erato—LYRIC POETRY IS NAMED FOR THE LYRE, A STRINGED INSTRUMENT USED BY THE ANCIENT GREEKS TO ACCOMPANY RECITATIONS OF POETRY. THE GREEKS DEPICTED THE GODDESS ERATO, SHOWN HERE PLAYING THE LYRE, AS THE MUSE OR PATRON OF LYRIC POETRY.

TU FU
(712–770) CHINESE

ONO KOMACHI
(c. 820–c. 900) JAPANESE

CHARLES BAUDELAIRE
(1821–1867) FRENCH

ALEXANDER PUSHKIN
(1799–1837) RUSSIAN

Comparing Literary Works

Poetry of William Wordsworth •
Lyric Poetry from Around the World

Comparing Lyric Poetry from Around the World

Lyric Poetry Lyric poetry began in song. In fact, the word *lyric* comes from *lyre*, the harplike instrument that ancient Greek poets like Sappho played to accompany their lyric poems. Even before the Greeks, however, people were singing poems expressing faith, love, sorrow, joy, and other strong emotions. Love lyrics survive from ancient Egypt's New Kingdom (c. 1570–1070 B.C.). The philosopher Confucius is said to have compiled the *Book of Songs*, collecting Chinese poetry written as early as 1100 B.C.

Lyric poetry typically has these characteristics:

- It is brief and concise.
- It is communicated by a single speaker expressing personal emotions and observations.
- It uses vivid images to convey ideas and evoke emotions.
- It is musical, often employing rhyme, alliteration, and repetition and following a pattern of rhythm (called meter) or a pattern of syllables.

For lyric poems that you read, fill in charts like this one. Then, use your charts to answer comparison-and-contrast questions about the poems.

**Common Core
State Standards**

Reading Literature
5. Analyze how an author's choices concerning how to structure specific parts of a text contribute to its overall structure and meaning as well as its aesthetic impact.

Language
4.c. Consult general and specialized reference materials, both print and digital, to find the pronunciation of a word or determine or clarify its precise meaning, its part of speech, its etymology, or its standard usage.

	"The World Is Too Much With Us"	"I Have Visited Again"
Form and/or lines	Petrarchan sonnet; 14 lines	
Speaker	Lover of nature	
Observations	Society is too materialistic; nature's beauty is unappreciated.	
Emotions	Unhappiness with society; joy and wonder in nature	
Images	Vivid sights and sounds of wild and pagan sea	
Sound devices	Rhyme, meter, some alliteration, assonance	

Gather Vocabulary Knowledge

These lyric poets use words such as *fathomless, treacherous,* and *splendor.* Use a **dictionary** to find each word's part of speech and definition. Then, employ the following references (printed or electronic) to explore these words:

- **History of Language:** Use a history of English to research each word's etymology, or origins.
- **Book of Quotations:** Use a collection of quotations to find a statement containing one of the words. In a paragraph, explain the nuances in meaning that are evident from the context of the quotation.

Comparing References Compare and contrast what you learn about the words from these specialized references.

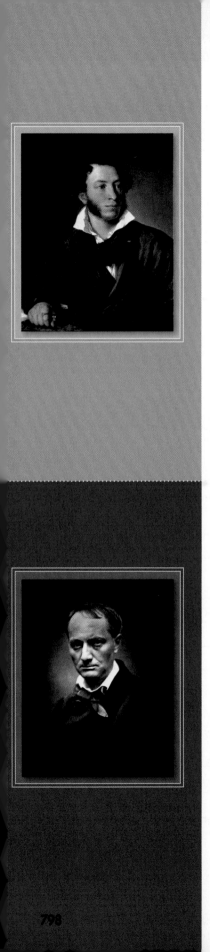

Alexander Pushkin (1799–1837)

Author of "I Have Visited Again"

Russian author Alexander Pushkin was born in Moscow into an aristocratic family. As a youth, he led a life of relative privilege and wrote with a skill that would hint at his eventual fame. While working in government service in St. Petersburg, he aroused suspicion by associating with political rebels and writing poems advocating government changes. In 1820, the government acted upon its suspicions by reappointing Pushkin to a post in a remote province in southern Russia. During the five years Pushkin spent there, he enhanced his reputation as a writer and began working on his masterpiece, the verse novel *Yevgeny Onegin* (1833). Unfortunately, his unrestrained and sometimes violent behavior resulted in his dismissal from civil service in 1824 and banishment to his family's estate.

Though isolated and unhappy on the estate, Pushkin channeled most of his energy into his writing. He spent much of his time interacting with the peasants who lived on the estate, learning about their lifestyles, and incorporating their legends and folklore into a number of his finest poems.

Acts of Rebellion Pushkin was allowed to return to Moscow in 1826. After marrying Natalya Goncharova in 1831, Pushkin grudgingly returned to government service. In a final act of rebellion, Pushkin entered into a duel that cost him his life.

Charles Baudelaire (1821–1867)

Author of "Invitation to the Voyage"

Charles Baudelaire (shȧrl bōd ler´) was one of the most colorful, startling, and innovative poets of the nineteenth century. Attempting to break away from the Romantic tradition, Baudelaire created poems that are objective rather than sentimental. Many of his works celebrate the city and the artificial rather than nature.

As a youth, Baudelaire rebelled against his family to pursue a career as a writer. To dissuade him from such a dissolute life, they sent him on an ocean voyage to India. Instead of completing the voyage, he returned to France to claim his share of his late father's fortune. Soon, extravagant living drove him into debt, a problem that would plague him for the rest of his life.

Baudelaire published short stories, translated works by Edgar Allan Poe into French, and both wrote and collected poems for *Flowers of Evil* (1857), which would become his signature work. Although his talents were not widely recognized during his lifetime, Baudelaire's reputation blossomed posthumously, and he came to be considered one of the finest nineteenth-century poets.

I Have Visited Again

Alexander Pushkin, translated by D. M. Thomas

BACKGROUND Initially, Alexander Pushkin found the inspiration to write in the politics of his homeland. His rebellious writings, as well as his unruly behavior, resulted in banishment to his family estate. Such a personality seems distantly related to the speaker of the gentle words and images in "I Have Visited Again." In this poem, the speaker revisits the estate to find that time and nature have hardly stood still in the intervening years.

. . . I have visited again
That corner of the earth where I spent two
Unnoticed, exiled years. Ten years have passed
Since then, and many things have changed for me,
5 And I have changed too, obedient to life's law—
But now that I am here again, the past
Has flown out eagerly to embrace me, claim me,
And it seems that only yesterday I wandered
Within these groves.

                Here is the cottage, sadly
10 Declined now, where I lived with my poor old nurse.
She is no more. No more behind the wall
Do I hear her heavy footsteps as she moved
Slowly, painstakingly about her tasks.

15   Here are the wooded slopes where often I
Sat motionless, and looked down at the lake,
Recalling other shores and other waves . . .
It gleams between golden cornfields and green meadows,
A wide expanse; across its fathomless waters
20 A fisherman passes, dragging an ancient net.
Along the shelving banks, hamlets are scattered
—Behind them the mill, so crooked it can scarcely
Make its sails turn in the wind . . .

                On the bounds
25 Of my ancestral acres, at the spot
Where a road, scarred by many rainfalls, climbs
The hill, three pine-trees stand—one by itself,
The others close together. When I rode
On horseback past them in the moonlit night,
30 The friendly rustling murmur of their crowns
Would welcome me. Now, I have ridden out
Upon that road, and seen those trees again.
They have remained the same, make the same murmur—
But round their ageing roots, where all before
35 Was barren, naked, a thicket of young pines
Has sprouted; like green children round the shadows
Of the two neighboring pines. But in the distance
Their solitary comrade stands, morose,
Like some old bachelor, and round its roots
40 All is barren as before.

Comparing Lyric Poetry

How is the speaker's experience here similar to that of the speaker in Wordsworth's "Lines Composed a Few Miles Above Tintern Abbey"? Do the two speakers share similar views of nature? Explain.

Vocabulary

ancestral (an ses′ trəl) *adj.* inherited

morose (mə rōs′) *adj.* gloomy; sullen

I greet you, young
And unknown tribe of pine-trees! I'll not see
Your mighty upward thrust of years to come
When you will overtop these friends of mine
45 And shield their ancient summits from the gaze
Of passers-by. But may my grandson hear
Your welcome murmur when, returning home
From lively company, and filled with gay
And pleasant thoughts, he passes you in the night,
50 And thinks perhaps of me . . .

And I have changed too,
obedient to life's law—

Critical Reading

1. **Key Ideas and Details (a)** Identify four familiar landmarks in the poem that have changed over the years. **(b) Infer:** How has the speaker changed in a similar fashion?

2. **Key Ideas and Details (a)** In stanza three, what thoughts occupy the speaker while he looks down at the lake? **(b) Infer:** What does the speaker mean by "other shores"? **(c) Hypothesize:** Why might the speaker have yearned to be in another place?

3. **Craft and Structure (a)** Where does the "unknown tribe of pine-trees" grow? **(b) Speculate:** What role will those pines play in the future? **(c) Interpret:** What do those pines symbolize?

4. **Integration of Knowledge and Ideas** Novelist Thomas Wolfe commented on how our lives change by saying that we "can't go home again," a theme shared by "I Have Visited Again." Do you agree or disagree with such a claim? Explain your answer.

Cite textual evidence to support your responses.

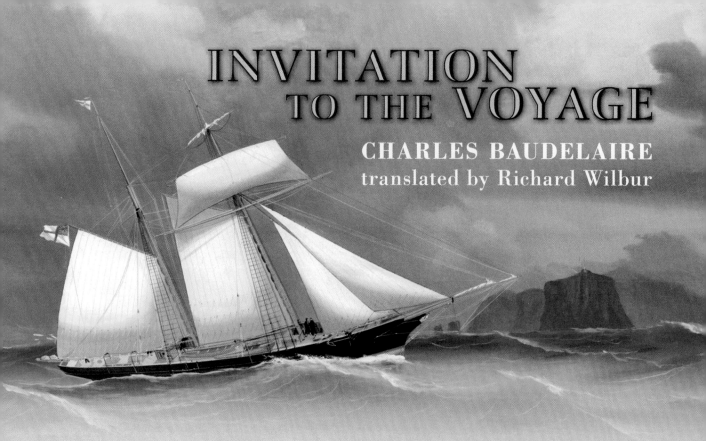

INVITATION TO THE VOYAGE

CHARLES BAUDELAIRE
translated by Richard Wilbur

BACKGROUND There is little doubt that Charles Baudelaire's ocean voyage to India was a significant event in his life. Although the journey was cut short—lasting only eight months instead of eighteen—the experience clearly inspired him as a poet. The voyage, his desire for a life of ease and luxury, and his yearning to escape reality all find expression in his poem "Invitation to the Voyage."

My child, my sister, dream
How sweet all things would seem
Were we in that kind land to live together
And there love slow and long,
5   There love and die among
Those scenes that image you, that sumptuous[1] weather.
Drowned suns that glimmer there
Through cloud-disheveled[2] air
Move me with such a mystery as appears
10   Within those other skies
Of your treacherous eyes
When I behold them shining through their tears.

---

1. sumptuous (sump´ chōō əs) *adj.* magnificent or splendid.
2. disheveled (di shev´ əld) *adj.* disarranged and untidy.

There, there is nothing else but grace and measure,
Richness, quietness, and pleasure.

15   Furniture that wears
      The luster of the years
Softly would glow within our glowing chamber,
      Flowers of rarest bloom
      Proffering their perfume
20 Mixed with the vague fragrances of amber;
      Gold ceilings would there be,
      Mirrors deep as the sea,
The walls all in an Eastern splendor hung—
      Nothing but should address
25   The soul's loneliness,
Speaking her sweet and secret native tongue.

There, there is nothing else but grace and measure,
Richness, quietness, and pleasure.

      See, sheltered from the swells
30   There in the still canals
Those drowsy ships that dream of sailing forth;
      It is to satisfy
      Your least desire, they ply
Hither through all the waters of the earth.
35   The sun at close of day
      Clothes the fields of hay,
Then the canals, at last the town entire
      In hyacinth and gold:
      Slowly the land is rolled
40 Sleepward under a sea of gentle fire.

There, there is nothing else but grace and measure,
Richness, quietness, and pleasure.

Vocabulary

proffering (präf´ ər iŋ)
v. offering

Comparing Lyric Poetry

How is the landscape described here unlike the landscape described in Pushkin's poem? What feelings does the speaker of each poem seem to have for the landscape he describes?

Critical Reading

1. **Key Ideas and Details (a)** Which details describe the "kind land" in "Invitation to the Voyage"? **(b) Interpret:** What impression of the land do these details convey?

2. **Integration of Knowledge and Ideas** How does the world described in "Invitation to the Voyage" compare to your ideal world?

Cite textual evidence to support your responses.

Chinese Poets

BOOK OF SONGS

The Book of Songs, also known as *The Book of Odes,* is an anthology of 305 ancient Chinese poems. The poems come from many different regions of China. Most of them were originally folk songs describing people's daily activities. Others, like "Thick Grow the Rush Leaves," focus on love or courtship. All of the songs were originally set to music.

TU FU (712–770)
Author of "Jade Flower Palace"

Tu Fu (dōō′ fōō′) is regarded as the supreme craftsman of Chinese shih (shǐ) poetry. In all of his poetry—poems dealing with social issues and those that focus on his personal experiences—Tu Fu shows a command of language and a mastery of the shih form. As a result, his poems are admired as much for their form as for their content.

Early in Tu Fu's career, China was relatively peaceful, but later the poet witnessed a major rebellion, the destruction of the capital city, and an invasion by tribes from the northwest. In his poems, Tu Fu gives some of the most vivid accounts of war and destruction in all of Chinese literature.

Japanese Poets

KI TSURAYUKI (died c. 945)

The chief aide of Emperor Daigo (dī′ gō′), Ki Tsurayuki (kē tsōōr′ ĭ ōō kē) was one of the leading poets, critics, and diarists of his time. Tsurayuki deserves much of the credit for assembling an anthology of over eleven hundred poems of the Heian (hā′ än′) Age. In addition, his *Tosa Diary* helped to establish the Japanese tradition of the literary diary.

ONO KOMACHI (c. 820–c. 900)

A great beauty with a strong personality, Ono Komachi (ō′ nō′ kō′ mä′ chē′) was an early tanka (täŋ′ kə) poet whose poems are characterized by their passion and energy. Few details of Ono Komachi's life are known.

PRIEST JAKUREN (1139?–1202)

Jakuren (jä′ kōō′ ren′) was a Buddhist priest and prominent tanka poet whose poems are filled with beautiful yet melancholic imagery. After entering the priesthood at the age of twenty-three, Jakuren spent much of his time traveling the Japanese countryside, writing poetry and seeking spiritual fulfillment.

FROM **THE BOOK OF SONGS**

Thick Grow the Rush Leaves

TRANSLATED BY ARTHUR WALEY

Thick grow the rush leaves;
Their white dew turns to frost.
He whom I love
Must be somewhere along this stream.
5 I went up the river to look for him,
But the way was difficult and long.
I went down the stream to look for him,
And there in mid-water
Sure enough, it's he!

10 Close grow the rush leaves,
Their white dew not yet dry.
He whom I love
Is at the water's side.
Up stream I sought him;
15 But the way was difficult and steep.
Down stream I sought him,
And away in mid-water
There on a ledge, that's he!

Very fresh are the rush leaves;
20 The white dew still falls.
He whom I love
Is at the water's edge.
Up stream I followed him;
But the way was hard and long.
25 Down stream I followed him,
And away in mid-water
There on the shoals is he!

▼ **Critical Viewing**

How is the river in this painting similar to or different from the one in the poem, along which "the way was difficult and long"? **COMPARE AND CONTRAST**

Jade Flower Palace

TU FU

TRANSLATED BY KENNETH REXROTH

Vocabulary

scurry (skʉr´ ē) *v.* to run hastily; to scamper

pathos (pā´ thəs´) *n.* quality that evokes sorrow or compassion

imperceptibly (im´ pər sep´ tə blē) *adv.* without being noticed

The stream swirls. The wind moans in
The pines. Gray rats scurry over
Broken tiles. What prince, long ago,
Built this palace, standing in
5 Ruins beside the cliffs? There are
Green ghost fires in the black rooms.
The shattered pavements are all
Washed away. Ten thousand organ
Pipes whistle and roar. The storm
10 Scatters the red autumn leaves.
His dancing girls are yellow dust.
Their painted cheeks have crumbled
Away. His gold chariots
And courtiers are gone. Only
15 A stone horse is left of his
Glory. I sit on the grass and
Start a poem, but the pathos of
It overcomes me. The future
Slips imperceptibly away.
20 Who can say what the years will bring?

▶ **Critical Viewing**

How is the building in this photo different from the palace described in "Jade Flower Palace"? How is the girl in the drawing on the facing page like the "dancing girls" found in the poem? **CONNECT**

BACKGROUND All three of the following poems are tanka. The tanka is the most prevalent verse form in traditional Japanese literature. In the original Japanese, each tanka consists of five lines of five, seven, five, seven, and seven syllables. Tanka usually tell a brief story or express a single thought or insight, usually relating to love or nature.

Priest Jakuren

TRANSLATED BY GEOFFREY BOWNAS

One cannot ask loneliness
How or where it starts.
On the cypress-mountain,[1]
Autumn evening.

Ki Tsurayuki

TRANSLATED BY GEOFFREY BOWNAS

When I went to visit
The girl I love so much,
That winter night
The river blew so cold
5   That the plovers[2] were crying.

---

1. **cypress-mountain** Cypress trees are cone-bearing evergreen trees, native to North America, Europe, and Asia.
2. **plovers** (pluv´ ərz) *n.* wading shorebirds with short tails, long, pointed wings, and short, stout beaks.

Ono Komachi

TRANSLATED BY GEOFFREY BOWNAS

Comparing Lyric Poetry
In which of the three tanka does the translator best retain the original syllabification?

Was it that I went to sleep
Thinking of him,
That he came in my dreams?
Had I known it a dream
5 I should not have wakened.

Critical Reading

Cite textual evidence to support your responses.

1. **Craft and Structure (a)** In "Thick Grow the Rush Leaves," which images in each stanza are repeated with slight variations? **(b) Infer:** What activity on the river do the images help capture? **(c) Interpret:** How do images help convey the speaker's feelings?

2. **Key Ideas and Details (a)** In "Jade Flower Palace," what remains of the long-gone prince's "glory"? **(b) Compare and Contrast:** In what way does this image contrast with the speaker's description of what used to be in the palace? **(c) Draw Conclusions:** What point might the speaker be making through this contrast?

3. **Craft and Structure (a)** What is the setting of Tsurayuki's poem? **(b) Infer:** What does the speaker's willingness to face that setting suggest about the depth of his love?

4. **Key Ideas and Details (a)** What question does the speaker of Ono Komachi's poem ask? **(b) Infer:** What do her question and her response to that question suggest about her feelings toward the man in her dreams?

Close Reading Activities

Poetry of William Wordsworth •
Lyric Poetry from Around the World

Comparing Lyric Poetry

1. **Key Ideas and Details** Compare "Thick Grow the Rush Leaves" to the first two tanka poems by Japanese writers. **(a)** What is similar and different about the feelings each poem expresses? **(b)** In which poem does imagery most effectively capture those feelings? Explain.

2. **Key Ideas and Details (a)** Compare and contrast the passage of time in "Tintern Abbey," the selection from *The Prelude*, "Jade Flower Palace," and "I Have Visited Again." **(b)** In which two poems are the speakers' experiences of the passage of time most similar? Explain.

3. **Craft and Structure** Of the translations presented here, which lyric poems do you find the most musical? Cite examples from the poems to support your evaluation.

 Common Core State Standards

Writing
2. Write informative/ explanatory texts to examine and convey complex ideas, concepts, and information clearly and accurately through the effective selection, organization, and analysis of content.

10. Write routinely over extended time frames and shorter time frames for a range of tasks, purposes, and audiences.

Timed Writing

Explanatory Text: Essay

Many of the lyric poems you have read in this section include descriptions of natural settings.

Assignment: Choose two poems by different authors that have vivid descriptions of nature. Write an **essay** in which you *compare and contrast* the two poems by addressing these questions. **[40 minutes]**

- What is the theme or central insight expressed in each poem?
- For each poem, how does the description of nature support the theme?
- What images does each speaker use to describe nature?
- For each poem, what feelings does the description of nature evoke?

As you write, follow the conventions of a strong explanatory essay. Organize your ideas logically. You might focus on the features of one poem and then the features of the other, or you might focus on points of similarity and difference, moving back and forth between the two poems.

5-Minute Planner

Complete these steps before you begin to write:

1. Read the assignment carefully. List key words and phrases.
2. To focus your analysis, scan the poems for evidence that relates to the questions.
3. Create a rough outline for your essay.
4. Reread the prompt, and draft your essay.

USE ACADEMIC VOCABULARY

As you write, use academic language, including the following words or their related forms:

correspond
insight
musicality
perspective

For more on academic language, see the vocabulary charts in the introduction to this book.

Analyzing Functional and Expository Texts

Government Report • Travel Guide

About the Texts

A **government report** is an account of work or a study completed by a government agency. These types of reports often include a description of events or an analysis of an issue; an explanation of how an issue affects different groups; and a description of problems, with proposed solutions, often including actions taken or planned by the government.

A **travel guide** is a document that provides information to people who are planning a trip to a particular destination. Travel guides generally provide an overview of an area and then go into detail about specific attractions, transportation, food, and lodging.

Preparing to Read Complex Texts

Reports and guides provide information in a logical order. Often, the textual information in these types of documents is supplemented by graphics, such as charts and photographs. Graphics may clarify the structure of the text and make it easier to read. They may also make the text more attractive and engaging. As you study these documents, **analyze information from charts, graphs, and illustrations** by evaluating these features:

- a heading or title of a graph that defines its information
- labels that classify different elements of charts and graphs
- captions explaining symbols and images

Use a checklist like the one shown to assess graphics in these texts. Analyze and evaluate how well these structures complement information presented verbally. Consider whether the graphic elements clarify ideas and make the text more interesting or useful to readers.

Common Core State Standards

Reading Informational Text
5. Analyze and evaluate the effectiveness of the structure an author uses in his or her exposition or argument, including whether the structure makes points clear, convincing, and engaging.

Language
4.d. Verify the preliminary determination of the meaning of a word or phrase. *(p. 817)*

Content-Area Vocabulary

These words may also appear in other subject-area texts:

district (dis´ trikt) *n.* a given area or selected geographical section on a map

trade (trād) *n.* the buying and selling of goods or services

policies (päl´ ə sēz´) *n.* plans of action by a government, business, or political party

geological (jē´ ə läj´ ik əl) *adj.* of or related to the structure of the earth

Features	Yes/No	Content
Graph and chart titles	☐ / ☐	
Graph and chart labels	☐ / ☐	
Photos or images	☐ / ☐	
Captions	☐ / ☐	
Explanations of symbols	☐ / ☐	

LAKE DISTRICT
National Park Authority

EDUCATION SERVICE TRAFFIC MANAGEMENT

The Lake **District** National Park is an area of outstandingly beautiful and varied landscape and the scenery is the reason most people give for visiting the Lake District (62%, 1994 All Parks Visitor Survey).

The Lake District remained relatively isolated until the 19th century when new railways allowed the large urban populations of Northwest England to visit the area easily. Both **trade** and early tourism flourished. In the 1940s, it was recognised that areas such as the Lake District would benefit from some kind of special protection. The Lake District was designated a National Park in 1951 to conserve and enhance its special landscape while providing opportunities for the public to enjoy that landscape. At this time, it was expected that "walkers, cyclists, riders and students of nature" would be the main users of the National Park rather than motorists, although National Parks were intended for all to enjoy.

Since then, car ownership has increased and now the vast majority of visitors come by car. Today, over 12 million people visit the National Park annually (staying for 22 million days) while 42,000 people live in the National Park. 89% of visitors come to the National Park by private motor vehicle.

The Lake District National Park Authority (LDNPA) and Cumbria County Council (CCC) have a number of automatic traffic counters around the National Park to help understand traffic movements. Traffic is greatest during the summer months when most visitors come to the National Park and mid-mornings and late afternoons can be exceptionally busy. In recent years, the rate of increase of traffic has slowed down, with recorded increases being largely confined to main roads such as the A591.

The heading "Lake District" and the words "Traffic Management" in the report's heading reveal the focus and purpose of the report.

This paragraph establishes the focus of the report on the issue of car traffic in the park.

Traffic Issues

Large volumes of traffic can lead to a number of issues, especially in an area like the Lake District where roads are often narrow.

- **Pollution:** Motor vehicles emit various pollutants which may reach high levels in certain weather conditions, especially within towns.

- **Noise:** 'Peace and Quiet' is often given as a reason for visiting, so this is an issue, especially when considering development.

- **Visual intrusion:** Lines of parked cars can detract from the natural beauty of the National Park.

- **Congestion:** Congestion can be a problem in certain areas and towns at peak times of day and the year.

- **Reducing visitor traffic:** Traffic Management aims to minimize the impact of traffic and encourage visitors to use public transport rather than private cars.

- **Parking:** A balance needs to be found between provision of parking for visitors and locals and impact on the landscape.

- **Hazards to vulnerable road users:** Walkers, cyclists and horse riders should be at ease on the roads in the Lake District. Actual and perceived hazards to these road users should be minimized.

The traffic problems are clearly described in this bulleted list.

The graph's clear title, different colors, and sidebar labels make information easy to interpret.

Annual Average Daily Traffic Flow

Source: LDNPA traffic counters

Number of vehicles in 24 hours

Year

— ◆ — Haweswater   — ■ — Langdale   — ▲ — Mungrisdale   — ✕ — Wasdale (Galesyke)

Traffic Management in the National Park

The guiding principle underpinning the **policies** of the LDNPA towards transport and traffic is that demand should be managed in order to:

- minimize its impact on the landscape
- improve the quality of life for local residents
- improve the quality of enjoyment for visitors
- encourage use of sustainable means of travel

The policies of the LDNPA are set out in the Lake District National Park Management Plan. These clearly state that increasing road capacity is not an appropriate solution to traffic management in the National Park. Instead, traffic management policy is to tailor traffic to existing roads.

A balance of interests is needed between the purposes of the National Park, local people and visitors to ensure the special qualities of the National Park are not compromised. For example, in 1966 the Lake District Special Planning Board published a "Report on Traffic in the Lake District National Park" suggesting that in the future it might become necessary to restrict all except local traffic along secondary routes. Objections were raised by local residents of Langdale and Borrowdale concerning the impact of these closures on the tourism trade.

> This paragraph addresses the different groups the traffic problem and proposed solutions affect.

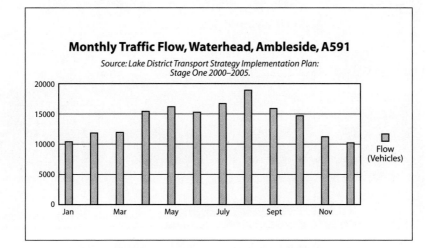

Monthly Traffic Flow, Waterhead, Ambleside, A591

Source: Lake District Transport Strategy Implementation Plan: Stage One 2000–2005.

Flow (Vehicles)

The North Country

Exploring Lancashire and the Lakes

The lake district's natural scenery outweighs any of its man-made attractions. Its natural features are the result of **geological** upheavals over millennia (see pp 340–41), and four of its peaks are more than 1,000 m (3,300 ft). Human influences have left their mark too: the main activities are quarrying, mining, farming and tourism.

The Lakes are most crowded in summer when activities include lake trips and hill-walking. The best bases are Keswick and Ambleside, while there are also good hotels on the shores of Windermere and Ullswater and in the Cartmel area.

Lancashire's Bowland Forest is an attractive place to explore on foot, with picturesque villages. Further south, Manchester and Liverpool have excellent museums and galleries.

This picture and caption give readers a clearer understanding of the area's "natural scenery" described in the text.

View over Crummock Water, north of Buttermere, one of the quieter Western Lakes

Preserved docks and Liver Building, Liverpool

Getting Around

For many, the first glimpse of the Lake District is from the M6 near Shap Fell, but the A6 is a more dramatic route. You can reach Windermere by train, but you need to change at Oxenholme, on the mainline route from Euston to Carlisle. Penrith also has rail services and bus links into the Lakes. L'al Ratty, the miniature railway up Eskdale, and the Lakeside & Haverthwaite railway, which connects with the steamers on Windermere, make for enjoyable outings. Regular buses link all the main centres where excursions are organized. One of the most enterprising is the Mountain Goat minibus, in Windermere and Keswick.

Lancaster, Liverpool and Manchester are on the main rail and bus routes and also have airports. For Blackpool, you need to change trains in Preston. Wherever you go in the area, one of the best means of getting around is on foot.

This section giving visitors information on traveling to different sites is supplemented by the map on the following page.

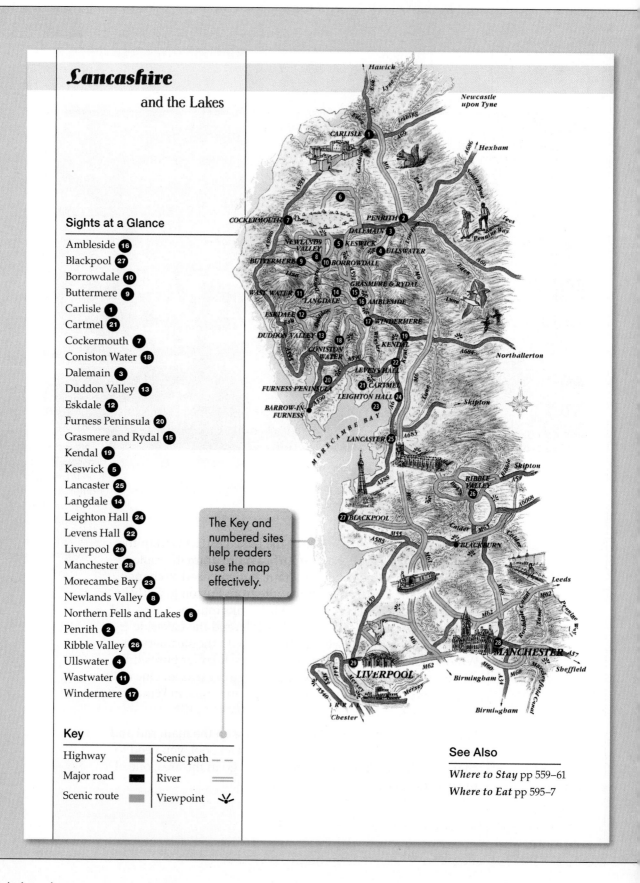

Lancashire
and the Lakes

Sights at a Glance

Ambleside **16**
Blackpool **27**
Borrowdale **10**
Buttermere **9**
Carlisle **1**
Cartmel **21**
Cockermouth **7**
Coniston Water **18**
Dalemain **3**
Duddon Valley **13**
Eskdale **12**
Furness Peninsula **20**
Grasmere and Rydal **15**
Kendal **19**
Keswick **5**
Lancaster **25**
Langdale **14**
Leighton Hall **24**
Levens Hall **22**
Liverpool **29**
Manchester **28**
Morecambe Bay **23**
Newlands Valley **8**
Northern Fells and Lakes **6**
Penrith **2**
Ribble Valley **26**
Ullswater **4**
Wastwater **11**
Windermere **17**

The Key and numbered sites help readers use the map effectively.

Key

Highway	▬▬	Scenic path	– – –
Major road	▬▬	River	══
Scenic route	▬▬	Viewpoint	⩘

See Also

Where to Stay pp 559–61
Where to Eat pp 595–7

Critical Reading

1. **Key Ideas and Details (a)** Based on the government report, what major change has taken place since 1951 in the way visitors tour the Lake District? **(b)** What problems has this change caused? **(c)** What solutions does the report propose?

2. **Key Ideas and Details (a)** Based on the travel guide, what are various transportation options in the Lake District? **(b)** Which option does the guide state is best? **(c)** How does the information in the government report support the opinion expressed in the travel guide?

3. **Craft and Structure** For each document, note at least one way in which its structure and organization reflect and support its content.

4. **Craft and Structure (a)** For each document, note a statement or fact presented verbally that is supported or enhanced by one or more graphics. **(b)** For each document, do the graphic elements make the ideas clearer and more engaging? Why or why not?

5. **Content-Area Vocabulary (a)** The word *policy* derives from the Greek root *-polis-/-polit-*, which means "city." Explain how the meaning of the root informs the meaning of *policy*. **(b)** Define the following words derived from the same root: *political, police,* and *cosmopolitan*. Use a dictionary to verify your definitions.

⏱ Timed Writing

Informative Text [40 minutes]

Format

In an **analytical essay,** you break a topic into smaller elements and show how these elements relate to the idea or ideas you are discussing.

> Although these documents have different purposes, they are about the same place. Write a brief **analytical essay** in which you use both documents to tell visitors what to expect on a trip to the Lake District. To accomplish your goal, **synthesize ideas and make logical connections** between the texts. Support your ideas with textual evidence, including evidence from the graphs and the map.

Academic Vocabulary

When you **synthesize and make logical connections,** you combine ideas and relate texts logically.

5-Minute Planner

Complete these steps before you begin to write.

1. Read the prompt carefully. Underline key words.

2. Draft a thesis that clearly responds to the prompt.

3. Scan the text for details that relate to the prompt. **TIP** Your scan will help provide the evidence you need to support your points.

4. Reread the prompt, and draft your essay.

Connecting to the Essential Question Romantics like Coleridge wrote about strange and faraway places. As you read, note details in the settings of these poems that seem unusual, even dreamlike. Finding such details will help you as you consider the Essential Question: **What is the relationship between literature and place?**

Close Reading Focus

Narrative Poetry; Poetic Sound Devices

Unlike *lyric poetry*, which expresses the thoughts and feelings of a speaker, **narrative poetry** tells a story. Narrative poems feature the storytelling elements of character, plot, and setting, but organize them with poetic structures. Romantics admired the storytelling of folk ballads, so it is no wonder Coleridge uses a *ballad stanza* (*abcb*) in much of his narrative poem *The Rime of the Ancient Mariner*. He also uses these **poetic sound devices** to heighten the music and *evoke emotions*:

- **Alliteration,** a repeated consonant sound at the beginnings of words: "The fair <u>br</u>eeze <u>bl</u>ew, the white <u>f</u>oam <u>fl</u>ew, . . ."

- **Consonance,** repeated similar final consonant sounds in stressed syllables with dissimilar vowel sounds: ". . . fie<u>nd</u> / . . . behi<u>nd</u>"

- **Assonance,** a repeated vowel sound in stressed syllables with dissimilar consonant sounds: "The western w<u>a</u>ve was all afl<u>a</u>me."

- **Internal rhyme,** the use of rhymes within a poetic line: "With heavy th<u>ump</u>, a lifeless l<u>ump</u>, . . ."

Comparing Literary Works Notice how, in both poems, the rhythms propel you forward. At the same time, Coleridge uses sound devices; *archaic,* or old-fashioned, words such as *eftsoons* ("immediately"); and exotic place names ("Xanadu") to create a riveting fantasy.

Preparing to Read Complex Texts By **comparing and contrasting sound devices** in two of his poems, you can understand how Coleridge evokes a range of moods. As you read, use a chart like the one shown to compare the effects of sound devices in the two poems.

Vocabulary

You will encounter the words below in the texts that follow. Copy the words into your notebook, noting which words are past-tense verbs.

averred	reverence
sojourn	sinuous
expiated	tumult

Common Core State Standards

Reading Literature
5. Analyze how an author's choices concerning how to structure specific parts of a text contribute to its overall structure and meaning as well as its aesthetic impact.

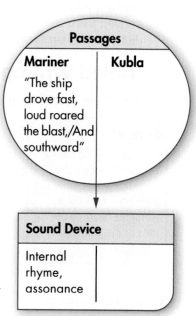

Passages

Mariner	Kubla
"The ship drove fast, loud roared the blast,/And southward"	

Sound Device

Internal rhyme, assonance	

Samuel Taylor Coleridge

(1772–1834)

Author of *The Rime of the Ancient Mariner* • "Kubla Khan"

The poetry of Samuel Taylor Coleridge stands at the place where real life slips into dreams and facts are reborn as fantasies. More than any other Romantic poet, he dared to journey inward—deep into the world of the imagination.

Early Fantasies Coleridge was born in Ottery St. Mary on the Devon coast of England, the last of ten children. At an early age, he retreated into a world of books and fantasy. When he was nine, his father died, and Coleridge was sent to school in London. Later, he went to Cambridge University.

Utopian Plans At Cambridge, Coleridge's hunger for new ideas led him into radical politics. He became a friend of the poet Robert Southey. Inspired by the early promise of the French Revolution, the two men planned to form a settlement in Pennsylvania based on their utopian political ideas. The plan collapsed, however, when Southey's aunt refused to fund their project.

A Literary Breakthrough In 1795, Coleridge and his wife, Sara Fricker, moved to Somerset, where he became a friend of poet William Wordsworth. In 1798, the two poets published *Lyrical Ballads*, a joint collection of their works. The four poems that make up Coleridge's contribution to the volume include his masterpiece *The Rime of the Ancient Mariner*. The collection of poems slowly gained critical attention. In the end, it caused a revolution in poetic style and thought, firmly establishing the movement known as Romanticism.

Success and Difficulty As Coleridge's fame grew, he suffered increasingly from asthma and rheumatism. He began to rely heavily on pain-killers, which dulled his creative powers. He sought relief from pain in the warmer climates of Malta and Italy. His travels, however, did not relieve his pain and caused the collapse of his marriage.

Though the end of his life was troubled, Coleridge left a great legacy in poetry and literary criticism. Above all, he helped establish the importance of the imagination in literature and in life.

> "Poetry:
> the best words
> in the best order."

The Rime of the
Ancient Mariner

Samuel Taylor Coleridge

Background

Coleridge used dreams as the basis of many of his great poems. "The Rime of the Ancient Mariner" was based on a dream reported by his friend John Cruikshank. Starting with the dream as raw material, Coleridge and Wordsworth began to elaborate upon it. Wordsworth suggested that the act that would drive the entire poem was a crime committed at sea. Using this idea and his own lively imagination, Coleridge wrote a poem that has chilled and enthralled audiences to this day. (The margin notes in italics were written by the poet.)

Argument

How a Ship having passed the Line[1] was driven by storms to the cold Country towards the South Pole: and how from thence she made her course to the tropical Latitude of the Great Pacific Ocean; and of the strange things that befell: and in what manner the Ancyent Marinere came back to his own Country.

◄ Critical Viewing

Identify two elements in this engraving that create a gloomy, suspense-filled atmosphere. **ANALYZE**

Part I ●━━━━━━

An ancient Mariner meeteth three Gallants bidden to a wedding feast and detaineth one.

It is an ancient Mariner,
And he stoppeth one of three.
"By thy long gray beard and glittering eye,
Now wherefore stopp'st thou me?"

5   "The Bridegroom's doors are opened wide,
And I am next of kin;
The guests are met, the feast is set:
May'st hear the merry din."

  He holds him with his skinny hand,
10 "There was a ship," quoth he.
"Hold off! unhand me, graybeard loon!"
Eftsoons[2] his hand dropped he.

The Wedding Guest is spellbound by the eye of the old seafaring man and constrained to hear his tale.

  He holds him with his glittering eye—
The Wedding Guest stood still,

Poetic Sound Devices

What examples of internal rhymes and assonance can you find in lines 5–8?

Comprehension

What effect does the ancient Mariner have on the Wedding Guest?

---

1. **Line** Equator.
2. **Eftsoons** immediately.

▶ **Critical Viewing**

From the expression on the Wedding Guest's face (figure on far left), what can you infer about his reaction to the ancient Mariner? **INFER**

15 And listens like a three years' child:
   The Mariner hath his will.

   The Wedding Guest sat on a stone:
   He cannot choose but hear;
   And thus spake on that ancient man,
20 The bright-eyed Mariner.

   "The ship was cheered, the harbor cleared,
   Merrily did we drop
   Below the kirk,³ below the hill,
   Below the lighthouse top.

25 "The Sun came up upon the left,
   Out of the sea came he!
   And he shone bright, and on the right
   Went down into the sea.

   "Higher and higher every day,
30 Till over the mast at noon⁴—"
   The Wedding Guest here beat his breast,
   For he heard the loud bassoon.

   The bride hath paced into the hall.
   Red as a rose is she;

*The Mariner tells
how the ship sailed
southward with
a good wind and
fair weather till it
reached the Line.*

*The Wedding Guest
heareth the bridal
music; but the
Mariner continueth
his tale.*

---

3. kirk church.
4. over . . . noon The ship has reached the equator.

35 Nodding their heads before her goes
The merry minstrelsy.

The Wedding Guest he beat his breast,
Yet he cannot choose but hear;
And thus spake on that ancient man
40 The bright-eyed Mariner.

"And now the Storm blast came, and he
Was tyrannous and strong:
He struck with his o'ertaking wings,
And chased us south along.

45 "With sloping masts and dipping prow,
As who pursued with yell and blow
Still treads the shadow of his foe,
And forward bends his head,
The ship drove fast, loud roared the blast,
50 And southward aye[5] we fled.

"And now there came both mist and snow.
And it grew wondrous cold;
And ice, mast-high, came floating by,
As green as emerald.

55 "And through the drifts the snowy clifts[6]
Did send a dismal sheen;
Nor shapes of men nor beasts we ken[7]—
The ice was all between.

"The ice was here, the ice was there,
60 The ice was all around;
It cracked and growled, and roared and howled,
Like noises in a swound![8]

"At length did cross an Albatross,
Thorough[9] the fog it came;
65 As if it had been a Christian soul,
We hailed it in God's name.

"It ate the food it ne'er had eat,[10]
And round and round it flew.

*The ship driven
by a storm toward
the South Pole.*

*The land of ice,
and of fearful sounds,
where no living
thing was to be seen.*

*Till a great sea
bird, called the
Albatross, came
through the snow-
fog, and was
received with great
joy and hospitality.*

Poetic Sound Devices

What archaic word-form appears in lines 37–40?

Comparing and Contrasting Sound Devices

Find one line in lines 51–54 that contains the long and the short sound of the same vowel. What emphasis does this alternation create?

Comprehension

In the Mariner's tale, what happens to the ship shortly after it sets out?

---

5. aye ever.
6. clifts icebergs.
7. ken knew.
8. swound swoon.
9. thorough through.
10. eat (et) old form of *eaten*.

The ice did split with a thunder-fit;
70 The helmsman steered us through!

"And a good south wind sprung up behind;
The Albatross did follow,
And every day, for food or play,
Came to the mariner's hollo!

75 "In mist or cloud, on mast or shroud,[11]
It perched for vespers[12] nine;
Whiles all the night, through fog-smoke
   white,
Glimmered the white Moonshine."

"God save thee, ancient Mariner!
80 From the fiends, that plague thee thus!—
Why look'st thou so?"[13] "With my crossbow
I shot the Albatross."

Part II ●━━━

"The Sun now rose upon the right:[14]
Out of the sea came he,
85 Still hid in mist, and on the left
Went down into the sea.

"And the good south wind still blew behind,
But no sweet bird did follow,
Nor any day for food or play
90 Came to the mariners' hollo!

"And I had done a hellish thing,
And it would work 'em woe:
For all averred, I had killed the bird
That made the breeze to blow.

95 Ah wretch! said they, the bird to slay,
That made the breeze to blow!

"Nor dim nor red, like God's own head,
The glorious Sun uprist;[15]
Then all averred, I had killed the bird
100 That brought the fog and mist.
'Twas right, said they, such birds to slay,
That bring the fog and mist.

---

11. shroud *n.* ropes stretching from the ship's side to the masthead.
12. vespers evenings.
13. God . . . so spoken by the Wedding Guest.
14. The Sun . . . right The ship is now headed north.
15. uprist arose.

▶ **Critical Viewing**
Based on the details of this illustration, how would you characterize the Albatross?
CONNECT

Comparing and Contrasting Sound Devices
How does the use of alliteration and internal rhyme in lines 91–94 give a fatal feeling to the Mariner's deed?

Vocabulary
averred (ə vʉrd´) *v.* stated to be true

And lo! the Albatross proveth a bird of good omen, and followeth the ship as it returned northward through fog and floating ice.

The ancient Mariner inhospitably killeth the pious bird of good omen.

His shipmates cry out against the ancient Mariner for killing the bird of good luck.

But when the fog cleared off, they justify the same, and thus make themselves accomplices in the crime.

Engraving by Gustave Doré for "The Rime of the Ancient Mariner" by Samuel Taylor Coleridge © 1970 by Dover Publications, Inc.

"The fair breeze blew, the white foam flew,
The furrow[16] followed free;
105   We were the first that ever burst
Into that silent sea.

"Down dropped the breeze, the sails
          dropped down,
'Twas sad as sad could be;
And we did speak only to break
110   The silence of the sea!

"All in a hot and copper sky,
The bloody Sun, at noon,
Right up above the mast did stand,
No bigger than the Moon.

Comparing and Contrasting Sound Devices

How does the repetition of words in lines 115–119 contribute to the image of the stilled ship?

115   "Day after day, day after day,
We stuck, nor breath nor motion;
As idle as a painted ship
Upon a painted ocean.

"Water, water, everywhere,
120   And all the boards did shrink;
Water, water, everywhere,
Nor any drop to drink.

"The very deep did rot: O Christ!
That ever this should be!
125   Yea, slimy things did crawl with legs
Upon the slimy sea.

Comparing and Contrasting Sound Devices

What effect does the increased concentration of sound devices in lines 127–130 have?

"About, about, in reel and rout[17]
The death fires[18] danced at night;
The water, like a witch's oils,
130   Burned green, and blue and white.

"And some in dreams assurèd were
Of the Spirit that plagued us so;
Nine fathom deep he had followed us
From the land of mist and snow.

135   "And every tongue, through utter drought,
Was withered at the root;
We could not speak, no more than if
We had been choked with soot.

The fair breeze continues; the ship enters the Pacific Ocean, and sails northward, even till it reaches the Line. The Ship hath been suddenly becalmed.

And the Albatross begins to be avenged.

A Spirit had followed them; one of the invisible inhabitants of this planet, neither departed souls nor angels. They are very numerous, and there is no climate or element without one or more.

---

16. furrow ship's wake.
17. rout disorderly crowd.
18. death fires St. Elmo's fire, a visible electrical discharge from a ship's mast, believed by sailors to be an omen of disaster.

Engraving by Gustave Doré for "The Rime of the Ancient Mariner" by Samuel Taylor Coleridge
© 1970 by Dover Publications, Inc.

◄ **Critical Viewing**
What effects does the artist, Gustave Doré, use to capture the eerie mood of the poem? **ANALYZE**

The shipmates, in their sore distress, would fain throw the whole guilt on the ancient Mariner: in sign whereof they hang the dead sea bird round his neck.

"Ah! well a-day! what evil looks
140 Had I from old and young!
Instead of the cross, the Albatross
About my neck was hung.

Part III ●━━━━━

"There passed a weary time. Each throat
Was parched, and glazed each eye.
145 A weary time! a weary time!
How glazed each weary eye,
When looking westward, I beheld
A something in the sky.

The ancient Mariner beholdeth a sign in the element afar off.

"At first it seemed a little speck,
150 And then it seemed a mist;
It moved and moved, and took at last
A certain shape, I wist.[19]

"A speck, a mist, a shape, I wist!
And still it neared and neared:
155 As if it dodged a water sprite,
It plunged and tacked and veered.

---

19. wist knew.

Comparing and Contrasting Sound Devices
What poetic effect does Coleridge use in lines 149–153 to build suspense?

Comprehension
What causes the sailors to suffer?

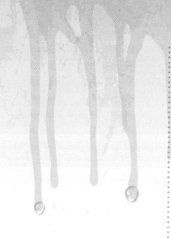

"With throats unslaked, with black lips baked,
We could nor laugh nor wail;
Through utter drought all dumb we stood!
160 I bit my arm, I sucked the blood,
And cried, A sail! a sail!

"With throats unslaked, with black lips baked,
Agape they heard me call:
Gramercy![20] for joy did grin,
165 And all at once their breath drew in,
As they were drinking all.

"See! see! (I cried) she tacks no more!
Hither to work us weal;[21]
Without a breeze, without a tide,
170 She steadies with upright keel!

"The western wave was all aflame.
The day was well nigh done!
Almost upon the western wave
Rested the broad bright Sun;
175 When that strange shape drove suddenly
Betwixt us and the Sun.

"And straight the Sun was flecked with bars,
(Heaven's Mother send us grace!)
As if through a dungeon grate he peered
180 With broad and burning face.

"Alas! (thought I, and my heart beat loud)
How fast she nears and nears!
Are those *her* sails that glance in the Sun,
Like restless gossameres?[22]

185 "Are those *her* ribs through which the Sun
Did peer, as through a grate?
And is that Woman all her crew?
Is that a Death? and are there two?
Is Death that woman's mate?

190 "*Her* lips were red, *her* looks were free,
Her locks were yellow as gold;
Her skin was as white as leprosy,

---

20. Gramercy (grə mʉr′ sē): great thanks.
21. work us weal assist us.
22. gossameres floating cobwebs.

Poetic Sound Devices

How does the line "Hither to work us weal" give the sense that these events are taking place in a strange, distant era?

▶ Critical Viewing

What reactions to the sighting of the other ship would you expect from the sailors? Can you find such reactions in the engraving? Explain. **CONNECT**

At its nearer approach, it seemeth him to be a ship; and at a dear ransom he freeth his speech from the bonds of thirst.

A flash of joy:

And horror follows. For can it be a ship that comes onward without wind or tide?

It seemeth him but the skeleton of a ship.

And its ribs are seen as bars on the face of the setting Sun.

The Specter Woman and her Death-mate, and no other on board the skeleton ship.

Like vessel, like crew! Death and Life-in-Death have diced for the ship's crew, and she (the latter) winneth the ancient Mariner.

Poetic Sound Devices

In what way does the name of the woman—Life-in-Death—add to the eerie, mysterious atmosphere of the story?

The Nightmare Life-in-Death was she,
Who thicks man's blood with cold.

195 "The naked hulk alongside came,
And the twain were casting dice;
'The game is done! I've won! I've won!'
Quoth she, and whistles thrice.

"The Sun's rim dips; the stars rush out:
200 At one stride comes the dark;
With far-heard whisper, o'er the sea,
Off shot the specter bark.

"We listened and looked sideways up!
Fear at my heart, as at a cup,
205 My lifeblood seemed to sip!
The stars were dim, and thick the night,
The steersman's face by his lamp
    gleamed white;
From the sails the dew did drip—
Till clomb²³ above the eastern bar
210 The hornèd²⁴ Moon, with one bright star
Within the nether tip.

"One after one, by the star-dogged Moon,²⁵
Too quick for groan or sigh,
Each turned his face with a ghastly pang,
215 And cursed me with his eye.

"Four times fifty living men,
(And I heard nor sigh nor groan)
With heavy thump, a lifeless lump,
They dropped down one by one.

220 "The souls did from their bodies fly—
They fled to bliss or woe!
And every soul, it passed me by,
Like the whizz of my crossbow!"

Part IV

"I fear thee, ancient Mariner!
225 I fear thy skinny hand!
And thou art long, and lank, and brown,
As is the ribbed sea sand.

*No twilight within
the courts of the Sun.*

*At the rising of the
Moon,*

One after another,

*His shipmates drop
down dead.*

*But Life-in-Death
begins her work on
the ancient Mariner.*

*The Wedding Guest
feareth that a Spirit
is talking to him;*

Poetic Sound Devices

How does Coleridge's unusual way of expressing numbers contribute to the fairy-tale atmosphere?

---

23. **clomb** climbed.
24. **hornèd** crescent.
25. **star-dogged Moon** omen of impending evil to sailors.

But the ancient Mariner assureth him of his bodily life, and proceedeth to relate his horrible penance.

"I fear thee and thy glittering eye,
And thy skinny hand, so brown."
230 "Fear not, fear not, thou Wedding Guest!
This body dropped not down.

"Alone, alone, all, all alone,
Alone on a wide wide sea!
And never a saint took pity on
235 My soul in agony.

He despiseth the creatures of the calm,

"The many men, so beautiful!
And they all dead did lie:
And a thousand thousand slimy things
Lived on; and so did I.

And envieth that they should live, and so many lie dead.

240 "I looked upon the rotting sea,
And drew my eyes away;
I looked upon the rotting deck,
And there the dead men lay.

"I looked to heaven, and tried to pray;
245 But or[26] ever a prayer had gushed,
A wicked whisper came, and made
My heart as dry as dust.

"I closed my lids, and kept them close,
And the balls like pulses beat;
250 For the sky and the sea, and the sea and the sky
Lay like a load on my weary eye,
And the dead were at my feet.

But the curse liveth for him in the eye of the dead men.

"The cold sweat melted from their limbs,
Nor rot nor reek did they;
255 The look with which they looked on me
Had never passed away.

"An orphan's curse would drag to hell
A spirit from on high;
But oh! more horrible than that
260 Is the curse in a dead man's eye!
Seven days, seven nights, I saw that curse,
And yet I could not die.

In his loneliness and fixedness he yearneth towards the journeying Moon, and the stars that still sojourn, yet still move onward; and everywhere the blue sky belongs to them,

"The moving Moon went up the sky,
And nowhere did abide:

---

26. or before.

Comparing and Contrasting Sound Devices

How does repetition in lines 240–243 emphasize the starkness of the Mariner's situation—the fact that he has "no way out"?

Vocabulary

sojourn (sō´ jərn) *v.* stay for a while

Comprehension

What has happened to the other sailors?

Spiral Review
Imagery How
does Coleridge's pattern
of imagery in lines
270–276 help set the
tone of the poem?

265 Softly she was going up,
   And a star or two beside—

   "Her beams bemocked the sultry main,[27]
   Like April hoarfrost spread;
   But where the ship's huge shadow lay,
270 The charmèd water burned alway
   A still and awful red.

   "Beyond the shadow of the ship,
   I watched the water snakes:
   They moved in tracks of shining white,
275 And when they reared, the elfish light
   Fell off in hoary flakes.

   "Within the shadow of the ship
   I watched their rich attire:
   Blue, glossy green, and velvet black,
280 They coiled and swam; and every track
   Was a flash of golden fire.

   "O happy living things! no tongue
   Their beauty might declare:
   A spring of love gushed from my heart,
285 And I blessed them unaware;
   Sure my kind saint took pity on me,
   And I blessed them unaware.

Poetic Sound Devices
What does the connection
of the two events in lines
288–291 add to the fairy-tale
quality of the story?

   "The selfsame moment I could pray;
   And from my neck so free
290 The Albatross fell off, and sank
   Like lead into the sea.

Part V ●━━━

   "Oh sleep! it is a gentle thing,
   Beloved from pole to pole!
   To Mary queen the praise be given!
295 She sent the gentle sleep from Heaven,
   That slid into my soul.

▶ **Critical Viewing**
How does Coleridge's
description of the creatures
of the great calm compare
and contrast with the
artist's representation of
them? **COMPARE AND
CONTRAST**

   "The silly[28] buckets on the deck.
   That had so long remained,
   I dreamed that they were filled with dew;
300 And when I awoke, it rained.

---

27. main open sea.
28. silly empty.

---

and is their appointed
rest, and their
native country and
their own natural
homes, which they
enter unannounced,
as lords that are
certainly expected
and yet there is
a silent joy at their
arrival.

By the light of the
Moon he beholdeth
God's creatures of
the great calm.

Their beauty and
their happiness.

He blesseth them in
his heart.

The spell begins
to break.

By grace of the holy
Mother, the ancient
Mariner is refreshed
with rain.

Poetic Sound Devices

Which repeated consonant sound in lines 303–304 creates alliteration?

"My lips were wet, my throat was cold,
My garments all were dank;
Sure I had drunken in my dreams,
And still my body drank.

305 "I moved, and could not feel my limbs:
I was so light—almost
I thought that I had died in sleep,
And was a blessèd ghost.

"And soon I heard a roaring wind:
310 It did not come anear;
But with its sound it shook the sails,
That were so thin and sere.[29]

"The upper air burst into life!
And a hundred fire flags sheen,[30]
315 To and fro they were hurried about!
And to and fro, and in and out,
The wan stars danced between.

"And the coming wind did roar more loud,
And the sails did sigh like sedge;[31]
320 And the rain poured down from one
        black cloud;
The Moon was at its edge.

"The thick black cloud was cleft, and still
The Moon was at its side:
Like waters shot from some high crag,
325 The lightning fell with never a jag,
A river steep and wide.

"The loud wind never reached the ship,
Yet now the ship moved on!
Beneath the lightning and the Moon
330 The dead men gave a groan.

"They groaned, they stirred, they all uprose,
Nor spake, nor moved their eyes;
It had been strange, even in a dream,
To have seen those dead men rise.

He heareth sounds and seeth strange sights and commotions in the sky and the element.

The bodies of the ship's crew are inspired[32] and the ship moves on;

Poetic Sound Devices

Find an example of assonance—the repetition of vowel sounds in unrhymed syllables—in lines 331–334.

---

29. **sere** dried up.
30. **fire flags sheen** the aurora australis, or southern lights, shone.
31. **sedge** *n.* rushlike plant that grows in wet soil.
32. **inspired** inspirited

335 "The helmsman steered, the ship moved on:
Yet never a breeze up-blew;
The mariners all 'gan work the ropes,
Where they were wont[33] to do;
They raised their limbs like lifeless tools—
340 We were a ghastly crew.

"The body of my brother's son
Stood by me, knee to knee;
The body and I pulled at one rope,
But he said nought to me."

345 "I fear thee, ancient Mariner!"
"Be calm, thou Wedding Guest!
'Twas not those souls that fled in pain,
Which to their corses[34] came again,
But a troop of spirits blessed:

350 "For when it dawned—they dropped their arms,
And clustered round the mast;
Sweet sounds rose slowly through
their mouths,
And from their bodies passed.

"Around, around, flew each sweet sound,
355 Then darted to the Sun;
Slowly the sounds came back again,
Now mixed, now one by one.

"Sometimes a-dropping from the sky
I heard the skylark sing;
360 Sometimes all little birds that are,
How they seemed to fill the sea and air
With their sweet jargoning![35]

"And now 'twas like all instruments,
Now like a lonely flute;
365 And now it is an angel's song,
That makes the heavens be mute.

"It ceased; yet still the sails made on
A pleasant noise till noon,
A noise like of a hidden brook
370 In the leafy month of June,

*But not by the souls
of the men, nor by
demons of earth or
middle air, but by
a blessed troop of
angelic spirits, sent
down by the invocation
of the guardian saint.*

Poetic Sound Devices
Find an example of
alliteration—the repetition of
initial consonant sounds—in
lines 350–353.

Comprehension
What happens to the
bodies of the Mariner's
shipmates?

33. **wont** accustomed.
34. **corses** corpses.
35. **jargoning** singing.

The Rime of the Ancient Mariner **835**

That to the sleeping woods all night
Singeth a quiet tune.

"Till noon we quietly sailed on,
Yet never a breeze did breathe;
375 Slowly and smoothly went the ship,
Moved onward from beneath.

"Under the keel nine fathom deep,
From the land of mist and snow,
The spirit slid; and it was he
380 That made the ship to go.
The sails at noon left off their tune,
And the ship stood still also.

"The Sun, right up above the mast,
Had fixed her to the ocean:
385 But in a minute she 'gan stir,
With a short uneasy motion—
Backwards and forwards half her length
With a short uneasy motion.

"Then like a pawing horse let go,
390 She made a sudden bound:
It flung the blood into my head,
And I fell down in a swound.

Comparing and Contrasting Sound Devices

How does the alliteration in lines 373–376 enhance the description of the boat's smooth progress?

The lonesome Spirit from the South Pole carries on the ship as far as the Line, in obedience to the angelic troop, but still requireth vengeance.

The Polar Spirit's fellow demons, the invisible inhabitants of the element, take part in his wrong; and two of them relate, one to the other, that penance long and heavy for the ancient Mariner hath been accorded to the Polar Spirit, who returneth southward.

Engraving by Gustave Doré for "The Rime of the Ancient Mariner" by Samuel Taylor Coleridge.
© 1970 by Dover Publications, Inc.

▶ **Critical Viewing**
Which details convey the mood of hopelessness in this illustration? **ANALYZE**

"How long in that same fit I lay,
I have not to declare;
395 But ere my living life returned,
I heard and in my soul discerned
Two voices in the air.

"'Is it he?' quoth one, 'Is this the man?
By him who died on cross,
400 With his cruel bow he laid full low
The harmless Albatross.

"'The spirit who bideth by himself
In the land of mist and snow,
He loved the bird that loved the man
405 Who shot him with his bow.'

"The other was a softer voice,
As soft as honeydew:
Quoth he, 'The man hath penance done,
And penance more will do.'

Part VI •━━━━

FIRST VOICE
410 "'But tell me, tell me! speak again,
Thy soft response renewing—
What makes that ship drive on so fast?
What is the ocean doing?'

SECOND VOICE
"'Still as a slave before his lord,
415 The ocean hath no blast;
His great bright eye most silently
Up to the Moon is cast—

"'If he may know which way to go;
For she guides him smooth or grim.
420 See, brother, see! how graciously
She looketh down on him.'

FIRST VOICE
"'But why drives on that ship so fast,
Without or wave or wind?'

SECOND VOICE
"'The air is cut away before,
425 And closes from behind.

Poetic Sound Devices

How do the two voices contribute to Coleridge's creation of a dream world?

Poetic Sound Devices

What instance of assonance can you find in lines 414–417?

Comprehension

What do the two voices discuss?

The Rime of the Ancient Mariner **837**

▶ **Critical Viewing**
How closely can you connect this illustration to the events in the poem? Is the image being portrayed from the Ancient Mariner's point of view? Why or why not?
CONNECT

"'Fly, brother, fly! more high, more high!
Or we shall be belated:
For slow and slow that ship will go,
When the Mariner's trance is abated.'

430 "I woke, and we were sailing on
As in a gentle weather:
'Twas night, calm night, the moon was high;
The dead men stood together.

"All stood together on the deck,
435 For a charnel dungeon³⁶ fitter;
All fixed on me their stony eyes,
That in the Moon did glitter.

"The pang, the curse, with which they died,
Had never passed away;
440 I could not draw my eyes from theirs,
Nor turn them up to pray.

"And now this spell was snapped; once more
I viewed the ocean green,
And looked far forth, yet little saw
445 Of what had else been seen—

The super-natural motion is retarded; the Mariner awakes, and his penance begins anew.

The curse is finally expiated.

Vocabulary
expiated (ēk´ spē āt´ əd)
v. atoned; made amends for, especially by suffering

---

36. charnel dungeon vault where corpses or bones are deposited.

"Like one, that on a lonesome road
Doth walk in fear and dread,
And having once turned round
    walks on,
And turns no more his head;
450 Because he knows, a frightful fiend
Doth close behind him tread.

"But soon there breathed a wind
    on me,
Nor sound nor motion made:
Its path was not upon the sea,
455 In ripple or in shade.

"It raised my hair, it fanned my cheek
Like a meadow-gale of spring—
It mingled strangely with my fears,
Yet it felt like a welcoming.

460 "Swiftly, swiftly flew the ship,
Yet she sailed softly too:
Sweetly, sweetly blew the breeze—
On me alone it blew.

"Oh! dream of joy! is this indeed
465 The lighthouse top I see?
Is this the hill? is this the kirk?
Is this mine own countree?

"We drifted o'er the harbor bar,
And I with sobs did pray—
470 O let me be awake, my God!
Or let me sleep alway.

"The harbor bay was clear as glass,
So smoothly it was strewn![37]
And on the bay the moonlight lay,
475 And the shadow of the Moon.

"The rock shone bright, the kirk
    no less,
That stands above the rock;
The moonlight steeped in silentness
The steady weathercock.

480 "And the bay was white with
    silent light,

*And the ancient
Mariner beholdeth
his native country.*

---

37. **strewn** spread.

The
BRITISH
TRADITION

The Tradition of Fantasy
Coleridge's *Rime of the Ancient Mariner*—written in a dreamlike language, set in an indeterminate past, and filled with supernatural events—is part of the British tradition of fantasy literature. Writers of works of fantasy set out to create a realm distinct from the everyday world of their readers—a never-never land ruled by strange laws.

    The fantasy tradition began as long ago as Sir Thomas Malory's *Morte d'Arthur* (p. 185), which is set in a vanished past that had become a myth by Malory's own day. The idea of a vanished past fascinated writers long after Malory, reappearing in the work of Alfred, Lord Tennyson, who resorted to Arthurian and mythological elements in many poems, as in "The Lady of Shalott" (p. 963).

    Fantasy writers like Coleridge use strange settings and supernatural tales to break the spell of ordinary life. By plunging us into a wild, unfamiliar world, they remind us that human imagination can always envision worlds beyond the one into which we are born—a power that enables scientific discoveries and social reforms as well as great poetry.

Connect to the Literature

What images in lines 480–499 contribute to the fantastical atmosphere in the poem?

Comprehension
What familiar things does the Mariner suddenly see from the ship?

Till rising from the same,
Full many shapes, that shadows were,
In crimson colors came.

"A little distance from the prow
485 Those crimson shadows were:
I turned my eyes upon the deck—
Oh, Christ! what saw I there!

"Each corse lay flat, lifeless and flat,
And, by the holy rood!³⁸
490 A man all light, a seraph³⁹ man,
On every corse there stood.

"This seraph band, each waved
        his hand:
It was a heavenly sight!
They stood as signals to the land,
495 Each one a lovely light;

"This seraph band, each waved
        his hand,
No voice did they impart—

---

38. rood cross.
39. seraph angel.

The angelic spirits leave the dead bodies,

And appear in their own forms of light.

Engraving by Gustave Doré for "The Rime of the Ancient Mariner" by Samuel Taylor Coleridge
© 1970 by Dover Publications, Inc.

▶ **Critical Viewing**
What event from the poem does this engraving represent? **CONNECT**

No voice; but oh! the silence sank
Like music on my heart.

500 "But soon I heard the dash of oars,
I heard the Pilot's cheer;
My head was turned perforce away
And I saw a boat appear.

"The Pilot and the Pilot's boy,
505 I heard them coming fast:
Dear Lord in Heaven! it was a joy
The dead men could not blast.

"I saw a third—I heard his voice:
It is the Hermit good!
510 He singeth loud his godly hymns
That he makes in the wood.
He'll shrieve[40] my soul, he'll
          wash away
The Albatross's blood.

Part VII ●━━━━━

*The Hermit of
the Wood,*

"This Hermit good lives in that wood
515 Which slopes down to the sea.
How loudly his sweet voice he rears!
He loves to talk with marineres
That come from a far countree.

"He kneels at morn, and noon,
          and eve—
520 He hath a cushion plump:
It is the moss that wholly hides
The rotted old oak-stump.

"The skiff boat neared; I heard them talk.
'Why, this is strange, I trow![41]
525 Where are those lights so many and fair,
That signal made but now?'

*Approacheth the ship
with wonder.*

"'Strange, by my faith!' the Hermit said—
'And they answered not our cheer!
The planks looked warped! and see those sails,
530 How thin they are and sere!
I never saw aught like to them,
Unless perchance it were

---

40. shrieve (shrēv) absolve from sin.
41. trow believe.

Comparing and Contrasting Sound Devices

These lines are less crowded with sound devices than the lines describing the Mariner's nightmarish sea journey. How does this shift in language match the shift in mood?

Poetic Sound Devices

Which word in lines 523–526 might Coleridge have borrowed from medieval tales of knights?

Comprehension

What does the Mariner think the Hermit will do for him?

"'Brown skeletons of leaves that lag
My forest brook along;
535 When the ivy tod[42] is heavy with snow,
And the owlet whoops to the wolf below,
That eats the she-wolf's young.'

"'Dear Lord! it hath a fiendish look'
(The Pilot made reply)
540 'I am a-feared'— 'Push on, push on!'
Said the Hermit cheerily.

"The boat came closer to the ship,
But I nor spake nor stirred;
The boat came close beneath the ship,
545 And straight[43] a sound was heard.

"Under the water it rumbled on,
Still louder and more dread:
It reached the ship, it split the bay;
The ship went down like lead.

550 "Stunned by that loud and dreadful sound,
Which sky and ocean smote,
Like one that hath been seven days drowned
My body lay afloat;
But swift as dreams, myself I found
555 Within the Pilot's boat.

"Upon the whirl, where sank the ship,
The boat spun round and round;
And all was still, save that the hill
Was telling of the sound.

560 "I moved my lips—the Pilot shrieked
And fell down in a fit;
The holy Hermit raised his eyes,
And prayed where he did sit.

"I took the oars; the Pilot's boy,
565 Who now doth crazy go,
Laughed loud and long, and all the while
His eyes went to and fro.
'Ha! ha!' quoth he, 'full plain I see,
The Devil knows how to row.'

---

42. **tod** bush.
43. **straight** immediately.

Engraving by Gustave Doré for "The Rime of the Ancient Mariner" by Samuel Taylor Coleridge © 1970 by Dover Publications, Inc.

The ship suddenly sinketh.

The ancient Mariner is saved in the Pilot's boat.

Comparing and Contrasting Sound Devices

Which poetic effects contribute to the impact of lines 556–559?

▶ **Critical Viewing**

Identify the Pilot, the Mariner, and the Hermit in this engraving. **CONNECT**

570
575
580
585
590
595
600
605

"And now, all in my own countree,
   I stood on the firm land!
The Hermit stepped forth from the boat,
   And scarcely he could stand.

"'O shrieve me, shrieve me, holy man!'
   The Hermit crossed his brow.[44]
     'Say, quick,' quoth he, 'I bid thee say—
     What manner of man art thou?'

"Forthwith this frame of mine was wrenched
   With a woeful agony,
Which forced me to begin my tale;
   And then it left me free.

"Since then, at an uncertain hour,
   That agony returns:
And till my ghastly tale is told,
   This heart within me burns.

"I pass, like night, from land to land;
   I have strange power of speech;
That moment that his face I see,
I know the man that must hear me:
   To him my tale I teach.

"What loud uproar bursts from that door!
   The wedding guests are there:
But in the garden bower the bride
   And bridemaids singing are:
And hark the little vesper bell,
   Which biddeth me to prayer!

"O Wedding Guest! this soul hath been
   Alone on a wide wide sea:
So lonely 'twas, that God himself
   Scarce seemèd there to be.

"O sweeter than the marriage feast,
   'Tis sweeter far to me,
To walk together to the kirk
   With a goodly company!—

"To walk together to the kirk,
   And all together pray,
While each to his great Father bends,

Comparing and Contrasting Sound Devices

What effect does the alliteration in line 590 featuring *tale*—a word that appears in each of the preceding two stanzas—have?

The ancient Mariner earnestly entreateth the Hermit to shrieve him; and the penance of life falls on him.

And ever and anon throughout his future life an agony constraineth him to travel from land to land;

---

44. **crossed his brow** made the sign of the cross on his forehead.

Old men, and babes, and loving friends
And youths and maidens gay!

610 "Farewell, farewell! but this I tell
To thee, thou Wedding Guest!
He prayeth well, who loveth well
Both man and bird and beast.

And to teach, by his own example, love and reverence *to all things that God made and loveth.*

"He prayeth best, who loveth best
615 All things both great and small;
For the dear God who loveth us,
He made and loveth all."

The Mariner, whose eye is bright,
Whose beard with age is hoar,
620 Is gone; and now the Wedding Guest
Turned from the bridegroom's door.

He went like one that hath been stunned
And is of sense forlorn:
A sadder and a wiser man,
625 He rose the morrow morn.

Vocabulary

reverence (rev´ ər əns)
n. deep respect

Critical Reading

Cite textual evidence to support your responses.

1. **Key Ideas and Details (a)** On what occasion does the Mariner tell his story? **(b) Interpret:** Why do you think Coleridge chose this occasion for the poem?

2. **Key Ideas and Details (a)** What contradictory connections does the crew make between the Albatross and the weather? **(b)** What does the Mariner do to the Albatross? **(c) Infer:** Why does the Mariner wear the Albatross around his neck?

3. **Key Ideas and Details (a)** What happens to the Mariner's shipmates after the appearance of the Specter Woman and her Death-mate? **(b) Generalize:** What might this symbolize about the effect of guilt on an individual's perceptions of and relations with others?

4. **Craft and Structure (a) Infer:** Why does the Albatross finally fall from the Mariner's neck? **(b) Interpret:** What do you think the Albatross symbolizes? Find evidence to support your answer.

5. **Integration of Knowledge and Ideas (a)** What is the Mariner's lifelong penance? **(b) Analyze:** How does his story affect his listener? **(c) Draw Conclusions:** What larger lesson about human life might his story suggest?

KUBLA KHAN

Samuel Taylor Coleridge

Box and Cover, Ming Dynasty, first half of 16th century, lacquer, black; mother of pearl; wood; fabric. H. 4 in. The Seattle Art Museum

▲ **Critical Viewing**

How do Coleridge's poetic images compare with the details on this sixteenth-century Chinese box cover? **COMPARE AND CONTRAST**

BACKGROUND

Coleridge claimed to have dreamed his poem "Kubla Khan" line for line after falling asleep while reading a passage from a work about the founder of the great Mongol dynasty. Upon awakening, he transcribed the lines as fast as he could. When he was interrupted by a visitor, however, the lines in his head disappeared, never to be remembered. As a result, Coleridge was unable to complete the poem.

In Xanadu[1] did Kubla Khan
A stately pleasure dome decree:
Where Alph,[2] the sacred river, ran
Through caverns measureless to man
5   Down to a sunless sea.
So twice five miles of fertile ground
With walls and towers were girdled round;
And there were gardens bright with sinuous rills,[3]
Where blossomed many an incense-bearing tree;
10 And here were forests ancient as the hills,
Enfolding sunny spots of greenery.

But oh! that deep romantic chasm which slanted
Down the green hill athwart[4] a cedarn cover![5]
A savage place! as holy and enchanted
15 As e'er beneath a waning moon was haunted
By woman wailing for her demon lover!
And from this chasm, with ceaseless turmoil seething,
As if this earth in fast thick pants were breathing,
A mighty fountain momently was forced;

Vocabulary
sinuous (sin´ yo͞o əs)
adj. bending; winding

Comparing and Contrasting Sound Devices
What alliteration in lines 15–16 helps you hear the cries of the haunted woman?

---

1. **Xanadu** (zan´ ə do͞o) indefinite area in China.
2. **Alph** probably derived from the Greek river Alpheus, the waters of which, it was believed in Greek mythology, joined with a stream to form a fountain in Sicily.
3. **rills** brooks.
4. **athwart** across.
5. **cedarn cover** covering of cedar trees.

20   Amid whose swift half-intermitted burst
      Huge fragments vaulted like rebounding hail,
      Or chaffy grain beneath the thresher's flail;
      And 'mid these dancing rocks at once and ever
      It flung up momently the sacred river.
25   Five miles meandering with a mazy motion
      Through wood and dale the sacred river ran,
      Then reached the caverns measureless to man,
      And sank in tumult to a lifeless ocean:
      And 'mid this tumult Kubla heard from far
30   Ancestral voices prophesying war!
          The shadow of the dome of pleasure
          Floated midway on the waves;
          Where was heard the mingled measure
          From the fountain and the caves.
35   It was a miracle of rare device.[6]
      A sunny pleasure dome with caves of ice!

---

6. device design.

A damsel with a dulcimer[7]
In a vision once I saw:
It was an Abyssinian[8] maid,
40　And on her dulcimer she played,
Singing of Mount Abora.[9]
Could I revive within me
Her symphony and song,
To such a deep delight 'twould win me,
45　That with music loud and long,
I would build that dome in air,
That sunny dome! those caves of ice!
And all who heard should see them there,
And all should cry, Beware! Beware!
50　His flashing eyes, his floating hair!
Weave a circle round him thrice,
And close your eyes with holy dread,
For he on honeydew hath fed,
And drunk the milk of Paradise.

---

7. dulcimer (dul′ sə mər) *n.* stringed musical instrument played with small hammers.
8. Abyssinian (ab ə sin′ ē ən) Ethiopian.
9. Mount Abora probably Mount Amara in Abyssinia.

Critical Reading

Cite textual evidence to support your responses.

1. **Key Ideas and Details (a)** Describe the pleasure dome and its setting. **(b) Analyze:** What makes the pleasure dome and its setting seem beautiful? What makes them sinister?

2. **Integration of Knowledge and Ideas (a)** What comes from the chasm, and what are its effects? **(b) Draw Conclusions:** The pleasure dome might be thought of as a work of art. What does the existence of the chasm on the site of the dome suggest about the relationship between constructive and "chaotic," or "wild," forces in art?

3. **Integration of Knowledge and Ideas (a)** What does the "holy dread" experienced by "all who heard" suggest about the power of art? **(b) Connect:** What connection can you find between this "dread" and the existence of the chasm at the site of the dome?

4. **Integration of Knowledge and Ideas** In what ways do the settings of these poems demonstrate the Romantics' rejection of the dreariness of everyday places and activities? In your response, use at least two of these Essential Question words: *exotic, fantastic, faraway.* **[Connecting to the Essential Question: What is the relationship between literature and place?]**

Literary Analysis

1. **Craft and Structure** What **sound device** does Coleridge use in the line "It cracked and growled, and roared and howled . . ." (*The Rime of the Ancient Mariner,* line 61)?

2. **Craft and Structure** Find an example of **alliteration** in lines 9–12 of *The Rime of the Ancient Mariner.*

3. **Craft and Structure** Which words in the following line create an **internal rhyme**: "Whiles all the night, through fog-smoke white..."? (*The Rime of the Ancient Mariner,* line 77)

4. **Craft and Structure** **(a)** Identify an example of **consonance** in lines 51–54 of *The Rime of the Ancient Mariner.* **(b)** Identify an example of **assonance** in the same lines.

5. **Key Ideas and Details** **(a)** Identify four words in "Kubla Khan" that contribute to the poem's exotic, or strange and faraway, atmosphere. **(b)** Do archaic words in *The Rime of the Ancient Mariner* also make the setting of this **narrative** poem seem exotic? Why or why not?

6. **Craft and Structure** What device dominates the first stanza of "Kubla Khan"? Give three examples.

7. **Craft and Structure** **(a)** What mood do lines 472–483 of *The Rime of the Ancient Mariner* create? **(b)** What poetic devices contribute to this mood? Explain.

8. **Comparing Literary Works** Using a chart like the one shown to gather details, explain how the characteristics of Coleridge's poetry, including its subjects, settings, events, and uses of language, suit the fantastic subjects he addresses. In discussing his uses of language, specifically consider sound devices.

Poem: _____

Subject	Setting	Events	Language	Why Suitable?

9. **Integration of Knowledge and Ideas** **Compare and contrast sound devices** in these poems by answering these questions. **(a)** Identify the mood, or feeling, that Coleridge evokes in lines 1–12 of *The Rime of the Ancient Mariner* and lines 1–11 of "Kubla Khan." **(b)** How do the sound devices and archaic words used in each poem allow Coleridge to create these moods?

Common Core State Standards

Reading Literature
9. Demonstrate knowledge of eighteenth-, nineteenth-, and early-twentieth-century foundational works of American literature, including how two or more texts from the same period treat similar themes or topics. (*p. 851*)

Writing
2.b. Develop the topic thoroughly by selecting the most significant and relevant facts, extended definitions, concrete details, quotations, or other information and examples appropriate to the audience's knowledge of the topic. (*p. 851*)

2.d. Use precise language, domain-specific vocabulary, and techniques such as metaphor, simile, and analogy to manage the complexity of the topic. (*p. 851*)

9.a. Apply grades 11–12 Reading standards to literature. (*p. 851*)

Vocabulary Acquisition and Use

Word Analysis: Latin Root *-journ-*

The verb *sojourn*, meaning "to visit for a while," contains the root *-journ-*, derived from French and Latin words meaning "day." In French, the root appears in such words and phrases as *bonjour* ("good day") and *soup du jour* ("soup of the day"). Explain how this root contributes to the meaning of each of these words. If you are unsure of the meaning of any of these words, you may consult a dictionary. Then use each word in an original sentence.

1. adjourn
2. journal
3. journalism
4. journey
5. journeyman

Vocabulary: Antonyms

An antonym is a word that has the opposite meaning of another word. *Freezing* and *boiling* are antonyms, as are *happy* and *sad*. For each word from the vocabulary list on page 818, choose the correct antonym. Then, write an original sentence using both the word and its antonym.

1. averred: **(a)** claimed, **(b)** denied, **(c)** wished
2. sojourn: **(a)** depart, **(b)** rest, **(c)** visit
3. expiated: **(a)** atoned, **(b)** sinned, **(c)** sold
4. reverence: **(a)** contempt, **(b)** hope, **(c)** respect
5. sinuous: **(a)** dark, **(b)** narrow, **(c)** straight
6. tumult: **(a)** peace, **(b)** pleasure, **(c)** wealth

Writing to Sources

Explanatory Text Coleridge was not the only nineteenth-century poet to fascinate readers with a mysterious symbolic bird. Find a copy of "The Raven" by the American author Edgar Allan Poe, and read it carefully. Then, write an **essay** comparing the Albatross in *The Rime of the Ancient Mariner* with Poe's Raven as poetic symbols.

Prewriting Gather details about the Albatross and the Raven, grouping them under headings such as "Appearance," "Actions," and "Influence." Remember that symbols are concrete images that stand for a cluster of ideas. For each specific quality or relationship you list in your chart, give the general ideas it suggests.

Drafting As you draft, discuss each category in your chart, linking the details you have listed to your conclusions about the symbolic meaning of each bird. Then, compare the two symbols. Support your ideas with quotations from the works.

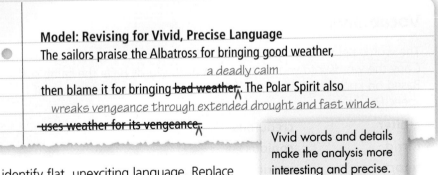

Model: Revising for Vivid, Precise Language

The sailors praise the Albatross for bringing good weather,
a deadly calm
then blame it for bringing ~~bad weather~~. The Polar Spirit also
wreaks vengeance through extended drought and fast winds.
~~uses weather for its vengeance.~~

> Vivid words and details make the analysis more interesting and precise.

Revising Review your draft to identify flat, unexciting language. Replace such language with vivid, specific descriptions or claims. Make sure that all quotations are accurate and properly cited.

Connecting to the Essential Question Like some Romantic poets, you may react with awe to nature's dramatic effects—a snow-covered mountain or a towering waterfall. As you read, note the feelings that the ocean calls up in the speaker of Byron's "Apostrophe to the Ocean." Identifying these feelings will help as you consider this Essential Question: **What is the relationship between literature and place?**

**Common Core
State Standards**

**Reading Literature
4.** Determine the meaning of words and phrases as they are used in the text, including figurative and connotative meanings.

Close Reading Focus

Figurative Language
Poetry often uses **figurative language,** or language not meant to be taken literally, to evoke emotions and state ideas in an imaginative way:

- **Similes**—direct comparisons of dissimilar things using the words *like* or *as:* "Her eyes glowed like the moon."
- **Metaphors**—comparisons in which one thing is identified with another, dissimilar thing: "All the world's a stage."
- **Personification**—giving human qualities to nonhuman subjects: "The trees danced in the wind."

Comparing Literary Works In two of these poems, Byron uses figurative language to express the *sublime*—a Romantic sense of overwhelming power and beauty in nature that escapes understanding. As you read, compare the impressions of nature's sublime beauty and power expressed in the first two lyrics with the sense of human limitations expressed in *Don Juan.*

Preparing to Read Complex Texts When you do not understand a difficult passage, **question** yourself to *repair your comprehension.* For example, to figure out the subject of a passage, ask yourself, "Whom is the speaker talking about?" Begin your questions with *who, what, where, when,* and *why.* Use a chart like the one shown to ask and answer questions as you read.

Passage
She walks in beauty, like the night Of cloudless climes and starry skies;...

Questions
1. *Who* is she?
2. *What* is her relationship with the speaker?
3. To *what* does the speaker compare her?

Vocabulary

The words below are important to understanding the texts that follow. Copy the words into your notebook. Which words have the same suffix? Based on knowledge of this suffix, can you infer the words' part of speech?

arbiter   credulous

torrid   copious

retort   avarice

Lord Byron (1788–1824)

Author of "She Walks in Beauty" • "Apostrophe to the Ocean" • *Don Juan*

As famous for the life he led as for the poems he wrote, George Gordon, Lord Byron, came from a long line of handsome but irresponsible aristocrats. Byron lived life in the "fast lane" and was looked on with disapproval by most of his contemporaries.

From Rags to Riches Byron was born in London to a poor but noble family. His father, a handsome ladies' man, died when Byron was just three years old. At the age of ten, Byron inherited his great-uncle's title, baron. He and his mother moved from Scotland to Nottingham, where Byron lived for a time in the ruins of the family hall. When he was seventeen, he left home to attend Trinity College at Cambridge.

A Zest for Life While at Cambridge, Byron made friends, played sports, and spent money. After graduating, he traveled to out-of-the-way corners of Europe and the Middle East. Byron returned home bearing two sections of a book-length poem entitled *Childe Harold's Pilgrimage*, which depicted a young hero not unlike himself—moody, sensitive, and reckless. The work was well received, and Byron became an overnight sensation.

For a time, Byron was the darling of London society. Byron became a celebrity, a public figure of literary genius who in turn thrilled and scandalized his contemporaries. "Mad, bad, and dangerous to know" was Lady Caroline Lamb's famous description of Lord Byron.

The Byronic Hero Although Byron could be quite charming and friendly, his admirers insisted on associating him with the dark, brooding hero, impassioned by a cause, whom he so often described. Because of this persona, or adopted personality, readers throughout the nineteenth century saw Byron as the quintessential Romantic poet.

Italy and Tragedy Byron's fame and infamy grew. When his marriage to Annabella Milbanke broke up, the resulting scandal drove Byron from England in 1816. He would never return to the country of his birth.

A Budding Revolutionary In 1823, Byron, a champion of liberty, joined a group of revolutionaries seeking to free Greece from Turkish rule. Soon after, while training Greek rebel troops, Byron died of a rheumatic fever. To this day he is revered in Greece as a national hero.

She Walks in Beauty

George Gordon,
Lord Byron

BACKGROUND Lord Byron became so identified with the rebellious heroes he created—brooding figures whose ironic attitude and hidden sorrow only added to their charm—that this kind of figure became known as a Byronic hero. Such heroes are a staple of Romantic literature. They survive in modern times as a Hollywood or rock-and-roll star.

The Byronic attitude may be ironic, but Byron the poet was certainly capable of direct, sincere appreciation of beauty, as this poem demonstrates.

She walks in beauty, like the night
    Of cloudless climes and starry skies;
And all that's best of dark and bright
    Meet in her aspect and her eyes:
5 Thus mellowed to that tender light
    Which heaven to gaudy day denies.

One shade the more, one ray the less,
    Had half impaired the nameless grace
Which waves in every raven tress,
10   Or softly lightens o'er her face;
Where thoughts serenely sweet express
    How pure, how dear their dwelling place.

And on that cheek, and o'er that brow,
    So soft, so calm, yet eloquent,
15 The smiles that win, the tints that glow,
    But tell of days in goodness spent,
A mind at peace with all below,
    A heart whose love is innocent!

Figurative Language
With what kind of poetic comparison does Byron capture the reader's imagination in the opening lines?

◀ **Critical Viewing**
How does the rendering of this woman suggest some of the qualities that Byron attributes to his cousin in the poem? **ANALYZE**

Critical Reading

1. **Key Ideas and Details (a)** To what does the speaker compare the lady's beauty? **(b) Interpret:** What might "that tender light" in line 5 be?

2. **Integration of Knowledge and Ideas (a) Connect:** In lines 11–18, what is the woman's appearance said to reveal about her character? **(b) Compare and Contrast:** How is the focus of the last six lines different from the focus of the opening lines? **(c) Draw Conclusions:** Does Byron's portrayal emphasize the spiritual or the physical aspect of the lady? Explain.

Cite textual evidence to support your responses.

FROM
CHILDE HAROLD'S PILGRIMAGE
APOSTROPHE TO THE *Ocean*

GEORGE GORDON,
LORD BYRON

Questioning

List three questions you might ask after reading the first stanza.

There is a pleasure in the pathless woods,
There is a rapture on the lonely shore,
There is society, where none intrudes,
By the deep sea, and music in its roar;
5   I love not man the less, but nature more,
From these our interviews, in which I steal
From all I may be, or have been before,
To mingle with the universe, and feel
What I can ne'er express, yet cannot all conceal.

10   Roll on, thou deep and dark blue ocean—roll!
Ten thousand fleets sweep over thee in vain;
Man marks the earth with ruin—his control
Stops with the shore; upon the watery plain
The wrecks are all thy deed, nor doth remain

▲ Critical Viewing

How does this painting capture the sublime nature of the ocean? **ANALYZE**

15 A shadow of man's ravage, save[1] his own,
 When, for a moment, like a drop of rain,
 He sinks into thy depths with bubbling groan,
Without a grave, unknelled, uncoffined, and unknown.

 His steps are not upon thy paths—thy fields
20 Are not a spoil for him—thou dost arise
 And shake him from thee; the vile strength he wields
 For earth's destruction thou dost all despise,
 Spurning him from thy bosom to the skies,
 And send'st him, shivering in thy playful spray
25 And howling, to his gods, where haply[2] lies
 His petty hope in some near port or bay,
And dashest him again to earth—there let him lay.[3]

Comprehension

According to the speaker, what impact does humanity's power have on the ocean?

---

1. save except.
2. haply perhaps.
3. lay A note on Byron's proof suggests that he intentionally made this grammatical error for the sake of the rhyme.

The armaments which thunderstrike the walls
Of rock-built cities, bidding nations quake,
And monarchs tremble in their capitals,
The oak leviathans,[4] whose huge ribs make
Their clay creator[5] the vain title take
Of lord of thee, and arbiter of war—
These are thy toys, and, as the snowy flake,
They melt into thy yeast of waves, which mar
Alike the Armada's[6] pride or spoils of Trafalgar.[7]

Thy shores are empires, changed in all save thee—
Assyria, Greece, Rome, Carthage, what are they?
Thy waters washed them power while they were free,
And many a tyrant since; their shores obey
The stranger, slave, or savage: their decay
Has dried up realms to deserts—not so thou,
Unchangeable, save to thy wild waves' play.
Time writes no wrinkle on thine azure brow;
Such as creation's dawn beheld, thou rollest now.

Vocabulary

arbiter (är´ bət ər) *n.*
judge; umpire

Figurative Language

Explain how the images
of destructive power in
lines 20–36 create a sense
of forces of nature beyond
human comprehension.

---

4. **leviathans** (lə vī´ ə thənz) monstrous sea creatures, described in the Old Testament. Here the word means giant ships.
5. **clay creator** human beings.
6. **Armada's** refers to the Spanish Armada, defeated by the English in 1588.
7. **Trafalgar** battle in 1805 during which the French and Spanish fleets were defeated by the British fleet led by Lord Nelson.

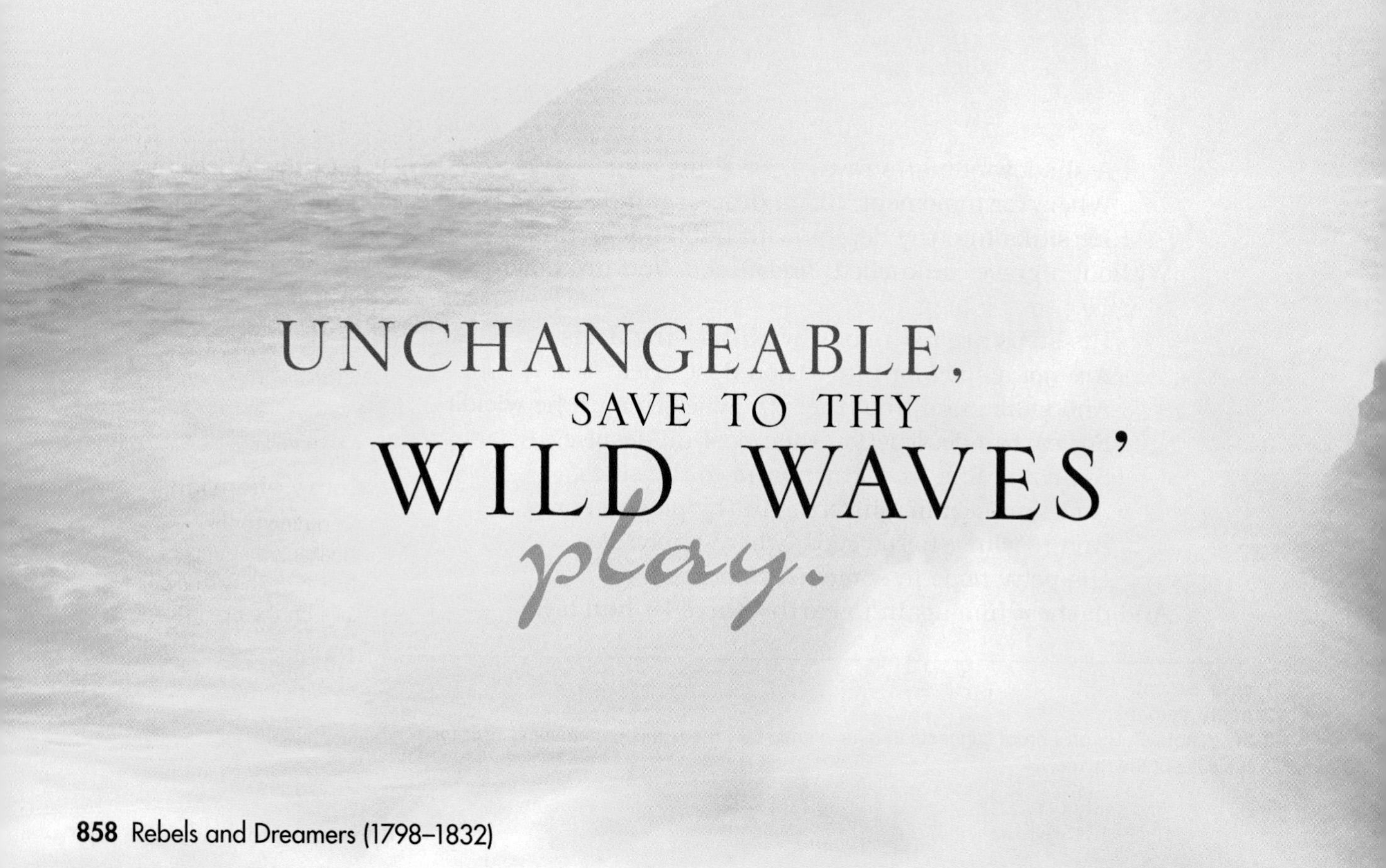

UNCHANGEABLE,
SAVE TO THY
WILD WAVES'
play.

Thou glorious mirror, where the Almighty's form
Glasses[8] itself in tempests: in all time,
Calm or convulsed—in breeze, or gale, or storm,
Icing the pole, or in the torrid clime
50 Dark-heaving—boundless, endless, and sublime;
The image of eternity, the throne
Of the Invisible; even from out thy slime
The monsters of the deep are made: each zone
Obeys thee; thou goest forth, dread, fathomless,[9] alone.

55 And I have loved thee, ocean! and my joy
Of youthful sports was on thy breast to be
Borne, like thy bubbles, onward; from a boy
I wantoned with thy breakers—they to me
Were a delight: and if the freshening sea
60 Made them a terror—'twas a pleasing fear,
For I was as it were a child of thee,
And trusted to thy billows far and near,
And laid my hand upon thy mane—as I do here.

8. Glasses mirrors.
9. fathomless (fath′ əm lis) *adj.* too deep to be measured or understood.

Vocabulary

torrid (tôr′ id) *adj.* very hot; scorching

Critical Reading

1. **Key Ideas and Details (a)** What natural settings does the speaker describe in the first lines? **(b) Interpret:** What attitude toward nature do his descriptions reveal?

2. **Craft and Structure (a)** In an apostrophe, a speaker addresses an absent person or personified quality or idea. Whom or what is the speaker addressing from line 10 on? **(b) Infer:** What is the speaker's attitude toward the subject he is addressing?

3. **Key Ideas and Details (a)** How does the ocean treat such human things as cities and warships? **(b) Compare and Contrast:** What contrast between the ocean and human governments does the speaker make in lines 37–45? **(c) Draw Conclusions:** In what sense is the ocean a power that dwarfs all human endeavors?

4. **Key Ideas and Details (a) Interpret:** In lines 46–54, what qualities make the ocean a reflection of "the Almighty's form"? **(b) Generalize:** What attitude toward nature do the lines encourage?

5. **Integration of Knowledge and Ideas** Is the sea still as mysterious and powerful today as it was in Byron's day? Explain.

Cite textual evidence to support your responses.

from

Don Juan

George Gordon, Lord Byron

Lord Byron, Shaking the Dust of England off His Shoes, from "The Poet's Corner" pub. William Heinemann, 1904 (engraving by Max Beerbohm) Central Saint Martin's College of Art and Design

BACKGROUND

Though it is unfinished, *Don Juan* (jōō´ ən) is regarded as Byron's finest work. A mock epic described by Shelley as "something wholly new and relative to the age," it satirizes the political and social problems of Byron's time.

Traditionally Don Juan, the poem's hero, is a wicked character driven by his obsession with beautiful women. In Byron's work, Don Juan is an innocent young man whose physical beauty, charm, and spirit prove to be alluring to ladies. As a result, he finds himself in many difficult situations.

During periodic pauses in the story, the narrator drifts away from the subject. In these digressions the narrator comments on the issues of the time and on life in general. In this excerpt the narrator sets aside the adventures of his hero to reflect on old age and death.

But now at thirty years my hair is gray
(I wonder what it will be like at forty?
I thought of a peruke¹ the other day)—
My heart is not much greener; and in short, I
5 Have squandered my whole summer while 'twas May,
And feel no more the spirit to retort; I
Have spent my life, both interest and principal,
And deem not, what I deemed, my soul invincible.

No more—no more—Oh! never more on me
10 The freshness of the heart can fall like dew,
Which out of all the lovely things we see
Extracts emotions beautiful and new,
Hived in our bosoms like the bag o' the bee:
Think'st thou the honey with those objects grew?
15 Alas! 'twas not in them, but in thy power
To double even the sweetness of a flower.

No more—no more—Oh! never more, my heart,
Canst thou be my sole world, my universe!
Once all in all, but now a thing apart,
20 Thou canst not be my blessing or my curse:
The illusion's gone forever, and thou art
Insensible,² I trust, but none the worse,
And in thy stead I've got a deal of judgment,
Though heaven knows how it ever found a lodgment.

Vocabulary

retort (ri tôrt´) *v.* respond with a clever answer or wisecrack

◀ Critical Viewing

What traits of the poem's narrator does this famous caricature of Byron share? **INTERPRET**

Comprehension

What type of experience will the speaker no longer undergo?

---

1. peruke (pə rook´) wig.
2. insensible (in sen´ sə bəl) *adj.* unable to feel or sense anything; numb.

World LITERATURE CONNECTION

Byron's Influence on World Literature

Byron's work was translated into many languages, and his fame quickly spread through Europe and beyond. Although the British dismissed Byron because of his wild life, the rest of Europe considered him the most important English poet. They were taken with the dark, brooding heroes described in his poems and were inspired by his life. Byron was a man of action. He made speeches in the House of Lords, defending the rights of workers and religious minorities. He traveled widely and he put his life on the line for liberty, joining the Greek revolutionaries in their fight against Turkish rule.

At a time when much of the world was embroiled in political and economic upheaval, writers found in Byron a model for passionate political and literary engagement. Byron's followers included some of the leading European and Russian poets: Alexander Pushkin and Mikhail Lermontov in Russia, Adam Mickiewicz in Poland, Heinrich Heine in Germany, Alfred de Musset in France, and José de Espronceda in Spain.

Connect to the Literature

What evidence of engagement with the world beyond Britain can you find in Byron's poems?

---

25 My days of love are over; me no more
The charms of maid, wife, and still less of widow
Can make the fool of which they made before—
In short, I must not lead the life I did do;
The credulous hope of mutual minds is o'er,
30 The copious use of claret is forbid too,
So for a good old-gentlemanly vice,
I think I must take up with avarice.

Ambition was my idol, which was broken
Before the shrines of Sorrow and of Pleasure;
35 And the two last have left me many a token
O'er which reflection may be made at leisure:
Now, like Friar Bacon's brazen head, I've spoken,
"Time is, Time was, Time's past,"[3] a chymic[4] treasure
Is glittering youth, which I have spent betimes—
40 My heart in passion, and my head on rhymes.

What is the end of fame? 'tis but to fill
A certain portion of uncertain paper:
Some liken it to climbing up a hill,
Whose summit, like all hills, is lost in vapor;
45 For this men write, speak, preach, and heroes kill,
And bards burn what they call their "midnight taper,"
To have, when the original is dust,
A name, a wretched picture, and worse bust.

What are the hopes of man? Old Egypt's King
50 Cheops erected the first pyramid
And largest, thinking it was just the thing
To keep his memory whole, and mummy hid:
But somebody or other rummaging
Burglariously broke his coffin's lid:
55 Let not a monument give you or me hopes,
Since not a pinch of dust remains of Cheops.

But I, being fond of true philosophy,
Say very often to myself, "Alas!
All things that have been born were born to die,
60 And flesh (which Death mows down to hay) is grass;
You've passed your youth not so unpleasantly,
And if you had it o'er again—'twould pass—
So thank your stars that matters are no worse,
And read your Bible, sir, and mind your purse."

---

3. **Friar Bacon's . . . Time's past** In Robert Greene's comedy *Friar Bacon and Friar Bungay* (1594), these words are spoken by a bronze bust, made by Friar Bacon.
4. **chymic** (kim´ ik) alchemic: counterfeit.

65　But for the present, gentle reader! and
　　　Still gentler purchaser! the bard—that's I—
　　　Must, with permission, shake you by the hand,
　　　And so your humble servant, and good-bye!
　　　We meet again, if we should understand
70　Each other; and if not, I shall not try
　　　Your patience further than by this short sample—
　　　'Twere well if others followed my example.

　　　"Go, little book, from this my solitude!
　　　I cast thee on the waters—go thy ways!
75　And if, as I believe, thy vein be good,
　　　The world will find thee after many days."[5]
　　　When Southey's read, and Wordsworth understood,
　　　I can't help putting in my claim to praise—
　　　The four first rhymes are Southey's, every line:
　　　For God's sake, reader! take them not for mine!

---

5. **Go . . . days** lines from the last stanza of Robert Southey's (1774–1843) Epilogue to *The Lay of the Laureate.*

What are the hopes of man?

Critical Reading

1. **Key Ideas and Details (a)** What subject does the speaker consider in the opening lines? **(b) Analyze:** How would you describe the mood of the speaker's reflections?

2. **Key Ideas and Details (a)** What does the speaker say was the focus of his youth? **(b) Interpret:** In lines 33–40, why does the speaker call "glittering youth" "chymic," or counterfeit, treasure?

3. **Key Ideas and Details (a) Draw Conclusions:** What do lines 65–80 suggest about Byron's attitude toward his own epic poem? **(b) Connect:** Is this attitude consistent with his "true philosophy"? Explain.

4. **Integration of Knowledge and Ideas** Identify a modern character who shares the disillusioned attitude of Byron's speaker.

5. **Integration of Knowledge and Ideas** Which poems express a sense of the sublime, a feeling of fear and wonder inspired by nature? Use at least two of these Essential Question words in your answer: *majestic, capture, preserve. [Connecting to the Essential Question: What is the relationship between literature and place?]*

Cite textual evidence to support your responses.

Literary Analysis

1. **Key Ideas and Details (a)** List the questions you asked as you read Byron's poems and the answers you found. **(b)** Did *repairing your comprehension* by **questioning** make your reading more active or focused? Explain.

2. **Key Ideas and Details** Ask and answer a series of questions to uncover the meaning of lines 9–16 of the excerpt from *Don Juan*.

3. **Craft and Structure** Use a chart to list examples from the poems of **figurative language,** finding at least one example each of **simile, metaphor,** and **personification.** Show how each example suggests a number of different associations for what is being described.

Figurative Language	What Is Being Described	Associations Suggested

4. **Craft and Structure (a)** Identify the simile in lines 10–18 of "Apostrophe to the Ocean." **(b)** What does the comparison suggest about the drowning man?

5. **Craft and Structure** Identify and interpret the types of figurative language in the following lines: **(a)** "Thou glorious mirror, where the Almighty's form / Glasses itself . . ." **(b)** "The freshness of the heart can fall like dew, . . ."

6. **Craft and Structure** In "Apostrophe to the Ocean," what effect does the personification of the ocean have on the poem as a whole?

7. **Craft and Structure** In *Don Juan*, the speaker says he "squandered [his] whole summer while 'twas May." **(a)** What type of figurative language is in this line? **(b)** What meaning does the comparison convey?

8. **Comparing Literary Works (a)** In "She Walks in Beauty," how does Byron use figures of speech and imagery of the night to convey the mysterious, endless power of Lady Horton's beauty? **(b)** Identify three images or figures of speech suggesting the sublime power of nature in "Apostrophe to the Ocean."

9. **Comparing Literary Works** Compare the feelings associated with infinite power or mystery in these two poems.

10. **Integration of Knowledge and Ideas** In what ways does Byron express the opposite of the sublime in the excerpt from *Don Juan*? Cite specific passages, figures of speech, and images to support your point.

Common Core State Standards

Writing

3.c. Use a variety of techniques to sequence events so that they build on one another to create a coherent whole and build toward a particular tone and outcome. *(p. 865)*

3.d. Use precise words and phrases, telling details, and sensory language to convey a vivid picture of the experiences, events, setting, and/or characters. *(p. 865)*

Language

4.a. Use context as a clue to the meaning of a word or phrase. *(p. 865)*

Vocabulary Acquisition and Use

Word Analysis: Latin Suffix *-ous*

The suffix *-ous* means "full of." The root of the word *credulous*, *cred-*, means "belief." Therefore, *credulous* means "full of belief" or "overly willing to believe." *Strenuous* exercise is "exercise that requires great exertion," or exercise that is "full of strain." Use the meaning of *-ous* to define the listed terms, checking a dictionary if necessary. Then, write an original sentence using each word.

1. furious
2. glorious
3. porous
4. plenteous
5. portentous
6. spacious
7. barbarous
8. querulous

Vocabulary: Context

An unfamiliar word's *context*—words, phrases, or sentences around it—can provide clues to its meaning. Identify the meaning of each italicized vocabulary word below and explain how the context makes that meaning clear.

1. Unable to agree on anything, the two brothers constantly relied on their sister as an *arbiter*.
2. The creek bed became dry after weeks of *torrid* weather.
3. The author's witty *retorts* to the host's questions left the audience laughing.
4. Unable to see her faults, he was always *credulous* with regard to her excuses.
5. The dutiful student filled the pages with *copious*, or plentiful, notes.
6. *Avarice* compelled him to accumulate wealth; selfishness led him to keep it all.

Writing to Sources

Narrative Text Write an **interior monologue**—words a character speaks to himself or herself—in which a modern Byronic hero tells his or her story. This type of hero is a brooding loner who may feel impassioned by a cause. If you like, use a real-life celebrity as a model.

Prewriting Jot down some opinions that a Byronic hero might hold today. Think about your hero's circumstances and how he or she might feel about them. Then, list words and phrases that convey this attitude.

Drafting Structure your monologue as the tale of a *sequence of events* that leads to your hero's strongest expression of his or her attitude. As you draft, use precise words to describe the character's feelings.

Revising Read through your draft and think about its *dramatic effect*. Rearrange or change words to intensify the dramatic effect.

Model: Revising to Structure Ideas for Effect

If I am a great actor, it is because my life has been great—not perfect. The films of my long career form an exhibition of my
mistakes, and crimes
flaws, ~~crimes and mistakes.~~
       ∧

Rearranging strengthens the dramatic effect by putting the more powerful word last.

Connecting to the Essential Question Romantic poets like Shelley were rebels who wanted to overthrow tyrants and bring in a new age of equality and justice. As you read, note which passages reveal Shelley as a political rebel. Finding such passages will help as you consider the Essential Question: **How does literature shape or reflect society?**

Close Reading Focus

Imagery; Romantic Philosophy
Imagery is descriptive language that re-creates sensory experience. Writers use imagery when they create metaphors and other figures of speech. Poetic imagery has these characteristics:

- It appeals to any or all of the five senses.
- It often creates patterns supporting a poem's theme.

The process of interpreting imagery requires you to make inferences, or educated guesses, about meaning. For example, in "Ode to the West Wind," Shelley uses wind images that appeal to sight, sound, and touch. Even though the poet does not explicitly state a theme, these images and their patterns suggest his message.

By gathering together powerful images of the west wind or of a skylark, Shelley links these elements of nature to the strivings of his own spirit. His images all depict concrete objects, such as leaves in the wind. Yet they also stir up longings and dreams. In the **Romantic philosophy** of the imagination, an image connects what is "outside" the mind with what is "inside," linking nature and spirit. As you read, think about the deeper meanings Shelley's imagery suggests.

Preparing to Read Complex Texts You can better understand an author's poetry by **comparing and contrasting elements** from different texts. For example, you might contrast the desert images of "Ozymandias," which suggest the bleakness of tyranny, with the wind images of "Ode to the West Wind," which suggest political rebellion. Use a chart like the one shown to compare the imagery in different poems by Shelley.

Vocabulary

You will encounter the words listed here in the texts that follow. Copy the words into your notebook, sorting them into words you know and words you do not know.

verge	blithe
sepulcher	profuse
impulse	satiety

Common Core State Standards

Reading Literature
1. Cite strong and thorough textual evidence to support analysis of what the text says explicitly as well as inferences drawn from the text, including determining where the text leaves matters uncertain.

Imagery	Poem

Percy Bysshe Shelley (1792–1822)

Author of **"Ozymandias"** • **"Ode to the West Wind"** • **"To a Skylark"**

When he died in a boating accident at 29, Percy Bysshe (bish) Shelley was eulogized by his fellow poet Lord Byron as "without exception the best and least selfish man I ever knew."

A Loner and Rebel Born into the British upper classes, Shelley was raised on a country estate in Sussex. He attended the finest schools, including the prestigious boarding school Eton, but he was never able to settle into the routine of a student. Instead, he spent most of his time wandering the countryside and performing private scientific experiments. At Oxford University, he became a friend of Thomas Jefferson Hogg, a student whose political views were as strong as his own. When, with Hogg's encouragement and support, Shelley published the radical tract *The Necessity of Atheism*, both he and Hogg were expelled from the university.

Love and Art The expulsion estranged Shelley from his father. Instead of going home, Shelley headed for London. There, he met Harriet Westbrook. An unhappy schoolgirl, Westbrook persuaded him to elope, and they married.

Shelley's development as a poet was already under way. In 1813, he had completed "Queen Mab," his first important poem. The work explored ideas of social justice that Shelley had encountered in the philosopher William Godwin's *Political Justice*.

Turmoil, Romance, and Tragedy Shelley's marriage, meanwhile, was in trouble. Harriet felt that she could not keep up with her husband. Then, Shelley fell in love with Mary Wollstonecraft Godwin, daughter of William Godwin and the feminist Mary Wollstonecraft. After Harriet's tragic death in 1816, Shelley married his beloved Mary Godwin.

A Poet and an Outcast His radical politics, his tract about atheism, his separation from his first wife—all helped make Shelley an outcast from England. He and Mary eventually settled in Italy, where Lord Byron, another famous exile, lived.

Shelley wrote many of his finest works in Italy, including "Ode to the West Wind" and "To a Skylark." His early death there, however, meant that he never saw his dreams of social progress come true.

Ozymandias

Percy Bysshe Shelley

rebels and Dreamers (1798–1832)

Background The Ozymandias of Shelley's poem is based on an actual Egyptian pharaoh, Ramses II ("Ozymandias" was his name in Greek). Ramses II ruled during the thirteenth century B.C. and figures in the biblical story of Moses. He sponsored ambitious building projects and called for huge statues of himself to be built. According to an ancient story, one of these colossal statues was inscribed with this boast about his bold deeds: "I am Ozymandias, king of kings; if anyone wishes to know what I am and where I lie, let him surpass me in some of my exploits."

I met a traveler from an antique land
Who said: Two vast and trunkless legs of stone
Stand in the desert. Near them, on the sand,
Half sunk, a shattered visage¹ lies, whose frown,
5 And wrinkled lip, and sneer of cold command,
Tell that its sculptor well those passions read
Which yet survive, stamped on these lifeless things,
The hand that mocked them and the heart that fed:
And on the pedestal these words appear:
10 "My name is Ozymandias, king of kings:
Look on my works, ye Mighty, and despair!"
Nothing beside remains. Round the decay
Of that colossal wreck, boundless and bare,
The lone and level sands stretch far away.

---

1. visage (viz′ ij) *n.* face.

◄ **Critical Viewing**
How is this Egyptian statue like and unlike the one in the poem? **COMPARE AND CONTRAST**

Critical Reading

1. **Key Ideas and Details (a)** How would you describe the expression on the face of Ozymandias? **(b) Infer:** What does his expression suggest about the kind of ruler he was?

2. **Key Ideas and Details (a) Interpret:** What attitude is conveyed by the words on the pedestal? **(b) Compare and Contrast:** Compare this attitude with the opening images of the poem. **(c) Analyze:** In what sense is the inscription ironic?

3. **Integration of Knowledge and Ideas (a) Draw Conclusions:** What is the message of this poem? **(b) Apply:** Do you think that the message is pertinent to today's world? Why or why not?

Cite textual evidence to support your responses.

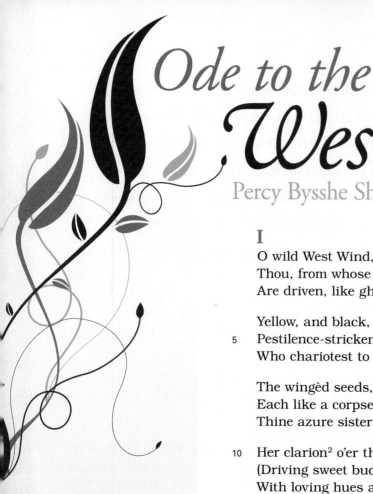

Ode to the West Wind

Percy Bysshe Shelley

I

O wild West Wind, thou breath of Autumn's being,
Thou, from whose unseen presence the leaves dead
Are driven, like ghosts from an enchanter fleeing,

Yellow, and black, and pale, and hectic red,
5   Pestilence-stricken multitudes: O thou,
Who chariotest to their dark and wintry bed

The wingèd seeds, where they lie cold and low,
Each like a corpse within its grave, until
Thine azure sister of the Spring[1] shall blow

10 Her clarion[2] o'er the dreaming earth, and fill
(Driving sweet buds like flocks to feed in air)
With loving hues and odors plain and hill:

Wild Spirit, which art moving everywhere;
Destroyer and preserver; hear, oh, hear!

II

15 Thou on whose stream, 'mid the steep sky's commotion,
Loose clouds like earth's decaying leaves are shed,
Shook from the tangled boughs of Heaven and Ocean,

Angels[3] of rain and lightning: there are spread
On the blue surface of thine aery surge,
20 Like the bright hair uplifted from the head

Of some fierce Maenad,[4] even from the dim verge
Of the horizon to the zenith's height,
The locks of the approaching storm. Thou dirge

Of the dying year, to which this closing night
25 Will be the dome of a vast sepulcher,
Vaulted with all thy congregated might

Imagery
To which sense does the image in lines 18–23 mostly appeal?

Vocabulary
verge (vʉrj) *n.* edge; rim
sepulcher (sep´ əl kər) *n.* tomb

---

1. **sister of the Spring** the wind prevailing during spring.
2. **clarion** *n.* trumpet producing clear, sharp tones.
3. **angels** messengers.
4. **Maenad** (mē´ nad) a priestess of Bacchus, the Greek and Roman god of wine and revelry.

Of vapors, from whose solid atmosphere
Black rain, and fire, and hail will burst: oh, hear!

III

Thou who didst waken from his summer dreams
30 The blue Mediterranean, where he lay,
Lulled by the coil of his crystalline streams,

Beside a pumice[5] isle in Baiae's bay,[6]
And saw in sleep old palaces and towers
Quivering within the wave's intenser day,

35 All overgrown with azure moss and flowers
So sweet, the sense faints picturing them!
For whose path the Atlantic's level powers

Cleave themselves into chasms, while far below
The sea-blooms and the oozy woods which wear
40 The sapless foliage of the ocean, know

Thy voice, and suddenly grow gray with fear,
And tremble and despoil themselves: oh, hear!

IV

If I were a dead leaf thou mightest bear;
If I were a swift cloud to fly with thee;
45 A wave to pant beneath thy power, and share

---

5. **pumice** (pum′ is) *n.* volcanic rock.
6. **Baiae's** (bā′ yēz) **bay** site of the ancient Roman resort near Naples, parts of which
lie submerged.

▲ Critical Viewing

Which elements in this painting match Shelley's evocation of the west wind in lines 1–8? **CONNECT**

Comparing Imagery

Contrast the images in lines 29–36 with those in lines 12–14 of "Ozymandias."

Comprehension

In the first three sections, what does the speaker ask the West Wind to do?

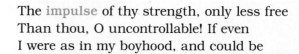

Vocabulary

impulse (im′ puls′) *n.* force
driving forward

The **impulse** of thy strength, only less free
Than thou, O uncontrollable! If even
I were as in my boyhood, and could be

The comrade of thy wanderings over Heaven,
50 As then, when to outstrip thy skyey speed
Scarce seemed a vision; I would ne'er have striven

As thus with thee in prayer in my sore need.
Oh, lift me as a wave, a leaf, a cloud!
I fall upon the thorns of life! I bleed!

55 A heavy weight of hours has chained and bowed
One too like thee: tameless, and swift, and proud.

**Imagery and Romantic
Philosophy**

How do the images
in lines 57–63 imply a
connection between the
speaker and nature?

V

Make me thy lyre,[7] even as the forest is:
What if my leaves are falling like its own!
The tumult of thy mighty harmonies

60 Will take from both a deep, autumnal tone,
Sweet though in sadness. Be thou, Spirit fierce,
My spirit! Be thou me, impetuous one!

Drive my dead thought over the universe
Like withered leaves to quicken a new birth!
65 And, by the incantation of this verse,

Scatter, as from an unextinguished hearth
Ashes and sparks, my words among mankind!
Be through my lips to unawakened earth

The trumpet of a prophecy! O Wind,
70 If Winter comes, can Spring be far behind?

---

7. **lyre** Aeolian (ē ō′ lē ən) lyre, or wind harp, a stringed instrument that produces musical
   sounds when the wind passes over it.

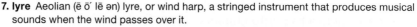

Critical Reading

1. **Key Ideas and Details (a)** What season does the poet associate
   with the west wind? **(b) Interpret:** What feelings does Shelley
   create around the west wind in sections II and III?

2. **Key Ideas and Details (a)** What does the speaker ask of the
   wind in section IV? **(b) Infer:** What change in his life prompts this
   question?

3. **Key Ideas and Details (a)** What does the final line of the poem
   mean? **(b)** How does it tie together the poem?

Woman and Bird in Moonlight, 1949, Joan Miro, Tate, London/Art Resource, NY. © Copyright ARS, NY.

To a Skylark

Percy Bysshe Shelley

▲ **Critical Viewing** Which details in this painting capture the freedom and independence of Shelley's skylark? **CONNECT**

Hail to thee, blithe spirit!
    Bird thou never wert,
That from heaven, or near it,
    Pourest thy full heart
5 In profuse strains of unpremeditated art.

    Higher still and higher,
    From the earth thou springest
Like a cloud of fire;
    The blue deep thou wingest,
10 And singing still dost soar, and soaring ever singest.

    In the golden lightning
    Of the sunken sun,
O'er which clouds are brightening,
    Thou dost float and run;
15 Like an unbodied joy whose race is just begun.

Vocabulary

blithe (blī*th*) *adj.* cheerful

profuse (prō fyo͞os′) *adj.* abundant; pouring out

Comprehension

To what type of cloud does Shelley compare the skylark?

To a Skylark **873**

The pale purple even[1]
    Melts around thy flight;
Like a star of heaven,
    In the broad daylight
20 Thou art unseen, but yet I hear thy shrill delight,

    Keen as are the arrows
      Of that silver sphere,[2]
    Whose intense lamp narrows
      In the white dawn clear,
25 Until we hardly see—we feel that it is there.

    All the earth and air
      With thy voice is loud,
    As, when night is bare,
      From one lonely cloud
30 The moon rains out her beams, and Heaven is overflowed.

    What thou art we know not;
      What is most like thee?
    From rainbow clouds there flow not
      Drops so bright to see,
35 As from thy presence showers a rain of melody.

    Like a poet hidden
      In the light of thought,
    Singing hymns unbidden,
      Till the world is wrought
40 To sympathy with hopes and fears it heeded not:

    Like a highborn maiden
      In a palace tower,
    Soothing her love-laden
      Soul in secret hour
45 With music sweet as love, which overflows her bower:

    Like a glowworm golden
      In a dell of dew,
    Scattering unbeholden
      Its aerial hue
50 Among the flowers and grass, which screen it from the view!

    Like a rose embowered
      In its own green leaves,

Spiral Review
Figurative Language
What type of figure of
speech appears throughout
these stanzas? How does
the repeated use of this
figure of speech to describe
the skylark emphasize the
bird's mystery?

1. even evening.
2. silver sphere the morning star.

By warm winds deflowered,[3]
   Till the scent it gives
55 Makes faint with too much sweet those heavy-wingèd thieves.[4]

Sound of vernal[5] showers
   On the twinkling grass,
Rain-awakened flowers,
   All that ever was
60 Joyous, and clear, and fresh, thy music doth surpass:

Teach us, sprite or bird,
   What sweet thoughts are thine:
I have never heard
   Praise of love or wine
65 That panted forth a flood of rapture so divine.

Chorus Hymeneal,[6]
   Or triumphal chant,
Matched with thine would be all
   But an empty vaunt,
70 A thing wherein we feel there is some hidden want.

What objects are the fountains[7]
   Of thy happy strain?
What fields, or waves, or mountains?
   What shapes of sky or plain?
75 What love of thine own kind? what ignorance of pain?

With thy clear keen joyance
   Languor cannot be;
Shadow of annoyance
   Never came near thee;
80 Thou lovest—but ne'er knew love's sad satiety.

Waking or asleep,
   Thou of death must deem[8]
Things more true and deep
   Than we mortals dream,
85 Or how could thy notes flow in such a crystal stream?

We look before and after,
   And pine for what is not;
Our sincerest laughter

---

3. deflowered fully open.

4. thieves the "warm winds."

5. vernal (vur′ nəl) *adj.* relating to spring.

6. Chorus Hymeneal (hī′ mə nē′ əl) marriage song, named after Hymen,
the Greek god of marriage.

7. fountains sources, inspiration.

8. deem know.

Comparing Imagery

Compare the images in lines 51–55 with those in lines 35–36 of "Ode to the West Wind."

Vocabulary

satiety (sə tī′ ə tē) *n.* state of being filled with enough or more than enough

Comprehension

Through what sense or senses does the speaker perceive the Skylark?

With some pain is fraught;
90 Our sweetest songs are those that tell of saddest thought.

Yet if[9] we could scorn
Hate, and pride, and fear;
If we were things born
Not to shed a tear,
95 I know not how thy joy we ever should come near.

Better than all measures
Of delightful sound,
Better than all treasures
That in books are found,
100 Thy skill to poet were,[10] thou scorner of the ground!

Teach me half the gladness
That thy brain must know,
Such harmonious madness
From my lips would flow,
105 The world should listen then, as I am listening now.

---

9. if even if.
10. were would be.

Critical Reading

Cite textual evidence to support your responses.

1. **Key Ideas and Details (a)** In the first stanza, what does the poet claim the skylark is not? **(b) Interpret:** What point is he making? **(c) Analyze:** How do the images of light in lines 6–35 reinforce the point?

2. **Key Ideas and Details (a)** To what four things does the speaker compare the bird in lines 36–55? **(b) Analyze:** What quality or power does each comparison suggest that the bird's song has?

3. **Key Ideas and Details (a)** What comparisons does the poet make between human song and the skylark's? **(b) Analyze:** Based on these comparisons, what does the speaker conclude about similarities and differences between the bird's life and human life?

4. **Craft and Structure** What does the speaker's use of the phrase "harmonious madness" (line 103) suggest about the difference between the skylark's song and human poetry?

5. **Integration of Knowledge and Ideas** In what ways does the sculpture in "Ozymandias" represent tyranny and the wind in "Ode to the West Wind" rebellion? In your response, use at least two of these Essential Question words: *independence, conform, limits.* [Connecting to the Essential Question: How does literature shape or reflect society?]

SHELLEY AND SCIENCE

Percy Bysshe Shelley was well educated in the science of his day. As a schoolboy, he studied with Adam Walker, a scientist who lectured on natural history, electricity, and meteorology. Later, Shelley, who was an avid reader, followed the latest scientific discoveries with great interest. For example, he read the work of meteorologist Luke Howard and incorporated Howard's theories of cloud formation into his poem "The Cloud":

This cloud sketch is by Luke Howard (1772–1864). Howard kept precise records of the weather in London for forty years and created a classification system for clouds that we still use today. His writings transformed the science of meteorology and inspired Shelley's poem "The Cloud."

. . . I am the daughter of Earth and Water,
And the nursling of the Sky;
I pass through the pores of the ocean and shores;
I change, but I cannot die.

CONNECT TO THE LITERATURE

What evidence of scientific influence can you find in the poems you have read by Shelley?

Literary Analysis

1. **Key Ideas and Details** Imagine filming the **imagery** of "Ozymandias." **(a)** Compare the camera placement you would use for lines 4–5, lines 9–11, and the final line. **(b)** Explain how each image helps convey Shelley's message.

2. **Craft and Structure (a)** In "Ode to the West Wind," find three images indicating the power of the wind, and explain to which senses each appeals. **(b)** How do these images support Shelley's message of renewal?

3. **Craft and Structure (a)** How do descriptions of sounds in "To a Skylark" *evoke emotions* by suggesting the bird's "unbodied joy"? **(b)** How does sound show the defect in human joy in lines 86–90?

4. **Comparing Literary Works** Compare Shelley's images of the statue, the west wind, and the skylark. **(a)** Which paints the strongest sensory picture of the object described? Explain. **(b)** Which provides the clearest sense of the ideas and feelings connected with the object? Explain.

5. **Comparing Literary Works** Using a chart like the one shown, compare two poems in which an image connects the speaker with nature.

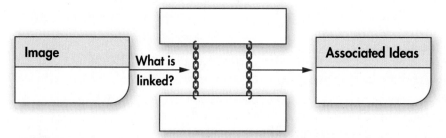

6. **Comparing Literary Works** In **Romantic philosophy,** the imagination connects nature and spirit. **(a)** What images in sections IV and V of "Ode to the West Wind" suggest such a connection? **(b)** Show how Shelley's use of *personification*—treating nonhuman things as if they were human—in two poems also helps link nature and spirit.

7. **Analyzing Visual Information** Using your knowledge of "Ozymandias," explain the humor of the cartoon shown on this page.

8. **Integration of Knowledge and Ideas Compare elements** in Shelley's poems by **contrasting** the desert imagery of "Ozymandias" with the wind imagery of "Ode to the West Wind." How does each of these patterns of imagery reveal Shelley as a political rebel?

9. **Integration of Knowledge and Ideas (a)** Using imagery from each poem, contrast the oppressive heaviness of the tyrant in "Ozymandias" with the lightness and ease of the bird in "To a Skylark." **(b)** To what extent do you think Shelley identifies the skylark with imagination itself? Explain.

Common Core State Standards

Writing
7. Conduct short research projects to answer a question or solve a problem. *(p. 879)*
8. Gather relevant information from multiple authoritative print and digital sources, using advanced searches effectively; assess the strengths and limitations of each source in terms of the task, purpose, and audience. *(p. 879)*

Language
4.d. Verify the preliminary determination of the meaning of a word or phrase. *(p. 879)*
5. Demonstrate understanding of figurative language, word relationships, and nuances in word meanings. *(p. 879)*

"My name is Ozymandias, king of kings: Look on my works, ye Mighty, and despair!" ▼

Vocabulary Acquisition and Use

Word Analysis: Latin Root -puls-

The Latin root -puls- means "push or drive." It is the base of some common words that are also used for *scientific concepts*. Using your knowledge of the root -puls-, write the definition of each numbered word below. Verify your definitions by checking a *dictionary*. Then, write three original sentences, each using a different word on the list.

1. compulsion
2. expulsion
3. impulse
4. propulsion
5. pulse
6. repulse

Vocabulary: Analogies

Analogies show the relationships between pairs of words. Complete each analogy using a word from the vocabulary list on page 866. In each, your choice should create a word pair that matches the relationship between the first two words given. Then, explain your answers.

1. *Penalty* is to *punishment* as _____ is to *brink*.
2. _____ is to *push* as *halt* is to *stop*.
3. *Sad* is to _____ as *ill* is to *healthy*.
4. *Glare* is to *sunlight* as _____ is to *fullness*.
5. _____ is to *building* as *dirge* is to *music*.
6. *Speed* is to *velocity* as _____ is to *excessive*.

Writing to Sources

Explanatory Text In lyric poems like "Ode to the West Wind," Shelley drew on the scientific and historical knowledge of his time. Develop a **research plan** for a report on Shelley's use of scientific or historical knowledge—or both—in his poetry. Include a *narrowed topic* to be investigated, *questions* to be answered, a *bibliography* of properly cited sources you will consult, and *annotations* stating the *appropriateness and objectivity* of each source.

Prewriting Use *creative research strategies* to formulate questions and develop a bibliography. Consider interviewing librarians and Shelley scholars. Also consider scanning biographies of Shelley and footnoted editions of his work to uncover scientific and historical influences.

Drafting Based on your reading, identify a narrow topic that could be answered adequately in a short paper. List your sources. Scan introductions, tables of contents, or opening paragraphs of the sources to see how appropriate and reliable each might be. Write specific annotations commenting on the relevance and objectivity of each.

Revising Review your questions to make sure they are clear and focused. Study your bibliography to make sure that you follow the format requested by your teacher.

> **Model: Making Evaluations Specific**
> Shelley, Mary. *Notes to the Complete Poetical Works of Percy Bysshe Shelley*. Sydney, Australia: ReadHowYouWant.com, 2006. Comments by his wife might show what reading in history and science Shelley had done.

> Use specific information in your evaluations for clarity.

Connecting to the Essential Question Keats adapted the ode—a poetic form designed to broadcast public concerns—to express personal emotions. As you read, note which lines in the odes reveal personal emotions. Locating these lines will help you explore the Essential Question: **What is the relationship of the writer to tradition?**

Close Reading Focus

Ode

An **ode** is a lyric poem, characterized by heightened emotion, that pays respect to a person or thing, usually directly addressed by the speaker.

- The **Pindaric ode** (named for the ancient Greek poet Pindar) uses groups of three stanzas, one of which differs in form from the other two. Pindar's odes celebrated victors at the Olympic Games.
- Roman poets later developed the **Horatian ode** (also called homostrophic), which contains only one type of stanza.
- The **irregular ode** has no set pattern.

Keats created his own form of the ode, using ten-line stanzas of iambic pentameter (lines containing ten beats with a repeated pattern of weak-strong). Often those stanzas begin with a heroic quatrain (four lines rhymed *abab*) followed by a sestet (six lines rhymed in various ways). As you read, note the various formal structures Keats uses in his odes.

Comparing Literary Works In his odes, Keats follows the tradition of paying respect to something. Yet his odes reveal as much about him as they do about his subjects. As you read, compare the ways in which his odes dramatize a conflict in the speaker. Also analyze how, in each case, the conflict is brought on by longings for what is unobtainable.

Preparing to Read Complex Texts You can **determine the main idea** of a passage by *paraphrasing* it—restating it in your own words. Doing so will not only help you clarify the meaning of the specific passage but will also help you see how the ideas in a work connect and develop. Use a chart like the one shown to paraphrase difficult passages in Keats's poems.

Vocabulary

You will encounter the words below in the texts that follow. Copy the words into your notebook, sorting them into words you know and words you do not know.

ken	teeming
surmise	vintage
gleaned	requiem

Common Core State Standards

Reading Literature
5. Analyze how an author's choices concerning how to structure specific parts of a text contribute to its overall structure and meaning as well as its aesthetic impact.

Original
"When I have fears that I may cease to be…"

Paraphrase
When I am afraid that I may die…

John Keats (1795–1821)

Author of **"On First Looking into Chapman's Homer"** • **"When I Have Fears That I May Cease to Be"** • **"Ode to a Nightingale"** • **"Ode on a Grecian Urn"**

Although he died at age twenty-five, Keats left his indelible mark on literature, and this makes us wonder what more he might have accomplished had he lived longer.

A Defender of Worthy Causes Unlike his contemporaries Byron and Shelley, John Keats was not an aristocrat. Instead, he was born to working-class Londoners. As a child, he received attention for his striking good looks and his restless spirit. Keats developed a reputation for fighting, but always for a worthy cause. It was not until he and his school-master's son, Charles Cowden Clarke, became friends that Keats developed an interest in poetry and became an avid reader.

From Medicine to Poetry In 1815, Keats began studying medicine at a London hospital. He had already begun writing poetry, but he earned his pharmacist's license before abandoning medicine for the literary world. In 1818, he published his first major work, *Endymion*, a long poem that the critics panned. Despite the critical rejection, Keats did not swerve from his new career.

A Year of Sorrow and Joy The year 1818 was significant for Keats in other ways as well. He lost his brother Tom to tuberculosis, but he also met the light of his life, Fanny Brawne, to whom he became engaged. The next year, 1819, was a period of feverish creativity. In just nine months, fired by grief, new-found love, and his own encroaching illness, Keats wrote the poems for which he is most famous, including "The Eve of St. Agnes," "La Belle Dame sans Merci," and his odes. Each is recognized as a masterpiece.

An Early Death Keats's engagement to Fanny and his burst of creativity might have been the prelude to a happy, productive life. Instead, Keats found his health deteriorating. Recognizing that like his brother, he had tuberculosis, Keats moved to Italy, hoping that the warmer climate would reverse the disease. Sadly, that hope proved false, and, in 1821, his battle with tuberculosis ended with his death.

Despite his early death, John Keats remains one of the major influences in English poetry.

On First Looking into Chapman's Homer

John Keats

BACKGROUND ROMANTIC POETS SUCH AS BYRON, SHELLEY, AND KEATS ADMIRED THE CULTURE OF ANCIENT GREECE AND DERIVED INSPIRATION FROM ITS ART AND LITERATURE. KEATS'S "ODE ON A GRECIAN URN" (P. 890), FOR INSTANCE, SHOWS HIS TENDENCY TO ASSOCIATE IDEAS ABOUT BEAUTY WITH ANTIQUITIES, SUCH AS THE BEAUTIFULLY ADORNED VASES THAT ANCIENT GREEK SOCIETY PRODUCED.

WHEN KEATS WAS TWENTY-ONE, HIS FRIEND AND FORMER SCHOOLMATE, CHARLES COWDEN CLARKE, INTRODUCED HIM TO A TRANSLATION OF HOMER BY ELIZABETHAN POET GEORGE CHAPMAN. THE TWO MEN SPENT THE EVENING READING THIS BOOK, AND EARLY THE NEXT MORNING KEATS PRESENTED THIS SONNET TO CLARKE.

Much have I traveled in the realms of gold,
    And many goodly states and kingdoms seen;
    Round many western islands have I been
Which bards in fealty to Apollo[1] hold.
5 Oft of one wide expanse had I been told
    That deep-browed Homer ruled as his demesne;[2]
    Yet did I never breathe its pure serene[3]
Till I heard Chapman speak out loud and bold:
Then felt I like some watcher of the skies
10   When a new planet swims into his ken;
Or like stout Cortez[4] when with eagle eyes
    He stared at the Pacific—and all his men
Looked at each other with a wild surmise—
    Silent, upon a peak in Darien.[5]

Paraphrasing
Paraphrase lines 5–6, paying special attention to the metaphor of a "demesne."

Vocabulary
ken (ken) *n.* range of sight or knowledge

surmise (sər mīz´) *n.* guess; assumption

---

1. **Apollo** in Greek and Roman mythology, the god of music, poetry, and medicine.
2. **demesne** (di mān´) realm.
3. **serene** clear air.
4. **Cortez** Here, Keats was mistaken. The Pacific was discovered in 1513 by Balboa, not Cortez.
5. **Darien** (der´ ē ən) the Isthmus of Panama.

◀ **Critical Viewing** How does this image of ships convey the feeling of exploration Keats describes in this sonnet? **CONNECT**

John Keats, 1821, Joseph Severn, by courtesy of the National Portrait Gallery, London

When I Have Fears That I May Cease to Be

John Keats

When I have fears that I may cease to be
　　Before my pen has gleaned my teeming brain,
Before high-piled books, in charactery,[1]
　　Hold like rich garners[2] the full ripened grain;
5　When I behold, upon the night's starred face,
　　Huge cloudy symbols of a high romance,
And think that I may never live to trace
　　Their shadows, with the magic hand of chance;
And when I feel, fair creature of an hour,
10　　That I shall never look upon thee more,
Never have relish in the fairy power
　　Of unreflecting love—then on the shore
Of the wide world I stand alone, and think
Till love and fame to nothingness do sink.

1. charactery written or printed letters of the alphabet.
2. garners storehouses for grain.

Vocabulary

gleaned (glēnd) *v.* collected from bit by bit, as when gathering stray grain after a harvest

teeming (tēm´ iŋ) *adj.* filled to overflowing

◄ **Critical Viewing**

From this rendering of Keats, how would you characterize him? **INFER**

Critical Reading

Cite textual evidence to support your responses.

1. **Key Ideas and Details** **(a)** In "On First Looking into Chapman's Homer," what feelings about Chapman's translation do lines 9–14 convey? **(b) Draw Conclusions:** How does the comparison of reading to a journey support these feelings?

2. **Key Ideas and Details** **(a)** In lines 1–4 of "When I Have Fears," what does the speaker fear he will not accomplish before he dies? **(b) Interpret:** In lines 5–12, what is he concerned about missing? **(c) Evaluate:** Do the last lines offer a convincing resolution to such fears? Explain.

3. **Integration of Knowledge and Ideas** What words describe Keats's character as revealed in these two poems?

4. **Integration of Knowledge and Ideas** Are most young people today as anxious about and thrilled by the future as Keats? Explain.

Ode to a Nightingale

John Keats

BACKGROUND Keats composed the following ode in 1819, while living in Hampstead with his friend Charles Brown. Brown wrote the following description about how the ode was composed: "In the spring of 1819 a nightingale had built her nest near my house. Keats felt a tranquil and continued joy in her song; and one morning he took his chair from the breakfast table to the grass plot under the plum tree, where he sat for two or three hours. When he came into the house, I perceived he had some scraps of paper in his hand, and these he was quietly thrusting behind the books. On inquiry, I found those scraps, four or five in number, contained his poetic feeling on the song of our nightingale."

I

My heart aches, and drowsy numbness pains
　　My sense, as though of hemlock[1] I had drunk,
Or emptied some dull opiate to the drains
　　One minute past, and Lethe-wards[2] had sunk:
5　'Tis not through envy of thy happy lot,
　　But being too happy in thine happiness,—
　　　That thou, light-winged Dryad[3] of the trees,
　　　　In some melodious plot
　　Of beechen green, and shadows numberless,
10　　Singest of summer in full-throated ease.

II

O, for a draft[4] of vintage! that hath been
　　Cooled a long age in the deep-delved earth,
Tasting of Flora[5] and the country green,
　　Dance, and Provençal[6] song, and sunburnt mirth!
15　O for a beaker full of the warm South,
　　Full of the true, the blushful Hippocrene,[7]
　　　With beaded bubbles winking at the brim,
　　　　And purple-stained mouth;
　　That I might drink, and leave the world unseen,
20　　And with thee fade away into the forest dim:

III

Fade far away, dissolve, and quite forget
　　What thou among the leaves hast never known,
The weariness, the fever, and the fret
　　Here, where men sit and hear each other groan;
25　Where palsy shakes a few, sad, last gray hairs,
　　Where youth grows pale, and specter-thin, and dies;[8]
　　　Where but to think is to be full of sorrow
　　　　And leaden-eyed despairs,
　　Where Beauty cannot keep her lustrous eyes,
30　　Or new Love pine at them beyond tomorrow.

---

1. **hemlock** poisonous herb.
2. **Lethe-wards** toward Lethe, the river of forgetfulness in Hades, the underworld, in classical mythology.
3. **Dryad** (drī´ əd) in classical mythology, a wood nymph.
4. **draft** drink.
5. **Flora** in classical mythology, the goddess of flowers, or the flowers themselves.
6. **Provençal** (prō´ vən säl´) pertaining to Provence, a region in Southern France, renowned in the late Middle Ages for its troubadours, who composed and sang love songs.
7. **Hippocrene** (hip´ ō krēn´) in classical mythology, the fountain of the Muses on Mt. Helicon. From this fountain flowed the waters of inspiration.
8. **youth . . . dies** Keats is referring to his brother, Tom, who had died from tuberculosis the previous winter.

◀ **Critical Viewing**
Compare the mood of this painting with that of stanza III. **COMPARE AND CONTRAST**

Vocabulary

vintage (vin´ tij) *n.* wine of fine quality

Paraphrasing
Restate lines 11–14 in your own words.

The Ode
Which passages in stanza III seem to express Keats's deep personal feelings? Explain.

Comprehension
What does the speaker wish to do along with the nightingale?

Ode to a Nightingale **887**

Pablo Neruda's Odes

Keats is considered the master of the 19th-century English ode. However, the master of the 20th-century ode is Pablo Neruda, who wrote in Spanish.

Neruda was born in Chile in 1904. At sixteen, he was already a published poet. As he grew older, Neruda realized that many of the uneducated poor in Latin America would have trouble understanding his ornate, complicated poems. Yet he wanted to reach everyone. "Poetry is like bread," he said. "It should be shared by all."

So Neruda began writing poems with short lines and vivid images. These new poems were tributes to everyday objects: a hat, a pair of socks, an onion, a tomato. Neruda called them odes. He described a watermelon as "a jewel box of water," and he described fire as "jumpy and blind but with studded eyes." Eventually, Neruda achieved his goal: hundreds of thousands of Spanish-speaking people, rich and poor, came to know and love his poetry.

Connect to the Literature

What sort of people do you think John Keats imagined would read "Ode to a Nightingale?"

Vocabulary

requiem (rek´ wē əm)
n. musical composition honoring the dead

IV

Away! away! for I will fly to thee,
    Not charioted by Bacchus[9] and his pards,
But on the viewless[10] wings of Poesy,[11]
    Though the dull brain perplexes and retards:
35 Already with thee! tender is the night,
    And haply[12] the Queen-Moon is on her throne,
      Clustered around by all her starry Fays;[13]
      But here there is no light,
    Save what from heaven is with the breezes blown
40   Through verdurous[14] glooms and winding mossy ways.

V

I cannot see what flowers are at my feet,
    Nor what soft incense hangs upon the boughs,
But, in embalmed[15] darkness, guess each sweet
    Wherewith the seasonable month endows
45 The grass, the thicket, and the fruit-tree wild;
    White hawthorn, and the pastoral eglantine;[16]
      Fast fading violets covered up in leaves;
      And mid-May's eldest child,
    The coming musk-rose, full of dewy wine,
50   The murmurous haunt of flies on summer eves.

VI

Darkling[17] I listen; and, for many a time
    I have been half in love with easeful Death,
Called him soft names in many a mused[18] rhyme,
    To take into the air my quiet breath;
55 Now more than ever seems it rich to die,
    To cease upon the midnight with no pain,
      While thou art pouring forth thy soul abroad
        In such an ecstasy!
    Still wouldst thou sing, and I have ears in vain—
60   To thy high requiem become a sod.

---

9. **Bacchus** (bak´ əs) in classical mythology, the god of wine, who was often represented in a chariot drawn by leopards ("pards").
10. **viewless** invisible.
11. **Poesy** poetic fancy.
12. **haply** perhaps.
13. **Fays** fairies.
14. **verdurous** green-foliaged.
15. **embalmed** perfumed.
16. **eglantine** (eg´ lən tīn´) sweetbrier or honeysuckle.
17. **Darkling** in the dark.
18. **mused** meditated.

VII

Thou wast not born for death, immortal Bird!
   No hungry generations tread thee down;
The voice I hear this passing night was heard
   In ancient days by emperor and clown:
65 Perhaps the selfsame song that found a path
   Through the sad heart of Ruth,[19] when, sick for home,
     She stood in tears amid the alien corn;
      The same that ofttimes hath
   Charmed magic casements, opening on the foam
70   Of perilous seas, in fairylands forlorn.

VIII

Forlorn! the very word is like a bell
   To toll me back from thee to my sole self!
Adieu! the fancy cannot cheat so well
   As she is famed[20] to do, deceiving elf.
75 Adieu! adieu! thy plaintive anthem fades
   Past the near meadows, over the still stream,
     Up the hillside; and now 'tis buried deep
     In the next valley-glades:
   Was it a vision, or a waking dream?
80   Fled is that music:—Do I wake or sleep?

---

19. Ruth in the Bible (Ruth 2:1–23), a widow who left her home and went to Judah to work in the corn (wheat) fields.
20. famed reported.

The Ode
What element of traditional odes appears in verse VII?

Past the near meadows,
   over the still stream,
Up the hillside;
   and now 'tis buried deep

Critical Reading

Cite textual evidence to support your responses.

1. **Key Ideas and Details (a)** How does the speaker describe his emotional state in stanza I? **(b) Infer:** What appears to have brought on this state?

2. **Key Ideas and Details (a)** What wish does the speaker express in lines 19–20? **(b) Compare and Contrast:** What differences does he see between the bird's life and his own that cause him to wish this?

3. **Craft and Structure (a) Analyze:** What is the viewpoint from which the speaker describes his surroundings in stanza V? **(b) Connect:** How does this viewpoint reflect the speaker's wish in line 21?

4. **Craft and Structure (a) Analyze:** How does stanza VII "answer" stanza VI? **(b) Synthesize:** What similarity between death and immortality does the speaker imply?

5. **Integration of Knowledge and Ideas** By writing a poem full of extreme feeling, is Keats just being dramatic, or is writing such a poem a way of making peace with strong feelings? Explain.

ODE ON A GRECIAN URN

JOHN KEATS

I

Thou still unravished bride of quietness
    Thou foster child of silence and slow time,
Sylvan[1] historian, who canst thus express
    A flowery tale more sweetly than our rhyme:
5 What leaf-fringed legend haunts about thy shape
    Of deities or mortals, or of both,
      In Tempe[2] or the dales of Arcady?[3]
    What men or gods are these? What maidens loath?[4]
What mad pursuit? What struggle to escape?
10   What pipes and timbrels?[5] What wild ecstasy?

II

Heard melodies are sweet, but those unheard
    Are sweeter; therefore, ye soft pipes, play on;
Not to the sensual[6] ear, but, more endeared,
    Pipe to the spirit ditties of no tone:
15 Fair youth, beneath the trees, thou canst not leave
    Thy song, nor ever can those trees be bare;
      Bold Lover, never, never canst thou kiss,
Though winning near the goal—yet, do not grieve;
    She cannot fade, though thou hast not thy bliss,
20   Forever wilt thou love, and she be fair!

III

Ah, happy, happy boughs! that cannot shed
    Your leaves, nor ever bid the Spring adieu;
And, happy melodist, unwearied,
    Forever piping songs forever new;
25 More happy love! more happy, happy love!
    Forever warm and still to be enjoyed,
      Forever panting, and forever young;
All breathing human passion far above,
    That leaves a heart high-sorrowful and cloyed,
30   A burning forehead, and a parching tongue.

IV

Who are these coming to the sacrifice?
    To what green altar, O mysterious priest,
Lead'st thou that heifer lowing at the skies,
    And all her silken flanks with garlands dressed?

---

1. **Sylvan** rustic, representing the woods or forest.
2. **Tempe** (tem´ pē) beautiful valley in Greece that has become a symbol of supreme rural beauty.
3. **Arcady** (är´ kə dē) region in Greece that has come to represent supreme pastoral contentment.
4. **loath** unwilling.
5. **timbrels** tambourines.
6. **sensual** involving the physical sense of hearing.

The Ode
What two figures on Keats's urn are directly addressed in stanza II?

Comprehension
Describe two scenes depicted on the urn.

◀ Critical Viewing
What stories can you see in the picture above and in the picture decorating the urn to the left? **SPECULATE**

The Ode

What do the speaker's questions reveal about his feelings or personality?

35 What little town by river or seashore,
 Or mountain-built with peaceful citadel,
  Is emptied of this folk, this pious morn?
And, little town, thy streets forevermore
 Will silent be; and not a soul to tell
40   Why thou art desolate, can e'er return.

V

O Attic[7] shape! Fair attitude! with brede[8]
 Of marble men and maidens overwrought,[9]
With forest branches and the trodden weed;
 Thou, silent form, dost tease us out of thought
45 As doth eternity: Cold[10] Pastoral!
 When old age shall this generation waste,
  Thou shalt remain, in midst of other woe
Than ours, a friend to man, to whom thou say'st,
 "Beauty is truth, truth beauty,"—that is all
50   Ye know on earth, and all ye need to know.

---

7. Attic Attica was the region of Greece in which Athens was located; the art of the region was characterized by grace and simplicity.
8. brede interwoven pattern.
9. overwrought adorned with.
10. Cold unchanging.

Critical Reading

1. **Key Ideas and Details (a)** Describe the scenes in stanzas I and II. **(b) Infer:** Why might the lover in stanza II grieve? **(c) Interpret:** Why does the speaker advise him not to grieve?

2. **Key Ideas and Details (a)** Which items are called "happy" in stanza III? **(b) Infer:** What is the reason for their happiness?

3. **Key Ideas and Details Infer:** What do the speaker's comments on these painted scenes indirectly suggest about real life?

4. **Key Ideas and Details (a) Interpret:** In line 49, what is the "truth" represented by the scenes on the urn? **(b) Connect:** How is this truth connected to the fact that the urn will remain after "old age shall this generation waste"? **(c) Make a Judgment:** Is the truth of the urn the "whole truth"? Explain.

5. **Integration of Knowledge and Ideas** In what ways are these poems traditional odes? In what ways has Keats personalized them? In your response, use at least two of these Essential Question words: *authentic, conventional, interpretation.* **[Connecting to the Essential Question: What is the relationship of the writer to tradition?]**

Cite textual evidence to support your responses.

Literary Analysis

1. **Key Ideas and Details** **Paraphrase** lines 9–10 from "Chapman's Homer" and, based on your paraphrasing, **determine** their **main idea.**

2. **Key Ideas and Details** Suppose you are telling a friend about Keats's sonnet "When I Have Fears." Paraphrase lines of the poem to explain to your friend exactly what Keats fears.

3. **Key Ideas and Details** Paraphrase at least one passage that you find difficult in stanza VII of "Ode to a Nightingale."

4. **Craft and Structure (a)** Identify the rhyme scheme of stanza I of "Ode on a Grecian Urn." **(b)** Is this rhyme scheme used throughout the poem? **(c)** Classify the **ode** as **Pindaric, Horatian,** or **irregular.** Then, explain your choice.

5. **Craft and Structure** What phrase does Keats use to directly address his subject in stanza I of "Ode to a Nightingale"? Identify another such phrase in the poem.

6. **Key Ideas and Details (a)** What do Keats's two odes honor? **(b)** Would you say he treats his subjects with heightened emotion? Why or why not?

7. **Integration of Knowledge and Ideas** What artifacts of today would speak most to the future about our culture, as the urn speaks of ancient Greece? Refer to the text as you draw parallels between the Grecian urn and a contemporary example.

8. **Comparing Literary Works (a)** Compare the speaker's attitude—wonder? fear? longing?—in each ode. **(b)** In each, an object or event represents something that the speaker desires but does not and perhaps cannot possess. Support this generalization with details from the poems.

9. **Comparing Literary Works** Both "Ode to a Nightingale" and "Ode on a Grecian Urn" show a speaker caught between eternal beauty and the realities of life. Using a chart like the one shown, collect details from each ode that compare the relationship between the eternal and the world of time.

10. **Comparing Literary Works** Explain how each ode contributes to the idea that a person's self is defined by his or her deepest conflicts.

11. **Integration of Knowledge and Ideas** In what ways are Keats's two sonnets as dramatic as his odes? Cite specific passages to support your argument.

Common Core State Standards

Writing
9.a. Apply *grades 11–12 Reading standards* to literature. [RL.11-12.5] *(p. 894)*

Language
5. Demonstrate understanding of figurative language, word relationships, and nuances in word meanings. *(p. 894)*

Close Reading Activities Continued

Vocabulary Acquisition and Use

Word Analysis: Multiple Meanings

Some words have both a literal and a figurative meaning. Literally, *vintage* is "wine of a particular place and season." Figuratively, though, the word *vintage* means "of a particular era" or "best of its class." As you can see, the figurative meaning draws on the literal one. Identify the figurative meaning of each word below and explain how it is related to the literal meaning. Consult a dictionary to verify your answers. Then, write two sentences for each word, one illustrating the literal meaning and one the figurative.

1. lamb, *n.*
2. varnish, *v.*
3. flak, *n.*
4. mouthpiece, *n.*
5. dim, *adj.*

Vocabulary: Sentence Completion

Using words from the vocabulary list on page 880, complete the sentences below. Use each word once. If necessary, change its form. Then, write original sentences with each word.

1. The storage room was _____ with supplies.
2. Despite the evidence, he remained convinced that his initial _____ was correct.
3. At the funeral, the organist played a mournful _____.
4. There are many mysteries beyond our _____.
5. The wine collector carefully organized his bottles according to _____.
6. At harvest time, the birds _____ stray grain from the reaped fields.

Writing to Sources

Explanatory Text Critics David Perkins and Walter Jackson Bate have pointed to the dramatic quality of Keats's odes, a quality also found in his lyrics. Write an **essay** analyzing how Keats uses *imagery, personification, figures of speech*, and *sound* to structure his poems, setting up dramatic situations and evoking readers' emotions. Bear in mind that drama springs from internal or external conflicts.

Prewriting Take notes on the poems, recording examples of the kinds of dramatic images and situations Keats presents. Annotate your notes to show how he evokes emotions. Then, use your notes to formulate a thesis statement.

Drafting Write your essay, explaining the techniques Keats uses and the effects they have. To make your essay more coherent, organize it to follow the sequence of ideas in your thesis statement.

Model: Annotating Notes	
Words or Passage	**Comment**
"Looked at each other with a wild surmise— / Silent, upon a peak in Darien." ("Chapman's Homer," lines 13–14)	Dramatic image: men stunned into silence by what they see.

Taking specific notes will help your writing flow more easily.

Revising Revise your draft to make sure you have organized it well, clearly stated your points, and supported your ideas with *accurate and detailed references* to the text.

Primary Sources

Parliamentary Debate
Speech by Lord John Russell
Speech by Sir Robert Peel

Letter
Thomas Babington Macaulay
to Thomas Flower Ellis

**Common Core
State Standards**

Reading Informational Text
4. Determine the meaning of words and phrases as they are used in a text, including figurative, connotative, and technical meanings; analyze how an author uses and refines the meaning of a key term or terms over the course of a text.

6. Determine an author's point of view or purpose in a text in which the rhetoric is particularly effective, analyzing how style and content contribute to the power, persuasiveness, or beauty of the text.

About the Text Forms

A **debate** is a formal argument in which speakers with opposing views try to persuade an audience to support their positions. Debates follow rules, especially if they take place in a legislative body like Parliament.

Those who viewed parliamentary proceedings might provide an eyewitness account of them in a **letter.** Such a communication can provide insights into public opinion as well as the writer's own views.

Preparing to Read Complex Texts

A speaker or author arguing for a position may use *rhetorical devices.*
Analyzing rhetorical devices like these will help you understand how authors try to make their case:

- *charged language and imagery:* words that carry strong emotional associations and stir up the audience's feelings
- *parallelism:* similar ideas expressed in similar grammatical forms
- *dramatic alternatives:* the posing of sharply contrasting alternatives
- *allusions:* references to well-known people, places, and events

As you read, notice how the two debaters and Macaulay use rhetorical devices to clarify their ideas, make them memorable, and engage the audience's emotions.

To fully appreciate rhetoric, first clarify the meaning of the writer's words:

- Be sensitive to word *connotations*—the positive or negative associations of words.

- Interpret words used in a *figurative sense,* such as *similes* (comparisons of unlike things using *like* or *as*).

- Consult references to determine the meaning of *technical terms*—terms specific to a discipline or profession, such as politics.

How does literature **shape or** reflect *society?*

Lord Russell and Sir Robert Peel were on opposite sides of the debate on the First Reform Bill. As you read, consider how the two served as spokesmen for different social interests. Also consider how the outcome of their argument, as reflected in Macaulay's letter, affected their society.

Note-Taking Guide

Primary source documents are a rich source of information for researchers. As you read these documents, use a note-taking guide like this one to organize relevant and accurate information.

1 Type of Document (check one)
☐ Newspaper ☐ Letter ☐ Diary ☐ Map ☐ Speech ☐ Government Form
☐ Advertisement ☐ Memorandum ☐ Other (Specify) _____

2 Date of Document _____

3 Author _____
Author's Position _____

4 Original Audience _____

5 Purpose and Importance

  a How does the author try to persuade his audience? _____
  Write down two details that support your answer. _____
  _____

  b List two important ideas, statements, or observations from this document. ___
  _____
  _____

  c What does this document show about life in the time and place in which it
  was written? _____
  _____
  _____

Analyzing Rhetorical Devices As you read, analyze rhetorical devices that authors of public documents, or of private documents relating to public issues, use to support their positions.

This guide was adapted from the **U.S. National Archives** document analysis worksheet.

Vocabulary

measure (mezh´ ər) *n.* a bill, resolution, or something else proposed or enacted to improve a situation (p. 900)

grievances (grēv´ əns əz) *n.* circumstances that cause people to complain (p. 900)

electors (ē lek´ tərz) *n.* those who vote (p. 900)

constituency (kən stich´ o͞o ən sē) *n.* the people making up a body of voters (p. 901)

extravagant (ek strav´ ə gənt) *adj.* going beyond reasonable limits; excessive (p. 902)

reverence (rev´ ər əns) *n.* deep respect (p. 902)

inauspicious (in´ ô spi´ shəs) *adj.* not promising a good outcome; unfavorable (p. 904)

orthodox (ôr´ thə däks´) *adj.* conforming to established beliefs (p. 907)

THE STORY BEHIND THE DOCUMENTS

Lord John Russell

Sir Robert Peel

Thomas Babington Macaulay

Lord John Russell (1792–1878) was the British statesman who introduced the Reform Bill of 1832 in Parliament. A champion of reform, Lord Russell was a leading member of the Whig party when it came to power in 1830 with Lord Grey as prime minister. Some years later, after the Whigs had evolved into the Liberal party, Russell himself served twice as Britain's prime minister. Among his later achievements was passage of a law limiting factory labor to ten hours a day.

Sir Robert Peel (1788–1850) helped lead the Tory party opposition to the Reform Bill of 1832. Peel later served as prime minister twice, first from 1834 to 1835 and later, after reorganizing the Tories as the modern Conservative party, for a much longer period in the 1840s. In 1829, while serving as home secretary in a Tory administration, he established London's police force, whose members are nicknamed "bobbies" in his honor.

Thomas Babington Macaulay (1800–1859) was a well-known nineteenth-century historian and literary critic. Trained as a lawyer, he was also a Whig member of Parliament who, like Lord Russell, spoke in favor of the Reform Bill of 1832. Macaulay first won literary fame with an essay on John Milton. His influential five-volume *History of England* (1849–1861) offered a Whig interpretation of British history, stressing the value of gradual democratic reform.

The Industrial Revolution brought great change to Britain. Large chunks of the population shifted from rural areas to newly emerging urban centers, where the middle class grew and prospered. Britain's political landscape, however, had not changed with the times. Sparsely populated rural areas had disproportionately large representation, while booming new industrial cities like Manchester had none. Some seats in Parliament were completely controlled by a single nobleman or by small self-interested groups. Additionally, landholding and financial restrictions kept much of the population from voting. The result was a Parliament that strongly favored the interests of landowners at the expense of everyone else. The Reform Bill of 1832—often called the First Reform Bill—was an attempt to correct that situation.

▶ **Primary Source: Photography** How does the arrangement of seats in the House of Commons suggest the idea of opposed parties? **[Analyze]**

SPEECH IN FAVOR OF REFORM

Lord John Russell

BACKGROUND When the Whigs came to power in 1830, the number one issue on the party's agenda was reform of Britain's election system. To that end, Lord Russell first proposed the Reform Bill on March 1, 1831. The Tory party opposed the bill, with Sir Robert Peel speaking effectively against it. Extracts from both those speeches are presented here.

On the second reading, the bill passed Parliament's House of Commons by just one vote. Recognizing the need for a greater majority, Lord Grey, the Whig prime minister, dissolved Parliament and called for a new election. The Whigs now won many more seats, and the Reform Bill readily passed in the House of Commons—but it was still rejected in Parliament's other chamber, the House of Lords. Finally, the prime minister forced King William IV to name several new members to the House of Lords—members sympathetic to the reforms—and in July of 1832 the bill passed both Houses of Parliament and became law.

Interior of the Commons Chambers Houses of Parliament, Westminster, United Kingdom

Vocabulary

measure (mezh′ ər) *n.* a bill, resolution, or something else proposed or enacted to improve a situation

grievances (grēv′ əns əz) *n.* circumstances that cause people to complain

Analyzing Rhetorical Devices

Identify the emotionally charged language in the first paragraph of Russell's speech.

An announcement for the first election following the passage of the Reform Bill

I come now to the utmost difficult part of this subject—the explanation of the measure, which, representing the King's Ministers,[1] I am about to propose to the House. . . . The chief grievances of which the people complain are these;—First, the nomination of Members by individuals. Second, the Elections by close Corporations;[2] third, the Expense of Elections. With regard to the first—the nomination by individuals—it may be exercised in one of two ways; either over a place containing scarcely any inhabitants, and with a very extensive right of election, or over a place of wide extent and numerous population, but where the franchise[3] is confined to very few residents. . . . We have addressed ourselves to both these evils, because we have thought it essential to apply a remedy to both; but they must, of course, be dealt with in different ways. With regard to Boroughs[4] where there are scarcely any inhabitants, . . . , it would be evidently a mere farce to take away the right from the person exercising it, and to give it to the borough; and the only Reform that can be justly recommended is, to deprive the borough of its franchise altogether. . . .

But, as I have already said, we do not mean to allow that the remaining boroughs should be in the hands of select Corporations—that is to say, in the possession of a small number of persons, to the exclusion of the great body of the inhabitants, who have property and interest in the place represented. . . . We therefore propose that the right of voting shall be given to householders paying rates[5] for, or occupying a house of, the yearly value of £10. and upwards. Whether he be the proprietor, or whether he only rent the house, the person rated will have the franchise, upon certain conditions hereafter to be named. At the same time, it is not intended to deprive the present electors of their privilege to vote, provided they be resident.

With regard to non-residence, we are of the opinion that it produces much expense, that it is the cause of a great deal of bribery, and that it occasions such manifold and manifest evils, that electors who do not live in a place ought not to be permitted to retain their votes. . . .

AN ACCOUNT

OF

𝕿𝖍𝖊 𝕻𝖗𝖔𝖈𝖊𝖊𝖉𝖎𝖓𝖌𝖘

AT THE

ELECTION OF MEMBERS

FOR THE BOROUGH OF

BURY ST. EDMUND'S,

Dec. 13 AND 14, 1832;

BEING THE FIRST ELECTION FOR THE BOROUGH SINCE THE PASSING OF THE "ACT FOR AMENDING THE REPRESENTATION OF THE PEOPLE."

BURY ST. EDMUND'S:

PRINTED AND PUBLISHED BY WALTER B. FROST.

MDCCCXXXIII.

Vocabulary

electors (ē lek′ tərz) *n.* those who vote

1. **King's Ministers** Having won the last election, members of Parliament from the Whig party become the King's ministers, taking charge of the different departments of government.
2. **close Corporations** small unelected groups of influential people who controlled all the votes in nearly 200 voting districts.
3. **franchise** (fran′ chīz′) *n.* the right to vote.
4. **Boroughs** (bʉr′ ōz) *n.* towns or voting districts that send members to Parliament.
5. **rates** *n.* local property taxes.

I now beg leave to direct the attention of the House to that part of the plan which relates to the expense of long-protracted Polls, and which, while it removes that evil also greatly facilitates the collection of the sense of the elective body. The names of electors are to be enrolled, by which means we hope that the disputes regarding qualification will be in a great measure avoided. We propose that all electors in counties, cities, towns, or boroughs, shall be registered. . . . These regulations are extremely simple, and will prevent all those vexatious and noisy scenes now so often witnessed, regarding disputed votes.

The means of ascertaining who are the electors being made thus easy, there will be no reason why the poll should be kept open for eight days, or for a longer period; and it is proposed that, nearly according to the present law, booths shall be erected for the voters of the different parishes, so that the whole poll may be taken in two days. . . . With respect to the manner of proceeding at Elections, we have it in view to introduce a measure which can hardly fail to be an improvement of the present system. Everybody knows, and must have lamented the enormous expense to which candidates are put in bringing voters to the poll. An election in Yorkshire has been known to cost nearly £150,000; and in Devonshire some of the electors are obliged to travel forty miles over rough cross-roads, which occupies one day; the next is consumed in polling, and the third in returning home; the whole scheme being a manifest source of vast expense, and most inconvenient delay. We propose, therefore, that the poll shall be taken in separate districts, into which the counties are to be divided, those districts to be arranged according to circumstances by the Magistrates at Quarter Sessions. . . .[6]

It is my opinion, therefore, that the whole measure will add to the constituency of the Commons House of Parliament, about half a million of Persons, and these all connected with the property of the country, having a valuable stake amongst us, and deeply interested in our institutions. They are the persons on whom we can depend in any future struggle in which this nation may be engaged, and who will maintain and support Parliament and the Throne in carrying that struggle to a successful termination. I think that those measures will produce a further benefit to the people, by the great incitement which it will occasion to industry and good conduct. For when a man finds, that by industrious exertion, and by punctuality, he will entitle himself to a place in the list of voters, he will have an additional motive to improve his circumstances, and to preserve his character amongst his neighbors. I think, therefore, that in adding to the constituency, we are providing for the moral as well as for the political improvement of the country. . . .

---

6. Magistrates (maj´ is trāts *or* trits) **at Quarter Sessions** judges in English local courts that sit four times a year.

Primary Sources
What do the details in Russell's next-to-last paragraph show about the actual process of holding elections in Russell's day?

Analyzing Rhetorical Devices
How does the phrase "Everybody knows" help persuade the audience to accept the statement that follows?

Vocabulary
constituency (kən stich´ ōo ən sē) *n.* the people making up a body of voters

Comprehension
To whom does Russell propose to give the right to vote?

Lord John Russell's Speech in Favor of Reform **901**

SPEECH AGAINST REFORM

Sir Robert Peel

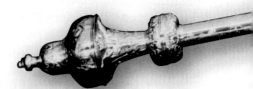

Vocabulary

extravagant (ek strav′ ə gənt) *adj.* going beyond reasonable limits; excessive

Analyzing Rhetorical Devices

In referring to the recent revolution in France, to what emotion does Peel appeal? Explain.

Primary Source

Debate What position on the Reform Bill does Peel state in his last paragraph?

Vocabulary

reverence (rev′ ər əns) *n.* deep respect

I expected that the present ministers would bring in a reform bill on their acceptance of office; but I believe, in my conscience, that the concessions made by them to the popular demands have been far more extensive than was at all necessary. I was not prepared for so extravagant a measure, still less could I have thought that they would venture to bring in so large a measure of reform within three months after they had taken office, and while the country was yet agitated by the events of the French Revolution.[7]

No issue of this discussion can be satisfactory, for, decide as we may, there must be much irreparable evil. I may be obliged to submit by necessity to a plan of reform which I cannot successfully oppose; but believing, as I do, that the people of this country are grossly deceived, grossly deluded, in their expectations of the practical benefits they will derive from reform, I shall not be precluded from declaring my opinion, and opposing that reform as long as I can. . . .

I am satisfied with the constitution under which I have lived hitherto, which I believe is adapted to the wants and habits of the people. I deplore a disposition, which seems too prevalent, to innovate unnecessarily upon all the institutions of the country. I admit, that to serve the sovereign, and the public in an office of honor and dignity, is an object of honorable ambition; but I am ready to sacrifice that object, rather than incur the responsibility of advocating measures which, I believe on my conscience, will tend to the destruction of the best interests of the country. I will continue my opposition to the last, believing, as I do, that this is the first step, not directly to revolution, but to a series of changes which will affect the property, and totally change the character, of the mixed constitution of this country. . . .

On this ground I take my stand, not opposed to a well-considered reform of any of our institutions which need reform, but opposed to this reform in our constitution, because it tends to root up the feelings of respect, the feelings of habitual reverence and attachment, which are the only sure foundations of government. . . .

---

7. French Revolution a second revolution in France, which took place in 1830 and replaced the reactionary monarch Charles X with Louis-Philippe, Duke of Orleans.

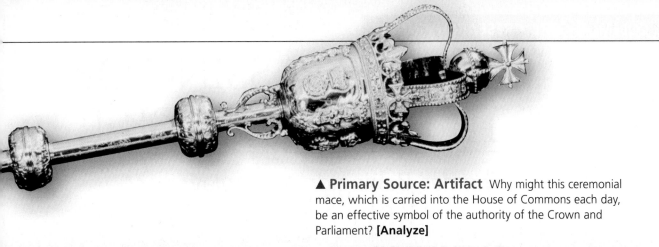

▲ **Primary Source: Artifact** Why might this ceremonial mace, which is carried into the House of Commons each day, be an effective symbol of the authority of the Crown and Parliament? **[Analyze]**

▲ **Primary Source: Art** In the 18th century, British artist William Hogarth created a series of paintings satirizing corrupt politicians. Which details in this depiction of a tavern dinner attended by Whig candidates serve Hogarth's satiric purpose? **[Infer]**

ON THE PASSING OF THE REFORM BILL

Thomas Babington Macaulay

BACKGROUND Macaulay was elected to Parliament in 1830, when his party, the Whigs, began the fight to pass the First Reform Bill. A talented writer and orator, he was in an excellent position to report on the great debate that was raging over the bill. The following letter, written to his good friend and fellow lawyer Thomas Flower Ellis, describes the excitement of the Reform Bill's passage—by just one vote—in Parliament's House of Commons.

Vocabulary
inauspicious (in´ ô spi´ shəs) *adj.* not promising a good outcome; unfavorable

Primary Source
What are two subjects you might learn something about by reading this letter?

Dear Ellis,

    I have little news for you, except what you will learn from the papers as well as from me. It is clear that the Reform Bill must pass, either in this or in another Parliament. The majority of one does not appear to me, as it does to you, by any means inauspicious. We should perhaps have had a better plea for a dissolution if the majority had been the other way. But surely a dissolution under such circumstances would have been a most alarming thing. If there should be a dissolution now there will not be that ferocity in the public mind which there would have been if the House of Commons had refused to entertain the Bill at all.—I confess that, till we had a majority, I was half inclined to tremble at the storm which we had raised. At present I think that we are absolutely certain of victory, and of victory without commotion.

    Such a scene as the division of last Tuesday I never saw, and never expect to see again. If I should live fifty years the impression of it will be as fresh and sharp in my mind as if it had just taken place. It was like seeing Caesar stabbed in the Senate House,[1] or seeing Oliver taking the mace from the table, a sight to be seen only once and never to be forgotten. The crowd overflowed the House in every part. When the strangers were cleared out and the doors locked we had six hundred and eight members present, more by fifty five than

---

1. Caesar (sē´ zər) **stabbed in the Senate House** Emperor Julius Caesar, assassinated in the legislative council of ancient Rome.

ever were at a division before. The Ayes and Noes were like two volleys of cannon from opposite sides of a field of battle. When the opposition went out into the lobby,—an operation by the by which took up twenty minutes or more,—we spread ourselves over the benches on both sides of the House. For there were many of us who had not been able to find a seat during the evening. When the doors were shut we began to speculate on our numbers. Everybody was desponding. "We have lost it. We are only two hundred and eighty at most. I do not think we are two hundred and fifty. They are three hundred. Alderman Thompson has counted them. He says they are two hundred and ninety-nine." This was the talk on our benches. I wonder that men who have been long in parliament do not acquire a better coup d'œil[2] for numbers. The House when only the Ayes were in it looked to me a very fair house,—much fuller than it generally is even

2. **coup d'œil** (kōō dëy´) glance.

▲ **Primary Source**

Art Does Hogarth's portrayal of voters attending the polling booth for an election suggest that the electoral process is fair? Why or why not? **[Infer]**

Comprehension

What scene does Macaulay describe in his letter?

On the Passing of the Reform Bill **905**

Vocabulary Connection

Government Terms

The following terms in the selection refer to British government:

Parliament the bicameral (two-house) legislative body of Britain

dissolution dismissal of Parliament in order to hold new elections; if major legislation fails, the prime minister resigns and Parliament is dissolved.

House of Commons the house of Parliament made up of elected members and led by the prime minister

House of Lords the house of Parliament whose membership is hereditary or by appointment

mace the symbol of the authority of the Speaker of the House of Commons. By demanding the removal of the mace in 1653, Puritan leader Oliver Cromwell (1599–1658) overrode Parliamentary authority and became virtual dictator of England.

Ayes and Noes respectively, votes in favor of and votes against a bill

tellers those appointed to count votes in Parliament

Connect to the Literature

What effect does a knowledge of the terminology have on your ability to understand the message of this work? Explain.

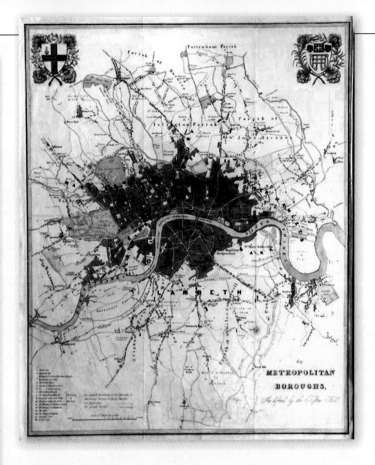

on debates of considerable interest. I had no hope however of three hundred. As the tellers passed along our lowest row on the left hand side the interest was insupportable,—two hundred and ninety-one:—two hundred and ninety-two:—we were all standing up and stretching forward, telling with the tellers. At three hundred there was a short cry of joy, at three hundred and two another—suppressed however in a moment. For we did not yet know what the hostile force might be. We knew however that we could not be severely beaten. The doors were thrown open and in they came. Each of them as he entered brought some different report of their numbers. It must have been impossible, as you may conceive, in the lobby, crowded as they must have been, to form any exact estimate. First we heard that they were three hundred and three—then the number rose to three hundred and ten, then went down to three hundred and seven. Alexander Baring told me that he had counted and that they were three hundred and four. We were all breathless with anxiety, when Charles Wood who stood near the door jumped on a bench and cried out, "They are only three hundred and one." We set up a shout that you might have heard to Charing Cross[3]—waving our hats—stamping against the floor and

---

3. **Charing Cross** London neighborhood some distance from the Houses of Parliament.

clapping our hands. The tellers scarcely got through the crowd:—for the house was thronged up to the table, and all the floor was fluctuating with heads like the pit of a theater. But you might have heard a pin drop as Duncannon read the numbers. Then again the shouts broke out—and many of us shed tears—I could scarcely refrain. And the jaw of Peel fell; and the face of Twiss[4] was as the face of a damned soul; and Herries[5] looked like Judas taking his neck-cloth off for the last operation. We shook hands and clapped each other on the back, and went out laughing, crying, and huzzaing into the lobby. And no sooner were the outer doors opened than another shout answered that within the house. All the passages and the stairs into the waiting rooms were thronged by people who had waited till four in the morning to know the issue. We passed through a narrow lane between two thick masses of them; and all the way down they were shouting and waving their hats; till we got into the open air. I called a cabriolet—and the first thing the driver asked was, "Is the Bill carried?"—"Yes, by one." "Thank God for it, Sir." And away I rode to Grey's Inn—and so ended a scene which will probably never be equalled till the reformed Parliament wants reforming; and that I hope will not be till the days of our grandchildren—till that truly orthodox and apostolical person Dr. Francis Ellis[6] is an archbishop of eighty.

---

4. Twiss Horace Twiss, another Tory who opposed the bill.
5. Herries J. C. Herries, another Tory who opposed the bill.
6. Francis Ellis six-year-old son of Thomas Ellis.

◄ Critical Viewing
The map shows London electoral boroughs as defined by the Reform Bill. Based on your knowledge of the bill, what can you assume about the voters in these boroughs? **APPLY**

Vocabulary
orthodox (ôr´ thə däks´)
adj. conforming to established beliefs

Critical Reading

1. **Key Ideas and Details (a)** To what two historic events does Macaulay compare the scene of division he witnessed in Parliament? **(b) Interpret:** What do these comparisons stress about the scene?

2. **Craft and Structure (a)** What was the outcome of the vote in the House of Commons for the Reform Bill, as reported by Macaulay? **(b) Analyze:** In what ways does he make the procedure exciting and dramatic?

3. **Integration of Knowledge and Ideas (a)** According to Macaulay, what was happening outside the House of Commons during and after the vote? **(b) Infer:** What do these details suggest about the public's view of the vote on the Reform Bill?

Cite textual evidence to support your responses.

Parliamentary Debate ▪ Letter

Comparing Primary Sources

Refer to your Note-Taking Guide to complete these questions.

1. (a) In his opening paragraph, what approach does Sir Robert Peel take to convince others not to support the Reform Bill? **(b)** In contrast, what basic approach does Lord Russell outline in his opening paragraph? **(c)** Which approach seems more effective to you? Why?

2. (a) Using a chart like the one below, compare the language that Russell and Peel use in their speeches. Explain the meaning of technical terms and figurative language and the connotations of charged language. **(b)** In your opinion, which man uses language more persuasively? Why?

Type of Language	Lord John Russell	Sir Robert Peel
Precise (including technical) language		
Charged language		
Imagery and figurative language		
Parallelism		

3. (a) Which rhetorical devices does Macaulay use? **(b)** Compare and contrast his use of these devices with that of the debaters. Does his purpose differ from theirs? Explain.

Vocabulary Acquisition and Use

Using Context Clues Revise each sentence so that the underlined word is used in a logical way.

1. The miser was typically quite <u>extravagant</u> with his money.

2. Most people show <u>reverence</u> for fools.

3. Her broad grin signaled an <u>inauspicious</u> outcome.

Content-Area Vocabulary For each item, choose the lettered word closest in meaning to the vocabulary word. Explain your answers.

1. electors: **(a)** candidates **(b)** voters **(c)** choices **(d)** elite

2. orthodox: **(a)** disobedient **(b)** spiritual **(c)** open-minded **(d)** conservative

3. grievances: **(a)** complaints **(b)** listings **(c)** armor **(d)** funerals

4. measure: **(a)** conclusion **(b)** question **(c)** remedy **(d)** contract

5. constituency: **(a)** candidates **(b)** voters **(c)** democracy **(d)** election

Etymology Study *Orthodox* combines the Greek word part *ortho-*, which means "straight," with the Greek word *doxa*, meaning "opinion." Someone or something that is *orthodox* conforms to the "straight" or established opinion. Why do you think certain dentists are called *orthodontists?*

Common Core State Standards

Reading Informational Text
8. Delineate and evaluate the reasoning in seminal U.S. texts, including the application of constitutional principles and use of legal reasoning and the premises, purposes, and arguments in works of public advocacy. *(p. 909)*

Writing
7. Conduct short as well as more sustained research projects to answer a question or solve a problem; narrow or broaden the inquiry when appropriate; synthesize multiple sources on the subject, demonstrating understanding of the subject under investigation. *(p. 909)*
9. Draw evidence from literary or informational texts to support analysis, reflection, and research. *(p. 909)*

Language
4.a. Use context as a clue to the meaning of a word or phrase.

Research Task

Topic: The Reform Bill Debate

The debate about reform was a battle between Britain's past and future. Greater representation in Parliament would mean greater economic benefits and more rights for many people, especially city dwellers.

Assignment: Stage a debate on the Reform Bill. Several students should take the roles of debating lords and members of the press, and others should act as the "commoners" who evaluate and judge the proceedings.

Plan your research, gather sources, and synthesize information. As a participant or an evaluator, list questions you need to answer, such as "What were the basic positions on reform?" Then, consult reliable primary and secondary sources, including the speeches and letter on pages 899–907, to gather and synthesize the answers.

Evaluate arguments. Review the arguments for and against reform, noting their strengths and weaknesses. Broaden the debate by consulting important United States works on government, such as the first section of Thomas Paine's *Common Sense*. Compare American arguments with those of the reformers. Debaters may incorporate or answer the strongest of them.

Listen responsively and frame inquiries. Listen carefully and respond effectively, whether as a debater or a member of the press. Take notes to identify the positions taken and the evidence in support of those positions.

Assess persuasiveness and formulate sound arguments. Identify each speaker's strong and weak arguments based on content; diction, or word choice; rhetorical strategies, such as appeals to logic or emotion; and delivery. Use a chart like the one shown.

Model: Questioning a Speaker's Appeal to Logic

Fact	Speaker' s Conclusion	My Question
Recent French Revolution	Too soon for major reform in England	Why? Maybe time is just right.

Speak clearly. As a debater, communicate your ideas effectively by using rhetorical devices such as appeals to logic and emotion. Make eye contact and control your speaking rate and volume. Pause for effect. Enunciate words clearly and use purposeful gestures.

The debate on the Reform Bill

RESEARCH TIP

As you do your own research, keep asking yourself, "Is this information my opponent can use against me?" Keep an index of facts and arguments that are "pro and con" (for and against) each issue.

Use a checklist like the one shown to ensure that you have prepared as well as possible.

Research Checklist

- ☐ Have I answered the basic questions about issues and positions?
- ☐ Have I gathered information from reliable sources?
- ☐ Have I organized the information in a useful way?
- ☐ Have I formulated sound arguments?
- ☐ Have I anticipated counter-arguments?

Connecting to the Essential Question These authors address issues surrounding women's role in society. As you read, find comments that suggest which of these two authors was more advanced for her time. Identifying such comments will help you as you explore the Essential Question: **How does literature shape or reflect society?**

Close Reading Focus

Social Commentary; Persuasive Techniques

Social commentary is writing or speech that offers insights into society. Social commentary can be *unconscious*, as when a writer points to a problem caused by social customs without explicitly challenging those customs. The commentary is *conscious* when a writer directly attributes a problem to social customs. As you read these selections, *analyze the political assumptions* about women that they expose, consciously or unconsciously.

Comparing Literary Works Austen and Wollstonecraft address widely different audiences for different purposes—Austen writes advice to her niece, and Wollstonecraft seeks to persuade the general reader. Both, however, use **persuasive techniques** that take the following forms:

- *Logical appeals:* arguments based on sound reasoning
- *Ethical appeals:* appeals to authority that establish credibility
- *Emotional appeals:* arguments that engage the reader's feelings

  As you read, consider each author's purpose for writing. Then, identify how the persuasive appeals each writer uses reflect and support that purpose.

Preparing to Read Complex Texts To **analyze the author's purpose,** or goals, use background knowledge and clues, such as the work's title. Then, determine how the purpose *affects the meaning* of passages. (Wollstonecraft's purpose explains her "indignation" in the first sentence.) Use a chart like the one shown.

Vocabulary

You will encounter the words below in the texts that follow. Copy the words into your notebook. Can you infer which word has a root that means "strong"?

amiable	specious
vindication	fortitude
fastidious	gravity

Common Core State Standards

Reading Informational Text
6. Determine an author's point of view or purpose in a text in which the rhetoric is particularly effective, analyzing how style and content contribute to the power, persuasiveness, or beauty of the text.

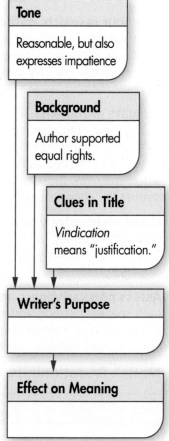

Tone
Reasonable, but also expresses impatience

Background
Author supported equal rights.

Clues in Title
Vindication means "justification."

Writer's Purpose

Effect on Meaning

Jane Austen (1775–1817)

Author of "On Making an Agreeable Marriage"

Modest about her own genius, Jane Austen lived a quiet life devoted to her family. Although she never married, she nonetheless explored love, beauty, and marriage in her six novels, which include *Pride and Prejudice, Emma*, and *Sense and Sensibility*.

A Reserved Life Austen was born in Steventon, Hampshire, the daughter of a clergyman. The seventh of eight children, she was educated largely at home by her father. In her teens, Austen began writing parodies and skits to amuse her family.

An Anonymous Novelist As an adult, Austen put her gift for keen observation to work in her novels. Capturing the absurdities of social life with satirical wit, she makes brilliant observations on human nature. Like most women writers of the time, Austen published anonymously. As her identity became more widely known, she was honored by the Prince Regent a few years before her death.

(1759–1797) Mary Wollstonecraft

Author of *A Vindication of the Rights of Woman*

Mary Wollstonecraft, the mother of writer Mary Wollstonecraft Shelley, is recognized as one of the first major feminists. She wrote revolutionary works attacking the restrictions on women's freedom and education. The movement for women's rights has been influenced by her writings ever since.

A Passionate Educator The daughter of a textile worker and sometime farmer, Mary Wollstonecraft grew up in poverty, yet she pursued an education. She worked at various times as a lady's companion and governess. With her sisters and a friend, she established a girls' school near London. In 1787, she wrote *Thoughts on the Education of Daughters*, criticizing the poor education given to most females of her day.

A Voice for Women In 1790, when the writer Edmund Burke attacked the French Revolution, Wollstonecraft defended it in *A Vindication of the Rights of Man*. Two years later, she produced her most important work, *A Vindication of the Rights of Woman*, a landmark book on women's rights.

On Making an
AGREEABLE
Marriage

Jane Austen

To Fanny Knight [1]

Friday 18–Sunday 20 November 1814

Chawton Nov: 18.—Friday

I feel quite as doubtful as you could be my dearest Fanny as to *when* my Letter may be finished, for I can command very little quiet time at present, but yet I must begin, for I know you will be glad to hear as soon as possible, & I really am impatient myself to be writing something on so very interesting a subject, though I have no hope of writing anything to the purpose.—I shall do very little more I dare say than say over again, what you have said before.—I was certainly a good deal surprised *at first*—as I had no suspicion of any change in your feelings, and I have no scruple in saying that you cannot be in Love. My dear Fanny, I am ready to laugh at the idea—and yet it is no laughing matter to have had you so mistaken as to your own feelings—And with all my heart I wish I had cautioned you on that point when first you spoke to me;—but tho' I did not think you then so *much* in love as you thought yourself, I did consider you as being attached in a degree—quite sufficiently for happiness, as I had no doubt it would increase with opportunity.—And from the time of our being in London together, I thought you really very much in love.— But you certainly are not at all—there is no concealing it.—What strange creatures we are!—It seems as if your being secure of him (as you say yourself) had made you Indifferent.—There was a little disgust I suspect, at the Races—& I do not wonder at it. His expressions then would not do for one who had rather more Acuteness, Penetration & Taste, than Love, which was your case. And yet, after all, I *am* surprised that the change in your feelings should be so great.—He is, just what he ever was, only more evidently & uniformly devoted to *you*. This is all the difference.—How shall we account for it?—My dearest Fanny, I am writing what will not be of the smallest use to you. I am feeling differently every moment, & shall not be able to suggest a single thing that can assist your Mind.—I could lament in one sentence & laugh in the next, but as to Opinion or Counsel I am sure none will [be] extracted worth having from this Letter.—I read yours through the very even[2] I received it—getting away by myself—I could not bear to leave off, when I had once begun.—I was full of curiosity & concern. Luckily Your Aunt C. dined at the other

---

1. Fanny Knight Fanny Austen Knight was the daughter of Austen's brother Edward.
2. even evening.

◄ **Critical Viewing** In what ways does William Hogarth's (1697–1764) satirical depiction of the signing of a wedding contract echo attitudes in Austen's letter? **COMPARE AND CONTRAST**

> *He is just what he ever was, only more evidently & uniformly devoted to you.*

Analyzing the Author's Purpose

What is Austen's purpose in claiming she has "no hope of writing anything to the purpose"?

Comprehension

What news from Fanny prompts Austen's reaction?

Social Commentary

What do these details reveal about the criteria for judging a suitor in Austen's day?

My dear Fanny, the more I write about him the warmer my feelings become...

Social Commentary

What assumptions about responsibility in courtship does this passage reveal?

house, therefore I had not to maneuver away from *her;*—& as to anybody else, I do not care.—Poor dear Mr J. P!^{3}—Oh! dear Fanny, Your mistake has been one that thousands of women fall into. He was the *first* young Man who attached himself to you. That was the charm, & most powerful it is.—Among the multitudes however that make the same mistake with Yourself, there can be few indeed who have so little reason to regret it;—*his* Character & *his* attachment leave you nothing to be ashamed of.—Upon the whole, what is to be done? You certainly *have* encouraged him to such a point as to make him feel almost secure of you—you have no inclination for any other person—His situation in life, family, friends, & above all his Character—his uncommonly amiable mind, strict principles, just notions, good habits—*all* that *you* know so well how to value, *All* that really is of the first importance—everything of this nature pleads his cause most strongly.—You have no doubt of his having superior Abilities—he has proved it at the University—he is I dare say such a Scholar as your agreeable, idle Brothers would ill bear a comparison with.—Oh! my dear Fanny, the more I write about him, the warmer my feelings become, the more strongly I feel the sterling worth of such a young Man & the desirableness of your growing in love with him again. I recommend this most thoroughly.—There *are* such beings in the World perhaps, one in a Thousand, as the Creature You & I should think perfection, where Grace & Spirit are united to Worth, where the Manners are equal to the Heart & Understanding, but such a person may not come in your way, or if he does, he may not be the eldest son of a Man of Fortune, the Brother of your particular friend, & belonging to your own County.—Think of all this Fanny. Mr J. P.– has advantages which do not often meet in one person. His only fault indeed seems Modesty. If he were less modest, he would be more agreeable, speak louder & look Impudenter;—and is not it a fine Character, of which Modesty is the only defect?—I have no doubt that he will get more lively & more like yourselves as he is more with you;—he will catch your ways if he belongs to you. And as to there being any objection from his *Goodness,* from the danger of his becoming even Evangelical,^{4} I cannot admit *that.* I am by no means convinced that we ought not all to be Evangelicals, & am at least persuaded that they who are so from Reason & Feeling, must be happiest & safest.—Do not be frightened from the connection by your Brothers having most wit. Wisdom is better than Wit, & in the long run will certainly have the laugh on her side; & don't be frightened by the idea of his acting more strictly up to the precepts of the New Testament than others.—And now, my dear Fanny, having written so much on one side of the question, I shall turn round & entreat you not to commit yourself farther, & not

---

3. **Mr J. P.** Fanny's suitor.
4. **Evangelical** of or relating to a group of earnest Church of England members active in social reform movements at the time of the letter.

Close Reading Activities

On Making an Agreeable Marriage • from *A Vindication of the Rights of Woman*

Literary Analysis

Common Core State Standards

Language
1.a. Apply the understanding that usage is a matter of convention, can change over time, and is sometimes contested.

1. **Key Ideas and Details** What unconscious **social commentary** does Austen's letter offer about the pressures that once limited women's choices?
2. **Key Ideas and Details** Which social and political assumptions about men and women does Wollstonecraft challenge in *A Vindication of the Rights of Woman*?
3. **Key Ideas and Details** Which assumptions about men's motives and desires does Wollstonecraft incorporate into her argument?
4. **Comparing Literary Works** Compare the kinds of appeals used by Wollstonecraft and Austen in a chart like the one shown.

Logic	Ethics	Emotion

5. **Comparing Literary Works** How does each writer's audience affect her choice of **persuasive techniques?**
6. **Integration of Knowledge and Ideas** Compare Wollstonecraft's and Austen's purposes in writing, explaining the clues you used to **analyze the author's purpose** in each work.
7. **Integration of Knowledge and Ideas** Explain how each author's purpose affected the meaning of a passage.

Vocabulary Acquisition and Use

From the vocabulary list on page 910, find a **synonym**—a word with the same or similar meaning—or an **antonym**—a word with the opposite meaning—for each of these words. Then, write an original sentence using each antonym or synonym pair.

1. justification
2. lightness
3. false
4. disagreeable
5. picky
6. cowardice

Writing to Sources

Explanatory Text Relatives still give well-meaning advice today, but they are more likely to do so in **e-mails** than in letters.

- Rewrite Austen's letter to her niece as an e-mail, keeping her ideas.
- Update the word choices, syntax, and situation to reflect modern times. For example, consider how you would update this sentence to reflect modern usage: "I read yours through the very even I received it . . . I could not bear to leave off, when I had once begun."

Multimedia Presentation of an Argument

Common Core State Standards

Writing
1. Write arguments to support claims in an analysis of substantive topics or texts, using valid reasoning and relevant and sufficient evidence.
2.a. Introduce a topic; organize complex ideas, concepts, and information so that each new element builds on that which precedes it to create a unified whole; include formatting, graphics, and multimedia when useful to aiding comprehension.
2.b. Develop the topic thoroughly by selecting the most significant and relevant facts, extended definitions, concrete details, quotations, or other information and examples appropriate to the audience's knowledge of the topic.
6. Use technology, including the Internet, to produce, publish, and update individual or shared writing products in response to ongoing feedback, including new arguments or information.
7. Conduct short as well as more sustained research projects to answer a question or solve a problem; narrow or broaden the inquiry when appropriate.

Argumentative Text Written text is only one way of communicating an argument. Claims and evidence can be communicated through a wide variety of other media, including film, radio, television, digital technology, and the Internet. In a multimedia presentation of an argument, a writer organizes words, images, and sounds into a coherent, informative, and lively presentation. Follow the steps in this workshop to create a compelling multimedia presentation of an argument.

Assignment Research, draft, revise, and present a multimedia presentation in which you present and defend a claim on a topic that is meaningful to you.

What to Include Your presentation should have these elements:

- an effective combination of words, images, and sounds
- a clear, consistent organization
- strong reasons and evidence, as well as consideration of counterclaims
- a coherent, well-paced flow of sounds, images, and information
- a variety of media appropriate to each aspect of the topic
- a strong, memorable conclusion

To preview the criteria on which your multimedia presentation may be assessed, see the rubric on page 927.

Media Types and Sources

Presentations can include existing media as well as media that you create yourself. You can use multimedia software to assemble your media elements. Ask your teacher which programs he or she recommends.

	Sources of Existing Media	Hardware to Generate New Media	Software to Edit Media
text	books, magazines, newspapers, Web sites, CD-ROMs, e-mails	keyboard; scanner; printer	word processor; multimedia software
photographs	books, magazines, newspapers, Web sites, CD-ROMs	digital camera; scanner; printer	photo-editing software
illustrations	books, magazines, newspapers, Web sites, CD-ROMs	keyboard; graphics tablet; scanner; printer	graphics programs
movies	television, DVDs, videos, Web sites, CD-ROMs	digital video camera	digital editor; animation software
sound	radio, CDs, Web sites, CD-ROMs	microphone; digital instruments	sound/music editor

Prewriting and Planning

Choosing Your Topic

Use one of these strategies to choose an appropriate topic:

- **Conduct a media flip-through.** Browse available sources, including magazines, television programs, and the Internet. As you scan for a topic, keep in mind that your presentation should present a valid claim and also include a variety of media.

- **List and itemize.** Begin with an issue that you care about, such as science trends, consumer issues, or environmental topics. Then, jot down specific ideas that come to mind. Review your list, considering the media you might use to present your ideas. Choose a topic.

Broad Category	Nature
Specific Ideas	National Parks: Yosemite, Zion, Grand Canyon
Media	slides and video of the park, music, audio of animal sounds park visitors might hear, video interviews
Claim	National parklands are a valuable national resource and must be maintained.

Developing Your Argument

Gather evidence. Find facts, statistics, and other relevant evidence to support your claim. Keep a list of ideas for media that might work well with each major piece of evidence you plan to use in your argument.

Review your research. Review your notes and ideas for media. Select the strongest ideas, including supporting arguments and counterarguments, to develop for your multimedia presentation.

Gathering Details

Organize your material. After you have gathered a variety of media, outline your presentation. Identify the media elements that best explain, illustrate, or set a mood for each aspect of your argument. Do a rough outline like the one shown, indicating where you expect to use each element.

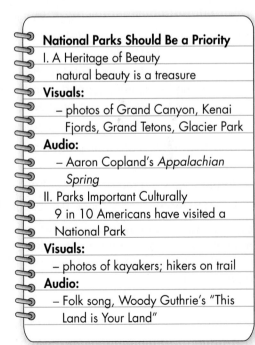

National Parks Should Be a Priority

I. A Heritage of Beauty
   natural beauty is a treasure

Visuals:
   – photos of Grand Canyon, Kenai Fjords, Grand Tetons, Glacier Park

Audio:
   – Aaron Copland's *Appalachian Spring*

II. Parks Important Culturally
   9 in 10 Americans have visited a National Park

Visuals:
   – photos of kayakers; hikers on trail

Audio:
   – Folk song, Woody Guthrie's "This Land is Your Land"

Drafting

Shaping Your Presentation

Select and position media elements. Your presentation should communicate information through both text and media elements. Using a two-column planning chart will help you to be sure that you achieve an effective balance.

Text	Audio and Video

Follow a logical flow and focus. Before you draft your presentation, try rehearsing it in your mind to make sure that your reasons and evidence follow a logical arc, or sequence. It can be tempting to include too many media elements. Make sure that each of your elements is relevant. Remember that your target duration should be ten to fifteen minutes. Create a timed outline to plan how much time you will devote to each media element.

Providing Elaboration

Consider both artistry and argumentation. As you draft, aim to create not only an interesting experience for your audience, but also a sound argument. As part of your argument, be sure to include a counterclaim and refute it, pointing out its strengths and weaknesses. Conclude your presentation with your strongest reason and evidence, supported by well-chosen images and audio.

Make sure that your presentation flows logically from idea to idea and that each media element supports the focus and mood. These tips will help you avoid some common problems.

Avoid: a series of photographs showing the same scene

Improvement: a photograph of a scene, followed by a map showing the scene's location

Avoid: one song repeated throughout the entire presentation

Improvement: shorter music clips or sound effects that set specific moods

Clarify and frame your media. As you introduce significant new multimedia elements, be sure to include an explanation so your audience can follow the connection. Transitional clauses can help you introduce media elements:

- As this chart indicates…
- In this footage, the speaker makes it clear that…
- Notice how this diagram connects to the photograph…

Writers on Writing

Elizabeth McCracken On the Writing Process

> Elizabeth McCracken is the author of "Creating a Legend" (p. 728).

I am a very inefficient writer. I do thousands of drafts and throw out a lot of pages. I keep a journal when I write, a place I can play around with ideas, and I often write a page in the voice of a minor character. I tried it with the librarian as I was writing *The Giant's House*. It turned out she wouldn't shut up. She was cranky and talkative and ended up narrating the entire story. The passage here is one of the oldest passages in the book, which is maybe why I'm fond of it. All around it, I tore out pages and pages and pages—I bet I write at least twice as many pages as ever gets into a book—and somehow it always worked.

"I keep a journal when I write, a place I can play around with ideas."
—*Elizabeth McCracken*

from *The Giant's House*

People think librarians are unromantic, unimaginative. This is not true. We are people whose dreams run in particular ways. Ask a mountain climber what he feels when he sees a mountain; a lion tamer what goes through his mind when he meets a new lion; a doctor confronted with a beautiful malfunctioning body. The idea of a library full of books, the books full of knowledge, fills me with fear and love and courage and endless wonder. I knew I would be a librarian in college as a student assistant at a reference desk, watching those lovely people at work. "I don't think there's such a book—" a patron would begin, and then the librarian would hand it to them, that very book.

> I worried about what my fellow librarians would make of my librarian, who's pretty stereotypically uptight and tweedy. I tried to make up for it by making her very romantic.

> I hear my sentences when I write them, and I love semi-colons—they're just another kind of music.

> Sometimes phrases stick in my mind for years before they come out in a book.

Revising

Revising Your Overall Structure

Improve your pacing. Practice your presentation, noting places where your pacing feels too rapid, too slow, or incompatible with the technology you are using. You may need to add more text to explain or support a point, or cut a media element that seems irrelevant.

Common Core State Standards

Writing

1.c. Use words, phrases, and clauses as well as varied syntax to link the major sections of the text, create cohesion, and clarify the relationships between claim(s) and reasons, between reasons and evidence, and between claim(s) and counterclaims.

Student Model: Revising for Smooth Flow

(Cue AUDIO) Many roads within National Parks are falling into disrepair,	AUDIO: sound effects, including the sound of rocks falling or a car braking
★ (Show SLIDE C) and some are changing from scenic to dangerous. Hiking trails need maintenance, too.	SLIDE C: Picture of eroded roadway
Show SLIDE C; pause, then back to (Show SLIDE B)	SLIDE B: Sign reading "Trail Closed"

The student postpones showing Slide C to make the delivery smoother and to provide better pacing for the audience.

Revising Your Media

Evaluate your media and delivery. Rehearsal is vital for a successful presentation. Do a run-through, focusing on smooth oral delivery and accurate matching of media elements to reasons and evidence. Become comfortable with your script so that you can maintain eye contact with your audience and not read word for word.

Revise media elements. You may decide to improve media elements to make them more effective. Here are some common revisions:

- Shorten video segments that feel too long.
- Add labels or captions to art to emphasize important evidence.
- Crop photos to focus more closely on the subject.
- Adjust sound levels of audio narration or music.

Peer Review: Hold a test run for a small group. Ask them to use the Evaluation Form shown here. Talk with your viewers about elements that were confusing or ineffective and revise accordingly.

Evaluation

Rate from 1 to 5 (5 = very; 1 = not at all)

____ How clear is the overall claim?

____ How logical is the organization of reasons and evidence?

____ How appropriate are the media elements?

____ How smooth are transitions between elements?

____ How effectively is the running time used?

Which media element is most effective?

_____

Which media element is least effective?

_____

What change would most improve the presentation?

_____

Developing Your Style

Integrating Media to Support Your Argument

It is important that all of the media elements work together. Use a chart like the one shown to help you evaluate the integration of these elements.

Media Element	Idea It Expresses or Supports	Is the idea clear? If not, consider how you can improve the way you handle this element or if you should replace it with something else.
Audio interview with Park Ranger	The public values our National Parks, but money is needed to keep them safe and enjoyable.	Clear
Video of heavy equipment clearing land	Development close to park lands can have an adverse effect on the park's environment.	Not very clear; add a line of narration to explain the connection.
Mozart's Requiem Mass in D Minor	Conveys a sense of loss and sadness	Too mournful and not connected to America; a better choice would be "America the Beautiful," which is more inspiring.

Find It in Your Reading

Review the Student Model on page 926.

1. Locate elements of the presentation that work together.

2. In particular, consider how the audio and video work together.

Apply It to Your Writing

Review the script for your multimedia presentation.

1. Evaluate each media element you have included in your presentation. Ask yourself, "Why did I include this element?"

2. Decide whether each element clearly connects to your argument. Consider adding narration and text labels or changing the order of media elements in order to make the ideas clearer.

3. Experiment with different combinations of images, music, and text. Preview combinations for a group and see if they work.

Student Model: Grace Ramsay, Maplewood, NJ

Preserve Our National Treasures; Fund Our National Parks

Text

Audio and Video

[Cue AUDIO.] American's national park-lands are awe-inspiring. [Cue VIDEO SLIDESHOW.] Ardent naturalists like John Muir fought to establish national protected parklands in the mid 1800s with the idea that they would be preserved for all time. [Fade music.]

AUDIO: Shaker theme from Copland's *Appalachian Spring*
VIDEO: rapid dissolve from one slide to the next: National Park vistas of Yellowstone, Glacier National Park, Yosemite, and Denali

> Stirring theme music and a sampling of scenery establish the tone and help to develop the claim of the presentation.

[Cue SLIDE A.] Hard economic times require sacrifices from everyone. However, budget cuts to the National Park Service have been deep. As this chart shows [Cue SLIDE A; pause], budget cuts lead to fewer services and less maintenance. [Cue SLIDE B] [Cue SLIDE C]. Yet 9 out of 10 Americans have visited a National Park. These destinations are an important part of our lives and memories.

SLIDE A: chart showing cuts to National Park Service Budget

SLIDE B: sign reading "Trail Closed"
SLIDE C: picture of crumbling roadway

> The text, audio, and visual elements clarify the relationship between the claim, reasons, and evidence.

[Cue AUDIO.] Opponents may say there are more pressing issues, but stewardship of our glorious natural treasures is worth the cost. Our parks benefit everyone, including local economies.

AUDIO: Woodie Guthrie's "This Land Is Your Land"
SLIDE D: pictures of outdoor activities: kayaking, hiking

> Grace chooses music to remind the audience of the connection between Americans and the land.

> Information is consistently organized, with each new main idea illustrated by a slide.

[Cue MUSIC.] [Cue VIDEO SLIDESHOW.] As John Muir, one of the early proponents of America's parks, once said, "In every walk with nature one receives far more than he seeks." We should preserve this natural heritage for the generations that will follow.

AUDIO: same as at opening
VIDEO SLIDESHOW: same as at opening

> Both the audiovisual and textual parts of Grace's conclusion are strong and memorable.

Editing and Proofreading

Check your presentation for errors in grammar, usage, punctuation, and spelling.

Focus on proper nouns and titles. Double-check the capitalization of names and places in your text elements, including labels and handouts.

Focus on spelling. Most words ending with the sound *seed* end with the spelling *cede,* as in *concede.* Three English words end in *ceed: exceed, proceed,* and *succeed.* Review your essay, circling words that end with this sound. Make sure your spelling of these words is correct.

Spiral Review: Conventions Earlier in this unit, you learned about correct subject-verb and pronoun-antecedent agreement. Check your presentation to make sure you have used these conventions correctly.

Publishing, Presenting, and Reflecting

Consider one of the following ways to share your writing:

Stage a showing. Deliver your multimedia presentation to your class. Speak slowly and confidently, and allow time for questions and answers.

Post your presentation. Create a final version of your report using multimedia software and post it to a class or school file-sharing site. If possible, invite visitors to post comments, and address readers' concerns or questions by posting updates with new evidence or additional arguments.

Reflect on your writing. Jot down your thoughts about creating a multimedia presentation. Answer these questions: What did you learn about presenting an argument using audio and visual elements as well as words? What surprised you about presenting the material to an audience?

Rubric for Self-Assessment

Evaluate your multimedia presentation using the following criteria and rating scale.

Common Core State Standards

Writing

1.a. Introduce precise, knowledgeable claim(s), establish the significance of the claim(s), distinguish the claim(s) from alternate or opposing claims, and create an organization that logically sequences claim(s), counterclaims, reasons, and evidence.

1.c. Use words, phrases, and clauses as well as varied syntax to link the major sections of the text, create cohesion, and clarify the relationships between claim(s) and reasons, between reasons and evidence, and between claim(s) and counterclaims.

5. Develop and strengthen writing as needed by editing, focusing on addressing what is most significant for a specific purpose and audience.

6. Use technology, including the Internet, to produce, publish, and update individual or shared writing products in response to ongoing feedback, including new arguments or information.

Language

2. Demonstrate command of the conventions of standard English capitalization, punctuation, and spelling when writing.

3. Apply knowledge of language to make effective choices for meaning or style.

Criteria	Rating Scale
	not very *very*
Purpose/Focus: How clearly do all of your media elements present your argument?	1 2 3 4
Organization: How well do you organize the presentation of your claim, reasons, and evidence?	1 2 3 4
Development of Ideas/Elaboration: How well do you integrate video and audio elements to support your claims?	1 2 3 4
Language: How effective are the words, phrases, and clauses that you use?	1 2 3 4
Conventions: How correct are the grammar, spelling, and punctuation in your presentation materials?	1 2 3 4

Analyze a Non-Print Political Advertisement

 **Common Core
State Standards**

Speaking and Listening
3. Evaluate a speaker's point
of view, reasoning, and use
of evidence and rhetoric,
assessing the stance, premises,
links among ideas, word
choice, points of emphasis,
and tone used.

During an election year, you may see advertisements promoting political
candidates in many different forms of media. Non-print political advertisements air on television, the radio, and the Internet. Because they reach a
vast audience, these ads can exert great influence on voters' decisions.

Identify Purpose of Political Advertising

Learning how political ads are designed will help you make informed
political choices. The goal of a political ad, like that of any ad, is to sell
something. However, instead of selling a product, a political ad sells a
candidate's ideas and image. Political ads create name recognition and cast
a candidate in a favorable light—or, in an attack ad, cast an opponent in a
negative light.

Negative Techniques Used in Political Ads

Campaign strategists determine advertising tactics based on their candidate's position in the polls. If a candidate is leading, strategists may simply
tout his or her accomplishments. When a race is very close, you may see
ads using **propaganda,** biased content that damages an opponent's credibility or image. Some ads use **wrong facts** to intentionally misrepresent
an opponent's stance on an issue. Other times, ads use **logical fallacies,**
appeals that sound convincing but are based on faulty reasoning.

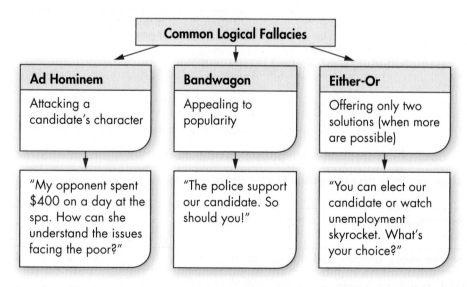

Common Logical Fallacies

Ad Hominem
Attacking a
candidate's character

"My opponent spent
$400 on a day at the
spa. How can she
understand the issues
facing the poor?"

Bandwagon
Appealing to
popularity

"The police support
our candidate. So
should you!"

Either-Or
Offering only two
solutions (when more
are possible)

"You can elect our
candidate or watch
unemployment
skyrocket. What's
your choice?"

Persuasive Techniques

Other strategies used in a non-print political ad include the following:

- *Editing*: arranging images and sound to create certain effects. A TV clip edited to show a candidate shaking hands with rival politicians creates the impression that he or she can negotiate successfully.
- *Camera Angles:* the direction from which a camera operator shoots images. A low-angle shot makes a person appear tall and confident.
- *Camera Shots:* different ways of framing a subject on camera. A close-up may make an ad feel more personal and intimate.
- *Symbols:* images with positive or negative associations. An ad that depicts a candidate's family suggests he or she understands issues affecting voters with families.
- *Charged Language:* words that carry very positive or negative connotations. A candidate might describe an opponent as a "waffler" to make him or her seem inconsistent.
- *Tone:* the general attitude conveyed by the words used. A phrase like "rising to the challenge" helps create a positive tone.

Activities: Analyze Non-Print Political Ads

Comprehension and Collaboration For both activities, use an evaluation form like the one shown below.

A. Watch a recent political ad on TV or online. Use the evaluation form to analyze the persuasive techniques included in the ad.

B. Using the Internet, find and analyze two opposing non-print political ads from a historical campaign.

Evaluating a Political Ad

Ad Title:_____
Name of Candidate:_____
Year of Production:_____
Primary Audience [pick one]: *Sympathetic* ☐   *Neutral* ☐   *Hostile* ☐
What makes you think so? Tone ☐   Language ☐   Images ☐
  Other_____
Visual and Sound Techniques: Angles ☐   Symbols ☐   Charged Language ☐
  Other_____
Negative Techniques: Yes ☐   No ☐
  If Yes, which ones? _____
How many of the claims made in this ad are true? Consult an unbiased
  source to find out._____

Language Study

Etymology of Scientific, Medical, and Mathematical Terms

 **Common Core State Standards**

Language

4.a. Use context as a clue to the meaning of a word or phrase.

4.c. Consult general and specialized reference materials (e.g., dictionaries, glossaries, thesauruses), both print and digital, to find the pronunciation of a word or determine or clarify its precise meaning, its part of speech, its etymology, or its standard usage.

During the Renaissance, English scholars gained much of their knowledge on medicine, mathematics, and science from ancient Greek and Roman texts. As they absorbed information from these works, the English naturally adopted many of the words they found. From the Renaissance onward, scholars have used these classical languages to describe new scientific and mathematical discoveries.

Study these other affixes and roots commonly found in science and math.

Prefixes	Roots	Suffixes
anthrop- (Greek): human *bio-* (Greek): life *cosmo-* (Greek): universe, world *epi-* (Greek): upon, over *equi-* (Latin): equal *geo-* (Greek): Earth *pseudo-* (Greek): false *quadr-* (Latin): four *thermo-* (Greek): heat	*angle* (Latin): intersecting lines *derma* (Greek): skin *morph* (Greek): form *photo* (Greek): light *pod* (Greek): foot *sphere* (Greek): ball, globe *stell* (Latin): star	*-al* (Latin): characterized by *-ar* (Latin): of or relating to, resembling *-ic* (Greek): of or relating to *-logy* (Greek): science, theory, study *-meter* (Greek): measure *-oid* (Greek): resembling, like *-phobia* (Greek): fear *-ty* (Anglo-Saxon): multiplied by ten

Practice

Directions: Combine the indicated affix or root with others from the chart to create additional terms related to science or math. Define them, using the meanings given in the chart. Check your definitions in a dictionary.

1. thermo
2. bio
3. geo
4. angle
5. sphere
6. anthrop

Directions: Provide an explanation for each question.

7. Why might an amoeba be called a *pseudopod?*
8. What is an *equilateral* triangle?
9. Why might a *photophobic* stay in the dark?
10. How can you protect your *epidermis?*

Vocabulary Acquisition and Use: Context Clues

Context clues are words or phrases that help readers clarify the meanings of unfamiliar words in a text. By using context clues, you can determine the word or words that complete a sentence. Sentence Completion questions appear in most standardized tests. In these types of questions, you are given sentences with one or more missing words. Your task is to choose the correct word or words to complete each sentence logically. Try this strategy: (1) Read the entire sentence and look for signal words that indicate whether a missing word is positive or negative. (2) Scan the answer choices and cross out those that do not fit your criteria. (3) Test the rest of the answer choices in the sentence.

Practice

This exercise is modeled after the Sentence Completion exercises that appear in the Critical Reading section of the SAT.

Directions: Each of the following sentences is missing one or two words. Choose the word or set of words that best completes each sentence.

> **Test-Taking Tip**
> Eliminate words you know are wrong. Test the rest in the sentence to determine what fits best.

1. William Blake studied painting at the Royal Academy yet was not considered one of the __?__ of art in his time.
   - **A.** sepulchers
   - **B.** roused
   - **C.** arbiters
   - **D.** torrid
   - **E.** morose

2. Blake was a visionary, but he lived in __?__ conditions, often at the edge of poverty.
   - **A.** sordid
   - **B.** vintage
   - **C.** orthodox
   - **D.** copious
   - **E.** ancestral

3. He existed on meager sales and the __?__ of his patrons.
   - **A.** reverence
   - **B.** symmetry
   - **C.** mundane
   - **D.** fortitude
   - **E.** recompense

4. Some of Blake's illustrations are childlike and __?__ while others are marked by __?__ and darkness.
   - **A.** incitement . . . sinuous
   - **B.** presumption . . . amiable
   - **C.** winsome . . . pathos
   - **D.** avarice . . . ungenial
   - **E.** platitudes . . . teeming

5. Blake used __?__ brushwork in his precise watercolors to create apocalyptic images, including __?__, and otherworldly creatures, giving shape to his poetic vision.
   - **A.** stagnant . . . vindications
   - **B.** expiated . . . discretions
   - **C.** blithe . . . requiems
   - **D.** acceded . . . discretions
   - **E.** fastidious . . . phantasms

From Text to Understanding

You have studied each part of Unit 4 as a set of connected texts. In this workshop, you will have the chance to further explore the fundamental connections among these texts and to deepen your essential understanding of the literature and its social and historical context.

PART 1: Fantasy and Reality

Writing: Argumentative Essay The relationship between fantasy and reality can be explored in the selections in Part 1. For example, Blake's "Chimney Sweep" blends the brutal reality of children's labor with the fantasy of release. In the Anchor Text, "The Introduction to *Frankenstein*," Mary Shelley explains the real event that inspired her startling work of fantasy. As you review the works in Part 1, take notes on the elements of fantasy and realism you see in these texts.

Assignment: Using Shelley's "Introduction to *Frankenstein*" as well as other works in Part 1, develop and defend a claim that explores how the authors incorporate fantasy and reality in their work. Consider how fantasy and reality often reverberate within the same text. As you write, refer to the notes you took as you reviewed the selections.

    Example: Literary works of the early nineteenth century illustrate how fantasy can be used to communicate feelings about reality.

Write a claim. In your introduction, include a clearly worded claim about the works. Identify the authors and selections you will discuss, and explain how fantasy and reality are used together to explore the texts' themes.

Provide support. Support your points by using quotations from the text. Make sure your textual evidence is clearly related to your argument.

Use transitions. Include strong transitions so readers can follow your argument within a paragraph as well as between paragraphs. Words such as *furthermore* extend your argument, while phrases such as *on the other hand* offer an alternative viewpoint.

Use precise words. As you write, experiment with targeted word choice. Words such as *colloquial*, *factual* and *pedestrian* might apply to reality and *Gothic*, *whimsical*, or *visionary* might pertain to fantasy.

**Common Core
State Standards**

Writing

1. Write arguments to support claims in an analysis of substantive topics or texts, using valid reasoning and relevant and sufficient evidence.

7. Conduct short as well as more sustained research projects to answer a question (including a self-generated question) or solve a problem; narrow or broaden the inquiry when appropriate; synthesize multiple sources on that subject, demonstrating understanding of the subject under investigation.

Speaking and Listening

3. Present information, findings, and supporting evidence, conveying a clear and distinct perspective, such that listeners can follow the line of reasoning, alternative or opposing perspectives are addressed, and the organization, development, substance, and style are appropriate to purpose, audience, and a range of formal and informal tasks.

Writing Checklist

☐ Clear claim

    Notes: _____

☐ Relevant textual evidence

    Notes: _____

☐ Effective transitions

    Notes: _____

☐ Strong vocabulary

    Notes: _____

PART 2: Lyric Poetry

Research: Slide Show/Poster Series Romanticism was the defining philosophy of early nineteenth-century Britain. Wordsworth's use of common language to celebrate nature was a revolutionary development in poetry. The cultural impact of the Romantic movement was profound: consider, for example, the lasting effects of the lyric poets' embrace of nature, and the introduction of the darkly brooding Byronic hero. The influence of Romanticism is visible in our culture today. Review the selections, especially the poetry by George Gordon, Lord Byron, along with background material in Unit 4. Consider the elements of Romanticism that are exemplified by the texts.

Assignment: Create a slide show or poster series showing a specific element of Romanticism in our culture today. You might opt for the rebellious hero, a sublime view of nature, or the expression of deep emotion. Consider the ways in which that Romantic ideal resonates in today's culture, including media, fashion, and the arts. Find examples in advertising, movies, television, and print media.

Use the Research Checklist as you prepare your slide show or posters. Accompany your visual examples with a script that explains the Romantic image and the philosophy behind it. Analyze the way in which the Romantic theme or image is used in modern society to inform, entertain, or persuade.

PART 3: The Reaction to Society's Ills

Listening and Speaking: Oral Report In addition to being an age of poetic expression, the Victorian era was also an age of reform. Industrialization and other modernizing forces were changing Britain's people and institutions. As you review the Anchor Texts, "On Making an Agreeable Marriage" and the excerpt from *A Vindication of the Rights of Women*, as well as the documents on the Parliament Reform Bill, think about how a society changes. Based on the perspectives offered in these texts, can you draw parallels between the Victorian era and our society?

Assignment: Working in small groups, deliver an oral report in which you analyze the excerpt from Mary Wollstonecraft's *A Vindication of the Rights of Women*. Discuss the central message of the piece. What did Wollstonecraft have to say about the position of women in society in 1792? Do her ideas seem relevant or out of date when applied to women today? In your report, be sure to do the following:

- Clearly identify the issues outlined by Wollstonecraft.
- Articulate Wollstonecraft's ideas about the issues.
- Effectively tie her thoughts to contemporary issues.

Present your ideas to the class and invite feedback and questions.

Research Checklist

☐ **Identify Romantic elements**
Decide which Romantic idea, image, or attitude you will explore.

☐ **Describe Romanticism**
Explain how the theme or image is representative of Romanticism.

☐ **Locate images**
Use drawings, photographs, illustrations or other images that reflect the Romantic element.

☐ **Explain influence today**
Analyze how this Romantic theme or image is used in today's culture. Capture the connection between Romanticism then and now.

☐ **Design slide show or posters**
Organize your work in an interesting, logical series of slides or posters. Include relevant, creative titles.

Test-Taking Practice

Reading Test: Long Reading Passages

The **long reading passages** of standardized tests present more substantial texts that require extended concentration. Passages can be as long as 850 words and can present narrative, persuasive, and expository styles. You should spend more time on answering the questions than reading the passages. You must read purposefully to cover the material, to which you can later return for details.

 Common Core State Standards

RI.11-12.1, RI.11-12.2, RI.11-12.3, RI.11-12.4, RI.11-12.6; L.11-12.1, L.11-12.2, L.11-12.3, L.11-12.4.a
[For the full wording of the standards, see the standards chart in the front of your textbook.]

Practice

The following exercise is modeled after the SAT Long Passage Critical Reading section. This section usually includes 48 questions.

Directions: Read the following passage, taken from *A Vindication of the Rights of Woman* by Mary Wollstonecraft. Then, choose the best answer to each question.

> Indeed the word *masculine* is only a bugbear; there is little reason to fear that women will acquire too much courage or fortitude, for their apparent inferiority with respect to bodily strength must render them in some degree dependent on men in the various relations of life; but
> 5   why should it be increased by prejudices that give a sex to virtue, and confound simple truths with sensual reveries?
>   Women are, in fact, so much degraded by mistaken notions of female excellence, that I do not mean to add a paradox when I assert that this artificial weakness produces a propensity to tyrannize and gives
> 10   birth to cunning, the natural opponent of strength, which leads them to play off those contemptible infantine airs that undermine esteem even whilst they excite desire. Let me become more chaste and modest, and if women do not grow wiser in the same ratio it will be clear that they have weaker understandings. It seems scarcely necessary to say that
> 15   I now speak of the sex in general. Many individuals have more sense than their male relatives; and, as nothing preponderates where there is a constant struggle for an equilibrium without it has naturally more gravity, some women govern their husbands without degrading themselves, because intellect will always govern.

Strategy

Identify opinions.

- **Scan the passage.** Notice "I" statements and charged language. These may indicate opinions.

- **Determine point of view.** Identify what the author wants readers to feel, understand, or do.

- Use this information to guide your answer choices.

1. Which of the following is the best statement of the overall purpose of the author's commentary in this passage?
   A. Most men are stronger than women and thus dominate.
   B. Some women dominate because they are smarter.
   C. Women are held back by a fear of their powers.
   D. Women should become more chaste and modest toward men.
   E. Men fear that women will gain too much strength and courage.

2. Which of the following persuasive techniques does the author employ?
   A. anticipating objections of her male readers and countering them
   B. suggesting that all women believe as she does and so should the reader
   C. offering questionable statistics and facts that support only her opinion
   D. challenging established opinions of both men and women of her day
   E. resorting to name-calling and mud-slinging to provoke male readers

3. In line 2, the word *fortitude* means
   A. attractiveness
   B. intelligence
   C. resistance
   D. weakness
   E. strength

4. Which social issue is this author attempting to address?
   A. forces in society that hold women back
   B. the struggle for equality among women
   C. men using physical force against women
   D. peer pressure on young women of the day
   E. career versus motherhood for young women

5. Which of the following quotations from the passage show the author attempting to persuade her audience?
   A. ". . . their apparent inferiority with respect to bodily strength . . ."
   B. ". . . I now speak of the sex in general . . ."
   C. ". . . there is a constant struggle for an equilibrium . . ."
   D. "Let me become more chaste and modest . . ."
   E. ". . . but why should it be increased by prejudices . . ."

6. Which choice best expresses the main idea of the first paragraph?
   A. Women have very little reason to fear men and should take comfort in their own feminine nature.
   B. Women will never be masculine, but their weaknesses should not be multiplied by turning them into virtues.
   C. Men are prejudiced against the virtues of women and have none of their own.
   D. Women will gradually gain power and courage, which poses a threat to men.
   E. Women lack strength and virtue, and always will.

Grammar and Writing: Improving Sentences

Improving Sentences exercises often appear in the writing sections of standardized tests. The test items show five different versions of a sentence. Your job is to choose the most effective version. This type of exercise tests your ability to recognize and correct flaws in grammar, usage, and sentence structure.

Practice

This exercise is modeled after the Improving Sentences portion of the SAT Writing Section. The full test has 25 such questions.

Directions: Part or all of each of the following sentences is underlined; beneath each sentence are five ways of phrasing the underlined portion. Choice A will always be the same as the original wording; B–E are different options. If you consider the original sentence to be the most effective sentence, select choice A; otherwise, select one of the other choices.

Strategy

Rely on your "ear."
Say possible choices quietly to yourself and let your natural "ear" for proper grammar distinguish what sounds correct.

1. John Keats's great poem "When I Have Fears" <u>represent his finest work and delight</u> millions of readers.
   - **A.** represent his finest work and delight
   - **B.** represents his finest work and delight
   - **C.** represents his finest work and delights
   - **D.** represent his finest work and delights
   - **E.** have represented his finest work and have delighted

2. <u>Readers of Wordsworth are lovers</u> of Romantic ideals.
   - **A.** Readers of Wordsworth are lovers
   - **B.** One of the readers of Wordsworth are lovers
   - **C.** Readers of Wordsworth is lovers
   - **D.** Reader of Wordsworth is a lover
   - **E.** Readers of Wordsworth is a lover

3. There <u>were, it seems in the varied life of Samuel Coleridge, few accomplishments</u> he didn't achieve.
   - **A.** were, it seems in the varied life of Samuel Coleridge, few accomplishments
   - **B.** were, it seem in the varied life of Samuel Coleridge, few accomplishments
   - **C.** were, it seems, in the varied life of Samuel Coleridge, few accomplishments
   - **D.** are, it seem in the varied life of Samuel Coleridge, few accomplishments
   - **E.** are, it seems in the varied lives of Samuel Coleridge, few accomplishments

4. Lord Byron, while at school, <u>have made friends, has played sports, and spends</u> money like a wastrel.

   A. have made friends, has played sports, and spends

   B. has made friends, has played sports, and has spent

   C. have made friends, have played sports, and spends

   D. made friends, played sports, and spent

   E. make friends, play sports, and spend

5. Percy Bysshe Shelley, <u>born into the British upper classes, were expelled from Oxford University with a friend and were forced</u> to live apart from his family.

   A. born into the British upper classes, were expelled from Oxford University with a friend and were forced

   B. born into the British upper classes, was expelled from Oxford University with a friend and were forced

   C. born into the British upper classes, was expelled from Oxford University with a friend and forced

   D. birthed into the British upper classes, were expelled from Oxford University with a friend and were forced

   E. born into the British upper classes, was expelled from Oxford University with a friend and was forced

6. <u>It were a tragedy that John Keats, like many poets, dies so young and writes</u> his major works in the space of only two years.

   A. It were a tragedy that John Keats, like many poets, dies so young and writes

   B. It was a tragedy that John Keats, like many poets, dies so young and writes

   C. It was a tragedy that John Keats, like many poets, died so young and wrote

   D. It was a tragedy that John Keats, like many poets, dies so young and writes

   E. It is a tragedy that John Keats, like many poets, dies so young and writes

7. *The Prelude*, which many students <u>memorize, and "Ozymandias" are poetry any reader loves</u> for a lifetime.

   A. memorize, and "Ozymandias" are poetry any reader loves

   B. memorizes, and "Ozymandias" are poetry any reader loves

   C. memorize, and "Ozymandias" is poetry any reader loves

   D. memorize, and "Ozymandias" is poetry any reader love

   E. memorize, and "Ozymandias" is poetry any readers loves

Timed Writing: Position Statement [25 minutes]

Mary Wollstonecraft wrote about the condition of women in the late eighteenth century. At that time few women enjoyed a formal education, and all women lacked basic legal rights. Things are entirely different today.

Write an essay in which you discuss whether education is the key to liberation for an oppressed group of people. You are free to take any side of the issue, but be sure to back up your opinions with observations and reasoning. This assignment is similar to the Essay portion of the SAT Writing Section.

> **Academic Vocabulary**
>
> Your **observations** come from things you have noticed or witnessed. You do not have to cite experts or recognized sources of research to include your observations in your essay.

Constructed Response

Directions: *Follow the instructions to complete the tasks below as required by your teacher. As you work on each task, incorporate both general academic vocabulary and literary terms you learned in this unit.*

Common Core State Standards

RL.11-12.1, RL.11-12.2, RL.11-12.4, RL.11-12.5; RI.11-12.5, RI.11-12.6; W.11-12.2.a, W.11-12.4, W.11-12.9.a; SL.11-12.1.a, SL.11-12.1.d, SL.11-12.4, SL.11-12.6; L.11-12.3.a

[For the full wording of the standards, see the standards chart in the front of your textbook.]

Writing

Task 1: Literature [RL.11-12.1, W.11-12.2.a, W.11-12.9.a]
Draw Inferences

Write an **essay** *in which you cite textual evidence to support inferences drawn from a poem in this unit.*

- Explain which poem you chose. Identify the poem's explicit meaning or key idea. Quote from the text to support your point.

- Identify any ideas or emotions that the speaker suggests but does not explicitly state. Cite details from the poem that help you draw inferences about the speaker's unstated ideas or feelings. Explain how you tied these details together to see connections that suggest implicit meanings.

- Discuss ideas or emotions the poem leaves uncertain or open to interpretation. Consider the reasons for and effects of this ambiguity.

- Organize your ideas so that each new idea builds on the one that precedes it to create a unified whole.

Task 2: Literature [RL.11-12.4, W.11-12.9.a]
Analyze the Impact of Word Choice

Write an **essay** *in which you analyze the impact of word choice in a poem from this unit.*

- Choose a poem in which the word choice is particularly interesting to you. Explain which poem you chose and why you chose it.

- Identify at least two words in the poem that carry connotative meanings that are essential to the poet's overall meaning. Explain the shades of meaning each word contributes to the poem as a whole.

- Explain the cumulative, or combined, impact these words have on the tone of the poem.

- Consider how word choices with similar denotations but different connotations would alter the meaning and tone of the poem.

Task 3: Literature [RL.11-12.5, W.11-12.4, L.11-12.3.a]
Analyze Text Structure

Write an **essay** *in which you analyze how a poet's choice of structure adds to the overall meaning and aesthetic impact of a poem in this unit.*

- Choose a poem from this unit in which the structure, or form, plays a key role in developing meaning. Explain which poem you chose and why.

- Analyze how the poet's choices of structure in sections of the poem contribute to the structure of the poem as a whole. Consider line length, rhyme scheme, and stanza lengths and divisions.

- Connect the author's choices concerning structure to the meaning as well as to the aesthetic, or artistic and emotional, impact of the poem.

- Clearly develop and organize your ideas while maintaining an appropriate, consistent style and tone in your writing.

- Vary your sentence length and structure to add interest and sophistication to your writing.

Speaking and Listening

Task 4: Literature [RL.11-12.2, SL.11-12.4]
Analyze Development of Theme

*Deliver an **oral presentation** in which you analyze the development of two or more themes in a poem in this unit.*

- State which poem you chose and briefly explain why you chose it.

- Clearly state the themes of your chosen poem. Discuss specific ways in which the author develops each theme throughout the poem. Identify specific details, figurative language, and images that contribute to the expression of each theme.

- Explain how the themes interact and build on one another as the poem progresses.

- Be sure to develop your ideas fully and present them in logical order.

- As you present, demonstrate your command of the conventions of Standard English grammar and usage. Choose language that expresses ideas precisely and concisely, eliminating wordiness.

Task 5: Informational Text [RI.11-12.6, SL.11-12.6]
Determine the Author's Point of View

*Deliver an **oral presentation** in which you examine the author's point of view, rhetoric, and style in a nonfiction work from this unit.*

- Introduce the work you chose. Explain the author's purpose, topic, and central idea.

- Describe the author's point of view. Explain how the author's stance affects his or her discussion of the topic and helps to shape the central idea.

- Discuss specific aspects of the author's rhetoric and style, explaining how they contribute to the power or persuasiveness of the text. Cite details and examples from the text to support your position.

- Be aware of your own uses of rhetoric and style. Use formal English appropriate to an academic discussion.

Task 6: Informational Text [RI.11-12.5, SL.11-12.1.a, SL.11-12.1.d]
Analyze Ideas or Events

*Participate in a **small-group discussion** in which you analyze the structure of an author's exposition or argument in a nonfiction work from this unit.*

- As a group, choose a nonfiction work from this unit. Prepare for the discussion by working independently to conduct your own analysis of the work.

- Identify the structure the author uses to present ideas. Consider whether the structure involves a formal pattern of organization, such as comparison-and-contrast, or combines various patterns.

- Evaluate the clarity and logic of the structure. Consider how the structure helps or hinders readers' understanding and whether it makes ideas more convincing and engaging.

- Discuss your ideas in a small group. Respond thoughtfully to each other's ideas, and work to resolve any contradictions in your interpretations.

 What is the relationship of the writer to tradition?

The Voice of a Romantic The voice of the Romantic writer is personal, passionate, and dedicated to expressing a personal imaginative vision. That personal vision colors the writer's reflections.

Assignment Write a **composition** in the voice of a Romantic. You may choose the voice of a particular author or any writer of the time. Use the form of an essay, a book introduction, or a letter to a friend.

Titles for Extended Reading

In this unit, you have read a variety of literature from the Romantic period. Continue to read works related to this era on your own. Select books that you enjoy, but challenge yourself to explore new topics, new authors, and works offering varied perspectives or approaches. The titles suggested below will help you get started.

LITERATURE

Frankenstein
Mary Shelley

Novel This classic story presents an epic battle between man and monster. Frankenstein, a medical student, fashions a creature from the body parts of the dead and brings it to life, setting in motion a chain of events that brings him to the brink of madness.

[Shelley's introduction to Frankenstein *appears on page 760 in this book. Build knowledge by reading the entire work.]*

Pride and Prejudice
Jane Austen   EXEMPLAR TEXT

Novel The setting is the English countryside in the eighteenth century, a world of comfortable homes, tidy fortunes, and respectable families. In this world, Mr. Darcy, handsome and wealthy, would seem to be the ideal match for the charming and pretty Elizabeth Bennet. Their courtship is one of the most treasured love stories of English literature.

The Portable Romantic Poets
Edited by W. H. Auden and Norman Holmes Pearson

Anthology This volume includes works by celebrated British and American poets, such as Robert Burns, William Wordsworth, and Edgar Allan Poe, as well as works by lesser-known writers.

[Poems by Burns and Wordsworth appear earlier in this unit. Build knowledge by reading additional works by these poets.]

The Complete Poetry and Prose of William Blake
Edited by David V. Erdman

Anthology All of Blake's great poetry, including *Songs of Innocence and Experience* and *The Marriage of Heaven and Hell*, appear in this volume. Also included are early poems and many illuminating letters.

[Poems by Blake appear on pages 748–752 of this book. Build knowledge by reading additional poems by Blake.]

INFORMATIONAL TEXT

Historical Texts

A Defence of Poetry and Other Essays
Percy Bysshe Shelley

Essays First published in 1821, "A Defence of Poetry" proclaimed a revolutionary idea—that poets are active political forces, or "the unacknowledged legislators of the world." In these essays, Shelley reflects on the art of poetry.

[Poems by Shelley appear on pages 868–876 of this book. Build knowledge by reading Shelley's essays.]

From Montrose to Culloden: Bonnie Prince Charlie & Scotland's Romantic Age
Sir Walter Scott

History Scott, one of the nineteenth century's most popular novelists, wrote these stories for his grandson. The historical tales bring to life Scotland's colorful and romantic history and feature memorable characters such as Bonnie Prince Charlie and the Duke of Cumberland.

Contemporary Scholarship

The Mirror and the Lamp: Romantic Theory and the Critical Tradition
M. H. Abrams
Oxford University Press, 1971

Scholarship Abrams explains a powerful contrast in the history of literary criticism. Pre-Romantic writers regarded literature as a mirror that reflects the real world. The Romantics, however, saw literature as a lamp that projects the writer's soul.

Romantic Poetry: Recent Revisionary Criticism
Edited by Karl Kroeber and G. Ruoff

Anthology These up-to-date essays reflect key critical views on the English Romantic poets: Blake, Wordsworth, Coleridge, Byron, Shelley, and Keats.

Preparing to Read Complex Texts

Reading for College and Career In both college and the workplace, readers must analyze texts independently, draw connections among works that offer varied perspectives, and develop their own ideas and informed opinions. The questions shown below, and others that you generate on your own, will help you more effectively read and analyze complex college-level texts.

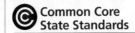 **Common Core
State Standards**

Reading Literature/Informational Text
10. By the end of grade 12, read and comprehend literature, including stories, dramas, and poems, and literary nonfiction at the high end of the grades 11-CCR text complexity band independently and proficiently.

When reading complex texts, ask yourself...

- What idea, experience, or story seems to have compelled the author to write? Has the author presented that idea, experience, or story in a way that I, too, find compelling?

- How might the author's era, social status, belief system, or personal experiences have affected the point of view he or she expresses in the text?

- What key idea does the author state explicitly? What key idea does he or she suggest or imply? Which details in the text help me to perceive implied ideas?

- Do I find multiple layers of meaning in the text? If so, what relationships do I see among these layers of meaning?

- How do details in the text connect or relate to one another? Do I find any details unconvincing, unrelated, or out of place?

- Do I find the text believable and convincing?

**© Key Ideas
and Details**

- What patterns of organization or sequences do I find in the text? Do these patterns help me understand the ideas better?

- What do I notice about the author's style, including his or her diction, uses of imagery and figurative language, and syntax?

- Do I like the author's style? Is the author's style memorable?

- What emotional attitude does the author express toward the topic, the story, or the characters? Does this attitude seem appropriate?

- What emotional attitude does the author express toward me, the reader? Does this attitude seem appropriate?

- What do I notice about the author's voice—his or her personality on the page? Do I like this voice? Does it make me want to read on?

 **Craft and
Structure**

- Is the work fresh and original?

- Do I agree with the author's ideas entirely or are there elements I find unconvincing?

- Do I disagree with the author's ideas entirely, or are there elements I can accept as true?

- How do the concerns, values, and assumptions of my own era shape my response to the text?

- Based on my knowledge of British literature, history, and culture, does this work reflect the British tradition? Why or why not?

 **Integration
of Ideas**

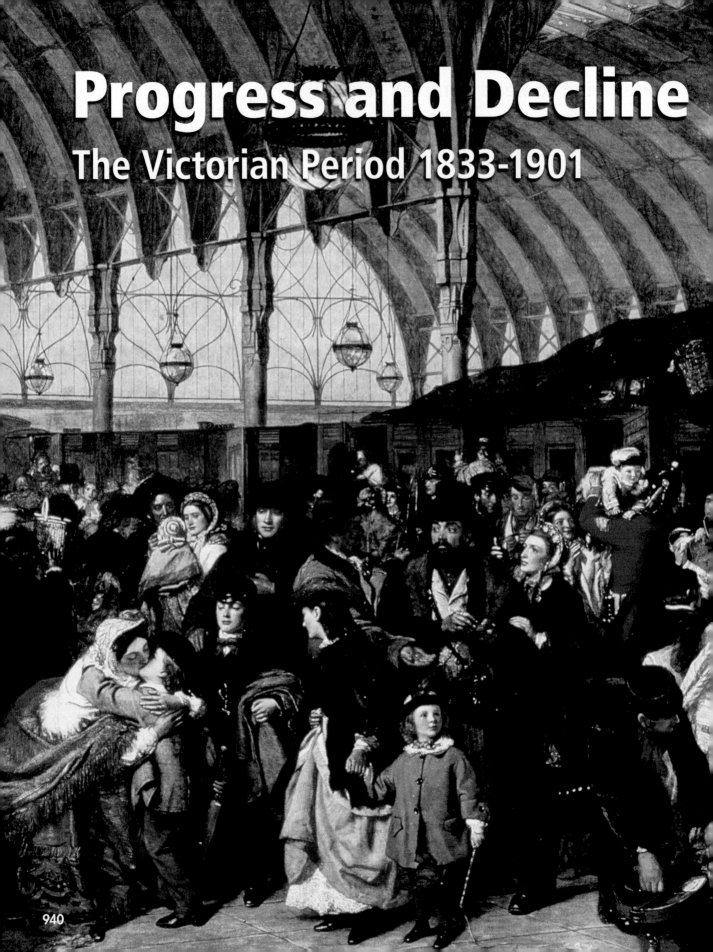

Progress and Decline
The Victorian Period 1833-1901

"It was the best of times, it was the worst of times . . . we were all going direct to Heaven, we were all going direct the other way . . ."

- Charles Dickens, from A Tale of Two Cities

Unit 5

PART 1 TEXT SET

RELATIONSHIPS

PART 2 TEXT SET

THE NOVEL

PART 3 TEXT SET

THE EMPIRE AND ITS DISCONTENTS

PART 4 TEXT SET

GLOOM AND GLORY

CLOSE READING TOOL

Use this tool to practice the close reading strategies you learn.

ONLINE WRITER'S NOTEBOOK

Easily capture notes and complete assignments online.

STUDENT eTEXT

Bring learning to life with audio, video, and interactive tools.

■ Find all Digital Resources at **pearsonrealize.com**.

Snapshot of the Period

The Crystal Palace, on the facing page, is a symbol of Victorian optimism and Victorian faith in progress, technology, and empire. It is true that this period witnessed dramatic technological advances, rapid industrialization, the growth of cities, political reforms, and the development of Britain into a worldwide empire. It is equally true that this era witnessed the spread of poverty, a division of Britain into two nations—one prosperous and the other poverty stricken—and advances in philosophy and science that threatened long-held beliefs. Above all, Victorians were aware that they were living—as a writer of the time put it—"in an age of transition." An old social and political order, dating back to medieval times, was being transformed into a modern democracy. The poet Matthew Arnold expressed the unease of this transition when he described himself as "Wandering between two worlds . . ."

This English cartoon of 1843 reflects the sharp contrast between the rich and the poor. The cartoon was inspired by a government report on the horrific state of workers in coal mines.

As you read the selections in this unit, you will be asked to think about them in view of three key questions:

What is the relationship between literature and *place?*

How does literature shape or reflect *society?*

What is the relationship of the writer to *tradition?*

Integration of Knowledge and Ideas The Crystal Palace (shown here), designed by Sir Joseph Paxton for Britain's Great Exhibition of 1851, was a large structure made of iron and glass. Stunningly advanced for its time, this "palace" housed exhibitions dramatizing the themes of empire and progress. If you were designing a Crystal Palace for today, what materials would you use, what would the structure look like, and what kind of exhibitions would it house?

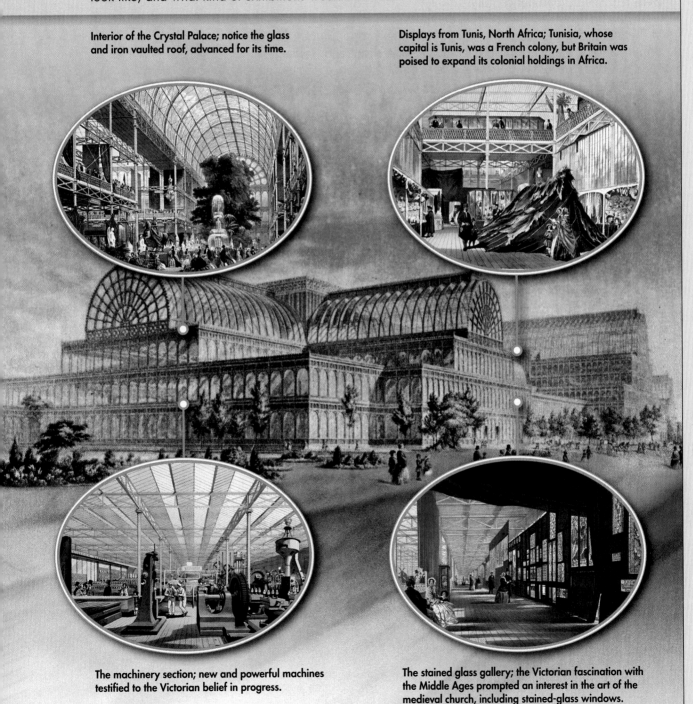

Interior of the Crystal Palace; notice the glass and iron vaulted roof, advanced for its time.

Displays from Tunis, North Africa; Tunisia, whose capital is Tunis, was a French colony, but Britain was poised to expand its colonial holdings in Africa.

The machinery section; new and powerful machines testified to the Victorian belief in progress.

The stained glass gallery; the Victorian fascination with the Middle Ages prompted an interest in the art of the medieval church, including stained-glass windows.

Historical Background

The Victorian Period (1833–1901)

Queen Victoria's reign (1837–1901) was marked by triumphs and tragedies. The consequences of some of them, like the mixed legacy of imperialism, were felt well beyond her century.

Shy and diminutive, the young queen set out to restore the reputation of the monarchy. Her marriage in 1840 to her first cousin, Albert of Saxe-Coburg and Gotha, whom she loved dearly, was a model of respectability. That quality, respectability, became a very important concept in her time.

Tragedies and Triumphs of Empire

The first blight on her reign came in 1845, when the potato crop failed in Ireland. The Famine grew worse until by 1849, half the population of Ireland had died or gone into exile. The British government did little or nothing for this quarter of the "United Kingdom." The events and the legends of the Famine fueled the hatred and violence in the relations between the British and the Irish for more than a hundred and fifty years.

The high point of Victoria's reign was the Great Exposition in the Crystal Palace, organized by her husband, the Prince Consort, in 1851. Built in a wholly new style, with iron girders holding over a million feet of glass panels, the building was the cathedral of commerce and empire. A combination of world's fair and industrial show, the Exposition trumpeted to the world the achievements of manufacturing England, colonizing England, and self-satisfied England.

Two works published during Victoria's reign proved as powerful as any of the machinery assembled for the Great Exposition. In 1848, as England watched while revolutions convulsed Europe, Karl Marx published *The Communist Manifesto*. This pamphlet warned that there was "a spectre haunting Europe." That "spectre" was communism, with its prophecy of political revolution. The other book, the work of a gentleman scientist who had seen evidence for biological evolution during his long sea voyage on the *H.M.S. Beagle*, was *On the Origin of Species*. Supporters and attackers alike

Queen Victoria

TIMELINE

1833: Slavery abolished in British empire.

1837: Victoria becomes queen. ▶

1839: Michael Faraday offers general theory of electricity. ▼

1832

1836 North America
The Alamo falls to the Mexican army. ▶

Odyssey who finally makes it home and reclaims his kingdom. In later legends, he is depicted as having had so many adventures that he cannot settle down to ordinary life. In these legends, he sails beyond the Pillars of Hercules, the Straits of Gibraltar, into the unknown sea. In Dante's medieval epic, the *Divine Comedy,* Ulysses is in hell, punished for his sin of going beyond an established boundary. To go beyond a limit—in Dante's structured, medieval world—was a grave sin. In Tennyson's fluid Victorian world, to accept a limit was a grave sin. The restless spirit that can never stop exploring, glorified in Tennyson's poem, is the spirit that created an empire.

Even a novel like Charlotte Brontë's *Jane Eyre,* set entirely in England, is connected with empire. When Jane Eyre grows up, she rejects one suitor who wants her to go with him as a missionary to India. She falls in love with the dark, brooding, Byronic Mr. Rochester, who has come back from Jamaica with a fortune and a terrible secret.

Empire's Poet The poet of empire was Rudyard Kipling. Born to British parents in India, he made that country, which he loved, vivid to his countrymen in poems and his panoramic novel *Kim.* Kipling delighted in describing British soldiers, the "Tommies," the thin, red line of heroes who carried the empire on their shoulders. In "The Widow at Windsor," one of those soldiers speaks of his pride and his problems in her service. "Recessional" is Kipling's own solemn warning against the arrogance of power.

The BRITISH TRADITION

CLOSE-UP ON ART

The Values of Empire and the Values of Art

While the British empire thrived on progress and expansion, an avant-garde group of Victorian painters sought purity and inward focus by moving backward in time. This group, founded by the painter and poet Dante Gabriel Rossetti (1828–1882), called itself the Pre-Raphaelite Brotherhood. Its members found inspiration in the Gothic style of the Middle Ages, before the time of the Renaissance painter Raphael (hence the group's name). Rossetti is known especially for his portraits of women, such as the one shown here. These portraits emphasize color, texture, and an earthy or sadly spiritual feminine beauty.

Critical Viewing Could this portrait by Rossetti, entitled *Day Dream,* be regarded as a comment on the Victorian belief in empire and progress? Why or why not?

1855: London sewers modernized after outbreak of cholera.

◄ 1857 **India** Sepoy Mutiny against British.

1859: Charles Darwin publishes *On the Origin of Species.* ▲

1860

How does literature shape or reflect *society?*

"It was the best of times, it was the worst of times...." That is how Charles Dickens begins his novel of the French Revolution, *A Tale of Two Cities.* He goes on to say that this is also true of Victorian England. He knew what he was talking about, and it is helpful to follow Dickens's words as a guide to the contradictions of Victorian society:

". . . it was the age of wisdom, it was the age of foolishness, it was the epoch of belief, it was the epoch of incredulity, it was the season of Light, it was the season of Darkness, it was the spring of hope, it was the winter of despair, we had everything before us, we had nothing before us, we were all going direct to Heaven, we were all going direct the other way . . ."

Charles Dickens

How did literature reflect Victorian contradictions?

"best of times" Sydney Smith's essay "Progress in Personal Comfort" lists some of the creature comforts invented in his lifetime. More important, however, is the attitude behind the essay: Life is getting better for more and more people. That optimistic spirit helped England make peaceful progress while Europe was torn by revolutions, assassinations, and war.

"worst of times" In the Irish Famine, two million people starved to death although there was food enough to feed them. From 1899 to 1902, the British fought the Dutch settlers of South Africa in the Boer War. The British army herded the women and children of the Boer guerillas into barbed-wire enclosures, thereby helping to invent the concentration camp.

"wisdom . . . foolishness" Wisdom includes Michael Faraday's experiments in electricity and Joseph Lister's introduction of sterile surgery. Matthew Arnold wrote essays urging his fellow citizens to enrich their minds with the same zeal with which they enriched their bank accounts.

TIMELINE

1861 Russia
Emancipation of serfs.

1865 Austria
Gregor Mendel proposes laws of heredity. ▶

1860

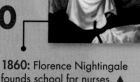

1860: Florence Nightingale founds school for nurses. ▲

1861 United States
Civil War begins. ▶

1865: London Fire Department established.

There were two varieties of foolishness. One was creative, a relief from the smug self-satisfaction of the time. Examples of this healthy foolishness are the operettas of W. S. Gilbert and Arthur Sullivan, with their amusing patter, and Lewis Carroll's fantastic tale *Alice in Wonderland* and his nonsense poem "Jabberwocky."

Unhealthy foolishness included using the Thames as an open sewer until one typhoid outbreak in 1861 killed Albert, Victoria's beloved Prince Consort. It also included sending British troops to fight in the Crimea so ill-fed, ill-clothed, and ill-led that the war is best remembered in Tennyson's poem "The Charge of the Light Brigade," which celebrates a suicidal cavalry charge.

"belief . . . incredulity" Problems of belief haunted the Victorians. At the very moment they wanted to think they were God's chosen people, they faced serious challenges to their belief in that God. Historical and scientific investigations undermined literal interpretations of the Bible, but it was Darwin who was the real villain for believers. Newton had distanced God from the universe; more frighteningly, Darwin seemed to distance God from human life.

"hope . . . despair" It is the spring of hope in Elizabeth Barrett Browning's Sonnet 43; it is the winter of despair in Matthew Arnold's "Dover Beach." It is the season of light in Gerard Manley Hopkins's "God's Grandeur"; it is the season of darkness in Emily Brontë's "Remembrance."

The BRITISH TRADITION

THE CHANGING ENGLISH LANGUAGE, BY RICHARD LEDERER

Euphemisms: The Fig Leaves of Language

Prudishness reached its golden age in the straitlaced Victorian era. Take the widely read *Lady Gough's Book of Etiquette.* Among Lady Gough's pronouncements was that under no circumstances should books written by male authors be placed on shelves next to books written by "authoresses." Married writers, however, such as Robert and Elizabeth Barrett Browning could be shelved together without impropriety.

So delicate were Victorian sensibilities that members of polite society would blush at the mention of anything physical. Instead of being *pregnant*, women were in a delicate condition, in a family way, or *expectant*. Their children were not born; rather, they were *brought by the stork* or *came into the world.*

Such words and expressions are called *euphemisms* (from two Greek roots that mean "pleasant speech," "words of good omen"). A euphemism is a mild, indirect word or phrase used in place of one that is more direct or that may have an unpleasant connotation for some people. Using a euphemism is "calling a spade a heart" . . . or "telling it like it isn't."

In the Victorian Age, prudery extended even to animals and things. *Bull* was considered an indecent word, and the proper substitute was *he cow, male cow,* or (gasp!) *gentleman cow.* Victorian standards were so exacting that Victorians could not refer to something as vulgar as legs. They had to call them *limbs*, even when talking about the legs on a chicken or a piano. Instead of asking for a leg of chicken, they would ask for dark meat, and they even went so far as to cover up piano legs with little skirts!

1869: Debtors' prisons abolished.

1872: Ballot Act in Britain introduces voting by secret ballot.

1874

◄ **1869 Egypt** Suez Canal, linking the Mediterranean Sea and the Red Sea, completed.

1872: First international soccer game, England vs. Scotland. ►

◀ **Critical Viewing**

In this scene from Charles Dickens's autobiographical novel *David Copperfield*, young David (shown at the center) is on a journey from Yarmouth to London. To what extent does the illustrator sentimentalize David? To what extent does the illustrator show David struggling to survive in a hostile world? **INTERPRET**

There was light and hope in The Crystal Palace; despair and darkness in the fetid slums with contaminated water.

"going direct to Heaven . . . going direct the other way" Nowhere is paradox more apparent than in the era's treatment of children. The Victorians frequently sentimentalized their children as little angels. However, in the novels of Dickens and Brontë and many others, we meet orphans and abandoned children struggling to survive in a hostile world. Often we see these children in school where the adults view them as, to use Dickens's phrase, "going direct the other way" unless they are rigorously and painfully kept in line.

All ages have their paradoxes, but the Victorians more than most felt, again in Dickens's words: ". . . we had everything before us, we had nothing before us."

ESSENTIAL QUESTION VOCABULARY

These Essential Question words will help you think and write about literature and society:

zeal (zēl) *n.* intense enthusiam

smug (smug´) *adj.* narrowly self-satisfied; overly contented

undermined (un´ dər mīnd) *v.* injured or weakened, especially in ways that are not immediately obvious

TIMELINE

1876 United States
Alexander Graham Bell patents telephone. ▶

— 1874

1875: Public Health Act is passed in Britain.

What is the relationship of the writer to *tradition?*

Literature turned inward in the Victorian period. As the Empire expanded and people talked of progress and prosperity, there was a brooding, melancholic tone to much of Victorian writing. Writers also used old forms in new ways or created new forms. Poets adapted traditional forms like the elegy and the sonnet to address contemporary questions of belief. Robert Browning's dramatic monologue, a new poetic form more vital than many stage plays of the era, reflected an up-to-date understanding of psychology. Novelists developed a genre created in an earlier century and found an eager audience. Published in serial form in magazines, novels generated the same excitement as popular TV sitcoms do today.

How did poets repurpose traditional forms and subjects?

An Elegy with Up-to-Date Themes Tennyson's *In Memoriam, A.H.H.,* his elegy for his friend Arthur Hallam, speaks to the problem of belief and doubt that was central to the age. In this poem, Tennyson struggles to come to terms with Hallam's death at the age of twenty-two, asking whether a benevolent God or an indifferent nature directs the universe. About ten years before Darwin, he writes of "nature red in tooth and claw." One of the most impressive aspects of this elegy is its engagement with the latest scientific discoveries. By the end of the poem, however, Tennyson has regained his belief and declares his faith in a divine plan for the universe.

Old and New Like the Pre-Raphaelite painters and many other artists of the era, Tennyson was fascinated by the Middle Ages. However, he combines this traditional subject with up-to-date concerns. In his epic poem *Idylls of the King*, which retells the story of King Arthur, he warns his contemporaries about what can happen to a powerful kingdom like Victoria's Britain.

A melancholy that is the opposite of faith in empire and progress informs Matthew Arnold's "Dover Beach." The speaker stands at the edge of the island kingdom and contemplates the chaos encroaching on the world. He hopes, almost desperately, that a personal relationship will survive that chaos.

1883: Joseph Swan produces synthetic fiber. ▶

◀ **1883 United States** First skyscraper built in Chicago.

1888: English Lawn Tennis Association founded at Wimbledon. ▶

1888

The Sonnet In Sonnet 43, Elizabeth Barrett Browning states her belief in the power of love, more positively than Matthew Arnold. She adds a distinctively Victorian note of piety, reverence, and religious belief to her love poem. Victorian poets were as committed to the sonnet as were the Romantics, and none more so than Gerard Manley Hopkins. A Catholic convert and Jesuit priest, he experimented boldly with the form. In "God's Grandeur," a traditional sonnet enhanced by experiments with meter, he proclaims his faith in a divine presence in the world.

What literary forms did the Victorians invent or perfect?

The Dramatic Monologue Robert Browning, Elizabeth Barrett's husband, perfected the dramatic monologue. In this poetic form, a character is speaking to a silent listener and in the process revealing more about himself than he realizes. Browning's strange and chilling speakers are the British cousins of Edgar Allan Poe's mad narrators in stories like "The Cask of Amontillado" and "The Tell-Tale Heart."

The Novel The dramatic monologue takes readers into the mind of a character, as does the popular Victorian genre, the novel. This genre was as central to the Victorian period as the drama was to the Elizabethan. Usually published serially in magazines, each new installment of a novel was eagerly awaited by all levels of society. The novel's social commentary and realistic descriptions presented the Victorians to themselves.

The great theme of these novels is education: the depiction of a hero or heroine learning how to secure a proper place in society.

Note of Melancholy At the end of the era, A. E. Housman does not react as Tennyson did to the premature death of a young man. He does not seek the meaning of such a death in cosmic terms. Rather, in "To an Athlete Dying Young," he offers ironic consolation.

In an age of prosperity and progress, pride and power, England's poets and novelists reminded their countrymen that empires crumble, individuals are fragile and vulnerable, and death awaits us.

> ### ESSENTIAL QUESTION VOCABULARY
>
> These Essential Question words will help you think and write about the writer and tradition:
>
> **chaos** (kā äs´) *n.* disorder and formlessness
>
> **piety** (pī´ ə tē) *n.* devotion to religious duties
>
> **reverence** (rev´ ər ens) *n.* feeling of deep respect, love, and awe

TIMELINE

1890: First English electrical power station opens in Deptford.

1888

1890 United States First entirely steel-framed building erected in Chicago.

1894 Asia Sino-Japanese War begins. ▲

CONTEMPORARY CONNECTION

The Brontës: Fantasy Forerunners

For today's readers, the name Brontë evokes two renowned classics, Emily Brontë's *Wuthering Heights* and her sister Charlotte's *Jane Eyre.* Less known is the fact that the Brontës—three sisters, including Anne, as well as their brother, Branwell—were among the pioneer writers of fantasy.

As children, the Brontës lived with their widowed clergyman father in a bleak and isolated region of northern England. Perhaps as a result of their isolation, they immersed themselves in a world of make-believe. Inspired by their play with Branwell's toy soldiers, they invented the lands of Angria and Gondal as settings for their fantasies.

They peopled their make-believe empires with fictional characters and real-life heroes, such as the Duke of Wellington, Napoleon, and various Arctic explorers. Also, they recorded the elaborate adventures of their characters in books, using tiny handwriting that adults needed a magnifying glass to read.

The Brontë children may not have intended their childhood tales to be widely read. These fantasies have been published, however, and have even inspired well-known authors. Not long ago, Joan Aiken published a book entitled *Dangerous Games* that, as she says, uses "bits and pieces" of the Brontës' Angria.

1896 Greece
First modern
Olympics held. ▶

1898 France
Marie and Pierre Curie
discover radium.

1901: Queen Victoria dies.

1901

◀ **1896 Austria**
Sigmund Freud
first uses the term
"psychoanalysis."

1900 China
Boxer Rebellion
against foreign
influence. ▶

Recent Scholarship

Growing up in Colonial Jamaica

James Berry

A British Colonial Child

I grew up as a British colonial child in Jamaica, British West Indies. I was made to feel that there was something special about being British: You were born into honoring the British flag and feeling that the British way of life was best. Yet you also knew in a strange way that there was something alien and inferior about you. I came to realize that this was to do with race. Because we were a black people, we knew that we were different from the rulers of our island, who were white.

We sang songs in praise of Britain, like "Land of Hope and Glory," which glorified Britain's colonial past and power. And once a year, on Empire Day, we sang "Rule Britannia," with its line: "Britons never, never, never shall be slaves." We sang with fervor because Britishness seemed to offer a sense of safety and belonging. But we also knew that our ancestors *had* been slaves and had been enslaved by the British.

As a child growing up, you had these two different histories to contend with. You felt and knew that your colonial existence was strongly influenced by your slave history. It made you feel almost an outsider in the world because there was nowhere you could appeal to.

Schooling

It was the British way of life that constructed our schooling. We received a good, basic education in ordinary subjects like English language, arithmetic, biology, history, and geography. The maps we used showed British territories colored in red, and we were proud of that. We were made to learn a little verse about Queen Victoria setting us free.

Our reading books were not based on Africa or Jamaica. They brought us the culture of the British Isles; the stories and poems in them were all British. Many of the poems were from the eighteenth or nineteenth centuries—they had all the weight of grand English usage.

About the Author

Born and raised in rural Jamaica, James Berry (b. 1925) now lives in London. His poetry and prose are enriched by both Creole language and more formal English. In 1993, Berry won the Coretta Scott King Award Honor Book and the Boston Globe–Horn Book Award for *Ajeeman and His Son,* a work of historical fiction set in Jamaica. Berry's books of poetry include *Fractured Circles* and *Lucy's Letters and Loving.*

Most Jamaican children spoke our island dialect every day at home, but if you spoke dialect at school, teachers would shame you. They would say, "This is not a place for bad talk." Speaking English properly was tremendously respected and was connected to further education.

The Mother Country

We grew up with the idea that all the best things came from England. On Sundays, my father liked to ride to church on an English saddle that he had sent to England for. People would save up to order shoes and wedding suits from England.

At church on Sundays, we prayed for the King and the Royal Family. These were our hopeful figureheads, possible sources of influence. On Empire Day, at school, we were issued with tins of sweets with pictures of the King on them. England was our mother country.

Our Jamaican colonial history is different from that of many other colonial peoples because our own mother country sold our ancestors as slaves, and we grew up disconnected from Africa. In this kind of situation, a country takes a long time to recover from its own history. But this history has given Jamaicans a unique status in the world: a connection with Europe as well as a link back to Africa.

"This is not a place for bad talk."

Speaking and Listening: Collaboration

James Berry discusses the positive and negative effects of British colonialism on Jamaica. With a partner, develop a research **plan for a presentation** on the pros and cons of colonialism for Jamaicans like Berry. In formulating your plan, take the following steps:

- Review Berry's essay, listing the pros and cons of colonialism from his perspective.
- Formulate *clear research questions* to explore this topic further.
- Develop *research strategies* that would help you answer these questions; consider such sources as *oral histories*, *interviews*, and *autobiographies*.
- Review sources, *evaluating them for objectivity or bias* and taking preliminary notes on your topic.

After reviewing sources, discuss what you have learned with your partner. Drawing on your reading, decide on a preliminary thesis. Present your plan and thesis to the class and ask for comments and suggestions for improving it.

Integrate and Evaluate Information

1. Use a chart like the one shown to determine the key ideas expressed in the Essential Question essays on pages 946–952. Fill in two ideas related to each Essential Question and note the authors most closely associated with each concept. An example has been provided for you.

Essential Questions	Key Concepts	Key Author
Place and Literature		
Literature and Society	pride in and cautions about empire	Rudyard Kipling
Writer and Tradition		

2. "It was the best of times, it was the worst of times," wrote Victorian novelist Charles Dickens. Review the images on pages 940–955, and choose one that evokes the "best" of this period and one that evokes the "worst." Describe each image and explain its significance.

3. When Queen Victoria celebrated her Diamond Jubilee in 1897, the theme was "The Empire." Which British citizens would have agreed that the Empire was a cause for celebration? Which citizens might have disagreed? Explain, citing evidence from the multiple sources on pages 942–953, as well as from other sources, such as online encyclopedias.

4. **Address a Question:** In his essay on pages 954–955, James Berry portrays Jamaican culture as a complex intersection of British tradition and local history. Choose an aspect of Jamaican culture, such as the Jamaican dialect of English. Integrating ideas from Berry's essay as well as from other sources, such as online encyclopedias, explain how the element reflects the intersection of—or struggle between—cultures.

Speaking and Listening: Multimedia Presentation

The British Empire was at its height in 1851, when the Crystal Palace was built. Create and deliver a **multimedia presentation** on the Palace, analyzing what its innovative construction and displays implied about Britain's place in the world.

Solve a Research Problem: To create an effective multimedia presentation, combine text, images, and sound from sources like these:

- TV documentaries
- Victorian newspapers
- Internet sites
- history books
- videos
- magazines

Formulate a plan to find and assemble the media you need. Determine how to access each type of source listed above. Then, select and use media strategically. Choose only pieces that clearly illustrate your points, and create pacing by distributing them evenly through the report.

Common Core State Standards

Reading Informational Text

7. Integrate and evaluate multiple sources of information presented in different media or formats as well as in words in order to address a question or solve a problem.

Speaking and Listening

1.a. Come to discussions prepared, having read and researched material under study; explicitly draw on that preparation by referring to evidence from texts and other research on the topic or issue to stimulate a thoughtful, well-reasoned exchange of ideas. *(p. 955)*

5. Make strategic use of digital media in presentations to enhance understanding of findings, reasoning, and evidence and to add interest.

ESSENTIAL QUESTION VOCABULARY

Use these words in your responses:

Literature and Place
empire
conquest
missionary

Literature and Society
zeal
smug
undermine

The Writer and Tradition
chaos
piety
reverence

Relationships

Building Knowledge and Insight

Connecting to the Essential Question *In Memoriam, A.H.H.* is a poem Tennyson wrote in memory of his best friend, Arthur Hallam. As you read, note the ideas Tennyson explores as a result of his friend's death. This focus will help you answer the Essential Question: **How does literature shape or reflect society?**

**Common Core
State Standards**

Reading Literature
1. Cite strong and thorough textual evidence to support analysis of what the text says explicitly as well as inferences drawn from the text, including determining where the text leaves matters uncertain.

Close Reading Focus

Speaker

The **speaker** in a poem—the person who "says" its words—is not necessarily the poet. Speakers fall into the following categories:

- Fictional or real
- Generalized (not described in specific detail) or with a specific identity

As you read, determine the identity of each speaker and analyze the speaker's conflict and motivation.

Comparing Literary Works Some of Tennyson's speakers have histories—they have undergone a change or suffered a loss. Using such speakers, he dramatizes different experiences of time, including the following:

- A perpetual present, in which nothing significant changes
- Restless movement from past achievement into an unknown future
- The loss of the past

Consider whether each poem creates its own "time"—a moment in which the speaker sums up the past, making way for the future.

Preparing to Read Complex Texts Analyzing an author's philosophical assumptions and beliefs will help you understand the meaning of a poem. For example, Tennyson's speaker in "Ulysses" expresses a desire "to seek a newer world." The speaker's restless drive to explore suggests that Tennyson, like many Victorians, valued progress. Use what is stated explicitly, or directly, in the text as the basis for making inferences about the author's assumptions and beliefs. As you read, use a chart like the one shown to identify the author's beliefs.

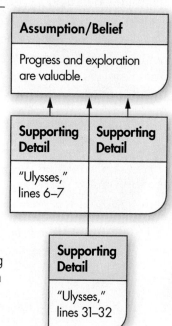

Vocabulary

The words below are important to understanding the texts that follow. Copy the words into your notebook, sorting them into words you know and words you do not know.

chrysalis	waning
diffusive	prudence
prosper	furrows

Author of *In Memoriam, A.H.H.* • "The Lady of Shalott" • "Tears, Idle Tears" • "Ulysses"

ALFRED, LORD **TENNYSON**

(1809–1892)

Tennyson was born in the rural town of Somersby in Lincolnshire, the fourth of twelve children. He was a sensitive boy who was charmed by the magical words "far, far away." His father, a clergyman, had a large library and supervised Tennyson's early education, predicting that his son would be "the greatest Poet of the Time." At the same time, Tennyson's father was extremely bitter, having been disinherited by his own father. His anger poisoned the atmosphere of the Tennyson household. As a teenager, Alfred was probably eager to escape to Cambridge University.

The Power of Friendship At first, Tennyson was disappointed by Cambridge. Then, he met the young man who became his closest friend, Arthur Henry Hallam. They were often together, and Hallam intended to marry Tennyson's sister Emily. In 1830, with Hallam's encouragement, Tennyson published *Poems, Chiefly Lyrical.*

A Stunning Tragedy In 1833, however, Hallam died suddenly, leaving a void in Tennyson's life that nearly destroyed him. Soon after Hallam's death, Tennyson began working on a series of short poems that considered questions of death, religious faith, and immortality. This series, which grew over seventeen years into an extended elegy for his friend, was published in 1850 under the title *In Memoriam, A.H.H.*

National Honor The elegy so impressed Prince Albert that in 1850, he encouraged Queen Victoria to appoint Tennyson the poet laureate of England, replacing the recently deceased Wordsworth.

In 1884, Queen Victoria made Tennyson a baron, and so added the title of Lord to his name.

Land, Literature, Long Life When royalties from *In Memoriam, A.H.H.* began to flow in, Tennyson bought a farm on the Isle of Wight. There, he and his wife Emily Sellwood raised two children. Tennyson continued to publish poems into his eighties.

The Stages of Life, Caspar David Friedrich, Museum der Bildenden Kunst, Leipzig

FROM In Memoriam, A.H.H.

ALFRED, LORD TENNYSON

▲ **Critical Viewing**

This painting, *The Stages of Life,* suggests that life is like a voyage. How would the speaker in the poem react to such a comparison? Explain. **SPECULATE**

1

I held it truth, with him who sings
    To one clear harp in divers¹ tones,
    That men may rise on stepping stones
Of their dead selves to higher things.

5   But who shall so forecast the years
    And find in loss a gain to match?
    Or reach a hand through time to catch
The far-off interest of tears?

---

1. divers (dī´ vərz) *adj.* varied; having many parts.

Let Love clasp Grief lest both be drowned,
    Let darkness keep her raven gloss.
10   Ah, sweeter to be drunk with loss,
To dance with death, to beat the ground,

Than that the victor Hours should scorn
    The long result of love, and boast,
15   "Behold the man that loved and lost,
But all he was is overworn."

7

Dark house, by which once more I stand
    Here in the long unlovely street,
    Doors, where my heart was used to beat
20 So quickly, waiting for a hand,

A hand that can be clasped no more—
    Behold me, for I cannot sleep,
    And like a guilty thing I creep
At earliest morning to the door.

25 He is not here; but far away
    The noise of life begins again,
    And ghastly through the drizzling rain
On the bald street breaks the blank day.

82

I wage not any feud with Death
30   For changes wrought on form and face;
    No lower life that earth's embrace
May breed with him, can fright my faith.

Eternal process moving on,
    From state to state the spirit walks;
35   And these are but the shattered stalks,
Or ruined chrysalis of one.

Nor blame I Death, because he bare
    The use of virtue out of earth;
    I know transplanted human worth
40 Will bloom to profit, otherwhere.

For this alone on Death I wreak
    The wrath that garners in my heart;
    He put our lives so far apart
We cannot hear each other speak.

He put our lives so far apart
We cannot hear each other speak.

The Speaker in Poetry
What do you learn about the speaker in lines 21–24?

Analyzing Philosophical Beliefs
In lines 29–44, what does the poet suggest about the consolations of faith and philosophy?

Vocabulary
chrysalis (kris´ l is)
n. the third stage in the development of a moth or butterfly

Comprehension
What are two of the main feelings Tennyson conveys in these stanzas?

I prosper, circled with thy voice;

I shall not lose thee though I die.

130

45 Thy voice is on the rolling air;
        I hear thee where the waters run;
        Thou standest in the rising sun,
And in the setting thou art fair.

What art thou then? I cannot guess;
50   But though I seem in star and flower
        To feel thee some diffusive power,
I do not therefore love thee less.

My love involves the love before;
        My love is vaster passion now;
55   Though mixed with God and Nature thou,
I seem to love thee more and more.

Far off thou art, but ever nigh;
        I have thee still, and I rejoice;
        I prosper, circled with thy voice;
60 I shall not lose thee though I die.

Vocabulary

diffusive (di fyoo′ siv) *adj.*
tending to spread out

prosper (präs′ pər) *v.*
thrive

Critical Reading

1. **Key Ideas and Details (a)** In section 1, what idea does the speaker say he once held as truth but now doubts?
(b) Interpret: The speaker rejects this truth in favor of a new view of grief. Paraphrase this view.

2. **Key Ideas and Details (a)** By what place is the speaker standing in section 7? **(b) Interpret:** What effect does the loss of his friend have on the scene?

3. **Integration of Knowledge and Ideas** Contrast the facts that, in section 82, the speaker says do not anger him with the one fact that does.

4. **Integration of Knowledge and Ideas (a) Interpret:** Explain the paradox in line 57: "Far off thou art, but ever nigh."
(b) Connect: How does section 130 answer the speaker's one reason for anger in section 82?

The Lady of SHALOTT

ALFRED, LORD TENNYSON

PART I

On either side the river lie
Long fields of barley and of rye,
That clothe the wold[1] and meet the sky;
And through the field the road runs by
5   To many-towered Camelot,[2]
And up and down the people go,
Gazing where the lilies blow[3]
Round an island there below,
     The island of Shalott.

10 Willows whiten, aspens quiver,
Little breezes dusk and shiver
Through the wave that runs forever
By the island in the river
     Flowing down to Camelot.
15 Four gray walls, and four gray towers,
Overlook a space of flowers,
And the silent isle imbowers
     The Lady of Shalott.

The Lady of Shalott, (detail), John Waterhouse, The Tate Gallery, London

The Speaker in Poetry

What does setting this poem in the days of King Arthur suggest about the poet's attitude toward the past?

---

1. **wold** rolling plains.
2. **Camelot** legendary English town where King Arthur had his court and Round Table.
3. **blow** bloom.

The Lady of Shalott, John Waterhouse, The Tate Gallery, London

▲ **Critical Viewing**
What symbols of the Lady of Shalott's occupation and eventual fate are in this painting? Explain why they are significant. **INTERPRET**

By the margin, willow-veiled,
20 Slide the heavy barges trailed
By slow horses; and unhailed
The shallop[4] flitteth silken-sailed
    Skimming down to Camelot:
But who hath seen her wave her hand?
25 Or at the casement seen her stand?
Or is she known in all the land,
    The Lady of Shalott?

Only reapers, reaping early
In among the bearded barley,
30 Hear a song that echoes cheerly,
From the river winding clearly,
    Down to towered Camelot:
And by the moon the reaper weary,
Piling sheaves in uplands airy,
35 Listening, whispers, "'Tis the fairy
    Lady of Shalott."

4. shallop light, open boat.

PART II

There she weaves by night and day
A magic web with colors gay.
She has heard a whisper say,
A curse is on her if she stay
    To look down to Camelot.
She knows not what the curse may be,
And so she weaveth steadily,
And little other care hath she,
    The Lady of Shalott.

And moving through a mirror[5] clear
That hangs before her all the year,
Shadows of the world appear.
There she sees the highway near
    Winding down to Camelot:
There the river eddy whirls,
And there the surly village churls,[6]
And the red cloaks of market girls,
    Pass onward from Shalott.

Sometimes a troop of damsels glad,
An abbot on an ambling pad,[7]
Sometimes a curly shepherd lad,
Or long-haired page in crimson clad,
    Goes by to towered Camelot;
And sometimes through the mirror blue
The knights come riding two and two:
She hath no loyal knight and true,
    The Lady of Shalott.

But in her web she still delights
To weave the mirror's magic sights,
For often through the silent nights
A funeral, with plumes and lights
    And music, went to Camelot:
Or when the moon was overhead,
Came two young lovers lately wed;
"I am half sick of shadows," said
    The Lady of Shalott.

Line numbers: 40, 45, 50, 55, 60, 65, 70

The Speaker in Poetry

Is the speaker who tells the Lady of Shalott's story also a character in the poem? How can you tell?

Comprehension

What does the Lady of Shalott do with her time?

---

5. mirror Weavers placed mirrors in front of their looms, so that they could view the progress of their work.

6. churls (churlz) *n.* farm laborers; peasants.

7. pad easy-paced horse.

PART III

A bow-shot from her bower eaves,
He rode between the barley sheaves,
75   The sun came dazzling through the leaves,
And flamed upon the brazen greaves[8]
      Of bold Sir Lancelot.
A red-cross knight[9] forever kneeled
To a lady in his shield,
80   That sparkled on the yellow field,
      Beside remote Shalott.

The gemmy[10] bridle glittered free,
Like to some branch of stars we see
Hung in the golden Galaxy.[11]
85   The bridle bells rang merrily
      As he rode down to Camelot:
And from his blazoned baldric[12] slung
A mighty silver bugle hung,
And as he rode his armor rung,
90   Beside remote Shalott.

All in the blue unclouded weather
Thick-jeweled shone the saddle leather,
The helmet and the helmet feather
Burned like one burning flame together,
95   As he rode down to Camelot.
As often through the purple night,
Below the starry clusters bright,
Some bearded meteor, trailing light,
      Moves over still Shalott.

100   His broad clear brow in sunlight glowed;
On burnish'd hooves his war horse trode;
From underneath his helmet flowed
His coal-black curls as on he rode,
      As he rode down to Camelot.
105   From the bank and from the river
He flashed into the crystal mirror,
"Tirra lirra," by the river
      Sang Sir Lancelot.

---

8. greaves armor that protects the legs below the kneecaps.
9. red-cross knight refers to the Redcrosse Knight from *The Faerie Queene* by Edmund Spenser. The knight is a symbol of holiness.
10. gemmy jeweled.
11. Galaxy the Milky Way.
12. blazoned baldric decorated sash worn diagonally across the chest.

She left the web, she left the loom,
110 She made three paces through the room,
She saw the waterlily bloom,
She saw the helmet and the plume,
　　She looked down to Camelot.
Out flew the web and floated wide;
115 The mirror cracked from side to side;
"The curse is come upon me," cried
　　The Lady of Shalott.

PART IV

In the stormy east wind straining,
The pale yellow woods were waning,
120 The broad stream in his banks complaining,
Heavily the low sky raining
　　Over towered Camelot;
Down she came and found a boat
Beneath a willow left afloat,
125 And round about the prow she wrote
　　The Lady of Shalott.

And down the river's dim expanse
Like some bold seër in a trance,
Seeing all his own mischance—
130 With a glassy countenance
　　Did she look to Camelot.
And at the closing of the day
She loosed the chain, and down she lay;
The broad stream bore her far away,
135 　　The Lady of Shalott.

Lying, robed in snowy white
That loosely flew to left and right—
The leaves upon her falling light—
Through the noises of the night
140 　　She floated down to Camelot:
And as the boathead wound along
The willowy hills and fields among,
They heard her singing her last song,
　　The Lady of Shalott.

145 Heard a carol, mournful, holy,
Chanted loudly, chanted lowly,
Till her blood was frozen slowly,
And her eyes were darkened wholly,
　　Turned to towered Camelot.

The Speaker in Poetry
How does the speaker create the sense that a decisive moment has arrived?

Vocabulary
waning (wān´ iŋ) *v.* gradually becoming dimmer or weaker

Comprehension
What does the Lady of Shalott do once she sees Sir Lancelot?

The Lady of Shalott **967**

150 For ere she reached upon the tide
    The first house by the waterside,
    Singing in her song she died,
        The Lady of Shalott.

    Under tower and balcony,
155 By garden wall and gallery,
    A gleaming shape she floated by,
    Dead-pale between the houses high,
        Silent into Camelot.
    Out upon the wharfs they came,
160 Knight and burgher, lord and dame,
    And round the prow they read her name,
        The Lady of Shalott.

    Who is this? and what is here?
    And in the lighted palace near
165 Died the sound of royal cheer;
    And they crossed themselves for fear,
        All the knights at Camelot:
    But Lancelot mused a little space;
    He said, "She has a lovely face;
170 God in his mercy lend her grace,
        The Lady of Shalott."

Critical Reading

Cite textual evidence to support your responses.

1. **Key Ideas and Details (a)** What does the Lady spend her time doing? Why? **(b) Interpret:** Why does the Lady glimpse only "shadows of the world"? **(c) Interpret:** Why might an artist share the complaint the Lady makes in lines 71–72?

2. **Key Ideas and Details (a)** What does the Lady do after seeing Sir Lancelot in the mirror? **(b) Analyze:** How does the long description of Sir Lancelot make the knight seem like the real-life embodiment of a vision? **(c) Draw Conclusions:** Given this description of Lancelot, explain why the Lady might be said to leave her room in pursuit of her visions.

3. **Key Ideas and Details (a) Draw Conclusions:** What does the fact that the Lady dies before meeting Lancelot suggest about her love for him? **(b) Make a Judgment:** Do you agree with Tennyson's implication that we can never realize our fantasies? Why or why not?

4. **Integration of Knowledge and Ideas** The poem suggests that the life of the imagination isolates one from reality. Do modern media outlets, such as television and the Internet, suggest otherwise? Explain.

TEARS, *Idle* TEARS

ALFRED, LORD TENNYSON

BACKGROUND *The Princess* (1847) is a long
narrative poem that contains a number of songs. Some
of these songs, including the one that follows, are
considered to be among the finest of Tennyson's lyrics.

Tears, idle tears, I know not what they mean,
Tears from the depth of some divine despair
Rise in the heart, and gather to the eyes,
In looking on the happy autumn fields,
5   And thinking of the days that are no more.

Fresh as the first beam glittering on a sail,
That brings our friends up from the underworld,
Sad as the last which reddens over one
That sinks with all we love below the verge;
10 So sad, so fresh, the days that are no more.

Ah, sad and strange as in dark summer dawns
The earliest pipe of half-awakened birds
To dying ears, when unto dying eyes
The casement slowly grows a glimmering square;
15 So sad, so strange, the days that are no more.

Dear as remembered kisses after death,
And sweet as those by hopeless fancy feigned
On lips that are for others; deep as love,
Deep as first love, and wild with all regret;
20 O Death in Life, the days that are no more.

Comprehension
What is the speaker's
reaction to the thought
of "the days that are
no more"?

ALFRED, LORD TENNYSON

Ulysses

BACKGROUND In this poem, Tennyson extends the story of Ulysses (yoo lis′ ez′), the hero of Homer's epic the *Odyssey*. Homer's writing ends after Ulysses' triumphant return home to Ithaca. Years later, Tennyson tells us, the hero has grown restless. Although he had been away for twenty long years—ten fighting in the Trojan War and another ten on a long and adventure-filled voyage back—Ulysses finds that he is contemplating yet another journey.

It little profits that an idle king,
By this still hearth, among these barren crags,
Matched with an aged wife, I mete and dole[1]
Unequal[2] laws unto a savage race,
5 That hoard, and sleep, and feed, and know not me.
I cannot rest from travel; I will drink
Life to the lees.[3] All times I have enjoyed
Greatly, have suffered greatly, both with those
That loved me, and alone; on shore, and when
10 Through scudding drifts the rainy Hyades[4]
Vexed the dim sea. I am become a name;
For always roaming with a hungry heart
Much have I seen and known—cities of men
And manners, climates, councils, governments,
15 Myself not least, but honored of them all—
And drunk delight of battle with my peers,
Far on the ringing plains of windy Troy.
I am a part of all that I have met;
Yet all experience is an arch wherethrough
20 Gleams that untraveled world, whose
     margin fades
Forever and forever when I move.
How dull it is to pause, to make an end,
To rust unburnished, not to shine in use!
As though to breathe were life. Life piled on life
25 Were all too little, and of one to me
Little remains; but every hour is saved
From that eternal silence, something more,
A bringer of new things; and vile it were
For some three suns to store and hoard myself,

The Speaker in Poetry
Who is speaking the words of this poem? How can you tell?

◀ **Critical Viewing**
Compare the character of Ulysses conveyed by this painting with the speaker in the poem. **COMPARE AND CONTRAST**

Comprehension
What has Ulysses encountered on his travels?

---

1. mete and dole measure and give out.
2. unequal unfair.
3. lees sediment.
4. Hyades (hī′ ə dēz′) group of stars whose rising was assumed to be followed by rain.

Analyzing Philosophical Beliefs

What do lines 22-32 suggest about Tennyson's philosophical beliefs?

Vocabulary

prudence (prōō′ ns) *n.* careful management of resources; economy

30   And this gray spirit yearning in desire
     To follow knowledge like a sinking star,
     Beyond the utmost bound of human thought.
          This is my son, mine own Telemachus,
     To whom I leave the scepter and the isle[5]
35   Well-loved of me, discerning to fulfill
     This labor, by slow prudence to make mild
     A rugged people, and through soft degrees
     Subdue them to the useful and the good.
     Most blameless is he, centered in the sphere
40   Of common duties, decent not to fail
     In offices of tenderness, and pay
     Meet[6] adoration to my household gods,
     When I am gone. He works his work, I mine.
          There lies the port; the vessel puffs her sail;
45   There gloom the dark broad seas. My mariners,
     Souls that have toiled and wrought, and thought with me—
     That ever with a frolic welcome took
     The thunder and the sunshine, and opposed
     Free hearts, free foreheads—you and I are old;
50   Old age hath yet his honor and his toil;
     Death closes all; but something ere the end,
     Some work of noble note, may yet be done,
     Not unbecoming men that strove with Gods.
     The lights begin to twinkle from the rocks;
55   The long day wanes; the slow moon climbs; the deep
     Moans round with many voices. Come, my friends,
     'Tis not too late to seek a newer world.
     Push off, and sitting well in order smite
     The sounding furrows; for my purpose holds

Vocabulary

furrows (fᴜr′ ōz) *n.* narrow grooves, such as those made by a plow

---

5. isle Ithaca, an island off the coast of Greece.
6. meet appropriate.

HOW DULL IT IS TO PAUSE, TO MAKE AN END, TO RUST UNBURNISHED, NOT TO **SHINE IN USE!**

60   To sail beyond the sunset, and the baths
    Of all the western stars, until I die.
    It may be that the gulfs will wash us down;
    It may be we shall touch the Happy Isles,[7]
    And see the great Achilles,[8] whom we knew.
65   Though much is taken, much abides; and though
    We are not now that strength which in old days
    Moved earth and heaven, that which we are, we are—
    One equal temper of heroic hearts,
    Made weak by time and fate, but strong in will
70   To strive, to seek, to find, and not to yield.

---

7. Happy Isles Elysium, or the Islands of the Blessed: in classical mythology, the place heroes went after death.

8. Achilles (ə kil′ ēz′) Greek hero of the Trojan War.

Critical Reading

1. **Key Ideas and Details (a)** What three comparisons in "Tears, Idle Tears" describe "the days that are no more"? **(b) Analyze:** What contrast does each comparison involve? **(c) Interpret:** What feelings does the line "Deep as first love, and wild with all regret" capture?

2. **Key Ideas and Details (a)** In "Ulysses," how does Ulysses describe his situation? **(b) Compare and Contrast:** How does this situation contrast with his previous experiences? **(c) Draw Conclusions:** What is Ulysses' attitude toward his experiences?

3. **Key Ideas and Details (a)** According to lines 58–61, what is Ulysses' purpose? **(b) Draw Conclusions:** What are Ulysses' feelings about aging? **(c) Draw Conclusions:** What is his attitude toward life in general?

4. **Integration of Knowledge and Ideas** What values do you think Tennyson celebrates in his poetry? Explain using two of these Essential Question words: *universe, rationalism, curiosity, challenge.* *[Connecting to the Essential Question: How does literature shape or reflect society?]*

Cite textual evidence to support your responses.

Literary Analysis

**Common Core
State Standards**

Writing
2. Write informative/
explanatory texts to
examine and convey
complex ideas, concepts,
and information clearly
and accurately through
the effective selection,
organization, and analysis
of content. *(p. 975)*

Language
4.a. Use context as a clue
to the meaning of a word
or phrase. *(p. 975)*

1. **Craft and Structure (a)** Who is the **speaker** of *In Memoriam, A.H.H.*? **(b)** Tennyson wrote the poem in direct response to his friend's death. How does the speaker's conflict reflect one that Tennyson might have felt?

2. **Key Ideas and Details Analyze the philosophical assumptions and beliefs** Tennyson expresses in *In Memoriam, A.H.H.* What attitudes toward faith and hope can you detect?

3. **Craft and Structure (a)** Who is the speaker of "The Lady of Shalott"? **(b)** Is the speaker fictional or real, generalized or specific? Explain.

4. **Integration of Knowledge and Ideas** Why might Tennyson have identified the situation of a poet with the Lady's situation?

5. **Key Ideas and Details** Tennyson's work is considered to be reflective of the Victorian period. What philosophical assumption about the spiritual condition of Victorian society is demonstrated in "The Lady of Shalott"?

6. **Integration of Knowledge and Ideas** Compare the speaker's relationship with the past in "Tears, Idle Tears" and in *In Memoriam, A.H.H.*

7. **Key Ideas and Details (a)** Describe the conflict faced by the speaker in "Ulysses." **(b)** Does Tennyson see Ulysses as heroic or as selfish and self-justifying? Support your answer by quoting from the poem.

8. **Key Ideas and Details** Tennyson lived in an age that accepted the idea of progress, believing the acquisition of knowledge would lead to a better world. Identify two passages in "Ulysses" that support this belief. Explain your choices.

9. **Integration of Knowledge and Ideas** Use a chart like the one shown to compare Ulysses' view of time with the Lady of Shalott's view.

	Past	Present	Future
Ulysses	Remembers it with satisfaction: "I am a part of all that I have met"		
The Lady of Shalott	Considers it identical with the present: "There she weaves by night and day"		

10. **Comparing Literary Works** Based on your understanding of his poems, which can you infer Tennyson values more—the timeless world of poetry or the perishable real world? Support your view.

Vocabulary Acquisition and Use

Word Analysis: Literal and Figurative Meanings

Many words have both a literal meaning and a figurative one. This is a broader or more symbolic meaning that often draws on the literal meaning. For instance, a *chrysalis* is the stage in the life of a butterfly in which the insect grows in a cocoon before emerging as an adult butterfly. Tennyson, in *In Memoriam, A.H.H.,* uses the word figuratively to refer to stages of human life. His image has a richer meaning, though. In the cocoon, the chrysalis changes from caterpillar to butterfly, just as death may transform a person from physical to spiritual life. Identify the literal and figurative meanings of these other words Tennyson uses:

1. doors (*In Memoriam, A.H.H.,* line 19)
2. bald (*In Memoriam, A.H.H.,* line 28)
3. lees ("Ulysses," line 7)
4. hungry ("Ulysses," line 12)
5. shine ("Ulysses," line 23)

Vocabulary: Context

The context of a word—the lines or phrases around it—can provide clues to the meaning of an unfamiliar word. Identify the contextual meaning of each italicized vocabulary word below and explain how context makes that meaning clear.

1. As the sun rose, its *diffusive* light reached into all the shadows of the night, revealing sharp edges and colors.
2. His popularity *waning,* the actor could no longer command starring roles.
3. When the *chrysalis* turns into the adult butterfly, the empty cocoon remains behind.
4. Her natural *prudence* prevented her from taking any rash action.
5. The *furrows* on his parents' foreheads showed their anxiety.
6. After launching the new business, she worked day and night to ensure it would *prosper.*

Writing to Sources

Informative Text Arthur Hallam's death had a decisive influence not only on Tennyson's life but also on his poetry. Writing *In Memoriam, A.H.H.* gave Tennyson the money he needed to buy his own land. Write a **biographical essay** that recounts the details of Tennyson's life and work, examining the *cause-and-effect relationships* between them.

Prewriting Research Tennyson's life and work. Outline the main events of his life and make a chart of his main accomplishments and literary themes. Take notes on ways his life and work affected each other.

Draft Draft your essay, following the *correct sequence of events* and locating incidents in specific places where they occurred. In your draft, explore the significance of major events in Tennyson's life, clarifying the way his life influenced his work and vice versa.

Revising Read through your draft to make sure that you present the correct sequence of events and clearly explain cause-and-effect relationships. Be sure that you have ample evidence or solid reasoning to claim such a relationship. If not, revise your text to support your claim.

Model: Charting Cause-and-Effect Relationships

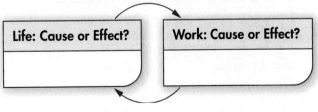

Life: Cause or Effect?	Work: Cause or Effect?

Connecting to the Essential Question Robert Browning's monologues were innovative in adapting dramatic devices to poetry. As you read, notice what makes these poems dramatic. This will help you address the Essential Question: **What is the relationship of the writer to tradition?**

Common Core State Standards

Reading Literature
3. Analyze the impact of the author's choices regarding how to develop and relate elements of a story or drama.

Close Reading Focus

Dramatic Monologue

Robert Browning perfected the **dramatic monologue,** in which a single character delivers a speech. His monologues contain these elements:

- A speaker who indirectly reveals his or her situation and character
- A silent listener, addressed by the speaker and implied in what the speaker says

Browning's decision to write "My Last Duchess" as a dramatic monologue allows him to develop a dramatic, tension-filled scene in which the reader does not immediately understand who is speaking, who is being addressed, and what has happened to the "last Duchess." Further, having only the duke speaking highlights his egotism. As you read, consider other ways that using the form of a dramatic monologue allows the author to develop the narrative and convey meaning.

Comparing Literary Works Robert Browning's monologues capture the rhythms of speech through **run-on lines**—lines whose natural flow goes past line endings:

> But to myself they turned (since none puts by
> The curtain I have drawn for you, but I)

He and Elizabeth Barrett also use **end-stopped lines,** which end just where a speaker would pause. Compare the poets' use of these devices.

Preparing to Read Complex Texts You can better understand the theme of a poem if you **compare and contrast speakers in multiple poems.** For example, you might gain insights into the selfish, possessive love of the speaker in one poem if you compare it to the deep, abiding love of the speaker in another. Use a diagram like the one shown to compare and contrast speakers in these poems.

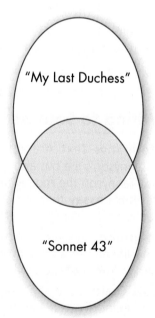

"My Last Duchess"

"Sonnet 43"

Vocabulary

The words below are important to understanding the texts that follow. Copy the words into your notebook, grouping them by number of syllables.

countenance	dowry
officious	eludes
munificence	sullen

Robert Browning

(1812–1889)

Author of "My Last Duchess" • "Life in a Love" • "Porphyria's Lover"

Young Robert Browning's best teacher may not have been a person, but his father's 6,000-book library. Although he had little schooling, he eagerly devoured those books, hungry for knowledge about history, art, and literature.

Inspiration and Discouragement By the time he was a teenager, Browning had decided to make poetry his life's pursuit. He published his first book, *Pauline,* at the age of twenty-one. Success was a while coming, though. A long and highly personal poem modeled after Shelley's work, *Pauline* did not sell a single copy.

Discouraged, Browning tried his hand at something less personal, a long dramatic poem called *Paracelsus.* He also wrote a play. His work still failed to attract much public notice, and his reputation was eclipsed by that of his wife, the poet Elizabeth Barrett Browning, whom he had married in 1846.

Lasting Fame In 1869, eight years after Elizabeth's death, the publication of *The Ring and the Book* turned Browning's career around. This long poem, based on an actual trial, tells the story of a murder in a series of dramatic monologues, or speeches by characters. *The Ring and the Book* achieved wide recognition for its author. It demonstrated the unique elements that Browning contributed to nineteenth-century poetry: a more down-to-earth, less "poetic" language and a renewal of the dramatic monologue, a literary form ideally suited to reveal character.

Today, Browning ranks with Tennyson as one of the great Victorian poets. His shorter dramatic monologues, such as "My Last Duchess," and "Porphyria's Lover," remain favorites of many.

My Last Duchess

Robert Browning

Background *This poem, set in the sixteenth century in a castle in northern Italy, is based on events from the life of the duke of Ferrara, a nobleman whose first wife died after just three years of marriage. Following his wife's death, the duke began making arrangements to remarry. In Browning's poem, the duke is showing a painting of his first wife to an agent who represents the father of the woman he hopes to marry.*

That's my last Duchess painted on the wall,
Looking as if she were alive. I call
That piece a wonder, now: Frà Pandolf's[1] hands
Worked busily a day, and there she stands.
5   Will't please you sit and look at her? I said
"Frà Pandolf" by design, for never read
Strangers like you that pictured countenance
The depth and passion of its earnest glance,
But to myself they turned (since none puts by
10 The curtain I have drawn for you, but I)
And seemed as they would ask me, if they durst,[2]
How such a glance came there; so, not the first
Are you to turn and ask thus. Sir, 'twas not
Her husband's presence only, called that spot

---

1. **Frà Pandolf's** work of Brother Pandolf, an imaginary painter.
2. **durst** dared.

◄ **Critical Viewing**
This portrait of the duke of Ferrara's wife inspired Browning to write "My Last Duchess." Compare the character of the duchess as conveyed by the painting with the character of the duchess as described by the duke in the poem. **COMPARE AND CONTRAST**

Vocabulary
countenance (koun´ tə nəns) *n.* face

Comprehension
What are the duke and his listener viewing?

Dramatic Monologue

How does the duke indirectly suggest his own deeply jealous nature?

Vocabulary

officious (ə fish´ əs)
adj. meddlesome

Compare and Contrast Speakers

Based on the speaker's description (lines 13–31), what sort of person was the duchess? In contrast, what do lines 32–34 show about the speaker?

Vocabulary

munificence (myoo nif´ ə
səns) *n.* lavish generosity

dowry (dou´ rē) *n.* property brought by a woman's family to her husband upon their marriage

15 Of joy into the Duchess' cheek: perhaps
Frà Pandolf chanced to say "Her mantle laps
Over my lady's wrist too much," or "Paint
Must never hope to reproduce the faint
Half-flush that dies along her throat"; such stuff
20 Was courtesy, she thought, and cause enough
For calling up that spot of joy. She had
A heart—how shall I say?—too soon made glad,
Too easily impressed; she liked whate'er
She looked on, and her looks went everywhere.
25 Sir, 'twas all one! My favor at her breast,
The dropping of the daylight in the West,
The bough of cherries some officious fool
Broke in the orchard for her, the white mule
She rode with round the terrace—all and each
30 Would draw from her alike the approving speech,
Or blush, at least. She thanked men—good! but thanked
  Somehow—I know not how—as if she ranked
My gift of a nine-hundred-year-old name
With anybody's gift. Who'd stoop to blame
35 This sort of trifling? Even had you skill
In speech—(which I have not)—to make your will
Quite clear to such an one, and say, "Just this
Or that in you disgusts me; here you miss,
Or there exceed the mark"—and if she let
40 Herself be lessoned so, nor plainly set
Her wits to yours, forsooth,[3] and made excuse,
—E'en then would be some stooping; and I choose
Never to stoop. Oh sir, she smiled, no doubt,
Whene'er I passed her; but who passed without
45 Much the same smile? This grew; I gave commands;
Then all smiles stopped together. There she stands
As if alive. Will 't please you rise? We'll meet
The company below, then. I repeat,
The Count your master's known munificence
50 Is ample warrant that no one just pretense
Of mine for dowry will be disallowed;
Though his fair daughter's self, as I avowed
At starting, is my object. Nay, we'll go
Together down, sir! Notice Neptune,[4] though,
55 Taming a sea horse, thought a rarity,
Which Claus of Innsbruck[5] cast in bronze for me!

---

3. **forsooth** in truth.
4. **Neptune** in Roman mythology, the god of the sea.
5. **Claus of Innsbruck** imaginary Austrian sculptor.

Life in a Love

Robert Browning

Escape me?
    Never—
    Beloved!
While I am I, and you are you,
5   So long as the world contains us both,
    Me the loving and you the loth,
While the one eludes, must the other pursue.
My life is a fault at last, I fear:
It seems too much like a fate, indeed!
10 Though I do my best I shall scarce succeed.
But what if I fail of my purpose here?
It is but to keep the nerves at strain,
To dry one's eyes and laugh at a fall,
And, baffled, get up and begin again,—
15 So the chase takes up one's life, that's all.
While, look but once from your farthest bound
At me so deep in the dust and dark,
No sooner the old hope goes to ground
Than a new one, straight to the self-same mark,
20 I shape me—
    Ever
    Removed!

Compare and Contrast Speakers

How is the speaker's attitude toward his beloved in this poem like and unlike the attitude toward his former wife of the speaker in "My Last Duchess"?

Vocabulary

eludes (ē loodz´) v. avoids or escapes

Critical Reading

1. **Key Ideas and Details (a)** What complaint does the speaker make about his first wife in lines 13–24 of "My Last Duchess"? **(b) Infer:** How did he respond to her behavior? **(c) Support:** Explain what has happened to the duchess, indicating where in the poem this is revealed.

2. **Key Ideas and Details (a)** To what new subject does the speaker turn in his last remark? **(b) Draw Conclusions:** What does this change of subject reveal about his character?

3. **Key Ideas and Details (a)** What does the speaker of "Life in a Love" do as his beloved eludes him? **(b) Interpret:** What causes his behavior?

4. **Integration of Knowledge and Ideas** Is the speaker's "love" truly love? Explain.

Cite textual evidence to support your responses.

PORPHYRIA'S LOVER

Robert Browning

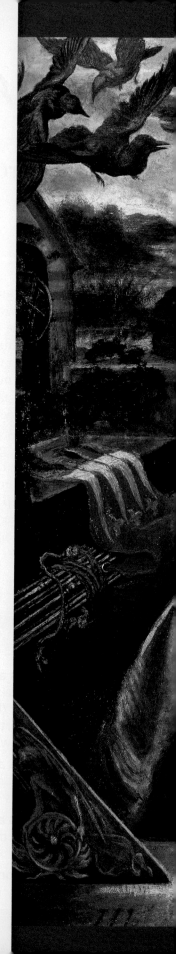

Vocabulary

sullen (səl´ ən) *adj.*
brooding; morose; sulky

The rain set early in tonight,
    The sullen wind was soon awake,
It tore the elm-tops down for spite,
    And did its worst to vex the lake:
5   I listened with heart fit to break.
When glided in Porphyria; straight
    She shut the cold out and the storm,
And kneeled and made the cheerless grate
    Blaze up, and all the cottage warm;
10   Which done, she rose, and from her form
Withdrew the dripping cloak and shawl,
    And laid her soiled gloves by, untied
Her hat and let the damp hair fall,
    And, last, she sat down by my side
15   And called me. When no voice replied,
She put my arm about her waist,
    And made her smooth white shoulder bare,
And all her yellow hair displaced,
    And, stooping, made my cheek lie there,
20   And spread, o'er all, her yellow hair,
Murmuring how she loved me—she
    Too weak, for all her heart's endeavor,
To set its struggling passion free
    From pride, and vainer ties dissever,

▶ **Critical Viewing**

Does the subject of this
painting seem to be in
love, as Porphyria is? Why
or why not? **INFER**

983

I AM QUITE
SURE SHE
FELT NO
PAIN

Compare and Contrast Speakers

From the contrast between the speaker's words and actions, what can you conclude about his mental state?

25   And give herself to me for ever.
         But passion sometimes would prevail,
             Nor could tonight's gay feast restrain
         A sudden thought of one so pale
             For love of her, and all in vain:
30   So, she was come through wind and rain.
         Be sure I looked up at her eyes
             Happy and proud; at last I knew
         Porphyria worshipped me; surprise
             Made my heart swell, and still it grew
35   While I debated what to do.
         That moment she was mine, mine, fair,
             Perfectly pure and good: I found
         A thing to do, and all her hair
             In one long yellow string I wound
40   Three times her little throat around,
         And strangled her. No pain felt she;
             I am quite sure she felt no pain.
         As a shut bud that holds a bee,
             I warily oped her lids: again
45   Laughed the blue eyes without a stain.
         And I untightened next the tress
             About her neck; her cheek once more
         Blushed bright beneath my burning kiss:
             I propped her head up as before,
50   Only, this time my shoulder bore
         Her head, which droops upon it still:
             The smiling rosy little head,
         So glad it has its utmost will,
             That all it scorned at once is fled,
55   And I, its love, am gained instead!
         Porphyria's love: she guessed not how
             Her darling one wish would be heard.
         And thus we sit together now,
             And all night long we have not stirred,
60   And yet God has not said a word!

Critical Reading

Cite textual evidence to support your responses.

1. **Craft and Structure** Does this monologue have such dramatic elements as conflict, resolution, dialogue, and stage directions? Explain.

2. **Craft and Structure** What makes the last line especially dramatic? Explain.

(1806–1861)

ELIZABETH
BARRETT
Browning

Author of Sonnet 43

Like her future husband, young Elizabeth Barrett had no formal education. However, her zest for knowledge spurred her to learn eight languages on her own. By the time she was ten, she had read plays by Shakespeare, passages of *Paradise Lost*, and histories of England, Greece, and Rome. The oldest of eleven children in an upper-middle-class family, she began writing poetry as a child. By the time she reached adulthood, she had published two volumes of verse.

Frailty and Romance Elizabeth Barrett's frail health, caused by a spinal injury, made her something of a recluse. But her poetry attracted much attention, including that of Robert Browning, who wrote her a letter of appreciation. After five months of correspondence, she and Browning met and fell in love. Her father objected to their romance, but Elizabeth and Robert married in 1846 and ran away to Florence, Italy, where they had a son they nicknamed Pen and lived in happy exile. In Italy, Elizabeth Barrett took an interest in politics and wrote denunciations of slavery in the United States. She died in Florence in 1861.

Shifting Reputations It is hard for us to believe today, when Robert Browning's reputation is so great, that Elizabeth was the more famous poet during her lifetime. Her love story in verse, *Aurora Leigh* (1857), was so popular that the income from it helped support the Brownings. Also popular was her *Sonnets from the Portuguese*, a sequence of forty-four love poems written to her husband. Sonnet 43, which comes from this collection, has appeared in countless anthologies and has assured her place in the history of English poetry.

Sonnet 43

ELIZABETH BARRETT BROWNING

Compare and Contrast Speakers

Compare and contrast the love expressed here with the speaker's love for Porphyria in "Porphyria's Lover." What, if anything, do the two types of love have in common? How are they different?

How do I love thee? Let me count the ways.
I love thee to the depth and breadth and height
My soul can reach, when feeling out of sight
For the ends of Being and ideal Grace.
5 I love thee to the level of every day's
Most quiet need, by sun and candlelight.
I love thee freely, as men strive for Right;
I love thee purely, as they turn from Praise.
I love thee with the passion put to use
10 In my old griefs, and with my childhood's faith.
I love thee with a love I seemed to lose
With my lost saints—I love thee with the breath,
Smiles, tears, of all my life!—and, if God choose,
I shall but love thee better after death.

Critical Reading

Cite textual evidence to support your responses.

1. **Key Ideas and Details (a)** In Sonnet 43, what question does the speaker ask? **(b) Paraphrase:** Briefly summarize the speaker's answers to her own question.

2. **Integration of Knowledge and Ideas** Cite a popular song that praises love, and compare its language, attitude, and images with those of Sonnet 43.

3. **Integration of Knowledge and Ideas** Which speakers in these poems are most dramatic? Explain, using three of these Essential Question words: *psychological, emotional, motivation, rationalize, confront.* *[Connecting to the Essential Question: What is the relationship of the writer to tradition?]*

Literary Analysis

1. **Craft and Structure (a)** Who delivers the **dramatic monologue** in "My Last Duchess," and who is the listener? **(b)** How can you tell when the listener interacts with the speaker? Give an example.

2. **Key Ideas and Details (a)** Cite two lines in which the speaker reveals something negative about himself. **(b)** Basing your answer on this monologue, do you think the speaker's next marriage will be successful? Explain.

3. **Key Ideas and Details (a)** Who are the speaker and the listener in "Life in a Love"? **(b)** Do they interact with each other? Explain.

4. **Key Ideas and Details (a)** Characterize the speaker in "Porphyria's Lover." **(b)** Whom do you think he might be addressing?

5. **Integration of Knowledge and Ideas Compare and contrast the speakers'** behavior in "My Last Duchess" and "Porphyria's Lover." What is similar about their actions? What is different about the reasons for their actions?

6. **Craft and Structure (a)** Use a chart like the one shown to analyze the places at which a speaker would naturally pause in lines 14–22 of "My Last Duchess." **(b)** How does the lack of **end-stopped lines** and the use of **run-on lines** and pauses within lines create a conversational rhythm?

Line 14:	Her hus-	-band's pre-	-sence on-	-ly, called	that spot
Natural Pauses	no pause	no pause	no pause	**pause**	no pause

7. **Craft and Structure** Use a similar chart to analyze the rhythms of Elizabeth Barrett Browning's Sonnet 43.

8. **Comparing Literary Works (a)** Compare the rhythms of speech in the two poems. **(b)** Which rhythm is more dramatic? Explain.

9. **Integration of Knowledge and Ideas (a)** What is similar about the mental state of the speakers in all three poems by Robert Browning? Cite details to support your comparisons. **(b)** How do the tones or attitudes of all three speakers differ?

10. **Analyzing Visual Information** What qualities in Robert Browning's work earned it the popularity suggested by this Victorian cartoon?

TRUE LITERARY EXCLUSIVENESS.
"Don't you admire Robert Browning as a poet, Mr. Fitzsnook?" "I used to, once; but everybody admires him now, don'tcherknow—so I've had to give him up!"▶

 **Common Core State Standards**

Writing
1. Write arguments to support claims in an analysis of substantive topics or texts, using valid reasoning and relevant and sufficient evidence. *(p. 988)*

1.d. Establish and maintain a formal style and objective tone while attending to the norms and conventions of the discipline in which they are writing. *(p. 988)*

Language
4.b. Identify and correctly use patterns of word changes that indicate different meanings or parts of speech. *(p. 988)*

Vocabulary Acquisition and Use

Word Analysis: Latin Suffix -ence

The Latin suffix -ence means "quality of," or "state of being." Words with this ending are often nouns that are closely related to adjectives. The adjective *munificent*, for example, means "very generous." Replacing the suffix -ent with -ence yields the noun *munificence*, "the state of being very generous." Write the noun forms of each of these words and then write an original sentence using each word.

1. innocent
2. intelligent
3. obedient
4. permanent
5. prominent
6. insistent

Vocabulary: Analogies

In an analogy, the relationship between two words is explained by comparing it to the relationship between two other words. Discern the meaning of the words from the vocabulary list on page 976 by using each word once to complete these analogies. Explain each choice.

1. *Building* is to *edifice* as *escapes* is to _____.
2. _____ is to *husband* as *gift* is to *charity*.
3. *Dialogue* is to *play* as _____ is to *portrait*.
4. *Silence* is to *noise* as _____ is to *happy*.
5. _____ is to *annoying* as *attentive* is to *pleasing*.
6. *Starting* is to *stopping* as _____ is to *greed*.

Writing to Sources

Argumentative Text The duke in "My Last Duchess" has proposed marriage to another woman. Her father has hired you, a detective, to investigate the duke's history and character. Your task is to write a **report** to the father recommending whether he should allow the marriage to take place.

Prewriting Begin by reviewing the poem, noting what it reveals about the duke's character and first marriage. Draw from it as many facts as you can; infer others that you think are logical outgrowths of the duke's character. Think about the steps you might take to verify these facts so that you can detail those actions in your report. Speculate about what might have caused the duke's behavior.

Drafting Write your report using the *format* a detective might employ. For instance, you might state the date of the assignment and the subject. Include technical words that a detective might use, such as *surveillance, eyewitnesses, suspicions,* or *charges.* Keep in mind that you are a professional working for a client. Choose words, such as *suspect,* that create a formal, businesslike tone, rather than informal words such as *guy.*

> **Model: Revising to Add Transitional Words**
>
> As a result of my observations,
> I have concluded the duke is a <u>cruel and dangerous</u>
>   Therefore,
> man. ~~and~~ I advise you to <u>reject</u> his proposal to marry
> your daughter.

Transitional words and phrases highlight causes and effects.

Revising Review your draft, drawing arrows between observations and the conclusions they support. Where needed, add missing transitional words to clarify causes and effects.

The Novel

—D. H. LAWRENCE

Defining the Novel

A novel is a long work of prose fiction. As a genre, the novel is comparatively recent, though it has roots in the narratives of earlier ages. The length of a novel allows a writer great scope, and from its beginnings, the novel tended to survey—and sometimes criticize—a society, a social class, or a way of life as a whole. The English novel began with the work of writers such as Henry Fielding in the eighteenth century and reached full flower during the Victorian era with such classics as *Hard Times* and *David Copperfield* by Charles Dickens.

Types of Novels While novels need not belong to a specific type, many do. The following are traditional types:

- **Picaresque Novel:** relates the adventures of a traveling hero in episodic form
- **Historical Novel:** features characters and events from history
- **Novel of Manners:** shows the effects of social customs on individuals
- **Social Novel:** presents a large-scale portrait of an age, showing the influence of social and economic conditions on characters and events
- *Bildungsroman* **(Novel of Growth):** traces a protagonist's passage to adulthood

Literary Elements Nearly all novels contain certain basic literary elements, including **plot,** or an ordered sequence of events; **setting,** or the specific time and place of the action; **characters,** or the people who take part in the action; and a **theme,** or the insight into life conveyed by the work. In addition, as the novel developed historically, it emphasized or led to innovations in the literary elements shown in the chart below.

Close Read: Novelistic Literary Elements
These literary elements are called out in the Model text at right.

Narrative Technique: the way in which a writer tells a story. **Example:** *In* Mrs. Dalloway, *Virginia Woolf tells the story through the thoughts of her characters.*	**Philosophical Themes:** general ideas about existence and values. **Example:** *In* Crime and Punishment, *Fyodor Dostoyevsky's main character tries to apply new philosophical ideas, rejecting traditional morality.*
Social Commentary: writing that poses questions about or suggests criticisms of life in a society. **Example:** *In* Oliver Twist, *Charles Dickens's portrayal of the plight of a poor orphan is a call for reforms in England's treatment of its poor.*	**Realistic Description:** writing that attempts to accurately capture life in its details. **Example:** *In* The Jungle, *Upton Sinclair described industrial conditions in his day with grim accuracy.*

Model

About the Text The Russian novelist Fyodor Dostoyevsky (1821–1881), is noted for keen psychological portraits, including that of Raskolnikov in *Crime and Punishment.*

from **Crime and Punishment**
Fyodor Dostoyevsky (translated by Constance Garnett)

On an exceptionally hot evening early in July a young man came out of the garret in which he lodged in S. Place and walked slowly, as though in hesitation, towards K. bridge.

He had successfully avoided meeting his landlady on the staircase. His garret was under the roof of a high, five-storied house and was more like a cupboard than a room. The landlady who provided him with garret, dinners, and attendance, lived on the floor below, and every time he went out he was obliged to pass her kitchen, the door of which invariably stood open. And each time he passed, the young man had a sick, frightened feeling, which made him scowl and feel ashamed. He was hopelessly in debt to his landlady, and was afraid of meeting her....

This evening, however, on coming out into the street, he became acutely aware of his fears.

"I want to attempt a thing *like that* and am frightened by these trifles," he thought, with an odd smile. "Hm... yes, all is in a man's hands and he lets it all slip from cowardice, that's an axiom. It would be interesting to know what it is men are most afraid of. Taking a new step, uttering a new word is what they fear most.... But I am talking too much. It's because I chatter that I do nothing. Or perhaps it is that I chatter because I do nothing. I've learned to chatter this last month, lying for days together in my den thinking...of Jack the Giant-killer. Why am I going there now? Am I capable of *that*? Is *that* serious? It is not serious at all. It's simply a fantasy to amuse myself; a plaything! Yes, maybe it is a plaything."

The heat in the street was terrible: and the airlessness, the bustle and the plaster, scaffolding, bricks, and dust all about him, and that special Petersburg stench, so familiar to all who are unable to get out of town in summer—all worked painfully upon the young man's already overwrought nerves. The insufferable stench from the pot-houses, which are particularly numerous in that part of the town, and the drunken men whom he met continually, although it was a working day, completed the revolting misery of the picture. An expression of the profoundest disgust gleamed for a moment in the young man's refined face. He was, by the way, exceptionally handsome, above the average in height, slim, well-built, with beautiful dark eyes and dark brown hair. Soon he sank into deep thought, or more accurately speaking into a complete blankness of mind; he walked along not observing what was about him and not caring to observe it. From time to time, he would mutter something, from the habit of talking to himself, to which he had just confessed. At these moments he would become conscious that his ideas were sometimes in a tangle and that he was very weak; for two days he had scarcely tasted food.

Realistic Description The details in this passage realistically depict a poor young man's life, without apology or an attempt to "dress things up."

Narrative Technique The interior monologue, or direct representation of a character's thoughts, in this passage helps to advance the plot: The young man is plotting something that will require daring. It also helps to develop his character: he is beset by doubts and confusion.

Philosophical Themes Here, Dostoevsky hints at key philosophical questions in the novel: What are the limits on a person's freedom of choice? Are these limits valid—a matter of morals—or invalid—a matter of fear?

Social Commentary Details in this passage point to the inhuman, alienating conditions in the city and prompt questions about the society that has created these conditions.

Literary History: Dickens's World

"Dickens compounded characters of peculiar turns of speech and singular mannerisms, some endearing, *some frightening.*"

The Curious Workshop of Charles Dickens: Making Myths

Even if you have never read a novel by Charles Dickens, you have encountered his work. Characters such as the miser Ebenezer Scrooge and the orphan Oliver Twist stepped out from Dickens's books long ago to take up a life as old friends in musicals and cartoons. The very word *Dickensian* conjures obscure city streets populated by leering villains, honest clerks, wide-eyed innocents, and a host of knotty eccentrics.

Defining Dickens This generalized picture of Dickens and his works is based on his novels and Christmas stories, most published in serial form in magazines. Dickens's popularity in his own lifetime was enormous. With his first major effort, *The Pickwick Papers* (1836–1837), and for decades after, he held Victorian England spellbound, raptly awaiting the publication of the next chapter of *Oliver Twist* (1837–1839) or *Great Expectations* (1860–1861). When his character Little Nell of *The Old Curiosity Shop* (1840–1841) died, England was torn by grief.

Reformer and Myth-Maker In Dickens's lifetime, the Industrial Revolution left England overcrowded with the new working class, living in slums and riddled with epidemic fatal diseases. Dickens's stories of hard times and injured innocents challenged the forces that smothered compassion and nursed vice in the new society.

A Curious Workshop Yet Dickens does more than tell stories about social injustice. The most distinctive characteristic of his work might be its mythical or fairy tale–like quality. In the shadow of the factories choking London with smoke and slums, Dickens set up a workshop of the imagination, where he developed new myths of crime and redemption.

"A Perpetual Summer of Being Themselves" There are no John Smiths or Jane Joneses among Dickens's characters. From Samuel Pickwick to Wilkins Micawber to Uriah Heep, each character's name is a distinctive concoction of syllables, a two-word poem. The names reflect the quirkiness of the characters themselves. From the Rumplestiltskin-like Daniel Quilp of *The Old Curiosity Shop* to the hopelessly optimistic Mr. Micawber of *David Copperfield* (1849–1850), Dickens compounded characters of peculiar turns of speech and mannerisms, some endearing, some frightening.

Wicked Woods, Safe Havens Under Dickens's fairy-tale pen, the economic and social challenges of Victorian times reappear as a grotesque landscape, the literary equivalent of the woods in which a wicked witch lives. Here is Dickens's description of landscape surrounding a new railroad:

> Everywhere were bridges that led nowhere; thoroughfares that were wholly impassable; Babel towers of chimneys, wanting half their height; temporary wooden houses and enclosures, in the most unlikely situations; carcasses of ragged tenements, and fragments of unfinished walls and arches, and piles of scaffolding, and wildernesses of bricks, and giant forms of cranes, and tripods straddling above nothing. There were a hundred thousand shapes and substances of incompleteness. . . *(Dombey and Son, 1846–1848).*

Yet Dickens also creates islands of safety and refuge, such as the permanently beached boat in which David Copperfield finds happiness with the Peggoty family. In settings such as these, both Dickens's social criticism and his childlike attunement to the fairy-tale dimension of life have a place.

Dickens and Victorian England Dickens ruled over the imagination of Victorian England as a kind of father figure, by turns jolly and stern. He amuses his readers even while reprimanding their faults. Though there is much that is simply sentimental in Dickens, there are also depths of realism, an unflagging faith in redemption, and the eternal exuberance in human variety. Modern readers can still warm themselves at the cheerful glow of his work.

Speaking and Listening: Discussion

Comprehension and Collaboration Message Art Dickens was a brilliant novelist and social critic who blended scathing critiques of Victorian society with first-class literary entertainment.

With a group, discuss your thoughts about how modern writers, musicians, and entertainers convey messages of social or political reform. Use these questions to guide your discussion:

- Of the writers, musicians, and entertainers you know, which ones use their art to send a message? What are their messages?

- What effect, if any, do popular entertainers' social or political messages have on others?

- Do you think artists have a responsibility to make public their social or political messages? Explain.

Choose a point person to share your thoughts with the class.

CHARLES *Dickens*

(1812–1870)

No writer since Shakespeare has occupied as important a place in popular culture as Charles Dickens. His novels have held a special appeal for critics and the public alike. They have also been dramatized time and again in plays and films.

A CHILDHOOD OF HARDSHIP

Born in Portsmouth on England's southern coast, Dickens had a generally unhappy childhood. His father was sent to debtors' prison, and the boy was sent to a "prison" of his own—a factory in which he worked long hours pasting labels. Similar experiences, dramatizing the ills of the newly industrialized society, were to figure prominently in Dickens's novels.

THE BIRTH OF A WRITER

As a young man, Dickens held jobs as a stenographer in the courts and as a reporter for London newspapers. At twenty-one, he began to apply his keen powers of observation to producing humorous literary sketches of everyday life in London. A collection of these, *Sketches by Boz* (1836), earned him a small following, but his first novel, *The Pickwick Papers* (1837), made him the most popular writer of his day. Closely following were *Oliver Twist* (1839) and *Nicholas Nickleby* (1839).

A SERIOUS NOVELIST

The young Dickens reveled in the variety and peculiarity of the human character. Memorable characters like the charming Mr. Pickwick and the evil Fagin abound in his early work, but they are perhaps more like cartoons or natural forces than full-blooded characters. Dickens shows his growing mastery of characterization in *Dombey and Son* (1848) and *David Copperfield* (1850), novels of greater psychological depth. Throughout his work, Dickens offers his distinctive brand of social criticism, which is especially prominent in his masterpiece *Hard Times* (1854).

SERIALIZATION

Many of Dickens's novels, beginning with *The Pickwick Papers,* were published serially in magazines—a common method of writing and producing fiction at the time. Monthly installments often ended with uncertain or dangerous situations, leaving readers eagerly awaiting the next installment.

IMMENSE POPULARITY

Dickens developed an avid following, and he thrived on the support of the public. He was widely read in Europe and the United States. Always fond of theater, he gave dramatic public readings from his novels. In 1842, he crossed the Atlantic for a five-month lecture tour in the United States. The American public welcomed him enthusiastically but were less happy with him when he criticized social issues in the United States.

Without doubt, Dickens was the preeminent nineteenth-century novelist. He was both imaginative and prolific. Despite his criticism of his age, he wrote to please his audience. So deeply did he affect his audiences, in fact, that the view of life in his novels has become a part of English tradition.

Dickens's

Bah, humbug!

"Bah, humbug!"

"Shake me up, Judy"

Characters—And Their Words—Live On!

"Very 'Eavy... Very 'Umble'"

What's in a name, Juliet asked in Shakespeare's *Romeo and Juliet*. She was making the point that names do not reveal anything about a person. Well, don't tell that to Charles Dickens. For him, there was a world of meaning in the names he gave his characters—989 in all. In fact, many of the names Dickens coined and the odd phrases he put into characters' mouths are still used today.

Scrooged!

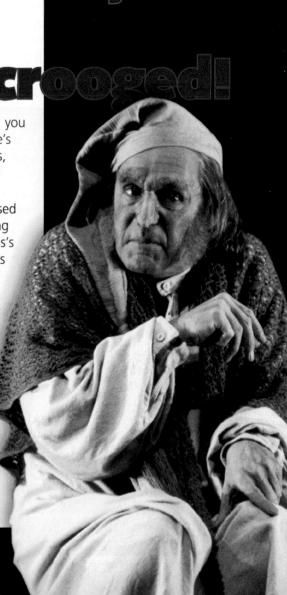

- Ever been Scrooged? Even if you are unfamiliar with *A Christmas Carol,* Dickens's tale about a miserly man whose experiences with three spirits on Christmas Eve change him into a kind and generous soul, you probably know how it feels to be the victim of someone else's stinginess. One of the unreformed Scrooge's favorite phrases, "Bah, humbug!," is still used today to express a Scrooge-like view of the world.

- Ever hear the optimistic phrase, "Something will turn up," used in a sarcastic way? If so, the speaker may be ironically quoting the ne'er-do-well Wilkins Micawber, a character from Dickens's autobiographical novel *David Copperfield*. Based on Dickens's father, Micawber was a perennial optimist, despite the evidence of reality.

- Ever listen to the music of the band Uriah Heep? The title of the band's first album, "Very 'Eavy . . . Very 'Umble," quotes a characteristic phrase spoken by the devious, obsequious clerk Uriah Heep, another character from *David Copperfield*. Young David memorably describes Heep as someone "who had hardly any eyebrows, and no eyelashes, and eyes of a red brown, so unsheltered and unshaded, that I remember wondering how he went to sleep." To this day, it is an insult to be called a falsely humble Uriah Heep.

These are just a few of the Dickens characters whose vivid names and twitchy phrases are still part of pop culture today.

Building Knowledge and Insight from *Hard Times*

Connecting to the Essential Question In *Hard Times*, Dickens criticizes education that is based on rote learning instead of imagination. As you read, notice how Dickens describes the educational approaches he is criticizing. Focusing on these descriptions will help you explore the Essential Question: **How does literature shape or reflect society?**

**Common Core
State Standards**

Reading Literature
3. Analyze the impact of the author's choices regarding how to develop and relate elements of a story or drama.

Close Reading Focus

Ethical and Social Influences

The novel, a long work of fiction, became popular in the nineteenth century, a period of disturbing social and economic changes. Like other novelists of the time, Dickens included social criticism in his works, calling attention to the **ethical and social influences** that resulted in society's ills.

   In *Hard Times*, Dickens focuses on misguided educational practices. Dickens makes clear to readers what his ethical leanings are from the first lines of Chapter 1, when a speaker, whose voice is "inflexible, dry, and dictatorial," states:

> *Now, what I want is, Facts. Teach these boys and girls nothing but Facts. Facts alone are wanted in life.*

   Through his characters and situations, Dickens reveals his own *philosophical assumptions*. As you read, notice how Dickens turns incidents into dramatizations—and criticisms—of ethical and social issues.

Preparing to Read Complex Texts Analyzing an author's purpose will help you understand how specific incidents relate to *meaning* in a novel. In *Hard Times*, note how Dickens develops elements such as characterization, setting, and dialogue to reveal the ethical and social influences that he is criticizing. Also note Dickens's use of comic exaggeration to achieve his purpose. Use a chart like the one shown to help you analyze Dickens's purpose and the meaning it reveals.

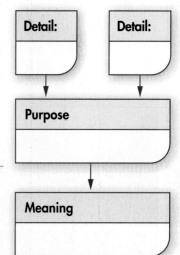

Vocabulary

You will encounter the words listed here in the text that follows. Copy the words into your notebook. Based on your knowledge of word origins, note which word contains the suffix meaning "the study of."

monotonous   indignant

obstinate   approbation

deficient   etymology

adversary   syntax

From HARD TIMES

CHARLES DICKENS

BACKGROUND OF THE MANY BELIEFS IN HIS SOCIETY WITH WHICH DICKENS TOOK ISSUE, THE UTILITARIANISM OF PHILOSOPHER JEREMY BENTHAM (1748–1832) PARTICULARLY IRRITATED HIM. BENTHAM BELIEVED THAT STATISTICS AND LOGIC COULD BE APPLIED TO ALL HUMAN AFFAIRS, AND HE VIEWED HUMAN BEINGS AS ESSENTIALLY INTERESTED ONLY IN THEIR OWN HAPPINESS. HE SAW THE PURPOSE OF SOCIETY AS "THE GREATEST HAPPINESS FOR THE GREATEST NUMBER," WITH HAPPINESS CALCULATED IN TERMS OF INDIVIDUAL PLEASURES AND PAINS. DICKENS BELIEVED UTILITARIANISM DISCOUNTED OR EVEN SOUGHT TO NEGATE VIRTUES LIKE IMAGINATION AND SYMPATHY. IN *HARD TIMES*, DICKENS USED HIS CHARACTER MR. GRADGRIND TO POKE FUN AT THIS PHILOSOPHY.

CHAPTER 1
THE ONE THING NEEDFUL

"Now, what I want is, Facts. Teach these boys and girls nothing but Facts. Facts alone are wanted in life. Plant nothing else, and root out everything else. You can only form the minds of reasoning animals upon Facts: nothing else will ever be of any service to them. This is the principle on which I bring up my own children, and this is the principle on which I bring up these children. Stick to Facts, sir!"

The scene was a plain, bare, monotonous vault of a schoolroom, and the speaker's square forefinger emphasized his observations by underscoring every sentence with a line on the schoolmaster's sleeve. The emphasis was helped by the speaker's square wall of a forehead, which had his eyebrows for its base, while his eyes found commodious cellarage in two dark caves, overshadowed by the wall. The emphasis was helped by the speaker's mouth, which was wide, thin, and hard set. The emphasis was helped by the speaker's voice, which was inflexible, dry, and dictatorial. The emphasis was helped by the speaker's hair, which bristled on the skirts of his bald head, a plantation of firs to keep the wind from its shining surface, all covered with knobs, like the crust of a plum pie, as if the head had scarcely warehouse-room for the hard facts stored inside. The speaker's obstinate carriage, square coat, square legs, square shoulders—nay, his very neckcloth, trained to take him by the throat with an unaccommodating grasp, like a stubborn fact, as it was—all helped the emphasis.

"In this life, we want nothing but Facts, sir; nothing but Facts!"

The speaker, and the schoolmaster, and the third grown person present, all backed a little, and swept with their eyes the inclined plane of little vessels, then and there arranged in order, ready to have imperial gallons of facts poured into them until they were full to the brim.

Vocabulary

monotonous (mə nät′ ən əs) *adj.* without variation

obstinate (äb′ stə nət) *adj.* stubborn; dogged

◀ **Critical Viewing**

Judging from the details in this illustration, what was school like in England during Victorian times? **SPECULATE**

Comprehension

What does Gradgrind aim to do for students?

from Hard Times **999**

In the nineteenth century, technological advances allowed newspaper and magazine publishers to print large runs at affordable prices. For the first time, this made reading material widely available to the middle classes. For these publications, writers contributed fiction that was serialized in weekly or monthly issues. British authors Charles Dickens, George Eliot, William Thackeray and Thomas Hardy, French authors Honoré de Balzac and Victor Hugo, and Russian authors Fyodor Dostoyevsky and Leo Tolstoy wrote their novels as serials.

Connect to the Literature

How do you think contemporary readers might have responded to the weekly installments of *Hard Times,* which Dickens joked were "teaspoon" servings?

Ethical and Social Influences

What outlook is Dickens criticizing through Gradgrind's identification of Sissy Jupe by a number?

CHAPTER 2
MURDERING THE INNOCENTS

Thomas Gradgrind, sir. A man of realities. A man of fact and calculations. A man who proceeds upon the principle that two and two are four, and nothing over, and who is not to be talked into allowing for anything over. Thomas Gradgrind, sir—peremptorily Thomas—Thomas Gradgrind. With a rule and a pair of scales, and the multiplication table always in his pocket, sir, ready to weigh and measure any parcel of human nature, and tell you exactly what it comes to. It is a mere question of figures, a case of simple arithmetic. You might hope to get some other nonsensical belief into the head of George Gradgrind, or Augustus Gradgrind, or John Gradgrind, or Joseph Gradgrind (all suppositious, non-existent persons), but into the head of Thomas Gradgrind—no, sir!

In such terms Mr. Gradgrind always mentally introduced himself, whether to his private circle of acquaintance, or to the public in general. In such terms, no doubt, substituting the words "boys and girls," for "sir," Thomas Gradgrind now presented Thomas Gradgrind to the little pitchers before him, who were to be filled so full of facts.

Indeed, as he eagerly sparkled at them from the cellarage before mentioned, he seemed a kind of cannon loaded to the muzzle with facts, and prepared to blow them clean out of the regions of childhood at one discharge. He seemed a galvanizing apparatus, too, charged with a grim mechanical substitute for the tender young imaginations that were to be stormed away.

"Girl number twenty," said Mr. Gradgrind, squarely pointing with his square forefinger, "I don't know that girl. Who is that girl?"

"Sissy Jupe, sir," explained number twenty, blushing, standing up, and curtseying.

"Sissy is not a name," said Mr. Gradgrind. "Don't call yourself Sissy. Call yourself Cecilia."

"It's father as calls me Sissy, sir," returned the young girl in a trembling voice, and with another curtsey.

"Then he has no business to do it," said Mr. Gradgrind. "Tell him he mustn't. Cecilia Jupe. Let me see. What is your father?"

"He belongs to the horse-riding, if you please, sir."

Mr. Gradgrind frowned, and waved off the objectionable calling with his hand.

"We don't want to know anything about that, here. You mustn't tell us about that, here. Your father breaks horses, don't he?"

"If you please, sir, when they can get any to break, they do break horses in the ring, sir."

"You mustn't tell us about the ring, here. Very well, then. Describe your father as a horsebreaker. He doctors sick horses, I dare say?"

"Oh yes, sir."

"Very well, then. He is a veterinary surgeon, a farrier and horse-breaker. Give me your definition of a horse."

(Sissy Jupe thrown into the greatest alarm by this demand.)

"Girl number twenty unable to define a horse!" said Mr. Gradgrind, for the general behoof of all the little pitchers. "Girl number twenty possessed of no facts, in reference to one of the commonest of animals! Some boy's definition of a horse. Bitzer, yours."

The square finger, moving here and there, lighted suddenly on Bitzer, perhaps because he chanced to sit in the same ray of sunlight which, darting in at one of the bare windows of the intensely white-washed room, irradiated Sissy. For, the boys and girls sat on the face of the inclined plane in two compact bodies, divided up the center by a narrow interval; and Sissy, being at the corner of a row on the sunny side, came in for the beginning of a sunbeam, of which Bitzer, being at the corner of a row on the other side, a few rows in advance, caught the end. But, whereas the girl was so dark-eyed and dark-haired, that she seemed to receive a deeper and more lustrous color from the sun when it shone upon her, the boy was so light-eyed and light-haired that the self-same rays appeared to draw out of him what little color he ever possessed. His cold eyes would hardly have been eyes, but for the short ends of lashes which, by bringing them into immediate contrast with something paler than themselves, expressed their form. His short-cropped hair might have been a mere continuation of the sandy freckles on his forehead and face. His skin was so unwhole-somely deficient in the natural tinge, that he looked as though, if he were cut, he would bleed white.

"Bitzer," said Thomas Gradgrind. "Your definition of a horse."

"Quadruped. Graminivorous. Forty teeth, namely twenty-four grinders, four eye-teeth, and twelve incisive. Sheds coat in the spring; in marshy countries, sheds hoofs, too. Hoofs hard, but requiring to be shod with iron. Age known by marks in mouth." Thus (and much more) Bitzer.

"Now girl number twenty," said Mr. Gradgrind. "You know what a horse is."

She curtseyed again, and would have blushed deeper, if she could have blushed deeper than she had blushed all this time. Bitzer, after rapidly blinking at Thomas Gradgrind with both eyes at once, and so catching the light upon his quivering ends of lashes that they looked like the antennae of busy insects, put his knuckles to his freckled fore-head, and sat down again.

The third gentleman now stepped forth. A mighty man at cutting and drying, he was; a government officer; in his way (and in most other people's too), a professed pugilist; always in training, always with a sys-tem to force down the general throat like a bolus,[1] always to be heard of at the bar of his little Public-office, ready to fight all England. To continue

---

1. **bolus** small, round mass, often of chewed food.

Vocabulary
deficient (di fish´ ent) *adj.* lacking an essential quality

Spiral Review
Plot How would you summarize the events of *Hard Times* up to this point in the plot?

Comprehension
What type of answer to his question does Gradgrind accept?

in fistic phraseology, he had a genius for coming up to the scratch, wherever and whatever it was, and proving himself an ugly customer. He would go in and damage any subject whatever with his right, follow up with his left, stop, exchange, counter, bore his opponent (he always fought All England[2]) to the ropes, and fall upon him neatly. He was certain to knock the wind out of common sense, and render that unlucky adversary deaf to the call of time. And he had it in charge from high authority to bring about the great public-office Millennium, when Commissioners should reign upon earth.

"Very well," said this gentleman, briskly smiling, and folding his arms. "That's a horse. Now, let me ask you girls and boys, Would you paper a room with representations of horses?"

After a pause, one half of the children cried in chorus, "Yes, sir!" Upon which the other half, seeing in the gentleman's face that Yes was wrong, cried out in chorus, "No, sir!"—as the custom is, in these examinations.

"Of course, No. Why wouldn't you?"

A pause. One corpulent slow boy, with a wheezy manner of breathing, ventured the answer, Because he wouldn't paper a room at all, but would paint it.

"You *must* paper it," said Thomas Gradgrind, "whether you like it or not. Don't tell *us* you wouldn't paper it. What do you mean, boy?"

"I'll explain to you, then," said the gentleman, after another and a dismal pause, "why you wouldn't paper a room with representations of horses. Do you ever see horses walking up and down the sides of rooms in reality—in fact? Do you?"

"Yes, sir!" from one half. "No, sir!" from the other.

"Of course no," said the gentleman, with an indignant look at the wrong half. "Why, then, you are not to see anywhere, what you don't see in fact; you are not to have anywhere, what you don't have in fact. What is called Taste, is only another name for Fact."

Thomas Gradgrind nodded his approbation.

"This is a new principle, a discovery, a great discovery," said the gentleman. "Now, I'll try you again. Suppose you were going to carpet a room. Would you use a carpet having a representation of flowers upon it?"

There being a general conviction by this time that "No, sir!" was always the right answer to this gentleman, the chorus of No was very strong. Only a few feeble stragglers said Yes; among them Sissy Jupe.

"Girl number twenty," said the gentleman, smiling in the calm strength of knowledge.

Sissy blushed, and stood up.

"So you would carpet your room—or your husband's room, if you were a grown woman, and had a husband—with representations of flowers, would you," said the gentleman. "Why would you?"

---

2. **fought All England** fought according to the official rules of boxing.

Analyzing the Author's Purpose

What does the reaction of the class hint about Dickens's purpose in this scene?

> **"WHAT
> IS
> CALLED
> TASTE,
> IS ONLY
> ANOTHER
> NAME FOR
> FACT."**

Vocabulary

indignant (in dig′ nənt)
adj. outraged; filled with righteous anger

approbation
(ap′ rə bā′ shən) *n.* official approval

"If you please, sir, I am very fond of flowers," returned the girl.

"And is that why you would put tables and chairs upon them, and have people walking over them with heavy boots?"

"It wouldn't hurt them, sir. They wouldn't crush and wither if you please, sir. They would be the pictures of what was very pretty and pleasant, and I would fancy—"

"Ay, ay, ay! but you mustn't fancy," cried the gentleman, quite elated by coming so happily to his point. "That's it! You are never to fancy."

"You are not, Cecilia Jupe," Thomas Gradgrind solemnly repeated, "to do anything of that kind."

"Fact, fact, fact!" said the gentleman. And "Fact, fact, fact!" repeated Thomas Gradgrind.

"You are to be in all things regulated and governed," said the gentleman, "by fact. We hope to have, before long, a board of fact, composed of commissioners of fact, who will force the people to be a people of fact, and of nothing but fact. You must discard the word Fancy altogether. You have nothing to do with it. You are not to have, in any object of use or ornament, what would be a contradiction in fact. You don't walk upon flowers in fact; you cannot be allowed to walk upon flowers in carpets. You don't find that foreign birds and butterflies come and perch upon your crockery. You never meet with quadrupeds going up and down walls; you must not have quadrupeds represented upon walls. You must use," said the gentleman, "for all these purposes, combinations and modifications (in primary colors) of mathematical figures which are susceptible of proof and demonstration. This is the new discovery. This is fact. This is taste."

The girl curtseyed, and sat down. She was very young, and she looked as if she were frightened by the matter of fact prospect the world afforded.

"Now, if Mr. M'Choakumchild," said the gentleman, "will proceed to give his first lesson here, Mr. Gradgrind, I shall be happy, at your request, to observe his mode of procedure."

Mr. Gradgrind was much obliged. "Mr. M'Choakumchild, we only wait for you."

So, Mr. M'Choakumchild began in his best manner. He and some one hundred and forty other schoolmasters, had been lately turned at the same time, in the same factory, on the same principles, like so many pianoforte legs. He had been put through an immense

Ethical and Social Influences

What point about imagination does Dickens make through the teacher's literal-minded understanding?

▼ **Critical Viewing**

What does this picture of Sissy suggest about her relationship with her classmates and Gradgrind? **INFER**

Comprehension

Why does the third gentleman object to horses on wallpaper and flowers on rugs?

from Hard Times **1003**

Vocabulary

etymology (et′ ə məl′ ə jē)
n. the study of word origins

syntax (sin′ taks) *n.* the
study of sentence structure

variety of paces, and had answered volumes of head-breaking questions. Orthography, etymology, syntax, and prosody, biography, astronomy, geography, and general cosmography, the sciences of compound proportion, algebra, land-surveying and leveling, vocal music, and drawing from models, were all at the ends of his ten chilled fingers. He had worked his stony way into Her Majesty's most Honorable Privy Council's Schedule B, and had taken the bloom off the higher branches of mathematics and physical science, French, German, Latin, and Greek. He knew all about all the Water Sheds of all the world (whatever they are), and all the histories of all the peoples, and all the names of all the rivers and mountains, and all the productions, manners, and customs of all the countries, and all their boundaries and bearings on the two-and-thirty points of the compass. Ah, rather overdone, M'Choakumchild. If he had only learnt a little less, how infinitely better he might have taught much more!

He went to work in this preparatory lesson, not unlike Morgiana in the Forty Thieves:[3] looking into all the vessels ranged before him, one after another, to see what they contained. Say, good M'Choakumchild. When from thy boiling store, thou shalt fill each jar brim full by and by, dost thou think that thou wilt always kill outright the robber Fancy lurking within—or sometimes only maim him and distort him!

---

3. Morgiana in the Forty Thieves In the tale "Ali Baba and the Forty Thieves," Ali Baba's clever servant, Morgiana, saves him from the thieves who are hiding in large jars.

> **"IF HE HAD ONLY LEARNT A LITTLE LESS... HE MIGHT HAVE TAUGHT MUCH MORE!"**

Cite textual evidence to support your responses.

Critical Reading

1. **Key Ideas and Details (a)** What does Mr. Gradgrind believe is the key to all learning? **(b) Connect:** In what ways does he put this belief into practice? **(c) Interpret:** What attitude does the description of the children as "little pitchers" reflect?

2. **Integration of Knowledge and Ideas (a) Compare and Contrast:** Compare and contrast Sissy's and Bitzer's performances in the classroom. **(b) Analyze:** With whom does Dickens expect the reader to sympathize? Why?

3. **Integration of Knowledge and Ideas** What values does Dickens believe a system of education should teach? Explain, using two of these Essential Question words: *imagination, sympathy, conform, society, fact.* **[Connecting to the Essential Question: How does literature shape or reflect society?]**

Critical Commentary

"Charles Dickens"
George Orwell

George Orwell (1903–1950), an important author in his own right (see p. 1317), wrote a brilliant and highly readable essay on Charles Dickens. In the essay, Orwell comments specifically on the criticism of Victorian education that Dickens made in Hard Times *and elsewhere.*

. . . Except for the universities and the big public schools, every kind of education then existing in England gets a mauling at Dickens's hands. . . . But as usual, Dickens's criticism is neither creative or destructive. He sees the idiocy of an educational system founded on the Greek lexicon and the wax-ended cane; on the other hand, he has no use for the new kind of school that is coming up in the 'fifties and 'sixties, the "modern" school, with its gritty insistence on "facts." What, then, *does* he want? As always, what he appears to want is a moralized version of the existing thing—the old type of school, but with no caning, no bullying or underfeeding, and not quite so much Greek.

Orwell also explains how he visualizes Dickens and what he values most about him.

When one reads any strongly individual piece of writing, one has the impression of seeing a face somewhere behind the page. It is not necessarily the actual face of the writer. . . . What one sees is the face that the writer *ought* to have. Well, in the case of Dickens I see a face that is not quite the face of Dickens's photographs, though it resembles it. It is the face of a man of about forty, with a small beard and a high color. He is laughing, with a touch of anger in his laughter, but no triumph, no malignity. It is the face of a man who is always fighting against something, but who fights in the open and is not frightened, the face of a man who is *generously angry*—in other words, of a nineteenth-century liberal, a free intelligence, a type hated with equal hatred by all the smelly little orthodoxies which are now contending for our souls.

> "Charity begins at home, and justice begins next door."

▼ Critical Viewing
Does this caricature of Dickens by David Levine capture any of the qualities Orwell discusses? Why or why not? **CONNECT**

Key Ideas and Details According to Orwell, what kind of a school does Dickens favor? What picture of Dickens does Orwell have in mind as he reads the Victorian author?

Close Reading Activities | from *Hard Times*

Literary Analysis

1. **Key Ideas and Details (a)** In the selection from *Hard Times,* which details make the setting vivid? **(b)** How do they contribute to a criticism of the **ethical and social influences** of the time?

2. **Key Ideas and Details (a)** Summarize the viewpoint that Dickens criticizes. **(b)** Do you think there is a positive side to this viewpoint that Dickens may have neglected or deliberately ignored? Why or why not?

3. **Key Ideas and Details** Choose an example of each of the following elements that help clarify the **author's purpose,** explaining your choice:
   (a) the name of a character
   (b) a character's statement or dialogue
   (c) a description of a place

4. **Craft and Structure (a)** Identify three examples in which Dickens uses comic exaggeration to criticize Gradgrind and his fellows.
   (b) What does Dickens accomplish through his use of exaggeration, both in characterization and in the character's words? Use a chart like the one shown to examine Dickens's techniques.

Passage	Intended Effect on Reader	Intended Message	Enjoyment Value

5. **Key Ideas and Details (a)** If Sissy and Bitzer grew up and became writers, which character would be likely to write social criticism and which might not? Explain. **(b)** What does your answer suggest about Dickens's purpose in including both characters?

6. **Integration of Knowledge and Ideas (a)** What conclusion does Dickens want the reader to draw about the three adults in the classroom? **(b)** What conclusions does Dickens want the reader to draw about the kind of students this type of education will produce?

7. **Integration of Knowledge and Ideas (a)** Identify the passage that you think is most effective in conveying Dickens's message about education. **(b)** Which details in this passage reveal the writer's desire to convey a message? Explain.

Common Core State Standards

Language

4.c. Consult general and specialized reference materials, both print and digital, to find the pronunciation of a word or determine or clarify its precise meaning, its part of speech, its etymology, or its standard usage. *(p. 1007)*

4.d. Verify the preliminary determination of the meaning of a word or phrase. *(p. 1007)*

Vocabulary Acquisition and Use

Word Analysis: Greek Prefix *mono-*

The Greek prefix *mono-* means "single" or "alone." Thus, someone who speaks in a *monotonous* way talks in a single, unchanging manner, without varying tone or subject. The prefix is used to form many common words as well as some scientific and technical words. Explain how the prefix *mono-* contributes to the meaning of each of these words. Use a dictionary to confirm the meaning of a word if you are unsure.

1. monochromatic

2. monogamy

3. monologue

4. monopoly

5. monorail

6. monotreme

Write two original sentences using these or any other words with the prefix *mono-*.

Vocabulary: Antonyms

Antonyms are words with opposite or nearly opposite meanings. *Bitter* and *sweet* are antonyms, as are *night* and *day*. For each of the following vocabulary words, identify an antonym. Then, write an original sentence using the word and its antonym.

> **Example:** reality
> **Antonym:** fantasy
> **Sentence:** Gradgrind did not believe in fantasy or the imagination, only in his cold, hard reality.

1. monotonous

2. obstinate

3. deficient

4. adversary

5. indignant

6. approbation

Using Resources to Build Vocabulary

Words for a Utilitarian Perspective

Charles Dickens gives Thomas Gradgrind a particular vocabulary that emphasizes his interest in only the utilitarian aspects of life. Near the beginning of the passage, he declares, "Facts alone are wanted in life." Review this list of utilitarian words that Dickens puts in Gradgrind's mouth—or thoughts.

reason	inflexible
observation	calculation
weigh	mechanical

Use a print or an electronic dictionary to find the **connotations** of these words. Connotations are ideas or emotions associated with a word. Then, use a print or an electronic dictionary or a thesaurus to find antonyms—words with the opposite connotation, such as *illogic* for *reason*. Explain why each word you choose is a suitable antonym.

Close Reading Activities Continued

Writing to Sources

Informative Text The excerpt from *Hard Times* presents a vivid picture of a Victorian school. Were the attitudes and methods used by Gradgrind typical of the period, or was Dickens painting an extreme picture? Answering that question requires a historical investigation.

Compile an **annotated bibliography** of works that could be used in a research paper on the topic. An annotated bibliography includes not only full bibliographic information on sources but also notes that describe the kinds of information each source can offer and an evaluation of its usefulness. In your bibliography, include works with different perspectives, and include both primary sources (books from Victorian times) and secondary sources (those from later periods).

Prewriting Use both print materials and the Internet to locate sources. You might ask a librarian for help in finding appropriate sources.

- Use relevant keywords like *education, Victorian,* and *Britain* to search for sources. Be sure to locate both primary and secondary sources.

- Scan the table of contents, introduction, first chapter, or other key elements of each source to learn what it says about the subject. Consider its scope, what type of education it addresses; its validity, how authoritative the observations seem to be; and its reliability, how free or absent of bias it is.

- Find a copy of the style guide, such as the MLA style guide, that your teacher wants you to use for presenting the bibliographic information for each source.

Drafting Write a draft of your annotated bibliography.

- Prepare an entry for each source you consulted, styling it properly according to the style guide.

- Add an annotation that addresses the scope, reliability, and validity of each source. Use your annotations to show the different perspectives you can gain from this variety of sources.

Revising Review your bibliographical entries for both format and content.

- Be sure the entries conform to the correct style. If not, make any needed changes.

- Review the annotations to make sure they clearly assess each work's usefulness.

Common Core State Standards

Writing

2. Write informative/explanatory texts to examine and convey complex ideas, concepts, and information clearly and accurately through the effective selection, organization, and analysis of content.

8. Gather relevant information from multiple authoritative print and digital sources, using advanced searches effectively; assess the strengths and limitations of each source in terms of the task, purpose, and audience; integrate information into the text selectively to maintain the flow of ideas, avoiding plagiarism and overreliance on any one source and following a standard format for citation.

Model: Drafting Annotations for Primary Sources

Timkins, Charles. *School Days.* London: Chapman, 1868.
Timkins's memoir narrates his life in a boarding, or private, school. It reveals the loneliness felt by the boys, the brutality of some teachers, and the tough academic standards students had to meet. Limited in scope to just one school but full of anecdotes.

The annotation shows the unique insight provided by this source.

Conventions and Style Shifts in Verb Tense

Use **verb tenses** in a logical sequence to show when actions happen in relation to one another. **Avoid shifting tenses** when the actions occur at the same time.

> **Shifted Tenses:** Mr. Gradgrind points to Sissy and asked her name.
> **Correct:** Mr. Gradgrind pointed to Sissy and asked her name.
> **Correct:** Mr. Gradgrind points to Sissy and asks her name.

Note the different forms of verb tenses:

Present:	wants, is wanting, does want, have wanted, have been wanting
Past:	wanted, was wanting, did want, had wanted, had been wanting
Future:	will want, will be wanting, will have wanted, will have been wanting

When actions occur at different times, use the sequence of tenses that indicates the correct times.

> **Mr. Gradgrind had learned Sissy's name, but he still called her "girl number twenty."**

Participle forms (*wanting, wanted, having wanted*) and infinitive forms (*to want, to have wanted*) can also indicate time. Use the form that indicates the timing in relation to the main verb.

Practice Decide whether a sentence uses verb tenses correctly. If it is correct, write *correct*. If it is incorrect, rewrite the sentence correctly

1. Bitzer had learned the definition of a horse, and so he recites it when called on.
2. The gentleman hopes commissioners of fact forced people to use only facts.
3. Once the children learn facts, they will be educated.
4. Having stated his beliefs about facts, Gradgrind begins to call on students.
5. The gentleman had been listening, but then he joins in the examining of students.
6. Half the class had called out "yes" before they see that the gentleman expected "no."
7. Sissy hadn't known the definition of *horse*, but she will be speaking up again.
8. In Mr. Gradgrind's opinion, children are like pitchers to have been filled with facts.
9. Educated with facts, the schoolmaster wanted to see what the children knew.
10. The schoolmaster had learned too many facts, and he is a poorer teacher as a result.

Writing and Speaking Conventions

A. Writing Use the two verbs in a sentence showing actions that happen at the same time. Use the tense given in parentheses.

1. ask, answer (*present*)
2. weigh, measure (*future*)
3. frown, wave (*past*)
4. fill, hold (*present*)

> **Example:** ask, answer
> **Sentence:** The adults ask questions, and the children answer.

B. Speaking Write and present to the class a persuasive argument in which you either agree or disagree with Mr. Gradgrind's point of view about education. Be sure to avoid shifts in verb tense and to include support for your argument.

The Novelist as Social Critic

Doris Lessing
(b. 1919)

John Steinbeck
(1902–1968)

Anton Chekhov
(1860–1904)

Émile Zola
(1840–1902)

Charles Dickens
(1812–1870)

Charlotte Brontë
(1816–1855)

CHILDREN of VIOLENCE

The Grapes of Wrath

Short STORIES

Germinal

Hard Times

JANE EYRE

END POVERTY

HIGHER WAGES

WOMEN'S RIGHTS

SAFER WORKING CONDITIONS

Comparing Literary Works

from *Hard Times* by Charles Dickens
• "An Upheaval" by Anton Chekhov

Comparing Social Criticism in Fiction

Social Criticism

In the nineteenth century, **social criticism** began to appear much more frequently in fiction. Writers like Charles Dickens and Anton Chekhov told stories that brought societal ills to public awareness. Slavery, unsafe work or living conditions, colonialism, the class system, injustices in the judicial and education systems—these are some of the issues that authors have criticized over the years. Social criticism often takes these forms:

- **Realism:** Reveals social ills by showing how life is really lived
- **Satire:** Ridicules individuals, institutions, groups, and so on
- **Utopian fiction:** Shows a perfect society, forcing readers to see what needs improvement in their own society
- **Dystopian fiction:** Depicts a dreadful society, forcing readers to see the dangers to which current social ills may lead

Some social criticism is **explicit,** stated directly in the work. More often in fiction, however, it is **implicit,** with readers expected to infer the criticisms based on the work's details. As you read "An Upheaval," compare it to the selection from *Hard Times,* using a chart like this to list your inferences.

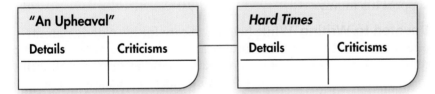

"An Upheaval"		*Hard Times*	
Details	Criticisms	Details	Criticisms

Gather Vocabulary Knowledge

Chekhov uses related forms of the words *shame, resentment,* and *dismay.* Use a **dictionary** to find each word's part of speech and definition. Then, employ the following references to further explore these words:

- **History of English:** Use this work to research each word's origin. Explain the word's emergence in English.
- **Book of Quotations:** Use this resource to find a quotation containing one of the words. Then, explain nuances in meaning that are evident from the context of the quotation.

Comparing References Compare and contrast what you learn about the words from these specialized references.

 **Common Core State Standards**

Reading Literature
1. Cite strong and thorough textual evidence to support analysis of what the text says explicitly as well as inferences drawn from the text, including determining where the text leaves matters uncertain.

Language
6. Demonstrate independence in gathering vocabulary knowledge when considering a word or phrase important to comprehension or expression.

(1860–1904)

ANTON CHEKHOV

Anton Chekhov (än tôn´ chek´ ôf) is one of only a few major writers who also studied and practiced medicine. By applying to his writing the same type of compassion and objectivity that are required of a good doctor, Chekhov was able to establish himself as one of the dominant figures in Russian Realism.

Beginnings The grandson of a serf who had purchased his freedom, Chekhov was born in the small coastal town of Taganrog in southern Russia. After the failure of his father's grocery business, his family moved to Moscow, while he remained in Taganrog to complete his schooling. In 1879, he moved to Moscow to be with his family, and he enrolled in medical school. As a medical student, he began writing comic sketches and light short stories to earn extra money to help support his family.

Devoted to Writing While helping to care for his elderly parents, offering medical treatment to local peasants, and becoming involved in community affairs, Chekhov managed to continue writing prolifically throughout the six years he lived in Melikhovo, a village south of Moscow. Among the most notable short stories that he produced during this period are "Ward Number Six" (1892), the story of a doctor who is ironically committed to the same grim, depressing mental ward that he had previously directed; and "An Anonymous Story" (1893) and "Peasant" (1897), two harshly realistic sketches of Russian peasant life. During this period, Chekhov also wrote one of his finest plays, *The Seagull* (1896), which focuses on the conflict between different generations of people.

> "YOU MUST TRUST AND BELIEVE IN PEOPLE OR LIFE BECOMES IMPOSSIBLE."

Poor Health and High Acclaim Toward the end of the nineteenth century, Chekhov's physical condition began to rapidly deteriorate. No longer able to withstand the cold climate of Melikhovo, he was forced to move to Yalta, a coastal resort on the Black Sea. His ill health did not impair his literary output, however, and in the final years of life he was able to produce two critically acclaimed plays, *The Sisters* (1901) and *The Cherry Orchard* (1904).

AN UPHEAVAL

BY ANTON CHEKHOV

TRANSLATED BY CONSTANCE GARNETT

BACKGROUND THE INDUSTRIAL REVOLUTION WAS SLOW IN COMING TO RUSSIA, BUT BY CHEKHOV'S DAY, TIMES WERE CHANGING. IN 1861, CZAR ALEXANDER II FREED THE SERFS—PEASANTS BOUND TO THE LAND SINCE MEDIEVAL TIMES—THOUGH MOST FREED SERFS REMAINED DESPERATELY POOR PEASANTS. STILL, AS THE NATION MOVED FROM AN AGRARIAN TO AN INDUSTRIAL ECONOMY, NEW OPPORTUNITIES AROSE FOR SOME WHOSE PARENTS OR GRANDPARENTS HAD NOT BEEN WELL BORN. HOWEVER, AMONG THE GENTRY, THOSE WHO COULD NOT ADAPT TO THE CHANGING ECONOMY WERE FINDING IT HARD TO STAY AFLOAT ECONOMICALLY.

M
ASHENKA PAVLETSKY, a young girl who had only just finished her studies at a boarding school, returning from a walk to the house of the Kushkins, with whom she was living as a governess, found the household in a terrible turmoil. Mihailo, the porter who opened the door to her, was excited and red as a crab.

Loud voices were heard from upstairs.

"Madame Kushkin is in a fit, most likely, or else she has quarrelled with her husband," thought Mashenka.

In the hall and in the corridor she met maidservants. One of them was crying. Then Mashenka saw, running out of her room, the master of the house himself, Nikolay Sergeitch, a little man with a flabby face and a bald head, though he was not old. He was red in the face and twitching all over. He passed the governess without noticing her, and throwing up his arms, exclaimed:

"Oh, how horrible it is! How tactless! How stupid! How barbarous! Abominable!"

Mashenka went into her room, and then, for the first time in her life, it was her lot to experience in all its acuteness the feeling that is so familiar to persons in dependent positions, who eat the bread of the rich and powerful, and cannot speak their minds. There was a search going on in her room. The lady of the house, Fedosya Vassilyevna,[1] a stout, broad-shouldered, uncouth woman with thick black eyebrows, a faintly perceptible moustache, and red hands, who was exactly like a plain, illiterate cook in face and manners, was standing, without her cap on, at the table, putting back into Mashenka's work-bag balls of wool, scraps of materials, and bits of papers. . . . Evidently the governess's arrival took her by surprise, since, on looking round and seeing the girl's pale and astonished face, she was a little taken aback, and muttered:

"*Pardon.* I . . . I upset it accidentally. . . . My sleeve caught in it . . ."

And saying something more, Madame Kushkin rustled her long skirts and went out. Mashenka looked round her room with wondering eyes, and, unable to understand it, not knowing what to think, shrugged her shoulders, and turned cold with dismay. What had Fedosya Vassilyevna been looking for in her workbag? If she really had, as she said, caught her sleeve in it and upset everything, why had Nikolay Sergeitch dashed out of her room so excited and red in the face? Why was one drawer of the table pulled out a little way? The moneybox, in which the governess put away ten kopeck pieces[2] and old stamps, was open. They had opened it, but did not know how to shut it, though they had scratched the lock all over. The whatnot[3]

---

1. Fedosya Vassilyevna Russian names traditionally include a patronymic, or father's name, with the ending *-evich/-ovich* meaning "son of" or *-evna/-ovna* meaning "daughter of"; *Fedosya Vassilyevna*, for example, means "Fedosya, daughter of Vassily."

2. kopeck pieces coins each worth a tenth of a **rouble** (roo´ bəl), the chief currency of Russia.

3. whatnot *n.* set of open shelves used to display miscellaneous items.

with her books on it, the things on the table, the bed—all bore fresh traces of a search. Her linen-basket, too. The linen had been carefully folded, but it was not in the same order as Mashenka had left it when she went out. So the search had been thorough, most thorough. But what was it for? Why? What had happened? Mashenka remembered the excited porter, the general turmoil which was still going on, the weeping servant-girl; had it not all some connection with the search that had just been made in her room? Was she not mixed up in something dreadful? Mashenka turned pale, and feeling cold all over, sank on to her linen-basket.

A maidservant came into the room.

"Liza, you don't know why they have been rummaging in my room?" the governess asked her.

"Mistress has lost a brooch worth two thousand," said Liza.

"Yes, but why have they been rummaging in my room?"

"They've been searching every one, miss. They've searched all my things, too. They stripped us . . . and searched us . . . God knows, miss, I never went near her toilet-table, let alone touching the brooch. I shall say the same at the police-station."

"But . . . why have they been rummaging here?" the governess still wondered.

"A brooch has been stolen, I tell you. The mistress has been rummaging in everything with her own hands. She even searched Mihailo, the porter, herself. It's a perfect disgrace! Nikolay Sergeitch simply looks on and cackles like a hen. But you've no need to tremble like that, miss. They found nothing here. You've nothing to be afraid of if you didn't take the brooch."

"But Liza, it's vile . . . it's insulting," said Mashenka, breathless with indignation. "It's so mean, so low! What right had she to suspect me and to rummage in my things?"

"You are living with strangers, miss," sighed Liza. "Though you are a young lady, still you are . . . as it were . . . a servant. . . . It's not like living with your papa and mamma."

Mashenka threw herself on the bed and sobbed bitterly. Never in her life had she been subjected to such an outrage, never had she been so deeply insulted. . . . She, well-educated, refined, the daughter of a teacher, was suspected of theft; she had been searched like a street-walker! She could not imagine a greater insult. And to this feeling of resentment was added an oppressive dread of what would come next. All sorts of absurd ideas came into her mind. If they could suspect her of theft, then they might arrest her . . . and search

Vocabulary

rummaging (rum´ ij in) v. thoroughly searching through

Comprehension

What is happening in the household where Mashenka is governess?

An Upheaval **1015**

▶ Critical Viewing
This nineteenth century Russian painting depicts a governess arriving at a merchant's house. What social commentary might the artist be offering? **INTERPRET**

"THEY WILL BELIEVE THAT
I COULD NOT BE A THIEF!"

Comparing Social Criticism What social criticism about the plight of young working women does Chekhov imply in this paragraph?

Vocabulary
kindred (kin´ drəd) *n.* family; relatives

her, then lead her through the street with an escort of soldiers, cast her into a cold, dark cell with mice and wood-lice, exactly like the dungeon in which Princess Tarakanov[4] was imprisoned. Who would stand up for her? Her parents lived far away in the Provinces; they had not the money to come to her. In the capital she was as solitary as in a desert, without friends or kindred. They could do what they liked with her.

"I will go to all the courts and all the lawyers," Mashenka thought, trembling. "I will explain to them, I will take an oath. . . . They will believe that I could not be a thief!"

Mashenka remembered that under the sheets in her basket she had some sweetmeats, which, following the habits of her schooldays, she had put in her pocket at dinner and carried off to her room. She

---

4. Princess Tarakanov daughter supposedly born to Russia's Empress Elizabeth (1709–1761) in a secret marriage to a commoner.

felt hot all over, and was ashamed at the thought that her little secret was known to the lady of the house; all this terror, shame, resentment, brought on an attack of palpitation of the heart, which set up a throbbing in her temples, in her heart, and deep down in her stomach.

"Dinner is ready," the servant summoned Mashenka.

"Shall I go, or not?"

Mashenka brushed her hair, wiped her face with a wet towel, and went into the dining-room. There they had already begun dinner. At one end of the table sat Fedosya Vassilyevna with a stupid, solemn, serious face; at the other end Nikolay Sergeitch. At the sides there were the visitors and the children. The dishes were handed by two footmen in swallowtails[5] and white gloves. Everyone knew that there was an upset in the house, that Madame Kushkin was in trouble, and everyone was silent. Nothing was heard but the sound of munching and the rattle of spoons on the plates.

The lady of the house, herself, was the first to speak.

"What is the third course?" she asked the footman in a weary, injured voice.

"*Esturgeon à la russe*,"[6] answered the footman.

"I ordered that, Fenya," Nikolay Sergeitch hastened to observe. "I wanted some fish. If you don't like it, *ma chère*,[7] don't let them serve it. I just ordered it. . . ."

Fedosya Vassilyevna did not like dishes that she had not ordered herself, and now her eyes filled with tears.

"Come, don't let us agitate ourselves," Mamikov, her household doctor, observed in a honeyed voice, just touching her arm, with a smile as honeyed. "We are nervous enough as it is. Let us forget the brooch! Health is worth more than two thousand roubles!"

"It's not the two thousand I regret," answered the lady, and a big tear rolled down her cheek. "It's the fact itself that revolts me! I cannot put up with thieves in my house. I don't regret it—I regret nothing; but to steal from me is such ingratitude! That's how they repay me for my kindness. . . ."

They all looked into their plates, but Mashenka fancied after the lady's words that every one was looking at her. A lump rose in her throat; she began crying and put her handkerchief to her lips.

"*Pardon*," she muttered. "I can't help it. My head aches. I'll go away."

And she got up from the table, scraping her chair awkwardly, and went out quickly, still more overcome with confusion.

"It's beyond everything!" said Nikolay Sergeitch, frowning. "What need was there to search her room? How out of place it was!"

---

5. **footmen in swallowtails** servants whose uniforms include full dress coats with long tapering tails in the back.

6. *Esturgeon à la russe* Russian sturgeon, the fish whose salted eggs are served as the costly Russian appetizer known as caviar.

7. *ma chère* (mä châr´) French for "my dear."

Vocabulary

palpitation (pal´ pə tā´ shən) *n.* rapid fluttering of the heart

Comparing Social Criticism What do the presence of "footmen in swallowtails" and so many other servants show about the Kushkin household?

Comprehension
What did Mashenka hide in her basket?

Comparing Social Criticism What does the disagreement about whether Mashenka's room should be searched reveal about attitudes toward social class in late-nineteenth-century Russia?

Spiral Review
Conflict There is disagreement about whether or not Mashenka's room should be searched. What does this reveal about ideas regarding social class in late-nineteenth-century Russia?

"I don't say she took the brooch," said Fedosya Vassilyevna, "but can you answer for her? To tell the truth, I haven't much confidence in these learned paupers."

"It really was unsuitable, Fenya. . . . Excuse me, Fenya, but you've no kind of legal right to make a search."

"I know nothing about your laws. All I know is that I've lost my brooch. And I will find the brooch!" She brought her fork down on the plate with a clatter, and her eyes flashed angrily. "And you eat your dinner, and don't interfere in what doesn't concern you!"

Nikolay Sergeitch dropped his eyes mildly and sighed. Meanwhile Mashenka, reaching her room, flung herself on her bed. She felt now neither alarm nor shame, but she felt an intense longing to go and slap the cheeks of this hard, arrogant, dull-witted, prosperous woman.

Lying on her bed she breathed into her pillow and dreamed of how nice it would be to go and buy the most expensive brooch and fling it into the face of this bullying woman. If only it were God's will that Fedosya Vassilyevna should come to ruin and wander about begging, and should taste all the horrors of poverty and dependence, and that Mashenka, whom she had insulted, might give her alms![8] Oh, if only she could come in for a big fortune, could buy a carriage, and could drive noisily past the windows so as to be envied by that woman!

But all these were only dreams, in reality there was only one thing left to do—to get away as quickly as possible, not to stay another hour in this place. It was true it was terrible to lose her place, to go back to her parents, who had nothing; but what could she do? Mashenka could not bear the sight of the lady of the house nor of her little room; she felt stifled and wretched here. She was so disgusted with Fedosya Vassilyevna, who was so obsessed by her illnesses and her supposed aristocratic rank, that everything in the world seemed to have become coarse and unattractive because this woman was living in it. Mashenka jumped up from the bed and began packing.

"May I come in?" asked Nikolay Sergeitch at the door; he had come up noiselessly to the door, and spoke in a soft, subdued voice. "May I?"

"Come in."

He came in and stood still near the door. His eyes looked dim and his red little nose was shiny. After dinner he used to drink beer, and the fact was perceptible in his walk, in his feeble, flabby hands.

"What's this?" he asked, pointing to the basket.

"I am packing. Forgive me, Nikolay Sergeitch, but I cannot remain in your house. I feel deeply insulted by this search!"

"I understand. . . . Only you are wrong to go. . . . Why should you? They've searched your things, but you . . . what does it matter to you? You will be none the worse for it."

---

8. **alms** (ämz) *n.* money, food, clothing, etc., given as charity to the poor.

Mashenka was silent and went on packing. Nikolay Sergeitch pinched his moustache, as though wondering what he should say next, and went on in an ingratiating voice:

"I understand, of course, but you must make allowances. You know my wife is nervous, headstrong; you mustn't judge her too harshly."

Mashenka did not speak.

"If you are so offended," Nikolay Sergeitch went on, "well, if you like, I'm ready to apologize. I ask your pardon."

Mashenka made no answer, but only bent lower over her box. This exhausted, irresolute man was of absolutely no significance in the household. He stood in the pitiful position of a dependent and hanger-on, even with the servants, and his apology meant nothing either.

"H'm . . . You say nothing! That's not enough for you. In that case, I will apologize for my wife. In my wife's name. . . . She behaved tact-lessly, I admit it as a gentleman. . . ."

Nikolay Sergeitch walked about the room, heaved a sigh, and went on:

"Then you want me to have it rankling here, under my heart. . . . You want my conscience to torment me. . . ."

"I know it's not your fault, Nikolay Sergeitch," said Mashenka, looking him full in the face with her big tearstained eyes. "Why should you worry yourself?"

"Of course, no. . . . But still, don't you . . . go away. I entreat you."

Mashenka shook her head. Nikolay Sergeitch stopped at the win-dow and drummed on a pane with his fingertips.

"Such misunderstandings are simply torture to me," he said. "Why, do you want me to go down on my knees to you, or what? Your pride is wounded, and here you've been crying and packing up to go; but I have pride, too, and you do not spare it! Or do you want me to tell you what I would not tell at Confession? Do you? Listen; you want me to tell you what I won't tell the priest on my deathbed?"

Mashenka made no answer.

"I took my wife's brooch," Nikolay Sergeitch said quickly. "Is that enough now? Are you satisfied? Yes, I . . . took it. . . . But, of course, I count on your discretion. . . . For God's sake, not a word, not half a hint to any one!"

Mashenka, amazed and frightened, went on packing; she snatched her things, crumpled them up, and thrust them anyhow into the box and the basket. Now, after this candid avowal on the part of Nikolay Sergeitch, she could not remain another minute, and could not understand how she could have gone on living in the house before.

Vocabulary

ingratiating
(in grā′ shē āt′ iŋ) *adj.* trying to win someone's favor or good opinion

Comprehension
What does Nikolay Sergeitch confess?

"I WILL APOLOGIZE FOR MY WIFE. IN MY WIFE'S NAME..."

"And it's nothing to wonder at," Nikolay Sergeitch went on after a pause. "It's an everyday story! I need money, and she . . . won't give it to me. It was my father's money that bought this house and everything, you know! It's all mine, and the brooch belonged to my mother, and . . . it's all mine! And she took it, took possession of everything. . . . I can't go to law with her, you'll admit. . . . I beg you most earnestly, overlook it . . . stay on. *Tout comprendre, tout pardonner.*[9] Will you stay?"

"No!" said Mashenka resolutely, beginning to tremble. "Let me alone, I entreat you!"

"Well, God bless you!" sighed Nikolay Sergeitch, sitting down on the stool near the box. "I must own I like people who still can feel resentment, contempt, and so on. I could sit here forever and look at your indignant face. . . . So you won't stay, then? I understand. . . . It's bound to be so. . . . Yes, of course. . . . It's all right for you, but for me—wo-o-o-o! . . . I can't stir a step out of this cellar. I'd go off to one of our estates, but in every one of them there are some of my wife's rascals . . . stewards, experts, damn them all! They mortgage and remortgage. . . . You mustn't catch fish, must keep off the grass, mustn't break the trees."

"Nikolay Sergeitch!" his wife's voice called from the drawing-room. "Agnia, call your master!"

"Then you won't stay?" asked Nikolay Sergeitch, getting up quickly and going toward the door. "You might as well stay, really. In the evenings I could come and have a talk with you. Eh? Stay! If you go, there won't be a human face left in the house. It's awful!"

Nikolay Sergeitch's pale, exhausted face besought her, but Mashenka shook her head, and with a wave of his hand he went out.

Half an hour later she was on her way.

---

9. ***Tout comprendre, tout pardonner*** (too′ kən prän′ dr too′ pär′ də nā′) a French proverb meaning "To understand all, to forgive all."

Critical Reading

1. **Key Ideas and Details (a)** Why is Mashenka's room searched? **(b) Infer:** Why does the search upset her?

2. **Key Ideas and Details (a)** What does Fedosya Vassilyevna say about her confidence in Mashenka? **(b) Infer:** Based on her remarks and behavior, what sort of person is Fedosya Vassilyevna?

3. **Integration of Knowledge and Ideas (a) Compare and Contrast:** In taking the brooch, how does Nikolay Sergeitch show himself to be unlike Mashenka? **(b) Analyze:** Why is it ironic that he has taken the brooch?

Cite textual evidence to support you responses.

Close Reading Activities from *Hard Times* • *An Upheaval*

Comparing Social Criticism

 Common Core State Standards

Writing
1. Write arguments to support claims in an analysis of substantive topics or texts, using valid reasoning and relevant and sufficient evidence.

1. **Key Ideas and Details (a)** What is similar about the plight of the schoolchildren in *Hard Times* and Mashenka in "An Upheaval"? **(b)** What is different about their backgrounds?

2. **Key Ideas and Details (a)** How does sticking to a particular social philosophy play a role in the behavior of the teachers in *Hard Times* and the behavior of Mashenka in "An Upheaval"? **(b)** In what way are the two philosophies nearly opposite?

3. **Key Ideas and Details (a)** Where in each selection do characters have trouble communicating? **(b)** What does each selection suggest about the importance of and barriers to communication in society?

4. **Integration of Knowledge and Ideas** What role does the title of the work play in stressing the social criticisms that each selection contains?

Timed Writing

Argumentative Text: Essay

Both Dickens and Chekhov take issue with ethical and social influences prevalent in their times.

Assignment: In an **essay,** compare and contrast the means that each author uses to express criticism of his society.

[40 minutes]

Address these questions, citing details from the selections to support your ideas:

- What main social criticisms does each selection make?
- Which selection uses more realism in its social criticism?
- Which writer uses more satire in his social criticism?
- Which text is more effective in its social criticism?

5-Minute Planner

Complete these steps before you begin to write:

1. Read the assignment carefully. Identify key words and phrases.

2. Weigh the similarities and differences between the two selections. **TIP** As you scan the texts, jot down quotations or details that you might use in your essay.

3. Create a rough outline for your essay.

4. Reread the prompt, and draft your essay.

Analyzing Functional and Expository Texts

Web Site Home Page • Brochure

About the Texts

A **Web site** consists of text and media that is divided into pages and accessed online, via a computer. A **Web site home page** is the opening page of a Web site. Serving as a table of contents, the home page displays links or connections to other pages on the site. In addition, it may provide information on the site's purpose and sponsoring organization.

A park or museum **brochure** is a pamphlet with information about an attraction, including contact and admission information. It also usually includes a map to guide visitors, historical background, and images meant to excite interest.

Preparing to Read Complex Texts

You can **predict the content and purpose** of home pages and brochures by scanning these *text features:*

- Simple section headings
- Introductions providing basic background information
- Sidebars, or sections of information presented in a column down the side of a page
- Captions or explanations of graphics

Once you have used text features to learn how a document is organized, you can more effectively use the text. To *evaluate the effectiveness of a document's organization,* consider how easy it is to follow the sequence of information and to locate specific items. Use a chart like this one to guide your review of the documents.

Checklist	Questions	Responses
☐ Introduction	How helpful is the overview provided?	
☐ Links or Headings	What ordering or subdivision of information do these present? Is this order logical?	
☐ Layout	How is information arranged on the page? Is this layout effective?	
☐ Graphics	How clear is the purpose for and labeling of graphics?	

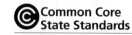

Common Core State Standards

Reading Informational Text
5. Analyze and evaluate the effectiveness of the structure an author uses in his or her exposition or argument, including whether the structure makes points clear, convincing, and engaging.

Language
4.d. Verify the preliminary determination of the meaning of a word or phrase.

Content-Area Vocabulary

These words appear in the selections that follow. They may also appear in other content-area texts.

manuscripts (man´ yoo skripts´) *n.* the unpublished versions of a written work

agricultural (ag´ ri kul´ chərəl) *adj.* pertaining to farming

tenant (ten´ ənt) *adj.* of or for someone who rents property

(The site's URL appears here.)

These links to other parts of the Web site help users quickly locate the information they need.

The Dickens Museum Home Page and Virtual Tour Link *London*

The Museum	Private Views	Books & Gifts	Media
Opening Hours	Events	Events	Research
Find Us	Teachers	Hire the Museum	Links
History	Access	Exhibitions	Access
Groups	Learning	Support	

The front of 48 Doughty Street.

© Adam Woolfitt/CORBIS

The Museum

The Charles Dickens Museum in London is the world's most important collection of material relating to the great Victorian novelist and social commentator. The only surviving London home of Dickens (from 1837 until 1839) was opened as a Museum in 1925 and is still welcoming visitors from all over the world in an authentic and inspiring surrounding. On four floors, visitors can see paintings, rare editions, **manuscripts**, original furniture and many items relating to the life of one of the most popular and beloved personalities of the Victorian age.

Gifts and Books

Here you will find gifts for all the family as well as a wide range of books by or about Charles Dickens.

Support

Click here to find out how you can support the Museum in its many educational, conservational and curatorial activities.

Events

For our program of events and educational activities, please click here.

Hire the Museum

The Museum can be hired for private functions, performances, soirees, book launches and many other social occasions. Click here to find out more.

This introduction provides a short history of the museum and a brief description of its holdings. To the left, you can see a photograph of the museum's entrance.

(The site's URL appears here.)

The Charles Dickens Museum *Virtual Tour*

| Main | Museum Map | Museum Guide | Tour Tutorial |

Basement
Library
Still room
Main Hallway
Wash House
Wine Cellar
Stairs to Ground Floor

Ground Floor
Front Hallway
Dining Room
Morning Room
Back Parlour
Stairs to First Floor

First Floor
Drawing Room
Study
Stairs to Second Floor

Second Floor
Dressing Room
Charles and Catherine
    Bedroom
Mary Hogarth Room

Welcome to the Virtual Tour of the Charles Dickens Museum!
What follows is a photographic tour of the former home of Charles Dickens, located at 48 Doughty Street, London. You can explore the house much as you would in an actual visit, going between rooms and focusing on items that catch your interest. This tour is meant to provide to you a feeling of actually exploring the house, from the comfort of any computer with access to the Internet.

As you make your way about the house you may notice some glare from light fixtures and windows present in pictures. This is a result of the fact that the purpose is to provide an accurate account of what a visitor to the actual museum experiences, and glare and reflections would be present in a real-life visit. It is also important to note that since the museum is constantly acquiring new items related to Charles Dickens, not everything currently on display at the museum will be present in this virtual tour. This tour was created during March and April of 2005, and since then some items may have been added, moved or removed.

The requirements to view this tour are minimal. It relies on providing an immersive experience through the use of pictures and text. File sizes are small enough so that visitors with low speed connections should be able to view it without problems, but please be patient, especially when viewing the panoramic photos.

To the left of this main section, you will see a column of links. These links will allow you to jump to specific rooms within the museum, and will be visible no matter what page within the tour you are currently viewing. If you are unsure of where to begin, you can start in The Morning Room and then follow the links at the bottom of each room's page. If you require more help making your way through the museum, check the tutorial which is also linked at the top.

The tour was developed at no cost to the museum by four college students in an effort to help The Charles Dickens Museum comply with the Disability Discrimination Act. Enjoy your visit!

© 2005 Charles Dickens Museum

> Users can take a virtual tour of the museum by clicking on the links in the left column. The text in the main column provides background on the tour.

ANDALUSIA

home of Flannery O'Connor

Milledgeville, Georgia

Andalusia is open on Monday, Tuesday and Saturday from 10:00 a.m. to 4:00 p.m. or by appointment. Guided trolly tours can be arranged by calling the Milledgeville, Baldwin County Visitors Center at 1-800-653-1804

2628 N. Columbia Street (Hwy 441 N)
Milledgeville, Georgia
www.andalusiafarm.org   478-454-4029

The brochure provides basic information in the form of frequently asked questions (FAQs) and answers.

Where was Flannery O'Connor born?

Flannery O'Connor was born in Savannah, Georgia on March 25, 1925, the only child of Edward F. O'Connor, Jr. and Regina Cline O'Connor.

Where did Flannery O'Connor attend school and college?

O'Connor attended St. Vincent's Grammar School and Sacred Heart Parochial School in Savannah, Georgia; St. Joseph's Parochial School and North Fulton High School in Atlanta, Georgia; Peabody High School and Georgia State College for Women in Milledgeville, Georgia; and the State University of Iowa in Iowa City.

How long did Flannery O'Connor live at Andalusia?

Flannery O'Connor lived at Andalusia with her mother, Regina Cline O'Connor, from early 1951 until Flannery's death in 1964. She completed all her published books while living here.

Why is the farm called Andalusia?

In the fall of 1946, before the death of Dr. Bernard Cline, Flannery O'Connor met on a bus to Atlanta a descendant of the original Hawkins family that owned Andalusia. It was the descendant who told her the original name of the place in the 19th century was Andalusia. She wrote her mother, and when her uncle Bernard heard of it, he was pleased and liked the name. From then on the name was Andalusia.

What happened to Flannery's peacocks?

None of the descendants of O'Connor's domestic flock has survived at the farm. Regina Cline O'Connor gave two pair of peafowl to Stone Mountain Mansion, one pair to Our Lady of Perpetual Help Cancer Home in Atlanta, and another pair to the Monastery of the Holy Spirit near Conyers, Georgia.

The cover page of the brochure features a photograph of O'Connor's home and provides contact information for the organization that administers the site.

Publications by Flannery O'Connor:

Wise Blood — 1952

A Good Man Is Hard To Find — 1955

The Violent Bear It Away — 1960

Everything That Rises Must Converge — 1965

Mystery and Manners — 1969

The Complete Stories, winner of the 1971 National Book Award for Fiction.

The Habit of Being — 1979, winner of the National Book Critics Circle Award.

Flannery O'Connor: Collected Works (Library of America) — 1988

Andalusia is the picturesque farm where American author Flannery O'Connor lived from 1951 until her death from lupus in 1964. Listed on the National Register of Historic Places, Andalusia is brought to life on many occasions in O'Connor's published letters. In the 1950s Andalusia was a dairy farm operated by O'Connor's mother, Regina Cline O'Connor. The **agricultural** setting of Andalusia provided for O'Connor not only a place to live and write, but also a landscape in which to set her fiction.

The farm complex consists of the 19th century Main House, Jack and Louise Hill's house (the home of farm workers), the cow barn, an equipment shed, the milk-processing shed, an additional smaller barn, a parking garage, a water tower, an old well house (storage), a horse stable, a pump house, several small **tenant** houses, a small pond, and nature trails.

Flannery O'Connor did not live a reclusive life at Andalusia. She traveled for various speaking engagements and made frequent visits into town for dining, social events, and to attend Mass regularly at Sacred Heart Catholic Church. She routinely wrote every morning until noon in her downstairs bedroom/study and spent her afternoons and evenings tending to her peafowl and other domestic birds or entertaining visitors.

The brochure provides background information about the house and the author.

Andalusia is located just north of the shopping center on Hwy 441 North of Milledgeville

The map helps visitors planning a trip to the site.

Critical Reading

**Common Core
State Standards**

Writing
2. Write informative/
explanatory texts to
examine and convey
complex ideas, concepts,
and information clearly
and accurately through
the effective selection,
organization, and analysis
of content.

1. **Key Ideas and Details (a)** Based on the Web site home page, where could you access views of Dickens's study? **(b)** How do the links at the top of the home page help visitors navigate the Web site?

2. **Key Ideas and Details (a)** Where in the brochure can you find information about O'Connor's publications and awards? **(b)** Where can you find contact information for the organization that sponsors the site?

3. **Craft and Structure (a)** How does the structure of each text, including the graphic elements, make points clear and engaging? **(b)** Which text has a more effective structure? Explain.

4. **Content-Area Vocabulary (a)** The word *tenant* derives from the Latin verb *tenere,* which means "to hold." Explain how the meaning of the Latin verb informs the meaning of *tenant.* **(b)** Define the following words derived from the same Latin verb: *tenable* and *tenacious.* Use a dictionary to verify your definitions.

⏱ Timed Writing

Explanatory Text [40 minutes]

> **Format**
> In an **analytical essay,** you present a clear thesis statement in an introductory paragraph and develop it in the body, following a clear organization.

> Write an **analytical essay** in which you explain the types of information preserved and published by museums and parks focused on authors' lives. Carefully select and organize information from the Web site home page and the museum brochure to support your explanation. Gather and develop ideas by **synthesizing ideas and making logical connections** between the Web site and the brochure.

> **Academic Vocabulary**
> When you **synthesize ideas and make logical connections,** you combine related ideas, focusing on ways in which they reinforce or build on one another, to reach new conclusions.

5-Minute Planner

Complete these steps before you begin to write.

1. Read the prompt carefully, and underline key words.

2. Scan the text for details that relate to the prompt. **TIP** As you consider the various types of information available at museums and parks, consider the types of information that a visitor might gather by inspecting an author's home in person, as well as information that the museum or park might provide in printed materials.

3. Before writing, create an outline to guide you.

4. Reread the prompt, and begin drafting your essay.

Connecting to the Essential Question In *Jane Eyre*, Charlotte Brontë criticizes harsh boarding schools like the one she attended as a girl. As you read, look for details that criticize conditions at the Lowood School. Doing so will help you answer the Essential Question: **How does literature shape or reflect society?**

Common Core State Standards

Reading Literature
3. Analyze the impact of the author's choices regarding how to develop and relate elements of a story or drama.

Close Reading Focus

Philosophical Assumptions

Works of fiction often reflect the author's philosophy—his or her assumptions about human nature and our relationships to each other and society. Such **philosophical assumptions** may influence the way the author develops and relates the elements of the story, including characters, settings, and events. For example, Charlotte Brontë develops Jane Eyre's character by contrasting the reactions that Jane and Helen Burns have to their harsh treatment at the Lowood School:

> **Jane**: "When we are struck at without a reason, we should strike back again very hard. . . . so hard as to teach the person who struck us never to do it again."

> **Helen**: " . . . Love your enemies; bless them that curse you; do good to them that hate you and despitefully use you. . . . Life appears to me to be too short to be spent in nursing animosity or registering wrongs."

When characters' philosophies conflict, the author may be criticizing one and accepting the other or may see some merit in both. As you read, consider the philosophical assumptions that drive Brontë's narrative.

Preparing to Read Complex Texts To **analyze the author's assumptions,** apply information you have about the author and time period to details in the selection itself. For example, if you consider the novel's presentation of the Lowood School along with the strong Victorian belief in social reform and Charlotte Brontë's experience, you can better understand the assumptions the author makes about such schools. As you read, use a chart like the one shown to help you analyze the author's assumptions.

How Characters Are Treated

Reactions to Wrongs | **Wrongs That Are Done**

Philosophical Assumptions

Vocabulary

The words below are important to understanding the text that follows. Copy the words into your notebook. Which word can you infer is a past tense verb?

obscure   tumult

comprised   truculent

sundry

Charlotte Brontë
(1816–1855)

Author of *Jane Eyre*

Charlotte Brontë was part of a renowned literary family: Her sisters Anne and Emily were also writers. Their father, an Anglican clergyman, moved his family to the moors in Yorkshire in 1820, and the children were educated largely at home. Raised without their mother, who had died in 1821, the sisters, together with their brother Branwell, led a rich fantasy life that nurtured their artistic development.

Early Failure With three of her sisters, Charlotte briefly attended a boarding school. Her experiences there provided material for the critical descriptions of boarding-school life at Lowood in *Jane Eyre*. Charlotte spent several years as a teacher, first of her own siblings and then at another school that she herself had briefly attended. She found this job difficult and unappealing, and in 1844 attempted to open her own school near her family home. The school's failure was quick and definite: No pupils enrolled.

Success In 1846, the three sisters published a volume of poems under the pseudonyms Currer, Ellis, and Acton Bell, but the book had little success. Charlotte had also written a novel, *The Professor,* but the book failed to find a publisher. Charlotte persevered, however, and when *Jane Eyre* was published in 1847, it met with immediate popular success.

Personal Struggle The final years of Charlotte Brontë's life were clouded by tragedy. Her brother died in 1848, and Emily and Anne died soon after. Despite her loneliness, Charlotte found the strength to complete the novels *Shirley* (1849) and *Villette* (1853). She married Arthur Bell Nicholls, her father's curate, and died about nine months later.

FROM **JANE EYRE**

Charlotte Brontë

CHAPTER 6

The next day commenced as before, getting up and dressing by rushlight; but this morning we were obliged to dispense with the ceremony of washing: the water in the pitchers was frozen. A change had taken place in the weather the preceding evening, and a keen northeast wind, whistling through the crevices of our bedroom windows all night long, had made us shiver in our beds, and turned the contents of the ewers to ice.

Before the long hour and a half of prayers and Bible reading was over, I felt ready to perish with cold. Breakfast time came at last, and this morning the porridge was not burnt; the quality was eatable, the quantity small; how small my portion seemed! I wished it had been doubled.

Analyzing an Author's Assumptions

Which details suggest Brontë thinks schools like Lowood are in need of reform?

In the course of the day I was enrolled a member of the fourth class, and regular tasks and occupations were assigned to me: hitherto, I had only been a spectator of the proceedings at Lowood, I was now to become an actor therein. At first, being little accustomed to learn by heart, the lessons appeared to me both long and difficult: the frequent change from task to task, too, bewildered me; and I was glad, when, about three o'clock in the afternoon, Miss Smith put into my hands a border of muslin two yards long, together with needle, thimble, etc., and sent me to sit in a quiet corner of the school room, with directions to hem the same. At that hour most of the others were sewing likewise; but one class still stood round Miss Scatcherd's chair reading, and as all was quiet, the subject of their lessons could be heard, together with the manner in which each girl acquitted herself, and the animadversions or commendations of Miss Scatcherd on the performance. It was English history; among the readers, I observed my acquaintance of the verandah; at the commencement of the lesson, her place had been at the top of the class, but for some error of pronunciation or some inattention to stops, she was suddenly sent to the very bottom. Even in that obscure position, Miss Scatcherd continued to make her an object of constant notice: she was continually addressing to her such phrases as the following:—

"Burns" (such it seems was her name: the girls here, were all called by their surnames, as boys are elsewhere), "Burns, you are standing on the side of your shoe, turn your toes out immediately." "Burns, you poke your chin most unpleasantly, draw it in." "Burns, I insist on your holding your head up: I will not have you before me in that attitude," etc. etc.

A chapter having been read through twice, the books were closed and the girls examined. The lesson had comprised part of the reign of Charles I, and there were sundry questions about tonnage and poundage, and ship-money, which most of them appeared unable to answer; still, every little difficulty was solved instantly when it reached Burns: her memory seemed to have retained the substance of the whole lesson, and she was ready with answers on every point. I kept expecting that Miss Scatcherd would praise her attention; but, instead of that, she suddenly cried out:—

"You dirty, disagreeable girl! you have never cleaned your nails this morning!"

Burns made no answer: I wondered at her silence.

"Why," thought I, "does she not explain that she could neither clean her nails nor wash her face, as the water was frozen?"

My attention was now called off by Miss Smith, desiring me to hold a skein of thread: while she was winding it, she talked to me from time to time, asking whether I had ever been at school before, whether I could mark, stitch, knit, etc.; till she dismissed me, I could not pursue my observations on Miss Scatcherd's movements. When I returned to my seat, that lady was just delivering an order, of which I did not catch the import; but Burns immediately left the class, and

Vocabulary

obscure (əb skyoor′) *adj.* not easily seen; not generally known

comprised (kəm prīzd′) *v.* consisted of; included

sundry (sun′ drē) adj. various, miscellaneous

Comprehension

How has the narrator's role at Lowood changed?

Author's Philosophical Assumptions

What does Miss Scatcherd's reaction suggest about Brontë's assumptions regarding an ideal teacher-student relationship?

Spiral Review

Point of View How does the novel's first-person narration affect the reader's connection with Jane?

Vocabulary

tumult (too̅′ mult) *n.* noise caused by a crowd

going into the small inner room where the books were kept, returned in half a minute, carrying in her hand a bundle of twigs tied together at one end. This ominous tool she presented to Miss Scatcherd with a respectful courtesy; then she quietly, and without being told, unloosed her pinafore, and the teacher instantly and sharply inflicted on her neck a dozen strokes with the bunch of twigs. Not a tear rose to Burns's eye; and, while I paused from my sewing, because my fingers quivered at this spectacle with a sentiment of unavailing and impotent anger, not a feature of her pensive face altered its ordinary expression.

"Hardened girl!" exclaimed Miss Scatcherd, "nothing can correct you of your slatternly habits: carry the rod away."

Burns obeyed: I looked at her narrowly as she emerged from the book closet; she was just putting back her handkerchief into her pocket, and the trace of a tear glistened on her thin cheek.

The play-hour in the evening I thought the pleasantest fraction of the day at Lowood: the bit of bread, the draught of coffee swallowed at five o'clock had revived vitality, if it had not satisfied hunger; the long restraint of the day was slackened; the school room felt warmer than in the morning: its fires being allowed to burn a little more brightly to supply, in some measure, the place of candles, not yet introduced; the ruddy gloaming,[1] the licensed uproar, the confusion of many voices gave one a welcome sense of liberty.

On the evening of the day on which I had seen Miss Scatcherd flog her pupil, Burns, I wandered as usual among the forms and tables and laughing groups without a companion, yet not feeling lonely: when I passed the windows, I now and then lifted a blind and looked out; it snowed fast, a drift was already forming against the lower panes; putting my ear close to the window, I could distinguish from the gleeful tumult within, the disconsolate moan of the wind outside.

Probably, if I had lately left a good home and kind parents, this would have been the hour when I should most keenly have regretted the separation: that wind would then have saddened my heart; this obscure chaos would have disturbed my peace: as it was I derived from both a strange excitement, and reckless and feverish, I wished the wind to howl more wildly, the gloom to deepen to darkness, and the confusion to rise to clamor.

Jumping over forms, and creeping under tables, I made my way to one of the fire-places: there, kneeling by the high wire fender, I found Burns, absorbed, silent, abstracted from all round her by the companionship of a book, which she read by the dim glare of the embers.

"Is it still 'Rasselas'?"[2] I asked, coming behind her.

"Yes," she said, "and I have just finished it."

And in five minutes more she shut it up. I was glad of this.

---

1. **ruddy gloaming** glowing twilight; the sunset.
2. **Rasselas** *The History of Rasselas, Prince of Abyssinia*, a moralizing novel by Samuel Johnson.

exclaimed Miss Scatcherd . . .

"Now," thought I, "I can perhaps get her to talk." I sat down by her on the floor.

"What is your name besides Burns?"

"Helen."

"Do you come a long way from here?"

"I come from a place further north; quite on the borders of Scotland."

"Will you ever go back?"

"I hope so; but nobody can be sure of the future."

"You must wish to leave Lowood?"

"No: why should I? I was sent to Lowood to get an education; and it would be of no use going away until I have attained that object."

"But that teacher, Miss Scatcherd, is so cruel to you?"

"Cruel? Not at all! She is severe: she dislikes my faults."

"And if I were in your place I should dislike her: I should resist her; if she struck me with that rod, I should get it from her hand; I should break it under her nose."

▲ **Critical Viewing**

How well does this still from a movie version of *Jane Eyre* match your vision of Jane and Burns? Explain.
EVALUATE

Comprehension

How does Burns react to her beating by Miss Scatcherd?

from Jane Eyre **1033**

"Probably you would do nothing of the sort: but if you did, Mr. Brocklehurst would expel you from the school; that would be a great grief to your relations. It is far better to endure patiently a smart which nobody feels but yourself, than to commit a hasty action whose evil consequences will extend to all connected with you—and, besides, the Bible bids us return good for evil."

"But then it seems disgraceful to be flogged, and to be sent to stand in the middle of a room full of people; and you are such a great girl: I am far younger than you, and I could not bear it."

"Yet it would be your duty to bear it, if you could not avoid it: it is weak and silly to say you *cannot bear* what it is your fate to be required to bear."

I heard her with wonder: I could not comprehend this doctrine of endurance; and still less could I understand or sympathize with the forbearance she expressed for her chastiser. Still I felt that Helen Burns considered things by a light invisible to my eyes. I suspected she might be right and I wrong; but I would not ponder the matter deeply: like Felix,[3] I put it off to a more convenient season.

"You say you have faults, Helen: what are they? To me you seem very good."

"Then learn from me, not to judge by appearances: I am, as Miss Scatcherd said, slatternly; I seldom put, and never keep, things in order; I am careless; I forget rules; I read when I should learn my lessons; I have no method; and sometimes I say, like you, I cannot *bear* to be subjected to systematic arrangements. This is all very provoking to Miss Scatcherd, who is naturally neat, punctual, and particular."

"And cross and cruel," I added; but Helen Burns would not admit my addition: she kept silence.

"Is Miss Temple as severe to you as Miss Scatcherd?"

At the utterance of Miss Temple's name, a soft smile flitted over her grave face.

"Miss Temple is full of goodness; it pains her to be severe to anyone, even the worst in the school: she sees my errors, and tells me of them gently; and, if I do anything worthy of praise, she gives me my meed liberally. One strong proof of my wretchedly defective nature is

---

3. **Felix** in the Bible, governor of Judea who released Paul from prison and deferred his trial until a more "convenient season" (Acts 24:25).

Author's Philosophical Assumptions

What do Jane's thoughts suggest about the author's assumptions regarding the relative importance of obedience and independence?

"... it is weak and silly to say you CANNOT BEAR what it is your fate to be required to bear."

that even her expostulations, so mild, so rational, have not influence to cure me of my faults; and even her praise, though I value it most highly, cannot stimulate me to continued care and foresight."

"That is curious," said I: "it is so easy to be careful."

"For *you* I have no doubt it is. I observed you in your class this morning, and saw you were closely attentive: your thoughts never seemed to wander while Miss Miller explained the lesson and questioned you. Now, mine continually rove away: when I should be listening to Miss Scatcherd, and collecting all she says with assiduity,[4] often I lose the very sound of her voice; I fall into a sort of dream. Sometimes I think I am in Northumberland, and that the noises I hear round me are the bubbling of a little brook which runs through Deepden, near our house;—then, when it comes to my turn to reply, I have to be wakened; and, having heard nothing of what was read for listening to the visionary brook, I have no answer ready."

"Yet how well you replied this afternoon."

"It was mere chance: the subject on which we had been reading had interested me. This afternoon, instead of dreaming of Deepden, I was wondering how a man who wished to do right could act so unjustly and unwisely as Charles the First sometimes did; and I thought what a pity it was that, with his integrity and conscientiousness, he could see no farther than the prerogatives of the crown. If he had but been able to look to a distance, and see how what they call the spirit of the age was tending! Still, I like Charles—I respect him—I pity him, poor murdered king! Yes, his enemies were the worst: they shed blood they had no right to shed. How dared they kill him!"

Helen was talking to herself now: she had forgotten I could not very well understand her—that I was ignorant, or nearly so, of the subject she discussed. I recalled her to my level.

"And when Miss Temple teaches you, do your thoughts wander then?"

"No, certainly, not often; because Miss Temple has generally something to say which is newer to me than my own reflections: her language is singularly agreeable to me, and the information she communicates is often just what I wished to gain."

"Well, then, with Miss Temple you are good?"

"Yes, in a passive way: I make no effort; I follow as inclination guides me. There is no merit in such goodness."

"A great deal: you are good to those who are good to you. It is all I ever desire to be. If people were always kind and obedient to those who are cruel and unjust, the wicked people would have it all their own way: they would never feel afraid, and so they would never alter, but would grow worse and worse. When we are struck at without a reason, we should strike back again very hard; I am sure we should—so hard as to teach the person who struck us never to do it again."

Analyzing an Author's Assumptions

To what extent is Brontë criticizing or supporting the ideas Helen shares about Charles the First? Explain.

Comprehension

What faults does Helen Burns attribute to herself?

---

4. assiduity (as´ ə dyo͞o´ ə tē) *n.* constant care and attention; diligence.

"You will change your mind, I hope, when you grow older: as yet you are but a little untaught girl."

"But I feel this, Helen: I must dislike those who, whatever I do to please them, persist in disliking me; I must resist those who punish me unjustly. It is as natural as that I should love those who show me affection, or submit to punishment when I feel it is deserved."

". . . Love your enemies; bless them that curse you; do good to them that hate you and despitefully use you."

"Then I should love Mrs. Reed, which I cannot do; I should bless her son John, which is impossible."

In her turn, Helen Burns asked me to explain; and I proceeded forthwith to pour out, in my way, the tale of my sufferings and resentments. Bitter and truculent when excited, I spoke as I felt, without reserve or softening.

Helen heard me patiently to the end: I expected she would then make a remark, but she said nothing.

"Well," I asked impatiently, "is not Mrs. Reed a hard-hearted, bad woman?"

"She has been unkind to you, no doubt; because, you see, she dislikes your cast of character, as Miss Scatcherd does mine: but how minutely you remember all she has done and said to you! What a singularly deep impression her injustice seems to have made on your heart! No ill usage so brands its record on my feelings. Would you not be happier if you tried to forget her severity, together with the passionate emotions it excited? Life appears to me too short to be spent in nursing animosity or registering wrongs. We are, and must be, one and all, burdened with faults in this world: but the time will soon come when, I trust, we shall put them off in putting off our corruptible bodies; when debasement and sin will fall from us with this cumbrous frame of flesh, and only the spark of the spirit will remain,—the impalpable principle of life and thought, pure as when it left the Creator to inspire the creature: whence[5] it came it will return; perhaps again to be communicated to some being higher than man—perhaps to pass through gradations of glory, from the pale human soul to brighten to the seraph![6] Surely it will never, on

Vocabulary

truculent (truk´ yə lənt) *adj.* cruel; fierce

Author's Philosophical Assumptions

Does the author favor one girl's argument over the other's? Explain.

---

5. whence the place from which.

the contrary, be suffered to degenerate from man to fiend? No; I cannot believe that: I hold another creed; which no one ever taught me, and which I seldom mention; but in which I delight, and to which I cling: for it extends hope to all: it makes Eternity a rest—a mighty home, not a terror and abyss. Besides, with this creed, I can so clearly distinguish between the criminal and his crime; I can so sincerely forgive the first while I abhor the last: with this creed revenge never worries my heart, degradation never too deeply disgusts me, injustice never crushes me too low: I live in calm, looking to the end."

Helen's head, always drooping, sank a little lower as she finished this sentence. I saw by her look she wished no longer to talk to me, but rather to converse with her own thoughts. She was not allowed much time for meditation: a monitor, a great rough girl, presently came up, exclaiming in a strong Cumberland accent—

"Helen Burns, if you don't go and put your drawer in order, and fold up your work this minute, I'll tell Miss Scatcherd to come and look at it!"

Helen sighed as her reverie fled, and getting up, obeyed the monitor without reply as without delay.

---

6. **seraph** angel of the highest order.

Critical Reading

1. **Key Ideas and Details (a)** For what offense does Miss Scatcherd punish Helen Burns? **(b) Infer:** When punished, why does Helen make every effort to hold back tears?

2. **Key Ideas and Details (a)** Which teacher does Helen particularly like? **(b) Analyze:** Why does Helen find that there is "no merit" in being good in this teacher's class?

3. **Key Ideas and Details** Describe Jane's personality in a few sentences.

4. **Integration of Knowledge and Ideas (a) Compare and Contrast:** Compare Jane's and Helen's reactions to mistreatment. **(b) Make a Judgment:** Do you think each has something to teach the other? Explain.

5. **Integration of Knowledge and Ideas** Might Helen and Jane be seen as two sides of the author's personality? Why or why not?

6. **Integration of Knowledge and Ideas** How do you think Brontë would like to reform schools like Lowood? In your response, use at least two of these Essential Question words: *education, independence, leadership*. *[Connecting to the Essential Question: How does literature shape or reflect society?]*

Cite textual evidence to support your responses.

Literary Analysis

Common Core State Standards

Writing
2. Write informative/ explanatory texts to examine and convey complex ideas, concepts, and information clearly and accurately through the effective selection, organization, and analysis of content.

1. **Key Ideas and Details (a)** Begin to **analyze the author's assumptions** in this selection by identifying three details Brontë uses to describe the setting. **(b)** What assumptions about children and education do these details suggest?

2. **Integration of Knowledge and Ideas (a)** Use a chart like the one shown to compare and contrast the two philosophies espoused by Jane and Helen in this excerpt. **(b)** Which do you think best reflects the underlying **philosophical assumptions** that Brontë brings to this story? Explain.

Character's view	of Miss Scatcherd's actions	of education	**Assumption**

3. **Integration of Knowledge and Ideas (a)** Based on their behavior, what different teaching philosophies do Miss Temple and Miss Scatcherd follow? **(b)** How does the author seem to feel about each teacher's philosophy? Cite details from the selection to support your evaluation.

4. **Integration of Knowledge and Ideas** Early Victorian society taught that women should be docile, domestic creatures with little concern for larger issues. Do Brontë's assumptions seem to agree with that view? Cite details to support your evaluation.

Vocabulary Acquisition and Use

For each word, choose the letter of its synonym, and explain your choice.

1. **tumult:** (a) ache (b) cruelty (c) satisfaction (d) excitement
2. **comprised:** (a) included (b) suggested (c) pried (d) attached
3. **truculent:** (a) forgetful (b) ferocious (c) driven (d) peaceful
4. **obscure:** (a) murky (b) noisy (c) arrogant (d) attentive
5. **sundry:** (a) shiny (b) outdoor (c) withered (d) diverse

Writing to Sources

Informative Text Write the **school conduct report** that Miss Scatcherd might have written about Helen Burns. From the selection, infer Miss Scatcherd's feelings about Helen. Then, set up a formal report with the Lowood School heading, your name (Miss Scatcherd), a date at the top, and an evaluation section that includes grades and comments in categories such as schoolwork, personal hygiene, posture, and effort.

The Empire and Its Discontents

Connecting to the Essential Question Matthew Arnold sees the world in terms of private loyalties, and Rudyard Kipling sees it in terms of public duties. As you read, notice Arnold's private settings and compare and contrast them with Kipling's public arenas. Doing so will help you explore the Essential Question: **What is the relationship between literature and place?**

Close Reading Focus

Mood; Theme

Poems contain emotional thoughts and thoughtful emotions. With thought and emotion so closely linked, the **mood,** or feeling, that a poem calls up is bound to be related to its **themes,** or messages about life, and to its *aesthetic impact*—its intended *emotional effect* on the reader. Read poetry with your feelings and you will find your way to its ideas.

In "Dover Beach," for example, the crash of waves brings "The eternal note of sadness in." This mood of sadness contributes to an important theme of the poem, which concerns a world with "neither joy, nor love, nor light." This theme interacts with other themes in the poem, such as the loss of certainty and faith, to produce a work with rich layers of meaning.

Comparing Literary Works The *"sound" of language* contributes to the mood and the intended effect on the reader. Compare the sounds of Arnold's and Kipling's language and consider their effects on the reader.

Preparing to Read Complex Texts **Connecting a poem to the historical period** will help you better understand its mood and themes. The Victorian era was marked by scientific progress, material prosperity, and British global domination, yet each success brought fresh anxieties with it:

- Scientific progress brought a greater questioning of religious faith.
- Material prosperity for some brought greater poverty for others.
- Expansion of Britain's empire brought heavy responsibilities as well as political and cultural tensions that often resulted in warfare.

Use a diagram like this to relate the poems to their historical period.

Vocabulary

The words below are important to understanding the texts that follow. Copy the words into your notebook. Which part of speech is signaled by the suffixes *-ence* and *-ion*?

tranquil	dominion
cadence	contrite
turbid	awe

Common Core State Standards

Reading Literature
2. Determine two or more themes or central ideas of a text and analyze their development over the course of the text, including how they interact and build on one another to produce a complex account.

Historical Background

The 1897 "Diamond Jubilee" celebrates the British Empire.

"Recessional" Mood/Themes

The speaker prays for the British Empire while recognizing its greatness is likely temporary.

(1822–1888)

MATTHEW ARNOLD

Author of "Dover Beach"

Much of Matthew Arnold's poetry concerns a theme as relevant today as it was in the nineteenth century: the isolation of individuals from one another and from society. In fact, in the 1960s, the American novelist Norman Mailer used a modified quotation from Arnold's poem "Dover Beach" for the title of his book about a Vietnam War protest, *Armies of the Night.*

A Social Conscience While attending Oxford University, Arnold developed the social conscience that was to guide his career as a public servant, poet, and literary critic. In 1851, he became Inspector of Schools, and in performing this job he did much to improve education throughout Great Britain. All the while, he remained a poet at heart, although his first two collections, published in 1849 and 1852, met with little success.

Literary Achievement Arnold's literary fortunes changed in 1853 when he published *Poems,* with its long preface that established him as a major critic. *New Poems,* published in 1867, contained Arnold's celebrated "Dover Beach."

A Return to Culture After completing this collection, Arnold believed that he had said everything he could in poetry. From that point on he wrote prose, such as the social criticism of the essays in *Culture and Anarchy* (1869). In this book, he attacks Victorian complacency and materialism, arguing that culture should open our minds to what is true and valuable. Arnold's idea of culture still influences critics today.

"CULTURE IS TO KNOW THE BEST THAT HAS BEEN SAID AND THOUGHT IN THE WORLD."

DOVER BEACH

MATTHEW ARNOLD

▲ **Critical Viewing**

Does this photograph capture the "eternal note of sadness" Arnold describes? Explain. **SUPPORT**

Vocabulary

tranquil (traŋ´ kwil) *adj.* calm; serene; peaceful

cadence (kād´ əns) *n.* measured movement

The sea is calm tonight.
The tide is full, the moon lies fair
Upon the straits;[1] on the French coast the light
Gleams and is gone; the cliffs of England stand,
5 Glimmering and vast, out in the tranquil bay.
Come to the window, sweet is the night air!

Only, from the long line of spray
Where the sea meets the moon-blanched land,
Listen! you hear the grating roar
10 Of pebbles which the waves draw back, and fling,
At their return, up the high strand,[2]
Begin, and cease, and then again begin,
With tremulous cadence slow, and bring
The eternal note of sadness in.

---

1. **straits** Straits of Dover, between England and France.
2. **strand** shore.

15 Sophocles[3] long ago
　　Heard it on the Aegean,[4] and it brought
　　Into his mind the turbid ebb and flow
　　Of human misery; we
　　Find also in the sound a thought,
20 Hearing it by this distant northern sea.

　　The Sea of Faith
　　Was once, too, at the full, and round earth's shore
　　Lay like the folds of a bright girdle furled.
　　But now I only hear
25 Its melancholy, long, withdrawing roar,
　　Retreating, to the breath
　　Of the night wind, down the vast edges drear
　　And naked shingles[5] of the world.

　　Ah, love, let us be true
30 To one another! for the world, which seems
　　To lie before us like a land of dreams,
　　So various, so beautiful, so new,
　　Hath really neither joy, nor love, nor light,
　　Nor certitude, nor peace, nor help for pain;
35 And we are here as on a darkling[6] plain
　　Swept with confused alarms of struggle and flight,
　　Where ignorant armies clash by night.

3. **Sophocles** (säf´ ə klēz´) Greek tragic dramatist (496?–406 B.C.).
4. **Aegean** (ē jē´ ən) arm of the Mediterranean Sea between Greece and Turkey.
5. **shingles** *n.* beaches covered with large, coarse, waterworn gravel.
6. **darkling** *adj.* in the dark.

Vocabulary

turbid (tʉr´ bid) *adj.* muddy or cloudy; not clear

Connecting to the Historical Period

How does the doubt expressed in lines 21–28 reflect the historical period in which the poem was written?

Mood as a Key to Theme

How do the feelings that the final stanza evokes relate to its message in lines 29–30?

Critical Reading

1. **Key Ideas and Details (a)** Where are the speaker and his "love," and what do they hear and see? **(b) Interpret:** Why do you think the scene suggests to the speaker "the eternal note of sadness"?

2. **Key Ideas and Details (a)** What does the speaker say has happened to "The Sea of Faith"? **(b) Interpret:** What does he mean by this remark?

3. **Key Ideas and Details (a)** In the last stanza, what does the speaker say that he and his "love" should do? **(b) Draw Conclusions:** What problem does the speaker believe that they can alleviate if they follow his urging?

4. **Integration of Knowledge and Ideas** Is Arnold's message in the final stanza a satisfactory response to "human misery" today? Why or why not?

Cite textual evidence to support your responses.

Rudyard Kipling

(1865–1936)

Author of "Recessional" • "The Widow at Windsor"

Rudyard Kipling's works are known for their celebration of the British Empire, yet they also warn of the costs of world dominion. While praising the benefits of imperialism, he emphasizes the responsibility of the British to bring their "civilized" ways to other parts of the world.

Early Success Kipling was born to British parents in India, one of Britain's largest colonies. At the age of six, he was placed by his parents in a foster home in England, and later, at a chaotic boarding school. One critic speculates that the theme of self-preservation in Kipling's work was inspired by experiences at the boarding school that tested his courage. Kipling would later immortalize his school days in a collection of stories called *Stalky and Co.* (1899). In 1882, Kipling returned to India to work as a journalist. During the next seven years, he published a number of witty poems and stories, and by the time he returned to England in 1889, he was a celebrity.

Kipling's Achievements Kipling is known as a Victorian author because he produced his best work before the death of Queen Victoria in 1901. In its great variety, that work includes poetry, short stories, and novels. Some of his books, such as *The Jungle Books* (1894, 1895), *Captains Courageous* (1897), and *Kim* (1901), have become children's classics.

For years, Kipling was the most popular English poet, and in 1907 he became the first English writer to receive the Nobel Prize for Literature.

RECESSIONAL[1]

Rudyard Kipling

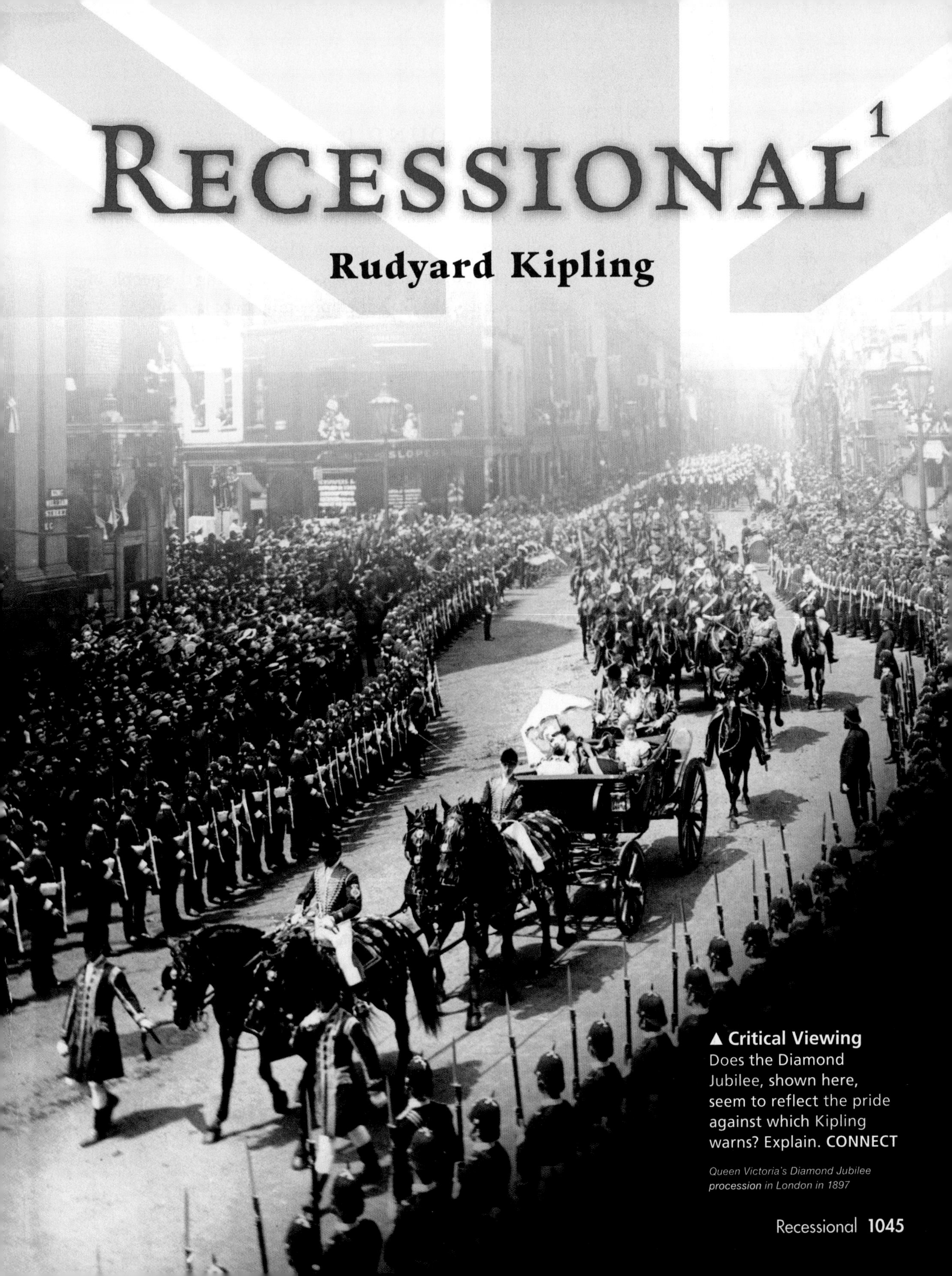

▲ **Critical Viewing**
Does the Diamond Jubilee, shown here, seem to reflect the pride against which Kipling warns? Explain. **CONNECT**

Queen Victoria's Diamond Jubilee procession in London in 1897

The
Diamond Jubilee March.

1837

1897

Composed by
J. Ord Hume.

Piano Solo 4/-

London.
E. Ascherberg & Co.
46 Berners Street, W.

New York. E. Schuberth & Co.

BACKGROUND In 1897, a national celebration called the "Diamond Jubilee" was held in honor of the sixtieth anniversary of Queen Victoria's reign. The occasion prompted a great deal of boasting about the strength and greatness of the empire. Kipling responded to the celebration by writing this poem, reminding the people of England that the British empire might not last forever.

God of our fathers, known of old—
    Lord of our far-flung battle-line—
Beneath whose awful Hand we hold
    Dominion over palm and pine—
5 Lord God of Hosts, be with us yet
Lest we forget—lest we forget!

The tumult and the shouting dies—
    The Captains and the Kings depart—
Still stands Thine ancient Sacrifice,
10   An humble and a contrite heart.[2]
Lord God of Hosts, be with us yet,
Lest we forget—lest we forget!

Far-called, our navies melt away—
    On dune and headland sinks the fire[3]—
15 Lo, all our pomp of yesterday
    Is one with Nineveh[4] and Tyre![5]
Judge of the Nations, spare us yet,
Lest we forget—lest we forget!
If, drunk with sight of power, we loose
20   Wild tongues that have not Thee in awe—
Such boasting as the Gentiles use

Vocabulary

dominion (də min′ yən) *n.*
rule; control

contrite (kən trīt′) *adj.*
willing to repent or atone

awe (ô) *n.* mixed feeling of
reverence, fear, and wonder

1. **Recessional** hymn sung at the end of a religious service. [footnote in title, previous page]
2. **An . . . heart** allusion to the Bible (Psalms 51:17) "The sacrifices of God are a broken spirit: a broken and contrite heart, O God, thou wilt not despise."
3. **On . . . fire** Bonfires were lit on high ground all over Britain as part of the opening ceremonies of the Jubilee celebration.
4. **Nineveh** (nin′ ə ve) ancient capital of the Assyrian Empire, the ruins of which were discovered buried in desert sands in the 1850s.
5. **Tyre** (tir) once a great port and the center of ancient Phoenician culture, now a small town in Lebanon.

Or lesser breeds without the Law—[6]
Lord God of Hosts, be with us yet,
Lest we forget—lest we forget!

25   For heathen heart that puts her trust
      In reeking tube[7] and iron shard[8]—
   All valiant dust that builds on dust,
      And guarding calls not Thee to guard—
   For frantic boast and foolish word,
30   Thy mercy on Thy People, Lord!

---

6. **Such boasting . . . Law** allusion to the Bible (Romans 2:14) "For when the Gentiles, which have not the law, do by nature the things contained in the law, these, having not the law, are a law unto themselves."
7. **tube** barrel of a gun.
8. **shard** fragment of a bombshell.

Mood as a Key to Theme

How does the refrain "Lest we forget," create a mood and support the poem's theme?

Critical Reading

1. **Key Ideas and Details (a)** To whom is this poem addressed? **(b) Interpret:** For whom is the message of the poem really meant?

2. **Key Ideas and Details (a)** What is the literal meaning of the title of the poem? **(b) Interpret:** What double meaning is contained in the title? **(c) Analyze:** How is this ambiguity appropriate to the mood of the poem?

3. **Key Ideas and Details (a)** Paraphrase the first stanza of the poem. **(b) Analyze:** According to this stanza, what is the relationship between God and empire? Explain.

4. **Key Ideas and Details (a)** In lines 15 and 16, what happens to "our pomp of yesterday"? **(b) Infer:** What qualities and actions does the speaker condemn? **(c) Draw Conclusions:** What is the theme of the poem?

5. **Integration of Knowledge and Ideas** Britain is no longer an empire. Does this fact bear out Kipling's warning? Explain.

6. **Integration of Knowledge and Ideas** Is Kipling condemning the very existence of the British empire, or is he advocating a more humble approach to the responsibilities of empire? Explain.

Cite textual evidence to support your responses.

The
Widow
at Windsor

Rudyard Kipling

▲ **Critical Viewing**
What elements of this portrait of Queen Victoria do you think the speaker of the poem might point out? Explain. **CONNECT**

'Ave you 'eard o' the Widow at Windsor
        With a hairy gold crown on 'er 'ead?
She 'as ships on the foam—she 'as millions at 'ome,
        An' she pays us poor beggars in red.
5   (Ow, poor beggars in red!)
There's 'er nick on the cavalry 'orses,
        There's 'er mark on the medical stores—
An' 'er troops you'll find with a fair wind be'ind
        That takes us to various wars.
10   (Poor beggars!—barbarious wars!)
            Then 'ere's to the Widow at Windsor,
                    An' 'ere's to the stores an' the guns,
        The men an' the 'orses what makes up the forces
                    O' Missis Victorier's sons.
15   (Poor beggars! Victorier's sons!)

Walk wide o' the Widow at Windsor,
        For 'alf o' Creation she owns:

We 'ave bought 'er the same with the sword an' the flame,
   An' we've salted it down with our bones.
20   (Poor beggars!—it's blue with our bones!)
   Hands off o' the sons o' the widow,
      Hands off o' the goods in 'er shop.
   For the kings must come down an' the emperors frown
      When the Widow at Windsor says "Stop!"
25   (Poor beggars!—we're sent to say "Stop!")
      Then 'ere's to the Lodge o' the Widow,
           From the Pole to the Tropics it runs—
      To the Lodge that we tile with the rank an' the file,
         An' open in form with the guns.
30   (Poor beggars!—it's always they guns!)

   We 'ave 'eard o' the Widow at Windsor,
      It's safest to leave 'er alone:
   For 'er sentries we stand by the sea an' the land
      Wherever the bugles are blown.
35   (Poor beggars!—an' don't we get blown!)
      Take 'old o' the Wings o' the Mornin',
      An' flop round the earth till you're dead;
   But you won't get away from the tune that they play
      To the bloomin' old rag over'ead.
40   (Poor beggars!—it's 'ot over'ead!)
      Then 'ere's to the sons o' the Widow,
           Wherever, 'owever they roam.
      'Ere's all they desire, an' if they require
         A speedy return to their 'ome.
45   (Poor beggars!—they'll never see 'ome!)

Mood as a Key to Theme

What do the remarks in parentheses suggest about the speaker's attitude toward the empire?

Critical Reading

1. **Key Ideas and Details (a)** Who is the "Widow at Windsor"? **(b) Infer:** What is surprising about the speaker's decision to use this description?

2. **Key Ideas and Details (a)** Who is the speaker of this poem? **(b) Analyze:** Would you describe the speaker's tone as disloyal or disrespectful? Explain.

3. **Key Ideas and Details (a)** What various remarks of the speaker's appear in parentheses? **(b) Make a Judgment:** How would the poem be different if the remarks in parentheses were deleted? Why?

4. **Integration of Knowledge and Ideas** What comment is the speaker making about the extent and power of the British Empire? Use two of these Essential Question words in your answer: *authority, consequence, domination.* [*Connecting to the Essential Question: What is the relationship between literature and place?*]

Cite textual evidence to support your responses.

Literary Analysis

1. **Craft and Structure** Fill in a chart like the one shown here by describing the **mood** evoked by images from "Dover Beach." Then, using what you have written as a clue, state the **theme** of the poem.

Image	Where It Appears	Mood It Evokes

2. **Craft and Structure** Review Arnold's descriptions of the night throughout "Dover Beach" and his use of the word "night" in line 37. Do you think his mood is ultimately pessimistic or optimistic? Explain.

3. **Craft and Structure** **Connect Arnold's work to the historical period** by considering how the phrases "ignorant armies" and "darkling plain" in "Dover Beach" might relate to advances in science and the decline of faith.

4. **Craft and Structure** Explain how the mood of sternness and solemnity in "Recessional" relates to the theme of the poem.

5. **Craft and Structure** Basing your answer on the concluding two lines of each stanza in "Recessional," what conclusion can you draw about Kipling's theme?

6. **Craft and Structure** Use the mood in "The Widow at Windsor" to explain which of these sentences best describes the theme of the poem: **(a)** Maintaining the Empire seems ridiculous to soldiers who must do it. **(b)** Maintaining the Empire is a deadly serious game, played at the expense of soldiers.

7. **Comparing Literary Works** Compare and contrast the effect of the sounds of words and lines of Arnold's and Kipling's poetry. **(a)** Which poet's work is more slow and somber? **(b)** Which poet's work is more clipped and lively? **(c)** Explain how the sound of the language contributes to the mood of each poem and to the poets' aesthetic purposes.

8. **Integration of Knowledge and Ideas** Relate "Recessional" and "The Widow at Windsor" to the historical period by explaining how the poems reflect different perspectives on the responsibilities and dangers that come with empire.

9. **Analyzing Visual Information** Use your knowledge of Arnold's "Dover Beach" to explain the humor of the cartoon on this page.

"Here as on a darkling plain swept with confused alarms of struggle and flight, where ignorant armies clash by night, Matthew Arnold, News." ▶

Common Core
State Standards

Writing
1. Write arguments to support claims in an analysis of substantive topics or texts, using valid reasoning and relevant and sufficient evidence. *(p. 1051)*
1.a. Introduce precise, knowledgeable claim(s), establish the significance of the claim(s), distinguish the claim(s) from alternate or opposing claims, and create an organization that logically sequences claim(s), counterclaims, reasons, and evidence. *(p. 1051)*

Vocabulary Acquisition and Use

Word Analysis: Word-Phrase Relationships

Some words have special meaning when used in phrases. *Dominion,* for instance, means "control." The phrase *dominion over,* which Kipling uses in "Recessional," suggests a responsibility for the beings that the person with dominion controls. Contrast the meanings of each of these words and the phrases in which they also appear. Then, write an original sentence using the phrase.

1. attend; attend on
2. awe; in awe of
3. closed; closed down
4. move; move on
5. see; see through
6. stand; stand by

Vocabulary: Antonyms

Antonyms are words with opposite meanings. *Love* and *hate* are antonyms. For each word from the vocabulary list on page 1040, choose the antonym. Then, write an original sentence using both the word and its antonym.

1. awe: **(a)** attrition **(b)** contempt **(c)** reverence
2. turbid: **(a)** clear **(b)** confused **(c)** separated
3. tranquil: **(a)** calm **(b)** rational **(c)** restless
4. contrite: **(a)** incomplete **(b)** respectful **(c)** unrepentant
5. cadence: **(a)** tempo **(b)** unevenness **(c)** vigor
6. dominion: **(a)** obedience **(b)** rule **(c)** sway

Writing to Sources

Argumentative Text Critic Walter E. Houghton writes that the Victorian Age was characterized by "widespread doubt about the nature of man, society, and the universe." Using *evidence* from the poems by Arnold and Kipling, write an **essay** to support or refute this general observation.

Prewriting Review the poems, using a chart like the one shown to gather evidence about the *theme* of Victorian doubt or self-confidence. Note uses of imagery, language, or stylistic devices that illustrate or contradict the doubts that Houghton cites. Based on your examples, decide whether you agree or disagree with Houghton's claim.

Drafting Begin your draft by summarizing Houghton's point and stating your position for or against it. Support your generalizations with evidence from Arnold's and Kipling's poems. Consider organizing your response by devoting a paragraph to each selection.

Model: Gathering Details

Poem:			
	Images	Mood(s)	Theme(s)
Doubt			
Self-confidence			

Revising Review your draft, highlighting generalizations and looking for supporting details for each. Where details are lacking, provide them. Make sure that all quotations are accurate and properly referenced. Also, be sure you have *acknowledged and refuted opposing arguments.*

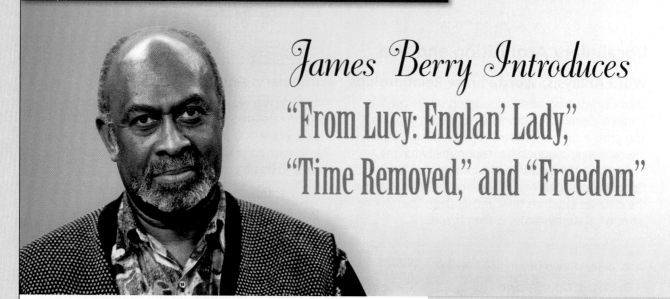

James Berry Introduces
"From Lucy: Englan' Lady,"
"Time Removed," and "Freedom"

On Growing Up British The poems in this selection reflect my different heritages: my Jamaican upbringing, my British identity, and to some extent, my African background. I was one of the peoples "of palm and pine" who grew up under the dominion of the British Empire that is the subject of Kipling's "Recessional" (p. 1045). As pompous as it sounds, Kipling's poem foresees some of the dangers of power and pomp and their likely end—those at the top will have to climb down. Empires are humbled, but sometimes, out of that, new relationships are made and changes happen.

Looking at England from a Caribbean Perspective When I grew up, the British Empire was fading fast, but my Caribbean people had become part of the British way of life. My poem "From Lucy: Englan' Lady" is one of a group of poems that I wrote in Caribbean Creole language and in the voice of Lucy, a Caribbean woman living in England.

Like Lucy, most people who came to Britain in the 1950s were royalists with a natural respect for the Royal Family. To them, the Queen was just like the church. Lucy treats the Queen like an ancient institution, something that will always be there, but at the same time she feels sympathy for her as a woman, for the hard time she has keeping up a show. She feels the Queen belongs to her, so she has a right to comment on her.

About the Author

James Berry has won numerous awards for his work as a poet, novelist, and short-story writer. Among his awards and honors are the Signal Poetry Award in 1989 for *When I Dance* and the Order of the British Empire in 1990.

Lucy represents the uncritical, unwavering admiration that so many ordinary people feel for royalty. She comes from the poverty-stricken context of the Caribbean, yet she would give her life for an institution that does nothing positive for her.

Traveling Back to Jamaica The poem "Time Removed" was one I wrote after I'd been in England for some years and following a visit I made back to Jamaica. I was saddened by how little had happened during my absence. My surroundings seemed to be more broken-down and less well maintained than before I went away.

Because I had a wider experience of life now, I could see what was not being done. In England, I had felt a kind of awe for all the work that had gone on over centuries to shape and tame the land. There was a sense of a managed landscape that was kept up and renewed continually through organization and the application of knowledge and skill. In Jamaica, the landscape and the roads were still very undeveloped.

▼ **Critical Viewing**
Which details in this photograph reflect Berry's recollections in his essay?
INTERPRET

"*I was saddened by how little had happened during my absence.*"

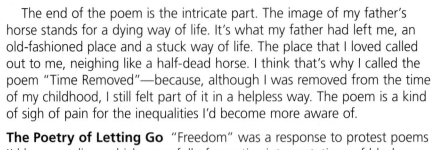

The end of the poem is the intricate part. The image of my father's horse stands for a dying way of life. It's what my father had left me, an old-fashioned place and a stuck way of life. The place that I loved called out to me, neighing like a half-dead horse. I think that's why I called the poem "Time Removed"—because, although I was removed from the time of my childhood, I still felt part of it in a helpless way. The poem is a kind of sigh of pain for the inequalities I'd become more aware of.

The Poetry of Letting Go "Freedom" was a response to protest poems I'd been reading, which were full of negative interpretations of black people's history. It was also an argument, an outcry against the backwardness I was born in and the inadequate political solutions that had been found for it. I was sick and tired of Jamaican leaders harping on in a helpless way about the terrible things Europeans had done to them. They were always hanging onto hurt instead of applying themselves in a positive way to change things.

I think you have to free yourself from your own pain and past. It's no good spending your energy on righteous indignation. For us to create something for ourselves as Caribbean people, we have to go beyond that, let go of a destructive past and create new structures. I hoped for a renaissance among Caribbean people. That's what my poems wanted to do—to stir people and show positive visions of possible futures.

Critical Reading

1. **Key Ideas and Details (a)** According to Berry, what often happens to those individuals or empires that reach the peak of their power? **(b) Interpret:** What changes in the relationship between the Empire and Jamaica might Berry have wanted after Britain's power diminished?

2. **Key Ideas and Details (a)** What reason does Berry give for naming his poem "Time Removed"? **(b) Apply:** What kind of inequalities around you echo Berry's concerns for Jamaica?

As You Read "From Lucy: Englan' Lady," "Time Removed," and "Freedom" . . .

3. **Key Ideas and Details** Look for images of Jamaica that Berry describes in his essay.

4. **Integration of Knowledge and Ideas** Note instances where Berry uses his poems to voice his frustration with Britain's treatment of Jamaica.

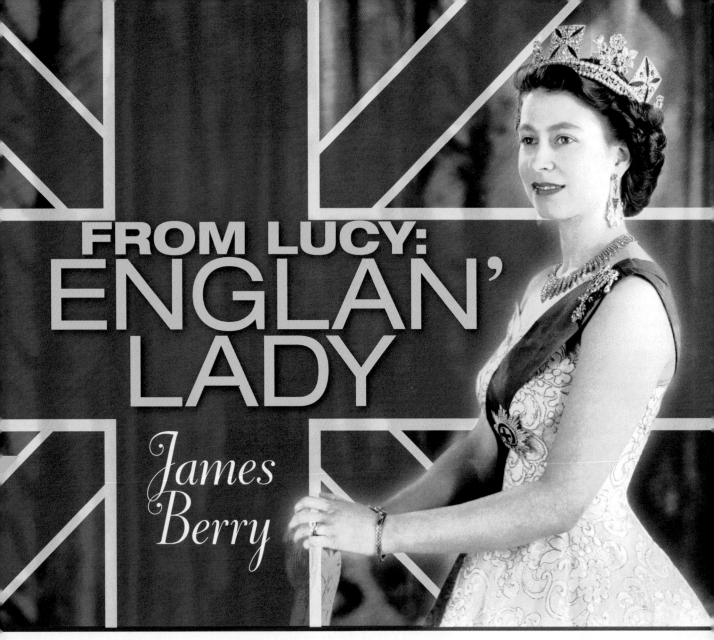

FROM LUCY: ENGLAN' LADY

James Berry

Queen Elizabeth II

You ask me 'bout the lady. Me dear,
old center here still shine
with Queen. She affec' the place
like the sun: not comin' out oft'n
5 an' when it happ'n everybody's out
smilin' as she wave a han'
like a seagull flyin' slow slow.

James Berry
Author's Insight Lucy has
been asked by Leela, her
friend back home, whether
she has seen the Queen.
Every time I go back to
the Caribbean people ask
me that!

An' you know she come from
dust free rooms an' velvet
10 an' diamond. She make you feel
this on-an'-on[1] town, London,
where long long time deeper than mind.[2]
An' han's after han's[3] die away,
makin' streets, putt'n' up bricks,
15 a piece of brass, a piece of wood
an' plantin' trees: an' it give
a car a halfday job gett'n' through.

An' Leela, darlin', no, I never
meet the Queen in flesh. Yet
20 sometimes, deep deep, I sorry for her.
Everybody expec' a show
from her, like she a space touris'
on earth. An' darlin', unless
you can go home an' scratch up[4]
25 you' husban', it mus' be hard
strain keepin' good graces for
all hypocrite faces.

Anyhow, me dear, you know what
ole time people say,
30 "Bird sing sweet for its nest."[5]

"BIRD SING SWEET FOR ITS NEST"

---

1. on-an'-on extraordinary.
2. deeper . . . mind more than can be comprehended.
3. han's after han's many generations.
4. scratch up lose your temper at.
5. "Bird . . . nest" Jamaican proverb, referring to the nightingale's
   habit of singing loudest near its nest. It means, "Those closest
   to home are the most contented."

Freedom

James Berry

Freedom is not
    a helpless grasping
    at a source of hurt
    or an outpour of oneself
5   to fixed ends others started

Freedom is not
    a hiding in the dust
    of righteous indignation
    or a merging with shadows

10 Freedom is not
    a becoming the model
    of destructive echoes
    or a walking in the hands of ghosts

Freedom is not
15   a reframing of oneself
    in the walls of the old prison
    or a becoming the tyrant's chain

Freedom is not
    excursions of energy
20   to nowhere
    driven and controlled
    by someone else's motivation

Freedom is
    a letting go like trees grow
25   a native self unravelling
    an adventure of a new
    self because of oneself

James Berry
Author's Insight This poem works through a series of images which all in some way suggest a failure to let go of a history of hurt and oppression.

James Berry
Author's Insight My argument in this poem is that people can continue their own imprisonment; if you live with hate and the desire for revenge, you replace one set of chains with another.

James Berry
Author's Insight This last verse sums up the adventure of living and striving to become more.

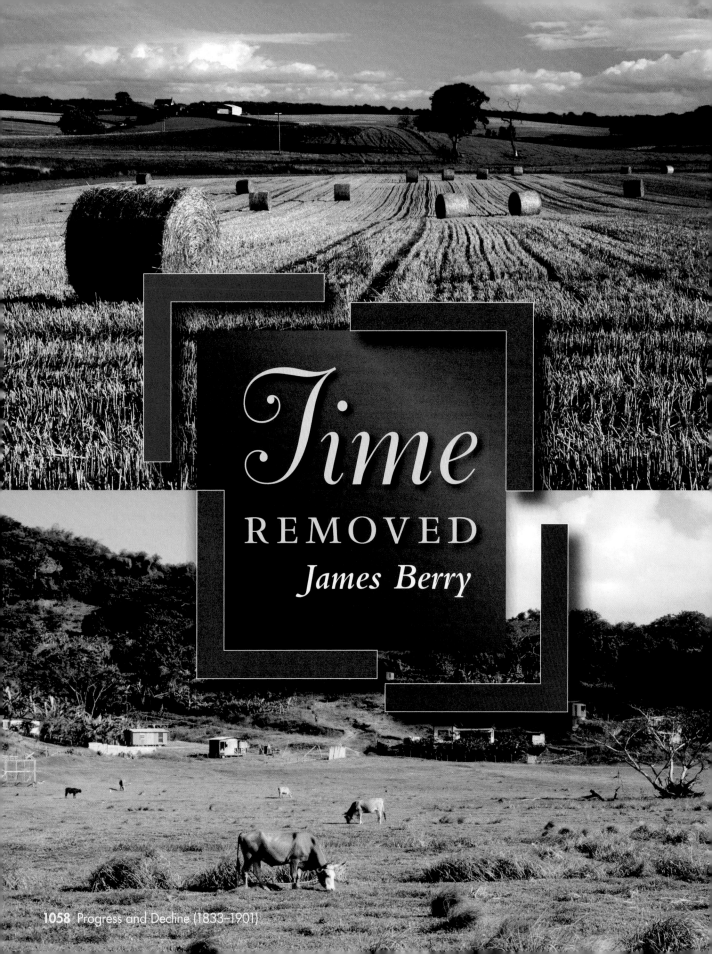

Time
REMOVED
James Berry

I go on and on in England
and walk no ground untrodden.

Landscapes are checkered —
tamed out of new years
5 and recurring generations.

Compulsive hands have shaped
bordered fields
out of scrub,
rivers' faces with bridge,
10 edifices for trees towering
lands now railed and tarred.

Animals are not bony and bare.
Wheels quicken time —
through a late summer
15 staying fresh as spring.

And here
just as jungles hold my love
every whiff of air evokes a time
like the horse my father left
20 and I after ten years away
found the greyhaired skeleton
neighing to me,
like these days do,
in memories too overlaid to touch.

James Berry
Author's Insight When I
first rode through England on
a train I was extraordinarily
moved by the organization
and variety of the landscape,
like an ordered checkerboard
of fields with different
colored crops.

◀ **Critical Viewing**
How do the two landscapes
in these photographs
dramatize the contrast that
Berry makes in the poem?
CONNECT

James Berry
Author's Insight Coming
from the Caribbean, I
wasn't used to the change
of seasons. I'd thought that
grass would go brown and
dry up in late summer, but it
stayed green all year round.

Critical Reading

1. **Key Ideas and Details (a)** According to Lucy, in what kind
   of environment does the Queen live? **(b) Summarize:** What
   challenges does Lucy think the Queen faces as a result of her
   position? **(c) Analyze:** How do Lucy's perceptions humanize
   the Queen?

Cite textual evidence to support your responses.

2. **Key Ideas and Details (a) Interpret:** In your own words,
   explain the meaning of lines 18–22 in "Freedom."
   (b) Support: Provide an example that illustrates your point.

3. **Integration of Knowledge and Ideas** In "Time Removed,"
   Berry writes in lines 3–5 that the landscapes around us are "tamed
   out" by each new generation. Do you think the landscape around
   you is improved by each generation or compromised by it? Provide
   examples to support your response.

CONNECTING VICTORIAN THEMES

Colin Meloy, frontman for lit-rock band The Decemberists, admits he reads a lot of Victorian novels. They have informed his writing style. His lyrics are often couched in the doubts and melancholy of the Victorians, harking back to the era's concerns about the passing of the natural world and the isolation ushered in by the new industrial age. Specifically, Meloy's "Eli, the Barrow Boy" lyrics echo the themes of love and loss in Matthew Arnold's "Dover Beach" as well as the working class voices in Kipling's poems.

COLIN MELOY SONGWRITER

Music is a necessity to Colin Meloy, something "that drives me completely," he says. He is the main songwriter for the indie group The Decemberists, whose music has been described as lit-rock. Meloy's background in literature qualifies him for the "lit" side of that description. He has a Master of Fine Arts (MFA) in creative writing and considers himself a writer of fictional song stories. The songs on the album *Picaresque,* for example, tell stories that seem to come straight out of Victorian Literature 101.

Sometimes, Meloy has to defend himself against charges of using too many big words! "I don't want to be the person who sends everyone to the diction- ary when they're listening to music," he said in a 2004 interview, "just because I think that pop music should be a populist thing."

ELI, THE BARROW BOY

Eli, the barrow boy of the old town
Sells coal and marigolds
And he cries out all down the day

Below the tamaracks he is crying.
"Corncobs and candlewax for the buying!"
All down the day

"Would I could afford to buy my love a fine robe
Made of gold and silk Arabian thread
But she is dead and gone and lying in a pine grove
And I must push my barrow all the day.
And I must push my barrow all the day."

Eli, the barrow boy—when they found him
Dressed all in corduroy, he had drowned in
The river down the way.

They laid his body down in the church yard
But still when the moon is out
With his push cart he calls down the day:

"Would I could afford to buy my love a fine robe
Made of gold and silk Arabian thread
But I am dead and gone and lying in a church ground
But still I push my barrow all the day.
Still I must push my barrow all the day."

"CORNCOBS AND CANDLEWAX FOR THE BUYING!"

Critical Reading

1. **(a)** What does Eli do to make a living? **(b) Summarize:** What is the story behind the poem?

2. **Compare and Contrast:** In what ways do the setting, characters, and details in these lyrics echo those of Victorian literary works? Explain.

Use this question to focus a group discussion of "Eli, The Barrow Boy":

3. What might a contemporary music group gain by connecting with literature from the past?

Primary Sources

**Newspaper Article
Progress in Personal
Comfort**

**Advertisement
Cook's Railroad
Advertisement**

 **Common Core
State Standards**

**Reading Informational
Text**

1. Cite strong and thorough textual evidence to support analysis of what the text says explicitly as well as inferences drawn from the text, including determining where the text leaves matters uncertain.

3. Analyze a complex set of ideas or sequence of events and explain how specific individuals, ideas, or events interact and develop over the course of the text.

About the Text Forms

A **newspaper article** is any short piece of prose writing that appears in a newspaper. It may contain straight news, opinions about recent events, or a combination of both.

An **advertisement** is a persuasive piece that attempts to sell people a product or service. Before the invention of radio and television, printed advertisements were the major means of publicizing products. Such advertisements appeared in a variety of formats, including leaflets, newspaper advertisements, billboards, posters, and product labels.

Preparing to Read Complex Texts

Analyze the techniques of media messages in advertisements and persuasive newspaper articles by focusing on the following *modes of persuasion:*

- **Logical:** presents factual evidence and arguments that make sense

- **Faulty:** presents arguments that upon close study are not fully sound

- **Deceptive:** presents intentionally misleading information

- **Emotional:** uses status symbols, peer pressure, patriotism, humor, or other appeals to the reader's emotions and desires

Look for these modes of appeal as you read or view the primary sources. To help you identify and analyze appeals in these modes,

- summarize what the text explicitly says

- draw conclusions about what the text implies, or suggests

- analyze the sequence of and interrelationships between ideas. For example, do they follow a logical order? Do they build on one another?

Support your summary and your analysis by citing relevant quotations and other details from the text.

How does literature **shape or** reflect *society?*

Both the newspaper article and the advertisement reflect changes to society in Victorian times. As you read, consider what each document reveals about its times and how each relates to the other.

Note-Taking Guide

Primary source documents are a rich source of information for researchers. As you read these documents, use a note-taking guide like the one shown to organize relevant and accurate information.

1 Type of Document (check one)
☐ Newspaper Article ☐ Letter ☐ Diary ☐ Speech ☐ Map
☐ Government Document ☐ Advertisement ☐ Memorandum ☐ Other

2 Date of Document _____

3 Author _____

Author's Position _____

4 Original Audience _____

5 Purpose and Importance

   a Does this document or image have a persuasive purpose?_____
   _____

   What techniques does it use to accomplish this purpose? Logical argument?
   Appeals to emotion? Attractive images?_____
   _____

   b List two important ideas, statements, or observations from this document.
   _____
   _____

   c What does this document show about life in the time and place in which it
   was composed? _____
   _____

Analyzing Media Messages Identifying a source's persuasive goals, target audience, and techniques is a key to analyzing its message.

This guide was adapted from the **U.S. National Archives** document analysis worksheet.

Vocabulary

depredation (dep′ rə dā′ shən) *n.* act or instance of robbing or laying waste (p. 1065)

Macadam (mə kad′ əm) *n.* road surfacing made of small stones bound with adhesive (p. 1065)

fracture (frak′ chər) *n.* a broken bone (p. 1065)

pulp (pulp) *n.* a soft, formless mass (p. 1065)

gout (gout) *n.* a type of arthritis characterized by painful attacks in the hands and especially the feet (p. 1066)

bilious (bil′ yəs) *adj.* suffering from or caused by too much bile or another liver problem (p. 1066)

privations (prī vā′ shənz) *n.* instances of being deprived; losses or absences of something (p. 1066)

THE STORY BEHIND THE DOCUMENTS

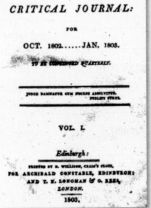

Sydney Smith

Sydney Smith (1771–1845) was an influential writer and preacher of his time. In 1802, he helped found the *Edinburgh Review,* a popular journal to which he frequently contributed articles. Many of these articles express progressive viewpoints on issues such as parliamentary reform, prisons, slavery, and religious freedom. Ordained in the Church of England, Smith nevertheless was a tireless champion of Catholic Emancipation, arguing that Roman Catholics should enjoy equal rights in Britain, at a time when many Britons still thought they should not.

THE
EDINBURGH REVIEW,

CRITICAL JOURNAL:

OCT. 1802......JAN. 1803.

VOL. I.

Edinburgh:

1803.

Volume I of *The Edinburgh Review,*
co-founded by Sydney Smith

The *Edinburgh Review,* which was published from 1802 to 1929, was a forerunner of today's magazines and journals. It was especially known for its progressive commentaries on politics and its criticism of literary works. Contributors to the journal included famous authors such as the essayist William Hazlitt and the historian Thomas Babington Macaulay (a letter of whose appears in this textbook). The relatively large circulation of this journal—13,500 in 1818—testifies to the growing interest in ideas and literature.

A pioneer of the modern travel industry, **Thomas Cook** (1808–1892) was a devout Baptist who organized his first tour to bring people to a meeting of the temperance movement, a movement to discourage the use of alcoholic beverages. Soon Cook was booking railway excursions all over Britain. He eventually expanded his tours to include Europe, the Middle East, and even North America. In 1872, he led a round-the-world tour that is said to have inspired Jules Verne's novel *Around the World in 80 Days.*

Smith's journal and Cook's tours are both evidence of the growth of Victorian Britain's middle class. An increasingly prosperous and literate middle class meant a greater audience for books, magazines, and newspapers. Having more money and leisure time also meant that middle-class Victorians could see a bit more of the world, enjoying the relatively safe and comfortable travel adventures that a Cook's tour provided.

New publications and new means of travel are just two examples of the kind of progress that Victorian Britain valued. Sydney Smith's newspaper article celebrates the innovations, large and small, that contributed to progress in the area of personal comfort—umbrellas, gas streetlights, and adhesive postage stamps, to name just a few. The great strides in transportation that Smith also describes—steamships, better roads, and most of all, railways—were the cornerstone of the new tourist industry promoted in Thomas Cook's advertisement.

Thomas Cook

PROGRESS IN PERSONAL COMFORT

Sydney Smith

It is of some importance at what period a man is born. A young man, alive at this period, hardly knows to what improvements of human life he has been introduced; and I would bring before his notice the following eighteen changes which have taken place in England since I first began to breathe in it the breath of life—a period amounting now to nearly seventy-three years.

Gas[1] was unknown: I groped about the streets of London in all but the utter darkness of a twinkling oil lamp, under the protection of watchmen in their grand climacteric,[2] and exposed to every species of depredation and insult.

I have been nine hours in sailing from Dover to Calais before the invention of steam. It took me nine hours to go from Taunton to Bath, before the invention of railroads, and I now go in six hours from Taunton to London! In going from Taunton to Bath, I suffered between 10,000 and 12,000 severe contusions,[3] before stone-breaking Macadam was born.

I paid £15 in a single year for repairs of carriage-springs on the pavement of London; and I now glide without noise or fracture, on wooden pavements.

I can walk, by the assistance of the police, from one end of London to the other, without molestation; or, if tired, get into a cheap and active cab, instead of those cottages on wheels, which the hackney coaches[4] were at the beginning of my life.

I had no umbrella! They were little used, and very dear. There were no waterproof hats, and *my* hat has often been reduced by rains into its primitive pulp.

---

1. **gas** coal gas, piped under the streets of London and used in streetlights after 1814.
2. **climacteric** (klī mak´ tər ik) *n.* a major turning point in life, referring here to old age.
3. **contusions** (kən tyoo´ or too´ zhənz) *n.* bruises.
4. **cheap and active cab . . . hackney coaches** Faster two-wheeled hansom cabs replaced hackney coaches as London's typical vehicles for hire to travel short distances.

Primary Sources:
Newspaper Article What does the article reveal to be the contrasting attitudes of younger and older Victorians toward the progress it describes?

Analyzing Media Messages

Identify the logical reasoning and emotional appeals in the third paragraph.

Vocabulary

depredation (dep´ rə dā´ shən) *n.* act or instance of robbing or laying waste

Macadam (mə kad´ əm) *n.* road surfacing made of small stones bound with adhesive

fracture (frak´ chər) *n.* a broken bone

pulp (pulp) *n.* a soft, formless mass

Primary Sources
Newspaper Article
Why do you think Smith does not relate the detailed history of the inventions he cites?

Vocabulary

gout (gout) *n.* a type of arthritis that especially affects the feet

bilious (bil′ yəs) *adj.* having a digestive ailment caused by too much bile or another liver problem

privations (prī vā′ shənz) *n.* losses or absences of something

I could not keep my smallclothes in their proper place, for braces were unknown.[5] If I had the gout, there was no colchicum. If I was bilious, there was no calomel. If I was attacked by ague, there was no quinine.[6] There were filthy coffee houses instead of elegant clubs. Game could not be bought. Quarrels about uncommuted tithes[7] were endless. The corruption of Parliament, before Reform, infamous.[8] There were no banks to receive the savings of the poor. The Poor Laws were gradually sapping the vitals of the country; and whatever miseries I suffered, I had no post to whisk my complaints for a single penny[9] to the remotest corners of the empire; and yet, in spite of all these privations, I lived on quietly, and am now ashamed that I was not more discontented, and utterly surprised that all these changes and inventions did not occur two centuries ago.

I forgot to add, that as the basket of stage coaches, in which luggage was then carried, had no springs, your clothes were rubbed all to pieces. . . .

---

5. **smallclothes . . . braces were unknown** There were no suspenders to hold up his trousers.

6. **gout . . . quinine** (kwī′ nīn′) Colchicum, calomel, and quinine were new, more effective medications used to treat the medical conditions mentioned. *Ague* (ā′ gyo͞o′) is an old word for a fever accompanied by chills—the kind of fever that recurs in people suffering from malaria.

7. **uncommuted tithes** (tīthz) Beginning with the Tithe Act of 1836, taxes paid to the Church of England in the form of produce were "commuted," or changed to, an equivalent payment in money.

8. **The corruption . . . infamous** Before passage of the Reform Bill of 1832, the House of Commons was dominated by a small number of wealthy, corrupt landowners.

9. **I had no post . . . single penny** Penny postage, in the form of an adhesive stamp, was first introduced to Britain in 1840.

Critical Reading

Cite textual evidence to support your responses.

1. **Key Ideas and Details** **(a)** How old was Smith when he wrote this newspaper article? **(b) Infer:** Why does he think a young man would "hardly know" the value of the improvements he describes?

2. **Key Ideas and Details** **(a) Classify:** What are two improvements in public safety and two in public transportation that Smith reports? **(b) Generalize:** What general picture does he draw of life before the various inventions and changes he describes?

3. **Integration of Knowledge and Ideas** **(a) Assess:** Does Smith consider the possibility that people in the future might find his world uncomfortable? Explain. **(b) Generalize:** What does Smith's attitude toward the past, present, and future show about human attitudes toward progress in general?

TECHNOLOGICAL ADVANCES
IN THE NINETEENTH CENTURY

As Sydney Smith describes, during the nineteenth century, technology developed at a rapid pace and changed people's lives in important ways. This timeline shows a few of these advances.

▲ 1824
Englishman **Joseph Aspin** patented Portland Cement, made from hydraulic lime. In 1843, cement was used to build the Thames Tunnel, the world's first underwater tunnel.

▼ 1835
Fox Talbot, an English chemist, published an article on his discovery of the paper negative, preparing the way for modern photography.

▲ 1862
French scientist **Louis Pasteur** discovered that, by heating milk, one could kill many harmful organisms in it, thus extending its shelf life. He called the process "pasteurization."

▲ 1895
The Frenchman **Louis Lumière** invented a portable all-in-one motion-picture camera, film processing unit, and projector called the Cinématographe, which began the era of motion pictures.

▶ 1834
The Analytic Engine—designed by **Charles Babbage,** a British scientist and mathematician—is a forerunner of modern digital computers.

▼ 1877
The cylinder phonograph, the earliest method of recording sound, was developed by **Thomas Edison.** Soon after, he recorded the voice of Alfred, Lord Tennyson.

CONNECT TO THE LITERATURE

How would you describe Sydney Smith's attitude toward the changes he witnessed during his lifetime?

RAILROAD ADVERTISEMENT

BACKGROUND This Victorian advertisement for a Cook's tour was aimed at Britain's growing middle class.

Analyzing Media Messages

For each of the following elements, indicate the intended audience, the message, and the method of persuasion:

- The use of a woman as the central figure
- The woman's position, body language, and dress
- Other images
- Featured words

Primary Source
Advertisement
What does this advertisement try to persuade people to do?

Critical Reading

1. **Key Ideas and Details (a)** Where does the ad say a Cook's tour will take you? **(b) Infer:** Why do you think the word *anywhere* is underlined?

2. **Integration of Knowledge and Ideas (a) Apply:** If this ad were used today, how would a contemporary reader react to it? Explain, citing specific elements of the ad. **(b) Evaluate:** Have the techniques of print advertising changed very much since Victorian times? Explain, giving examples in support.

Cite textual evidence to support your responses.

Newspaper Article • Advertisement

Comparing Primary Sources

Refer to your Note-Taking Guide to answer these questions.

1. (a) Summarize the **newspaper article.** Support your answer with quotations from the text. **(b)** What attitudes and ideas does Smith implicitly promote? Explain, citing relevant details. **(c)** Explain how the main ideas in the article reinforce one another.

2. (a) What does the appearance of the people in the **advertisement** show about the background, class, and interests of its audience? **(b)** Which details in Smith's article appeal to a similar audience? Organize details in a diagram like the one shown.

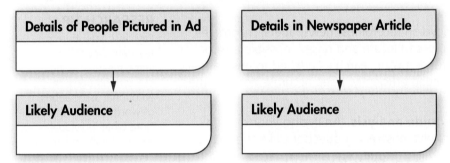

Details of People Pictured in Ad	Details in Newspaper Article
Likely Audience	Likely Audience

3. Write a paragraph comparing the modes of persuasion used in the two sources.

Vocabulary Acquisition and Use

New Vocabulary Is each statement true or false? Explain.

1. A generous philanthropist will often engage in *depredation*.

2. The *pulp* of the tooth is the hard enamel on the outside.

3. Someone camping in the wild is likely to experience *privations*.

Content-Area Vocabulary Use the italicized vocabulary words to help you answer each question. Then, explain your answer.

1. A person with *gout* would probably **(a)** cough a lot **(b)** sleep a lot **(c)** rest his or her feet on a cushion.

2. A person would most likely feel *bilious* after **(a)** eating **(b)** resting **(c)** trying on shoes.

3. To heal a *fracture*, a person would most likely need **(a)** a cast **(b)** a flu shot **(c)** a warm drink.

4. Supplying new *Macadam* would be the job of **(a)** a chef **(b)** a road builder **(c)** a travel agent.

Etymology Study Macadam is named for John Macadam, the engineer who developed it. Use a dictionary to trace the etymology of these words based on a person's name: *boycott, maverick, silhouette, watt.*

 **Common Core State Standards**

Writing
7. Conduct short as well as more sustained research projects to answer a question or solve a problem; narrow or broaden the inquiry when appropriate; synthesize multiple sources on the subject, demonstrating understanding of the subject under investigation. *(p. 1070)*

8. Gather relevant information from multiple authoritative print and digital sources, using advanced searches effectively; assess the strengths and limitations of each source in terms of the task, purpose, and audience; integrate information into the text selectively to maintain the flow of ideas, avoiding plagiarism and overreliance on any one source and following a standard format for citation. *(p. 1070)*

Language
6. Acquire and use accurately general academic and domain-specific words and phrases, sufficient for reading, writing, speaking, and listening at the college and career readiness level; demonstrate independence in gathering vocabulary knowledge when considering a word or phrase important to comprehension or expression.

Research Task

Topic: The Theme of "Progress" in the Media

In the centuries separating Victorian England from the present, the idea of progress—measured with terms such as "faster," "farther," and "easier"—has acquired a large shadow side. Concerned about everything from pollution to poor diet to cell phones, people today may associate progress with threats to the environment, to health, and even to civility. These days, "progress" may even mean taking a step back.

Assignment: Present a research report in which you analyze the treatment of the theme of "progress" in a television and a print advertisement. Then, evaluate how these media reflect cultural and social views different from those in Sydney Smith's essay and in the Cook's tour advertisement.

Gather sources. Use television recordings, newspapers, magazines, and online and library sources to locate and review possible ads for your report. Narrow or broaden your search as needed to ensure that you find the material you need efficiently. Keep accurate notes of the sources of all material.

Develop questions to guide analysis. Analyzing your chosen advertisements should involve answering questions like these:

- What is the purpose of and audience for the ad?
- What media techniques does the ad use to convey the theme of progress?
- What view of progress—positive, negative, or mixed—does the advertisement present?

Synthesize information. Review each ad, analyzing individual elements such as words, images, graphic elements, and sounds. Create a chart like the one shown to help synthesize your insights.

Model: Synthesizing Information in Media

Words	Images	Graphics	Sounds
Simpler and *purer* suggest progress —away from "progress"!	Images of an elderly farmer suggest tradition.	Logo of a mill suggests return to the past.	Theme played on banjo suggests simpler times.

Conclusion: Ad suggests that the product helps consumers escape the confusion and stress of "progress" to return to simpler times.

Organize and present ideas. Present your analysis of the ads and your comparison of the social and cultural views they reflect with the views found in Smith's essay and the Cook's tour advertisement. To ensure flow, select the strongest examples for each point you make. Avoid plagiarism, citing your sources for images and ideas.

RESEARCH TIP

Pay close attention to the denotations, or literal meanings, and the connotations, or emotional associations, of words used in the ads. Note what individual words literally mean and what connotations they take on in the context of the ads.

Use a checklist like the one shown to evaluate your work.

Research Checklist

☐ Have I answered all the questions in my guidelines for analysis?

☐ Have I fully analyzed the words and the images?

☐ Have I evaluated the impact of the graphics and the sounds?

☐ Have I articulated the overall meaning of each ad?

☐ Have I successfully compared the social and cultural views reflected in the ads with the views of optimistic Victorians?

Gloom and Glory

Connecting to the Essential Question Brontë and Hardy express the feeling of not being at home in the world. As you read, note the ways in which the speakers in these poems indicate dissatisfaction with the places in which they find themselves. Doing so will help you think about the Essential Question: **What is the relationship between literature and place?**

Close Reading Focus

Stanza; Stanza Structure; Irony

Poets have a number of ways of addressing a reader's expectations. **Stanzas,** for instance, are repeated groupings of two or more verse lines with a definite pattern of line length, rhythm, and, frequently, rhyme. The **stanza structure** of a poem is the pattern of stanzas from which it is built. While stanza structure creates an expectation of a regular pattern, **irony** challenges expectations by creating a contradiction between reality and appearance or between what is said and what is meant.

Both stanza structure and irony may set up and then fulfill or not fulfill expectations. In reading these poems, for example, notice these patterns:

- The arrangement of the first stanza leads you to expect a similar arrangement in the others.
- Irony surprises you by not fulfilling expectations.

Comparing Literary Works Brontë's and Hardy's poems deal in different ways with the theme of absence—the sense of something missing. Compare the ways in which the speakers in these poems feel about an absence and succeed or fail in handling it.

Preparing to Read Complex Texts Many poetic stanzas express a single main idea, as paragraphs do in prose. You can **analyze the pattern of stanzas** and how it affects the meaning and aesthetic impact of the poem if you notice how each stanza builds on the preceding one. Use a chart like this one to understand the logical progression of stanzas in each poem.

Vocabulary

You will encounter the words listed here in the texts that follow. Copy the words into your notebook, sorting them into words you know and words you do not know.

obscure	gaunt
languish	terrestrial
rapturous	prodding

Common Core State Standards

Reading Literature
5. Analyze how an author's choices concerning how to structure specific parts of a text contribute to its overall structure and meaning as well as its aesthetic impact.

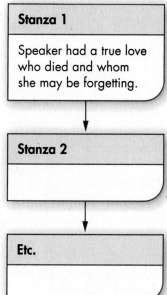

"Remembrance"

Stanza 1

Speaker had a true love who died and whom she may be forgetting.

↓

Stanza 2

↓

Etc.

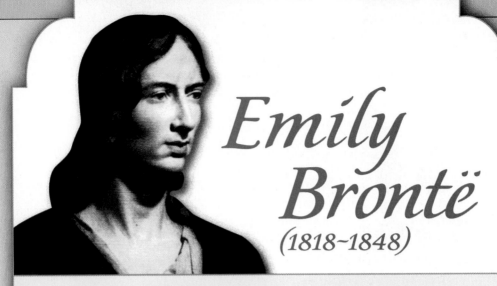

Emily Brontë
(1818~1848)

Author of "Remembrance"

Although some literary critics of the time attacked Emily Brontë for the violent passions expressed in her novel *Wuthering Heights* (1847), her dark Romanticism is now regarded as the essence of her genius.

A Writer's Beginnings Brontë grew up in the Yorkshire moorlands, a barren wasteland in the north of England, where her father was a clergyman. When Emily was just three, her mother died. Emily and her sisters, Charlotte and Anne, were educated at home for the most part and were often on their own.

Homesickness In 1835, Charlotte became a teacher at a school some distance from her home. Emily accompanied her as a pupil, but she quickly returned home. Three years later, she took a teaching position herself but resigned after six months.

Several years later, Charlotte and Emily devised another plan to support themselves as teachers. They would establish and run a school for girls in their own town of Haworth. To learn the skills they needed for this enterprise, they traveled to Brussels, Belgium. There, many people they met admired Emily for her Romantic temperament. However, Emily became homesick again and, after learning of her aunt's death, went home for good.

A Career Cut Short As adults, the three sisters published a book of poetry. The twenty-one poems that Emily contributed are considered the best of the collection. Emily's first and only novel, *Wuthering Heights,* was published in 1847. It tells the story of a tragic love affair played out against the mysterious landscape of the Yorkshire moors. The book is now considered a classic.

Wuthering Heights is the culminating expression of Emily's fiery imagination. A year after the book was published, she died of tuberculosis.

REMEMBRANCE

Emily Brontë

BACKGROUND Victorian poets wrote in many voices and many styles. Some writers, like Emily Brontë, are classified as Romantic because they explore and celebrate the human soul, the wildness of nature, and the powers of the imagination. Thomas Hardy, however, focused on the victimization of ordinary people by social and natural forces.

Cold in the earth, and the deep snow piled above thee!
Far, far removed, cold in the dreary grave!
Have I forgot, my Only Love, to love thee,
Severed at last by Time's all-wearing wave?

5　Now, when alone, do my thoughts no longer hover
Over the mountains, on that northern shore;
Resting their wings where heath and fern-leaves cover
Thy noble heart for ever, ever more?

Cold in the earth, and fifteen wild Decembers
10　From those brown hills have melted into spring—
Faithful indeed is the spirit that remembers
After such years of change and suffering!

Sweet Love of youth, forgive if I forget thee
While the World's tide is bearing me along:

The Soul of the Rose, 1908, John William Waterhouse, Private Collection/Julian Hartnoll, London, UK

◄ **Critical Viewing**
In what ways might the woman in this painting represent the poem's speaker? **ANALYZE**

Comprehension
What is troubling the poem's speaker?

Vocabulary

obscure (əb skyoor´)
v. make difficult to see

Analyzing Patterns of Organization

How do lines 25–28 elaborate on the idea in lines 21–24?

Vocabulary

languish (laŋ´ gwish)
v. become weak; suffer from longing

rapturous (rap´ chər əs)
adj. filled with joy and love; ecstatic

15 Other desires and other hopes beset me,
    Hopes which obscure but cannot do thee wrong.

    No later light has lightened up my heaven,
    No second morn has ever shone for me:
    All my life's bliss from thy dear life was given—
20 All my life's bliss is in the grave with thee.

    But when the days of golden dreams had perished
    And even Despair was powerless to destroy,
    Then did I learn how existence could be cherished,
    Strengthened and fed without the aid of joy;

25 Then did I check the tears of useless passion,
    Weaned my young soul from yearning after thine;
    Sternly denied its burning wish to hasten
    Down to that tomb already more than mine!

    And even yet, I dare not let it languish,
30 Dare not indulge in Memory's rapturous pain;
    Once drinking deep of that divinest anguish,
    How could I seek the empty world again?

Critical Reading

Cite textual evidence to support your responses.

1. **Key Ideas and Details (a)** How long ago did the speaker's love die? **(b) Interpret:** What does the speaker mean by, "No later light has lightened up my heaven"?

2. **Key Ideas and Details (a)** What does the speaker plan to do? **(b) Interpret:** Why is the speaker afraid to give in to his or her old feelings?

3. **Key Ideas and Details (a) Draw Conclusions:** In your own words, express the basic conflict of the poem's speaker. **(b) Analyze:** How does the speaker handle this conflict?

4. **Integration of Knowledge and Ideas** Can it be desirable in some circumstances to lead an existence "without . . . joy"? Explain.

5. **Integration of Knowledge and Ideas** In ancient times, lyric poems like this one were accompanied by music. Which of these types of music would make the best accompaniment for this poem: country, jazz, folk, rock, or rap? Explain your choice.

Thomas Hardy

(1840–1928)

Author of "The Darkling Thrush" • "Ah, Are You Digging on My Grave?"

Thomas Hardy, who was unusual in being both a great novelist and a great poet, was born in Dorset, a region of southwest England. He used this region as the basis for the imaginary county of Wessex that is the setting of many of his novels.

Early Life The son of a stonemason, Hardy grew up in a rural cottage near a tract of wasteland. He received a fine education at a local school, although he never went on to study at a university. As a teenager, he began working for a local architect, and he eventually became a draftsman for an architect who specialized in churches.

While on a business trip to Cornwall, at the southwestern tip of England, Hardy met the woman who later became his first wife. She encouraged him in his literary activities, and soon he committed himself entirely to writing.

The Novelist When Hardy's early poetry did not gain notice, he turned to writing novels. *Far From the Madding Crowd* was the first to gain success.

Hardy used his fiction writing to elaborate his own pessimistic view of life. In tragic novels like *Tess of the D'Urbervilles* (1891) and *Jude the Obscure* (1895), he showed the difficulty people experience when trying to rise above their circumstances.

The Poet The bleakness of Hardy's fiction disturbed readers, and the response to *Jude the Obscure* was so hostile that Hardy abandoned fiction and returned to writing poetry, a form of writing he had pursued in the 1860s.

A Poetic Legacy Hardy's poetry marks a transition from Victorian verse to the Modernist movement of the twentieth century. In his use of strict meter and stanza structure, Hardy was unmistakably Victorian. However, his nonpoetic language and odd rhymes, his devotion to English characters and the English countryside, and his fatalistic outlook inspired twentieth-century poets like Philip Larkin.

"Time changes everything except something within us which is always surprised by change."

The Darkling¹ Thrush

THOMAS HARDY

▶ **Critical Viewing**

How does the thrush shown in this painting provide a hopeful contrast to the bleak winter landscape? **INTERPRET**

I leant upon a coppice gate²
    When Frost was specter-gray,
And Winter's dregs made desolate
    The weakening eye of day.
5 The tangled bine-stems³ scored the sky
    Like strings of broken lyres,
And all mankind that haunted nigh
    Had sought their household fires.

The land's sharp features seemed to be
10   The Century's corpse⁴ outleant,
His crypt the cloudy canopy,
    The wind his death-lament.
The ancient pulse of germ⁵ and birth
    Was shrunken hard and dry,
15 And every spirit upon earth
    Seemed fervorless as I.

---

1. **darkling** *adj.* in the dark.
2. **coppice** (kop´ is) **gate** gate leading to a thicket, or small wood.
3. **bine-stems** twining stems.
4. **Century's corpse** This poem was written on December 31, 1900, the last day of the nineteenth century.
5. germ seed or bud.

At once a voice arose among
    The bleak twigs overhead
In a full-hearted evensong
20   Of joy illimited;
An aged thrush, frail, gaunt, and small,
    In blast-beruffled plume,
Had chosen thus to fling his soul
    Upon the growing gloom.

25 So little cause for carolings
    Of such ecstatic sound
Was written on terrestrial things
    Afar or nigh around,
That I could think there trembled through
30   His happy good-night air
Some blessed Hope, whereof he knew
    And I was unaware.

Vocabulary

gaunt (gônt) *adj.* thin and bony, as from great hunger or age

terrestrial (tə res′ trē əl) *adj.* relating to the earth or to this world

Critical Reading

Cite textual evidence to support your responses.

1. **Key Ideas and Details (a)** In which season and time of year is this poem set? **(b) Classify:** In the first two stanzas, what details and images does Hardy use to convey the mood of the setting?

2. **Key Ideas and Details (a)** What does the speaker suddenly hear and see in the third stanza? **(b) Compare and Contrast:** How does the mood in the third stanza differ from that in the first two?

3. **Integration of Knowledge and Ideas (a)** Summarize what the speaker says in the final stanza. **(b) Draw Conclusions:** Do you agree with critics who assert that Hardy longs to believe there is reason for hope but does not really think so? Why or why not?

4. **Integration of Knowledge and Ideas** If Hardy had seen the end of the twentieth century, do you think he would have felt the same way that he did at the end of the nineteenth? Explain.

"Ah, Are You Digging on My Grave?" Thomas Hardy

"Ah, are you digging on my grave
    My loved one?—planting rue?"
—"No: yesterday he went to wed
One of the brightest wealth has bred.
5 'It cannot hurt her now,' he said,
    'That I should not be true.'"

"Then who is digging on my grave?
    My nearest dearest kin?"
—"Ah, no: they sit and think, 'What use!
10 What good will planting flowers produce?
No tendance of her mound can loose
    Her spirit from Death's gin.'"[1]

"But some one digs upon my grave?
    My enemy?—prodding sly?"
15 —"Nay: when she heard you had passed the Gate
That shuts on all flesh soon or late,
She thought you no more worth her hate,
    And cares not where you lie."

---

1. **gin** *n.* trap.

Analyzing Patterns of Organization
What pattern do you see developing in these first stanzas?

Vocabulary
prodding (präd´ iŋ)
adj. poking; jabbing; seeking

Comprehension
Who is the speaker of this poem?

The Greek Anthology
Hardy was not the first poet to write in the voice of a deceased person. Many of the poems in *The Greek Anthology*, compiled in the tenth century, are ancient Greek epitaphs written in the voice of the person who died. Like most well-educated people in nineteenth-century Britain, Hardy owned a copy of *The Greek Anthology*. He probably spent hours poring over the little tombstone poems, which commemorate the lives of men, women, children, and even dogs.

Connect to the Literature

Do you think Hardy expresses traditional sentiments about remembering the dead? Why or why not?

"Then, who is digging on my grave?
20   Say—since I have not guessed!"
—"O it is I, my mistress dear,
Your little dog, who still lives near,
And much I hope my movements here
        Have not disturbed your rest?"

25 "Ah, yes! *You* dig upon my grave . . .
        Why flashed it not on me
That one true heart was left behind!
What feeling do we ever find
To equal among human kind
30   A dog's fidelity!"

"Mistress, I dug upon your grave
        To bury a bone, in case
I should be hungry near this spot
When passing on my daily trot.
35 I am sorry, but I quite forgot
        It was your resting-place."

Critical Reading

Cite textual evidence to support your responses.

1. **Key Ideas and Details (a)** In each of the first three stanzas, who does the speaker think is digging? **(b) Infer:** What do the responses tell you about the people thought to be digging?

2. **Key Ideas and Details (a)** Who is actually digging on the grave? **(b) Draw Conclusions:** What point about human vanity and self-esteem is Hardy making in this poem?

3. **Integration of Knowledge and Ideas** How do the places in which the Hardy's speakers find themselves limit their knowledge? Use two of these Essential Question words in your answer: *pessimism, insignificant, humorous, ironic. [Connecting to the Essential Question: What is the relationship between literature and place?]*

Close Reading Activity

Remembrance • *The Darkling Thrush* • "Ah, Are You Digging on My Grave?"

Literary Analysis

Common Core State Standards

Writing
2.b. Develop the topic thoroughly by selecting the most significant and relevant facts, extended definitions, concrete details, quotations, or other information and examples appropriate to the audience's knowledge of the topic. *(p. 1084)*

5. Develop and strengthen writing as needed by planning, revising, editing, rewriting, or trying a new approach, focusing on addressing what is most significant for a specific purpose and audience. *(p. 1084)*

Language
5. Demonstrate understanding of figurative language, word relationships, and nuances in word meaning. *(p. 1084)*

1. **Craft and Structure (a)** Complete a chart like the one shown to determine whether each poem uses a consistent **stanza structure.** **(b)** Summarize the pattern of stanzas in each of these poems.

Stanza	Number of lines	Rhyme scheme	Meter
1			
2			
3			

2. **Craft and Structure Analyze the pattern of stanzas** in "Remembrance" to show how the speaker gradually works out an answer to the question in the first stanza.

3. **Craft and Structure** What is ironic about the phrases "rapturous pain" and "divinest anguish" in the final stanza of "Remembrance"?

4. **Craft and Structure** Explain the function of each stanza in "The Darkling Thrush."

5. **Craft and Structure (a)** In "The Darkling Thrush," which stanza introduces a shift in meaning? Explain. **(b)** In "Ah, Are You Digging on My Grave?," what important shift in meaning occurs between the last two stanzas?

6. **Craft and Structure** Explain how repetition in the stanza structure of "Ah, Are You Digging on My Grave?" contributes to Hardy's ironic—and aesthetic—purpose.

7. **Craft and Structure (a)** How do lines 25–30 of "Ah, Are You Digging on My Grave?" disappoint a reader's expectations for an established stanza structure? **(b)** How does the last stanza use **irony** to disappoint a character's expectations in a drastic way?

8. **Integration of Knowledge and Ideas** Compare and contrast the types of absence that these poems address.

9. **Integration of Knowledge and Ideas** Which of the three speakers seems to experience the sorrow of loss most keenly? Why?

10. **Integration of Knowledge and Ideas** Which speaker seems best able to handle the absence of a sign of remembrance or hope? Explain.

11. **Analyzing Visual Information** What qualities of Hardy's poetry—for example, its moods and themes—does the artist capture in the caricature of Hardy on this page? Explain.

Vocabulary Acquisition and Use

Word Analysis: Latin Root -terr(a)-

The Latin root -terr(a)- comes from the Latin word for "earth." *Terrestrial*, which contains this root, means "of the earth" or "of this world." Write the definition for each -terr(a)- word below based on the meaning of the root. Explain how you arrived at your meaning. Then, write an original sentence for each of the words.

1. extraterrestrial
2. subterranean
3. terrace
4. terrain
5. territory

Vocabulary: Analogies

In an analogy, the relationship between two words is compared to the relationship between two other words. To complete these analogies, choose the word from the vocabulary list on page 1072 that creates a word pair that matches the relationship in the other pair. Explain your choices.

1. *Explain* is to *clarify* as _____ is to *conceal*.
2. _____ is to *ecstasy* as *miserable* is to *depression*.
3. _____ is to *emaciated* as *vigorous* is to *fitness*.
4. *Arrival* is to *departure* as _____ is to *heavenly*.
5. *Withdrawn* is to *shy* as *pushy* is to _____.
6. *Longing* is to _____ as *sympathy* is to *assist*.

Writing to Sources

Informative Text Brontë's and Hardy's poems deal in different ways with the theme of absence, the sense of something missing, whether that is a loved one, a sign of hope, or the knowledge that people remember the speaker. Write a **comparative analysis** in which you examine the ways in which the speakers in these poems feel about an absence and succeed or fail in handling it.

Prewriting Review the poems, using a chart to take notes on how each speaker perceives and responds to absence. Note uses of *imagery, language, or stylistic devices* that reveal the speaker's feelings. Review your examples to determine whether the speakers' attitudes and feelings are more similar or different. Then develop a thesis statement that expresses your view.

Drafting Begin your draft by stating your thesis. As you write, support your generalizations with quotations from Brontë's and Hardy's poems. Consider analyzing all the similarities first and then the differences if you think the differences are more important—and vice versa.

Model: Revising to Signal Similarities and Differences

The speaker in Hardy's "Ah, Are You Digging on My Grave?" learns that family and friends have gone on with their lives.

In contrast,

Brontë's speaker points out that she lives "without the aid of joy" in an "empty world."

Use of expressions like in *the same way* or *in contrast* calls attention to key similarities and differences.

Revising Review your draft, making sure that you signal similarities and differences. Make sure that all quotations are accurate and properly referenced.

Conventions and Style: Active, Not Passive, Voice

When you write, you can make your sentences more energetic and powerful by using active-voice verbs. A verb is in the **active-voice** when the subject is the doer of the action. A verb is in the **passive voice** when it receives the action of the verb.

The active voice is more direct and concise than the passive voice. However, the passive voice can be appropriate and effective in the following situations:

- You wish to emphasize the receiver of the action rather than the doer.

   Hope was symbolized by the tiny thrush.

- The doer of the action is not known or is unimportant to your meaning.

   The poem had been written on the last day of the nineteenth century.

The passive voice is constructed from the past participle of the main verb and a form of the verb *be*. Review these examples of active and passive voice.

	Active	Passive
Present	*is digging, digs*	*is dug, is being dug*
Past	*dug, was digging, had dug*	*was dug, was being dug, had been dug*
Future	*will dig, will have dug*	*will be dug, will have been dug*

Practice Identify whether the verb in each sentence is in the active or passive voice. If a sentence in the passive voice should be in the active voice, rewrite it. If the passive voice is appropriate, explain why.

1. Fires were hurried to by people who wanted to sit by them on a winter night.
2. A tiny bird was heard to sing in the middle of the gloomy evening.
3. The branches of a tree are compared to the broken strings of a musical instrument by the speaker.
4. The bird's joy cannot be understood.
5. The speaker, surprised by the joyful singing, believes that something giving hope is known by the bird.
6. The woman buried in the grave was not mourned by her loved one.
7. Flowers won't be planted by relatives.
8. The dead one was disturbed by the digging.
9. The dead are quickly forgotten by the living.
10. Can anyone overlook the faithfulness expressed by a friendly dog?

Writing and Speaking Conventions

A. Writing Use each subject-verb pair in a sentence with the verb in the active voice.

1. **S:** poet, **V:** lean
2. **S:** relatives, **V:** plant
3. **S:** voice, **V:** sing
4. **S:** dog, **V:** disturb
5. **S:** thrush, **V:** know

   Example: S: poet, **V:** lean.
   Sentence: The poet leans on a gate and sees a winter landscape.

B. Speaking Write and present to the class a brief scene for a play based on the poem "Ah, Are You Digging on My Grave?" Describe the setting, list the character(s) in your scene, and include at least one speech written in the active voice.

ANCHOR TEXT
God's Grandeur • Spring and Fall: To a Young Child • To an Athlete Dying Young •When I Was One-and-Twenty

Connecting to the Essential Question Hopkins coined words and invented new rhythms for his poetry. As you read, notice how Hopkins is innovative and Housman is traditional. This distinction will help you explore the Essential Question: **What is the relationship of the writer to tradition?**

Close Reading Focus

Rhythm; Feet

Poetry with a regular **rhythm,** or movement, is **metrical verse,** which is divided into combinations of syllables called **feet.** The following are types of feet and the pattern of stressed and unstressed syllables they contain:

- **Iambic:** unstressed, stressed, as in *the time*
- **Trochaic:** stressed, unstressed, as in *grandeur*

Lines with three, four, and five feet are **trimeter, tetrameter,** and **pentameter,** respectively. Iambic pentameter, for example, is a five-foot line with iambic feet. Housman uses regular meters like iambic and trochaic tetrameter, but Hopkins invents rhythms like these:

- **Counterpoint rhythm:** two opposing rhythms appear together; for example, two trochaic feet in an iambic line:
  The world is charged with the grandeur of God.
- **Sprung rhythm:** all feet begin with a stressed syllable and contain a varying number of unstressed syllables. Sprung rhythm creates densely stressed lines with many echoing consonant and vowel sounds.

As you read, notice which words the poets choose to stress. Consider why the authors may have placed special emphasis on these words and determine if such emphasis adds to the meaning of the poems.

Comparing Literary Works Beauty and mortality are two connected themes these poets explore. Analyze how these themes interact.

Preparing to Read Complex Texts **Analyzing the author's beliefs** will help you understand the ideas and feelings in the poems. Consider details in the author's biography along with details of the poems. Use a diagram like this to analyze the poets' beliefs.

Vocabulary

You will encounter the words listed here in the texts that follow. Copy the words into your notebook. What clue can help you infer the meaning of the word *grandeur*?

grandeur	blight
smudge	lintel
brink	rue

Common Core State Standards

Reading Literature
5. Analyze how an author's choices concerning how to structure specific parts of a text contribute to its overall structure and meaning as well as its aesthetic impact.

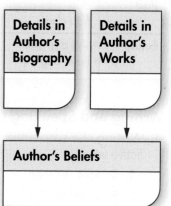

Details in Author's Biography

Details in Author's Works

Author's Beliefs

GERARD MANLEY HOPKINS

(1844—1889)

Author of "God's Grandeur" • "Spring and Fall: To a Young Child"

Although he was the most innovative poet of the Victorian period, Hopkins never published a collection of his work during his lifetime. It was not until 1918 that his work was published and a generation of poets could read and be influenced by his startling poetry.

Devotion to God and Nature This quietly rebellious poet was born just outside London, the oldest of nine children in a prosperous middle-class family. Although physically slight, he would perch fearlessly at the top of a tree and sway in the wind while observing the landscape. He began to write poetry in grammar school, a practice he continued at Oxford University, where he studied the classics.

During his third year at Oxford, Hopkins decided to become a Catholic priest in the Jesuit order—a decision that dismayed his parents, who were devout Anglicans. The discipline of Hopkins's religious vocation was sometimes at odds with his writing of verse. He temporarily gave up poetry but continued to keep detailed notebooks that recorded his fascination with words and his love of nature.

Inscape In the mid-1870s, while studying theology in Wales, he began to write poetry again, stimulated by the Welsh language and encouraged by his religious mentor. Somewhat earlier, Hopkins had found in the medieval theologian Duns Scotus a verification of his own ideas about the individuality of all things. Hopkins called this precious individuality *inscape*, and he tried to capture it in highly original poems like "God's Grandeur." He also experimented with new rhythms in his verse.

From early 1884 on, he taught at a Jesuit college in Dublin. There, he died of typhoid fever just before his forty-fifth birthday. Although in many ways he was not typical of the other poets of his age, he is now considered one of the greatest Victorian poets.

God's Grandeur

Gerard Manley Hopkins

Surprisingly, when Gerard Manley Hopkins died, none of his obituaries mentioned that he was a poet and only a few friends were aware of this fact. One of these friends was Robert Bridges, an Oxford classmate and later the British poet laureate. Bridges had corresponded with Hopkins and took an interest in his experiments with rhythm. It was through Bridges's efforts that a volume of Hopkins's poetry was published for the first time in 1918. Today, Bridges is little known, but his once-obscure friend Gerard Manley Hopkins is a famous Victorian poet.

The world is charged with the grandeur of God.
    It will flame out, like shining from shook foil;[1]
    It gathers to a greatness, like the ooze of oil
Crushed.[2] Why do men then now not reck his rod?[3]
5 Generations have trod, have trod, have trod;
    And all is seared with trade; bleared, smeared with toil;
    And wears man's smudge and shares man's smell: the soil
Is bare now, nor can foot feel, being shod.

And for all this, nature is never spent;
10   There lives the dearest freshness deep down things;
And though the last lights off the black West went
    Oh, morning, at the brown brink eastward, springs—
Because the Holy Ghost over the bent
    World broods with warm breast and with ah! bright wings.

Vocabulary

grandeur (gran´ jər)
n. splendor; magnificence

smudge (smŭj) *n.* a smear or stain of dirt

brink (brĭngk) *n.* edge; margin

◀ **Critical Viewing**
How does this painting reflect Hopkins's ideas in "God's Grandeur"? **APPLY**

---

1. foil *n.* tinsel.
2. crushed squeezed from olives.
3. reck his rod heed God's authority.

SPRING AND FALL:
TO A YOUNG CHILD
GERARD MANLEY HOPKINS

Márgarét, áre you gríeving
Over Goldengrove unleaving?
Leáves, líke the things of man, you
With your fresh thoughts care for, can you?
5 Áh! ás the heart grows older
It will come to such sights colder
By and by, nor spare a sigh
Though worlds of wanwood[1] leafmeal[2] lie;
And yet you wíll weep and know why.
10 Now no matter, child, the name:
Sórrow's spríngs áre the same.
Nor mouth had, no nor mind, expressed
What heart heard of, ghost[3] guessed:
It ís the blight man was born for,
15 It is Margaret you mourn for.

---

1. wanwood (wän' wood) pale wood.
2. leafmeal ground-up decomposed leaves.
3. ghost spirit.

Rhythm and Meter
Identify a visual clue that proves that this poem is written in sprung rhythm.

Vocabulary
blight (blīt) *n.* condition of withering

Critical Reading

Cite textual evidence to support your responses.

1. **Key Ideas and Details (a)** According to Hopkins in "God's Grandeur," what has been the impact on nature of humanity's behavior? **(b) Analyze:** What opposition or conflict does he explore in lines 1–8 of "God's Grandeur"? **(c) Draw Conclusions:** How does Hopkins resolve that opposition?

2. **Key Ideas and Details (a)** What makes Margaret unhappy in "Spring and Fall"? **(b) Interpret:** Explain how the poem's speaker suggests that Margaret will both outgrow and not outgrow this sadness.

3. **Key Ideas and Details (a)** According to the speaker, how will Margaret change as she grows older? **(b) Draw Conclusions:** What lesson does the speaker offer to Margaret in this poem?

4. **Integration of Knowledge and Ideas** Judging by "God's Grandeur," would Hopkins support the ecology movement if he were alive today? Explain.

A. E. Housman

Author of "To an Athlete Dying Young" • "When I Was One-and-Twenty"

A man of solitary habits and harsh self-discipline, Housman was also capable of creating delicately crafted poems, full of gentle regret.

Challenges of Youth Housman grew up in Worcestershire, a region northwest of London. His childhood came to an end on his twelfth birthday, when his mother died. Later, at Oxford University, his despair over an unrequited love darkened his life still further. Perhaps because of this double grief, his poetry has bitter undertones.

Upon leaving Oxford, where he had studied classical literature and philosophy, Housman went to work in the Patent Office. Determined to prove himself in the classics, he studied Greek and Latin at night and wrote scholarly articles. In 1892, his hard work paid off when he was appointed to a position as professor of Latin at University College in London.

Literary Success Although Housman spent most of his life engaged in teaching and in scholarly pursuits, he is most remembered for three slender volumes of poetry that are as romantic and melancholy as any ever written. His first and most famous collection of verse, *A Shropshire Lad* (1896), has as its central character a young man named Terence. In later years, Housman claimed, ironically, that he had "never spent much time" in Shropshire.

Housman's image is that of an emotionless intellectual, but his poems display deep feelings. In his view, the goal of poetry is to "transfuse emotion," not to transmit thought. A well-written poem, he maintained, should affect the reader like a shiver down the spine or a punch in the stomach.

To an Athlete Dying Young

A. E. Housman

The time you won your town the race
We chaired you through the marketplace;
Man and boy stood cheering by,
And home we brought you shoulder-high.

5 Today, the road all runners come,
Shoulder-high we bring you home,
And set you at your threshold down,
Townsman of a stiller town.

Smart lad, to slip betimes away
10 From fields where glory does not stay
And early though the laurel[1] grows
It withers quicker than the rose.

Eyes the shady night has shut
Cannot see the record cut,
15 And silence sounds no worse than cheers
After earth has stopped the ears:

Now you will not swell the rout
Of lads that wore their honors out,
Runners whom renown outran
20 And the name died before the man.

So set, before its echoes fade,
The fleet foot on the sill of shade.
And hold to the low lintel up
The still-defended challenge cup.

25 And round that early-laureled head
Will flock to gaze the strengthless dead,
And find unwithered on its curls
The garland briefer than a girl's.

Vocabulary
lintel (lĭn′ tl) *n.* horizontal
bar above a door

---

1. laurel symbol of victory.

When I Was One-and-Twenty

A. E. Housman

When I was one-and-twenty
    I heard a wise man say,
"Give crowns and pounds and guineas[1]
    But not your heart away;
5 Give pearls away and rubies
    But keep your fancy free."
But I was one-and-twenty,
    No use to talk to me.

When I was one-and-twenty
10   I heard him say again,
"The heart out of the bosom
    Was never given in vain;
'Tis paid with sighs a plenty
    And sold for endless rue."
15 And I am two-and-twenty,
    And oh, 'tis true, 'tis true.

---

1. **crowns . . . guineas** denominations of money.

Analyzing an Author's Beliefs

In this poem, do the speaker's beliefs about youth correspond with the author's? Why or why not?

Vocabulary

rue (rōō) *n.* sorrow; regret

Critical Reading

Cite textual evidence to support your responses.

1. **Key Ideas and Details (a)** In "To an Athlete," what are three advantages of dying young, according to the speaker?
   (b) Interpret: Does the speaker entirely mean what he says about these advantages? Explain.

2. **Key Ideas and Details (a)** In "When I Was One-and-Twenty," what advice does the speaker receive, and how does he react?
   (b) Interpret: What clues are there in the poem that Housman is mocking his speaker?

3. **Integration of Knowledge and Ideas** Which are more effective, Hopkins's inventive rhythms or Housman's more traditional ones? Explain, using two of these Essential Question terms: *meter, sprung rhythm, innovation.* **[Connecting to the Essential Question: What is the relationship of the writer to tradition?]**

Literary Analysis

1. **Craft and Structure (a)** Use scansion symbols (˘ ´) to identify the **feet** in line 5 of "God's Grandeur," inserting symbols over syllables on a slip of paper like the one shown below. **(b)** Explain how your scan demonstrates that the line uses **counterpoint rhythm.**

   > Generations have trod, have trod, have trod;…

2. **Key Ideas and Details** **Analyze the author's beliefs** by finding a passage in "God's Grandeur" that reflects Hopkins's love of nature. Then, explain your choice.

3. **Craft and Structure** "Spring and Fall" is written with **sprung rhythm.** Using the stresses in line 11, indicate how many feet that line has.

4. **Craft and Structure (a)** How does the counterpoint rhythm in line 5 of "God's Grandeur" support the meaning of the line? **(b)** In "Spring and Fall," how do the three stresses in line 11 reinforce the meaning of the line?

5. **Integration of Knowledge and Ideas (a)** In "God's Grandeur," does Hopkins think the beauty of nature is enduring? Explain. **(b)** In "Spring and Fall," does he express the same perspective on the endurance of nature's beauty as he does in "God's Grandeur"? Explain.

6. **Craft and Structure (a)** Show that in lines 1–8 of "To an Athlete," the **meter** includes five **iambic tetrameter** lines and three **trochaic tetrameter** lines. **(b)** How do the trochaic lines reinforce the idea of a "stiller town"?

7. **Key Ideas and Details** Find a passage in "To an Athlete" that reflects Housman's underlying sadness. Explain your choice.

8. **Integration of Knowledge and Ideas** Would the speakers in "Spring and Fall" and "To an Athlete" agree that deep sorrow is the right response to the realization that life and earthly beauty are fleeting? Explain.

9. **Integration of Knowledge and Ideas** Hopkins was inspired by his idea of "inscape"—that special individual quality that distinguished one person, object, or emotion from every other. Find a passage that reflects this belief, and explain how this passage conveys the idea of inscape.

10. **Comparing Literary Works** Which poem conveys the most compassionate view of human mortality—"Spring and Fall," "To an Athlete," or "When I Was One-and-Twenty"? Explain.

Common Core State Standards

Writing

1. Write arguments to support claims in an analysis of substantive topics or texts, using valid reasoning and relevant and sufficient evidence. *(p. 1095)*

1.d. Establish and maintain a formal style and objective tone while attending to the norms and conventions of the discipline in which they are writing. *(p. 1095)*

Language

3. Apply knowledge of language to understand how language functions in different contexts, to make effective choices for meaning or style, and to comprehend more fully when reading or listening. *(p. 1095)*

Vocabulary Acquisition and Use

Word Analysis: Coined Words

Hopkins's fascination with language can be seen in the way he coins, or invents, words. For example, he combines *wan*, meaning "pale," and *wood* to make *wanwood*, a new word to describe pale autumn trees. Similarly, he coins *leafmeal* to describe fallen dead leaves ground into a kind of meal. Imitate Hopkins and *create new words from familiar words* to replace each of these phrases. Use concrete or vivid words so that others will understand the meaning you are trying to convey.

1. the very end of summer

2. chilly mornings right after dawn

3. snow-covered lawns

4. tall, bare trees

Vocabulary: Analogies

Analogies compare the relationships between pairs of words. To complete these analogies, choose the word from the vocabulary list on page 1086 that creates a word pair that matches the relationship in the other pair. Explain your choices.

1. *Roof* is to *car* as _____ is to *doorway*.

2. _____ is to *squalor* as *summer* is to *winter*.

3. _____ is to *cliff* as *balcony* is to *building*.

4. *Joy* is to *happiness* as _____ is to *regret*.

5. *Remove* is to *stain* as *wash* is to _____.

6. *Starvation* is to *hunger* as _____ is to *damage*.

Writing to Sources

Argumentative Text Hopkins's poetry was virtually unknown during his life. The poet became more widely read only after Robert Bridges, a long-time friend, had his work published in 1918, long after the poet's death. Take the role of Bridges in 1918 and write a **business letter** to a British publishing company recommending that the publisher issue a collected edition of the poetry of Hopkins.

Prewriting Review the background information about Hopkins's theory of sprung rhythm, his idea of inscape, and his use of coined words. Find passages from his poems that illustrate these ideas and Hopkins's unique poetic voice.

Drafting Use the proper format of a business letter, with the date, the name and address of a fictional publisher, salutation, body, and closing. In the body of your letter, give reasons why the publisher should issue the volume you propose. Explain Hopkins's ideas and cite passages from Hopkins's poetry that show his use of *imagery, figures of speech, and sound* to *evoke reader's emotions*.

Revising Review your letter to make sure that it is persuasive, and strengthen parts that need more emphasis. Use the formal language of business and not the less formal tone of everyday speech.

> **Model: Revising to Use Formal Language**
>
> In sum, Hopkins's poetry deserves to reach a wider public.
> unique poetic voice
> His ~~awesome style~~ must be heard.
>
> The use of formal language in business letters establishes credibility.

Historical Investigation Report

Common Core State Standards

Writing

2. Write informative/explanatory texts to examine and convey complex ideas, concepts, and information clearly and accurately through the effective selection, organization, and analysis of content.

7. Conduct short as well as more sustained research projects to answer a question or solve a problem; narrow or broaden the inquiry when appropriate; synthesize multiple sources on the subject, demonstrating understanding of the subject under investigation.

8. Gather relevant information from multiple authoritative print and digital sources, using advanced searches effectively; assess the strengths and limitations of each source in terms of the task, purpose, and audience.

Historical Investigation Conducting a historical investigation can help you analyze and evaluate the historical background of literary works. You can record your findings in a research report. Remember that an effective report does more than simply list facts: it synthesizes information from a variety of primary, secondary, and tertiary sources and connects ideas to present a coherent analysis, explaining any differences in sources. Follow the steps outlined in this workshop to write a historical investigation.

Assignment Write a **historical investigation report** on an event, figure, or topic that relates to the historical context of a work or works of literature.

What to Include Your research report should have these elements:

- A clear thesis statement, supported by a variety of formats and rhetorical strategies
- An analysis that supports and develops personal opinions, as opposed to restating existing information
- Incorporation of the complexities of and discrepancies in information from multiple sources, with anticipation and refutation of counter-arguments
- Proper documentation and listing of sources, using a style manual
- Sufficient length and complexity to address the topic

To preview the criteria on which your research report may be assessed, see the rubric on page 1107.

Focus on Research

When you conduct research, you should keep the following strategies in mind:

- Use both print and electronic sources.
- Be sure you use information from reliable sources.
- If you are doing research online, look for sources that have *.gov* or *.edu* in their addresses.
- When possible and appropriate, use primary sources.

Be sure to note all sources you use in your research, and credit appropriately. Refer to the Conducting Research pages in the Introductory Unit (pp. lxxii–lxxvii) as well pages 1102–1103 in this workshop and the Citing Sources and Preparing Manuscript pages in the Resource section for information on citation.

Prewriting and Planning

Choosing Your Topic

To choose a topic suitable for the research sources that are available to you, use one of the following strategies:

- **Notebook and Textbook Review** Reviewing school notebooks, textbooks, and writing journals, list topics that interest you. Also review the selections you have read in this textbook, and consider specific questions you have about the historical context for your favorite works.

- **Research Preview** When you have two good topic choices, spend 10–15 minutes researching each topic on the Internet or at the library. This quick research preview will help you identify how much information is available on each topic. Look for both primary and secondary sources.

  Primary sources: letters, diaries, interviews, eyewitness accounts
  Secondary sources: encyclopedias, nonfiction books, and articles

Narrowing Your Topic

Freewrite to find your focus. If your topic can be divided into significant subheads, each with its own focus, it is probably too broad. Using what you already know or have learned in preliminary research, write freely on your topic for two or three minutes. Review your writing and circle the most important or interesting idea. Continue this process until you arrive at a topic that is narrow enough for your paper.

Gathering Details

Do the research. Use both library and Internet resources to locate information. Evaluate sources for validity and reliability before citing them. Be especially critical of Internet sources, checking that the authors have followed careful academic procedures.

Use source cards and note cards. For every source you consult, create a source card with the author's name, title, publisher, city, and date of publication. Then, create a note card for each relevant fact or opinion. Write the general subject at the top. Then, write the fact or quotation, followed by a keyword, such as the author's name, that links the fact with its source.

Source Card
[Ament]
Ament, Phil. "Charles Babbage." The Great Idea Finder. 15 Jan. 2008 <http://www.ideafinder.com/history/inventors/babbage.htm>

Note card
[Babbage's importance]
he's often called the "Father of Computing"
Source: Ament

Drafting

Shaping Your Writing

Develop a thesis statement. Review your notes and draft a statement that reflects a theme in the material you have collected. Your thesis statement should introduce your topic and the point you will develop.

Establish your organizational plan. Decide whether you will present conclusions about your sources as part of your introduction, or build toward your conclusions throughout the paper. Use one of these plans.

Effective Methods of Organization		
Introduction	present historical context give thesis statement DRAW CONCLUSION	present historical context establish issue in thesis statement
Body	PROVE CONCLUSION present/analyze/compare sources	present/analyze/compare sources LEAD TO CONCLUSION
Closing	summarize	DRAW CONCLUSION

Write a powerful introduction and conclusion. Use your opening paragraph to introduce the issue, to define unfamiliar terms, and to clarify background details such as the time, place, and relevant social conditions. In your conclusion, emphasize the significance of your findings.

Maintain a formal style and objective tone. As you draft, choose words consistent with a formal style, such as *supplies*, rather than informal words, such as *stuff*. In addition, keep your tone objective. Rather than choosing words that express opinions, such as *outrageous*, choose objective words and phrases such as *widely condemned*.

Providing Elaboration

Handle your sources well. Follow these guidelines when presenting sources:

- Use a mix of paraphrases and direct quotations. Do not string quotations together without interpretation. Instead, frame your quotations so that a reader understands why you chose them.
- Describe and analyze your sources. Explain whether or not primary resources reflect consensus, or general agreement, about a topic. When primary resources offer different perspectives, try to account for these differences. If a writer's perspective is unique, explain it, if possible, by analyzing the writer's circumstances and motives.
- As you draft, underline sentences you will need to document. After you finish drafting, you can format the appropriate citations.
- Be aware of what constitutes *plagiarism*, especially in using media and digital sources. Clearly attribute the words and ideas of others.

Common Core State Standards

Writing

2.c. Use appropriate and varied transitions and syntax to link the major sections of the text, create cohesion, and clarify the relationships among complex ideas and concepts.

2.e. Establish and maintain a formal style and objective tone while attending to the norms and conventions of the discipline in which they are writing.

2.f. Provide a concluding statement or section that follows from and supports the information or explanation presented.

4. Produce clear and coherent writing in which the development, organization, and style are appropriate to task, purpose, and audience.

Developing Your Style

Check for Coherence

Examine your draft for coherence, the logical, smooth connections of ideas. Vary your syntax and consider adding transitional words and phrases to show the relationships between your thoughts.

Transitional Words and Phrases			
above all	aside from	however	on the whole
accordingly	because	in other words	otherwise
alternatively	consequently	instead	particularly
although	for example	likewise	similarly
as a result	for that reason	on the contrary	therefore
as well as	furthermore	on the other hand	usually

Integrate source material. Another aspect of a coherent report is the careful integration of source material. Be aware of discrepancies among sources and account for them. Also, connect paraphrases or quotations to the subject being discussed and show how they support your point.

Find It in Your Reading

Read the student model research report "Visionaries" on page 1104.

1. Identify and evaluate transitional words and phrases.
2. Analyze how the writer integrates information from other sources.

Try It in Your Writing

To check your sentences for coherence, follow these steps:

1. Circle any transitional words and phrases in your writing. Check that each transition is effective and appropriate.

2. Read each paragraph aloud, listening for how the ideas connect. Sudden shifts may indicate that a transition is needed.

3. Review sentences in which you present information from your research. For paraphrases, be sure you have not copied wording. For direct quotations, check that you have introduced and analyzed the quotation effectively.

Revising

 Common Core
State Standards

Writing
5. Develop and strengthen writing as needed by planning, revising, editing, rewriting, or trying a new approach, focusing on addressing what is most significant for a specific purpose and audience.

Revising Your Overall Structure

Organize ideas effectively. Review the flow of ideas in your historical investigation report. This chart shows some common organizational methods you can use throughout your report or in specific sections. For example, you might follow an overall chronological order, but within one section, a problem/solution order may help you clarify an important relationship.

Method	Description
Chronological	Discuss events in time order.
Cause/Effect	Analyze the causes and/or effects of an event.
Problem/Solution	Identify a specific problem or conflict and tell how it was or was not solved.
Parts to Whole	Relate elements of a single event or topic to a whole.
Order of Importance	Present your support from most to least important, or from least to most important.
Comparison and Contrast	When comparing two topics, discuss their similarities and then their differences, or discuss each topic separately.

Peer Review: Ask a partner to review your draft and describe your organizational plan. Did your partner identify the plan you intended to follow? Discuss how you can improve the flow of ideas throughout your report.

Revising Your Paragraphs

Place topic sentences effectively. Each key paragraph should contain a topic sentence and supporting details, but the topic sentence can appear in the first sentence, in the last sentence, or in the body of the paragraph.

Reread each paragraph in your essay. Place brackets around the topic sentence. Then, review the placement of each topic sentence, considering moving it for maximum impact.

Model: Revising Placement of Topic Sentence

Original: In contrast to Babbage and Da Vinci, Bill Gates has been able to directly affect the world in which he lives. He is a visionary of our own time. It seems that this man can literally predict future technology and then develop it.

Revised: A visionary of our own time is Bill Gates. In contrast to Babbage and Da Vinci, Gates has been able to directly affect the world in which he lives. It seems that this man can literally predict future technology and then develop it.

> Moving the topic sentence to the beginning of the paragraph presents a clearer focus.

Writers on Writing

James Berry On Research-Based Writing

James Berry is the author of *"From Lucy: Englan' Lady"* (p. 1055).

James Berry on Research-Based Writing

I deliberately set this novel of slavery in the period 1807–1840, so as to take in both the end of the slave trade and life after Emancipation. Writing it, for me, was like traveling through the experiences of my ancestors. My childhood home was only minutes from the ruins of a big slave plantation, so I grew up surrounded by landmarks of slavery. To learn more about these times, I read obsessively, consulting books, maps, and old pictures.

"To learn more about these times, I read obsessively. . . ."

—James Berry

from *Ajeemah and His Son*

Atu saw his father leaving, being taken away by a planter while he was held, already bought by another plantation owner. Led along, Ajeemah looked back, calling desperately, "Atu, my son Atu—freedom! Freedom! Or let us meet in the land of spirits!"

Two hours' ride from Kingston, in the back of the estate horse-drawn carriage with two other male slaves bought with him, and Ajeemah came to his big and busy New World sugar plantation. Nearly four hundred slaves lived and worked here.

Everybody stepped down from the carriage in the center of the estate work yard in a blaze of sunlight. The estate work yard buildings spread out like a little village. The huge windmill that powered the grinding of the sugarcane was near the millhouse where the cane was crushed and where its juice was taken and boiled into the wealth-making sugar, and also rum. Then in a close cluster there were the boiling house, curing house, distilling house and trash house. Ajeemah stared at the windmill; he'd never seen a windmill. He then glanced at the many workshop buildings, the animal houses and the overseer's and headmen's houses. And he could see, separated some good distance away, the huts—the slaves' quarters. . . .

I wanted to show here how family members could be separated forever at the kind of barbaric sales, called "scrambles," where purchasers rushed in and grabbed slaves to gain the right to buy them.

I researched in Jamaican libraries for pictures of how four broken-down old estates near my home would have looked when they were flourishing.

I used Eric Williams's *Capitalism and Slavery* as a reference in writing this book.

Just at the top of my lane were the ruins of an old slave estate. As a boy, I climbed up inside the windmill tower to look out over the landscape.

Providing Appropriate Citations

Common Core State Standards

Writing
8. Integrate information into the text selectively to maintain the flow of ideas, avoiding plagiarism and overreliance on any one source and following a standard format for citation.

You must cite the source for the information and ideas you use in your report. In the body of your paper, include a footnote, an endnote, or a parenthetical citation to identify the source of each fact, opinion, and quotation. At the end of your paper, provide a bibliography or a Works Cited list, a list of all the sources you cite. Follow the format your teacher recommends, such as Modern Language Association (MLA) style or American Psychological Association (APA) style. See page 1103 for more information about how to prepare citations for different kinds of sources.

If you do not give credit for the information you found, you commit the serious offense of plagiarism, presenting someone else's work as your own. Plagiarism is stealing someone else's ideas, so it is both illegal and dishonest. It's easy to prevent this problem by fairly and thoroughly citing every source you use.

Deciding What to Cite

A fact that can be found in three or more reference sources is probably common knowledge and does not need to be cited. However, do cite facts and opinions that are not common knowledge. This chart distinguishes between common knowledge and facts that should be cited.

Reading/Writing Connection
To read the complete student model, see page 1104.

Common Knowledge
• Charles Babbage was born in 1791 and died in 1871.   • He was a mathematician and a philosopher.   • He invented a machine called The Difference Engine.

Facts to be Cited
• Babbage's early computer greatly impressed some forward-thinking scientists as early as 1833.   Source: "Wonderful Machinery." *New York Weekly Messenger.* 13 Feb, 1833.   • Babbage was fascinated by machinery and even went backstage at the theater to find out how the staging was created.   Source: Lee, J.A.N. "Charles Babbage." 15 Jan. 2008.   <http://ei.cs.vt.edu/~history/Babbage.html>.

In your report, you will give credit for the following ideas, opinions, or theories presented by other writers:

- Any facts or statistics that are not common knowledge
- Direct quotations of spoken or written words
- Paraphrases of spoken or written words

Notice that you must still provide a citation even if you paraphrase someone else's ideas. It is appropriate to give credit to someone else's thoughts, whether or not you use his or her exact words. In general, it is a good idea to provide too many citations rather than too few.

Developing Your Style

Avoiding Plagiarism

Give proper credit. In a research paper, commonly known facts need not be credited. However, lesser-known facts, as well as quotations and the opinions of other writers, must be acknowledged with proper citations.

> *Common knowledge: Charles Babbage was a nineteenth-century British scientist.*
>
> *Requires citation: Charles Babbage planned a calculating machine with [describe the design].*

Never present someone else's ideas or words as though they were your own. To avoid plagiarism—the act of repeating other people's words or ideas without crediting them—follow these steps:

1. Avoid taking notes verbatim, or word for word. Instead, jot down a main idea. When you copy from a source, use quotation marks.

2. Have a partner read your draft and mark any statements that need documentation. Write legibly to avoid miscommunication.

3. Add credits and documentation, as needed.

Find It in Your Reading

Read or review the writing model on page 1104. Notice the way in which this writer gives credit to specific individuals whose ideas she uses.

Sample Works-Cited List

Indicate the date you accessed information from an Internet site. Content and addresses at Web sites change frequently.

> Swade, Doron. *The Difference Engine: Charles Babbage and the Quest to Build the First Computer.* Penguin, 2002.
>
> Ament, Phil. "Charles Babbage." *The Great Idea Finder.* 15 Jan. 2008. <http://www.ideafinder.com/history/inventors/babbage.htm>.
>
> *The Life of Leonardo Da Vinci.* Dir. Renato Castellani. Questar, 2003.
>
> "Wonderful Machinery." *New York Weekly Messenger.* 13 Feb. 1833.

List an anonymous work by title.

Apply It to Your Writing

Review the draft of your research paper. Be sure that your citations are accurate and follow a consistent format. Underline statements in your draft if they are not common knowledge. Then, provide a complete citation for each underlined statement.

Visionaries

The world has seen many visionaries whose inventions and concepts would change the world forever and shape the way we live our lives today. Despite the fact that their ideas were not necessarily accepted right away, many people like Charles Babbage, Leonardo Da Vinci, and even Bill Gates, are now regarded as some of the most amazing minds the world has ever seen.

> Nicole states her thesis in the opening paragraph.

One who is not very well known but incredibly influential was Charles Babbage. He was born in 1791 and died in 1871 in the UK. Babbage was a well-known mathematician, philosopher, and engineer who invented the first computer and was so far ahead of the technology of his time that he was unable to complete his machine due to lack of sufficient machinery to build the parts needed. Babbage is now considered the "Father of Computing," but during the early 1800s—the period in which he lived—his plans for the first programmable computer seemed unattainable to most people despite his credibility as a leading mathematician and engineer (Ament). His life was so consumed by his work that even when he went to the theater "[He] went behind the scenes to look at the mechanism" (Lee). In the 1820s and 1830s it was impossible to build his precisely engineered Difference Engine with the technology available to him and the lack of funding that he experienced (Ament). However, more than a century later in the 1990s, several scientists decided to build his machine according to his original plans. The machine was made up of four thousand parts and weighed over three metric tons, but size was not the most impressive part (Ament). His Difference machine worked to perfection and effectively eliminated the high rate of human error in math problems, which was his original motivation for the project.

> Next, Nicole provides readers with general background on her subject.

It's hard to imagine how different the world would be if Babbage had finished his machine and given us the first programmable computer. However, it was not until a century later in the 1940s that Howard Aiken created the Harvard Mark I Calculator, which is the first modern digital computer. Aiken used several ideas from Babbage's original design, including a push card and vacuum tube, both of which were unheard of at the time Babbage envisioned them.

> Nicole provides readers with a sense of Babbage's accomplishments by linking them to modern computer technology.

Another visionary working past simpler innovation was Leonardo Da Vinci. Da Vinci is best known for his paintings that seem to pop off the canvas. He was one of the first painters to use the technique of perspective to achieve this type of picture, which was radically different from the flat paintings of the Middle Ages. He often used mathematics, geometry, and shading to help him plan out the perspective. His paintings show something else that is truly remarkable. They show no brush strokes because of his skill level as well as his use of oil paints while the rest of the painting world was using tempera paints (O'Connor 27).

> Nicole cites sources on her Works Cited list properly, following MLA style.

However, Da Vinci's legacy is more than just his artwork. As he sketched and painted, Da Vinci often drew scientific instruments on the side of his paper. He had a fascination with studying the way things worked and most of all creating his own inventions, ranging from war machines to musical instruments (O'Connor 44). Soon his study and experimentation distracted him from his painting. He began to study the nature of light and how it affects shading and the inner workings of optics. As he studied the human body more closely, he found that human eyes received light rather than giving off particles, which was the common belief at the time. Through this experimentation, Da Vinci began to develop theories that linked sound waves and light. He also studied the way muscles work and greatly contributed to the medical science of his day. These concepts were well ahead of their time.

Da Vinci's study of the human body fit in perfectly with his inventions; he noted that joints were like hinges and muscles were like gears and levers. He was fascinated with the thought of motion and how things move. In fact, he once expressed the idea that "motion is the principle of all life" (O'Connor 58). Da Vinci devoted much of his study to how things could move by themselves. He drew several sketches of motors and flying machines that came from his study of the wings of a variety of birds. One of his sketches of his flying machines, called an aerial screw, resembles the modern-day helicopter.

Overall, Leonardo Da Vinci's devotion to the study of the human body, scientific observations, and inventions, and his ground-breaking artistic work became the foundation that many after him would build on.

Another visionary who has directly affected the world is Bill Gates. In contrast to Babbage and Da Vinci, Gates has been able to directly affect the world in which he lives. It seems that this man can literally predict future technology and then develop it.

In the 1980s, Bill Gate's company focused on producing products for individual computer use. Three years later, Microsoft developed a word-processing tool called Word that put words on the screen exactly how they would be printed on paper (Lesinski 41). Later, he made use of a piece of hardware called the mouse, which had been invented by Douglas C. Englebart and Bill English. At that time, the mouse was a breakthrough innovation that made interaction with a computer screen easier for many people.

This, however, was just the beginning. Gates's company went international as he continued to innovate and create new technology. The new technologies he developed have changed the way we communicate, do business, teach, and learn. Due to the contributions of Bill Gates, we can now use computers at home and at school. We can communicate with amazing speed. Recently, Microsoft has expanded into the creation of voice-activated technology to be put in cars. With this technology, driving may become safer and the number of accidents may be reduced. After so many years of creating and innovating, Bill Gates continues to influence the evolution of technology, bringing products to market that people before him could not even imagine.

It is hard to imagine how the world would be without Bill Gates and his contributions to technology. It is truly amazing that in a matter of seconds

Nicole provides specific information on Da Vinci's study of optics.

Notice how Nicole creates a transition between Gates and the previous "visionaries": "In contrast to Babbage and Da Vinci . . ." Such a transition makes the report more coherent.

Notice how Nicole uses language to show causes and effects: "Due to . . ."

anyone could pull up a Web site about Charles Babbage or Leonardo Da Vinci or communicate incredibly quickly with someone on the other side of the world.

There is no doubt that the world would be a different place if it were not for visionaries like these. These men were not afraid of the limitations of their time. They pursued the what-ifs their minds developed, imagining things that were science fiction in their day. For Babbage and Da Vinci, their ideas would be brought to fruition in future generations. Gates has been able to bring his imaginings from sketch to prototype to best-seller, consistently moving technology past what even he might have thought possible.

> Nicole summarizes her report in the final paragraph.

Works Cited

Ament, Phil [pseudonym for employees at Vaunt Design Group, an Internet consulting company in Troy, Michigan]. "Charles Babbage." The Great Idea Finder. 4 May 2006. 15 Jan. 2008
    <http://www.ideafinder.com/history/inventors/babbage.htm>.

Lee, J.A.N. "Charles Babbage." History of Computing site. Department of Computer Science at Virginia Tech. Sep. 1994. 15 Jan. 2008.
    <http://ei.cs.vt.edu/~history/Babbage.html>.

Lesinski, Jeanne M. *Bill Gates*. Minneapolis: Lerner Publications, 2000.

O'Connor, Barbara. *Leonardo Da Vinci: Renaissance Genius.* Minneapolis: Carolrhoda Books, Inc., 2003.

> Nicole provides a complete, detailed, and properly formatted list of all the works she has cited in her report.

Editing and Proofreading

Check your report to eliminate grammatical or spelling errors. Also, be sure that your report is neatly presented and legible.

Focus on quotations. Compare each direct quotation in your essay with its source. Make sure that you have recorded exactly what your source said or wrote. To avoid plagiarism, use quotation marks around words, phrases, and sentences that come directly from your sources.

Spiral Review: Conventions Earlier in this unit, you learned about verb tense (p. 1009) and active voice (p. 1085). Check your report to be sure you have used those conventions correctly.

Publishing, Presenting, and Reflecting

Consider one of the following ways to share your writing:

Prepare your Works-Cited list. Your paper is ready for presentation only after you add your Works-Cited list, which provides full bibliographical information on each source you cite. Identify the format your teacher prefers. Then, follow that accepted style to assemble your list. (For more information, see Citing Sources, pp. R21–R23.)

Apply principles of design. Make sure the text of your investigation is appealing to the eye. The lines should be evenly spaced, and the margins of the page should be even, not ragged.

Present your report orally. Use your report as the basis for an oral presentation. Be sure to rehearse well, using clear syntax and accessible diction.

Reflect on your writing. Jot down your thoughts on the experience of writing a research report. Begin by answering these questions. What have you learned in this workshop about differing points of view on the same event? What aspects of researching one topic in depth surprised you?

Rubric for Self-Assessment

Evaluate your reflective essay using the following criteria and rating scale:

Criteria	Rating Scale
	not very very
Purpose/Focus: How clearly does your thesis statement guide your report?	1 2 3 4
Organization: How logical and well documented is your presentation?	1 2 3 4
Development of Ideas/Elaboration: How well do you use a variety of primary and secondary sources to support your thesis?	1 2 3 4
Language: How clear is your writing, and how precise is your word choice?	1 2 3 4
Conventions: According to an accepted format, how complete and accurate are your citations?	1 2 3 4

Common Core State Standards

Writing
5. Develop and strengthen writing as needed by editing, focusing on addressing what is most significant for a specific purpose and audience.

Language
2. Demonstrate command of the conventions of standard English capitalization, punctuation, and spelling when writing.

Analyze and Evaluate Entertainment Media

Our culture is saturated with **entertainment media**—movies, TV shows, music videos, and other programming designed primarily for enjoyment rather than for instruction or information. While providing entertainment is the core goal, these media also appeal to our values, offering representations of society that both reinforce those values and shape our perceptions of reality. As a consumer of media, you should determine whether the portrait of reality they present is flawed or misleading.

Evaluating Media Credibility

In addition to seeking the primary goal of entertaining audiences, entertainment media makers often influence viewers in these ways:

- *Informing them* and providing a new understanding of historical or current events. Dramatic interpretations of history or current issues, however, may not always be reliable factual accounts.

- *Persuading them* to accept particular viewpoints. By providing only certain perspectives or depicting groups or actions as positive or negative, media can present a *biased* view of an issue.

Entertainment media also cater to audiences' values. For instance, when they tell tales of families reunited, criminals punished, and underdogs who become winners, they are forming a picture of how we think life should be. In this way, they *transmit our own cultural values* back to us. You might envision the relationship between media and culture as a cycle:

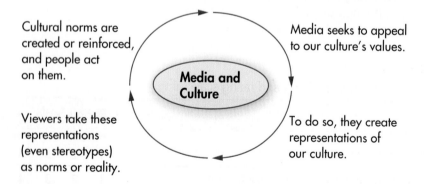

Cultural norms are created or reinforced, and people act on them.

Media seeks to appeal to our culture's values.

Media and Culture

Viewers take these representations (even stereotypes) as norms or reality.

To do so, they create representations of our culture.

Along with the transmission of values, however, come representations of groups of people. Scholars who study the media have examined the effects these representations have upon public perception. They have found that the way groups are portrayed in the media can create **stereotypes,** assumptions about race, gender, or religion that influence a person's attitude and behavior toward individuals who belong to certain groups.

**Common Core
State Standards**

**Speaking and Listening
2.** Integrate multiple sources of information presented in diverse formats and media in order to make informed decisions and solve problems, evaluating the credibility and accuracy of each source and noting any discrepancies among the data.

Media Tools and Techniques

The makers of entertainment media use the following *editing techniques*:

- **Special Effects**—technological tricks of sight and sound that produce images, such as flying superheroes and roaming dinosaurs
- **Camera Angles**—the different positions from which a scene is recorded to create different effects
- **Reaction Shots**—close-up shots of an actor's face as he or she responds to another actor or to action in the script
- **Sequencing**—the arrangement of a story's events, such as chronological order or a series of flashbacks
- **Music**—sound added to visual sequences to complement the action or create a particular mood

Activities: Evaluate a Movie, TV Episode, or Skit

Comprehension and Collaboration For both activities, use an evaluation form like the one shown below.

A. Find a movie, show, or skit you like to watch on television or the Internet. Examine the main ideas it presents and analyze how it conveys these ideas. Record your observations on a form like the one below.

B. Search the Internet to find episodes of a television show from the 1960s or 1970s. Consider how a particular group is represented in this show. Then, compare this representation with representations of the same group on television today. Share your observations with your class.

Evaluation Form

Type of Entertainment Media: Movie ☐ TV Episode ☐ Skit ☐

Name of Movie, Show, or Skit: _____

What story does this movie, episode, or clip tell? _____

What cultural values does it appeal to? Idealism ☐ Fear ☐ Family ☐

    Justice ☐ Other _____

    How does it appeal to these values? _____

Are there stereotypes in this representation? Yes ☐ No ☐

    If yes, what are they? _____

Identify techniques used in this film: Special effects ☐ Editing ☐

    Camera angles ☐ Reaction shots ☐ Sequencing ☐ Music ☐

    Explain the effect of two of these techniques. _____

Idioms

**Common Core
State Standards**

Language
4.a. Use context as a clue to the meaning of a word or phrase.
5. Demonstrate understanding of figurative language, word relationships, and nuances in word meanings.

Idioms are figurative expressions that do not mean what the words literally say. For example, describing the weather as *raining cats and dogs* means the rain is torrential. To recognize an idiom, you have to understand *word-phrase relationships*—to realize that in the phrase *raining cats and dogs,* the words have a figurative meaning rather than their usual literal ones.

Idioms can be effective tools in some kinds of writing to convey character or to evoke a particular time period or setting. For example, an American detective of the 1940s might jump in a taxi and growl to the driver, "Step on it." Idioms can also help set a particular mood or tone.

Relying on idioms consistently in your own writing is not always a good idea, however. Because they have been used so often, many of them have lost their originality. Look at the examples below. Note how replacing the idioms can help to communicate meaning in a more precise and lively way.

Idioms	Alternatives
After ten hours of driving in heavy traffic, the trucker <u>ran out of steam.</u>	☐ collapsed over his steering wheel. ☐ sighed and pulled into a rest stop. ☐ radioed his boss and told her he quit.
She was <u>down in the dumps.</u>	☐ too lethargic to get out of bed. ☐ apt to burst into tears if anyone looked at her the wrong way. ☐ in need of a friend to listen to her problems.

Practice

Directions: An analogy shows the relationship between sets of words. Each of the analogies below pairs a word with an idiomatic phrase. Complete each analogy with one of the lettered words provided, creating a pair that matches the other pair in the analogy. Then, write an explanation of the idiomatic expression and the relationships in each pairing.

1. upset : "bent out of shape" :: _____ : "under the weather"
   a. cloudy   **b.** sick   **c.** wet   **d.** forgetful

2. "jump the gun" : _____ :: "shoot the breeze" : deliberate
   a. run quickly   **b.** rush   **c.** chat   **d.** consider

3. "over the moon" : ecstatic :: "fit to be tied" : _____
   a. furious   **b.** delighted   **c.** sad   **d.** fastened

Vocabulary Acquisition and Use: Context Clues

Context clues are words or phrases that help readers clarify the meanings of unfamiliar words in a text. By using context clues, you can determine the word or words that complete a sentence. Sentence Completion questions appear in most standardized tests. In these types of questions, you are given sentences with one or more missing words. Your task is to use the context to choose the correct word or words to complete each sentence logically. Try this strategy: (1) Read the sentence. (2) Scan the answer choices. Find synonyms that are simple words or phrases for the choices. (3) Test the synonyms and determine which makes the most sense.

Practice

This exercise is modeled after the Sentence Completion questions that appear in the Reading Comprehension section of the SAT.

Directions: Each of the following sentences is missing one or two words. Choose the word or set of words that best completes each sentence.

> **Test-Taking Tip**
> Eliminate any words with similar meanings because a single correct answer choice should be obvious.

1. Charlotte Brontë's work might have remained ___?___ without the popular success of *Jane Eyre*.
   A. truculent
   B. obscure
   C. rapturous
   D. monotonous
   E. obstinate

2. Charlotte and her gifted siblings can be called ___?___ spirits.
   A. agricultural
   B. terrestrial
   C. gaunt
   D. rapturous
   E. kindred

3. Her close-knit family ___?___ six children and a widowed father.
   A. blanched
   B. eluded
   C. comprised
   D. assessed
   E. clasped

4. The ___?___ Charlotte witnessed at boarding school inspired her to write *Jane Eyre*.
   A. depredation
   B. contusion
   C. adversary
   D. approbation
   E. etymology

5. She would never ___?___ her days as a governess, for they led her to write a popular novel from which she would ___?___ .
   A. impel . . . profundity
   B. fracture . . . officious
   C. rue . . . prosper
   D. languish . . . deficient
   E. elude . . . diffusive

6. In the ___?___ years of her life she married, enjoying a brief time of happiness after the ___?___ of her siblings' deaths.
   A. waning . . . turmoil
   B. ingratiating . . . inculcation
   C. ravenous . . . rendezvous
   D. wily . . . malevolence
   E. gaudy . . . predilection

From Text to Understanding

You have studied each part of Unit 5 as a set of connected texts. In this workshop, you will have the chance to further explore the fundamental connections among these texts and to deepen your essential understanding of the literature and its social and historical context.

PART 1: Relationships

Writing: Argumentative Essay The Victorians embraced progress but also looked to the past for inspiration and comfort. Eras such as the early Renaissance and ancient Greece caught the Victorian imagination. Review the poems of Part 1, focusing on the Anchor Texts by Robert Browning and Elizabeth Barrett Browning, noting which works look to the past and which remain fixed in the present. Consider how a historical setting helps to convey a poem's theme.

Assignment: Develop and defend a claim about the significance of setting a poem in a historical time versus the present day, using examples of both from Part 1.

> **Example:** Historical setting can buffer a poem's emotional impact, as shown in a comparison of "My Last Duchess" and "Sonnet 43."

Interpret the Literature: Use the Writing Checklist to help organize your thinking. Once you have decided on your claim, develop and support it with strong analysis and textual evidence.

PART 2: The Novel

Writing: Writing to Sources The Victorian novel reflects nineteenth-century values but also reflects a changing society. Thus, some aspects of the Victorian worldview remain relevant in the twenty-first century. Review the excerpt from Charlotte Brontë's *Jane Eyre,* as well as the other selections in Part 2. As you read, identify Victorian values and themes that are still present and powerful today.

Assignment: Develop an essay that makes connections between contemporary American values and themes and those of the British Victorian era.

Develop your ideas. Present your observations in a clear thesis statement. Keep your discussion of the Victorian period grounded in the novels, and use details from the texts for support.

Draw valid parallels. Make sure the comparisons you make to the modern world are relevant and engaging.

**Common Core
State Standards**

Writing

1. Write arguments to support claims in an analysis of substantive topics or texts, using valid reasoning and relevant and sufficient evidence.

7. Conduct short as well as more sustained research projects to answer a question (including a self-generated question) or solve a problem; narrow or broaden the inquiry when appropriate; synthesize multiple sources on that subject, demonstrating understanding of the subject under investivation.

9. Draw evidence from literary or informational texts to support analysis, reflection, and research.

Speaking and Listening

1. Initiate and participate effectively in a range of collaborative discussions (one-on-one, in groups, and teacher-led) with diverse partners on *grades 11–12 topics, texts, and issues,* building on others' ideas and expressing their own clearly and persuasively.

Writing Checklist

☐ Poems that look to the past.

　Notes: _____

☐ Poems set in the present.

　Notes: _____

☐ Clear claim.

　Notes: _____

☐ Relevant textual evidence.

　Notes: _____

PART 3: The Empire and Its Discontents

Research: Historical Introduction The Anchor Texts "Dover Beach," "Recessional," and "The Widow at Windsor" contain commentary about the power of government, the cost of war, and social inequality. As you review these poems, think about the social and political questions they raise about the British Empire.

Assignment: Write a historical introduction to the Anchor Text poems of Part 3, explaining their background and significance. Working in a small group, use a variety of sources and research the British Empire during the Victorian period. Consider these questions:

- What topics of protest, controversy, or celebration were prevalent in late nineteenth-century Britain?

- What did it mean when people said that the sun never sets on the British Empire?

- How did society change at home as Britain expanded around the world?

Take notes on your findings. Then, use the information you have learned to write an introduction to the poems by Arnold and Kipling. Include a works cited list with your finished work.

PART 4: Gloom and Glory

Listening and Speaking: Dialogue What would Brontë or Hardy, Hopkins or Housman say to us now, if only he or she could sit down for a conversation? Review the texts and background information in Part 4, paying special attention to the Anchor Texts, the poems by Gerard Manley Hopkins and A. E. Housman. Identify the messages about melancholy or the soaring soul—about gloom or glory—these poets convey.

Assignment: With a partner, present a dialogue between a 21st-century interviewer and one of the poets from Part 4. To prepare, do some biographical research on the poet of your choice. Discuss the poet's likely opinions about life and death, eternity and redemption, joy and regret. Then, write a partial script with questions and responses, along with other topics on which you can improvise. Have the class listen to the dialogue. Using the checklists shown on this page, the audience can assess both the interviewer's responsiveness to the Victorian writer and the overall presentation.

Listening Responsively

☐ Has the interviewer asked questions that show an understanding of what the speaker said?

☐ Has the interviewer identified the positions the speaker has taken and the evidence offered in support of those positions?

Assessing a Presentation
Score 1 (low) to 4 (high)

How highly do I rate the speaker's content, or message? 1 2 3 4

How highly do I rate the speaker's diction, or word choice? 1 2 3 4

How highly do I rate the speaker's rhetorical strategies, such as appeals to logic and emotion? 1 2 3 4

How highly do I rate the speaker's delivery, including such elements as making eye contact and using purposeful gestures? 1 2 3 4

Test-Taking Practice

Reading Test: Prose Fiction

Some standardized tests include lengthy prose fiction reading passages drawn from novels and short stories. You will have to demonstrate your basic comprehension as well as your analytical skills. Questions will focus on topics such as main ideas, significant details, causes and effects, and themes. In addition, you may be asked to show understanding of words, statements, and the author's perspective.

Common Core State Standards

RL.11-12.1, RL.11-12.3, RL.11-12.4; L.11-12.1, L.11-12.2, L.11-12.3

[For the full wording of the standards, see the standards chart in the front of your textbook.]

Practice

The following exercise is modeled after the ACT Reading Test, Prose Fiction section.

Directions: Read the following passage, taken from *Jane Eyre,* by Charlotte Brontë. Then, choose the best answer to each question.

It was English history: among the readers I observed my acquaintance of the verandah: at the commencement of the lesson, her place had been at the top of the class, but for some error of pronunciation, or some inattention to stops, she was suddenly sent to the very bottom.
5   Even in that obscure position, Miss Scatcherd continued to make her an object of constant notice: she was continually addressing to her such phrases as the following:—
"Burns" (such it seems was her name: the girls here were all called by their surnames, as boys are elsewhere), "Burns, you are
10   standing on the side of your shoe; turn your toes out immediately."
"Burns, you poke your chin most unpleasantly; draw it in." "Burns, I insist on your holding your head up; I will not have you before me in that attitude," etc. etc.
A chapter having been read through twice, the books were closed
15   and the girls examined. The lesson had comprised part of the reign of Charles I, and there were sundry questions about tonnage and poundage and ship-money, which most of them appeared unable to answer; still, every little difficulty was solved instantly when it reached Burns: her memory seemed to have retained the substance
20   of the whole lesson, and she was ready with answers on every point. I kept expecting that Miss Scatcherd would praise her attention; but, instead of that, she suddenly cried out—
"You dirty, disagreeable girl! you have never cleaned your nails this morning!"
25   Burns made no answer: I wondered at her silence. "Why," thought I, "does she not explain that she could neither clean her nails nor wash her face, as the water was frozen?"

Strategy:

- **Underline time words,** such as dates and time of day, and **transition words,** such as "then," and "afterwards," to clarify sequence.

- As you read, **make a chronological list of the story's events.**

- Refer to your list as you answer the questions.

1. Which of the following quotes from the passage demonstrates emotive language and not informative language?
   A. "there were sundry questions about tonnage and poundage"
   B. "she was suddenly sent to the very bottom"
   C. "'You dirty, disagreeable girl!'"
   D. "the girls here were all called by their surnames"

2. The author provides precise dialogue to increase the reader's understanding of her characters' motivations because she wants:
   F. readers to understand what Burns is really like.
   G. to show how the setting affects the characters.
   H. readers to experience the shock the narrator feels.
   J. to show how Burns forces Miss Scatcherd to act.

3. As it is used in line 9, the word *surnames* most nearly means:
   A. nicknames.
   B. last names.
   C. first names.
   D. official titles.

4. Which of the following would be included in a summary of this selection?

   I. Burns was an acquaintance of Jane's.
   II. The lesson they read was about Charles I.
   III. Burns did not mention the frozen wash water.
   F. I and II
   G. I only
   H. III only
   J. I, II, and III

5. Considering the events of the entire passage, it is most reasonable to infer that
   A. Jane would soon become a favorite of the teacher.
   B. Burns knew how to deal with Miss Scatcherd.
   C. Burns would one day be recognized as intelligent.
   D. Jane thought Burns deserved the way she was treated.

6. Which elements of the author's beliefs are demonstrated in her description of Miss Scatcherd's response to Burns's answers?
   F. Good students deserve praise.
   G. Boarding schools are good for character.
   H. Teachers need to be firm with their students.
   J. Cleanliness is an important personal trait.

7. The details and events in the passage suggest that the relationship between Jane and Burns would most accurately be described as:
   A. a misunderstanding.
   B. a rivalry.
   C. sympathetic.
   D. jealousy.

GO ON

Grammar and Writing: Editing in Context

Editing-in-context segments appear in some standardized tests. They are made up of a passage with underlined and numbered areas, some of which contain errors in grammar, style, and usage. For each question, you must choose the best way to correct a given sentence.

Practice

This exercise is modeled after the ACT English Test.

Directions: For each underlined sentence or portion of a sentence, choose the best alternative. If an item asks a question about the underlined portion or a numbered sentence, choose the best answer to the question.

Strategy

Try out each answer.

Examine the answer choices with an eye to what makes them different. Various aspects of writing can vary in multiple answers. Make sure each part is effective.

[1]

Boarding schools first began in England when boys <u>go</u> to a local monastery
          ₁
for their education. Monks and lay staff would provide a variety of instruction while **<u>the boys' housing would be provided by the order that sponsored the monastery.</u>** Often a local nobleman would make his estate available to the sons of other nobles. **<u>Employing a literate priest from the</u>**
                                                       ₃
<u>area.</u> These makeshift academies often became boarding houses for the elite.

[2]

In the twelfth century, **<u>all Benedictine monasteries were ordered by the</u>**
                                                            ₄
<u>Pope to provide what were known as "charity schools." Followed by</u>
<u>what we know today as public schools.</u> Students **<u>began to pay their</u>**
                          ₅   ₆
<u>way and attended</u> in greater numbers than ever before.

[3]

Aristocratic families continued to favor private instruction in their homes.[7]
The great universities of Cambridge and Oxford provided models. As the British Empire began to expand, the boarding school became well established.[8]

    1. **A.** NO CHANGE
        B. goes
        C. have gone
        D. went

2. Which of the following sentences would best make this statement more forceful?
   F. NO CHANGE
   G. the order that sponsored the monastery would provide the boys' housing.
   H. the boys' housing would be sponsored by the order the monastery provided.
   J. the order that sponsored the monastery would be provided by the boys' housing.

3. **A.** NO CHANGE
   B. attach it to previous sentence
   C. attach it to next sentence
   D. OMIT

4. **F.** NO CHANGE
   G. all Benedictine monasteries were ordered to provide what were known as "charity schools" by the Pope.
   H. the Pope ordered all Benedictine monasteries to provide what were known as "charity schools."
   J. the Pope was ordered by all Benedictine monasteries to provide what were known as "charity schools."

5. **A.** NO CHANGE
   B. These were soon followed by what we know today as public schools.
   C. Followed soon is what we know today as public schools.
   D. Public schools what we know today followed soon.

6. **F.** NO CHANGE
   G. began to pay their way and attending
   H. begin to pay their way and attend
   J. begin paying their way and attending

7. The writer wishes to add the following sentence without creating a run-on sentence:
   However, elite boarding schools also became fashionable.
   If added, this would best be placed:
   A. as part of the previous sentence, at its beginning, with new punctuation.
   B. as part of the previous sentence, at its end, joined by a semicolon and a conjunction.
   C. as part of the following sentence at its beginning joined by a comma.
   D. as is, standing alone as a sentence.

8. Which of these alternatives provides the most direct conclusion of Paragraph 3?
   F. To stay attuned to their own culture and attend boarding school, children of British administrators were sent back to England.
   G. Children of British administrators attended boarding school, going back to England and stay attuned to their own culture.
   H. Children of British administrators went back to England attending boarding school and staying attuned to their own culture.
   J. British administrators sent their children back to England to attend boarding school and stay attuned to their own culture.

⏱ Timed Writing: Position Statement [30 minutes]

> **Academic Vocabulary**
>
> A position statement is a form of argumentation in which you present and support your position on a topic. As part of your argument, state and refute opposing points.

Jane Eyre is sent to Lowood, a private boarding school, and has to deal with strict teachers and harsh conditions. Charlotte Brontë briefly attended a school like Lowood and clearly did not enjoy the experience. But for many students, boarding school life became a wonderful home away from home and a memorable academic experience.

Write an essay in which you discuss the benefits or drawbacks of boarding school. Support your opinions with sound reasoning, and try to anticipate and address counterarguments.

Constructed Response

 **Common Core State Standards**

RL.11-12.2, RL.11-12.3, RL.11-12.5; RI.11-12.5; W.11-12.2, W.11-12.9.a, W.11-12.4; SL.11-12.1, SL.11-12.4, SL.11-12.6; L.11-12.3.a
[For the complete wording of the standards, see the standards chart in the front of your textbook.]

Directions: *Follow the instructions to complete the tasks below as required by your teacher. As you work on each task, incorporate both general academic vocabulary and literary terms you learned in this unit.*

Writing

Task 1: Literature [RL.11-12.2; W.11-12.2, W.11-12.9.a]
Analyze Development of Themes

Write an **essay** *in which you analyze the development of two themes in a work of fiction from this unit.*

- Choose a story or a novel excerpt from this unit that expresses multiple themes.
- Briefly summarize the story. Identify two themes that develop in the story.
- Analyze how the author introduces and develops those themes over the course of the story.
- Note ways in which the themes interact and build on one another, and discuss how this interaction creates deeper meaning.
- Use transitions to clearly show the relationships and interactions among story elements.
- Use active, not passive, voice.
- Accurately use academic vocabulary in your writing.

Task 2: Literature [RL.11-12.5; W.11-12.4; L.11-12.3.a]
Analyze Text Structure

Write an **essay** *in which you analyze how a poet's choice of structure adds to the overall meaning and aesthetic impact of a poem in this unit.*

- Choose a poem from this unit in which the structure, or form, plays a key role in developing the poem's meaning. Explain which poem you chose and why.
- Analyze how the poet's choices of structure in sections of the poem contribute to the structure of the poem as a whole. Consider line length, rhyme scheme, and meter, as well as stanza lengths and divisions.

- Connect the author's choices concerning structure to the meaning as well as to the aesthetic, or artistic and emotional, impact of the poem. Cite examples from the text to support your thinking.
- Develop and present your ideas while maintaining an appropriate, consistent style and tone in your writing.
- Vary your sentence length and structure to add interest and sophistication to your writing.

Task 3: Literature [RL.11-12.3; W.11-12.2, W.11.12.9.a]
Analyze Character Development

Write an **essay** *in which you analyze the impact of the author's choices regarding how to introduce and develop characters in a work of fiction from this unit.*

- State which fictional characters you will be discussing in your essay and the reasons for your choice.
- Describe each character, including the points at which important information is revealed. Determine what kinds of details the author provides about each character.
- Analyze the role each character plays in the story and explain each character's goals and motivations.
- Explain the connection between characters and theme.
- Sum up your analysis with a conclusion about how the author's choices regarding character development shaped the work of fiction.
- In your writing, use technical academic vocabulary, standard English grammar, and correct spelling.

Speaking and Listening

Task 4: Literature [RL.11-12.2, SL.11-12.6]
Analyze Related Themes

*Prepare and deliver an **oral presentation** in which you analyze two themes expressed in a literary work in this unit and the way in which those themes interact.*

- Select a work that expresses multiple, related themes. Briefly summarize the work and explain why you chose it.
- Explain how the author develops themes over the course of the work. Consider narrative elements such as plot, setting, and character. Also consider literary elements such as symbolism and imagery.
- Explain how the two themes interact and build on each other during the course of the work.
- Cite specific evidence from the text to support your points.
- As you present, use adequate volume and clear pronunciation. Demonstrate a command of formal English.

Task 5: Literature [RL.11-12.3; SL.11-12.1]
Analyze and Compare Speakers

Prepare and conduct a group discussion comparing speakers in two poems in this unit.

- Choose two poems with distinctive speakers that have a good basis for comparison.
- Analyze the speaker in each poem. Consider the choices the poet made as to the speaker. For example, the speaker may be real or fictional, specific or general. Determine each speaker's motivation and conflict. Draw inferences about the character of each speaker based on evidence from the poems.
- Prepare for the discussion. Create a list of questions designed to promote discussion. Make charts on which to record the main points that are brought up during the discussion.
- During the discussion, clarify or challenge ideas; respond thoughtfully to diverse perspectives; and propel conversation by posing and responding to questions.

Task 6: Informational Text [RI.11-12.5; SL.11-12.4]
Analyze Structure

*Prepare and deliver an **oral presentation** in which you analyze an author's use of text structure as part of exposition in a nonfiction work from this unit.*

- Select a work of nonfiction from this unit in which the structure helps to communicate the author's ideas or argument. Briefly explain why you chose this work.
- Define the text's structure. Explain how it enhances or helps to develop the author's ideas or argument. Consider how the text structure serves the author's purpose as well as how it might affect an audience.
- Be sure to provide examples from the text to support your points. Check the pronunciation of challenging words from the text.
- Present your ideas clearly and completely so that your listeners can follow your reasoning.
- While presenting, use formal English, good pronunciation, and adequate volume.

How does literature shape or reflect society?

Victorian Views in Today's World Which aspects of the Victorian Age have meaning and value for us now?

Assignment Imagine that you are compiling a book of Victorian wit and wisdom to be sold today. It will include nuggets of literature that reflect Victorian values. First, select some quotations you would include. Then, write a **preface to the book,** convincing the reader of the value and relevance of the quotations in today's world.

Titles for Extended Reading

In this unit, you have read a variety of British literature from the Victorian period. Continue to read works related to this era on your own. Select books that you enjoy, but challenge yourself to explore new topics, new authors, and works offering varied perspectives or approaches. The titles suggested below will help you get started.

LITERATURE

Wuthering Heights
Emily Brontë

Novel Set on the wild and windy moors of northern Yorkshire, *Wuthering Heights* tells the story of Heathcliff and Catherine, who are desperately in love. The thwarting of their love prompts Heathcliff to seek revenge.

[The poem "Remembrance" by Emily Brontë begins on page 1075. Build knowledge by reading a novel by this author.]

Jane Eyre
Charlotte Brontë   EXEMPLAR TEXT

Novel The title character in this classic novel endures many challenges that give readers insight into the life of a single, middle-class woman in Victorian Britain. After a lonely, difficult childhood, Jane Eyre becomes a governess at the home of Mr. Rochester, a man with a terrible secret.

[An excerpt from Jane Eyre *begins on page 1030 of this book. Build knowledge by reading the complete novel.]*

Hard Times
Charles Dickens

Novel While exposing the harsh realities of poverty in nineteenth-century England, Dickens tells the story of Thomas Gradgrind, a teacher and parent who believes facts alone are all that are needed in life. As life unfolds around him, his views change.

[An excerpt from Hard Times *begins on page 998 of this book. Build knowledge by reading the complete novel.]*

Crime and Punishment
Fyodor Dostoyevsky   EXEMPLAR TEXT

Novel Ex-student Raskolnikov is poor and starving. Though he thinks of himself as a good person, he rationalizes robbing and murdering an old woman by telling himself that she is morally corrupt. His actions soon begin to haunt him, however, and he is forced to face their consequences.

INFORMATIONAL TEXTS

Historical Texts

The Essays of Virginia Woolf
Virginia Woolf
Mariner Books, 1990

Essay This four-volume text includes essays written by Woolf from her early twenties until her death in 1941. Woolf's essays present a personal view of her life, as well as her views on women, writing, literature, and politics.

[Selected works by Virginia Woolf appear on page 1192 of this book. Build knowledge by reading the full text.]

Queen Victoria
Lytton Strachey
Nabu Press, 2010

Biography Get to know Britain's long-reigning and influential queen in this comprehensive and engaging biography—her willful childhood, her joyful marriage to Albert, her sorrow at his death, and her devotion to her servant John Brown.

Contemporary Scholarship

Dickens
Peter Ackroyd

Biography This award-winning biography describes in detail the life of famed British novelist Charles Dickens. Read about his difficult childhood and his rise to popular and critical acclaim as one of the most important writers of his time.

The Ghost Map
Steven Johnson
Riverhead, 2007

Scientific History It is the summer of 1854 and a devastating cholera outbreak has seized London. Dr. John Snow—whose ideas about contagious disease have been dismissed by the scientific community—is spurred into action when his neighbors begin dying.

Preparing to Read Complex Texts

Reading for College and Career In both college and the work-place, readers must analyze texts independently, draw connections among works that offer varied perspectives, and develop their own ideas and informed opinions. The questions shown below, and others that you generate on your own, will help you more effectively read and analyze complex college-level texts.

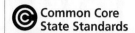

**Common Core
State Standards**

Reading Literature/Informational Text
10. By the end of grade 12, read and comprehend literature, including stories, dramas, and poems, and literary nonfiction at the high end of the grade 11-CCR text complexity band independently and proficiently.

When reading analytically, ask yourself...

- What idea, experience, or story seems to have compelled the author to write? Has the author presented that idea, experience, or story in a way that I, too, find compelling?

- How might the author's era, social status, belief system, or personal experiences have affected the point of view he or she expresses in the text?

- How do my circumstances affect what I understand and feel about this text?

- What key idea does the author state explicitly? What key idea does he or she suggest or imply? Which details in the text help me to perceive implied ideas?

- Do I find multiple layers of meaning in the text? If so, what relationships do I see among these layers of meaning?

- How do details in the text connect or relate to one another? Do I find any details unconvincing, unrelated, or out of place?

- Do I find the text believable and convincing?

**© Key Ideas
and Details**

- What patterns of organization or sequences do I find in the text? Do these patterns help me understand the ideas better?

- What do I notice about the author's style, including his or her diction, uses of imagery and figurative language, and syntax?

- Do I like the author's style? Is the author's style memorable?

- What emotional attitude does the author express toward the topic, the story, or the characters? Does this attitude seem appropriate?

- What emotional attitude does the author express toward me, the reader? Does this attitude seem appropriate?

- What do I notice about the author's voice—his or her personality on the page? Do I like this voice? Does it make me want to read on?

**© Craft and
Structure**

- Is the work fresh and original?

- Do I agree with the author's ideas entirely, or are there elements I find unconvincing?

- Do I disagree with the author's ideas entirely, or are there elements I can accept as true?

- Based on my knowledge of British literature, history, and culture, does this work reflect the British tradition? Why or why not?

**© Integration
of Ideas**

A Time of Rapid Change
The Modern and Postmodern Periods
1901–Present

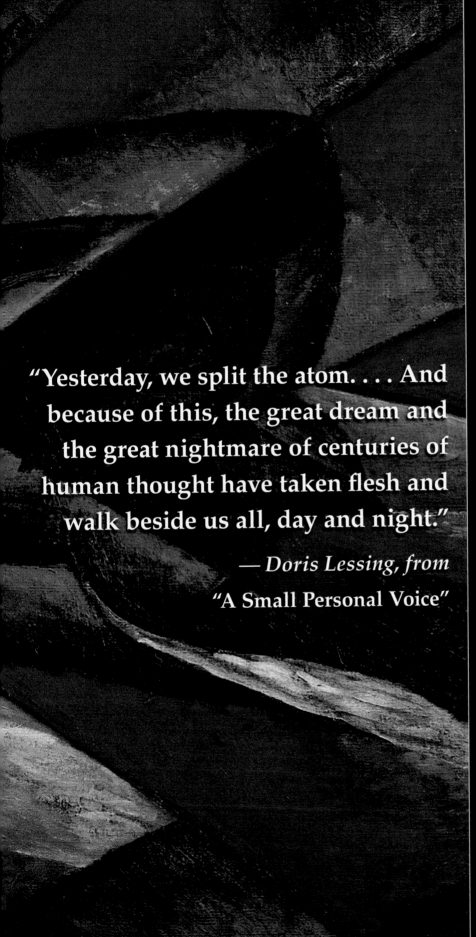

"Yesterday, we split the atom. . . . And because of this, the great dream and the great nightmare of centuries of human thought have taken flesh and walk beside us all, day and night."

— *Doris Lessing, from*
"A Small Personal Voice"

Unit 6

PART 1 TEXT SET

FORGING MODERNISM

PART 2 TEXT SET

MODERNISM IN FICTION

PART 3 TEXT SET

CONFLICTS AT HOME AND ABROAD

PART 4 TEXT SET

THE POSTMODERN AND BEYOND

CLOSE READING TOOL

Use this tool to practice the close reading strategies you learn.

ONLINE WRITER'S NOTEBOOK

Easily capture notes and complete assignments online.

STUDENT eTEXT

Bring learning to life with audio, video, and interactive tools.

■ Find all Digital Resources at **pearsonrealize.com**.

Snapshot of the Period

A Ride on the London Eye

England celebrated the new millennium with the London Eye, a 443-foot Ferris wheel beside the Thames (see page to the right). Picture this wheel as the symbol of a 2,000-year cycle in time. Looking out from it, we might view England's history—waves of invaders from the Romans to the Normans, performances at Shakespeare's Globe, the changing versions of London known to Dr. Johnson, Charles Dickens, and Virginia Woolf. From the top, we might see how England's empire stretched across the globe in the nineteenth century and how, in the twentieth, two world wars led to the loss of that empire. The ride over, we would step onto the soil of twenty-first-century England, once more a nation rather than an empire. It is a nation, however, whose language is spoken across the globe and whose literature is enriched by writers from St. Lucia to Singapore.

These two maps dramatize Britain's loss of its empire in the twentieth century.

British Empire, 1900

Britain Today

As you read the selections in this unit, you will be asked to think about them in view of three key questions:

What is the **relationship** between literature and *place?*

How does literature **shape or** reflect *society?*

What is the relationship of the **writer** to *tradition?*

Integration of Knowledge and Ideas As this London Eye timeline indicates, the end of the British empire was also marked by a renewal of English literature as writers from former colonies made—and are still making—important contributions to the tradition. During what postwar decade did Britain lose most of its colonies? What are three former colonies that have produced Nobel Prize-winning authors who write in English?

GAINING INDEPENDENCE

1947   India and Pakistan

1948   Burma (Myanmar); Sri Lanka

1957   Ghana

1960   Nigeria; Cyprus

1961   Sierra Leone; Tanzania

1962   Jamaica; Trinidad & Tobago; Uganda

1963   Kenya; Malaysia

1964   Malawi; Malta; Zambia

1965   The Gambia; Singapore

1966   Guyana; Botswana; Lesotho

NOBEL PRIZE WINNERS

Rabindrinath Tagore (India)   1913

William Butler Yeats (Ireland)   1923

Samuel Beckett (Ireland)   1969

Wole Soyinka (Nigeria)   1986

Nadine Gordimer (South Africa)   1991

Derek Walcott (St. Lucia)   1992

V.S. Naipaul (Trinidad)   2001

J.M. Coetzee (South Africa)   2003

Doris Lessing (Rhodesia/Zimbabwe)   2007

Historical Background

The Modern and Postmodern Periods (1901–Present)

At dusk on August 3, 1914, Sir Edward Grey, the British Foreign Secretary, clutching the telegram announcing the German invasion of Belgium, walked to the window, looked over a darkening London and said: "The lamps are going out all over Europe; we shall not see them lit again in our lifetime." The next day, Britain declared war on Germany.

World War I and Its Long-Lasting Effects

Many said that the war would be brief, with the troops coming home by Christmas. Instead, the war lasted four long years and 750,000 British soldiers never came home at all. World War I, and the flaws in the treaty with which it was finally settled, influenced much of what followed in the twentieth century.

Germany, for example, wanting to get Russia out of the war and thereby win a victory on the Western Front, transported Lenin to St. Petersburg. There, he led the Bolshevik Revolution that altered the course of Russian and European history.

The war also encouraged Irish nationalists to fight for independence in 1916 while the British army was engaged in France. Their attempted rebellion failed and deepened the hatred between the British and Irish. In 1922, the Irish achieved a measure of independence in the south, but fighting between Catholics and Protestants in the northern, British provinces prolonged the bloodshed for the rest of the century.

The Treaty of Versailles, which settled World War I, led to economic collapse and near-anarchy in Germany, paving the way for Hitler to exact revenge on the Allies.

The horrific slaughter of the war and the crippling effects of the Great Depression forced England into a passive role in the 1930s. Once the mightiest nation in the world, England looked on as a re-armed Germany amassed territory in Europe, and as Japan, perceiving Western powers as weak, occupied much of China.

World War I recruiting poster

TIMELINE

1901: Edward VII becomes king. ▶

1905: Germany Albert Einstein proposes theory of relativity. ▶

1901

1903: Orville and Wilbur Wright build first successful airplane.

1914: Britain enters World War I ▶

World War II and the Loss of the Empire

The aggression of Germany and Japan led inevitably to World War II. When Hitler's armies overran Europe, the English stood defiantly alone, shielded by the English Channel and the Royal Air Force. It was, Winston Churchill said, "their finest hour."

In 1942, Russia blunted the German advance, America was in the war, and the tide turned against the aggressors. After nearly six years of struggle, England emerged from the war victorious, battered, and impoverished.

England's former colonies became independent countries. The Indian subcontinent, where Gandhi had led an independence movement, was divided into the nations of India and Pakistan in 1947.

The imperial British lion gave a dying gasp in 1956 when Britain, France, and Israel invaded Egypt to keep control of the Suez Canal. However, the United States intervened, the Egyptians kept the Canal, and British troops came home to a country ashamed of its government's actions.

Suez was forgotten in the cultural upheaval of the nineteen sixties when British fashion and British rock musicians carried the flag around the world in a kind of cultural conquest. Also, writers from England's former colonies were engaged in their own re-conquest, enriching English literature.

As the century closed, the violence in Northern Ireland seemed to be ending. Also, England pondered its involvement with Europe, not accepting the common currency, the Euro, but cooperating in drilling a tunnel under the English Channel.

Do Sir Edward Grey's words still have a prophetic ring? Many thought the lamps came on again when the Berlin Wall fell. However, countries cobbled together in the aftermath of World War I—Yugoslavia and Iraq— have been the sites of bitter conflict.

The Spitfire fighter played a major role in defending Britain during World War II.

Key Historical Theme: Conflicts and the Loss of Empire

• England emerged victorious but weakened from World War I, which influenced events in Europe for years to come.

• England was on the winning side in World War II as well, but it was weakened further and gradually lost all its colonies.

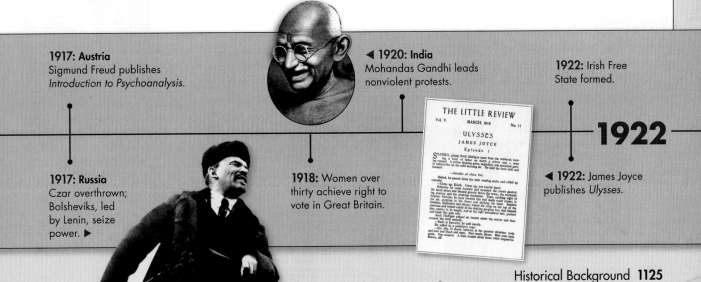

1917: Austria
Sigmund Freud publishes
Introduction to Psychoanalysis.

◀ **1920: India**
Mohandas Gandhi leads
nonviolent protests.

1922: Irish Free
State formed.

1917: Russia
Czar overthrown;
Bolsheviks, led
by Lenin, seize
power. ▶

1918: Women over
thirty achieve right to
vote in Great Britain.

◀ **1922:** James Joyce
publishes *Ulysses.*

1922

Essential Questions Across Time

A Time of Rapid Change (1901–Present)

What is the relationship between literature and *place*?

England in the twentieth century is, of course, a geographic place—an island nation ravaged and rebuilt to an unprecedented degree. It is also a geopolitical place—a "mother country" that stood as a land of hope and glory to many citizens of her far-flung empire. Lastly, it is a place of imagination, a realm of letters and literature fed by the ever-changing English language.

In what ways are the "three Englands" reflected in literature?

The Land Itself The English landscape was untouched by the terrible destruction of World War I. However, the real devastation was human, as an entire generation of young men was wiped out. The physical and psychological damage of the war is documented in poems by soldier poets.

Postwar Growth and Materialism The most obvious change in the landscape after the war came with the automobile. More people could afford cars, and ribbons of highway covered the landscape. Accompanying this economic growth was a materialistic attitude on the part of many, perhaps inspired by the war's devastation. In his story "The Rocking-Horse Winner" (1926), D. H. Lawrence criticizes such materialism and reveals a stylish home as a place haunted by the need for "more money."

World War II and the Blitz The Blitz, from the German *blitzkrieg*, "lightning warfare," refers to the German bombing of English cities during World War II. Large sections of London were destroyed by bombs and rockets, but nothing could break what a song hailed as "London Pride." Elizabeth Bowen's story "The Demon Lover" reflects not so much the actual damage as

---

ESSENTIAL QUESTION VOCABULARY

These Essential Question words will help you think and write about literature and place:

generation (jen´ ər ā´ shən) *n.* all the people born and living at the same time

materialism (mə tir´ ē əl iz´ əm) *n.* belief in comfort, pleasure, and wealth as the highest values

colonial (kə lō´ nē əl) *adj.* of or relating to the colony or colonies of a mother country

TIMELINE

1927: United States
Charles Lindbergh flies solo to Paris. ▼

1939: Europe
Hitler invades Poland; World War II begins. ▶

1922

1939: Britain enters World War II. ▼

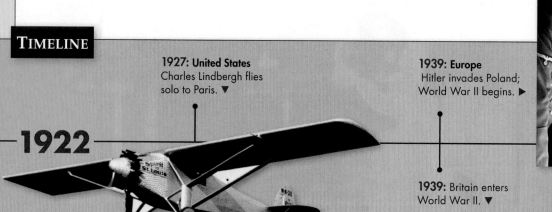

the psychological aftershocks of this assault. Her wartime London is truly a haunted place.

From the ashes, a new London emerged. Other changes were more problematic. The mill and mining country of the north was no longer the economic heart of the country. Wealth concentrated in the south as banking and technology took command. The economic divide between the rusting north and the booming south grew wider as the century ended. The poet Ted Hughes, a northerner, portrays in his work a vision of nature as both glorious and cruel. That vision may be related to the north-south divide.

The England of Hope and Glory In addition to an economic divide, Britain felt the effects of racial and colonial divisions. In V. S. Naipaul's story "B. Wordsworth," England is the distant land of hope and glory to those living in colonial Trinidad, but the dream may be an empty one.

Until 1950, the typical English man or woman was seen as fair-haired, blue eyed, and Anglican. When people of color, British citizens from the former colonies, began to move to England, the English had to deal with unprecedented diversity. In "Midsummer XXIII," Caribbean poet Derek Walcott writes about riots prompted by racial prejudice.

The Realm of the English Language Walcott also raises questions about the English language itself. To whom does the language and its literary tradition belong? Can writers from former colonies and elsewhere in the world find a home in that language and tradition? The evidence, starting with Walcott's own brilliant work, indicates that the answer is yes.

The BRITISH TRADITION

CLOSE-UP ON HISTORY

Planned Town, Unplanned Poet

Sir Ebenezer Howard (1850–1928) was a British social thinker who helped invent the concept of the suburbs. In *Garden Cities of Tomorrow* (1902), Howard described a new kind of planned town surrounded by a ring of farmland. This garden city, as he called it, would combine the advantages of a city with those of the country. Welwyn Garden City, one of the first examples, was built after World War I and inspired the "new towns" that the British government built after World War II. Howard's ideas also inspired Walt Disney's original design for the Experimental Prototype Community of Tomorrow (EPCOT) in Florida.

Unplanned by Howard was the fact that Glyn Maxwell, a talented young poet and playwright, would grow up in a planned town. Humorously calling himself the "Shakespeare of Welwyn Garden City," Maxwell often alludes to Welwyn in his poetry. He has also been known to stage what he calls "large pageant-like shows" in his parents' garden. Given Maxwell's skilled use of poetic forms, perhaps it is true that Sir Ebenezer's talent for planning influenced him after all.

1940: Winston Churchill becomes prime minister. ▶

REMEMBER PEARL HARBOR

1943

1941: United States
Japan bombs Pearl Harbor; United States enters World War II. ▲

How does literature **shape or** reflect *society?*

In what ways did literature reflect new social freedoms?

Women as Bicyclists At the end of the nineteenth and beginning of the twentieth century, the craze for cycling swept England and the Continent. Cycling required a drastic change in the way women dressed. The new freedom in clothing was, however, only a part of the change in pre-World War I England. The strongest social movement of the time was the campaign for women's right to vote. The Suffragettes, women who crusaded for the vote, chained themselves to buildings and went on hunger strikes when arrested. Their victory was slow in coming, but by 1918 women over the age of thirty could vote.

Women as Writers The work of novelist Virginia Woolf revealed a new freedom that women were finding in literature as well. Woolf's experimental fiction broke new ground, and her nonfiction explored the social conditions that would help women succeed in the arts.

The bicycle as product and the right to vote as principle were part of the century-long process of loosening the rigid rules of class, propriety, and morality that had bound the Victorians. This process applied to such areas as access to higher education, health care, marriage laws and customs for ordinary people and the monarchy, home ownership, pensions, and working conditions.

How did writers respond to social crises?

War and Social Change The war of 1914 put most questions of social change on hold, but the men who were "demobbed" (demobilized or discharged) and the women who had coped without them were not going to settle for the old ways. As soldier-poet Siegfried Sassoon wrote of one patrol, "night's misery is ended." However, the years-long "misery" of the war would not be forgotten by those who returned. The

TIMELINE

1945: Japan The United States drops atomic bombs on Hiroshima and Nagasaki. World War II ends as Japan surrenders. ▼

1948: Middle East Israel established.

1943

1947: India and Pakistan gain independence.

1949: China Mao Zedong establishes People's Republic. ▲

aristocracy would have to make do with many fewer servants as men and women found work in new industries (automotive), new jobs (radio), and new forms of entertainment (movies). Higher hemlines and shorter hair signaled that women were freer than ever.

Writers and Politics Then came the 1930s, called by poet W. H. Auden "a low dishonest decade." Auden and fellow poets Louis MacNeice and Stephen Spender responded to such crises as The Great Depression and the Spanish Civil War. In that conflict, the Communist and Fascist tyrannies sparred, foreshadowing the conflict that would come in World War II. Especially shocking was the Nazi-Soviet treaty, a cynical pretense at peace by the totalitarian powers. Men and women on the left and the right were sickened by the callousness of it. Left-wing writer George Orwell, who fought in Spain, would later attack totalitarianism of all kinds in books like *Animal Farm* and *1984*.

Speeches and Poems When war broke out, British Prime Minister Winston Churchill rallied the people for the supreme effort required of them. His radio broadcasts and other speeches— "I have nothing to offer but blood, toil, tears, and sweat"—were classics of their kind. The war indeed brought blood and tears, and the bombs and rockets made all the British combatants and casualties. Literary descendants of the World War I soldier poets, writers like Keith Douglas and Alun Lewis, recorded the cost of conflict.

The BRITISH TRADITION

THE CHANGING ENGLISH LANGUAGE, BY RICHARD LEDERER

Britspeak, A to Zed

At the end of World War II, Winston Churchill tells us, the Allied leaders nearly came to blows over a single word during their negotiations when some diplomats suggested that it was time to "table" an important motion. For the British, table meant that the motion should be put on the table for discussion. For the Americans it meant just the opposite—that it should be put on the shelf and dismissed from discussion.

This confusion serves to illustrate the truth of George Bernard Shaw's pronouncement that "England and America are two countries divided by a common language."

When an American exclaims, "I'm mad about my flat," he is upset about his tire. When a Brit exclaims, "I'm mad about my flat," she's not bemoaning the puncture of her "tyre"; she is delighted with her apartment. When a Brit points out that you have "a ladder in your hose," the situation is not as bizarre as you might at first think. Quite simply, you have a run in your stocking.

With the increasing influence of film, radio, television, and international travel, the two main streams of the English language are rapidly converging like the streets of a circus (British for "traffic circle"). Nonetheless, there are scores of words, phrases, and spellings about which Brits and Yanks still do not agree.

1955: United States
Martin Luther King, Jr., leads civil rights bus boycott. ▶

1961: Germany
Berlin Wall built.

1964: Vietnam
American involvement in the Vietnam War grows.

1964

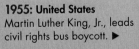

◀ **1957: Russia**
Sputnik I, first satellite, launched.

1963: United States
President John F. Kennedy assassinated. ▶

As soon as the war had ended, however, Churchill was voted out of office and the returning veterans and the survivors of the bombings demanded a new kind of welfare state. Recovery was slow and England was struggling when the twenty-five-year-old Elizabeth became Queen in 1952. She reminded many of Victoria, another shy young woman who had become queen more than a century before, and suddenly things looked brighter.

How did music and literature respond to social changes?

Music and Literature in the Sixties Things were at their brightest in the next decade: the swinging sixties. The Greek philosopher Plato once said: "When the modes of music change, the walls of the city are shaken." The walls were rocked by the Beatles and the Rolling Stones. Not as famous as these songwriters and singers, poets like Ted Hughes and Peter Redgrove nevertheless opened their minds and their styles to a wide range of new influences.

The pendulum slowed in the eighties. Margaret Thatcher, a Conservative Party member and the first female prime minister, reversed many of the socio-economic changes of the previous twenty-five years. Early in her administration, the army and navy crushed Argentina's attempt to seize the Falkland Islands in the South Atlantic. This was the final flick of the imperial lion's tail. She was succeeded by fellow Conservative John Major, but the Labor Party came back into power with Tony Blair's election in 1997.

Literature Celebrates Diversity More capitalistic, more technological, and much more multiracial, the England of Tony Blair entered the twenty-first century in style. That style was maintained in literature as well, as Zadie Smith's acclaimed first novel, *White Teeth* (2000), welcomed the new millennium with a comic celebration of diversity.

The Rolling Stones in performance

ESSENTIAL QUESTION VOCABULARY

These Essential Question words will help you think and write about literature and society:

propriety (prō prī´ ə tē) *n.* display of proper manners or behavior

aristocracy (ar i stä´ krə sē) *n.* ruling class; nobility

fascism (fash´ iz´ əm) *n.* type of government ruled by one party, which puts down all opposition

TIMELINE

1964

1967: The Beatles release *Sgt. Pepper's Lonely Hearts Club Band.* ▲

1969: United States Apollo 11 lands on moon. ▼

1972: Britain imposes direct rule on Northern Ireland.

1975: North Sea oil production begins.

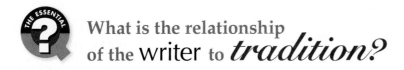

What is the relationship of the writer to *tradition?*

In the twentieth century, the English literary tradition became more accessible and more inclusive. It was more accessible because inexpensive editions of books and the Internet made all of English literature instantly available for writers and readers. It was more inclusive because writers from the former colonies were now enriching the tradition.

How did writers connect with and renew traditions?

Poet as Prophet It was an "outsider," for example, who, following the examples of Romantic poets Blake and Shelley, continued the tradition of prophetic poetry. Irish poet William Butler Yeats summed up the fears of the century in "The Second Coming": "Things fall apart; the center cannot hold . . ."

New Uses for Traditional Forms Twentieth-century writers found new uses for traditional forms such as the sonnet. In twentieth-century hands, the sonnet dealt with experiences undreamed of by the Elizabethans. The radical change in subject matter and tone can be seen by comparing sonnets written by two different World War I poets. The young and dashing Rupert Brooke wrote, in "The Soldier," of the idealism that spurred many of his generation. However, Wilfred Owen's sonnet "Anthem for Doomed Youth" tells what happened when those idealistic young men encountered the turmoil of the Western Front: "What passing bells for those who die as cattle?"

Echoes of Romanticism Although Ted Hughes's lyric "The Horses" differs in many ways from William Wordsworth's "Tintern Abbey," we can still hear an echo of Wordsworth in Hughes's celebration of nature and his distrust of cities.

The Blossoming of the Modern Short Story The modern short story was invented in the nineteenth century. In the twentieth century, however, it became a global genre. Just a few examples will show how authors were setting their tales everywhere and anywhere in the world: James

◀ **1977: Africa**
Djibouti, last remaining European colony, granted independence.

1979: Iran
Ayatollah Khomeini overthrows Shah. ▶

1985

◀ **1979:** Margaret Thatcher becomes first woman prime minister.

Joyce in the streets of Dublin, Joseph Conrad in the jungles of the Malay Archipelago, and Doris Lessing on the Rhodesian veldt.

The subjects of these stories are as varied as their settings. Joyce writes about the coming of age of an infatuated boy. D. H. Lawrence, in "The Rocking-Horse Winner, tells a chilling story of twisted love and destructive greed. Elizabeth Bowen's "The Demon Lover" links both of the World Wars in a few evocative pages. Doris Lessing and Nadine Gordimer deal with the thorny cultural and racial problems of a fading empire.

How did well-crafted poetry capture an unruly world?

A Sestina on "The Troubles" Poets Seamus Heaney, from Northern Ireland, and Derek Walcott, from St. Lucia, both use well-ordered poetry to express the world's disorder. In the sestina "Two Lorries," Heaney writes of the lingering violence in Ireland resulting from an incomplete separation, violence known as "the Troubles." At first glance, a sestina, with its intricate pattern of repeated end words, seems like the wrong form for capturing such a gritty reality. In this poet's hands, however, the repetitions evoke a repeated nightmare of violence that cannot be shaken.

In "Midsummer XXIII," Walcott writes about the violent racism experienced by people of color in "antic England." Like Heaney's, his poem is deeply rooted in the English poetic tradition—it is filled with allusions to earlier work—but also expresses bitter contemporary realities.

What happens to literary traditions in tumultuous times?

Traditions change, especially in times of conflict, but they also endure and connect a living present with a vital past. T. S. Eliot said that any individual talent is best understood in terms of the tradition within which that talent is working. Eliot, who served as an air-raid warden during the Blitz, wrote his poem "Little Gidding" during that dark time. This work links a perilous present to the literary past by invoking Shelley and Milton and the recently deceased Joyce and Yeats, a communion of writers. It invokes them at "the intersection of" a "timeless moment" that somehow contains both past and present—"the timeless moment" of a work of art.

TIMELINE

1985

1989: Germany
Berlin Wall torn down; reunification of East and West Germany follows. ▶

1994: South Africa
Nelson Mandela elected president. ▶

1986: Soviet Union
Nuclear accident occurs in Chernobyl. ▶

1991: Eastern Europe
Soviet Union dissolved.

CONTEMPORARY CONNECTION

George Orwell: More Relevant Than Ever!

Big Brother, Newspeak, and *doublethink* are words that probably sound familiar because you hear them frequently. They were all coined in the 1940s by British author George Orwell for his novel *1984* (published in 1949). After World War II, Orwell was alarmed by a trend toward repressive totalitarian rule. Believing that language is the first weapon dictators use to seize power, he employed his own words as a warning. In the futuristic tyranny portrayed in his novel, words are used to obscure and destroy meaning:

- The official language, *Newspeak,* has been stripped of meaning.

- The tyrannical ruler is deceptively named *Big Brother.*

- Dissenters face torture in the innocently named *Room 101.*

- Citizens are adept at *doublethink,* the ability to accept blatant contradictions, as in the government declaration "War is Peace."

Sixty years later, these terms and others coined by Orwell still ring true. In fact, Orwell's own name is used as an adjective, *Orwellian,* to describe this kind of abuse of language. Pundits, reporters, citizens, and bloggers alike use Orwell's words to criticize Orwellian practices. The year 1984 has come and gone, but Orwell's words live on.

ROOM 101

THAT'S ORWELLIAN!

BIG BROTHER IS WATCHING
>

1997: United Kingdom signs Kyoto Protocol against global warming.

2001: United States Hijacked planes crash into the World Trade Center in New York, the Pentagon in Washington, D.C., and a field in rural Pennsylvania. Thousands of lives are lost. ▶

Present

1997: Tony Blair becomes Prime Minister.

◀ **2004:** Tsunami devastates Southeast Asia.

Recent Scholarship

ANITA DESAI

The English Language Takes Root in India

The Portuguese, the Dutch, and the French all came to India as traders. So did the British, but they stayed to govern. To trade and to govern, you need a common language with the people. In the French colony of Pondicherry, people were taught French; in the Portuguese colony of Goa, Portuguese. In the rest of India, a few English people did learn some Indian languages—in order to compile dictionaries and to translate the Bible—but it was largely left to Indians to learn English if they wanted jobs or to do business. So schools were set up across the country to teach the English language and also its literature.

Two Languages and Two Worlds to Occupy

I went to such a school myself, Queen Mary's School for Girls in Old Delhi. I was taught to read and write English before my own language, Hindi, and my first books were of English nursery rhymes and fairy stories. This was curious because they had nothing at all to do with our Indian world—its plants and animals, its festivals and seasons—but they did provide me with a rich, imagined world, in addition to the one we lived in and knew. And at home, with our families and neighbors, we spoke our own language. So there were always two languages and two worlds to occupy.

About the Author

Introducing Anita Desai (b. 1937) Born to a German mother and an Indian father, Desai spoke German at home in New Delhi, conversed in Hindi with friends, and learned English in school. Her works, written in English, often deal with the conflict between tradition and contemporary life.

THE REAL MOTHER GOOSE

I went on to read the English classics—Jane Austen and George Eliot, Charles Dickens and Henry James—as well as other literatures translated into English. And all the time, I was writing my own books about my own world—but in this other language, English.

Expressing Indian Thoughts in This Foreign Language, English

There were other Indian writers in those years who were also doing so, while continuing to draw upon the rich Indian-language literatures. Each of us had to experiment to find out how to express Indian thoughts and experiences in this foreign language. Sometimes, we had to combine the languages if, say, we were describing an Indian ceremony or a meal for which there were no English words.

After India won independence in 1947, writing in English was looked on with scorn. The English were gone, so why were we still using their language? We found ourselves having to explain how, after three hundred years, a language could not simply vanish or be thrown aside. It had established roots in India and by now had a tradition—not as old as the literary traditions in the Indian languages but still, a living, growing one that belonged to our own complicated times.

A New Form of the Language: Indian English

Then, in 1980, a book called *Midnight's Children* by Salman Rushdie was published. It was based

on our own themes—the fight for freedom and the birth of two nations, India and Pakistan—and used our own epics, the *Mahabharata* and the *Ramayana* as sources. But it was written in the polyglot language of the Indian streets, of newspapers and shop signs, the cinema and school grounds. It was a bold, noisy, loud, and funny language. Rushdie's work won the Booker Prize, which showed that the English, too, were ready to read this new form of their language—Indian English.

It gave many young writers in India the confidence to use Indian English. So things came together at last, and now there is as lively a literature in English as in Bengali and Tamil, Urdu and Hindi, to name just a few of the Indian languages. If you look into it, I think you will find it as crowded and colorful and bustling as an Indian market or fair.

Speaking and Listening: Collaboration

Anita Desai describes the language she uses in her work as a new form of English—Indian English. With a group of classmates, develop a **presentation** on the varieties of English in your school or community. These varieties may include versions of English with different degrees of formality, types of English used by different age groups, and types of English influenced by other languages. Develop a *comprehensive flexible search plan,* using *clear research questions* and *strategies* like these:

- Oral histories—in-depth interviews with individuals
- Field studies—observation and notetaking in public places
- Surveys—use of questionnaires to obtain information from numbers of people

Take steps to ensure that your interviews, observations, and questionnaires are *objective* and *free from bias*—that they don't reflect prejudice against any language uses. Finally, summarize your findings in a presentation to your classmates.

Indian women cheer Lord and Lady Mountbatten, who are followed by Pandit Nehru, the Indian prime minister. This ceremony marks the British departure from India, a newly independent nation (June 25, 1948).

Integrate and Evaluate Information

1. Use a chart like the one shown to determine the key ideas expressed in the Essential Question essays on pages 1126–1132. Fill in two ideas related to each Essential Question and note the author or group most closely associated with each concept. One example has been done for you.

Essential Question	Key Concept	Author or Group
Literature and Place	Bombing of England in WWII	Winston Churchill
Literature and Society		
Writer and Tradition		

2. For England, as for much of the world, the twentieth century was a time of dramatic social, political, and technological change. Choose three visual sources from this section, one reflecting each kind of change. Describe the image and explain its impact on England during this period.

3. In "The Second Coming," William Butler Yeats wrote that "Things fall apart; the center cannot hold…." How do these words describe the British Empire over the course of the twentieth century? Explain, citing evidence from the multiple sources presented on pages 1122–1133.

4. **Address a Question:** Anita Desai grew up speaking three different languages—German at home, Hindi with friends, and English at school. Even if you speak only one language, you probably use different versions of that language in various social contexts. Explain how you use different "languages" in your life, using information from "Britspeak, A to Zed" on page 1129 as well as other sources to support your ideas.

Speaking and Listening: Book Talk

Authors from former British colonies who write in English often use language that reflects their countries of origin. With a partner, prepare a **book talk** illustrating this idea. Choose four or five contemporary writers from countries such as India, Jamaica, Nigeria, Pakistan, and South Africa. Prepare a talk in which you discuss connections between the authors' cultural experiences and their writing.

Solve a Research Problem: This assignment requires you to research and synthesize a great deal of complex material. Work with your partner to formulate a research plan that includes the authors' writings, biographical materials, and reviews. Consult both print and electronic sources. For each author you cover, provide the following content:

- Name, with correct pronunciation; date of birth; native country
- Titles of one or two books, with brief summaries
- Clear explanation, using formal English, of the author's style, subject matter, and cultural influences
- Brief recitation from the author's work to show the influence of place

 **Common Core State Standards**

Reading Informational Text
7. Integrate and evaluate multiple sources of information presented in different media or formats as well as in words in order to address a question or solve a problem.

Speaking and Listening
4. Present information, findings, and supporting evidence, conveying a clear and distinct perspective.

6. Adapt speech to a variety of contexts and tasks, demonstrating a command of formal English when indicated or appropriate.

ESSENTIAL QUESTION VOCABULARY

Use these words in your responses:

Literature and Place
generation
materialism
colonial

Literature and Society
propriety
aristocracy
fascism

Writer and Tradition
inclusive
evocative
allusions

Forging Modernism

Connecting to the Essential Question Yeats felt a deep connection to Ireland. As you read, note details in Yeats's poems that evoke a sense of place. Noticing these details will help you think about the Essential Question: **What is the relationship between literature and place?**

Close Reading Focus

Philosophical System; Symbol

Yeats created a unique **philosophical system,** or set of ideas about fundamental truths, woven from his own insights and the ideas of many thinkers. To express his philosophy in his poetry, Yeats used symbols. A **symbol** is an image, character, object, or action with these functions:

- It stands for something beyond itself, such as an abstract idea.
- It gives rise to a number of associations.
- It intensifies feelings and adds complexity to meaning by concentrating these associations together.

The swans in "The Wild Swans at Coole," for example, combine associations of beauty (they are attractive), purity (they are white), freedom (they are wild), and the eternal (they return every year). Over time, Yeats consistently used certain symbols to express his philosophical system, which is described in more detail in the graphic Literature in Context feature on page 1144. As you read, consider how this philosophy shapes the meaning of his poems, particularly "The Second Coming" and "Sailing to Byzantium."

Preparing to Read Complex Texts

As a poet, Yeats uses vivid language and rich symbols to make his philosophical arguments, relying on the emotional impact of specific word choices and symbolic images to convey meaning and "convince" his readers. As you read, **analyze Yeats's philosophical assumptions** by analyzing the emotional impact of his word choices and symbolic images. Use a chart like the one shown. To ensure that you appreciate his word choice, consult a dictionary as needed to determine the connotations as well as the literal meanings of unfamiliar words.

Vocabulary

The words below are important to understanding the texts that follow. Copy the words into your notebook, sorting them into words you know and words you do not know.

clamorous	conviction
conquest	paltry
anarchy	artifice

**Common Core
State Standards**

Reading Literature
4. Determine the meaning of words and phrases as they are used in the text, including figurative and connotative meanings; analyze the impact of specific word choices on meaning and tone, including words with multiple meanings or language that is particularly fresh, engaging, or beautiful.

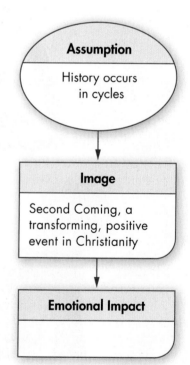

Assumption

History occurs in cycles

Image

Second Coming, a transforming, positive event in Christianity

Emotional Impact

Author of **Poetry of William Butler Yeats**

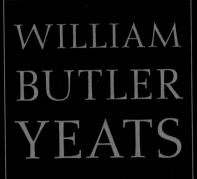

The twentieth century was a time of change, marked by unprecedented world wars, revolutions, technological innovations, and a mass media explosion. Even as the winds of change threatened to sweep away old traditions, the Irish poet William Butler Yeats delved deep into his nation's mythological past for insight. Winner of the Nobel Prize for Literature in 1923, Yeats is generally regarded as one of the finest poets of the century. His return to the past helped earn him an abiding place in the future.

Born in Dublin, Ireland, Yeats was educated there and in London. His heart lay to the west, though, in County Sligo, where he spent childhood vacations with his grandparents. In the shadow of Sligo's barren mountains, the young Yeats was immersed in the mythology and legends of Ireland. This experience led to a lifelong enthusiasm for the roots of Irish culture.

Philosophical Influences After three years of studying painting in Dublin, Yeats moved to London to pursue a literary career. He became a friend of the poet Arthur Symons, who awakened his interest in the symbolic, visionary poetry of William Blake and the delicate, musical verse of the French Symbolists. Yeats's early poems show Symbolist influences as well as an affinity with the Pre-Raphaelites, a group of nineteenth-century British painters and writers who turned to medieval art as they strove for simplicity and beauty.

From Poetry to Plays to Poetry As the century turned, Yeats became interested in drama. He joined with his friend Lady Augusta Gregory in founding the Irish National Theatre Society. In 1892, Yeats had written *The Countess Cathleen,* a play that was to become one of his most popular dramatic works. With the acquisition and opening of the Abbey Theatre in Dublin, Yeats turned increasingly to writing plays. When Yeats returned to poetry, it was with a new voice, subtler and more powerful than the one he had used before. The poems in *The Tower* (1928) show Yeats at the height of his abilities. "Sailing to Byzantium" dates from this period of his work.

Ireland's Hero On his seventieth birthday, he was hailed by his nation as the greatest living Irishman. Though Yeats's quarrels with the tastes and politics of middle-class Ireland were often fierce, no one could deny his stature. He continued to write up until a day or two before his death in France. One of his last poems contains his famous epitaph: "Cast a cold eye / On life, on death. / Horseman, pass by!"

(1865–1939)

"THINGS FALL APART; THE CENTER CANNOT HOLD..."

WHEN YOU ARE OLD

WILLIAM BUTLER YEATS

When you are old and gray and full of sleep,
And nodding by the fire, take down this book,
And slowly read, and dream of the soft look
Your eyes had once, and of their shadows deep;

5 How many loved your moments of glad grace,
And loved your beauty with love false or true,
But one man loved the pilgrim soul in you,
And loved the sorrows of your changing face;

And bending down beside the glowing bars,
10 Murmur, a little sadly, how Love fled
And paced upon the mountains overhead
And hid his face amid a crowd of stars.

The Lake Isle of Innisfree

WILLIAM BUTLER YEATS

I will arise and go now, and go to Innisfree,
And a small cabin build there, of clay and wattles[1] made:
Nine bean-rows will I have there, a hive for the honeybee,
And live alone in the bee-loud glade.

5   And I shall have some peace there, for peace comes dropping slow,
Dropping from the veils of the morning to where the cricket sings;
There midnight's all a glimmer, and noon a purple glow,
And evening full of the linnet's wings.[2]

I will arise and go now, for always night and day
10 I hear lake water lapping with low sounds by the shore:
While I stand on the roadway, or on the pavements gray,
I hear it in the deep heart's core.

---

1. **wattles** stakes interwoven with twigs or branches.
2. **linnet's wings** wings of a European singing bird.

Analyzing Philosophical Assumptions

What kind of ideal life does Yeats envision in the first stanza?

Critical Reading

1. **Key Ideas and Details (a)** What "comes dropping slow" at Innisfree? **(b) Infer:** How does life at Innisfree contrast with the speaker's current life?

2. **Integration of Knowledge and Ideas Compare and Contrast:** Do you think that "Innisfree" and "When You Are Old" suggest that writing poetry is a way of compensating for disappointments? Why or why not?

Cite textual evidence to support your responses.

THE WILD SWANS AT COOLE

WILLIAM BUTLER YEATS

▲ **Critical Viewing**
Why might Yeats describe swans such as this one as "mysterious" and "beautiful"? **INFER**

The trees are in their autumn beauty,
The woodland paths are dry,
Under the October twilight the water
Mirrors a still sky;
5   Upon the brimming water among the stones
Are nine-and-fifty swans.

The nineteenth autumn has come upon me
Since I first made my count;
I saw, before I had well finished,
10   All suddenly mount
And scatter wheeling in great broken rings
Upon their clamorous wings.

Vocabulary
clamorous (klam´ ər əs) *adj.*
loud and confused; noisy

I have looked upon those brilliant creatures,
And now my heart is sore.

15 All's changed since I, hearing at twilight,
The first time on this shore,
The bell-beat of their wings above my head,
Trod with a lighter tread.

Unwearied still, lover by lover,
20 They paddle in the cold
Companionable streams or climb the air;
Their hearts have not grown old;
Passion or conquest, wander where they will,
Attend upon them still.

25 But now they drift on the still water,
Mysterious, beautiful;
Among what rushes will they build,
By what lake's edge or pool
Delight men's eyes when I awake some day
30 To find they have flown away?

Vocabulary
conquest (kän´ kwest´) *n.*
the winning of the sub-
mission or affection of

Symbolism
What might the swans
symbolize?

Critical Reading

Cite textual evidence to support your responses.

1. **Key Ideas and Details (a) Where** is the poem set? **(b) Interpret:**
   How does the time of year reflect the speaker's place in life?
   (c) Analyze: Which details suggest the passing of time?

2. **Key Ideas and Details (a)** When the speaker first counted the
   swans, what did they suddenly do? **(b) Interpret:** What reflection does the memory of their action prompt in the speaker?

3. **Key Ideas and Details (a) Infer:** What has changed in the
   speaker since he first heard the swans? **(b) Compare and
   Contrast:** How does the swans' condition contrast with that of
   the speaker?

4. **Integration of Knowledge and Ideas (a) Interpret:** The
   speaker says he will "awake some day / To find they have
   flown away?" What event might this flight represent for him?
   (b) Draw Conclusions: How does this imagined absence
   increase the poignancy of the sight of the swans?

5. **Integration of Knowledge and Ideas (a) Interpret:** In what
   way does the sight of the swans help the speaker measure the
   passage of time? **(b) Apply:** Compare this experience with
   another way in which people measure the passage of time.

YEATS'S PHILOSOPHY

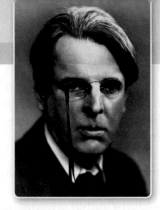

Yeats developed a philosophy that united his interest in history, art, personality, and society. His basic insight was that, in all these fields, conflicting forces are at work. In history, for example, as one kind of civilization grows and eventually dies, an opposite kind of civilization is born to take its place. Similarly, human personalities can be defined as opposites: the creative or subjective person versus the active or objective person.

Gyres
To visualize the conflict of opposites, Yeats uses gyres [jierz]. In two dimensions, these look like triangles.

Objectivity
Subjectivity

Circles and Wheels
Because Yeats wanted to imagine completion as well as conflict, he placed a circle around the two gyres. This circle he called The Great Wheel. He labeled it with compass points, qualities, and phases of the moon. He said this wheel is "every completed movement of thought or life."

However, Yeats pictured them as helixes, whirling forms of motion.

Interpenetrating gyres showed how two different forces struggled against one another, moving from left to right, and back again. This movement could describe the development of a personality or the rise and fall of civilizations.

Byzantium: Perfect Place and Time
For Yeats, the perfect era in the cycle was the Byzantine Empire in the early sixth century A.D. It stands for an escape from time's wheel because "in early Byzantium, maybe never before or since . . ., religious, aesthetic and practical life were one." Artists' work spoke directly to the people.

CONNECT TO THE LITERATURE

Does knowing some of Yeats's philosophical ideas help you better understand poems like "The Second Coming" and "Sailing to Byzantium"? Explain.

The Second Coming

WILLIAM BUTLER YEATS

BACKGROUND In 1925, Yeats published *A Vision*, a work that explained the mythology, symbolism, and philosophy that he strove to express in his poetry. Yeats believed that history occurs in two-thousand-year cycles, during which a particular civilization is born, grows, and decays. Each civilization then gives way to a new one that is the direct opposite of it. Yeats believed that the society of the early twentieth century was decaying and would lead to another sort of rebirth, very different from the birth of Christ. These ideas are vividly expressed in the poem "The Second Coming."

Turning and turning in the widening gyre
The falcon cannot hear the falconer;
Things fall apart; the center cannot hold;
Mere anarchy is loosed upon the world,
5　The blood-dimmed tide is loosed, and everywhere
The ceremony of innocence is drowned;
The best lack all conviction, while the worst
Are full of passionate intensity.[1]

---

1. Mere . . . intensity refers to the Russian Revolution of 1917.

Vocabulary
anarchy (an´ ər kē) *n.* absence of government; disorder

conviction (kən vik´ shən) *n.* belief; faith

Surely some revelation is at hand;
10 Surely the Second Coming is at hand.
The Second Coming! Hardly are those words out
When a vast image out of *Spiritus Mundi*[2]
Troubles my sight: somewhere in sands of the desert
A shape with lion body and the head of a man,[3]
15 A gaze blank and pitiless as the sun,
Is moving its slow thighs, while all about it
Reel shadows of the indignant desert birds.
The darkness drops again; but now I know
That twenty centuries[4] of stony sleep
20 Were vexed to nightmare by a rocking cradle,[5]
And what rough beast, its hour come round at last,
Slouches towards Bethlehem to be born?

Philosophical System

What elements of Yeats's philosophy does "The Second Coming" contain?

---

2. Spiritus Mundi (spir´ i təs moon´ dē) Universal Spirit or Soul, in which the memories of the entire human race are forever preserved.

3. A . . . man the Sphinx, a monster in Greek mythology that posed a riddle to passing travelers and destroyed those who could not answer it. The answer to the riddle was "man."

4. twenty centuries historical cycle preceding the birth of Christ.

5. rocking cradle cradle of Jesus Christ.

Critical Reading

Cite textual evidence to support your responses.

1. **Key Ideas and Details** **(a)** In the first two lines of the poem, why does the falcon not return to the falconer, as it ordinarily would? **(b) Analyze:** Why is the image of the falcon an effective introduction to Yeats's ideas about order and innocence?

2. **Key Ideas and Details** **(a)** At the beginning of the second stanza, what does the speaker believe is at hand? **(b) Interpret:** What era of history might the vision in lines 11–17 represent? Explain. **(c) Interpret:** In what sense did a past birth in Bethlehem bring this era to an end?

3. **Key Ideas and Details** **(a) Analyze:** What birth does the speaker predict will end the modern era? **(b) Draw Conclusions:** How does the traditional idea of the Second Coming differ from what the speaker is envisioning?

4. **Integration of Knowledge and Ideas** Yeats draws on his own theories of history for the theme and imagery of this poem. Why might the poem be appreciated even by readers who do not share his beliefs?

5. **Integration of Knowledge and Ideas** In your opinion, do any contemporary events bear out Yeats's vision of history? Explain.

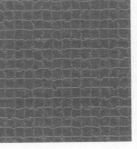

SAILING TO BYZANTIUM

William Butler Yeats

I

That is no country for old men. The young
In one another's arms, birds in the trees
—Those dying generations—at their song,
The salmon-falls, the mackerel-crowded seas,
5 Fish, flesh, or fowl, commend all summer long
Whatever is begotten, born, and dies.
Caught in that sensual music all neglect
Monuments of unaging intellect.

II

An aged man is but a paltry thing,
10 A tattered coat upon a stick, unless
Soul clap its hands and sing, and louder sing
For every tatter in its mortal dress,
Nor is there singing school but studying
Monuments of its own magnificence;
15 And therefore I have sailed the seas and come
To the holy city of Byzantium.[1]

III

O sages standing in God's holy fire
As in the gold mosaic of a wall,[2]

Vocabulary
paltry (pôl′ trē) *adj.*
practically worthless;
insignificant

Comprehension
What does the speaker's age
motivate him to do?

---

1. **Byzantium** (bi zan′ shē əm) ancient capital of the Eastern Roman (or Byzantine) Empire
and the seat of the Greek Orthodox Church; today, Istanbul, Turkey. For Yeats, Byzantium
symbolized the world of art as opposed to the world of time and nature.
2. **sages . . . wall** wise men portrayed in mosaic on the walls of Byzantine churches.

Come from the holy fire, perne in a gyre,[3]
20 And be the singing-masters of my soul.
Consume my heart away; sick with desire
And fastened to a dying animal
It knows not what it is; and gather me
Into the artifice of eternity.

IV

25 Once out of nature I shall never take
My bodily form from any natural thing,
But such a form as Grecian goldsmiths make
Of hammered gold and gold enameling
To keep a drowsy Emperor awake;
30 Or set upon a golden bough to sing[4]
To lords and ladies of Byzantium
Of what is past, or passing, or to come.

Analyzing Philosophical Assumptions

What does the last stanza suggest about the artist's relationship to nature and time?

---

3. **perne . . . gyre** spin in a spiraling motion.
4. **To . . . sing** Yeats wrote, "I have read somewhere that in the Emperor's palace at Byzantium was a tree made of gold and silver, and artificial birds that sang."

Critical Reading

Cite textual evidence to support your responses.

1. **Key Ideas and Details (a)** What do the people and things of the country referred to in the first stanza "commend"? What do they "neglect"? **(b) Interpret:** What "country" is Yeats describing in the first stanza?

2. **Key Ideas and Details (a)** What is an "aged man," according to the second stanza? **(b) Interpret:** Why might the aged not belong to the "country" of the first stanza?

3. **Key Ideas and Details (a) Interpret:** In the third stanza, what does the speaker ask the sages to change in him? **(b) Draw Conclusions:** What does this request reveal about the speaker's faith in artistic production?

4. **Integration of Knowledge and Ideas Make a Judgment:** In your view, which is a "dream"—Byzantium or the world of what "is begotten, born, and dies"?

5. **Integration of Knowledge and Ideas** How is Yeats's poetry affected by both real and imagined places? Use at least three of these Essential Question words in your response: *ideal, locate, occur, affect, significance, constant.* *[Connecting to the Essential Question: What is the relationship between literature and place?]*

Literary Analysis

1. **Key Ideas and Details (a)** In "When You Are Old," Yeats refers to "Love" as a person. What ideas are traditionally associated with love? **(b)** How does the behavior of Love in the poem compare to that traditional image?

2. **Craft and Structure (a)** What associations does the speaker in "The Lake Isle of Innisfree" build around the **symbol** of Innisfree? **(b)** Explain two things Innisfree might symbolize.

3. **Key Ideas and Details (a)** What emotions does the speaker in "The Lake Isle of Innisfree" express? **(b)** What does the speaker in "The Wild Swans at Coole" express? **(c)** Explain how Yeats's word choice helps convey these feelings.

4. **Key Ideas and Details** Explain what the dry "woodland paths," the "October twilight," and the "still sky" symbolize in "The Wild Swans at Coole."

5. **Key Ideas and Details** "The Second Coming" is a poem strongly influenced by Yeats's **philosophical system. (a)** In the poem, how does Yeats characterize the period of transition between the end of one civilization and the beginning of another? **(b)** How does humanity respond to these times of crisis?

6. **Craft and Structure** Use a chart like the one below to compare the birds in the first and second stanzas of "The Second Coming." How do these symbols contribute to the meaning of the poem?

Symbol	Associations	Effect on Meaning
Falcon		

7. **Craft and Structure (a)** In "Sailing to Byzantium," what do the monuments in lines 8 and 14 symbolize? **(b)** Find two examples in this poem of Yeats's use of Byzantine art to symbolize perfection.

8. **Craft and Structure** How does Yeats use the symbol of the "gyre" in "The Second Coming" and "Sailing to Byzantium"?

9. **Integration of Knowledge and Ideas Analyze Yeats's philosophical assumptions** by assessing the emotional impact of his symbols. **(a)** Compare the emotional effect and meaning of the swans in "The Wild Swans at Coole" and the birds in "Sailing to Byzantium." **(b)** Based on those meanings, what conclusion could you draw about how Yeats's attitude toward nature changed during his life?

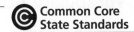

Common Core State Standards

Writing

1. Write arguments to support claims in an analysis of substantive topics or texts, using valid reasoning and relevant and sufficient evidence. *(p. 1150)*

5. Develop and strengthen writing as needed by planning, revising, editing, rewriting, or trying a new approach, focusing on addressing what is most significant for a specific purpose and audience. *(p. 1150)*

Language

4.d. Verify the preliminary determination of the meaning of a word or phrase. *(p. 1150)*

Vocabulary Acquisition and Use

Word Analysis: Words with the Greek Root -archy-

In "The Second Coming," Yeats uses the word *anarchy*. The word combines the prefix *an-*, meaning "not," and the Greek root *-archy*, which means "ruler." *Anarchy*, then, is the condition of having no ruler, or government. Use context to determine the meanings of the italicized words. Explain those meanings in a sentence. You may consult a dictionary to confirm the meanings.

1. In a *matriarchy*, mothers own the land and pass it on to their daughters.
2. The oldest surviving child of the king gains the throne in a *monarchy*.
3. In the army's *hierarchy*, each member obeys the orders of those with higher rank.
4. The Council of Ten was a powerful *oligarchy* that led a country of millions.
5. The family was a *patriarchy*, and the father's word had to be followed.

Vocabulary: Synonyms

A synonym is a word that has a meaning similar to that of another word. Replace each italicized word below with a synonym from the vocabulary list on page 1138. Use each vocabulary word only once. Then write two original sentences, each using one of the vocabulary words.

1. His *trickery* managed to convince the gullible victim.
2. *Chaos* resulted when the government leaders fled.
3. She had the power gained from certainty in her *beliefs*.
4. The *insignificant* sum was hardly sufficient recompense for the damage done.
5. With her final victory in the chess tournament, her *triumph* was complete.
6. The *noisy* crowd shouted the speaker down.

Writing to Sources

Argumentative Text Critic Richard Ellmann writes that Yeats's poetry is based on the opposition between "the world of change" and a world of "changelessness." Write a **response** in which you find evidence of this opposition in Yeats's poems.

Prewriting Note uses of imagery, language, or ideas that represent change or changelessness. Review your examples to see if they mainly support or refute Ellmann's claim, and decide whether you agree or disagree with his view.

Drafting Begin your draft by summarizing Ellmann's position and stating your response to it. Support your generalizations with quotations from Yeats's writing. Introduce each quotation and explain how it supports the point you are making.

Revising Review your draft, highlighting generalizations and looking for supporting details. Where details are lacking, look back at Yeats's poems to find supporting details. Be sure that the titles of Yeats's poems and the quotations you use from them are accurate.

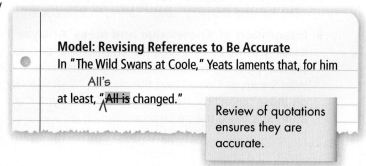

Model: Revising References to Be Accurate
In "The Wild Swans at Coole," Yeats laments that, for him
                                    All's
at least, "~~All is~~ changed."

Review of quotations ensures they are accurate.

Conventions and Style: Sentence Fragments and Run-ons

In most writing, except for dialogue in fiction, it is important to avoid sentence fragments and run-on sentences. A **sentence fragment** is an incomplete sentence punctuated as a sentence. It may be missing a subject, a verb, or both, and it fails to express a complete thought. Fragments are often phrases or subordinate clauses.

Fragment (lacking a verb): The lover old and gray sitting by the fire.

Add a verb: The lover grew old and gray sitting by the fire.

A **run-on sentence** is two or more sentences punctuated as one. **Fused sentences** and **comma splices** are two types of run-ons:

Fused sentence: The trees are beautiful in the fall the still water reflects the sky.

Corrected by rewriting: The trees are beautiful in the fall when the still water reflects the sky.

Comma splice: Many love a woman's beauty, few will love the inner person.

Corrected by adding a conjunction: Many love a woman's beauty, but few will love the inner person.

Punctuation Tip If the two parts of a run-on sentence are related, you can connect them with a semicolon.

Practice: Identify each of the following items as a fragment, a run-on, or a complete sentence. If an item is a fragment or a run-on, rewrite it.

1. The sound of water remains in the memory it gives calm in a cold, gray world.
2. Swans do not seem to weary from the cares of the world as humans do.
3. The swans swim across the water. Or take off and fly through the air.
4. On the still water, swans mysterious and lovely.
5. In fall, swans migrate. In noisy flight.
6. Things that live and breathe must one day die it is the way of the world.
7. When there is no order, things collapse disorder rules the world.
8. People grow old and worthless, monuments are timeless.
9. Art that captures the sound of birds hammered in gold. Lives on through time.
10. Yeats believed in historical cycles of twenty centuries.

Writing and Speaking Conventions

A. Writing Find three fragments and two run-ons in the paragraph below. Rewrite the paragraph so that each sentence is complete.

A small cabin at Innisfree. The cabin is built of clay and sticks, the cabin provides shelter and peace. A place for a garden and hive for the bees. In the morning the cricket sings in the evening songbirds fill the air with music. Outside the water against the shore.

Example: A small cabin at Innisfree.

Rewritten: There's a small cabin at Innisfree.

B. Speaking Write and present to the class a brief explanation of whether you believe Yeats's predictions are proving true or false in the twenty-first century. Be sure to check your writing for fragments and run-ons.

Literary History:
T. S. Eliot's World

Modernists like T. S. Eliot responded to an increasingly complex and fragmented world with art that was also complex, dark, and multifaceted.

Modernism and Beyond

At the beginning of the twentieth century, the world woke up and discovered that it had changed. Electricity, engines, telephones, radios—the globe crackled with new energy. Airplanes, machine guns, and chemical warfare enabled human beings to destroy each other with horrendous efficiency. The First World War (1914–1918) claimed twenty million lives. Disillusionment with politics and society was common.

In this climate of change and uncertainty, artists broke with the past and began to pursue new ideals and visions. They began to see themselves not just as preservers of culture but as creators of culture; they did not simply follow traditions, they created new ones. These dramatic trends in the arts in the early twentieth century are collectively known as Modernism (1890–1945).

Images of Modernism When you take a photograph, you record and preserve what is happening now. Modernism could be thought of as a complex response to what photographs imply. Some Modernists, such as the American poet Ezra Pound (1885–1972) and the British poet T. S. Eliot (1888–1965), wrote poetry as if they were taking snapshots of the world and then cutting and pasting them into collages. Eliot celebrated what he called objectivity in poetry. He relied on images, well chosen and artfully rendered, to encapsulate a feeling or perspective.

On the other hand, the British Modernist novelist Virginia Woolf (1882–1941) perfected techniques for conveying an individual's moment-by-moment experience. For Woolf, the mind is like a camera filming continuously. Her writing records what the moment looks like to an individual. A photograph shows us exactly what the world looks like; Woolf suggests that what the world looks like depends on who is looking.

Visual Arts Photography makes a good analogy for Modernist literary developments. It had a clear impact on painting. Photography now had the job of recording literal appearances, so artists were freed from the necessity of directly imitating the look of things. The revolutionary French painter Paul Cézanne (1839–1906) began to emphasize the canvas as a two-dimensional arrangement of form and color. His work led to the innovations of Modernists such as Pablo Picasso (1881–1973), whose

Les Desmoiselles d'Avignon is the first Cubist painting—a picture in which multiple perspectives on the subject are depicted simultaneously.

Past, Present, and Future Time is a central theme of Modernism. To a photographer, every moment in time is equal to every other, another present to be captured. Yet Eliot was deeply preoccupied with the thought that the past and present are quite unequal. In a poem like "Journey of the Magi" (p. 1158), Eliot portrays the present as a time of despair, an emptiness left behind when the past has disappeared.

Making the New At the same time that Eliot seemed to mourn the past, Modernism also turned toward the future. Modernist fiction writers broke with traditional narrative methods. Describing how characters saw their lives became more important than constructing a traditional plot, and endings were sometimes unresolved. Modernist poets, too, favored experimentation over traditional forms and rhyme schemes. Their poems draw images from a variety of sources, such as history, everyday life, and other texts and cultures.

Beyond Modernism The Modernist literary movement climaxed in 1922, when both James Joyce's *Ulysses* and T. S. Eliot's *The Waste Land* were published. In ensuing decades, the arts took another turn in the developments known as Postmodernism, a movement that replaced the hopes Modernism placed on innovative artistic breakthroughs with a sometimes cynical questioning of the nature of art and perception. The Modernist legacy lives on, though, in the continuing drive for the new.

Speaking and Listening: Discussion

Comprehension and Collaboration Photography was invented in the nineteenth century and evolved aesthetically and technologically through the twentieth century. Today, photography is both an art form and a technology accessible to nearly everyone. With a group, discuss photography's changing role in art and culture. Use the list of questions provided to guide your discussion.

Prepare by researching photography as both popular hobby and art form. Assign group members to specific research tasks, using these questions to focus the work:

- How has digital technology changed photography?
- With the technology to retouch photographs, have we strayed completely from the Modernist idea that an image captures a moment forever?
- If anyone can take a picture, what makes photography an art form?

As a group, assign roles for the discussion, such as moderator and note-taker. Agree upon a set of rules to ensure all members participate fully. Choose a point person to share your conclusions with the class.

Connecting to the Essential Question T. S. Eliot broke dramatically with traditional poetry. As you read, notice details in Eliot's poems that show differences from traditional poetic themes, meter, or language. Doing so will help you think about the Essential Question: **What is the relationship of the writer to tradition?**

Close Reading Focus

Modernism

Modernism was an early-twentieth-century movement in the arts. The movement responded to the fragmented modern world created by industrialization, rapid transportation and communication, and a feeling of alienation caused by mass society and the growth of cities. Eliot led the movement for Modernism in poetry, which had several features:

- A new objectivity or impersonality in poetry, in which a work is built from images and allusions rather than from direct statements of thoughts and feelings
- A rejection of realistic depictions of life in favor of the use of images for artistic effect
- Critical attention to the social conditions and spiritual troubles of modern life, often accompanied by a sense of displacement and despair

As you read, look for details that reflect Modernism in Eliot's poems.

Preparing to Read Complex Texts Modernist writers found their society bleak and lifeless. They saw crowded cities as places of isolation and loneliness. They believed that the new emphasis on material goods and technology left people adrift spiritually, while factory work dehumanized them. Modernist works do not state these ideas directly. Instead, their emphasis is on the oblique, suggested meanings, requiring readers to draw inferences, or interpret ideas, from images and details. As you read, use a chart like the one shown to **relate Eliot's literary works to the historical period** by identifying images that suggest the Modernist worldview.

Vocabulary

You will encounter the words listed here in the texts that follow. Copy them into your notebook, separating them into words you know and words you do not know.

galled	supplication
refractory	tumid
dispensation	

Common Core State Standards

Reading Literature
1. Cite strong and thorough textual evidence to support analysis of what the text says explicitly as well as inferences drawn from the text.

Speaking and Listening
1.a. Come to discussions prepared, having read and researched material under study.

1.b. Work with peers to promote civil, democratic discussions and decision making, set clear goals and deadlines, and establish individual roles as needed. (p. 1162)

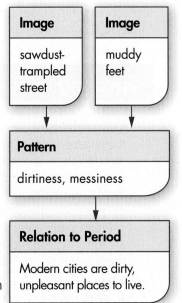

T. S. ELIOT

Author of "Preludes" • "Journey of the Magi" • "The Hollow Men"

T. S. Eliot was the most famous English poet of his time. He was also the most influential. His distinctive style and novel ideas affected not only poets, but also critics, fiction writers, playwrights, and even philosophers. From the 1920s on, he was a leader of the artistic movement called Modernism. Eliot and fellow Modernist Ezra Pound transformed English-language poetry, grounding their work in the power of images.

Crossing the Atlantic Born Thomas Stearns Eliot in St. Louis, Missouri, he was educated at Harvard University. He went on to study at Oxford University in England and at the Sorbonne in Paris. The outbreak of World War I in 1914 found Eliot in England, where he settled and eventually became a citizen.

In 1915, Eliot married the sensitive, intelligent, and witty Vivien Haigh-Wood. While writing poetry and critical reviews, Eliot taught school, worked for the banking firm of Lloyd's, and eventually took a position with a publishing company.

Early Work Because of its unconventional style, Eliot's earliest work was greeted with less than universal acclaim, although the American poet Ezra Pound was a vocal supporter from the beginning. Pound saw that Eliot spoke in an authentic new voice and offered an original, if bleak, vision. From *Prufrock and Other Observations* (1917) through *The Waste Land* (1922) and "The Hollow Men" (1925), Eliot portrayed the modern world as one of fragmented experiences and despair. Eliot may have been responding to World War I, an event that damaged the faith of many. At the same time, the war may have prompted readers to catch up with Eliot, who had written works such as "Preludes" and "The Love Song of J. Alfred Prufrock" before the war.

A Spiritual Rebirth Eventually, Eliot found an answer to despair in religion. In 1927, he joined the Church of England and became a devout Anglican. His new faith shaped the writing of "Journey of the Magi" (1927), *Ash Wednesday* (1930), and the *Four Quartets* (1935–1943).

As a literary critic, Eliot had a profound influence on his contemporaries. His re-evaluations of past poetry shaped the tastes of a generation. In 1948, Eliot received the Nobel Prize for Literature.

"WE SHALL NOT CEASE FROM EXPLORATION."

Preludes

T. S. ELIOT

I

The winter evening settles down
With smell of steaks[1] in passageways.
Six o'clock.
The burnt-out ends of smoky days.
5 And now a gusty shower wraps
The grimy scraps
Of withered leaves about your feet
And newspapers from vacant lots;
The showers beat
10 On broken blinds and chimney-pots,
And at the corner of the street
A lonely cab-horse steams and stamps.
And then the lighting of the lamps.

II

The morning comes to consciousness
15 Of faint stale smells of beer
From the sawdust-trampled street
With all its muddy feet that press
To early coffee-stands.
With the other masquerades
20 That time resumes,
One thinks of all the hands
That are raising dingy shades
In a thousand furnished rooms.

III

You tossed a blanket from the bed,
25 You lay upon your back, and waited;
You dozed, and watched the night revealing
The thousand sordid images
Of which your soul was constituted;

Modernism in Poetry

What fragmented images of city life appear in this stanza?

---

1. steaks In 1910, when this poem was composed, steaks were inexpensive and were commonly eaten by members of the lower class.

They flickered against the ceiling.
30 And when all the world came back
And the light crept up between the shutters
And you heard the sparrows in the gutters,
You had such a vision of the street
As the street hardly understands;
35 Sitting along the bed's edge, where
You curled the papers from your hair,
Or clasped the yellow soles of feet
In the palms of both soiled hands.

IV

His soul stretched tight across the skies
40 That fade behind a city block,
Or trampled by insistent feet
At four and five and six o'clock;
And short square fingers stuffing pipes,
And evening newspapers, and eyes
45 Assured of certain certainties,
The conscience of a blackened street
Impatient to assume the world.

I am moved by fancies that are curled
Around these images, and cling:
50 The notion of some infinitely gentle
Infinitely suffering thing.

Wipe your hand across your mouth, and laugh;
The worlds revolve like ancient women
Gathering fuel in vacant lots.

Relating Poetry to Historical Period

What view of modern life do the last lines in this stanza convey?

Critical Reading

Cite textual evidence to support your responses.

1. **Key Ideas and Details (a)** In Prelude I, what is the time of year and the time of day? **(b) Interpret:** What cycle of time takes place from Prelude I to Prelude IV? **(c) Support:** What effect does the poet achieve by representing this complete cycle?

2. **Key Ideas and Details (a) Draw Conclusions:** What is the character of modern life as Eliot depicts it? **(b) Compare and Contrast:** Contrast this character with "The notion of some infinitely gentle / Infinitely suffering thing" (lines 50–51). **(c) Speculate:** Based on this contrast, what do you think the "thing" might be?

3. **Integration of Knowledge and Ideas** Think of a sight in a modern city that conveys joy. How might Eliot have reacted to that image?

JOURNEY
OF THE MAGI

T. S. ELIOT

BACKGROUND "Journey of the Magi" is a dramatic monologue spoken by one of the wise men ("magi") who, according to the Bible, visited the infant Jesus. In the poem, the speaker uses modern conversational language to describe events, making vividly present the spiritual agony of a man who lived long ago.

> "A cold coming we had of it,
> Just the worst time of the year
> For a journey, and such a long journey:
> The ways deep and the weather sharp,
> 5   The very dead of winter."[1]
> And the camels galled, sore-footed, refractory,
> Lying down in the melting snow.
> There were times we regretted
> The summer palaces on slopes, the terraces,
> 10   And the silken girls bringing sherbet.
> Then the camel men cursing and grumbling
> And running away, and wanting their liquor and women,
> And the night-fires going out, and the lack of shelters,
> And the cities hostile and the towns unfriendly
> 15   And the villages dirty and charging high prices:
> A hard time we had of it.

---

1. **"A . . . winter"** Adapted from a part of a sermon delivered by 17th-century Bishop Lancelot Andrewes: "A cold coming they had of it at this time of year, just the worst time of the year to take a journey, and specially a long journey in. The ways deep, the weather sharp, the days short, the sun farthest off . . . the very dead of winter."

Vocabulary

galled (gôld) *adj.* injured or made sore by rubbing or chafing

refractory (ri frak´ tər ē) *adj.* hard to manage; stubborn

Relating Poetry to Historical Period

What picture of society do these images convey?

At the end we preferred to travel all night,
Sleeping in snatches,
With the voices singing in our ears, saying
20 That this was all folly.

    Then at dawn we came down to a temperate valley,
Wet, below the snow line, smelling of vegetation;
With a running stream and a water-mill beating the darkness,
And three trees on the low sky,
25 And an old white horse galloped away in the meadow.
Then we came to a tavern with vine-leaves over the lintel,
Six hands at an open door dicing for pieces of silver,
And feet kicking the empty wine-skins.
But there was no information, and so we continued
30 And arrived at evening, not a moment too soon
Finding the place; it was (you may say) satisfactory.

    All this was a long time ago, I remember,
And I would do it again, but set down
This set down
35 This: were we led all that way for
Birth or Death? There was a Birth, certainly,
We had evidence and no doubt. I had seen birth and death,
But had thought they were different; this Birth was
Hard and bitter agony for us, like Death, our death.
40 We returned to our places, these Kingdoms,
But no longer at ease here, in the old dispensation,
With an alien people clutching their gods.
I should be glad of another death.

Vocabulary
dispensation (dis´ pən sā´
shən) *n.* religious system
or belief

Critical Reading

1. **Key Ideas and Details (a)** What event has the speaker in "Journey of the Magi" gone to witness? **(b) Compare and Contrast:** How does the description of the journey compare to the description of the event? **(c) Interpret:** Why might the speaker say so little about one and so much about the other?

2. **Key Ideas and Details** How has the event changed the speaker's relation to his own people?

3. **Integration of Knowledge and Ideas (a) Compare and Contrast:** In what way is Eliot's choice of details similar in the first stanzas of "Preludes" and "Journey of the Magi"? **(b) Draw Conclusions:** What do you think Eliot was trying to achieve in each case?

Cite textual evidence to support your responses.

Literary History: Eliot's "The Hollow Men"

"Eliot's allusions create a distinctive, dreamlike world for a reader to explore."

How "The Hollow Men" Was Written

In 1921, T. S. Eliot began a long poem called *The Waste Land*. He later used sections that had been edited out of *The Waste Land* as the basis for "The Hollow Men." He often worked this way, building a poem from pieces that had been written independently and using discarded fragments of one poem to create the next. He explained this process of working in an interview with Donald Hall (*The Paris Review*, No. 21):

Interviewer: Are any of your minor poems actually sections cut out of longer works? There are two that sound like "The Hollow Men."

Eliot: Oh, those were the preliminary sketches. Those things were earlier. Others I published in periodicals but not in my collected poems . . .

Interviewer: You seem often to have written poems in sections. Did they begin as separate poems? I am thinking of "Ash Wednesday," in particular.

Eliot: Yes, like "The Hollow Men," it originated out of separate poems. As I recall, one or two early drafts of parts of *Ash Wednesday* appeared in *Commerce* [magazine] and elsewhere. Then gradually I came to see it as a sequence. That's one way in which my mind does seem to have worked throughout the years poetically—doing things separately and then seeing the possibility of fusing them together, altering them, and making a kind of whole of them.

The Theme of "The Hollow Men"

It makes sense to assume that "The Hollow Men" and *The Waste Land* are thematically related. *The Waste Land*, as its title suggests, deals with a sense of emotional and spiritual barrenness after the destruction wrought by World War I. "The Hollow Men," published in 1925, also deals with a barren and empty (hollow) existence. It resembles *The Waste Land* in its use of literary allusions to convey this theme of barrenness and to compare the present with other historical eras.

Using Allusions to Interpret the Poem

Critics have identified four key allusions in the poem:

Joseph Conrad's "Heart of Darkness" Kurtz, referred to in a line introducing the poem, is a mysterious character in Conrad's "Heart of Darkness." He travels to the Belgian Congo on a mission to uplift and educate the Congolese people. However, he develops his own little kingdom in which he exercises absolute power over the people he intended to save. It is only when he is dying that he sees the "horror" of what he has done and how he has been, in Conrad's words, a "hollow sham," or fake. His tragic downfall exposes the hollowness of his noble ideals and of the whole colonial enterprise. That enterprise is supported by a host of administrators and clerks who are most like the speakers in Eliot's poem, a chorus of paralyzed nonentities: "We are the hollow men. . . ." Eliot may also be suggesting that this chorus includes his readers.

The Gunpowder Plot The hollow men are also like the effigies of Guy Fawkes, burned to commemorate the uncovering of the Gunpowder Plot of 1605. Fawkes himself was tortured until he revealed the names of his co-conspirators who plotted a powerful explosion that would destroy the king of England and Parliament. As Eliot writes at the end of the poem, "This is the way the world ends / Not with a bang but a whimper." Like Fawkes, so the speakers of Eliot's poem are as helpless and ineffective as straw dummies: "Leaning together / Headpiece filled with straw. Alas!"

Shakespeare's *Julius Caesar* This play deals with another conspiracy to betray a leader. Brutus, a high-minded Roman, is lured by flattery into a plot to assassinate the Roman ruler Julius Caesar. Section V of "The Hollow Men" quotes lines from Shakespeare's play in which Brutus experiences the nightmarelike emptiness of the time before the deed. Like Kurtz in Conrad's story, Brutus is a tragic figure, a self-deluded man who commits murder in the name of high ideals. In this sense, he too is a form of hollow man.

Dante's *Divine Comedy* Dante's medieval poems describe the three realms of the afterlife according to Roman Catholic belief: *Inferno, Purgatorio,* and *Paradiso*—hell, purgatory, and heaven. The speakers in Eliot's poem are being punished for their spiritual emptiness in a kind of inferno: a "dead land" (line 39); a "cactus land" (line 40); a "valley of dying stars" (line 54). It does not appear that these speakers will gain salvation, but Eliot uses images drawn from Dante's description of paradise to suggest the existence of higher realms: " . . . the perpetual star / Multifoliate rose . . ." (lines 63–64). In terms of Dante's work, "The Hollow Men" is like an inferno (a realm of punishment) that is almost without the promise of a purgatory or a paradise.

Eliot's Theory of Tradition

Eliot's allusions create a distinctive, dreamlike world for a reader to explore. They also reflect his theory of poetry. In an essay, Eliot compares the poet to a catalyst in a chemical reaction. A catalyst adds nothing of itself, but without it, the reaction will not take place. The poet's mind is the catalyst that causes images and feelings to combine in a poem, but the poem does not necessarily reflect the poet's own life. For Eliot, a tradition of past literature was a key source of ingredients for the reaction. Eliot's allusions reflect both of these values: impersonality and tradition.

Speaking and Listening: Discussion

Comprehension and Collaboration An **allusion** is a device used by many creative artists, not just poets. Filmmakers and composers sometimes incorporate cinematic or musical allusions into their work to enrich the audience's experience. As "The Hollow Men" demonstrates, allusions add depth to a work but can also make it more difficult to understand.

With a group, discuss your thoughts about films and musical works that feature allusions. Set a twenty-minute time limit for the discussion, and use these questions to help you set clear goals:

- Identify a movie or song that alludes to or quotes from another source. What is that source, and what point does the artist make through the allusion?

- In what way does understanding allusions enhance your enjoyment of a work?

- Is it always necessary to fully understand an allusion? Explain.

Encourage each group member to participate. Remind participants to be courteous as they interact. Appoint one person to take notes on the ideas and issues presented. After the discussion, choose a point person to share your thoughts with the class.

THE HOLLOW MEN

T. S. ELIOT

BACKGROUND As in "Journey of the Magi," Eliot uses allusions at the beginning of "The Hollow Men" to help him contrast the past with the present. For example, "A penny for the Old Guy" is a traditional cry of children on Guy Fawkes Day. Fawkes was executed for attempting to blow up the king and Parliament on November 5, 1605. He is one of the "lost / Violent souls" of the past who contrast with the "hollow men" of today.

Mistah Kurtz[1]—he dead.

A penny for the Old Guy[2]

I

We are the hollow men
We are the stuffed men
Leaning together
Headpiece filled with straw. Alas!
5   Our dried voices, when
We whisper together
Are quiet and meaningless
As wind in dry grass

Le Maitre d'ecole. 1955, Rene Magritte, Photothèque R. Magritte-ADAGP / Art Resource, NY, © 1998 C. Herscovici, Brussels / Artists Rights Society (ARS), New York.

Comprehension

How does the speaker characterize the sounds made by the hollow men?

---

1. ***Mistah Kurtz*** character in Joseph Conrad's "Heart of Darkness" who hopes to improve the lives of native Africans, but who finds instead that he is corrupted by his power over them.
2. ***A . . . Guy*** traditional cry used by children on Guy Fawkes Day (November 5), celebrating the execution of a famous English traitor of the same name. The "Old Guy" refers to stuffed dummies representing Fawkes.

Or rats' feet over broken glass
10   In our dry cellar

Shape without form, shade without color,
Paralyzed force, gesture without motion;
Those who have crossed
With direct eyes, to death's other Kingdom[3]
15   Remember us—if at all—not as lost
Violent souls, but only
As the hollow men
The stuffed men.

II

Eyes I dare not meet in dreams
20   In death's dream kingdom
These do not appear:
There, the eyes are
Sunlight on a broken column
There, is a tree swinging
25   And voices are
In the wind's singing
More distant and more solemn
Than a fading star.
Let me be no nearer
30   In death's dream kingdom
Let me also wear
Such deliberate disguises
Rat's coat, crowskin, crossed staves
In a field[4]
35   Behaving as the wind behaves
No nearer—

Not that final meeting
In the twilight kingdom

III

This is the dead land
40   This is cactus land
Here the stone images
Are raised, here they receive
The supplication of a dead man's hand
Under the twinkle of a fading star.

Modernism in Poetry

In what ways does this poem reflect the fragmentation characteristic of Modernism?

Vocabulary

supplication (sup′ lə kā′ shən) *n.* act of praying or pleading

SHAPE WITHOUT FORM, SHADE WITHOUT COLOR

---

3. Those . . . kingdom allusion to Dante's *Paradiso*, in which those "with direct eyes" are blessed by God in heaven.
4. crossed . . . field scarecrows.

Is it like this
In death's other kingdom
Waking alone
At the hour when we are
Trembling with tenderness
Lips that would kiss
Form prayers to broken stone.

IV

The eyes are not here
There are no eyes here
In this valley of dying stars
In this hollow valley
This broken jaw of our lost kingdoms

In this last of meeting places
We grope together
And avoid speech
Gathered on this beach of the **tumid** river[5]

Sightless, unless
The eyes reappear
As the perpetual star[6]
Multifoliate rose[7]
Of death's twilight kingdom
The hope only
Of empty men.

V

Here we go round the prickly pear
Prickly pear prickly pear
Here we go round the prickly pear
At five o'clock in the morning.[8]

Between the idea
And the reality
Between the motion
And the act[9]
Falls the Shadow

---

5. **river** from Dante's *Inferno*, the river Acheron, which the dead cross on the way to hell.
6. **star** traditional symbol for Christ.
7. **Multifoliate rose** rose with many leaves. Dante describes paradise as such a rose in his *Paradiso*. The rose is a traditional symbol for the Virgin Mary.
8. **Here . . . morning** adaptation of a common nursery rhyme. A prickly pear is a cactus.
9. **Between . . . act** reference to *Julius Caesar*, Act II, Scene i, 63–65: "Between the acting of a dreadful thing / And the first motion, all the interim is / Like a phantasma or hideous dream."

The British Tradition

The Literary Magazine

No institution played a more important role in the development of Modernism than the literary magazine. These modest periodicals were published on both sides of the Atlantic. In England, Eliot founded *The Criterion* (later called *The New Criterion*) in 1922. In the United States, *The Dial* published the work of Eliot, W. B. Yeats, Ezra Pound, and D. H. Lawrence. Another important journal, *The Egoist*, serialized *A Portrait of the Artist as a Young Man*, James Joyce's first major work, from 1914 to 1915.

These Modernist periodicals dedicated themselves to promoting new trends in art. The profound impact of Eliot's work would perhaps not have been as great if it had not found a home in such journals.

Connect to the Literature

What kinds of readers might enjoy literary magazines featuring poems like "The Hollow Men"?

Vocabulary

tumid (to͞o′ mid) *adj.* swollen

Comprehension

To what kingdoms does the speaker refer?

For Thine is the Kingdom[10]

Between the conception
And the creation
80　Between the emotion
And the response
Falls the Shadow

Life is very long[11]

Between the desire
85　And the spasm
Between the potency
And the existence
Between the essence
And the descent
90　Falls the Shadow

For Thine is the Kingdom

For Thine is
Life is
For Thine is the

95　This is the way the world ends
This is the way the world ends
This is the way the world ends
Not with a bang but a whimper.

---

10. For . . . Kingdom from the ending of the Lord's Prayer.
11. Life . . . long Quotation from Joseph Conrad's *An Outcast of the Islands*.

Modernism in Poetry
How does Eliot's handling of the line from the Lord's Prayer reflect modernist techniques?

BETWEEN
THE IDEA

AND THE
REALITY

Cite textual evidence to support your responses.

Critical Reading

1. **Craft and Structures (a)** Which words are used to describe the hollow men in the first ten lines? **(b) Infer:** What do the images of wind in Parts I and II suggest about the hollow men?

2. **Key Ideas and Details (a)** In Part V, what repeatedly "falls"? **(b) Interpret:** How is this action related to the poem's theme?

3. **Integration of Knowledge and Ideas** In what ways do Eliot's poems both break with tradition and connect to tradition? Use at least two of these Essential Question words in your response: *free verse, fragmentation, allusion, imagery.* **[Connecting to the Essential Question: What is the relationship of the writer to tradition?]**

Literary Analysis

1. **Craft and Structure** Identify three images in the "Preludes" that suggest the **Modernist** view that modern life is empty. Explain your choices.

2. **Key Ideas and Details** **(a)** What escape from modern despair does "Journey of the Magi" suggest? **(b)** What despair appears in the poem?

3. **Integration of Knowledge and Ideas** "The Journey of the Magi" is set in ancient times. What aspects of the poem reflect on Eliot's contemporary society? Explain your answer.

4. **Craft and Structure** **(a)** Quoting passages in support, identify two aspects of Modernism illustrated by the "Preludes." **(b)** Does "Journey of the Magi" also illustrate these aspects? Explain, quoting from the poem.

5. **Craft and Structure** What Modernist qualities characterize "The Hollow Men"? Use a chart like the one shown to help you in answering.

Passage	Fragmented Images/ Realistic Pictures	Critical of Modern Life?

6. **Craft and Structure** Compare the use of *allusion*—brief references to literature—in "The Hollow Men" with the use of images in the "Preludes." **(a)** How are they similar? **(b)** Which poem is more relatable, or accessible? Explain.

7. **Integration of Knowledge and Ideas** **(a)** What similarities are there in the way Eliot describes people in "Preludes" and "The Hollow Men"? **(b) Relate Eliot's work to the historical period** by determining what vision of modern life these similar images provide.

8. **Integration of Knowledge and Ideas** Why might Eliot have found it necessary to turn to past literature to make a point about what is missing in the present?

9. **Integration of Knowledge and Ideas** The Christian religion had been a source of spiritual comfort to various cultures for many centuries. Both "The Journey of the Magi" and "The Hollow Men" refer to Christian events or ideas. What does Eliot's treatment of these events or ideas suggest about his view of the role of Christianity in his society?

Common Core State Standards

Writing
2. Write informative/ explanatory texts to examine and convey complex ideas, concepts, and information clearly and accurately through the effective selection, organization, and analysis of content. *(p. 1168)*
4. Produce clear and coherent writing in which the development, organization, and style are appropriate to task, purpose, and audience. *(p. 1168)*

Language
3.a. Vary syntax for effect. *(p. 1169)*
5. Demonstrate understanding of figurative language, word relationships, and nuances in word meanings. *(p. 1168)*

Vocabulary Acquisition and Use

Word Analysis: Latin Root -fract-

The Latin root -fract- means "to break." A *refractory* animal is one that "breaks away," making it difficult to manage. A *fraction* is a part broken away from a larger whole. Explain how the root contributes to the meaning of the italicized words in these sentences.

1. When white light is *refracted* by a prism, it produces a spectrum.

2. Her motives were good, but she was guilty of an *infraction* of the rules.

3. Computer scenery may be formed of *fractals* so tiny you cannot see them.

4. The *fractured* bone needed time to mend.

Vocabulary: Analogies

In an analogy, the relationship between two words is explained by comparing it to the relationship between two other words. Discern the meaning of the words from the vocabulary list on page 1154 by using each word once to complete these analogies. Explain each choice.

1. *Thin* is to *slender* as _____ is to *bloated*.

2. *Emotional* is to *rational* as *obedient* is to _____.

3. *Order* is to *inferior* as _____ is to *superior*.

4. *Belief* is to _____ as *citizenship* is to *nation*.

5. *Medicine* is to *scraped* as *ointment* is to _____.

Writing to Sources

Informative Text Eliot's poetry reflects the Modernist movement that swept through other arts as well. He uses words to achieve effects similar to those attained by such artists as Pablo Picasso and Paul Cézanne. Write a **multi-genre response** that responds to Eliot's Modernism in poetry. Analyze his techniques, showing how they contribute to a *comment on life*, and present the art of a Modernist painter, showing how he or she uses comparable devices.

Prewriting Review Eliot's poems to identify imagery, rhythms, and other techniques that reflect Modernism. Take notes on his Modernist themes as well. Using a history of art, find a Modernist work of art that shows comparable techniques or themes in visual form.

Drafting Begin with a thesis statement explaining your main point about Modernism in literature and art. Then, discuss the Modernist techniques in Eliot's poetry and write a caption for the work of art explaining similar Modernist techniques it uses.

> **Model: Revising to Clarify Generalizations**
>
>   *a verbal form of*
> Eliot's poetry is ‸ like Picasso's cubism. He breaks the soul into a "thousand sordid images"; Picasso breaks the face into dozens of different pieces.
>
> Using vivid language clarifies generalizations.

Revising Review your draft, highlighting generalizations. Where supporting details are lacking, look back at the poems or the artwork to find relevant support. Make sure that all quotations are accurate and properly referenced.

Conventions and Style: Transitional Expressions

To write coherently and smoothly, you must show how your ideas relate to one another. **Transitional expressions** can help you do this by making clear the connection between ideas.

Conjunctive adverbs make a transition between two independent clauses and show the relationship between the ideas in the clauses.

The examples demonstrate how conjunctive adverbs combine choppy sentences and make clear the relationship between ideas.

Choppy: The Magi's journey was long. It was at the worst time of year.

Conjunctive adverb: The Magi's journey was long; *moreover,* it was at the worst time of year.

Below is a chart of some common transitional expressions used as conjunctive adverbs.

Cause-effect	consequently, because of this
Time	in time, afterwards, at present
To illustrate	in other words, for instance
To add to	also, moreover, in addition
Compare	similarly, in like manner
Contrast	however, on the contrary

Punctuation Tip Remember to use a semicolon before the transitional expression.

Practice Rewrite each item using a conjunctive adverb to make a transition and show the relationship between the ideas.

1. Nighttime was dark and dismal. A new day dawned.
2. The modern world appeared lifeless. Former times seemed filled with emotion.
3. Cities, towns, and villages were unwelcoming. The travelers chose to keep on through the night.
4. The journey was long ago. The speaker would make it again.
5. The Magi returned to their homes. They no longer felt comfortable there.
6. Eliot alluded to Mistah Kurtz. He wanted to emphasize that power corrupts.
7. Hollow men had heads filled with straw. They were unthinking and unfeeling.
8. People spoke with dry voices. Their words were meaningless.
9. On Earth, people gathered but avoided speaking. They lived in a world of shadows.
10. Sightless eyes were symbols. They stood for emptiness.

Writing and Speaking Conventions

A. Writing Write an independent clause followed by a semicolon to fill each blank.

1. _____ that is, they had no shape or form.
2. _____ for this reason, he used the cactus image.
3. _____ in other words, it will go out with a quiet groan.

Example: _____ that is, they had no shape or form.

Complete Sentence: Eliot wrote of hollow men; that is, they had no shape or form.

B. Speaking Briefly explain to the class why Eliot's poems continue to have meaning. Include at least two conjunctive adverbs as transitional expressions.

Connecting to the Essential Question These poems reveal a profound sense of place. As you read, notice details in these poems that highlight the special character of the places being described. These observations will help you think about the Essential Question: **What is the relationship between literature and place?**

Close Reading Focus

Allegory; Pastoral

Allegory and pastoral are two subgenres of literature with long traditions. They are called subgenres because these approaches to writing can be found in each major genre—poetry, prose, fiction, and drama.

- In an **allegory,** a writer uses symbolic characters to stand for abstract qualities or traits. In "In Memory of W. B. Yeats," for instance, Auden embodies poetry in a brief allegory. Allegories often teach a moral or lesson.

- In the **pastoral,** writers celebrate nature and those who live in the natural world. In this subgenre, farmers and shepherds are often seen as being wiser or more virtuous than city dwellers.

Comparing Literary Works Many modernist writers rejected traditional forms and styles. These poets may explore allegory or the pastoral not by embracing them but by rejecting them. As you read, look for both positive and negative attitudes.

Preparing to Read Complex Texts Both Auden poems address the role of art in the world. The speakers in the MacNeice and Spender poems react in different ways to the traditional pastoral world and the modern human-made one. You can enrich your understanding by **comparing and contrasting elements** that appear in the same poem or different poems. Comparing and contrasting MacNeice's and Spender's presentations of the natural world, for instance, highlights the different themes of their poems and how each poet develops them. As you read, use a chart like the one shown to record similarities and differences in the poems.

Vocabulary

You will encounter the words listed here in the texts that follow. Copy the words into your notebook, and determine which one is most likely connected to the idea of birth.

sequestered	affinities
topographical	prenatal
	intrigues

Common Core State Standards

Reading Literature
1. Cite strong and thorough textual evidence to support analysis of what the text says explicitly as well as inferences drawn from the text, including determining where the text leaves matters uncertain.

MacNeice on Nature

"The child's astonishment not yet cured"

Spender on Nature

"Leave your gardens"

Conclusion

MacNeice is tied to the place and the past; Spender rejects the natural for the new.

W. H. AUDEN
(1907–1973)

Author of "In Memory of W. B. Yeats" • "Musée des Beaux Arts"

Much as T. S. Eliot became established as the poetic voice of the 1920s, so Wystan Hugh Auden emerged as the voice of the 1930s. As a young poet, Auden was greatly influenced by Eliot's work, particularly *The Waste Land*. He soon developed his own poetic style, however, characterized by versatility, wit, and dazzling technique.

Born in York, England, Auden had early dreams of becoming an engineer but gravitated to poetry instead. His commitment to social justice and his opposition to fascism made him a poetic spokesperson for the political left. In 1939, Auden left England for the United States, where he taught at a number of universities. He became an American citizen in 1946. From 1956 to 1960, he taught at Oxford as professor of poetry.

Achievements in Poetry Auden's early poems, along with works by his friends Louis MacNeice and Stephen Spender, appeared in *Oxford Poetry*, a series of annual collections of verse by the university's undergraduates. Auden's first published collection, entitled *Poems*, appeared in 1930. Full of cryptic images and references, Auden's verse struck some readers of the day as impenetrable. His more straightfoward second collection, *On This Island* (1937), generated greater enthusiasm. In 1948, Auden won a Pulitzer Prize for the collection *The Age of Anxiety*.

A Versatile Poet Auden wrote equally well in the idiom of the street or in the archaic measures of *Beowulf*. His voice is original, achieving a kind of personable intimacy even as he makes polished pronouncements on the general human condition. With Yeats and Eliot, he is among the most highly regarded British poets of the twentieth century.

> "A REAL BOOK IS NOT ONE THAT WE READ, BUT ONE THAT READS US."

In Memory of W. B. YEATS

W. H. AUDEN

BACKGROUND THE 1930S WAS A DECADE OF ECONOMIC COLLAPSE AND POLITICAL TURMOIL THAT ENDED WITH THE WORLD PLUNGED INTO ANOTHER GREAT WAR. THE COMPLEX CONCERNS OF THE PERIOD ARE REFLECTED IN THE POEMS OF THE AUDEN CIRCLE, WHICH INCLUDED AUDEN HIMSELF, SPENDER, MACNEICE, AND C. DAY LEWIS. THE POLITICAL URGENCIES OF THE TIMES—THE OPPOSITION TO FASCISM AND THE MOVEMENT FOR SOCIAL JUSTICE FOR THE WORKING CLASSES—SHAPED MUCH OF THE POETRY THE AUDEN CIRCLE WROTE THEN. YET ALONG WITH THEIR SOCIAL CONCERNS, EACH OF THESE POETS SHARED A DEEP SENSE OF A SPECIFICALLY POETIC VOCATION—TO MAKE SOMETHING HAPPEN IN LANGUAGE.

1

He disappeared in the dead of winter:
The brooks were frozen, the airports almost deserted,
And snow disfigured the public statues;
The mercury sank in the mouth of the dying day.
O all the instruments agree
The day of his death was a dark cold day.

Far from his illness
The wolves ran on through the evergreen forests,
The peasant river was untempted by fashionable quays;[1]
By mourning tongues
The death of the poet was kept from his poems.

But for him it was his last afternoon as himself,
An afternoon of nurses and rumors;
The provinces of his body revolted,
The squares of his mind were empty,
Silence invaded the suburbs,
The current of his feeling failed: he became his admirers.

Now he is scattered among a hundred cities
And wholly given over to unfamiliar affections;
To find his happiness in another kind of wood
And be punished by another code of conscience.
The words of a dead man
Are modified in the guts of the living.

But in the importance and noise of tomorrow
When the brokers are roaring like beasts on the floor
of the Bourse,[2]
And the poor have the sufferings to which they are
fairly accustomed,

◀ Critical Viewing
Does this photograph of Yeats present him as the mortal man described in parts 1 and 2 of Auden's poem or as the great writer eulogized in part 3? Explain. **INTERPRET**

Compare and Contrast Elements
How does Auden use images of different locations to dramatize Yeats's death?

Comprehension
According to the speaker, where is Yeats now?

1. quays (kēz) wharfs with facilities for loading or unloading ships.
2. Bourse (bo͝ors) Paris Stock Exchange.

And each in the cell of himself is almost convinced of
    his freedom;
A few thousand will think of this day
As one thinks of a day when one did something
    slightly unusual.
30 O all the instruments agree
The day of his death was a dark cold day.

2

You were silly like us: your gift survived it all;
The parish of rich women, physical decay,
Yourself; mad Ireland hurt you into poetry.
35 Now Ireland has her madness and her weather still,
For poetry makes nothing happen: it survives
In the valley of its saying where executives
Would never want to tamper; it flows south
From ranches of isolation and the busy griefs,
40 Raw towns that we believe and die in; it survives,
A way of happening, a mouth.

3

Earth, receive an honored guest;
William Yeats is laid to rest:
Let the Irish vessel lie
45 Emptied of its poetry.

Time that is intolerant
Of the brave and innocent,
And indifferent in a week
To a beautiful physique,

50 Worships language and forgives
Everyone by whom it lives;
Pardons cowardice, conceit
Lays its honors at their feet.

Time that with this strange excuse
55 Pardoned Kipling and his views,[3]
And will pardon Paul Claudel,[4]
Pardons him for writing well.

Allegory

How does Auden create a mini-allegory, or symbolic narrative, in lines 36–41 to describe the creation and progress of poetry?

---

3. Kipling . . . views English writer Rudyard Kipling (1865–1936) was a supporter of imperialism.

4. pardon Paul Claudel (klō del′) French poet, dramatist, and diplomat. Paul Claudel (1868–1955) had antidemocratic political views, which Yeats at times shared.

In the nightmare of the dark
All the dogs of Europe bark,
60 And the living nations wait,
Each sequestered in its hate;

Intellectual disgrace
Stares from every human face,
And the seas of pity lie
65 Locked and frozen in each eye.

Follow, poet, follow right
To the bottom of the night,
With your unconstraining voice
Still persuade us to rejoice;

70 With the farming of a verse
Make a vineyard of the curse,
Sing of human unsuccess
In a rapture of distress;

In the deserts of the heart
75 Let the healing fountain start,
In the prison of his days
Teach the free man how to praise.

Vocabulary

sequestered (si kwes′ tərd)
adj. kept apart from others

FOLLOW, POET,

FOLLOW RIGHT

TO THE BOTTOM

OF THE *Night*

Critical Reading

1. **Key Ideas and Details** What does the speaker mean by saying Yeats "became his admirers"?

2. **Key Ideas and Details** What does the second section suggest about the sources and effects of poetry?

3. **Integration of Knowledge and Ideas (a) Interpret:** Considering the kind of fame great past poets enjoy, why does the speaker say that time "Worships language and forgives / Everyone by whom it lives . . ."? **(b) Synthesize:** What kind of poetry might "Sing of human unsuccess / In a rapture of distress . . ."?

4. **Integration of Knowledge and Ideas** Summarize the view of poetry presented in the poem.

5. **Craft and Structure** In phrases such as "ranches of isolation," Auden combines the abstract and the specific. Identify three other images that combine abstract ideas and concrete details.

6. **Craft and Structure** Is Auden's style suited to a poem of mourning? Explain.

Cite textual evidence to support your responses.

▲ **Critical Viewing** In this painting by Brueghel, which inspired Auden's poem, the drowning Icarus appears in the lower right. What is Brueghel implying about the place of suffering in life? **[Interpret]**

Musée des Beaux Arts[1]

W. H. Auden

About suffering they were never wrong,
The Old Masters: how well they understood
Its human position; how it takes place
While someone else is eating or opening a window or just
    walking dully along;
5   How, when the aged are reverently, passionately waiting
For the miraculous birth, there always must be
Children who did not specially want it to happen, skating

Comprehension
What did the Old Masters understand about suffering?

---

1. **Musée des Beaux Arts** Museum of Fine Arts in Brussels, Belgium, which contains
Brueghel's *Icarus*.

On a pond at the edge of the wood:
They never forgot

10 That even the dreadful martyrdom must run its course
Anyhow in a corner, some untidy spot
Where the dogs go on with their doggy life and the
    torturer's horse
Scratches its innocent behind on a tree.

In Brueghel's *Icarus*,[2] for instance: how everything turns away

15 Quite leisurely from the disaster; the ploughman may
Have heard the splash, the forsaken cry,
But for him it was not an important failure; the sun shone
As it had to on the white legs disappearing into the green
Water; and the expensive delicate ship that must have seen

20 Something amazing, a boy falling out of the sky,
Had somewhere to get to and sailed calmly on.

Allegory

In what way does Brueghel's picture depict an allegorical landscape for Auden? What is the moral of this allegory?

---

2. Brueghel's (brü′ gəlz) *Icarus* (ik′ ə rəs) *The Fall of Icarus,* a painting by Flemish painter Pieter Brueghel (1525?–1569). In Greek mythology, Icarus flies too close to the sun. The wax of his artificial wings melts, and he falls into the sea.

Critical Reading

Cite textual evidence to support your responses.

1. **Key Ideas and Details** **(a)** Who are the "Old Masters"? **(b) Interpret:** What general device used by the Old Masters does the speaker discuss?

2. **Key Ideas and Details** **(a)** What disaster do the "ploughman" and the "ship" witness? **(b) Compare and Contrast:** How do their responses contrast with the gravity of the event?

3. **Key Ideas and Details** **(a) Infer:** What is the relation of the children to the important events near them? **(b) Connect:** Is the attitude of the ploughman to Icarus's fall similar? Explain.

4. **Key Ideas and Details** **(a) Analyze:** Look at Brueghel's *The Fall of Icarus* (p. 1176). What does the artist imply by showing only Icarus's legs in the right corner of the picture? **(b) Infer:** What does Brueghel, an Old Master, realize about the place of suffering in the world?

5. **Integration of Knowledge and Ideas** Consider these two statements: (1) *A person's suffering belongs to him or her in a way that not even pity can change.* (2) *Suffering gives meaning to innocent everyday life, and vice versa.* Which statement better captures the sense of the poem? Support your choice.

6. **Integration of Knowledge and Ideas** **(a) Apply:** Identify two examples of indifference to suffering today. **(b) Relate:** What might Auden say about them?

(1907–1963)

Louis MacNeice

Author of **"Carrick Revisited"**

Louis MacNeice was the son of a Protestant clergyman in Belfast, Northern Ireland. A gifted youth, he began to write poetry at age seven, about the time his mother died. His first collection, *Blind Fireworks*, appeared in 1929, followed six years later by *Poems*, the volume that established his reputation. During the 1930s, MacNeice taught classical literature. In 1941, he joined the British Broadcasting Corporation, writing radio plays in verse.

In a period when Auden and others embraced leftist politics, MacNeice was unwilling to commit to a rigid political program. He once dismissed Marxism by writing that "the evil of the means obscures the good of the end." Proudly Irish, he often returned to the island to enjoy its land and people. At the same time, he lived most of his adult life in England and tried to achieve a balance between the pulls of those two places and Europe as a whole.

T. S. Eliot praised MacNeice as a "poet of genius whose virtuosity can be fully appreciated only by other poets." Critics of his time viewed him less favorably, though. His reputation has since shifted more toward Eliot's judgment. Today, many consider MacNeice second only to Auden among the poets of their generation. His poetry is restrained and precise, with overtones of melancholy. It is the poetry of a man who, as the poet Edwin Muir put it, "is never swept off his feet."

> " The evil of the means obscures the good of the end."

Carrick Revisited

Louis MacNeice

Back to Carrick,[1] the castle as plumb assured
As thirty years ago—Which war was which?
Here are new villas, here is a sizzling grid
But the green banks are as rich and the lough[2] as hazily lazy
5   And the child's astonishment not yet cured.

Who was—and am—dumbfounded to find myself
In a topographical frame—here, not there—
The channels of my dreams determined largely
By random chemistry of soil and air;
10   Memories I had shelved peer at me from the shelf.

Fog-horn, mill-horn, corncrake and church bell
Half-heard through boarded time as a child in bed
Glimpses a brangle of talk from the floor below
But cannot catch the words. Our past we know
15   But not its meaning—whether it meant well.

---

1. **Carrick** shortened form of Carrickfergus, a town in Northern Ireland.
2. **lough** (läkh) lake, specifically Belfast Lough. Carrickfergus is situated on the northern shore of Belfast Lough.

Time and place—our bridgeheads into reality
But also its concealment! Out of the sea
We land on the Particular and lose
All other possible bird's-eye views, the Truth
20 That is of Itself for Itself—but not for me.

Torn before birth from where my fathers dwelt,
Schooled from the age of ten to a foreign voice,
Yet neither western Ireland nor southern England
Cancels this interlude; what chance misspelt
25 May never now be righted by my choice.

Whatever then my inherited or acquired
Affinities, such remains my childhood's frame
Like a belated rock in the red Antrim[3] clay
That cannot at this era change its pitch or name—
30 And the prenatal mountain is far away.

◄ Carrickfergus Castle, shown on the facing page, was built in 1177.

Vocabulary

affinities (ə fin′ i tēz) *n.* family connections; sympathies

prenatal (prē nāt′ əl) *adj.* existing or taking place before birth

---

3. Antrim county in Northern Ireland in which Carrickfergus is located.

Critical Reading

Cite textual evidence to support your responses.

1. **Key Ideas and Details (a)** Where does the speaker find himself at the beginning of the poem? **(b) Compare and Contrast:** According to the first stanza, what has changed and what has remained the same?

2. **Key Ideas and Details (a)** What discovery dumbfounds the speaker? **(b) Interpret:** What relationship does the speaker discover between the imagination—which enables us to picture ourselves in any circumstances—and the facts of his personal history?

3. **Key Ideas and Details (a) Interpret:** What effect do the specifics of the place have on the speaker's imagination? **(b) Interpret:** What does the speaker mean in saying "Our past we know / But not its meaning . . ."? **(c) Speculate:** What task concerning the past might MacNeice assign to poetry?

4. **Integration of Knowledge and Ideas (a) Interpret:** Why does the speaker call his childhood in Carrick an "interlude"? **(b) Draw Conclusions:** How is MacNeice's identity, as described in this poem, influenced by two cultures but separate from both?

5. **Integration of Knowledge and Ideas** Name two ways in which issues of identity are just as complex for people today.

Stephen Spender

(1909–1995)

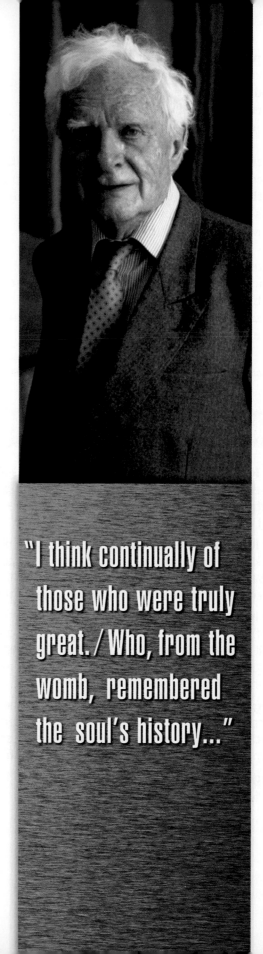

"I think continually of those who were truly great./Who, from the womb, remembered the soul's history..."

Author of "Not Palaces"

No poet of the 1930s provided a more honest picture of the era between the wars than did Stephen Spender. Much of his early poetry deals with the world of the thirties, the "low dishonest decade"—in W. H. Auden's phrase—that saw many countries struggle with economic depression, experiment with extremist ideologies, and drift inexorably toward war. Yet Spender, never a pessimist, celebrates technology at the same time as he confronts the problems of industrial progress. While many of his poems had political themes, they also reflect his deeply personal responses to the world.

Born in London and educated at Oxford, Spender published his first important book, *Poems* (1933), while he was living in Germany. Early in life, Spender was politically active and—like many other young English college men of the time—embraced communism. He promoted antifascist propaganda in Spain during that country's civil war (1936–1939) but abandoned communism during World War II. In 1949, he joined with others in publishing a work that criticized communism called *The God That Failed*.

Even in his college years, Spender was more than a poet. It was he who published Auden's first collection of poems, privately printing an edition of thirty copies. Starting in the 1940s, Spender became a highly regarded literary critic and commentator. He later coedited the literary magazine *Horizon* and the political, cultural, and literary review *Encounter*. Along with writing poetry, Spender wrote short stories, a novel, verse plays, and volumes of criticism and essays. He continued working at poetry, though, publishing his last collection of poems a year before his death.

Not Palaces

Stephen Spender

BACKGROUND In this poem's unifying metaphor, Spender says that he will not build old-fashioned poems that are like palaces—beautiful, ornate structures remote from the masses. Instead, he hopes to build active, modern poetry, more like the steel and glass skyscrapers that began with the International and Bauhaus architectural styles of the 1920s and 1930s. These buildings create dynamic spaces by combining strikingly simple forms with superior industrial craftsmanship. Walter Gropius, the founder of the Bauhaus school, sought to integrate architecture and the other arts.

Not palaces, an era's crown
Where the mind dwells, **intrigues**, rests:
Architectural gold-leaved flower
From people ordered like a single mind,
5 I build: this only what I tell:
It is too late for rare accumulation,
For family pride, for beauty's filtered dusts;

I say, stamping the words with emphasis,
Drink from here energy and only energy
10   To will this time's change.
Eye, gazelle, delicate wanderer,
Drinker of horizon's fluid line;
Ear that suspends on a chord
The spirit drinking timelessness;
15   Touch, love, all senses;
Leave your gardens, your singing feasts,
Your dreams of suns circling before our sun,
Of heaven after our world.
Instead, watch images of flashing glass
20   That strike the outward sense, the polished will,
Flag of our purpose which the wind engraves.
No spirit seek here rest. But this: No one
Shall hunger: Man shall spend equally;
Our goal which we compel: Man shall be man.

Compare and Contrast Elements

Contrast Spender's definite rejection of pastoral images in lines 16–18 with MacNeice's mixed feelings about the pastoral of childhood.

Critical Reading

Cite textual evidence to support your responses.

1. **Key Ideas and Details (a)** In lines 1–7, what does the speaker say he will not do? **(b) Interpret:** What vision of art is he rejecting?

2. **Key Ideas and Details (a)** What reason does the speaker give for rejecting the "accumulation" of rarities? **(b) Interpret:** What connection does the speaker make between his poem and social progress in lines 9–10?

3. **Key Ideas and Details (a) Interpret:** What might the speaker mean by "images of flashing glass"? **(b) Compare and Contrast:** How does this image contrast with the palaces described in the poem's opening?

4. **Integration of Knowledge and Ideas (a) Analyze:** What does Spender think the job of poetry once was? **(b) Analyze:** What does he think it should be now?

5. **Integration of Knowledge and Ideas** Do these poems reflect a sense of a particular place or time? Explain. In your response, use at least two of these Essential Question words: *unique, aware, consciousness, permanence.* *[Connecting to the Essential Question: What is the relationship between literature and place?]*

Literary Analysis

1. **Craft and Structure** Is it reasonable to say that Auden builds an **allegory** out of Yeats's work and life in the poem "In Memory of W. B. Yeats"? Explain.

2. **Craft and Structure** Auden uses similar images in lines 27 and 76–77 in "In Memory of W. B. Yeats." How do the differences in these two images help carry the meaning of the poem?

3. **Craft and Structure** Use a chart like the one shown to trace the use of **pastoral** images in "In Memory of W. B. Yeats," "Carrick Revisited," and "Not Palaces." Then, summarize the way each writer uses pastoral elements in his poems.

Poem	Pastoral Images	Poet's Attitude Toward Pastoral
"In Memory of W. B. Yeats"	Frozen brook; wolves running wild	
"Carrick Revisited"		
"Not Palaces"		

4. **Key Ideas and Details** **(a)** What does MacNeice say we gain from being born in a particular time and place? **(b)** What do we lose?

5. **Comparing Literary Works** Pastoral writers often look to the past, cherishing a time when life was simpler and sometimes portraying that time as a "golden age." **(a)** Does Auden reflect this perspective in "Musée des Beaux Arts"? Explain your answer. **(b)** Does Spender reflect this view in "Not Palaces"? Explain your answer.

6. **Integration of Knowledge and Ideas** **(a) Compare and contrast** Auden's portrayal of the contemporary world in "In Memory of W. B. Yeats" with Spender's view of the modern world in "Not Palaces." **(b)** With which of these views do you think MacNeice would most agree? Explain your answer.

7. **Craft and Structure** **(a)** How do the language and tone of "Musée des Beaux Arts" and "Not Palaces" differ? **(b)** How do those differences contribute to the feeling and meaning of the poems?

8. **Integration of Knowledge and Ideas** Both "In Memory of W. B. Yeats" and "Carrick Revisited" question the connection between the particulars of an artist's life and his or her work. Compare their answers.

9. **Integration of Knowledge and Ideas** **(a)** Which of these poets believe that art in some sense rises above life? **(b)** Which do not? Explain, using examples. **(c)** With which poet's view of art do you agree? Include details from the texts to support your argument.

Common Core State Standards

Writing
5. Develop and strengthen writing as needed by planning, revising, editing, rewriting, or trying a new approach, focusing on addressing what is most significant for a specific purpose and audience. *(p. 1186)*

Language
3. Apply knowledge of language to understand how language functions in different contexts, to make effective choices for meaning or style, and to comprehend more fully when reading or listening. *(p. 1186)*

Vocabulary Acquisition and Use

Word Analysis: Greek Root *-top-*

The Greek root *-top-* means "place" or "surface." The word *topographical*, which MacNeice uses in "Carrick Revisited," means "relating to a map of the surface features of a place." Explain how the root contributes to the meaning of the italicized words in these sentences.

1. The nurse used a *topical* ointment on the bee sting to reduce the swelling.

2. The *topocentric* distances were all measured from the same point of origin.

3. Mapmakers use precise measures to learn the *topography* of a place.

4. *Topology* is only one branch of geography.

Vocabulary: Synonyms

A synonym is a word that has a meaning similar to that of another word. Answer each question below. In your answer, use a word from the vocabulary list on page 1170 that is a synonym for the italicized word in each question.

1. Were the *schemes* of the plotters successful?

2. Were the different conspirators *isolated* from each other or held together?

3. What kind of detail did the *elevation* map show?

4. Do experts agree on the importance of *prebirth* nutrition?

5. Did her *sympathies* affect what charities she gave to?

Writing to Sources

Poem Auden's poem "Musée des Beaux Arts" was inspired by a Brueghel painting. Choose another painting or a photograph and respond to it in a **poem** of your own. To convey one main impression, establish and maintain a strong, consistent tone. Demonstrate your understanding of the style of the poets in this collection by using the free verse and conversational tone of Auden or the more energetic, rhythmic style of Spender.

Prewriting Begin by choosing an artwork that you either admire or dislike. Jot notes about what the artwork shows—the use of shapes and colors—and how it makes you feel. Is the work dramatic and stirring? Or is it peaceful and calming? Review your notes, circling important details.

Drafting Choose a logical organization. You might begin with a physical description of the artwork and then reveal your emotional response to it. As you draft, concentrate on choosing natural, fresh, and vivid language that will result in a strong, consistent tone, whether that is wonder, amusement, or disappointment.

Revising Ask a partner to read your poem and share the main impression he or she received. Revise your poem if your partner's impression does not match the one you wanted to convey. Pay special attention to your word choice, revising language as needed to more clearly convey your intended impression.

Model: Revising to Add Descriptive Language

bold   mocking, laughing—

A blue stripe splits the canvas in two, ~~challenging the viewer,~~
"On which side are you?"

Flatly descriptive language is revised to portray stronger images.

Virginia Woolf

(1882–1941)

Virginia Woolf, one of the early practitioners of Modernism, was instrumental in revolutionizing modern fiction. Abandoning traditional plot and structure in fiction, she was one of the pioneers of the stream-of-consciousness technique. This device allows readers to tune in directly to the flow of thoughts and images in a character's mind.

A Literary Life

Born Virginia Stephen, Woolf came from a prim and proper Victorian family, but it was one in which literature was prized. Her father, the renowned editor Leslie Stephen, made sure that his daughter grew up surrounded by books. Woolf always knew that she wanted to be a writer. At the age of twenty-three, Woolf was writing articles and essays and contributing book reviews to the *Times Literary Supplement*.

Bloomsbury

After their father died in 1904, Virginia moved with her sister Vanessa and her brothers to a home in the Bloomsbury neighborhood of London. Their house became a meeting place for writers, artists, and thinkers, who gathered to discuss literature, art, and politics. This influential group, known as the Bloomsbury Group, generally rejected the values and morals of Victorianism, instead promoting artistic and personal freedoms.

In 1912, Virginia married Leonard Woolf, a member of this group, who was a journalist, author, and literary editor. Together they founded the Hogarth Press in 1917. Along with Virginia's works, they published the works of other notable writers, including T. S. Eliot, E. M. Forster, and Katherine Mansfield.

Revolutionizing Fiction

Woolf's first two novels were not unusual, but she soon established herself as one of the leading writers of Modernism. *Jacob's Room* (1922) shattered the conventions of fiction by telling the story of a young man's life entirely through an examination of his room. (She also uses this device in "The Lady in the Looking Glass: A Reflection.") Woolf continued to refine her fluid, inward-looking style with three more stream-of-consciousness novels—*Mrs. Dalloway* (1925), *To the Lighthouse* (1927), and *The Waves* (1931). In her more revolutionary works, she virtually abolishes a traditional plot, preferring to concentrate on what she called "an ordinary mind on an ordinary day." In *Mrs. Dalloway*, for example, there is little action. The central character, Clarissa Dalloway, spends a day in London preparing for an evening party. Her thoughts move from the present to the past and back to the present.

Depression and Tragedy

Throughout her life, Woolf suffered episodes of severe depression brought on by poor health. She had frequent periods when she was unable to focus enough to read or write. The turmoil of World War II worsened her depression. In 1941, she drowned in the River Ouse near the Woolfs' home in Sussex.

In addition to the considerable number of critical essays she produced in her life, Woolf wrote about fifteen novels. Today she is recognized as one of the greatest contributors to modern fiction.

Virginia Woolf & Pop Culture

Who's afraid of Virginia Woolf? That punning question—based on the jingle, Who's Afraid of the Big Bad Wolf—was the title of a famous Edward Albee play. Part of the joke behind it is that the author of such sophisticated stream-of-consciousness novels as *Mrs. Dalloway* and *To the Lighthouse* does seem like a forbidding intellectual figure.

Surprisingly, however, this great Modernist author turns up frequently on the Internet. Apparently, no one on the World Wide Web is afraid of her.

Some Woolf sites, such as that of The Virginia Woolf Society, are devoted to a serious-minded discussion of her as an important literary figure. Others, however, blur the line between high and low culture, bringing the upper-class British author into the democracy of the Internet. Another way to view her online popularity would be to say that somehow she has entered into our culture's stream of consciousness.

One of the sites showing no fear of the Woolf is that of the Cosmic Baseball Association, a self-described art project that had the Bloomsbury author playing on one of the league's teams. A dispute between Woolf and her manager, however, led to her being traded.

As these Web shenanigans reveal, Woolf has gone beyond her role as a writer to become a cultural icon—a figure in whom many online constituencies see their own interests and obsessions reflected. In this respect, Woolf is not unlike Marilyn Monroe, another iconic female who has achieved immortality in the culture's stream of consciousness.

Marilyn Monroe, as depicted by Andy Warhol

Director Mike Nichols (left) and part of the cast of the film version of *Who's Afraid of Virginia Woolf* (1966): (from left to right, after Nichols) George Segal, Elizabeth Taylor, and Richard Burton

Nicole Kidman, playing Virginia Woolf in the film *The Hours* (2002)

Connecting to the Essential Question Think of a song you like. Freewrite about your associations with the song—your thoughts, your feelings, and why you like it. As you read, find details in the fictional selections by Virginia Woolf that differ from the traditional way of telling a story. This will help you think about the Essential Question: **What is the relationship of the writer to tradition?**

Close Reading Focus

Point of View; Stream of Consciousness

Searching for forms suited to modern experience, writers tested different **points of view,** the perspective from which a story is told.

- A **first-person** narrator tells his or her own story. With this technique, authors can probe the thoughts of the narrator.
- A **third-person** narrator tells what happened to others. An **omniscient third person** has the ability to reveal the thoughts of several characters. A narrator with **limited omniscience** sees only into the mind of one or few characters.
- **Stream-of-consciousness** narration follows the flowing, branching currents of thought in a character's mind.

Writers began using the stream-of-consciousness technique under the influence of the emerging science of psychology. As in psychology, the free association of ideas in stream-of-consciousness narration reveals the dynamic nature of people's minds. As you read, consider how Woolf uses this technique to develop character.

Preparing to Read Complex Texts Experimental works offer great rewards but also place demands on readers. If you lose your way in a stream-of-consciousness story, you can **repair your comprehension by asking questions** to restore your focus. Use a chart such as the one shown.

Vocabulary

You will encounter the words listed here in the texts that follow. Copy the words into your notebook, grouping them by number of syllables.

suffused	reticent
transient	vivacious
upbraidings	irrevocable
evanescence	escapade

Common Core State Standards

Reading Literature
3. Analyze the impact of the author's choices regarding how to develop and relate elements of a story or drama.

Passage

"The room that afternoon was full of such shy creatures..."

↓

Question

Why is the narrator talking about creatures filling the drawing room?

↓

Answer

She is comparing the movements in the room to the movements of shy animals that do not know they are being observed.

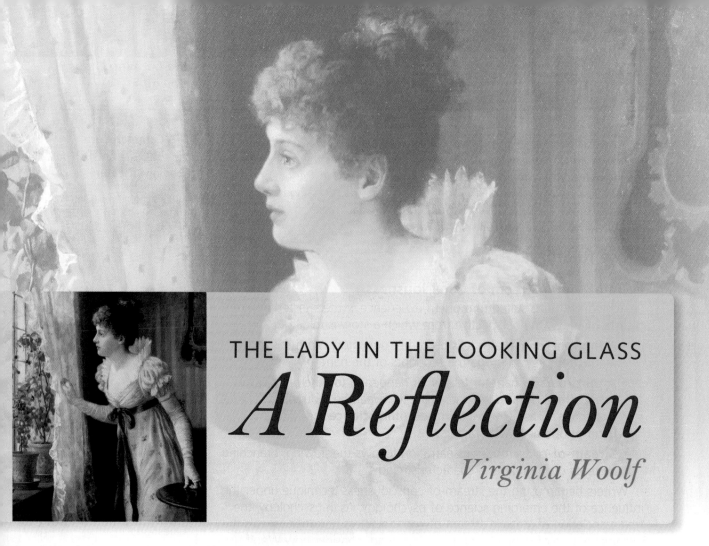

THE LADY IN THE LOOKING GLASS
A Reflection
Virginia Woolf

BACKGROUND Virginia Woolf was part of an artistic and intellectual circle called the Bloomsbury Group, named for the section of London where they met. The circle included Woolf's husband, her brother, her sister and brother-in-law, and such intellectual stars as novelist E. M. Forster and economist John Maynard Keynes. Like others in the Modernist movement, group members rejected tradition and sought new answers in their efforts to define artistic beauty and morality.

People should not leave looking glasses hanging in their rooms any more than they should leave open checkbooks or letters confessing some hideous crime. One could not help looking, that summer afternoon, in the long glass that hung outside in the hall. Chance had so arranged it. From the depths of the sofa in the drawing room one could see reflected in the Italian glass not only the marble-topped table opposite, but a stretch of the garden beyond. One could see a long grass path leading between banks of tall flowers until, slicing off an angle, the gold rim cut it off.

The house was empty, and one felt, since one was the only person in the drawing room, like one of those naturalists who, covered with grass and leaves, lie watching the shyest animals—badgers, otters, king-fishers—moving about freely, themselves unseen. The room that afternoon was full of such shy creatures, lights and shadows, curtains blowing, petals falling—things that never happen, so it seems, if someone is looking. The quiet old country room with its rugs and stone chimney pieces, its sunken bookcases and red and gold lacquer cabinets, was full of such nocturnal creatures. They came pirouetting across the floor, stepping delicately with high-lifted feet and spread tails and pecking allusive beaks as if they had been cranes or flocks of elegant flamingoes whose pink was faded, or peacocks whose trains were veiled with silver. And there were obscure flushes and darkening too, as if a cuttlefish had suddenly suffused the air with purple; and the room had its passions and rages and envies and sorrows coming over it and clouding it, like a human being. Nothing stayed the same for two seconds together.

But, outside, the looking glass reflected the hall table, the sunflowers, the garden path so accurately and so fixedly that they seemed held there in their reality unescapably. It was a strange contrast—all changing here, all stillness there. One could not help looking from one to the other. Meanwhile, since all the doors and windows were open in the heat, there was a perpetual sighing and ceasing sound, the voice of the transient and the perishing, it seemed, coming and going like human breath, while in the looking glass things had ceased to breathe and lay still in the trance of immortality.

Half an hour ago the mistress of the house, Isabella Tyson, had gone down the grass path in her thin summer dress, carrying a basket, and had vanished, sliced off by the gilt rim of the looking glass. She had gone presumably into the lower garden to pick flowers; or as it seemed more natural to suppose, to pick something light and fantastic and leafy and trailing, traveler's-joy, or one of those elegant sprays of convolvulus that twine round ugly walls and burst here and there into white and violet blossoms. She suggested the fantastic and the tremulous convolvulus rather than the upright aster, the starched zinnia, or her own burning roses alight like lamps on the straight posts of their rose trees. The comparison showed how very little, after all these years, one knew about her; for it is impossible that any woman of flesh and blood of fifty-five or sixty should be really a wreath or a tendril. Such comparisons are worse than idle and superficial—they are cruel even, for they come like the convolvulus itself trembling between one's eyes and the truth. There must be truth; there must be a wall. Yet it was strange that after knowing her all these years one could not say what the truth about Isabella was; one still made up phrases like this about convolvulus and traveler's-joy. As for facts, it was a fact that she was a spinster; that she was rich; that she had bought this house and collected with her own hands—often in the

Repairing Comprehension

Is your impression of the narrator clear? Ask a question to clarify your impression.

Vocabulary

suffused (sə fyo͞ozd′) v. spread throughout; filled

Vocabulary

transient (tran′ shənt) n. that which passes quickly

Comprehension

Where is the narrator?

The Lady in the Looking Glass: A Reflection **1193**

most obscure corners of the world and at great risk from poisonous stings and Oriental diseases—the rugs, the chairs, the cabinets
which now lived their nocturnal life before one's eyes. Sometimes it
seemed as if they knew more about her than we, who sat on them,
wrote at them, and trod on them so carefully, were allowed to know.
In each of these cabinets were many little drawers, and each almost
certainly held letters, tied with bows of ribbon, sprinkled with sticks
of lavender or rose leaves. For it was another fact—if facts were what
one wanted—that Isabella had known many people, had had many
friends; and thus if one had the audacity to open a drawer and read
her letters, one would find the traces of many agitations, of appointments to meet, of upbraidings for not having met, long letters of intimacy and affection, violent letters of jealousy and reproach, terrible
final words of parting—for all those interviews and assignations had
led to nothing—that is, she had never married, and yet, judging from
the masklike indifference of her face, she had gone through twenty
times more of passion and experience than those whose loves are
trumpeted forth for all the world to hear. Under the stress of thinking about Isabella, her room became more shadowy and symbolic;
the corners seemed darker, the legs of chairs and tables more spindly
and hieroglyphic.

Suddenly these reflections were ended violently and yet without a
sound. A large black form loomed into the looking glass; blotted out
everything, strewed the table with a packet of marble tablets veined
with pink and gray, and was gone. But the picture was entirely
altered. For the moment it was unrecognizable and irrational and
entirely out of focus. One could not relate these tablets to any human
purpose. And then by degrees some logical process set to work on
them and began ordering and arranging them and bringing them
into the fold of common experience. One realized at last that they
were merely letters. The man had brought the post.

There they lay on the marble-topped table, all dripping with light
and color at first and crude and unabsorbed. And then it was strange
to see how they were drawn in and arranged and composed and made
part of the picture and granted that stillness and immortality which
the looking glass conferred. They lay there invested with a new reality and significance and with a greater heaviness, too, as if it would
have needed a chisel to dislodge them from the table. And, whether
it was fancy or not, they seemed to have become not merely a handful of casual letters but to be tablets graven with eternal truth—if one
could read them, one would know everything there was to be known
about Isabella, yes, and about life, too. The pages inside those marble-
looking envelopes must be cut deep and scored thick with meaning.
Isabella would come in, and take them, one by one, very slowly, and
open them, and read them carefully word by word, and then with a
profound sigh of comprehension, as if she had seen to the bottom of
everything, she would tear the envelopes to little bits and tie the letters
together and lock the cabinet drawer in her determination to conceal
what she did not wish to be known.

Vocabulary

upbraidings (up brād′ iŋz)
n. stern words of disapproval;
scoldings

Point of View

What effect does the
narrator's attention to the
workings of his or her own
mind have on the narration?

▶ **Critical Viewing**

What aspects of this painting
mirror the story's setting?
CONNECT

The thought served as a challenge. Isabella did not wish to be known—but she should no longer escape. It was absurd, it was monstrous. If she concealed so much and knew so much one must prize her open with the first tool that came to hand—the imagination. One must fix one's mind upon her at that very moment. One must fasten her down there. One must refuse to be put off any longer with sayings and doings such as the moment brought forth—with dinners and visits and polite conversations. One must put oneself in her shoes. If one took the phrase literally, it was easy to see the shoes in which she stood, down in the lower garden, at this moment. They were very narrow and long and fashionable—they were made of the softest and most flexible leather. Like everything she wore, they were exquisite. And she would be standing under the high hedge in the lower part of the garden, raising the scissors that were tied to her waist to cut some dead flower, some overgrown branch. The sun would beat down on her face, into her eyes; but no, at the critical moment a veil of cloud covered the sun, making the expression of her eyes doubtful—was it mocking or tender, brilliant or dull? One could only see the indeterminate outline of her rather faded, fine face looking at the sky. She was thinking, perhaps, that she must order a new net for the strawberries; that she must send flowers to Johnson's widow; that it was time she drove over to see the Hippesleys in their new house. Those were the things she talked about at dinner certainly. But one was tired of the things that she talked about at dinner. It

Stream of Consciousness

In what way does this paragraph illustrate the use of stream-of-consciousness narration?

Comprehension

What do the "marble tablets" turn out to be?

THE THOUGHT SERVED AS A CHALLENGE. *Isabella did not wish to be known— but she should no longer escape.*

The Garden of Love, (detail), Walter Richard Sickert, The Fitzwilliam Museum, Cambridge

AND THERE WAS NOTHING.

Isabella was perfectly empty. She had no thoughts. She had no friends.

Vocabulary

evanescence (ev´ ə nes´ əns) *n.* vanishing or tendency to vanish

reticent (ret´ ə sənt) *adj.* silent; reserved

was her profounder state of being that one wanted to catch and turn to words, the state that is to the mind what breathing is to the body, what one calls happiness or unhappiness. At the mention of those words it became obvious, surely, that she must be happy. She was rich; she was distinguished; she had many friends; she traveled—she bought rugs in Turkey and blue pots in Persia. Avenues of pleasure radiated this way and that from where she stood with her scissors raised to cut the trembling branches while the lacy clouds veiled her face.

Here with a quick movement of her scissors she snipped the spray of traveler's-joy and it fell to the ground. As it fell, surely some light came in too, surely one could penetrate a little farther into her being. Her mind then was filled with tenderness and regret. . . . To cut an overgrown branch saddened her because it had once lived, and life was dear to her. Yes, and at the same time the fall of the branch would suggest to her how she must die herself and all the futility and evanescence of things. And then again quickly catching this thought up, with her instant good sense, she thought life had treated her well; even if fall she must, it was to lie on the earth and molder sweetly into the roots of violets. So she stood thinking. Without making any thought precise—for she was one of those reticent people whose minds hold their thoughts enmeshed in clouds of silence—she was filled with thoughts. Her mind was like her room, in which lights advanced and retreated, came pirouetting and stepping delicately, spread their tails, pecked their way; and then her whole being was suffused, like the room again, with a cloud of some profound knowledge, some unspoken regret, and then she was full of locked drawers, stuffed with letters, like her cabinets. To talk of "prizing her open" as if she were an oyster, to use any but the finest and subtlest and most pliable tools upon her was impious and absurd. One must imagine—here was she in the looking glass. It made one start.

She was so far off at first that one could not see her clearly. She came lingering and pausing, here straightening a rose, there lifting a pink to smell it, but she never stopped; and all the time she became larger and larger in the looking glass, more and more completely the person into whose mind one had been trying to penetrate. One verified her by degrees—fitted the qualities one had discovered into this visible body. There were her gray-green dress, and her long shoes, her basket, and something sparkling at her throat. She came so gradually that she did not seem to derange the pattern in the glass, but only to bring in some new element which gently moved and altered the other objects as if asking them, courteously, to make room for her. And the letters and the table and the grass walk and the sunflowers which had been waiting in the looking glass separated and opened out so that she might be received among them. At last there she was, in the hall. She stopped dead. She stood by the table. She stood perfectly still. At once the looking glass began to pour over her a light that seemed to fix her; that seemed like some acid to bite off the unessential and superficial and to leave only the truth. It was an enthralling spectacle. Everything dropped from her—clouds, dress, basket, diamond—all that one had called the creeper and convolvulus. Here was the hard wall beneath. Here was the woman herself. She stood naked in that pitiless light. And there was nothing. Isabella was perfectly empty. She had no thoughts. She had no friends. She cared for nobody. As for her letters, they were all bills. Look, as she stood there, old and angular, veined and lined, with her high nose and her wrinkled neck, she did not even trouble to open them.

People should not leave looking glasses hanging in their rooms.

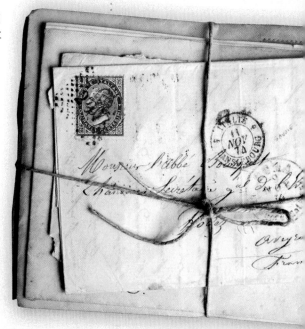

▼ **Critical Viewing**
Make an analogy comparing an unopened letter like this one with Isabella as seen by the narrator. **CONNECT**

Critical Reading

Cite textual evidence to support your responses.

1. **Key Ideas and Details** **(a)** Where are the narrator and Isabella, respectively, at the opening of the story? **(b) Infer:** From what perspective does the narrator observe Isabella? **(c) Speculate:** Who might the narrator be? Explain.

2. **Key Ideas and Details** **(a)** Briefly describe the layout and furnishings of the room in the story. **(b) Summarize:** How does the looking glass "guide" the narrator to an understanding of Isabella? **(c) Interpret:** What does the last sentence of the story, repeated from the beginning, mean?

from
Mrs. Dalloway

Virginia Woolf

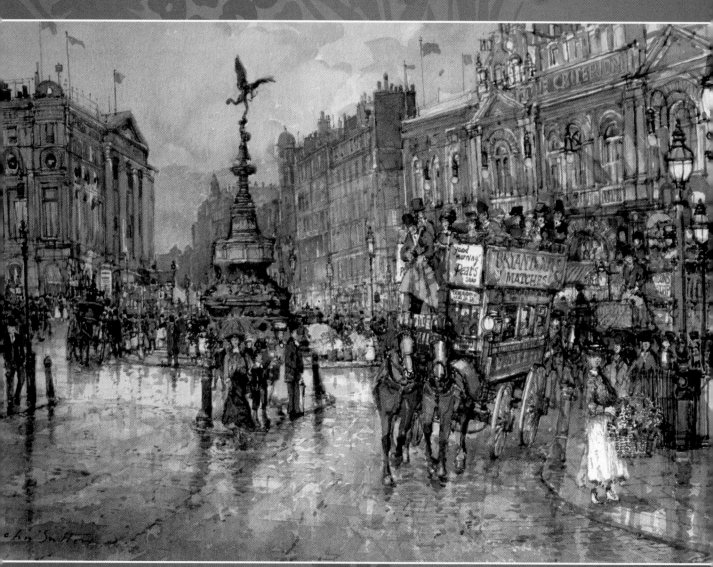

M rs. Dalloway said she would buy the flowers herself. For Lucy had her work cut out for her. The doors would be taken off their hinges; Rumpelmayer's men were coming. And then, thought Clarissa Dalloway, what a morning—fresh as if issued to children on a beach.

What a lark! What a plunge! For so it had always seemed to her, when, with a little squeak of the hinges, which she could hear now, she had burst open the French windows and plunged at Bourton into the open air. How fresh, how calm, stiller than this of course, the air was in the early morning; like the flap of a wave; the kiss of a wave; chill and sharp and yet (for a girl of eighteen as she then was) solemn, feeling as she did, standing there at the open window, that something awful was about to happen; looking at the flowers, at the trees with the smoke winding off them and the rooks[1] rising, falling; standing and looking until Peter Walsh said, "Musing among the vegetables?"— was that it?—"I prefer men to cauliflowers"—was that it? He must have said it at breakfast one morning when she had gone out on to the terrace—Peter Walsh. He would be back from India one of these days, June or July, she forgot which, for his letters were awfully dull; it was his sayings one remembered; his eyes, his pocket-knife, his smile, his grumpiness and, when millions of things had utterly vanished—how strange it was!—a few sayings like this about cabbages.

She stiffened a little on the kerb,[2] waiting for Durtnall's van to pass. A charming woman, Scrope Purvis thought her (knowing her as one does know people who live next door to one in Westminster); a touch of the bird about her, of the jay, blue-green, light, vivacious, though she was over fifty, and grown very white since her illness. There she perched, never seeing him, waiting to cross, very upright.

For having lived in Westminster—how many years now? over twenty,—one feels even in the midst of the traffic, or waking at night, Clarissa was positive, a particular hush, or solemnity; an indescribable pause; a suspense (but that might be her heart, affected, they said, by influenza) before Big Ben strikes. There! Out it boomed. First a warning, musical; then the hour, irrevocable. The leaden circles dissolved in the air. Such fools we are, she thought, crossing Victoria Street. For Heaven only knows why one loves it so, how one sees it so, making it up, building it round one, tumbling it, creating it every moment afresh; but the veriest frumps,[3] the most dejected of miseries sitting on doorsteps (drink their downfall) do the same; can't be dealt with, she felt positive, by Acts of Parliament for that very reason: they love life. In

---

1. **rooks** crows.
2. **kerb** the curb.
3. **veriest frumps** most plain, unfashionable women.

◀ **Critical Viewing**
How do the bustle and vividness of this painting mirror the stream-of-consciousness narration of the story? **DEDUCE**

Vocabulary

vivacious (və vā′ shəs)
adj. lively, spirited
irrevocable (i re′ və kə bəl)
adj. not possible to revoke or change

Comprehension

Where does Mrs. Dalloway live?

people's eyes, in the swing, tramp, and trudge; in the bellow and the uproar; the carriages, motor cars, omnibuses,[4] vans, sandwich men shuffling and swinging; brass bands; barrel organs; in the triumph and the jingle and the strange high singing of some aeroplane overhead was what she loved; life; London; this moment of June.

---

4. omnibuses buses

Julian Barrow

▶ **Critical Viewing**
What might Mrs. Dalloway think about on a London street like this?
CONNECT

Critical Reading

1. **Key Ideas and Details** **(a)** What does Mrs. Dalloway remember of Peter Walsh? **(b)** How does the narrator call into question Scrope Purvis's understanding of Mrs. Dalloway? **(c) Infer:** What do these comments suggest about the ability of one person to understand another?

2. **Key Ideas and Details** **(a)** What details suggest that Mrs. Dalloway has not been in the best of health? **(b) Infer:** How might that history affect her outlook on life?

3. **Key Ideas and Details** **(a) Summarize:** What happens in the passage? **(b) Draw Conclusions:** How important are those events?

4. **Integration of Knowledge and Ideas** How effectively do you think Woolf portrays the inner thoughts of Mrs. Dalloway?

Critical Commentary

from a Speech on Virginia Woolf

Michael Cunningham

Michael Cunningham is an American writer whose Pulitzer Prize–winning novel The Hours *features Virginia Woolf as a character. In this speech delivered at a PEN America Virginia Woolf tribute, Cunningham describes how, as a high-school student, he first fell in love with her work.*

Michael Cunningham

Mrs. Dalloway is the first great book I ever read. I was fifteen . . . One day I . . . suddenly found myself standing beside the pirate queen of our school. She was beautiful and mean and smart, she had long red fingernails, and long straight hair. Fringe, pretty much everywhere. I found myself standing next to her, and I thought, "Uh oh, uh oh . . . Think fast, be suave, say something that will make her love you forever." So I said something that I thought then—and I think today—was very winning, about the poetry of Bob Dylan and Leonard Cohen. She was kind to me. . . . and said, "Well, yes, they're very good, but how do you feel about T. S. Eliot and Virginia Woolf?"

. . . I never expected I'd have to read either one of them. I went to the library, the Bookmobile, the little trailer where the books were. They didn't have any Eliot, but they did have one book of Woolf's, and it was *Mrs. Dalloway.* I took it out, and I took it home and read it, tried to read it, and I didn't know what was going on. In another way I did get it. I did get the depth and density, and the sentences, and it did turn on some little light inside my stupid skull.

Everybody who reads has a first book—maybe not the first book you read, but the first book that shows you what literature can be. Like a first kiss. And you read other books, you kiss other people, but especially for those who are romantically inclined, that first book stays with you. I felt wedded to *Mrs. Dalloway* in a way I've never felt about any other book. I finally, finally, finally grew up and wrote *The Hours,* in which I tried to take an existing work of great art and make another work of art out of it, the way a jazz musician might play improvisations on a great piece of music.

I learned so much from Woolf as a writer. I think what I learned most importantly was her conviction that the whole of human existence, while it is copiously contained in foreign wars and the death of kings, and the other big subjects for big novels, is also contained in every hour in the life of everybody, very much the way the blueprint for the whole organism is contained in every strand of its DNA. If you look with sufficient penetration, and sufficient art, at any hour in the life of anybody, you can crack it open. And get everything. Virginia Woolf understood that every character, no matter how minor, in a novel she wrote was visiting the novel, from a novel of his or her own, where he or she was the hero of another great tragic and comic tale.

Key Ideas and Details What did Cunningham as a writer learn from reading Virginia Woolf?

Shakespeare's Sister

Virginia Woolf

Vocabulary

escapade (es´ kə pād)
n. a wild and reckless adventure

Be that as it may, I could not help thinking, as I looked at the works of Shakespeare on the shelf, that the bishop was right[1] at least in this; it would have been impossible, completely and entirely, for any woman to have written the plays of Shakespeare in the age of Shakespeare. Let me imagine, since facts are so hard to come by, what would have happened had Shakespeare had a wonderfully gifted sister, called Judith, let us say. Shakespeare himself went, very probably—his mother was an heiress—to the grammar school, where he may have learned Latin—Ovid, Virgil and Horace—and the elements of grammar and logic. He was, it is well known, a wild boy who poached[2] rabbits, perhaps shot a deer, and had, rather sooner than he should have done, to marry a woman in the neighborhood, who bore him a child rather quicker than was right. That escapade sent him to seek his fortune in London. He had, it seemed, a taste for the theater; he began by holding horses at the stage door. Very soon he got work in the theater, became a successful actor, and lived at the hub of the universe, meeting everybody, knowing everybody, practicing his art on the boards, exercising his wits in the streets, and even getting access to the palace of the queen. Meanwhile his extraordinarily gifted sister, let us suppose, remained at home. She was as adventurous, as imaginative, as agog to see the world as he was. But she was not sent to school. She had no chance of learning grammar and logic, let alone of reading Horace and Virgil. She picked up a book now and then, one of her brother's perhaps, and read a few pages. But then her parents came in and told her to mend the stockings or mind the stew and not moon about with books and papers. They would have spoken sharply but kindly, for they were substantial people who knew the conditions of life for a woman and loved their daughter—indeed, more likely than not she was the apple of her father's eye. Perhaps she scribbled some pages up in an apple loft on the sly, but was careful to hide them or set fire to them. Soon, however, before she was out of her teens, she was to be betrothed to the son

---

1. **the bishop was right** In the paragraph prior to this one, Woolf recalls that a bishop, whom she does not name, once wrote to a newspaper to say "it was impossible for any woman, past, present, or to come, to have the genius of Shakespeare."
2. **poached** hunted illegally.

of a neighboring wool-stapler. She cried out that marriage was hateful to her, and for that she was severely beaten by her father. Then he ceased to scold her. He begged her instead not to hurt him, not to shame him in this matter of her marriage. He would give her a chain of beads or a fine petticoat, he said; and there were tears in his eyes. How could she disobey him? How could she break his heart? The force of her own gift alone drove her to it. She made up a small parcel of her belongings, let herself down by a rope one summer's night and took the road to London. She was not seventeen. The birds that sang in the hedge were not more musical than she was. She had the quickest fancy, a gift like her brother's, for the tune of words. Like him, she had a taste for the theater. She stood at the stage door; she wanted to act,[3] she said. Men laughed in her face. The manager—a fat, loose-lipped man—guffawed. He bellowed something about poodles dancing and women acting—no woman, he said, could possibly be an actress. He hinted—you can imagine what. She could get no training in her craft. Could she even seek her dinner in a tavern or roam the streets at midnight? Yet her genius was for fiction and lusted to feed abundantly upon the lives of men and women and the study of their ways. At last—for she was very young, oddly like Shakespeare the poet in her face, with the same grey eyes and rounded brows—at last Nick Greene the actor-manager took pity on her; she found herself with child by that gentleman and so—who shall measure the heat and violence of the poet's heart when caught and tangled in a woman's body?—killed herself one winter's night and lies buried at some cross-roads where the omnibuses now stop outside the Elephant and Castle.

That, more or less, is how the story would run, I think, if a woman in Shakespeare's day had had Shakespeare's genius.

Repairing Comprehension

If you were wondering whether these events actually occurred, what questions might you ask to clarify that point?

Like him, She had a taste for the theater.

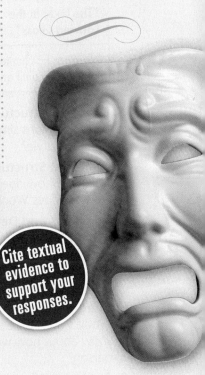

3. **she wanted to act** In Shakespeare's time, women were not allowed to act on stage. Men, dressed as women, played female roles.

Critical Reading

1. **Key Ideas and Details (a)** What details does Woolf include to give an identity to Shakespeare's sister? **(b) Infer:** What does she hope to accomplish by doing so?

2. **Integration of Knowledge and Ideas** Would Woolf say that the same obstacles blocking Shakespeare's sister existed in Woolf's own time?

3. **Integration of Knowledge and Ideas** How do the selections by Woolf reveal her to be a writer interested in changing tradition? In your response, use at least two of these Essential Question words: *convention, defy, credible, narrative, stream of consciousness.* **[Connecting to the Essential Question: What is the relationship of the writer to tradition?]**

Cite textual evidence to support your responses.

Literary Analysis

1. **Craft and Structure** Give three examples of the use of the **stream-of-consciousness** technique in "The Lady in the Looking Glass."

2. **Key Ideas and Details (a)** In "The Lady in the Looking Glass," what **questions** about the narrator might you ask? **(b)** What answers does the story suggest?

3. **Craft and Structure (a)** How does the literal reflection of Isabella in the mirror serve as a climax for the narrator's mental reflections? **(b)** What does the climax reveal about Isabella?

4. **Craft and Structure (a)** How would you describe Woolf's narrative **point of view** in the essay "Shakespeare's Sister"? **(b)** How does that point of view compare to those of the narrators of the other two selections? Use a chart like the one shown to list details about each narrator.

**Common Core
State Standards**

Language
4.d. Verify the preliminary determination of the meaning of a word or phrase. *(p. 1205)*

"The Lady in the Looking Glass"	*Mrs. Dalloway*	"Shakespeare's Sister"
Narrator has limited knowledge until end	Omniscient narrator	

5. **Craft and Structure (a)** How is the writing style in all three selections similar? **(b)** What does Woolf gain by using this style?

6. **Craft and Structure (a)** In the excerpt from *Mrs. Dalloway*, how does the narrative point of view shift? **(b)** How does Woolf's style make that shift possible?

7. **Key Ideas and Details (a)** What impression did you have of Mrs. Dalloway after reading the first long paragraph in the passage? **(b)** What questions would you ask about her to confirm that impression? **(c)** Did you have the same impression after reading the entire passage?

8. **Integration of Knowledge and Ideas** What does Woolf's use of the stream-of-consciousness technique show about how we construct a picture of another person?

9. **Analyzing Visual Information** In the caricature of Woolf on this page, what qualities of Woolf or her work does David Levine capture?

▲ David Levine caricature of Woolf from November 20, 1980

Vocabulary Acquisition and Use

Word Analysis: Latin Root -trans-

The Latin root -trans-, meaning "through" or "across," appears in the word *transient*, which Woolf uses in "The Lady in the Looking Glass." In that word, the root conveys the idea that an emotion or thought passes quickly, moving *through* a person rapidly. Use the meaning of -trans- to define these phrases that include the root.

1. transnational corporation

2. business transaction

3. transatlantic communication

4. transparent proceedings

5. transfer station

6. transformational experience

After defining the phrases, check your meanings by looking up the words in a dictionary.

Vocabulary: Sentence Completions

Use a word from the vocabulary list on page 1191 to complete each sentence, and explain your choice. Use each word only once.

1. The _____ hostess helped everyone at her party have a good time.

2. Constant _____ from his boss convinced the harried worker to resign.

3. The decisions of the Supreme Court are _____ and cannot be appealed.

4. How did the trickster manage to avoid the consequences of that particular _____?

5. The setting sun _____ the room with red-orange light.

6. The shy man was _____ to speak at the crowded meeting.

7. "It is just a passing fad, a _____ movement," declared the critic.

8. The preacher contrasted the _____ of worldly goods with the eternal nature of the spirit.

Using Resources to Build Vocabulary

Precise Words for Movement

Many words have synonyms, or other words with a similar meaning, but each word has a precise meaning. Woolf uses several words to describe the movements of light or objects in "The Lady in the Looking Glass":

pirouetting (p. 1193)   trembling (p. 1193)

pecking (p. 1193)   loomed (p. 1194)

Use a print or electronic dictionary or thesaurus to find synonyms of these words. State whether you think Woolf used the most effective word or whether you would recommend that she use one of the synonyms. Explain your reasoning.

Writing to Sources

Informative Text While a traditional omniscient third-person narrator can penetrate the thoughts of characters, the stream-of-consciousness technique gives the author an opportunity to show those thoughts in more complex ways. At the same time, this technique puts demands on readers. Choose a passage from "The Lady in the Looking Glass" or *Mrs. Dalloway* that you think is a good representative of the stream-of-consciousness technique. Then "translate" that passage into the style of a traditional omniscient third-person narrator. Finally, write a brief essay in which you state whether you prefer the original version or your "translation" and explain why.

Prewriting Begin by choosing a passage to "translate."

- Look for a passage that effectively presents the flow of the character's thoughts and feelings.
- Pick a passage that you found difficult to understand.

Drafting Write a "translation" of the passage that converts it to that of a traditional omniscient narrator.

- Remember that an omniscient narrator can reveal the inner thoughts of a character but does not use the fragmented words and phrases or association of ideas that mark stream-of-consciousness narration.
- Draft a brief **essay** that compares the two techniques. You might think about the different opportunities each gives to writers and the demands each places on readers. You might use a graphic organizer like the one below to take notes on the two points of view.

Common Core State Standards

Writing
2. Write informative/explanatory texts to examine and convey complex ideas, concepts, and information clearly and accurately through the effective selection, organization, and analysis of content.

Language
1. Demonstrate command of the conventions of standard English grammar and usage when writing or speaking. *(p. 1207)*
2.b. Spell correctly.

Stream of Consciousness Simulates the way people think | **Both reveal characters' thoughts** | **Traditional Narrator** More coherent; easier to follow

Revising Revise your essay to make it clear and effective:

- Review the draft of your "translation," making sure it is true to the traditional narrative style.
- Review the draft of your essay to ensure that you clearly state your position and cite evidence to support your points.
- Read both drafts carefully to make sure they are grammatically correct and all words are spelled correctly.

Conventions and Style: Parallel Structure

Good writers use **parallel structure,** or similar grammatical forms, to express similar ideas. Parallel structure gives your writing rhythm and emphasizes key ideas. To create parallel structure, use nouns with nouns, phrases with phrases, and clauses with clauses.

Look at the examples below. Notice that coordinating conjunctions *(and, or)* join items of equal importance.

Nonparallel: Look past the room *with its rugs, with its bookcases, and the night creatures that were dancing around.*	**Parallel:** Look past the room *with its rugs, with its bookcases, and with its dancing night creatures.*
Nonparallel: It was a fact *that Isabella was rich, and she took risks to collect objects.*	**Parallel:** It was a fact *that Isabella was rich and that she took risks to collect objects.*
Nonparallel: Isabella went into the garden *because of its flowers rather than because she wanted quiet.*	**Parallel:** Isabella went into the garden *because of its flowers rather than because of its quiet.*

As you edit your writing, check for parallel structure.

Practice Rewrite each item to correct the non-parallel structure.

1. Lights and shadows moved across the room, curtains blew, and there were petals that fell.
2. Rage, envy, and sorrowing seemed to fill the room.
3. Isabella went from the house, down the grass path, and she walked into the garden.
4. Isabella would choose a trailing plant rather than it was an upright, sturdy flower.
5. Because it was hot, the windows and doors were open, letting in sounds of life and to contrast with the scene in the mirror.
6. Isabella bought the house, traveled to far off places, and choosing furnishings.
7. The envelopes lay on the marble table, seeming to be out of order and not focusing.
8. Letters can reveal a person's past— appointments, dates not kept, and breaking promises.
9. She was seen in the looking glass, pausing, straightening a rose, and to lift a bloom to smell it.
10. Was her expression scornful or sensitive, shining or in a dull way?

Writing and Speaking Conventions

A. Writing Use the following items to write sentences with parallel structure:

1. feet, tails, beaks
2. of affection, of jealousy, of parting
3. marble-topped table, long grass path, the sunflowers
4. raising, looking, thinking

> **Example:** feet, tails, beaks
> **Sentence:** The birds lifted their feet, spread their tails, and tapped their beaks.

B. Speaking Consider the letters mentioned in "The Lady in the Looking Glass." Compose and present to the class a letter that might be written by the narrator who is imagining the contents of the drawers. Use at least three examples of parallel structure.

Stream-of-Consciousness
IN WORLD LITERATURE

James Joyce
(1882–1941)

Ulysses

Virginia Woolf
(1882–1941)

Mrs. Dalloway

YES I SAID YES I WILL YES

William Faulkner
(1897–1962)

AS I LAY DYING

WHAT A LARK!
WHAT A PLUNGE

MY MOTHER IS A FISH

PEDRO PÁRAMO

HERE I LIE, FLAT ON MY BACK

Rosario Castellanos
(1925–1974)

The Nine Guardians

Juan Rulfo
(1918–1986)

NANA LEADS ME

Comparing Literary Works

"The Lady in the Looking Glass"
by Virginia Woolf • from *Pedro Páramo by Juan Rulfo* • from *The Nine Guardians by Rosario Castellanos*

Comparing Stream-of-Consciousness Narratives

Stream-of-Consciousness Narration

In the early twentieth century, writers like James Joyce and Virginia Woolf tried to capture all the layers of consciousness observed in the groundbreaking work of Austrian psychoanalyst Sigmund Freud—visual and auditory perceptions, associations, memories, dreams, unconscious impulses—all flowing through the mind in what psychologist William James called the stream of consciousness. **Stream-of-consciousness narration** has these traits:

- Whether it uses first- or third-person point of view, it presents the external world through one or more characters' impressions.
- It leaps abruptly to new mental associations.
- It may shift in time, presenting memories or flashbacks.
- It may include fantasy elements or even dreams.
- It may use symbols that can be interpreted to reveal character.
- It may use long sentences or irregular grammar or punctuation to capture the flow of thoughts.

As you read, use a form like the one shown to help you compare the stream-of-consciousness narration in these selections.

> Selection: _____
> Character(s) Portrayed: _____
> Leaps to New Associations: _____
> Time Shifts/Memories or Flashbacks: _____
> Fantasies or Dreams: _____
> Symbols and Interpretations: _____
> Unusual Grammar/Usage/Punctuation: _____

Common Core State Standards

Reading Literature
3. Analyze the impact of the author's choices regarding how to develop and relate elements of a story or drama.

Language
4.c. Consult general and specialized reference materials, both print and digital, to find the pronunciation of a word or determine or clarify its precise meaning, its part of speech, its etymology, or its standard usage.

Gather Vocabulary Knowledge

Rulfo and Castellanos use related forms of the words *sweeping, swirling,* and *lashing.* Use a **dictionary** to find each word's part of speech and definition. Then, employ the following references to further explore these words:

- **History of Language:** Use a history of English to research each word's origins. Write a paragraph about the word's emergence in English.
- **Book of Quotations:** Use an online or print collection of quotations to find a quotation containing one of the words. In a paragraph, explain nuances in meaning that are evident from the context of the quotation.

Comparing References Compare and contrast what you learn about the words from these and other related references (printed or electronic), such as **books of roots and affixes.**

JUAN RULFO (1918–1986)

The son of wealthy landowners, Juan Rulfo (hwän ro̅o̅l' fo̅) grew up at a time when violent rebellion was tearing the Mexican countryside apart. When his father was killed and his mother died soon after, he lived for a time in an orphanage before moving to Mexico City. There he held a variety of jobs and also wrote fiction and screenplays, drawing on the tormented landscape of his childhood to produce the story collection *The Burning Plain* and the short novel *Pedro Páramo*.

A Literary Pioneer Although he wrote only two major works, Rulfo's influence on Latin American literature has been enormous. One of the first Spanish-language writers to use stream-of-consciousness narration, he also blended reality and fantasy to pioneer the magical realism that became so popular in Latin American fiction. The great magical realist Gabriel García Márquez recognized his debt to Rulfo by including a line from *Pedro Páramo* in his famous novel *One Hundred Years of Solitude*.

ROSARIO CASTELLANOS (1925–1974)

Rosario Castellanos (ro̅ sär' e̅ o̅ käs tel yä' no̅s) grew up in the southern Mexican region of Chiapas, where her family owned sugar and coffee plantations. Here she saw firsthand the poverty of the indigenous Mayan population whose plight she would later portray in her writing. After graduating from college in Mexico City, she began publishing essays and poetry. She won fame with her novel *The Nine Guardians*, published in 1957.

Battling for Justice A champion of social and economic justice, Rosario Castellanos wrote with deep concern about women's rights and the rights of Mexico's indigenous peoples. She also held several government posts and, as a member of the National Indigenous Institute, worked to promote literacy in impoverished parts of the country. She was serving as Mexico's ambassador to Israel when she died in an accident there in 1974.

Pedro Páramo
Juan Rulfo

BACKGROUND To fulfill his mother's deathbed request of vengeance against the man who abandoned their family, Juan Preciado goes in search of his father, Pedro Páramo. He travels to Comala, his mother's home town, only to learn that his father has died years before. Comala itself is a ghost town—literally, for the reader gradually comes to realize that all of the people Preciado encounters there are ghosts. The book shifts point of view to some of those people; in the following passage, the voice talking is probably that of Doña Susanita, Pedro Páramo's last wife.

I am lying in the same bed where my mother died so long ago; on the same mattress, beneath the same black wool coverlet she wrapped us in to sleep. I slept beside her, her little girl, in the special place she made for me in her arms.

I think I can still feel the calm rhythm of her breathing; the palpitations and sighs that soothed my sleep. . . . I think I feel the pain of her death. . . . But that isn't true.

Here I lie, flat on my back, hoping to forget my loneliness by remembering those times. Because I am not here just for a while. And I am not in my mother's bed but in a black box like the ones for burying the dead. Because I am dead.

Vocabulary
palpitations
(pal´ pə tā´ shənz) *n.*
rapid beating of the heart

Comparing Stream-of-Consciousness Narratives Which details indicate that this narrative, like that in *Mrs. Dalloway*, uses the stream-of-consciousness technique?

Vocabulary

tendrils (ten´ drəlz) *n.* climbing plants' clinging or coiling stemlike parts

I sense where I am, but I can think. . . .

I think about the limes ripening. About the February wind that used to snap the fern stalks before they dried up from neglect. The ripe limes that filled the overgrown patio with their fragrance.

The wind blew down from the mountains on February mornings. And the clouds gathered there waiting for the warm weather that would force them down into the valley. Meanwhile the sky was blue, and the light played on little whirlwinds sweeping across the earth, swirling the dust and lashing the branches of the orange trees.

The sparrows were twittering; they pecked at the wind-blown leaves, and twittered. They left their feathers among the thorny branches, and chased the butterflies, and twittered. It was that season.

February, when the mornings are filled with wind and sparrows and blue light. I remember. That is when my mother died.

I should have wailed. I should have wrung my hands until they were bleeding. That is how you would have wanted it. But in fact, wasn't that a joyful morning? The breeze was blowing in through the open door, tearing loose the ivy tendrils.

Critical Reading

Cite textual evidence to support your responses.

1. **Key Ideas and Details (a)** What has happened to the narrator to cause her to lie in the black box? **(b) Infer:** What is the black box? **(c) Analyze:** Why does she pretend to be a little girl in her mother's bed?

2. **Key Ideas and Details (a) Compare and Contrast:** Contrast the narrator's attitude toward the morning her mother died with the attitude she thinks she is supposed to have. **(b) Analyze:** Why do you think she feels the way she does about the morning?

3. **Integration of Knowledge and Ideas (a) Interpret:** What does the passage suggest about death in general? **(b) Support:** Cite details to support your interpretation.

from
The Nine Guardians
Rosario Castellanos

BACKGROUND Set in the remote towns and countryside of 1930s Chiapas, Mexico, *The Nine Guardians* depicts the harsh poverty of the area's Mayan Indians and the changes to society brought about by government efforts to improve economic conditions. Most of the book is narrated by a nameless seven-year-old girl from a family of ranch owners, through whose eyes and mind we see the social landscape mixed together with the nursery tales and fantasies of childhood. In this passage from early in the book, the narrator walks through the nearby town with Nana, the devoted Indian servant who has cared for her since birth.

Nana leads me through the street by the hand. The pavements are flagstones, polished and slippery. The street is cobbled. Little stones are arranged like petals in a flower. From between the joints grows short grass which the Indians tear up with the points of their machetes.[1] There are carts drawn by sleepy bullocks;[2] and ponies that strike sparks with their hoofs; and old horses tied to posts by their halters. All day they remain there, heads hanging, ears sadly twitching. We've just passed one. I held my breath and pressed close to the wall, afraid that any minute the horse would bare its great yellow teeth—and he has such lots of them—and bite my arm. I'd be ashamed, because my arms are very skinny and the horse might laugh.

The balconies are forever staring into the street, watching it go uphill and down and the way it turns the corners. Watching the gentlemen pass with their mahogany canes; the ranchers dragging their spurs as they walk; the Indians running under their heavy burdens. And at all times the diligent trotting donkeys loaded with water in wooden tubs. It must be nice to be like the balconies, always idle, absent-minded, just looking on. When I'm grown up. . . .

Vocabulary

diligent (dil´ ə jənt) *adj.* persevering and careful

---

1. **machetes** (mə shet´ *or* chet´ əz) *n.* large, heavy blades used for cutting down sugar cane, dense underbrush, or other plants.
2. **bullocks** (bool´ ə ks) *n.* bulls that have been neutered.

Now we begin climbing down Market Hill. The butchers' hatchets are ringing inside, and the stupid, sated flies are buzzing. We trip over the Indian women sitting on the ground weaving palm. They are talking together in their odd language, panting like hunted deer. And suddenly they let their sobs fly into the air, high-pitched, without tears. They always frighten me though I've heard them so often.

We skirt past the puddles. Last night came the first shower, the one that brings out the little ants with wings that go *tzisim*. We pass in front of the shops smelling of freshly dyed cloth. Behind the counter the assistant is measuring with a yard-stick. We can hear the grains of rice pattering against the metal scales. Someone is crumbling a handful of cocoa. And through the open street doors goes a girl with a basket on her head, and she screams, afraid that either the dogs or the owners will let fly at her:

"Dumplings—come buy!"

Nana urges me on. Now the only person in the street is a man with squeaking yellow shoes he can't have worn very often. A large door is wide open, and in front of the lighted forge[3] stands the blacksmith, dark from his trade. His chest shows bare and sweating as he hammers. An old maid opens her window just wide enough to watch us furtively. Her mouth is clamped tight as if she'd locked some secret in. She is sad because she knows her hair is turning white.

"Say how-do-you-do, child, she's a friend of your mother."

But we're already some distance off. The last few steps I almost run. I mustn't be late for school.

---

3. forge *n.* the place where a blacksmith heats metal and hammers it into shape.

Critical Reading

Cite textual evidence to support your responses.

1. **Key Ideas and Details (a)** Where is the narrator going? **(b) Infer:** Why does Nana accompany her? **(c) Infer:** What does the presence of Nana suggest about the social or economic standing of the narrator's family?

2. **Key Ideas and Details (a)** List some of the people, animals, or things the narrator observes as she walks through the town. **(b) Draw Conclusions:** From the details, what can you conclude the town is like?

3. **Key Ideas and Details (a)** With what emotions does the narrator react to the world around her? **(b) Evaluate:** Would you say she has a vivid imagination? Why or why not?

Comparing Stream-of-Consciousness Narration

1. **Craft and Structure** In your estimation, in which of the three selections does the **stream-of-consciousness narration** best capture the way the human mind works? Cite examples to support your opinion.

2. **Integration of Knowledge and Ideas (a)** Contrast the point of view in the Woolf story with that of the selections by Rulfo and Castellanos. **(b)** Which narrative has the strongest sense of immediacy, making you feel as if you are there? Why?

3. **Integration of Knowledge and Ideas (a)** What do the narrator in Woolf's story and the narrators of the other two selections have in common? **(b)** What are some of their chief differences? **(c)** Which of the three characters seems most in touch with reality? Why?

 Timed Writing

Informative Text: Analytical Essay

Each of these stream-of-consciousness narratives has to meet a challenge: how to use a character's thought processes, which are often chaotic, to convey a sense of the world around the character.

Assignment: Write an **analytical essay** in which you compare and contrast the ways in which the exterior world is conveyed in the three stream-of-consciousness narratives. **[40 minutes]**

Your essay should address these questions:

- Through whose eyes is the setting conveyed?
- What memories or other associations do the details of setting prompt in this person's mind?
- How do the character's perceptions and memories color your impression of the exterior world?

As you write, follow the conventions of a strong analytical essay:

- Advance a clear thesis statement.
- Support your ideas with relevant and substantial evidence and well-chosen details from the texts.

Remember to write legibly and use appropriate capitalization and punctuation conventions.

5-Minute Planner

Complete these steps before you begin to write:

1. Read the assignment carefully. Identify key words and phrases.

2. Weigh the similarities and differences in the ways in which each selection conveys the setting. **TIP** As you scan the texts, jot down quotations or details that you might use in your essay.

3. Create a rough outline for your essay.

4. Reread the prompt, and draft your essay.

Common Core State Standards

Writing

2. Write informative/ explanatory texts to examine and convey complex ideas, concepts, and information clearly and accurately through the effective selection, organization, and analysis of content.

10. Write routinely over extended time frames and shorter time frames for a range of tasks, purposes, and audiences.

USE ACADEMIC VOCABULARY

As you write, use academic language, including the following words or their related forms:

approximates
clarify
coherent
emerge

For more on academic language, see the vocabulary charts in the introduction to this book.

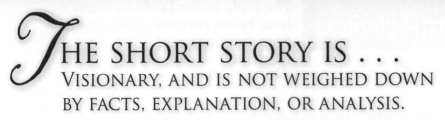

THE SHORT STORY IS . . .
VISIONARY, AND IS NOT WEIGHED DOWN BY FACTS, EXPLANATION, OR ANALYSIS.

— ELIZABETH BOWEN

Defining the Contemporary Short Story

A short story is a brief work of fiction that usually features a plot with a distinct beginning, middle, and end. In the late nineteenth century, most writers used a formulaic structure that involved a suspenseful climax and a dramatic ending. In the twentieth century, British writers like Virginia Woolf, Henry Green, and Katherine Mansfield strove to depict life more truthfully and modernized the short story. Later writers such as D. H. Lawrence, Graham Greene, and Doris Lessing continued to develop the form.

Literary Elements The short story and the novel share basic narrative elements:

• **Plot:** the ordered sequence of events that explores characters in conflict in many modern stories. The plot builds to a crucial moment in which the conflict is altered, but not necessarily resolved.

• **Conflict:** a struggle between opposing forces

• **Setting:** the time and place of a story's action

• **Character:** a person or creature that participates in the action of a story

• **Theme:** the central idea, message, or insight expressed in a story

• **Point of view:** the vantage point from which a story is told. In *first-person point of view*, the narrator is a character in the story who speaks in the first person. In *third-person point of view*, the narrator is a voice outside the action. A *third-person omniscient* narrator is all-knowing and can reveal all the characters' thoughts and feelings. A *third-person limited* narrator reveals only what a single character experiences, thinks, and feels.

Close Read: Literary Elements

These additional narrative elements appear in the Model text at right.

Irony: a discrepancy between appearance and reality, between what is said and what is meant, or between expectation and outcome Example: *"The scientist, who all the time had been leaning back in a big chair, sipping his coffee and smiling with skeptical good humor, chipped in and explained . . . about . . . the progress of science."* (Doris Lessing)	**Flashback:** a type of plot device in which a scene from the past interrupts an ongoing sequence of events Example: *"The young girl talking to the soldier in the garden had not ever completely seen his face. It was dark; they were saying goodbye under a tree."* (Elizabeth Bowen)
Dialogue: the words characters speak; dialogue may advance the story's action and show what characters are like Example: *"Oh!" said the boy. "Then what is luck, mother?"* *"It's what causes you to have money. . . ."* (D.H. Lawrence)	**Characterization:** the revelation of characters' personalities through descriptions of their appearances, feelings, thoughts, and actions Example: *"There was a woman who was beautiful, who started with all the advantages, yet she had no luck."* (D.H. Lawrence)

Model

About the Text One of the dominant figures in Russian Realism, Anton Chekhov (1860–1904) excelled at two literary forms: drama and the short story. His work is noted for both its compassion and objectivity.

---

from "Home"

by Anton Chekhov (translated by Constance Garnett)

"Someone came from the Grigoryevs' to fetch a book, but I said you were not at home. The postman brought the newspaper and two letters. By the way, Yevgeny Petrovitch, I should like to ask you to speak to Seryozha. To-day, and the day before yesterday, I have noticed that he is smoking. When I began to expostulate with him, he put his fingers in his ears as usual, and sang loudly to drown my voice."

Yvgeny Petrovitch Bykovsky, the prosecutor of the circuit court, who had just come back from a session and was taking off his gloves in his study, looked at the governess as she made her report, and laughed.

"Seryozha smoking . . ." he said, shrugging his shoulders. "I can picture the little cherub with a cigarette in his mouth! Why, how old is he?"

"Seven. You think it is not important, but at his age smoking is a bad and pernicious habit, and bad habits ought to be eradicated in the beginning."

"Perfectly true. And where does he get the tobacco?"

"He takes it from the drawer in your table."

"Yes? In that case, send him to me."

When the governess had gone out, Bykovsky. . . called up memories of the long past, half-forgotten time when smoking aroused in his teachers and parents a strange, not quite intelligible horror. . . . Yvegeny Petrovitch remembered the head-master of the high school, a very cultured and good-natured old man, who was so appalled when he found a high-school boy with a cigarette in his mouth that he turned pale, immediately summoned an emergency committee of the teachers, and sentenced the sinner to expulsion. . . .

"What am I to say to him, though?" Yvgeny Petrovitch wondered.

But before he had time to think of anything whatever his son Seryozha, a boy of seven, walked into the study. . . .

"Good evening, papa!" he said, in a soft voice, clambering on to his father's knee and giving him a rapid kiss on his neck. "Did you send for me?" . . .

"Natalya Semyonovna has just been complaining to me that you have been smoking. . . . Is it true? Have you been smoking?"

"Yes, I did smoke once. . . . That's true. . . ."

"Now you see you are lying as well," said the prosecutor, frowning to disguise a smile. "Natalya Semyonovna has seen you smoking twice. So you see you have been detected in three misdeeds: smoking, taking someone else's tobacco, and lying. Three faults."

Characterization The passage begins to develop Bilovsky's character—he is a successful lawyer who does not seem to view life, or child rearing, with too much gravity.

Dialogue The conversation between the governess and Bilovsky both reveals differences in the two characters' personalities and sets up the action that is to follow.

Flashback As Bilovsky prepares to scold his son, a flashback in the form of a memory interrupts the narrative. The information it provides helps readers understand Bilovsky's mild reaction to his son's behavior.

Irony The discrepancy between Bilovsky's feelings of amusement and his stern statements is ironic. The irony emphasizes both Bilovsky's understanding of his paternal role and the tenderness he feels toward his son.

Connecting to the Essential Question Conrad and Joyce tried to find new ways to explore language and human relationships. As you read, find details in these stories that show new approaches to storytelling. These details will help you think about the Essential Question: **What is the relationship of the writer to tradition?**

Close Reading Focus

Plot Devices

Both Conrad and Joyce use **plot devices** to achieve aesthetic effects as they relate the events of a story.

- In "The Lagoon," Conrad tells a **story within a story**—a tale told by a character within a framing fictional narrative.
- In "Araby," Joyce builds toward an **epiphany**—a character's sudden insight—which forms the climax of the story.

Comparing Literary Works Plot devices have a close connection with the **themes,** or central meaning, of a story. "The Lagoon" is told by a neutral narrator outside the story—but the story within this story is told in the first person, with passion. By juxtaposing these two points of view, Conrad reveals one of his themes: the relation of passion to the act of storytelling. Similarly, Joyce's epiphany depends on the contrast between the narrator's passion at the time of the story and his detachment later, when he tells the story. As you read, compare the implications that these plot devices have for the themes of the stories in which they are used.

Preparing to Read Complex Texts Plots are a sequence of causally connected events. That is, one event usually causes another, which in turn triggers yet another effect. The sequence continues until the action closes. **Identifying cause-and-effect relationships** in a plot can help you understand the author's themes. As you read, use a graphic organizer like the one shown.

Vocabulary

The words below are important to understanding the texts that follow. Copy the words into your notebook and note which two have prefixes that share the same meaning.

invincible	imperturbable
propitiate	garrulous
conflagration	derided

Common Core State Standards

Reading Literature
5. Analyze how an author's choices regarding how to structure specific parts of a text contribute to its overall structure and meaning as well as its aesthetic impact.

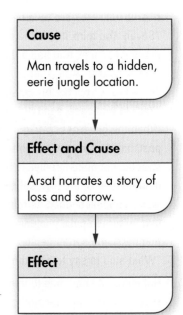

Cause

Man travels to a hidden, eerie jungle location.

Effect and Cause

Arsat narrates a story of loss and sorrow.

Effect

Joseph Conrad

(1857–1924)

Author of "The Lagoon"

It is accomplishment enough to become one of the most distinguished novelists of your age, but to do so in your third language is an achievement almost without parallel. Born in Poland, Joseph Conrad mastered English only after acquiring Polish, his native language, and French.

At Sea in the World Orphaned at the age of eleven, Conrad fled his Russian-occupied homeland when he was sixteen. He landed first in France and later in England. He spent the next six years as an apprentice seaman. The voyages Conrad made to the corners of the globe—Asia, Africa, and South America—became the vivid settings of much of his fiction. In 1886, he became a master mariner and an English citizen.

A Storytelling Life Conrad published his first novel, *Almayer's Folly,* when he was in his late thirties. Three masterpieces followed: *Lord Jim* (1900); *Youth,* a collection of shorter pieces that includes his famous short story "Heart of Darkness" (1902); and *Nostromo* (1904).

Although many of Conrad's works may be read as thrilling tales of the sea, the notion of "voyage" in a work by Conrad translates to a voyage of self-discovery. The question of loyalty, so crucial for the survival of a ship's crew, appears as a question of the general frailty of human relationships and the limits of self-knowledge. The menacing jungles, vast oceans, and exotic people that confront the characters become metaphors for the hidden depths of the self. Telling tales set around the globe, Conrad charts a geography of the human soul.

THE
LAGOON

Joseph Conrad

BACKGROUND Between 1883 and 1888, Conrad sailed the Malay Archipelago—a group of Pacific islands that includes the Philippines and Indonesia—in British merchant ships. He used the knowledge he acquired of the region—of its language, landscape, and customs—to enrich his seafaring tales. It is likely that Captain William Lingard, revered as a spellbinding storyteller among sailors of the Malay settlements, was the model for Marlowe, who appears as the narrator of several Conrad stories.

The white man, leaning with both arms over the roof of the little house in the stern of the boat, said to the steersman—

"We will pass the night in Arsat's clearing. It is late."

The Malay[1] only grunted, and went on looking fixedly at the river. The white man rested his chin on his crossed arms and gazed at the wake of the boat. At the end of the straight avenue of forests cut by the intense glitter of the river, the sun appeared unclouded and dazzling, poised low over the water that shone smoothly like a band of metal. The forests, somber and dull, stood motionless and silent on each side of the broad stream. At the foot of big, towering trees trunkless nipa palms rose from the mud of the bank, in bunches of leaves enormous and heavy, that hung unstirring over the brown swirl of eddies. In the stillness of the air every tree, every leaf, every bough, every tendril of creeper and every petal of minute blossoms seemed to have been bewitched into an immobility perfect and final. Nothing moved on the river but the eight paddles that rose flashing regularly, dipped together with a single splash; while the steersman swept right and left with a periodic and sudden flourish of his blade describing a glinting semicircle above his head. The churned-up water frothed alongside with a confused murmur. And the white man's canoe, advancing up stream in the short-lived disturbance of its own making,

---

1. **Malay** (mā´ lā) native of the Malay peninsula in Southeast Asia.

seemed to enter the portals[2] of a land from which the very memory of motion had forever departed.

The white man, turning his back upon the setting sun, looked along the empty and broad expanse of the sea-reach. For the last three miles of its course the wandering, hesitating river, as if enticed irresistibly by the freedom of an open horizon, flows straight into the sea, flows straight to the east—to the east that harbors both light and darkness. Astern of the boat the repeated call of some bird, a cry discordant and feeble, skipped along over the smooth water and lost itself, before it could reach the other shore, in the breathless silence of the world.

The steersman dug his paddle into the stream, and held hard with stiffened arms, his body thrown forward. The water gurgled aloud; and suddenly the long straight reach seemed to pivot on its center, the forests swung in a semicircle, and the slanting beams of sunset touched the broadside of the canoe with a fiery glow, throwing the slender and distorted shadows of its crew upon the streaked glitter of the river. The white man turned to look ahead. The course of the boat had been altered at right-angles to the stream, and the carved dragonhead of its prow was pointing now at a gap in the fringing bushes of the bank. It glided through, brushing the overhanging twigs, and disappeared from the river like some slim and amphibious creature leaving the water for its lair in the forests.

---

2. **portals** (pôr′təlz) *n.* doors.

▲ **Critical Viewing**
Judging from this photograph, would it be difficult to escape from an enemy in jungle territory? Why or why not?
MAKE A JUDGMENT

Comprehension
What is the white man's destination?

The narrow creek was like a ditch: tortuous, fabulously deep; filled with gloom under the thin strip of pure and shining blue of the heaven. Immense trees soared up, invisible behind the festooned draperies of creepers. Here and there, near the glistening blackness of the water, a twisted root of some tall tree showed amongst the tracery of small ferns, black and dull, writhing and motionless, like an arrested snake. The short words of the paddlers reverberated loudly between the thick and somber walls of vegetation. Darkness oozed out from between the trees, through the tangled maze of the creepers, from behind the great fantastic and unstirring leaves; the darkness, mysterious and invincible; the darkness scented and poisonous of impenetrable forests.

The men poled in the shoaling[3] water. The creek broadened, opening out into a wide sweep of a stagnant lagoon. The forests receded from the marshy bank, leaving a level strip of bright green, reedy grass to frame the reflected blueness of the sky. A fleecy pink cloud drifted high above, trailing the delicate coloring of its image under the floating leaves and the silvery blossoms of the lotus. A little house, perched on high piles, appeared black in the distance. Near it, two tall nibong palms, that seemed to have come out of the forests in the background, leaned slightly over the ragged roof, with a suggestion of sad tenderness and care in the droop of their leafy and soaring heads.

The steersman, pointing with his paddle, said, "Arsat is there. I see his canoe fast between the piles."

Identifying Cause-and-Effect Relationships

Why is the boat coming to Arsat's? What is the reaction of the Malays to coming here?

The polers ran along the sides of the boat glancing over their shoulders at the end of the day's journey. They would have preferred to spend the night somewhere else than on this lagoon of weird aspect and ghostly reputation. Moreover, they disliked Arsat, first as a stranger, and also because he who repairs a ruined house, and dwells in it, proclaims that he is not afraid to live amongst the spirits that haunt the places abandoned by mankind. Such a man can disturb the course of fate by glances or words; while his familiar ghosts are not easy to propitiate by casual wayfarers upon whom they long to wreak the malice of their human master. White men care not for such things, being unbelievers and in league with the Father of Evil, who leads them unharmed through the invisible dangers of this world. To the warnings of the righteous they oppose an offensive pretense of disbelief. What is there to be done?

Vocabulary

propitiate (prō pish′ ē āt′)
v. win the good will of; appease

So they thought, throwing their weight on the end of their long poles. The big canoe glided on swiftly, noiselessly, and smoothly, toward Arsat's clearing, till, in a great rattling of poles thrown down, and the loud murmurs of "Allah[4] be praised!" it came with a gentle knock against the crooked piles below the house.

---

3. shoaling shallow.
4. Allah (al′ ə) Muslim name for God.

The boatmen with uplifted faces shouted discordantly, "Arsat! O Arsat!" Nobody came. The white man began to climb the rude ladder giving access to the bamboo platform before the house. The juragan[5] of the boat said sulkily, "We will cook in the sampan,[6] and sleep on the water."

"Pass my blankets and the basket," said the white man curtly.

He knelt on the edge of the platform to receive the bundle. Then the boat shoved off, and the white man, standing up, confronted Arsat, who had come out through the low door of his hut. He was a man young, powerful, with a broad chest and muscular arms. He had nothing on but his sarong.[7] His head was bare. His big, soft eyes stared eagerly at the white man, but his voice and demeanor were composed as he asked, without any words of greeting—

"Have you medicine, Tuan?"[8]

"No," said the visitor in a startled tone. "No. Why? Is there sickness in the house?"

"Enter and see," replied Arsat, in the same calm manner, and turning short round, passed again through the small doorway. The white man, dropping his bundles, followed.

In the dim light of the dwelling he made out on a couch of bamboos a woman stretched on her back under a broad sheet of red cotton cloth. She lay still, as if dead; but her big eyes, wide open, glittered in the gloom, staring upward at the slender rafters, motionless and unseeing. She was in a high fever, and evidently unconscious. Her cheeks were sunk slightly, her lips were partly open, and on the young face there was the ominous and fixed expression—the absorbed, contemplating expression of the unconscious who are going to die. The two men stood looking down at her in silence.

"Has she been long ill?" asked the traveler.

"I have not slept for five nights," answered the Malay, in a deliberate tone. "At first she heard voices calling her from the water and struggled against me who held her. But since the sun of today rose she hears nothing—she hears not me. She sees nothing. She sees not me—me!"

---

5. **juragan** (jōō rä′ gän) captain or master.
6. **sampan** small flat-bottomed boat with a cabin formed by mats.
7. **sarong** long, brightly colored strip of cloth worn like a skirt.
8. **Tuan** (twan) Malayan for "sir."

Comprehension

What is wrong in Arsat's house?

SHE LAY STILL
AS IF DEAD...

He remained silent for a minute, then asked softly—

"Tuan, will she die?"

"I fear so," said the white man sorrowfully. He had known Arsat years ago, in a far country in times of trouble and danger, when no friendship is to be despised. And since his Malay friend had come unexpectedly to dwell in the hut on the lagoon with a strange woman, he had slept many times there, in his journeys up and down the river. He liked the man who knew how to keep faith in council and how to fight without fear by the side of his white friend. He liked him—not so much perhaps as a man likes his favorite dog—but still he liked him well enough to help and ask no questions, to think sometimes vaguely and hazily in the midst of his own pursuits, about the lonely man and the long-haired woman with audacious face and triumphant eyes, who lived together by the forests—alone and feared.

The white man came out of the hut in time to see the enormous conflagration of sunset put out by the swift and stealthy shadows that, rising like a black and impalpable vapor above the treetops, spread over the heaven, extinguishing the crimson glow of floating clouds and the red brilliance of departing daylight. In a few moments all the stars came out above the intense blackness of the earth, and the great lagoon gleaming suddenly with reflected lights resembled an oval patch of night sky flung down into the hopeless and abysmal night of the wilderness. The white man had some supper out of the basket, then collecting a few sticks that lay about the platform, made up a small fire, not for warmth, but for the sake of the smoke, which would keep off the mosquitos. He wrapped himself in his blankets and sat with his back against the reed wall of the house, smoking thoughtfully.

Arsat came through the doorway with noiseless steps and squatted down by the fire. The white man moved his outstretched legs a little.

"She breathes," said Arsat in a low voice, anticipating the expected question. "She breathes and burns as if with a great fire. She speaks not; she hears not—and burns!" He paused for a moment, then asked in a quiet, incurious tone—

"Tuan . . . will she die?"

The white man moved his shoulders uneasily, and muttered in a hesitating manner—

"If such is her fate."

"No, Tuan," said Arsat calmly. "If such is my fate. I hear, I see, I wait. I remember . . . Tuan, do you remember the old days? Do you remember my brother?"

"Yes," said the white man. The Malay rose suddenly and went in.

Plot Devices

Is the narrator of the story closer in point of view to the white man or Arsat? Explain.

Vocabulary

conflagration (kän′ flə grā′ shən) n. great fire

The other, sitting still outside, could hear the voice in the hut. Arsat said: "Hear me! Speak!" His words were succeeded by a complete silence. "O Diamelen!" he cried suddenly. After that cry there was a deep sigh. Arsat came out and sank down again in his old place.

They sat in silence before the fire. There was no sound within the house, there was no sound near them; but far away on the lagoon they could hear the voices of the boatmen ringing fitful and distinct on the calm water. The fire in the bows of the sampan shone faintly in the distance with a hazy red glow. Then it died out. The voices ceased. The land and the water slept invisible, unstirring and mute. It was as though there had been nothing left in the world but the glitter of stars streaming, ceaseless and vain, through the black stillness of the night.

The white man gazed straight before him into the darkness with wide-open eyes. The fear and fascination, the inspiration and the wonder of death—of death near, unavoidable, and unseen, soothed the unrest of his race and stirred the most indistinct, the most intimate of his thoughts. The ever-ready suspicion of evil, the gnawing suspicion that lurks in our hearts, flowed out into the stillness round him—into the stillness profound and dumb, and made it appear untrustworthy and infamous, like the placid and impenetrable mask of an unjustifiable violence. In that fleeting and powerful disturbance of his being the earth enfolded in the starlight peace became a shadowy country of inhuman strife, a battlefield of phantoms terrible and charming, august[9] or ignoble[10], struggling ardently for the possession of our helpless hearts. An unquiet and mysterious country of inextinguishable desires and fears.

A plaintive murmur rose in the night; a murmur saddening and startling, as if the great solitudes of surrounding woods had tried to whisper into his ear the wisdom of their immense and lofty indifference. Sounds hesitating and vague floated in the air round him, shaped themselves slowly into words; and at last flowed on gently in a murmuring stream of soft and monotonous sentences. He stirred like a man waking up and changed his position slightly. Arsat, motionless and shadowy, sitting with bowed head under the stars, was speaking in a low and dreamy tone—

". . . for where can we lay down the heaviness of our trouble but in a friend's heart? A man must speak of war and of love. You, Tuan, know what war is, and you have seen me in time of danger seek death as other men seek life! A writing may be lost; a lie may be written; but what the eye has seen is truth and remains in the mind!"

---

9. august (ô gust´) *adj.* worthy of great respect; inspiring awe.
10. ignoble (ig nō´ bəl) *adj.* of the common people; dishonorable.

Identifying Cause-and-Effect Relationships

What causes Arsat to speak to the white man?

Comprehension

What does Arsat tell Tuan about the woman's health?

"I remember," said the white man quietly. Arsat went on with mournful composure—

"Therefore I shall speak to you of love. Speak in the night. Speak before both night and love are gone—and the eye of day looks upon my sorrow and my shame; upon my blackened face; upon my burnt-up heart."

A sigh, short and faint, marked an almost imperceptible pause, and then his words flowed on, without a stir, without a gesture.

"After the time of trouble and war was over and you went away from my country in the pursuit of your desires, which we, men of the islands, cannot understand, I and my brother became again, as we had been before, the sword bearers of the Ruler. You know we were men of family, belonging to a ruling race, and more fit than any to carry on our right shoulder the emblem of power. And in the time of prosperity Si Dendring showed us favor, as we, in time of sorrow, had showed to him the faithfulness of our courage. It was a time of peace. A time of deer hunts and cock fights; of idle talks and foolish squabbles between men whose bellies are full and weapons are rusty. But the sower watched the young rice shoots grow up without fear, and the traders came and went, departed lean and returned fat into the river of peace. They brought news too. Brought lies and truth mixed together, so that no man knew when to rejoice and when to be sorry. We heard from them about you also. They had seen you here and had seen you there. And I was glad to hear, for I remembered the stirring times, and I always remembered you, Tuan, till the time came when my eyes could see nothing in the past, because they had looked upon the one who is dying there—in the house."

He stopped to exclaim in an intense whisper, "O Mara bahia! O Calamity!" then went on speaking a little louder.

"There's no worse enemy and no better friend than a brother, Tuan, for one brother knows another, and in perfect knowledge is strength for good or evil. I loved my brother. I went to him and told him that I could see nothing but one face, hear nothing but one voice. He told me: 'Open your heart so that she can see what is in it—and wait. Patience is wisdom. Inchi Midah may die or our Ruler may throw off his fear of a woman!'. . . I waited!. . . You remember the lady with the veiled face, Tuan, and the fear of our Ruler before her cunning and temper. And if she wanted her servant, what could I do?

But I fed the hunger of my heart on short glances and stealthy words. I loitered on the path to the bath houses in the daytime, and when the sun had fallen behind the forest I crept along the jasmine hedges of the women's courtyard. Unseeing, we spoke to one another through the scent of flowers, through the veil of leaves, through the blades of long grass that stood still before our lips; so great was our prudence, so faint was the murmur of our great longing. The time passed swiftly . . . and there were whispers amongst women—and our enemies watched—my brother was gloomy, and I began to think of killing and of a fierce death. . . . We are of a people who take what they want—like you whites. There is a time when a man should forget loyalty and respect. Might and authority are given to rulers, but to all men is given love and strength and courage. My brother said, 'You shall take her from their midst. We are two who are like one.' And I answered, 'Let it be soon, for I find no warmth in sunlight that does not shine upon her.' Our time came when the Ruler and all the great people went to the mouth of the river to fish by torchlight. There were hundreds of boats, and on the white sand, between the water and the forests, dwellings of leaves were built for the households of the Rajahs.[11] The smoke of cooking fires was like a blue mist of the evening, and many voices rang in it joyfully. While they were making the boats ready to beat up the fish, my brother came to me and said, 'Tonight!' I looked to my weapons, and when the time came our canoe took its place in the circle of boats carrying the torches. The lights blazed on the water, but behind the boats there was darkness. When the shouting began and the excitement made them like mad we dropped out. The water swallowed our fire, and we floated back to the shore that was dark with only here and there the glimmer of embers. We could hear the talk of slave girls amongst the sheds. Then we found a place deserted and silent. We waited there. She came. She came running along the shore, rapid and leaving no trace, like a leaf driven by the wind into the sea. My brother said gloomily, 'Go and take her; carry her into our boat.' I lifted her in my arms. She panted. Her heart was beating against my breast. I said, 'I take you from those people. You came to the cry of my heart, but my arms take you into my boat against the will of the great!' 'It is right,' said my brother. 'We are men who take what we want and can hold it against many. We should have taken her in daylight.' I said, 'Let us be off'; for since she was in my boat I began to think of our Ruler's many men.

Identifying Cause-and-Effect Relationships
What causes Arsat to speak to the woman? What is the result of that action?

Comprehension
What do Arsat and his brother decide to do?

---

11. Rajahs (ra´ jəz) Malayan chiefs.

"LET IT BE SOON, FOR I FIND NO WARMTH IN SUNLIGHT THAT DOES NOT SHINE UPON HER."

'Yes. Let us be off,' said my brother. 'We are cast out and this boat is our country now—and the sea is our refuge.' He lingered with his foot on the shore, and I entreated him to hasten, for I remembered the strokes of her heart against my breast and thought that two men cannot withstand a hundred. We left, paddling downstream close to the bank; and as we passed by the creek where they were fishing, the great shouting had ceased, but the murmur of voices was loud like the humming of insects flying at noonday. The boats floated, clustered together, in the red light of torches, under a black roof of smoke; and men talked of their sport. Men that boasted, and praised, and jeered—men that would have been our friends in the morning, but on that night were already our enemies. We paddled swiftly past. We had no more friends in the country of our birth. She sat in the middle of the canoe with covered face; silent as she is now; unseeing as she is now—and I had no regret at what I was leaving because I could hear her breathing close to me—as I can hear her now."

He paused, listened with his ear turned to the doorway, then shook his head and went on.

"My brother wanted to shout the cry of challenge—one cry only—to let the people know we were freeborn robbers who trusted our arms and the great sea. And again I begged him in the name of our love to be silent. Could I not hear her breathing close to me? I knew the pursuit would come quick enough. My brother loved me. He dipped his paddle without a splash. He only said, 'There is half a man in you now—the other half is in that woman. I can wait. When you are a whole man again, you will come back with me here to shout defiance. We are sons of the same mother.' I made no answer. All my strength and all my spirit were in my hands that held the paddle—for I longed to be with her in a safe place beyond the reach of men's anger and of women's spite. My love was so great, that I thought it could guide me to a country where death was unknown,

Identifying Cause-and-Effect Relationships

What is the effect of the brothers' action? What do you think might happen next?

Plot Devices

What do the pauses in Arsat's story indicate to the white man and the reader about Arsat's emotional state?

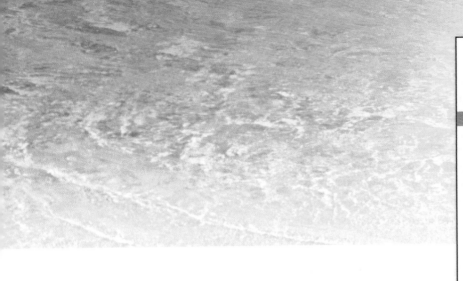

if I could only escape from Inchi Midah's fury and from our Ruler's sword. We paddled with haste, breathing through our teeth. The blades bit deep into the smooth water. We passed out of the river; we flew in clear channels amongst the shallows. We skirted the black coast; we skirted the sand beaches where the sea speaks in whispers to the land; and the gleam of white sand flashed back past our boat, so swiftly she ran upon the water. We spoke not. Only once I said, 'Sleep, Diamelen, for soon you may want all your strength.' I heard the sweetness of her voice, but I never turned my head. The sun rose and still we went on. Water fell from my face like rain from a cloud. We flew in the light and heat. I never looked back, but I knew that my brother's eyes, behind me, were looking steadily ahead, for the boat went as straight as a bushman's dart, when it leaves the end of the sumpitan.[12] There was no better paddler, no better steersman than my brother. Many times, together, we had won races in that canoe. But we never had put out our strength as we did then—then, when for the last time we paddled together! There was no braver or stronger man in our country than my brother. I could not spare the strength to turn my head and look at him, every moment I heard the hiss of his breath getting louder behind me. Still he did not speak. The sun was high. The heat clung to my back like a flame of fire. My ribs were ready to burst, but I could no longer get enough air into my chest. And then I felt I must cry out with my last breath. 'Let us rest!' . . . 'Good!' he answered; and his voice was firm. He was strong. He was brave. He knew not fear and no fatigue . . . My brother!"

---

12. **sumpitan** (sump′ ə tän) Malayan blowgun that discharges poisonous darts.

World LITERATURE Connection

Joseph Conrad, International Author

As a child, Jozeph Konrad Nalecz Korzeniowski (1857-1924) moved between cultures and languages. He was born in Berdichev, a city once part of Poland, that was under Russian rule. Polish was his first language, but he also spoke French and Russian.

When he was eleven, Jozeph was orphaned and went to live with his uncle in Switzerland. There he picked up some Italian and German. At seventeen, he shipped out with the French merchant marine. When he was 29, he earned British citizenship and changed his name to Joseph Conrad. Soon after, he settled in Britain.

Conrad did not begin writing until his early thirties, and when he did, he wrote in English. His first novel, *Almayer's Folly*, was published in 1895. Soon Conrad's fiction was published in French translation too. His work influenced leading French writers including André Gide, Marcel Proust, Louis-Ferdinand Céline, André Malraux, and Jean-Paul Sartre.

Connect to the Literature

What evidence of Conrad's ability to learn languages can you find in "The Lagoon"?

Comprehension

Have Arsat, his brother, and Diamelen escaped the Rajah? Explain.

Plot Devices

How do the descriptions of the setting in which Arsat tells his tale provide a kind of commentary on his tale?

A murmur powerful and gentle, a murmur vast and faint; the murmur of trembling leaves, of stirring boughs, ran through the tangled depths of the forests, ran over the starry smoothness of the lagoon, and the water between the piles lapped the slimy timber once with a sudden splash. A breath of warm air touched the two men's faces and passed on with a mournful sound—a breath loud and short like an uneasy sigh of the dreaming earth.

Arsat went on in an even, low voice:

"We ran our canoe on the white beach of a little bay close to a long tongue of land that seemed to bar our road; a long wooded cape going far into the sea. My brother knew that place. Beyond the cape a river has its entrance, and through the jungle of that land there is a narrow path. We made a fire and cooked rice. Then we lay down to sleep on the soft sand in the shade of our canoe, while she watched. No sooner had I closed my eyes than I heard her cry of alarm. We leaped up. The sun was halfway down the sky already, and coming in sight in the opening of the bay we saw a prau[13] manned by many paddlers. We knew it at once; it was one of our Rajah's praus. They were watching the shore, and saw us. They beat the gong, and turned the head of the prau into the bay. I felt my heart become weak within my breast. Diamelen sat on the sand and covered her face. There was no escape by sea. My brother laughed. He had the gun you had given him, Tuan, before you went away, but there was only a handful of

---

13. **prau** (prou) swift Malayan boat with a large sail.

powder. He spoke to me quickly: 'Run with her along the path. I shall keep them back, for they have no firearms, and landing in the face of a man with a gun is certain death for some. Run with her. On the other side of that wood there is a fisherman's house—and a canoe. When I have fired all the shots I will follow. I am a great runner, and before they can come up we shall be gone. I will hold out as long as I can, for she is but a woman—that can neither run nor fight, but she has your heart in her weak hands.' He dropped behind the canoe. The prau was coming. She and I ran, and as we rushed along the path I heard shots. My brother fired—once—twice—and the booming of the gong ceased. There was silence behind us. That neck of land is narrow. Before I heard my brother fire the third shot I saw the shelving shore, and I saw the water again: the mouth of a broad river. We crossed a grassy glade. We ran down to the water. I saw a low hut above the black mud, and a small canoe hauled up. I heard another shot behind me. I thought, 'That is his last charge.' We rushed down to the canoe; a man came running from the hut, but I leaped on him, and we rolled together in the mud. Then I got up, and he lay still at my feet. I don't know whether I had killed him or not. I and Diamelen pushed the canoe afloat. I heard yells behind me, and I saw my brother run across the glade. Many men were bounding after him. I took her in my arms and threw her into the boat, then leaped in myself.

▼ **Critical Viewing**
What aspects of Conrad's story does this photograph capture? **CONNECT**

Comprehension
What instructions does Arsat's brother give him?

"WE RAN OUR CANOE

ON THE WHITE BEACH
OF A LITTLE BAY..."

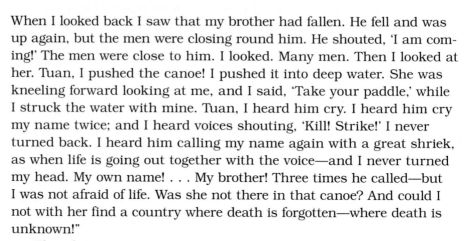

When I looked back I saw that my brother had fallen. He fell and was up again, but the men were closing round him. He shouted, 'I am coming!' The men were close to him. I looked. Many men. Then I looked at her. Tuan, I pushed the canoe! I pushed it into deep water. She was kneeling forward looking at me, and I said, 'Take your paddle,' while I struck the water with mine. Tuan, I heard him cry. I heard him cry my name twice; and I heard voices shouting, 'Kill! Strike!' I never turned back. I heard him calling my name again with a great shriek, as when life is going out together with the voice—and I never turned my head. My own name! . . . My brother! Three times he called—but I was not afraid of life. Was she not there in that canoe? And could I not with her find a country where death is forgotten—where death is unknown!"

The white man sat up. Arsat rose and stood, an indistinct and silent figure above the dying embers of the fire. Over the lagoon a mist drifting and low had crept, erasing slowly the glittering images of the stars. And now a great expanse of white vapor covered the land; it flowed cold and gray in the darkness, eddied in noiseless whirls round the tree-trunks and about the platform of the house, which seemed to float upon a restless and impalpable illusion of a sea. Only far away the tops of the trees stood outlined on the twinkle of heaven, like a somber and forbidding shore—a coast deceptive, pitiless and black.

Arsat's voice vibrated loudly in the profound peace.

"I had her there! I had her! To get her I would have faced all mankind. But I had her—and—"

His words went out ringing into the empty distances. He paused, and seemed to listen to them dying away very far—beyond help and beyond recall. Then he said quietly—

"Tuan, I loved my brother."

A breath of wind made him shiver. High above his head, high above the silent sea of mist the drooping leaves of the palms rattled together with a mournful and expiring sound. The white man stretched his legs. His chin rested on his chest, and he murmured sadly without lifting his head—

"We all love our brothers."

THEN HE SAID—
"SHE BURNS
NO MORE."

Arsat burst out with an intense whispering violence—
"What did I care who died? I wanted peace in my own heart."

He seemed to hear a stir in the house—listened—then stepped in noiselessly. The white man stood up. A breeze was coming in fitful puffs. The stars shone paler as if they had retreated into the frozen depths of immense space. After a chill gust of wind there were a few seconds of perfect calm and absolute silence. Then from behind the black and wavy line of the forests a column of golden light shot up into the heavens and spread over the semicircle of the eastern horizon. The sun had risen. The mist lifted, broke into drifting patches, vanished into thin flying wreaths; and the unveiled lagoon lay, polished and black, in the heavy shadows at the foot of the wall of trees. A white eagle rose over it with a slanting and ponderous flight, reached the clear sunshine and appeared dazzlingly brilliant for a moment, then soaring higher, became a dark and motionless speck before it vanished into the blue as if it had left the earth forever. The white man, standing gazing upward before the doorway, heard in the hut a confused and broken murmur of distracted words ending with a loud groan. Suddenly Arsat stumbled out with outstretched hands, shivered, and stood still for some time with fixed eyes. Then he said—

"She burns no more."

Before his face the sun showed its edge above the treetops, rising steadily. The breeze freshened; a great brilliance burst upon the lagoon, sparkled on the rippling water. The forests came out of the clear shadows of the morning, became distinct, as if they had rushed nearer—to stop short in a great stir of leaves, of nodding boughs, of swaying branches. In the merciless sunshine the whisper of unconscious life grew louder, speaking in an incomprehensible voice round the dumb darkness of that human sorrow. Arsat's eyes wandered slowly, then stared at the rising sun.

"I can see nothing," he said half aloud to himself.

"There is nothing," said the white man, moving to the edge of the platform and waving his hand to his boat. A shout came faintly over the lagoon and the sampan began to glide toward the abode of the friend of ghosts.

"If you want to come with me, I will wait all the morning," said the white man, looking away upon the water.

Identifying Cause-and-Effect Relationships

What event causes Arsat to shiver? What else might have caused that reaction?

Comprehension

What happens to Arsat's brother?

The Lagoon **1233**

"No, Tuan," said Arsat softly. "I shall not eat or sleep in this house, but I must first see my road. Now I can see nothing—see nothing! There is no light and no peace in the world; but there is death—death for many. We were sons of the same mother—and I left him in the midst of enemies; but I am going back now."

He drew a long breath and went on in a dreamy tone:

"In a little while I shall see clear enough to strike—to strike. But she has died, and . . . now . . . darkness."

He flung his arms wide open, let them fall along his body, then stood still with unmoved face and stony eyes, staring at the sun. The white man got down into his canoe. The polers ran smartly along the sides of the boat, looking over their shoulders at the beginning of a weary journey. High in the stern, his head muffled up in white rags, the juragon sat moody, letting his paddle trail in the water. The white man, leaning with both arms over the grass roof of the little cabin, looked back at the shining ripple of the boat's wake. Before the sampan passed out of the lagoon into the creek he lifted his eyes. Arsat had not moved. He stood lonely in the searching sunshine; and he looked beyond the great light of a cloudless day into the darkness of a world of illusions.

Critical Reading

1. **Key Ideas and Details (a)** Why does Arsat ask the white man if he has medicine? **(b) Infer:** What is Arsat's state of mind?

2. **Key Ideas and Details (a)** What does Arsat's brother do while Arsat and Diamelen run to the canoe? **(b) Analyze Cause and Effect:** What motivates Arsat to leave his brother behind? **(c) Speculate:** How else could he have responded, and what might have been the results?

3. **Key Ideas and Details (a) Interpret:** Following Diamelen's death, Arsat says, "I can see nothing," and the white man replies, "There is nothing." What does each statement mean? **(b) Connect:** How might this dialogue relate to the story's final line?

4. **Craft and Structure (a) Analyze:** Find three examples of Conrad's descriptions of sounds, including descriptions of silence and speech. What do these images suggest about the act of storytelling? **(b) Draw Conclusions:** What is Arsat's purpose in telling his story? **(c) Evaluate:** Does he achieve it? Explain.

5. **Integration of Knowledge and Ideas (a) Draw Conclusions:** What do you think Conrad would recommend to people as a way to deal with past mistakes or regrets? **(b) Make a Judgment:** Would you agree? Explain.

Cite textual evidence to support your responses.

JAMES JOYCE

(1882–1941)

Author of **"Araby"**

The Dublin writer James Joyce's innovations in plot, character, and language make him one of the most challenging and distinguished writers of the twentieth century.

Experimentation Joyce's family and teachers wanted him to become a priest, but he pursued his own way as a writer. In 1904, he left Ireland for the continent. Ten years later, he published a landmark collection of short stories entitled *Dubliners*. These deceptively simple tales focus on the psychological conflicts of ordinary people. In the course of each story, the main character is forced to alter his or her perspective on life.

In 1916, Joyce published *A Portrait of the Artist as a Young Man*, a semiautobiographical work. Like Joyce, the novel's main character is in conflict with his Irish roots and chooses to become a writer.

Mature Fiction *A Portrait of the Artist* reveals a heightened awareness of language and an immersion in the minds of characters. Joyce carried these characteristics to a new level in *Ulysses* (1922). A stream-of-consciousness novel that roughly parallels Homer's *Odyssey*, the work presents a day in the life of three Dubliners. *Ulysses* represents a liberation of the novel from old ideas. Using a variety of styles and techniques, it places a new and thoroughly modern emphasis on the play of language.

In his final novel, *Finnegans Wake* (1939), Joyce took his fascination with words a step further. Written in what one scholar terms "a dream language of Joyce's own invention," it explores the author's view of human existence. With such radical innovations, Joyce guaranteed his place as one of the re-inventors of modern fiction.

> "A MAN'S ERRORS ARE HIS PORTALS OF DISCOVERY."

Araby

JAMES JOYCE

North Richmond Street, being blind,[1] was a quiet street except at the hour when the Christian Brothers' School set the boys free. An uninhabited house of two stories stood at the blind end, detached from its neighbors in a square ground. The other houses of the street, conscious of decent lives within them, gazed at one another with brown imperturbable faces.

The former tenant of our house, a priest, had died in the back drawing room. Air, musty from having been long enclosed, hung in all the rooms, and the waste room behind the kitchen was littered with old useless papers. Among these I found a few paper-covered books, the pages of which were curled and damp: *The Abbot,* by Walter Scott, *The Devout Communicant* and *The Memoirs of Vidocq.*[2] I liked the last best because its leaves were yellow. The wild garden behind the house contained a central apple tree and a few straggling bushes under one of which I found the late tenant's rusty bicycle pump. He had been a very charitable priest: in his will he had left all his money to institutions and the furniture of his house to his sister.

When the short days of winter came dusk fell before we had well eaten our dinners. When we met in the street the houses had grown somber. The space of sky above us was the color of ever-changing violet and toward it the lamps of the street lifted their feeble lanterns. The cold air stung us and we played till our bodies glowed. Our shouts echoed in the silent street. The career of our play brought us through the dark muddy lanes behind the houses where we ran the gantlet of the rough tribes from the cottages, to the back doors of the dark dripping gardens where odors arose from the ashpits, to the dark odorous stables where a coachman smoothed and combed the horse or shook music from the buckled harness. When we returned to the street, light from the kitchen windows had filled the areas. If my uncle was seen turning the corner we hid in the shadow until we had seen him safely housed. Or if Mangan's sister came out on the doorstep to call her brother in to his tea we watched her from our shadow peer up and down the street. We waited to see whether she would remain or go in and, if she remained, we left our shadow and walked up to Mangan's steps resignedly. She was waiting for us, her figure defined by the light from the half-opened door. Her brother always teased her before he obeyed and I stood by the railings looking at her. Her dress swung as she moved her body and the soft rope of her hair tossed from side to side.

Every morning I lay on the floor in the front parlor watching her door. The blind was pulled down to within an inch of the sash so that I could not be seen. When she came out on the doorstep my heart leaped. I ran to the hall, seized my books and followed her. I kept her brown figure always in my eye and, when we came near the point at

---

1. **blind** a dead end.
2. ***The Abbot . . . Vidocq*** a historical tale, a religious manual, and the remembrances of a French adventurer, respectively.

Vocabulary
imperturbable (im´ pər tʉr´ bə bel) *adj.* calm; not easily ruffled

◀ **Critical Viewing**
Why might the prospect of a fair or bazaar appeal to someone living on a street like this? **INFER**

Plot Devices
What effect does the use of first-person point of view have on your impression of Mangan's sister?

Comprehension
When and where does the story take place?

which our ways diverged, I quickened my pace and passed her. This happened morning after morning. I had never spoken to her, except for a few casual words, and yet her name was like a summons to all my foolish blood.

Her image accompanied me even in places the most hostile to romance. On Saturday evenings when my aunt went marketing I had to go to carry some of the parcels. We walked through the flaring streets, jostled by drunken men and bargaining women, amid the curses of laborers, the shrill litanies[3] of shop-boys who stood on guard by the barrels of pigs' cheeks, the nasal chanting of street singers, who sang a *come-all-you* about O'Donovan Rossa,[4] or a ballad about the troubles in our native land. These noises converged in a single sensation of life for me: I imagined that I bore my chalice safely through a throng of foes. Her name sprang to my lips at moments in strange prayers and praises which I myself did not understand. My eyes were often full of tears (I could not tell why) and at times a flood from my heart seemed to pour itself out into my bosom. I thought little of the future. I did not know whether I would ever speak to her or not or, if I spoke to her, how I could tell her of my confused adoration. But my body was like a harp and her words and gestures were like fingers running upon the wires.

One evening I went into the back drawing room in which the priest had died. It was a dark rainy evening and there was no sound in the house. Through one of the broken panes I heard the rain impinge upon the earth, the fine incessant needles of water playing in the sodden beds. Some distant lamp or lighted window gleamed below me. I was thankful that I could see so little. All my senses seemed to desire to veil themselves and, feeling that I was about to slip from them, I pressed the palms of my hands together until they trembled, murmuring: *"O love! O love!"* many times.

At last she spoke to me. When she addressed the first words to me I was so confused that I did not know what to answer. She asked me was I going to *Araby.* I forget whether I answered yes or no. It would be a splendid bazaar, she said; she would love to go.

"And why can't you?" I asked.

While she spoke she turned a silver bracelet round and round her wrist. She could not go, she said, because there would be a retreat[5] that week in her convent.[6] Her brother and two other boys were fighting for their caps and I was alone at the railings. She held one of the spikes, bowing her head towards me. The light from the lamp opposite our door caught the white curve of her neck, lit up her hair that rested there and, falling, lit up the hand upon the railing. It fell over one side of her dress and caught the white border of a petticoat, just visible as she stood at ease.

Identifying Cause-and-Effect Relationships

What is causing the narrator's distracted behavior? What do you think will happen to him?

Plot Devices and Epiphany

In what way might the narrator's comments on his own past thoughts and feelings prepare for an epiphany?

---

3. litanies (lit´ ən ēz) *n* prayers in which a congregation repeats a fixed response; repetitive recitations.

4. *come-all-you* **. . . Rossa** opening of a ballad about an Irish hero.

5. retreat *n.* period of retirement or seclusion for prayer, religious study, and meditation.

6. convent *n.* school run by an order of nuns.

"It's well for you," she said.

"If I go," I said, "I will bring you something."

What innumerable follies laid waste my waking and sleeping thoughts after that evening! I wished to annihilate the tedious intervening days. I chafed against the work of school. At night in my bedroom and by day in the classroom her image came between me and the page I strove to read. The syllables of the word *Araby* were called to me through the silence in which my soul luxuriated and cast an Eastern enchantment over me. I asked for leave to go to the bazaar on Saturday night. My aunt was surprised and hoped it was not some Freemason[7] affair. I answered few questions in class. I watched my master's face pass from amiability to sternness; he hoped I was not beginning to idle. I could not call my wandering thoughts together. I had hardly any patience with the serious work of life which, now that it stood between me and my desire, seemed to me child's play, ugly monotonous child's play.

On Saturday morning I reminded my uncle that I wished to go to the bazaar in the evening. He was fussing at the hallstand, looking for the hat brush, and answered me curtly:

"Yes, boy, I know."

As he was in the hall I could not go into the front parlor and lie at the window. I left the house in bad humor and walked slowly toward the school. The air was pitilessly raw and already my heart misgave me.

When I came home to dinner my uncle had not yet been home. Still it was early. I sat staring at the clock for some time and, when its ticking began to irritate me, I left the room. I mounted the staircase and gained the upper part of the house. The high cold empty gloomy rooms liberated me and I went from room to room singing. From the front window I saw my companions playing in the street. Their cries reached me weakened and indistinct and, leaning my forehead against the cool glass, I looked over at the dark house where she lived. I may have stood there for an hour, seeing nothing but the brown-clad figure cast by my imagination, touched discreetly by the lamplight at the curved neck, at the hand upon the railings and at the border below the dress.

When I came downstairs again I found Mrs. Mercer sitting at the fire. She was an old garrulous woman, a pawnbroker's widow, who collected used stamps for some pious purpose. I had to endure the gossip of the tea table. The meal was prolonged beyond an hour and still my uncle did not come. Mrs. Mercer stood up to go: she was sorry she couldn't wait any longer, but it was after eight o'clock and she did not like to be out late, as the night air was bad for her. When she had gone I began to walk up and down the room, clenching my fists. My aunt said:

"I'm afraid you may put off your bazaar for this night of Our Lord."

---

7. **Freemason** Free and Accepted Masons, an international secret society.

Spiral Review

Character Summarize the paragraph that begins "What innumerable follies. . . ." What can you conclude about the narrator's emotional state?

Identifying Cause-and-Effect Relationships

Why does the narrator have to wait to go to the bazaar? What effect does his waiting have on his mood?

Vocabulary

garrulous (gar′ ə ləs) *adj.* talkative

Comprehension

What does the narrator promise Mangan's sister?

The Irish Tradition

Joyce's stories are a modern addition to the rich cultural legacy of Ireland. Irish literature began with an oral tradition of epics and flourished through the medieval period. Bede's *History* is a culminating testament to the Irish preservation of learning on the islands—Irish books and Irish teaching flowing into Bede's England made the work possible.

Although the Irish cultural tradition is strong, centuries of rule by the English in Ireland and the Irish struggles against that rule have raised questions of cultural identity. When W. B. Yeats reinvigorated Irish poetry, he helped to launch the Irish Literary Revival. This literary assertion of Irish identity was also a political gesture reinforcing the movement to free Ireland. Since Yeats, writers such as Joyce, Louis MacNeice, and Seamus Heaney have made the Irish identity, as well as the splits it suffered under English rule, a theme for literary exploration.

Connect to the Literature

Which reflects more Irish details: the setting or the narrator? Explain.

At nine o'clock I heard my uncle's latchkey in the hall door. I heard him talking to himself and heard the hall-stand rocking when it had received the weight of his overcoat. I could interpret these signs. When he was midway through his dinner I asked him to give me the money to go to the bazaar. He had forgotten.

"The people are in bed and after their first sleep now," he said.

I did not smile. My aunt said to him energetically:

"Can't you give him the money and let him go? You've kept him late enough as it is."

My uncle said he was very sorry he had forgotten. He said he believed in the old saying: *All work and no play makes Jack a dull boy.* He asked me where I was going and, when I had told him a second time he asked me did I know *The Arab's Farewell to His Steed.*[8] When I left the kitchen he was about to recite the opening lines of the piece to my aunt.

I held a florin[9] tightly in my hand as I strode down Buckingham Street toward the station. The sight of the streets thronged with buyers and glaring with gas recalled to me the purpose of my journey. I took my seat in a third-class carriage of a deserted train. After an intolerable delay the train moved out of the station slowly. It crept onward among ruinous houses and over the twinkling river. At Westland Row Station a crowd of people pressed to the carriage doors; but the porters moved them back, saying that it was a special train for the bazaar. I remained alone in the bare carriage. In a few minutes the train drew up beside an improvised wooden platform. I passed out onto the road and saw by the lighted dial of a clock that it was ten minutes to ten. In front of me was a large building which displayed the magical name.

I could not find any sixpenny entrance and, fearing that the bazaar would be closed, I passed in quickly through a turnstile, handing a shilling to a weary-looking man. I found myself in a big hall girdled at half its height by a gallery. Nearly all the stalls were closed and the greater part of the hall was in darkness. I recognized a silence like that which pervades a church after a service. I walked into the center of the bazaar timidly. A few people were gathered about the stalls which were still open. Before a curtain, over which the words *Café Chantant*[10] were written in colored lamps, two men were counting money on a salver.[11] I listened to the fall of the coins.

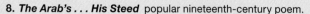

8. ***The Arab's . . . His Steed*** popular nineteenth-century poem.
9. **florin** two shilling coin of the time.
10. ***Café Chantant*** café with musical entertainment.
11. **salver** tray usually used for the presentation of letters or visiting cards.

Remembering with difficulty why I had come I went over to one of the stalls and examined porcelain vases and flowered tea sets. At the door of the stall a young lady was talking and laughing with two young gentlemen. I remarked their English accents and listened vaguely to their conversation.

"O, I never said such a thing!"

"O, but you did!"

"O, but I didn't!"

"Didn't she say that?"

"Yes. I heard her."

"O, there's a . . . fib!"

Observing me the young lady came over and asked me did I wish to buy anything. The tone of her voice was not encouraging; she seemed to have spoken to me out of a sense of duty. I looked humbly at the great jars that stood like Eastern guards at either side of the dark entrance to the stall and murmured:

"No, thank you."

The young lady changed the position of one of the vases and went back to the two young men. They began to talk of the same subject. Once or twice the young lady glanced at me over her shoulder.

I lingered before her stall, though I knew my stay was useless, to make my interest in her wares seem the more real. Then I turned away slowly and walked down the middle of the bazaar. I allowed the two pennies to fall against the sixpence in my pocket. I heard a voice call from one end of the gallery that the light was out. The upper part of the hall was now completely dark.

Gazing up into the darkness I saw myself as a creature driven and derided by vanity; and my eyes burned with anguish and anger.

▲ **Critical Viewing**
What inferences can you make about people who value objects like the ones shown here? **MAKE INFERENCES**

Vocabulary
derided (di rīd′ id) v. made fun of; ridiculed

Critical Reading ©

1. **Key Ideas and Details (a)** What does Mangan's sister do to make a trip to the bazaar so important to the narrator? **(b) Analyze:** Describe three scenes that establish the narrator's feelings for her.

2. **Key Ideas and Details** What features of the Araby bazaar conflict with the narrator's expectations?

3. **Key Ideas and Details (a) Draw Conclusions:** What has the narrator lost by the end of the story? **(b) Draw Conclusions:** What might he have gained?

4. **Integration of Knowledge and Ideas** Do the plot devices these writers use, story-within-a-story and epiphany, help convey the pain of wanting something very much and then failing to get it? Explain, using at least three of these Essential Question words: *imply, process, realization, epiphany, story-within-a-story.* [**Connecting to the Essential Question: What is the relationship of the writer to tradition?**]

Cite textual evidence to support your responses.

Literary Analysis

1. **Craft and Structure** Conrad uses the **plot device** of a **story within a story** in "The Lagoon." What specific information would you lack if "The Lagoon" had been narrated entirely in the first person by Arsat?

2. **Craft and Structure** Why do you think Conrad chose to have Arsat narrate his own story? Support your thinking with details from the text.

3. **Craft and Structure** Contrast the mood of the parts of "The Lagoon" narrated by Arsat with the mood of the framing story, narrated in the third person.

4. **Key Ideas and Details** Identify an effect that the "story within a story" has upon the frame story that surrounds it.

5. **Key Ideas and Details** **(a)** Where in "Araby" does the **epiphany** occur? **(b)** What does the narrator in "Araby" suddenly realize?

6. **Key Ideas and Details** What is the cause of the epiphany in "Araby"?

7. **Integration of Knowledge and Ideas** Explain in what sense the narrator's epiphany in "Araby" is as much a loss of vision as it is a gain of insight.

8. **Key Ideas and Details** **Identify cause and effect** in both stories. **(a)** What causes Arsat and the youngster in "Araby" to act? **(b)** In each case, what are the results of those actions?

9. **Comparing Literary Works** Use a chart like the one shown to compare how each story uses plot devices to establish distance between an experience of passion and the act of telling a story about passion.

Common Core State Standards

Reading Literature
9. Demonstrate knowledge of eighteenth-, nineteenth- and early-twentieth-century foundational works of American literature, including how two or more texts from the same period treat similar themes or topics. *(p. 1243)*

Writing
2. Write informative/explanatory texts to examine and convey complex ideas, concepts, and information clearly and accurately through the effective selection, organization, and analysis of content. *(p. 1243)*

2.b. Develop the topic thoroughly by selecting the most significant and relevant facts, extended definitions, concrete details, quotations, or other information and examples appropriate to the audience's knowledge of the topic. *(p. 1243)*

5. Develop and strengthen writing as needed by planning, revising, editing, rewriting, or trying a new approach, focusing on addressing what is most significant for a specific purpose and audience. *(p. 1243)*

9.a. Apply *grades 11–12 Reading standards* to literature. [RL.11-12.9] *(p. 1243)*

Language
5.b. Analyze nuances in the meaning of words with similar denotations. *(p. 1243)*

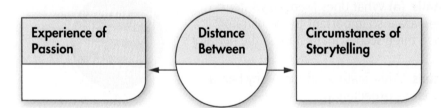

Experience of Passion	Distance Between	Circumstances of Storytelling

10. **Integration of Knowledge and Ideas** **(a)** Compare the way that each story creates an "outsider's" perspective on a narrator's obsessive, passionate concerns. **(b)** Explain how plot devices add to the **theme** of each story. Remember to cite details from the texts in support of your explanation.

Vocabulary Acquisition and Use

Word Analysis: Latin Root -vinc-

Early in "The Lagoon," you will find the word *invincible,* which means "unconquerable." *Invincible* is formed with the Latin root *-vinc-,* which comes from a Latin verb meaning "to conquer" and "to show conclusively." Some words use a variant spelling such as *-vict-,* which has the same meanings. Use the meaning of the root to define each of the following words. Then, write a sentence using each word appropriately.

1. convict
2. victory
3. vanquish
4. convince
5. evince
6. evict

Vocabulary: Synonyms

Synonyms are words with nearly the same meaning. Write the letter of the word that is a synonym of each word from the vocabulary list on page 1218. Then, explain the differences in meaning between the synonyms.

1. derided: **(a)** ejected, **(b)** exaggerated, **(c)** ridiculed
2. imperturbable: **(a)** calm, **(b)** indifferent, **(c)** ruthless
3. invincible: **(a)** facile, **(b)** warlike, **(c)** unconquerable
4. garrulous: **(a)** coy, **(b)** rich, **(c)** talkative
5. conflagration: **(a)** dispute, **(b)** fire, **(c)** battle
6. propitiate: **(a)** appease, **(b)** refuse, **(c)** resign

Writing to Sources

Informative Text James Joyce, an Irish author, and Ernest Hemingway, an American author, wrote several early twentieth-century masterpieces. Find a copy of Hemingway's short story "In Another Country," and read it carefully. Then, write an **essay** comparing and contrasting the first-person narrators in "Araby" and "In Another Country."

Prewriting Start by jotting down your impressions of the narrator in "Araby." Then jot down your impressions of the narrator in "In Another Country." Consider these questions: In what way is each narrator "wounded"? In each story, what events trigger an epiphany, or a moment of sudden insight?

Drafting As you draft your essay, use your prewriting notes as a guide, addressing the details you listed for each narrator. Link these details to broader considerations about how one narrator's characteristics are similar to or different from the other's. Support your ideas with quotations from each story.

Revising Review your draft, making sure that the sentences flow logically and that your ideas are well supported with details. Where evidence is lacking, review the stories to find relevant details to strengthen the support.

Model: Revising to Add Relevant Support

In "Araby," the narrator rushes off to the bazaar, but he is disappointed. Nearly all the stalls are closed, and he remembers only "with difficulty why I had come. . . ."

Citing specific textual details strengthens writing about literature.

Building Knowledge and Insight

Connecting to the Essential Question Both of these stories involve conflicts centering on issues of wealth and class. As you read, find details that show the effect of social position on the characters. These details will help you think about the Essential Question: **How does literature shape or reflect society?**

**Common Core
State Standards**

**Reading Literature
3.** Analyze the impact of the author's choices regarding how to develop and relate elements of a story.

Close Reading Focus

Theme; Symbol

In most short stories, the writer explores a **theme,** a central idea or question. Writers often reveal theme through a **symbol,** a person, object, or action that suggests deeper meanings. To identify symbols, look for descriptions that carry special emphasis, such as the underlined words in this passage from "The Rocking-Horse Winner."

> He knew *the horse could take him to where
> there was luck*, if only he forced it. So he
> would mount again, and start on his furious
> ride, hoping at last to get there.

Comparing Literary Works Each of these stories is told from a **third-person point of view,** meaning that the narrator does not take part in the action. As you read, compare how both authors use this point of view to develop their themes—for example, in the way they disclose the thoughts of characters and create symbols to suggest meanings. In addition, ask yourself how the third-person point of view differs in the two stories. Consider, for instance, whether Greene's narrative has the same intensity as Lawrence's.

Preparing to Read Complex Texts As you read, use the descriptions, events, and dialogue in the text—and your own background knowledge—to **make predictions** about what might happen. As you continue reading and learn more, you can confirm or revise those predictions. Use a graphic organizer like the one shown.

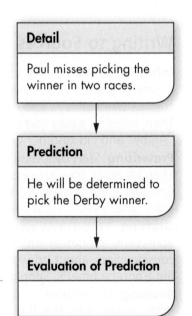

Detail

Paul misses picking the winner in two races.

Prediction

He will be determined to pick the Derby winner.

Evaluation of Prediction

Vocabulary

The words below are important to understanding the texts that follow. Copy the words into your notebook and note which ones are adverbs.

discreet   apprehension

obstinately   embarked

uncanny   intrinsically

D. H. Lawrence

(1885–1930)

Author of "The Rocking-Horse Winner"

During his lifetime, D. H. Lawrence's literary achievements were overshadowed by controversy. Like Percy Bysshe Shelley and Lord Byron in their day, Lawrence took unorthodox positions on politics and morality that shocked mainstream society.

Early Years Lawrence was born in Eastwood, Nottinghamshire, the son of an almost illiterate coal miner father and a more educated mother. Through her influence, he pursued a scholarship to the Nottingham High School, where he studied from 1898 to 1901. After leaving school for a job as a clerk, he contracted pneumonia and, on recovering, became a teacher.

Lawrence also began to write poems, stories, and novels, and his poetry attracted the attention of the well-known writer and editor Ford Madox Ford. In 1913, Lawrence published his first major novel, *Sons and Lovers,* a thinly disguised autobiography. Two years later, he published *The Rainbow,* which was banned in Britain.

Travels Abroad During World War I, Lawrence and his German wife, Frieda, lived in poverty in England and were unreasonably suspected of being German spies. At the end of the war, they left England and never returned. They traveled to Italy, Ceylon, Australia, Mexico, and the United States, and Lawrence used many of these locales in his fiction. In 1920, he published *Women in Love,* one of his greatest novels. A few years later, although suffering from tuberculosis, he completed *Lady Chatterley's Lover.* Shortly afterward, in the south of France, he died from that disease.

In the years since Lawrence's death, society's views of his writings have changed profoundly. Today, his fiction is widely admired for its vivid settings, fine craftsmanship, and psychological insight.

"THE HUMAN SOUL NEEDS ACTUAL BEAUTY MORE THAN bread."

The Rocking-Horse Winner

Winner

D. H. Lawrence

BACKGROUND

DURING THE FIRST HALF OF THE TWENTIETH CENTURY, BRITAIN HAD A RIGID CLASS STRUCTURE. ITS UPPER CLASSES TRIED TO LIVE AT THE "RIGHT" ADDRESSES, ATTEND THE "RIGHT" SCHOOLS, AND HAVE THE "RIGHT" FRIENDS. IN "THE ROCKING-HORSE WINNER," PAUL'S MOTHER IS DESPERATE TO MAINTAIN UPPER-CLASS APPEARANCES DESPITE HER HUSBAND'S "SMALL INCOME." IN "A SHOCKING ACCIDENT," JEROME ATTENDS AN "EXPENSIVE PREPARATORY SCHOOL"—PRIVATE SCHOOLS IN BRITAIN ARE REFERRED TO AS PUBLIC SCHOOLS—AND MUST DEAL WITH CLASSMATES' REACTIONS TO A TRAGEDY THAT IS BIZARRELY IMPROPER.

There was a woman who was beautiful, who started with all the advantages, yet she had no luck. She married for love, and the love turned to dust. She had bonny children, yet she felt they had been thrust upon her, and she could not love them. They looked at her coldly, as if they were finding fault with her. And hurriedly she felt she must cover up some fault in herself. Yet what it was that she must cover up she never knew. Nevertheless, when her children were present, she always felt the center of her heart go hard. This troubled her, and in her manner she was all the more gentle and anxious for her children, as if she loved them very much. Only she herself knew that at the center of her heart was a hard little place that could not feel love, no, not for anybody. Everybody else said of her: "She is such a good mother. She adores her children." Only she herself, and her children themselves, knew it was not so. They read it in each other's eyes.

There were a boy and two little girls. They lived in a pleasant house, with a garden and they had discreet servants, and felt themselves superior to anyone in the neighborhood.

Although they lived in style, they felt always an anxiety in the house. There was never enough money. The mother had a small income and the father had a small income, but not nearly enough for the social position which they had to keep up. The father went into town to some office. But though he had good prospects, these prospects never materialized. There was always the grinding sense of the shortage of money, though the style was always kept up.

At last the mother said, "I will see if *I* can't make something." But she did not know where to begin. She racked her brains, and tried this thing and the other, but could not find anything successful. The failure made deep lines come into her face. Her children were growing

◀ **Critical Viewing**
What could someone riding a rocking horse like this one win? **SPECULATE**

Theme and Symbol
What ideas about the story's theme does this first paragraph suggest?

Vocabulary
discreet (di skrēt´) *adj.* wise; prudent

Comprehension
What does the mother feel toward her children?

up, they would have to go to school. There must be more money, there must be more money. The father, who was always very handsome and expensive in his tastes, seemed as if he never *would* be able to do anything worth doing. And the mother, who had a great belief in herself, did not succeed any better, and her tastes were just as expensive.

And so the house came to be haunted by the unspoken phrase: *There must be more money! There must be more money!* The children could hear it all the time, though nobody said it aloud. They heard it at Christmas, when the expensive and splendid toys filled the nursery. Behind the shining modern rocking horse, behind the smart doll's house, a voice would start whispering: "There *must* be more money! There *must* be more money!" And the children would stop playing, to listen for a moment. They would look into each other's eyes to see if they had all heard. And each one saw in the eyes of the other two that they too had heard. "There *must* be more money! There *must* be more money!"

It came whispering from the springs of the still-swaying rocking horse, and even the horse, bending his wooden, champing head, heard it. The big doll, sitting so pink and smirking in her new pram,[1] could hear it quite plainly, and seemed to be smirking all the more self-consciously because of it. The foolish puppy, too, that took the place of the teddy bear, he was looking so extraordinarily foolish for no other reason but that he heard the secret whisper all over the house: "There *must* be more money."

Yet nobody ever said it aloud. The whisper was everywhere, and therefore no one spoke it. Just as no one ever says: "We are breathing!" in spite of the fact that breath is coming and going all the time.

"Mother!" said the boy Paul one day. "Why don't we keep a car of our own? Why do we always use uncle's, or else a taxi?"

"Because we're the poor members of the family," said the mother.

"But why *are* we, mother?"

"Well—I suppose," she said slowly and bitterly, "it's because your father has no luck."

The boy was silent for some time.

"Is luck money, mother?" he asked, rather timidly.

"No, Paul! Not quite. It's what causes you to have money."

"Oh!" said Paul vaguely. "I thought when Uncle Oscar said *filthy lucker,* it meant money."

"*Filthy lucre* does mean money," said the mother. "But it's lucre, not luck."

"Oh!" said the boy. "Then what *is* luck, mother?"

"It's what causes you to have money. If you're lucky you have money. That's why it's better to be born lucky than rich. If you're rich, you may lose your money. But if you're lucky, you will always get more money."

---

1. pram baby carriage.

"Oh! Will you! And is father not lucky?"

"Very unlucky, I should say," she said bitterly.

The boy watched her with unsure eyes.

"Why?" he asked.

"I don't know. Nobody ever knows why one person is lucky and another unlucky."

"Don't they? Nobody at all? Does *nobody* know?"

"Perhaps God! But He never tells."

"He ought to, then. And aren't you lucky either, mother?"

"I can't be, if I married an unlucky husband."

"But by yourself, aren't you?"

"I used to think I was, before I married. Now I think I am very unlucky indeed."

"Why?"

"Well—never mind! Perhaps I'm not really," she said.

The child looked at her, to see if she meant it. But he saw, by the lines of her mouth, that she was only trying to hide something from him.

"Well, anyhow," he said stoutly, "I'm a lucky person."

"Why?" said his mother, with a sudden laugh.

He stared at her. He didn't even know why he had said it.

"God told me," he asserted, brazening[2] it out.

"I hope He did, dear!" she said, again with a laugh, but rather bitter.

"He did, mother!"

"Excellent!" said the mother, using one of her husband's exclamations.

The boy saw she did not believe him; or rather, that she paid no attention to his assertion. This angered him somewhere, and made him want to compel her attention.

He went off by himself, vaguely, in a childish way, seeking for the clue to "luck." Absorbed, taking no heed of other people, he went about with a sort of stealth, seeking inwardly for luck. He wanted luck, he wanted it, he wanted it. When the two girls were playing dolls, in the nursery, he would sit on his big rocking horse, charging madly into space, with a frenzy that made the little girls peer at him uneasily. Wildly the horse careered, the waving dark hair of the boy tossed, his eyes had a strange glare in them. The little girls dared not speak to him.

When he had ridden to the end of his mad little journey, he climbed down and stood in front of his rocking horse, staring fixedly into its lowered face. Its red mouth was slightly open, its big eye was wide and glassy bright.

"Now!" he would silently command the snorting steed. "Now take me to where there is luck! Now take me!"

And he would slash the horse on the neck with the little whip he had asked Uncle Oscar for. He *knew* the horse could take him to

Making and Confirming Predictions

Based on what you have read, what do you think Paul will do? Why do you think so?

Comprehension

What does Paul do to find "the clue to 'luck'"?

---

2. brazening (brā′ zən iŋ) *v.* daring boldly or shamelessly.

where there was luck, if only he forced it. So he would mount again, and start on his furious ride, hoping at last to get there. He knew he could get there.

"You'll break your horse, Paul!" said the nurse.

"He's always riding like that! I wish he'd leave off!" said his elder sister Joan.

But he only glared down on them in silence. Nurse gave him up. She could make nothing of him. Anyhow he was growing beyond her.

One day his mother and his Uncle Oscar came in when he was on one of his furious rides. He did not speak to them.

"Hallo! you young jockey! Riding a winner?" said his uncle.

"Aren't you growing too big for a rocking horse? You're not a very little boy any longer, you know," said his mother.

But Paul only gave a blue glare from his big, rather close-set eyes. He would speak to nobody when he was in full tilt. His mother watched him with an anxious expression on her face.

At last he suddenly stopped forcing his horse into the mechanical gallop, and slid down.

"Well, I got there!" he announced fiercely, his blue eyes still flaring, and his sturdy long legs straddling apart.

"Where did you get to?" asked his mother.

"Where I wanted to go to," he flared back at her.

"That's right, son!" said Uncle Oscar. "Don't you stop till you get there. What's the horse's name?"

"He doesn't have a name," said the boy.

"Gets on without all right?" asked the uncle.

"Well, he has different names. He was called Sansovino last week."

"Sansovino, eh? Won the Ascot.[3] How did you know his name?"

"He always talks about horse races with Bassett," said Joan.

"AREN'T YOU GROWING TOO BIG FOR A *rocking horse?*"

The uncle was delighted to find that his small nephew was posted with all the racing news. Bassett, the young gardener who had been wounded in the left foot in the war, and had got his present job through Oscar Cresswell, whose batman[4] he had been, was a perfect blade of the "turf."[5] He lived in the racing events, and the small boy lived with him.

Oscar Cresswell got it all from Bassett.

"Master Paul comes and asks me, so I can't do more than tell him, sir," said Bassett, his face terribly serious, as if he were speaking of religious matters.

"And does he ever put anything on a horse he fancies?"

"Well—I don't want to give him away—he's a young sport, a fine sport, sir. Would you mind asking him yourself? He sort of takes a

Theme and Symbol

Bassett and the small boy "lived" in the racing events. What might this detail suggest about their lives?

---

3. **Ascot** major English horse race.
4. **batman** British military officer's orderly.
5. **blade . . . "turf"** horse-racing fan.

pleasure in it, and perhaps he'd feel I was giving him away, sir, if you don't mind."

Bassett was serious as a church.

The uncle went back to his nephew, and took him off for a ride in the car.

"Say, Paul, old man, do you ever put anything on a horse?" the uncle asked.

The boy watched the handsome man closely.

"Why, do you think I oughtn't to?" he parried.

"Not a bit of it! I thought perhaps you might give me a tip for the Lincoln."[6]

The car sped on into the country, going down to Uncle Oscar's place in Hampshire.

"Honor bright?" said the nephew.

"Honor bright, son!" said the uncle.

"Well, then, Daffodil."

"Daffodil! I doubt it, sonny. What about Mirza?"

"I only know the winner," said the boy. "That's Daffodil!"

"Daffodil, eh?"

There was a pause. Daffodil was an obscure horse comparatively.

"Uncle!"

"Yes, son?"

"You won't let it go any further, will you? I promised Bassett."

"Bassett be hanged, old man! What's he got to do with it?"

"We're partners! We've been partners from the first! Uncle, he lent me my first five shillings, which I lost. I promised him, honor bright, it was only between me and him: only you gave me that ten-shilling note I started winning with, so I thought you were lucky. You won't let it go any further, will you?"

The boy gazed at his uncle from those big, hot, blue eyes, set rather close together. The uncle stirred and laughed uneasily.

"Right you are, son! I'll keep your tip private. Daffodil, eh! How much are you putting on him?"

"All except twenty pounds," said the boy. "I keep that in reserve."

The uncle thought it a good joke.

"You keep twenty pounds in reserve, do you, you young romancer? What are you betting, then?"

"I'm betting three hundred," said the boy gravely. "But it's between you and me, Uncle Oscar! Honor bright?"

The uncle burst into a roar of laughter.

"It's between you and me all right, you young Nat Gould,"[7] he said, laughing. "But where's your three hundred?"

Making and Confirming Predictions
Which horse do you think will do better? Why?

Comprehension
What kind of a partnership does Paul have with Bassett?

---

6. Lincoln major English horse race.
7. Nat Gould famous English sportswriter and authority on horse racing.

"Bassett keeps it for me. We're partners."

"You are, are you! And what is Bassett putting on Daffodil?"

"He won't go quite as high as I do, I expect. Perhaps he'll go a hundred and fifty."

"What, pennies?" laughed the uncle.

"Pounds," said the child, with a surprised look at his uncle. "Bassett keeps a bigger reserve than I do."

Between wonder and amusement, Uncle Oscar was silent. He pursued the matter no further, but he determined to take his nephew with him to the Lincoln races.

"Now, son," he said, "I'm putting twenty on Mirza, and I'll put five for you on any horse you fancy. What's your pick?"

"Daffodil, uncle!"

"No, not the fiver on Daffodil!"

"I should if it was my own five," said the child.

"Good! Good! Right you are! A fiver for me and a fiver for you on Daffodil."

The child had never been to a race meeting before, and his eyes were blue fire. He pursed his mouth tight, and watched. A Frenchman just in front had put his money on Lancelot. Wild with excitement, he flayed his arms up and down, yelling *Lancelot! Lancelot!* in his French accent.

Daffodil came in first, Lancelot second, Mirza third. The child, flushed and with eyes blazing, was curiously serene. His uncle brought him five five-pound notes: four to one.

"What am I to do with these?" he cried, waving them before the boy's eyes.

"I suppose we'll talk to Bassett," said the boy. "I expect I have fifteen hundred now; and twenty in reserve; and this twenty."

His uncle studied him for some moments.

"Look here, son!" he said. "You're not serious about Bassett and that fifteen hundred, are you?"

"Yes, I am. But it's between you and me, uncle! Honor bright!"

"Honor bright all right, son! But I must talk to Bassett."

"If you'd like to be a partner, uncle, with Bassett and me, we could all be partners. Only you'd have to promise, honor bright, uncle, not to let it go beyond us three. Bassett and I are lucky, and you must be lucky, because it was your ten shillings I started winning with. . . ."

Uncle Oscar took both Bassett and Paul into Richmond Park for an afternoon, and there they talked.

"It's like this, you see, sir," Bassett said. "Master Paul would get me talking about racing events, spinning yarns, you know, sir. And he was always keen on knowing if I'd made or if I'd lost. It's about a year since, now, that I put five shillings on Blush of Dawn for him— and we lost. Then the luck turned, with that ten shillings he had

Theme, Symbol, and Third-Person Point of View

What does the narrator suggest about Paul's need by describing his eyes as "blue fire"?

Making and Confirming Predictions

Based on what you have read, who do you think picks the winning horses? Why?

▶ **Critical Viewing**

Which details in this picture convey the feverish excitement that Paul and Bassett feel about horse racing? **ANALYZE**

"Daffodil CAME IN FIRST, LANCELOT SECOND, MIRZA THIRD."

from you, that we put on Singhalese. And since that time, it's been pretty steady, all things considering. What do you say, Master Paul?"

"We're all right when we're *sure*," said Paul. "It's when we're not quite sure that we go down."

"Oh, but we're careful then," said Bassett.

"But when are you *sure?*" smiled Uncle Oscar.

"It's Master Paul, sir," said Bassett, in a secret, religious voice. "It's as if he had it from heaven. Like Daffodil now, for the Lincoln. That was as sure as eggs."

"Did you put anything on Daffodil?" asked Oscar Cresswell.

"Yes, sir. I made my bit."

"And my nephew?"

Bassett was obstinately silent, looking at Paul.

"I made twelve hundred, didn't I, Bassett? I told uncle I was putting three hundred on Daffodil."

"That's right," said Bassett, nodding.

"But where's the money?" asked the uncle.

"I keep it safe locked up, sir. Master Paul, he can have it any minute he likes to ask for it."

"What, fifteen hundred pounds?"

"And twenty! And *forty*, that is, with the twenty he made on the course."

"It's amazing!" said the uncle.

"If Master Paul offers you to be partners, sir, I would, if I were you; if you'll excuse me," said Bassett.

Oscar Cresswell thought about it.

"I'll see the money," he said.

They drove home again, and sure enough, Bassett came round to the garden house with fifteen hundred pounds in notes. The twenty pounds reserve was left with Joe Glee, in the Turf Commission deposit.

"You see, it's all right, uncle, when I'm *sure!* Then we go strong, for all we're worth. Don't we, Bassett?"

"We do that, Master Paul."

"And when are you sure?" said the uncle, laughing.

"Oh, well, sometimes I'm *absolutely* sure, like about Daffodil," said the boy, "and sometimes I have an idea; and sometimes I haven't even an idea, have I, Bassett? Then we're careful, because we mostly go down."

"You do, do you! And when you're sure, like about Daffodil, what makes you sure, sonny?"

"Oh, well, I don't know," said the boy uneasily. "I'm sure, you know, uncle; that's all."

"It's as if he had it from heaven, sir," Bassett reiterated.

"I should say so!" said the uncle.

But he became a partner. And when the Leger was coming on, Paul was "sure" about Lively Spark, which was a quite inconsiderable horse. The boy insisted on putting a thousand on the horse, Bassett went for five hundred, and Oscar Cresswell two hundred. Lively

Vocabulary

obstinately (äb´ stə nət lē) *adv.* in a determined way; stubbornly

Spark came in first, and the betting had been ten to one against him. Paul had made ten thousand.

"You see," he said. "I was absolutely sure of him."

Even Oscar Cresswell had cleared two thousand.

"Look here, son," he said, "this sort of thing makes me nervous."

"It needn't, uncle! Perhaps I shan't be sure again for a long time."

"But what are you going to do with your money?" asked the uncle.

"Of course," said the boy, "I started it for mother. She said she had no luck, because father is unlucky, so I thought if *I* was lucky, it might stop whispering."

"What might stop whispering?"

"Our house! I *hate* our house for whispering."

"What does it whisper?"

"Why—why"—the boy fidgeted—"why, I don't know! But it's always short of money, you know, uncle."

"I know it, son, I know it."

"You know people send mother writs, don't you, uncle?"

"I'm afraid I do," said the uncle.

"And then the house whispers like people laughing at you behind your back. It's awful, that is! I thought if I was lucky . . ."

"You might stop it," added the uncle.

The boy watched him with big blue eyes, that had an uncanny cold fire in them, and he said never a word.

"Well then!" said the uncle. "What are we doing?"

"I shouldn't like mother to know I was lucky," said the boy.

"Why not, son?"

"She'd stop me."

"I don't think she would."

"Oh!"—and the boy writhed in an odd way—"I *don't* want her to know, uncle."

"All right, son! We'll manage it without her knowing."

They managed it very easily. Paul, at the other's suggestion, handed over five thousand pounds to his uncle, who deposited it with the family lawyer, who was then to inform Paul's mother that a relative had put five thousand pounds into his hands, which sum was to be paid out a thousand pounds at a time, on the mother's birthday, for the next five years.

"So she'll have a birthday present of a thousand pounds for five successive years," said Uncle Oscar. "I hope it won't make it all the harder for her later."

Paul's mother had her birthday in November. The house had been "whispering" worse than ever lately, and even in spite of his luck, Paul could not bear up against it. He was very anxious to see the effect of the birthday letter, telling his mother about the thousand pounds.

When there were no visitors, Paul now took his meals with his parents, as he was beyond the nursery control. His mother went into

" OUR HOUSE!

I **HATE** OUR HOUSE FOR

whispering."

Vocabulary

uncanny (un kan′ ē) *adj.*
mysterious; hard to explain

Comprehension
Why does Paul want to win money?

Making and Confirming Predictions

How do you think Paul's mother will react to the letter about the money? Why?

town nearly every day. She had discovered that she had an odd knack of sketching furs and dress materials, so she worked secretly in the studio of a friend who was the chief "artist" for the leading drapers. She drew the figures of ladies in furs and ladies in silk and sequins for the newspaper advertisements. This young woman artist earned several thousand pounds a year, but Paul's mother only made several hundreds, and she was again dissatisfied. She so wanted to be first in something, and she did not succeed, even in making sketches for drapery advertisements.

She was down to breakfast on the morning of her birthday. Paul watched her face as she read her letters. He knew the lawyer's letter. As his mother read it, her face hardened and became more expressionless. Then a cold, determined look came on her mouth. She hid the letter under the pile of others, and said not a word about it.

"Didn't you have anything nice in the post for your birthday, mother?" said Paul.

"Quite moderately nice," she said, her voice cold and absent.

She went away to town without saying more.

But in the afternoon Uncle Oscar appeared. He said Paul's mother had had a long interview with the lawyer, asking if the whole five thousand could not be advanced at once, as she was in debt.

"What do you think, uncle?" said the boy.

"I leave it to you, son."

"Oh, let her have it, then! We can get some more with the other," said the boy.

"A bird in the hand is worth two in the bush, laddie!" said Uncle Oscar.

"But I'm sure to *know* for the Grand National; or the Lincolnshire; or else the Derby.[8] I'm sure to know for *one* of them," said Paul.

So Uncle Oscar signed the agreement, and Paul's mother touched the whole five thousand. Then something very curious happened. The voices in the house suddenly went mad, like a chorus of frogs on a spring evening. There were certain new furnishings, and Paul had a tutor. He was *really* going to Eton,[9] his father's school, in the following autumn. There were flowers in the winter, and a blossoming of the luxury Paul's mother had been used to. And yet the voices in the house, behind the sprays of mimosa and almond blossom, and from under the piles of iridescent cushions, simply trilled and screamed in a sort of ecstasy: "There *must* be more money! Oh-h-h! There *must* be more money! Oh, now, now-w! now-w-w—there *must* be more money!—more than ever! More than ever!"

It frightened Paul terribly. He studied away at his Latin and Greek with his tutors. But his intense hours were spent with Bassett. The

"DIDN'T YOU HAVE ANYTHING NICE IN THE POST FOR YOUR BIRTHDAY, mother?"

Making and Confirming Predictions

How accurate was your prediction about Paul's mother's reaction? How do you think Paul will respond to this result?

8. Grand National . . . Derby major English horse races.
9. Eton prestigious private school in England.

Grand National had gone by: he had not "known," and had lost a hundred pounds. Summer was at hand. He was in agony for the Lincoln. But even for the Lincoln he didn't "know," and he lost fifty pounds. He became wild-eyed and strange, as if something were going to explode in him.

"Let it alone, son! Don't you bother about it!" urged Uncle Oscar. But it was as if the boy couldn't really hear what his uncle was saying.

"I've got to know for the Derby! I've *got* to know for the Derby!" the child reiterated, his big blue eyes blazing with a sort of madness.

His mother noticed how overwrought he was.

"You'd better go to the seaside. Wouldn't you like to go now to the seaside, instead of waiting? I think you'd better," she said, looking down at him anxiously, her heart curiously heavy because of him.

But the child lifted his uncanny blue eyes.

"I couldn't possibly go before the Derby, mother!" he said. "I couldn't possibly!"

"Why not?" she said, her voice becoming heavy when she was opposed. "Why not? You can still go from the seaside to see the Derby with your Uncle Oscar, if that's what you wish. No need for you to wait here. Besides, I think you care too much about these races. It's a bad sign. My family has been a gambling family, and you won't know till you grow up how much damage it has done. But it has done damage. I shall have to send Bassett away, and ask Uncle Oscar not to talk racing to you, unless you promise to be reasonable about it; go away to the seaside and forget it. You're all nerves!"

"I'll do what you like, mother, so long as you don't send me away till after the Derby," the boy said.

"Send you away from where? Just from this house?"

"Yes," he said, gazing at her.

"Why, you curious child, what makes you care about this house so much, suddenly? I never knew you loved it!"

He gazed at her without speaking. He had a secret within a secret, something he had not divulged, even to Bassett or to his Uncle Oscar.

But his mother, after standing undecided and a little bit sullen for some moments, said:

"Very well, then! Don't go to the seaside till after the Derby, if you don't wish it. But promise me you won't let your nerves go to pieces! Promise you won't think so much about horse racing and *events*, as you call them!"

"Oh, no!" said the boy, casually. "I won't think much about them, mother. You needn't worry. I wouldn't worry, mother, if I were you."

"If you were me and I were you," said his mother, "I wonder what we should do!"

"But you know you needn't worry, mother, don't you?" the boy repeated.

"I should be awfully glad to know it," she said wearily.

Theme, Symbol, and Third-Person Point of View

If the story were told from Paul's point of view, would you know about the mother's "curiously heavy" feelings concerning Paul? Why or why not?

Comprehension

What present does Paul give his mother?

Theme and Symbol

In the paragraph beginning, "Paul's secret . . . ," which words or phrases suggest that the rocking horse is a symbol?

"Oh, well, you *can*, you know. I mean you *ought* to know you needn't worry!" he insisted.

"Ought I? Then I'll see about it," she said.

Paul's secret of secrets was his wooden horse, that which had no name. Since he was emancipated from a nurse and a nursery governess, he had had his rocking horse removed to his own bedroom at the top of the house.

"Surely you're too big for a rocking horse!" his mother had remonstrated.

"Well, you see, mother, till I can have a *real* horse, I like to have *some* sort of animal about," had been his quaint answer.

"Do you feel he keeps you company?" she laughed.

"Oh, yes! He's very good, he always keeps me company, when I'm there," said Paul.

So the horse, rather shabby, stood in an arrested prance in the boy's bedroom.

The Derby was drawing near, and the boy grew more and more tense. He hardly heard what was spoken to him, he was very frail, and his eyes were really uncanny. His mother had sudden strange seizures of uneasiness about him. Sometimes, for half an hour, she would feel a sudden anxiety about him that was almost anguish. She wanted to rush to him at once, and know he was safe.

Two nights before the Derby, she was at a big party in town, when one of her rushes of anxiety about her boy, her firstborn, gripped her heart till she could hardly speak. She fought with the feeling, might and main, for she believed in common sense. But it was too strong. She had to leave the dance and go downstairs to telephone to the country. The children's nursery governess was terribly surprised and startled at being rung up in the night.

"Are the children all right, Miss Wilmot?"

"Oh yes, they are quite all right."

"Master Paul? Is he all right?"

"He went to bed as right as a trivet.[10] Shall I run up and look at him?"

"No!" said Paul's mother reluctantly. "No! Don't trouble. It's all right. Don't sit up. We shall be home fairly soon." She did not want her son's privacy intruded upon.

"Very good," said the governess.

It was about one o'clock when Paul's mother and father drove up to their house. All was still. Paul's mother went to her room and slipped off her white fur cloak. She had told her maid not to wait up for her. She heard her husband downstairs, mixing a whisky-and-soda.

And then, because of the strange anxiety at her heart, she stole upstairs to her son's room. Noiselessly she went along the upper corridor. Was there a faint noise? What was it?

Theme, Symbol, and Third-Person Point of View

Does the third-person narrator's insight into the mother's anxiety make you feel more sympathy for her? Explain.

---

10. right as a trivet perfectly right.

She stood, with arrested muscles, outside his door, listening. There was a strange, heavy, and yet not loud noise. Her heart stood still. It was a soundless noise, yet rushing and powerful. Something huge, in violent, hushed motion. What was it? What in God's name was it? She ought to know. She felt that she *knew* the noise. She knew what it was.

Yet she could not place it. She couldn't say what it was. And on and on it went, like madness.

Softly, frozen with anxiety and fear, she turned the door handle.

The room was dark. Yet in the space near the window, she heard and saw something plunging to and fro. She gazed in fear and amazement.

Then suddenly she switched on the light, and saw her son, in his green pajamas, madly surging on his rocking horse. The blaze of light suddenly lit him up, as he urged the wooden horse, and lit her up, as she stood, blond, in her dress of pale green and crystal, in the doorway.

"Paul!" she cried. "Whatever are you doing?"

"It's Malabar!" he screamed, in a powerful, strange voice. "It's Malabar!"

His eyes blazed at her for one strange and senseless second, as he ceased urging his wooden horse. Then he fell with a crash to the ground, and she, all her tormented motherhood flooding upon her, rushed to gather him up.

But he was unconscious, and unconscious he remained, with some brain fever. He talked and tossed, and his mother sat stonily by his side.

"Malabar! It's Malabar! Bassett, Bassett, I *know* it's Malabar!"

So the child cried, trying to get up and urge the rocking horse that gave him his inspiration.

"What does he mean by Malabar?" asked the heart-frozen mother.

"I don't know," said the father, stonily.

"What does he mean by Malabar?" she asked her brother Oscar.

"It's one of the horses running for the Derby," was the answer.

And, in spite of himself, Oscar Cresswell spoke to Bassett, and himself put a thousand on Malabar: at fourteen to one.

The third day of the illness was critical: they were watching for a change. The boy, with his rather long, curly hair, was tossing ceaselessly on the pillow. He neither slept nor regained consciousness, and his eyes were like blue stones. His mother sat, feeling her heart had gone, turned actually into a stone.

Theme and Symbol

In what way is the rocking horse connected with the whispering of the house?

Making and Confirming Predictions

What do you think will happen to Paul?

Comprehension

Why is Paul especially tense just before the Derby?

"It's Malabar!

BASSETT, BASSETT, I KNOW

IT'S MALABAR!"

In the evening, Oscar Cresswell did not come, but Bassett sent a message, saying could he come up for one moment, just one moment? Paul's mother was very angry at the intrusion, but on second thoughts she agreed. The boy was the same. Perhaps Bassett might bring him to consciousness.

The gardener, a shortish fellow with a little brown moustache and sharp little brown eyes, tiptoed into the room, touched his imaginary cap to Paul's mother, and stole to the bedside, staring with glittering, smallish eyes at the tossing, dying child.

"Master Paul!" he whispered. "Master Paul! Malabar came in first all right, a clean win. I did as you told me. You've made over seventy thousand pounds, you have; you've got over eighty thousand. Malabar came in all right, Master Paul."

"Malabar! Malabar! Did I say Malabar, mother? Did I say Malabar? Do you think I'm lucky, mother? I knew Malabar, didn't I? Over eighty thousand pounds! I call that lucky, don't you, mother? Over eighty thousand pounds! I knew, didn't I know I knew? Malabar came in all right. If I ride my horse till I'm sure, then I tell you, Bassett, you can go as high as you like. Did you go for all you were worth, Bassett?"

"I went a thousand on it, Master Paul."

"I never told you, mother, that if I can ride my horse, and *get there*, then I'm absolutely sure—oh, absolutely! Mother, did I ever tell you? I *am* lucky!"

"No, you never did," said the mother.

But the boy died in the night.

And even as he lay dead, his mother heard her brother's voice saying to her: "My God, Hester, you're eighty-odd thousand to the good, and a poor devil of a son to the bad. But, poor devil, poor devil, he's best gone out of a life where he rides his rocking horse to find a winner."

Spiral Review
Character What difficult problem does Paul face throughout the story?

Critical Reading

1. **Key Ideas and Details (a)** From the point of view of Paul's mother, what is the main problem of the family? **(b) Infer:** What does the mother's statement that the father is "unlucky" suggest about her values?

2. **Key Ideas and Details (a)** Over the course of the story, how does Paul react to the house's "whispers"? **(b) Analyze Cause and Effect:** Why is he affected as he is?

3. **Key Ideas and Details (a)** What does Uncle Oscar say at the end of the story? **(b) Interpret:** Do you think Uncle Oscar is speaking for the author? Why or why not?

4. **Integration of Knowledge and Ideas** What, if anything, is more important than the luck and money that Paul's mother wanted so desperately?

Cite textual evidence to support your responses.

GRAHAM GREENE

(1904-1991)

Author of "A Shocking Accident"

The search for salvation, a theme addressed by poets like T. S. Eliot, is a central concern in the fiction of novelist Graham Greene. Like Eliot, Greene was a religious convert who wrote works exploring pain, fear, despair, and alienation.

Journalism and Travel The son of a school-master, Greene was born in Berkhamsted in Hertfordshire. He converted to Roman Catholicism after studying at Oxford University. Then, he began working as a copy editor in London and married. Eventually, he became a traveling freelance journalist.

Thrillers and More His journalism helped him develop the powers of observation, sensitivity to atmosphere, and simplicity of language that became hallmarks of his fiction. While traveling, he was able to scout out locations for his stories and novels.

Some of these novels, such as *Orient Express* (1932), he called "entertainments." These were an unusual type of thriller that went beyond the genre in its concern with moral issues.

Even more deeply involved with spiritual crisis, however, were such Greene classics as *Brighton Rock* (1938), *The Power and the Glory* (1940), and two novels set in Africa, *The Heart of the Matter* (1948) and *A Burnt-Out Case* (1961). In these works, Greene's concern with salvation burns with intensity.

Psychological Insight Greene's best fiction focuses on the psychology of human character rather than on plot. Many of his protagonists are people without roots or beliefs—people in pain. They may be odd, but they almost always excite the reader's curiosity and pity—and, almost always, Greene treats them with compassion as they strive to achieve salvation.

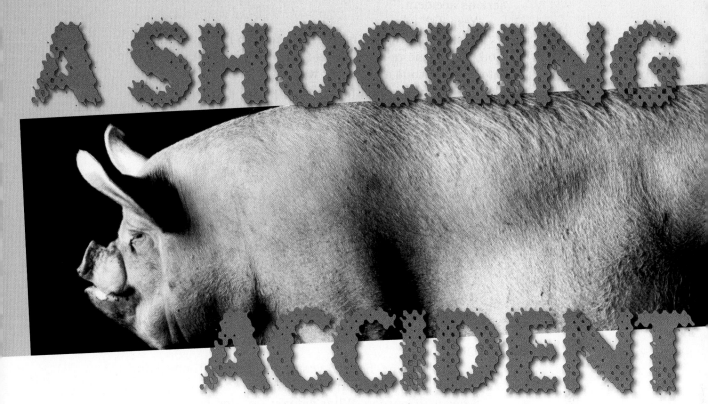

A SHOCKING ACCIDENT

GRAHAM GREENE

I

Jerome was called into his housemaster's room in the break between the second and the third class on a Thursday morning. He had no fear of trouble, for he was a warden—the name that the proprietor and headmaster of a rather expensive preparatory school had chosen to give to approved, reliable boys in the lower forms (from a warden one became a guardian and finally before leaving, it was hoped for Marlborough or Rugby, a crusader). The housemaster, Mr. Wordsworth, sat behind his desk with an appearance of perplexity and apprehension. Jerome had the odd impression when he entered that he was a cause of fear.

"Sit down, Jerome," Mr. Wordsworth said. "All going well with the trigonometry?"

"Yes, sir."

"I've had a telephone call, Jerome. From your aunt. I'm afraid I have bad news for you."

"Yes, sir?"

"Your father has had an accident."

"Oh."

▲ **Critical Viewing**
What role do you think a pig like the one shown will play in this story? **PREDICT**

Vocabulary
apprehension (ap´ rē hen´ shən) *n.* anxious feeling of foreboding; dread

Comprehension
Why is Jerome not afraid of being called to the housemaster's room?

Mr. Wordsworth looked at him with some surprise. "A serious accident."

"Yes, sir?"

Jerome worshipped his father: the verb is exact. As man re-creates God, so Jerome re-created his father—from a restless widowed author into a mysterious adventurer who traveled in far places—Nice, Beirut, Majorca, even the Canaries. The time had arrived about his eighth birthday when Jerome believed that his father either "ran guns" or was a member of the British Secret Service. Now it occurred to him that his father might have been wounded in "a hail of machine-gun bullets."

Mr. Wordsworth played with the ruler on his desk. He seemed at a loss how to continue. He said, "You knew your father was in Naples?"

"Yes, sir."

"Your aunt heard from the hospital today."

"Oh."

Mr. Wordsworth said with desperation, "It was a street accident."

"Yes, sir?" It seemed quite likely to Jerome that they would call it a street accident. The police, of course, had fired first; his father would not take human life except as a last resort.

"I'm afraid your father was very seriously hurt indeed."

"Oh."

"In fact, Jerome, he died yesterday. Quite without pain."

"Did they shoot him through the heart?"

"I beg your pardon. What did you say, Jerome?"

"Did they shoot him through the heart?"

Theme and Symbol

Do you think that the way Jerome's father died could be symbolic? Why or why not?

"Nobody shot him, Jerome. A pig fell on him." An inexplicable convulsion took place in the nerves of Mr. Wordsworth's face; it really looked for a moment as though he were going to laugh. He closed his eyes, composed his features, and said rapidly, as though it were necessary to expel the story as rapidly as possible, "Your father was walking along a street in Naples when a pig fell on him. A shocking accident. Apparently in the poorer quarters of Naples they keep pigs on their balconies. This one was on the fifth floor. It had grown too fat. The balcony broke. The pig fell on your father."

Mr. Wordsworth left his desk rapidly and went to the window, turning his back on Jerome. He shook a little with emotion.

Jerome said, "What happened to the pig?"

"WHAT HAPPENED TO THE PIG?"

2

This was not callousness on the part of Jerome as it was interpreted by Mr. Wordsworth to his colleagues (he even discussed with them whether, perhaps, Jerome was not yet fitted to be a warden). Jerome was only attempting to visualize the strange scene and to get the details right. Nor was Jerome a boy who cried; he was a boy who brooded, and it never occurred to him at his preparatory school that the circumstances of his father's death were comic—they were still part of the mystery of life. It was later in his first term at his public school, when he told the story to his best friend, that he began to realize how it affected others. Naturally, after that disclosure he was known, rather unreasonably, as Pig.

Unfortunately his aunt had no sense of humor. There was an enlarged snapshot of his father on the piano: a large sad man in an unsuitable dark suit posed in Capri with an umbrella (to guard him against sunstroke), the Faraglioni rocks forming the background. By the age of sixteen Jerome was well aware that the portrait looked more like the author of *Sunshine and Shade* and *Rambles in the Balearics* than an agent of the Secret Service. All the same, he loved the memory of his father: he still possessed an album filled with picture-postcards (the stamps had been soaked off long ago for his other collection), and it pained him when his aunt embarked with strangers on the story of his father's death.

"A shocking accident," she would begin, and the stranger would compose his or her features into the correct shape for interest and commiseration. Both reactions, of course, were false, but it was terrible for Jerome to see how suddenly, midway in her rambling discourse, the interest would become genuine. "I can't think how such things can be allowed in a civilized country," his aunt would say. "I suppose one has to regard Italy as civilized. One is prepared for all kinds of things abroad, of course, and my brother was a great traveler. He always carried a water-filter with him. It was far less expensive, you know, than buying all those bottles of mineral water. My brother always said that his filter paid for his dinner wine. You can see from that what a careful man he was, but who could possibly have expected when he was walking along the Via Dottore Manuele Panucci on his way to the Hydrographic Museum that a pig would fall on him?" That was the moment when the interest became genuine.

Jerome's father had not been a distinguished writer, but the time always seems to come, after an author's death, when somebody thinks it worth his while to write a letter to *The Times Literary Supplement* announcing the preparation of a biography and asking to see any letters or documents or receive any anecdotes from friends of the dead man. Most of the biographies, of course, never appear—one

Spiral Review

Context What conclusions can you draw about the nuances in meaning of the word *disclosure* by analyzing the paragraph?

Vocabulary

embarked (em bärkt´) *v.* engaged in something, such as a conversation

Comprehension
What happened to Jerome's father?

wonders whether the whole thing may not be an obscure form of blackmail and whether many a potential writer of a biography or thesis finds the means in this way to finish his education at Kansas or Nottingham. Jerome, however, as a chartered accountant, lived far from the literary world. He did not realize how small the menace really was, nor that the danger period for someone of his father's obscurity had long passed. Sometimes he rehearsed the method of recounting his father's death so as to reduce the comic element to its smallest dimensions—it would be of no use to refuse information, for in that case the biographer would undoubtedly visit his aunt, who was living to a great old age with no sign of flagging.

It seemed to Jerome that there were two possible methods—the first led gently up to the accident, so well prepared that the death came really as an anticlimax. The chief danger of laughter in such a story was always surprise. When he rehearsed this method Jerome began boringly enough.

"You know Naples and those high tenement buildings? Somebody once told me that the Neapolitan always feels at home in New York just as the man from Turin feels at home in London because the river runs in much the same way in both cities. Where was I? Oh, yes, Naples, of course. You'd be surprised in the poorer quarters what things they keep on the balconies of those skyscraping tenements—not washing, you know, or bedding, but things like livestock, chickens or even pigs. Of course the pigs get no exercise whatever and fatten all the quicker." He could imagine how his hearer's eyes would have glazed by this time. "I've no idea, have you, how heavy a pig can be, but those old buildings are all badly in need of repair. A balcony on the fifth floor gave way under one of those pigs. It struck the third-floor balcony on its way down and sort of ricocheted into the street. My father was on the way to the Hydrographic Museum when the pig hit him. Coming from that height and that angle it broke his neck." This was really a masterly attempt to make an intrinsically interesting subject boring.

The other method Jerome rehearsed had the virtue of brevity.

"My father was killed by a pig."

"Really? In India?"

"No, in Italy."

"How interesting. I never realized there was pig-sticking in Italy. Was your father keen on polo?"

In course of time, neither too early nor too late, rather as though, in his capacity as a chartered accountant, Jerome had studied the statistics and taken the average, he became engaged to be married: to a pleasant fresh-faced girl of twenty-five whose father was a doctor in Pinner. Her name was Sally, her favorite author was still Hugh

Vocabulary

intrinsically (in trin′ sik lē) *adv.* at its core; inherently; innately

Walpole, and she had adored babies ever since she had been given a doll at the age of five which moved its eyes and made water. Their relationship was contented rather than exciting, as became the love affair of a chartered accountant; it would never have done if it had interfered with the figures.

One thought worried Jerome, however. Now that within a year he might himself become a father, his love for the dead man increased; he realized what affection had gone into the picture-postcards. He felt a longing to protect his memory, and uncertain whether this quiet love of his would survive if Sally were so insensitive as to laugh when she heard the story of his father's death. Inevitably she would hear it when Jerome brought her to dinner with his aunt. Several times he tried to tell her himself, as she was naturally anxious to know all she could that concerned him.

"You were very small when your father died?"

"Just nine."

"Poor little boy," she said.

"I was at school. They broke the news to me."

"Did you take it very hard?"

"I can't remember."

"You never told me how it happened."

"It was very sudden. A street accident."

"You'll never drive fast, will you, Jemmy?" (She had begun to call him "Jemmy.") It was too late then to try the second method—the one he thought of as the pig-sticking one.

They were going to marry quietly at a registry-office and have their honeymoon at Torquay. He avoided taking her to see his aunt until a week before the wedding, but then the night came, and he could not have told himself whether his apprehension was more for his father's memory or the security of his own love.

The moment came all too soon. "Is that Jemmy's father?" Sally asked, picking up the portrait of the man with the umbrella.

"Yes, dear. How did you guess?"

"He has Jemmy's eyes and brow, hasn't he?"

"Has Jerome lent you his books?"

"No."

"I will give you a set for your wedding. He wrote so tenderly about his travels. My own favorite is *Nooks and Crannies*. He would have had a great future. It made that shocking accident all the worse."

"Yes?"

Making and Confirming Predictions

How do you think Sally will react to the story of Jerome's father's death? What impact will that have on Jerome?

Comprehension

What two methods of narrating his father's death does Jerome rehearse?

"IT WAS VERY SUDDEN. A STREET ACCIDENT."

How Jerome longed to leave the room and not see that loved face crinkle with irresistible amusement.

"I had so many letters from his readers after the pig fell on him." She had never been so abrupt before.

And then the miracle happened. Sally did not laugh. Sally sat with open eyes of horror while his aunt told her the story, and at the end, "How horrible," Sally said. "It makes you think, doesn't it? Happening like that. Out of a clear sky."

Theme and Symbol

What does the contrast between Sally's reaction and those of other characters suggest about the theme?

Jerome's heart sang with joy. It was as though she had appeased his fear forever. In the taxi going home he kissed her with more passion than he had ever shown, and she returned it. There were babies in her pale blue pupils, babies that rolled their eyes and made water.

"A week today," Jerome said, and she squeezed his hand. "Penny for your thoughts, my darling."

"I was wondering," Sally said, "what happened to the poor pig?"

"They almost certainly had it for dinner," Jerome said happily and kissed the dear child again.

"WHAT HAPPENED TO THE POOR PIG?"

Critical Reading

1. **Key Ideas and Details** How does Jerome protect himself from the embarrassing aspects of the death?

2. **Key Ideas and Details (a)** How does Sally react when she hears the story? **(b) Infer:** What does Sally's reaction reveal to Jerome about her character? **(c) Draw Conclusions:** Are Jerome's conflicts about his father's death resolved at the end of the story? Why or why not?

3. **Integration of Knowledge and Ideas** One implication of the "shocking accident" might be that what happens in life is basically beyond our control. Do you agree with this idea? Why or why not?

4. **Integration of Knowledge and Ideas** Does the uniqueness of the main character in either or both of the stories suggest a message about society? Explain. In your response, use at least two of these Essential Question words: *emotion, spontaneity, conventional, trait.* [Connecting to the Essential Question: How does literature shape or reflect society?]

Cite textual evidence to support your responses.

Close Reading Activities

The Rocking-Horse Winner • A Shocking Accident

Literary Analysis

1. **Key Ideas and Details** Using the terms *love* and *money,* state a central question, issue, or concern that expresses one of the **themes** in "The Rocking-Horse Winner."

2. **Craft and Structure** Complete a chart like this with **(a)** passages illustrating the **symbolic** meanings of the rocking horse and **(b)** explanations linking these meanings to the theme.

Symbolic Meanings	Passages That Illustrate	Links to Overall Theme
• Frantic effort to satisfy an unsatisfiable need • Frightening power of desires and wishes		

3. **Integration of Knowledge and Ideas (a)** If "The Rocking-Horse Winner" continued, **predict** how Paul's mother might act in the future. **(b)** What information in the story and in your own *background knowledge* leads you to make that prediction?

4. **Craft and Structure** For "A Shocking Accident," explain how the accident might symbolize either of these meanings: **(a)** that which makes no sense; **(b)** that which is unacceptable according to upper-class notions.

5. **Key Ideas and Details** Use the symbolic meanings of the accident to state the theme of "A Shocking Accident."

6. **Craft and Structure** For both "The Rocking-Horse Winner" and "A Shocking Accident," identify two passages that show the use of the **third-person point of view.**

7. **Comparing Literary Works** In which story does the third-person point of view work more effectively to reveal the theme? Explain, citing details from the stories.

8. **Comparing Literary Works** In which story is the third-person narrative more like a fairy tale and in which is it more like an anecdote? Explain.

9. **Integration of Knowledge and Ideas** Which story ending surprised you more? What did the author do to make the ending surprising?

Common Core State Standards

Writing
3. Write narratives to develop real or imagined experiences or events using effective technique, well-chosen details, and well-structured event sequences. *(p. 1270)*

5. Develop and strengthen writing as needed by planning, revising, editing, rewriting, or trying a new approach, focusing on addressing what is most significant for a specific purpose and audience. *(p. 1270)*

Language
4.a. Use context as a clue to the meaning of a word or phrase. *(p. 1270)*

Close Reading Activities Continued

Vocabulary Acquisition and Use

Word Analysis: Anglo-Saxon prefix *un-*

Lawrence describes Paul's eyes as having an "uncanny" fire. The prefix *un-* means "not" or "the opposite or reversal of an action." It is used with adjectives, such as *unavailable* ("not available"), and verbs, such as *unlock* ("to reverse the action of locking"). The prefix comes from Anglo-Saxon, a Germanic language that is the basis for English. Write an original sentence that shows your understanding of the meaning of each of these words that begin with the prefix *un-*:

1. unhinge
2. unavoidable
3. unrecognized
4. unclasp
5. unsure
6. unchecked

Vocabulary: Context Clues

The context in which an unfamiliar word appears can give you clues to the word's meaning. For each sentence, explain how a context clue helps you identify the meaning of the italicized word from the vocabulary listed on page 1244.

1. The story was *intrinsically* boring, but the storyteller's style made it gripping.
2. The investigator's *discreet* queries raised no suspicions.
3. The camel *obstinately* refused to budge despite the owner's many efforts.
4. Reunited after ten years, the two sisters *embarked* on recounting their lives.
5. The dark clouds gave the worried farmer a feeling of *apprehension*.
6. Her *uncanny* ability to predict the future defied all logic.

Writing to Sources

Narrative Text Filmmakers use dialogue, images, and sounds to create symbols in films. Write a **script for a scene** from one of the stories. Include descriptions of the scenery, dialogue, and directions regarding shots, camera movement, and scene changes. Use some of the terms explained in the chart below.

Shots	Camera Movement	Scene Changes
• **Wide shot:** Camera captures a large area • **Medium shot:** Camera sees objects and surroundings • **Close-up:** Camera focuses on one object	• **Crane:** Camera moves in and out and up and down • **Pan:** Camera moves from side to side • **Zoom:** Camera moves in for a closer view	• **Dissolve:** Image grows faint as new image emerges • **Fade-out:** Image fades to black • **Montage:** Quick succession of unrelated images

Prewriting Choose the scene to script. Identify the symbols in that scene and their meaning. Decide how you want those symbols to appear.

Drafting Write a draft of your script. Be sure to describe what the camera sees, the movements of the characters, and the way the symbols will look. Include dialogue, indicating which character is speaking. Embellish your script with notes on how the scene should be shot and edited.

Revising Review your draft, making sure that the scene flows well, that directions are clear, and that you use the symbols effectively. Ensure that the descriptions and dialogue accurately and faithfully present the story.

Conflicts at Home and Abroad

Connecting to the Essential Question War can lead soldiers to write powerful prose and poetry. As you read, notice details that show the impact of the war on these poets. Doing so will help you think about the Essential Question: **How does literature shape or reflect society?**

Close Reading Focus

Tone

The **tone** of a literary work is the writer's attitude toward the readers and the subject. A writer's choice of words and details conveys the tone of the work. For example, in these lines from Rupert Brooke's "The Soldier," the underlined words and phrases communicate a tone of patriotic devotion and wistful memory:

> Her sights and sounds; <u>dreams happy as her day</u>;
> And <u>laughter</u>, learnt of <u>friends</u>; and <u>gentleness</u>,
> In <u>hearts at peace</u>, under an <u>English heaven</u>.

Comparing Literary Works In a way, these selections are like letters sent home by soldiers during World War I. These "letters" each contain central messages, or **themes,** about the war for those back in England, removed from the fighting. In figuring out these messages, use tone as a clue. Identify words and phrases that reveal each writer's attitude about the war and toward civilian readers. Then, compare and contrast the different writers' messages.

Preparing to Read Complex Texts Because writers often suggest rather than state elements like theme and speaker, readers must **infer the essential message,** or make educated guesses based on clues in the text. Use a chart like the one shown to make inferences about the essential messages of these poems.

Vocabulary

You will encounter the words listed here in the texts that follow. Copy these words into your notebook, sorting them into words you know and words you do not know.

stealthy   mockeries

ghastly   pallor

desolate

**Common Core
State Standards**

Reading Literature
4. Analyze the impact of specific word choices on meaning and tone, including words with multiple meanings or language that is particularly fresh, engaging, or beautiful.

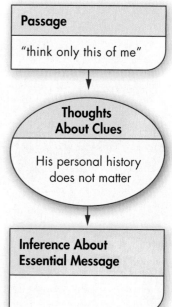

Passage
"think only this of me"

Thoughts About Clues

His personal history does not matter

Inference About Essential Message

RUPERT BROOKE   *(1887–1915)*

Author of **"The Soldier"**

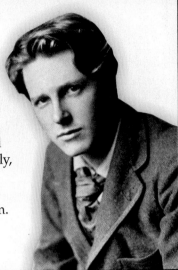

Rupert Brooke had striking good looks, personal charm, and high intelligence. Before World War I began, Brooke had already established himself as a serious poet. He traveled a great deal, writing essays as well as poetry. When war broke out in 1914, he joined the Royal Navy. Tragically, he died from blood poisoning while on a mission to defeat the Turks.

Brooke's war sonnets, traditional and idealistic, were among the last from the soldier-poets of World War I to express wholehearted patriotism. The prolonged, inhuman slaughter of trench warfare extinguished the idealism of many of them.

SIEGFRIED SASSOON   *(1886–1967)*

Author of **"Wirers"**

Born into a wealthy family in Kent, England, Siegfried Sassoon published poetry while still in his twenties. In 1914, he joined the army and showed such reckless courage in battle that he earned the nickname "Mad Jack," along with a medal for gallantry.

By 1916 or 1917, though, Sassoon's attitude toward war had changed. He began to write starkly realistic "trench poems" about war's agonies. He was wounded early in 1917 and, while recovering, wrote a statement condemning the war. Partly to defuse his criticism and partly to protect him from its consequences, he was placed in a hospital for victims of shell shock.

Sassoon survived the war and lived almost fifty years longer, but he wrote little to match his wartime verses.

WILFRED OWEN   *(1893–1918)*

Author of **"Anthem for Doomed Youth"**

Always interested in literature, Wilfred Owen studied at London University and joined the army in 1915. He was wounded three times in 1917 and won a medal for outstanding bravery in 1918. Owen's work became grittier and angrier under the influence of Siegfried Sassoon, whom he had met at a military hospital in 1917. It was a terrible loss to English poetry when Owen was killed in battle just one week before the end of the war.

Owen was unknown as a poet until Sassoon published a collection of his work, *Poems*, in 1920. Today, Owen is regarded as one of the greatest war poets in the English language.

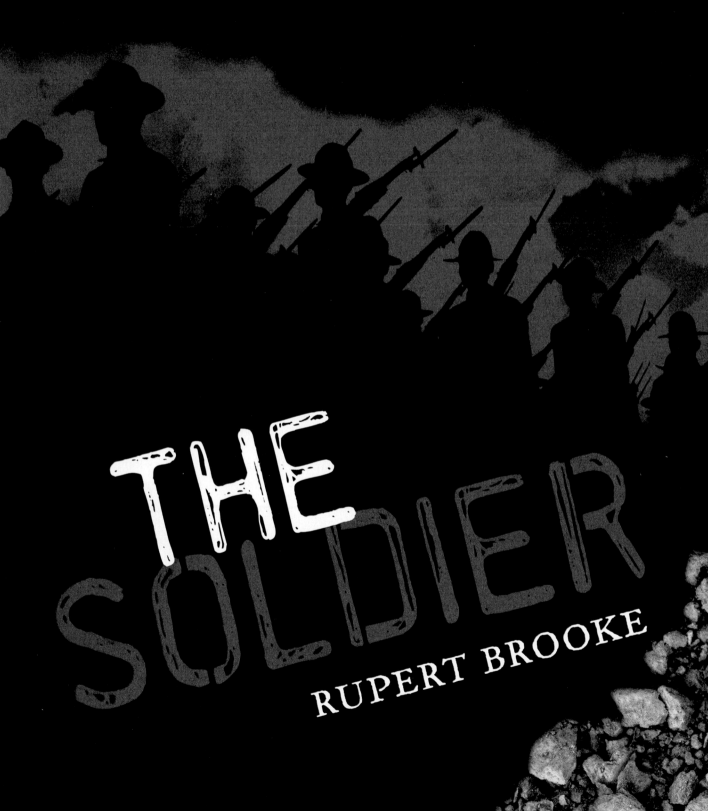

THE SOLDIER

RUPERT BROOKE

BACKGROUND World War I (1914–1918) pitted Great Britain, France, Russia, Japan, Italy, and, later, the United States (the Allies) against Germany, Austria-Hungary, and Turkey (the Central Powers). The war was fought not only in Europe but also in regions like the Middle East and Asia Minor. Typical of this conflict, especially in Western Europe, was trench warfare. Armies faced each other in defensive trenches protected by barbed wire. Periodically, one army would attack another in the face of machine-gun and artillery fire. Such warfare and the illnesses resulting from life in filthy trenches led to a total loss of about 8.5 million soldiers.

> If I should die, think only this of me:
>   That there's some corner of a foreign field
> That is forever England. There shall be
>   In that rich earth a richer dust concealed;
> 5 A dust whom England bore, shaped, made aware,
>   Gave, once, her flowers to love, her ways to roam,
>   A body of England's, breathing English air,
>   Washed by the rivers, blest by suns of home.
>
>   And think, this heart, all evil shed away,
> 10   A pulse in the eternal mind, no less
>   Gives somewhere back the thoughts by England given;
>   Her sights and sounds; dreams happy as her day;
>   And laughter, learnt of friends; and gentleness,
>   In hearts at peace, under an English heaven.

Tone

What are three adjectives that describe the tone of this poem? Explain.

Critical Reading ©

1. **Key Ideas and Details (a)** How does the speaker ask his readers to remember him, should he die? **(b) Infer:** Why would the speaker go off to war, knowing he could be killed?

2. **Key Ideas and Details (a)** Name some of the things England has given the speaker. **(b) Interpret:** What is the "richer dust" to which the speaker refers?

3. **Key Ideas and Details (a)** In lines 9 and 10, what does the speaker say his "heart" will become? **(b) Interpret:** What does the speaker mean by this statement?

4. **Integration of Knowledge and Ideas** Brooke's attitude has been called a "ridiculous anachronism"—something outdated—in the face of modern warfare. Do you agree or disagree? Why?

Cite textual evidence to support your responses.

WIRERS[1]

SIEGFRIED SASSOON

▲ **Critical Viewing**
Which details in this photograph support Sassoon's depiction of warfare? Explain. **CONNECT**

Vocabulary
stealthy (stel´ thē)
adj. secretive; furtive

ghastly (gast´ lē)
adj. extremely horrible; frightening

desolate (des´ ə lit)
adj. deserted; forlorn

"Pass it along, the wiring party's going out"—
And yawning sentries mumble, "Wirers going out."
Unraveling; twisting; hammering stakes with muffled thud,
They toil with stealthy haste and anger in their blood.

5　The Boche[2] sends up a flare. Black forms stand rigid there,
Stock-still like posts; then darkness, and the clumsy ghosts
Stride hither and thither, whispering, tripped by clutching
　　　　snare
Of snags and tangles.
　　　　　　Ghastly dawn with vaporous coasts
10　Gleams desolate along the sky, night's misery ended.

Young Hughes was badly hit; I heard him carried away,
Moaning at every lurch; no doubt he'll die today.
But *we* can say the front-line wire's been safely mended.

---

1. **Wirers** soldiers who were responsible for repairing the barbed-wire fences that protected the trenches in World War I.
2. **Boche** (bōsh) French slang for a German soldier.

ANTHEM FOR DOOMED YOUTH

WILFRED OWEN

What passing-bells for these who die as cattle?
Only the monstrous anger of the guns.
Only the stuttering rifles' rapid rattle
Can patter out their hasty orisons.[1]
5 No mockeries for them from prayers or bells,
Nor any voice of mourning save the choirs—
The shrill, demented choirs of wailing shells;
And bugles calling for them from sad shires.[2]

What candles may be held to speed them all?
10 Not in the hands of boys, but in their eyes
Shall shine the holy glimmers of good-byes.
The pallor of girls' brows shall be their pall;
Their flowers the tenderness of patient minds,
And each slow dusk a drawing-down of blinds.

---

1. **orisons** (ôr´ i zəns) *n.* prayers.
2. **shires** (shīrz) *n.* any of the counties of England.

Inferring the Essential Message

Based on the first line of the poem, what can you infer about Owen's attitude toward the war?

Vocabulary

mockeries (mäk´ ər ēz) *n.* futile or disappointing efforts; ridicule

pallor (pal´ ər) *n.* lack of color; paleness

Critical Reading

1. **Key Ideas and Details (a)** In "Wirers," what happens in the course of the mission? **(b) Draw Conclusions:** What is the speaker's attitude toward the mission and toward the war? Explain.

2. **Key Ideas and Details (a)** In lines 9–14 of "Anthem for Doomed Youth," what conventional signs of mourning are mentioned? **(b) Analyze:** What do Owen's suggested replacements for these signs have in common?

3. **Integration of Knowledge and Ideas** Do you think Sassoon's poem affected the attitude of British readers toward the war? Explain your answer, using two of these Essential Question words: *position, destructive, factors, influence, support. [Connecting to the Essential Question: How does literature shape or reflect society?]*

Cite textual evidence to support your responses.

Literary Analysis

1. **Key Ideas and Details** Infer the essential message of "Wirers," explaining what details led you to your conclusion.

2. **Key Ideas and Details** What do you think Owen's purpose is in altering funeral rituals in lines 9–14 of "Anthem for Doomed Youth"? Explain your reasoning.

3. **Key Ideas and Details** (a) Infer the essential message of "The Soldier" and "Anthem for Doomed Youth" and explain what details led you to that conclusion. (b) If Brooke had lived longer and experienced more of the war, do you think he would have produced poetry more like Owen's? Explain your answer.

4. **Craft and Structure** Using a chart like the one shown, briefly describe the **tone** in two or three key passages from each poem.

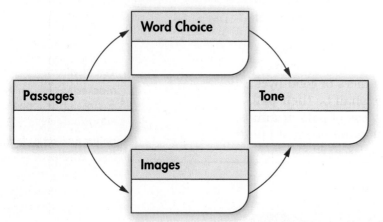

5. **Craft and Structure** (a) Of the three selections, which is the least angry in tone? Explain. (b) Which is the most sarcastic? Explain.

6. **Craft and Structure** (a) Which of the selections has the most surprising tone or mixture of tones? Why? (b) What is less surprising about the tone or tones of the other selections?

7. **Integration of Knowledge and Ideas** For English civilians of the time, which of these selections probably conveyed the most positive message about the war? Explain.

8. **Integration of Knowledge and Ideas** (a) Which poems are most concerned with war's destruction? Explain. (b) Which criticize how the war is being run? Explain.

9. **Comparing Literary Works** Compare the attitudes these writers have toward civilian readers.

Common Core State Standards

Writing
1. Write arguments to support claims in an analysis of substantive topics or texts, using valid reasoning and relevant and sufficient evidence. (p. 1279)

Language
5. Demonstrate understanding of figurative language, word relationships, and nuances in word meanings. (p. 1279)

Vocabulary Acquisition and Use

Word Analysis: Anglo-Saxon roots -ghast-, -ghost-

In "Wirers," Sassoon refers to the "ghastly" dawn. *Ghastly* comes from an Anglo-Saxon root, *-ghast-*, that means "to terrify." The same root also appears as *-ghost-*, which means "the spirit of a dead person," which can terrify the living. Use your understanding of these roots to determine the meaning of these words. Then use them in a sentence.

1. aghast
2. ghostly
3. ghosting
4. ghastful

Vocabulary: Synonyms

Synonyms are words that have similar meanings. Write the letter of the word that is the synonym of each word from the vocabulary list on page 1272. Then, explain the differences in meaning between the synonyms.

1. desolate: **(a)** crowded, **(b)** forlorn, **(c)** happy
2. ghastly: **(a)** frightening, **(b)** ghostly, **(c)** shocking
3. mockeries: **(a)** bravery, **(b)** praise, **(c)** ridicule
4. pallor: **(a)** care, **(b)** paleness, **(c)** friends
5. stealthy: **(a)** furtive, **(b)** honest, **(c)** smart

Writing to Sources

Argumentative Text When Irish poet William Butler Yeats selected poems for an anthology of modern English poetry, he left out Brooke, Sassoon, and Owen. Yeats explained his action this way: "I have a distaste for certain poems written in the midst of the great war. . . . The writers . . . were . . . officers of exceptional courage . . . but . . . passive suffering is not a theme for poetry." Write an **essay** that responds to Yeats based on your reading of these poets, particularly Sassoon and Owen. Cite evidence from the poems to support your point about the merits—or lack of merit—of these poets.

Prewriting Note uses of imagery, language, or ideas in the poems that reflect poetic skill or communicate important messages. Review your examples to see if they mainly support or refute Yeats's claim, and decide whether you agree or disagree with his view.

Drafting Begin your draft by summarizing Yeats's position and stating your response to it. Use detailed evidence and examples from the poems to support your points.

Revising Review your draft, highlighting generalizations and looking for supporting details for each. Where details are lacking, add them. Make sure that all quotations are accurate and properly referenced.

Clearly Stating Your Response

As I will demonstrate, Yeats misreads poems like "Wirers" when he dismisses them as representing "passive suffering."

Stating a position early and supporting it with evidence gives a clear picture of the argument.

CONTEMPORARY CONNECTION

CONNECTING WAR WRITINGS PAST AND PRESENT

Wilfred Owen, British soldier and poet killed in battle one week before the end of World War I in 1918, wrote that "War and the Pity of War" were his chosen subject. The blogger Riverbend's subject is also the pity of war, a war that has forced her and her family, Iraqi Muslims, to realize that they must abandon their home in Baghdad, a city that in 2007 has all but disappeared into violence. Owen uses the traditional poetic form to describe the threat of "The shrill, demented choirs of wailing shells" in "Anthem for Doomed Youth." Riverbend's April 26, 2007 Web journal entry may be prose, yet it is just as fear-based: "It's difficult to decide which is more frightening—car bombs and militias, or having to leave everything you know and love. . . ."

Both writers are in their 20's when they confront the reality of war. Worlds of difference separate them—gender, religion, geography, technology, the patriotism of an enlisted soldier versus the witness a civilian woman must bear to the chaos surrounding her home—yet their concerns are remarkably similar: death, and the death of a way of life. Riverbend, 24 when she began to chronicle the details of daily life in her gripping blog, known in book form as *Baghdad Burning*, writes anonymously because, "I wouldn't feel free to write otherwise. . . ." Owen, at least, knows nothing of that kind of fear and publishes signed poetry describing the horror of what he witnesses. Both doomed soldier-poet and determined prose writer document events that overtake them, in the most effective and persuasive style they know.

RIVERBEND, AUTHOR OF

BAGHDAD BURNING

"I am female, Iraqi, and 24. I survived the war." With these words, the blogger who calls herself Riverbend begins her online journal one Sunday in August 2003. "That's all you need to know. That's all that matters these days," she writes. Her postings have been compiled into two books, *Baghdad Burning*, published in 2005, and *Baghdad Burning II*, which appeared the following year. Riverbend has become something of a blog celebrity, supplying her readers with a comprehensive local Iraqi view of the war. In fact, her blog has journeyed from cyberspace to the printed page to the stage, debuting in New York in 2005 in a blending of documentary drama and blog that became a play.

No journalist, Riverbend, who explains that she was forced from her job as a computer programmer, nonetheless exhibits a journalist's ability to describe everything around her, from the horror of looking for a missing neighbor to power failures that keep her from her computer. Her perspective is personal and her weapons are words, which survive beyond immediate events, just as the words of the war poets of World War I do.

"RIVERBEND" IS A STORYTELLER. HER "BAGHDAD BURNING" BLOG IS ONE PART ANNE FRANK, ANOTHER PART SCHEHERAZADE AND "A THOUSAND AND ONE ARABIAN NIGHTS."

— FROM CYBERSPACE
[PROMOTION BY HER PUBLISHER]

BAGHDAD BURNING

... I'LL MEET YOU 'ROUND THE BEND MY FRIEND,
WHERE HEARTS CAN HEAL AND SOULS CAN MEND...

FROM THURSDAY, APRIL 26, 2007

I remember Baghdad before the war—one could live anywhere. We didn't know what our neighbors were—we didn't care. No one asked about religion or sect. No one bothered with what was considered a trivial topic: are you Sunni or Shia? You only asked something like that if you were uncouth and backward. Our lives revolve around it now. Our existence depends on hiding it or highlighting it—depending on the group of masked men who stop you or raid your home in the middle of the night.

On a personal note, we've finally decided to leave. I guess I've known we would be leaving for a while now. We discussed it as a family dozens of times. At first, someone would suggest it tentatively because, it was just a preposterous idea—leaving one's home and extended family—leaving one's country—and to what? To where?

Since last summer, we had been discussing it more and more. It was only a matter of time before what began as a suggestion—a last case scenario—soon took on solidity and developed into a plan. For the last couple of months, it has only been a matter of logistics. Plane or car? Jordan or Syria? Will we all leave together as a family? Or will it be only my brother and I at first?

After Jordan or Syria—where then? Obviously, either of those countries is going to be a transit to something else. They are both overflowing with Iraqi refugees, and every single Iraqi living in either country is complaining of the fact that work is difficult to come by, and getting a residency is even more difficult. There is also the little problem of being turned back at the border. Thousands of Iraqis aren't being let into Syria or Jordan—and there are no definite criteria for entry, the decision is based on the whim of the border patrol guard checking your passport.

An airplane isn't necessarily safer, as the trip to Baghdad International Airport is in itself risky and travelers are just as likely to be refused permission to enter the country (Syria and Jordan) if they arrive by airplane. And if you're wondering why Syria or Jordan, because they are the only two countries that will let Iraqis in without a visa. Following up visa issues with the few functioning embassies or consulates in Baghdad is next to impossible.

So we've been busy. Busy trying to decide what part of our lives to leave behind. Which memories are dispensable? We, like many Iraqis,

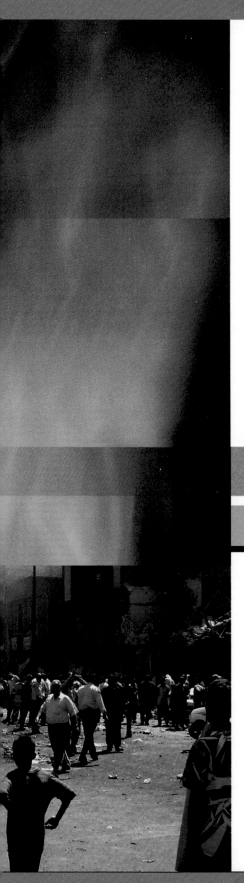

are not the classic refugees—the ones with only the clothes on their backs and no choice. We are choosing to leave because the other option is simply a continuation of what has been one long nightmare—stay and wait and try to survive.

On the one hand, I know that leaving the country and starting a new life somewhere else—as yet unknown—is such a huge thing that it should dwarf every trivial concern. The funny thing is that it's the trivial that seems to occupy our lives. We discuss whether to take photo albums or leave them behind. Can I bring along a stuffed animal I've had since the age of four? Is there room for E.'s guitar? What clothes do we take? Summer clothes? The winter clothes too? What about my books? What about the CDs, the baby pictures?

The problem is that we don't even know if we'll ever see this stuff again. We don't know if whatever we leave, including the house, will be available when and if we come back. There are moments when the injustice of having to leave your country, simply because someone got it into his head to invade it, is overwhelming. It is unfair that in order to survive and live normally, we have to leave our home and what remains of family and friends… And to what?

It's difficult to decide which is more frightening—car bombs and militias, or having to leave everything you know and love, to some unspecified place for a future where nothing is certain.

… WE'VE FINALLY DECIDED TO LEAVE

Critical Reading

1. **(a)** Why did Riverbend's family originally think leaving Iraq was a "preposterous" idea? **(b) Assess:** Was their idea to leave Iraq "preposterous"? Explain.

2. **(a)** What are the difficulties Riverbend anticipates her family will encounter as they try to leave Iraq?
   (b) Infer: How does Riverbend feel about these difficulties? Explain.

3. **(a)** What items might Riverbend's family take when they leave Iraq? **(b) Interpret:** Why does Riverbend's family want to bring these items?

Use these questions to focus a class discussion of "Baghdad Burning":

4. What can readers who are not involved in a war learn from the writings of Riverbend?

5. How is a blog posted on the Internet different from published essays, stories, or memoirs? How is it similar?

Primary Sources

Speech   **Memorandum**
Wartime Speech   **Evacuation Scheme**

About the Text Forms

A **speech** is an oral presentation on an important issue. Three elements of a speech are its *purpose,* the reason for its presentation; its *occasion,* the event that inspires it; and its *audience,* those who hear it at the time it is delivered or who hear or read it later. In the World War II era, before television, radio listeners were the largest audience for the speeches of national leaders and other important figures. Such speeches can be valuable primary sources in showing how both the authorities and the general public perceived and responded to events.

  A **government memorandum** is a brief official message that summarizes reasons for a particular action and gives instructions on how it is to be performed. Since they affected large numbers of people, government memorandums from the past can be valuable primary sources about events and practices of those times.

Preparing to Read Complex Texts

The central idea, or essential message, of a text is the main point the author expresses. It is closely tied to the author's purpose and his or her point of view on the issue. These texts, written during a period of crisis, reflect their authors' urgent purposes, including the need to ensure the public's willingness to endure hardship for the sake of survival and victory.

  As you **determine the essential messages** of these documents, notice the *rhetorical devices and features* that the writers use to emphasize their *main points.*

  For example, analyze Churchill's speech for **rhetorical devices** like *parallelism,* the use of similar grammatical structures to express ideas in a memorable way. Also analyze the speech for *emotional appeals,* such as the use of charged words like "victory." Analyze the memorandum for **text features** like headings and lists. Use a chart like the one shown to identify the essential message and the supporting devices and features.

How does literature **shape or** reflect *society?*

Winston Churchill was an inspirational leader at a time of great suffering for the British people. As you read, consider how his speech helped shape the public reaction to the hardships of World War II.

 **Common Core
State Standards**

Reading Informational Text
2. Determine two or more central ideas of a text and analyze their development over the course of the text, including how they interact and build on one another to provide a complex analysis; provide an objective summary of the text.
6. Determine an author's point of view or purpose in a text in which the rhetoric is particularly effective, analyzing how style and content contribute to the power, persuasiveness, or beauty of the text.

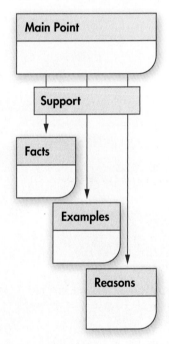

Note-Taking Guide

Primary-source documents are a rich source of information for researchers. As you read these documents, use a note-taking guide like the one shown here to organize relevant and accurate information.

1 Type of Document
   ☐ Newspaper Article   ☐ Letter   ☐ Diary   ☐ Speech   ☐ Map
   ☐ Government Document   ☐ Advertisement   ☐ Memorandum   ☐ Other

2 Date of Document _____

3 Author _____
   Author's Position _____

4 Original Audience _____

5 Purpose and Importance

   a What was the original purpose? _____
      Write down two details that support your answer. _____
      _____

   b List two important ideas, statements, or observations from this document.
      _____
      _____

   c What does this document show about the time and place in which it
      was composed? _____
      _____
      _____

Determine the Essential Message
Identifying the sources' main points and supporting features and devices will help you appreciate their purposes.

This guide was adapted from the **U.S. National Archives** document analysis worksheet.

Vocabulary

intimidated (in tim′ ə dāt əd) *v.* made afraid; frightened (p. 1288)

endurance (en door′ əns) *n.* ability to last or continue (p. 1288)

formidable (fôr′ mə də bəl) *adj.* causing fear or dread; hard to overcome (p. 1288)

invincible (in vin′ sə bəl) *adj.* unconquerable (p. 1288)

retaliate (ri tal′ ē āt′) *v.* fight in order to pay back an injury or wrong (p. 1289)

humanitarian (hyoo man′ ə ter′ ē ən) *adj.* acting to help humanity, especially by easing pain and suffering (p. 1291)

allocation (al′ ō kā′ shən) *n.* setting apart for a specific purpose; fixing the location of (p. 1291)

THE STORY BEHIND THE DOCUMENTS

Sir Winston Churchill

Sir Winston Churchill (1874–1965) first won fame as a soldier and journalist in colonial India and South Africa. His war-hero status earned him a seat in Parliament and several government posts, but he was out of power by the 1930s, when his repeated warnings about the dangers of Nazi Germany went unheeded. Only after World War II broke out did the British turn to the man who had been right about the Nazis all along. Churchill became prime minister in May of 1940 and went on to play a key role in the Allied victory five years later.

Churchill was a gifted orator who made dozens of memorable **speeches.** Many of these were delivered to Parliament or other live audiences and also broadcast on the radio; others were radio addresses made directly to the public. In the dark days of the war, when most of Europe had fallen and Britain faced the Nazis alone, it sometimes seemed that the fate of freedom itself depended on the gruff voice of the prime minister, infusing his fellow citizens with the strength and courage to endure.

In the autumn of 1940, a few months after the fall of France, the Germans concentrated their efforts on air attacks on Britain, hoping to bomb the nation into submission. In anticipation of the bombing attacks—and before the war actually began—the British government made plans for the evacuation of children, hospital patients, and some others in the urban areas likely to be targeted by German bombs. The British Ministry of Health outlined the evacuation plan in a 1939 **government memorandum.**

Evacuation was voluntary, but with the bombs flying, few families refused to participate. Because the likely targets for German bombs were factories, docks, and other industrial areas, the majority of the evacuated children were from poor working-class families who generally live in such areas. They were sent to the less populated countryside to live with farmers and villagers of the more prosperous middle class. The result was culture shock—but a culture shock that ultimately brought Britain closer together.

WARTIME SPEECH

Sir Winston Churchill

BBC, London, 19 May 1940

I speak to you for the first time as Prime Minister in a solemn hour for the life of our country, of our Empire, of our Allies, and, above all, of the cause of Freedom. A tremendous battle is raging in France and Flanders.[1] The Germans, by a remarkable combination of air bombing and heavily armored tanks, have broken through the French defenses north of the Maginot Line,[2] and strong columns of their armored vehicles are ravaging the open country, which for the first day or two was without defenders. They have penetrated deeply and spread alarm and confusion in their track. Behind them there are now appearing infantry in lorries,[3] and behind them, again, the large masses are moving forward. The regroupment of the French armies to make head against, and also to strike at, this intruding wedge has

---

1. **Flanders** (flan´ dərz) region in northwest Europe, on the North Sea, that includes northern France and much of Belgium.
2. **Maginot** (mazh´ ə nō´) **Line** heavy fortifications built before World War II on the eastern frontier of France, in an unsuccessful effort to prevent a German invasion.
3. **infantry in lorries** (lôr´ ēz) foot soldiers in trucks.

is for **FRANCE** which we helped to defend

Vocabulary

intimidated (in tim′ ə dāt əd)
v. made afraid; frightened

endurance (en dŏŏr′ əns)
n. ability to last or continue

formidable (fôr′ mə də bəl)
adj. causing fear or dread;
hard to overcome

invincible (in vin′ sə bəl)
adj. unconquerable

Primary Source

Speech What do Churchill's
words in the third paragraph
show about his opinion of
the "concrete lines"
of defense?

been proceeding for several days, largely assisted by the magnificent efforts of the Royal Air Force.

We must not allow ourselves to be intimidated by the presence of these armored vehicles in unexpected places behind our lines. If they are behind our Front, the French are also at many points fighting actively behind theirs. Both sides are therefore in an extremely dangerous position. And if the French Army, and our own Army, are well handled, as I believe they will be; if the French retain that genius for recovery and counterattack for which they have so long been famous; and if the British Army shows the dogged endurance and solid fighting power of which there have been so many examples in the past—then a sudden transformation of the scene might spring into being.

It would be foolish, however, to disguise the gravity of the hour. It would be still more foolish to lose heart and courage or to suppose that well-trained, well-equipped armies numbering three or four millions of men can be overcome in the space of a few weeks, or even months, by a scoop, or raid of mechanized vehicles, however formidable. We may look with confidence to the stabilization of the Front in France, and to the general engagement of the masses, which will enable the qualities of the French and British soldiers to be matched squarely against those of their adversaries. For myself, I have invincible confidence in the French Army and its leaders. Only a very small part of that splendid army has yet been heavily engaged; and only a very small part of France has yet been invaded. There is good evidence to show that practically the whole of the specialized and mechanized forces of the enemy have been already thrown into the battle; and we know that very heavy losses have been inflicted upon them. No officer or man, no brigade or division,[4] which grapples at close quarters with the enemy, wherever encountered, can fail to make a worthy contribution to the general result. The Armies must cast away the idea of resisting behind concrete lines or natural obstacles, and must realize that mastery can only be regained by furious and unrelenting assault. And this spirit must not only animate the High Command, but must inspire every fighting man.

In the air—often at serious odds—often at odds hitherto[5] thought overwhelming—we have been clawing down three or four to one of our enemies; and the relative balance of the British and German Air Forces is now considerably more favorable to us than at the beginning of the battle. In cutting down the German bombers, we are fighting our own battle as well as that of France. My confidence in our ability to fight it out to the finish with the German Air Force has

---

4. brigade or division large units of soldiers.
5. hitherto (hith′ ər tōō) *adv.* until this time.

been strengthened by the fierce encounters which have taken place and are taking place. At the same time, our heavy bombers are striking nightly at the taproot of German mechanized power, and have already inflicted serious damage upon the oil refineries on which the Nazi effort to dominate the world directly depends.

We must expect that as soon as stability is reached on the Western Front, the bulk of that hideous apparatus of aggression which gashed Holland into ruin and slavery in a few days, will be turned upon us. I am sure I speak for all when I say we are ready to face it; to endure it; and to retaliate against it—to any extent that the unwritten laws of war permit. There will be many men, and many women, in this island who when the ordeal comes upon them, as come it will, will feel comfort, and even a pride—that they are sharing the perils of our lads at the Front—soldiers, sailors and airmen, God bless them—and are drawing away from them a part at least of the onslaught they have to bear. Is not this the appointed time for all to make the utmost exertions in their power? If the battle is to be won, we must provide our men with everincreasing quantities of the weapons and ammunition they need. We must have, and have quickly, more airplanes, more tanks, more shells, more guns. There is imperious need for these vital munitions.[6] They increase our strength against the powerfully armed enemy. They replace the wastage of the obstinate struggle; and the knowledge that wastage will speedily be replaced enables us to draw more readily upon our reserves and throw them in now that everything counts so much.

Our task is not only to win the battle—but to win the War. After this battle in France abates its force, there will come the battle for

◀▲ Primary Source: Art and Photographs What mood about the war does the poster (left page) convey to British citizens? Does the photo above show Churchill conveying a similar mood? Explain. **[Compare and Contrast]**

Vocabulary

retaliate (ri tal′ ē ət′) *v.* fight in order to pay back an injury or wrong

Comprehension

What does Churchill say is the advantage of "the general engagement of the masses"?

---

6. imperious (im pir′ ē əs) . . . **munitions** (myoo nish′ ənz) urgent need for these vital weapons and ammunition.

our island—for all that Britain is, and all that Britain means. That will be the struggle. In that supreme emergency we shall not hesitate to take every step, even the most drastic, to call forth from our people the last ounce and the last inch of effort of which they are capable. The interests of property, the hours of labor, are nothing compared with the struggle for life and honor, for right and freedom, to which we have vowed ourselves.

I have received from the Chiefs of the French Republic, and in particular from its indomitable Prime Minister, M. Reynaud,[7] the most sacred pledges that whatever happens they will fight to the end, be it bitter or be it glorious. Nay, if we fight to the end, it can only be glorious.

Having received His Majesty's commission, I have found an administration of men and women of every party and of almost every point of view. We have differed and quarreled in the past; but now one bond unites us all—to wage war until victory is won, and never to surrender ourselves to servitude and shame, whatever the cost and the agony may be. This is one of the most awe-striking periods in the long history of France and Britain. It is also beyond doubt the most sublime. Side by side, unaided except by their kith and kin in the great Dominions and by the wide Empires which rest beneath their shield—side by side, the British and French peoples have advanced to rescue not only Europe but mankind from the foulest and most soul-destroying tyranny which has ever darkened and stained the pages of history. Behind them—behind us—behind the armies and fleets of Britain and France—gather a group of shattered States and bludgeoned[8] races: the Czechs, the Poles, the Norwegians, the Danes, the Dutch, the Belgians—upon all of whom the long night of barbarism will descend, unbroken even by a star of hope, unless we conquer, as conquer we must; as conquer we shall.

Today is Trinity Sunday.[9] Centuries ago words were written to be a call and a spur to the faithful servants of Truth and Justice; "Arm yourselves, and be ye men of valor, and be in readiness for the conflict; for it is better for us to perish in battle than to look upon the outrage of our nation and our altar. As the Will of God is in Heaven, even so let it be."[10]

Determining the Essential Message

What is the main point of this paragraph? What rhetorical devices does Churchill use to convey this point?

▼ Primary Source: Photograph

What does Churchill say have been the effects of having a strong air force with planes like the spitfire pictured here? **[Analyze Causes and Effects]**

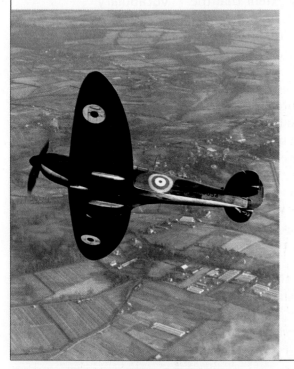

---

7. **M. Reynaud** (rā nō´) Paul Reynaud (1878-1966), French politician who served as France's prime minister from March to June of 1940, when France fell to the Germans.
8. **bludgeoned** (bluj´ ənd) *adj.* beaten. Churchill goes on to name the people of nations that have been overrun by the Germans.
9. **Trinity Sunday** Christian holy day on the eighth Sunday after Easter.
10. **"Arm . . . be"** a quotation from the first book of Maccabees 3:58, a book that is part of Roman Catholic versions of the Bible but not Jewish and Protestant versions.

EVACUATION SCHEME

Memo. Ev. 4

GOVERNMENT EVACUATION SCHEME

MEMORANDUM.

4. The objective has been therefore to provide facilities for the removal from certain large crowded areas, in which the effects of air attack would be most serious, of certain groups of people whose removal is desirable on both national and humanitarian grounds, and to transfer them to districts where the primary purpose of dispersal can be achieved. This has involved an order of priority as regards both the classes of persons to be transferred and the towns to be evacuated, and the provisional allocation of other districts as receiving areas.

Priority classes.

5. The classes of person to whom priority is to be given under the Government Scheme are:—

    (1) school children in organized units in charge of their teachers;
    (2) children of pre-school age accompanied by their mothers or other persons responsible for looking after them;
    (3) expectant mothers;
    (4) the adult blind and cripple population so far as removal may be feasible.

The information to be given should include information as to the points of assembly and the amount and kind of hand luggage which can be conveyed. A full list should include the child's gas mask, a change of underclothing, night-clothes, house-shoes or plimsolls, spare stockings or socks, a toothbrush, comb, towel and handerkerchiefs, a warm coat or mackintosh, and a packet of food for the day. The children should be sent away wearing their thickest and warmest footwear.

Determining the Essential Message

What text features, such as fonts, heads, and design, are used to convey the essential message of this memorandum?

Vocabulary

humanitarian (hyo͞o man′ ə ter′ ē ən) *adj.* acting to help humanity, especially by easing pain and suffering

allocation (al′ ō kā′ shən) *n.* setting apart for a specific purpose; fixing the location of

Critical Reading

1. **Key Ideas and Details (a)** What major new development in the war does Churchill report in the beginning of his speech? **(b) Analyze:** What answer does Churchill provide to any concerns that this development might cause?

2. **Key Ideas and Details (a)** According to the memorandum, what is the "primary purpose" of the evacuation? **(b) Interpret:** What are the "national and humanitarian grounds" for the evacuation?

Cite textual evidence to support your responses.

PHOTOGRAPHS
OF THE LONDON BLITZ

Churchill's promise of "conflict" in his Wartime Speech of May 19, 1940, was grimly fulfilled during the German bombing attack on London known as the Blitz (from the German *blitzkrieg*, meaning "lightning warfare"). The Blitz, which lasted from September 7, 1940, to May 11, 1941, caused many casualties and resulted in the damage or destruction of more than a million houses. Nevertheless, this bombardment strengthened rather than undermined Britain's resolve to fight. The photographs on this page show some of the physical effects of the Blitz.

V is for **VICTORY**
we never shall
be slaves

▶ **Primary Source: Art and Photographs** What story do the poster (above) and the photographs (right) tell you about the effects of the Blitz on England and its citizens? **[Interpret]**

Speech ▪ Memorandum

Comparing Primary Sources

Refer to your Note-Taking Guide to complete these questions:

1. **(a)** What is the specific occasion and purpose for Churchill's **speech** and the events to which the **government memorandum** responds? **(b)** What future occasion do both documents anticipate?

2. **(a)** Summarize one or more essential messages expressed in each document. **(b)** How is each document, in its own way, part of the British war effort?

3. **(a)** Who was the intended audience for each document? **(b)** What details and language used in each document reflect that audience? Use this chart to gather ideas and examples.

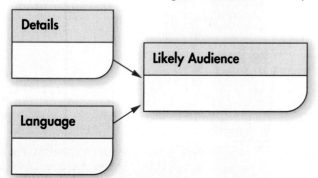

Vocabulary Acquisition and Use

Antonyms For each word, choose the letter of its antonym, or opposite, and explain your choice.

1. intimidated: **(a)** astounded **(b)** soothed **(c)** yelled **(d)** arose
2. endurance: **(a)** disobedience **(b)** devotion **(c)** stability **(d)** brevity
3. formidable: **(a)** strong **(b)** weak **(c)** scary **(d)** lengthy
4. invincible: **(a)** conquerable **(b)** triumphant **(c)** wise **(d)** printable

Content-Area Vocabulary Indicate whether each statement is true or false and explain your answer.

5. Someone who wants revenge will not seek to *retaliate*.
6. A *humanitarian* effort does little to help others.
7. When you make an *allocation* of funds, you put the money aside for a specific purpose.

Etymology Study *Allocation* contains the Latin root -*loc*-, which means "place." When you make an *allocation*, you set something apart in a particular place or location. Explain the meaning of the following words, which also contain the Latin root -*loc*-. Then, use each word in a sentence.

dislocate	locality	locomotive
local	locomotion	relocate

Common Core State Standards

Writing
7. Conduct short as well as more sustained research projects to answer a question or solve a problem; narrow or broaden the inquiry when appropriate; synthesize multiple sources on the subject, demonstrating understanding of the subject under investigation. *(p. 1295)*
8. Gather relevant information from multiple authoritative print and digital sources, using advanced searches effectively; assess the strengths and limitations of each source in terms of the task, purpose, and audience; integrate information into the text selectively to maintain the flow of ideas, avoiding plagiarism and overreliance on any one source and following a standard format for citation. *(p. 1295)*

Language
6. Acquire and use accurately general academic and domain-specific words and phrases, sufficient for reading, writing, speaking, and listening at the college and career readiness level.

Research Task

Topic: Great Speeches

When Winston Churchill's speech beamed out on radio waves in 1940, it relied solely on the power of spoken words to connect with listeners. Twenty-five years later, Lyndon Johnson's "we shall overcome" speech to Congress, urging passage of civil rights legislation, was televised. Today, politicians' speeches can also be viewed on the Internet. How do various media affect the coverage—and the formality and tone—of major speeches like these?

Assignment: Create a **multimedia presentation** in which you analyze media coverage of a major contemporary speech. Focus on how the presentation varies in different media—newspapers, magazines, radio, television, and the Internet. Consider such factors as bias and different audiences and purposes for the coverage.

Formulate a research plan. First, select the speech on which you will focus. Identify the different types of media used to cover the speech. Choose three types of media coverage you wish to research. Then, formulate questions such as these:

- Which medium is most complete and clear in its coverage?
- For each medium, how do different audiences and purposes affect the bias, formality, and tone of the coverage?
- Which medium seems the most unbiased? Explain.

Gather sources. Using print, broadcast, library, and online sources, research coverage of the speech. Keep accurate notations of the sources of all written, visual, and audio material to document your research.

Synthesize information. Based on your research plan, compare and contrast coverage of the speech. Pay special attention to changes in formality and tone across the various media.

Organize and present ideas. Use visuals, such as stills from a television report; sound, such as recording of a radio broadcast; and text to present your analysis. Tell the audience what to look for before showing each example. Then, present your analyses and conclusions.

On March 15, 1965, President Lyndon Johnson urged Congress to pass a major civil rights bill.

RESEARCH TIP

In addition to the verbal commentary on the speech, pay attention to nonverbal elements such as music, sound effects, and displayed symbols.

Use a checklist like the one shown to prepare a well-organized multimedia presentation.

Model: Presenting a Media Analysis

Step 1: Introduction	Listen for words: "thrilling occasion."
Step 2: Example	Show video clip.
Step 3: Analysis	Denotation and connotation of "thrilling occasion" show reporter may favor the speaker.
Step 4: Conclusion	This news outlet may be biased.

Research Checklist

- ☐ Have I answered all the questions in my research plan?
- ☐ Have I properly identified every visual and audio excerpt in my presentation?
- ☐ Have I analyzed each medium's coverage objectively?
- ☐ Do my conclusions proceed logically from my analyses?

Connecting to the Essential Question In this story, a woman's state of mind is affected by wartime conditions. As you read, note details of wartime conditions in the story. These details will help you think about the Essential Question: **What is the relationship between literature and place?**

Close Reading Focus

Ghost Story; Flashback; Ambiguity

During World War II, life in England was severely disrupted. Routines were changed, and anxiety replaced trust. The usual sights and sounds of daily life became doubtful, dangerous, even deadly.

In this historical context, a ghost story is right at home. A **ghost story** is a tale in which part of the past—typically, a dead person—seems to appear in the present. Ghost stories include these elements:

- An eerie or mysterious atmosphere
- The suggestion that supernatural forces are at work
- Eerie events that may have a natural explanation

A ghost story may include a **flashback,** a scene that interrupts a narrative to relate events that occurred in the past. Ghost stories may create uncertainty or an unresolved tension through **ambiguity**—the effect of two or more different possible interpretations. As you read, note how Bowen uses flashback and ambiguity to develop elements of the story.

Preparing to Read Complex Texts "The Demon Lover" enables you to **relate a literary work to a primary-source document.** Bowen's fiction takes place in the real world described by Winston Churchill in his speech beginning on page 1287. As you read Bowen's story, use a graphic organizer like the one shown to relate Mrs. Drover's private battle to the public battle in Churchill's speech.

Vocabulary

The words below are important to understanding the text that follows. Copy the words into your notebook. What are some other forms of the word *dislocation*?

spectral   circumscribed

dislocation   aperture

arboreal

Common Core State Standards

Reading Literature
3. Analyze the impact of the author's choices regarding how to develop and relate elements of a story or drama.

	Literary Work: Demon Lover	Primary Source: Wartime Speech
Source of Fear	Ghostly lover	German army
Atmosphere		
Weapons		
Tactics		
Main Goal		
End Result		

Author of "The Demon Lover"

The fiction of Elizabeth Bowen is distinguished by her subtle observation of landscape, by her innovative and believable use of the supernatural, and by her haunting portrayal of England during one of the darkest eras of the country's history—World War II.

From Life Into Art Early in life, Bowen suffered serious losses. Her father had a breakdown when she was seven years old and was confined to an institution. When Bowen was thirteen, her mother died. As an adult, Bowen was to write about such experiences of the denial of emotion and the helplessness of the heart to understand itself or others in the absence of love. In her characters' insecure lives, in the damage that is done them when their feelings are not acknowledged, one can still trace the marks left by Bowen's own early abandonment.

A Writer's Life Bowen's one ambition was to write, and her family's money was enough to support her as she wrote her first short stories. Her first collection, published in 1923, received little attention. Through the 1930s, she perfected her craft, publishing regularly. In 1938, she completed *The Death of the Heart,* one of her best-known works. The novel is about the disillusionment of an innocent teenage girl, taken in by uncaring relatives after her mother's death.

The War and After During the war, Bowen observed England's hardships keenly and with compassion. She incorporated the brutal realities of the war—air raids, blackouts, betrayal—into some of her best stories. By using a wartime setting and playing on the heightened emotions and perceptions people have at such times, Bowen exposed the innermost workings of her characters' minds.

After the war, Bowen widened her literary activities to include literary criticism and book reviews. Her later novels exhibit a more symbolic, more poetic style than her earlier works. Bowen defined the novel as the "non-poetic statement of poetic truth." Guided by the hardships she had undergone, working in a deceptively simple style, she achieved this goal admirably.

Elizabeth
BOWEN
(1899–1973)

The DEMON LOVER

Elizabeth Bowen

BACKGROUND World War II was a fact of daily life in the London of the 1940s. After decisive victories in Europe, Germany determined to break Britain with a steady bombardment focused on London. During the Blitz, from September 1940 to May 1941, German planes dropped bombs on the city almost every night. Whole communities were evacuated periodically, leaving street after street of deserted buildings. Elizabeth Bowen lived in London during this time, and the eerie quality of "The Demon Lover" stems from her experience of a time when war's horrors had become all too "ordinary."

Toward the end of her day in London Mrs. Drover went round to her shut-up house to look for several things she wanted to take away. Some belonged to herself, some to her family, who were by now used to their country life. It was late August; it had been a steamy, showery day: at the moment the trees down the pavement glittered in an escape of humid yellow afternoon sun. Against the next batch of clouds, already piling up ink-dark, broken chimneys and parapets stood out. In her once familiar street, as in any unused channel, an unfamiliar queerness had silted up; a cat wove itself in and out of railings, but no human eye watched Mrs. Drover's return. Shifting some parcels under her arm, she slowly forced round her latchkey in an unwilling lock, then gave the door, which had warped, a push with her knee. Dead air came out to meet her as she went in.

The staircase window having been boarded up, no light came down into the hall. But one door, she could just see, stood ajar, so she went quickly through into the room and unshuttered the big window in there. Now the prosaic woman, looking about her, was more perplexed than she knew by everything that she saw, by traces of her long former habit of life—the yellow smoke stain up the white marble mantel-piece, the ring left by a vase on the top of the escritoire,[1] the bruise in the wallpaper where, on the door being thrown open widely, the china handle had always hit the wall. The piano, having gone away to be stored, had left what looked like claw marks on its part of the parquet.[2] Though not much dust had seeped in, each object wore a film of another kind; and, the only ventilation being the chimney, the whole drawing room smelled of the cold hearth. Mrs. Drover put down her parcels on the escritoire and left the room to proceed upstairs; the things she wanted were in a bedroom chest.

She had been anxious to see how the house was—the part-time caretaker she shared with some neighbors was away this week on his holiday, known to be not yet back. At the best of times he did not look in often, and she was never sure that she trusted him. There were some cracks in the structure, left by the last bombing, on which she was anxious to keep an eye. Not that one could do anything—

A shaft of refracted daylight now lay across the hall. She stopped dead and stared at the hall table—on this lay a letter addressed to her.

She thought first—then the caretaker *must* be back. All the same, who, seeing the house shuttered, would have dropped a letter in at the box? It was not a circular, it was not a bill. And the post office redirected, to the address in the country, everything for her that came through the post. The caretaker (even if he *were* back) did not know she was due in London today—her call here had been planned to be a surprise—so his negligence in the manner of this letter, leaving it to wait in the dusk and the dust, annoyed her. Annoyed, she picked up the letter, which bore no stamp. But it cannot be important, or they would know . . . She took the letter rapidly upstairs with her, without a stop to look at the writing till she reached what had been her bedroom, where she let in light. The room looked over the garden and other gardens: the sun had gone in; as the clouds sharpened and lowered, the trees and rank lawns seemed already to smoke with dark. Her reluctance to look again at the letter came from the fact that she felt intruded upon—and by someone contemptuous of her ways. However, in the tenseness preceding the fall of rain she read it: it was a few lines.

DEAR KATHLEEN,
You will not have forgotten that today is our anniversary, and the day we said. The years have gone by at once slowly and fast. In view of the fact that nothing has changed, I shall rely upon you to

---

1. escritoire (es′ krə twär′) *n.* a writing desk or table.
2. parquet (pär kā′) *n.* flooring of inlaid woodwork in geometric forms.

Relate to Primary Source Documents
Winston Churchill described "the gravity of the hour." How does the historical situation contribute to Mrs. Drover's anxiety?

The Ghost Story
How does Bowen prepare the reader for the suggestion that there is something supernatural about the letter?

Comprehension
What does Mrs. Drover unexpectedly discover in her vacant house?

Flashback

What clues in the text signal the beginning of the flashback?

Vocabulary

spectral (spek' trəl) *adj.* ghostly

keep your promise. I was sorry to see you leave London, but was satisfied that you would be back in time. You may expect me, therefore, at the hour arranged. Until then . . . K.

Mrs. Drover looked for the date: it was today's. She dropped the letter onto the bedsprings, then picked it up to see the writing again—her lips, beneath the remains of lipstick, beginning to go white. She felt so much the change in her own face that she went to the mirror, polished a clear patch in it and looked at once urgently and stealthily in. She was confronted by a woman of forty-four, with eyes starting out under a hatbrim that had been rather carelessly pulled down. She had not put on any more powder since she left the shop where she ate her solitary tea. The pearls her husband had given her on their marriage hung loose round her now rather thinner throat, slipping into the V of the pink wool jumper her sister knitted last autumn as they sat round the fire. Mrs. Drover's most normal expression was one of controlled worry, but of assent. Since the birth of the third of her little boys, attended by a quite serious illness, she had had an intermittent muscular flicker to the left of her mouth, but in spite of this she could always sustain a manner that was at once energetic and calm.

Turning from her own face as precipitately as she had gone to meet it, she went to the chest where the things were, unlocked it, threw up the lid and knelt to search. But as rain began to come crashing down she could not keep from looking over her shoulder at the stripped bed on which the letter lay. Behind the blanket of rain the clock of the church that still stood struck six—with rapidly heightening apprehension she counted each of the slow strokes. "The hour arranged . . . My God," she said, "*What hour*? How should I . . .? After twenty-five years. . . ."

The young girl talking to the soldier in the garden had not ever completely seen his face. It was dark; they were saying good-bye under a tree. Now and then—for it felt, from not seeing him at this intense moment, as though she had never seen him at all—she verified his presence for these few moments longer by putting out a hand, which he each time pressed, without very much kindness, and painfully, on to one of the breast buttons of his uniform. That cut of the button on the palm of her hand was, principally, what she was to carry away. This was so near the end of a leave from France that she could only wish him already gone. It was August 1916. Being not kissed, being drawn away from and looked at intimidated Kathleen till she imagined spectral glitters in the place of his eyes. Turning away and looking back up the lawn she saw, through branches of trees, the drawing-room window alight; she caught a breath for the

▲ **Critical Viewing** In what ways is the mood or atmosphere of the story reflected in this painting? **INTERPRET**

▲ **Critical Viewing**

Which details in this painting suggest the dusty, abandoned quality of Mrs. Drover's room?
ANALYZE

Ambiguity

In what two ways might Kathleen's fiancé's remarks be interpreted?

moment when she could go running back there into the safe arms of her mother and sister, and cry: "What shall I do, what shall I do? He has gone."

Hearing her catch her breath, her fiancé said, without feeling: "Cold?"

"You're going away such a long way."

"Not so far as you think."

"I don't understand?"

"You don't have to," he said. "You will. You know what we said."

"But that was—suppose you—I mean, suppose."

"I shall be with you," he said, "sooner or later. You won't forget that. You need do nothing but wait."

Only a little more than a minute later she was free to run up the silent lawn. Looking in through the window at her mother and sister, who did not for the moment perceive her, she already felt that unnatural promise drive down between her and the rest of all humankind. No other way of having given herself could have made her feel so apart, lost and foresworn. She could not have plighted a more sinister troth.

Kathleen behaved well when, some months later, her fiancé was reported missing, presumed killed. Her family not only supported her but were able to praise her courage without stint because they could not regret, as a husband for her, the man they knew almost nothing about. They hoped she would, in a year or two, console herself—and had it been only a question of consolation things might have gone much straighter ahead. But her trouble, behind just a little grief, was a complete dislocation from everything. She did not reject other lovers, for these failed to appear: for years she failed to attract men—and with the approach of her thirties she became natural enough to share her family's anxiousness on this score. She began to put herself out, to wonder; and at thirty-two she was very greatly relieved to find herself being courted by William Drover. She married him, and the two of them settled down in this quiet, arboreal part of Kensington; in this house the years piled up, her children were born and they all lived till they were driven out by the bombs of the next war. Her movements as Mrs. Drover were circumscribed, and she dismissed any idea that they were still watched.

As things were—dead or living the letter writer sent her only a threat. Unable, for some minutes, to go on kneeling with her back exposed to the empty room, Mrs. Drover rose from the chest to sit on an upright chair whose back was firmly against the wall. The desuetude[3] of her former bedroom, her married London home's whole air of being a cracked cup from which memory, with its reassuring power, had either evaporated or leaked away, made a crisis—and at just this crisis the letter writer had, knowledgeably, struck. The hollowness of the house this evening canceled years on years of voices, habits and steps. Through the shut windows she only heard rain fall on the roofs around. To rally herself, she said she was in a mood—and, for two or three seconds shutting her eyes, told herself that she imagined the letter. But she opened them—there it lay on the bed.

On the supernatural side of the letter's entrance she was not permitting her mind to dwell. Who, in London, knew she meant to call at the house today? Evidently, however, this had been known. The caretaker, *had* he come back, had had no cause to expect her: he would have taken the letter in his pocket, to forward it, at his own time, through the post. There was no other sign that the caretaker had been in—but, if not? Letters dropped in at doors of deserted houses do not fly or walk to tables in halls. They do not sit on the dust of empty tables with the air of certainty that they will be found. There is needed some human hand—but nobody but the caretaker had a key. Under circumstances she did not care to consider, a house can be entered without a key. It was possible that she was not alone now. She might be being waited for, downstairs. Waited for—until when? Until "the hour arranged." At least that was not six o'clock; six has struck.

She rose from the chair and went over and locked the door.

The thing was, to get out. To fly? No, not that: she had to catch

---

3. **desuetude** (des´ wi tood´) *adj.* condition of not being used any more.

Vocabulary

dislocation (dis´ lō kā´ shən) *n.* condition of being out of place

arboreal (är bòr´ ē´ əl) *adj.* of, near, or among trees

circumscribed (sur´ kəm skrībd´) *adj.* limited; having a definite boundary

Comprehension

What happens to Kathleen's fiancé after he returns to war?

The Demon Lover **1303**

her train. As a woman whose utter dependability was the keystone of her family life she was not willing to return to the country, to her husband, her little boys and her sister, without the objects she had come up to fetch. Resuming work at the chest she set about making up a number of parcels in a rapid, fumbling-decisive way. These, with her shopping parcels, would be too much to carry; these meant a taxi—at the thought of the taxi her heart went up and her normal breathing resumed. I will ring up the taxi now; the taxi cannot come too soon; I shall hear the taxi out there running its engine, till I walk calmly down to it through the hall. I'll ring up—But no: the telephone is cut off . . . She tugged at a knot she had tied wrong.

The idea of flight . . . He was never kind to me, not really. I don't remember him kind at all. Mother said he never considered me. He was set on me, that was what it was—not love. Not love, not meaning a person well. What did he do, to make me promise like that? I can't remember—But she found that she could.

She remembered with such dreadful acuteness that the twenty-five years since then dissolved like smoke and she instinctively looked for the weal[4] left by the button on the palm of her hand. She remembered not only all that he said and did but the complete suspension of *her* existence during that August week. I was not myself—they all told me so at the time. She remembered—but with one white burning blank as where acid has dropped on a photograph: *under no conditions* could she remember his face.

So wherever he may be waiting, I shall not know him. You have no time to run from a face you do not expect.

The thing was to get to the taxi before any clock struck what could be the hour. She would slip down the street and round the side of the square to where the square gave on the main road. She would return in the taxi, safe, to her own door, and bring the driver into the house with her to pick up the parcels from room to room. The idea of the taxi driver made her decisive, bold; she unlocked her door, went to the top of the staircase and listened down.

She heard nothing—but while she was hearing nothing the passé[5] air of the staircase was disturbed by a draft that traveled up to her face. It emanated from the basement: down there a door or window was being opened by someone who chose this moment to leave the house.

The rain had stopped; the pavements steamily shone as Mrs. Drover let herself out by inches from her own front door into the empty street. The unoccupied houses opposite continued to meet her look with their damaged stare. Making toward the thoroughfare and the taxi, she tried not to keep looking behind. Indeed, the silence was so intense—one of those creeks of London silence exaggerated this summer by the damage of war—that no tread could have gained on hers unheard. Where her street debouched on the square where people went on living, she

---

4. **weal** *n.* raised mark, line, or ridge on the skin caused by an injury.
5. **passé** (pa sä´) *adj.* stale.

The Ghost Story

In this paragraph, how do Mrs. Drover's fear of the supernatural and her attention to practical details blur the lines between the familiar world and the unknown?

grew conscious of, and checked, her unnatural pace. Across the open end of the square two buses impassively passed each other; women, a perambulator,[6] cyclists, a man wheeling a barrow signalized, once again, the ordinary flow of life. At the square's most populous corner should be—and was—the short taxi rank. This evening, only one taxi —but this, although it presented its blank rump, appeared already to be alertly waiting for her. Indeed, without looking round the driver started his engine as she panted up from behind and put her hand on the door. As she did so, the clock struck seven. The taxi faced the main road. To make the trip back to her house it would have to turn—she had settled back on the seat and the taxi *had* turned before she, surprised by its knowing movement, recollected that she had not "said where." She leaned forward to scratch at the glass panel that divided the driver's head from her own.

The driver braked to what was almost a stop, turned round and slid the glass panel back. The jolt of this flung Mrs. Drover forward till her face was almost into the glass. Through the aperture driver and passenger, not six inches between them, remained for an eternity eye to eye. Mrs. Drover's mouth hung open for some seconds before she could issue her first scream. After that she continued to scream freely and to beat with her gloved hands on the glass all round as the taxi, accelerating without mercy, made off with her into the hinterland of deserted streets.

---

6. **perambulator** *n.* baby carriage.

Critical Reading

1. **Key Ideas and Details** **(a)** Why is the appearance of the letter in Mrs. Drover's house unexpected? **(b) Infer:** Why is she so upset by it?

2. **Key Ideas and Details** **(a)** Before returning to the war, what had Mrs. Drover's fiancé promised her? **(b) Analyze:** Identify three points at which she feels she is being watched, and describe what each moment adds to the story.

3. **Key Ideas and Details** **(a) Analyze:** Identify three references in the story to "traces," marks left behind by objects or actions. **(b) Interpret:** In what sense are ghosts and memories also traces? **(c) Draw Conclusions:** How do the references to traces suggest and support the story's theme?

4. **Integration of Knowledge and Ideas** Beyond the physical effects of war on the home front, what emotional effects of the war does Bowen's story suggest? In your response, use at least two of these Essential Question words: *alter, vulnerable, unresolved.* [Connecting to the Essential Question: *What is the relationship between literature and place?*]

Cite textual evidence to support your responses.

Literary Analysis

1. **Key Ideas and Details** Bowen uses a historical period—the World War II home front—to create a haunting atmosphere of silence and emptiness. Identify three eerie details that show how ordinary life was affected during this period.

2. **Craft and Structure** A **ghost story** often suggests that supernatural forces are at work. Explain how Bowen creates that suggestion with each of the following sentences:

   a) ". . . no human eye watched Mrs. Drover's return."

   b) "Dead air came out to meet her as she went in."

   c) "On the supernatural side of the letter's entrance she was not permitting her mind to dwell."

3. **Craft and Structure** The **flashback** that returns Mrs. Drover and the reader to 1916 suggests an explanation for her state of mind in 1940. **(a)** What does the flashback tell you about Mrs. Drover? **(b)** In what sense is she "haunted" by an unresolved problem in her past?

4. **Craft and Structure** Bowen maintains **ambiguity**—the effect of two or more different interpretations—throughout the story. Use a chart like the one shown to interpret a word, an action, and an image in more than one way.

	Interpretation 1	Interpretation 2
Word		
Action		
Image		

5. **Integration of Knowledge and Ideas** A ghost story often keeps open the possibility that its eerie events have a rational explanation. Propose rational causes for the events of "The Demon Lover."

6. **Integration of Knowledge and Ideas Relate a literary work to a primary-source document** by assessing Churchill and Bowen's sense of the power of the spoken word. **(a)** What do you think some of the effects of a wartime radio broadcast were? **(b)** What effect does Bowen create by emphasizing the intense silence of the city?

7. **Integration of Knowledge and Ideas** In his wartime speech, Churchill says, "We must not allow ourselves to be intimidated by the presence of these armored vehicles in unexpected places behind our lines." Explain how Bowen, in her wartime story of terror, uses an "armored vehicle" and "unexpected" events to intimidate her main character.

Common Core State Standards

Writing

3.c. Use a variety of techniques to sequence events so that they build on one another to create a coherent whole and build toward a particular tone and outcome. *(p. 1307)*

3.d. Use precise words and phrases, telling details, and sensory language to convey a vivid picture of the experiences, events, setting, and/or characters. *(p. 1307)*

Language

4.a. Use context as a clue to the meaning of a word or phrase. *(p. 1307)*

Vocabulary Acquisition and Use

Word Analysis: Cognates

Cognates are words derived from the same original form. Cognates are often easy to spot because they have parts that look and sound alike.

Spectral, meaning "ghostly," is a cognate of *specter*, a word for "ghost." Both *specter* and *spectral* derive from the Latin word *spectrum*, meaning "appearance." When Isaac Newton experimented with light, he examined the spectrum, the colored bands that are visible when white light is refracted through a prism. Now a spectrum refers to any wide range, such as a spectrum of opinions.

Answer these questions:

1. Would you expect a *specter* to have a lively and vivid appearance? Why or why not?

2. If a store offers you a *spectrum* of choices, would you be a happier shopper? Explain.

3. If a landscape is described as *spectral,* what might it look like?

Vocabulary: Context Clues

Words take on meaning depending upon context—the meanings of the words around them. You can often use context clues to determine the meaning of an unfamiliar word.

Review the vocabulary list on page 1296. Then, in your notebook, explain whether the italicized word in each of the sentences below is used correctly, based on its context.

1. I was relieved when I touched not a *spectral* presence, but solid flesh.

2. Given the pollution in the world's waterways, I am surprised that more *arboreal* species are not endangered.

3. Take whatever you wish; my generosity is strictly *circumscribed*.

4. The letter fit through the *aperture*.

5. The doctor has caused a permanent *dislocation* of your shoulder; you should feel fine in a day or two.

Writing to Sources

Narrative Text Write a **sequel** to "The Demon Lover," answering the question *What happened next?* Continue the narrative logically. To ensure that your sequel also maintains the uneasy atmosphere that Bowen creates, use plenty of sensory details. Include an *interior monologue*—a speech that occurs only silently in a character's mind—to depict a character's feelings.

Prewriting Jot down questions that "The Demon Lover" leaves unanswered. Then, suggest answers to these questions. Select a few of these answers as a starting point.

Drafting Outline the events in your story in a logical way. As you draft, fill in background from the original story wherever you think it is necessary. In the interior monologue, include only what the character might know or feel.

Model: Revising to Add Sensory Details

fog-enshrouded   blood-curdling
As the taxi went down the ∧street, the driver gave a ∧laugh.

Sensory details make writing more vivid and interesting for the reader.

Revising Make sure that the events in your story are in the correct order. If you have used a *flashback*, make sure the reader knows where it begins and ends. Add sensory details to make the sights, sounds, and smells of a scene and the specific actions, movements, gestures, and feelings of the characters as vivid as possible.

Connecting to the Essential Question Each of these poets juxtaposes an image of war with an image of another kind. As you read, notice images in the poems that reveal wartime attitudes. Recognizing these attitudes will help you think about the Essential Question: **How does literature shape or reflect society?**

Close Reading Activities

Universal Theme; Irony

A **theme** is the central idea, message, or insight that a literary work reveals. A **universal theme** is a message about life that is expressed regularly in many different cultures and time periods. For example, the power of love amid the horror of war is a universal theme because every culture and age has experienced it. In every war, the fierce fighter who kills and dies on a battlefield is also someone's beloved, someone's parent, someone's friend. As Keith Douglas expresses it,

> *For here the lover and killer are mingled*
> *who had one body and one heart.*

Comparing Literary Works In the twentieth century, authors who use the universal theme of love and war often express the theme with irony. **Irony** is a discrepancy or a contradiction between appearance and reality, between expectation and outcome, or between what is directly stated and what is really meant. As you read, identify examples of irony and consider what they suggest about the author's point of view.

Preparing to Read Complex Texts Each poet has a purpose in juxtaposing contrasting images of love and war. By understanding the **author's purpose,** you will gain an insight into love, war, or life in general. For example, the poet may want to celebrate the power of an undying love or lament the power of a death-dealing war. Use a graphic organizer like this one to help clarify each author's purpose.

Vocabulary

The words below are important to understanding the texts that follow. Copy the words into your notebook. What are some other forms of the vocabulary words?

combatants   abide

sprawling   eloquent

**Common Core
State Standards**

Reading Literature
6. Analyze a case in which grasping point of view requires distinguishing what is directly stated in a text from what is really meant.

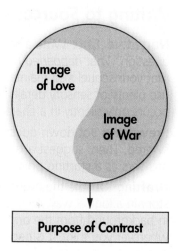

Image of Love

Image of War

Purpose of Contrast